THE TIMES

Book of Quotations

TIMES BOOKS

HarperCollins Publishers
Westerhill Road, Glasgow G64 2QT

www.**fire**and**water**.com

First published 2000

Reprint 10 9 8 7 6 5 4 3 2 1 0

ISBN 0 00 710296 8

A catalogue record for this book is available from the British Library

Printed by the Bath Press

CONTENTS

INTRODUCTION

Quotation is our national vice (*Evelyn Waugh*), the parole of literary men all over the world (*Sam Johnson*), and the act of repeating erroneously the words of another (*Ambrose Bierce*). But quotation is also the most enduring form of immortality.

Quotable lines bring to pass a monument with a longer shelf-life than brass (the poet Horace, coarsely translated). Every hour of every day, billions of words are spoken and written. And those are just in English, the world language. Almost all of these words have been said many times before. Most language is repetition, slop, pudder, jargon – conventional noises that pass through the ears of the audience without creating a ripple. It is almost impossible to think a new thought or make an original statement that has not been thought or made many times before. Originality is the business of poets and philosophers. It is the last thing we expect (or want?) from our politicians, football managers, pop stars, television readers of the autocue, and other celebrities who are famous for being famous, not for being original.

But in the ceaseless chatter of language, just occasionally something original is said. And the astonishing revolution in communication that rages around us means that Everyman (and Everywoman) can at last get their voices heard. Until this generation, politicians and ruling elites in other fields were those who were heard and published. In the future everyone will be famous for fifteen minutes (*Andy Warhol*). I'm bored with that line. My new line is, 'In fifteen minutes everybody will be famous.' Today everybody can be quoted. And is.

There are already many excellent quotation dictionaries, from Oxford and Collins to Penguin and Bartletts. So why do we need another one? The distinctive feature of *The Times Book of Quotations* is that it catches the rascal quotations when they are just hatched. Other dictionaries record the great sayings of the past. One of my favourite bits in *The Times* is the 'Quotes of the Week' at the back of the Weekend section. My observation suggests that other people also turn to them first on Saturdays. They are included. So here we find the witty, wise and weird sayings made yesterday by the famous and the infamous, by Everyman and (that oxymoronic newspaper construct) the Ordinary Man. The surest way to make a monkey of a man is to quote him (*Benchley*).

There are many uses for a quotation dictionary. A bad one is for a hack in a hurry to decorate his prose with other men's flowers (*Archie Wavell*). A good one is to verify your references, sir (*Routh*). But the best is to open the door we never opened into the rose-garden (*Eliot*, Thomas Stearns, not George). The best choice of a single book for a desert island (perhaps even before Shakespeare and the Authorized Version) is a good dictionary of quotations. With it you can remember old friends and meet new ones. It is an immortal possession (*Thucydides*). Words are man's defining characteristic and our only true immortality. *The Times Book of Quotations* is a running commentary on current affairs, as well as a treasury of the past, and a window into future reading. And it is also, of course, the best book yet published for browsing like a butterfly and stinging like a bee.

Philip Howard

LIST OF THEMES

LIST OF THEMES

LIST OF THEMES

A

abortion

Brooks, Gwendolyn (1917–)
> Abortions will not let you forget you remember the children you got that you did not get.
> *Selected Poems* (1963)

Parker, Dorothy (1893–1967)
US writer, poet, critic and wit
> It serves me right for putting all my eggs in one bastard.
> *You Might As Well Live*

absence

Ashford, Daisy (1881–1972)
English child author
> My life will be sour grapes and ashes without you.
> *The Young Visiters* (1919)

Bayly, Thomas Haynes (1797–1839)
English songwriter, writer and dramatist
> Absence make the heart grow fonder.
> *Isle of Beauty*

Behan, Brendan (1923–1964)
Irish dramatist, writer and Republican
> When I came back to Dublin, I was court-martialled in my absence and sentenced to death in my absence, so I said they could shoot me in my absence.
> *The Hostage* (1958)

Bowen, Elizabeth (1899–1973)
Irish writer
> The heart may think it knows better: the senses know that absence blots people out. We have really no absent friends.
> *The Death of the Heart*

Clough, Arthur Hugh (1819–1861)
English poet and letter writer
> That out of sight is out of mind
> Is true of most we leave behind.
> *Songs in Absence* (1849)

La Rochefoucauld (1613–1680)
French writer
> Absence diminishes mediocre passions and increases great ones, as the wind extinguishes candles and kindles fire.
> *Maximes* (1678)

Norton, Caroline (1808–1877)
English poet
> I do not love thee! – no! I do not love thee!
> And yet when thou art absent I am sad;
> And envy even the bright blue sky above thee,
> Whose quiet stars may see thee and be glad.
> *The Sorrows of Rosalie* (1829)

Proverbs
> Long absent, soon forgottten.
>
> Out of sight, out of mind.
>
> When the cat's away, the mice will play.

Rushdie, Salman (1947–)
Indian-born English author
> Most of what matters in your life takes place in your absence.
> *Midnight's Children* (1981)

Shah, Idries (1924–1996)
English writer
> A certain person may have, as you say, a wonderful presence: I do not know. What I do know is that he has a perfectly delightful absence.
> *Reflections*

Shakespeare, William (1564–1616)
English dramatist, poet and actor
> Give me to drink mandragora
> That I might sleep out this great gap of time
> My Antony is away.
> *Antony and Cleopatra*
>
> How like a winter hath my absence been
> From thee, the pleasure of the fleeting year!
> What freezings have I felt, what dark days seen!
> What old December's bareness everywhere!
> Sonnet 97

Trollope, Anthony (1815–1882)
English writer, traveller and post office official
> To think of one's absent love is very sweet; but it becomes monotonous after a mile or two of a towing-path, and the mind will turn away to Aunt Sally, the Cremorne Gardens, and financial questions. I doubt whether any girl would be satisfied with her lover's mind if she knew the whole of it.
> *The Small House at Allington* (1864)

▶▶ SEPARATION

accidents

Arno, Peter (1904–1968)
> Well, back to the old drawing board.
> *The New Yorker*, caption to cartoon of designers walking away from crashed plane

Benchley, Robert (1889–1945)
US essayist, humorist and actor
> My only solution for the problem of habitual accidents is for everybody to stay in bed all day. Even then, there is always the chance that you will fall out.
>> *Chips off the Old Bentley*

Chesterfield, Lord (1694–1773)
English politician and letter writer
> The chapter of knowledge is very short, but the chapter of accidents is a very long one.
>> *Letter to Solomon Dayrolles, 1753*

Coren, Alan (1938–)
British humorist, writer and broadcaster
> The Act of God designation on all insurance policies; which means, roughly, that you cannot be insured for the accidents that are most likely to happen to you.
>> *The Lady from Stalingrad Museum* (1977)

Graham, Harry (1874–1936)
English writer
> 'There's been an accident!' they said,
> 'Your servant's cut in half; he's dead!'
> 'Indeed!' said Mr Jones, 'and please
> Send me the half that's got my keys.'
>> *Ruthless Rhymes for Heartless Homes* (1899)

Marquis, Don (1878–1937)
US columnist, satirist and poet
> now and then
> there is a person born
> who is so unlucky
> that he runs into accidents
> which started out to happen
> to somebody else.
>> *archys life of mehitabel* (1933)

McGonagall, William (c.1830–1902)
Scottish poet, tragedian and actor
> Beautiful Railway Bridge of the Silv'ry Tay!
> Alas, I am very sorry to say
> That ninety lives have been taken away
> On the last Sabbath day of 1879,
> Which will be remember'd for a very long time.
>> *'The Tay Bridge Disaster'* (1890)

Potter, Beatrix (1866–1943)
English children's writer
> You may go into the field or down the lane, but don't go into Mr McGregor's garden: your Father had an accident there; he was put in a pie by Mrs McGregor.
>> *The Tale of Peter Rabbit* (1902)

Punch
> What is better than presence of mind in a railway accident? Absence of body.
>> 1849

Simpson, N.F. (1919–)
English dramatist
> Knocked down a doctor? With an ambulance? How could she? It's a contradiction in terms!
>> *One-Way Pendulum* (1960)

Smollett, Tobias (1721–1771)
Scottish writer, satirist, historian, traveller and physician
> I have met with so many axidents, suprisals, and terrifications, that I am in a pafeck fantigo, and I believe I shall never be my own self again.
>> *The Expedition of Humphry Clinker* (1771)

Wiesel, Elie (1928–)
Romanian-born US writer
> I don't believe in accidents. There are only encounters in history. There are no accidents.
>> *International Herald Tribune, 1992*

Wilkes, John (1727–1797)
English politician
> The chapter of accidents is the longest chapter in the book.
>> Attr.

▶▶ ADVERSITY; CHANCE

achievement

Anonymous
> Be not afraid of growing slowly, be afraid only of standing still.
>> Chinese Proverb

Confucius (c.550–c.478 BC)
Chinese philosopher and teacher of ethics
> Our greatest glory is not in never falling, but in rising every time we fall.
>> *Analects*

Huxley, Aldous (1894–1963)
English writer, poet and critic
> Those who believe that they are exclusively in the right are generally those who achieve something.
>> *Proper Studies* (1927)

Longfellow, Henry Wadsworth (1807–1882)
US poet and writer
> Let us, then, be up and doing,
> With a heart for any fate;
> Still achieving, still pursuing,
> Learn to labour and to wait.
>> *'A Psalm of Life'* (1838)

> The heights by great men reached and kept
> Were not attained by sudden flight,
> But they, while their companions slept,

Were toiling upward in the night.
'The Ladder of Saint Augustine' (1850)

Stevenson, Robert Louis (1850–1894)
Scottish writer, poet and essayist
Is there anything in life so disenchanting as attainment?
New Arabian Nights (1882)

▶▶ SUCCESS

acting

Alda, Alan (1936–)
US actor and director
Laugh at yourself, but don't ever aim your doubt at yourself. Be bold. When you embark for strange places, don't leave any of yourself safely on shore. Have the nerve to go into unexplored territory.
Connecticut College News, 1980

Astor, Mary (1906–1987)
US actress
A painter paints, a musician plays, a writer writes – but a movie actor waits.
A Life on Film (1967)

Bankhead, Tallulah (1903–1968)
US actress
Acting is a form of confusion.
Tallulah (1952)

Barrymore, Ethel (1879–1959)
US actress
There is as much difference between the stage and the film as between a piano and a violin. Normally you can't become a virtuoso in both.
The New York Post, 1956

Baylis, Lilian (1874–1937)
English theatrical manager
On a less than adequate performance in *King Lear*
Quite a sweet little Goneril, don't you think?
The Guardian, 1976

The Bible (King James Version)
But be ye doers of the word, and not hearers only.
James, 1:22

Brando, Marlon (1924–)
US actor
To grasp the full significance of life is the actor's duty, to interpret it is his problem, and to express it his dedication.
In David Shipman, *Marlon Brando* (1974)

Chaplin, Charlie (1889–1977)
English comedian, actor, director and satirist
You have to believe in yourself, that's the secret. Even when I was in the orphanage, when I was roaming the street trying to find enough to eat, even then I thought of myself as the greatest actor in the world.
Reader's Digest, 1982

Cusack, John (1966–)
US actor
Acting should be like punk in the best way. It should be a full-on expression of self – only without the broken bottles.
Uncut magazine, 2000

Davis, Bette (1908–1989)
US actress
Without wonder and insight, acting is just a trade. With it, it becomes creation.
The Lonely Life (1962)

Duras, Marguerite (1914–1996)
French author and filmmaker
Acting doesn't bring anything to a text. On the contrary, it detracts from it.
International Herald Tribune, 1990

Fielding, Henry (1707–1754)
English writer, dramatist and journalist
He the best player! … Why, I could act as well as he myself. I am sure, if I had seen a ghost, I should have looked in the very same manner, and done just as he did … The king for my money! He speaks all his words distinctly, half as loud again as the other. Anybody may see he is an actor.
Tom Jones (1749)

Fonda, Jane (1937–)
US actress and political activist
You spend all your life trying to do something they put people in asylums for.
In Halliwell *Filmgoer's Book of Quotes* (1973)

Gielgud, Sir John (1904–2000)
English actor
Being another character is more interesting than being yourself.
Attr.

Hull, Josephine (1886–1957)
US actress
Playing Shakespeare is very tiring. You never get to sit down, unless you're a King.
In Cooper and Hartman, *Violets and Vinegar* (1980)

Jackson, Glenda (1936–)
English actress and Labour politician
Acting is not about dressing up. Acting is about stripping bare. The whole essence of learning lines is to forget them so you can make them sound like you thought of them that instant.
Sunday Telegraph, 1992

Lunt, Alfred (1892–1977)
US actor

On acting
> Speak in a loud clear voice and try not to bump into the furniture.
>> In Halliwell, *Filmgoer's Book of Quotes* (1973)

Moore, George (1852–1933)
Irish writer, dramatist and critic
> Acting is therefore the lowest of the arts, if it is an art at all.
>> *Impressions and Opinions* (1891)

MacLaine, Shirley (1934–)
US actress
> I've made so many movies playing a hooker that they don't pay me in the regular way any more. They leave it on the dresser.
>> *Out on a Limb* (1983)

Newman, Paul (1925–)
US actor
> Acting is a question of absorbing other people's personalities and adding some of your own experience.
>> In Halliwell *Filmgoer's Companion* (1984)

Olivier, Sir Laurence (1907–1989)
English actor and director
> The actor should be able to create the universe in the palm of his hand.
>> *New York Times*, 1986

Richardson, Sir Ralph (1902–1983)
English actor
> The art of acting consists in keeping people from coughing.
>> *The Observer*

> The most precious things in speech are pauses.
>> Attr.

Russell, Rosalind (1911–1976)
US actress
> Acting is standing up naked and turning around slowly.
>> *Life Is a Banquet* (1977)

Shakespeare, William (1564–1616)
English dramatist, poet and actor
On the power of acting
> He would drown the stage with tears,
> And cleave the general ear with horrid speech;
> Make mad the guilty, and appal the free,
> Confound the ignorant, and amaze indeed
> The very faculties of eyes and ears.
>> *Hamlet*, II.ii

Sheridan, Richard Brinsley (1751–1816)
Irish dramatist, politician and orator
> *Burleigh comes forward, shakes his head, and exit.*
> *Sneer*: He is very perfect indeed. Now pray, what did he mean by that?
> *Puff*: Why, by that shake of the head, he gave

you to understand that even though they had more justice in their cause and wisdom in their measures, yet, if there was not a greater spirit shown on the part of the people, the country would at last fall a sacrifice to the hostile ambition of the Spanish monarchy.
> *Sneer*: The devil! – did he mean all that by shaking his head?
> *Puff*: Every word of it. If he shook his head as I taught him.
>> *The Critic* (1779)

> I wish, sir, you would practise this without me. I can't stay dying here all night.
>> *The Critic* (1779)

Terry, Dame Ellen (1847–1928)
English actress, theatrical manager and memoirist
> Imagination! imagination! I put it first years ago, when I was asked what qualities I thought necessary for success upon the stage.
>> *The Story of My Life* (1933)

Wayne, John (1907–1979)
US actor
> I am a just an ordinary goddamn American and I talk for all the ordinary goddamn Americans, the butchers and bakers and plumbers. I know these people; I know what they think.
>> In Barry Norman, *The Film Greats* (1985)

> I've spent my whole career playing myself.
>> In Barry Norman, *The Film Greats* (1985)

Ze Ami (1363–1443)
> In the act of imitation there is the level of no-imitation. When the act of imitation is perfectly accomplished and the actor becomes the thing itself, the actor will no longer have the desire to imitate.
>> *Fúshi kaden* (1400–1418)

▶▶ ACTORS; THEATRE

action

Amiel, Henri-Frédéric (1821–1881)
Swiss philosopher and writer
> Action is but coarsened thought – thought become concrete, obscure, and unconscious.
>> *Journal*, 1850

Aristotle (384–322 BC)
Greek philosopher
> Our actions determine our dispositions.
>> *Nicomachean Ethics*

Beerbohm, Sir Max (1872–1956)
English satirist, cartoonist, critic and essayist
> Anything that is worth doing has been done frequently. Things hitherto undone should be

given, I suspect, a wide berth.

Mainly on the Air (1946)

Canetti, Elias (1905–1994)

Bulgarian-born English writer, dramatist and critic

Was immer ihre Tätigkeit ist, die Tätigen halten sich für besser.

Whatever their activity is, the active think they are better.

The Human Province (1969)

Carlyle, Thomas (1795–1881)

Scottish historian, biographer, critic, and essayist

The end of man is an Action and not a Thought, though it were the noblest.

Sartor Resartus (1834)

Cernuda, Luis (1902–1963)

Spanish poet

¿Es toda acción humana, como estimas ahora,
Fruto de imitación y de inconsciencia?

Is every human action, as you now think,
The fruit of imitation and thoughtlessness?

La realidad y el deseo (1964)

Chesterfield, Lord (1694–1773)

English politician and letter writer

It is an undoubted truth, that the less one has to do, the less time one finds to do it in. One yawns, one procrastinates, one can do it when one will, and therefore one seldom does it at all.

Letter

Confucius (c.550–c.478 BC)

Chinese philosopher and teacher of ethics

Chi Wen Tzu always thought three times before taking action. Twice would have been quite enough.

Analects

Cornford, F.M. (1874–1943)

English Platonic scholar

Every public action which is not customary, either is wrong or, if it is right, is a dangerous precedent. It follows that nothing should ever be done for the first time.

Microcosmographia Academica (1908)

De Gaulle, Charles (1890–1970)

French general and statesman

Deliberation is the work of many men. Action, of one alone.

War Memoirs

Eliot, George (1819–1880)

English writer and poet

Our deeds determine us, as much as we determine our needs.

Adam Bede (1859)

Emerson, Ralph Waldo (1803–1882)

US poet, essayist, transcendentalist and teacher

The manly part is to do with might and main what you can do.

Conduct of Life (1860)

We are taught by great actions that the universe is the property of every individual in it.

Nature (1836)

The reward of a thing well done, is to have done it.

'New England Reformers' (1844)

Fletcher, John (1579–1625)

English dramatist

Deeds, not words shall speak me.

The Lover's Progress (1647)

Gide, André (1869–1951)

French writer, critic, dramatist and poet

M'est avis … que le profit n'est pas toujours ce qui mène l'homme; qu'il y a des actions désintéressées. … Par désintéressé j'entends: gratuit. Et que le mal, ce que l'on appelle: le mal, peut être aussi gratuit que le bien.

I believe … that profit is not always what motivates man; that there are disinterested actions. … By disinterested I mean: gratuitous. And that evil acts, what people call evil, can be as gratuitous as good acts.

Les Caves du Vatican (1914)

Hazlitt, William (1778–1830)

English writer and critic

We never do anything well till we cease to think about the manner of doing it.

Atlas (1830)

Herbert, Sir A.P. (1890–1971)

English humorist, writer, dramatist and politician

Let's find out what everyone is doing,
And then stop everyone from doing it.

Ballads for Broadbrows (1930)

Huxley, T.H. (1825–1895)

English biologist, Darwinist and agnostic

The great end of life is not knowledge but action.

Science and Culture (1877)

Johnson, Samuel (1709–1784)

English lexicographer, poet, critic, conversationalist and essayist

The love of life is necessary to the vigorous prosecution of any undertaking.

The Rambler (1750–1752)

Jowett, Benjamin (1817–1893)

English scholar, translator, essayist and priest

The way to get things done is not to mind who gets the credit for doing them.

Attr.

Kant, Immanuel (1724–1804)

German idealist philosopher

I should always act in such a way that I may want my maxim to become a general law.

Outline of the Metaphysics of Morals (1785)

Kempis, Thomas à (c.1380–1471)
German mystic, monk and writer

Certe adveniente die iudicii non quaeretur a nobis quid legimus sed quid fecimus.

Truly, when the day of judgement comes, it will not be a question of what we have read, but what we have done.

De Imitatione Christi (1892)

La Rochefoucauld (1613–1680)
French writer

Nous aurions souvent honte de nos plus belles actions, si le monde voyait les motifs qui les produisent.

We would often be ashamed of our finest actions if the world could see the motives behind them.

Maximes (1678)

Pérez Galdos, Benito (1843–1920)

El hombre de pensamiento descubre la Verdad; pero quien goza de ella y utiliza sus celestiales dones es el hombre de acción.

The man of reflection discovers Truth; but the one who enjoys it and makes use of its heavenly gifts is the man of action.

Friend Manso (1882)

Proverbs

Doing is better than saying.

Easier said than done.

Saying is one thing, and doing another.

Barking dogs seldom bite.

Sartre, Jean-Paul (1905–1980)
French philosopher, writer, dramatist and critic

I know perfectly well that I don't want to do anything; to do something is to create existence – and there is quite enough existence as it is.

Nausea (1938)

Shaw, George Bernard (1856–1950)
Irish socialist, writer, dramatist and critic

Activity is the only road to knowledge.

Man and Superman (1903)

Shenstone, William (1714–1763)

People in high or in distinguished life ought to have a greater circumspection in regard to their most trivial actions. For instance, I saw Mr Pope … to the best of my memory, he was picking his nose.

The Selected Works in Verse and Prose of William Shenstone (1770)

Spinoza, Baruch (1632–1677)
Dutch philosopher and theologian

Sedula curavi, humanas actiones non ridere, non lugere, neque detestare, sed intelligere.

I have taken great care not to laugh at human actions, not to weep at them, nor to hate them, but to understand them.

Tractatus Politicus (1677)

Szasz, Thomas (1920–)
Hungarian-born US psychiatrist and writer

Men are rewarded and punished not for what they do, but rather for how their acts are defined. This is why men are more interested in better justifying themselves than in better behaving themselves.

The Second Sin (1973)

Tawney, R.H. (1880–1962)
British economic historian and Christian socialist

It is a commonplace that the characteristic virtue of Englishmen is their power of sustained practical activity, and their characteristic vice a reluctance to test the quality of that activity by reference to principles.

The Acquisitive Society (1921)

Whitefield, George (1714–1770)
English evangelist

I had rather wear out than rust out.

Attr.

actors

Anonymous
On a performance of Cleopatra by Sarah Bernhardt

How different, how very different from the home life of our own dear Queen!

Remark

Totus mundus agit histrionem.
The whole world plays the actor.

Motto of Globe playhouse

Benchley, Robert (1889–1945)
US essayist, humorist and actor
Suggesting an epitaph for an actress

She sleeps alone at last.

Attr.

Bernhardt, Sarah (1844–1923)
French actress

For the theatre one needs long arms; it is better to have them too long than too short. An artiste with short arms can never, never make a fine gesture.

Attr.

Betterton, Thomas (1635–1710)
English actor and dramatist
Reply to the Archbishop of Canterbury

Actors speak of things imaginary as if they were real, while you preachers too often speak of things real as if they were imaginary.

Attr.

Brando, Marlon (1924–)
US actor

An actor's a guy who, if you ain't talking about him, ain't listening.

The Observer, 1956

Brown, John Mason (1900–1969)
On Tallulah Bankhead's performance as Shakespeare's Cleopatra in 1937

Tallulah Bankhead barged down the Nile last night and sank. As the Serpent of the Nile she proves to be no more dangerous than a garter snake.

In Current Biography (1941)

Burns, George (1896–1996)
US comedian

If it's a good script I'll do it. And if it's a bad script, and they pay me enough, I'll do it.

International Herald Tribune, 1988

Caine, Michael (1933–)
English actor
Commenting on the patronizing attitude of the British press to his work as an actor

I'm every bourgeois' nightmare. A Cockney with intelligence and a million dollars. They think they should have done it – but then why didn't they, if they were so much smarter and more intelligent than this stupid Cockney git?

The Times, 2000

Comment at the Golden Globe awards ceremony

I'm shocked. My career must have slipped. This is the first time I've been able to pick up an award.

The Times, 1999

Campbell, Mrs Patrick (1865–1940)
English actress

Watching Tallulah Bankhead on stage is like watching somebody skating over very thin ice – and the English want to be there when she falls through.

In Gavin Lambert, On Cukor

Coleridge, Samuel Taylor (1772–1834)
English poet, philosopher and critic
Of Edmund Kean

To see him act is like reading Shakespeare by flashes of lightning.

Table Talk (1835)

Coward, Sir Noël (1899–1973)
English dramatist, actor, producer and composer
Comment on a child star, in a long-winded play

Two things should be cut: the second act and the child's throat.

In Richards, The Wit of Noël Coward

Diller, Phyllis (1917–1974)
US comedian
Of Arnold Schwarzenegger

He has so many muscles that he has to make an appointment to move his fingers.

Attr.

Dundy, Elaine (1927–)
US writer

The question actors most often get asked is how they can bear saying the same things over and over again night after night, but God knows the answer to that is, don't we all anyway; might as well get paid for it.

The Dud Avocado (1958)

Field, Eugene (1850–1895)
US columnist, children's poet, translator and humorist
Of Creston Clarke as *King Lear*

He played the King as though under momentary apprehension that someone else was about to play the ace.

Attr.

Ford, John (1895–1973)
Irish-American film director

It is easier to get an actor to be a cowboy than to get a cowboy to be an actor.

Attr.

Goldsmith, Oliver (c.1728–1774)
Irish dramatist, poet and writer
Of Garrick

Here lies David Garrick, describe me who can,
An abridgment of all that was pleasant in man …
On the stage he was natural, simple, affecting,
'Twas only that, when he was off, he was acting …
He cast off his friends as a huntsman his pack,
For he knew, when he pleased, he could whistle them back.

'Retaliation' (1774)

Head, Edith (1898–1981)
US costume designer

I have yet to see one completely unspoiled star, except for the animals – like Lassie.

Saturday Evening Post, 1963

Hitchcock, Alfred (1899–1980)
English film director

I deny that I ever said that actors are cattle. What I said was, 'Actors should be treated like cattle'.

Attr.

Nobody can really like an actor.

The New Yorker, 1992

Hopper, Hedda (1890–1966)
US actress and writer

At one time I thought he wanted to be an actor. He had certain qualifications, including no money and a total lack of responsibility.

From Under My Hat (1953)

Johnson, Samuel (1709–1784)
English lexicographer, poet, critic, conversationalist and essayist

Players, Sir! I look upon them as no better than creatures set upon tables and joint stools to make faces and produce laughter, like dancing dogs.

In Boswell, *The Life of Samuel Johnson* (1791)

To Garrick

I'll come no more behind your scenes, David: for the silk stockings and white bosoms of your actresses excite my amorous propensities.

In Boswell, *The Life of Samuel Johnson* (1791)

Kaufman, George S. (1889–1961)
US scriptwriter, librettist and journalist
On Raymond Massey's interpretation of Abraham Lincoln

Massey won't be satisfied until somebody assassinates him.

In Meredith, *George S. Kaufman and the Algonquin Round Table* (1974)

Lanchester, Elsa (1902–1986)
US film actress
Of Maureen O'Hara

She looked as though butter wouldn't melt in her mouth – or anywhere else.

Attr.

Levant, Oscar (1906–1972)
US pianist and autobiographer

Romance on the High Seas was Doris Day's first picture; that was before she became a virgin.

Memoirs of an Amnesiac (1965)

Lloyd, Robert (1733–1764)
English poet

Who teach the mind its proper face to scan, And hold the faithful mirror up to man.

'The Actor'

Malouf, David (1934–)
Australian writer and poet

Actors don't pretend to be other people; they become themselves by finding other people inside them.

Harland's Half Acre (1984)

Olivier, Sir Laurence (1907–1989)
English actor and director

To Dustin Hoffman, who had stayed up all night to play a character in the film *Marathon Man* (1976) who had stayed up all night

Why not try acting? It's much easier.

Attr.

Paglia, Camille (1947–)
US academic and writer

Rumours of Ralph Fiennes's acting ability are wildly exaggerated. He is as asexual as an adenoid.

The Times, 1998

Parker, Dorothy (1893–1967)
US writer, poet, critic and wit
Remark on a performance by Katherine Hepburn

She ran the whole gamut of the emotions from A to B.

In Carey, *Katherine Hepburn* (1985)

Scratch an actor and you'll find an actress.

Attr.

Richardson, Sir Ralph (1902–1983)
English actor

There are lots of reasons why people become actors. Some to hide themselves, and some to show themselves.

In K. Tynan, *Show People*

Shakespeare, William (1564–1616)
English dramatist, poet and actor

Like a dull actor now, I have forgot my part and I am out, Even to a full disgrace.

Coriolanus, V.iii

Tree, Sir Herbert Beerbohm (1853–1917)
English actor and theatre manager
Directing a group of sophisticated actresses

Ladies, just a little more virginity, if you don't mind.

In H. Teichmann, *Smart Aleck*

Warhol, Andy (c.1926–1987)
US painter, graphic designer and filmmaker
Of James Dean

He is not our hero because he was perfect. He is our hero because he perfectly represented the damaged and beautiful soul of our time.

In Brandreth, *Great Theatrical Disasters*

Wilde, Oscar (1854–1900)
Irish poet, dramatist, writer, critic and wit
Referring to Beerbohm Tree's unconscious adoption of some of the mannerisms of a character he was playing in one of Wilde's plays

Ah, every day dear Herbert becomes *de plus en plus Oscarié*. It is a wonderful case of nature imitating art.

Attr.

Williamson, Nicol (1938–)
Scottish actor
Of Sean Connery

Guys like him and Caine talk about acting as if they knew what it was.

Interview, Daily *Mail*, 1996

Winchell, Walter (1897–1972)
US drama critic, columnist and broadcaster
Referring to a show starring Earl Carroll
> I saw it at a disadvantage – the curtain was up.
>> In Whiteman, *Come to Judgement*

Windsor, Barbara (1937–)
English actress
Comment on being named a top BBC personality
> They say an actor is only as good as his parts. Well, my parts have done me pretty well, darling.
>> *The Times*, 1999

▶▶ ACTING; THEATRE

addiction

Auden, W.H. (1907–1973)
English poet, essayist, critic, teacher and dramatist
> All sin tends to be addictive, and the terminal point of addiction is what is called damnation.
>> *A Certain World* (1970)

Bankhead, Tallulah (1903–1968)
US actress
> Cocaine isn't habit-forming. I know, because I've been taking it for years.
>> Attr.

Burroughs, William S. (1914–1999)
US writer
> Junk is the ideal product… the ultimate merchandise. No sales talk necessary. The client will crawl through a sewer and beg to buy.
>> *Naked Lunch* (1959)

Jung, Carl Gustav (1875–1961)
Swiss psychiatrist and pupil of Freud
> Every form of addiction is a bad thing, irrespective of whether it is to alcohol, morphine or idealism.
>> *Memories, Dreams, Thoughts* (1962)

▶▶ DRUGS

admiration

Addison, Joseph (1672–1719)
English essayist, poet, playwright and statesman
> Admiration is a very short-lived passion that immediately decays upon growing familiar with its object, unless it be still fed with fresh discoveries, and kept alive by a perpetual succession of miracles rising into view.
>> *The Spectator*, 1711

Boileau-Despréaux, Nicolas (1636–1711)
French writer
> A fool always finds a greater fool to admire him.
>> *L'Art poétique*

adolescence

Frank, Anne (1929–1945)
Jewish diarist; died in Nazi concentration camp
> I think what is happening to me is so wonderful, and not only what can be seen on my body, but all that is taking place inside. I never discuss myself or any of these things with anybody; that is why I have to talk to myself about them.
>> *Diary of a Young Girl*

Searle, Ronald William Fordham (1920–)
English cartoonist
> In the spring your lovely Chloë lightly turns to one mass of spots.
>> *The Terror of St Trinian's* (1952)

adultery

Austen, Jane (1775–1817)
English writer
> I am proud to say that I have a very good eye at an Adultress, for tho' repeatedly assured that another in the same party was the She, I fixed upon the right one from the first.
>> Letter to Cassandra Austen, 1801

Bardot, Brigitte (1934–)
French actress
> It is better to be unfaithful than faithful without wanting to be.
>> *The Observer*, 1968

Benchley, Robert (1889–1945)
US essayist, humorist and actor
Comment on an office shared with Dorothy Parker
> One cubic foot less of space and it would have constituted adultery.
>> Attr.

Byron, Lord (1788–1824)
English poet satirist and traveller
> What men call gallantry, and gods adultery,
> Is much more common where the climate's sultry.
>> *Don Juan* (1824)

> Merely innocent flirtation.
> Not quite adultery, but adulteration.
>> *Don Juan* (1824)

Carter, Jimmy (1924–)
US Democrat statesman and President

I've looked on a lot of women with lust. I've committed adultery in my heart many times. God recognizes I will do this and forgives me.

Interview with Playboy, *1976*

Cary, Joyce (1888–1957)
English novelist

Sara could commit adultery at one end and weep for her sins at the other, and enjoy both operations at once.

The Horse's Mouth (1944)

Dring, Philip (1924–)
US preacher

I may commit adultery again if God moves me to it.

The Observer, 1980

Ekland, Britt (1942–)
Swedish actress

I say I don't sleep with married men, but what I mean is that I don't sleep with happily married men.

Attr.

Huxley, Aldous (1894–1963)
English writer, poet and critic

There are few who would not rather be taken in adultery than in provincialism.

Antic Hay (1923)

John Paul II (1920–)
Polish pope

Adultery in your heart is committed not only when you look with excessive sexual desire at a woman who is not your wife, but also if you look in the same manner at your wife.

The Observer, 1990

Maugham, William Somerset (1874–1965)
English writer, dramatist and physician

You know, of course, that the Tasmanians, who never committed adultery, are now extinct.

The Bread-Winner

Rabelais, François (c.1494–c.1553)
French monk, physician, satirist and humanist

This is a great year for cuckolds.

Pantagruel (1532)

Richelieu, Duc de (1766–1822)
French courtier, soldier and Prime Minister
On discovering his wife with her lover

Madame, you must really be more careful. Suppose it had been someone else who found you like this.

In Wallechinsky, The Book of Lists (1977)

Shakespeare, William (1564–1616)
English dramatist, poet and actor

Adultery?
Thou shalt not die. Die for adultery? No.
The wren goes to't, and the small gilded fly

Does lecher in my sight.
Let copulation thrive.

King Lear, IV.vi

▶▶ MARRIAGE; SEX

adults

Beauvoir, Simone de (1908–1986)
French writer, feminist critic and philosopher

Qu'est-ce qu'un adulte? Un enfant gonflé d'âge.
What is an adult? A child blown up by age.

The Woman Destroyed (1969)

Harris, Sydney J. (1917–)
US journalist

We have not passed that subtle line between childhood and adulthood until we move from the passive voice to the active voice – that is, until we have stopped saying 'It got lost', and say, 'I lost it'.

Attr.

Millay, Edna St Vincent (1892–1950)
US poet and dramatist

Was it for this I uttered prayers,
And sobbed and cursed and kicked the stairs,
That now, domestic as a plate,
I should retire at half-past eight?

'Grown-up' (1920)

Rostand, Jean (1894–1977)
French biologist

Etre adulte, c'est être seul.
To be an adult is to be alone.

Thoughts of a Biologist (1939)

Saint-Exupéry, Antoine de (1900–1944)
French author and aviator

Les grandes personnes ne comprennent rien toutes seules, et c'est fatigant, pour les enfants, de toujours et toujours leur donner des explications.
Grown-ups never understand anything for themselves, and it is tiresome for children to be always and forever explaining things to them.

The Little Prince (1943)

Shakespeare, William (1564–1616)
English dramatist, poet and actor

Your lordship, though not clean past your youth, hath yet some smack of age in you, some relish of the saltness of time.

Henry IV, Part 2, I.ii

Szasz, Thomas (1920–)
Hungarian-born US psychiatrist and writer

A child becomes an adult when he realizes that he has a right not only to be right but also to be wrong.

The Second Sin (1973)

adventure

Churchill, Jennie Jerome (1854–1921)
US-born English hostess and author
> … and we owe something to extravagance, for thrift and adventure seldom go hand in hand …
> *Pearson's*, 1915

Dukes, Ashley (1885 –1959)
> Adventure must be held in delicate fingers. It should be handled, not embraced. It should be sipped, not swallowed at a gulp.
> *The Man with a Load of Mischief* (1924)

Least-Heat Moon, William (1939–)
US author
> There are two kinds of adventurers: those who go truly hoping to find adventure and those who go secretly hoping they won't.
> *Blue Highways* (1983)

adversity

Carlyle, Thomas (1795–1881)
Scottish historian, biographer, critic, and essayist
> Adversity is sometimes hard upon a man; but for one man who can stand prosperity, there are a hundred that will stand adversity.
> *On Heroes, Hero-Worship, and the Heroic in History* (1841)

Chaucer, Geoffrey (c.1340–1400)
English poet, public servant and courtier
> For of fortunes sharpe adversitee
> The worste kynde of infortune is this,
> A man to han ben in prosperitee,
> And it remembren, whan it passed is.
> *Troilus and Criseyde*, III

Shakespeare, William (1564–1616)
English dramatist, poet and actor
> Sweet are the uses of adversity;
> Which, like the toad, ugly and venomous,
> Wears yet a precious jewel in his head.
> *As You Like It*, II.i

advertising

Acheson, Dean (1893–1971)
US Democrat politician
> Time spent in the advertising business seems to create a permanent deformity like the Chinese habit of foot-binding.
> David S. McLellan and David C. Acheson, *Among Friends* (1980)

Allen, Fred (1894–1956)
US vaudeville performer and comedian
> An advertising agency is 85 per cent confusion and 15 per cent commission.
> *Treadmill to Oblivion* (1954)

Barton, Bruce (1886–1967)
US advertising agent and writer
> In good times, people want to advertise; in bad times, they have to.
> *Town & Country*, 1955

Beatty, Warren (1937–)
US actor and director
On refusing to grant television rights for his films because of cuts made for commercial breaks
> When you mutilate movies for mass media, you tamper with the hearts and minds of America.
> *New York Times*, 1985

Britt, Steuart Henderson (1907–)
> Doing business without advertising is like winking at a girl in the dark. You know what you are doing, but nobody else does.
> *New York Herald Tribune*, 1956

Douglas, Norman (1868–1952)
Austrian-born Scottish writer
> You can tell the ideals of a nation by its advertisements.
> *South Wind* (1917)

Fincher, David (1963–)
US film director
> Advertising has us chasing cars and clothes, working jobs we hate, so we can buy shit we don't need.
> *Fight Club* (film, 1999)

Fitzgerald, Zelda (1900–1948)
US writer
> We grew up founding our dreams on the infinite promise of American advertising. I still believe that one can learn to play the piano by mail and that mud will give you a perfect complexion.
> *Save Me the Waltz* (1932)

Huxley, Aldous (1894–1963)
English writer, poet and critic
> It is far easier to write ten passably effective Sonnets, good enough to take in the not too inquiring critic, than one effective advertisement that will take in a few thousand of the uncritical buying public.
> *On the Margin* (1923)

Jefferson, Thomas (1743–1826)
US Democrat statesman and President
> Advertisements contain the only truths to be relied on in a newspaper.
> Letter, 1819

Johnson, Samuel (1709–1784)
English lexicographer, poet, critic, conversationalist and essayist

Promise, large promise, is the soul of an
advertisement.

The Idler (1758–1760)

Lahr, John (1941–)
Society drives people crazy with lust and calls it
advertising.

The Guardian, 1989

Leacock, Stephen (1869–1944)
English-born Canadian humorist, writer and economist
Advertising may be described as the science of
arresting the human intelligence long enough to
get money from it.

In Prochow, *The Public Speaker's Treasure Chest*

Leverhulme, Lord (1851–1925)
English soap manufacturer and philanthropist
Half the money I spend on advertising is wasted,
and the trouble is I don't know which half.

In Ogilvy, *Confessions of an Advertising Man* (1963)

McDermott, John W. (1937–)
Hawaiian travel writer
Ninety-Mile Beach was obviously named by one
of New Zealand's first advertising copywriters …
It is fifty-six miles long.

How to Get Lost and Found in New Zealand (1976)

McLuhan, Marshall (1911–1980)
Canadian communications theorist
Ads are the cave art of the twentieth century.

Culture Is Our Business (1970)

Nash, Ogden (1902–1971)
US poet
I think that I shall never see
A billboard lovely as a tree.
Indeed, unless the billboards fall
I'll never see a tree at all.

'Song of the Open Road' (1933)

Beneath this slab
John Brown is stowed.
He watched the ads,
And not the road.

'Lather as You Go' (1942)

Packard, Vance (1914–)
US writer
The Hidden Persuaders.

Title of book, 1957

advertising slogans

Access takes the waiting out of wanting.

Access credit card, UK, 1973

Access – your flexible friend.

Access credit card, UK, 1981

A Mars a day helps you work, rest and play.

Mars bars, from 1960

And all because the lady loves Milk Tray.

Cadbury's Milk Tray chocolates, 1968 onwards

Any time, any place, anywhere.

Martini, UK, 1970s

Apple – The Power to be Your best.

Apple Computers, US, 1986

Ask the man who owns one.

Packard, USA, 1902

Australians wouldn't give a XXXX for anything
else.

Castlemaine lager, 1986 onwards

Beanz means Heinz.

Heinz baked beans

Bounty – The Taste of Paradise.

Breakfast of champions.

Wheaties cereal, USA, 1950

Can you tell Stork from butter?

Stork margarine

Chocolates with the less fattening centres.

Maltesers chocolates, UK, 1965

Cool as a mountain stream.

Consulate menthol cigarettes

Does she … or doesn't she?

Harmony hairspray, 1980s

Don't be vague – ask for Haig.

Haig whisky, c.1936

Don't forget the fruit gums, Mum.

Rowntree's Fruit Gums, 1958 onwards

Don't just book it – Thomas Cook it.

Thomas Cook Travel Agents

Don't leave home without it.

American Express card, US, 1981

Drinka Pinta Milka Day.

British Milk Marketing Board, 1958

Eight out of ten cats prefer Whiskas.

Whiskas catfood, 1970s

Everyone's a fruit and nut case.

Cadbury's Fruit and Nut chocolate, 1964 onwards

Everything you hear is true.

Pioneer hi-fi equipment, 1970s

For Mash Get Smash.

Smash instant mashed potato

Full of Eastern promise.

Fry's Turkish Delight, 1950s onwards

Good to the last drop.
Remark made by Theodore Roosevelt, 1907, about Maxwell House coffee; later used as an advertising slogan

Go to work on an egg.
British Egg Marketing Board

Guinness is good for you.
Guinness, c.1930s

Happiness is a cigar called Hamlet.
Hamlet cigars, UK

Have a break, have a Kit-Kat.
Rowntree's Kit-Kat chocolate bars, from c.1955

Heineken refreshes the parts other beers cannot reach.
Heineken lager, 1975 onwards

Horlicks guards against night starvation.
Horlicks milk drink

I'd like to buy the world a Coke.
Coca-Cola, 1971

If we don't have the lowest fare, we probably don't fly there.
Continental Airlines, US

If you want to get ahead, get a hat.
UK Hat Council, 1965

I like Aeroplane Jelly … Aeroplane Jelly for me, I like it for dinner, I like it for tea.
Originally sung by five year old Joy King, it began in 1938 and was in use in the 1980s

I'm only here for the beer.
Double Diamond beer

Inter-City makes the going easy, and the coming back.
British Rail, 1980

It beats as it sweeps as it cleans.
Advertising slogan for Hoover vacuum cleaners, 1919

It's a lot less bovver with a hover.
Qualcast Lawnmowers, UK

It's fingerlickin' good.
Kentucky Fried Chicken Co., US, 1950s

It's good to listen.
British Telecom, from 1997

It's good to talk.
British Telecom, from 1994

It's the real thing.
Coca-Cola, 1970

Just do it.
Nike

Kills all known germs.
Domestos bleach, 1959

Let Hertz put you in the driver's seat.
Hertz car rental, 1962

Let the train take the strain.
British Rail, 1970

Let your fingers do the walking.
Yellow Pages, from American Telephone and Telegraph Company, 1960s

Live life to the Max.
Pepsi

Lucozade refreshes you through the ups and downs of the day.
Beecham Foods, c.1978

Make today a Heinz Souperday.
Heinz soups, 1968

Man invented time – Seiko perfected it.
Seiko watches, 1980s

Mean! Moody! Magnificent!
Promotional slogan for the film The Outlaw, 1943

Milk from contented cows.
Carnation Milk, 1906

Murray Mints! Murray Mints!
Too-good-to-hurry-Mints.
Advertising jingle for Murray Mints, UK from late 1950s

My goodness, my Guinness.
Guinness, c.1930s

Nine out of ten screen stars use Lux toilet soap.
Lux soap, USA, late 1920s

Nothing over sixpence.
Woolworth stores, UK, from 1909

Now hands that do dishes can be soft as your face.
Jingle for Fairy washing-up liquid

Player's please.
John Player and Sons cigarettes

P-p-p-pick up a Penguin.
Penguin chocolate biscuits

Pure Genius.
Guinness, 1994

Put a tiger in your tank.
Esso, US, 1964

Say it with flowers.
Advertisement for the Society of American florists, late 1920s

Sch … you know who.
Schweppes mineral drinks, 1960s

Size matters.
Renault Clio

Snap! Crackle! Pop!
Kellogg's Rice Crispies, USA, c.1928

Stop me and buy one.
> Wall's ice-cream, 1922

Test drive a Macintosh.
> Apple Computers, US, 1984

Tetley make tea-bags make tea.
> Tetley's tea

That'll do nicely, Sir!
> American Express card, UK, late 1970s onwards

The bank that likes to say yes.
> Trustee Savings Bank

The customer is always right.
> Slogan devised by Gordon Selfridge (1858–1947) to advertise Selfridge's department store

The future's bright, the future's Orange.
> Orange mobile phones

The greatest motion picture ever made.
> Promotional slogan for the film *Gone with the Wind*, 1939

The greatest show on earth.
> Barnum and Bailey's circus, from 1881

The mint with the hole.
> Life-Savers, US, 1920; Rowntree's Polo mints, UK from 1947

They're g-r-r-r-eat!
> Long-running slogan for Kellogg's Frosties cereal

Things go better with Coke.
> Coca-Cola, 1963

Think Different.
> Apple Computers, US, 1998

Top breeders recommend it.
> Pedigree Chum dog food, UK 1964

Tunes help you breathe more easily.
> Tunes throat lozenges

Progress through technology
Vorsprung durch Technik.
> Audi cars, from 1986

We're Getting There.
> British Rail, 1980s

We're with the Woolwich.
> Woolwich Equitable Building Society, UK, from late 1970s

Where do you want to go today?
> Microsoft

Where's the beef?
> Wendy's Hamburgers

Worth a guinea a box.
> Beechams pills, c.1940

You can be sure of Shell.
> Shell UK, c.1931

You'll look a little lovelier each day

With fabulous pink Camay.
> Camay soap, c.1960

You'll wonder where the yellow went
When you brush your teeth with Pepsodent.
> Advertising jingle for Pepsodent toothpaste, USA, 1950s

You only fit double glazing once, so fit the best.
> Everest Double Glazing, UK

You press the button, and we'll do the rest.
> Kodak cameras and film

You too can have a body like mine.
> Charles Atlas body-building courses

You've come a long way baby.
> Virginia Slims cigarettes

advice

Adams, Douglas (1952–)
English writer
> Don't panic.
> > *The Hitch Hiker's Guide to the Galaxy* (1979)

Addison, Joseph (1672–1719)
English essayist, poet, playwright and statesman
> A woman seldom asks advice before she has bought her wedding clothes.
> > *The Spectator*, September 1712

Auden, W.H. (1907–1973)
English poet, essayist, critic, teacher and dramatist
> Read *The New Yorker*, trust in God;
> And take short views.
> > *Collected Poems, 1939–1947*

Avery, Oswald Theodore (1877–1955)
Canadian bacteriologist
> Whenever you fall, pick up something.
> > Attr.

Bierce, Ambrose (1842–c.1914)
US writer, verse writer and soldier
> *Advice*: The smallest current coin.
> > *The Cynic's Word Book* (1906)

Bismarck, Prince Otto von (1815–1898)
First Chancellor of the German Reich
> To youth I have but three words of counsel – work, work, work.
> > Attr.

Borrow, George (1803–1881)
English writer and linguist
> Fear God, and take your own part.
> > *The Romany Rye* (1857)

Burns, Robert (1759–1796)
Scottish poet and song writer
> Ah! gentle dames, it gars me greet,

To think how monie counsels sweet,
How monie lengthen'd, sage advices
The husband frae the wife despises!

'Tam o' Shanter' (1790)

Burton, Robert (1577–1640)
English clergyman and writer
Who cannot give good counsel? 'tis cheap, it costs them nothing.

Anatomy of Melancholy (1621)

Chesterfield, Lord (1694–1773)
English politician and letter writer
In matters of religion and matrimony I never give any advice; because I will not have anybody's torments in this world or the next laid to my charge.

Letter to A.C. Stanhope, 1765

Advice is seldom welcome; and those who want it the most, always like it the least.

Letter to his son, 1748

Collins, John Churton (1848–1908)
English scholar, critic and essayist
To ask advice is in nine cases out of ten to tout for flattery.

In L.C. Collins, Life of John Churton Collins (1912)

Edward VIII (later Duke of Windsor) (1894–1972)
King of the United Kingdom; abdicated 11 December 1936
Perhaps one of the only positive pieces of advice that I was ever given was that supplied by an old courtier who observed: 'Only two rules really count. Never miss an opportunity to relieve yourself; never miss a chance to sit down and rest your feet.'

A King's Story (1951)

Emerson, Ralph Waldo (1803–1882)
US poet, essayist, transcendentalist and teacher
It was a high counsel that I once heard given to a young person, – 'Always do what you are afraid to do.'

Essays, First Series (1841)

Gay, John (1685–1732)
English poet, dramatist and librettist
Can Love be controll'd by advice?

The Beggar's Opera (1728)

Groening, Matt
US cartoonist
Instruction in Homer Simpson's brain to Homer during communal crisis
Keep looking shocked and move slowly towards the cakes.

The Simpsons, TV cartoon series

Harris, George (1844–1922)
US churchman and educator
In his address to students at the start of a new academic year

I intended to give you some advice but now I remember how much is left over from last year unused.

In Braude, Braude's Second Encyclopedia (1957)

Jong, Erica (1942–)
US writer
Advice is what we ask for when we already know the answer but wish we didn't.

How to Save Your Own Life (1977)

La Rochefoucauld (1613–1680)
French writer
On ne donne rien si libéralement que ses conseils.
One gives nothing so generously as advice.

Maximes (1678)

Proverbs
A good scare is worth more than good advice.

Don't teach your grandmother to suck eggs.

Pythagoras (6th century BC)
Greek philosopher and mathematician
Abstain from beans.

Attr.

Runcie, Robert (1921–2000)
On his discussions with the Prince and Princess of Wales prior to marrying them
My advice was delicately poised between the cliché and the indiscretion.

The Times, 1981

Saki (1870–1916)
Burmese-born British writer
In baiting a mouse-trap with cheese, always leave room for the mouse.

The Square Egg (1924), 'The Infernal Parliament'

Smith, Sydney (1771–1845)
English clergyman, essayist, journalist and wit
Take short views, hope for the best, and trust in God.

In Holland, A Memoir of the Reverend Sydney Smith (1855)

Sorkin, Aaron (1961–)
US screenwriter
Walk softly and carry an armoured tank division, I always say.

A Few Good Men (film, 1992)

Steinbeck, John (1902–1968)
US writer
No one wants advice – only corroboration.

Attr.

Sullivan, Annie (1866–1936)
US lecturer, writer and teacher
It's queer how ready people always are with advice in any real or imaginary emergency, and no matter how many times experience has shown them to be wrong, they continue to set

forth their opinions, as if they had received them from the Almighty!

Letter, 1887

Thackeray, William Makepeace (1811–1863)
Indian-born English writer
> They tell me not to drink, and I do drink ... They tell me not to eat, and I do eat.
>> *The Letters and Private Papers of William Makepeace Thackeray* (1946)

Thoreau, Henry David (1817–1862)
US essayist, social critic and writer
> I have lived some thirty years on this planet, and I have yet to hear the first syllable of valuable or even earnest advice from my seniors.
>> *Walden* (1854)

Walden, George (1939–)
British Conservative politician and diplomat
Advice for those travelling with the Queen
> Never turn down a drink, unless it is of local manufacture.
>> *The Times*, 1999

Wellington, Duke of (1769–1852)
Irish-born British military commander and statesman
Advice when asked by Queen Victoria how to remove sparrows from the Crystal Palace
> Sparrowhawks, Ma'am.
>> Attr.

West, Nathaniel (1903–1940)
US novelist
> Are you in trouble? Do you need advice? Write to Miss Lonelyhearts and she will help.
>> *Miss Lonelyhearts* (1933)

Wilde, Oscar (1854–1900)
Irish poet, dramatist, writer, critic and wit
> It is always a silly thing to give advice, but to give good advice is absolutely fatal.
>> Attr.

affairs

Maclaine, Shirley (1934–)
US actress
On her friendship with Andrew Peacock
> I thought as long as he's Minister for Foreign Affairs I might as well give him one he'd never forget.
>> *Melbourne Herald*, 1979

Parker, Dorothy (1893–1967)
US writer, poet, critic and wit
Reviewing Asquith's *Lay Sermons*
> The affair between Margot Asquith and Margot

Asquith will live as one of the prettiest love stories in all literature.
>> *New Yorker*, 1927

▶▶ ADULTERY; MARRIAGE; SEX

africa

Macmillan, Harold (1894–1986)
British Conservative Prime Minister
> The most striking of all the impressions I have formed since I left London a month ago is of the strength of this African national consciousness. The wind of change is blowing through this continent.
>> Speech, 1960, written by Sir David Hunt

Malcolm X (1925–1965)
US black leader
> The soul of Africa is still reflected in the music played by the black man. In everything else we do we still are African in color, feeling, everything. And we will always be that whether we like it or not.
>> Speech, Harvard Law School, 1964

Mugabe, Robert (1924–)
President of Zimbabwe
On violence against white farm owners
> This is Africa. This isn't Little Puddleton-in-the-Marsh. They behave differently. They think nothing of sticking tent poles up each other's what-not and doing filthy beastly things to each other. It does happen. I'm afraid.
>> *The Sunday Times*, 2000

Pliny the Elder (AD 23–79)
Roman scholar
> *Ex Africa semper aliquid novi.*
> There is always something new out of Africa.
>> *Historia Naturalis*

Plomer, William (1903–1973)
South African-born British writer and editor
> Men being absent, Africa is good.
>> 'The Wild Doves at Louis Trichardt' (1960)

> Africa is not the white man's country.
>> *Turbott Wolfe* (1926)

Schweitzer, Albert (1875–1965)
French Protestant theologian, physician and musician
> The African is my brother – but he is my younger brother by several centuries.
>> *The Observer*, 1955

Van der Post, Sir Laurens (1906–1996)
South African explorer and writer
> Africa has always walked in my mind proudly upright, an African giant among the other continents, toes well dug into the final ocean of one hemisphere, rising to its full height in the

greying skies of the other; head and shoulders broad, square and enduring, making light of the bagful of blue Mediterranean slung over its back as it marches patiently through time.

Flamingo Feather (1955)

the afterlife

Beckett, Samuel (1906–1989)
Irish dramatist, writer and poet
Clov: Do you believe in the life to come?
Hamm: Mine was always that.

Endgame (1958)

Coward, Sir Noël (1899–1973)
English dramatist, actor, producer and composer
We have no reliable guarantee that the afterlife will be any less exasperating than this one, have we?

Blithe Spirit (1941)

Gregory, Lady Isabella Augusta (1852–1932)
Irish dramatist, writer and translator
I believe we shall meet again after death ... but if we don't you will have the worst of it, for you can't say anything to me, and if we do, I will say 'I told you so!'.

In Mary-Lou Kohfeldt, *Lady Gregory* (1985)

Pope, Alexander (1688–1744)
English poet, translator and editor
Go, like the Indian, in another life
Expect thy dog, thy bottle, and thy wife.

Essay on Man, IV (1734)

Shinran (1173–1263)
Even good people achieve their rebirth in the Land of Perfect Bliss; then how much more so should the case be with evil persons!

Tannishó (c.1290)

Updike, John (1932–)
US writer, poet and critic
In fact we do not try to picture the afterlife, nor is it ourselves in our nervous tics and optical flecks that we wish to perpetuate; it is the self as the window on the world that we can't bear to think of shutting.

Self-Consciousness: Memoirs (1989)

▶▶ DEATH; HEAVEN

age

Adams, John Quincy (1767–1848)
US lawyer, diplomat and President
I inhabit a weak, frail, decayed tenement; battered by the winds and broken in on by the storms, and, from all I can learn, the landlord

does not intend to repair.

Attr.

Adenauer, Konrad (1876–1967)
German Chancellor
To his doctor
I haven't asked you to make me young again. All I want is to go on getting older.

Attr.

Aimeé, Anouk (1932–)
French actress
You can only perceive real beauty in a person as they get older.

The Guardian, 1988

Allen, Dave (1936–)
Irish comedian and television personality
I still think of myself as I was 25 years ago. Then I look in a mirror and see an old bastard and I realise it's me.

The Independent, 1993

Allen, Woody (1935–)
US film director, writer, actor and comedian
I recently turned sixty. Practically a third of my life is over.

The Observer Review, 1996

Anonymous
In ancient times a woman was considered old at the age of forty. Today a woman of that age is only twenty-nine.

The editors are well under thirty and intend to remain so.

Editorial, *The Canadian Mercury*, 1928

Aristophanes (c.445–385 BC)
Greek playwright
Old age is a second childhood.

Clouds, 1417

Arnold, Matthew (1822–1888)
English poet, critic, essayist and educationist
I am past thirty, and three parts iced over.

Letter to A.H. Clough, 1853

Auber, Daniel François Esprit (1782–1871)
French opera composer
Ageing seems to be the only available way to live a long time.

Attr.

Bainbridge, Beryl (1934–)
English novelist
The older one becomes the quicker the present fades into sepia and the past looms up in glorious technicolour.

The Observer, 1998

Baker, Tom (1934–)
English actor and writer
On becoming a pensioner

I am saving up for my own hospital trolley.

The Times, 1999

Baruch, Bernard (1870–1965)
US financier, government advisor and writer
> I will never be an old man. To me, old age is always fifteen years older than I am.

The Observer, 1955

Beauvoir, Simone de (1908–1986)
French writer, feminist critic and philosopher
> Since it is the Other within us who is old, it is natural that the revelation of our age should come to us from outside – from others. We do not accept it willingly.

The Coming of Age (1970)

Benny, Jack (1894–1974)
US comedian
> Age is strictly a case of mind over matter. If you don't mind, it doesn't matter.

New York Times, 1974

Billings, Josh (1818–1885)
US writer, philosopher and lecturer
> I've never known a person to live to 110 or more, and then die, to be remarkable for anything else.

Attr.

Binyon, Laurence (1869–1943)
English poet, art historian and critic
> They shall grow not old, as we that are left grow old:
> Age shall not weary them, nor the years condemn.
> At the going down of the sun and in the morning
> We will remember them.

'For the Fallen' (1914)

Blake, Eubie (1883–1983)
US jazz performer and songwriter
He died five days after his hundredth birthday
> If I'd known I was gonna live this long, I'd have taken better care of myself.

The Observer, 1983

Blythe, Ronald (1922–)
English writer
> To be old is to be part of a huge and ordinary multitude … the reason why old age was venerated in the past was because it was extraordinary.

The View in Winter (1979)

Brenan, Gerald (1894–1987)
English writer
> Old age takes away from us what we have inherited and gives us what we have earned.

Thoughts in a Dry Season (1978)

Browning, Robert (1812–1889)
English poet
> Grow old along with me!
> The best is yet to be,
> The last of life for which the first was made:
> Our times are in His hand
> Who saith, 'A whole I planned,
> Youth shows but half; trust God: see all, nor be afraid!'.

'Rabbi Ben Ezra' (1864)

Buck, Pearl S. (1892–1973)
US writer and dramatist
> Ah well, perhaps one has to be very old before one learns how to be amused rather than shocked.

China, Past and Present (1972)

Burchill, Julie (1960–)
English writer
> Fame is no sanctuary from the passing of youth … suicide is much easier and more acceptable in Hollywood than growing old gracefully.

Girls on Film (1986)

Burke, Edmund (1729–1797)
Irish-born British statesman and philosopher
> The arrogance of age must submit to be taught by youth.

Letter to Fanny Burney, 1782

Burns, Robert (1759–1796)
Scottish poet and song writer
> John Anderson my jo, John,
> When we were first acquent,
> Your locks were like the raven,
> Your bonie brow was brent
> John Anderson, my jo, John,
> We clamb the hills thegither;
> And mony a cantie day, John,
> We've had wi ane anither;
> Now we maun totter down, John:
> And hand in hand we'll go,
> And sleep thegither at the foot,
> John Anderson, my jo.

'John Anderson My Jo' (1790)

Byron, Lord (1788–1824)
English poet satirist and traveller
> What is the worst of woes that wait on age?
> What stamps the wrinkle deeper on the brow?
> To view each loved one blotted from life's page,
> And be alone on earth, as I am now.

Childe Harold's Pilgrimage (1818)

> I am ashes where once I was fire.

'To the Countess of Blessington' (1823)

> Years steal
> Fire from the mind as vigour from the limb;
> And life's enchanted cup but sparkles near the brim.

Childe Harold's Pilgrimage (1818)

Calment, Jeanne (1875–1997)
Frenchwoman, renowned for her longevity
Reply to someone who asked what she would like for her
121st birthday
> Respect.

The Mail on Sunday, 1996

Campbell, Joseph (1879–1944)
Irish poet and republican
> As a white candle
> In a holy place,
> So is the beauty
> Of an aged face.

'The Old Woman' (1913)

Carroll, Lewis (1832–1898)
English writer and photographer
> 'You are old, Father William,' the young man
> said,
> 'And your hair has become very white;
> And yet you incessantly stand on your head –
> Do you think, at your age, it is right?'

> 'In my youth,' Father William replied to his son,
> 'I feared it might injure the brain;
> But now that I'm perfectly sure I have none,
> Why, I do it again and again.'

Alice's Adventures in Wonderland (1865)

Chevalier, Maurice (1888–1972)
French singer and actor
> I'm over eighty in a world where the young
> reject the old with more intensity than ever
> before … Now I'd like my old age to be my best
> performance. Death is the best exit.

In Behr, *Thank Heaven for Little Girls* (1993)

> I prefer old age to the alternative.

Attr.

Christina of Sweden (1626–1689)
Queen of Sweden
> We grow old more through indolence, than
> through age.

Pensées de Christine, reine de Suede (1825)

Churchill, Charles (1731–1764)
English poet, political writer and clergyman
> Old-age, a second child, by Nature curs'd
> With more and greater evils than the first,
> Weak, sickly, full of pains; in ev'ry breath
> Railing at life, and yet afraid of death.

Gotham (1764)

Cicero (106–43 BC)
Roman orator, statesman, essayist and letter writer
> No man is so old as to think he cannot live one
> more year.

Attr.

Collins, Mortimer (1827–1876)
English poet and writer
> A man is as old as he's feeling,

> A woman as old as she looks.

'The Unknown Quantity'

Compton-Burnett, Dame Ivy (1884–1969)
English novelist
Describing a certain woman's age
> Pushing forty? She's clinging on to it for dear
> life.

Attr.

Day, Doris (1924–)
US singer and actress
> The really frightening thing about middle age is
> the knowledge that you'll grow out of it.

A. E. Hotchner, *Doris Day: Her Own Story* (1976)

Depardieu, Gérard (1948–)
French actor
> At twenty you have many desires which hide the
> truth, but beyond forty there are only real and
> fragile truths – your abilities and your failings.

The Daily Mail, 1991

Dewey, John (1859–1952)
US educationist, philosopher and reformer
> It is strange that the one thing that every person
> looks forward to, namely old age, is the one
> thing for which no preparation is made.

Attr.

Disraeli, Benjamin (1804–1881)
English statesman and writer
> When a man fell into his anecdotage it was a
> sign for him to retire from the world.

Lothair (1870)

Dryden, John (1631–1700)
English poet, satirist, dramatist and critic
> None would live past years again,
> Yet all hope pleasure in what yet remain;
> And, from the dregs of life, think to receive,
> What the first sprightly running could not give.

Aureng-Zebe (1675)

Durrell, Lawrence (1912–1990)
Indian-born British poet and writer
> Old age is an insult. It's like being smacked.

The Sunday Times, 1988

Edmond, James (1859–1933)
Scottish-born Australian writer and editor
Caption to a drawing of three women by Norman Lindsay
> We walk along the gas-lit street in a dreadful
> row, we three,
> The woman I was, the woman I am, and the
> woman I'll one day be.

In Moore, *The Story of Australian Art*

Eliot, T.S. (1888–1965)
US-born British poet, verse dramatist and critic
> I grow old … I grow old …
> I shall wear the bottoms of my trousers
> rolled.

Shall I part my hair behind? Do I dare to eat a peach?
I shall wear white flannel trousers, and walk upon the beach.
I have heard the mermaids singing, each to each.
I do not think that they will sing to me.
> 'The Love Song of J. Alfred Prufrock' (1917)

The years between fifty and seventy are the hardest You are always being asked to do things, and you are not yet decrepit enough to turn them down.
> *Time*, 1950

Elizabeth, the Queen Mother (1900–)
Queen of the United Kingdom and mother of Elizabeth II
On the retouching of a photograph to disguise wrinkles
> I would not want it to be thought that I had lived for all these years without having anything to show for it.
> In *The Guardian*, 2000

Emerson, Ralph Waldo (1803–1882)
US poet, essayist, transcendentalist and teacher
> Old age brings along with its ugliness the comfort that you will soon be out of it, – which ought to be a substantial relief to such discontented pendulums as we are. To be out of the war, out of debt, out of the drouth, out of the blues, out of the dentist's hands, out of the second thoughts, mortifications, and remorses that inflict such twinges and shooting pains, – out of the next winter, and the high prices, and company below your ambition, – surely these are soothing hints.
> *Journals*, 1864

> Spring still makes spring in the mind,
> When sixty years are told.
> *Poems* (1847)

Engel, Sigmund (b. 1869)
> The age of a woman doesn't mean a thing. The best tunes are played on the oldest fiddles.
> *Newsweek*, 1949

Estienne, Henri (1531–1598)
French scholar, lexicographer and publisher
> *Si jeunesse savoit; si vieillesse pouvoit.*
> If only youth knew; if only age could.
> *Les Prémices* (1594)

Fairburn, A.R.D. (1904–1957)
New Zealand poet
> The years have stolen
> all her loveliness,
> her days are fallen
> in the long wet grass
> like petals shaken
> from the lilac's bosom.
> *Collected Poems* (1966)

Feiffer, Jules (1929–)
US cartoonist
> At sixteen I was stupid, confused, insecure and indecisive. At twenty-five I was wise, self-confident, prepossessing and assertive. At forty-five I am stupid, confused, insecure and indecisive. Who would have supposed that maturity is only a short break in adolescence?
> *The Observer*, 1974

Fonda, Jane (1937–)
US actress and political activist
> A man has every season while a woman only has the right to spring. That disgusts me.
> *Daily Mail*, 1989

Franklin, Benjamin (1706–1790)
US statesman, scientist, political critic and printer
> At twenty years of age, the will reigns; at thirty, the wit; and at forty, the judgement.
> *Poor Richard's Almanac* (1741)

Gibbon, Edward (1737–1794)
English historian, politician and memoirist
> I must reluctantly observe that two causes, the abbreviation of time, and the failure of hope, will always tinge with a browner shade the evening of life.
> *Memoirs of My Life and Writings* (1796)

Gielgud, Sir John (1904–2000)
English actor
> When you're my age, you just never risk being ill – because then everyone says: Oh, he's done for.
> *Sunday Express Magazine*, 1988

Gogol, Nicolai Vasilyevich (1809–1852)
Russian writer and soldier
> Threatening, terrifying is oncoming old age, but nothing will reverse and return!
> *Dead Souls* (1835–1842)

Goldsmith, Oliver (c.1728–1774)
Irish dramatist, poet and writer
> I love every thing that's old: old friends, old times, old manners, old books, old wine.
> *She Stoops to Conquer* (1773)

Gonne, Maud (1865–1953)
Irish patriot and philanthropist
> Oh how you hate old age – well so do I … but I, who am more a rebel against man than you, rebel less against nature, and accept the inevitable and go with it gently into the unknown.
> Letter to W.B. Yeats

Grant, Cary (1904–1986)
English-born US film actor
Responding to a telegram received by his agent inquiring: 'How old Cary Grant?'

'Old Cary Grant fine. How you?'.

> In Halliwell, *Filmgoer's Book of Quotes* (1973)

Hall, Sir Peter (1930–)
English theatre director

> We do not necessarily improve with age: for better or worse we become more like ourselves.
>
> *The Observer*, 1988

Hamilton, Elizabeth (1758–1816)
Scottish poet and novelist

> With expectation beating high,
> Myself I now desired to spy;
> And straight I in a glass surveyed
> An antique lady, much decayed.
>
> In Sarah Hale, *Biography of Distinguished Women* (1876)

Harrison, Tony (1937–)
English poet

> Perhaps with age I've learned to let go of things and people, not to possess or confine them.
>
> Attr.

Hilton, James (1900–1954)
English writer and screenwriter

> Anno domini … that's the most fatal complaint of all, in the end.
>
> *Goodbye, Mr Chips* (1934)

Holmes, Oliver Wendell (1809–1894)
US physician, poet, writer and scientist

> For him in vain the envious seasons roll
> Who bears eternal summer in his soul.
>
> 'The Old Player' (1861)

> To be seventy years young is sometimes far more cheerful and hopeful than to be forty years old.
>
> 'On the Seventieth Birthday of Julia Ward Howe' (1889)

Holmes, Oliver Wendell, Jr (1841–1935)
US jurist and judge
At the age of 86, on seeing a pretty girl

> Oh, to be seventy again!
>
> In Fadiman, *The American Treasury*

Hope, Bob (1903–)
US comedian

> I don't generally feel anything until noon, then it's time for my nap.
>
> *International Herald Tribune*, 1990

Irving, Washington (1783–1859)
US writer and diplomat

> Whenever a man's friends begin to compliment him about looking young, he may be sure that they think he is growing old.
>
> *Bracebridge Hall* (1822)

James, Alice (1848–1892)
US diarist

> It is so comic to hear oneself called old, even at ninety I suppose!
>
> In Leon Edel (ed.), *The Diary of Alice James*, 1889

Johnson, Samuel (1709–1784)
English lexicographer, poet, critic, conversationalist and essayist

> At seventy-seven it is time to be in earnest.
>
> *A Journey to the Western Islands of Scotland* (1775)

> There is a wicked inclination in most people to suppose an old man decayed in his intellects. If a young or middle-aged man, when leaving a company, does not recollect where he laid his hat, it is nothing; but if the same inattention is discovered in an old man, people will shrug up their shoulders, and say, 'His memory is going.'
>
> In Boswell, *The Life of Samuel Johnson* (1791)

Lang, Andrew (1844–1912)
Scottish poet, writer, mythologist and anthropologist

> Our hearts are young 'neath wrinkled rind:
> Life's more amusing than we thought.
>
> 'Ballade of Middle Age'

Larkin, Philip (1922–1985)
English poet, writer and librarian

> Perhaps being old is having lighted rooms
> Inside your head, and people in them, acting.
> People you know, yet can't quite
> name.
>
> 'The Old Fools' (1974)

Laurence, Margaret (1926–1987)
Canadian novelist
Address at Trent University, 1983

> If, as you grow older, you feel you are also growing stupider, do not worry. This is normal, and usually occurs around the time when your children, now grown, are discovering the opposite – they now see that you aren't nearly as stupid as they had believed when they were young teenagers. Take heart from that.
>
> Quoted in *The Globe and Mail*, 1989

Lenclos, Ninon de (1620–1705)
French courtesan

> *La vieillesse est l'enfer des femmes.*
> Old age is woman's hell.
>
> Attr.

Lloyd, Harold (1893–1971)
Film comedian
Reply when, aged 77, he was asked his age

> I am just turning forty and taking my time about it.
>
> *The Times*, 1970

Marx, Groucho (1895–1977)
US comedian

> Age is not a particularly interesting subject.

Anyone can get old. All you have to do is live long enough.

Groucho and Me (1959)

Maugham, William Somerset (1874–1965)
English writer, dramatist and physician
Said on his ninetieth birthday

I am sick of this way of life. The weariness and sadness of old age make it intolerable. I have walked with death in hand, and death's own hand is warmer than my own. I don't wish to live any longer.

In M.B. Strauss, *Familiar Medical Quotations*

From the earliest times the old have rubbed it into the young that they are wiser than they, and before the young had discovered what nonsense this was they were old too, and it profited them to carry on the imposture.

Cakes and Ale (1930)

Meir, Golda (1898–1978)
Russian-born Israeli stateswoman and Prime Minister

Being seventy is not a sin.

Reader's Digest, 1971

Mencken, H.L. (1880–1956)
US writer, critic, philologist and satirist

The best years are the forties. After fifty a man begins to deteriorate, but in his forties he is at the maximum of his villainy.

In Lieberman, *3,500 Good Quotes for Speakers* (1983)

Molière (1622–1673)
French dramatist, actor and director

*L'âge amènera tout, et ce n'est pas le temps,
Madame, comme on sait, d'être prude à vingt ans.*
Everything comes with age, and everyone knows, Madame, that twenty is not the time to be a prude.

Le Misanthrope (1666)

Nash, Ogden (1902–1971)
US poet

I prefer to forget both pairs of glasses and pass my declining years
Saluting strange women and grandfather clocks.

The Private Dining Room and Other New Verses (1952)

Do you think my mind is maturing late,
Or simply rotted early?

'Lines on Facing Forty' (1942)

Naylor, James Ball (1860–1945)
US physician and writer

King David and King Solomon
Led merry, merry lives,
With many, many lady friends
And many, many wives;
But when old age crept over them,
With many, many qualms,
King Solomon wrote the Proverbs

And King David wrote the Psalms.

'King David and King Solomon' (1935)

Orwell, George (1903–1950)
English writer and critic

At 50, everyone has the face he deserves.

Notebook, 1949

Parkes, Sir Henry (1815–1896)
Australian politician, writer and poet
On being congratulated when he was eighty years old on the birth of his last child

Don't say my last, you damned fool! Say my latest.

In Randolph Bedford, *Naught to Thirty-three*

Paterson, Jennifer (1928–1999)
English food writer and TV chef

At 70, I'm in fine fettle for my age, sleep like a babe and feel around 12. The secret? Lots of meat, drink and cigarettes and not giving in to things.

The Times, 1998

Patten, Brian (1946–)
British poet

Mr Old Age, would catch you in his deadly trap
And come finally to polish you off,
His machine-gun dripping with years.

'where are you now, Batman?'

Pattison, Ian (1950–)
Scottish actor

Rab C. Nesbitt: I hate middle age. Too young for the bowling green, too old for Ecstasy.

Rab C. Nesbitt, television series

Peele, George (c.1558–c.1597)
English dramatist and poet

His golden locks time hath to silver turn'd;
O time too swift, O swiftness never ceasing!
His youth 'gainst time and age hath ever spurn'd
But spurn'd in vain; youth waneth by increasing:
Beauty, strength, youth, are flowers but fading seen;
Duty, faith, love, are roots, and ever green.

His helmet now shall make a hive for bees,
And, lovers' sonnets turn'd to holy psalms,
A man-at-arms must now serve on his knees,
And feed on prayers, which are age his alms:
But though from court to cottage he depart,
His saint is sure of his unspotted heart ...

Goddess, allow this aged man his right,
To be your beadsman now that was your knight.

'Sonnet. A Farewell to Arms' (1590)

Phillips, Stephen (1864–1915)
English poet

A man not old, but mellow, like good wine.

Ulysses (1902)

Picasso, Pablo (1881–1973)
Spanish painter, sculptor and graphic artist
> Age only matters when one is ageing. Now that
> I have arrived at a great age, I might just as well
> be twenty.
>> In J. Richardson, *The Observer, Shouts and Murmurs*

> One starts get young at the age of sixty and
> then it is too late.
>> *The Sunday Times*, 1963

Pinero, Sir Arthur Wing (1855–1934)
English dramatist
> From forty to fifty a man is at heart either a stoic
> or a satyr.
>> *The Second Mrs Tanqueray* (1893)

Pitkin, William B. (1878–1953)
> Life Begins at Forty.
>> Title of book, 1932

Pound, Ezra (1885–1972)
US poet
> One of the pleasures of middle age is to find out
> that one WAS right, and that one was much
> righter than one knew at say 17 or 23.
>> *ABC of Reading* (1934)

Powell, Anthony (1905–2000)
English writer and critic
> Growing old is like being increasingly penalized
> for a crime you haven't committed.
>> *A Dance to the Music of Time* (1973)

Power, Marguerite, Countess of Blessington
(1789–1849)
English writer
> Tears fell from my eyes – yes, weak and foolish
> as it now appears to me, I wept for my departed
> youth; and for that beauty of which the faithful
> mirror too plainly assured me, no remnant
> existed.
>> *The Confessions of an Elderly Lady* (1838)

> … it is better to die young than to outlive all
> one loved, and all that rendered one lovable.
>> *The Confessions of an Elderly Gentleman* (1836)

Proverbs
> Man fools himself. He prays for a long life, and
> he fears an old age.
>> Chinese saying

> Never too late to learn.

Reagan, Ronald (1911–)
US actor, Republican statesman and President
On his challenger, Walter Mondale, in the 1984 election
campaign
> I will not make age an issue of this campaign. I
> am not going to exploit for political purposes
> my opponent's youth and inexperience.
>> TV debate, 1984

> I am delighted to be with you. In fact, at my
> age, I am delighted to be anywhere.
>> Speech at the Oxford Union, 1992

Reed, Henry (1914–1986)
English poet, radio dramatist and translator
> As we get older we do not get any younger.
> Seasons return, and today I am fifty-five,
> And this time last year I was fifty-four,
> And this time next year I shall be sixty-two.
>> 'Chard Whitlow (Mr Eliot's Sunday Evening
>> Postscript)' (1941)

Rexford, Eben (1848–1916)
English songwriter
> Darling, I am growing old,
> Silver threads among the gold.
>> 'Silver Threads Among the Gold' (1873)

Rochester, Earl of (1647–1680)
English poet, satirist, courtier and libertine
> Ancient person, for whom I
> All the flattering youth defy,
> Long be it ere thou grow old,
> Aching, shaking, crazy, cold;
> But still continue as thou art,
> Ancient person of my heart.
>> 'A Song of a Young Lady to her Ancient Lover' (1691)

Ronsard, Pierre de (1524–1585)
> *Quand vous serez bien vieille, au soir à la chandelle,*
> *Assise auprès du feu dévidant et filant,*
> *Direz, chantant mes vers, en vous émerveillant,*
> *Ronsard me célébrait du temps que j'étais belle.*
> When you are very old, at night, in the candle-
> light, sitting spinning by the fire, you will say as
> you sing my verses, marvelling, 'Ronsard sang of
> me in the time of my beauty.'
>> *Sonnets pour Hélène* (1578)

Roosevelt, Franklin Delano (1882–1945)
US Democrat statesman and President
After Churchill had congratulated him on his 60th birthday
> It is fun to be in the same decade with you.
>> In Winston S. Churchill, *The Hinge of Fate*

Rubinstein, Helena (1872–1965)
Polish-born US cosmetician and businesswoman
> I have always felt that a woman has a right to
> treat the subject of her age with ambiguity until,
> perhaps, she passes into the realm of over
> ninety. Then it is better she be candid with
> herself and with the world.
>> *My Life for Beauty* (1965)

Saki (1870–1916)
Burmese-born British writer
> The young have aspirations that never come to
> pass, the old have reminiscences of what never
> happened. It's only the middle-aged who are
> really conscious of their limitations.
>> *Reginald* (1904)

Santayana, George (1863–1952)

Spanish-born US philosopher and writer

> The young man who has not wept is a savage, and the old man who will not laugh is a fool.
>
> *Dialogues in Limbo* (1925)

Sarton, May (1912–1995)

US poet and writer

> Old age is not an illness, it is a timeless ascent. As power diminishes, we grow toward the light.
>
> *Ms* magazine, 1982

Satie, Erik (1866–1925)

French composer

> When I was young, I was told: 'You'll see, when you're fifty.' I am fifty and I haven't seen a thing.
>
> In Pierre-Daniel Templier, *Erik Satie*, 2, Letter to his brother

Sexton, Anne (1928–1974)

US poet

> In a dream you are never eighty.
>
> 'Old' (1962)

Shakespeare, William (1564–1616)

English dramatist, poet and actor

> Unregarded age in corners thrown.
>
> *As You Like It*, II.iii

> Therefore my age is as a lusty winter,
> Frosty, but kindly.
>
> *As You Like It*, II.iii

> And so, from hour to hour, we ripe and ripe,
> And then, from hour to hour, we rot and rot;
> And thereby hangs a tale.
>
> *As You Like It*, II.vii

> O, sir, you are old;
> Nature in you stands on the very verge
> Of her confine.
>
> *King Lear*, II.iv

> Though age from folly could not give me freedom,
> It does from childishness.
>
> *Antony and Cleopatra*, I.iii

> A good old man, sir, he will be talking; as they say 'When the age is in the wit is out.'
>
> *Much Ado About Nothing*, III.v

> The satirical rogue says here that old men have grey beards; that their faces are wrinkled; their eyes purging thick amber and plum-tree gum; and that they have a plentiful lack of wit, together with most weak hams – all of which, sir, though I most powerfully and potently believe, yet I hold it not honesty to have it thus set down.
>
> *Hamlet*, II.ii

> That time of year thou mayst in me behold
> When yellow leaves, or none, or few, do hang
> Upon those boughs which shake against the cold,
> Bare ruin'd choirs where late the sweet birds sang.
> In me thou seest the twilight of such day
> As after sunset fadeth in the west,
> Which by and by black night doth take away,
> Death's second self, that seals up all in rest.
>
> Sonnet 73

> Crabbed age and youth cannot live together:
> Youth is full of pleasance, age is full of care ...
>
> Age, I do abhor thee; youth, I do adore thee.
>
> *The Passionate Pilgrim*, xii

Shaw, George Bernard (1856–1950)

Irish socialist, writer, dramatist and critic

> Old men are dangerous: it doesn't matter to them what is going to happen to the world.
>
> *Heartbreak House* (1919)

> Every man over forty is a scoundrel.
>
> *Man and Superman* (1903)

Smith, Logan Pearsall (1865–1946)

US-born British epigrammatist, critic and writer

> There is more felicity on the far side of baldness than young men can possibly imagine.
>
> 'Last Words' (1933)

Solon (c.638–c.559 BC)

Athenian statesman, reformer and poet

> I grow old ever learning many things.
>
> In Bergk (ed.), *Poetae Lyrici Graeci*

Southey, Robert (1774–1843)

English poet, essayist, historian and letterwriter

> You are old, Father William, the young man cried,
> The few locks which are left you are grey;
> You are hale, Father William, a hearty old man,
> Now tell me the reason, I pray ...
>
> In the days of my youth I remembered my God!
> And He hath not forgotten my age.
>
> 'The Old Man's Comforts, and how he Gained them' (1799)

Spark, Muriel (1918–)

Scottish writer, poet and dramatist

> Being over seventy is like being engaged in a war. All our friends are going or gone and we survive amongst the dead and the dying as on a battlefield.
>
> *Memento Mori*

Sparrow, John (1906–1992)

English lawyer and writer

> Chill on the brow and in the breast
> The frost of years is spread –
> Soon we shall take our endless rest

With the unfeeling dead.
Insensibly, ere we depart,
We grow more cold, more kind:
Age makes a winter in the heart,
An autumn in the mind.

'Grave Epigrams'

Steele, Sir Richard (1672–1729)
Irish-born English writer, dramatist and politician
There are so few who can grow old with a good grace.

The Spectator, 263, 1712

Stephen, James Kenneth (1859–1892)
English writer and poet
Ah! Matt: old age has brought to me
Thy wisdom, less thy certainty:
The world's a jest, and joy's a trinket:
I knew that once: but now – I think it.

Lapsus Calami (1891), 'Senex to Matt. Prior'

Stephens, James (1882–1950)
Irish poet and writer
Men come of age at sixty, women at fifteen.

The Observer, 1944

Stevenson, Robert Louis (1850–1894)
Scottish writer, poet and essayist
By the time a man gets well into the seventies his continued existence is a mere miracle.

Virginibus Puerisque (1881)

Our frailties are invincible, our virtues barren; the battle goes sore against us to the going down of the sun.

Across the Plains (1892)

Stone, I.F. (1907–1989)
US writer
If you live long enough, the venerability factor creeps in; you get accused of things you never did and praised for virtues you never had.

In Laurence J. Peter, *Peter's Quotations*

Swift, Jonathan (1667–1745)
Irish satirist, poet, essayist and cleric
Old men and comets have been reverenced for the same reason; their long beards, and pretences to foretell events.

Thoughts on Various Subjects (1711)

Every man desires to live long; but no man would be old.

Thoughts on Various Subjects (1711)

I'm as old as my tongue, and a little older than my teeth.

Polite Conversation (1738)

Talleyrand, Charles-Maurice de (1754–1838)
French statesman, memoirist and prelate
Remark to young man who boasted that he did not play whist
Quelle triste vieillesse vous vous préparez.

What a sad old age you are preparing for yourself.

In J. Amédée Pichot, *Souvenirs intimes sur M. de Talleyrand* (1870)

Thomas, Dylan (1914–1953)
Welsh poet, writer and radio dramatist
Do not go gentle into that good night,
Old age should burn and rave at close of day;
Rage, rage against the dying of the light.

'Do Not Go Gentle into that Good Night' (1952)

Trotsky, Leon (1879–1940)
Russian revolutionary and Communist theorist
Old age is the most unexpected of all the things that happen to a man.

Diary in Exile, 8 May 1935

Tucker, Sophie (1884–1966)
Russian-born US vaudeville singer
Asked, when 80, the secret of longevity
Keep breathing.

Attr.

Ustinov, Sir Peter (1921–)
English actor, director, dramatist, writer and raconteur
There are no old men any more. *Playboy* and *Penthouse* have between them made an ideal of eternal adolescence, sunburnt and saunaed, with the grey dorianed out of it.

Dear Me (1977)

Wall, Max (1908–1990)
English comedian
To me Adler will always be Jung.

Telegram to Larry Adler on his 60th birthday

Walpole, Horace (1717–1797)
English writer and politician
What has one to do, when one grows tired of the world, as we both do, but to draw nearer and nearer, and gently waste the remains of life with friends with whom one began it?

Letter to George Montagu, 1765

Old age is no such uncomfortable thing if one gives oneself up to it with a good grace, and doesn't drag it about 'To midnight dances and the public show'.

Letter, 1774

Webb, Sidney (1859–1947)
English reformer, historian and socialist
Old people are always absorbed in something, usually themselves; we prefer to be absorbed in the Soviet Union.

Attr.

White, Patrick (1912–1990)
English-born Australian writer and dramatist
The aged are usually tougher and more calculating than the young, provided they keep enough of their wits about them. How could

they have lived so long if there weren't steel buried inside them?

The Eye of the Storm (1973)

Whitman, Walt (1819–1892)
US poet and writer

Women sit or move to and fro, some old, some young.
The young are beautiful – but the old are more beautiful than the young.

'Beautiful Women' (1871)

Wilde, Oscar (1854–1900)
Irish poet, dramatist, writer, critic and wit

One should never trust a woman who tells one her real age. A woman who would tell one that would tell one anything.

A Woman of No Importance (1893)

Mrs Allonby: I delight in men over seventy. They always offer one the devotion of a lifetime.

A Woman of No Importance (1893)

The old believe everything: the middle-aged suspect everything: the young know everything.

The Chameleon, 1894

No woman should ever be quite accurate about her age. It looks so calculating.

The Importance of Being Earnest (1895), IV

Williams, William Carlos (1883–1963)
US poet, writer and paediatrician

In old age
the mind
casts off
rebelliously
an eagle
from its crag.

Paterson (1946–1958)

Wodehouse, P.G. (1881–1975)
English humorist and writer

He was either a man of about a hundred and fifty who was rather young for his years or a man of about a hundred and ten who had been aged by trouble.

In Usborne, *Wodehouse at Work to the End* (1976)

Wordsworth, William (1770–1850)
English poet

The wiser mind
Mourns less for what age takes away
Than what it leaves behind.

'The Fountain' (1800)

Yeats, W.B. (1865–1939)
Irish poet, dramatist, editor, writer and senator

I thought no more was needed
Youth to prolong
Than dumb-bell and foil
To keep the body young.
O who could have foretold

That the heart grows old?

'A Song' 1918

An aged man is but a paltry thing,
A tattered coat upon a stick, unless
Soul clap its hands and sing, and louder sing
For every tatter in its mortal dress.

'Sailing to Byzantium' (1927)

You think it horrible that lust and rage
Should dance attention upon my old age;
They were not such a plague when I was young;
What else have I to spur me into song?

In the *London Mercury*, 1938

►► LONGEVITY; MATURITY; YOUTH

agnosticism

Darrow, Clarence (1857–1938)
US lawyer, reformer and writer
At the trial of John Thomas Scopes for teaching Darwin's theory of evolution in school

I do not consider it an insult, but rather a compliment to be called an agnostic. I do not pretend to know where many ignorant men are sure – that is all that agnosticism means.

Speech, 1925

agony

Macaulay, Lord (1800–1859)
English Liberal statesman, essayist and poet
Reply, aged four, after hot coffee had been spilt on his legs

Thank you, madam, the agony is abated.

In G.O. Trevelyan, *Life and Letters of Macaulay* (1876)

agreement and disagreement

The Bible (King James Version)

Can two walk together, except they be agreed?

Amos, 3:3

Gibran, Kahlil (1883–1931)
Lebanese poet, mystic and painter

Disagreement may be the shortest cut between two minds.

Sand and Foam

Hampton, Christopher (1946–)
English dramatist

It's possible to disagree with someone about the ethics of non-violence without wanting to kick his face in.

Treats (1976), Scene iv

Inge, William Ralph (1860–1954)
English divine, writer and teacher
> It takes in reality only one to make a quarrel. It is useless for the sheep to pass resolutions in favour of vegetarianism while the wolf remains of a different opinion.
>> *Outspoken Essays: First Series* (1919)

La Rochefoucauld (1613–1680)
French writer
> *Nous ne trouvons guère de gens de bon sens que ceux qui sont de notre avis.*
> We rarely think people have good sense unless they agree with us.
>> *Maximes* (1678)

Spaak, Paul Henri (1899–1972)
Belgian Prime Minister
Concluding the first General Assembly meeting of the United Nations, 1946
> Our agenda is now exhausted. The secretary general is exhausted. All of you are exhausted. I find it comforting that, beginning with our very first day, we find ourselves in such complete unanimity.
>> Attr.

Waugh, Evelyn (1903–1966)
English writer and diarist
> When Lord Copper was right he said, 'Definitely, Lord Copper'; when he was wrong, 'Up to a point'.
>> *Scoop* (1938)

Wilde, Oscar (1854–1900)
Irish poet, dramatist, writer, critic and wit
> Ah! Don't say that you agree with me. When people agree with me I always feel that I must be wrong.
>> *Intentions* (1891)

agriculture

Charles, Prince of Wales (1948–)
Son and heir of Elizabeth II and Prince Philip
> I believe agriculture has lost its soul. Organic farming can put its soul back.
>> *The Times*, 1998

Crabbe, George (1754–1832)
English poet, clergyman, surgeon and botanist
> Our farmers round, well pleased with constant gain,
> Like other farmers, flourish and complain.
>> *The Parish Register* (1807)

Dickens, Charles (1812–1870)
English writer
> Cows are my passion.
>> *Dombey and Son* (1848)

Goldsmith, Oliver (c.1728–1774)
Irish dramatist, poet and writer
> A time there was, ere England's griefs began,
> When every rood of ground maintained its man;
> For him light labour spread her wholesome store,
> Just gave what life required, but gave no more.
> His best companions, innocence and health;
> And his best riches, ignorance of wealth.
>> *The Deserted Village* (1770)

Mill, John Stuart (1806–1873)
English philosopher, economist and reformer
> When the land is cultivated entirely by the spade and no horses are kept, a cow is kept for every three acres of land.
>> *Principles of Political Economy* (1848)

Ruskin, John (1819–1900)
English art critic, philosopher and reformer
> Soldiers of the ploughshare as well as soldiers of the sword.
>> *Unto this Last* (1862), Preface

Swift, Jonathan (1667–1745)
Irish satirist, poet, essayist and cleric
> And he gave it for his opinion, that whoever could make two ears of corn or two blades of grass to grow upon a spot of ground where only one grew before, would deserve better of mankind, and do more essential service to his country than the whole race of politicians put together.
>> *Gulliver's Travels* (1726)

Thomas, Dylan (1914–1953)
Welsh poet, writer and radio dramatist
> This bread I break was once the oat,
> This wine upon a foreign tree
> Plunged in its fruit;
> Man in the day or wind at night
> Laid the crops low, broke the grape's joy.
>> 'This bread I break' (1936)

Virgil (70–19 BC)
Roman poet
> *O fortunatos nimium, sua si bona norint, Agricolas!*
> O happy are farmers, too happy if they knew their blessings.
>> *Georgics*

▶▶ COUNTRY

aids

Anne, the Princess Royal (1950–)
Daughter of Elizabeth II
> It could be said that the Aids pandemic is a classic own-goal scored by the human race against itself.
>> Remark, 1988

Anonymous

Every time you sleep with a boy you sleep with all his old girlfriends.

Government slogan, anti-Aids campaign, 1987

Currie, Edwina (1946–)

My message to the businessmen of this country when they go abroad on business is that there is one thing above all they can take with them to stop them catching Aids, and that is the wife.

The Observer, 1987

Perkins, Anthony (1932–1992)

US actor

I have learned more about love, selflessness and human understanding in this great adventure in the world of Aids than I ever did in the cutthroat, competitive world in which I spent my life.

Independent on Sunday, 1992

Sontag, Susan (1933–)

US critic and writer

Societies need to have one illness which becomes identified with evil, and attaches blame to its 'victims'

AIDS and Its Metaphors (1989)

alcohol

Aga Khan III (1877–1957)

Leader of Ismaili Muslims

Justifying his liking for alcohol

I'm so holy that when I touch wine, it turns into water.

Attr. in Compton Miller, Who's Really Who (1983)

Aldrich, Henry (1647–1710)

English scholar, divine and composer of songs

If all be true that I do think,
There are five reasons we should drink;
Good wine – a friend – or being dry –
Or lest we should be by and by –
Or any other reason why.

'Five Reasons for Drinking' (1689)

Amis, Kingsley (1922–1995)

English writer, poet and critic

A dusty thudding in his head made the scene before him beat like a pulse. His mouth had been used as a latrine by some small creature of the night and then as its mausoleum.

Lucky Jim (1958)

Anonymous

Bring us in no browne bred, for that is made of brane,

Nor bring us in no white bred, for therein is no gane,
But bring us in good ale!

'Bring us in Good Ale'

I feel no pain dear mother now
But oh, I am so dry!
O take me to a brewery
And leave me there to die.

Parody of Edward Farmer, 'The Collier's Dying Child'

Hath wine an oblivious power?
Can it pluck out the sting from the brain?
The draught might beguile for an hour,
But still leaves behind it the pain.

'Farewell to England'; sometimes attr. to Byron

Menu translation

Our wines leave you nothing to hope for.

The Times, 1999

Said by the secretary of the Residents' Association after the council voted to allow the Essex resort its first pub

It's the worst day for Frinton since the Luftwaffe beat up the town in 1944.

The Times, 1999

Archpoet of Cologne (fl. c.1205)

Meum est propositum in taberna mori,
ut sint vina proxima morientis ori.
Tunc cantabunt laetius angelorum chori:
'sit Deus propitius huic potatori!'

I am resolved to die in a tavern, so that wine will be very near to my dying mouth. Then the bands of angels will chant with greater joy 'May God forgive this drinker.'

The Confession of Golias

Becon, Thomas (1512–1567)

English Protestant divine

For when the wine is in, the wit is out.

Catechism (1560)

Behan, Brendan (1923–1964)

Irish dramatist, writer and Republican

I only take a drink on two occasions – when I'm thirsty and when I'm not.

In McCann, The Wit of Brendan Behan

Bell, Ian

Scottish journalist

There is no hangover on earth like the single malt hangover. It roars in the ears, burns in the stomach and sizzles in the brain like a short circuit. Death is the easy way out.

The Observer, 1991

Belloc, Hilaire (1870–1953)

English writer of verse, essayist and critic; Liberal MP

Strong Brother in God and last Companion: Wine.

Short Talks with the Dead and Others (1926)

Benchley, Robert (1889–1945)
US essayist, humorist and actor
Reply when asked if he realised that drinking was a
slow death
> So who's in a hurry?
>
> Attr.

Bentley, Richard (1662–1742)
English classical scholar
Of claret
> It would be port if it could.
>
> Attr.

Borrow, George (1803–1881)
English writer and linguist
> Good ale, the true and proper drink of Englishmen. He is not deserving of the name of Englishman who speaketh against ale, that is good ale.
>
> *Lavengro* (1851)

Brigid of Kildare (453–523)
Irish abbess
> I should like a great lake of ale
> For the King of Kings.
>
> *The Feast of St Brigid of Kildare*

Breslin, Jimmy (1930–)
US talk show host and columnist
> When you stop drinking, you have to deal with this marvelous personality that started you drinking in the first place.
>
> *Table Money* (1986)

Burns, Robert (1759–1796)
Scottish poet and song writer
> Freedom and whisky gang thegither,
> Tak aff your dram!
>
> 'The Author's Earnest Cry and Prayer' (1786)

Burton, Robert (1577–1640)
English clergyman and writer
> I may not here omit those two main plagues, and common dotages of human kind, wine and women, which have infatuated and besotted myriads of people. They go commonly together.
>
> *Anatomy of Melancholy* (1621)

Calverley, C.S. (1831–1884)
English poet, parodist, scholar and lawyer
> The heart which grief hath canker'd
> Hath one unfailing remedy – the Tankard.
>
> 'Beer' (1861)

Cervantes, Miguel de (1547–1616)
Spanish writer and dramatist
> Under a bad cloak there is often a good drinker.
>
> *Don Quixote* (1605–15)

Chandler, Raymond (1888–1959)
US crime writer
> Alcohol is like love: the first kiss is magic, the second is intimate, the third is routine. After that

you just take the girl's clothes off.
>
> *The Long Good-bye* (1953)

Churchill, Sir Winston (1874–1965)
English Conservative Prime Minister
Said during a lunch with the Arab leader Ibn Saud, when he heard that the king's religion forbade smoking and alcohol
> I must point out that my rule of life prescribed as an absolutely sacred rite smoking cigars and also the drinking of alcohol before, after, and if need be during all meals and in the intervals between them.
>
> *Triumph and Tragedy*

Clarke, Marcus (1846–1881)
English-born Australian writer
> No man has a right to inflict the torture of bad wine upon his fellow-creatures.
>
> *The Peripatetic Philosopher* (1867–1870)

Connolly, Billy (1942–)
Scottish comedian and actor
> A well-balanced person has a drink in each hand.
>
> *Gullible's Travels*

Cooper, Derek (1925–)
Highland saying
> One whisky is all right; two is too much; three is too few.
>
> *A Taste of Scotch* (1989)

Cope, Wendy (1945–)
English poet
> All you need is love, love
> or, failing that, alcohol.
>
> Variation on a Lennon and McCartney song

Coren, Alan (1938–)
British humorist, writer and broadcaster
> Apart from cheese and tulips, the main product of the country Holland is advocaat, a drink made from lawyers.
>
> *The Sanity Inspector* (1974)

Crabbe, George (1754–1832)
English poet, clergyman, surgeon and botanist
> Lo! the poor toper whose untutor'd sense,
> Sees bliss in ale, and can with wine dispense;
> Whose head proud fancy never taught to steer,
> Beyond the muddy ecstasies of beer.
>
> *Inebriety* (1774)

De Quincey, Thomas (1785–1859)
English writer
> It is most absurdly said, in popular language, of any man, that he is disguised in liquor; for, on the contrary, most men are disguised by sobriety.
>
> *Confessions of an English Opium Eater* (1822)

Dibdin, Charles (1745–1814)
English songwriter, dramatist and actor
> Then trust me, there's nothing like drinking

So pleasant on this side the grave;
It keeps the unhappy from thinking,
And makes e'en the valiant more brave.

'Nothing like Grog'

Dickens, Charles (1812–1870)
English writer
Bring in the bottled lightning, a clean tumbler,
and a corkscrew.

Nicholas Nickleby (1839)

Disraeli, Benjamin (1804–1881)
English statesman and writer
'I rather like bad wine, ' said Mr Mountchesney;
'one gets so bored with good wine.'

Sybil (1845)

Dom Perignon
On discovering champagne
Come quickly, I am tasting stars!

Attr.

Dunne, Finley Peter (1867–1936)
US writer
There is wan thing an' on'y wan thing to be said
in favour iv dhrink, an' that is that it has caused
manny a lady to be loved that otherwise
might've died single.

Mr Dooley Says (1910)

Duras, Marguerite (1914–1996)
French author and filmmaker
No other human being, no woman, no poem or
music, book or painting can replace alcohol in its
power to give man the illusion of real creation.

Practicalities (1987)

Farquhar, George (1678–1707)
Irish dramatist
I have fed purely upon ale; I have eat my ale,
drank my ale, and I always sleep upon ale.

The Beaux' Stratagem (1707)

Fitzgerald, Edward (1809–1883)
English poet, translator and letter writer
Drink! for you know not whence you came, nor
why:
Drink! for you know not why you go, nor where.

The Rubáiyát of Omar Khayyám (1879)

The Grape that can with Logic absolute
The Two-and-Seventy jarring Sects confute.

The Rubáiyát of Omar Khayyám (1859)

And much as Wine has play'd the Infidel,
And robb'd me of my Robe of Honour – Well,
I often wonder what the Vintners buy
One half so precious as the Goods they sell.

The Rubáiyát of Omar Khayyám (1859)

Here with a Loaf of Bread beneath the Bough,
A Flask of Wine, a Book of Verse – and Thou
Beside me singing in the Wilderness –

And Wilderness is Paradise enow.

The Rubáiyát of Omar Khayyám (1859)

Fitzgerald, F. Scott (1896–1940)
US writer
First you take a drink, then the drink takes a
drink, then the drink takes you.

In Jules Feiffer, *Ackroyd*

Fletcher, John (1579–1625)
English dramatist
And he that will go to bed sober,
Falls with the leaf still in October.

The Bloody Brother (1616)

Fuller, Thomas (1654–1734)
English churchman and antiquary
Bacchus hath drowned more men than Neptune.

Gnomologia, 1732

Goldsmith, Oliver (c.1728–1774)
Irish dramatist, poet and writer
Let school-masters puzzle their brain,
With grammar, and nonsense, and learning,
Good liquor, I stoutly maintain,
Gives genius a better discerning.

She Stoops to Conquer (1773)

Harris, Joel Chandler (1848–1908)
US author
Licker talks mighty loud w'en it git loose fum de
jug.

Uncle Remus (1881)

Herbert, George (1593–1633)
English poet and priest
Drink not the third glasse, – which thou canst
not tame
When once it is within thee.

The Temple (1633)

Holmes, Oliver Wendell (1809–1894)
US physician, poet, writer and scientist
Man wants but little drink below,
But wants that little strong.

'A Song of other Days' (1848)

Home, John (1722–1808)
Scottish clergyman and dramatist
On the high duty on French wine, claret being 'the only wine
drunk by gentlemen in Scotland'
Firm and erect the Caledonian stood,
Old was his mutton, and his claret good;
Let him drink port, an English statesman cried –
He drank the poison and his spirit died.

In Mackenzie, *An Account of the Life and Writings of
John Home, Esq.* (1822)

Hoover, Herbert Clark (1874–1964)
US Republican statesman and President
On the Eighteenth Amendment, enacting Prohibition
Our country has deliberately undertaken a great
social and economic experiment, noble in motive

and far-reaching in purpose.

Letter to Senator Borah, 1928

Housman, A.E. (1859–1936)
English poet and scholar
> Oh many a peer of England brews
> Livelier liquor than the Muse,
> And malt does more than Milton can
> To justify God's ways to man.
> Ale, man, ale's the stuff to drink
> For fellows whom it hurts to think.

A Shropshire Lad (1896)

Howkins, Alun (1947–)
British historian and writer
> Real ale is an odd concept, linked more to an imagined real pub with real fire and real bread and cheese, as much as to a scientific definition of a brewing process.

New Statesman and Society, 1989

Howse, Christopher
> It is difficult to speak about proper beer, because its friends (just like the friends of G.K. Chesterton) are its worst enemies. 'Real ale' fans are just like train-spotters – only drunk.

The Spectator, 1992

Irving, Washington (1783–1859)
US writer and diplomat
> They who drink beer will think beer.

The Sketch Book (1820)

Johnson, Samuel (1709–1784)
English lexicographer, poet, critic, conversationalist and essayist
> Claret is the liquor for boys; port for men; but he who aspires to be a hero must drink brandy.

In Boswell, *The Life of Samuel Johnson* (1791)

> Wine gives a man nothing. It neither gives him knowledge nor wit; it only animates a man, and enables him to bring out what a dread of the company has repressed.

In Boswell *The Life of Samuel Johnson* (1791)

Calling for a gill of whisky
> Come, let me know what it is that makes a Scotchman happy!

In Boswell, *Journal of a Tour to the Hebrides* (1785)

> He said that few people had intellectual resources sufficient to forgo the pleasures of wine. They would not otherwise contrive to fill the interval between dinner and supper.

In Boswell, *The Life of Samuel Johnson* (1791)

Joyce, James (1882–1941)
Irish writer
> I was blue mouldy for the want of that pint. Declare to God I could hear it hit the pit of my stomach with a click.

Ulysses (1922)

Kamprad, Ingvar (1926–)
Swedish businessman; founder of IKEA
Putting his alcohol problems down to frequent business trips to Poland
> In the 1960s it was almost compulsory to drink vodka.

The Times, 1998

Keats, John (1795–1821)
English poet
> Souls of poets dead and gone,
> What Elysium have ye known,
> Happy field or mossy cavern,
> Choicer than the Mermaid Tavern?
> Have ye tippled drink more fine
> Than mine host's Canary wine?

'Lines on the Mermaid Tavern' (1818)

> O for a beaker full of the warm South,
> Full of the true, the blushful Hippocrene,
> With beaded bubbles winking at the brim,
> And purple-stainèd mouth;
> That I might drink, and leave the world unseen;
> And with thee fade away into the forest dim.

'Ode to a Nightingale' (1819)

Kerr, Jean (1923–)
US writer and dramatist
> Even though a number of people have tried, no one has yet found a way to drink for a living.

Poor Richard (1963)

Lardner, Ring (1885–1933)
US humorist and writer
> Frenchmen drink wine just like we used to drink water before Prohibition.

In R.E. Drennan, *Wit's End*

Lauder, Sir Harry (1870–1950)
Scottish music-hall entertainer
> Just a wee deoch-an-duoris
> Before we gang awa' …
> If y' can say
> It's a braw brecht moonlecht necht,
> Yer a' recht, that's a'.

Song, 1912

Lawson, Henry (1867–1922)
Australian writer and poet
> Beer makes you feel as you ought to feel without beer.

In David Low, *Low's Autobiography*

Lemmon, Jack (1925–)
US actor
> You'd be surprised how much fun you can have sober. When you get the hang of it.

In *Days of Wine and Roses* (film, 1962)

Lloyd George, David (1863–1945)
British Liberal statesman
To a deputation of ship owners urging a campaign for

prohibition during the First World War
> We are fighting Germany, Austria, and drink, and so far as I can see the greatest of these deadly foes is drink.
>> *Speech, 1915*

Mackenzie, Sir Compton (1883–1972)
Scottish writer and broadcaster
> Love makes the world go round? Not at all. Whisky makes it go round twice as fast.
>> *Whisky Galore (1947)*

Map, Walter (c.1140–c.1209)
Welsh clergyman and writer
> If die I must, let me die drinking in an inn.
>> *De Nugis Curialium (1182)*

Martin, Dean (1917–1995)
US singer
> I feel sorry for people who don't drink. When they wake up in the morning, that's the best they are going to feel all day.
>> Attr.

Marx, Groucho (1895–1977)
US comedian
> I was T.T. until prohibition.
>> Attr.

Mencken, H.L. (1880–1956)
US writer, critic, philologist and satirist
> I've made it a rule never to drink by daylight and never to refuse a drink after dark.
>> *New York Post, 1945*

Nash, Ogden (1902–1971)
US poet
> Candy
> Is dandy
> But liquor
> Is quicker.
>> 'Reflections on Ice-Breaking' (1931)

O'Brien, Flann (1911–1966)
Irish novelist and journalist
> When things go wrong and will not come right,
> Though you do the best you can,
> When life looks black as the hour of night ñ
> A PINT OF PLAIN IS YOUR ONLY MAN.
>> *At Swim-Two-Birds (1939)*

O'Sullivan, John L. (1813–1895)
US editor and diplomat
Of whisky
> A torchlight procession marching down your throat.
>> Attr.

Osler, Sir William (1849–1919)
Canadian physician
His description of alcohol
> Milk of the elderly.
>> *The Globe and Mail, 1988*

Pascal, Blaise (1623–1662)
French philosopher and scientist
> Too much and too little wine. Give him none, he cannot find truth; give him too much, the same.
>> *Pensées, 1670*

Peacock, Thomas Love (1785–1866)
English writer and poet
> There are two reasons for drinking; one is, when you are thirsty, to cure it; the other, when you are not thirsty, to prevent it … Prevention is better than cure.
>> *Melincourt (1817)*

Pliny the Elder (AD 23–79)
Roman scholar
> *In vino veritas.*
> Wine brings out the truth!
>> *Historia Naturalis*

Potter, Stephen (1900–1969)
English writer, critic and lecturer
> It is WRONG to do what everyone else does – namely, to hold the wine list just out of sight, look for the second cheapest claret on the list, and say, 'Number 22, please'.
>> *One-Upmanship (1952)*

> A good general rule is to state that the bouquet is better than the taste, and vice versa.
>> *One-Upmanship (1952)*

Proverbs
> A cask of wine works more miracles than a church full of saints.

> Adam's ale is the best brew.

> A good drink makes the old young.

> He who drinks a little too much drinks much too much.

Rabelais, François (c.1494–c.1553)
French monk, physician, satirist and humanist
> I drink for the thirst to come.
>> *Gargantua (1534)*

> No noble man ever hated good wine.
>> *Gargantua (1534)*

Russell, George William (1867–1935)
Irish poet
Refusing a drink that was offered him
> No, thank you, I was born intoxicated.
>> *In L. Copeland, 10, 000 Jokes, Toasts, and Stories*

Saintsbury, George (1845–1933)
English critic and historian
> It is the unbroken testimony of all history that alcoholic liquors have been used by the strongest, wisest, handsomest, and in every way best races of all times.
>> Attr.

Selden, John (1584–1654)
English historian, jurist and politician
'Tis not the drinking that is to be blamed, but the excess.

Table Talk (1689)

Shakespeare, William (1564–1616)
English dramatist, poet and actor
Drink, sir, is a great provoker of three things – nose-painting, sleep, and urine. Lechery, sir, it provokes, and unprovokes: it provokes the desire, but it takes away the performance.

Macbeth, II.iii

I have very poor and unhappy brains for drinking; I could well wish courtesy would invent some other custom of entertainment.

Othello, II.iii

Shaw, George Bernard (1856–1950)
Irish socialist, writer, dramatist and critic
I'm only a beer teetotaller, not a champagne teetotaller.

Candida (1898)

Alcohol is a very necessary article … It enables Parliament to do things at eleven at night that no sane person would do at eleven in the morning.

Major Barbara (1907)

Sheridan, Richard Brinsley (1751–1816)
Irish dramatist, politician and orator
On being warned that his drinking would destroy the coat of his stomach
Well, then, my stomach must just digest in its waistcoat.

In L. Harris, *The Fine Art of Political Wit* (1965)

Sitwell, Dame Edith (1887–1964)
English poet, anthologist, critic and biographer
Another little drink wouldn't do us any harm.

'Scotch Rhapsody' (1922)

Stevenson, Robert Louis (1850–1894)
Scottish writer, poet and essayist
Fifteen men on the dead man's chest
Yo-ho-ho, and a bottle of rum!
Drink and the devil had done for the rest –
Yo-ho-ho, and a bottle of rum!

Treasure Island (1883)

Stevenson, William (1546?–1575)
English scholar
I can not eat but little meat,
My stomach is not good;
But sure I think, that I can drink
With him that wears a hood.
Though I go bare, take ye no care,
I am nothing a-cold:
I stuff my skin, so full within,
Of jolly good ale and old.

Gammer Gurton's Needle, Song

Still, John (c.1543–c.1608)
Back and side go bare, go bare,
Both foot and hand go cold;
But, belly, God send thee good ale enough,
Whether it be new or old.

Gammer Gurton's Needle, song

Surtees, R.S. (1805–1864)
English writer
Champagne certainly gives one werry gentlemanly ideas, but for a continuance, I don't know but I should prefer mild hale.

Jorrocks's Jaunts and Jollities (1838)

Tarkington, Booth (1869–1946)
US writer and dramatist
There are two things that will be believed of any man whatsoever, and one of them is that he has taken to drink.

Penrod (1914)

Thatcher, Denis (1915–)
English businessman, husband of Margaret Thatcher
Reply to someone who asked if he had a drinking problem.
Yes, there's never enough.

Daily Mail, 1996

Thomas, Dylan (1914–1953)
Welsh poet, writer and radio dramatist
An alcoholic is someone you don't like who drinks as much as you do.

Attr.

Thurber, James (1894–1961)
US humorist, writer and dramatist
It's a naïve domestic Burgundy, without any breeding, but I think you'll be amused by its presumption.

Cartoon caption in *The New Yorker*, 1937

Ward, Artemus (1834–1867)
US humorist, journalist, editor and lecturer
I prefer temperance hotels – although they sell worse kinds of liquor than any other kind of hotels.

Wilde, Oscar (1854–1900)
Irish poet, dramatist, writer, critic and wit
I have made an important discovery … that alcohol, taken in sufficient quantities, produces all the effects of intoxication.

Attr.

Wodehouse, P.G. (1881–1975)
English humorist and writer
It was my Uncle George who discovered that alcohol was a food well in advance of modern medical thought.

The Inimitable Jeeves (1923)

I hadn't the heart to touch my breakfast. I told Jeeves to drink it himself.

My Man Jeeves

Wright, Ian
English footballer
On his Arsenal teammate's alcoholism
> It took a lot of bottle for Tony Adams to own up.
>> *Attr.*

Young, George W. (1846–1919)
British writer
> Your lips, on my own, when they printed
> 'Farewell',
> Had never been soiled by the 'beverage of hell';
> But they come to me now with the bacchanal
> sign,
> And the lips that touch liquor must never touch
> mine.
>> 'The lips that touch liquor must never touch mine' (c.1870)

▶▶ DRUNKENNESS

ambition

Aeschylus (525–456 BC)
Greek dramatist and poet
> He wishes not to seem but to be the best.
>> *The Seven against Thebes*, 592

Alexander the Great (356–323 BC)
Macedonian king and conquering army commander
> Alexander wept on hearing from Anaxarchus
> that there was an infinite number of worlds …
> 'Do you not think it lamentable that with such an
> infinite number, we have not yet conquered
> one?'.
>> In Plutarch, *On the Tranquillity of the Mind*

Bernieres, Louis de (1954–)
English author
> The trouble with fulfilling your ambitions is you
> think you will be transformed into some sort of
> archangel and you're not. You still have to wash
> your socks.
>> *The Times*, 1999

Blake, William (1757–1827)
English poet, engraver, painter and mystic
> Ambition is the growth of ev'ry clime.
>> *Poetical Sketches* (1783)

Browning, Robert (1812–1889)
English poet
> 'Tis not what man does which exalts him, but
> what a man would do!
>> 'Saul' (1855)

Burke, Edmund (1729–1797)
Irish-born British statesman and philosopher
> Well is it known that ambition can creep as well
> as soar.
>> *Third Letter … on the Proposals for Peace with the*
>> *Regicide Directory of France* (1797)

Caesar, Gaius Julius (c.102–44 BC)
Roman statesman, historian and army commander
> I would rather be the first man here (in Gaul)
> than second in Rome.
>> *Attr. in Plutarch,* Lives

Conrad, Joseph (1857–1924)
Polish-born British writer, sailor and explorer
> All ambitions are lawful except those which
> climb upward on the miseries or credulities of
> mankind.
>> *A Personal Record* (1912)

Dali, Salvador (1904–1989)
Spanish painter and writer
> At the age of six are wanted to be a cook.
> At seven I wanted to be Napoleon. And my
> ambition has been growing steadily ever
> since.
>> *The Secret Life of Salvador Dali* (1948)

Gilbert, W.S. (1836–1911)
English dramatist, humorist and librettist
> If you wish in this world to advance
> Your merits you're bound to enhance,
> You must stir it and stump it,
> And blow your own trumpet,
> Or, trust me, you haven't a chance!
>> *Ruddigore* (1887)

Herbert, George (1593–1633)
English poet and priest
> Who aimeth at the sky
> Shoots higher much than he that means a tree.
>> *The Temple* (1633)

Herford, Oliver (1863–1935)
When asked if he really had no ambition beyond making
people laugh
> I would like to throw an egg into an electric fan.
>> *Attr.*

Juvenal (c.60–130)
Roman verse satirist and Stoic
> Go climb the Alps, ambitious fool,
> To please the boys, and be a theme at school.
>> *Satires*

Keats, John (1795–1821)
English poet
> I am ambitious of doing the world some good: if
> I should be spared, that may be the work of
> maturer years – in the interval I will assay to
> reach to as high a summit in Poetry as the nerve
> bestowed upon me will suffer.
>> Letter to Richard Woodhouse, 1818

Keneally, Thomas (1935–)
Australian writer and screenwriter
> It's only when you abandon your ambitions that
> they become possible.
>> *Australian*, 1983

Kennedy, Joseph P. (1888–1969)
US financier and diplomat
> I have no political ambitions for myself or my children.
>> *Quoted in an obituary, 18 November 1969*

Longfellow, Henry Wadsworth (1807–1882)
US poet and writer
> If you would hit the mark, you must aim a little above it;
> Every arrow that flies feels the attraction of earth.
>> *'Elegiac Verse' (1880)*

Massinger, Philip (1583–1640)
English dramatist and poet
> Ambition, in a private man a vice,
> Is, in a prince, the virtue.
>> *The Bashful Lover (1636)*

Pope, Alexander (1688–1744)
English poet, translator and editor
> Get Place and Wealth, if possible, with Grace;
> If not, by any means get Wealth and Place.
>> *Imitations of Horace (1737–1738)*

Raleigh, Sir Walter (c.1552–1618)
English courtier, explorer, military commander, poet, historian and essayist
Written on a window-pane, and referring to his ambitions at the court of Elizabeth I
> Fain would I climb, yet fear I to fall.
>> Attr.

Shakespeare, William (1564–1616)
English dramatist, poet and actor
> I charge thee, fling away ambition:
> By that sin fell the angels. How can man then,
> The image of his Maker, hope to win by it?
>> *Henry VIII, III.ii*

> 'Tis a common proof
> That lowliness is young ambition's ladder,
> Whereto the climber-upward turns his face;
> But when he once attains the upmost round,
> He then unto the ladder turns his back,
> Looks in the clouds, scorning the base degrees
> By which he did ascend.
>> *Julius Caesar, II.i*

> Thou wouldst be great;
> Art not without ambition, but without
> The illness should attend it. What thou wouldst highly,
> That wouldst thou holily; wouldst not play false,
> And yet wouldst wrongly win.
>> *Macbeth, I.v*

> I have no spur
> To prick the sides of my intent, but only
> Vaulting ambition, which o'er-leaps itself,
> And falls on th' other.
>> *Macbeth, I.vii*

Shaw, George Bernard (1856–1950)
Irish socialist, writer, dramatist and critic
> The Gospel of Getting On.
>> *Mrs Warren's Profession (1898)*

Sidney, Sir Philip (1554–1586)
English poet, critic, soldier, courtier and diplomat
> Who shoots at the midday sun, though he be sure he shall never hit the mark, yet as sure he is he shall shoot higher than who aims but at a bush.
>> *New Arcadia (1590)*

Smith, Adam (1723–1790)
Scottish economist, philosopher and essayist
> And thus, place, that great object which divides the wives of aldermen, is the end of half the labours of human life; and is the cause of all the tumult and bustle, all the rapine and injustice, which avarice and ambition have introduced into this world.
>> *The Theory of Moral Sentiments (1759)*

Spenser, Edmund (c.1522–1599)
English poet
> And he that strives to touch the starres,
> Oft stombles at a strawe.
>> *The Shepheardes Calender (1579)*

Wagner, Jane (1927–)
> All my life I always wanted to be somebody.
> Now I see that I should have been more specific.
>> Attr.

Webster, Daniel (1782–1852)
US statesman, orator and lawyer
On being advised not to join the overcrowded legal profession
> There is always room at the top.
>> Attr.

▶▶ DESIRE

america

> A man went looking for America and couldn't find it anywhere.
>> *Advertisement for the film Easy Rider, 1969*

Adams, Henry Brooks (1838–1918)
US historian and memoirist
> American society is a sort of flat, fresh-water pond which absorbs silently, without reaction, anything which is thrown into it.
>> *Letter, 1911*

Adams, John (1735–1826)
US lawyer, diplomat and President
> I always consider the settlement of America with reverence and wonder, as the opening of a grand scene and design in providence, for the

illumination of the ignorant and the emancipation of the slavish part of mankind all over the earth.

> *Notes for A Dissertation on the Canon and Feudal Law* (1765)

The Revolution was effected before the War commenced. The Revolution was in the minds and hearts of the people; a change in their religious sentiments of their duties and obligations.

> *The Works of John Adams* (1856), letter, 1818

Appleton, Thomas Gold (1812–1884)
US epigrammatist

> Good Americans, when they die, go to Paris.
>
> In Oliver Wendell Holmes, *The Autocrat of the Breakfast Table* (1858)

Arnold, Matthew (1822–1888)
English poet, critic, essayist and educationist

> Our society distributes itself into Barbarians, Philistines, and Populace; and America is just ourselves, with the Barbarians quite left out, and the Populace nearly.
>
> *Culture and Anarchy* (1869)

Auden, W.H. (1907–1973)
English poet, essayist, critic, teacher and dramatist

> God bless the U.S.A., so large,
> So friendly, and so rich.
>
> 'On the Circuit'

Aykroyd, Dan (1952–)
US film actor

> What the American public doesn't know is what makes it the American public.
>
> *Tommy Boy* (film, 1995)

Bailey, Philip James (1816–1902)

> America, thou half-brother of the world;
> With something good and bad of every land.
>
> *Festus* (1839)

Baker, Russell (1925–)
US writer

> In America nothing dies easier than tradition.
>
> *New York Times*, 1991

Bates, Katherine Lee (1859–1929)
US writer and poet

> America! America!
> God shed His grace on thee
> And crown thy good with brotherhood
> From sea to shining sea!
>
> 'America the Beautiful', song, 1895

Bloom, Allan (1930–1992)
US academic and critic

> American nihilism is nihilism without the abyss.
>
> In *The Observer*, 2000

Burroughs, William S. (1914–1999)
US writer

> America is not a young land: it is old and dirty and evil before the settlers, before the Indians. The evil is there waiting.
>
> *Naked Lunch* (1959)

Butler, Nicholas Murray (1862–1947)
US teacher, lecturer, politican and writer

> … a society like ours USA of which it is truly said to be often but three generations 'from shirt-sleeves to shirt-sleeves'.
>
> *True and False Democracy*

Canning, George (1770–1827)
English Prime Minister, orator and poet

> I called the New World into existence, to redress the balance of the Old.
>
> Speech, 1826

Cheever, John (1912–1982)
US novelist

> We travel by plane, oftener than not, and yet the spirit of our country seems to have remained a country of railroads.
>
> *Bullet Park* (1969)

Clarkson, Jeremy
English motoring journalist

> The Americans have a proud and noble tradition of being utterly hopeless in warfare. They lost in Vietnam, they lost in Somalia, they lost in the Bay of Pigs, and though they won the Gulf war they managed to kill more British soldiers than the Iraqis.
>
> *The Sunday Times*, 1999

Clemenceau, Georges (1841–1929)
French Prime Minister and journalist

> America is the only nation in history which miraculously has gone directly from barbarism to degeneration without the usual interval of civilization.
>
> Attr.

Clinton, William ('Bill') (1946–)
US Democrat President

> Though our challenges are fearsome, so are our strengths. Americans have ever been a relentless, questioning, hopeful people.
>
> Inauguration speech, 20 January 1993

Coleman, Ornette (1930–)
US jazz musician

> Only America makes you feel that everybody wants to be like you. That's what success is: everybody wants to be like you.
>
> In Arthur Taylor, *Notes and Tones* (1977)

Coolidge, Calvin (1872–1933)
US President

> The business of America is business.
>
> Speech, 1925

Díaz, Porfirio (1830–1915)
Mexican general and statesman
> Poor Mexico, so far from God and so near to the United States!

> Attr.

Edward VIII (later Duke of Windsor) (1894–1972)
King of the United Kingdom; abdicated 11 December 1936
> The thing that impresses me most about America is the way parents obey their children.

> In *Look*, 1957

Eisenhower, Dwight D. (1890–1969)
US Republican President and general
> Whatever America hopes to bring to pass in this world must first come to pass in the heart of America.

> Inaugural address, 1953

Emerson, Ralph Waldo (1803–1882)
US poet, essayist, transcendentalist and teacher
> America is a country of young men.

> *Society and Solitude* (1870)

> The Americans have little faith. They rely on the power of a dollar.

> Lecture, 1841, 'Man the Reformer'

Fitzgerald, F. Scott (1896–1940)
US writer
> Americans, while willing, even eager, to be serfs, have always been obstinate about being peasantry.

> *The Great Gatsby* (1926)

Ford, Gerald R. (1913–)
US Republican President
Referring to his own appointment as President
> I guess it proves that in America anyone can be President.

> In Reeves, *A Ford Not a Lincoln*

Freud, Sigmund (1856–1939)
Austrian physicist; founder of psychoanalysis
> Yes, America is gigantic, but a gigantic mistake.

> In Peter Gay, *Freud: A Life for Our Time* (1988)

Fuentes, Carlos (1928–)
Mexican novelist and playwright
> What America does best is to understand itself. What it does worst is to understand others.

> *Time*, 1986

George, Dan (1899–1982)
Canadian Indian chief
> When the white man came we had the land and they had the Bibles; now they have the land and we have the Bibles.

> Attr.

Goering, Hermann (1893–1946)
Nazi leader and military commander

Assurance to Hitler
> The Americans cannot build aeroplanes. They are very good at refrigerators and razor blades.

> In Alistair Cooke, *America*

Grey, Edward, Viscount of Fallodon (1862–1933)
English statesman and writer
> The United States is like a gigantic boiler. Once the fire is lighted under it there is no limit to the power it can generate.

> In Winston S. Churchill, *Their Finest Hour*

Harding, Gilbert (1907–1960)
English writer and broadcaster
> Before he [Gilbert Harding] could go to New York he had to get a US visa at the American consulate in Toronto. He was called upon to fill in a long form with many questions, including 'Is it your intention to overthrow the Government of the United States by force?' By the time Harding got to that one he was so irritated that he answered: 'Sole purpose of visit.'

> In W. Reyburn, *Gilbert Harding* (1978)

Harding, Warren G. (1865–1923)
US statesman and Republican President
> America's present need is not heroics but healing, not nostrums but normalcy.

> Speech, Boston, May 1920

Hobson, Sir Harold (1904–1992)
British critic and writer
> The United States, I believe, are under the impression that they are twenty years in advance of this country; whilst, as a matter of actual verifiable fact, of course, they are just about six hours behind it.

> *The Devil in Woodford Wells*

Hopkins, Anthony (1937–)
Welsh actor
> It created in me a yearning for all that is wide and open and expansive. Something that will never allow me to fit in in my own country, with its narrow towns and narrow roads and narrow kindnesses and narrow reprimands.

> *Independent*, 1994

James, Henry (1843–1916)
US-born British writer, critic and letter writer
> It's a complex fate, being an American.

> Letter, 1872

Johnson, Samuel (1709–1784)
English lexicographer, poet, critic, conversationalist and essayist
> I am willing to love all mankind, except an American.

> In Boswell, *The Life of Samuel Johnson* (1791)

Kennedy, John F. (1917–1963)
US Democrat President

The United States has to move very fast to even stand still.

The Observer, 1963

And so, my fellow Americans: ask not what your country can do for you – ask what you can do for your country. My fellow citizens of the world: ask not what America will do for you, but what together we can do for the freedom of man.

Inaugural address, 1961

Lawrence, D.H. (1885–1930)
English writer, poet and critic
> And suddenly she craved again for the more absolute silence of America. English stillness was so soft, like an inaudible murmur of voices, of presences.

St Mawr (1925)

Lewis, Sinclair (1885–1951)
US writer
> In other countries, art and literature are left to a lot of shabby bums living in attics and feeding on booze and spaghetti, but in America the successful writer or picture-painter is indistinguishable from any other decent business man.

Babbit (1922)

Lorca, Federico Garcia (1898–1936)
Spanish poet and dramatist
> The only things that the United States has given to the world are skyscrapers, jazz, and cocktails. That is all. And in Cuba, in our America, they make much better cocktails.

Poet in New York (1940, trans 1988)

McCarthy, Joseph (1908–1957)
US Republican politician
> McCarthyism is Americanism with its sleeves rolled.

Speech, 1952

McCarthy, Mary (1912–1989)
US writer and critic
> The happy ending is our national belief.

Attr.

> An interviewer asked me what book I thought best represented the modern American woman. All I could think of to answer was: *Madame Bovary*.

On the Contrary (1961)

Madariaga, Salvador de (1886–1978)
Spanish writer, diplomat and teacher
> First, the sweetheart of the nation, then her aunt, woman governs America because America is a land where boys refuse to grow up.

'Americans are Boys'

Martineau, Harriet (1802–1876)
English writer
> If there is any country on earth where the course of true love may be expected to run smooth, it is America.

Society in America (1837)

Mencken, H.L. (1880–1956)
US writer, critic, philologist and satirist
> No one ever went broke underestimating the intelligence of the American people.

Attr.

Minifie, James M. (1900–1974)
Canadian broadcaster
> The United States is the glory, jest, and terror of mankind.

In Purdy (ed.), *The New Romans* (1988)

Mitford, Jessica (1917–1996)
English writer
> Things on the whole are much faster in America; people don't 'stand for election', they 'run for office.'

Sons and Rebels (1960)

Pitt, William (1708–1778)
English politician and Prime Minister
> I rejoice that America has resisted. Three millions of people, so dead to all the feelings of liberty, as voluntarily to submit to be slaves, would have been fit instruments to make slaves of the rest.

Speech, House of Commons, 1766

Roosevelt, Eleanor (1884–1962)
US writer and lecturer
> I think if the people of this country can be reached with the truth, their judgment will be in favour of the many, as against the privileged few.

Ladies' Home Journal

Roosevelt, Theodore (1858–1919)
US Republican President
> There can be no fifty-fifty Americanism in this country. There is room here for only hundred per cent Americanism, only for those who are Americans and nothing else.

Speech, 1918

> We have room in this country for but one flag, the Stars and Stripes … We have room for but one loyalty, loyalty to the United States … We have room for but one language, the language of the Declaration of Independence and the Gettysburg speech.

In Lord Charnwood, *Theodore Roosevelt* (1923)

> There is no room in this country for hyphenated Americanism.

Speech, 1915

Russell, Bertrand (1872–1970)
English philosopher, mathematician, essayist and social reformer

America … where law and custom alike are based upon the dreams of spinsters.

Marriage and Morals (1929)

In America everybody is of the opinion that he has no social superiors, since all men are equal, but he does not admit that he has no social inferiors.

'Ideas that have harmed mankind' (1950)

Smith, Samuel Francis (1808–1895)
American Baptist clergyman and poet
My country, 'tis of thee,
Sweet land of liberty,
Of thee I sing:
Land where my fathers died,
Land of the pilgrims' pride,
From every mountain-side
Let freedom ring.

'America' (1832)

Stapledon, Olaf (1886–1950)
British philosopher and writer
That strange blend of the commercial traveller, the missionary, and the barbarian conqueror, which was the American abroad.

Last and First Men (1930)

Stein, Gertrude (1874–1946)
US writer, dramatist, poet and critic
In the United States there is more space where nobody is than where anybody is. That is what makes America what it is.

The Geographical History of America (1936)

Talleyrand, Charles-Maurice de (1754–1838)
French statesman, memoirist and prelate
Of America
I found there a country with thirty-two religions and only one sauce.

In Pedrazzini, *Autant en apportent les mots*

Toynbee, Arnold (1889–1975)
English historian
America is a large, friendly dog in a very small room. Ever time it wags its tail it knocks over a chair.

Broadcast news summary, 1954

Trinder, Tommy (1909–1989)
English comedian and actor
Referring to the GIs in World War II
Overpaid, overfed, oversexed and over here.

The Sunday Times, 1976

Trollope, Anthony (1815–1882)
English writer, traveller and post office official
On Frances Trollope's *Domestic Manners of the Americans*
What though people had plenty to eat and clothes to wear, if they put their feet upon the tables and did not reverence their betters? The Americans were to her rough, uncouth, and

vulgar, – and she told them so.

An Autobiography (1883)

Vidal, Gore (1925–)
US writer, critic and poet
The land of the dull and the home of the literal.

Reflections upon a Sinking Ship (1969)

Walpole, Horace (1717–1797)
English writer and politician
The next Augustan age will dawn on the other side of the Atlantic. There will, perhaps, be a Thucydides at Boston, a Xenophon at New York, and, in time, a Virgil at Mexico, and a Newton at Peru. At last, some curious traveller from Lima will visit England and give a description of the ruins of St Paul's, like the editions of Balbec and Palmyra.

Letter to Sir Horace Mann, 1774

Wells, H.G. (1866–1946)
English writer
Every time Europe looks across the Atlantic to see the American eagle, it observes only the rear end of an ostrich.

America

Whitman, Walt (1819–1892)
US poet and writer
The United States themselves are essentially the greatest poem.

Leaves of Grass (1855 edition), Preface

Wilde, Oscar (1854–1900)
Irish poet, dramatist, writer, critic and wit
Of course, America had often been discovered before, but it had always been hushed up.

Personal Impressions of America (1883)

The youth of America is their oldest tradition. It has been going on now for three hundred years.

A Woman of No Importance (1893)

Wilson, Woodrow (1856–1924)
US Democrat President
America lives in the heart of every man everywhere who wishes to find a region where he will be free to work out his destiny as he chooses.

Speech, 1912

America … is the prize amateur nation of the world. Germany is the prize professional nation.

Speech, 1917

America is the only idealistic nation in the world.

Speech, 1919

Zangwill, Israel (1864–1926)
English writer and Jewish spokesman
America is God's Crucible, the great

Melting-Pot where all the races of Europe are melting and re-forming!

The Melting Pot (1908)

anarchy

Anonymous
> Anarchy may not be the best form of government, but it's better than no government at all.

Bennett, Alan (1934–)
English dramatist, actor and diarist
> We started off trying to set up a small anarchist community, but people wouldn't obey the rules.

Getting On (1972)

Cary, Joyce (1888–1957)
English novelist
> Anarchists who love God always fall for Spinoza because he tells them that God doesn't love them. This is just what they need. A poke in the eye. To a real anarchist a poke in the eye is better than a bunch of flowers. It makes him see stars.

The Horse's Mouth (1944)

Shaw, George Bernard (1856–1950)
Irish socialist, writer, dramatist and critic
> All men are anarchists with regard to laws which are against their consciences.
> In London our worst anarchists are the magistrates, because many of them are so old and ignorant that when they are called upon to administer any law that is based on ideas or knowledge less than half a century old, they disagree with it, and naively set the example of violating it.

Major Barbara (1907), Preface

▶▶ GOVERNMENT; POLITICS

ancestors

Adams, John Quincy (1767–1848)
US lawyer, diplomat and President
> Think of your forefathers! Think of your posterity!

Speech, December 1802

Cervantes, Miguel de (1547–1616)
Spanish writer and dramatist
> *Dos linajes solos hay en el mundo, como decía una agüela mía, que son el tener y el no tener.*
> There are only two lineages in the world, as a grandmother of mine used to say, the Haves and the Have-nots.

Don Quixote, II (1615)

Forro, (Rev. Fr) Francis Stephen (1914–1974)
Response to a journalist's comment on the scruffiness of Hungarian refugees arriving at Mascot aerodrome, Australia, in 1956
> Ah, yes, but they will make fine ancestors.

Attr.

Gilbert, W.S. (1836–1911)
English dramatist, humorist and librettist
> I can trace my ancestry back to a protoplasmal primordial atomic globule. Consequently, my family pride is something inconceivable.

The Mikado (1885)

Junot, Andoche, Duc d'Abrantes (1771–1813)
On being made a duke
> I am my own ancestor.

Attr.

Plutarch (c.46–c.120)
Greek biographer and philosopher
> It is indeed desirable to be well descended, but the glory belongs to our ancestors.

On the Training of Children

Seneca (c.4 BC–AD 65)
Roman philosopher, poet, dramatist, essayist, rhetorician and statesman
> *Qui genus joctat suum*
> *Aliena laudat.*
> Who boasts his ancestry, praises others' worth.

Hercules Furens, line 340, trans. Milton

Sheridan, Richard Brinsley (1751–1816)
Irish dramatist, politician and orator
> Our ancestors are very good kind of folks; but they are the last people I should choose to have a visiting acquaintance with.

The Rivals (1775)

Squire, Sir J.C. (1884–1958)
English poet, critic, writer and editor
> At last incapable of further harm.
> The lewd forefathers of the village sleep.

'If Gray had had to write his Elegy in the Cemetery of Spoon River'

Stevenson, Robert Louis (1850–1894)
Scottish writer, poet and essayist
> Each has his own tree of ancestors, but at the top of all sits Probably Arboreal.

Memories and Portraits (1887)

▶▶ ARISTOCRACY; FAMILY

angels

The Bible (King James Version)
> And he dreamed, and behold a ladder set up on the earth, and the top of it reached to heaven: and behold the angels of God ascending and

descending on it.

Genesis, 28:12

Chesterton, G.K. (1874–1936)
English writer, poet and critic
> Angels can fly because they can take themselves lightly.

Orthodoxy (1908)

Firbank, Ronald (1886–1926)
English writer
> There was a pause – just long enough for an angel to pass, flying slowly.

Vainglory (1915)

Gregory I (540–604)
Pope and saint
> Answer was given that they were called Angles. But he remarked, 'They are well named, for they have the countenance of angels, and as such should be coheirs with the angels in heaven.'

In Bede, Historia Ecclesiastica (731)

Pope, Alexander (1688–1744)
English poet, translator and editor
> Men would be Angels, Angels would be Gods.
> Aspiring to be Gods, if Angels fell,
> Aspiring to be Angels, Men rebel.

An Essay on Man (1733)

Shakespeare, William (1564–1616)
English dramatist, poet and actor
> Angels are bright still, though the brightest fell.

Macbeth, IV.iii

anger

Albertano of Brescia (c.1190–c.1270)
Jurist, philosopher and politician
> *Iratus semper plus putat posse facere quam possit.*
> The angry man always thinks he can do more than he can.

Liber Consolationis

Aristotle (384–322 BC)
Greek philosopher
> The man who is angry on the right grounds and with the right people, and in the right manner and at the right moment and for the right length of time, is to be praised.

Nicomachean Ethics

Bacon, Francis (1561–1626)
English philosopher, essayist, politician and courtier
> Anger makes dull men witty, but it keeps them poor.

'Apophthegms' (1679)

Beckford, William (1760–1844)
English writer, collector and politician
> When he was angry, one of his eyes became so terrible, that no person could bear to behold it; and the wretch upon whom it was fixed, instantly fell backward, and sometimes expired. For fear, however, of depopulating his dominions and making his palace desolate, he but rarely gave way to his anger.

Vathek (1787)

The Bible (King James Version)
> A soft answer turneth away wrath.

Proverbs, 15: 1

> Be ye angry, and sin not; let not the sun go down upon your wrath.

Ephesians, 4: 26

Blake, William (1757–1827)
English poet, engraver, painter and mystic
> The tygers of wrath are wiser than the horses of instruction.

The Marriage of Heaven and Hell (c.1790–1793)

> I was angry with my friend:
> I told my wrath, my wrath did end.
> I was angry with my foe:
> I told it not, my wrath did grow.

Songs of Experience (1794)

Burns, Robert (1759–1796)
Scottish poet and song writer
> We think na on the lang Scots miles,
> The mosses, waters, slaps, and styles,
> That lie between us and our hame,
> Whare sits our sulky, sullen dame,
> Gathering her brows like gathering storm,
> Nursing her wrath to keep it warm.

'Tam o' Shanter' (1790)

Congreve, William (1670–1729)
English dramatist
> Heav'n has no rage, like love to hatred turned,
> Nor Hell a fury, like a woman scorn'd.

The Mourning Bride (1697)

Connolly, Cyril (1903–1974)
English literary editor, writer and critic
> There is no fury like an ex-wife searching for a new lover.

The Unquiet Grave (1944)

Diller, Phyllis (1917–1974)
US comedian
> Never go to bed mad. Stay up and fight.

Phyllis Diller's Housekeeping Hints

Dryden, John (1631–1700)
English poet, satirist, dramatist and critic
> Beware the fury of a patient man.

Absalom and Achitophel (1681)

Fuller, Thomas (1608–1661)
English churchman and antiquary
> Anger is one of the sinews of the soul; he that

wants it hath a maimed mind.

The Holy State and the Profane State
(1642)

Halifax, Lord (1633–1695)
English politician, courtier, pamphleteer and epigrammatist
>Anger is never without an Argument, but seldom with a good one.

Thoughts and Reflections (1750)

Hazlitt, William (1778–1830)
English writer and critic
>Spleen can subsist on any kind of food.

'On Wit and Humour' (1819)

Irving, Washington (1783–1859)
US writer and diplomat
>A tart temper never mellows with age, and a sharp tongue is the only edged tool that grows keener with constant use.

'Rip Van Winkle' (1820)

Louis XIV (1638–1715)
King of France
>Ah, if I were not king, I should lose my temper.

Attr.

Proverb
>If you are patient in one moment of anger, you will escape a hundred days of sorrow.

Chinese Proverb

Shaw, George Bernard (1856–1950)
Irish socialist, writer, dramatist and critic
>Beware of the man who does not return your blow: he neither forgives you nor allows you to forgive yourself.

Man and Superman (1903)

Sidney, Sir Philip (1554–1586)
English poet, critic, soldier, courtier and diplomat
>O heavenly Foole, thy most kisse worthy face
>Anger invests with such a lovely grace,
>That Anger's selfe I needes must kisse againe.

Astrophel and Stella (1591)

Spyri, Johanna (1827–1901)
Swiss writer
>Anger has overpowered him, and driven him to a revenge which was rather a stupid one, I must acknowledge, but anger makes us all stupid.

Heidi, 23

Twain, Mark (1835–1910)
US humorist, writer, journalist and lecturer
>When angry count four; when very angry swear.

Pudd'nhead Wilson's Calendar (1894)

Wilde, Oscar (1854–1900)
Irish poet, dramatist, writer, critic and wit
>Man is a rational animal who always loses his temper when he is called upon to act in

accordance with the dictates of reason.

Intentions (1891)

animals

Anonymous
>The rabbit has a charming face;
>Its private life is a disgrace.

'The Rabbit'

>This animal is very wicked,
>When it is attacked it defends itself.

La Ménagerie (1868)

Archilochus (fl. c.650 BC)
Greek poet
>The fox knows many things but the hedgehog one big one.

In Plutarch, *Moralia*

Blake, William (1757–1827)
English poet, engraver, painter and mystic
>Tyger Tyger, burning bright
>In the forests of the night:
>What immortal hand or eye
>Could frame thy fearful symmetry?

'The Tyger' (1794)

Canetti, Elias (1905–1994)
Bulgarian-born English writer, dramatist and critic
>*Immer wenn man ein Tier genau betracht, hat man das Gefühl, ein Mensch, der drin sitzt, macht sich über einen lustig.*
>Whenever you observe an animal closely, you have the feeling that a person sitting inside is making fun of you.

The Human Province

Chesterton, G.K. (1874–1936)
English writer, poet and critic
>When fishes flew and forests walked
>And figs grew upon thorn,
>Some moment when the moon was blood
>Then surely I was born.

>With monstrous head and sickening cry
>And ears like errant wings,
>The devil's walking parody
>On all four-footed things …

>Fools! For I also had my hour;
>One far fierce hour and sweet:
>There was a shout about my ears,
>And palms before my feet.

The Wild Knight and Other Poems
(1900)

Coleridge, Samuel Taylor (1772–1834)
English poet, philosopher and critic
>Poor little Foal of an oppressed race!

I love the languid patience of thy face.
> 'To a Young Ass' (1794)

Donne, John (1572–1631)
English poet
> Nature's great masterpiece, an Elephant,
> The only harmless great thing –
> Still sleeping stood; vexed not his fantasy
> Black dreams; like an unbent bow, carelessly,
> His sinewy proboscis did remissly lie.
>> 'The Progress of the Soul' (1601

Eliot, George (1819–1880)
English writer and poet
> Animals are such agreeable friends – they ask no
> questions, they pass no criticisms.
>> Scenes of Clerical Life (1858)

Ennius, Quintus (239–169 BC)
> Simia, quam similis turpissima bestia, nobis.
> How like us is the ape, most horrible of beasts.
>> In Cicero, De Natura Deorum

Fleming, Ian (1908–1964)
English writer
> A horse is dangerous at both ends and
> uncomfortable in the middle.
>> The Sunday Times, 1966

Foyle, Christina (1911–1999)
Member of famous British bookselling family
> Animals are always loyal and love you, whereas
> with children you never know where you are.
>> The Times, 1993

Froude, James Anthony (1818–1894)
English historian and scholar
> Wild animals never kill for sport. Man is the only
> one to whom the torture and death of his fellow
> creatures is amusing in itself.
>> Oceana, or England and her Colonies
>> (1886)

Goldsmith, Oliver (c.1728–1774)
Irish dramatist, poet and writer
> Brutes never meet in bloody fray,
> Nor cut each other's throats, for pay.
>> 'Logicians Refuted' (1759)

Keats, John (1795–1821)
English poet
> I go among the Fields and catch a glimpse of a
> Stoat or a fieldmouse peeping out of the
> withered grass – the creature hath a purpose
> and its eyes are bright with it. I go amongst the
> buildings of a city and I see a Man hurrying
> along – to what? the Creature has a purpose
> and his eyes are bright with it.
>> Letter to George and Georgiana Keats,
>> 14 February–3 May 1819

Lawrence, D.H. (1885–1930)
English writer, poet and critic

Be a good animal, true to your animal instincts.
> The White Peacock (1911)

Nash, Ogden (1902–1971)
US poet
> The turtle lives 'twixt plated decks
> Which practically conceal its sex.
> I think it clever of the turtle
> In such a fix to be so fertile.
>> Hard Lines (1931)

> The cow is of the bovine ilk;
> One end is moo, the other, milk.
>> Free Wheeling (1931)

Nerval, Gérard de (1808–1855)
French poet and writer
Justifying his habit of walking a lobster, on a lead, in the
gardens of the Palais Royal
> Why is a lobster any more ridiculous than a dog –
> or any other creature one chooses to take for a
> walk? I have a liking for lobsters: they are
> peaceful and solemn, they know the secrets of
> the sea, they do not bark, and they do not eat
> into the essential privacy of one's soul the way
> dogs do. And Goethe had an aversion to dogs,
> and he was not mad.
>> In T. Gautier, Portraits et Souvenirs Littéraires (1875)

Peacock, Thomas Love (1785–1866)
English writer and poet
> Nothing can be more obvious than that all
> animals were created solely and exclusively for
> the use of man.
>> Headlong Hall (1816)

Pope, Alexander (1688–1744)
English poet, translator and editor
> The spider's touch, how exquisitely fine!
> Feels at each thread, and lives along the line.
>> An Essay on Man 1733)

Punch
> Cats is 'dogs' and rabbits is 'dogs' and so's
> Parrats, but this 'ere 'Tortis' is an insect, and
> there ain't no charge for it.
>> 1869

Quiller-Couch, Sir Arthur (**'Q'**) (1863–1944)
English man of letters
> The lion is the beast to fight:
> He leaps along the plain,
> And if you run with all your might,
> He runs with all his mane.
>> 'Sage Counsel'

Shakespeare, William (1564–1616)
English dramatist, poet and actor
> No beast so fierce but knows some touch of pity.
>> Richard III, I.ii

Solzhenitsyn, Alexander (1918–)
Russian writer, dramatist and historian

Nowadays we don't think much of a man's love for an animal; we mock people who are attached to cats. But if we stop loving animals, aren't we bound to stop loving humans too?

Cancer Ward (1968)

Spencer, Herbert (1820–1903)

English philosopher and journalist

People are beginning to see that the first requisite to success in life, is to be a good animal.

Education (1861)

Thackeray, William Makepeace (1811–1863)

Indian-born English writer

The leopard follows his nature as the lamb does, and acts after leopard law; she can neither help her beauty, nor her courage, nor her cruelty; nor a single spot on her shining coat; nor the conquering spirit which impels her; nor the shot which brings her down.

The History of Henry Esmond (1852)

Voltaire (1694–1778)

French philosopher, dramatist, poet, historian writer and critic

There are two things for which animals are to be envied: they know nothing of future evils, or of what people say about them.

Letter, 1739

Whitman, Walt (1819–1892)

US poet and writer

I think I could turn and live with animals, they are so placid and self-contain'd,
I stand and look at them long and long.
They do not sweat and whine about their condition,
They do not lie awake in the dark and weep for their sins,
They do not make me sick discussing their duty to God,
Not one is dissatisfied, not one is demented with the mania of owning things,
Not one kneels to another, nor to his kind that lived thousands of years ago,
Not one is respectable or unhappy over the whole earth.

'Song of Myself' (1855), 32

Sellar, Walter (1898–1951) and **Yeatman, Robert Julian** (1897–1968)

British writers

To confess that you are totally Ignorant about the Horse, is social suicide: you will be despised by everybody, especially the horse.

Horse Nonsense (1933)

▶▶ BIRDS; CATS; DOGS

apathy

The Bible (King James Version)

Because thou art lukewarm, and neither cold nor hot, I will spue thee out of my mouth.

Revelation, 3:16

Keller, Helen (1880–1968)

US writer and educator of the blind and deaf

Science may have found a cure for most evils; but it has found no remedy for the worst of them all – the apathy of human beings.

My Religion (1927)

Whitelaw, William (1918–)

English Conservative politician

I am not prepared to go about the country stirring up apathy.

Attr.

apologies

Dickens, Charles (1812–1870)

English writer

'Not to put too fine a point upon it' – a favourite apology for plain-speaking with Mr Snagsby.

Bleak House (1853)

Shaw, George Bernard (1856–1950)

Irish socialist, writer, dramatist and critic

I never apologise.

Arms and the Man (1898)

Wodehouse, P.G. (1881–1975)

English humorist and writer

It is a good rule in life never to apologize. The right sort of people do not want apologies, and the wrong sort take a mean advantage of them.

The Man Upstairs (1914)

▶▶ REGRET

appearance

Aesop (6th century BC)

Legendary Greek writer of fables

It is not only fine feathers that make fine birds.

Fables

Appearances are often deceiving.

'The Wolf in Sheep's Clothing'

Amis, Kingsley (1922–1995)

English writer, poet and critic

Outside every fat man there was an even fatter man trying to close in.

One Fat Englishman (1963)

Auden, W.H. (1907–1973)
English poet, essayist, critic, teacher and dramatist
> Only God can tell the saintly from the suburban,
> Counterfeit values always resemble the true;
> Neither in Life nor Art is honesty bohemian,
> The free behave much as the respectable
> do.
>> 'New Year Letter' (1941)

Brown, James (1933–)
US singer
> Hair is the first thing. And teeth the second. Hair and teeth. A man got those two things he's got it all.
>> The Godfather of Soul (1986)

Camus, Albert (1913–1960)
Algerian-born French writer
> *Hélas! après un certain âge, tout homme est responsable de son visage.*
> Alas! after a certain age every man is responsible for the face he has.
>> The Fall, 1956

Coward, Sir Noël (1899–1973)
English dramatist, actor, producer and composer
> Sunburn is very becoming – but only when it is even – one must be careful not to look like a mixed grill.
>> Lido Beach

Crawford, Joan (1908–1977)
US film actress
> I think the most important thing a woman can have – next to talent, of course, is – her hairdresser.
>> Esquire, 1957

Daniels, R.G. (1916–1993)
English magistrate
> The most delightful advantage of being bald – one can hear snowflakes.
>> The Observer, 1976

Dickens, Charles (1812–1870)
English writer
> He might have brought an action against his countenance for libel, and won heavy damages.
>> Oliver Twist (1838)

Goldsmith, Oliver (c.1728–1774)
Irish dramatist, poet and writer
> Is it one of my well looking days, child? Am I in face to-day?
>> She Stoops to Conquer (1773)

Lardner, Ring (1885–1933)
US humorist and writer
Speaking to a flamboyantly dressed stranger who walked into the club where he was drinking
> How do you look when I'm sober?
>> In J. Yardley, Ring

Lincoln, Abraham (1809–1865)
US statesman and President
> The Lord prefers common-looking people. That is why he makes so many of them.
>> In James Morgan, Our President (1928)

Ovid (43 BC–AD 18)
Roman poet
> *Delectant etiam castas praeconia formae;*
> *Virginibus curae grataque forma sua est.*
> Even respectable girls delight in hearing their beauty praised; even the innocent are worried and pleased by their appearance.
>> Ars Amatoria, I, line 623

Plato (c.429–347 BC)
Greek philosopher
> The imitator or maker of the images knows nothing of true existence; he knows appearances only.
>> The Republic, X

Proverbs
> Fine feathers make fine birds.
>
> Handsome is as handsome does.

Robinson, Robert (1927–)
English broadcaster
> Certain people are born with natural false teeth.
>> Stop the Week, BBC radio programme, 1977

Rostand, Edmond (1868–1918)
French poet and dramatist
> Enormous, my nose! Vile pug-nose, flat-nose, flat-head, let me inform you that I pride myself in such an appendage, considering that a big nose is the proper sign of a friendly, good, courteous, witty, liberal, courageous brave man, such as I am.
>> Cyrano de Bergerac (1897)

Rubinstein, Helena (1872–1965)
Polish-born US cosmetician and businesswoman
Recalling her arrival in America on a cold day in 1914
> All the American women had purple noses and gray lips and their faces were chalk white from terrible powder. I recognized that the United States could be my life's work.
>> In Time, 1965

Sartre, Jean-Paul (1905–1980)
French philosopher, writer, dramatist and critic
> Things are entirely what they appear to be and behind them … there is nothing.
>> La Nausée, 1938

Wilde, Oscar (1854–1900)
Irish poet, dramatist, writer, critic and wit
It is only shallow people who do not judge by appearances.
>> The Picture of Dorian Gray (1891)

Windsor, Duchess of (Wallis Simpson) (1896–1986)
Wife of Duke of Windsor (formerly Edward VIII)
> One can never be too thin or too rich.

Attr.

▶▶ BEAUTY; EYES; VANITY

architecture

Austen, Jane (1775–1817)
English writer
> Nothing can be said in his vindication, but that his abolishing Religious Houses and leaving them to the ruinous depredations of time has been of infinite use to the landscape of England in general.

The History of England (1791)

Bacon, Francis (1561–1626)
English philosopher, essayist, politician and courtier
> Houses are built to live in and not to look on; therefore let use be preferred before uniformity, except where both may be had.

Essays (1625)

Bentley, Edmund Clerihew (1875–1956)
English writer
> Sir Christopher Wren
> Said, 'I am going to dine with some men.
> If anybody calls
> Say I am designing St Paul's.'

Biography for Beginners

Betjeman, Sir John (1906–1984)
English poet laureate
> Ghastly Good Taste, or A Depressing Story of the Rise and Fall of English Architecture.

Title of book, 1933

Boyd, Robin Gerard Penleigh (1919–1971)
Australian architect
> The Australian town-dweller spent a century in the acquisition of his toy: an emasculated garden, a five-roomed cottage of his very own, different from its neighbours by a minor contortion of window or porch – its difference significant to no-one but himself.

Australia's Home (1952)

Buckminster Fuller, Richard (1895–1983)
US architect and engineer
Lines to the tune of 'Home on the Range'
> Let architects sing of aesthetics that bring
> Rich clients in hordes to their knees;
> Just give me a home, in a great circle dome
> Where stresses and strains are at ease.

Time, 1964

Charles, Prince of Wales (1948–)
Son and heir of Elizabeth II and Prince Philip

On the proposed extension to the National Gallery
> A kind of vast municipal fire station ... like a monstrous carbuncle on the face of a much-loved and elegant friend.

Speech, 1984, to the Royal Institute of British Architects

Coward, Sir Noël (1899–1973)
English dramatist, actor, producer and composer
Of the Taj Mahal
> It didn't look like a biscuit box did it? I've always felt that it might.

Private Lives (1930)

De Wolfe, Elsie (1865–1950)
US interior designer
On first sighting the Acropolis
> It's beige! My color!

In J. Smith, Elsie De Wolfe

Fuller, Thomas (1608–1661)
English churchman and antiquary
> Light (God's eldest daughter) is a principal beauty in building.

The Holy State and the Profane State (1642)

Goethe (1749–1832)
German poet, writer, dramatist and scientist
> *Ich nenne die Baukunst eine erstarrte Musik.*
> I call architecture a kind of petrified music.

Gespräche mit Eckermann, 1829.

Gogol, Nicolai Vasilyevich (1809–1852)
Russian writer and soldier
> I always feel sad when I look at new buildings which are constantly being built and on which millions are spent ... Has the age of architecture passed without hope of return?

Attr.

Lancaster, Sir Osbert (1908–1986)
English writer, cartoonist and stage designer
> 'Fan vaulting' ... an architectural device which arouses enormous enthusiasm on account of the difficulties it has all too obviously involved but which from an aesthetic standpoint frequently belongs to the 'Last-supper-carved-on-a-peach-stone' class of masterpiece.

Pillar to Post (1938)

> A hundred and fifty accurate reproductions of Anne Hathaway's cottage, each complete with central heating and garage.

Pillar to Post (1938)

Le Corbusier (1887–1965)
French architect
> *Une maison est une machine-à-habiter.*
> A house is a machine for living in.

Vers une architecture (1923)

Lette, Kathy (1959–)
Australian novelist

Inner-city council estates make you believe the world was really built in six days.

Mad Cows (1996)

Levin, Bernard (1928–)
British author and journalist
What has happened to architecture since the second world war that the only passers-by who can contemplate it without pain are those equipped with a white stick and a dog?

The Times, 1983

McGregor, Craig (1933–)
Australian writer
A house is a machine for loving in.

In Ian McKay et al., *Living and Partly Living*

Mies van der Rohe, Ludwig (1886–1969)
German-born US architect and designer

A chair is a very difficult object. A skyscraper is almost easier. That is why Chippendale is famous.

Time, 1957

Less is more.

New York Herald Tribune, 1959

Architecture starts when you carefully put two bricks together. There it begins.

New York Herald Tribune, 1959

Nairn, Ian (1930–1983)
English writer on architecture and journalist
If what is called development is allowed to multiply at the present rate, then by the end of the century Great Britain will consist of isolated oases of preserved monuments in a desert of wire, concrete roads, cosy plots and bungalows … Upon this new Britain the Review bestows a name in the hope that it will stick – SUBTOPIA.

Architectural Review, 1955

Pringle, John Martin Douglas (1912–)
Scottish-born Australian writer
On Sydney Opera House
There it stands, like Santa Maria della Salute on the lagoon in Venice, a perfect symbol linking the city to the sea … I believe it is a building of which all Australians may rightly be proud, perhaps the only true work of architecture on this continent.

On Second Thoughts (1971)

Reynolds, Malvina (1900–1978)
US singer-songwriter
Describing newly built houses south of San Francisco
They're all made out of ticky-tacky,
And they all look just the same.

'Little Boxes', song, 1962

Ruskin, John (1819–1900)
English art critic, philosopher and reformer

Better the rudest work that tells a story or records a fact, than the richest without meaning. There should not be a single ornament put upon great civic buildings, without some intellectual intention.

The Seven Lamps of Architecture (1849)

When we build, let us think that we build for ever.

The Seven Lamps of Architecture (1849)

You know there are a great many odd styles of architecture about; you don't want to do anything ridiculous; you hear of me, among others, as a respectable architectural man-milliner; and you send for me, that I may tell you the leading fashion.

The Crown of Wild Olive (1866)

No person who is not a great sculptor or painter can be an architect. If he is not a sculptor or painter, he can only be a builder.

Lectures on Architecture and Painting (1854)

Schelling, Friedrich von (1775–1854)
German philosopher
Architektur … ist gleichsam die erstarrte Musik.
Architecture is, as it were, petrified music.

Philosophy of Art (1803)

Wotton, Sir Henry (1568–1639)
English diplomat, traveller and poet
In Architecture as in all other Operative Arts, the end must direct the Operation. The end is to build well. Well building hath three Conditions: Commodity, Firmness, and Delight.

Elements of Architecture (1624)

Wright, Frank Lloyd (1869–1959)
US architect and writer
The physician can bury his mistakes, but the architect can only advise his client to plant vines.

New York Times Magazine, 1953

▶▶ ART; TRAGEDY

argument

Addison, Joseph (1672–1719)
English essayist, poet, playwright and statesman
Our disputants put me in mind of the skuttle fish, that when he is unable to extricate himself, blackens all the water about him, till he becomes invisible.

The Spectator, 1712

Arguments out of a pretty mouth are unanswerable.

Women and Liberty

Anonymous

This is a rotten argument, but it should be good enough for their lordships on a hot summer afternoon.

Annotation in ministerial brief

Billings, Josh (1818–1885)
US writer, philosopher and lecturer

Thrice is he armed that hath his quarrel just,
But four times he who gets his blow in fust.

Josh Billings, his Sayings (1865)

Essex, Robert Devereux, Earl of (1566–1601)
Elizabethan soldier and courtier
To Lord Willoughby

Reasons are not like garments, the worse for wearing.

Attr., c.1599

Fergusson, Sir James (1832–1907)
Scottish Conservative statesman

I have heard many arguments which influenced my opinion, but never one which influenced my vote.

Attr.

FitzGerald, Edward (1809–1883)
English poet, translator and letter writer

Myself when young did eagerly frequent
Doctor and Saint, and heard great argument
About it and about: but evermore
Came out by the same Door as in I went.

The Rubáiyát of Omar Khayyám (1859)

Gay, John (1685–1732)
English poet, dramatist and librettist

Those, who in quarrels interpose,
Must often wipe a bloody nose.

Fables (1727)

Herbert, George (1593–1633)
English poet and priest

Be calm in arguing; for fiercenesse makes
Errour a fault, and truth discourtesie.

The Temple (1633)

Inge, William Ralph (1860–1954)
English divine, writer and teacher

It takes in reality only one to make a quarrel. It is useless for the sheep to pass resolutions in favour of vegetarianism while the wolf remains of a different opinion.

Outspoken Essays (1919)

Johnson, Samuel (1709–1784)
English lexicographer, poet, critic, conversationalist and essayist

I dogmatize and am contradicted, and in this conflict of opinions and sentiments I find delight.

In Sir John Hawkins, Life of Samuel Johnson (1787)

Though we cannot out-vote them we will out-argue them.

In Boswell, The Life of Samuel Johnson (1791)

La Rochefoucauld (1613–1680)
French writer

Les querelles ne dureraient pas longtemps si le tort n'était que d'un côté.
Quarrels would not last long if the fault were on one side only.

Maximes (1678)

Lowell, James Russell (1819–1891)
US poet, editor, abolitionist and diplomat

There is no good in arguing with the inevitable. The only argument available with an east wind is to put on your overcoat.

Democracy and Other Addresses (1887)

Potter, Stephen (1900–1969)
English writer, critic and lecturer
A blocking phrase for conversation

'Yes, but not in the South', with slight adjustments will do for any argument about any place, if not about any person.

Lifemanship (1950)

Rostand, Jean (1894–1977)
French biologist

A married couple are well suited when both partners usually feel the need for a quarrel at the same time.

Le Mariage

Shakespeare, William (1564–1616)
English dramatist, poet and actor

In a false quarrel there is no true valour.

Much Ado About Nothing, V.i

Sheridan, Richard Brinsley (1751–1816)
Irish dramatist, politician and orator

The quarrel is a very pretty quarrel as it stands – we should only spoil it by trying to explain it.

The Rivals (1775)

Sterne, Laurence (1713–1768)
Irish-born English writer and clergyman

Heat is in proportion to the want of true knowledge.

Tristram Shandy (1759–1767)

Thatcher, Margaret (1925–)
English Conservative Prime Minister

I love argument, I love debate. I don't expect anyone just to sit there and agree with me, that's not their job.

The Times, 1980

Yeats, W.B. (1865–1939)
Irish poet, dramatist, editor, writer and senator

We make out of the quarrel with others, rhetoric; but of the quarrel with ourselves, poetry.

'Anima Hominis' (1917)

aristocracy

Ailesbury, Maria, Marchioness of (d. 1893)
English aristocrat
> My dear, my dear, you never know when any
> beautiful young lady may not blossom into a
> Duchess!
>
> In Portland, *Men, Women, and Things* (1937)

Austen, Jane (1775–1817)
English writer
> Sir Walter Elliot, of Kellynch Hall, in
> Somersetshire, was a man who, for his own
> amusement, never took up any book but the
> Baronetage; there he found occupation for an
> idle hour and consolation in a distressed one …
> this was the page at which the favourite volume
> always opened: – ELLIOT OF KELLYNCH-HALL.
>
> *Persuasion* (1818)

Beaumarchais (1732–1799)
French dramatist
> Because you are a great lord, you think yourself
> a great genius! You took the trouble to be born,
> but nothing more.
>
> *Mariage de Figaro* (1784)

Burke, Edmund (1729–1797)
Irish-born British statesman and philosopher
> Nobility is a graceful ornament to the civil order.
> It is the Corinthian capital of polished society.
>
> *Reflections on the Revolution in France and on the
> Proceedings in Certain Societies in London* (1790)

Charles, Prince of Wales (1948–)
Son and heir of Elizabeth II and Prince Philip
> The one advantage about marrying a princess –
> or someone from a royal family – is that they do
> know what happens.
>
> Attr.

Haldane, J.B.S. (1892–1964)
British biochemist, geneticist and popularizer of science
> If human beings could be propagated by
> cutting, like apple trees, aristocracy would be
> biologically sound.
>
> *The Inequality of Man and Other Essays* (1932)

Hope, Anthony (1863–1933)
English writer, dramatist and lawyer
> 'Bourgeois, ' I observed, 'is an epithet which the
> riff-raff apply to what is respectable, and the
> aristocracy to what is decent.'
>
> *The Dolly Dialogues* (1894)

Lévis, Duc de (1764–1830)
French writer and soldier
> Noblesse oblige.
> Nobility has its obligations.
>
> *Maximes et réflexions* (1812)

Lloyd George, David (1863–1945)
British Liberal statesman
> A fully equipped duke costs as much to keep up
> as two Dreadnoughts; and dukes are just as
> great a terror and they last longer.
>
> Speech, 1909

Machiavelli (1469–1527)
Florentine statesman, political theorist and historian
> For titles do not reflect honour on men, but
> rather men on their titles.
>
> *Dei Discorsi*

Manners, Lord (1818–1906)
English Conservative politician and writer
> Let wealth and commerce, laws and learning die,
> But leave us still our old nobility!
>
> *England's Trust* (1841)

Mill, John Stuart (1806–1873)
English philosopher, economist and reformer
> Persons require to possess a title, or some other
> badge of rank, or of the consideration of people
> of rank, to be able to indulge somewhat in the
> luxury of doing as they like without detriment to
> their estimation.
>
> *On Liberty* (1859)

Mitford, Nancy (1904–1973)
English writer
> An aristocracy in a republic is like a chicken
> whose head had been cut off: it may run about
> in a lively way, but in fact it is dead.
>
> *Noblesse Oblige* (1956)

Mosley, Charles
> Did you know that a peer condemned to death
> had the right to be hanged with a silken cord? A
> bit like insisting that the electric chair had to be
> Chippendale.
>
> *The Observer*, 1999

Northcliffe, Lord (1865–1922)
Irish-born British newspaper proprietor
> When I want a peerage, I shall buy one like an
> honest man.
>
> Attr.

Pearson, Hesketh (1887–1964)
English biographer
> There is no stronger craving in the world than
> that of the rich for titles, except that of the
> titled for riches.
>
> Attr.

Seitz, Raymond
> In the British aristocracy, the gene pool has
> always had a shallow end.
>
> *The Observer*, 1998

Shaw, George Bernard (1856–1950)
Irish socialist, writer, dramatist and critic
> Titles distinguish the mediocre, embarrass the

superior, and are disgraced by the inferior.

Man and Superman (1903)

I've been offered titles, but I think they get one into disreputable company.

In Barrow, *Gossip*

Talleyrand, Charles-Maurice de (1754–1838)
French statesman, memoirist and prelate
Comment on exiled French aristocrats

Ils n'ont rien appris, ni rien oublié.
They have learnt nothing, and forgotten nothing.

Attr.

Tennyson, Alfred, Lord (1809–1892)
English lyric poet

From yon blue heavens above us bent
The gardener Adam and his wife
Smile at the claims of long descent.
Howe'er it be, it seems to me,
'Tis only noble to be good.
Kind hearts are more than coronets,
And simple faith than Norman blood.

'Lady Clara Vere de Vere' (c.1835)

Thackeray, William Makepeace (1811–1863)
Indian-born English writer

Nothing like blood, sir, in hosses, dawgs, and men.

Vanity Fair (1848)

Wellington, Duke of (1769–1852)
Irish-born British military commander and statesman

I believe I forgot to tell you I was made a Duke.

Postscript to a letter to his nephew, 1814

Wilde, Oscar (1854–1900)
Irish poet, dramatist, writer, critic and wit

You should study the Peerage, Gerald. It is the one book a young man about town should know thoroughly, and it is the best thing in fiction the English have ever done.

A Woman of No Importance (1893), III

Wodehouse, P.G. (1881–1975)
English humorist and writer

Unlike the male codfish which, suddenly finding itself the parent of three million five hundred thousand little codfish, cheerfully resolves to love them all, the British aristocracy is apt to look with a somewhat jaundiced eye on its younger sons.

In R. Usborne, *Wodehouse at Work to the End* (1976)

Woolf, Virginia (1882–1941)
English writer and critic

Those comfortably padded lunatic asylums which are known, euphemistically, as the stately homes of England.

The Common Reader (1925)

▶▶ CLASS

the army

Anonymous
Definition of NAAFI

Where you can eat dirt cheap.

In Frank Muir, *A Kentish Lad* (1997)

Any officer who shall behave in a scandalous manner, unbecoming the character of an officer and a gentleman shall … be CASHIERED.

Articles of War

The words of a soldier in the Peninsular War

I looked along the line; it was enough to assure me. The steady determined scowl of my companions assured my heart and gave me determination.

In Richardson, *Fighting Spirit: Psychological Factors in War* (1978)

Baxter, James K. (1926–1972)
New Zealand poet and playwright

The boy who volunteered at seventeen
At twenty-three is heavy on the booze.

'Returned Soldier' (1946)

Brodsky, Joseph (1940–1996)
Russian poet, essayist, critic and exile

It is the army that finally makes a citizen of you; without it, you still have a chance, however slim, to remain a human being.

'Less Than One' (1986)

Cambronne, General (1770–1842)

La Garde meurt, et ne se rend pas.
The Guard dies and does not surrender.

Attr., Waterloo, June 1815

Churchill, Sir Winston (1874–1965)
English Conservative Prime Minister
On the Chiefs of Staffs system, 1943

You may take the most gallant sailor, the most intrepid airman, or the most audacious soldier, put them at a table together – what do you get? The sum of their fears.

In Macmillan, *The Blast of War*

Frederick the Great (1712–1786)
King of Prussia

An army, like a serpent, goes on its belly.

Attr.

Gerrish, Theodore (1712–1786)
US soldier

The ties that bound us together were of the most sacred nature: they had been gotten in hardship and baptised in blood.

Army Life: A Private's Reminiscence of the Civil War (1882)

Gerry, Elbridge (1744–1814)
US Vice-President

A standing army is like a standing member: an excellent assurance of domestic tranquillity but a dangerous temptation to foreign adventure.

The *Observer*, 'Soundbites', 1998

Green, Michael (1927–)
English writer and playwright

Fortunately, the army has had much practice in ignoring impossible instructions.

The Boy Who Shot Down an Airship (1988)

Heller, Joseph (1923–1999)
US writer

I had examined myself pretty thoroughly and discovered that I was unfit for military service.

Catch-22 (1961)

Hoffmann, Max (1869–1927)
German general
Referring to the performance of the British army in World War I

Ludendorff: The English soldiers fight like lions. Hoffman: True. But don't we know that they are lions led by donkeys.

In Falkenhayn, *Memoirs*

Hull, General Sir Richard, (1907–)

National Service did the country a lot of good but it darned near killed the army.

Attr.

Kipling, Rudyard (1865–1936)
Indian-born British poet and writer

O, it's Tommy this, an' Tommy that, an' 'Tommy, go away';
But it's 'Thank you, Mister Atkins, ' when the band begins to play …

Then it's Tommy this, an' Tommy that, an' 'Tommy 'ow's yer soul?'
But it's 'Thin red line of 'eroes' when the drums begin to roll …

For it's Tommy this, an' Tommy that, an' 'Chuck him out, the brute!'
But it's 'Saviour of 'is country' when the guns begin to shoot.

Barrack-Room Ballads and Other Verses (1892)

Kissinger, Henry (1923–)
German-born US Secretary of State

The conventional army loses if it does not win. The guerilla wins if he does not lose.

'Foreign Affairs', XIII (1969)

Lincoln, Abraham (1809–1865)
US statesman and President

If you don't want to use the army, I should like to borrow it for a while. Yours respectfully, A. Lincoln.

Letter to General George B. McClellan during the US Civil War, 1862

Manning, Frederic (1882–1935)
Australian writer
Of the men in his battalion

These apparently rude and brutal natures comforted, encouraged, and reconciled each other to fate, with a tenderness and tact which was more moving than anything in life.

Her Privates We (1929)

Marlborough, Duke of (1650–1722)
English soldier

No soldier can fight unless he is properly fed on beef and beer.

Attr.

Milligan, Spike (1918–)
Irish comedian and writer

The Army works like this: if a man dies when you hang him, keep hanging him until he gets used to it.

Attr.

Monash, Sir John (1865–1931)
Australian military commander

Leadership counts for something, of course, but it cannot succeed without the spirit, élan and morale of those led. Therefore I count myself the most fortunate of men in having been placed at the head of the finest fighting machine the world has ever known.

Argus, 1927

A man of character in peace is a man of courage in war.

The Anatomy of Courage (1945)

Napier, Sir William (1785–1860)
British general and historian

Then was seen with what a strength and majesty the British soldier fights.

History of the War in the Peninsula

Napoleon I (1769–1821)
French emperor

An army marches on its stomach.

Attr.

Of his generals

I made most of mine *de la boue* out of mud. Wherever I found talent and courage, I rewarded it. My principle was *la carrière ouverte aux talens* sic career open to talent, without asking whether there were any quarters of nobility to show.

In O'Meara, *Napoleon in Exile* (1822)

Napoleon III (1808–1873)
French emperor

The army is the true nobility of our country.

Speech, March 1855

Patton, George S. (1885–1945)
US general

Untutored courage is useless in the face of
educated bullets.

Cavalry Journal, 1922

Quarles, Francis (1592–1644)
English poet, writer and royalist
> Our God and soldiers we alike adore
> Ev'n at the brink of danger; not before:
> After deliverance, both alike requited,
> Our God's forgotten, and our soldiers slighted.

'Of Common Devotion' (1632)

Rosten, Norman (1914–)
> And there's the outhouse poet, anonymous:
> Soldiers who wish to be a hero
> Are practically zero
> But whose who wish to be civilians
> Jesus they run into millions.

'The Big Road'

Sassoon, Siegfried (1886–1967)
English poet and writer
> Soldiers are citizens of death's gray land,
> Drawing no dividend from time's tomorrows …
>
> Soldiers are dreamers; when the guns begin
> They think of firelit homes, clean beds, and wives.
> I see them in foul dug-outs, gnawed by rats,
> And in the ruined trenches, lashed with rain,
> Dreaming of things they did with balls and bats.

'Dreamers' (1917)

Sellar, Walter (1898–1951) and **Yeatman, Robert
Julian** (1897–1968)
British writers
> Napoleon's armies always used to march on
> their stomachs, shouting: 'Vive l'Intérieur!' and
> so moved about very slowly.

1066 And All That (1930)

Shakespeare, William (1564–1616)
English dramatist, poet and actor
> That in the captain's but a choleric word
> Which in the soldier is flat blasphemy.

Measure For Measure, II.ii

Shaw, George Bernard (1856–1950)
Irish socialist, writer, dramatist and critic
> I never expect a soldier to think.

The Devil's Disciple (1901)

> When the military man approaches, the world
> locks up its spoons and packs off its womankind.

Man and Superman (1903)

> You can always tell an old soldier by the inside
> of his holsters and cartridge boxes. The young
> ones carry pistols and cartridges: the old ones,
> grub.

Arms and the Man (1898)

Smithers, Alan Jack (1919–)
Of Sir John Monash, Australian military commander

He was, above all, the first twentieth-century
general, a man with petrol in his veins and a
computer in his head.

Sterne, Laurence (1713–1768)
Irish-born English writer and clergyman
> 'A soldier, ' cried my uncle Toby, interrupting the
> corporal, 'is no more exempt from saying a
> foolish thing, Trim, than a man of letters.' – 'But
> not so often, and please your honour, ' replied
> the corporal.

Tristram Shandy (1759–1767)

Tolstoy, Leo (1828–1910)
Russian writer, essayist, philosopher and moralist
> The chief attraction of military service has been
> and will remain this compulsory and
> irreproachable idleness.

War and Peace (1868–1869)

Truman, Harry S. (1884–1972)
US Democrat President
Of General MacArthur
> I didn't fire him because he was a dumb son of a
> bitch, although he was, but that's not against
> the law for generals. If it was, half to three-
> quarters of them would be in gaol.

In Miller, *Plain Speaking* (1974)

Tucholsky, Kurt (1890–1935)
German satirist and writer
> *Der französische Soldat ist ein verkleideter Zivilist, der
> deutsche Zivilist ist ein verkleideter Soldat.*
> The French soldier is a civilian in disguise, the
> German civilian is a soldier in disguise.

'Ocean of Pain' (1973)

Ustinov, Sir Peter (1921–)
English actor, director, dramatist, writer and raconteur
> As for being a General, well, at the age of four
> with paper hats and wooden swords we're all
> Generals. Only some of us never grow out of it.

Romanoff and Juliet (1956)

Vigny, Alfred de (1797–1863)
French writer
> *L'armée est une nation dans la nation; c'est un vice de
> notre temps.*
> The army is a nation within the nation; it is one
> of the vices of our times.

The Military Condition, 1835

Washington, George (1732–1799)
US general, statesman and President
> Discipline is the soul of an army. It makes small
> numbers formidable; procures success to the
> weak, and esteem to all.

Letter of Instructions to the Captains of the
Virginia Regiments, 1759

Wellington, Duke of (1769–1852)
Irish-born British military commander and statesman

When I reflect upon the characters and attainments of some of the general officers of this army, and consider that these are the persons on whom I am to rely to lead columns against the French, I tremble; and as Lord Chesterfield said of the generals of his day, 'I only hope that when the enemy reads the list of their names, he trembles as I do.'

Letter to Torrens, 29 August 1810; usually quoted as 'I don't know what effect these men will have upon the enemy, but, by God, they frighten me.'

Of his troops
> The mere scum of the earth.

In Stanhope, *Conversations with the Duke of Wellington* (1888)

Wells, H.G. (1866–1946)
English writer
> The army ages men sooner than the law and philosophy; it exposes them more freely to germs, which undermine and destroy, and it shelters them more completely from thought, which stimulates and preserves.

Bealby (1915)

Wilde, Lady Jane (1826–1896)
Irish poet and society hostess, mother of Oscar Wilde
English poet and writer
> There's a proud array of soldiers –
> what do they round your door?
> They guard our master's granaries
> from the thin hands of the poor.

'The Famine Years'

▶▶ NAVY; WAR; WEAPONS

art

Adams, Scott (1957–)
US cartoonist
> Creativity is allowing yourself to make mistakes. Art is knowing which ones to keep.

The Dilbert Principle

Albert, Prince Consort (1819–1861)
German-born husband of Queen Victoria
> The works of art, by being publicly exhibited and offered for sale, are becoming articles of trade, following as such the unreasoning laws of markets and fashion; and public and even private patronage is swayed by their tyrannical influence.

Speech to the Royal Academy, May 1851

Alexander, Hilary (1818–1895)
> To the accountants, a true work of art is an investment that hangs on the wall.

Sunday Telegraph, 1993

Anonymous
> We would prefer to see the Royal Opera House run by a philistine with the requisite financial acumen than by the succession of opera and ballet lovers who have brought a great and valuable institution to its knees.

Select Committe Report into the Royal Opera House, 1997

Anouilh, Jean (1910–1987)
French dramatist and screenwriter
> *C'est très jolie la vie, mais elle n'a pas de forme. L'art a pour objet de lui en donner une précisément.*
> Life is very nice, but it has no shape. It is the purpose of art to give it shape.

The Rehearsal (1950)

Artaud, Antonin (1896–1948)
French actor, dramatist and theorist
> No one has ever written, painted, sculpted, modelled, built or invented except literally to get out of hell.

In Lewis Wolpert, *Malignant Sadness* (1999)

Bacon, Francis (1909–1993)
English philosopher, essayist, politician and courtier
> The job of the artist is always to deepen the mystery.

Sunday Telegraph, 1964

Baryshnikov, Mikhail (1948–)
Latvian-born ballet dancer
> The essence of all art is to have pleasure in giving pleasure.

Time, 1975

Beaverbrook, Lord (1879–1964)
Canadian-born British newspaper owner
> Buy old masters. They fetch a better price than old mistresses.

Attr.

Beerbohm, Sir Max (1872–1956)
English satirist, cartoonist, critic and essayist
> The lower one's vitality, the more sensitive one is to great art.

'Enoch Soames' (1912)

Bell, Clive (1881–1964)
English art critic
> It would follow that 'significant form' was form behind which we catch a sense of ultimate reality.

Art (1914)

Bellow, Saul (1915–)
Canadian-born US Jewish writer
> I feel that art has something to do with the achievement of stillness in the midst of chaos. A stillness which characterizes prayer, too, and the eye of the storm. I think that art has something to do with an arrest of

attention in the midst of distraction.

In Plimpton (ed.), Writers at Work (1967)

On the perception that time seems to speed up as we grow older

Art is one rescue from this chaotic acceleration. Metre in poetry, tempo in music, form and colour in painting. But we do feel that we are speeding earthward, crashing into our graves.

Ravelstein (2000)

Berenson, Bernard (1865–1959)
Lithuanian-born US art critic

Art is mind and heart and touch as much and more than it is mere instrument, technique – without which however it cannot exist at all.

The Bernard Berenson Treasury (1962)

Bernstein, Leonard (1918–1990)
US composer and conductor

Any great work of art … revives and readapts time and space, and the measure of its success is the extent to which it makes you an inhabitant of that world – the extent to which it invites you in and lets you breathe its strange, special air.

Vogue, 1958

Bing, Rudolf (1902–)
Director of the New York Metropolitan Opera

It is so much worse to be a mediocre artist than to be a mediocre post office clerk.

5000 Nights at the Opera (1972)

Bowen, Elizabeth (1899–1973)
Irish writer

Art is the only thing that can go on mattering once it has stopped hurting.

The Heat of the Day (1949)

Bowen, Stella (1893–1947)
Australian writer

Any artist knows that after a good bout of work one is both too tired and too excited to be of any use to anyone. … What one wants … is for other people to occupy themselves with one's own moods and requirements; to lie on a sofa and listen to music, and to have things brought to one on a tray!

Drawn from Life (1941)

Brack, (Cecil) John (1920–)
Australian artist

I know all about art, but I don't know what I like.

In Stephen Murray-Smith (ed.), The Dictionary of Australian Quotations

Braque, Georges (1882–1963)
French painter

L'Art est fait pour troubler, la Science rassure.
Art is meant to disturb, science reassures.

Day and Night, Notebooks (1952)

Brodsky, Joseph (1940–1996)
Russian poet, essayist, critic and exile

Art is not a better, but an alternative existence; it is not an attempt to escape reality but the opposite, an attempt to animate it. It is a spirit seeking flesh but finding words.

Less Than One (1986)

Buñuel, Luis (1900–1983)
Spanish film director

In any society, the artist has a responsibility. His effectiveness is certainly limited and a painter or writer cannot change the world. But they can keep an essential margin of non-conformity alive. Thanks to them, the powerful can never affirm that everyone agrees with their acts. That small difference is very important.

Quoted by Anthony Hill in Contemporary Artists (1977)

Butler, Samuel (1835–1902)
English writer, painter, philosopher and scholar

An art can only be learned in the workshop of those who are winning their bread by it.

Erewhon (1872)

Calman, Mel (1931–1994)
English cartoonist

In answer to the criticism of his cartoons that 'any child could do better'

Yes, but it takes courage for an adult to draw as badly as that.

The Independent, 1994

Cary, Joyce (1888–1957)
English novelist

Remember I'm an artist. And you know what that means in a court of law. Next worst to an actress.

The Horse's Mouth (1944)

Chagall, Marc (1887–1985)
Russian-born French painter

Art is the unceasing effort to compete with the beauty of flowers – and never succeeding.

In Frank S. Pepper The Wit and Wisdom of the 20th Century (1987)

Great art picks up where nature ends.

Time, 1985

Chekhov, Anton (1860–1904)
Russian writer, dramatist and doctor

The artist may not be a judge of his characters, only a dispassionate witness.

Attr.

Chesterton, G.K. (1874–1936)
English writer, poet and critic

The artistic temperament is a disease that afflicts amateurs.

Heretics (1905)

Art, like morality, consists in drawing the line somewhere.

Orthodoxy (1908)

Connolly, Cyril (1903–1974)
English literary editor, writer and critic
It is closing time in the gardens of the West and from now on an artist will be judged only by the resonance of his solitude or the quality of his despair.

Horizon, 1949–1950)

There is no more sombre enemy of good art than the pram in the hall.

Enemies of Promise (1938)

Conrad, Joseph (1857–1924)
Polish-born British writer, sailor and explorer
A work that aspires, however humbly, to the condition of art should carry its justification in every line.

The Nigger of the Narcissus (1897)

Constant, Benjamin (1767–1834)
Swiss-born French writer and politician
Dîner avec Robinson, écolier de Schelling. Son travail sur l'esthétique du Kant. Idées très ingénieuses. L'art pour l'art et sans but; tout but dénature l'art. Mais l'art atteint au but qu'il n'a pas.
Dinner with Robinson, a pupil of Schelling. His work on the aesthetics of that man Kant. Very ingenious ideas. Art for art's sake, without a purpose; every purpose distorts the true nature of art. But art achieves a purpose which it does not have.

Journal intime, 1804

Correggio (c.1489–1534)
Italian painter
On seeing Raphael's 'St Cecilia' in Bologna, c.1525
Anchí io sono pittore!
I, too, am an artist.

In L. Pungileoni, *Memorie Istoriche de … Correggio* (1817)

Croce, Benedetto (1866–1952)
Italian philosopher, historian and critic
Art is ruled uniquely by the imagination.

Esthetic

Davy, Sir Humphry (1778–1829)
English chemist and inventor
His opinion of the art galleries in Paris
The finest collection of frames I ever saw.

Attr.

Debussy, Claude (1862–1918)
French composer and critic
L'art est le plus beau des mensonges.
Art is the most beautiful of all lies.

Monsieur Croche, antidilettante

Degas, Edgar (1834–1917)
French painter and sculptor
Art is vice. You don't marry it legitimately, you rape it.

In Paul Lafond, *Degas* (1918)

Demarco, Richard (1930–)
Scottish exhibition and theatre director, art patron and teacher
Art is for everyone – paint, like a piece of music, is the most international thing I know.

Attr.

Duchamp, Marcel (1887–1968)
French-born US artist
I don't believe in art. I believe in artists.

The World of Marcel Duchamp (1966)

Eliot, T.S. (1888–1965)
US-born British poet, verse dramatist and critic
The only way of expressing emotion in the form of art is by finding an 'objective correlative'; in other words, a set of objects, a situation, a chain of events which shall be the formula of that particular emotion; such that when the external facts, which must terminate in sensory experience, are given, the emotion is immediately evoked.

'Hamlet' (1919)

No poet, no artist of any sort, has his complete meaning alone. His significance, his appreciation is the appreciation of his relation to the dead poets and artists.

'Tradition and the Individual Talent' (1919)

No artist produces great art by a deliberate attempt to express his own personality.

'Four Elizabethan Dramatists' (1924)

Ellis, Havelock (1859–1939)
English sexologist and essayist
Every artist writes his own autobiography.

The New Spirit (1890)

Emerson, Ralph Waldo (1803–1882)
US poet, essayist, transcendentalist and teacher
Art is a jealous mistress, and, if a man have a genius for painting, poetry, music, architecture, or philosophy, he makes a bad husband and an ill provider.

Conduct of Life (1860)

Artists must be sacrificed to their art. Like bees, they must put their lives into the sting they give.

Letters and Social Aims (1875)

Eyre, Richard (1943–)
English film, theatre and television director
I would like to see the good in art made popular and the popular made good.

BBC radio interview, 1998

Commenting on the Government's decision to freeze spending on the arts.

> Art is all the things that politics isn't: it's passionate, ambiguous, complex, mysterious and thrilling. It's our means of redemption, it's the image of our humanity.
>
> *The Observer*, 1996

Fadiman, Clifton (1904–)
US writer, editor and broadcaster
Of Gertrude Stein

> I encountered the mama of dada again.
>
> *Appreciations* (1955)

Fellini, Federico (1920–1993)
Italian film director

> All art is autobiographical; the pearl is the oyster's autobiography.
>
> *Atlantic*, 1965

Fielding, Henry (1707–1754)
English writer, dramatist and journalist

> It hath been thought a vast commendation of a painter to say his figures seem to breathe; but surely it is much greater and nobler applause, that they appear to think.
>
> *Joseph Andrews* (1742)

Flaubert, Gustave (1821–1880)
French writer

> *L'artiste doit être dans son œuvre comme Dieu dans la création, invisible et tout-puissant; qu'on le sente partout, mais qu'on ne le voie pas.*
> The artist must be in his work as God is in creation, invisible and all-powerful; his presence should be felt everywhere, but he should never be seen.
>
> Letter to Mlle Leroyer de Chantepie, 1857

Fonteyn, Margot (1919–)
English dancer

> Great artists are people who find the way to be themselves in their art. Any sort of pretension induces mediocrity in art and life alike.
>
> *Margot Fonteyn: Autobiography* (1976)

Forster, E.M. (1879–1970)
English writer, essayist and literary critic

> To make us feel small in the right way is a function of art. Men can only make us feel small in the wrong way.
>
> Attr.

> Works of art, in my opinion, are the only objects in the material universe to possess internal order, and that is why, though I don't believe that only art matters, I do believe in Art for Art's sake.
>
> *Two Cheers for Democracy* (1951)

Friel, Brian (1929–)
Irish dramatist and writer

> The hell of it seems to be, when an artist starts saving the world, he starts losing himself.
>
> *Extracts from a Sporadic Diary*

Fry, Roger (1866–1934)
English art critic, philosopher and painter

> Mr Fry … brought out a screen upon which there was a picture of a circus. The interviewer was puzzled by the long waists, bulging necks and short legs of the figures. 'But how much wit there is in those figures, ' said Mr Fry. 'Art is significant deformity.'
>
> In Virginia Woolf, *Roger Fry* (1940)

Gauguin, Paul (1848–1903)
French Post-Impressionist painter

> Art is either a plagiarist or a revolutionist.
>
> In Huneker, *Pathos of Distance* (1913)

Gautier, Théophile (1811–1872)
French poet, writer and critic

> *Oui, l'œuvre sort plus belle*
> *D'une forme au travail*
> *Rebelle,*
> *Vers, marbre, onyx, émail.*
> Yes, creation comes out more beautiful from a form rebellious to work: verse, marble, onyx, enamel.
>
> *Emaux et Camées* (1932)

George I (1660–1727)
KIng of Great Britain and Ireland

> I hate all Boets and Bainters.
>
> In Campbell, *Lives of the Chief Justices* (1849)

Goethe (1749–1832)
German poet, writer, dramatist and scientist

> *Wenn es eine Freude ist, das Gute zu geniessen, so ist es eine grössere, das Bessere zu empfinden, und in der Kunst ist das Beste gut genug. Neapel, den 3. März, 1787.*
> If it is a joy to enjoy what is good, then it is a greater one to feel what is better, and in art the best is good enough. Naples, 3rd March, 1787.
>
> *Italian Journey* (published 1816–17)

> *Im übrigen ist es zuletzt die grösste Kunst, sich zu beschränken und zu isolieren.*
> Incidentally, however, ultimately the greatest art is in limiting and isolating oneself.
>
> *Gespräche mit Eckermann*, 1825

> *Das Klassische nenne ich das Gesunde, and das Romantische das Kranke.*
> Classicism I call health, and romanticism disease.
>
> *Gespräche mit Eckermann*, 1829

Hepworth, Dame Barbara (1903–1975)
English sculptor

> I rarely draw what I see. I draw what I feel in my body.
>
> Attr.

Herbert, Sir A.P. (1890–1971)
English humorist, writer, dramatist and politician
> A highbrow is the kind of person who looks at a sausage and thinks of Picasso.
>
> Attr.

> As my poor father used to say
> In 1863,
> Once people start on all this Art
> Good-bye, moralitee!
> And what my father used to say
> Is good enough for me.
>
> 'Lines for a Worthy Person' (1930)

Hershaw, William (1957–)
Scottish poet
On Damien Hirst's entry for the Turner Prize for contemporary art
> A coo and a cauf
> Cut in hauf.
>
> *The Cowdenbeath Man*

Heysen, Sir Hans William (1877–1968)
German-born Australian artist
> Why don't they draw, draw and draw? Their one idea is to cultivate the emotional sense, under the plea that they are expressing their personality.
>
> In Colin Thiele, *Heysen of Hahndorf*

Hirst, Damien (1965–)
British artist
On winning the Turner Prize
> It's amazing what you can do with an E in A-level art, twisted imagination and a chainsaw.
>
> *The Observer Review*, 1995

> I sometimes feel that I have nothing to say and I want to communicate this.
>
> Attr.

Huxley, Aldous (1894–1963)
English writer, poet and critic
> In the upper and the lower churches of St Francis, Giotto and Cimabue showed that art had once worshipped something other than itself.
>
> *Those Barren Leaves* (1925)

Ingres, J.A.D. (1780–1867)
French painter
> *Le dessin est la probité de l'art.*
> Drawing is the true test of art.
>
> *Pensées d'Ingres* (1922)

James, Henry (1843–1916)
US-born British writer, critic and letter writer
> It is art that makes life, makes interest, makes importance, for our consideration and application of these things, and I know of no substitute whatever for the force and beauty of its process.
>
> Letter to H.G. Wells, 1915

Joyce, James (1882–1941)
Irish writer
> The artist, like the God of creation, remains within or behind or beyond or above his handiwork, invisible, refined out of existence, indifferent, paring his fingernails.
>
> *A Portrait of the Artist as a Young Man* (1916)

Keats, John (1795–1821)
English poet
> The excellence of every art is its intensity, capable of making all disagreeables evaporate, from their being in close relationship with Beauty and Truth.
>
> Letter to George and Tom Keats, 21 December 1817

Kennedy, John F. (1917–1963)
US Democrat President
> In free society art is not a weapon … Artists are not engineers of the soul.
>
> Speech, 1963

Kipling, Rudyard (1865–1936)
Indian-born British poet and writer
> Till the Devil whispered behind the leaves,
> 'It's pretty, but is it Art?' …

> We know that the tail must wag the dog, for the horse is drawn by the cart;
> But the Devil whoops, as he whooped of old:
> 'It's clever, but is it Art?'.
>
> 'The Conundrum of the Workshops' (1890)

Klee, Paul (1879–1940)
Swiss painter, engraver and teacher
> *Eine aktive Linie, die sich frei ergeht, ein Spaziergang um seiner selbst willen, ohne Ziel. Das Agens ist ein Punkt, der sich verschiebt.*
> An active line going for a stroll, freely, aimlessly, a walk for its own sake. The agent is a point which moves around.
>
> *Pedagogical Sketchbook*, 1925

> *Kunst gibt nicht das Sichtbare wieder, sondern macht sichtbar.*
> Art does not reproduce what is visible; it makes things visible.
>
> 'Creative Credo' (1920)

Kraus, Karl (1874–1936)
Austrian scientist, critic and poet
> *Künstler ist nur einer, der aus der Lösung ein Rätsel machen kann.*
> The only person who is an artist is the one that can make a puzzle out of the solution.
>
> *By Night* (1919)

Lawrence, D.H. (1885–1930)
English writer, poet and critic
> Never trust the artist. Trust the tale. The proper function of a critic is to save the tale from the

artist who created it.

Studies in Classic American Literature (1923)

Low, Sir David (1891–1963)
New Zealand-born British political cartoonist
> I do not know whether he draws a line himself.
> But I assume that his is the direction … It makes
> Disney the most significant figure in graphic art
> since Leonardo.

In R. Schickel, *Walt Disney*

Marlborough, Sarah, First Duchess of (1660–1744)
Wife of John Churchill, First Duke of Marlborough
> For painters, poets and builders have very high
> flights, but they must be kept down.

Letter to the Duchess of Bedford, 1734

Maron, Monika (1941–)
German writer
> *Der Künstler als Bürger kann Demokrat sein, so gut und
> so schlecht wie alle anderen. Der Künstler als Künstler
> darf kein Demokrat sein.*
> The artist as a citizen can be a democrat, just as
> well and as badly as everybody else. The artist
> as an artist may not be a democrat.

Interview in *Der Spiegel*, 1994

Mayakovsky, Vladimir (1893–1930)
Russian poet, dramatist and artist
> Art is not a mirror to reflect the world, but a
> hammer with which to shape it.

The Guardian, 1974

Moore, George (1852–1933)
Irish writer, dramatist and critic
> Art must be parochial in the beginning to be
> cosmopolitan in the end.

Hail and Farewell: Ave (1911)

Mumford, Lewis (1895–1990)
US sociologist and writer
> The artist has a special task and duty
> – the task of reminding men of their humanity
> and the promise of their creativity.

Attr.

Murdoch, Iris (1919–1999)
Irish-born British writer, philosopher and dramatist
> All art deals with the absurd and aims at the
> simple. Good art speaks truth, indeed is truth,
> perhaps the only truth.

The Black Prince (1989)

Musset, Alfred de (1810–1857)
French dramatist and poet
> *Les grands artistes n'ont pas de patrie.*
> Great artists have no homeland.

Lorenzaccio (1834)

Nietzsche, Friedrich Wilhelm (1844–1900)
German philosopher, critic and poet
> *Als Artist hat man keine Heimat in Europa ausser in
> Paris.*

As an artist, one has no home in Europe except
Paris.

Ecco Homo (1888)

Nolan, Sir Sidney Robert (1917–1992)
Australian artist
> A successful artist would have no trouble being
> a successful member of the Mafia.

Good Weekend, 1985

Opie, John (1761–1807)
Asked how he mixed his colours
> I mix them with my brains, sir.

In Samuel Smiles, *Self-Help* (1859)

Ortega y Gasset, José (1883–1955)
> *El arte es incapaz de soportar el peso de nuestra vida.
> Cuando lo intenta, fracasa, perdiendo su gracia
> esencial.*
> Art is incapable of bearing the burden of our
> lives. When it tries, it fails, losing its essential
> grace.

The Theme of our Time, 1923

Paolozzi, Eduardo (1924–)
Scottish sculptor
> Modernism is the acceptance of the concrete
> landscape and the destruction of the human
> soul.

'Junk and the new Arts and Crafts Movement'

Pater, Walter (1839–1894)
English critic, writer and lecturer
> The love of art for art's sake.

Studies in the History of the Renaissance (1873)

> All art constantly aspires towards the condition
> of music.

Studies in the History of the Renaissance
(1873)

Rossetti, Dante Gabriel (1828–1882)
English poet, painter, translator and letter-writer
> Conception, my boy, fundamental brainwork, is
> what makes the difference in all art.

Letter to Hall Caine

Rowse, A.L. (1903–1997)
English historian, writer and poet
> Burning of people and (what was more valuable)
> works of art.

In H.R. Trevor-Roper, *Historical Essays*

Rückriem, Ulrich (1938–)
German sculptor
> People don't want art, they want football.

Scala, 1992

Ruskin, John (1819–1900)
English art critic, philosopher and reformer
> I believe the right question to ask, respecting
> all ornament, is simply this: Was it done with
> enjoyment – was the carver happy while

he was about it?

The Seven Lamps of Architecture (1849)

Nobody cares much at heart about Titian; only there is a strange undercurrent of everlasting murmur about his name, which means the deep consent of all great men that he is greater than they.

The Two Paths (1859)

Fine art is that in which the hand, the head, and the heart of man go together.

The Two Paths (1859)

Saatchi, Charles (1943–)
Co-founder of Saatchi & Saatchi advertising agency
Ninety per cent of the art I buy will probably be worthless in ten years' time.

The Observer, 1997

Sand, George (1804–1876)
French writer and dramatist
L'art n'est pas une étude de la réalité positive; c'est une recherche de la vérité idéale.
Art is not a study of positive reality; it is a search for ideal truth.

The Devil's Pond (1846)

L'art est une démonstration dont la nature est la preuve.
Art is a demonstration of which nature is the proof.

François le Champi

Santayana, George (1863–1952)
Spanish-born US philosopher and writer
Nothing is really so poor and melancholy as art that is interested in itself and not in its subject.

The Life of Reason (1906)

Schiller, Johann Christoph Friedrich (1759–1805)
German writer, dramatist, poet and historian
Ernst ist das Leben, heiter ist die Kunst.
Life is serious, art is serene.

Wallenstein I (1798–1801), Prologue

Shaw, George Bernard (1856–1950)
Irish socialist, writer, dramatist and critic
The true artist will let his wife starve, his children go barefoot, his mother drudge for his living at seventy, sooner than work at anything but his art.

Man and Superman (1903)

I believe in Michael Angelo, Velasquez, and Rembrandt; in the might of design, the mystery of color, the redemption of all things by Beauty everlasting, and the message of Art that has made these hands blessed. Amen.

The Doctor's Dilemma (1908)

Smith, Logan Pearsall (1865–1946)
US-born British epigrammatist, critic and writer

How often my soul visits the National Gallery, and how seldom I go there myself!

Afterthoughts (1931)

Sontag, Susan (1933–)
US critic and writer
A photograph is not only an image (as a painting is an image), an interpretation of the real; it is also a trace, something directly stencilled off the real, like a footprint or a death mask.

New York Review of Books, 1977

Spalding, Julian (1948–)
English art administrator
The professional art world is becoming a conspiracy against the public.

The Daily Mail, 1996

Stoppard, Tom (1937–)
British dramatist
Skill without imagination is craftsmanship and gives us many useful objects such as wickerwork picnic baskets. Imagination without skill gives us modern art.

Artist Descending a Staircase (1973)

What is an artist? For every thousand people there's nine hundred doing the work, ninety doing well, nine doing good, and one lucky bastard who's the artist.

Travesties (1975)

Storr, Dr Anthony (1920–)
British writer and psychiatrist
By creating a new unity in a poem or other work of art, the artist is attempting to restore a lost unity, or to find a new unity, within the inner world of the psyche, as well as producing work which has a real existence in the external world.

Solitude (1989)

Tertz, Abram (1925–1997)
Russian writer and dissident
Fairy-tales interest me as a manifestation of pure art, perhaps the very first instance of art detaching itself from real life, and also because – like pure art – they enhance reality, remaking it in their own likeness, separating good from evil, and bringing all fears and terrors to a happy conclusion.

A Voice From the Chorus (1973)

Thurber, James (1894–1961)
US humorist, writer and dramatist
He knows all about art, but he doesn't know what he likes.

Cartoon caption

Tolstoy, Leo (1828–1910)
Russian writer, essayist, philosopher and moralist
Art is not a handicraft, it is a transmission of

feeling which the artist has experienced.

What is Art? (1898)

Art is a human activity which has as its purpose the transmission to others of the highest and best feelings to which men have risen.

What is Art? (1898)

Ustinov, Sir Peter (1921–)

English actor, director, dramatist, writer and raconteur

If Botticelli were alive today he'd be working for Vogue.

The Observer, 1962

Vidal, Gore (1925–)

US writer, critic and poet

He will lie even when it is inconvenient, the sign of the true artist.

Two Sisters (1970)

Warhol, Andy (c.1926–1987)

US painter, graphic designer and filmmaker

An artist is someone who produces things that people don't need to have but that he – for some reason – thinks it would be a good idea to give them.

From A to B and Back Again (1975)

West, Dame Rebecca (1892–1983)

English writer, critic and feminist

… any authentic work of art must start an argument between the artist and his audience.

The Court and the Castle (1958)

Wharton, Edith (1862–1937)

US writer

Another unsettling element in modern art is that common symptom of immaturity, the dread of doing what has been done before.

The Writing of Fiction (1925)

Whistler, James McNeill (1834–1903)

US painter, etcher and pamphleteer

Listen! There never was an artistic period. There never was an Art-loving nation.

Mr Whistler's 'Ten O'Clock' (1885)

To a lady who said the two greatest painters were himself and Velasquez

'Why, ' answered Whistler in dulcet tones, 'why drag in Velasquez?'.

Seitz, Whistler Stories (1913)

Replying to the question 'For two days' labour, you ask two hundred guineas?'

No, I ask it for the knowledge of a lifetime.

Seitz, Whistler Stories (1913)

Whitehead, A.N. (1861–1947)

English mathematician and philosopher

Art is the imposing of a pattern on experience, and our aesthetic enjoyment is recognition of

the pattern.

Dialogues (1954)

Wilde, Oscar (1854–1900)

Irish poet, dramatist, writer, critic and wit

Art never expresses anything but itself.

The Nineteenth Century, 1889

Art is the most intense mode of individualism that the world has known.

The Fortnightly Review, 1891, 'The Soul of Man under Socialism'

All art is quite useless.

The Picture of Dorian Gray (1891)

Wyllie, George (1921–)

Scottish artist

On modern art

Art is like soup. There will be some vegetables you don't like but as long as you get some soup down you it doesn't matter.

The Daily Mail, 1996

Public art is art that the public can't avoid.

Attr.

Yevtushenko, Yevgeny (1933–)

Russian poet

A tremendous part in strengthening friendship between our peoples must be played by art, whose eternal role is the uniting of human hearts in the name of goodness and justice.

Yevtushenko Poems (1966)

▶▶ DESIGN; NATURE

artificial intelligence

Anonymous

Artificial Intelligence is the study of how to make real computers act like the ones in movies.

Artificial Intelligence is no match for natural stupidity.

Computers are not intelligent. They only think they are.

▶▶ COMPUTERS

assassination

Agate, James (1877–1947)

English drama critic and writer

On the failed attempt to assassinate Hitler

The worst of failure of this kind is that it spoils the market for more competent performers.

Ego 7, 1944

Shaw, George Bernard (1856–1950)
Irish socialist, writer, dramatist and critic
> Assassination is the extreme form of censorship.
> > *The Showing-Up of Blanco Posnet* (1911)

atheism

Bacon, Francis (1561–1626)
English philosopher, essayist, politician and courtier
> I had rather believe all the fables in the legend, and the Talmud, and the Alcoran, than that this universal frame is without a mind.
> > *Essays* (1625)

> God never wrought miracle to convince atheism, because his ordinary works convince it.
> > *Essays* (1625)

> It is true, that a little philosophy inclineth man's mind to atheism; but depth in philosophy bringeth men's minds about to religion.
> > *Essays* (1625)

Buchan, John (1875–1940)
Scottish writer, lawyer and Conservative politician
> An atheist is a man who has no invisible means of support.
> > Attr.

Buñuel, Luis (1900–1983)
Spanish film director
> I am still an atheist, thank God.
> > Attr.

Burke, Edmund (1729–1797)
Irish-born British statesman and philosopher
> Man is by his constitution a religious animal; … atheism is against, not only our reason, but our instincts.
> > *Reflections on the Revolution in France …* (1790)

Burns, Robert (1759–1796)
Scottish poet and song writer
> An atheist-laugh's a poor exchange
> For Deity offended!
> > 'Epistle to a Young Friend' (1786)

Cowper, William (1731–1800)
English poet, hymn and letter writer
> Blind unbelief is sure to err,
> And scan his work in vain;
> God is his own interpreter,
> And he will make it plain.
> > *Olney Hymns* (1779)

Cummings, William Thomas (1903–1945)
US priest
> There are no atheists in the foxholes.
> > In Romulo, *I Saw the Fall of the Philippines* (1943)

Diderot, Denis (1713–1784)
French philosopher, encyclopaedist, writer and dramatist
> *Voyez-vous cet œuf. C'est avec cela qu'on renverse toutes les écoles de théologie, et tous les temples de la terre.*
> See this egg. It is with this that one overturns all the schools of theology and all the temples on earth.
> > *Le Rêve de d'Alembert* (1769)

Orwell, George (1903–1950)
English writer and critic
> He was an embittered atheist (the sort of atheist who does not so much disbelieve in God as personally dislike Him).
> > *Down and Out in Paris and London* (1933)

Otway, Thomas (1652–1685)
English dramatist and poet
> These are rogues that pretend to be of a religion now!
> Well, all I say is, honest atheism for my money.
> > *The Atheist* (1683)

Proust, Marcel (1871–1922)
French writer and critic
> *On a même pu dire que la louange la plus haute de Dieu est dans la négation de l'athée qui trouve la Création assez parfaite pour se passer d'un créateur.*
> It has been said that the highest praise of God consists in the denial of Him by the atheist, who finds creation so perfect that he has no need of a creator.
> > *Le Côté de Guermantes* (1921)

Proverb
> An atheist is one point beyond the devil.

Rossetti, Dante Gabriel (1828–1882)
English poet, painter, translator and letter-writer
> The worst moment for the atheist is when he is really thankful and has nobody to thank.
> > Attr.

Russell, Bertrand (1872–1970)
English philosopher, mathematician, essayist and social reformer
> I was told that the Chinese say they would bury me by the Western Lake and build a shrine to my memory. I have some slight regret that this did not happen, as I might have become a god, which would have been very chic for an atheist.
> > *The Autobiography of Bertrand Russell* (1969)

Santayana, George (1863–1952)
Spanish-born US philosopher and writer
> My atheism, like that of Spinoza, is true piety towards the universe.
> > *Soliloquies in England* (1922)

Sartre, Jean-Paul (1905–1980)
French philosopher, writer, dramatist and critic

Elle ne croyait à rien; seul, son scepticisme l'empêchait d'être athée.
She didn't believe in anything; only her scepticism kept her from being an atheist.

Words (1964)

Turgenev, Ivan (1818–1883)
Russian writer and dramatist
The courage to believe in nothing.

Fathers and Sons (1862)

Young, Edward (1683–1765)
English poet, dramatist, satirist and clergyman
By Night an Atheist half believes a God.

Night-Thoughts on Life, Death and Immortality (1742–1745)

▶▶ GOD; RELIGION

australia

Blainey, Geoffrey Norman (1930–)
Australian writer
The Tyranny of Distance: How Distance Shaped Australia's History.

Title of book, 1966

The physical mastering of Australia was swift and often dramatic, but the emotional conquest was slow.

A Land Half Won

Boyd, Robin Gerard Penleigh (1919–1971)
Australian architect
The ugliness I mean is skin deep. If the visitor to Australia fails to notice it immediately, fails to respond to the surfeit of colour, the love of advertisements, the dreadful language, the ladylike euphemisms outside public lavatory doors, the technical competence, but the almost uncanny misjudgement in floral arrangements, or if he thinks that things of this sort are too trivial to dwell on, then he is unlikely to enjoy modern Australia.

The Australian Ugliness (1960)

Bragg, William Henry (1862–1942)
English scientist and academic
Going to Australia was like sunshine and fresh invigorating air.

In G.M. Caroe, William Henry Bragg (1978)

Cusack, Dymphna (1902–1981)
If the Spirit of the Bush walked down Martin Place it would be raped before it got ten feet.

Remark at the Adelaide Arts Festival, March 1964

Ellis, Havelock (1859–1939)
English sexologist and essayist
But for my everlasting good fortune I was flung into the wide sea of Australian bush alone, to

sink or to swim.

My Life (1940)

Esson, Louis (1879–1943)
Scots-born Australian dramatist
Australia is the only country in the world where the peasantry make the laws.

The Time Is Not Yet Ripe (1912)

Fitzgerald, Alan John (1935–)
Australian writer, Director of Planning
In Canberra, even the mistakes are planned by the National Capital Development Commission.

Life in Canberra

Galbraith, J.K. (1908–)
Canadian-born US economist, diplomat and writer
The Australians were wise to choose such a large country, for of all the people in the world they clearly require the most space.

Annals of an Abiding Liberal (1980)

Green, Marshall (1916–)
Lyndon B. Johnson always thought that Australia was the next large rectangular State beyond El Paso, and treated it accordingly.

Interview in film Allies

Hancock, Sir William Keith (1898–1988)
Australian historian
The little exclusive circles, which in Melbourne and Sydney had politely imitated English gentility, looked askance at the lucky upstarts – and intermarried with them. In the second half of the nineteenth century Australia became familiar with a new vulgarity and a new vigour.

Australia (1930)

Herbert, Xavier (1901–1984)
Australian writer, poet and social critic
On returning from the war
There's no place like home, Mum. Have me head read if ever I leave this gawd's own lovely land again. You dunno what a lovely land it is till you've seen them other crowded, foggy, frozen, furrin holes.

Capricornia (1938)

On the plight of the Aborigines
Until we give back to the Blackman just a bit of the land that was his and give it back without provisos, without strings to snatch it back, without anything but complete generosity of spirit in concession for the evil we have done him – until we do that, we shall remain what we have always been so far, a people without integrity; not a nation but a community of thieves.

Poor Fellow My Country (1975

Hogan, Paul (1939–)
Australian actor

We're a nation of punters and party-goers.
Bicentenary television programme, 'Australia Live', 1988

Hope, Alec (Derwent) (1907–)
Australian poet and critic

And her five cities, like teeming sores,
Each drains her: a vast parasite robber-state
Where second-hand Europeans pullulate
Timidly on the edge of alien shores.

'Australia' (1939)

Horne, Donald Richmond (1921–)
Australian novelist

Australia is a lucky country run mainly by
second-rate people who share its luck.

The Lucky Country: Australia in the Sixties (1964)

Humphries, Barry (1934–)
Australian entertainer

I think one of the highest compliments ever paid
to Australia was the imminent Japanese
invasion. To think the Japanese would [think] of
coming to Australia [to] live! They did change
their mind, with a little persuasion.

Men in Vogue, 1976

Lawrence, D.H. (1885–1930)
English writer, poet and critic

And all lying mysteriously within the Australian
underdark, that peculiar, lost weary aloofness of
Australia. There was the vast town of Sydney.
And it didn't seem to be real, it seemed to be
sprinkled on the surface of a darkness into which
it never penetrated.

Kangaroo (1923)

Lawson, Henry (1867–1922)
Australian writer and poet

And the sun sank on the grand Australian bush –
the nurse and tutor of eccentric minds, the
home of the weird, and of much that is different
from things in other lands.

'Rats' (1893)

Lenin, V.I. (1870–1924)
Russian revolutionary, Marxist theoretician and first
leader of the USSR
On Australia

What sort of peculiar capitalist country is this, in
which the workers' representatives predominate
in the Upper House and, till recently, did so in
the Lower House as well, and yet the capitalist
system is in no danger?

Collected Works (1963)

Moffitt, Ian Lawson (1929–)
Australian journalist and novelist

The Australian's loving relationship with his car
has become a commonplace: he fondles each
nut and bolt in interminable conversations in the
pub; strips it, lays it on the lawn, and greases its
nipples while his wife wonders whether he will

ever better his indoor average of one-a-month.

The U-Jack Society (1972)

Murray, Les A. (1938–)
Australian poet and writer

Much of the hostility to Australia ... shown by
English people above a certain class can be
traced to the fact that we are, to a large extent,
the poor who got away.

Sydney Morning Herald, 1974

Palmer, Vance (1885–1959)
Australian writer
On Australia in the Second World War

I believe we will survive; that what is significant
in us will survive; that we will come out of this
struggle battered, stripped to the bone, but
spiritually sounder than we went in, surer of our
essential character, adults in a wider world than
the one we lived in hitherto. These are great,
tragic days. Let us accept them stoically, and
make every yard of Australian earth a battle-
station.

Meanjin Papers, 1942

Phillip, Arthur (1738–1814)
English naval officer and Colonial Governor
From a letter to Lord Sydney, 1788

Nor do I doubt but that this country will prove
the most valuable acquisition Great Britain ever
made.

Historical Records of New South Wales

Phillips, Arthur Angell (1900–1985)
Australian critic

Above our writers – and other artists – looms
the intimidating mass of Anglo-Saxon culture.
Such a situation almost inevitably produces the
characteristic Australian Cultural Cringe –
appearing either as the Cringe Direct, or as the
Cringe Inverted, in the attitude of the Blatant
Blatherskite, the God's-Own-Country and I'm-a-
better-man-than-you-are Australian bore.

Meanjin, 1950, 'The Cultural Cringe'

Pringle, John Martin Douglas (1912–)
Scottish-born Australian writer

Only one profound book has been written about
Australia. It is D. H. Lawrence's novel *Kangaroo.*
... Most of it is as true today as when it was
written thirty-five years ago. I can think of no
more convincing proof of the superiority of the
creative writer over the journalist or historian.

Australian Accent

Royce, Phillip (1903–)

... as an Australian I was brought up in an Anglo-
Irish country – part of the weirdness of our
personality is that inside every Australian there's
an Irishman fighting an Englishman.

The Independent, 1992

Schulz, Charles (1922–2000)
US cartoonist
> Don't worry about the world coming to an end today. It's already tomorrow in Australia.
> > Attr.

White, Patrick (1912–1990)
English-born Australian writer and dramatist
> The ideal Australia I visualised during any exile and which drew me back, was always, I realise, a landscape without figures.
> > *Flaws in the Glass* (1981)

Wilde, Oscar (1854–1900)
Irish poet, dramatist, writer, critic and wit
> Do you know, Mr Hopper, dear Agatha and I are so much interested in Australia. It must be so pretty with all the dear little kangaroos flying about.
> > *Lady Windermere's Fan* (1892)

authority

Ayer, A.J. (1910–1989)
English philosopher
> No moral system can rest solely on authority.
> > *Humanist Outlook* (1968)

D'Souza, Dinesh (1961–)
Indeian-born US writer
> The rejection of authority can sometimes result, paradoxically, in an embrace of authoritarianism. Indeed, it can happen with insidious ease.
> > *Atlantic Monthly*, 1991

Kempis, Thomas à (c.1380–1471)
German mystic, monk and writer
> *Multo tutius est stare in subiectione; quam in praelatura.*
> It is much safer to be in a subordinate position than in one of authority.
> > *De Imitatione Christi* (1892 ed.)

Shakespeare, William (1564–1616)
English dramatist, poet and actor
> Man, proud man,
> Dress'd in a little brief authority,
> Most ignorant of what he's most assur'd,
> His glassy essence, like an angry ape,
> Plays such fantastic tricks before high heaven

As makes the angels weep.
> > *Measure For Measure*, II.ii

awards

Faraday, Michael (1791–1867)
English chemist and physicist
On being offered the Presidency of the Royal Society
> Tyndall, I must remain plain Michael Faraday to the last; and let me now tell you, that if I accepted the honour which the Royal Society desires to confer upon me, I would not answer for the integrity of my intellect for a single year.
> > In J. Tyndall, *Faraday as a Discoverer* (1868)

Lamb, Charles (1775–1834)
English essayist, critic and letter writer
> I have made a little scale, supposing myself to receive the following various accessions of dignity from the king, who is the fountain of honour – As at first, 1, Mr C. Lamb; – 10th, Emperor Lamb; 11th Pope Innocent, higher than which is nothing but the Lamb of God.
> > Letter to Thomas Manning, 1810

Osborne, John (1929–1994)
English dramatist and actor
> He really deserves some sort of decoration – a medal inscribed 'For Vaguery in the Field'.
> > *Look Back in Anger* (1956)

Place, Godfrey
> I fear that as time goes on – great deeds no linger impress. In the age of the common man, decorations may be frowned upon.
> > In *The Times*, 2000

Twain, Mark (1835–1910)
US humorist, writer, joumalist and lecturer
> The cross of the Legion of Honour has been conferred upon me. However, few escape that distinction.
> > *A Tramp Abroad* (1880)

Yeats, W.B. (1865–1939)
Irish poet, dramatist, editor, writer and senator
On being told how great an honour it was for himself and his country to win the Nobel Prize
> How much is it, Smyllie, how much is it?
> > Attr. in W.R. Rodgers (ed.), *Irish Literary Portraits* (1972)

B

babies

Churchill, Sir Winston (1874–1965)
English Conservative Prime Minister
> There is no finer investment for any community than putting milk into babies.
>> *Radio broadcast, March 1943*

Coleridge, Samuel Taylor (1772–1834)
English poet, philosopher and critic
> So for the mother's sake the child was dear,
> And dearer was the mother for the child.
>> *'Sonnet to a Friend Who Asked How I felt When the Nurse First Presented My Infant to Me'* (1797)

Dickens, Charles (1812–1870)
English writer
> Every baby born into the world is a finer one than the last.
>> *Nicholas Nickleby* (1839)

Jonson, Ben (1572–1637)
English dramatist and poet
> Rest in soft peace, and, ask'd say here doth lye
> Ben Jonson his best piece of poetrie.
>> *Epigrams* (1616)

Marryat, Frederick (1792–1848)
English naval officer and writer
Of an illegitimate baby
> If you please, ma'am, it was a very little one.
>> *Mr Midshipman Easy* (1836)

Nash, Ogden (1902–1971)
US poet
> A bit of talcum
> Is always walcum.
>> *Free Wheeling* (1931)

Plath, Sylvia (1932–1963)
US poet, writer and diarist
On seeing her newborn baby
> What did my fingers do before they held him?
> What did my heart do, with its love?
> I have never seen a thing so clear.
> His lids are like the lilac flower
> And soft as a moth, his breath.
> I shall not let go.
> There is no guile or warp in him. May he keep so.
>> *'Three Women: A Poem for Three Voices'* (1962)

Runyon, Damon (1884–1946)
US writer
> I once knew a chap who had a system of just hanging the baby on the clothes line to dry and he was greatly admired by his fellow citizens for having discovered a wonderful innovation on changing a diaper.
>> *Short Takes* (1946)

▶▶ BIRTH; CHILDREN; PREGNANCY

bad company

Machiavelli (1469–1527)
Florentine statesman, political theorist and historian
> And they are right, those who say that bad company leads to the gallows.
>> *The Mandrake* (1518)

baths

Plath, Sylvia (1932–1963)
US poet, writer and diarist
> There must be quite a few things a hot bath won't cure, but I don't know many of them.
>> *The Bell Jar* (1963)

Smith, Dodie (1896–1990)
English dramatist
> Noble deeds and hot baths are the best cures for depression.
>> *I Capture the Castle* (1948)

beauty

Bacon, Francis (1561–1626)
English philosopher, essayist, politician and courtier
> There is no excellent beauty, that hath not some strangeness in the proportion.
>> *Essays* (1625)

Beerbohm, Sir Max (1872–1956)
English satirist, cartoonist, critic and essayist
> Beauty and the lust for learning have yet to be allied.
>> *Zuleika Dobson* (1911)

Blake, William (1757–1827)
English poet, engraver, painter and mystic
> Exuberance is Beauty.
>> *'Proverbs of Hell'* (1793)

Bridges, Robert (1844–1930)
English poet, dramatist, essayist and doctor
> I love all beauteous things,
> I seek and adore them;

God hath no better praise,
And man in his hasty days
Is honoured for them.

I too will something make
And joy in the making;
Altho' to-morrow it seem
Like the empty words of a dream
Remembered on waking.

'I Love All Beauteous Things' (1890)

For beauty being the best of all we know
Sums up the unsearchable and secret aims
Of nature.

'The Growth of Love' (1876)

Buchanan, Robert Williams (1841–1901)
British poet, writer and dramatist
All that is beautiful shall abide,
All that is base shall die.

'Balder the Beautiful' (1877)

Beauty and Truth, though never found, are
worthy to be sought.

'To David in Heaven' (1865)

Buck, Pearl S. (1892–1973)
US writer and dramatist
It is better to be first with an ugly woman than
the hundredth with a beauty.

The Good Earth (1931)

Burchill, Julie (1960–)
English writer
It has been said that a pretty face is a passport.
But it's not, it's a visa, and it runs out fast.

Mail on Sunday, 1988

Burke, Edmund (1729–1797)
Irish-born British statesman and philosopher
Beauty in distress is much the most affecting
beauty.

*A Philosophical Enquiry into the Origin of our Ideas
of the Sublime and Beautiful* (1757)

Byron, Lord (1788–1824)
English poet satirist and traveller
She walks in beauty, like the night
Of cloudless climes and starry skies;
And all that's best of dark and bright
Meet in her aspect and her eyes.

'She Walks in Beauty' (1815)

Confucius (c.550–c.478 BC)
Chinese philosopher and teacher of ethics
Everything has its beauty but not everyone sees it.

Analects

Congreve, William (1670–1729)
English dramatist
Beauty is the lover's gift.

The Way of the World (1700)

Constable, John (1776–1837)
English painter
There is nothing ugly; I never saw an ugly thing
in my life: for let the form of an object be what
it may, – light, shade, and perspective will always
make it beautiful.

In C.R. Leslie, *Memoirs of the Life of John Constable* (1843)

Cousin, Victor (1792–1867)
*Il faut de la religion pour la religion, de la morale pour
la morale, comme de l'art pour l'art ... le beau ne peut
être la voie ni de l'utile, ni du bien, ni du saint; il ne
conduit qu'à lui-même.*
There must be religion for religion's sake,
morality for morality's sake, as there is art for
art's sake ... the beautiful cannot be the way to
what is useful, nor to what is good, nor to what
is holy; it leads only to itself.

Lecture, 1818

Dryden, John (1631–1700)
English poet, satirist, dramatist and critic
When beauty fires the blood, how love exalts
the mind.

Cymon and Iphigenia (1700)

Ellis, Havelock (1859–1939)
English sexologist and essayist
Beauty is the child of love.

The New Spirit (1890)

The absence of flaw in beauty is itself a flaw.

Impressions and Comments (1914)

Emerson, Ralph Waldo (1803–1882)
US poet, essayist, transcendentalist and teacher
Though we travel the world over to find the
beautiful we must carry it with us or we find it
not.

Essays, First Series (1841)

Farquhar, George (1678–1707)
Irish dramatist
No woman can be a beauty without a fortune.

The Beaux' Stratagem (1707)

Gainsbourg, Serge (1928–1991)
French singer, songwriter and director
Ugliness is, in a way, superior to beauty because
it lasts.

The Scotsman, 1998

Galsworthy, John (1867–1933)
English writer and dramatist
He Jolyon was afflicted by the thought that
where Beauty was, nothing ever ran quite
straight, which, no doubt, was why so many
people looked on it as immoral.

In Chancery (1920)

Hopkins, Gerard Manley (1844–1889)
English Jesuit priest, poet and classicist
Glory be to God for dappled things ...

All things counter, original, spare, strange;
Whatever is fickle, freckled (who knows how?)
With swift, slow; sweet, sour; adazzle, dim;
He fathers-forth whose beauty is past change:
Praise him.

'Pied Beauty' (1877)

Hugo, Victor (1802–1885)
French poet, writer, dramatist and politician
> Le beau est aussi utile que l'utile. Plus peut-être.
> Beauty is as useful as usefulness. Maybe more so.

Les Misérables (1862)

Hume, David (1711–1776)
Scottish philosopher and political economist
> Beauty is no quality in things themselves: It exists merely in the mind which contemplates them; and each mind perceives a different beauty.

Essays, Moral, Political, and Literary (1742)

Hungerford, Margaret Wolfe (c.1855–1897)
Irish novelist
> Beauty is altogether in the eye of the beholder.

Molly Bawn (1878)

Johnson, Samuel (1709–1784)
English lexicographer, poet, critic, conversationalist and essayist
> What ills from beauty spring.

The Vanity of Human Wishes (1749)

Keats, John (1795–1821)
English poet
> 'Beauty is truth, truth beauty, ' – that is all
> Ye know on earth, and all ye need to know.

'Ode on a Grecian Urn' (1819)

> A thing of beauty is a joy for ever:
> Its loveliness increases; it will never
> Pass into nothingness; but still will keep
> A bower quiet for us, and a sleep
> Full of sweet dreams, and health, and quiet breathing.

'Endymion' (1818)

> I never can feel certain of any truth but from a clear perception of its Beauty.

Letter to George and Georgiana Keats,
16 December 1818–4 January 1819

King, William (1663–1712)
English judge and writer
> Beauty from order springs.

Art of Cookery (1708)

Marlowe, Christopher (1564–1593)
English poet and dramatist
> Was this the face that launch'd a thousand ships,
> And burnt the topless towers of Ilium?

Doctor Faustus (1604)

> O, thou art fairer than the evening's air
> Clad in the beauty of a thousand stars.

Doctor Faustus (1604)

Molière (1622–1673)
French dramatist, actor and director
> La beauté du visage est un frêle ornement,
> Une fleur passagère, un éclat d'un moment,
> Et qui n'est attaché qu'à la simple épiderme.
> The beauty of a face is a frail ornament, a passing flower, a moment's brightness belonging only to the skin.

Les Femmes savantes (1672)

Mortimer, John (1923–)
English lawyer, dramatist and writer
> Beauty is handed out as undemocratically as inherited peerages, and beautiful people have done nothing to deserve their astonishing reward.

The Observer, 1999

Pascal, Blaise (1623–1662)
French philosopher and scientist
> If Cleopatra's nose had been shorter the whole face of the earth would have changed.

Pensées (1670)

Philips, Ambrose (c.1675–1749)
English poet and politician
> The flowers anew, returning seasons bring!
> But beauty faded has no second spring.

The First Pastoral (1710)

Picasso, Pablo (1881–1973)
Spanish painter, sculptor and graphic artist
> I hate that aesthetic game of the eye and the mind, played by these connoisseurs, these mandarins who 'appreciate' beauty. What is beauty, anyway? There's no such thing. I never 'appreciate', any more than I 'like'. I love or I hate.

In Françoise Gilot and Carlton Lake, Life with
Picasso (1964)

Proverbs
> Beauty is potent but money is omnipotent.

> A good face is a letter of recommendation.

> Beauty is only skin-deep.

> A good face is a letter of recommendation.

Pushkin, Aleksandr (1799–1837)
Russian poet, novelist and playwright
> I remember a wonderful moment:
> Before me you appeared,
> Like a fleeting apparition,
> Like a spirit of pure beauty.

'To –' (1825)

Rodó, José Enrique (1872–1917)
> Lo bello nace de la muerte de lo útil; lo útil se convierte

en bello cuando ha caducado su utilidad.
What is beautiful has its origin in the death of what is useful; what is useful becomes beautiful when it has outlived its usefulness.

Letter to Miguel de Unamuno, 19 July 1903

Rourke, M.E. (20th century)
US songwriter
> And when I told them how beautiful you are
> They didn't believe me! They didn't believe me!

'They Didn't Believe Me', song, 1914

Ruskin, John (1819–1900)
English art critic, philosopher and reformer
> Remember that the most beautiful things in the world are the most useless; peacocks and lilies for instance.

The Stones of Venice (1851)

Russell, Bertrand (1872–1970)
English philosopher, mathematician, essayist and social reformer
> Mathematics, rightly viewed, possesses not only truth, but supreme beauty –a beauty cold and austere, like that of sculpture.

Mysticism and Logic (1918)

Sainte-Beuve, Charles-Augustin (1804–1869)
French writer and critic
> One of the greatest satisfactions for a man is when the woman he passionately desired and who obstinately refused to give herself to him ceases to be beautiful.

Notebooks (1834–1847)

Saki (1870–1916)
Burmese-born British writer
> I always say beauty is only sin deep.

'Reginald's Choir Treat' (1904)

Sappho (fl. 7th–6th centuries BC)
Greek poet
> Beauty endures for only as long as it can be seen; goodness, beautiful today, will remain so tomorrow.

In Naim Attallah, Women (1987)

Schiller, Johann Christoph Friedrich (1759–1805)
German writer, dramatist, poet and historian
> Die Schönheit ist das Produkt der Zusammenstimmung zwischen dem Geist und den Sinnen.
> Beauty is the product of harmony between the mind and the senses.

'On Naive and Sentimental Poetry' (1795–1796)

Shakespeare, William (1564–1616)
English dramatist, poet and actor
> Beauty itself doth of itself persuade
> The eyes of men without an orator.

'The Rape of Lucrece'

Spenser, Edmund (c.1522–1599)
English poet

> That Beautie is not, as fond men misdeeme,
> An outward shew of things, that onely seeme …
>
> For of the soule the bodie forme doth take:
> For soule is forme, and doth the bodie make.

Fowre Hymnes (1596)

Stevens, Wallace (1879–1955)
US poet, essayist, dramatist and lawyer
> I do not know which to prefer,
> The beauty of inflections
> Or the beauty of innuendoes,
> The blackbird whistling
> Or just after.

'Thirteen Ways of Looking at a Blackbird' (1923)

> Beauty is momentary in the mind –
> The fitful tracing of a portal;
> But in the flesh it is immortal.
> The body dies; the body's beauty lives.
> So evenings die, in their green going,
> Aware, interminably flowing.

'Peter Quince at the Clavier' (1923)

Tolstoy, Leo (1828–1910)
Russian writer, essayist, philosopher and moralist
> It is amazing how complete is the delusion that beauty is goodness.

The Kreutzer Sonata (1890)

Virgil (70–19 BC)
Roman poet
> O formose puer, nimium ne crede colori.
> O beautiful boy, do not put too much trust in your beauty.

Eclogues, II, line 17

Wallace, Lew (1827–1905)
US novelist and statesman
> Beauty is altogether in the eye of the beholder.

The Prince of India (1893)

Wollstonecraft, Mary (1759–1797)
English feminist, writer and teacher
> Taught from their infancy that beauty is woman's sceptre, the mind shapes itself to the body, and roaming round its gilt cage, only seeks to adorn its prison.

A Vindication of the Rights of Woman (1792)

Woolf, Virginia (1882–1941)
English writer and critic
> She bore about with her, she could not help knowing it, the torch of her beauty; she carried it erect into any room that she entered; and after all, veil it as she might, and shrink from the monotony of bearing that it imposed on her, her beauty was apparent. She had been admired. She had been loved.

To the Lighthouse (1927)

Yeats, W.B. (1865–1939)
Irish poet, dramatist, editor, writer and senator
> O heart, we are old;
> The living beauty is for younger men:
> We cannot pay its tribute of wild tears.
>> In the *Little Review*, 1918

▶▶ APPEARANCE

bed

Benjamin, Walter (1892–1940)
German writer, philosopher and critic
> *Bücher und Dirnen kann man ins Bett nehmen.*
> Books and bimbos can be taken to bed.
>> *One-way street*, 1928

Breton, Nicholas (c.1545–c.1626)
English writer and poet
> We rise with the lark and go to bed with the lamb.
>> 'The Court and Country' (1618)

Brooke, Rupert (1887–1915)
English poet
> The cool kindliness of sheets, that soon
> Smooth away trouble; and the rough male kiss
> of blankets.
>> 'The Great Lover' (1914)

Dickens, Charles (1812–1870)
English writer
> 'It would make any one go to sleep, that
> bedstead would, whether they wanted to or
> not.'
> 'I should think, ' said Sam, … 'poppies was
> nothing to it.'
>> *The Pickwick Papers* (1837), 41

Franklin, Benjamin (1706–1790)
US statesman, scientist, political critic and printer
> Early to bed and early to rise,
> Makes a man healthy, wealthy and wise.
>> *Poor Richard's Almanac* (1758)

Fry, Christopher (1907–)
English verse dramatist, theatre director and translator
> It doesn't do a man any good, daylight.
> It means up and doing, and that means up to no
> good.
> The best life is led horizontal.
>> *Thor, with Angels* (1949)

Herbert, George (1593–1633)
English poet and priest
> When boyes go first to bed,
> They step into their voluntarie graves.
>> *The Temple* (1633)

Huxley, Aldous (1894–1963)
English writer, poet and critic

Lady Capricorn, he understood, was still keeping
open bed.
>> *Antic Hay* (1923)

'Bed, ' as the Italian proverb succinctly puts it, 'is
the poor man's opera.'
>> *Heaven and Hell* (1956)

Jennings, Elizabeth (1926–)
English poet
> Now deep in my bed I turn
> And the world turns on the other side.
>> 'In the Night'

Johnson, Samuel (1709–1784)
English lexicographer, poet, critic, conversationalist and essayist
> I have, all my life long, been lying till noon; yet I
> tell all young men, and tell them with great
> sincerity, that nobody who does not rise early
> will ever do any good.
>> In Boswell, *Journal of a Tour to the Hebrides* (1785)

Lauder, Sir Harry (1870–1950)
Scottish music-hall entertainer
> O! it's nice to get up in the mornin',
> But it's nicer to stay in bed.
>> Song, 1913

Pepys, Samuel (1633–1703)
English diarist, naval administrator and politician
> And mighty proud I am (and ought to be
> thankful to God Almighty) that I am able to have
> a spare bed for my friends.
>> *Diary*, August 1666

Proust, Marcel (1871–1922)
French writer and critic
> *Longtemps, je me suis couché de bonne heure.*
> For a long time I used to go to bed early.
>> *Du côté de chez Swann* (1913)

Proverbs
> Go to bed with the lamb, and rise with the lark.

> Early to bed and early to rise, makes a man
> healthy, wealthy and wise.

Rabelais, François (c.1494–c.1553)
French monk, physician, satirist and humanist
> *Lever matin n'est poinct bon heur;*
> *Boire matin est le meilleur.*
> Getting up in the morning is no pleasure;
> Drinking in the morning is the best.
>> *Gargantua* (1534)

Runyon, Damon (1884–1946)
US writer
> At such an hour the sinners are still in bed
> resting up from their sinning of the night before,
> so they will be in good shape for more sinning a
> little later on.
>> *Runyon à la carte* (1944), 'The Idyll of Miss Sarah
>> Brown'

Sidney, Sir Philip (1554–1586)
English poet, critic, soldier, courtier and diplomat
> Take thou of me smooth pillows, sweetest bed;
> A chamber deaf to noise and blind to light,
> A rosy garland and a weary head.
>> *Astrophel and Stella* (1591)

Sterne, Laurence (1713–1768)
Irish-born English writer and clergyman
> 'My brother Toby, ' quoth she, 'is going to be married to Mrs Wadman.'
> 'Then he will never, ' quoth my father, 'be able to lie diagonally in his bed again as long as he lives.'
>> *Tristram Shandy* (1759–1767)

Stevenson, Robert Louis (1850–1894)
Scottish writer, poet and essayist
> Must we to bed indeed? Well then,
> Let us arise and go like men,
> And face with an undaunted tread
> The long black passage up to bed.
>> *A Child's Garden of Verses* (1885)

Surtees, R.S. (1805–1864)
English writer
> When at length they rose to go to bed, it struck each man as he followed his neighbour upstairs that the one before him walked very crookedly.
>> *Mr Sponge's Sporting Tour* (1853)

Thomas, Dylan (1914–1953)
Welsh poet, writer and radio dramatist
> He was sitting straight up in bed and rocking from side to side as though the bed were on a rough road; the knotted edges of the counterpane were his reins; his invisible horses stood in a shadow beyond the bedside candle. Over a white flannel nightshirt he was wearing a red waistcoat with walnut-sized brass buttons.
>> *Portrait of the Artist as a Young Dog* (1940)

Thurber, James (1894–1961)
US humorist, writer and dramatist
> I suppose that the high-water mark of my youth in Columbus, Ohio, was the night the bed fell on my father.
>> *My Life and Hard Times* (1933)

> A man's bed is his resting-place, but a woman's is often her rack.
>> *Further Fables for Our Time* (1956)

> Early to rise and early to bed makes a male healthy and wealthy and dead.
>> *The New Yorker*, 1939

Waugh, Evelyn (1903–1966)
English writer and diarist
> I haven't been to sleep for over a year. That's why I go to bed early. One needs more rest if one doesn't sleep.
>> *Decline and Fall* (1928)

►► IDLENESS AND UNEMPLOYMENT; SLEEP

beginning

Carroll, Lewis (1832–1898)
English writer and photographer
> 'Begin at the beginning, ' the King said, very gravely, 'and go on till you come to the end: then stop.'
>> *Alice's Adventures in Wonderland* (1865)

Churchill, Sir Winston (1874–1965)
English Conservative Prime Minister
On the Battle of Egypt
> This is not the end. It is not even the beginning of the end. But it is, perhaps, the end of the beginning.
>> Speech, Mansion House, November 1942.

Du Deffand, Marquise (1697–1780)
French noblewoman
Commenting on the legend of St Denis, who is believed to have carried his severed head for six miles after his execution
> The distance isn't important; it is only the first step that is difficult.
>> Letter to d'Alembert, 1763

Horne, Richard Henry (1803–1884)
English writer
> 'Tis always morning somewhere in the world.
>> *Orion* (1843

Keats, John (1795–1821)
English poet
> There is an old saying 'well begun is half done' – 'tis a bad one. I would use instead – 'Not begun at all until half done'.
>> Letter to B.R. Haydon, 10–11 May, 1817

Lao-Tzu (c.604–531 BC)
Chinese philosopher
> A journey of a thousand miles must begin with a single step.
>> *Tao Te Ching*

Mary, Queen of Scots (1542–1587)
Daughter of James V, mother of James VI and I; executed by Elizabeth I of England
> *En ma fin git mon commencement.*
> In my end is my beginning.
>> Motto embroidered with her mother's emblem

Proverbs
> A journey of a thousand leagues begins with a single step.
>> Chinese Proverb

> Fingers were made before forks, and hands

before knives.

From small beginnings come great things.

Great oaks from little acorns grow.

belief

Amiel, Henri-Frédéric (1821–1881)
Swiss philosopher and writer
A belief is not true because it is useful.

Journal, 1876

Augustine, Saint (354–430)
Numidian-born Christian theologian and philosopher
Nisi credideritis, non intelligitis.
Unless you believe, you will not understand.

De Libero Arbitrio

Bagehot, Walter (1826–1877)
English economist and political philosopher
So long as there are earnest believers in the
world, they will always wish to punish opinions,
even if their judgement tells them it is unwise, and
their conscience that it is wrong.

Literary Studies (1879)

The Bible (King James Version)
Lord, I believe; help thou mine unbelief.

Mark, 9: 24

Blessed are they that have not seen, and yet
have believed.

John, 20: 29

Caesar, Gaius Julius (c.102–44 BC)
Roman statesman, historian and army commander
Fere libenter homines id quod volunt credunt.
Men generally believe what they wish.

De Bello Gallico

Carlyle, Thomas (1795–1881)
Scottish historian, biographer, critic, and essayist
The difference between Orthodoxy or My-doxy
and Heterodoxy or Thy-doxy.

History of the French Revolution
(1837)

Carroll, Lewis (1832–1898)
English writer and photographer
If you'll believe in me, I'll believe in you.

Through the Looking-Glass (1872)

'There's no use trying, ' she said: 'one can't
believe impossible things.'
'I dare say you haven't had much practice, ' said
the Queen. 'When I was your age, I always did it
for half an hour a day. Why, sometimes I've
believed as many as six impossible things before
breakfast.'

Through the Looking-Glass (1872)

Chesterton, G.K. (1874–1936)
English writer, poet and critic
The men who really believe in themselves are all
in lunatic asylums.

Orthodoxy (1908)

Ellis, Havelock (1859–1939)
English sexologist and essayist
A man must not swallow more beliefs than he
can digest.

The Dance of Life

Forster, E.M. (1879–1970)
English writer, essayist and literary critic
I do not believe in Belief ... Lord I disbelieve –
help thou my unbelief.

Two Cheers for Democracy (1951)

Frank, Anne (1929–1945)
Jewish diarist; died in Nazi concentration camp
In spite of everything I still believe that people
are good at heart.

The Diary of Anne Frank (1947)

Freud, Sigmund (1856–1939)
Austrian physicist; founder of psychoanalysis
The more the fruits of knowledge become
accessible to men, the more widespread is the
decline of religious belief.

The Future of an Illusion (1927)

Grant, George (1918–)
We listen to others to discover what we
ourselves believe.

CBC Times, 1959

Greene, Graham (1904–1991)
English writer and dramatist
My belief certainly seems to get stronger in the
presence of people whose goodness seems of
almost supernatural origin.

Attr.

Haskins, Minnie Louise (1875–1957)
English teacher and writer
Quoted by King George VI in his Christmas broadcast, 1939
And I said to a man who stood at the gate of
the year: 'Give me a light that I may tread safely
into the unknown.' And he replied: 'Go out into
the darkness and put your hand into the hand of
God. That shall be to you better than a light,
and safer than a known way.'

The Desert (1908)

Ibsen, Henrik (1828–1906)
Norwegian writer, dramatist and poet
It's not just what we inherit from our mothers
and fathers that haunts us. It's all kinds of old
defunct theories, all sorts of old defunct beliefs,
and things like that. It's not that they actually
live on in us; they are simply lodged there, and
we cannot get rid of them. I've only to pick up a

newspaper and I seem to see ghosts gliding between the lines.

> *Ghosts* (1881)

Jenkins, David (1925–)
English Bishop of Durham
> As I get older I seem to believe less and less and yet to believe what I do believe more and more.

> *The Observer*, 1988

Jowett, Benjamin (1817–1893)
English scholar, translator, essayist and priest
> My dear child, you must believe in God in spite of what the clergy tell you.

> In M. Asquith, *Autobiography* (1922)

Kant, Immanuel (1724–1804)
German idealist philosopher
> *Es ist nur eine (wahre) Religion; aber es kann vielerlei Arten des Glaubens geben.*
> There is only one (true) religion; but there can be many different kinds of belief.

> *Religion within the Boundaries of Mere Reason* (1793)

Lamb, Charles (1775–1834)
English essayist, critic and letter writer
> Credulity is the man's weakness, but the child's strength.

> *Essays of Elia* (1823)

Madan, Geoffrey (1895–1947)
English bibliophile
> The dust of exploded beliefs may make a fine sunset.

> *Livre sans nom: Twelve Reflections* (1934)

Newman, John Henry, Cardinal (1801–1890)
English Cardinal, theologian and poet
> Though you can believe what you choose, you must believe what you ought.

> Letter, 1848

> It is as absurd to argue men, as to torture them, into believing.

> Sermon, 1831

> We can believe what we choose. We are answerable for what we choose to believe.

> Letter to Mrs Froude, 1848

Orwell, George (1903–1950)
English writer and critic
> Doublethink means the power of holding two contradictory beliefs in one's mind simultaneously, and accepting both of them.

> *Nineteen Eighty-Four* (1949)

Pope, Alexander (1688–1744)
English poet, translator and editor
> The most positive men are the most credulous.

> *Miscellanies* (1727)

Proverbs
> Believe nothing of what you hear, and only half

of what you see.

> Seeing is believing.

Russell, Bertrand (1872–1970)
English philosopher, mathematician, essayist and social reformer
> It is undesirable to believe a proposition when there is no ground whatever for supposing it true.

> *Sceptical Essays* (1928)

> Every man, wherever he goes, is encompassed by a cloud of comforting convictions, which move with him like flies on a summer day.

> *Sceptical Essays* (1928)

On being asked if he would be willing to die for his beliefs
> Of course not. After all, I may be wrong.

> Attr.

Sitwell, Dame Edith (1887–1964)
English poet, anthologist, critic and biographer
> During the writing … of this book, I realized that the public will believe anything – so long as it is not founded on truth.

> *Taken Care Of* (1965), Preface

Turgenev, Ivan (1818–1883)
Russian writer and dramatist
> The courage to believe in nothing.

> *Fathers and Sons* (1862)

Unamuno, Miguel de (1864–1936)
Spanish philosopher, poet and writer
> *Creer en Dios es anhelar que le haya y es además conducirse como si le hubiera.*
> To believe in God is to yearn for his existence and, moreover, it is to behave as if he did exist.

> *The Tragic Sense of Life* (1913)

Valéry, Paul (1871–1945)
French poet, mathematician and philosopher
> *Ce qui a été cru par tous, et toujours, et partout, a toutes les chances d'être faux.*
> What has always been believed by everyone, everywhere, will most likely turn out to be false.

> *Moralities*, 1932

Warburton, William (1698–1779)
English cleric and controversialist
> Orthodoxy is my doxy; heterodoxy is another man's doxy.

> In Joseph Priestley, *Memoirs* (1807)

▶▶ FAITH; RELIGION

benefactors

Bagehot, Walter (1826–1877)
English economist and political philosopher

The most melancholy of human reflections, perhaps, is that, on the whole, it is a question whether the benevolence of mankind does most good or harm.

Physics and Politics (1872)

Chamfort, Nicolas (1741–1794)
French writer

Our gratitude to most benefactors is the same as our feeling for dentists who have pulled our teeth. We acknowledge the good they have done and the evil from which they have delivered us, but we remember the pain they occasioned and do not love them very much.

Maximes et pensées (1796)

Compton-Burnett, Dame Ivy (1884–1969)
English novelist

At any time you might act for my good. When people do that, it kills something precious between them.

Manservant and Maidservant (1947)

Connolly, Billy (1942–)
Scottish comedian and actor
Of Andrew Carnegie

It was said that he gave money away as silently as a waiter falling down a flight of stairs with a tray of glasses.

Gullible's Travels

Creighton, Mandell (1843–1901)
English churchman, historian and biographer

No people do so much harm as those who go about doing good.

The Life and Letters of Mandell Creighton (1904)

Donne, John (1572–1631)
English poet

There is a hook in every benefit, that sticks in his jaws that takes that benefit, and draws him whither the benefactor will.

Sermon, c.1625

Gilbert, W.S. (1836–1911)
English dramatist, humorist and librettist

I love my fellow creatures – I do all the good I can –
Yet everybody says I'm such a disagreeable man!

Princess Ida (1884)

Goldsmith, Oliver (c.1728–1774)
Irish dramatist, poet and writer

And learn the luxury of doing good.

'The Traveller' (1764)

Johnson, Samuel (1709–1784)
English lexicographer, poet, critic, conversationalist and essayist

Patron. Commonly a wretch who supports with insolence, and is paid with flattery.

A Dictionary of the English Language (1755)

Is not a Patron, my Lord, one who looks with unconcern on a man struggling for life in the water, and, when he has reached ground, encumbers him with help? The notice which you have been pleased to take of my labours, had it been early, had been kind; but it has been delayed till I am indifferent, and cannot enjoy it; till I am solitary, and cannot impart it; till I am known, and do not want it.

Letter to Lord Chesterfield, 1755

Machiavelli (1469–1527)
Florentine statesman, political theorist and historian

It is the nature of men to be bound by the benefits they confer as much as by those they receive.

The Prince (1532)

Titus Vespasianus (AD 39–81)

Recordatus quondam super cenam, quod nihil cuiquam toto die praestitisset, memorabilem illam meritoque laudatam vocem edidit: 'Amici, diem perdidi.'
Recalling once after dinner that he had done nothing to help anyone all that day, he gave voice to that memorable and praiseworthy remark: 'Friends, I have lost a day.'

In Suetonius, *Lives of the Caesars*

Turner, Ted (1938–)
US media tycoon
On donating $1 billion to the UN, 1997

I'm only giving up nine months' earnings. It's not that big a deal.

The Guardian, 1999

Wordsworth, William (1770–1850)
English poet

On that best portion of a good man's life;
His little, nameless, unremembered acts
Of kindness and of love.

'Lines composed a few miles above Tintern Abbey' (1798)

▶▶ GOODNESS

betrayal

The Bible (King James Version)

Yea, mine own familiar friend, in whom I trusted, which did eat of my bread, hath lifted up his heel against me.

Psalms, 41:9

Churchill, Sir Winston (1874–1965)
English Conservative Prime Minister

It is all right to rat, but you can't re-rat.

Attr.

Congreve, William (1670–1729)
English dramatist

Man was by Nature Woman's cully made:
We never are, but by ourselves, betrayed.
The Old Bachelor (1693)

Nixon, Richard (1913–1994)
US Republican politician and President
　　I let down my friends, I let down my country. I
　　let down our system of government.
The Observer, 1977

Shakespeare, William (1564–1616)
English dramatist, poet and actor
　　Why, as a woodcock, to mine own springe,
　　Osric;
　　I am justly kill'd with mine own treachery.
Hamlet, V.ii

bible

Anonymous
　　It's just called 'The Bible' now. We dropped the
　　word 'Holy' to give it a more mass-market
　　appeal.
Editor at Hodder & Stoughton quoted
in *Daily Telegraph*, 1989

Chillingworth, William (1602–1644)
English theologian and scholar
　　The Bible and the Bible only is the religion of
　　Protestants.
The Religion of Protestants (1637)

Selden, John (1584–1654)
English historian, jurist and politician
　　Scrutamini scripturas. Let us look at the Scriptures.
　　These two words have undone the world.
Table Talk (1689)

Whately, Richard (1787–1863)
English philosopher, theologian, educationist and writer
To a meeting of his diocesan clergy
　　'Never forget, gentlemen, ' he said, to his
　　astonished hearers, as he held up a copy of the
　　'Authorised Version' of the Bible, 'never forget
　　that this is not the Bible, ' then, after a
　　moment's pause, he continued, 'This, gentlemen,
　　is only a translation of the Bible.'
In H. Solly, *These Eighty Years* (1893)

▶▶ RELIGION

bigotry

Tagore, Rabindranath (1861–1941)
Indian poet and philosopher
　　Bigotry tries to keep truth safe in its hand
　　With a grip that kills it.
Fireflies (1928)

▶▶ RACISIM

biography

Amis, Martin (1949–)
English writer
Of biography
　　To be more interested in the writer than the
　　writing is just eternal human vulgarity.
The Observer Review, 1996

Andersen, Hans Christian (1805–1875)
Danish writer and dramatist
　　Every man's life is a fairy-tale written by God's
　　fingers.
Works (c.1843), Preface

Arbuthnot, John (1667–1735)
Scottish physician, pamphleteer and wit
Of biography
　　One of the new terrors of death.
In Carruthers, *Life of Pope* (1857)

Bentley, Edmund Clerihew (1875–1956)
English writer
　　The art of Biography
　　Is different from Geography.
　　Geography is about Maps,
　　But Biography is about chaps.
Biography for Beginners (1905)

Brontë, Rev. Patrick (1777–1861)
About her agreeing to write the life of Charlotte Brontë
　　No quailing, Mrs Gaskell! no drawing back!
Letter to Ellen Nussey, 1855

Carlyle, Thomas (1795–1881)
Scottish historian, biographer, critic, and essayist
　　There is no life of a man, faithfully recorded, but
　　is a heroic poem of its sort, rhymed or
　　unrhymed.
Critical and Miscellaneous Essays (1839)

　　A well-written Life is almost as rare as a well-
　　spent one.
Critical and Miscellaneous Essays (1839)

Crisp, Quentin (1908–1999)
English writer, publicist and model
　　An autobiography is an obituary in serial form
　　with the last instalment missing.
The Naked Civil Servant (1968)

Davies, Robertson (1913–1995)
Canadian playwright, writer and critic
　　Biography at its best is a form of fiction.
The Lyre of Orpheus (1988)

Disraeli, Benjamin (1804–1881)
English statesman and writer
　　Read no history: nothing but biography, for that

is life without theory.

Contarini Fleming (1832)

Emerson, Ralph Waldo (1803–1882)
US poet, essayist, transcendentalist and teacher
There is properly no history; only biography.

Essays, First Series (1841)

Frye, Northrop (1912–1991)
Canadian critic and academic
There's only one story, the story of your life.

In Ayre, *Northrop Frye: A Biography* (1989)

Gladstone, William (1809–1898)
English statesman and reformer
On J.W. Cross's *Life of George Eliot*
It is not a Life at all. It is a Reticence, in three volumes.

In E.F. Benson, *As We Were* (1930)

Grant, Cary (1904–1986)
English-born US film actor
Nobody is ever truthful about his own life. There are always ambiguities.

The Observer, 1981

Guedalla, Philip (1889–1944)
English historian, writer and lawyer
Biography, like big-game hunting, is one of the recognized forms of sport, and it is as unfair as only sport can be.

Supers and Supermen (1920)

Johnson, Samuel (1709–1784)
English lexicographer, poet, critic, conversationalist and essayist
Nobody can write the life of a man, but those who have eat and drunk and lived in social intercourse with him.

In Boswell, *The Life of Samuel Johnson* (1791)

Lee, Robert E. (1807–1870)
US general
Refusing to write his memoirs
I should be trading on the blood of my men.

In M. Ringo, *Nobody Said It Better*

Macaulay, Lord (1800–1859)
English Liberal statesman, essayist and poet
Biographers, translators, editors, all, in short, who employ themselves in illustrating the lives or writings of others, are peculiarly exposed to the Lues Boswelliana, or disease of admiration.

Collected Essays (1843)

Pétain, Marshal (1856–1951)
French soldier and statesman
To write one's memoirs is to speak ill of everybody except oneself.

The Observer, 1946

Salinger, J.D. (1919–)
US writer

If you really want to hear about it, the first thing you'll probably want to know is where I was born and what my lousy childhood was like, and how my parents were occupied and all before they had me, and all that David Copperfield kind of crap.

The Catcher in the Rye (1951)

Stocks, Mary, Baroness (1891–1975)
English educationist, broadcaster and biographer
Biographies are like anthologies, especially anthologies of poetry. One's eyes are magnetically directed to what ought to be there but isn't, as well as to what oughtn't to be there but is.

Still More Commonplace (1973)

Trollope, Anthony (1815–1882)
English writer, traveller and post office official
In these days a man is nobody unless his biography is kept so far posted up that it may be ready for the national breakfast-table on the morning after his demise.

Doctor Thorne (1858)

Walpole, Horace (1717–1797)
English writer and politician
The life of any man written under the direction of his family, did nobody honour.

Letter, 1778

West, Dame Rebecca (1892–1983)
English writer, critic and feminist
Just how difficult it is to write biography can be reckoned by anybody who sits down and considers just how many people know the real truth about his or her love affairs.

Vogue, 1952

Wilde, Oscar (1854–1900)
Irish poet, dramatist, writer, critic and wit
Every great man has his disciples, but it is always Judas who writes the biography.

Attr.

birds

Aristophanes (c.445–385 BC)
Greek playwright
Suggestion for the name of the Birds' capital city
What do you think of 'Cloudcuckooland'?

Birds

Arlen, Michael (1895–1956)
There is a tale that is told in London about a nightingale, how it did this and that and, finally for no apparent reason, rested and sang in Berkeley Square.

These Charming People (1924)

BIRDS

Bridges, Robert (1844–1930)

English poet, dramatist, essayist and doctor

> I heard a linnet courting
> His lady in the spring.

> 'I heard a linnet' (1890)

Browning, Elizabeth Barrett (1806–1861)

English poet; wife of Robert Browning

> Near all the birds
> Will sing at dawn, – and yet we do not take
> The chaffering swallow for the holy lark.

> *Aurora Leigh* (1857)

Clarke, Kenneth (1940–)

English Conservative politican

> When asked to name my favourite bird I usually name the bar-tailed godwit.

> *The Times*, 1999

Clare, John (1793–1864)

English rural poet; died in an asylum

> The crow will tumble up and down
> At the first sight of spring
> And in old trees around the town
> Brush winter from its wing.

> 'Crows in Spring'

Cuppy, Will (1884–1949)

US humorist

> The Dodo never had a chance. He seems to have been invented for the sole purpose of becoming extinct and that was all he was good for.

> *How to Become Extinct* (1941)

Gibbons, Orlando (1583–1625)

English organist and composer of church music

> The silver swan, who, living had no note,
> When death approached unlocked her silent throat.

> 'The Silver Swan' (1612)

Gilmore, Dame Mary (1865–1962)

Australian poet and journalist

> I never knew how wide the dark,
> I never knew the depth of space,
> I never knew how frail a bark,
> How small is man within his place,
>
> Not till I heard the swans go by,
> Not till I marked their haunting cry,
> Not till, within the vague on high,
> I watched them pass across the sky.

> 'Swans at Night'

Hardy, Thomas (1840–1928)

English writer and poet

> A little ball of feather and bone.

> 'Shelley's Skylark' (1887)

> At once a voice arose among
> The bleak twigs overhead

> In a full-hearted evensong
> Of joy illimited;
> An aged thrush, frail, gaunt, and small,
> In blast-beruffled plume,
> Had chosen thus to fling his soul
> Upon the growing gloom.
>
> So little cause for carolings
> Of such ecstatic sound
> Was written on terrestrial things
> Afar or nigh around,
> That I could think there trembled through
> His happy good-night air
> Some blessed Hope, whereof he knew
> And I was unaware.

> 'The Darkling Thrush' (1900)

Hawes, Stephen (d. c.1523)

English allegorical poet

> Whan the lytell byrdes swetely dyde synge
> Laudes to theyr maker erly in the mornynge.

> *The Passetyme of Pleasure* (1509)

Isherwood, Christopher (1904–1986)

English novelist

> The common cormorant or shag
> Lays eggs inside a paper bag
> The reason you will see no doubt
> It is to keep the lightning out.
>
> But what these unobservant birds
> Have never noticed is that herds
> Of wandering bears may come with buns
> And steal the bags to hold the crumbs.

> 'The Common Cormorant' (c.1925)

Jeffers, Robinson (1887–1962)

US poet

> … I gave him the lead gift in the twilight. What fell was relaxed,
> Owl-downy, soft feminine feathers; but what
> Soared: the fierce rush: the night-heron by the flooded river cries fear at its rising
> Before it was quite unsheathed from reality.

> *Hurt Hawks* (1928)

Keats, John (1795–1821)

English poet

> Where the nightingale doth sing
> Not a senseless, trancèd thing,
> But divine melodious truth.

> 'Ode' (1818)

> Thou wast not born for death, immortal Bird!
> No hungry generations tread thee down;
> The voice I hear this passing night was heard
> In ancient days by emperor and clown:
> Perhaps the self-same song that found a path
> Through the sad heart of Ruth, when sick for home,
> She stood in tears amid the alien corn;

The same that oft-times hath
Charm'd magic casements, opening on the foam
Of perilous seas, in faery lands forlorn.

'Ode to a Nightingale' (1819)

Lear, Edward (1812–1888)
English artist and writer

There was an Old Man with a beard,
Who said, 'It is just as I feared! –
Two Owls and a Hen,
Four Larks and a Wren,
Have all built their nests in my beard!'.

A Book of Nonsense (1846)

Lee, Harper (1926–)
US writer

Shoot all the bluejays you want, if you can hit
'em, but remember it's a sin to kill a
mockingbird.

To Kill a Mockingbird (1960)

Lyly, John (c.1554–1606)
English dramatist and politician

What bird so sings, yet does so wail?
O 'tis the ravish'd nightingale.
Jug, jug, jug, jug, tereu, she cries,
And still her woes at midnight rise.

Campaspe (1584)

The lark

How at heaven's gates she claps her wings,
The morn not waking till she sings.

Campaspe (1584)

Mansfield, Katherine (1888–1923)
New Zealand writer

The ostrich burying its head in the sand does at
any rate wish to convey the impression that its
head is the most important part of it.

Journal of Katherine Mansfield (1954)

Meredith, George (1828–1909)
English writer, poet and critic

Lovely are the curves of the white owl sweeping
Wavy in the dusk lit by one large star.
Lone in the fir-branch, his rattle-note unvaried,
Brooding o'er the gloom, spins the brown eve-
jar.

'Love in the Valley' (1883)

Merritt, Dixon Lanier (1879–1972)
US editor

A wonderful bird is the pelican,
His bill will hold more than his belican.
He can take in his beak
Food enough for a week,
But I'm damned if I see how the helican.

Nashville Banner, 1913

Nash, Ogden (1902–1971)
US poet

The song of canaries
Never varies,

And when they're moulting
They're pretty revolting.

The Face is Familiar (1940)

Roche, Sir Boyle (1743–1807)
Irish politician

He regretted that he was not a bird, and could
not be in two places at once.

Attr.

Shakespeare, William (1564–1616)
English dramatist, poet and actor

And now this pale swan in her wat'ry nest
Begins the sad dirge of her certain ending.

'The Rape of Lucrece'

Shelley, Percy Bysshe (1792–1822)
English poet, dramatist and essayist

Hail to thee, blithe Spirit!
Bird thou never wert,
That from Heaven, or near it,
Pourest thy full heart
In profuse strains of unpremeditated art.

'To a Skylark' (1820)

Spenser, Edmund (c.1522–1599)
English poet

The merry Cuckow, messenger of Spring,
His trompet shrill hath thrise already sounded.

Amoretti, and Epithalamion (1595), Sonnet 19

Thoreau, Henry David (1817–1862)
US essayist, social critic and writer

I once had a sparrow alight upon my shoulder
for a moment while I was hoeing in a village
garden, and I felt that I was more distinguished
by that circumstance than I should have been by
any epaulet I could have worn.

Walden (1854)

Webster, John (c.1580–c.1625)
English dramatist

We think caged birds sing, when indeed they
cry.

The White Devil (1612)

Call for the robin redbreast and the wren,
Since o'er shady groves they hover,
And with leaves and flowers do cover
The friendless bodies of unburied men.

The White Devil (1612)

Williams, Tennessee (1911–1983)
US dramatist and writer

Caged birds accept each other but flight is what
they long for.

Camino Real (1953)

Williams, William Carlos (1883–1963)
US poet, writer and paediatrician

On a tissue-thin monotone of blue-grey buds
two blue-grey birds, chasing a third,
at full cry! Now they are

flung outward and up – disappearing suddenly!

'Spring Strains' (1917)

Wordsworth, William (1770–1850)
English poet

O blithe new-comer! I have heard,
I hear thee and rejoice.
O Cuckoo! Shall I call thee bird,
Or but a wandering voice?

'To the Cuckoo' (1807)

birth

Ackerley, J.R. (1896–1967)
English writer

I was born in 1896, and my parents were
married in 1919.

My Father and Myself (1968)

Austen, Jane (1775–1817)
English writer

The stain of illegitimacy, unbleached by nobility
or wealth, would have been a stain indeed.

Emma (1816)

Bhagavadgita

For that which is born death is certain, and for
the dead birth is certain. Therefore grieve not
over that which is unavoidable.

Ch. II

Blake, William (1757–1827)
English poet, engraver, painter and mystic

My mother groand! my father wept.
Into the dangerous world I leapt:
Helpless, naked, piping loud:
Like a fiend hid in a cloud.

Struggling in my father's hands:
Striving against my swadling bands:
Bound and weary I thought best
To sulk upon by mothers breast.

Songs of Experience (1794)

Calderón de la Barca, Pedro (1600–1681)
Spanish dramatist and poet

Pues el delito mayor del hombre es haber nacido.
For man's greatest offence is to have been born.

Life is a Dream (1636)

Congreve, William (1670–1729)
English dramatist

I came upstairs into the world; for I was born in
a cellar.

Love for Love (1695)

Fromm, Erich (1900–1980)
US psychologist and philosopher

Man's main task in life is to give *birth* to himself.

Man for Himself

Guest, Edgar A. (1945–)

Whoe'er has paced the floor
And lived those years of fearful thoughts, and
then been swept from woe
Up to the topmost height of bliss that's given
man to know,
Will tell you there's no phrase so sweet, so
charged with human joy
As that the doctor brings from God – that
message: 'It's a boy!'.

'It's a Boy'

Lette, Kathy (1959–)
Australian novelist

Childbirth was the moment of truth in my life.
Suddenly you realise that you are having the
greatest love affair of your life (but you also
realise that God's a bloke).

The Observer, June 1999

Lillie, Beatrice (1894–1989)
Canadian-born English actress

I'll simply say here that I was born Beatrice
Gladys Lillie at an extremely tender age because
my mother needed a fourth at meals.

Every Other Inch a Lady (1973)

Macneice, Louis (1907–1963)
Belfast-born poet, writer, radio producer, translator and
critic

I am not yet born; O fill me
With strength against those who would freeze
my
humanity, would dragoon me into a lethal
automaton,
would make me a cog in a machine, a thing
withone face, a thing, and against all those
who would dissipate my entirety, would
blow me like thistledown hither and
thither or hither and thither
like water held in the
hands would spill me.

Let them not make me a stone and let them not
spill me.
Otherwise kill me.

'Prayer before Birth' (1944)

Madonna (1958–)
US singer
Requesting an epidural in advance of childbirth, 1996

I'm not interested in being Wonder Woman in
the delivery room. Give me drugs.

Attr.

Mitchell, Margaret (1900–1949)
US author

Death and taxes and childbirth! There's never
any convenient time for any of them.

Gone With The Wind (1936)

Plato (c.429–347 BC)
Greek philosopher
> You must consider this too, that we are born, each of us, not for ourselves alone but partly for our country, partly for our parents and partly for our friends.
>> *Epistles*, IX

Shakespeare, William (1564–1616)
English dramatist, poet and actor
> *Don Pedro*: Out o' question, you were born in a merry hour.
> *Beatrice*: No, sure, my lord, my mother cried; but then there was a star danc'd, and under that was I born.
>> *Much Ado About Nothing*, II.i

Sophocles (496–406 BC)
Greek dramatist
> Not to be born is the best of all; next best is, having been born, to return as quickly as possible whence we came.
>> *Oedipus at Colonus*, line 1225

Stowe, Harriet Beecher (1811–1896)
US writer and reformer
> 'Who was your mother?' 'Never had none!' said the child, with another grin. 'Never had any mother? What do you mean? Where were you born?' 'Never was born!' persisted Topsy.
>> *Uncle Tom's Cabin* (1852)

Wisdom, Norman (1918–)
English comic actor
> I was born in very sorry circumstances. My mother was sorry and my father was sorry as well.
>> *The Observer*, 1998

Wordsworth, William (1770–1850)
English poet
> Our birth is but a sleep and a forgetting.
> The Soul that rises with us, our life's Star,
> Hath had elsewhere its setting,
> And cometh from afar;
> Not in entire forgetfulness,
> And not in utter nakedness,
> But trailing clouds of glory do we come
> From God, who is our home.
>> 'Ode: Intimations of Immortality' (1807)

▶▶ BABIES; PREGNANCY

the body

Blake, William (1757–1827)
English poet, engraver, painter and mystic
> Man has no Body distinct from his Soul for that called Body is a portion of Soul discernd by the five Senses, the chief inlets of Soul in this age.
>> *The Marriage of Heaven and Hell* (c.1790–1793)

Fry, Christopher (1907–)
English verse dramatist, theatre director and translator
> I travel light; as light,
> That is, as a man can travel who will
> Still carry his body around because
> Of its sentimental value.
>> *The Lady's not for Burning* (1949)

Hawking, Stephen (1942–)
English theoretical physicist
> I don't think there is a distinction between the body and soul. Which means that although I may take pride in my intelligence, I have to accept that the disability is also part of me and not something I can blame on a poor body I happened to pick up at an auction.
>> Interview in *The Times*, 1998

Hunter, William (1718–1783)
Scottish anatomist and physician
> Some physiologists will have it that the stomach is a mill; – others, that it is a fermenting vat; – others again that it is a stew-pan; – but in my view of the matter, it is neither a mill, a fermenting vat, nor a stew-pan – but a stomach, gentlemen, a stomach.
>> *A Treatise on Diet* (1826)

Lawrence, D.H. (1885–1930)
English writer, poet and critic
> The mind's terror of the body has probably driven more men mad than ever could be counted.
>> *The Plumed Serpent* (1926)

Orton, Joe (1933–1967)
English dramatist and writer
> I'd the upbringing a nun would envy and that's the truth. Until I was fifteen I was more familiar with Africa than my own body.
>> *Entertaining Mr Sloane* (1964)

Sanger, Margaret (1879–1966)
> No woman can call herself free who does not own and control her own body.
>> In Rosalind Miles, *The Women's History of the World* (1988)

Shakespeare, William (1564–1616)
English dramatist, poet and actor
> Virtue? A fig!
> 'Tis in ourselves that we are thus or thus. Our bodies are our gardens to the which our wills are gardeners.
>> *Othello*, I.iii

Sterne, Laurence (1713–1768)
Irish-born English writer and clergyman
> A man's body and his mind … are exactly like a

jerkin and a jerkin's lining; – rumple the one, –
you rumple the other.

Tristram Shandy (1759–1767)

Swift, Jonathan (1667–1745)
Irish satirist, poet, essayist and cleric
Thus finishing his grand survey,
The swain disgusted slunk away,
Repeating in his amorous fits,
'Oh! Celia, Celia, Celia shits!'.

'The Lady's Dressing Room' (1732)

Traherne, Thomas (c.1637–1674)
English religious writer and clergyman
The hands are a sort of feet, which serve us in
our passage towards Heaven, curiously
distinguished into joints and fingers, and fit to
be applied to any thing which reason can
imagine or desire.

Meditations on the Six Days of Creation
(1717)

Wheeler, Hugh (1912–1987)
English-born US writer
To lose a lover or even a husband or two during
the course of one's life can be vexing. But to
lose one's teeth is a catastrophe.

A Little Night Music (1974)

Whitman, Walt (1819–1892)
US poet and writer
If anything is sacred the human body is sacred.

'I Sing the Body Electric' (1855)

▶▶ APPEARANCE; VANITY

boldness

Koestler, Arthur (1905–1983)
British writer, essayist and political refugee
If the creator had a purpose in equipping us with
a neck, he surely meant us to stick it out.

Encounter, 1970

Livy (59 BC–AD 17)
Roman historian
*In rebus asperis et tenui spe fortissima quaeque consilia
tutissima sunt.*
In harsh circumstances when there is little hope,
the boldest measures are the safest.

History

Marmion, Shackerley (1603–1639)
English dramatist and poet
Familiarity begets boldness.

The Antiquary (1641)

Spenser, Edmund (c.1522–1599)
English poet
And as she lookt about, she did behold,
How over that same dore was likewise writ,

Be bold, be bold, and every where Be bold …
At last she spyde at that roome's upper end,
Another yron dore, on which was writ,
Be not too bold.

The Faerie Queene (1596)

Swift, Jonathan (1667–1745)
Irish satirist, poet, essayist and cleric
He was a bold man that first eat an oyster.

Polite Conversation (1738)

Virgil (70–19 BC)
Roman poet
Audentis Fortuna iuvat.
Fortune helps those who dare.

Aeneid

books

Addison, Joseph (1672–1719)
English essayist, poet, playwright and statesman
A reader seldom peruses a book with pleasure
until he knows whether the writer of it be a
black man or a fair man, of a mild or choleric
disposition, married or a bachelor.

The Spectator, 1711

Arnold, Matthew (1822–1888)
English poet, critic, essayist and educationist
He the translator will find one English book and
one only, where, as in the Iliad itself, perfect
plainness of speech is allied with perfect
nobleness; and that book is the Bible.

On Translating Homer (1861)

Auden, W.H. (1907–1973)
English poet, essayist, critic, teacher and dramatist
Some books are undeservedly forgotten; none
are undeservedly remembered.

The Dyer's Hand (1963)

Bacon, Francis (1561–1626)
English philosopher, essayist, politician and courtier
Books will speak plain when counsellors blanch.

'Of Counsel' (1625)

Some books are to be tasted, others to be
swallowed, and some few to be chewed and
digested; that is, some books are to be read
only in parts; others to be read but not
curiously; and some few to be read wholly, and
with diligence and attention.

'Of Studies' (1625)

Barnes, Julian (1946–)
English writer
Books say: she did this because. Life says: she
did this. Books are where things are explained
to you; life is where things aren't.

Flaubert's Parrot (1984)

Beauvoir, Simone de (1908–1986)
French writer, feminist critic and philosopher
> Few books are more thrilling than certain
> confessions, but they must be honest, and the
> author must have something to confess.
>> *The Second Sex* (1953)

Beecher, Henry Ward (1813–1887)
US clergyman, lecturer, editor and writer
> Books are not made for furniture, but there is
> nothing else that so beautifully furnishes a
> house.
>> *Life Thoughts* (1858)

Belloc, Hilaire (1870–1953)
English writer of verse, essayist and critic; Liberal MP
> When I am dead, I hope it may be said:
> 'His sins were scarlet, but his books were
> read.'
>> *Sonnets and Verse* (1923)

Bennett, Alan (1934–)
English dramatist, actor and diarist
> Definition of a classic: a book everyone is
> assumed to have read and often thinks they
> have.
>> *Independent on Sunday*, 1991

The Bible (King James Version)
> Of making many books there is no end; and
> much study is a weariness of the flesh.
>> *Ecclesiastes*, 12:12

Boorstin, Daniel (1914–)
US librarian, historian, lawyer and writer
> A best-seller was a book which somehow sold
> well simply because it was selling well.
>> *The Image* (1962)

Bradbury, Ray (1920–)
US science fiction writer
> You don't have to burn books to destroy a
> culture. Just get people to stop reading them.
>> *Reader's Digest*, 1994

Brodsky, Joseph (1940–1996)
Russian poet, essayist, critic and exile
> There are worse crimes than burning books. One
> of them is not reading them.
>> Remark, 1991

Browne, Sir Thomas (1605–1682)
English physician, author and antiquary
> They do most by Books, who could do much
> without them, and he that chiefly owes himself
> unto himself, is the substantial man.
>> *Christian Morals* (1716)

Browning, Elizabeth Barrett (1806–1861)
English poet; wife of Robert Browning
> Of writing many books there is no end.
>> *Aurora Leigh* (1857)

Burgess, Anthony (1917–1993)
English writer, linguist and composer
> The possession of a book becomes a substitute
> for reading it.
>> *New York Times Book Review*

Byron, Lord (1788–1824)
English poet satirist and traveller
> 'Tis pleasant, sure, to see one's name in print;
> A Book's a Book, altho' there is nothing in't.
>> *English Bards and Scotch Reviewers* (1809)

Callimachus (c.305–c.240 BC)
Cyrene-born Alexandrian poet and epigrammatist
> A great book is like great evil.
>> In R. Pfeiffer (ed.), *Fragments*

Calvino, Italo (1923–1985)
Italian writer
> A classic is a book that has never finished saying
> what it has to say.
>> *The Literature Machine* (1987)

Campbell, Baron (1799–1861)
Scottish lawyer and politician
> So essential did I consider an Index to be to
> every book, that I proposed to bring a Bill into
> parliament to deprive an author who publishes a
> book without an Index of the privilege of
> copyright; and, moreover, to subject him, for his
> offence, to a pecuniary penalty.
>> *Lives of the Chief Justices*, Preface to Vol. III

Campbell, Thomas (1777–1844)
Scottish poet, ballad writer and journalist
Excusing himself in proposing a toast to Napoleon at a literary
dinner
> Gentlemen you must not mistake me. I admit
> that the French Emperor is a tyrant. I admit that
> he is a monster. I admit that he is the sworn foe
> of our own nation, and, if you will, of the whole
> human race. But, gentlemen, we must be just to
> our great enemy. We must not forget that he
> once shot a bookseller.
>> Attr. in a footnote in G.O. Trevelyan, *The Life and Letters of
>> Lord Macaulay* (1876)

Carroll, Lewis (1832–1898)
English writer and photographer
> 'What is the use of a book,' thought Alice,
> 'without pictures or conversations?'.
>> *Alice's Adventures in Wonderland* (1865)

Chamfort, Nicolas (1741–1794)
French writer
> The success of many books is due to the affinity
> between the mediocrity of the author's ideas
> and those of the public.
>> In J. R. Solly *A Cynic's Breviary* (1925)

Chandler, Raymond (1888–1959)
US crime writer

If my books had been any worse I should not have been invited to Hollywood, and ... if they had been any better, I should not have come.

Letter to C.W. Morton, 1945

Chesterfield, Lord (1694–1773)
English politician and letter writer

Due attention to the inside of books, and due contempt for the outside, is the proper relation between a man of sense and his books.

Letter to his son, 1749

Cowper, William (1731–1800)
English poet, hymn and letter writer

Books are not seldom talismans and spells.

The Task (1785)

Crabbe, George (1754–1832)
English poet, clergyman, surgeon and botanist

Books cannot always please, however good;
Minds are not ever craving for their food.

The Borough (1810)

Lo! all in silence, all in order stand,
And mighty folios first, a lordly band,
Then quartos, their well-order'd ranks maintain,
And light octavos fill a spacious plain;
See yonder, ranged in more frequented rows,
A humbler band of duodecimos.

The Library (1808)

With awe around these silent walks I tread:
These are the lasting mansions of the dead.

The Library (1808)

This, books can do – nor this alone: they give
New views to life, and teach us how to live;
They soothe the grieved, the stubborn they chastise;
Fools they admonish, and confirm the wise,
Their aid they yield to all: they never shun
The man of sorrow, nor the wretch undone;
Unlike the hard, the selfish, and the proud,
They fly not from the suppliant crowd;
Nor tell to various people various things,
But show to subjects, what they show to kings.

The Library (1808)

Davies, Robertson (1913–1995)
Canadian playwright, writer and critic

A truly great book should be read in youth, again in maturity, and once more in old age, as a fine building should be seen by morning light, at noon, and by moonlight.

In Grant, The Enthusiasms of Robertson Davies

Descartes, René (1596–1650)
French philosopher and mathematician

La lecture de tous les bons livres est comme une conversation avec les plus honnêtes gens des siècles passés.
The reading of all good books is like a conversation with the finest men of past centuries.

Discours de la Méthode (1637)

Diodorus Siculus (c.1st century BC)
Greek historian
Inscription over library door in Alexandria

Medicine for the soul.

History

Eddington, Sir Arthur (1882–1944)
English astronomer, physicist and mathematician

If an army of monkeys were strumming on typewriters they might write all the books in the British Museum.

The Nature of the Physical World (1928)

Evans, Dame Edith (1888–1976)
English actress
On being told that Nancy Mitford had been lent a villa to enable her to finish a book

Oh really. What exactly is she reading?

Attr.

Flaubert, Gustave (1821–1880)
French writer

Les livres ne se font pas comme les enfants, mais comme les pyramides ... et ça ne sert à rien! et ça reste dans le désert! ... Les chacals pissent au bas et les bourgeois montent dessus.
Books are made not like children but like the pyramids ... and they're good for nothing! and they stay in the desert! Jackals piss at their foot and the bourgeois climb up on them.

Letter to Ernest Feydeau, 1857

Forster, E.M. (1879–1970)
English writer, essayist and literary critic

I suggest that the only books that influence us are those for which we are ready, and which have gone a little farther down our particular path than we have yet got ourselves.

Two Cheers for Democracy (1951)

Frank, Anne (1929–1945)
Jewish diarist; died in Nazi concentration camp

If I read a book that impresses me, I have to take myself firmly in hand before I mix with other people; otherwise they would think my mind rather queer.

The Diary of Anne Frank (1947)

Franklin, Benjamin (1706–1790)
US statesman, scientist, political critic and printer

If you would not be forgotten as soon as you are dead, either write things worth reading or do things worth writing.

Attr.

Frye, Northrop (1912–1991)
Canadian critic and academic

The book is the world's most patient medium.
The Scholar in Society (film, 1984)

Fuller, Thomas (1608–1661)
English churchman and antiquary
　Learning hath gained most by those books by which the printers have lost.
The Holy State and the Profane State (1642)

Gloucester, William, Duke of (1743–1805)
English Field Marshal; brither of George III
　Another damned, thick, square book. Always scribble, scribble, scribble! Eh! Mr. Gibbon?
In Henry Best, *Personal and Literary Memorials* (1829)

Goldsmith, Oliver (c.1728–1774)
Irish dramatist, poet and writer
　I...shewed her that books were sweet unreproaching companions to the miserable, and that if they could not bring us to enjoy life, they would at least teach us to endure it.
The Vicar of Wakefield (1766)

　A book may be amusing with numerous errors, or it may be very dull without a single absurdity.
The Vicar of Wakefield (1766)

Hemingway, Ernest (1898–1961)
US author
　For a true writer each book should be a new beginning, where he tries again for something that is beyond attainment.
Speech for the presentation of the Nobel Prize, 1954

Horace (65–8 BC)
Roman poet
Delere licebit
Quod non edideris; nescit vox missa reverti.
You can destroy what you haven't published; the word once out cannot be recalled.
Ars Poetica

Howell, John
　The Reason why there is no table or Index added hereunto, is, that every Page in this Work is so full of Signal Remarks, that were they couched in an Index, it would make a volume as big as the Book, and so make the Postern Gate bear no proportion with the Building.
Note in the front of *Proedria Basilike* (1664)

Huxley, Aldous (1894–1963)
English writer, poet and critic
　A bad book is as much of a labour to write as a good one; it comes as sincerely from the author's soul ... its sincerities will be ... uninterestingly expressed, and the labour expended on the expression will be wasted. Nature is monstrously unjust. There is no substitute for talent. Industry and all the virtues

are of no avail.
Point Counter Point (1928)

The proper study of mankind is books.
Crome Yellow (1921)

Innes, Hammond (1913–1998)
English novelist
On growing trees
　I'm replacing some of the timber used up by my books. Books are just trees with squiggles on them.
Radio Times, 1984

James, Brian (1892–1972)
Australian writer
　The book of my enemy has been remaindered And I am pleased.
'The Book of My Enemy Has Been Remaindered'

Johnson, Samuel (1709–1784)
English lexicographer, poet, critic, conversationalist and essayist
　Books that you may carry to the fire, and hold readily in your hand, are the most useful after all.
In Sir John Hawkins, *Life of Samuel Johnson* (1787)

Jowett, Benjamin (1817–1893)
English scholar, translator, essayist and priest
　One man is as good as another until he has written a book.
In E. Abbott and L. Campbell (eds), *Life and Letters of Benjamin Jowett* (1897)

Kafka, Franz (1883–1924)
Czech-born German-speaking writer
Ich glaube, man sollte überhaupt nur solche Bücher lesen, die einen beissen und stechen.
I think you should only read those books which bite and sting you.
Letter to Oskar Pollak, 1904

... ein Buch muss die Axt sein für das gefrorene Meer in uns.
... a book must be the axe for the frozen sea within us.
Letter to Oskar Pollak, 1904

Kennedy, A.L. (1965–)
Scottish novelist
Definition of a classic
　... a book which in some manner celebrates and encourages the human imagination, which renders possible the impossible, which sustains the interior life of the reader and which speaks to and of the human spirit.
What makes a classic a classic? The test of time

Koran
　Every age hath its book.
Chapter 13

La Bruyère, Jean de (1645–1696)
French satirist
> *C'est un métier que de faire un livre, comme de faire une pendule: il faut plus que de l'esprit pour être auteur.*
> The making of a book, like the making of a clock, is a craft; it takes more than wit to be an author.
>> *Les caractères ou les moeurs de ce siècle* (1688)

Laing, R.D. (1927–1989)
Scottish psychiatrist, psychoanalyst and poet
> Few books today are forgivable.
>> *The Politics of Experience* (1967)

Lamb, Charles (1775–1834)
English essayist, critic and letter writer
> I mean your borrowers of books – those mutilators of collections, spoilers of the symmetry of shelves, and creators of odd volumes.
>> *Essays of Elia* (1823)

> I love to lose myself in other men's minds. When I am not walking, I am reading; I cannot sit and think. Books think for me.
>> *Last Essays of Elia* (1833)

> She unbent her mind afterwards – over a book.
>> *Essays of Elia* (1823), 'Mrs Battle's Opinions on Whist'

Larkin, Philip (1922–1985)
English poet, writer and librarian
> Get stewed:
> Books are a load of crap.
>> 'A Study of Reading Habits' (1964)

Lebowitz, Fran (1946–)
US writer
> Never judge a book by its cover.
>> *Metropolitan Life* (1978)

On self-help books
> Wealth and power are much more likely to be the result of breeding than they are of reading.
>> *Social Studies* (1981)

Lichtenberg, Georg (1742–1799)
German physicist, satirist and writer
> There can hardly be a stranger commodity in the world than books. Printed by people who don't understand them; sold by people who don't understand them; bound, criticized and read by people who don't understand them, and now even written by people who don't understand them.
>> A Doctrine of Scattered Occasions

Lynton, Michael
British publishing executive
> The book is the greatest interactive medium of all time. You can underline it, write in the margins, fold down a page, skip ahead. And you can take it anywhere.
>> *Daily Telegraph*, 1996

Macaulay, Dame Rose (1881–1958)
English writer
> It was a book to kill time for those who like it better dead.
>> Attr.

Madonna (1958–)
US singer and actress
> Everyone probably thinks that I'm a raving nymphomaniac, that I have an insatiable sexual appetite, when the truth is I'd rather read a book.
>> *Q Magazine*, 1991

Marx, Groucho (1895–1977)
US comedian
> I did toy with the idea of doing a cook-book ... I think a lot of people who hate literature but love fried eggs would buy it if the price was right.
>> *Groucho and Me* (1959)

Martial (c.AD 40–c.104)
Spanish-born Latin epigrammatist and poet
> *Lasciva est nobis pagina, vita proba.*
> My book is licentious, but my life is pure.
>> *Epigrammata*

Maugham, William Somerset (1874–1965)
English writer, dramatist and physician
> There is an impression abroad that everyone had it in him to write one book; but if by this is implied a good book the impression is false.
>> *The Summing Up* (1938)

Milton, John (1608–1674)
English poet, libertarian and pamphleteer
> As good almost kill a Man as kill a good Book; who kills a Man kills a reasonable creature, God's Image; but hee who destroyes a good Booke, kills reason it selfe, kills the Image of God, as it were in the eye. Many a man lives a burden to the Earth; but a good Booke is the pretious life-blood of a master spirit, imbalm'd and treasur'd up on purpose to a life beyond life.
>> *Areopagitica* (1644)

Murdoch, Sir Walter Logie Forbes (1874–1970)
Australian writer and broadcaster
> A second-hand bookshop is the sign and symbol of a civilized community ... and the number and quality of these shops give you the exact measure of a city's right to be counted among the great cities of the world ... Show me a city's second-hand bookshops, and I will tell you what manner of citizens dwell there, and of what ancestry sprung.
>> *Collected Essays* (1940)

Powell, Anthony (1905–2000)
English writer and critic
> Books Do Furnish a Room.
>
> *Title of novel, 1971*

Proverb
> Books and friends should be few but good.

Raleigh, Sir Walter A. (1861–1922)
English scholar, critic and essayist
> An anthology is like all the plums and orange peel picked out of a cake.
>
> *Letter to Mrs Robert Bridges, 1915*

Reed, Henry (1914–1986)
English poet, radio dramatist and translator
> I have known her pass the whole evening without mentioning a single book, or in fact anything unpleasant, at all.
>
> *A Very Great Man Indeed* (1953)

Rogers, Samuel (1763–1855)
British poet
> When a new book is published, read an old one.
>
> Attr.

Roosevelt, Franklin Delano (1882–1945)
US Democrat President
> We all know that books burn – yet we have the greater knowledge that books cannot be killed by fire. People die, but books never die. No man and no force can abolish memory … In this war, we know, books are weapons.
>
> *Publisher's Weekly*, 1942, 'Message to the American Booksellers Association'

Rushdie, Salman (1947–)
Indian-born English author
> A book is a version of the world. If you do not like it, ignore it; or offer your own version in return.
>
> *Independent on Sunday*, 1990

Ruskin, John (1819–1900)
English art critic, philosopher and reformer
> All books are divisible into two classes: the books of the hour, and the books of all time.
>
> *Sesame and Lilies* (1865)

> What do we, as a nation, care about books? How much do you think we spend altogether on our libraries, public or private, as compared with what we spend on our horses?
>
> *Sesame and Lilies* (1865)

> If a book is worth reading, it is worth buying.
>
> *Sesame and Lilies* (1865)

> How long most people would look at the best book before they would give the price of a large turbot for it!
>
> *Sesame and Lilies* (1865)

Samuel, Lord (1870–1963)
English Liberal statesman, philosopher and administrator
> A library is thought in cold storage.
>
> *A Book of Quotations* (1947)

Singer, Isaac Bashevis (1904–1991)
Polish-born US Yiddish writer
> Children… have no use for psychology. They detest sociology. They still believe in God, the family, angels, devils, witches, goblins, logic, clarity, punctuation, and other such obsolete stuff … When a book is boring, they yawn openly. They don't expect their writer to redeem humanity, but leave to adults such childish illusions.
>
> *Nobel Prize acceptance speech, 1978*

Smith, Logan Pearsall (1865–1946)
US-born British epigrammatist, critic and writer
> A best-seller is the gilded tomb of a mediocre talent.
>
> *Afterthoughts* (1931)

Smith, Sydney (1771–1845)
English clergyman, essayist, journalist and wit
> No furniture so charming as books, even if you never open them, or read a single word.
>
> In Holland, *A Memoir of the Reverend Sydney Smith* (1855)

Spenser, Edmund (c.1522–1599)
English poet
> The generall end therefore of all the booke is to fashion a gentleman or noble person in vertuous and gentle discipline.
>
> *The Faerie Queene* (1596)

Steinbeck, John (1902–1968)
US writer
> It is wonderful that even today, with all the competition of radio, television, films, and records, the book has kept its precious character. A book is somehow sacred. A dictator can kill and maim people, can sink to any kind of tyranny, and only be hated. But when books are burnt the ultimate in tyranny has happened. This we cannot forgive.
>
> Attr.

Stevenson, Robert Louis (1850–1894)
Scottish writer, poet and essayist
> Books are good enough in their own way, but they are a mighty bloodless substitute for life.
>
> *Virginibus Puerisque* (1881)

Swift, Jonathan (1667–1745)
Irish satirist, poet, essayist and cleric
> Books, like men their authors, have no more than one way of coming into the world, but there are ten thousand to go out of it, and return no more.
>
> *A Tale of a Tub* (1704)

Trilling, Lionel (1905–1975)
US critic
> Youth is a time when we find the books we give up but do not get over.
>> *New York Times*, 1966

Trollope, Anthony (1815–1882)
English writer, traveller and post office official
> Of all the needs a book has the chief need is that it be readable.
>> *Autobiography* (1883)

Tupper, Martin (1810–1889)
English writer, lawyer and inventor
> A good book is the best of friends, the same today and for ever.
>> *Proverbial Philosophy* (1838)

Valéry, Paul (1871–1945)
French poet, mathematician and philosopher
> *Les livres ont les mêmes ennemis que l'homme: le feu, l'humide, les bêtes, le temps; et leur propre contenu.*
> Books have the same enemies as man: fire, damp, animals, time; and their own contents.
>> *Littérature*

Waugh, Evelyn (1903–1966)
English writer and diarist
> Particularly against books the Home Secretary is. If we can't stamp out literature in the country, we can at least stop it being brought in from outside.
>> *Vile Bodies* (1930)

Wesley, John (1703–1791)
English theologian and preacher
> Beware you be not swallowed up in books! An ounce of love is worth a pound of knowledge.
>> In Southey, *Life of Wesley* (1820)

West, Dame Rebecca (1892–1983)
English writer, critic and feminist
> God forbid that any book should be banned. The practice is as indefensible as infanticide.
>> *The Strange Necessity* (1928)

Wilde, Oscar (1854–1900)
Irish poet, dramatist, writer, critic and wit
> There is no such thing as a moral or an immoral book. Books are well written, or badly written. That is all.
>> *The Picture of Dorian Gray* (1891)

Wodehouse, P.G. (1881–1975)
English humorist and writer
Dedication
> To my daughter Leonora without whose never-failing sympathy and encouragement this book would have been finished in half the time.
>> *The Heart of a Goof* (1926)

Wordsworth, William (1770–1850)
English poet
> Up! up! my friend, and quit your books;

> Or surely you'll grow double –
> Books! 'tis a dull and endless strife:
> Come, hear the woodland linnet,
> How sweet his music! on my life,
> There's more of wisdom in it.
>> 'The Tables Turned' (1798)

▶▶ CENSORSHIP; CRITICISM; FICTION; LITERATURE; PUBLISHING; READING; WRITERS; WRITING

boredom

Adler, Renata
US film critic and writer
> Idle people are often bored and bored people, unless they sleep a lot, are cruel. It is not accident that boredom and cruelty are great preoccupations in our time.
>> *Speedboat* (1976)

Austin, Warren Robinson (1877–1962)
First US ambassador to the UN
On being asked if he found long debates at the UN tiring
> It is better for aged diplomats to be bored than for young men to die.
>> Attr.

Beaton, Cecil (1904–1980)
English photographer
> Perhaps the world's second-worst crime is boredom; the first is being a bore.
>> Attr.

Bernanos, Georges (1888–1948)
French novelist and essayist
> The world is eaten up by boredom ... It is like dust. You go about and never notice, you breathe it in ... It is sifted so fine, it doesn't even grit on your teeth. But stand still for an instant and there it is, coating your face and hands.
>> *The Diary of a Country Priest* (1936)

Bierce, Ambrose (1842–c.1914)
US writer, verse writer and soldier
> *Bore*: A person who talks when you wish him to listen.
>> *The Cynic's Word Book* (1906)

Bridie, James (1888–1951)
Scottish dramatist, writer and physician
> Boredom is a sign of satisfied ignorance, blunted apprehension, crass sympathies, dull understanding, feeble powers of attention and irreclaimable weakness of character.
>> *Mr Bolfry* (1943)

Bryson, Bill (1951–)
US travel writer
> I mused for a few moments on the question of which was worse, to lead a life so boring that

you are easily enchanted or a life so full of stimulus that you are easily bored.

The Lost Continent (1989)

Byron, Lord (1788–1824)
English poet satirist and traveller
Society is now one polish'd horde,
Form'd of two mighty tribes, the Bores and Bored.

Don Juan (1819–1824)

Carter, Angela (1940–1992)
English writer
Rationalization of the Japanese veneration of boredom
He loved to be bored; don't think he was contemptuously dismissive of the element of boredom inherent in sexual activity. He adored and venerated boredom. He said that dogs, for example, were never bored, nor birds, so, obviously, the capacity that distinguished man from the other higher mammals, from the scaled and feathered things, was that of boredom. The more bored one was, the more one expressed one's humanity.

'The Quilt Maker'

Chesterton, G.K. (1874–1936)
English writer, poet and critic
There is no such thing on earth as an uninteresting subject; the only thing that can exist is an uninterested person.

Heretics (1905)

De Vries, Peter (1910–1993)
US novelist
I wanted to be bored to death, as good a way to go as any.

Comfort me with Apples (1956)

Durrell, Lawrence (1912–1990)
Indian-born British poet and writer
No more about sex, it's too boring.

Tunc (1968)

Emerson, Ralph Waldo (1803–1882)
US poet, essayist, transcendentalist and teacher
Every hero becomes a bore at last.

Representative Men (1850)

Freud, Clement (1924–)
British Liberal politician, broadcaster and writer
If you resolve to give up smoking, drinking and loving, you don't actually live longer; it just seems longer.

The Observer, 1964

Gautier, Théophile (1811–1872)
French poet, writer and critic
Plutôt la barbarie que l'ennui.
Sooner barbarity than boredom.

Attr.

Halsey, Margaret (1910–)
US writer

… it takes a great deal to produce ennui in an Englishman and if you do, he only takes it as convincing proof that you are well-bred.

With Malice Toward Some (1938)

Howells, W.D. (1837–1920)
US writer, critic, editor and poet
Some people can stay longer in an hour than others can in a week.

In Esar, *Treasury of Humorous Quotations (1951)*

Hugo, Victor (1802–1885)
French poet, writer, dramatist and politician
La symétrie, c'est l'ennui, et l'ennui est le fond même du deuil. Le désespoir bâille.
Symmetry is boredom, and boredom is the very source of death. Despair yawns.

Les Misérables (1862)

Huxley, Aldous (1894–1963)
English writer, poet and critic
I can sympathize with people's pains, but not with their pleasures. There is something curiously boring about somebody else's happiness.

Limbo (1920)

Inge, William Ralph (1860–1954)
English divine, writer and teacher
The effect of boredom on a large scale in history is underestimated. It is a main cause of revolutions, and would soon bring to an end all the static Utopias and the farmyard civilization of the Fabians.

End of an Age (1948)

Jerrold, Douglas William (1803–1857)
English dramatist, writer and wit
Remark to a small thin man who was boring him
Sir, you are like a pin, but without either its head or its point.

Attr.

La Rochefoucauld (1613–1680)
French writer
On s'ennuie presque toujours avec les gens avec qui il n'est pas permis de s'ennuyer.
We are almost always bored by the very people whom we are not allowed to find boring.

Maximes (1678)

Nietzsche, Friedrich Wilhelm (1844–1900)
German philosopher, critic and poet
Ist das Leben nicht hundert Mal zu kurz, sich in ihm – zu langweilen?
Is life not a hundred times too short – to get bored?

Beyond Good and Evil (1886)

Saki (1870–1916)
Burmese-born British writer
'I believe I take precedence, ' he said coldly;

'you are merely the club Bore; I am the club Liar.'

Beasts and Super-Beasts (1914)

Shakespeare, William (1564–1616)
English dramatist, poet and actor

Life is as tedious as a twice-told tale
Vexing the dull ear of a drowsy man.

King John, III.iv

O, he is as tedious
As a tired horse, a railing wife;
Worse than a smoky house; I had rather live
With cheese and garlic in a windmill, far,
Than feed on cates and have him talk to me
In any summer house in Christendom.

Henry IV, Part 1, III.i

Steele, Sir Richard (1672–1729)
Irish-born English writer, dramatist and politician

It is to be noted, That when any Part of this Paper appears dull, there is a Design in it.

The Tatler, 38, 1709

Taylor, Bert Leston (1866–1921)
US journalist

A bore is a man who, when you ask him how he is, tells you.

The So-Called Human Race (1922)

Thomas, Dylan (1914–1953)
Welsh poet, writer and radio dramatist

Dylan talked copiously, then stopped. 'Somebody's boring me, ' he said, 'I think it's me.'

In Heppenstall, *Four Absentees* (1960)

Tree, Sir Herbert Beerbohm (1853–1917)
English actor and theatre manager
Of Israel Zangwill

He is an old bore; even the grave yawns for him.

In Pearson, *Beerbohm Tree* (1956)

Updike, John (1932–)
US writer, poet and critic

A healthy male adult bore consumes one and a half times his own weight in other people's patience.

Assorted Prose (1965)

Voltaire (1694–1778)
French philosopher, dramatist, poet, historian writer and critic

Le secret d'ennuyer est celui de tout dire.
The secret of being boring is to say everything.

Discours en vers sur l'homme (1737)

borrowing and lending

Benchley, Robert (1889–1945)
US essayist, humorist and actor

I don't trust a bank that would lend money to such a poor risk.

Attr.

Lamb, Charles (1775–1834)
English essayist, critic and letter writer

The human species, according to the best theory I can form of it, is composed of two distinct races, the men who borrow, and the men who lend.

Essays of Elia (1823)

Proverbs

Lend only what you can afford to lose.

Borrowed garments never fit well.

Shakespeare, William (1564–1616)
English dramatist, poet and actor

Neither a borrower nor a lender be;
For loan oft loses both itself and friend,
And borrowing dulls the edge of husbandry.

Hamlet, I.iii

Surtees, R.S. (1805–1864)
English writer

Three things I never lends – my 'oss, my wife, and my name.

Hillingdon Hall (1845)

Tusser, Thomas (c.1524–1580)
English writer, poet and musician

Who goeth a borrowing
Goeth a sorrowing.
Few lend (but fools)
Their working tools.

Five Hundred Points of Good Husbandry (1557)

boxing

Ali, Muhammad (1942–)
US heavyweight boxer

It's just a job. Grass grows, birds fly, waves pound the sand. I beat people up.

The New York Times, 1977

Bruno, Frank (1961–)
English heavyweight boxer

Boxing is just show business with blood.

The Guardian, 1991

boys

Byron, Lord (1788–1824)
English poet satirist and traveller

Ah! happy years! once more who would not be a boy?

Childe Harold's Pilgrimage

Causley, Charles (1917–)
English poet and teacher
> Ears like bombs and teeth like splinters:
> A blitz of a boy is Timothy Winters.
>> *Union Street* (1957), 'Timothy Winters'

Carroll, Lewis (1832–1898)
English writer and photographer
> I am fond of children (except boys).
>> Letter to Kathleen Eschwege, 1879

O'Brien, Flann (1911–1966)
Irish novelist and journalist
> Do engine drivers, I wonder, eternally wish they
> were small boys?
>> *The Best of Myles Na Gopaleen* (1990)

Shakespeare, William (1564–1616)
English dramatist, poet and actor
> Two lads that thought there was no more behind
> But such a day tomorrow as today,
> And to be boy eternal.
>> *The Winter's Tale*, I.ii

Thomas, Dylan (1914–1953)
Welsh poet, writer and radio dramatist
> And the wild boys as innocent as strawberries.
>> 'The Hunchback in the Park'

> The boys are dreaming wicked or of the bucking
> ranches of the night and the jollyrodgered sea.
>> *Under Milk Wood* (1954)

brevity

Brabazon of Tara, Lord (1910–1974)
English businessman and Conservative politician
> I take the view, and always have done, that if
> you cannot say what you have to say in twenty
> minutes, you should go away and write a book
> about it.
>> Attr.

Horace (65–8 BC)
Roman poet
> *Brevis esse laboro,*
> *Obscurus fio.*
> I labour to be brief, and I become obscure.
>> *Ars Poetica*, line 25

Jonson, Ben (1572–1637)
English dramatist and poet
> In small proportions we just beauties see;
> And in short measures, life may perfect be.
>> *The Underwood* (1640)

> In all pointed sentences, some degree of
> accuracy must be sacrificed to conciseness.
>> 'The Bravery of the English Common Soldier'
>> (1760)

La Fontaine, Jean de (1621–1695)
French poet and fabulist
> *Mais les ouvrages les plus courts*
> *Sont toujours les meilleurs.*
> But the shortest works are always the best.
>> *Fables*, 'Les lapins'

Thoreau, Henry David (1817–1862)
US essayist, social critic and writer
> Not that the story need be long, but it will take
> a long while to make it short.
>> Letter to Harrison Blake, 1857

Wellington, Duke of (1769–1852)
Irish-born British military commander and statesman
Responding to a vicar's enquiry as to whether there was
anything he would like his forthcoming sermon to be about
> Yes, about ten minutes.
>> Attr.

▶▶ DEBT

bribery

Greene, Graham (1904–1991)
English writer and dramatist
> I have often noticed that a bribe … has that
> effect – it changes a relation. The man who
> offers a bribe gives away a little of his own
> importance; the bribe once accepted, he
> becomes the inferior, like a man who has paid
> for a woman.
>> *The Comedians* (1966)

Penn, William (1644–1718)
English Quaker, founder of state of Pennsylvania
> The taking of a Bribe or Gratuity, should be
> punished with as severe Penalties as the
> defrauding of the State.
>> *Some Fruits of Solitude, in Reflections and Maxims*
>> *relating to the Conduct of Humane Life* (1693)

Reed, Joseph (1741–1785)
American Revolutionary statesman
Reply on being offered money to act on behalf of the British
Crown
> I am not worth purchasing, but such as I am, the
> King of Great Britain is not rich enough to do it.
>> In W.B. Reed, *Life and Correspondence of*
>> *Joseph Reed* (1847)

britain

Acheson, Dean (1893–1971)
US Democrat politician
> Great Britain … has lost an Empire and not yet
> found a role. The attempt to play a separate

power role – that is, a role apart from Europe, a role based on a 'special relationship' with the United States, a role based on being the head of a Commonwealth ... this role is about to be played out ... Her Majesty's Government is now attempting, wisely in my opinion, to re-enter Europe.

Speech, 1962

Artley, Alexandra
British writer
On the reprocessing of foreign nuclear waste in Britain
This is not 'polite and tidy Britain' ... It's Widow Twankey's Nuclear Laundry.

In Britain in the Eighties *(1989)*

Attlee, Clement (1883–1967)
English statesman and Prime Minister
I think the British have the distinction above all other nations of being able to put new wine into old bottles without bursting them.

Hansard, 1950

Benn, Tony (1925–)
English Labour politician
Britain today is suffering from galloping obsolescence.

Speech, 1963

Borrow, George (1803–1881)
English writer and linguist
There are no countries in the world less known by the British than these selfsame British Islands.

Lavengro (1851)

Bullock, Alan, Baron (1914–)
English historian
The people Hitler never understood, and whose actions continued to exasperate him to the end of his life, were the British.

Hitler, A Study in Tyranny (1952)

Callaghan, James (1912–)
English Labour statesman and Prime Minister
Britain has lived for too long on borrowed time, borrowed money and even borrowed ideas.

The Observer, 1976

Camp, William (1926–)
What annoys me about Britain is the rugged will to lose.

Attr.

Casson, Sir Hugh (1910–)
English architect and writer
The British love permanence more than they love beauty.

The Observer, 1964

Chesterfield, Lord (1694–1773)
English politician and letter writer
It must be owned that the Graces do not seem to be natives of Great Britain; and, I doubt, the

best of us here have more of the rough than the polished diamond.

Letter to his son, 1748

Churchill, Sir Winston (1874–1965)
English Conservative Prime Minister
Of the British
They are the only people who like to be told how bad things are – who like to be told the worst.

Speech, 1921

When I warned them the French Government that Britain would fight on alone whatever they did, their Generals told their Prime Minister and his divided Cabinet, 'In three weeks England will have her neck wrung like a chicken'. Some chicken! Some neck!

Speech, December 1941

The British Empire and the United States will have to be somewhat mixed up together in some of their affairs for mutual and general advantage. For my own part, looking out for the future, I do not view the process with any misgivings. I could not stop it if I wished; no one can stop it. Like the Mississippi, it just keeps rolling along. Let it roll. Let it roll on full flood, inexorable, irresistible, benignant, to broader lands and better days.

Speech, House of Commons, August 1940

The maxim of the British people is 'Business as usual'.

Speech, November 1914

Coleridge, Samuel Taylor (1772–1834)
English poet, philosopher and critic
Of Britain
A vain, speech-mouthing, speech-reporting guild,
One benefit-club for mutual flattery.

'Fears in Solitude' (1798)

Edmond, James (1859–1933)
Scottish-born Australian writer and editor
I had been told by Jimmy Edmond in Australia that there were only three things against living in Britain: the place, the climate and the people.

In Low, Low Autobiography

Gaitskell, Hugh (1906–1963)
English Labour politician
On Britain's joining the European Community
It does mean, if this is the idea, the end of Britain as an independent European state ... it means the end of a thousand years of history.

Speech, 1962

Hamilton, William (Willie) (1917–)
English politician, teacher and antiroyalist
Britain is not a country that is easily rocked by

revolution … In Britain our institutions evolve. We are a Fabian Society writ large.

My Queen and I (1975)

Harlech, Lord (1918–1985)
English politician, and TV company chairman
In the end it may well be that Britain will be honoured by historians more for the way she disposed of an empire than for the way in which she acquired it.

New York Times, 1962

Levin, Bernard (1928–)
British writer
Once, when a British Prime Minister sneezed, men half a world away would blow their noses. Now when a British Prime Minister sneezes nobody else will even say 'Bless You'.

The Times, 1976

Lloyd George, David (1863–1945)
British Liberal statesman
What is our task? To make Britain a fit country for heroes to live in.

Speech, 1918

Palmerston, Lord (1784–1865)
British Prime Minister
I therefore fearlessly challenge the verdict which this House … is to give … whether, as the Roman, in days of old, held himself free from indignity, when he could say *Civis Romanus sum*; so also a British subject, in whatever land he may be, shall feel confident that the watchful eye and the strong arm of England will protect him against injustice and wrong.

Speech, House of Commons, 1850

Shaw, George Bernard (1856–1950)
Irish socialist, writer, dramatist and critic
He the Briton is a barbarian, and thinks that the custom of his tribe and island are the laws of nature.

Caesar and Cleopatra (1901)

Smith, Adam (1723–1790)
Scottish economist, philosopher and essayist
If any of the provinces of the British empire cannot be made to contribute towards the support of the whole empire, it is surely time that Great Britain should free herself from the expense of defending those provinces in time of war, and of supporting any part of their civil or military establishments in time of peace, and endeavour to accommodate her future views and designs to the real mediocrity of her circumstances.

Wealth of Nations (1776)

Somerville, William (1675–1742)
Hail, happy Britain! highly favoured isle,

And Heaven's peculiar care!

The Chase (1735)

Thomson, James (1700–1748)
Scottish poet and dramatist
When Britain first, at heaven's command,
Arose from out the azure main,
This was the charter of the land,
And guardian angels sung this strain:
'Rule, Britannia, rule the waves;
Britons never will be slaves.'

Alfred: A Masque (1740)

Thoreau, Henry David (1817–1862)
US essayist, social critic and writer
The government of the world I live in was not framed, like that of Britain, in after-dinner conversations over the wine.

Walden (1854), 'Economy'

▶▶ EMPIRE; ENGLAND; IRELAND; PATRIOTISM; SCOTLAND; WALES

bureaucracy

Acheson, Dean (1893–1971)
US Democrat politician
A memorandum is written not to inform the reader but to protect the writer.

Attr.

Adenauer, Konrad (1876–1967)
German Chancellor
There's nothing which cannot be made a mess of again by officials.

Der Spiegel, 1975

Allen, Fred (1894–1956)
US vaudeville performer and comedian
A conference is a gathering of important people who singly can do nothing, but together can decide that nothing can be done.

Attr.

Anonymous
A committee is a cul-de-sac down which ideas are lured and then quietly strangled.

New Scientist, 1973

A camel is a horse designed by a committee.

Berle, Milton (1908–)
US comedian
Committee – a group of men who keep minutes and waste hours.

Attr.

Dickens, Charles (1812–1870)
English writer
Whatever was required to be done, the Circumlocution Office was beforehand with all the

public departments in the art of perceiving –
HOW NOT TO DO IT.

Little Dorrit (1857)

Fonda, Jane (1937–)
US actress and activist
> You can run the office without a boss, but you
> can't run an office without the secretaries.

The Observer, 1981

Foot, Michael (1913–)
British Labour politician
> A Royal Commission is a broody hen sitting on a
> china egg.

Speech, House of Commons, 1964

Gowers, Sir Ernest (1880–1966)
English civil servant, champion of plain language
> It is not easy nowadays to remember anything
> so contrary to all appearances as that officials
> are the servants of the public; and the official
> must try not to foster the illusion that it is the
> other way round.

Plain Words

Harkness, Richard
> What is a committee? A group of the unwilling,
> picked from the unfit, to do the unnecessary.

Attr.

Huxley, Aldous (1894–1963)
English writer, poet and critic
> Official dignity tends to increase in inverse ratio
> to the importance of the country in which the
> office is held.

Beyond the Mexique Bay (1934)

Kelly, Bert (1912–1997)
Australian politician
> Always remember that if a civil servant had the
> ability to … correctly foresee the demand
> situation for any product he would not be
> working for the government for long. He would
> shortly be sitting in the south of France with his
> feet in a bucket of champagne!

Economics Made Easy

McCarthy, Eugene (1916–)
US politician
> The only thing that saves us from bureaucracy is
> its inefficiency. An efficient bureaucracy is the
> greatest threat to freedom.

Time, 1979

McCarthy, Mary (1912–1989)
US writer and critic
> Bureaucracy, the rule of no one, has become the
> modern form of despotism.

The New Yorker, 1958

McLuhan, Marshall (1911–1980)
Canadian communications theorist
> An administrator in a bureaucratic world is a

man who can feel big by merging his non-entity
with an abstraction. A real person in touch with
real things inspires terror in him.

Letter to Ezra Pound, 1951

Sampson, Anthony (1926–)
British writer
Of the Civil Service
> Members rise from CMG (known sometimes in
> Whitehall as 'Call Me God') to the KCMG ('Kindly
> Call Me God') to … the GCMG ('God Calls Me
> God').

The Anatomy of Britain (1962)

Samuel, Lord (1870–1963)
English Liberal statesman, philosopher and administrator
Referring to the Civil Service
> A difficulty for every solution.

Attr.

Santayana, George (1863–1952)
Spanish-born US philosopher and writer
> The working of great institutions is mainly the
> result of a vast mass of routine, petty malice,
> self interest, carelessness, and sheer mistake.
> Only a residual fraction is thought.

The Crime of Galileo

Schumpeter, Joseph A. (1883–1950)
US economist
> Bureaucracy is not an obstacle to democracy but
> an inevitable complement to it.

Capitalism, Socialism and Democracy (1942)

Thomas, Gwyn (1913–1981)
Welsh writer, dramatist and teacher
> My life's been a meeting, Dad, one long
> meeting. Even on the few committees I don't
> yet belong to, the agenda winks at me when I
> pass.

The Keep (1961)

Tree, Sir Herbert Beerbohm (1853–1917)
English actor and theatre manager
> A committee should consist of three men, two
> of whom are absent.

In Pearson, *Beerbohm Tree*

Vidal, Gore (1925–)
US writer, critic and poet
> There is something about a bureaucrat that does
> not like a poem.

Sex, Death and Money (1968)

business

Anonymous
> A Company for carrying on an undertaking of
> Great Advantage, but no one to know what it is.

The South Sea Company Prospectus

Our company absorbs the cost.

> Useful Arab phrase in modern Arab–English phrase book for American oil engineers

In no event shall the author be liable for any damage whatsoever including loss of business profits.

> On a CD of the Bible

Austen, Jane (1775–1817)
English writer
> Business, you know, may bring money, but friendship hardly ever does.
>
> *Emma* (1816)

Bagehot, Walter (1826–1877)
English economist and political philosopher
> Business is really more agreeable than pleasure; it interests the whole mind, the aggregate nature of man more continuously, and more deeply. But it does not look as if it did.
>
> *The English Constitution* (1867)

Balzac, Honoré de (1799–1850)
French writer
> Generous people make bad shopkeepers.
>
> *Illusions perdues* (1843)

Barnum, Phineas T. (1810–1891)
US showman and writer
> Every crowd has a silver lining.
>
> Attr.

> Every man's occupation should be beneficial to his fellow-man as well as profitable to himself. All else is vanity and folly.
>
> *The Humbugs of the World* (1866)

Barton, Bruce (1886–1967)
US advertising agent and writer
> Jesus picked up twelve men from the bottom ranks of business and forged them into an organization that conquered the world.
>
> *The Man Nobody Knows: A Discovery of the Real Jesus* (1924)

Betjeman, Sir John (1906–1984)
English poet laureate
> You ask me what it is I do. Well actually, you know,
> I'm partly a liaison man and partly P.R.O.
> Essentially I integrate the current export drive
> And basically I'm viable from ten o'clock till five.
>
> 'Executive' (1974)

Charles, Prince of Wales (1948–)
Son and heir of Elizabeth II and Prince Philip
> British management doesn't seem to understand the importance of the human factor.
>
> Speech, 1979

Cohen, Sir Jack (1898–1979)
Supermarket magnate
> Pile it high, sell it cheap.
>
> Business motto

Dennis, C.J. (1876–1938)
Australian writer and poet
> It takes one hen to lay an egg,
> But seven men to sell it.
>
> 'The Regimental Hen'

Dickens, Charles (1812–1870)
English writer
> Here's the rule for bargains. 'Do other men, for they would do you.' That's the true business precept. All others are counterfeit.
>
> *Martin Chuzzlewit* (1844)

Ford, Henry (1863–1947)
US car manufacturer
> A business that makes nothing but money is a poor kind of business.
>
> Interview

Franklin, Benjamin (1706–1790)
US statesman, scientist, political critic and printer
> No nation was ever ruined by trade.
>
> *Essays*

Galbraith, J.K. (1908–)
Canadian-born US economist, diplomat and writer
> The salary of the chief executive of the large corporation is not a market award for achievement. It is frequently in the nature of a warm personal gesture by the individual to himself.
>
> *Annals of an Abiding Liberal* (1980)

Gandhi (1869–1948)
Indian political leader
> It is difficult but not impossible to conduct strictly honest business. What is true is that honesty is incompatible with the amassing of a large fortune.
>
> *Non-Violence in Peace and War* (1948)

Getty, John Paul (1892–1976)
US oil billionaire and art collector
> The meek shall inherit the earth, but not the mineral rights.
>
> In Robert Lenzner, *The Great Getty* (1985)

> No one can possibly achieve any real and lasting success or 'get rich' in business by being a conformist.
>
> *International Herald Tribune*, 1961

Goldwyn, Samuel (1882–1974)
Polish-born US film producer
> Chaplin is no business man – all he knows is that he can't take anything less.
>
> Attr.

Khrushchev, Nikita (1894–1971)
Russian statesman and Premier of the USSR
Remark to British businessmen
> When you are skinning your customers, you should leave some skin on to heal so that you can skin them again.
>
> *The Observer*, 1961

Lloyd George, David (1863–1945)
British Liberal statesman
> Love your neighbour is not merely sound Christianity; it is good business.
>
> *The Observer*, 1921

Macmillan, Harold (1894–1986)
British Conservative Prime Minister
> Macmillan and Company Limited propose to carry on their business at St Martin's Street, London W.C.2 until they are either taxed, insured, ARP'd or bombed out of existence.
>
> Announcement, 17 September 1939

Mencken, H.L. (1880–1956)
US writer, critic, philologist and satirist
Referring to the businessman
> He is the only man who is ever apologizing for his occupation.
>
> *Prejudices* (1927)

Napoleon I (1769–1821)
French emperor
> *L'Angleterre est une nation de boutiquiers.*
> England is a nation of shopkeepers.
>
> In O'Meara, *Napoleon in Exile* (1822)

Onassis, Aristotle (1906–1975)
Turkish-born Greek shipping magnate
> The secret of business is to know something that nobody else knows.
>
> *The Economist*, 1991

Puzo, Mario (1920–)
US writer
> He's a businessman. I'll make him an offer he can't refuse.
>
> *The Godfather* (1969)

Revson, Charles (1906–1975)
US cosmetic company executive
> In the factory we make cosmetics. In the store we sell hope.
>
> In Tobias, *Fire and Ice* (1976)

Rockefeller, John D. (1839–1937)
US oil magnate and philanthropist
> A friendship founded on business is better than a business founded on friendship.
>
> Attr.

Roddick, Anita (1942–)
English businesswoman, founder of The Body Shop
> I am still looking for the modern equivalent of those Quakers who ran successful businesses, made money because they offered honest products and treated their people decently ... This business creed, sadly, seems long forgotten.
>
> *Body and Soul* (1991)

Roosevelt, Theodore (1858–1919)
US Republican President
> We demand that big business give the people a square deal; in return we must insist that when any one engaged in big business honestly endeavors to do right he shall himself be given a square deal.
>
> *Theodore Roosevelt: an Autobiography* (1913)

Selfridge, Harry Gordon (1858–1947)
US-born British merchant
> The customer is always right.
>
> Slogan adopted at his shops

Sheen, J. Fulton (1895–1979)
US Catholic bishop, broadcaster and writer
Referring to his contract for a television appearance
> The big print giveth and the fine print taketh away.
>
> Attr.

Smiles, Samuel (1812–1904)
English writer
> Cecil's despatch of business was extraordinary, his maxim being, 'The shortest way to do many things is to do only one thing at once.'
>
> *Self-Help* (1859)

Smith, Adam (1723–1790)
Scottish economist, philosopher and essayist
> People of the same trade seldom meet together, even for merriment and diversion, but the conversation ends in a conspiracy against the public, or in some contrivance to raise prices.
>
> *Wealth of Nations* (1776)

Stevenson, Robert Louis (1850–1894)
Scottish writer, poet and essayist
> Everyone lives by selling something.
>
> *Across the Plains* (1892), 'Beggars'

Thurlow, Edward, First Baron (1731–1806)
English lawyer, politician and Lord Chancellor
> Did you ever expect a corporation to have a conscience, when it has no soul to be damned, and no body to be kicked?
>
> Attr.

Trump, Donald (1946–)
US billionaire property developer
> Deals are my art form. Other people paint beautifully on canvas or write wonderful poetry. I like making deals, preferably big deals. That's how I get my kicks.
>
> *Trump: The Art of the Deal* (1987)

Warhol, Andy (c.1926–1987)
US painter, graphic designer and filmmaker

Being good in business is the most fascinating kind of art.

The Observer, 1987

Wells, H.G. (1866–1946)
English writer
Of Max Beaverbrook
If Max gets to Heaven he won't last long. He will be chucked out for trying to pull off a merger between Heaven and Hell … after having secured a controlling interest in key subsidiary compames in both places, of course.

In A.J.P. Taylor, *Beaverbrook* (1972)

Wilder, Thornton (1897–1975)
US author and playwright
A living is made, Mr Kemper, by selling something that everybody needs at least once a year. Yes, sir! And a million is made by producing something that everybody needs every day. You artists produce something that nobody needs at any time.

The Merchant of Yonkers (1939)

Wilson, Charles E. (1890–1961)
US industrialist, car manufacturer and politician
What is good for the country is good for General Motors, and vice versa.

Remark to Congressional Committee, 1953

Wilson, Woodrow (1856–1924)
US Democrat President
Business underlies everything in our national life, including our spiritual life. Witness the fact that in the Lord's Prayer the first petition is for daily bread. No one can worship God or love his neighbour on an empty stomach.

Speech, 1912

Young, Andrew (1932–)
US politician and civil rights campaigner
Nothing is illegal if one hundred businessmen decide to do it.

Attr.

▶▶ CAPITALISM; ECONOMICS; MONEY AND WEALTH

C

calm

Herbert, George (1593–1633)
English poet and priest
> Calmnesse is great advantage. He that lets
> Another chafe, may warm him at his fire.
>> *The Temple* (1633),
>> 'The Church-Porch'

Holmes, Oliver Wendell (1809–1894)
US physician, poet, writer and scientist
> Wisdom has taught us to be calm and meek,
> To take one blow, and turn the other cheek;
> It is not written what a man shall do
> If the rude caitiff smite the other too!
>> 'Non-Resistance' (1861)

Spenser, Edmund (c.1522–1599)
English poet
> Calm was the day, and through the trembling air
> Sweet-breathing Zephyrus did softly play.
>> *Prothalamion* (1596)

Waller, Edmund (1606–1687)
English poet and politician
> The seas are quiet, when the winds give o'er:
> So calm are we, when passions are no
> more.
>> 'Of the Last Verses in the
>> Book' (1596)

Yeats, W.B. (1865–1939)
Irish poet, dramatist, editor, writer and senator
> And I shall have some peace there, for peace
> comes dropping slow,
> Dropping from the veils of the morning to where
> the cricket sings;
> There midnight's all a glimmer, and noon a
> purple glow,
> And evening full of the linnet's wings.
>> In the *National Observer*, 1890, 'The Lake Isle
>> of Innisfree'

camping

Sackville-West, Vita (1892–1962)
English poet and novelist
> Those who have never dwelt in tents have no
> idea either of the charm or of the discomfort of
> a nomadic existence. The charm is purely
> romantic, and consequently very soon proves to
> be fallacious.
>> *Twelve Days* (1928)

canada

Capone, Al (1899–1947)
Chicago gangster
> I don't even know what street Canada is on.
>> Attr.

Mahy, Margaret (1936–)
> Canadians are Americans with no Disneyland.
>> *The Changeover* (1984)

capitalism

Anonymous
> Capitalism is the exploitation of man by man.
> Communism is the complete opposite.
>> Described by Laurence J. Peter as a 'Polish proverb'

Connolly, James (1868–1916)
Irish labour leader
> Governments in a capitalist society are but
> committees of the rich to manage the affairs of
> the capitalist class.
>> *Irish Worker*, 1914

Galbraith, J.K. (1908–)
Canadian-born US economist, diplomat and writer
> You must now speak always of the market
> system. The word 'capitalism', once the common
> reference, has acquired a deleterious Marxist
> sound.
>> *The Observer*, 1998

Gonne, Maud (1865–1953)
Irish patriot and philanthropist
> To me judges seem the well paid watch-dogs of
> Capitalism, making things safe and easy for the
> devil Mammon.
>> Letter to W.B. Yeats

Hampton, Christopher (1946–)
English dramatist
> If I had to give a definition of capitalism I would
> say: the process whereby American girls turn
> into American women.
>> *Savages* (1973)

Heath, Sir Edward (1916–)
English Conservative Prime Minister
On the Lonrho affair (involving tax avoidance)
> The unpleasant and unacceptable face of
> capitalism.
>> Speech, House of Commons, 1973

Illich, Ivan (1926–)
Austrian-born US educator, sociologist, writer and priest

In a consumer society there are inevitably two kinds of slaves: the prisoners of addiction and the prisoners of envy.

Tools for Conviviality (1973)

Keller, Helen (1880–1968)
US writer and educator of the blind and deaf
Militarism ... is one of the chief bulwarks of capitalism, and the day that militarism is undermined, capitalism will fail.

The Story of My Life (1902)

Keynes, John Maynard (1883–1946)
English economist
I think that Capitalism, wisely managed, can probably be made more efficient for attaining economic ends than any alternative system yet in sight, but that in itself it is in many ways extremely objectionable.

'The End of Laissez-Faire' (1926)

Lenin, V.I. (1870–1924)
Russian revolutionary, Marxist theoretician and first leader of the USSR
Under capitalism we have a state in the proper sense of the word, that is, a special machine for the suppression of one class by another.

The State and Revolution (1917)

Malcolm X (1925–1965)
US black leader
You show me a capitalist, I'll show you a bloodsucker.

Malcolm X Speaks, 1965

Marcuse, Herbert (1898–1979)
German-born US philosopher
Not every problem someone has with his girlfriend is necessarily due to the capitalist mode of production.

The Listener

Marx, Karl (1818–1883)
German political philosopher and economist; founder of Communism
Capitalist production creates, with the inexorability of a law of nature, its own negation.

Das Kapital (1867)

Ortega spottorno, José (1870–1924)
Estoy ... convencido de que la forma actual del capitalismo dejará paso a otra más humana y menos especulativa.
I'm convinced that the present form of capitalism will make way for another one which will be more human and less speculative.

El País, 1994

Pankhurst, Sylvia (1882–1960)
English suffragette, pacifist and internationalist
I have gone to war too ... I am going to fight capitalism even if it kills me. It is wrong that

people like you should be comfortable and well fed while all around you people are starving.

In David Mitchell, *The Fighting Pankhursts*

Richler, Mordecai (1931–)
Canadian novelist
Remember this, Griffin. The revolution eats its own. Capitalism re-creates itself.

Cocksure (1968)

Saki (1870–1916)
Burmese-born British writer
When she inveighed eloquently against the evils of capitalism at drawing-room meetings and Fabian conferences she was conscious of a comfortable feeling that the system, with all its inequalities and iniquities, would probably last her time. It is one of the consolations of middle-aged reformers that the good they inculcate must live after them if it is to live at all.

Beasts and Super-Beasts (1914)

Schumpeter, Joseph A. (1883–1950)
US economist
Capitalism inevitably and by virtue of the very logic of its civilization creates, educates and subsidizes a vested interest in social unrest.

Capitalism, Socialism and Democracy (1942)

Economic progress, in capitalist society, means turmoil.

Capitalism, Socialism and Democracy (1942)

Stretton, Hugh (1924–)
Australian political scientist and historian
Is it really good for policy-makers to act as if everything has its price, and as if policies should be judged chiefly by their effects in delivering material benefits to selfish citizens? ... It does not ask those individuals whether they also have other values which are not revealed by their shopping.

Capitalism, Socialism and the Environment (1976)

Taylor, A.J.P. (1906–1990)
English historian, writer, broadcaster and lecturer
Lenin was the first to discover that capitalism 'inevitably' caused war; and he discovered this only when the First World War was already being fought. Of course he was right. Since every great state was capitalist in 1914, capitalism obviously 'caused' the First World War; but just as obviously it had 'caused' the previous generation of Peace.

The Origins of the Second World War (1961)

Waugh, Evelyn (1903–1966)
English writer and diarist
Pappenhacker says that every time you are polite to a proletarian you are helping to bolster up the capitalist system.

Scoop (1938)

Welsh, Irvine (1957–)
Scottish novelist
> Consumer capitalism has eaten up the Church, the state, trade unions, extended families, everywhere that people learn morality.
>> *The Observer*, 1998

▶▶ BUSINESS

careers

Adams, Scott (1957–)
US cartoonist
> It is better for your career to do nothing, than to do something and attract criticism.
>> *Building a Better Life by Stealing Office Supplies: Dogbert's Big Book of Business* (1991)

Bacon, Francis (1561–1626)
English philosopher, essayist, politician and courtier
> I hold every man a debtor to his profession.
>> *The Elements of Common Law* (1596)

Balfour, A.J. (1848–1930)
British Conservative Prime Minister
On being asked whether he was going to marry Margot Tennant
> I rather think of having a career of my own.
>> In Asquith, *Autobiography* (1920)

Bentley, Nicolas (1907–1978)
English publisher and artist
> His was the sort of career that made the Recording Angel think seriously about taking up shorthand.
>> Attr.

Colby, Frank Moore (1865–1925)
US editor, historian and economist
> I have found some of the best reasons I ever had for remaining at the bottom simply by looking at the men at the top.
>> *Essays*

Disraeli, Benjamin (1804–1881)
English statesman and writer
> To do nothing and get something, formed a boy's ideal of a manly career.
>> *Sybil* (1845)

Dos Passos, John (1896–1970)
US writer
> People don't choose their careers; they are engulfed by them.
>> *New York Times*, 1959

Eames, Emma (1865–1952)
Chinese-born US opera singer
On giving up her operatic career at 47
> I would rather be a brilliant memory than a curiosity.
>> Attr.

Franklin, Miles (1879–1954)
Australian writer
> This was life – my life – my career, my brilliant career! I was fifteen – fifteen! A few fleeting hours and I would be old as those around me. I looked at them as they stood there, weary, and turning down the other side of the hill of life. When young, no doubt they had hoped for, and dreamed of, better things – had even known them, but here they were. This had been their life; this was their career. It was, and in all probability would be, mine too. My life – my career – my brilliant career!
>> *My Brilliant Career* (1901)

▶▶ AMBITION; WORK

cars

Allen, Woody (1935–)
US film director, writer, actor and comedian
> My life is passing in front of my eyes. The worst part is I'm driving a used car.
>> *Manhattan Murder Mystery* (film, 1993)

Barthes, Roland (1915–1980)
French writer, critic and teacher
> I think that cars today are almost the exact equivalent of the great Gothic cathedrals ... the supreme creation of an era, conceived with passion by unknown artists.
>> Attr.

McLuhan, Marshall (1911–1980)
Canadian communications theorist
> The car has become the carapace, the protective and aggressive shell, of urban and suburban man.
>> *Understanding Media* (1964)

Morton, J.B. (1893–1979)
English humorist
> *Rush hour*: that hour when traffic is almost at a standstill.
>> *Morton's Folly*

O'Rourke, P.J. (1947–)
US writer
> There are a number of mechanical devices which increase sexual arousal, particularly in women. Chief among these is the Mercedes-Benz 380SL convertible.
>> Attr.

▶▶ TRAVEL

catastrophe

Greer, Germaine (1939–)
Australian feminist, critic, English scholar and writer
> Perhaps catastrophe is the natural human environment, and even though we spend a good deal of energy trying to get away from it, we are programmed for survival amid catastrophe.
>> *Sex and Destiny* (1984)

cats

Arnold, Matthew (1822–1888)
English poet, critic, essayist and educationist
> Cruel, but composed and bland,
> Dumb, inscrutable and grand,
> So Tiberius might have sat,
> Had Tiberius been a cat.
>> 'Poor Matthias'

Chaucer, Geoffrey (c.1340–1400)
English poet, public servant and courtier
> Lat take a cat, and fostre hym wel with milk
> And tendre flessh, and make his couche of silk,
> And lat hym seen a mous go by the wal,
> Anon he weyveth milk and flessh and al,
> And every deyntee that is in that hous,
> Swich appetit hath he to ete a mous.
>> *The Canterbury Tales* (1387)

De La Mare, Walter (1873–1956)
> In Hans' old Mill his three black cats
> Watch the bins for the thieving rats.
> Whisker and claw, they crouch in the night,
> Their five eyes smouldering green and bright: …
>
> Then up he climbs to his creaking mill
> Out come his cats all grey with meal –
> Jekkel, and Jessup, and one-eyed Jill.
>> 'Five Eyes' (1913)

Eliot, T.S. (1888–1965)
US-born British poet, verse dramatist and critic
> Macavity, Macavity, there's no one like Macavity,
> There never was a Cat of such deceitfulness and suavity.
> He always has an alibi, and one or two to spare:
> At whatever time the deed took place –
> MACAVITY WASN'T THERE!
>> 'Macavity: the Mystery Cat' (1939)
>
> The Naming of Cats is a difficult matter,
> It isn't just one of your holiday games;
> You may think at first I'm as mad as a hatter
> When I tell you a cat must have THREE DIFFERENT NAMES …

> When you notice a cat in profound meditation,
> The reason, I tell you, is always the same:
> His mind is engaged in a rapt contemplation
> Of the thought, of the thought, of the thought of his name:
> His ineffable effable
> Effanineffable
> Deep and inscrutable singular Name.
>> 'The Naming of Cats' (1939)

Hare, Maurice Evan (1886–1967)
English limerick writer
> Alfred de Musset
> Used to call his cat Pusset.
> His accent was affected.
> That was only to be expected.
>> 'Byway in Biography'

Household, Geoffrey (1900–1988)
English writer
> I have noticed that what cats most appreciate in a human being is not the ability to produce food which they take for granted – but his or her entertainment value.
>> *Rogue Male* (1939)

Johnson, Samuel (1709–1784)
English lexicographer, poet, critic, conversationalist and essayist
> When I observed he was a fine cat, saying, 'why yes, Sir, but I have had cats whom I liked better than this'; and then as if perceiving Hodge to be out of countenance, adding, 'but he is a very fine cat, a very fine cat indeed.'
>> In Boswell, *The Life of Samuel Johnson* (1791)

Marquis, Don (1878–1937)
US columnist, satirist and poet
> the great open spaces
> where cats are cats.
>> *archys life of mehitabel* (1927)

Montaigne, Michel de (1533–1592)
French essayist and moralist
> *Quand je me joue à ma chatte, qui sait si elle passe son temps de moi plus que je ne fais d'elle?*
> When I play with my cat, who knows whether she isn't amusing herself with me more than I am with her?
>> *Essais* (1580)

Porter, Peter Neville Frederick (1929–)
> Moving one paw out and yawning,
> he closes his eyes. Everywhere
> people are in despair. And he is dancing.
>> *Collected Poems* (1983)

Proverbs
> A cat may look at a king.
>
> All cats are grey in the dark.
>
> A cat has nine lives.

Rowbotham, David Harold (1924–)
Australian journalist, critic and poet
> Let some of the tranquillity of the cat
> Curl into me.
>> 'The Creature in the Chair'

Sackville-West, Vita (1892–1962)
English poet and novelist
> The greater cats with golden eyes
> Stare out between the bars.
> Deserts are there, and different skies,
> And night with different stars.
>> *The King's Daughter* (1929)

Smart, Christopher (1722–1771)
English poet and translator
> For I will consider my Cat Jeoffry.
> For he is the servant of the Living God, duly and
> daily serving Him.
> For at the first glance of the glory of God in the
> East he worships in his way.
> For this is done by wreathing his body seven
> times round with elegant quickness.
>> *Jubilate Agno*

> For the English Cats are the best in Europe.
>> *Jubilate Agno*

> For he counteracts the powers of darkness by
> his electrical skin and glaring eyes.
> For he counteracts the Devil, who is death, by
> brisking about the life.
>> *Jubilate Agno*

Smith, Stevie (1902–1971)
English poet and writer
> Oh I am a cat that likes to
> Gallop about doing good.
>> 'The Galloping Cat' (1972)

Tessimond, A.S.J. (1902–1962)
English poet
> Cats, no less liquid than their shadows,
> Offer no angles to the wind.
> They slip, diminished, neat, through loopholes
> Less than themselves.
>> *Cats* (1934)

▶▶ ANIMALS

caution

Adler, Alfred (1870–1937)
Austrian psychiatrist and psychologist
> The chief danger in life is that you may take too
> many precautions.
>> Attr.

Anonymous
> *Quidquid agas, prudenter agas, et respice finem.*
> Whatever you do, do it warily, and take account

> of the end.
>> *Gesta Romanorum*

Armstrong, Dr John (1709–1779)
Scottish physician, poet and writer
> Distrust yourself, and sleep before you fight.
> 'Tis not too late tomorrow to be brave.
>> *The Art of Preserving Health* (1744)

Bacon, Francis (1561–1626)
English philosopher, essayist, politician and courtier
> A man ought warily to begin charges which once
> begun will continue.
>> 'Of Expense' (1625)

Belloc, Hilaire (1870–1953)
English writer of verse, essayist and critic; Liberal MP
> And always keep a-hold of Nurse
> For fear of finding something worse.
>> *Cautionary Tales* (1907)

Cowper, William (1731–1800)
English poet, hymn and letter writer
> To combat may be glorious, and success
> Perhaps may crown us; but to fly is safe.
>> *The Task* (1785)

Dryden, John (1631–1700)
English poet, satirist, dramatist and critic
> But now the world's o'er stocked with prudent
> men.
>> *The Medal* (1682)

La Fontaine, Jean de (1621–1695)
French poet and fabulist
> *Il m'a dit qu'il ne faut jamais*
> *Vendre la peau de l'ours qu'on ne l'ait mis par terre.*
> He told me never to sell the bear's skin before
> killing the beast.
>> Fables, 'L'ours et les deux compagnons'

Lincoln, Abraham (1809–1865)
US statesman and President
> When you have got an elephant by the hind leg,
> and he is trying to run away, it's best to let him
> run.
>> Remark, 1865

Proverbs
> Better be safe than sorry.

> Don't put all your eggs in one basket.

> He that fights and runs away, may live to fight
> another day.

> He who sups with the devil should have a long
> spoon.

> If you trust before you try, you may repent
> before you die.

> Keep your mouth shut and your eyes open.

> Look before you leap.

Shaw, George Bernard (1856–1950)
Irish socialist, writer, dramatist and critic
> Self-denial is not a virtue: it is only the effect of prudence on rascality.
>> *Man and Superman* (1903)

Twain, Mark (1835–1910)
US humorist, writer, journalist and lecturer
> It is by the goodness of God that in our country we have those three unspeakably precious things: freedom of speech, freedom of conscience, and the prudence never to practise either of them.
>> *Following the Equator* (1897)

celebrity

Alcott, Louisa May (1832–1888)
US writer
> It takes very little fire to make a great deal of smoke nowadays, and notoriety is not real glory.
>> *Jo's Boys* (1886)

Allen, Fred (1894–1956)
US vaudeville performer and comedian
> A celebrity is a person who works hard all his life to become well known, and then wears dark glasses to avoid being recognized.
>> In Laurence Peter, *Quotations for Our Time* (1977)

Boorstin, Daniel (1914–)
US librarian, historian, lawyer and writer
> A sign of a celebrity is that his name is often worth more than his services.
>> *The Image* (1962)

Jackson, Michael (1958–)
US singer
> I was a veteran, before I was a teenager.
>> Attr.

Kissinger, Henry (1923–)
German-born US Secretary of State
> The nice thing about being a celebrity is that, if you bore people, they think it's their fault.
>> Attr.

Mencken, H.L. (1880–1956)
US writer, critic, philologist and satirist
> A celebrity is one who is known to many persons he is glad he doesn't know.
>> Attr.

Temple, Shirley (1928–)
US child actress and diplomat
> I stopped believing in Santa Claus when I was six. Mother took me to see him in a department store and he asked for my autograph.
>> Attr.

Updike, John (1932–)
US writer, poet and critic
> Celebrity is a mask that eats into the face.
>> *Memoirs* (1989)

▶▶ FAME; REPUTATION

censorship

Bentham, Jeremy (1748–1832)
English writer and philosopher
> As to the evil which results from censorship, it is impossible to measure it, because it is impossible to tell where it ends.
>> *On Liberty of the Press and Public Discussion*

Borovoy, A. Alan
Canadian writer and civil liberties advocate
> It is usually better to permit a piece of trash than to suppress a work of art.
>> *When Freedoms Collide* (1988)

Cronenberg, David (1943–)
Canadian film director
> Censors tend to do what only psychotics do: they confuse reality with illusion.
>> *Cronenberg on Cronenberg* (1992)

Emerson, Ralph Waldo (1803–1882)
US poet, essayist, transcendentalist and teacher
> Every burned book enlightens the world.
>> Attr.

Gordimer, Nadine (1923–)
South African writer
> Censorship is never over for those who have experienced it. It is a brand on the imagination that affects the individual who has suffered it, forever.
>> Lecture, June 1990

Griffith-Jones, Mervyn (1909–1979)
English lawyer
At the trial of D.H. Lawrence's novel *Lady Chatterley's Lover*
> Is it a book you would even wish your wife or your servants to read?
>> *The Times*, 1960

Heine, Heinrich (1797–1856)
German lyric poet, essayist and journalist
> *Dort, wo man Bücher*
> *Verbrennt, verbrennt man auch am Ende Menschen.*
> It is there, where they
> Burn books, that eventually they burn people too.
>> *Almansor: A Tragedy* (1821)

Mill, John Stuart (1806–1873)
English philosopher, economist and reformer
> We can never be sure that the opinion we are endeavouring to stifle is a false opinion; and if

we were sure, stifling it would be an evil still.

On Liberty (1859)

Milton, John (1608–1674)
English poet, libertarian and pamphleteer

As good almost kill a Man as kill a good Book; who kills a Man kills a reasonable creature, God's Image; but hee who destroyes a good Booke, kills reason it selfe, kills the Image of God, as it were in the eye. Many a man lives a burden to the Earth; but a good Booke is the pretious life-blood of a master spirit, imbalm'd and treasur'd up on purpose to a life beyond life.

Areopagitica (1644)

Pinter, Harold (1930–)
English dramatist, poet and screenwriter
On the execution of Nigerian writer Ken Saro-Wiwa

Murder is the most brutal form of censorship.

The Observer, 1995

Censorship in the UK reveals a deeply conservative country still in thrall to its strict Protestant values.

Index on Censorship, 1996

Rushdie, Salman (1947–)
Indian-born English author

Means of artistic expression that require large quantities of finance and sophisticated technology – films, plays, records – become, by virtue of that dependence, easy to censor and to control. But what one writer can make in the solitude of one room is something no power can easily destroy.

Index on Censorship, 1996

Siddique, Dr Kalim

We cannot live in this country together with *The Satanic Verses* and Salman Rushdie. They will have to go.

The Independent, 1989

Stromme, Sigmund (1946–)
Norwegian publisher

Strict censorship cannot be maintained without terrorism.

Index on Censorship, 1996

▶▶ BOOKS; PORNOGRAPHY

certainty

Barnfield, Richard (1574–1627)
English poet

Nothing more certain than incertainties;
Fortune is full of fresh variety:
Constant in nothing but inconstancy.

'The Shepherd's Content'
(1594)

Bissell, Claude T. (1916–)
Canadian writer

I prefer complexity to certainty, cheerful mysteries to sullen facts.

Address, University of Toronto, 1969

Camus, Albert (1913–1960)
Algerian-born French writer

*Là était la certitude, dans le travail de tous les jours…
L'essentiel était de bien faire son métier.*
That was where certainty lay, in everyday work … The essential thing was to do one's job well.

The Plague (1947)

Franklin, Benjamin (1706–1790)
US statesman, scientist, political critic and printer

But in this world nothing can be said to be certain, except death and taxes.

Letter to Jean Baptiste Le Roy, 1789

Guedalla, Philip (1889–1944)
English historian, writer and lawyer

People who jump to conclusions rarely alight on them.

The Observer, 1924

Johnson, Samuel (1709–1784)
English lexicographer, poet, critic, conversationalist and essayist

He is no wise man who will quit a certainty for an uncertainty.

The Idler (1758–1760)

Pliny the Elder (AD 23–79)
Roman scholar

The only certainty is that nothing is certain.

Attr.

Tertullian (c.AD 160–c.225)
Carthaginian theologian

Certum est quia impossibile.
It is certain because it is impossible.

De Carne Christi

Yeats, W.B. (1865–1939)
Irish poet, dramatist, editor, writer and senator

The best lack all conviction, while the worst
Are full of passionate intensity.

'The Second Coming' (1920)

▶▶ DOUBT

challenge

Mallory, George Leigh (1886–1924)
English mountaineer
Asked why he wished to climb Mt Everest

Because it is there.

New York Times, 1923

chance

France, Anatole (1844–1924)
French writer and critic

> *Le hasard c'est peut-être le pseudonyme de Dieu, quand il ne veut pas signer.*
> Chance might be God's pseudonym when He does not want to sign his name.
>> *Le Jardin d'Epicure* (1894)

Ovid (43 BC–AD 18)
Roman poet

> Chance is always powerful. Let your hook be always cast. In the pool where you least expect it, will be fish.
>> Attr.

Proverb

> Throw out a sprat to catch a mackerel.

▶▶ ACCIDENTS; LUCK; OPPORTUNITY

change

Anonymous

> Change imposed is change opposed.
>> Management slogan, Deloitte and Touche, 1999

> *Tempora mutantur, et nos mutamur in illis.*
> Times change, and we change with them.
>> In Harrison, *Description of Britain* (1577)

Arnold, Matthew (1822–1888)
English poet, critic, essayist and educationist

> Wandering between two worlds, one dead,
> The other powerless to be born,
> With nowhere yet to rest my head,
> Like these, on earth I wait forlorn …
>
> Years hence, perhaps, may dawn an age,
> More fortunate, alas! than we,
> Which without hardness will be sage,
> And gay without frivolity.
>> 'The Grande Chartreuse' (1855)

Aurelius, Marcus (121–180)
Roman emperor and Stoic philosopher

> The universe is change; life is what thinking makes of it.
>> *Meditations*

Bacon, Francis (1561–1626)
English philosopher, essayist, politician and courtier

> That all things are changed, and that nothing really perishes, and that the sum of matter remains exactly the same, is sufficiently certain.
>> *Thoughts on the Nature of Things* (1604)

Beauvoir, Simone de (1908–1986)
French writer, feminist critic and philosopher

> *Si l'on vit assez longtemps, on voit que toute victoire se change un jour en défaite.*
> If you live long enough, you'll find that every victory turns into a defeat.
>> *All Men are Mortal* (1955)

Brittain, Vera (1893–1970)
English writer and pacifist

> It is probably true to say that the largest scope for change still lies in men's attitude to women, and in women's attitude to themselves.
>> *Lady into Woman* (1953)

> It is said I am against change. I am not against change. I am in favour of change in the right circumstances. And those circumstances are when it can no longer be resisted.
>> Attr. by Paul Johnson in *The Spectator*, May 1996

Chesterton, G.K. (1874–1936)
English writer, poet and critic

> All conservatism is based upon the idea that if you leave things alone you leave them as they are. But you do not. If you leave a thing alone you leave it to a torrent of change.
>> *Orthodoxy* (1908)

Confucius (c.550–c.478 BC)
Chinese philosopher and teacher of ethics

> They must often change who would be constant in happiness or wisdom.
>> *Analects*

Disraeli, Benjamin (1804–1881)
English statesman and writer

> Change is inevitable. In a progressive country change is constant.
>> Speech, Edinburgh, 1867

Falkland, Viscount (c.1610–1643)
English politician and writer

> When it is not necessary to change, it is necessary not to change.
>> Speech concerning Episcopacy, 1641

Heraclitus (c.540–c.480 BC)
Greek philosopher

> You cannot step twice into the same river.
>> In Plato, *Cratylus*

Hooker, Richard (c.1554–1600)
English theologian and churchman

> Change is not made without inconvenience, even from worse to better.
>> In Johnson, *Dictionary of the English Language* (1755)

Horace (65–8 BC)
Roman poet

> *Immortalia ne speres, monet annus et almum
> Quae rapit hora diem.*
> The changing year and the passing hour that takes away genial day warns you

not to build everlasting hopes.

Odes

Irving, Washington (1783–1859)
US writer and diplomat

There is a certain relief in change, even though it be from bad to worse; as I have found in travelling in a stage-coach, that it is often a comfort to shift one's position and be bruised in a new place.

Tales of a Traveller (1824)

Karr, Alphonse (1808–1890)
French writer and editor

Plus ça change, plus c'est la même chose.
The more things change the more they remain the same.

Les Guêpes (1849)

Keats, John (1795–1821)
English poet

There is nothing stable in the world; uproar's your only music.

Letter to George and Tom Keats, 13 January 1818

Lloyd George, David (1863–1945)
British Liberal statesman
On being asked how he maintained his cheerfulness when beset by numerous political obstacles

Well, I find that a change of nuisances is as good as a vacation.

Attr.

Lucretius (c.95–55 BC)
Roman philosopher

Augescunt aliae gentes, aliae minuuntur,
Inque brevi spatio mutantur saecla animantum
Et quasi cursores vitai lampada tradunt.
Some groups increase, others diminish, and in a short space the generations of living creatures are changed and like runners pass on the torch of life.

De Rerum Natura

Malcolm X (1925–1965)
US black leader

Usually when people are sad, they don't do anything. They just cry over their condition. But when they get angry, they bring about a change.

Malcolm X Speaks, 1965

Proverb

To change and to change for the better are two different things.

German proverb

Rochester, Earl of (1647–1680)
English poet, satirist, courtier and libertine

Since 'tis Nature's law to change,
Constancy alone is strange.

'A Dialogue between Strephon and Daphne' (1691)

Russell, Bertrand (1872–1970)
English philosopher, mathematician, essayist and social reformer

'Change' is scientific, 'progress' is ethical; change is indubitable, whereas progress is a matter of controversy.

Unpopular Essays (1950)

Southwell, Robert (1561–1595)
English poet and Jesuit martyr

Times go by turns, and chances change by course,
From foul to fair, from better hap to worse.

'Times go by Turns' (1595)

Spenser, Edmund (c.1522–1599)
English poet

What man that sees the ever-whirling wheele
Of Change, the which all mortall things doth sway,
But that therby doth find, and plainly feele,
How Mutability in them doth play
Her cruell sports, to many men's decay?

The Faerie Queene (1596)

Swift, Jonathan (1667–1745)
Irish satirist, poet, essayist and cleric

There is nothing in this world constant, but inconstancy.

A Critical Essay upon the Faculties of the Mind (1709)

Tennyson, Alfred, Lord (1809–1892)
English lyric poet

Forward, forward let us range,
Let the great world spin for ever down the ringing grooves of change.

'Locksley Hall' (1838)

The old order changeth, yielding place to new,
And God fulfils himself in many ways,
Lest one good custom should corrupt the world.

The Idylls of the King

Thoreau, Henry David (1817–1862)
US essayist, social critic and writer

Things do not change; we change.

Walden (1854)

Toffler, Alvin (1928–)

Future shock ... the shattering stress and disorientation that we induce in individuals by subjecting them to too much change in too short a time.

Future Shock (1970)

Tusser, Thomas (c.1524–1580)
English writer, poet and musician

The stone that is rolling can gather no moss;
For master and servant oft changing is loss.

Five Hundred Points of Good Husbandry (1557)

▶▶ CONSERVATISM; TIME

character

Beerbohm, Sir Max (1872–1956)
English satirist, cartoonist, critic and essayist
> Men of genius are not quick judges of character. Deep thinking and high imagining blunt that trivial instinct by which you and I size people up.
>> *And Even Now* (1920)

Edgeworth, Maria (1767–1849)
English-born Irish writer
> We cannot judge either of the feelings or of the characters of men with perfect accuracy, from their actions or their appearance in public; it is from their careless conversations, their half-finished sentences, that we may hope with the greatest probability of success to discover their real character.
>> *Castle Rackrent* (1800)

Eliot, George (1819–1880)
English writer and poet
> 'Character', says Novalis, in one of his questionable aphorisms – 'character is destiny.'
>> *The Mill on the Floss* (1860)

Emerson, Ralph Waldo (1803–1882)
US poet, essayist, transcendentalist and teacher
> Character is nature in the highest form. It is of no use to ape it, or to contend with it.
>> *Essays, Second Series* (1844)

Frank, Anne (1929–1945)
Jewish diarist; died in Nazi concentration camp
> Parents can only give good advice or put them on the right paths, but the final forming of a person's character lies in their own hands.
>> *The Diary of Anne Frank* (1947)

Frisch, Max (1911–1991)
Swiss dramatist, writer and architect
> *Jede Uniform verdirbt den Charakter.*
> Every uniform corrupts one's character.
>> *Diary*, 1948

Goethe (1749–1832)
German poet, writer, dramatist and scientist
> Talent is formed in quiet retreat,
> Character in the headlong rush of life.
>> *Torquato Tasso* (1790)

James, Henry (1843–1916)
US-born British writer, critic and letter writer
> What is character but the determination of incident? What is incident but the illustration of character?
>> *Partial Portraits* (1888)

Karr, Alphonse (1808–1890)
French writer and editor
> Every man has three characters: that which he exhibits, that which he has, and that which he thinks he has.
>> Attr.

King, Martin Luther (1929–1968)
US civil rights leader and Baptist minister
> The ultimate measure of a man is not where he stands in moments of comfort and convenience, but where he stands at times of challenge and controversy.
>> *Strength to Love*, 1963

Lincoln, Abraham (1809–1865)
US statesman and President
> Character is like a tree and reputation like its shadow. The shadow is what we think of it; the tree is the real thing.
>> In Gross, *Lincoln's Own Stories*

Murray, Les A. (1938–)
Australian poet and writer
> In the defiance of fashion is the beginning of character.
>> *The Boy who Stole the Funeral* (1979)

Reagan, Ronald (1911–)
US actor, Republican statesman and President
> You can tell a lot about a fellow's character by the way he eats jelly beans.
>> *Daily Mail*, 1981

Sheridan, Richard Brinsley (1751–1816)
Irish dramatist, politician and orator
> I'm called away by particular business. But I leave my character behind me.
>> *The School for Scandal* (1777)

Simpson, O.J. (1947–)
US footballer and actor
Following his acquittal on murder charges
> The only thing that endures is character. Fame and wealth – all that is illusion. All that endures is character.
>> *The Guardian*, 1995

Wilson, Woodrow (1856–1924)
US Democrat President
> Character is a by-product; it is produced in the great manufacture of daily duty.
>> Speech, 1915

▶▶ REPUTATION

charity

Arnold, George (1834–1865)
US poet
> The living need charity more than the dead.
>> *The Jolly Old Pedagogue* (1866)

Bacon, Francis (1561–1626)

English philosopher, essayist, politician and courtier

In charity there is no excess.

'Of Goodness, and Goodness of Nature'
(1625)

Browne, Sir Thomas (1605–1682)

English physician, author and antiquary

Charity begins at home, is the voice of the world.

Religio Medici (1643)

Carnegie, Andrew (1835–1919)

Scottish-born US millionaire and philanthropist

Of every thousand dollars spent in so-called charity today, it is probable that nine hundred and fifty dollars is unwisely spent.

'Wealth' (1889)

Fuller, Thomas (1608–1661)

English churchman and antiquary

He that feeds upon charity has a cold dinner and no supper.

Attr.

Geldof, Bob (1954–)

Irish rock musician

Emotional appeal during the Live Aid concert to raise funds for famine victims in Ethiopia.

Give us your fucking money.

BBC TV broadcast, 3 July 1985

Peron, Eva (1919–1952)

Argentinian actress and politician

Keeping books on charity is capitalist nonsense! I just use the money for the poor. I can't stop to count it.

In Fleur Cowles, *Bloody Precedent: the Peron Story* (1952)

Pope, Alexander (1688–1744)

English poet, translator and editor

For Forms of Government let fools contest;
Whate'er is best administer'd is best:
For Modes of Faith, let graceless zealots fight;
His can't be wrong whose life is in the right:
In Faith and Hope the world will disagree,
But all Mankind's concern is Charity.

Essay on Man (1733)

In Faith and Hope the world will disagree,
But all Mankind's concern is Charity.

Essay on Man (1733)

Proverb

Charity begins at home.

Publilius, Syrus (1st century BC)

Roman writer

Inopi beneficium bis dat qui dat celeriter.

He does the poor man two favours who gives quickly.

Sententiae

Rousseau, Jean-Jacques (1712–1778)

Swiss-born French philosopher educationist and essayist

The feigned charity of the rich man is for him no more than another luxury; he feeds the poor as he feeds dogs and horses.

Letter to M. Moulton

Sheridan, Richard Brinsley (1751–1816)

Irish dramatist, politician and orator

Rowley: I believe there is no sentiment he has more faith in than that 'charity begins at home'.
Sir Oliver Surface: And his, I presume, is of that domestic sort which never stirs abroad at all.

The School for Scandal (1777)

Smart, Christopher (1722–1771)

English poet and translator

Charity is cold in the multitude of possessions, and the rich are covetous of their crumbs.

Jubilate Agno (c.1758–63)

Voltaire (1694–1778)

French philosopher, dramatist, poet, historian writer and critic

The man who leaves money to charity in his will is only giving away what no longer belongs to him.

Letter, 1769

West, Dame Rebecca (1892–1983)

English writer, critic and feminist

Of charity

It is an ugly trick. It is a virtue grown by the rich on the graves of the poor. Unless it is accompanied by sincere revolt against the present social system, it is cheap moral swagger.

The Clarion

▶▶ BENEFACTORS; GENEROSITY

charm

Barrie, Sir J.M. (1860–1937)

Scottish dramatist and writer

On charm

It's a sort of bloom on a woman. If you have it, you don't need to have anything else; and if you don't have it, it doesn't much matter what else you have.

What Every Woman Knows (1908)

Bierce, Ambrose (1842–c.1914)

US writer, verse writer and soldier

Please: To lay the foundation for a superstructure of imposition.

The Enlarged Devil's Dictionary (1961)

Camus, Albert (1913–1960)

Algerian-born French writer

Vous savez ce que c'est le charme: une manière de

*s'entendre répondre oui sans avoir posé aucune
question claire.*
You know what charm is: a way of getting the
answer yes without having asked any clear
question.

The Fall (1956)

Connolly, Cyril (1903–1974)
English literary editor, writer and critic
All charming people have something to conceal,
usually their total dependence on the
appreciation of others.

Enemies of Promise (1938)

Farquhar, George (1678–1707)
Irish dramatist
Charming women can true converts make,
We love the precepts for the teacher's sake.

The Constant Couple (1699)

Lerner, Alan Jay (1918–1986)
US lyricist and screenwriter
Oozing charm from every pore,
He oiled his way around the floor.

My Fair Lady (1956)

Macnally, Leonard (1752–1820)
Irish lawyer, dramatist and political informer
On Richmond Hill there lives a lass,
More sweet than May day morn,
Whose charms all other maids surpass,
A rose without a thorn.

'The Lass of Richmond Hill' (1789)

Waugh, Evelyn (1903–1966)
English writer and diarist
Charm is the great English blight. It does not
exist outside these damp islands. It spots and
kills anything it touches. It kills love, it kills art.

Brideshead Revisited (1945)

Wilde, Oscar (1854–1900)
Irish poet, dramatist, writer, critic and wit
It is absurd to divide people into good and bad.
People are either charming or tedious.

Lady Windermere's Fan (1892)

Wollstonecraft, Mary (1759–1797)
English feminist, writer and teacher
The woman who has only been taught to please
will soon find that her charms are oblique
sunbeams, and that they cannot have much
effect on her husband's heart when they are
seen every day.

A Vindication of the Rights of Woman (1792)

chastity

Augustine, Saint (354–430)
Numidian-born Christian theologian and philosopher

Da mihi castitatem et continentiam, sed noli modo.
Give me chastity and continency, but not yet.

Confessions (397–398)

Congreve, William (1670–1729)
English dramatist
You are all camphire and frankincense, all
chastity and odour.

The Way of the World (1700)

Pope, Alexander (1688–1744)
English poet, translator and editor
How happy is the blameless Vestal's lot?
The world forgetting, by the world forgot.

'Eloisa to Abelard' (1717)

Shakespeare, William (1564–1616)
English dramatist, poet and actor
Your virginity, your old virginity, is like one of our
French wither'd pears: it looks ill, it eats drily.

All's Well That Ends Well, I.i

Chaste as the icicle
That's curdied by the frost from purest snow,
And hangs on Dian's temple.

The Comedy of Errors, V.iii

Why should a man whose blood is warm within
Sit like his grandsire cut in alabaster?

The Merchant of Venice, I.i

Voltaire (1694–1778)
French philosopher, dramatist, poet, historian writer and
critic
It is amusing that the vice of chastity is made
into a virtue; and it's an odd sort of chastity at
that, which leads men straight to the sin of
Onan, and girls to the fading of their colours.

Letter to M. Mariott, 1766

West, Mae (1892–1980)
US actress and scriptwriter
I used to be Snow White – but I drifted.

*In J. Weintraub (ed.), The Wit and Wisdom of
Mae West (1967)*

childhood

O'Connor, Flannery (1925–1964)
US writer
Anybody who has survived his childhood has
enough information about life to last him the
rest of his days.

In New York Times Book Review, 1989

Wordsworth, William (1770–1850)
English poet
Sweet childish days, that were as long
As twenty days are now.

'To a Butterfly' (1807)

children

Agee, James (1909–1955)
US novelist and poet
> In every child who is born, under no matter what circumstances, and no matter what parents, the potentiality of the human race is born again.
>> *Let Us Now Praise Famous Men* (1941)

Amis, Kingsley (1922–1995)
English writer, poet and critic
> It was no wonder that people were so horrible when they started life as children.
>> *One Fat Englishman* (1963)

Anonymous
> Children are natural mimics who act like their parents despite every effort to teach them good manners.

Auden, W.H. (1907–1973)
English poet, essayist, critic, teacher and dramatist
> Only those in the last stages of disease could believe that children are true judges of character.
>> *The Orators* (1932)

Austen, Jane (1775–1817)
English writer
> On every formal visit a child ought to be of the party, by way of provision for discourse.
>> *Sense and Sensibility* (1811)

Bacon, Francis (1561–1626)
English philosopher, essayist, politician and courtier
> Children sweeten labours, but they make misfortunes more bitter.
>> *Essays* (1625)

Baldwin, James (1924–1987)
US writer, dramatist, poet and civil rights activist
> Children have never been very good at listening to their elders, but they have never failed to imitate them. They must, they have no other models.
>> *Nobody Knows My Name* (1961)

Behan, Brendan (1923–1964)
Irish dramatist, writer and Republican
> I am married to Beatrice Salkeld, a painter. We have no children, except me.
>> Attr.

The Bible (King James Version)
> Train up a child in the way he should go: and when he is old, he will not depart from it.
>> *Proverbs*, 22:6

> Suffer the little children to come unto me, and forbid them not: for of such is the kingdom of God.
>> *Mark*, 10:14

Bowen, Elizabeth (1899–1973)
Irish writer
> There is no end to the violations committed by children on children, quietly talking alone.
>> *The House in Paris* (1935)

Browning, Elizabeth Barrett (1806–1861)
English poet; wife of Robert Browning
> Do you hear the children weeping, O my brothers,
> Ere the sorrow comes with years?
>> 'The Cry of the Children' (1844)

Campbell, David (1915–1979)
Australian poet, rugby player and wartime pilot
> In the heart of dew we lie
> Drowned in brief immortality
> And watch our fair-haired children play.
>> 'Hearts and Children'

Carter, ('Miz') Lillian (1902–1983)
Mother of US President Jimmy Carter
> I love all my children, but some of them I don't like.
>> In *Woman*, 1977

> Sometimes when I look at my children I say to myself, 'Lillian, you should have stayed a virgin.'
>> Remark, 1980

Connolly, Cyril (1903–1974)
English literary editor, writer and critic
> Boys do not grow up gradually. They move forward in spurts like the hands of clocks in railway stations.
>> *Enemies of Promise* (1938)

De Gaulle, Charles (1890–1970)
French general and statesman
After the death of his retarded daughter Anne
> And now she is like everyone else.
>> Attr.

De La Mare, Walter (1873–1956)
> Angel of Words, in vain I have striven with thee,
> Nor plead a lifetime's love and loyalty;
> Only, with envy, bid thee watch this face,
> That says so much, so flawlessly,
> And in how small a space!
>> 'A Child Asleep'

Dickens, Charles (1812–1870)
English writer
> In the little world in which children have their existence … there is nothing so finely perceived and so finely felt as injustice.
>> *Great Expectations* (1861)

Diller, Phyllis (1917–1974)
US comedian

We spend the first twelve months of our children's lives teaching them to walk and talk and the next twelve telling them to sit down and shut up.

Attr.

Dumas, Alexandre (Fils) (1824–1895)

It is only rarely that one can see in a little boy the promise of a man, but one can almost always see in a little girl the threat of a woman.

Attr.

Frost, David (1939–)

English broadcaster

Having one child makes you a parent; having two you are a referee.

Independent, 1989

Gandhi, Indira (1917–1984)

Indian statesman and Prime Minister

To bear many children is considered not only a religious blessing but also an investment. The greater their number, some Indians reason, the more alms they can beg.

In Fallaci, *New York Review of Books*

George V (1865–1936)

My father was frightened of his mother. I was frightened of my father, and I'm damned well going to make sure that my children are frightened of me.

In R. Churchill, *Lord Derby – 'King of Lancashire'* (1959)

Gibbon, Edward (1737–1794)

English historian, politician and memoirist

Few, perhaps, are the children who, after the expiration of some months or years, would sincerely rejoice in the resurrection of their parents.

Memoirs of My Life and Writings (1796)

Gibran, Kahlil (1883–1931)

Lebanese poet, mystic and painter

Your children are not your children.
They are the sons and daughters of Life's longing for itself.
They came through you but not from you,
And though they are with you yet they belong not to you.

You may give them your love but not your thoughts,
For they have their own thoughts.
You may house their bodies but not their souls,
For their souls dwell in the house of tomorrow, which you cannot visit, not even in your dreams.
You may strive to be like them, but seek not to make them like you.
For life goes not backward nor tarries with yesterday.
You are the bows from which your children as

living arrows are sent forth.

The Prophet (1923)

Graves, Robert (1895–1985)

English poet, writer, critic, translator and mythologist

Children are dumb to say how hot the day is,
How hot the scent is of the summer rose.

'The Cool Web' (1927)

Harwood, Gwen (1920–)

Australian poet and music teacher

'It's so sweet
to hear their chatter, watch them grow and thrive,'
she says to his departing smile. Then, nursing the youngest child, sits staring at her feet.
To the wind she says, 'They have eaten me alive.'

Poems (1968)

Inge, William Ralph (1860–1954)

English divine, writer and teacher

The proper time to influence the character of a child is about a hundred years before he is born.

The Observer, 1929

Jonson, Ben (1572–1637)

English dramatist and poet

Rest in soft peace, and, ask'd say here doth lye
Ben Jonson his best piece of poetrie.

'On My First Son' (1616)

Key, Ellen (1849–1926)

Swedish feminist, writer and lecturer

At every step the child should be allowed to meet the real experiences of life; the thorns should never be plucked from his roses.

The Century of the Child (1909)

Kipling, Rudyard (1865–1936)

Indian-born British poet and writer

These were our children who died for our lands …
But who shall return us the children?

'The Children' (1917)

Knox, Ronald (1888–1957)

English Catholic priest and biblical translator

Definition of a baby

A loud noise at one end and no sense of responsibility at the other.

Attr.

Lamb, Charles (1775–1834)

English essayist, critic and letter writer

Boys are capital fellows in their own way, among their mates; but they are unwholesome companions for grown people.

Essays of Elia (1823)

Riddle of destiny, who can show
What thy short visit meant, or know
What thy errand here below?

'On an Infant Dying as soon as Born'

Lamb, Mary (1764–1847)
English prose writer
>A child's a plaything for an hour.
>> *Parental Recollections*

Lebowitz, Fran (1946–)
US writer
>Remember that as a teenager you are at the last stage in your life when you will be happy to hear that the phone is for you.
>> *Social Studies* (1981)

Longfellow, Henry Wadsworth (1807–1882)
US poet and writer
>You are better than all the ballads
>That ever were sung or said;
>For ye are living poems,
>And all the rest are dead.
>> 'Children' (1849)

The Mental Health Foundation
Commenting on over-protective parents
>Children need to get into trouble to learn how to get out of trouble.
>> *The Times*, 1999

Millay, Edna St Vincent (1892–1950)
US poet and dramatist
>Childhood is not from birth to a certain age and at a certain age
>The child is grown, and puts away childish things,
>Childhood is the kingdom where nobody dies.
>Nobody that matters, that is.
>> *Wine from these Grapes* (1934)

Miller, Alice
Swiss-born US psychotherapist and writer
>Society chooses to disregard the mistreatment of children, judging it to be altogether normal because it is so commonplace.
>> *Pictures of a Childhood* (1986)

Mitford, Nancy (1904–1973)
English writer
>I love children – especially when they cry, for then someone takes them away.
>> Attr.

Montaigne, Michel de (1533–1592)
French essayist and moralist
>*Il faut noter, que les jeux d'enfants ne sont pas jeux: et les faut juger en eux, comme leurs plus sérieuses actions.*
>It should be noted that children at play are not merely playing; their games should be seen as their most serious actions.
>> *Essais* (1580)

Nash, Ogden (1902–1971)
US poet
>Children aren't happy with nothing to ignore,

And that's what parents were created for.
>> 'The Parent' (1933)

Patten, Brian (1946–)
British poet
>Growing up's wonderful if you keep your eyes closed tightly,
>and, if you manage to grow,
>take your soul with you,
>nobody wants it..
>> *Grinning Jack* (1990)

Pavese, Cesare (1908–1950)
Italian writer and translator
>One stops being a child when one realizes that telling one's trouble does not make it better.
>> *The Business of Living: Diaries 1935–50*

Penn, William (1644–1718)
English Quaker, founder of state of Pennsylvania
>Men are generally more careful of the breed of their horses and dogs than of their children.
>> *Some Fruits of Solitude, in Reflections and Maxims relating to the Conduct of Humane Life* (1693)

Pope, Alexander (1688–1744)
English poet, translator and editor
>Behold the child, by Nature's kindly law,
>Pleas'd with a rattle, tickled with a straw.
>> *An Essay on Man* (1733)

Proverbs
>Spare the rod and spoil the child.

>There's only one pretty child in the world, and every mother has it.

Saki (1870–1916)
Burmese-born British writer
>Children with Hyacinth's temperament don't know better as they grow older; they merely know more.
>> *The Toys of Peace* (1919)

Smith, Sir Sydney (1883–1969)
New Zealand-born British forensic scientist and writer
English politician
>No child is born a criminal: no child is born an angel: he's just born.
>> Remark

Spock, Dr Benjamin (1903–1998)
US pediatrician and psychiatrist
>There are only two things a child will share willingly – communicable diseases and his mother's age.
>> Attr.

Stevenson, Robert Louis (1850–1894)
Scottish writer, poet and essayist
>The child that is not clean and neat,
>With lots of toys and things to eat,
>He is a naughty child, I'm sure –

Or else his dear papa is poor.
A Child's Garden of Verses (1885)

A child should always say what's true,
And speak when he is spoken to,
And behave mannerly at table:
At least as far as he is able.
A Child's Garden of Verses (1885)

Swift, Jonathan (1667–1745)
Irish satirist, poet, essayist and cleric
I have been assured by a very knowing American of my acquaintance in London, that a young healthy child well nursed is, at a year old, a most delicious, nourishing, and wholesome food, whether stewed, roasted, baked, or boiled; and I make no doubt that it will equally serve in a fricassee, or a ragout.
A Modest Proposal for Preventing the Children of Ireland from being a Burden to their Parents or Country (1729)

Taylor, Bishop Jeremy (1613–1667)
English divine and writer
No man can tell but he that loves his children, how many delicious accents make a man's heart dance in the pretty conversation of those dear pledges; their childishness, their stammering, their little angers, their innocence, their imperfections, their necessities are so many little emanations of joy and comfort to him that delights in their persons and society.
XXV Sermons Preached at Golden Grove (1653)

Tyler, Anne (1941–)
US writer
It seems to me that since I've had children, I've grown richer and deeper. They may have slowed down my writing for a while, but when I did write, I had more of a self to speak from.
Attr.

Vidal, Gore (1925–)
US writer, critic and poet
Never have children, only grandchildren.
Two Sisters (1970)

Watts, Isaac (1674–1748)
English hymn-writer, poet and minister
Birds in their little nests agree
And 'tis a shameful sight,
When children of one family
Fall out, and chide, and fight.
Divine Songs for Children (1715)

Wilde, Oscar (1854–1900)
Irish poet, dramatist, writer, critic and wit
Children begin by loving their parents. After a time they judge them. Rarely, if ever, do they forgive them.
A Woman of No Importance (1893)

Wood, Anne
We are gearing our programmes at two to eight-year-olds. We feel that nine-year-olds can no longer be considered children.
The Times, 'Quotes of the Week', 1999

Yankwich, Léon R. (1888–1975)
Decision, State District Court, Southern District of California, June 1928, quoting columnist O.O. McIntyre
There are no illegitimate children – only illegitimate parents.
Attr.

▶▶ BABIES; BOYS; FAMILIES; INNOCENCE; PARENTS; YOUTH

china

Buck, Pearl S. (1892–1973)
US writer and dramatist
Nothing and no one can destroy the Chinese people. They are relentless survivors. They are the oldest civilized people on earth. Their civilization passes through phases but its basic characteristics remain the same. They yield, they bend to the wind, but they never break.
China, Past and Present (1972)

Saki (1870–1916)
Burmese-born British writer
Even the Hooligan was probably invented in China centuries before we thought of him.
Reginald (1904)

Smith, Adam (1723–1790)
Scottish economist, philosopher and essayist
China, though it may perhaps stand still, does not seem to go backwards.
Wealth of Nations (1776)

choice

Ford, Henry (1863–1947)
US car manufacturer
On the Model T Ford motor car
People can have it any colour – so long as it's black.
In Allan Nevins, *Ford* (1957)

Punch
You pays your money and you takes your choice.
1846

Ward, Thomas (1577–1639)
English controversialist and poet
Where to elect there is but one, 'Tis Hobson's choice, – take that or none.
England's Reformation (1630)

christianity

Arnold, Matthew (1822–1888)
English poet, critic, essayist and educationist
> But there remains the question: what righteousness really is. The method and secret and sweet reasonableness of Jesus.
>
> *Literature and Dogma* (1873)

Barton, Bruce (1886–1967)
US advertising agent and writer
> Jesus picked up twelve men from the bottom ranks of business and forged them into an organization that conquered the world.
>
> *The Man Nobody Knows: A Discovery of the Real Jesus* (1924)

Brecht, Bertolt (1898–1956)
German dramatist
> *Da konnt unser Herr auch verlangen, dass man seinen Nächsten liebt, denn man war satt. Heutzutage ist das anders.*
> In those days our Lord could demand that men love their neighbour, because they'd had enough to eat. Nowadays it's different.
>
> *Mother Courage and her Children* (1941)

Bruce, Lenny (1925–1966)
US comedian
Referring to the Crucifixion
> It was just one of those parties which got out of hand.
>
> *The Guardian*, 1979

Butler, Samuel (1835–1902)
English writer, painter, philosopher and scholar
> They would have been equally horrified at hearing the Christian religion doubted, and at seeing it practised.
>
> *The Way of All Flesh* (1903)

Caen, Herb (1916–1997)
> The trouble with born-again Christians is that they are an even bigger pain the second time around.
>
> *San Francisco Chronicle*, 1981

Carlyle, Thomas (1795–1881)
Scottish historian, biographer, critic, and essayist
> If Jesus Christ were to come to-day, people would not even crucify him. They would ask him to dinner, and hear what he had to say, and make fun of it.
>
> In Wilson, *Carlyle at his Zenith* (1927)

Chesterton, G.K. (1874–1936)
English writer, poet and critic
> Carlyle said that men were mostly fools. Christianity, with a surer and more reverend realism, says that they are all fools.
>
> *Heretics* (1905)

> The Christian ideal has not been tried and found wanting. It has been found difficult; and left untried.
>
> *What's Wrong with the World* (1910)

Coleridge, Samuel Taylor (1772–1834)
English poet, philosopher and critic
> He who begins by loving Christianity better than Truth will proceed by loving his own sect or church better than Christianity, and end by loving himself better than all.
>
> *Aids to Reflection* (1825)

Constantine, Emperor (c.288–337)
His motto, in memory of a vision of the Cross which appeared to him on the eve of his defeat of Maxentius and victorious entry into Rome, 312
> *In hoc signo vinces.*
> In this sign thou shalt conquer.
>
> In Eusebius, *Vita Constantini*

De Blank, Joost (1908–1968)
Of South Africa
> Christ in this country would quite likely have been arrested under the Suppression of Communism Act.
>
> *The Observer*, 1963

Disraeli, Benjamin (1804–1881)
English statesman and writer
> His Christianity was muscular.
>
> *Endymion* (1880)

> A Protestant, if he wants aid or advice on any matter, can only go to his solicitor.
>
> *Lothair* (1870)

Dunbar, William (c.1460–c.1525)
Scottish poet, satirist and courtier
> Done is a battell on the dragon blak;
> Our campioun Christ counfoundit hes his force;
> The yettis of hell ar brokin with a crak,
> The signe triumphall rasit is of the croce.
>
> 'On the Resurrection of Christ'

Ellis, Bob (1942–)
Australian dramatist
> Show me a Wednesday wencher and a Sunday saint, and I'll show you a Roman Catholic.
>
> *The Legend of King O'Malley* (1974)

France, Anatole (1844–1924)
French writer and critic
> *Le Christianisme a beaucoup fait pour l'amour en en faisant un péché.*
> Christianity has done a great deal for love by making a sin of it.
>
> *Le Jardin d'Epicure* (1894)

Glashan, John (1931–)
Caption to cartoon of Christ descended from the cross
> On second thoughts, they knew exactly what

they were doing.

The Spectator, Easter 1991

Greene, Graham (1904–1991)
English writer and dramatist

I wouldn't recommend anyone to be a Catholic, unless they had to be.

Attr.

Hale, Sir Matthew (1609–1676)
English judge and writer

Christianity is part of the laws of England.

In Blackstone, *Commentaries on the Laws of England* (1769)

Hardy, Thomas (1840–1928)
English writer and poet

A local cult called Christianity.

The Dynasts, Part I (1903)

Hood, Thomas (1799–1845)
English poet, editor and humorist
Of Quakers

The sedate, sober, silent, serious, sad-coloured sect.

The Comic Annual (1839)

Huxley, Aldous (1894–1963)
English writer, poet and critic

Christianity accepted as given a metaphysical system derived from several already existing and mutually incompatible systems.

Grey Eminence (1941)

Kingsley, Charles (1819–1875)
English writer, poet, lecturer and clergyman

We have used the Bible as if it was a constable's handbook – an opium-dose for keeping beasts of burden patient while they are being overloaded.

'Letters to Chartists' (1848)

Kipling, Rudyard (1865–1936)
Indian-born British poet and writer

The Three in One, the One in Three? Not so!
To my own Gods I go.
It may be they shall give me greater ease
Than your cold Christ and tangled Trinities.

Plain Tales from the Hills (1888)

Lennon, John (1940–1980)
English rock musician

We're more popular than Jesus Christ now. I don't know which will go first. Rock and roll or Christianity.

The Beatles Illustrated Lyrics

Luther, Martin (1483–1546)
German Protestant theologian and reformer

Be a sinner and sin strongly, but believe and rejoice in Christ even more strongly.

Letter to Melanchton

McCarthy, Mary (1912–1989)
US writer and critic

I don't believe in God – that's just a fact, it's not an act of will … But ethics came to me in the frame of Christian teaching, and even though I don't believe in an afterlife, I'm still concerned with the salvation of my soul.

In Carol Gelderman, *Mary McCarthy* (1988)

Melville, Herman (1819–1891)
US writer and poet

Better sleep with a sober cannibal than a drunken Christian.

Moby Dick (1851)

Mencken, H.L. (1880–1956)
US writer, critic, philologist and satirist

Puritanism – The haunting fear that someone, somewhere, may be happy.

A Mencken Chrestomathy (1949)

The chief contribution of Protestantism to human thought is its massive proof that God is a bore.

Notebooks (1956)

Montesquieu, Charles (1689–1755)
French philosopher and jurist

Il n'y a jamais eu de royaume où il y ait eu tant de guerres civiles que dans celui du Christ.
No kingdom has ever had as many civil wars as the kingdom of Christ.

Lettres persanes (1721)

Nietzsche, Friedrich Wilhelm (1844–1900)
German philosopher, critic and poet

Ich heisse das Christentum den einen grossen Fluch, die eine grosse innerlichste Verdorbenheit, den einen grossen Instinkt der Rache, dem kein Mittel giftig, heimlich, unterirdisch, klein genug ist – ich heisse es den einen unsterblichen Schandfleck der Menschheit.
I call Christianity the one great curse, the one great innermost form of depravity, the one great instinct for revenge, for which no means is poisonous, furtive, underground, petty enough – I call it the one immortal blemish of humanity.

Der Antichrist (1888)

Der christliche Entschluss, die Welt hässlich und schlecht zu finden, hat die Welt hässlich und schlecht gemacht.
The Christian decision to find the world ugly and bad has made the world ugly and bad.

The Gay Science (1887)

Penn, William (1644–1718)
English Quaker, founder of state of Pennsylvania

No pain, no palm; no thorns, no throne; no gall, no glory; no cross, no crown.

No Cross, No Crown (1669)

Russell, Bertrand (1872–1970)
English philosopher, mathematician, essayist and social reformer
> There's a Bible on that shelf there. But I keep it next to Voltaire – poison and antidote.
>> In Harris, *Kenneth Harris Talking To:* (1971)

Saki (1870–1916)
Burmese-born British writer
> People may say what they like about the decay of Christianity; the religious system that produced green Chartreuse can never really die.
>> *Reginald* (1904)

Santayana, George (1863–1952)
Spanish-born US philosopher and writer
> The Bible is literature, not dogma.
>> Introduction to Spinoza's *Ethics*

Shaw, George Bernard (1856–1950)
Irish socialist, writer, dramatist and critic
> It is the protest of the individual soul against the interference of priest or peer between the private man and his God. I should call it Protestantism if I had to find a name for it.
>> *Saint Joan* (1924)

Sitwell, Dame Edith (1887–1964)
English poet, anthologist, critic and biographer
> Who dreamed that Christ has died in vain?
> He walks again on the Seas of Blood, he comes in the terrible Rain.
>> *The Shadow of Cain* (1947)

Strachey, John St Loe (1901–1963)
English politican
> Becoming an Anglo-Catholic must surely be a sad business – rather like becoming an amateur conjurer.
>> *The Coming Struggle for Power*

Swift, Jonathan (1667–1745)
Irish satirist, poet, essayist and cleric
> I conceive some scattered notions about a superior power to be of singular use for the common people, as furnishing excellent materials to keep children quiet when they grow peevish, and providing topics of amusement in a tedious winter-night.
>> *An Argument Against Abolishing Christianity* (1708)

Temple, William (1881–1944)
Anglican prelate, social reformer and writer
> Christianity is the most materialistic of all great religions.
>> *Readings in St John's Gospel* (1939)

Tutu, Archbishop Desmond (1931–)
South African churchman and anti-apartheid campaigner
> For the Church in any country to retreat from politics is nothing short of heresy. Christianity is political or it is not Christianity.
>> *The Observer*, 1994

Twain, Mark (1835–1910)
US humorist, writer, journalist and lecturer
> Most people are bothered by those passages in Scripture which they cannot understand; but as for me, I always noticed that the passages in Scripture which trouble me most are those that I do understand.
>> In Simcox, *Treasury of Quotations on Christian Themes*

Van der Post, Sir Laurens (1906–1996)
South African explorer and writer
> Organized religion is making Christianity political rather than making politics Christian.
>> *The Observer*, 1986

Wilson, Sir Angus (1913–1991)
English novelist and critic
> 'God knows how you Protestants can be expected to have any sense of direction, ' she said. 'It's different with us. I haven't been to mass for years, I've got every mortal sin on my conscience, but I know when I'm doing wrong. I'm still a Catholic.'
>> *The Wrong Set* (1949)

Ybarra, Thomas Russell (1880–1971)
US writer and poet
> A Christian is a man who feels
> Repentance on a Sunday
> For what he did on Saturday
> And is going to do on Monday.
>> 'The Christian' (1909)

Zangwill, Israel (1864–1926)
English writer and Jewish spokesman
> Scratch the Christian and you find the pagan – spoiled.
>> *Children of the Ghetto* (1892)

▶▶ BIBLE; RELIGION

christmas

Band Aid song written to raise money for the relief of famine in Ethiopia
> Feed the World
> Let them know it's Christmas.
>> 'Do They Know It's Christmas?' (song, 1985)

Addison, Joseph (1672–1719)
English essayist, poet, playwright and statesman
> I have often thought, says Sir Roger, it happens very well that Christmas should fall out in the Middle of Winter.
>> *The Spectator*, January 1712

Barry, Dave
US columnist and journalist

> In the old days, it was not called the Holiday Season; the Christians called it 'Christmas' and went to church; the Jews called it 'Hanukka' and went to synagogue; the atheists went to parties and drank. People passing each other on the street would say 'Merry Christmas!' or 'Happy Hanukka!' or (to the atheists) 'Look out for the wall!'.

Christmas Shopping: A Survivor's Guide

Berlin, Irving (1888–1989)
Russian-born US musical and songwriter

> I'm dreaming of a white Christmas, just like the ones I used to know.

'White Christmas' (song, 1942)

Betjeman, Sir John (1906–1984)
English poet laureate

> And girls in slacks remember Dad,
> And oafish louts remember Mum,
> And sleepless children's hearts are glad,
> And Christmas morning bells say 'Come!'
> Even to shining ones who dwell
> Safe in the Dorchester Hotel.
>
> And is it true? And is it true,
> This most tremendous tale of all,
> Seen in a stained-glass window's hue,
> A Baby in an ox's stall?

A Few Late Chrysanthemums (1954)

Castro, Fidel (1927–)
President of Cuba
On Santa Claus

> The leading symbol of the hagiography of US mercantilism.

The Times, 1998

Clarke, Marcus (1846–1881)
English-born Australian writer

> A very merry Christmas, with roast beef in a violent perspiration, and the thermometer 110° in the shade!

Australasian, 1868

Cope, Wendy (1945–)
English poet

> Bloody Christmas, here again,
> Let us raise a loving cup:
> Peace on earth, goodwill to men,
> And make them do the washing-up.

'Another Christmas Poem'

Cupitt, Don (1934–)
English theologian

> Christmas is the Disneyfication of Christianity.

Independent, 1996

Franklin, Benjamin (1706–1790)
US statesman, scientist, political critic and printer

> How many observe Christ's birthday! How few, his precepts! O! 'tis easier to keep holidays than commandments.

Poor Richard's Almanack, 1732–57

Fry, Stephen (1957–)
British comedian and writer

> Christmas to a child is the first terrible proof that to travel hopefully is better than to arrive.

Paperweight

Hardy, Thomas (1840–1928)
English writer and poet

> If someone said on Christmas Eve,
> 'Come; see the oxen kneel
>
> In the lonely barton by yonder coomb
> Our childhood used to know, '
> I should go with him in the gloom,
> Hoping it might be so.

'The Oxen' (1915)

Milligan, Spike (1918–)
Irish comedian and writer

> I'm walking backwards for Christmas.

The Goon Show

Moore, Clement C. (1779–1863)

> 'Twas the night before Christmas, when all through the house
> Not a creature was stirring, not even a mouse;
> The stockings were hung by the chimney with care,
> In hopes that St Nicholas soon would be there …
>
> 'Happy Christmas to all, and to all a goodnight!'.

'A Visit from St Nicholas' (1823)

Nash, Ogden (1902–1971)
US poet

> People can't concentrate properly on blowing other people to pieces properly if their minds are poisoned by thoughts suitable to the twenty-fifth of December.

'I'm a Stranger Here Myself' (1938)

Proverb

> Christmas comes but once a year.

Scott, Sir Walter (1771–1832)
Scottish writer and historian

> Heap on more wood! – the wind is chill;
> But let it whistle as it will,
> We'll keep our Christmas merry still …
>
> England was merry England, when
> Old Christmas brought his sports again.
> 'Twas Christmas broach'd the mightiest ale;
> 'Twas Christmas told the merriest tale;
> A Christmas gambol oft could cheer
> The poor man's heart through half the year.

Marmion (1808)

Sims, George R. (1847–1922)
English dramatist and novelist
> It is Christmas Day in the Workhouse.
> > 'In the Workhouse – Christmas Day' (1879)

Tusser, Thomas (c.1524–1580)
English writer, poet and musician
> At Christmas play and make good cheer,
> For Christmas comes but once a year.
> > *Five Hundred Points of Good*
> > *Husbandry* (1557)

White, E.B. (1899–1985)
US humorist and writer
> To perceive Christmas through its wrapping
> becomes more difficult with every year.
> > *The Second Tree from the Corner* (1954)

Zarnack, August (1777–1827)
> *O Tannenbaum, O Tannenbaum,*
> *Wie treu sind deine Blätter!*
> O Christmas tree, O Christmas tree,
> How faithful are thy branches!
> > Adaptation of an old folk-song, 1820

▶▶ CHRISTIANITY

the church

Ambrose, Saint (c.340–397)
French-born churchman; writer of music and hymns
> *Ubi Petrus, ibi ergo ecclesia.*
> Where Peter is, there of necessity is the Church.
> > *Explanatio psalmi 40*

Andrewes, Bishop Lancelot (1555–1626)
English churchman
> The nearer the Church the further from God.
> > Sermon 15, *Of the Nativity* (1629)

Anonymous
E-mail address offered to and rejected by the Archbishop of Wales
> Archbishop@demon.net.
> > *The Times*, 1999

Augustine, Saint (354–430)
Numidian-born Christian theologian and philosopher
> *Salus extra ecclesiam non est.*
> Outside the church there is no salvation.
> > *De Baptismo*

Bancroft, Richard (1544–1610)
English churchman
> Where Christ erecteth his Church, the devil in
> the same churchyard will have his chapel.
> > Sermon, 1588

Belloc, Hilaire (1870–1953)
English writer of verse, essayist and critic; Liberal MP
> I always like to associate with a lot of priests

> because it makes me understand anti-clerical
> things so well.
> > Attr.

The Bible (King James Version)
> Thou art Peter, and upon this rock I will build my
> church; and the gates of hell shall not prevail
> against it.
> > *Matthew*, 16: 18

Blake, William (1757–1827)
English poet, engraver, painter and mystic
> But if at the Church they would give us some
> Ale,
> And a pleasant fire our souls to regale:
> We'd sing and we'd pray all the live-long day;
> Nor ever once wish from the Church to stray.
> > *Songs of Experience* (1794)

Blythe, Ronald (1922–)
English writer
> As for the British churchman, he goes to church
> as he goes to the bathroom, with the minimum
> of fuss and no explanation if he can help it.
> > *The Age of Illusion* (1963)

Brontë, Charlotte (1816–1855)
English writer
> Of late years an abundant shower of curates has
> fallen upon the North of England.
> > *Shirley* (1849)

Bruce, Lenny (1925–1966)
US comedian
> Every day, people are straying away from the
> church and going back to God.
> > In John Cohen, *The Essential Lenny Bruce* (1967)

Burke, Edmund (1729–1797)
Irish-born British statesman and philosopher
> Politics and the pulpit are terms that have little
> agreement. No sound ought to be heard in the
> church but the healing voice of Christian charity.
> > *Reflections on the Revolution in France ...* (1790)

Charles II (1630–1685)
King of Great Britain and Ireland
> He told me, he had a chaplain Woolly, later
> made a bishop ... a very great blockhead ... he
> said he was a very silly fellow: but that, he
> believed, his nonsense suited their nonsense, for
> he had brought them all the non-conformists to
> church.
> > In Burnet, *The History of His Own Time* (1724)

Chesterfield, Lord (1694–1773)
English politician and letter writer
When asked what could be done to control the evangelical
preacher George Whitefield
> Make him a bishop, and you will silence him at
> once.
> > Attr.

Cyprian, Saint (c.200–258)
Carthaginian churchman, theological writer and martyr
> *Salus extra ecclesiam non est.*
> There is no salvation outside the Church.
>> Letter

> *Habere non potest Deum patrem qui ecclesiam non habet matrem.*
> Who has not the Church as his mother cannot have God as his father.
>> *De Unitate Ecclesiae*

D'Alpuget, Blanche (1944–)
Australian writer
> Convent girls never leave the church, they just become feminists. I learned that in Australia.
>> *Turtle Beach* (1981)

Devlin, Bernadette (1947–)
Irish politician
> Among the best traitors Ireland has ever had, Mother Church ranks at the very top, a massive obstacle in the path to equality and freedom.
>> *The Price of My Soul*

Emerson, Ralph Waldo (1803–1882)
US poet, essayist, transcendentalist and teacher
> I like the silent church before the service begins, better than any preaching.
>> *Essays, First Series* (1841)

Fielding, Henry (1707–1754)
English writer, dramatist and journalist
> For clergy are men as well as other folks.
>> *Joseph Andrews* (1742)

> There is not in the universe a more ridiculous, nor a more contemptible animal, than a proud clergyman.
>> *Amelia* (1751)

Goldman, Emma (1869–1940)
US anarchist
> Religion is a superstition that originated in man's mental ability to solve natural phenomena. The Church is an organized institution that has always been a stumbling block to progress.
>> *What I Believe*

Herbert, George (1593–1633)
English poet and priest
> Kneeling ne're spoil'd silk stocking. Quit thy state.
> All equall are within the churches gate.
>> *The Temple* (1633)

Higton, Tony (19th century)
Church of England evangelical
> The church is not a mere ecclesiastical wing of the state which benignly blesses what an increasingly secular society does. Its function is primarily to represent God to the nation.
>> *The Times*, 1992

Jowett, Benjamin (1817–1893)
English scholar, translator, essayist and priest
> Nowhere probably is there more true feeling, and nowhere worse taste, than in a churchyard – both as regards the monuments and the inscriptions. Scarcely a word of the true poetry anywhere.
>> In E. Abbott and L. Campbell (eds), *Life and Letters of Benjamin Jowett* (1897)

Lamb, William, Lord (1779–1848)
> While I cannot be regarded as a pillar, I must be regarded as a buttress of the church, because I support it from the outside.
>> Attr.

Macaulay, Lord (1800–1859)
English Liberal statesman, essayist and poet
Of the Roman Catholic Church
> She may still exist in undiminished vigour when some traveller from New Zealand shall, in the midst of a vast solitude, take his stand on a broken arch of London Bridge to sketch the ruins of St Paul's.
>> *Collected Essays* (1843)

Miller, Arthur (1915–)
US dramatist and screenwriter
> There are many who stay away from church these days because you hardly ever mention God any more.
>> *The Crucible* (1952)

Muggeridge, Malcolm (1903–1990)
English writer
On *Punch*, which he once edited
> Very much like the Church of England. It is doctrinally inexplicable but it goes on.
>> Attr.

Paisley, Rev. Ian (1926–)
> The Roman Catholic Church is getting nearer to communism every day.
>> *The Irish Times*, 1969

Priestley, J.B. (1894–1984)
English writer, dramatist and critic
> It is hard to tell where the MCC ends and the Church of England begins.
>> *New Statesman*, 1962

Proverb
> If there's a hen or a goose, it's on the priest's table you'll find it.
>> Irish proverb

Runcie, Robert (1921–2000)
Archbishop of Canterbury 1980–91
> I hope I can persuade the church to loosen its stays a bit and perhaps rock the boat a little.
>> In *The Guardian*, 2000

Sabia, Laura (1903–1990)
Canadian feminist writer

I'm a Roman Catholic and I take a dim view of 2,500 celibates shuffling back and forth to Rome to discuss birth control and not one woman to raise a voice.

The Toronto Star, 1975

Shorthouse, J.H. (1834–1903)
English novelist
'The Church of England, ' I said, seeing that Mr Inglesant paused, 'is no doubt a compromise.'

John Inglesant (1880)

Smith, Sydney (1771–1845)
English clergyman, essayist, journalist and wit
A Curate – there is something which excites compassion in the very name of a Curate!!!

Edinburgh Review, 1822

What Bishops like best in their Clergy is a droppingdown-deadness of manner.

The Works of the Rev. Sydney Smith (1839)

I have seen nobody since I saw you, but persons in orders. My only varieties are vicars, rectors, curates, and every now and they (by way of turbot) an archdeacon.

Letters, To Miss Berry, 1843

As the French say, there are three sexes – men, women, and clergymen.

In Holland, *A Memoir of the Reverend Sydney Smith* (1855)

Stalin, Joseph (1879–1953)
Soviet Communist leader
Reply to Laval, French Foreign Minister, who asked Stalin in 1935 to do something to encourage the Catholic religion in Russia in order to help him gain the support of the Pope
The Pope! How many divisions has he got?

In W.S. Churchill, *The Gathering Storm* (1948)

Swift, Jonathan (1667–1745)
Irish satirist, poet, essayist and cleric
I never saw, heard, nor read, that the clergy were beloved in any nation where Christianity was the religion of the country. Nothing can render them popular, but some degree of persecution.

Thoughts on Religion (1765)

Temple, Frederick, Archbishop (1821–1902)
English churchman
There is a certain class of clergyman whose mendicity is only equalled by their mendacity.

Attr.

Temple, William (1881–1944)
Anglican prelate, social reformer and writer
The Church exists for the sake of those outside it.

Attr.

I believe in the Church, One Holy, Catholic and

Apostolic, and I regret that it nowhere exists.

Attr.

Tucholsky, Kurt (1890–1935)
German satirist and writer
Was die Kirche nicht verhindern kann, das segnet sie.
What the church can't prevent, it blesses.

Scraps (1973)

Updike, John (1932–)
US writer, poet and critic
In general the churches, visited by me too often on weekdays … bore for me the same relation to God that billboards did to Coca-Cola: they promoted thirst without quenching it.

A Month of Sundays (1975)

Waugh, Evelyn (1903–1966)
English writer and diarist
There is a species of person called a 'Modern Churchman' who draws the full salary of a beneficed clergyman and need not commit himself to any religious belief.

Decline and Fall (1928)

I have noticed again and again since I have been in the Church that lay interest in ecclesiastical matters is often a prelude to insanity.

Decline and Fall (1928)

Wotton, Sir Henry (1568–1639)
English diplomat, traveller and poet
The itch of disputing will prove the scab of churches.

A Panegyric to King Charles (1651)

▶▶ RELIGION

cinema

Adler, Renata
US film critic and writer
People have been modelling their lives after films for years, but the medium is somehow unsuited to moral lessons, cautionary tales or polemics of any kind.

A Year in the Dark: A Year in the Life of a Film Critic (1971)

Altman, Robert (1922–)
US film director
What's a cult? It just means not enough people to make a minority.

The Observer, 1981

Berryman, John (1914–1972)
US poet and author
I seldom go to films. They are too exciting,
Said the Honourable Possum.

Dream Songs (1964), 53

Brown, Geoff (1949–)
Film critic and writer

Dictators needed a talking cinema to twist nations round their fingers: remove the sound from Mussolini and you are left with a puffing bullfrog.

The Times, 1992

Cameron, James (1954–)
US film director
On winning an oscar for Best Director for *Titanic*

I'm the king of the world!

Scotland on Sunday

Coltrane, Robbie (1950–)
Scottish comedian and actor
On film acting

If anyone asked me what I was doing, I'd say 'I've come 1500 miles to a foreign country to pretend to be someone else in front of a machine'.

Arena, 1991

Disney, Walt (1901–1966)
US filmmaker and pioneer of animated films

Girls bored me – they still do. I love Mickey Mouse more than any woman I've ever known.

In Wagner, *You Must Remember This*

Doyle, Roddy (1958–)
Irish writer

There's a big trend in Hollywood of taking very good European films and turning them into very bad American films. I've been offered a few of those, but it's really a peverse activity, I'd rather go on the dole.

The Independent, 1994

Fellini, Federico (1920–1993)
Italian film director

Sono vent'anni che sempre più stancamente tento di dire che 'La dolce vita' era un titolo goffo e patetico.
I have been trying to say for over twenty years that 'La dolce vita' was a pathetic and awkward title.

In *Corriere della Sera*, 1993

Gibson, Mel (1956–)
Australian actor

I'll tell you what really turns my toes up – love scenes with 68-year-old men and young actresses. I promise you, when I get to that age I will say no.

The Observer, 1999

Godard, Jean-Luc (1930–)
French film director and writer

Of course a film should have a beginning, a middle and an end. But not necessarily in that order.

Attr.

La photographie, c'est la vérité. Le cinéma: la vérité vingt-quatre fois par seconde.
Photography is truth. Cinema is truth twenty-four times a second.

Le Petit Soldat (film, 1960)

Goldwyn, Samuel (1882–1974)
Polish-born US film producer
On being warned that a story was too caustic

To hell with the cost. If it's a sound story, we'll make a picture of it.

In Zierold, *Moguls* (1969)

Tell me, how did you love my picture?

Attr.

A wide screen just makes a bad film twice as bad.

Attr.

Before the opening of his film *The Best Years of Our Lives* in 1946

I don't care if it doesn't make a nickel, I just want every man, woman, and child in America to see it.

In Zierold, *Moguls* (1969)

Why should people go out and pay money to see bad films when they can stay at home and see bad television for nothing?

The Observer, 1956

The trouble with this business is the dearth of bad pictures.

Attr.

Grade, Lew (1906–1994)
Russian-born British film, TV and theatrical producer.
To Franco Zeffirelli who had explained that the high cost of the film Jesus of Nazareth was partly because there had to be twelve apostles

Twelve! So who needs twelve! Couldn't we make do with six?

Radio Times, 1983

Griffith, D.W. (1874–1948)
US film director
Said when directing an epic film

Move those ten thousand horses a trifle to the right. And that mob out there, three feet forward.

Attr.

Hitchcock, Alfred (1899–1980)
English film director

Cinema is life with the dull bits cut out.
The length of a film should be directly related to the endurance of the human bladder.

In Simon Rose, *Classic Film Guide* (1995)

Jung, Carl Gustav (1875–1961)
Swiss psychiatrist and pupil of Freud

The cinema, like the detective story, makes it

possible to experience without danger all the excitement, passion and desire which must be repressed in a humanitarian ordering of life.

Attr.

Kaufman, George S. (1889–1961)
US scriptwriter, librettist and journalist
At a rehearsal of *Animal Crackers* (1930), for which he wrote the script
> Excuse me for interrupting but I actually thought I heard a line I wrote.
> In Meredith, *George S. Kaufman and the Algonquin Round Table* (1974)

Lucas, George (1944–)
US film director
On *Star Wars*
> I thought it was too wacky for the general public.
> Attr.

Marx, Groucho (1895–1977)
US comedian
Explaining why he didn't go to films starring Victor Mature
> I never go to movies where the hero's bust is bigger than the heroine's.
> Attr.

> We in this industry know that behind every successful screenwriter stands a woman. And behind her stands his wife.
> Attr.

Minghella, Anthony (1954–)
English film director
On winning an oscar for Best Director for *The English Patient*
> It's a great day for the Isle of Wight.
> *Scotland on Sunday*, 1999

Rogers, Will (1879–1935)
US humorist, actor, rancher, writer and wit
> The movies are the only business where you can go out front and applaud yourself.
> In Halliwell, *Filmgoer's Book of Quotes* (1973)

Tracy, Spencer (1900–1967)
US film actor
Defending his demand for equal billing with Katherine Hepburn
> This is a movie, not a lifeboat.
> Attr.

Tree, Sir Herbert Beerbohm (1853–1917)
English actor and theatre manager
Objecting to the presence of a camera while performing in a silent film
> Take that black box away. I can't act in front of it.
> In K. Brownlow, *Hollywood: The Pioneers*

Ustinov, Sir Peter (1921–)
English actor, director, dramatist, writer and raconteur
> Thanks to the movies, gunfire has always

sounded unreal to me, even when being fired at.
> *Dear Me* (1977)

Wallach, Eli (1915–)
US actor
Remarking upon the long line of people at the box office before one of his performances
> There's something about a crowd like that that brings a lump to my wallet.
> Attr.

▶▶ HOLLYWOOD; SHOWBUSINESS

cities

Anonymous
Inscription in the armoury of Venice
> Happy is that city which in time of peace thinks of war.
> In Robert Burton, *Anatomy of Melancholy* (1621–1651)

Arnold, Matthew (1822–1888)
English poet, critic, essayist and educationist
> And that sweet city with her dreaming spires,
> She needs not June for beauty's heightening.
> 'Thyrsis' (1866)

Burgon, John William (1813–1888)
English churchman
> Match me such marvel save in Eastern clime,
> A rose-red city 'half as old as Time'!
> 'Petra' (1845)

Caesar, Augustus (63 BC–AD 14)
First Roman emperor
> He so beautified the city that he justly boasted that he found it brick and left it marble.
> In Suetonius, *Lives of the Caesars*

Colton, Charles Caleb (c.1780–1832)
English clergyman and satirist
> If you would be known, and not know, vegetate in a village; if you would know, and not be known, live in a city.
> *Lacon* (1820)

Cowper, William (1731–1800)
English poet, hymn and letter writer
> God made the country, and man made the town.
> *The Task* (1785)

Keats, John (1795–1821)
English poet
> To one who has been long in city pent,
> 'Tis very sweet to look into the fair
> And open face of heaven.
> 'To one who has been long in city pent' (1816)

Kipling, Rudyard (1865–1936)
Indian-born British poet and writer
> Cities and Thrones and Powers,

Stand in Time's eye,
Almost as long as flowers,
Which daily die:
But, as new buds put forth,
To glad new men,
Out of the spent and unconsidered Earth,
The Cities rise again.
'Cities and Thrones and Powers'
(1906)

Lorca, Federico Garcia (1898–1936)
Spanish poet and dramatist
The two elements the traveller first captures in
the big city are extrahuman architecture and
furious rhythm. Geometry and anguish.
Poet in New York (1940, trans 1988)

Milton, John (1608–1674)
English poet, libertarian and pamphleteer
Towred Cities please us then,
And the busie humm of men.
'L'Allegro' (1645)

Moore, Brian (1921–1999)
Canadian writer
This city was full of lunatics, people who went
into muttering fits on the bus, others who
shouted obscenities in automats, lost souls who
walked the pavements alone, caught up in
imaginary conversations.
An Answer From Limbo (1994)

Morris, Charles (1745–1838)
English songwriter and soldier
A house is much more to my taste than a tree,
And for groves, oh! a good grove of chimneys
for me.
'Country and Town' (song, 1840)

If one must have a villa in summer to dwell,
Oh, give me the sweet shady side of Pall Mall!
'The Contrast' (song, 1840)

Morris, Desmond (1928–)
English anthropologist and broadcaster
Clearly, then, the city is not a concrete jungle, it
is a human zoo.
The Human Zoo (1969)

Mumford, Lewis (1895–1990)
US sociologist and writer
The city is a fact in nature, like a cave, a run of
mackerel or an ant-heap. But it is also a
conscious work of art, and it holds within its
communal framework many simpler and more
personal forms of art.
The Culture of Cities (1938)

Thomson, James (1834–1882)
Scottish poet and dramatist
The City is of Night; perchance of Death,
But certainly of Night; for never there

Can come the lucid morning's fragrant breath
After the dewy dawning's cold grey air ...

The City is of Night, but not of Sleep;
There sweet sleep is not for the weary brain;
The pitiless hours like years and ages creep,
A night seems termless hell.
The City of Dreadful Night (1880)

Wright, Frank Lloyd (1869–1959)
US architect and writer
The screech and mechanical uproar of the big
city turns the citified head, fills citified ears – as
the song of birds, wind in the trees, animal cries,
or as the voices and songs of his loved ones
once filled his heart. He is sidewalk-happy.
The Living City (1958)

cities: aberdeen

Anonymous
A day oot o' Aiberdeen is a day oot o' life.
Traditional Scottish saying

cities: bath

Austen, Jane (1775–1817)
English writer
Oh! who can ever be tired of Bath?
Northanger Abbey (1818)

cities: belfast

Craig, Maurice James (1919–)
Poet and historian
Red bricks in the suburbs, white horse on the
wall,
Eyetalian marbles in the City Hall:
O stranger from England, why stand so aghast?
May the Lord in his mercy be kind to Belfast.
'Ballad to a traditional Refrain'

cities: birmingham

Austen, Jane (1775–1817)
English writer
One has not great hopes from Birmingham. I
always say there is something direful in the
sound.
Emma (1816)

cities: boston

Appleton, Thomas Gold (1812–1884)
US epigrammatist
> A Boston man is the east wind made flesh.
>
> *Attr.*

Bossidy, John Collins (1860–1928)
US oculist
> And this is good old Boston,
> The home of the bean and the cod,
> Where the Lowells talk only to Cabots,
> And the Cabots talk only to God.
>
> *Toast at Harvard dinner, 1910*

Emerson, Ralph Waldo (1803–1882)
US poet, essayist, transcendentalist and teacher
> We say the cows laid out Boston. Well, there are worse surveyors.
>
> *Conduct of Life (1860)*

cities: cambridge

Baedeker, Karl (1801–1859)
> Oxford is on the whole more attractive than Cambridge to the ordinary visitor; and the traveller is therefore recommended to visit Cambridge first, or to omit it altogether if he cannot visit both.
>
> *Baedeker's Great Britain (1887)*

Raphael, Frederic (1931–)
> This is the city of perspiring dreams.
>
> *The Glittering Prizes (1976)*

cities: chicago

Capone, Al (1899–1947)
Chicago gangster
Talking about suburban Chicago
> This is virgin territory for whorehouses.
>
> *In Kenneth Allsop, The Bootleggers (1961)*

cities: edinburgh

Garioch, Robert (1909–1981)
> In simmer, whan aa sorts foregether
> in Embro to the ploy,
> fowk seek out friens to hae a blether,
> or faes they'd fain annoy;
> smorit wi British Railways' reek
> frae Glesca or Glen Roy
> or Wick, they come to hae a week
> of cultivatit joy,

or three,
in Embro to the ploy.
>
> *Selected Poems (1966)*

Goebbels, Joseph (1897–1945)
Nazi politician
Of Edinburgh
> Enchanting … it shall make a delightful summer capital when we invade Britain.
>
> *Attr.*

cities: glasgow

Bridie, James (1888–1951)
Scottish dramatist, writer and physician
> You must not look down on … Glasgow which gave the world the internal combustion engine, political economy, antiseptic and cerebral surgery, the balloon, the mariner's compass, the theory of Latent Heat, Tobias Smollett and James Bridie.
>
> *Letter to St John Ervine*

Cernuda, Luis (1902–1963)
Spanish poet
On leaving Glasgow, where he had lived from 1939 to 1943
> *Rara vez me he ido tan a gusto de sitio alguno.*
> Rarely have I been so pleased to leave a place.
>
> *Chronicle of a book (1958)*

McGonagall, William (c.1830–1902)
Scottish poet, tragedian and actor
> Beautiful city of Glasgow, I now conclude my muse,
> And to write in praise of thee my pen does not refuse;
> And, without fear of contradiction, I will venture to say
> You are the second grandest city in Scotland at the present day.
>
> *'Glasgow' (1890)*

Smith, Alexander (1830–1867)
Scottish poet and writer
> City! I am true son of thine;
> Ne'er dwelt I where great mornings shine
> Around the bleating pens;
> Ne'er by the rivulets I strayed,
> And ne'er upon my childhood weighed
> The silence of the glens.
> Instead of shores where ocean beats,
> I hear the ebb and flow of streets.
> Thou hast my kith and kin:
> My childhood, youth, and manhood brave;
> Thou hast that unforgotten grave
> Within thy central din.
> A sacredness of love and death
> Dwells in thy noise and smoky breath.
>
> *City Poems (1857)*

cities: liverpool

Ginsberg, Allen (1926–1997)
US poet
> Liverpool is at the present moment the centre of the consciousness of the human universe.
>> Attr.

cities: london

Austen, Jane (1775–1817)
English writer
> Nobody is healthy in London. Nobody can be.
>> *Emma* (1816)

Blake, William (1757–1827)
English poet, engraver, painter and mystic
> I wander thro' each charter'd street,
> Near where the charter'd Thames does flow
> And mark in every face I meet
> Marks of weakness, marks of woe.
>> 'London' (1794)

Blücher, Prince (1742–1819)
Prussian field marshal
Remark made on seeing London in June, 1814
> *Was für Plunder!*
> What junk!
>> Attr.

Bridie, James (1888–1951)
Scottish dramatist, writer and physician
> London! Pompous Ignorance sits enthroned there and welcomes Pretentious Mediocrity with flattery and gifts. Oh, dull and witless city! Very hell for the restless, inquiring, sensitive soul. Paradise for the snob, the parasite and the prig; the pimp, the placeman and the cheapjack.
>> *The Anatomist* (1931)

Chamberlain, Joseph (1836–1914)
English politician
> Provided that the City of London remains as it is at present, the clearing-house of the world, any other nation may be its workshop.
>> Speech, London, 1904

Cobbett, William (1762–1835)
English politician, reformer, writer, farmer and army officer
Of London
> But what is to be the fate of the great wen of all? The monster, called…'the metropolis of the empire'?
>> 'Rural Rides', 1822

Colman, the Younger, George (1762–1836)
English dramatist and Examiner of Plays
> Oh, London is a fine town,

> A very famous city,
> Where all the streets are paved with gold,
> And all the maidens pretty.
>> *The Heir at Law* (1797)

Disraeli, Benjamin (1804–1881)
English statesman and writer
> London; a nation, not a city.
>> *Lothair* (1870)

Doyle, Sir Arthur Conan (1859–1930)
Scottish writer and war correspondent
> London, that great cesspool into which all the loungers of the Empire are irresistibly drained.
>> *A Study in Scarlet* (1887)

Dunbar, William (c.1460–c.1525)
Scottish poet, satirist and courtier
> London, thou art the flower of cities all!
> Gemme of all joy, jasper of jocunditie.
>> 'London' (1834)

Gibbon, Edward (1737–1794)
English historian, politician and memoirist
> Crowds without company, and dissipation without pleasure.
>> *Memoirs of My Life and Writings* (1796)

Gregg, Hubert (1914–)
> Maybe it's because I'm a Londoner
> That I love London so.
>> 'Maybe It's Because I'm a Londoner' (song, 1947)

Johnson, Samuel (1709–1784)
English lexicographer, poet, critic, conversationalist and essayist
> By seeing London, I have seen as much of life as the world can show.
>> In Boswell, *Journal of a Tour to the Hebrides* (1785)

> When a man is tired of London, he is tired of life; for there is in London all that life can afford.
>> In Boswell, *The Life of Samuel Johnson* (1791)

Meynell, Hugo (1727–1780)
Frequenter of London society, acquaintance of Dr Johnson
> The chief advantage of London is, that a man is always so near his burrow.
>> In Boswell, *The Life of Samuel Johnson* (1791)

Morris, William (1834–1896)
English poet, designer, craftsman, artist and socialist
> Forget six counties overhung with smoke,
> Forget the snorting steam and piston stroke,
> Forget the spreading of the hideous town;
> Think rather of the pack-horse on the down,
> And dream of London, small and white and clean,
> The clear Thames bordered by its gardens green.
>> *The Earthly Paradise* (1868–1870)

Swift, Jonathan (1667–1745)
Irish satirist, poet, essayist and cleric
> It is the folly of too many to mistake the echo of a London coffee house for the voice of the kingdom.
>> *The Conduct of the Allies* (1711)

Wordsworth, William (1770–1850)
English poet
> Earth has not anything to show more fair;
> Dull would he be of soul who could pass by
> A sight so touching in its majesty:
> This city now doth, like a garment, wear
>
> The beauty of the morning; silent, bare,
> Ships, towers, domes, theatres, and temples lie
> Open unto the fields, and to the sky,
> All bright and glittering in the smokeless air …
>
> Dear God! the very houses seem asleep;
> And all that mighty heart is lying still!
>> 'Sonnet composed upon Westminster Bridge' (1807)

cities: manchester

Bolitho, William (1890–1930)
South African-born British writer
> The shortest way out of Manchester is notoriously a bottle of Gordon's gin.
>> *The Treasury of Humorous Quotations*

cities: melbourne

Beven, Rodney Allan (1916–1982)
> The people of Melbourne
> Are frightfully well-born.
>> 'Observation Sociologique'

Bygraves, Max (1922–)
English singer and entertainer
> I've always wanted to see a ghost town. You couldn't even get a parachute to open here after 10 p.m.
>> *Melbourne Sun*, 1965

Jillett, Neil (1933–)
A phrase wrongly attributed to Ava Gardner, who starred in the film *On the Beach*, adapted from Nevil Shute's novel of that name (1957)
> *On the Beach* is a story about the end of the world, and Melbourne sure is the right place to film it.
>> Attr.

cities: naples

Gladstone, William (1809–1898)
English statesman and reformer
> This is a negation of God erected into a system of government.
>> *Letter to Lord Aberdeen*, 1851

cities: new york

Gilman, Charlotte Perkins (1860–1935)
US writer, social reformer and feminist
> New York … that unnatural city where every one is an exile, none more so than the American.
>> *The Living of Charlotte Perkins Gilman* (1935)

Koch, Ed (1924–)
US politician and jurist; Mayor of New York 1978–89
> Being a New Yorker is a state of mind. If, after living there for six months, you find that you walk faster, talk faster and think faster, you are a New Yorker.
>> *The Observer*, 1999

McAllister, Ward (1827–1895)
> There are only about four hundred people in New York society.
>> Interview with Charles H. Crandall in the *New York Tribune*, 1888

Simon, Neil (1927–)
US playwright
> New York … is not Mecca. It just smells like it.
>> *California Suite* (1976)

Stout, Rex (1886–1975)
> I like to walk around Manhattan, catching glimpses of its wild life, the pigeons and cats and girls.
>> *Three Witnesses*, 'When a Man Murders'

Weiss, Anita
> I moved to New York City for my health. I'm paranoid and New York was the only place where my fears were justified.
>> Attr.

cities: oxford

Arnold, Matthew (1822–1888)
English poet, critic, essayist and educationist
> Beautiful city! so venerable, so lovely, so unravaged by the fierce intellectual life of our century, so serene! … whispering from her towers the last enchantments of the Middle Age … home of lost causes, and forsaken beliefs,

and unpopular names, and impossible loyalties!

Essays in Criticism (1865)

cities: paris

Elms, Robert (1927–)

Paris is the paradise of the easily-impressed –
the universal provincial mind.

In Burchill, *Sex and Sensibility* (1992)

Hammerstein II, Oscar (1895–1960)
US lyricist

The last time I saw Paris,
Her heart was warm and gay,
I heard the laughter of her heart in ev'ry street
café.

'The Last Time I Saw Paris', song, 1940, from *Lady
Be Good*

Hemingway, Ernest (1898–1961)
US author

If you are lucky enough to have lived in Paris as
a young man, then wherever you go for the rest
of your life, it stays with you, for Paris is a
moveable feast.

A Moveable Feast (1964)

Henri IV (1553–1610)
King of France

Paris vaut bien une messe.
Paris is well worth a mass.

Attr.

Kurtz, Irma (1935–)
English writer and 'agony aunt'

Cities are only human. And I had begun to see
Paris for the bitch she is: a stunning transvestite
– vain, narrow-minded and all false charm.

Daily Mail, 1996

cities: philadelphia

Fields, W.C. (1880–1946)
US film actor

Last week, I went to Philadelphia, but it was
closed.

Attr.

cities: prague

Prowse, William Jeffrey (1836–1870)
English poet

Though the latitude's rather uncertain,
And the longitude also is vague,
The persons I pity who know not the city,

The beautiful city of Prague.

'The City of Prague'

cities: rome

Alcott, Louisa May (1832–1888)
US writer

Rome took all the vanity out of me; for after
seeing the wonders there, I felt too insignificant
to live, and gave up all my foolish hopes in
despair.

Little Women (1869)

Burgess, Anthony (1917–1993)
English writer, linguist and composer

Rome's just a city like anywhere else. A vastly
overrated city, I'd say. It trades on belief just as
Stratford trades on Shakespeare.

Inside Mr Enderby (1968)

Caesar, Augustus (63 BC–AD 14)
First Roman emperor

I found Rome a city of bricks and left it a city of
marble.

In Suetonius, *Lives of the Caesars*

Clough, Arthur Hugh (1819–1861)
English poet and letter writer

Rome, believe me, my friend, is like its own
Monte Testaceo,
Merely a marvellous mass of broken and
castaway wine-pots.

Amours de Voyage (1858)

Horace (65–8 BC)
Roman poet

Fumum et opes strepitumque Romae.
The smoke and wealth and noise of Rome.

Odes

cities: st andrews

Lang, Andrew (1844–1912)
Scottish poet, writer, mythologist and anthropologist

St Andrews by the Northern Sea,
A haunted town it is to me!

'Almae Matres' (1884)

cities: sydney

Slessor, Kenneth (1901–1971)
Australian poet and journalist

On Sydney's ferry-boats

At sunset, when the Harbour is glazed with
pebbles of gold and white, and the sun is

burning out like a bushfire behind Balmain, the ferry-boats put on their lights. They turn into luminous water-beetles, filed with a gliding, sliding reflected glitter that bubbles on the water like phosphorus.

Bread and Wine (1970)

cities: venice

Benchley, Robert (1889–1945)
US essayist, humorist and actor
Telegram sent on arriving in Venice
Streets flooded. Please advise.

Attr.

Capote, Truman (1924–1984)
US writer
Venice is like eating an entire box of chocolate liqueurs in one go.

The Observer, 1961

Morris, Jan (1926–)
Welsh travel writer
There's romance for you! There's the lust and dark wine of Venice! No wonder George Eliot's husband fell into the Grand Canal.

Venice (1960)

▶▶ COUNTRY

citizens

Auden, W.H. (1907–1973)
English poet, essayist, critic, teacher and dramatist
Our researchers into Public Opinion are content That he held the proper opinions for the time of year;
When there was peace, he was for peace; when there was war, he went.

Collected Poems, 1939–1947

Bryan, William Jennings (1860–1925)
US Democrat politician and editor
The humblest citizen of all the land, when clad in the armour of a righteous cause is stronger than all the hosts of error.

Speech, Chicago, 1896

Socrates (469–399 BC)
Athenian philosopher
I am not an Athenian nor a Greek, but a citizen of the world.

Attr. in Plutarch, *On Exile*, 600

Vizinczey, Stephen (1933–)
Hungarian-born writer, editor and broadcaster
I was told I am a true cosmopolitan. I am

unhappy everywhere.

The Guardian, 1968

civilization

Addams, Jane (1860–1935)
US sociologist and writer
Civilization is a method of living, an attitude of equal respect for all men.

Speech, Honolulu, 1933

Alcott, Bronson (1799–1888)
US educator, reformer and transcendentalist
Civilization degrades the many to exalt the few.

Table Talk (1877)

Anonymous
Local resident on the opening of the first Russian McDonalds Restaurant, Moscow, 1990
It's like the coming of civilization.

Bagehot, Walter (1826–1877)
English economist and political philosopher
The whole history of civilization is strewn with creeds and institutions which were invaluable at first, and deadly afterwards.

Physics and Politics (1872)

Bancroft, George (1800–1891)
US historian
The exact measure of the progress of civilization is the degree in which the intelligence of the common mind has prevailed over wealth and brute force.

Address to The Historical Society, New York, 1854

Bates, Daisy May (1863–1951)
Irish-born journalist, anthropologist and reformer
The Australian native can withstand all the reverses of nature, fiendish droughts and sweeping floods, horrors of thirst and enforced starvation – but he cannot withstand civilisation.

The Passing of the Aborigines ... (1938)

Buck, Pearl S. (1892–1973)
US writer and dramatist
Nothing and no one can destroy the Chinese people. They are relentless survivors. They are the oldest civilized people on earth. Their civilization passes through phases but its basic characteristics remain the same. They yield, they bend to the wind, but they never break.

China, Past and Present (1972)

Carlyle, Thomas (1795–1881)
Scottish historian, biographer, critic, and essayist
The three great elements of modern civilization, Gunpowder, Printing, and the Protestant Religion.

Critical and Miscellaneous Essays (1839)

Disraeli, Benjamin (1804–1881)
English statesman and writer
> Increased means and increased leisure are the two civilizers of man.
>> Speech, Manchester, 1872

Ellis, Havelock (1859–1939)
English sexologist and essayist
> The more rapidly a civilisation progresses, the sooner it dies for another to rise in its place.
>> *The Dance of Life*

Fowles, John (1926–)
English writer
> In essence the Renaissance was simply the green end of one of civilization's hardest winters.
>> *The French Lieutenant's Woman* (1969)

Gandhi (1869–1948)
Indian political leader
When asked what he thought of Western civilization
> I think it would be an excellent idea.
>> Attr.

Garrod, Heathcote William (1878–1960)
English scholar, academic and essayist
In response to criticism that, during World War I, he was not fighting to defend civilization
> Madam, I am the civilization they are fighting to defend.
>> In Balsdon, *Oxford Now and Then* (1970)

Gauguin, Paul (1848–1903)
French Post-Impressionist painter
> Civilization is paralysis.
>> In Cournos, *Modern Plutarch* (1928)

Hillary, Sir Edmund (1919–)
New Zealand mountaineer, explorer and apiarist
> There is precious little in civilization to appeal to a Yeti.
>> *The Observer*, 1960

Hugo, Victor (1802–1885)
French poet, writer, dramatist and politician
> *Jésus a pleuré, Voltaire a souri; c'est de cette larme divine et de ce sourire humain qu'est faite la douceur de la civilisation actuelle.*
> Jesus cried; Voltaire smiled. From that divine tear, from that human smile was born the sweetness of civilisation today.
>> Centenary oration on Voltaire, 1878

James, William (1842–1910)
US psychologist and philosopher
> Our civilization is founded on the shambles, and every individual existence goes out in a lonely spasm of helpless agony.
>> *Varieties of Religious Experience* (1902)

Knox, Ronald (1888–1957)
English Catholic priest and biblical translator
> It is so stupid of modern civilization to have

given up believing in the devil when he is the only explanation of it.
>> Attr.

Levi, Carlo (1902–1975)
Italian writer and journalist
> And I thought with affectionate anguish of that motionless time, of that dark civilization that I had abandoned.
>> *Christ stopped at Eboli* (1945)

Mansfield, Katherine (1888–1923)
New Zealand writer
> How idiotic civilization is! Why be given a body if you have to keep it shut up in a case like a rare, rare fiddle?
>> *Bliss and Other Stories* (1920)

Mill, John Stuart (1806–1873)
English philosopher, economist and reformer
> I am not aware that any community has a right to force another to be civilized.
>> *On Liberty* (1859)

Paglia, Camille (1947–)
US academic and writer
> If civilisation had been left in female hands, we would still be living in grass huts.
>> *Sex, Art and American Culture: Essays* (1992)

Pankhurst, Emmeline (1858–1928)
English suffragette
> If civilization is to advance at all in the future, it must be through the help of women, women freed of their political shackles, women with full power to work their will in society.
>> *My Own Story* (1914)

Park, Mungo (1771–1806)
Scottish explorer, writer and physician
Remark on finding a gibbet in an unexplored part of Africa
> The sight of it gave me infinite pleasure, as it proved that I was in a civilized society.
>> Attr.

Popper, Sir Karl (1902–1994)
Austrian-born British philosopher
> Our civilization ... has not yet fully recovered from the shock of its birth – the transition from the tribal or 'closed society', with its submission to magical forces, to the 'open society' which sets free the critical powers of man.
>> *The Open Society and its Enemies* (1945)

Rand, Ayn (1905–1982)
Russian-born US writer
> Civilization is the progress toward a society of privacy. The savage's whole existence is public, ruled by the laws of his tribe. Civilization is the process of setting man free from men.
>> *The Fountainhead* (1943)

Rogers, Will (1879–1935)
US humorist, actor, rancher, writer and wit
> You can't say civilization don't advance, however, for in every war they kill you a new way.
>> *New York Times*, 1929

Santayana, George (1863–1952)
Spanish-born US philosopher and writer
> Civilisation is perhaps approaching one of those long winters that overtake it from time to time. Romantic Christendom – picturesque, passionate, unhappy episode – may be coming to an end. Such a catastrophe would be no reason for despair.
>> *Characters and Opinions in the United States*

Trevelyan, G.M. (1876–1962)
English historian and writer
> Disinterested intellectual curiosity is the life blood of real civilization.
>> *English Social History* (1942)

Yeats, W.B. (1865–1939)
Irish poet, dramatist, editor, writer and senator
> A civilisation is a struggle to keep self-control.
>> *A Vision* (1925)

▶▶ CULTURE

class

Arnold, Matthew (1822–1888)
English poet, critic, essayist and educationist
> *Philistine* gives the notion of something particularly stiff-necked and perverse in the resistance to light and its children; and therein it specially suits our middle class.
>> *Culture and Anarchy* (1869

> I often, therefore, when I want to distinguish clearly the aristocratic class from the Philistines proper, or middle class, name the former, in my own mind, the Barbarians.
>> *Culture and Anarchy* (1869)

> But that vast portion, lastly, of the working-class which, raw and half-developed, has long lain half-hidden amidst its poverty and squalor, and is now issuing from its hiding-place to assert an Englishman's heaven-born privilege of doing as he likes, and is beginning to perplex us by marching where it likes, meeting where it likes, bawling what it likes, breaking what it likes – to this vast residuum we may with great propriety give the name of Populace.
>> *Culture and Anarchy* (1869)

> One has often wondered whether upon the whole earth there is anything so unintelligent, so unapt to perceive how the world is really going,

as an ordinary young Englishman of our upper class.
>> *Culture and Anarchy* (1869)

Ashford, Daisy (1881–1972)
English child author
> My dear Clincham, The bearer of this letter is an old friend of mine not quite the right side of the blanket as they say in fact he is the son of a first rate butcher but his mother was a decent family called Hyssopps of the Glen so you see he is not so bad and is desireus of being the correct article.
>> *The Young Visiters* (1919)

Belloc, Hilaire (1870–1953)
English writer of verse, essayist and critic; Liberal MP
> Like many of the Upper Class
> He liked the Sound of Broken Glass.
>> *New Cautionary Tales* (1930)

Brenan, Gerald (1894–1987)
English writer
> Poets and painters are outside the class system, or rather they constitute a special class of their own, like the circus people and the gipsies.
>> *Thoughts in a Dry Season* (1978)

Brough, Robert Barnabas (1828–1860)
English journalist and writer
> My Lord Tomnoddy is thirty-four;
> The Earl can last but a few years more.
> My Lord in the Peers will take his place:
> Her Majesty's councils his words will grace.
> Office he'll hold and patronage sway;
> Fortunes and lives he will vote away;
> And what are his qualifications? – ONE!
> He's the Earl of Fitzdotterel's eldest son.
>> 'My Lord Tomnoddy' (1855)

Brougham, Lord Henry (1778–1868)
Scottish politician, abolitionist and journalist
> The great Unwashed.
>> Attr.

Burgess, Anthony (1917–1993)
English writer, linguist and composer
> Without class differences, England would cease to be the living theatre it is.
>> Remark, 1985

Calverley, C.S. (1831–1884)
English poet, parodist, scholar and lawyer
> For I've read in many a novel that, unless they've souls that grovel,
> Folks prefer in fact a hovel to your dreary marble halls.
>> 'In the Gloaming' (1872)

Cartland, Barbara (1902–2000)
English writer
When asked in a radio interview whether she thought that

British class barriers had broken down
> Of course they have, or I wouldn't be sitting here talking to someone like you.
> *In J. Cooper, Class (1979)*

Chelsea, Jenny, Viscountess
Introducing a seminar on upper class behaviour
> So many people don't know how to behave at a shooting party.
> *The Observer, 1998*

Curzon, Lord (1859–1925)
English statesman and scholar
On seeing some soldiers bathing
> I never knew the lower classes had such white skins.
> *Attr.*

Defoe, Daniel (c.1661–1731)
English writer and critic
> He bid me observe ... that the calamities of life were shared among the upper and lower part of mankind; but that the middle station had the fewest disasters.
> *The Life and Adventures of Robinson Crusoe (1719)*

Doyle, Roddy (1958–)
Irish writer
> 'You're working class, right?'
> 'We would be if there was any work.'
> *The Commitments (film, 1991)*

Edward, Prince (1964–)
Son of Queen Elizabeth II
> We are forever being told we have a rigid class structure. That's a load of codswallop.
> *Daily Mail, 1996*

Elizabeth, the Queen Mother (1900–)
Queen of the United Kingdom and mother of Elizabeth II
> My favourite programme is 'Mrs Dale's Diary'. I try never to miss it because it is the only way of knowing what goes on in a middle-class family.
> *Attr.*

Engels, Friedrich (1820–1895)
German socialist and political philosopher
> The history of all hitherto existing society is the history of class struggles.
> *The Communist Manifesto (1848)*

Friel, Brian (1929–)
Irish dramatist and writer
> The result is that people with a culture of poverty suffer much less repression than we of the middle-class suffer and indeed, if I may make the suggestion with due qualification, they often have a lot more fun than we have.
> *The Freedom of the City (1973)*

Hailsham, Quintin Hogg, Baron (1907–)
English Conservative politician and Lord Chancellor
> I don't see any harm in being middle class, I've been middle class all my life and have benefited from it.
> *The Observer, 1983*

Hope, Anthony (1863–1933)
English writer, dramatist and lawyer
> 'Bourgeois, ' I observed, 'is an epithet which the riff-raff apply to what is respectable, and the aristocracy to what is decent.'
> *The Dolly Dialogues (1894)*

Howard, Philip (1933–)
English journalist
> Every time an Englishman opens his mouth, he enables other Englishmen if not to despise him, at any rate to place him in some social and class pigeonhole.
> *The Times, 1992*

Iphicrates (419–353 BC)
Athenian general
Responding to a descendant of Harmodius (an Athenian hero), who had mocked Iphicrates for being the son of a shoemaker
> The difference between us is that my family begins with me, whereas yours ends with you.
> *Attr.*

Lawrence, D.H. (1885–1930)
English writer, poet and critic
> How beastly the bourgeois is
> especially the male of the species.
> *Pansies (1929), 'How Beastly the Bourgeois Is'*

Lerner, Alan Jay (1918–1986)
US lyricist and screenwriter
> An Englishman's way of speaking absolutely classifies him.
> *My Fair Lady (1956)*

Lewis, John Llewellyn (1880–1969)
> I'm not interested in classes ... Far be it from me to foster inferiority complexes among the workers by trying to make them think they belong to some special class. That has happened in Europe but it hasn't happened here yet.
> *In A.M. Schlesinger Jr., The Coming of the New Deal*

Lillie, Beatrice (1894–1989)
Canadian-born English actress
Commenting on her childhood in Toronto
> We were located half way up the social ladder. Or half way down. It depends on which way you're looking.
> *The Toronto Star, 1989*

Macneice, Louis (1907–1963)
Belfast-born poet, writer, radio producer, translator and critic
> Take, for instance, the question of class. There were many undergraduates like myself who theoretically conceded that all men were equal, but who, in practice, while only too willing to

converse, or attempt to, with say Normandy peasants or shopkeepers, would wince away in their own college halls from those old grammar school boys who with impure vowels kept admiring Bernard Shaw or Noël Coward while grabbing their knives and forks like dumb-bells.

The Saturday Book (1961)

Marx, Karl (1818–1883)
German political philosopher and economist; founder of Communism

What I did that was new was prove ... that the class struggle necessarily leads to the dictatorship of the proletariat.

Letter, 1852

Mikes, George (1912–1987)
Hungarian-born British writer

The one class you do not belong to and are not proud of at all is the lower-middle class. No one ever describes himself as belonging to the lower-middle class.

How to be an Inimitable

Parsons, Tony (1953–)
British journalist and author

The working class has come a long way in recent years, all of it downhill. They look like one big Manson family.

Arena, 1989

Of the working class in the 1980s

They are the real class traitors, betrayers of the men who fought the Second World War, those men who fought for Churchill but voted for Clement Attlee. But in the tattooed jungle they have no sense of history. The true unruly children of Thatcherism, they know their place and wallow in their peasanthood.

Arena, 1989

Rattigan, Terence (1911–1977)
English dramatist and screenwriter

You can be in the Horse Guards and still be common, dear.

Separate Tables (1955)

Renard, Jules (1864–1910)
French writer and dramatist

Les bourgeois, ce sont les autres.
The bourgeois are other people.

Journal, 1890

Scargill, Arthur (1941–)
English trade union leader
On John Prescott's description of himself as middle class

I have little or no time for people who aspire to be members of the middle class.

Remark at the launch of the Socialist Labour Party, 1996

Scott, Walter-Montagu-Douglas, Duke of Buccleuch (1923–)
British Conservative politician and landowner

On the proposal to ban hunting in Scotland

This is 95 per cent about class warfare and 5 per cent animal welfare.

In *The Observer*, 1999

Sitwell, Sir Osbert (1892–1969)
English poet and writer

The British Bourgeoisie
Is not born,
And does not die,
But, if it is ill,
It has a frightened look in its eyes.

'At the House of Mrs Kinfoot' (1921)

Stanton, Elizabeth Cady (1815–1902)
US suffragist, abolitionist, feminist, editor and writer

It is impossible for one class to appreciate the wrongs of another.

In Anthony and Gage, *History of Woman Suffrage* (1881)

Thatcher, Margaret (1925–)
English Conservative Prime Minister

The charm of Britain has always been the ease with which one can move into the middle class.

The Observer, 1974

Theroux, Paul (1941–)
US writer

The ship follows Soviet custom: it is riddled with class distinctions so subtle, it takes a trained Marxist to appreciate them.

The Great Railway Bazaar (1975)

Thiers, Louis Adolphe (1797–1877)
French statesman and historian
Defending his social status after someone had remarked that his mother had been a cook

She was – but I assure you that she was a very bad cook.

Attr.

Thompson, E.P. (1924–1993)
English historian

I am seeking to rescue the poor stockinger, the Luddite cropper, the 'obsolete' handloom weaver, the 'utopian' artisan, and even the deluded follower of Joanna Southcott, from the enormous condescension of posterity.

The Making of the English Working Class, quoted in *The Guardian*

Waugh, Auberon (1939–)
English writer and critic

The mistake in voting Labour, as 13.5 million people so foolishly did in 1997, was that it gave the wrong sort of people ideas above themselves.

The Observer, 1999

Wilde, Oscar (1854–1900)
Irish poet, dramatist, writer, critic and wit

Really, if the lower orders don't set us a good example, what on earth is the use of them? They seem, as a class, to have absolutely no sense of moral responsibility.

The Importance of Being Earnest (1895)

Wran, Neville Kenneth (1926–)
Australian lawyer and politician
> There's what being in the working-class is all about – how to get out of it.

Sydney Morning Herald, 1982

▶▶ ARISTOCRACY; EQUALITY; SNOBBERY

cloning

Anonymous
After Scottish scientists pioneered the cloning of a sheep, Dolly.
> There'll never be another ewe? Don't count on it!

Newspaper headline, 1997

Marchi, John (1948–)
After Scottish scientists pioneered the cloning of a sheep, Dolly.
> We ought not to permit a cottage industry in the God business.

The Guardian, 1997

clubs

Dickens, Charles (1812–1870)
English writer
Of the House of Commons
> I think … that it is the best club in London.

Our Mutual Friend (1865)

Johnson, Samuel (1709–1784)
English lexicographer, poet, critic, conversationalist and essayist
> Boswell is a very clubbable man.

In Boswell, *The Life of Samuel Johnson* (1791)

Marx, Groucho (1895–1977)
US comedian
> Please accept my resignation. I don't want to belong to any club that would have me as a member.

Groucho and Me (1959)

Mortimer, John (1923–)
English lawyer, dramatist and writer
> One enlightened member said that in the past the Garrick Club excluded lunatics, gays and women: now the first two classes have been let in there's no conceivable reason to bar the third.

Attr.

Surtees, R.S. (1805–1864)
English writer
> Every man shouting in proportion to the amount of his subscription.

Jorrock's Jaunts and Jollities (1838)

Wilde, Oscar (1854–1900)
Irish poet, dramatist, writer, critic and wit
Refusing to attend a function at a club whose members were hostile to him
> I should be like a lion in a cage of savage Daniels.

Attr.

▶▶ BOREDOM

coffee

Chelebi, Katib (1609–1657)
> Coffee is a cold dry food, suited to the ascetic life and sedative of lust.

In G.L. Lewis (trans.), *The Balance of Truth* (1957)

Lynch, David (1947–)
US film director
> Damned fine cup of coffee!

Frequent remark by Agent Dale Cooper in *Twin Peaks* TV series (1989–91)

Pope, Alexander (1688–1744)
English poet, translator and editor
> Coffee, which makes the politician wise, And see through all things with his half-shut eyes.

The Rape of the Lock (1712)

Thackeray, William Makepeace (1811–1863)
Indian-born English writer
> Why do they always put mud into coffee on board steamers? Why does the tea generally taste of boiled boots?

The Kickleburys on the Rhine (1850)

Twain, Mark (1835–1910)
US humorist, writer, journalist and lecturer
> The best coffee in Europe is Vienna coffee, compared to which all other coffee is fluid poverty.

Greatly Exaggerated

comedy

Carter, Angela (1940–1992)
English writer
> Comedy is tragedy that happens to *other* people.

Wise Children (1991)

Chaplin, Charlie (1889–1977)
English comedian, film actor, director and satirist
> All I need to make a comedy is a park, a
> policeman and a pretty girl.
>> *My Autobiography* (1964)

> I remain just one thing, and one thing only – and
> that is a clown. It places me on a far higher
> plane than any politician.
>> *The Observer*, 1960

Feldman, Marty (1933–1982)
English comedian
> Comedy, like sodomy, is an unnatural act.
>> *The Times*, 1969

Molière (1622–1673)
French dramatist, actor and director
> *C'est une étrange entreprise que celle de faire rire les*
> *honnêtes gens.*
> It's a strange job, making decent people laugh.
>> *L'Ecole des Femmes* (1662)

Priestley, J.B. (1894–1984)
English writer, dramatist and critic
> Comedy, we may say, is society protecting itself
> – with a smile.
>> *George Meredith* (1926)

Rivers, Joan (1937–)
US comedian
> My routines come out of total unhappiness. My
> audiences are my group therapy.
>> Television program, BBC2, 23 February 1990

Rogers, Will (1879–1935)
US humorist, actor, rancher, writer and wit
> A comedian can only last till he either takes
> himself serious or his audience takes him
> serious.
>> Newspaper article, 1931

commercialism

Miller, Arthur (1915–)
US dramatist and screenwriter
> When any creativity becomes useful, it is sucked
> into the vortex of commercialism, and when a
> thing becomes commercial, it becomes the
> enemy of man.
>> *The New Yorker*, 1961

Vidal, Gore (1925–)
US writer, critic and poet
> Commercialism is doing well that which should
> not be done at all.
>> *Listener* (1975)

▶▶ BUSINESS; ECONOMICS; MONEY

commitment

Navratilova, Martina (1956–)
US tennis player
> Do you know the difference between involvement
> and commitment? Think of ham and eggs. The
> chicken is involved. The pig is committed.
>> *The Observer*, 1982

commonsense

Descartes, René (1596–1650)
French philosopher and mathematician
> *Le bon sens est la chose du monde la mieux partagée,*
> *car chacun pense en être bien pourvu.*
> Common sense is the best distributed thing in
> the world, for we all think we possess a good
> share of it.
>> *Discours de la Méthode* (1637)

Einstein, Albert (1879–1955)
German-born US mathematical physicist
> Common sense is the collection of prejudices
> acquired by age eighteen.
>> Attr.

Emerson, Ralph Waldo (1803–1882)
US poet, essayist, transcendentalist and teacher
> Nothing astonishes men so much as common-
> sense and plain dealing.
>> 'Art' (1841)

La Bruyère, Jean de (1645–1696)
French satirist
> *Entre le bon sens et le bon goût il y a la différence de*
> *la cause et son effet.*
> Between good sense and good taste there is the
> same difference as between cause and effect.
>> *Les caractères ou les moeurs de ce siècle* (1688)

Salisbury, Lord (1830–1903)
English Conservative Prime Minister
> No lesson seems to be so deeply inculcated by
> the experience of life as that you never should
> trust experts. If you believe the doctors, nothing
> is wholesome: if you believe the theologians,
> nothing is innocent: if you believe the soldiers,
> nothing is safe. They all require to have their
> strong wine diluted by a very large admixture of
> insipid common sense.
>> Letter to Lord Lytton, 1877

communism

Attlee, Clement (1883–1967)
English statesman and Prime Minister

Russian Communism is the illegitimate child of Karl Marx and Catherine the Great.

The Observer, 1956

Bevan, Aneurin (1897–1960)
Welsh Labour politician, miner and orator
Of the Communist Party

Its relationship to democratic institutions is that of the death watch beetle – it is not a Party, it is a conspiracy.

Attr.

Churchill, Sir Winston (1874–1965)
English Conservative Prime Minister

Beware, for the time may be short. A shadow has fallen across the scenes so lately lighted by the Allied victory. Nobody knows what Soviet Russia and its Communist international organization intend to do in the immediate future. From Stettin in the Baltic to Trieste in the Adriatic an Iron Curtain has descended across the Continent.

Speech, Fulton, Missouri, March 1946

Elliott, Ebenezer (1781–1849)
English poet and merchant

What is a communist? One who hath yearnings
For equal division of unequal earnings.

Epigram, 1850

Engels, Friedrich (1820–1895)
German socialist and political philosopher

A spectre is haunting Europe – the spectre of Communism.

The Communist Manifesto (1848)

Gallacher, William (1881–1965)
Scottish Communist politician

We are for our own people. We want to see them happy, healthy and wise, drawing strength from cooperation with the peoples of other lands, but also contributing their full share to the general well-being. Not a broken-down pauper and mendicant, but a strong, living partner in the progressive advancement of civilization.

The Case for Communism (1949)

Khrushchev, Nikita (1894–1971)
Russian statesman and Premier of the USSR
On the possibility that the Soviet Union might one day reject communism

Those who wait for that must wait until a shrimp learns to whistle.

Attr.

Lenin, V.I. (1870–1924)
Russian revolutionary, Marxist theoretician and first leader of the USSR

Communism is Soviet power plus the electrification of the whole country.

Report at the Congress of Soviets, 1920

McCarthy, Joseph (1908–1957)
US Republican politician

I have here in my hand a list of two hundred and five people that were known to the Secretary of State as being members of the Communist Party and who nevertheless are still working and shaping the policy of the State Department.

Speech, Wheeling, West Virginia, Febuary 9, 1950

Of someone alleged to have communist sympathies

It makes me sick, sick, sick way down inside.

In Lewis, *The Fifties* (1978)

On how to spot a communist

It looks like a duck, walks like a duck, and quacks like a duck.

Attr.

Mencken, H.L. (1880–1956)
US writer, critic, philologist and satirist

The trouble with Communism is the Communists, just as the trouble with Christianity is the Christians.

Life, 1946

Morley, Robert (1908–1992)
British actor

There's no such thing in Communist countries as a load of old cod's wallop, the cod's wallop is always fresh made.

Punch, 1974

Rogers, Will (1879–1935)
US humorist, actor, rancher, writer and wit

Communism is like prohibition, it's a good idea but it won't work.

Weekly Articles (1981)

Smith, F.E. (1872–1930)
English politician and Lord Chancellor
On Bolshevism

Nature has no cure for this sort of madness, though I have known a legacy from a rich relative work wonders.

Law, Life and Letters (1927)

Solzhenitsyn, Alexander (1918–)
Russian writer, dramatist and historian

For us in Russia, communism is a dead dog, while for many people in the West, it is still a living lion.

The Listener, 1979

Spark, Muriel (1918–)
English novelist

Every communist has a fascist frown, every fascist a communist smile.

The Girls of Slender Means

Stalin, Joseph (1879–1953)
Soviet Communist leader

The party is the rallying-point for the best elements of the working class.

Attr.

Taylor, A.J.P. (1906–1990)

English historian, writer, broadcaster and lecturer

Communism continued to haunt Europe as a spectre – a name men gave to their own fears and blunders. But the crusade against Communism was even more imaginary than the spectre of Communism.

The Origins of the Second World War (1961)

▶▶ CAPITALISM; SOCIALISM

company

Austen, Jane (1775–1817)

English writer

'My idea of good company, Mr Elliot, is the company of clever, well-informed people, who have a great deal of conversation; that is what I call good company.' 'You are mistaken, ' said he gently, 'that is not good company; that is the best.'

Persuasion (1818)

Cervantes, Miguel de (1547–1616)

Spanish writer and dramatist

Tell me the company you keep, and I'll tell you who you are.

Don Quixote, II (1615)

Chesterfield, Lord (1694–1773)

English politician and letter writer

Take the tone of the company you are in.

Letter to his son, 1747

Machiavelli (1469–1527)

Florentine statesman, political theorist and historian

And they are right, those who say that bad company leads to the gallows.

The Mandrake (1518)

Proust, Marcel (1871–1922)

French writer and critic

I have sometimes regretted living so close to Marie – because I may be very fond of her, but I am not quite so fond of her company.

Sodome et Gomorrhe (1922)

Shakespeare, William (1564–1616)

English dramatist, poet and actor

Company, villainous company, hath been the spoil of me.

Henry IV, Part 1, III.iii

compassion

The Bible (King James Version)

Blessed are the merciful: for they shall obtain mercy.

Matthew, 5: 7

Blake, William (1757–1827)

English poet, engraver, painter and mystic

Can I see anothers woe,
And not be in sorrow too?
Can I see anothers grief,
And not seek for kind relief?

Songs of Innocence (1789)

Can I see another's woe,
And not be in sorrow too?
Can I see another's grief,
And not seek for kind relief?

'On Another's Sorrow' (1789)

Bradford, John (c.1510–1555)

English Protestant martyr and writer

Remark on criminals going to the gallows

But for the grace of God there goes John Bradford.

Attr.

Burns, Robert (1759–1796)

Scottish poet and song writer

Then gently scan your brother man,
Still gentler sister woman;
Tho' they may gang a kennin wrang,
To step aside is human.

'Address to the Unco Guid' (1786)

Chaucer, Geoffrey (c.1340–1400)

English poet, public servant and courtier

For pitee renneth soone in gentil herte.

The Canterbury Tales (1387)

Cromwell, Oliver (1599–1658)

English general, statesman and Puritan leader

The dimensions of this mercy are above my thoughts. It is, for aught I know, a crowning mercy.

Letter to William Lenthall, 1651

Dalai Lama (1935–)

Compassion and love are not mere luxuries. As the source of both inner and external peace, they are fundamental to the continued survival of our species.

The Times, June 1999

Desmoulins, Camille (1760–1794)

French pamphleteer, orator and revolutionary

La clémence aussi est une mesure révolutionnaire.
Clemency is also a revolutionary measure.

Speech, 1793

Eliot, George (1819–1880)

English writer and poet
> We hand folks over to God's mercy, and show none ourselves.
>> *Adam Bede* (1859)

Gay, John (1685–1732)
English poet, dramatist and librettist
> He best can pity who has felt the woe.
>> *Dione* (1720)

Gibbon, Edward (1737–1794)
English historian, politician and memoirist
> Our sympathy is cold to the relation of distant misery.
>> *Decline and Fall of the Roman Empire* (1788)

Hopkins, Gerard Manley (1844–1889)
English Jesuit priest, poet and classicist
> My own heart let me more have pity on; let
> Me live to my sad self hereafter kind,
> Charitable; not live this tormented mind
> With this tormented mind tormenting yet.
>> 'My own Heart let me more have Pity on' (c.1885)

Huxley, Aldous (1894–1963)
English writer, poet and critic
> She was a machine-gun riddling her hostess with sympathy.
>> *Mortal Coils* (1922)

Kinnock, Neil (1942–)
Welsh Labour politician
> Compassion is not a sloppy, sentimental feeling for people who are underprivileged or sick ... it is an absolutely practical belief that, regardless of a person's background, ability or ability to pay, he should be provided with the best that society has to offer.
>> Maiden speech, House of Commons, 1970

Lazarus, Emma (1849–1887)
US poet and translator
> Give me your tired, your poor,
> Your huddled masses yearning to breathe free.
>> 'The New Colossus' (1883); verse inscribed on the Statue of Liberty

Nietzsche, Friedrich Wilhelm (1844–1900)
German philosopher, critic and poet
> *Mitleiden äussern wird als ein Zeichen der Verachtung empfunden, weil man ersichtlich aufgehört hat, ein Gegenstand der Furcht zu sein, sobald einem Mitleiden erwiesen wird.*
> To show pity is felt to be a sign of scorn, because one has obviously stopped being an object of fear as soon as one is pitied.
>> *Human, All too Human* (1886)

Richardson, Samuel (1689–1761)
English novelist
> Pity is but one remove from love.
>> *The History of Sir Charles Grandison* (1754)

Shakespeare, William (1564–1616)
English dramatist, poet and actor
> The quality of mercy is not strain'd;
> It droppeth as the gentle rain from heaven
> Upon the place beneath. It is twice blest:
> It blesseth him that gives and him that takes.
>> *The Merchant of Venice*, IV.i

> Is there no pity sitting in the clouds
> That sees into the bottom of my grief?
>> *Romeo and Juliet*, III.v

Smollett, Tobias (1721–1771)
Scottish writer, satirist, historian, traveller and physician
> Any man of humane sentiments ... would have been prompted to offer his services to the forlorn stranger: but ... our hero was devoid of all these infirmities of human nature.
>> *The Adventures of Ferdinand Count Fathom* (1753)

Villon, François (1431–1485)
> *Frères humains qui après nous vivez,*
> *N'ayez les coeurs contre nous endurcis,*
> *Car, si pitié de nous pauvres avez,*
> *Dieu en aura plus tôt de vous mercis ...*
> *Mais priez Dieu que tous nous veuille absoudre!*
> Brothers in humanity who live after us, don't let your hearts be hardened against us, for, if you take pity on us poor souls, God will be more likely to have mercy on you. But pray to God that he may be willing to absolve us all!
>> 'Ballad of the Hanged Men' (1462)

Virgil (70–19 BC)
Roman poet
> *Non ignara mali miseris succurrere disco.*
> No stranger to misery myself, I am learning to befriend the wretched.
>> *Aeneid*

White, Patrick (1912–1990)
English-born Australian writer and dramatist
> And remember Mother's practical ethics: *one can drown in compassion if one answers every call it's another way of suicide.*
>> *The Eye of the Storm* (1973)

Wilde, Oscar (1854–1900)
Irish poet, dramatist, writer, critic and wit
> I can sympathize with everything, except suffering.
>> *The Picture of Dorian Gray* (1891)

> Anybody can sympathise with the sufferings of a friend, but it requires a very fine nature to sympathise with a friend's success.
>> 'The Soul of Man under Socialism' (1881)

competence

Peter, Laurence J. (1919–1990)
Canadian educationist and writer
> Competence, like truth, beauty and contact lenses, is in the eye of the beholder.
>
> *The Peter Principle* (1969)

complaint

Berkeley, Bishop George (1685–1753)
Irish philosopher and scholar
> We have first raised a dust and then complain we cannot see.
>
> *A Treatise Concerning the Principles of Human Knowledge* (1710)

Disraeli, Benjamin (1804–1881)
English statesman and writer
> Never complain, never explain.
>
> Attr.

Gilmore, Dame Mary (1865–1962)
> Never admit the pain,
> Bury it deep;
> Only the weak complain,
> Complaint is cheap.
>
> *The Wild Swan* (1930)

Marx, Groucho (1895–1977)
US comedian
> I want to register a complaint. Do you know who sneaked into my room at three o'clock this morning? – Who?
> Nobody, and that's my complaint.
>
> *Monkey Business* (film, 1931)

Melbourne, Lord (1779–1848)
English statesman
After his dismissal by William IV
> I have always thought complaints of ill-usage contemptible, whether from a seduced disappointed girl or a turned out Prime Minister.
>
> In a letter from Emily Eden to Mrs Lister, 1834

Saki (1870–1916)
Burmese-born British writer
> There are so many things to complain of in this household that it would never have occurred to me to complain of rheumatism.
>
> *The Chronicles of Clovis* (1911)

Scott, Robert Falcon (1868–1912)
English explorer
> We took risks, we knew we took them; things have come out against us, and therefore we have no cause for complaint.
>
> 'The Last Message' in *Scott's Last Expedition* (1913)

Semple, Robert (1873–1955)
New Zealand politician
A favourite term of abuse for whingeing complainants or opponents
> Snivelling snufflebusters.
>
> A Semple-ism, first recorded 1905

computers

Adams, Joey (b. 1911)
US comedian and author
> The computer can do more work faster than a human because it doesn't have to answer the phone.
>
> Attr.

Adams, Scott (1957–)
US cartoonist
> Methods for predicting the future:
> 1) read horoscopes, tea leaves, tarot cards, or crystal balls … collectively known as 'nutty methods';
> 2) put well-researched facts into sophisticated computer … commonly referred to as 'a complete waste of time'.
>
> *The Dilbert Future*

Anderson, Jeremy S.
> There are two major products that come out of Berkeley: LSD and UNIX. We don't believe this to be a coincidence.
>
> Attr.

Anonymous
> Putting a computer in front of a child and expecting it to teach him is like putting a book under his pillow, only more expensive.

> Applying computer technology is simply finding the right wrench to pound in the correct screw.

> WARNING: Keyboard Not Attached. Press F10 to Continue.

> Press any key … no, no, no, NOT THAT ONE!

> What goes up must come down. Ask any system administrator.

> Intel has announced its next chip: the Repentium.

> I speak BASIC to clients, 1-2-3 to management, and mumble to myself.

> A program is a spell cast over a computer, turning input into error messages.

> There are two ways to write error-free programs. Only the third one works.

Any given program, when running, is obsolete.

Laws of Computer Programming I

Any given program costs more and takes longer.

Laws of Computer Programming II

If a program is useful, it will have to be changed.

Laws of Computer Programming, III

If a program is useless, it will have to be documented.

Laws of Computer Programming, IV

Any program will expand to fill available memory.

Laws of Computer Programming, V

The value of a program is proportional to the weight of its output.

Laws of Computer Programming, VI

Program complexity grows until it exceeds the capabilities of the programmer who must maintain it.

Laws of Computer Programming, VII

Any non-trivial program contains at least one bug.

Laws of Computer Programming, VIII

Undetectable errors are infinite in variety, in contrast to detectable errors, which by definition are limited.

Laws of Computer Programming, IX

Adding manpower to a late software project makes it later.

Laws of Computer Programming, X

If a computer cable has one end, then it has another.

Lyall's Conjecture

Avishai, Bernard

The danger from computers is not that they will eventually get as smart as men, but we will meanwhile agree to meet them halfway.

Attr.

Bush, Vannevar (1890–1974)
US engineer and physicist

The world has arrived at an age of cheap complex devices of great reliability, and something is bound to come of it.

Attr.

Crichton, Michael (1942–)
US writer

In the information society, nobody thinks. We expect to banish paper, but we actually banish thought.

Jurassic Park (1991)

Cringely, Robert X. (1953–)
US computer journalist and author

If the automobile had followed the same development cycle as the computer, a Rolls-Royce would today cost $100, get one million miles to the gallon, and explode once a year, killing everyone inside.

Attr.

Dawkins, Richard (1941–)
English biologist and author

Personally, I rather look forward to a computer program winning the world chess championship. Humanity needs a lesson in humility.

Attr.

Gates, Bill (1955–)
US businessman; co-founder of Microsoft Corporation

The past twenty years have been an incredible adventure for me. It started on a day when, as a college sophomore, I stood in Harvard Square with my friend Paul Allen and pored over the description of a kit computer in *Popular Electronics* magazine.

Attr.

Hawking, Stephen (1942–)
English theoretical physicist

I think computer viruses should count as life. I think it says something about human nature that the only form of life we have created so far is purely destructive. We've created life in our own image.

Attr.

Kulawiec, Rich

Any sufficiently advanced bug is indistinguishable from a feature.

Attr.

Minor, Janet
US poet

I have a spelling checker
It came with my PC;
It plainly marks four my revue
Mistakes I cannot sea.
I've run this poem threw it,
I'm sure your pleased too no,
Its letter perfect in it's weigh,
My checker tolled me sew.

Attr.

Ondaatje, Michael (1943–)
Canadian writer
Comment after accepting a computer at the Wang International Festival of Authors; the author writes with a fountain pen

I think giving this computer to the last Luddite is ridiculous. It's like giving a Porsche to someone who just discovered the bicycle.

Attr.

Salomom, Dan

Sometimes it pays to stay in bed on Monday,

rather than spending the rest of the week debuging Monday's code.

Attr.

Segal, Erich (1937–)
US academic
> The OED database is one of the wonders of the modern world – to paraphrase Christopher Marlowe, 'infinite riches in a little ROM'.
> *The Times Literary Supplement, 1992*

Stoll, Clifford
> Why is it drug addicts and computer afficionados are both called users?
> *Attr.*

Stroustrup, Bjarne (1950–)
Danish computer scientist
> C makes it easy to shoot yourself in the foot. C++ makes it harder, but when you do, it blows away your whole leg.
> *Attr.*

Watson, Thomas J. (1874–1956)
The founder of IBM on the prospects for desktop computers
> I think there's a world market for about five computers.
> In Martin Moskovits, *Science and Society, 1995*

Wozniak, Steve
Co-founder of Apple Computers
> Never trust a computer you can't throw out a window.
> *Attr.*

▶▶ ARTIFICIAL INTELLIGENCE; INNOVATION; TECHNOLOGY

conception

Orton, Joe (1933–1967)
English dramatist and writer
> It's all any reasonable child can expect if the dad is present at the conception.
> *Entertaining Mr Sloane (1964)*

confession

Mitchell, Joni (1943–)
Canadian singer and songwriter
> There are things to confess that enrich the world, and things that need not be said.
> *The Independent, 1988*

conformity

Brown, Rita Mae (1944–)
US writer and poet

> I think the reward for conformity is that everyone likes you except yourself.
> *Bingo*

Mill, John Stuart (1806–1873)
English philosopher, economist and reformer
> … mere conformers to commonplace, or time-servers for truth, whose arguments on all great subjects are meant for their hearers, and are not those which have convinced themselves.
> *On Liberty (1859)*

Taylor, A.J.P. (1906–1990)
English historian, writer, broadcaster and lecturer
> All change in history, all advance, comes from nonconformity. If there had been no trouble-makers, no dissenters, we should still be living in caves.
> *The Trouble-makers*

Wilde, Oscar (1854–1900)
Irish poet, dramatist, writer, critic and wit
> He who would be free – must not conform.
> *The Fortnightly Review, 1891*

conscience

Anonymous
> Conscience is what hurts when everything else feels so good.

Bradley, Omar (1893–1981)
US general
> The world has achieved brilliance without conscience. Ours is a world of nuclear giants and ethical infants.
> Speech, Armistice Day, 1948

De Quincey, Thomas (1785–1859)
English writer
> Better to stand ten thousand sneers than one abiding pang, such as time could not abolish, of bitter self-reproach.
> *Confessions of an English Opium Eater (1822)*

Heine, Heinrich (1797–1856)
German lyric poet, essayist and journalist
> Mental torture is more readily endured, alas, than physical pain; and if I were forced to choose between a bad conscience and an aching tooth, I would settle for the bad conscience.
> *Letter on the French Stage (1837)*

Henderson, Arthur (1863–1935)
Scottish politician
> The plural of conscience is conspiracy.
> *The Independent, 1992*

Hobbes, Thomas (1588–1679)
Political philosopher

> A man's conscience and his judgement is the same thing, and as the judgement, so also the conscience, may be erroneous.
>
> *Attr.*

Mencken, H.L. (1880–1956)
US writer, critic, philologist and satirist

> Conscience is the inner voice that warns us somebody may be looking.
>
> *A Mencken Chrestomathy* (1949)

Nash, Ogden (1902–1971)
US poet

> He who is ridden by a conscience
> Worries about a lot of nonscience;
> He without benefit of scruples
> His fun and income soon quadruples.
>
> 'Reflection on the Fallibility of Nemesis' (1940)

Shakespeare, William (1564–1616)
English dramatist, poet and actor

> A peace above all earthly dignities,
> A still and quiet conscience.
>
> *Henry VIII*, III.ii

> My conscience hath a thousand several tongues,
> And every tongue brings in a several tale,
> And every tale condemns me for a villain.
>
> *Richard III*, V.iii

> Conscience is but a word that cowards use,
> Devis'd at first to keep the strong in awe.
>
> *Richard III*, V.iii

> Thus conscience does make cowards of us all;
> And thus the native hue of resolution
> Is sicklied o'er with the pale cast of thought.
>
> *Hamlet*, III:1

Sheridan, Richard Brinsley (1751–1816)
Irish dramatist, politician and orator

> Conscience has no more to do with gallantry than it has with politics.
>
> *The Duenna* (1775)

Washington, George (1732–1799)
US general, statesman and President

> Labour to keep alive in your breast that little spark of celestial fire, called conscience.
>
> *Rules of Civility and Decent Behaviour*

conservatism

Disraeli, Benjamin (1804–1881)
English statesman and writer

> Conservatism discards Prescription, shrinks from Principle, disavows Progress: having rejected all respect for antiquity, it offers no redress for the present, and makes no preparation for the future.
>
> *Coningsby* (1844)

> A sound Conservative government … Tory men and Whig measures.
>
> *Coningsby* (1844)

> It seems to me a barren thing this Conservatism – an unhappy cross-breed, the mule of politics that engenders nothing.
>
> *Coningsby* (1844)

> A Conservative government is an organized hypocrisy.
>
> *Speech, 1845*

Emerson, Ralph Waldo (1803–1882)
US poet, essayist, transcendentalist and teacher

> Men are conservatives when they are least vigorous, or when they are most luxurious. They are conservatives after dinner. … when they hear music, or when they read poetry, they are radicals.
>
> *Essays, Second Series* (1844)

Lilley, Peter
English Conservative politician

> Conservatism is not, never has been, and never will be, solely about the free market.
>
> *The Times, 1999*

Lincoln, Abraham (1809–1865)
US statesman and President

> What is conservatism? Is it not adherence to the old and tried, against the new and untried?
>
> *Speech, 1860*

Montaigne, Michel de (1533–1592)
French essayist and moralist

> *Pour les affaires publiques, il n'est aucun si mauvais train, pourvu qu'il ait de l'âge et de la constance, qui ne vaille mieux que le changement et le remuement.*
> There is, in public affairs, no state so bad, provided it has age and stability on its side, that is not preferable to change and disturbance.
>
> *Essais* (1580)

Parker, Dorothy (1893–1967)
US writer, poet, critic and wit

> You can't teach an old dogma new tricks.
>
> In R. E. Drennan, *Wit's End*

Twain, Mark (1835–1910)
US humorist, writer, journalist and lecturer

> The radical invents the views. When he has worn them out, the conservative adopts them.
>
> *Notebooks* (1935)

Watson, Sir William (1858–1936)

> The staid conservative,
> Came-over-with-the-Conqueror type of mind.
>
> 'A Study in Contrasts' (1905)

▶▶ CHANGE; CONVENTION; POLITICIANS

consistency

Berenson, Bernard (1865–1959)
Lithuanian-born US art critic
> Consistency requires you to be as ignorant today as you were a year ago.
>
> *Notebook* (1892)

Huxley, Aldous (1894–1963)
English writer, poet and critic
> Consistency is contrary to nature, contrary to life. The only completely consistent people are the dead.
>
> *Do What You Will* (1929)

Maugham, William Somerset (1874–1965)
English writer, dramatist and physician
> Like all weak men he laid an exaggerated stress on not changing one's mind.
>
> *Of Human Bondage* (1915)

Pope, Alexander (1688–1744)
English poet, translator and editor
> Some praise at morning what they blame at night;
> But always think the last opinion right.
>
> *An Essay on Criticism* (1711)

Shakespeare, William (1564–1616)
English dramatist, poet and actor
> Now the melancholy god protect thee;
> and the tailor make thy doublet of changeable taffeta, for thy mind is a very opal.
>
> *Twelfth Night*, II.iv

Whitman, Walt (1819–1892)
US poet and writer
> Do I contradict myself?
> Very well then I contradict myself,
> (I am large, I contain multitudes).
>
> 'Song of Myself' (1855)

consumer society

Galbraith, J.K. (1908–)
Canadian-born US economist, diplomat and writer
> In a community where public services have failed to keep abreast of private consumption things are very different. Here, in an atmosphere of private opulence and public squalor, the private goods have full sway.
>
> *The Affluent Society* (1958)

Gitlin, Todd
US sociologist
> There is a misunderstanding by marketers in our culture about what freedom of choice is. In the market, it is equated with multiplying choice. This is a misconception. If you have infinite choice, people are reduced to passivity.
>
> *New York Times*, 1990

Iacocca, Lee (1924–)
US businessman; President of Ford Motor Company
> People want economy and they will pay any price to get it.
>
> *New York Times*, 1974

Illich, Ivan (1926–)
Austrian-born US educator, sociologist, writer and priest
> In both rich and poor nations consumption is polarized while expectation is equalized.
>
> *Celebration of Awareness* (1970)

James, Clive (1939–)
Australian writer and broadcaster
> The last stage of fitting the product to the market is fitting the market to the product.
>
> *The Observer*, 1989

Larkin, Philip (1922–1985)
English poet, writer and librarian
> Recognising that if you haven't got the money for something you can't have it – this is a concept that's vanished for many years.
>
> Interview, *The Observer*, 1979

Marcuse, Herbert (1898–1979)
German-born US philosopher
> The people recognize themselves in their commodities; they find their soul in their automobile, hi-fi set, split-level home, kitchen equipment.
>
> *One-Dimensional Man* (1964)

Nicholson, Vivian (1936–)
Reply when asked what she would do with the £152,000 she won on the pools in 1961
> I'm going to spend, spend, spend, that's what I'm going to do.
>
> In V. Nicholson and S. Smith, *I'm Going to Spend, Spend, Spend*

Stretton, Hugh (1924–)
Australian political scientist and historian
> Is it really good for policy-makers to act as if everything has its price, and as if policies should be judged chiefly by their effects in delivering material benefits to selfish citizens? … It does not ask those individuals whether they also have other values which are not revealed by their shopping.
>
> *Capitalism, Socialism and the Environment* (1976)

Theroux, Paul (1941–)
US writer
> There must be something in the Japanese character that saves them from the despair

Americans feel in similar throes of consuming. The American, gorging himself on merchandise, develops a sense of guilty self-consciousness; if the Japanese have these doubts they do not show them. Perhaps hesitation is not part of the national character, or perhaps the ones who hesitate are trampled by the crowds of shoppers – that natural selection that capitalist society practises against the reflective.

The Great Railway Bazaar (1975)

Veblen, Thorstein (1857–1929)
US economist and sociologist
Conspicuous consumption of valuable goods is a means of reputability to the gentleman of leisure.

The Theory of the Leisure Class (1899)

▶▶ CAPITALISM; GREED; MONEY AND WEALTH; SHOPPING

contempt

Albertano of Brescia (c.1190–c.1270)
Jurist, philosopher and politician
Qui omnes despicit, omnibus displicet.
Who despises all, displeases all.

Liber Consolationis

Ashford, Daisy (1881–1972)
English child author
Ethel patted her hair and looked very sneery.

The Young Visiters (1919)

Austen, Jane (1775–1817)
English writer
She was nothing more than a mere good-tempered, civil and obliging young woman; as such we could scarcely dislike her – she was only an Object of Contempt.

Love and Freindship (1791)

Belloc, Hilaire (1870–1953)
English writer of verse, essayist and critic; Liberal MP
Godolphin Horne was Nobly Born;
He held the Human Race in Scorn –
Alas! That such Affected Tricks
Should flourish in a Child of Six!

Cautionary Tales (1907), 'Godolphin Horne'

Bierce, Ambrose (1842–c.1914)
US writer, verse writer and soldier
Contempt: The feeling of a prudent man for an enemy who is too formidable safely to be oppoosed.

The Enlarged Devil's Dictionary (1961)

Carew, Thomas (c.1595–1640)
English poet, musician and dramatist
I was foretold, your rebell sex,
Nor love, nor pitty knew.
And with what scorne, you use to vex
Poore hearts, that humbly sue.

'A deposition from love'

Chateaubriand, François-René (1768–1848)
French writer and statesman
One is not superior merely because one sees the world in an odious light.

Attr.

Congreve, William (1670–1729)
English dramatist
A little disdain is not amiss; a little scorn is alluring.

The Way of the World (1700)

Johnson, Samuel (1709–1784)
English lexicographer, poet, critic, conversationalist and essayist
Of all the griefs that harrass the distress'd,
Sure the most bitter is a scornful jest;
Fate never wounds more deep the gen'rous heart,
Than when a blockhead's insult points the dart.

London: A Poem (1738)

Paley, Rev. William (1743–1805)
English theologian and philosopher
Who can refute a sneer?

Principles of Moral and Political Philosophy (1785)

Proverb
Familiarity breeds contempt.

Roosevelt, Theodore (1858–1919)
US Republican President
The poorest way to face life is to face it with a sneer.

Attr.

Shaw, George Bernard (1856–1950)
Irish socialist, writer, dramatist and critic
I have never sneered in my life. Sneering doesn't become either the human face or the human soul.

Pygmalion (1916)

Steinbeck, John (1902–1968)
US writer
Okie use' ta mean you was from Oklahoma. Now it means you're a dirty son-of-a-bitch. Okie means you're scum. Don't mean nothing itself, it's the way they say it.

The Grapes of Wrath (1939)

▶▶ RIDICULE

contentment

Aesop (6th century BC)
Legendary Greek writer of fables

Be content with your lot; one cannot be first in everything.

Attr.

Aurelius, Marcus (121–180)
Roman emperor and Stoic philosopher
'Live with the gods'
But he is living with the gods who constantly shows them that his soul is satisfied with what is assigned to him.

Meditations

Barnes, Barnabe (c.1569–1609)
English poet
Ah, sweet Content! where doth thine harbour hold?

'Parthenophil and Parthenophe' (1593)

Burns, Robert (1759–1796)
Scottish poet and song writer
Contented wi' little and cantie wi' mair,
Whene'er I forgather wi' Sorrow and Care,
I gie them a skelp, as they're creepin alang,
Wi' a cog o' guid swats and an auld Scottish sang.

'Contented wi' Little and Cantie wi' Mair' (1794)

Cowper, William (1731–1800)
English poet, hymn and letter writer
I crown thee king of intimate delights,
Fire-side enjoyments, home-born happiness.

The Task (1785) 'The Winter Evening'

Dunbar, William (c.1460–c.1525)
Scottish poet, satirist and courtier
Gif thou has micht, be gentle and free;
And gif thou stands in povertie,
Of thine awn will to it consent;
And riches sall return to thee:
He has eneuch that is content.

'Of Content' (1834 edition)

Kipling, Rudyard (1865–1936)
Indian-born British poet and writer
The toad beneath the harrow knows
Exactly where each tooth-point goes;
The butterfly upon the road
Preaches contentment to that toad.

Departmental Ditties and Other Verses (1886)

Pope, Alexander (1688–1744)
English poet, translator and editor
Happy the man, whose wish and care
A few paternal acres bound,
Content to breathe his native air,
In his own ground.

'Ode on Solitude' (c.1700)

Traherne, Thomas (c.1637–1674)
English religious writer and clergyman
Contentment is a sleepy thing
If it in death alone must die;

A quiet mind is worse than poverty,
Unless it from enjoyment spring!

'Of Contentment'

contraception

Adler, Larry (1914–)
US musician
Vasectomy means not ever having to say you're sorry.

Attr.

Allen, Woody (1935–)
US film director, writer, actor and comedian
I want to tell you a terrific story about oral contraception. I asked this girl to sleep with me and she said 'no'.

Attr.

Anonymous
Comment made by a judge in the case of a doctor who had supplied condoms at the weekend when chemists' shops were closed
Anyone without condoms at the weekend will have to wait until Monday.

In Michael Solomon, *Pro Life?*

Remark by a delegate at the International Planned Parenthood Federation Conference
The best contraceptive is a glass of cold water: not before or after, but instead.

Lowry, Malcolm (1909–1957)
English writer and poet
Where are the children I might have had? You may suppose I might have wanted them. Drowned to the accompaniment of the rattling of a thousand douche bags.

Under the Volcano (1947)

Mencken, H.L. (1880–1956)
US writer, critic, philologist and satirist
It is now quite lawful for a Catholic woman to avoid pregnancy by a resort to mathematics, though she is still forbidden to resort to physics and chemistry.

Notebooks (1956)

Milligan, Spike (1918–)
Irish comedian and writer
Contraceptives should be used on every conceivable occasion.

The Last Goon Show of All

Russell, Dora (1894–1986)
British author and campaigner
We want far better reasons for having children than not knowing how to prevent them.

Hypatia

Sharpe, Tom (1928–)
English writer
> Skullion had little use for contraceptives at the best of times. Unnatural, he called them, and placed them in the lower social category of things along with elastic-sided boots and made-up bow ties. Not the sort of attire for a gentleman.
>> *Porterhouse Blue* (1974)

Thomas, Irene (1920–)
English writer and broadcaster
> Protestant women may take the Pill. Roman Catholic woman must keep taking *The Tablet*.
>> *The Guardian*, 1990

▶▶ SEX

controversy

Acheson, Dean (1893–1971)
US Democrat politician
> Controversial proposals, once accepted, soon become hallowed.
>> Speech, Independence, Missouri, 1962

convention

Brontë, Charlotte (1816–1855)
English writer
> Conventionality is not morality. Self-righteousness is not religion. To attack the first is not to assail the last. To pluck the mask from the face of the Pharisee, is not to lift an impious hand to the Crown of Thorns.
>> *Jane Eyre* (1847)

conversation

Achebe, Chinua (1930–)
Nigerian writer, poet and critic
> Among the Ibo the art of conversation is regarded very highly and proverbs are the palm-oil with which words are eaten.
>> *Things Fall Apart* (1958)

Ade, George (1866–1944)
US fabulist and playwright
> For parlor use, the vague generality is a life saver.
>> Attr.

Bagehot, Walter (1826–1877)
English economist and political philosopher
> The habit of common and continuous speech is a symptom of mental deficiency.
>> *Literary Studies* (1879)

Boswell, James (1740–1795)
Scottish biographer
> *Johnson*: Well, we had a good talk.
> *Boswell*: Yes, Sir; you tossed and gored several persons.
>> *The Life of Samuel Johnson* (1791)

Bryan, William Jennings (1860–1925)
US Democrat politician and editor
> An orator is a man who says what he thinks and feels what he says.
>> Attr.

Carlyle, Thomas (1795–1881)
Scottish historian, biographer, critic, and essayist
> Speech is human, silence is divine, yet also brutish and dead: therefore we must learn both arts.
>> Attr.

Churchill, Sir Winston (1874–1965)
English Conservative Prime Minister
Of Lord Charles Beresford
> He is one of those orators of whom it was well said, 'Before they get up they do not know what they are going to say; when they are speaking, they do not know what they are saying; and when they sit down, they do not know what they have said.'
>> Speech, House of Commons, 1912

> To jaw-jaw is better than to war-war.
>> Speech, Washington, 1954

Coleridge, Samuel Taylor (1772–1834)
English poet, philosopher and critic
> I am glad you came in to punctuate my discourse, which I fear has gone on for an hour without any stop at all.
>> *Table Talk* (1835), 29 June 1833

Confucius (c.550–c.478 BC)
Chinese philosopher and teacher of ethics
> For one word a man is often deemed to be wise, and for one word he is often deemed to be foolish. We should be careful indeed what we say.
>> *Analects*

Darwin, Erasmus (1731–1802)
Dutch scholar and humanist
Reply when asked whether he found his stammer inconvenient
> No, Sir, because I have time to think before I speak, and don't ask impertinent questions.
>> In Sir Francis Darwin, *Reminiscences of My Father's Everyday Life*

Disraeli, Benjamin (1804–1881)
English statesman and writer
> I grew intoxicated with my own eloquence.
>> *Contarini Fleming* (1832)

Dryden, John (1631–1700)
English poet, satirist, dramatist and critic
> But far more numerous was the herd of such
> Who think too little and who talk too much.
>> *Absalom and Achitophel* (1681)

Eliot, George (1819–1880)
English writer and poet
> Half the sorrows of women would be averted if
> they could repress the speech they know to be
> useless; nay, the speech they have resolved not
> to make.
>> *Felix Holt* (1866)

Emerson, Ralph Waldo (1803–1882)
US poet, essayist, transcendentalist and teacher
> Conversation is a game of circles. In
> conversation we pluck up the termini which
> bound the common of silence on every side.
>> *Essays, First Series* (1841)

Halifax, Lord (1633–1695)
English politician, courtier, pamphleteer and
epigrammatist
> Most Men make little other use of their Speech
> than to give evidence against their own
> Understanding.
>> 'Of Folly and Fools' (1750)

Hobbes, Thomas (1588–1679)
Political philosopher
> True and false are attributes of speech, not of
> things. And where speech is not, there is neither
> truth nor falsehood.
>> *Leviathan* (1651)

Holmes, Oliver Wendell (1809–1894)
US physician, poet, writer and scientist
> And, when you stick on conversation's burrs,
> Don't strew your pathway with those dreadful
> urs.
>> 'A Rhymed Lesson' (1848)

Johnson, Samuel (1709–1784)
English lexicographer, poet, critic, conversationalist and
essayist
> That is the happiest conversation where there is
> no competition, no vanity, but a calm quiet
> interchange of sentiments.
>> In Boswell, *The Life of Samuel Johnson* (1791)

> Questioning is not the mode of conversation
> among gentlemen.
>> In Boswell, *The Life of Samuel Johnson* (1791)

Jonson, Ben (1572–1637)
English dramatist and poet
> Talking and eloquence are not the same: to
> speak, and to speak well, are two things.
>> *Timber, or Discoveries made upon Men and Matter* (1641)

La Bruyère, Jean de (1645–1696)
French satirist

> *Il y a des gens qui parlent un moment avant que d'avoir pensé.*
> There are people who speak one moment
> before they think.
>> *Les caractères ou les moeurs de ce siècle* (1688)

Macaulay, Lord (1800–1859)
English Liberal statesman, essayist and poet
> The object of oratory alone is not truth, but
> persuasion.
>> 'Essay on Athenian Orators' (1898)

Meredith, George (1828–1909)
English writer, poet and critic
> Speech is the small change of silence.
>> *The Ordeal of Richard Feverel* (1859)

Moore, Lorrie (1957–)
US novelist
> Overheard or recorded, all marital conversation
> sounds as if someone must be joking, though
> usually no one is.
>> *Birds of America* (1998)

Morley, Robert (1908–1992)
British actor
> Beware of the conversationalist who adds 'in
> other words'. He is merely starting afresh.
>> *The Observer*, 1964

O'Brian, Patrick (1914–2000)
Irish writer
> Question and answer is not a civilized form of
> conversation.
>> *Clarissa Oakes* (1992)

Post, Emily (1873–1960)
US writer
> Ideal conversation must be an exchange of
> thought, and not, as many of those who worry
> most about their shortcomings believe, an
> eloquent exhibition of wit or oratory.
>> *Etiquette* (1922)

Proverb
> Although there exist many thousand subjects for
> elegant conversation, there are persons who
> cannot meet a cripple without talking about
> feet.
>> Chinese Proverb

Seneca (c.4 BC–AD 65)
Roman philosopher, poet, dramatist, essayist, rhetorician
and statesman
> Conversation has a kind of charm about it, an
> insinuating and insidious something that elicits
> secrets from us just like love or liquor.
>> *Epistles*

Shakespeare, William (1564–1616)
English dramatist, poet and actor
> He draweth out the thread of his verbosity finer

than the staple of his argument.

Love's Labour Lost, V.i

Smith, Sydney (1771–1845)
English clergyman, essayist, journalist and wit
One of the greatest pleasures in life is
conversation.

Essays (1877)

Talleyrand, Charles-Maurice de (1754–1838)
French statesman, memoirist and prelate
*La parole a été donnée à l'homme pour déguiser sa
pensée.*
Speech was given to man to disguise his
thoughts.

Attr.

Tannen, Deborah (1945–)
US linguist and academic
Each person's life is lived as a series of
conversations.

The Observer, 1992

Trollope, Anthony (1815–1882)
English writer, traveller and post office official
For the most of us, if we do not talk of
ourselves, or at any rate of the individual circles
of which we are the centres, we can talk of
nothing. I cannot hold with those who wish to
put down the insignificant chatter of the world.

Framley Parsonage (1860)

West, Dame Rebecca (1892–1983)
English writer, critic and feminist
There is no such thing as conversation. It is an
illusion. There are intersecting monologues, that
is all.

There is No Conversation (1935)

▶▶ SILENCE

cookery

Acton, Eliza (1799–1859)
The difference between good cookery and bad
cookery can scarcely be more strikingly shown
than in the manner in which sauces are prepared
and served.

*Modern Cookery for Private
Families* (1845)

Brillat-Savarin, Anthelme (1755–1826)
French jurist and gastronome
*La découverte d'un mets nouveau fait plus pour le
bonheur du genre humain que la découverte d'une
étoile.*
The discovery of a new dish does more for the
happiness of mankind than the discovery of a
star.

Physiologie du Goût (1825)

Cleese, John (1939–)
British comedian, actor and writer
The English contribution to world cuisine – the
chip.

A Fish Called Wanda (film, 1988)

David, Elizabeth (1913–1992)
British cookery writer
Even more than long hours in the kitchen, fine
meals require ingenious organization and
experience which is a pleasure to acquire. A
highly developed shopping sense is important,
so is some knowledge of the construction of a
menu with a view to the food in season, the
manner of cooking, the texture and colour of the
dishes to be served in relation to each other.

French Country Cooking (1951)

Delicious meals can, as everybody knows, be
cooked with the sole aid of a blackened frying-
pan over a primus stove, a camp fire, a gas-ring,
or even a methylated spirit lamp.

French Country Cooking (1951)

Fern, Fanny (Sara Payson Parton) (1811–1872)
US writer
The way to a man's heart is through his stomach.

Willis Parton

Galsworthy, John (1867–1933)
English writer and dramatist
The French cook; we open tins.

Treasury of Humorous Quotations

Gauguin, Paul (1848–1903)
French Post-Impressionist painter
Many excellent cooks are spoiled by going into
the arts.

In Cournos, *Modern Plutarch* (1928)

Harney, Bill (1895–1962)
Australian writer
Advice on bush cooking
You always want to garnish it when it's orf.

'Talkabout', c.1960

Hood, Thomas (1799–1845)
English poet, editor and humorist
Home-made dishes that drive one from home.

Miss Kilmansegg and her Precious Leg (1840)

King, William (1663–1712)
'Tis by his cleanliness a cook must please.

Art of Cookery (1708)

Landor, Walter Savage (1775–1864)
English poet and writer
Having thrown his cook out of an open window into the
flowerbed below
Good God, I forgot the violets!

In F. Muir, *An Irreverent Companion to Social History*
(1976)

Leith, Prue (1940–)
English cookery writer and businesswoman
>Cuisine is when things taste like what they are.
>>Lecture, 'The Fine Art of Food', 1987

Meredith, George (1828–1909)
English writer, poet and critic
>Kissing don't last: cookery do!
>>*The Ordeal of Richard Feverel* (1859)

Meredith, Owen (1831–1891)
English statesman and poet
>We may live without poetry, music and art;
>We may live without conscience, and live
>without heart;
>We may live without friends; we may live without
>books;
>But civilized man cannot live without cooks.
>>'Lucile' (1860)

Post, Emily (1873–1960)
US writer
>To the old saying that man built the house but
>woman made of it a 'home' might be added the
>modern supplement that woman accepted
>cooking as a chore but man has made of it a
>recreation.
>>*Etiquette* (1922)

Robinson, Robert (1927–)
>The national dish of America is menus.
>>BBC TV programme, *Robinson's Travels*, 1977

Saki (1870–1916)
Burmese-born British writer
>The cook was a good cook, as cooks go; and as
>cooks go she went.
>>*Reginald* (1904)

Sala, G.A.
>The Milanese, be it remarked, are undoubtedly
>the best cooks in Italy.
>>*The Thorough Good Cook*

Scott, Sir Walter (1771–1832)
Scottish writer and historian
>Man is a cooking animal.
>>*St Ronan's Well* (1823)

Shakespeare, William (1564–1616)
English dramatist, poet and actor
>'Tis an ill cook that cannot lick his own fingers.
>>*Romeo and Juliet*, IV.ii

Slater, Nigel
English food writer
>Cooking is about not cheating yourself of
>pleasure.
>>*Slice of Life*, BBC TV programme

Smith, Delia (1941–)
English food writer
>If you look at France now, after *nouvelle cuisine*

and all the rest, you find that they are going
crazy about what they call *cuisine grandmère*:
just like granny used to make. I suppose that's
what I'm about.
>>Interview by Libby Purves,
>>*The Times*, 1990

I truly have tried and we had a microwave to
heat things in the filming – but, actually, we
mainly use it to keep the ashtrays in. I think it
takes the soul out of food. Cooking is about
ingredients being put together, and having time
to amalgamate.
>>Interview, *The Times*, 1990

Ullman, Tracey
English comedian
>The most remarkable thing about my mother is
>that for 30 years she served nothing but
>leftovers. The original meal was never found.
>>*The Observer*, 1999

▶▶ DIETS; DINING; FOOD

the country

Broderick, John (1927–)
Irish writer
>The city dweller who passes through a country
>town, and imagines it sleepy and apathetic is
>very far from the truth: it is watchful as the
>jungle.
>>*The Pilgrimage* (1961)

Congreve, William (1670–1729)
English dramatist
>I nauseate walking; 'tis a country diversion, I
>loathe the country.
>>*The Way of the World* (1700)

Conn, Stewart (1936–)
Scottish poet
On John Muir, naturalist
>What better than a Wilderness, to liberate the
>mind.
>>*In the Blood* (1995)

Cowper, William (1731–1800)
English poet, hymn and letter writer
>God made the country, and man made the town.
>>*The Task* (1785)

Doyle, Sir Arthur Conan (1859–1930)
Scottish writer and war correspondent
>It is my belief, Watson, founded upon my
>experience, that the lowest and vilest alleys of
>London do not present a more dreadful record
>of sin than does the smiling and beautiful
>countryside.
>>'Copper Beeches' (1892)

Gibbon, Lewis Grassic (1901–1935)
> Nothing endured at all, nothing but the land …
> The land was forever, it moved and changed
> below you, but was forever.
>> *Sunset Song* (1932)

Hazlitt, William (1778–1830)
English writer and critic
> When I am in the country, I wish to vegetate like
> the country.
>> *Table-Talk* (1822)

> There is nothing good to be had in the country,
> or, if there is, they will not let you have it.
>> *The Round Table* (1817)

Hopkins, Gerard Manley (1844–1889)
English Jesuit priest, poet and classicist
> What would the world be, once bereft
> Of wet and of wildness? Let them be left,
> O let them be left, wildness and wet;
> Long live the weeds and the wilderness yet.
>> 'Inversnaid' (1881)

Kilvert, Francis (1840–1879)
English curate and diarist
> It is a fine thing to be out on the hills alone. A
> man could hardly be a beast or a fool alone on a
> great mountain.
>> *Diary*, 1871

Sackville-West, Vita (1892–1962)
English poet and novelist
> The country habit has me by the heart,
> For he's bewitched for ever who has seen,
> Not with his eyes but with his vision, Spring
> Flow down the woods and stipple leaves with
> sun.
>> 'Winter' (1926)

Smith, Sydney (1771–1845)
English clergyman, essayist, journalist and wit
> It is a place with only one post a day … In the
> country I always fear that creation will expire
> before tea-time.
>> In H. Pearson, *The Smith of Smiths*
>> (1934)

> I have no relish for the country; it is a kind of
> healthy grave.
>> Letter to Miss G. Harcourt,
>> 1838

Stevenson, Robert Louis (1850–1894)
Scottish writer, poet and essayist
> In the highlands, in the country places,
> Where the old plain men have rosy faces,
> And the young fair maidens
> Quiet eyes.
>> *Songs of Travel* (1896)

Wilde, Oscar (1854–1900)
Irish poet, dramatist, writer, critic and wit

> Anybody can be good in the country.
>> *The Picture of Dorian Gray* (1891)

▶▶ CITIES

courage

Anonymous
> Never share a foxhole with anyone braver than
> you are.

Aristotle (384–322 BC)
Greek philosopher
> I count him braver who overcomes his desires
> than him who overcomes his enemies.
>> In Stobaeus, *Florilegium*

Barrie, Sir J.M. (1860–1937)
Scottish dramatist and writer
> Courage is the thing. All goes if courage goes.
>> Address, St Andrews University, 1922

Blair, Robert (1699–1746)
Scottish poet
> The schoolboy, with his satchel in his hand,
> Whistling aloud to bear his courage up.
>> 'The Grave' (1743)

Carroll, Lewis (1832–1898)
English writer and photographer
> 'I'm very brave generally, ' he went on in a low
> voice: 'only to-day I happen to have a
> headache.'
>> *Through the Looking-Glass (and What Alice Found*
>> *There)* (1872)

Chandler, Raymond (1888–1959)
US crime writer
> Down these mean streets a man must go who is
> not himself mean, who is neither tarnished nor
> afraid.
>> *Atlantic Monthly* (1944)

Day Lewis, C. (1904–1972)
Irish-born British academic, writer and critic
> I sang as one
> Who on a tilting deck sings
> To keep men's courage up, though the wave
> hangs
> That shall cut off their sun.
>> 'The Conflict' (1935)

Earhart, Amelia (1898–1937)
US aviator
> Courage is the price that Life exacts for granting
> peace.
>> 'Courage' (1927)

Hemingway, Ernest (1898–1961)
US author
Definition of 'guts'

Grace under pressure.

Attr.

Howard, Michael (1922–)
English historian and writer
The important thing when you are going to do something brave is to have someone on hand to witness it.

The Observer, 1980

Ibárruri, Dolores ('La Pasionaria') (1895–1989)
Basque Communist leader
Il vaut mieux mourir debout que vivre à genoux!
It is better to die on your feet than to live on your knees.

Speech, Paris, 1936

Ingersoll, Robert G. (1833–1899)
US lawyer, soldier and writer
Courage without conscience is a wild beast.

Speech, 1882

Kierkegaard, Søren (1813–1855)
Danish philosopher
It takes moral courage to grieve, but it takes religious courage to rejoice.

Attr. by Jonathan Sacks in *The Times,* 1998

Leacock, Stephen (1869–1944)
English-born Canadian humorist, writer and economist
It takes a good deal of physical courage to ride a horse. This, however, I have. I get it at about forty cents a flask, and take it as required.

Literary Lapses (1910)

Marie-Antoinette (1755–1793)
Queen of France
Remark on the way to the guillotine, 16 October 1793
Courage! I have shown it for years; think you I shall lose it at the moment when my sufferings are to end?

Attr.

Meredith, George (1828–1909)
English writer, poet and critic
Want of courage is want of sense.

The Tragic Comedians

Napoleon I (1769–1821)
French emperor
Quant au courage moral, il avait trouvé fort rare, disait-il, celui de deux heures après minuit; c'est-à-dire le courage de l'improviste.
As for moral courage, he said he had very rarely encountered two o'clock in the morning courage; that is, the courage of the unprepared.

Mémorial de Sainte Hélène

Nixon, Richard (1913–1994)
US Republican politician and President
Courage – or putting it more accurately, lack of fear – is a result of discipline. By an act of will, a man refuses to think of the reasons for fear, and

so concentrates entirely on winning the battle.

The Independent, 1994

Scott, Sir Walter (1771–1832)
Scottish writer and historian
The stubborn spear-men still made good
Their dark impenetrable wood,
Each stepping where his comrade stood,
The instant that he fell.

Marmion (1808)

Shakespeare, William (1564–1616)
English dramatist, poet and actor
Courage mounteth with occasion.

King John, II.i

Sheridan, Richard Brinsley (1751–1816)
Irish dramatist, politician and orator
My valour is certainly going! – it is sneaking off! – I feel it oozing out as it were at the palms of my hands!

The Rivals (1775)

Thoreau, Henry David (1817–1862)
US essayist, social critic and writer
The three-o'-clock in the morning courage, which Bonaparte thought was the rarest.

Walden (1854)

Trollope, Anthony (1815–1882)
English writer, traveller and post office official
Those who have courage to love should have courage to suffer.

The Bertrams (1859)

Ustinov, Sir Peter (1921–)
English actor, director, dramatist, writer and raconteur
Courage is often lack of insight, whereas cowardice in many cases is based on good information.

Attr.

Walpole, Sir Hugh (1884–1941)
New Zealand-born English writer
'Tisn't life that matters! 'Tis the courage you bring to it.

Fortitude (1913)

▶▶ PATRIOTISM

courtesy

Bacon, Francis (1561–1626)
English philosopher, essayist, politician and courtier
If a man be gracious and courteous to strangers, it shews he is a citizen of the world.

Essays

Duhamel, Georges (1884–1966)
French writer, poet, dramatist and physician
Courtesy is not dead – it has merely taken

refuge in Great Britain.

The Observer, 1953

Mankiewicz, Herman J. (1897–1953)
US journalist and screenwriter
Commenting on the fact that he had not been harmed when swimming in shark-infested waters
> I think that's what they call professional courtesy.
>> Attr.

Proverb
> Civility costs nothing.

▶▶ MANNERS; RESPECT

courtship

Braisted, Harry (19th century)
> If you want to win her hand,
> Let the maiden understand
> That's she's not the only pebble on the beach.
>> 'You're Not the Only Pebble on the Beach'

Bray, John Jefferson (1912–)
Australian lawyer and poet
> When your grape was green you denied me.
> When your grape was ripe you despised me.
> Can I have a nibble at the old sultana?
>> 'After Long Absence'

Campbell, Thomas (1777–1844)
Scottish poet, ballad writer and journalist
> Better be courted and jilted
> Than never be courted at all.
>> 'The Jilted Nymph' (1843)

Congreve, William (1670–1729)
English dramatist
> Courtship to marriage, as a very witty prologue to a very dull Play.
>> *The Old Bachelor* (1693)

Dacre, Harry (d. 1922)
> Daisy, Daisy, give me your answer, do!
> I'm half crazy, all for the love of you!
> It won't be a stylish marriage,
> I can't afford a carriage,
> But you'll look sweet upon the seat
> Of a bicycle made for two!
>> 'Daisy Bell', song, 1892

Gay, John (1685–1732)
English poet, dramatist and librettist
> Would you gain the tender Creature?
> Softly, gently, kindly treat her;
> Suff'ring is the Lover's Part.
> Beauty by Constraint possessing,
> You enjoy but half the Blessing,
> Lifeless Charms, without the Heart.
>> *Acis and Galatea* (1718)

Jonson, Ben (1572–1637)
English dramatist and poet
> Follow a shadow, it still flies you,
> Seem to fly it, it will pursue:
> So court a mistress, she denies you;
> Let her alone, she will court you.
> Say, are not women truly, then,
> Styl'd but the shadows of us men?
>> *The Forest* (1616)

Meredith, George (1828–1909)
English writer, poet and critic
> She whom I love is hard to catch and conquer,
> Hard, but O the glory of the winning were she won!
>> 'Love in the Valley' (1883)

Perelman, S.J. (1904–1979)
US humorist, writer and dramatist
> I tried to resist his overtures, but he plied me with symphonies, quartets, chamber music and cantatas.
>> *Crazy Like a Fox* (1944), 'The Love Decoy'

Prior, Matthew (1664–1721)
> I court others in verse: but I love thee in prose:
> And they have my whimsies, but thou hast my heart.
>> 'A Better Answer' (1718)

Shakespeare, William (1564–1616)
English dramatist, poet and actor
> Your brother and my sister no sooner met but they look'd;
> no sooner look'd but they lov'd;
> no sooner lov'd but they sigh'd;
> no sooner sigh'd but they ask'd one another the reason;
> no sooner knew the reason but they sought the remedy –
> and in these degrees have they made a pair of stairs to marriage,
> which they will climb incontinent, or else be incontinent before marriage.
>> *As You Like, It* V.ii

> She's beautiful, and therefore to be woo'd;
> She is a woman, therefore to be won.
>> *Henry VI, Part 1*, V.iii

> Women are angels, wooing:
> Things won are done;
> joy's soul lies in the doing.
> That she belov'd knows nought that knows not this:
> Men prize the thing ungain'd more than it is.
>> *Troilus and Cressida*, I.ii

Wilde, Oscar (1854–1900)
Irish poet, dramatist, writer, critic and wit
> I am not in favour of long engagements. They give people the opportunity of finding out each

other's character before marriage, which I think is never advisable.

The Importance of Being Earnest (1895)

▶▶ MARRIAGE; SEX

cowardice

Brontë, Emily (1818–1848)
English poet and writer
> No coward soul is mine,
> No trembler in the world's storm-troubled sphere:
> I see Heaven's glories shine,
> And faith shines equal, arming me from fear.

'Last Lines' (1846)

Elizabeth I (1533–1603)
Queen of England
> If thy heart fails thee, climb not at all.

In Fuller, *The History of the Worthies of England* (1662)

Granville, George (1666–1735)
English poet, dramatist and politician
> Cowards in scarlet pass for men of war.

The She Gallants (1696)

Housman, A.E. (1859–1936)
English poet and scholar
> The man that runs away
> Lives to die another day.

A Shropshire Lad (1896)

Johnson, Samuel (1709–1784)
English lexicographer, poet, critic, conversationalist and essayist
> It is thus that mutual cowardice keeps us in peace. Were one half of mankind brave and one half cowards, the brave would be always beating the cowards. Were all brave, they would lead a very uneasy life; all would be continually fighting; but being all cowards, we go on very well.

In Boswell, *The Life of Samuel Johnson* (1791)

Johnston, Brian (1912–1994)
British broadcaster
When asked by his commanding officer what steps he would take if he came across a German battalion
> Long ones, backwards.

Quoted in his obituary, *The Sunday Times*, 1994

Kipling, Rudyard (1865–1936)
Indian-born British poet and writer
> I could not look on Death, which being known,
> Men led me to him, blindfold and alone.

The Years Between (1919)

Rochester, Earl of (1647–1680)
English poet, satirist, courtier and libertine
> For all men would be cowards if they durst.

'A Satire Against Reason and Mankind' (1679)

Shakespeare, William (1564–1616)
English dramatist, poet and actor
> Instinct is a great matter: I was now a coward on instinct.

Henry IV, Part 1, II.iv

> Cowards die many times before their deaths:
> The valiant never taste of death but once.

Julius Caesar, II.ii

Shaw, George Bernard (1856–1950)
Irish socialist, writer, dramatist and critic
> As an old soldier I admit the cowardice: it's as universal as sea sickness, and matters just as little.

Man and Superman (1903)

Voltaire (1694–1778)
French philosopher, dramatist, poet, historian writer and critic
> Marriage is the only adventure open to the cowardly.

Attr.

Webster, John (c.1580–c.1625)
English dramatist
> Cowardly dogs bark loudest.

The White Devil (1612)

cricket

Grace, W.G. (1848–1915)
English cricketer, physician and surgeon
Refusing to leave the crease after being bowled first ball in front of a large crowd
> They came to see me bat not to see you bowl.

Attr.

Hughes, Thomas (1822–1896)
Of cricket
> It's more than a game. It's an institution.

Tom Brown's Schooldays (1857)

Johnston, Brian (1912–1994)
British broadcaster
> The bowler's Holding, the batsman's Willey.

Quoted in his obituary, *Sunday Times*

> We're going to see Afaq to Knight at the Nursery End.

Quoted in his obituary, *Sunday Times*

Mancroft, Lord (1914–1987)
> Cricket – a game which the English, not being a spiritual people, have invented in order to give

themselves some conception of eternity.

Bees in Some Bonnets (1979)

Mugabe, Robert (1924–)

President of Zimbabwe

Cricket civilizes people and creates good gentlemen. I want everyone to play cricket in Zimbabwe; I want ours to be a nation of gentlemen.

The Sunday Times, 1984

Temple, William (1881–1944)

Anglican prelate, social reformer and writer

Remark to parents when headmaster of Repton School

Personally, I have always looked on cricket as organized loafing.

Attr.

Thompson, Francis (1859–1907)

English poet

And I look through my tears at a soundless-clapping host

As the run-stealers flicker to and fro.

To and fro:

O my Hornby and my Barlow long ago!

'At Lord's'

▶▶ SPORT AND GAMES

crime

Adler, Freda (1934–)

US educator and writer

On rape

Perhaps it is the only crime in which the victim becomes the accused and, in reality, it is she who must prove her good reputation, her mental soundness, and her impeccable propriety.

Sisters in Crime (1975)

Allen, Fred (1894–1956)

US vaudeville performer and comedian

He's a good boy; everything he steals he brings right home to his mother.

Attr.

Anonymous

The fault is great in man or woman

Who steals a goose from off a common;

But what can plead that man's excuse

Who steals a common from a goose?

The Tickler Magazine, 1821

Don't steal. The government hates competition.

Bacon, Francis (1561–1626)

English philosopher, essayist, politician and courtier

Opportunity makes a thief.

Letter to Essex, 1598

The Bible (King James Version)

Whoso sheddeth man's blood, by man shall his blood be shed.

Genesis, 9: 6

Blair, Tony (1953–)

British Labour Prime Minister

Speech as Shadow Home Secretary

Labour is the party of law and order in Britain today. Tough on crime and tough on the causes of crime.

Speech at the Labour Party Conference, 1993

Bocca, Giorgio (1920–)

Italian writer

The mafia is rational, it wants to reduce homicides to the minimum.

Hell (1992)

Boyle, Jimmy (1944–)

Society has a choice: it either has a prison system based on punitive measures or one that rehabilitates. Do people want to sleep with a shotgun under their bed and go shopping in an armoured van, or do they want to live in a safer, fairer community?

Interview, *The Big Issue*, May 1996

When you've got nothing, being a great thief or a respected fighter really counts for something.

Interview, *The Big Issue*, May 1996

Brecht, Bertolt (1898–1956)

German dramatist

Was ist ein Einbruch in eine Bank gegen die Gründung einer Bank?

What is robbing a bank compared with founding a bank?

The Threepenny Opera (1928)

Bulwer-Lytton, Edward (1803–1873)

English novelist, dramatist, poet and politician

In other countries poverty is a misfortune – with us it is a crime.

England and the English (1833)

Camus, Albert (1913–1960)

Algerian-born French writer

Combien de crimes commis simplement parce que leur auteur ne pouvait supporter d'être en faute!

How many crimes committed simply because their authors could not endure being wrong!

The Fall, 1956

Capone, Al (1899–1947)

Chicago gangster

I've been accused of every death except the casualty list of the World War.

In Allsop, *The Bootleggers* (1961)

Chaucer, Geoffrey (c.1340–1400)

English poet, public servant and courtier

Mordre wol out, that se we day by day.

The Canterbury Tales (1387)

Chesterton, G.K. (1874–1936)
English writer, poet and critic
Thieves respect property; they merely wish the property to become their property that they may more perfectly respect it.

Attr.

Congreve, William (1670–1729)
English dramatist
He that first cries out stop thief, is often he that has stolen the treasure.

Love for Love (1695)

De Quincey, Thomas (1785–1859)
English writer
If a man once indulges himself in murder, very soon he comes to think little of robbing; and from robbing he comes next to drinking and sabbath-breaking, and from that to incivility and procrastination.

'Murder Considered as One of the Fine Arts' (1839)

Dinkins, David (1927–)
US politician; Mayor of New York 1989–93
Answering accusations that he failed to pay his taxes.
I haven't committed a crime. What I did was fail to comply with the law.

Attr.

Doyle, Sir Arthur Conan (1859–1930)
Scottish writer and war correspondent
Singularity is almost invariably a clue. The more featureless and commonplace a crime is, the more difficult it is to bring it home.

'The Boscombe Valley Mystery' (1892)

Farber, Barry (1859–1930)
Crime expands according to our willingness to put up with it.

Attr.

Farquhar, George (1678–1707)
Irish dramatist
Crimes, like virtues, are their own rewards.

The Inconstant (1702)

Fry, Elizabeth (1780–1845)
English social and prison reformer
Punishment is not for revenge, but to lessen crime and reform the criminal.

Journal entry

Goldman, Emma (1869–1940)
US anarchist
Crime is naught but misdirected energy.

Anarchism (1910)

Greene, Graham (1904–1991)
English writer and dramatist

Catholics and Communists have committed great crimes, but at least they have not stood aside, like an established society, and been indifferent. I would rather have blood on my hands than water like Pilate.

The Comedians (1966)

Hancock, Sir William Keith (1898–1988)
Australian historian
Were it possible to compel the prison warders of this past age to produce for our inspection a 'typical' transported convict, they would show us, not the countryman who snared rabbits, but the Londoner who stole spoons.

Australia (1930)

Hawthorne, Nathaniel (1804–1864)
US allegorical writer
By the sympathy of your human hearts for sin ye shall scent out all the places – whether in church, bedchamber, stret, field or forest – where crime has been committed, and shall exult to behold the whole earth one stain of guilt, one mighty blood spot.

Young Goodman Brown (1835)

Henry, O. (1862–1910)
US short-story writer
A burglar who respects his art always takes his time before taking anything else.

Makes the Whole World Kin

La Bruyère, Jean de (1645–1696)
French satirist
Si la pauvreté est la mère des crimes, le défaut d'esprit en est le père.
If poverty is the mother of crime, lack of intelligence is its father.

Les caractères ou les moeurs de ce siècle (1688)

Lewes, G.H. (1817–1878)
English writer, philosopher, critic and scientist
Murder, like talent, seems occasionally to run in families.

The Physiology of Common Life (1859)

Lightner, Candy (1946–)
US estate agent and founder of MADD (Mothers Against Drunk Driving)
Death by drunken driving is a socially acceptable form of homicide.

San José Mercury, April 1981

Meir, Golda (1898–1978)
Russian-born Israeli stateswoman and Prime Minister
Replying to a member of her Cabinet who proposed a curfew on women after dark in response to a recent outbreak of assaults on women
But it's the men who are attacking the women. If there's to be a curfew, let the men stay at home, not the women.

Attr.

Racine, Jean (1639–1699)
French tragedian and poet
> *Ainsi que la vertu, le crime a ses degrés.*
> Crime has its degrees, as virtue does.
>> *Phèdre* (1677)

Rains, Claude (1889–1967)
British actor
> Major Strasser has been shot. Round up the usual suspects.
>> *Casablanca* (film, 1942)

Roosevelt, Theodore (1858–1919)
US Republican President
Dismissing a cowboy who had put Roosevelt's brand on a steer belonging to a neighbouring ranch
> A man who will steal for me will steal from me.
>> In Hagedorn, *Roosevelt in the Bad Lands* (1921)

Ross, Nick (1947–)
British broadcaster
> We're barking mad about crime in this country. We have an obsession with believing the worst, conning ourselves that there was a golden age – typically forty years before the one we're living in.
>> *Radio Times*, 1993

Rostand, Jean (1894–1977)
French biologist
> *Tue un homme, on est un assassin. On tue des millions d'hommes, on est conquérant. On les tue tous, on est un dieu.*
> Kill one man, and you are a murderer. Kill millions of men, and you are a conqueror. Kill them all, and you are a god.
>> *Thoughts of a Biologist* (1939)

Schwarzenegger, Arnold (1947–)
Austrian-born US film actor
> Crime has nothing to do with movies or guns, or TV. It has to do with Washington not creating an environment where one of the parents stays home to bring up children, so they point the finger at Hollywood.
>> *The Observer*, 1999

Shakespeare, William (1564–1616)
English dramatist, poet and actor
Of stealing
> Why, Hal, 'tis my vocation, Hal; 'tis no sin for a man to labour in his vocation.
>> *Henry IV, Part 1*, I.ii

> The robb'd that smiles steals something from the thief.
>> *Othello*, I.iii

Spencer, Herbert (1820–1903)
English philosopher and journalist
> A clever theft was praiseworthy amongst the Spartans; and it is equally so amongst Christians, provided it be on a sufficiently large scale.
>> *Social Statics* (1850)

Takayama, Tokutaro
Kyoto mob boss defending the reputation of Japan's yakuza following the attack on film director Juzo Itami
> We haven't used our power only for doing bad things. I myself personally wounded the head of the local Communist party after the police asked us for help.
>> *Newsweek*, 1992

Waugh, Evelyn (1903–1966)
English writer and diarist
> I came to the conclusion many years ago that almost all crime is due to the repressed desire for aesthetic expression.
>> *Decline and Fall* (1928)

▶▶ MURDER; PUNISHMENT; THEFT

criticism

Antiphanes of Macedonia (fl. 360 BC)
Greek comic dramatist
> Idly inquisitive tribe of grammarians, who dig up the poetry of others by the roots … Get away, bugs that secretly bite the eloquent.
>> *Greek Anthology*

Arnold, Matthew (1822–1888)
English poet, critic, essayist and educationist
> I am bound by my own definition of criticism: a disinterested endeavour to learn and propagate the best that is known and thought in the world.
>> *Essays in Criticism* (1865)

Atwood, Margaret (1939–)
Canadian writer, poet and critic
> Once upon a time I thought there was an old man with a grey beard somewhere who knew the truth, and if I was good enough, naturally he would tell me that this was it. That person doesn't exist, but that's who I write for. The great critic in the sky.
>> In Ingersoll, *Margaret Atwood: Conversations* (1990)

Auden, W.H. (1907–1973)
English poet, essayist, critic, teacher and dramatist
> One cannot review a bad book without showing off.
>> *The Dyer's Hand and Other Essays* (1963)

Bell, Clive (1881–1964)
English art critic
> I will try to account for the degree of my aesthetic emotion. That, I conceive, is the function of the critic.
>> *Art* (1914)

Browne, Sir Thomas (1605–1682)
English physician, author and antiquary
> He who discommendeth others obliquely commendeth himself.
>> *Christian Morals* (1716)

Bullet, Gerald (1893–1958)
English writer, poet and critic
> So, when a new book comes his way,
> By someone still alive to-day,
> Our Honest John, with right good will,
> Sharpens his pencil for the kill.
>> 'A Reviewer'

Burgess, Anthony (1917–1993)
English writer, linguist and composer
> I know how foolish critics can be, being one myself.
>> *The Observer*, 1980

Butler, Samuel (1835–1902)
English writer, painter, philosopher and scholar
> Talking it over, we agreed that Blake was no good because he learnt Italian at over 60 to study Dante, and we knew Dante was no good because he was so fond of Virgil, and Virgil was no good because Tennyson ran him, and as for Tennyson – well, Tennyson goes without saying.
>> *The Note-Books of Samuel Butler* (1912)

Byron, Lord (1788–1824)
English poet satirist and traveller
> A man must serve his time to every trade
> Save censure – critics all are ready made.
> Take hackney'd jokes from Miller, got by rote,
> With just enough of learning to misquote.
>> *English Bards and Scotch Reviewers* (1809)

Castro, Fidel (1927–)
President of Cuba
> All criticism is opposition. All opposition is counter-revolutionary.
>> In John Newhouse, 'Socialism of Death', *The New Yorker*, 1992

Chesterton, G.K. (1874–1936)
English writer, poet and critic
> A great deal of contemporary criticism reads to me like a man saying: 'Of course I do not like green cheese; I am very fond of brown sherry.'
>> *All I Survey* (1933)

Churchill, Charles (1731–1764)
English poet, political writer and clergyman
> Though by whim, envy, or resentment led,
> They damn those authors whom they never read.
>> *The Candidate* (1764)

Churchill, Sir Winston (1874–1965)
English Conservative Prime Minister
> I do not resent criticism, even when, for the sake of emphasis, it parts for the time with reality.
>> Speech, 1941

Coleridge, Samuel Taylor (1772–1834)
English poet, philosopher and critic
> That passage is what I call the sublime dashed to pieces by cutting too close with the fiery four-in-hand round the corner of nonsense.
>> *Table Talk* (1835), 20 January 1834

> Reviewers are usually people who would have been poets, historians, biographers, etc., if they could; they have tried their talents at one or at the other, and have failed; therefore they turn critics.
>> *Seven Lectures on Shakespeare and Milton* (1856)

Collins, Jackie
English-born US popular novelist
> The biggest critics of my books are people who never read them.
>> Attr.

Collins, William (1721–1759)
> Too nicely Jonson knew the critic's part,
> Nature in him was almost lost in Art.
>> 'Verses Addressed to Sir Thomas Hanmer' (1743)

Conran, Shirley (1932–)
English writer
On Julie Burchill
> I cannot take seriously the criticism of someone who doesn't know how to use a semicolon.
>> Attr.

Disraeli, Benjamin (1804–1881)
English statesman and writer
> You know who the critics are? The men who have failed in literature and art.
>> *Lothair* (1870)

> This shows how much easier it is to be critical than to be correct.
>> Speech, 1860

> Cosmopolitan critics, men who are the friends of every country save their own.
>> Speech, 1877

Donatus, Aelius (fl. 4th century AD)
Roman Latin grammarian and teacher
Donatus was a commentator on texts
> *Pereant, inquit, qui ante nos nostra dixerunt.*
> Confound those who have made our comments before us.
>> In St Jerome, *Commentaries on Ecclesiastes*

Eliot, T.S. (1888–1965)
US-born British poet, verse dramatist and critic
> The critic, one would suppose, if he is to justify his existence, should endeavour to discipline his personal prejudices and cranks – tares to which we are all subject – and compose his differences

with as many of his fellows as possible, in the common pursuit of true judgement.

'The Function of Criticism' (1923)

France, Anatole (1844–1924)
French writer and critic
Le bon critique est celui qui raconte les aventures de son âme au milieu des chefs-d'oeuvre.
A good critic is one who tells of his own soul's adventures among masterpieces.
La Vie Littéraire (1888)

Fry, Christopher (1907–)
English verse dramatist, theatre director and translator
I sometimes think
His critical judgement is so exquisite
It leaves us nothing to admire except his opinion.
The Dark is Light Enough (1954)

Hampton, Christopher (1946–)
English dramatist
Asking a working writer what he thinks about critics is like asking a lamp-post how it feels about dogs.
The Sunday Times Magazine, 1977

Heller, Joseph (1923–1999)
US writer
When I read something saying I've not done anything as good as *Catch 22* I'm tempted to reply, 'who has?'.
The Times, 1993

Hood, Thomas (1799–1845)
English poet, editor and humorist
What is a modern poet's fate?
To write his thoughts upon a slate;
The critic spits on what is done,
Gives it a wipe – and all is gone.
In Hallam Tennyson, *Alfred Lord Tennyson, A Memoir* (1897)

Huxley, Aldous (1894–1963)
English writer, poet and critic
Parodies and caricatures are the most penetrating of criticisms.
Point Counter Point (1928)

James, Henry (1843–1916)
US-born British writer, critic and letter writer
We must grant the artist his subject, his idea, his donnée: our criticism is applied only to what he makes of it.
Partial Portraits (1888)

Johnson, Samuel (1709–1784)
English lexicographer, poet, critic, conversationalist and essayist
Replying to Maurice Morgann who asked him whether Derrick or Smart was the better poet
Sir, there is no settling the point of precedence

between a louse and a flea.
In Boswell, *The Life of Samuel Johnson* (1791)

There are two things which I am confident I can do very well: one is an introduction to any literary work, stating what it is to contain, and how it should be executed in the most perfect manner; the other is a conclusion, shewing from various causes why the execution has not been equal to what the author promised himself and to the public.
In Boswell, *The Life of Samuel Johnson* (1791)

Of literary criticism
You may abuse a tragedy, though you cannot write one, You may scold a carpenter who has made you a bad table, though you cannot make a table. It is not your trade to make tables.
In Boswell, *The Life of Samuel Johnson* (1791)

The man who is asked by an author what he thinks of his work, is put to the torture, and is not obliged to speak the truth.
In Boswell, *The Life of Samuel Johnson* (1791)

Kael, Pauline (1919–)
US film critic
In the arts, the critic is the only independent source of information. The rest is advertising.
Newsweek, 1973

La Bruyère, Jean de (1645–1696)
French satirist
Le plaisir de la critique nous ôte celui d'être vivement touchés de très belles choses.
The pleasure of criticizing takes away from us the pleasure of being moved by some very fine things.
Les caractères ou les moeurs de ce siècle (1688)

Landor, Walter Savage (1775–1864)
English poet and writer
Fleas know not whether they are upon the body of a giant or upon one of ordinary size.
Imaginary Conversations (1824)

He who first praises a good book becomingly, is next in merit to the author.
Imaginary Conversations (1824–1829)

Leavis, F.R. (1895–1978)
English critic, lecturer and writer
Literary criticism provides the test for life and concreteness; where it degenerates, the instruments of thought degenerate too, and thinking, released from the testing and energizing contact with the full living consciousness, is debilitated, and betrayed to the academic, the abstract and the verbal.
Towards Standards in Criticism (1930)

Lerner, Alan Jay (1918–1986)
US lyricist and screenwriter

Coughing in the theatre is not a respiratory ailment. It is a criticism.

The Street Where I Live (1978)

Lowell, James Russell (1819–1891)
US poet, editor, abolitionist and diplomat
A wise skepticism is the first attribute of a good critic.

Among My Books

Marx, Groucho (1895–1977)
US comedian
I was so long writing my review that I never got around to reading the book.

Attr.

Maugham, William Somerset (1874–1965)
English writer, dramatist and physician
People ask you for criticism, but they only want praise.

Of Human Bondage (1915)

Moore, George (1852–1933)
Irish writer, dramatist and critic
The lot of critics is to be remembered by what they failed to understand.

Impressions and Opinions (1891)

Murdoch, Iris (1919–1999)
Irish-born British writer, philosopher and dramatist
A bad review is even less important than whether it is raining in Patagonia.

The Times, 1989

Orwell, George (1903–1950)
English writer and critic
Prolonged, indiscriminate reviewing of books … not only involves praising trash … but constantly inventing reactions towards books about which one has no spontaneous feelings whatever.

Shooting an Elephant (1950)

Parker, Dorothy (1893–1967)
US writer, poet, critic and wit
On A. A. Milne's *The House at Pooh Corner* in her column 'Constant Reader'
Tonstant Weader fwowed up.

Attr.

This is not a novel to be tossed aside lightly. It should be thrown with great force.

In Gaines, *Wit's End*

Pope, Alexander (1688–1744)
English poet, translator and editor
Turn what they will to Verse, their toil is vain,
Critics like me shall make it Prose again.

The Dunciad (1742)

Nor in the Critic let the Man be lost.
Good-nature and good-sense must ever join;
To err is human, to forgive, divine.

An Essay on Criticism (1711)

Porson, Richard (1759–1808)
English scholar
Giving his opinion of Southey's poems
Your works will be read after Shakespeare and Milton are forgotten – and not till then.

In Meissen, *Quotable Anecdotes*

Potter, Stephen (1900–1969)
English writer, critic and lecturer
Donsmanship … 'the art of criticizing without actually listening'.

Lifemanship (1950)

Priestley, J.B. (1894–1984)
English writer, dramatist and critic
They will review a book by a writer much older than themselves as if it were an over-ambitious essay by a second-year student … It is the little dons I complain about, like so many corgis trotting up, hoping to nip your ankles.

Outcries and Asides

Quiller-Couch, Sir Arthur ('Q') (1863–1944)
English man of letters
The best is the best, though a hundred judges have declared it so.

Oxford Book of English Verse (1900)

Reger, Max (1873–1916)
German composer, conductor, teacher and pianist
Letter written to Rudolf Louis in response to his criticism of Reger's *Sinfonietta*, 1906
Ich sitze in dem kleinsten Zimmer in meinem Hause. Ich habe Ihre Kritik vor mir. Im nächsten Augenblick wird sie hinter mir sein.
I am sitting in the smallest room in my house. I have your review in front of me. In a moment it will be behind me.

In Slonimsky, *The Lexicon of Musical Invective*

Rivarol, Antoine de (1753–1801)
French writer and wit
On a couplet by a mediocre poet
C'est bien, mais il y a des longueurs.
Very good, but it has its longueurs.

Rivaroliana

Shaw, George Bernard (1856–1950)
Irish socialist, writer, dramatist and critic
A dramatic critic … leaves no turn unstoned.

New York Times, 1950

You don't expect me to know what to say about a play when I don't know who the author is, do you? … If it's by a good author, it's a good play, naturally. That stands to reason.

Fanny's First Play (1911)

Sibelius, Jean (1865–1957)
Finnish composer
Pay no attention to what the critics say. No

statue has ever been put up to a critic.

Attr.

Smith, Sydney (1771–1845)
English clergyman, essayist, journalist and wit
>I never read a book before reviewing it; it prejudices a man so.

In Pearson, *The Smith of Smiths* (1934)

Sontag, Susan (1933–)
US critic and writer
>Interpretation is the revenge of the intellect upon art.

Evergreen Review, 1964

Steinbeck, John (1902–1968)
US writer
On critics
>Unless the bastards have the courage to give you unqualified praise, I say ignore them.

In J.K. Galbraith, *A Life in Our Times* (1981)

Sterne, Laurence (1713–1768)
Irish-born English writer and clergyman
>Of all the cants which are canted in this canting world, – though the cant of hypocrites may be the worst, – the cant of criticism is the most tormenting!

Tristram Shandy (1759–1767)

Stoppard, Tom (1937–)
British dramatist
>I doubt that art needed Ruskin any more than a moving train needs one of its passengers to shove it.

The Times Literary Supplement, 1977

Stravinsky, Igor (1882–1971)
Russian composer and conductor
>I had another dream the other day about music critics. They were small and rodent-like with padlocked ears, as if they had stepped out of a painting by Goya.

The Evening Standard, 1969

Swift, Jonathan (1667–1745)
Irish satirist, poet, essayist and cleric
>So, naturalists observe, a flea
>Hath smaller fleas that on him prey;
>And these have smaller fleas to bite 'em,
>And so proceed ad infinitum.
>Thus every poet, in his kind,
>Is bit by him that comes behind.

'On Poetry' (1733)

Tynan, Kenneth (1927–1980)
English drama critic, producer and essayist
>A good drama critic is one who perceives what is happening in the theatre of his time. A great drama critic also perceives what is not happening.

Tynan Right and Left (1967)

A critic is a man who knows the way but can't drive the car.

New York Times Magazine, 1966

Voltaire (1694–1778)
French philosopher, dramatist, poet, historian writer and critic
Reviewing Rousseau's poem 'Ode to Posterity'
>I do not think this poem will reach its destination.

Attr.

Vorster, John (1915–1983)
South African Nationalist politician, Prime Minister and President
>As far as criticism is concerned, we don't resent that unless it is absolutely biased, as it is in most cases.

The Observer, 1969

Whistler, James McNeill (1834–1903)
US painter, etcher and pamphleteer
>You shouldn't say it is not good. You should say, you do not like it; and then, you know, you're perfectly safe.

In D.C. Seitz, *Whistler Stories* (1913)

Wilde, Oscar (1854–1900)
Irish poet, dramatist, writer, critic and wit
On a notice at a dancing saloon
>I saw the only rational method of art criticism I have ever come across … 'Please do not shoot the pianist. He is doing his best.' The mortality among pianists in that place is marvellous.

'Impressions of America' (1906)

>The man who sees both sides of a question is a man who sees absolutely nothing at all.

'The Critic as Artist' (1891)

▶▶ ACTORS; INSULTS; POETS; WRITERS

cruelty

Blake, William (1757–1827)
English poet, engraver, painter and mystic
>Cruelty has a Human Heart
>And Jealousy a Human Face,
>Terror the Human Form Divine,
>And Secrecy the Human Dress.

'A Divine Image' (c.1832)

Caligula (12–41)
Roman emperor
>*Ita feri ut se mori sentiat.*
>Strike him so that he may feel that he is dying.

In Suetonius, *Lives of the Caesars*

Cowper, William (1731–1800)
English poet, hymn and letter writer
>I would not enter on my list of friends Tho'

grac'd with polish'd manners
and fine sense,
Yet wanting sensibility) the man
Who needlessly sets foot upon a
worm.

The Task (1785)

Daniels, Dr Anthony
Cruelty is like hope: it springs eternal.

The Observer, 1998

Froude, James Anthony (1818–1894)
English historian and scholar
Fear is the parent of cruelty.

Short Studies on Great Subjects (1877)

Gide, André (1869–1951)
French writer, critic, dramatist and poet
La cruauté, c'est le premier des attributs de Dieu.
Cruelty is the first of God's attributes.

The Counterfeiters

Shelley, Percy Bysshe (1792–1822)
English poet, dramatist and essayist
Cruel he looks, but calm and strong,
Like one who does, not suffers wrong.

Prometheus Unbound (1820)

Trotsky, Leon (1879–1940)
Russian revolutionary and Communist theorist
In a serious struggle there is no worse cruelty
than to be magnanimous at an inappropriate
time.

The History of the Russian Revolution (1933)

▶▶ PURITANS; VIOLENCE

crying

Blake, William (1757–1827)
English poet, engraver, painter and mystic
For a Tear is an Intellectual thing!
And a Sigh is the Sword of an Angel King
And the bitter groan of a Martyrs woe
Is an Arrow from the Almighties Bow.

Jerusalem (1804–1820)

Byron, Lord (1788–1824)
English poet satirist and traveller
English Romantic poet, satirist and traveller
Oh! too convincing – dangerously dear –
In woman's eye the unanswerable tear!

The Corsair (1814)

Churchill, Charles (1731–1764)
English poet, political writer and clergyman
With the persuasive language of a tear.

'The Times' (1764)

Crisp, Quentin (1908–1999)
English writer, publicist and model

Tears were to me what glass beads are to
African traders.

The Naked Civil Servant (1968)

Crompton, Richmal (1890–1969)
English writer and teacher
Violet Elizabeth dried her tears. She saw that
they were useless and she did not believe in
wasting her effects. 'All right, ' she said calmly,
'I'll thcream then. I'll thcream, an' thcream, an'
thcream till I'm thick.'

Still William (1925)

Dickens, Charles (1812–1870)
English writer
We need never be ashamed of our tears.

Great Expectations (1861)

'It opens the lungs, washes the countenance,
exercises the eyes, and softens down the
temper', said Mr Bumble. 'So cry away.'

Oliver Twist (1838)

Fletcher, Phineas (1582–1650)
English poet and clergyman
Drop, drop, slow tears,
And bathe those beauteous feet,
Which brought from Heav'n
The news and Prince of Peace.

Poetical Miscellanies (1633), 'An Hymn'

Liberace, Wladziu Valentino (1919–1987)
US pianist and showman
Remark made after hostile criticism
I cried all the way to the bank.

Autobiography (1973)

Musset, Alfred de (1810–1857)
French dramatist and poet
*Le seul bien qui me rest au monde
Est d'avoir quelquefois pleuré.*
The only good things the world has left me are
the times that I have wept.

'Tristesse' (1841)

Rhys, Jean (1894–1979)
West Indian-born English writer
I often want to cry. That is the only advantage
women have over men – at least they can cry.

Good Morning, Midnight (1939)

Saint-Exupéry, Antoine de (1900–1944)
C'est tellement mystérieux, le pays des larmes.
It is such a mysterious place, the land of tears.

The Little Prince (1943)

Shakespeare, William (1564–1616)
English dramatist, poet and actor
The big round tears
Cours'd one another down his innocent nose
In piteous chase.

As You Like It, II.i

Touch me with noble anger,
And let not women's weapons, water-drops,
Stain my man's cheeks!
No, you unnatural hags,
I will have such revenges on you both
That all the world shall – I will do such things –
What they are yet I know not; but they shall be
The terrors of the earth.
You think I'll weep.
No, I'll not weep.
I have full cause of weeping; but this heart
Shall break into a hundred thousand flaws
Or ere I'll weep.
O fool, I shall go mad!

King Lear, II.iv

Indeed the tears live in an onion that should water this sorrow.

Antony and Cleopatra, I.ii

Webster, John (c.1580–c.1625)
English dramatist
There's nothing sooner dry than women's tears.

The White Devil (1612)

West, Dame Rebecca (1892–1983)
English writer, critic and feminist
But there are other things than dissipation that thicken the features. Tears, for example.

Black Lamb and Grey Falcon
(1942)

▶▶ EYES

culture

Arnold, Matthew (1822–1888)
English poet, critic, essayist and educationist
Philistinism! – We have not the expression in English. Perhaps we have not the word because we have so much of the thing.

Essays in Criticism (1865)

… the aim which is the great aim of culture, the aim of setting ourselves to ascertain what perfection is and to make it prevail.

Culture and Anarchy (1869)

The pursuit of perfection, then, is the pursuit of sweetness and light. He who works for sweetness and light, works to make reason and the will of God prevail.

Culture and Anarchy (1869)

The men of culture are the true apostles of equality.

Culture and Anarchy (1869)

Hebraism and Hellenism – between these two points of influence moves our World … they are, each of them, contributions to human development.

Culture and Anarchy (1869)

The governing idea of Hellenism is spontaneity of consciousness; that of Hebraism, strictness of conscience.

Culture and Anarchy (1869)

Culture being a pursuit of our total perfection by means of getting to know, on all the matters which most concern us, the best which has been thought and said in the world.

Culture and Anarchy (1869)

Culture, the acquainting ourselves with the best that has been known and said in the world, and thus the history of the human spirit.

Literature and Dogma

Banda, Dr Hastings (1905–1997)
Malawian politician and President
I wish I could bring Stonehenge to Nyasaland to show there was a time when Britain had a savage culture.

The Observer, 1963

Baudelaire, Charles (1821–1867)
French poet, translator and critic
Il faut épater le bourgeois.
One must shock the bourgeois.

Attr.

Bellow, Saul (1915–)
Canadian-born US Jewish writer
If culture means anything, it means knowing what value to set upon human life; it's not somebody with a mortarboard reading Greek. I know a lot of facts, history. That's not culture. Culture is the openness of the individual psyche … to the news of being.

The Glasgow Herald, 1985

We are in the position of savage men who have been educated into believing there are no mysteries.

The Independent, 1990

Berlin, Isaiah (1909–1997)
To belong to a given community, to be connected with its members by indissoluble and impalpable ties of a common language, historical memory, habit, tradition and feeling, is a basic human need no less natural than that for food or drink and security or procreation. One nation can under-stand and sympathize with the institutions of another only because it knows how much its own mean to itself.
Cosmopolitanism is the shedding of all that makes one most human, most oneself.

'The Counter-Enlightenment'

Carlyle, Thomas (1795–1881)
Scottish historian, biographer, critic, and essayist

The great law of culture is: let each become all that he was created capable of being.

'Jean Paul Friedrich Richter' (1839)

Darwin, Charles (1809–1882)
English naturalist

The highest possible stage in moral culture is when we recognize that we ought to control our thoughts.

The Descent of Man (1871)

Frye, Northrop (1912–1991)
Canadian critic and academic

Creative culture is infinitely porous – it absorbs influences from all over the world.

Maclean's, 1991

Goering, Hermann (1893–1946)
Nazi leader and military commander

When I hear anyone talk of Culture, I reach for my revolver.

Attr.

Helpman, Sir Robert Murray (1909–1986)
Australian choreographer and director

I don't despair about the cultural scene in Australia because there isn't one here to despair about.

In Dunstan, *Knockers* (1972)

Johst, Hanns (1890–1978)

Wenn ich Kultur höre … entsichere ich meinen Browning!

When I hear the word 'culture' … I take the safety-catch off my Browning!

Schlageter (1933)

Kenny, Mary (1944–)
Irish writer and broadcaster

Decadent cultures usually fall in the end, and robust cultures rise to replace them. Our own cultural supermarket may eventually be subject to a takeover bid: the most likely challenger being, surely, Islam.

Sunday Telegraph, 1993

Koestler, Arthur (1905–1983)
British writer, essayist and political refugee

Two half-truths do not make a truth, and two half-cultures do not make a culture.

The Ghost in the Machine (1961)

Lawless, Emily (1845–1913)
Irish novelist and poet

We are all children of our environment – the good no less than the bad, – products of that particular group of habits, customs, traditions, ways of looking at things, standards of right and wrong, which chance has presented to our still growing and expanding consciousness.

Hurrish (1886)

McLuhan, Marshall (1911–1980)
Canadian communications theorist

In a culture like ours, long accustomed to splitting and dividing all things as a means of control, it is sometimes a bit of a shock to be reminded that, in operational and practical fact, the medium is the message.

Understanding Media (1964)

Mantel, Hilary (1952–)
English writer
On travel

I saw the world as some sort of exchange scheme for my ideals, but the world deserves better than this. When you come across an alien culture you must not automatically respect it. You must sometimes pay it the compliment of hating it.

'Last Months in Al Hamra' (1987)

Menand, Louis (1953–)

Culture isn't something that comes with one's race or sex. It comes only through experience; there isn't any other way to acquire it. And in the end everyone's culture is different, because everyone's experience is different.

The New Yorker, 1992

Mussolini, Benito (1883–1945)
Italian fascist dictator

In un uomo di stato, la cosidetta 'cultura' è in fin dei conti un lusso inutile.

In a statesman so-called 'culture' is, after all, a useless luxury.

Il Populo d'Italia, 1919

Shaffer, Peter (1926–)
English dramatist

All my wife had ever taken from the Mediterranean – from that whole vast intuitive culture – are four bottles of Chianti to make into lamps, and two china condiment donkeys labelled Sally and Peppy.

Equus (1973)

Wallace, Edgar (1875–1932)
English writer and dramatist

What is a highbrow? He is a man who has found something more interesting than women.

New York Times, 1932

Weil, Simone (1909–1943)
French philosopher, essayist and mystic

La culture est un instrument manié par des professeurs pour fabriquer des professeurs qui à leur tour fabriqueront des professeurs.

Culture is an instrument wielded by teachers to manufacture teachers, who, in their turn, will manufacture teachers.

The Need for Roots (1949)

Wharton, Edith (1862–1937)
US writer

Mrs Ballinger is one of the ladies who pursue Culture in bands, as though it were dangerous to meet it alone.

Xingu and Other Stories (1916)

▶▶ CIVILIZATION; SCIENCE

cunning

Blake, William (1757–1827)
English poet, engraver, painter and mystic

The weak in courage is strong in cunning.

The Marriage of Heaven and Hell (c.1790–1793)

Chesterfield, Lord (1694–1773)
English politician and letter writer

Cunning is the dark sanctuary of incapacity.

Letter to his godson and heir (to be delivered after his own death)

curiosity

Bacon, Francis (1561–1626)
English philosopher, essayist, politician and courtier

They are ill discoverers that think there is no land, when they can see nothing but sea.

The Advancement of Learning (1605)

The Bible (King James Version)

Be not curious in unnecessary matters: for more things are shewed unto thee than men understand.

Apocrypha, Ecclesiasticus, 3: 23

Bax, Sir Arnold (1883–1953)
English composer

One should try everything once, except incest and folk-dancing.

Farewell my Youth (1943)

Carroll, Lewis (1832–1898)
English writer and photographer

'If everybody minded their own business, ' said the Duchess in a hoarse growl, 'the world would go round a deal faster than it does.'

Alice's Adventures in Wonderland (1865)

Johnson, Samuel (1709–1784)
English lexicographer, poet, critic, conversationalist and essayist

A generous and elevated mind is distinguished by nothing more certainly than an eminent degree of curiosity.

In Boswell, *The Life of Samuel Johnson* (1791)

Lamb, Charles (1775–1834)
English essayist, critic and letter writer

Not many sounds in life, and I include all urban and all rural sounds, exceed in interest a knock at the door.

'Valentine's Day' (1823)

Morita, Akio (1921–1999)
Japanese businessman, chief executive of Sony

Curiosity is the key to creativity.

Made in Japan (1986)

Perelman, S.J. (1904–1979)
US humorist, writer and dramatist

Giving his reasons for refusing to see a priest as he lay dying

I am curious to see what happens in the next world to one who dies unshriven.

Attr.

Proverbs

Ask no questions, and hear no lies.

Curiosity killed the cat.

curses

Blake, William (1757–1827)
English poet, engraver, painter and mystic

Damn braces: Bless relaxes.

The Marriage of Heaven and Hell (c.1790–1793)

Lipman, Maureen (1946–)
English actress

After criticism for swearing on TV

The word I used was 'bloody' which, where I come from in Yorkshire, is practically the only surviving adjective.

The Times, 1999

Shaw, George Bernard (1856–1950)
Irish socialist, writer, dramatist and critic

If ever I utter an oath again may my soul be blasted to eternal damnation!

Saint Joan (1924)

Sidney, Sir Philip (1554–1586)
English poet, critic, soldier, courtier and diplomat

Though I will not wish unto you the Ass's eares of Midas, nor to be driven by a Poet's verses as Bubonax was, to hang himselfe, nor to be rimed to death as is said to be done in Ireland; yet thus much Curse I must send you in the behalfe of all Poets, that while you live, you live in love, and never get favour, for lacking skill of a Sonet, and when you die, your memorie die from the earth for want of an Epitaphe.

The Defence of Poesie (1595)

Southey, Robert (1774–1843)
English poet, essayist, historian and letterwriter

Curses are like young chickens, they always

come home to roost.

The Curse of Kehama (1810)

And Sleep shall obey me,
And visit thee never,
And the Curse shall be on thee
For ever and ever.

The Curse of Kehama (1810)

Synge, J.M. (1871–1909)
Irish dramatist, poet and letter writer
To the sister of an enemy of the author who disapproved of
The Playboy of the Western World

Lord, confound this surly sister,
Blight her brow with blotch and blister,
Cramp her larynx, lung and liver,
In her guts a galling give her.

Let her live to earn her dinners
In Mountjoy with seedy sinners:
Lord, this judgement quickly bring,
And I'm your servant, J.M. Synge.

'The Curse'

Theroux, Paul (1941–)
US writer

A foreign swear-word is practically inoffensive
except to the person who has learnt it early in
life and knows its social limits.

Saint Jack

Twain, Mark (1835–1910)
US humorist, writer, journalist and lecturer

Some of his words were not Sunday-school
words.

A Tramp Abroad (1880)

curtains

Anonymous

The first pull on the cord ALWAYS sends the
curtains in the wrong direction.

Boyle's Other Law

Pope, Alexander (1688–1744)
English poet, translator and editor

Lo! thy dread empire, Chaos! is restored;
Light dies before thy uncreating word:
Thy hand, great Anarch! lets the curtain fall;
And universal darkness buries all.

The Dunciad (1742)

Rabelais, François (c.1494–c.1553)
French monk, physician, satirist and humanist
Last words

I am going to seek a great perhaps …Bring
down the curtain, the farce is played out.

Attr.

custom

Baillie, Joanna (1762–1851)
Scottish dramatist and poet

What custom hath endear'd
We part with sadly, though we prize it not.

Basil (1798)

Beckett, Samuel (1906–1989)
Irish dramatist, writer and poet

The air is full of our cries. But habit is a great
deadener.

Waiting for Godot (1955)

Benedict, Ruth (1887–1948)
US anthropologist

No man ever looks at the world with pristine
eyes. He sees it edited by a definite set
of customs and institutions and ways of
thinking.

Patterns of Culture (1934)

Burke, Edmund (1729–1797)
Irish-born British statesman and philosopher

Custom reconciles us to everything.

*A Philosophical Enquiry into the Origin of our Ideas
of the Sublime and Beautiful* (1757)

Crabbe, George (1754–1832)
English poet, clergyman, surgeon and botanist

Habit with him was all the test of truth,
'It must be right: I've done it from my youth.'

The Borough (1810)

Habit with him was all the test of truth,
'It must be right: I've done it from my youth.'

The Borough (1810)

Davenant, Charles (1656–1714)
English politician and dramatist

Custom, that unwritten law,
By which the people keep even kings in awe.

Circe (1677)

Hume, David (1711–1776)
Scottish philosopher and political economist

Custom, then, is the great guide of human life.

*Philosophical Essays Concerning Human
Understanding* (1748)

James, William (1842–1910)
US psychologist and philosopher

Habit is the enormous fly-wheel of society, its
most precious conservative agent.

Principles of Psychology (1890)

More, Hannah (1745–1833)
English poet, dramatist and religious writer

Small habits, well pursued betimes,
May reach the dignity of crimes.

Florio (1786)

Péguy, Charles (1873–1914)
French Catholic socialist, poet and writer

> *La mémoire et l'habitude sont les fourriers de la mort.*
> Memory and habit are the harbingers of death.
>
> *Note conjointe sur M. Descartes*

Shakespeare, William (1564–1616)
English dramatist, poet and actor

> Age cannot wither her, nor custom stale
> Her infinite variety. Other women cloy
> The appetites they feed, but she makes hungry
> Where most she satisfies.
>
> *Antony and Cleopatra*, II.ii

> Custom calls me to't.
> What custom wills, in all things should we do't.
>
> *Coriolanus* II.iii

> It is a custom
> More honour'd in the breach than the observance.
>
> *Hamlet*, I.iv

> How use doth breed a habit in a man!
>
> *The Two Gentlemen of Verona*, V.iv

Sheridan, Richard Brinsley (1751–1816)
Irish dramatist, politician and orator

> There's nothing like being used to a thing.
>
> *The Rivals* (1775)

Wordsworth, William (1770–1850)
English poet

> Not choice
> But habit rules the unreflecting herd.
>
> 'Grant that by this unsparing hurricane' (1822)

▶▶ HABIT

cynicism

Allen, Woody (1935–)
US film director, writer, actor and comedian

> The lion and the calf shall lie down together but the calf won't get much sleep.
>
> *Without Feathers* (1976)

Bierce, Ambrose (1842–c.1914)
US writer, verse writer and soldier

> *Cynic*: A blackguard whose faulty vision sees things as they are, not as they ought to be.
>
> *The Enlarged Devil's Dictionary* (1961)

Chekhov, Anton (1860–1904)
Russian writer, dramatist and doctor

> After all, the cynicism of real life can't be outdone by any literature: one glass won't get someone drunk when he's already had a whole barrel.
>
> Letter to M.V. Kiseleva, 1887

Cozzens, James Gould 1903–1978)
US writer

> A cynic is just a man who found out when he was about ten that there wasn't any Santa Claus, and he's still upset.
>
> Attr.

Harris, Sydney J. (1917–)
US journalist

> A cynic is not merely one who reads bitter lessons from the past, he is one who is prematurely disappointed in the future.
>
> *On the Contrary* (1962)

Hellman, Lillian (1907–1984)
US dramatist and screenwriter

> Cynicism is an unpleasant way of saying the truth.
>
> *The Little Foxes* (1939)

Hurst, Fannie (1889–1968)
US writer and playwright

> It takes a clever man to turn cynic, and a wise man to be clever enough not to.
>
> Attr.

Meredith, George (1828–1909)
English writer, poet and critic

> Cynicism is intellectual dandyism.
>
> *The Egoist* (1879)

Wilde, Oscar (1854–1900)
Irish poet, dramatist, writer, critic and wit
In a lecture on Dickens

> One would have to have a heart of stone to read the death of Little Nell without laughing.
>
> In H. Pearson, *Lives of the Wits*

> Cecil Graham: What is a cynic?
> Lord Darlington: A man who knows the price of everything and the value of nothing.
>
> *Lady Windermere's Fan* (1892)

D

dancing

Auden, W.H. (1907–1973)
English poet, essayist, critic, teacher and dramatist
> The desires of the heart are as crooked as corkscrews,
> Not to be born is the best for man;
> The second-best is a formal order,
> Thy dance's pattern; dance while you can.
> Dance, dance, for the figure is easy,
> The tune is catching and will not stop;
> Dance till the stars come down from the rafters;
> Dance, dance, dance till you drop.
>> *Collected Poems, 1933–1938,* 'Death's Echo'

Austen, Jane (1775–1817)
English writer
> Fine dancing, I believe, like virtue, must be its own reward.
>> *Emma* (1816)

Bankhead, Tallulah (1903–1968)
US actress
Said on dropping fifty dollars into a tambourine held out by a Salvation Army collector
> Don't bother to thank me. I know what a perfectly ghastly season it's been for you Spanish dancers.
>> Attr.

Burney, Fanny (1752–1840)
English diarist
> Dancing? Oh, dreadful! How it was ever adopted in a civilized country I cannot find out; 'tis certainly a Barbarian exercise, and of savage origin.
>> *Cecilia* (1782)

Burns, Robert (1759–1796)
Scottish poet and song writer
> But the ae best dance ere cam to the land
> Was The Deil's Awa wi' th' Exciseman!
>> 'The Deil's Awa wi' th' Exciseman' (1792)

Chesterfield, Lord (1694–1773)
English politician and letter writer
> Custom has made dancing sometimes necessary for a young man; therefore mind it while you learn it, that you may learn to do it well, and not be ridiculous, though in a ridiculous act.
>> Letter to his son, 1746

Cicero (106–43 BC)
Roman orator, statesman, essayist and letter writer
> *Nemo enim fere saltat sobrius, nisi forte insanit.*
> No sober man dances, unless he happens to be mad.
>> *Pro Murena*

De Valois, Dame Ninette (1898–1998)
> Ladies and gentlemen, it takes more than one to make a ballet.
>> *The New Yorker*

Duncan, Isadora (1878–1927)
US modern dance pioneer
> I have discovered the dance. I have discovered the art which has been lost for two thousand years.
>> *My Life* (1927)

Harris, Charles (1865–1930)
US songwriter
> Many a heart is aching, if you could read them all,
> Many the hopes that have vanished, after the ball.
>> 'After the Ball', 1892

Helpman, Sir Robert Murray (1909–1986)
Australian choreographer and director
> Aren't all ballets sexy? I think they should be. I can thing of nothing more kinky than a prince chasing a swan around all night.
>> In Jonathon Green (ed.), *A Dictionary of Contemporary Quotations* (1982)

Pavlova, Anna (1881–1931)
Russian ballet dancer
> Although one may fail to find happiness in theatrical life, one never wishes to give it up after having once tasted its fruits. To enter the School of the Imperial Ballet is to enter a convent whence frivolity is banned, and where merciless discipline reigns.
>> In A.H. Franks (ed.), *Pavlova: A Biography*

Sallust (86–c.34 BC)
Roman historian and statesman
> *Psallere et saltare elegantius, quam necesse est probae.*
> To play the lyre and dance more beautifully than a virtuous woman need.
>> *Catiline*

Shakespeare, William (1564–1616)
English dramatist, poet and actor
> You and I are past our dancing days.
>> *Romeo and Juliet,* I.v

> When you do dance, I wish you
> A wave o' th' sea, that you might ever do
> Nothing but that; move still, still so,
> And own no other function.
>> *The Winter's Tale,* IV.iv

Suckling, Sir John (1609–1642)
English poet and dramatist
> Her feet beneath her petticoat,
> Like little mice, stole in and out,

As if they fear'd the light:
But O she dances such a way!
No sun upon an Easter-day
Is half so fine a sight.

'A Ballad upon a Wedding' (1646)

Surtees, R.S. (1805–1864)
English writer
These sort of boobies think that people come to balls to do nothing but dance; whereas everyone knows that the real business of a ball is either to look out for a wife, to look after a wife, or to look after somebody else's wife.

Mr Facey Romford's Hounds (1865)

Yeats, W.B. (1865–1939)
Irish poet, dramatist, editor, writer and senator
When I play on my fiddle in Dooney,
Folk dance like a wave of the sea …

For the good are always the merry,
Save by an evil chance,
And the merry love the fiddle,
And the merry love to dance.

In the *Bookman*, 1892

All men are dancers and their tread
Goes to the barbarous clangour of a gong.

'Nineteen Hundred and Nineteen' (1921)

O chestnut-tree, great-rooted blossomer,
Are you the leaf, the blossom or the bole?
O body swayed to music, O brightening glance,
How can we know the dancer from the dance?

'Among School Children' (1927)

danger

Burke, Edmund (1729–1797)
Irish-born British statesman and philosopher
Dangers by being despised grow great.

Speech on the Petition of the Unitarians, 1792

Chapman, George (c.1559–c.1634)
English poet, dramatist and translator
Danger (the spurre of all great mindes) is ever
The curbe to your tame spirits.

Revenge of Bussy D'Ambois (1613)

Corneille, Pierre (1606–1684)
French dramatist, poet and lawyer
A vaincre sans péril, on triomphe sans gloire.
When we conquer without danger our triumph is without glory.

Le Cid (1637)

Curnow, Allen (1911–)
New Zealand poet and editor
Always to islanders danger

Is what comes over the sea.

Collected Poems 1933–1973 (1974)

Earhart, Amelia (1898–1937)
US aviator
Of her flight in the 'Friendship'
Of course I realized there was a measure of danger. Obviously I faced the possibility of not returning when first I considered going. Once faced and settled there really wasn't any good reason to refer to it.

20 Hours: 40 Minutes – Our Flight in the Friendship (1928)

Emerson, Ralph Waldo (1803–1882)
US poet, essayist, transcendentalist and teacher
In skating over thin ice, our safety is in our speed.

'Prudence' (1841)

As soon as there is life there is danger.

Society and Solitude (1870)

Gay, John (1685–1732)
English poet, dramatist and librettist
How, like a moth, the simple maid,
Still plays about the flame!

The Beggar's Opera (1728)

Jordan, Thomas (c.1612–1685)
Our God and soldier we alike adore,
Just at the brink of ruin, not before:
The danger past, both are alike requited;
God is forgotten, and our soldier slighted.

Epigram

MacCarthy, Cormac (1933–)
US writer
There are dragons in the wings of the world.

The Guardian, 1995

Proverb
Danger and delight grow on one stalk.

Salinger, J.D. (1919–)
US writer
What I have to do, I have to catch everybody if they start to go over the cliff – I mean if they're running and they don't look where they're going I have to come out from somewhere and catch them … I'd just be the catcher in the rye and all.

The Catcher in the Rye (1951)

Salvandy, Narcisse Achille (1795–1856)
French statesman and man of letters
Nous dansons sur un volcan.
We are dancing on a volcano.

Remark made before July Revolution, 1830

Scott, Sir Walter (1771–1832)
Scottish writer and historian
Look back, and smile at perils past.

The Bridal of Triermain (1813), Introduction

Shakespeare, William (1564–1616)
English dramatist, poet and actor
> Out of this nettle, danger, we pluck this flower, safety.

Henry IV, Part 1, II.iii

Stevenson, Robert Louis (1850–1894)
Scottish writer, poet and essayist
> The bright face of danger.

'The Lantern-Bearers' (1892)

Tertullian (c.AD 160–c.225)
Carthaginian theologian
> *Pervenimus igitur de calcaria, quod dici solet, in carbonarium.*
> We come therefore, as the Proverb has it, out of the frying pan into the fire [literally, from the limekiln to the charcoal furnace].

De Carne Christi

Washington, George (1732–1799)
US general, statesman and President
> I heard the bullets whistle, and believe me, there is something charming in the sound.

In P. Boller, *Presidential Anecdotes*

dawn

FitzGerald, Edward (1809–1883)
English poet, translator and letter writer
> Awake! for Morning in the Bowl of Night
> Has flung the Stone that puts the Stars to Flight:
> And Lo! the Hunter of the East has caught
> The Sultan's Turret in a Noose of Light.

The Rubáiyát of Omar Khayyám (1859)

Homer (fl. c.8th century BC)
Greek epic poet
> Rosy-fingered dawn.

Iliad, passim

Masefield, John (1878–1967)
English poet, writer and critic
> I have seen dawn and sunset on moors and windy hills
> Coming in solemn beauty like slow old tunes of Spain.

'Beauty' (1903)

Shakespeare, William (1564–1616)
English dramatist, poet and actor
> Hark, hark! the lark at heaven's gate sings,
> And Phoebus 'gins arise,
> His steeds to water at those springs
> On chalic'd flow'rs that lies;
> And winking Mary-buds begin
> To ope their golden eyes.
> With everything that pretty bin,
> My lady sweet, arise.

Cymbeline, II.iii

> But look, the morn, in russet mantle clad,
> Walks o'er the dew of yon high eastward hill.

Hamlet, I.i

> The glowworm shows the matin to be near,
> And gins to pale his uneffectual fire.

Hamlet, I.v

> *Juliet*: Wilt thou be gone? It is not yet near day;
> It was the nightingale, and not the lark,
> That pierc'd the fearfull hollow of thine ear;
> Nightly she sings on yond pomegranate tree.
> Believe me, love, it was the nightingale.
> *Romeo*: It was the lark, the herald of the morn,
> No nightingale. Look, love, what envious streaks
> Do lace the severing clouds in yonder east;
> Night's candles are burnt out, and jocund day
> Stands tiptoe on the misty mountain tops.
> I must be gone and live, or stay and die.

Romeo and Juliet, III.v

Wilde, Oscar (1854–1900)
Irish poet, dramatist, writer, critic and wit
> And down the long and silent street,
> The dawn, with silver-sandalled feet,
> Crept like a frightened girl.

'The Harlot's House' (1881)

Wilder, Thornton (1897–1975)
US author and playwright
> For what human ill does dawn not seem to be an alleviation?

The Bridge of San Luis Rey

deadlines

Adams, Scott (1957–)
> I love deadlines. I especially love the swooshing sound they make as they go flying by.

The Dilbert Principle

Anonymous
> The remaining work to finish in order to reach your goal increases as the deadline approaches.

Bove's Theorem

death

Addison, Joseph (1672–1719)
English essayist, poet, playwright and statesman
> When I read the several dates of the tombs, of some that died yesterday, and some six hundred years ago, I consider that great day when we shall all of us be contemporaries, and make our appearance together.

Thoughts in Westminster Abbey

Anonymous
    Enjoy life. There's plenty of time to be dead.

Auber, Daniel François Esprit (1782–1871)
French opera composer
Remark made at a funeral
    This is the last time I will take part as an
    amateur.
                                                    Attr.

Bacon, Francis (1561–1626)
English philosopher, essayist, politician and courtier
    Men fear death as children fear to go in the
    dark; and as that natural fear in children is
    increased with tales, so is the other.
                                        Essays (1625)

    I have often thought upon death, and I find it
    the least of all evils.
                    The Remaines of ... Lord Verulam (1648)

Balzac, Honoré de (1799–1850)
French writer
    *La fin est le retour de toutes choses à l'unite qui est
    Dieu.*
    The end is when all things return to unity, that is
    to say, God.
                                Louis Lambert (1832)

    *Que signifie adieu, à moins de mourir? Mais la mort
    serait-elle un adieu?*
    What does farewell mean, unless one is dying?
    But is death itself a farewell?
                                Louis Lambert (1832)

Baudelaire, Charles (1821–1867)
French poet, translator and critic
    O Mort, vieux capitaine, il est temps! levons l'ancre!
    O Death, old captain, the time has come! Let us
    weigh anchor!
                    Les Fleurs du mal (1857), 'Le Voyage'

Bhagavadgita
    I am become death, the destroyer of worlds.
        Quoted by J. Robert Oppenheimer on seeing the
        first nuclear explosion

The Bible (King James Version)
    The last enemy that shall be destroyed is death.
                            I Corinthians, 15:26

    O death, where is thy sting? O grave, where is
    thy victory?
                            I Corinthians, 15:55

Bion (fl. 280 BC)
    Though boys throw stones at frogs in sport, the
    frogs do not die in sport, but in earnest.
                            Quoted by *Plutarch*

Bowra, Sir Maurice (1898–1971)
English scholar
    Any amusing deaths lately?
                                                    Attr.

Bridges, Robert (1844–1930)
English poet, dramatist, essayist and doctor
    When Death to either shall come, –
    I pray it be first to me.
                    'When Death to Either Shall Come'

Brontë, Emily (1818–1848)
English poet and writer
    I lingered round them, under that benign sky:
    watched the moths fluttering among the heath
    and harebells; listened to the soft wind
    breathing through the grass; and wondered how
    anyone could ever imagine unquiet slumbers for
    the sleepers in that quiet earth.
                    Wuthering Heights (1847), last lines

Brooke, Rupert (1887–1915)
English poet
    Oh! Death will find me long before I tire
    Of watching you; and swing me suddenly
    Into the shade and loneliness and mire
    Of the last land!
                    'Oh! Death will find me' (1909)

Browne, Sir Thomas (1605–1682)
English physician, author and antiquary
    He forgets that he can die who complains of
    misery – we are in the power of no calamity
    while death is in our own.
                            Religio Medici (1643)

    I am not so much afraid of death, as ashamed
    thereof; 'tis the very disgrace and ignominy of
    our natures, that in a moment can so disfigure
    us that our nearest friends, wife, and children,
    stand afraid and start at us.
                            Religio Medici (1643)

Buck, Pearl S. (1892–1973)
US writer and dramatist
    Euthanasia is a long, smooth-sounding word,
    and it conceals its danger as long, smooth words
    do, but the danger is there, nevertheless.
                    The Child Who Never Grew (1950)

Burchill, Julie (1960–)
English writer
    Tears are sometimes an inappropriate response
    to death. When a life has been lived completely
    honestly, completely successfully, or just
    completely, the correct response to death's
    perfect punctuation mark is a smile.
                    The Independent, 1989

Burke, Edmund (1729–1797)
Irish-born British statesman and philosopher
    I would rather sleep in the southern corner of a
    little country church-yard, than in the tomb of
    the Capulets. I should like, however, that my
    dust should mingle with kindred dust.
                    Letter to Matthew Smith, 1750

Burns, Robert (1759–1796)
Scottish poet and song writer
> O death, the poor man's dearest friend,
> The kindest and the best!
>> 'Man was made to Mourn, a Dirge' (1784)

Butler, Samuel (1835–1902)
English writer, painter, philosopher and scholar
> When you have told anyone you have left him a legacy the only decent thing to do is to die at once.
>> In Festing Jones, *Samuel Butler: A Memoir*

Catullus (84–c.54 BC)
Roman poet
> *Qui nunc it per iter tenebricosum*
> *Illuc, unde negant redire quemquam.*
> Now he goes along the shadowy path, there, from which they say no one returns.
>> *Carmina*

Cervantes, Miguel de (1547–1616)
Spanish writer and dramatist
> *Ahora bien: todas las cosas tienen remedio, si no es la muerte.*
> Well, now: there's a remedy for everything, except death.
>> *Don Quixote* (1615)

Chateaubriand, François-René (1768–1848)
French writer and statesman
> *On n'apprend pas à mourir en tuant les autres.*
> One does not learn how to die by killing others.
>> *Memoirs* (1826–1841)

Chesterfield, Lord (1694–1773)
English politician and letter writer
Said when Tyrawley was old and infirm
> Tyrawley and I have been dead these two years; but we don't choose to have it known.
>> In Boswell, *The Life of Samuel Johnson* (1791)

Clare, John (1793–1864)
English rural poet; died in an asylum
> Pale death, the grand physician, cures all pain;
> The dead rest well who lived for joys in vain.
>> 'Child Harold' (1841)

Dibdin, Charles (1745–1814)
English songwriter, dramatist and actor
> What argufies pride and ambition?
> Soon or late death will take us in tow:
> Each bullet has got its commission,
> And when our time's come we must go.
>> 'Each Bullet has its Commission'

Dickinson, Emily (1830–1886)
US poet
> Because I could not stop for Death –
> He kindly stopped for me –
> The Carriage held but just Ourselves –
> And Immortality.
>> 'Because I could not stop for Death' (c.1863)

> This quiet Dust was Gentlemen and Ladies
> And Lads and Girls –
> Was laughter and ability and Sighing
> And Frocks and Curls.
>> 'This quiet Dust was Gentlemen and Ladies' (c.1864)

Donne, John (1572–1631)
English poet
> Think then, my soul, that death is but a groom,
> Which brings a taper to the outward room.
>> *Of the Progress of the Soul* (1612)

> One short sleep past, we wake eternally,
> And death shall be no more; death, thou shalt die.
>> *Holy Sonnets* (1609–1617)

On Death
> It comes equally to us all, and makes us all equal when it comes. The ashes of an Oak in the Chimney, are no epitaph of that Oak, to tell me now high or how large that was; It tells me not what flocks it sheltered while it stood, nor what men it hurt when it fell. The dust of great persons' graves is speechless too, it says nothing, it distinguishes nothing: As soon the dust of a wretch whom thou wouldest not, as of a Prince whom thou couldest not look upon, will trouble thine eyes, if the wind blow it thither; and when a whirlwind hath blown the dust of the Churchyard into the Church, and the man sweeps out the dust of the Church into the Churchyard, who will undertake to sift those dusts again, and to pronounce, This is the Patrician, this is the noble flower, and this is the yeomanly, this the Plebeian bran.
>> *LXXX Sermons* (1640)

Dryden, John (1631–1700)
English poet, satirist, dramatist and critic
> Death, in itself, is nothing; but we fear,
> To be we know not what, we know not where.
>> *Aureng-Zebe* (1675)

Dunbar, William (c.1460–c.1525)
Scottish poet, satirist and courtier
> I that in heill wes and gladnes
> Am trublit now with gret seiknes
> And feblit with infirmitie:
> Timor mortis conturbat me …
> Our plesance here is all vain glory,
> This fals world is but transitory,
> The flesh is bruckle, the Feynd is slee:
> Timor Mortis conturbat me …
>
> Unto the deid gois all Estatis,
> Princis, prelatis, and potestatis,
> Baith rich and poor of all degree:

Timor Mortis conturbat me.

'Lament for the Makaris' (1834)

Eliot, T.S. (1888–1965)
US-born British poet, verse dramatist and critic
Webster was much possessed by death
And saw the skull beneath the skin;
And breastless creatures under ground
Leaned backward with a lipless grin.

'Whispers of Immortality' (1920)

Phlebas the Phoenician, a fortnight dead,
Forgot the cry of gulls, and the deep sea swell
And the profit and loss.

The Waste Land (1922)

Fitzgerald, Edward (1809–1883)
English poet, translator and letter writer
Strange, is it not? that of the myriads who
Before us pass'd the door of Darkness through,
Not one returns to tell us of the Road,
Which to discover we must travel too.

The Rubáiyát of Omar Khayyám (1879)

Fletcher, John (1579–1625)
English dramatist
Death hath so many doors to let out life.

The Custom of the Country (1647)

Forster, E.M. (1879–1970)
English writer, essayist and literary critic
Death destroys a man; the idea of Death saves
him.

Howard's End (1910)

Goldsmith, Oliver (c.1728–1774)
Irish dramatist, poet and writer
I'm told he makes a very handsome corpse, and
becomes his coffin prodigiously.

The Good Natur'd Man (1768)

Gordon, Adam Lindsay (1833–1870)
 Australian poet and ballad writer
Let me slumber in the hollow where the wattle
blossoms wave,
With never stone or rail to fence my bed;
Should the sturdy station children pull the bush
flowers on my grave,
I may chance to hear them romping overhead.

'The Sick Stockrider'

Gray, John
British academic
There are nearly as many human beings alive as
ever lived up to the start of this century. Soon,
the Greek catchword for death – joining the
majority – will cease to be accurate.

The Observer, 1998

Gray, Patrick (d. 1612)
Scottish courtier, ambassador at the court of Elizabeth I
of England
Advocating the execution of Mary, Queen of Scots

A dead woman bites not.

Oral tradition, 1587

Gray, Thomas (1716–1771)
English poet and scholar
The boast of heraldry, the pomp of pow'r,
And all that beauty, all that wealth e'er gave,
Awaits alike th' inevitable hour,
The paths of glory lead but to the grave.

'Elegy Written in a Country Churchyard' (1751)

Hastings, Lady Flora (1806–1839)
Scottish poet
Grieve not that I die young. Is it not well
To pass away ere life hath lost its brightness?

'Swan Song'

Hawthorne, Nathaniel (1804–1864)
US allegorical writer
We sometimes congratulate ourselves at the
moment of waking from a troubled dream; it
may be so the moment after death.

American Notebooks

Hendrix, Jimi (1942–1970)
US rock singer, songwriter and guitarist
It's funny the way most people love the dead.
Once you're dead, you're made for life.

In Rolling Stone, 1976

Henley, William Ernest (1849–1903)
English poet, dramatist and critic
Madam Life's a piece in bloom
Death goes dogging everywhere:
She's the tenant of the room,
He's the ruffian on the stair.

Echoes (1877)

Herbert, George (1593–1633)
English poet and priest
Death is still working like a mole,
And digs my grave at each remove.

The Temple (1633)

Holland, Canon Henry Scott (1847–1918)
English cleric, Professor of Divinity and Christian social
reformer
Death is nothing at all. It does not count. I
have only slipped away into the next room.
Nothing has happened. Everything remains
exactly as it was. I am I, and you are you, and
the old life that we lived so fondly together is
untouched, unchanged. Whatever we were to
each other, that we are still. Call me by the old
familiar name. Speak of me in the easy way
which you always used. Put no difference into
your tone. Wear no forced air of solemnity or
sorrow. Laugh as we always laughed at the
little jokes that we enjoyed together. Play,
smile, think of me, pray for me. Let my name
be ever the household word that it always was.
Let my name be ever the household word that

it always was. Let it be spoken without an effort, without the ghost of a shadow upon it. Life means all that it ever meant. It is the same as it ever was. There is absolute and unbroken continuity. What is death but a negligible accident? Why should I be out of mind because I am out of sight? I am but waiting for you, for an interval, somewhere very near, just round the corner. All is well.

Facts of the faith (1919)

Horace (65–8 BC)
Roman poet

Pallida Mors, aequo pulsat pede pauperum tabernas
Regumque turris.
Pale Death strikes with impartial foot at the cottages of the poor and the turrets of kings.

Odes

Huxley, Aldous (1894–1963)
English writer, poet and critic
Death … It's the only thing we haven't succeeded in completely vulgarizing.

Eyeless in Gaza (1936)

Huxley, Henrietta (1825–1915)
English writer and poet; wife of T.H. Huxley
And if there be no meeting past the grave,
If all is darkness, silence, yet 'tis rest.
Be not afraid ye waiting hearts that weep;
For still He giveth His beloved sleep,
And if an endless sleep He wills, so best.

Lines on the grave of her husband, 1895

Juvenal (c.60–130)
Roman verse satirist and Stoic

Mors sola fatetur
Quantula sint hominum corpuscula.
Death only this mysterious truth unfolds,
The mighty soul, how small a body holds.

Satires

Keats, John (1795–1821)
English poet
Darkling I listen; and, for many a time
I have been half in love with easeful Death,
Call'd him soft names in many a musèd rhyme,
To take into the air my quiet breath;
Now more than ever seems it rich to die,
To cease upon the midnight with no pain,
While thou art pouring forth thy soul abroad
In such an ecstasy!
Still wouldst thou sing, and I have ears in vain –
To thy high requiem become a sod.

'Ode to a Nightingale' (1819)

Keyes, Sidney (1922–1943)
English poet and soldier
At this twelfth hour of unrelenting summer
I think of those whose ready mouths are
stopped,
I remember those who crouch in narrow graves,
I weep for those whose eyes are full of sand.

Two Offices of a Sentry (1942)

Kipling, Rudyard (1865–1936)
Indian-born British poet and writer
To a magazine which incorrectly reported his death
I've just read that I am dead. Don't forget to delete me from your list of subscribers.

Attr.

Koestler, Arthur (1905–1983)
British writer, essayist and political refugee
Of the atomic bomb
Hitherto man had to live with the idea of death as an individual; from now onward mankind will have to live with the idea of its death as a species.

Attr.

Kübler-Ross, Elisabeth (1926–)
Watching the peaceful death of a human being reminds us of a falling star; one of a million lights in a vast sky that flares up for a brief moment only to disappear into the endless night forever.

On Death and Dying (1969)

La Fontaine, Jean de (1621–1695)
French poet and fabulist

La Mort ne surprend point le sage;
Il est toujours prêt à partir.
Death does not take the wise man by surprise, he is always prepared to leave.

'La Mort et le mourant'

Lamb, Charles (1775–1834)
English essayist, critic and letter writer
Gone before
To that unknown and silent shore.

'Hester' (1803)

Landor, Walter Savage (1775–1864)
English poet and writer
Death stands above me, whispering low
I know not what into my ear;
Of his strange language all I know
Is, there is not a word of fear.

Epigrams (1853)

I strove with none; for none was worth my strife;
Nature I loved, and next to Nature, Art;
I warmed both hands before the fire of life;
It sinks, and I am ready to depart.

'Finis'

Larkin, Philip (1922–1985)
English poet, writer and librarian
On death
The anaesthetic from which none come round.

'Aubade' (1988)

Lawrence, D.H. (1885–1930)
English writer, poet and critic
>The dead don't die. They look on and help.
>
>>Letter to J. Middleton Murry, 1923

>Now it is autumn and the falling fruit
>and the long journey towards oblivion –
>Have you built your ship of death,
>O have you?
>O build your ship of death, for you will need it.
>
>>*Last Poems* (1932), 'The Ship of Death'

Lewis, D.B. Wyndham (1891–1969)
British writer and biographer
>I am one of those unfortunates to whom death
>is less hideous than explanations.
>
>>*Welcome to All This*

Lucretius (c.95–55 BC)
Roman philosopher
>*Nil igitur mors est ad nos neque pertinet hilum,*
>*Quandoquidem natura animi mortalis habetur.*
>What has this bugbear death to frighten man
>If souls can die as well as bodies can?
>
>>*De Rerum Natura*

>*Scire licet nobis nil esse in morte timendum*
>*Nec miserum fieri qui non est posse neque hilum*
>*Differre an nullo fuerit iam tempore natus,*
>*Mortalem vitam mors cum immortalis ademit.*
>And since the man who is not, feels not woe,
>(For death exempts him, and wards off the blow,
>Which we, the living, only feel and bear,)
>What is there left for us in death to fear?
>When once that pause of life has come between
>'Tis just the same as we had never been.
>
>>*De Rerum Natura*

Macaulay, Lord (1800–1859)
English Liberal statesman, essayist and poet
>With the dead there is no rivalry. In the dead
>there is no change. Plato is never sullen.
>Cervantes is never petulant. Demosthenes never
>comes unseasonably. Dante never stays too
>long. No difference of political opinion can
>alienate Cicero. No heresy can excite the horror
>of Bossuet.
>
>>*Collected Essays* (1843),
>>'Lord Bacon'

Maeterlinck, Maurice (1862–1949)
Belgian poet, playwright and essayist
>The living are just the dead on holiday.
>
>>Attr.

Mankiewicz, Herman J. (1897–1953)
US journalist and screenwriter
Of death
>It is the only disease you don't look forward to
>being cured of.
>
>>*Citizen Kane* (film, 1941)

Mann, Thomas (1875–1955)
German writer and critic
>*Vom Tode wüsste Ihnen keiner, der wiederkäme, was*
>*Rechtes zu erzählen, denn man erlebt ihn nicht. Wir*
>*kommen aus dem Dunkel und gehen ins Dunkel,*
>*dazwischen liegen Erlebnisse, aber Anfang und Ende,*
>*Geburt und Tod, werden von uns nicht erlebt, sie haben*
>*keinen subjektiven Charakter.*
>No one who could come back from death would
>be able to tell you anything about it, because
>we do not experience it. We come out of the
>dark and go into the dark, and in between we
>have experiences, but beginning and end, birth
>and death, are not experienced by us, they have
>no subjective character.
>
>>*The Magic Mountain* (1924)

Marvell, Andrew (1621–1678)
English poet and satirist
>The grave's a fine and private place,
>But none I think do there embrace.
>
>>'To His Coy Mistress' (1681)

Marx, Groucho (1895–1977)
US comedian
>Either he's dead or my watch has stopped.
>
>>*A Day at the Races* (film, 1937)

Masefield, John (1878–1967)
English poet, writer and critic
>Death opens unknown doors. It is most grand to
>die.
>
>>*Pompey the Great* (1910)

Massinger, Philip (1583–1640)
English dramatist and poet
>Death has a thousand doors to let out life:
>I shall find one.
>
>>*A Very Woman* (1634)

Millay, Edna St Vincent (1892–1950)
US poet and dramatist
>Down, down, down into the darkness of the
>grave
>Gently they go, the beautiful, the tender, the
>kind;
>Quietly they go, the intelligent, the witty, the
>brave.
>I know. But I do not approve. And I am not
>resigned.
>
>>'Dirge without Music' (1928)

Molière (1622–1673)
French dramatist, actor and director
>*On ne meurt qu'une fois, et c'est pour si longtemps!*
>One dies only once, and then for such a long
>time!
>
>>*Le Dépit Amoureux* (1656)

Montaigne, Michel de (1533–1592)
French essayist and moralist
>*Je veux ... que la mort me trouve plantant mes choux,*

mais nonchalant d'elle, et encore plus de mon jardin imparfait.
I want death to find me planting my cabbages, but caring little for it, and even less for my imperfect garden.

Essais (1580)

Napoleon I (1769–1821)
French emperor
Oh well, no matter what happens, there's always death.

Attr.

Ouida (1839–1908)
English writer and critic
Even of death Christianity has made a terror which was unknown to the gay calmness of the Pagan.

Views and Opinions (1895)

Owen, Wilfred (1893–1918)
English poet
What passing-bells for these who die as cattle?
Only the monstrous anger of the guns.
Only the stuttering rifles' rapid rattle
Can patter out their hasty orisons.

'Anthem for Doomed Youth' (1917)

Patten, Brian (1946–)
British poet
Death is the only grammatically correct full-stop ...

'Schoolboy' (1990)

Between himself and the grave his parents stand,
monuments that will crumble.

'Schoolboy' (1990)

Death does not necessarily diminish us,
it also deepens our awareness of what it means to be alive.

'Grave gossip'

Petronius Arbiter (d. AD 66)
Speaking of someone who has died
Abiit ad plures.
He has joined the great majority.

Satyricon

Power, Marguerite, Countess of Blessington (1789–1849)
English writer
It is better to die young than to outlive all one loved, and all that rendered one lovable.

The Confessions of an Elderly Gentleman (1836)

Proverbs
Death is the great leveller.

Fear of death is worse than death itself.

A man can die but once.

Raleigh, Sir Walter (c.1552–1618)
English courtier, explorer, military commander, poet, historian and essayist
Only we die in earnest, that's no jest.

'On the Life of Man'

O eloquent, just and mighty Death! ... thou hast drawn together all the far-stretched greatness, all the pride, cruelty, and ambition of man, and covered it all over with these two narrow words, *Hic jacet.*

The History of the World (1614)

Robinson, Edwin Arlington (1869–1935)
US poet
I shall have more to say when I am dead.

The Three Taverns (1920)

Ros, Amanda (1860–1939)
Irish novelist and poet
Holy Moses! Have a look!
Flesh decayed in every nook.
Some rare bits of brain lie here,
Mortal loads of beef and beer.

'Lines on Westminster Abbey'

Ross, Sir Ronald (1857–1932)
Indian-born British physician
O Death, where is thy sting?
Thy victory, O Grave?

Philosophies (1910)

Rossetti, Christina (1830–1894)
English poet
O Earth, lie heavily upon her eyes;
Seal her sweet eyes weary of watching, Earth.

'Rest' (1862)

Rowe, Nicholas (1674–1718)
English dramatist
Death is the privilege of human nature,
And life without it were not worth our taking.

The Fair Penitent (1703)

Saki (1870–1916)
Burmese-born British writer
Waldo is one of those people who would be enormously improved by death.

Beasts and Super-Beasts (1914)

Sassoon, Siegfried (1886–1967)
English poet and writer
Stumbling along the trench in the dusk, dead men and living lying against the sides of the trenches – one never knew which were dead and which living. Dead and living were nearly one, for death was in all our hearts.

Diary, April 1917

The place was rotten with dead: green clumsy legs
High-booted, sprawled and grovelled along the saps

And trunks, face downward, in the sucking mud
Wallowed like trodden sandbags loosely filled;
And naked sodden buttocks, mats of hair,
Bulged, clotted heads slept in the plastering
slime.
And then the rain began – the jolly old rain!

'Counter-Attack' (1917)

Schopenhauer, Arthur (1788–1860)
German philosopher

After your death you will be what you were
before your birth.

Parerga and Paralipomena (1851)

Scott, Ridley
English film director
Dying speech of replicant Roy Batty

I've seen things you wouldn't believe. Attack
ships on fire off the shoulder of Orion. I watched
C-beams glitter in the dark near the Tannhauser
gate. All those moments will be lost in time, like
tears in rain. Time to die.

Blade Runner (film, 1982)

Scott, Sir Walter (1771–1832)
Scottish writer and historian

And come he slow, or come he fast,
It is but Death who comes at last.

Marmion (1808)

His morning walk was beneath the elms in the
churchyard; 'for death, ' he said, 'had been his
next-door neighbour for so many years, that he
had no apology for dropping the acquaintance.'

A Legend of Montrose (1819)

Seeger, Alan (1888–1916)
US poet

I have a rendezvous with Death,
At some disputed barricade,
At midnight in some flaming town.

'I Have a Rendezvous with Death' (1916)

Seneca (c.4 BC–AD 65)
Roman philosopher, poet, dramatist, essayist, rhetorician
and statesman

Eripere vitam nemo non homini potest,
At nemo mortem; mille ad hanc aditus patent.
Anyone can take away a man's life, but no one
his death; to this a thousand doors lie open.

Phoenissae

Illi mors gravis incubat
Qui notus nimis omnibus
Ignotus moritur sibi.
For him death grippeth right hard by the crop
That know of all, but to himself, alas
Doth die unknown, dazed with dreadful face.

Thyestes

Sévigné, Marquise de (1626–1696)

Je trouve la mort si terrible, que je hais plus la vie parce
qu'elle m'y mène, que par les épines qui s'y
rencontrent.
I find death so terrible that I hate life more for
leading me towards it than for the thorns
encountered on the way.

Letter to Mme de Grignan, 1672

Shakespeare, Nicholas
English writer

The dead are surprised by too many friends.

Sunday Telegraph, 1993

Shakespeare, William (1564–1616)
English dramatist, poet and actor

Fear no more the heat o' th' sun
Nor the furious winter's rages;
Thou thy worldly task hast done,
Home art gone, and ta'en thy wages.
Golden lads and girls all must,
As chimney-sweepers, come to dust.

Cymbeline, IV.ii

O, that this too too solid flesh would melt,
Thaw, and resolve itself into a dew!
Or that the Everlasting had not fix'd
His canon 'gainst self-slaughter! O God! God!
How weary, stale, flat, and unprofitable,
Seem to me all the uses of this world!
Fie on't! Ah, fie! 'tis an unweeded garden,
That grows to seed; things rank and gross in
nature
Possess it merely.

Hamlet, I.ii

To be, or not to be – that is the question;
Whether 'tis nobler in the mind to suffer
The slings and arrows of outrageous fortune,
Or to take arms against a sea of troubles,
And by opposing end them? To die, to sleep –
No more; and by a sleep to say we end
The heart-ache and the thousand natural shocks
That flesh is heir to. 'Tis a consummation
Devoutly to be wish'd. To die, to sleep;
To sleep, perchance to dream. Ay, there's the
rub;
For in that sleep of death what dreams may
come,
When we have shuffled off this mortal coil,
Must give us pause.

Hamlet, III.i

This fell sergeant Death
Is strict in his arrest.

Hamlet, V.ii

Cowards die many times before their deaths:
The valiant never taste of death but once.

Julius Caesar, II.ii

Men must endure
Their going hence, even as their coming hither:
Ripeness is all.

King Lear, V.ii

The weariest and most loathed worldly life
That age, ache, penury, and imprisonment,
Can lay on nature is a paradise
To what we fear of death.

Measure For Measure, III.i

If thou and nature can so gently part,
The stroke of death is as a lover's pinch,
Which hurts and is desir'd.

Antony and Cleopatra, V.ii

Nothing in his life
Became him like the leaving it: he died
As one that had been studied in his death
To throw away the dearest thing he ow'd
As 'twere a careless trifle.

Macbeth, I.iv

Out, alas! she's cold;
Her blood is settled, and her joints are stiff.
Life and these lips have long been separated.
Death lies on her like an untimely frost
Upon the sweetest flower of all the field.

Romeo and Juliet IV.v

Shaw, George Bernard (1856–1950)
Irish socialist, writer, dramatist and critic
Life levels all men: death reveals the eminent.

Man and Superman (1903)

Shelley, Percy Bysshe (1792–1822)
English poet, dramatist and essayist
Death is the veil which those who live call life:
They sleep, and it is lifted.

Prometheus Unbound (1820)

Shirley, James (1596–1666)
English poet and dramatist
The glories of our blood and state
Are shadows, not substantial things;
There is no armour against fate;
Death lays his icy hand on kings:
Sceptre and crown
Must tumble down,
And in the dust be equal made
With the poor crooked scythe and spade.

The Contention of Ajax and Ulysses (1659)

How little room
Do we take up in death that living know
No bounds!

The Wedding (1629)

Slessor, Kenneth (1901–1971)
Australian poet and journalist
Softly and humbly to the Gulf of Arabs
The convoys of dead sailors come;
At night they sway and wander in the waters far
under,
But morning rolls them in the foam.

Between the sob and clubbing of the gunfire

Someone, it seems, has time for this,
To pluck them from the shallows and bury them
in burrows
And tread the sand upon their
nakedness;

And each cross, the driven stake of tidewood,
Bears the last signature of men,
Written with such perplexity, with such
bewildered pity,
The words choke as they begin –

'Unknown seaman' - the ghostly pencil
Wavers and fades, the purple drips,
The breath of the wet season has washed their
inscriptions
As blue as drowned men's lips,

Dead seamen, gone in search of the same
landfall,
Whether as enemies they fought,
Or fought with us, or neither; the sand joins
them together,
Enlisted on the other front.

'Beach Burial' (1942)

Smith, Stevie (1902–1971)
English poet and writer
If there wasn't death, I think you couldn't go on.

The Observer, 1969

Smith, Sydney (1771–1845)
English clergyman, essayist, journalist and wit
Death must be distinguished from dying, with
which it is often confused.

In H. Pearson, *The Smith of Smiths*
(1934)

Socrates (469–399 BC)
Athenian philosopher
Death is one of two things. Either it is
nothingness, and the dead have no
consciousness of anything; or, as people say, it is
a change and migration of the soul from this
place to another.

Attr. in Plato, *Apology*

Sophocles (496–406 BC)
Greek dramatist
Death is not the worst thing; rather, when one
who craves death cannot attain even that wish.

Electra

Southey, Robert (1774–1843)
English poet, essayist, historian and letterwriter
My name is Death: the last best friend am I.

Carmen Nuptiale (1816)

Spooner, William (1844–1930)
English churchman and university warden
Poor soul, very sad; her late husband, you know,

a very sad death – eaten by missionaries – poor soul!

In William Hayter, Spooner (1977)

Swift, Jonathan (1667–1745)
Irish satirist, poet, essayist and cleric

You think, as I ought to think, that it is time for me to have done with the world, and so I would if I could get into a better before I was called into the best, and not die here in a rage, like a poisoned rat in a hole.

Letter to Bolingbroke, 1729

Tate, Allen (1899–1979)
US poet

Row upon row with strict impunity
The headstones yield their names to the element.

'Ode to the Confederate Dead' (1926)

Tennyson, Alfred, Lord (1809–1892)
English lyric poet

Do we indeed desire the dead
Should still be near us at our side?
Is there no baseness we would hide?
No inner vileness that we dread?

In Memoriam A. H. H. (1850)

Thomas, Dylan (1914–1953)
Welsh poet, writer and radio dramatist

Though they go mad they shall be sane,
Though they sink through the sea they shall rise again;
Though lovers be lost love shall not;
And death shall have no dominion.

'And death shall have no dominion' (1936)

Turgenev, Ivan (1818–1883)
Russian writer and dramatist

Go and try to disprove death. Death will disprove you, and that's all there is to it!

Fathers and Sons (1862), 27

Death is an old jest but it comes to everyone.

In Jennifer Johnston, The Old Jest

Twain, Mark (1835–1910)
US humorist, writer, journalist and lecturer

Whoever has lived long enough to find out what life is, knows how deep a debt of gratitude we owe to Adam, the first great benefactor of our race. He brought death into the world.

Pudd'nhead Wilson (1894)

The report of my death was an exaggeration.

Cable, 1897

Vaughan, Henry (1622–1695)
Welsh poet and physician

Dear, beauteous death! the Jewel of the Just,
Shining nowhere, but in the dark;
What mysteries do lie beyond thy dust;

Could man outlook that mark!

Silex Scintillans (1650–1655)

Voltaire (1694–1778)
French philosopher, dramatist, poet, historian writer and critic

On doit des égards aux vivants; on ne doit aux morts que la vérité.
We owe respect to the living; we owe nothing but truth to the dead.

'Première Lettre sur Oedipe' (1785)

Webster, John (c.1580–c.1625)
English dramatist

I know death hath ten thousand several doors
For men to take their exits.

The Duchess of Malfi (1623)

O, that it were possible,
We might but hold some two days' conference
With the dead!

The Duchess of Malfi (1623)

Weiss, Peter (1916–1982)
German dramatist, painter and film producer

Jeder Tod auch der grausamste
ertrinkt in der völligen Gleichgültigkeit der Natur
Nur wir verleihen unserm Leben irgendeinen Wert.
Every death, even the cruellest, drowns in Nature's complete indifference. We are the only ones who bestow a value on our lives.

The Hunting Down and Murder of Jean Paul Marat (1964)

West, Dame Rebecca (1892–1983)
English writer, critic and feminist
Cable sent to Noël Coward after learning they had both been on a Nazi death list

My dear – the people we should have been seen dead with.

Times Literary Supplement, 1982

Whitman, Walt (1819–1892)
US poet and writer

Has anyone supposed it lucky to be born?
I hasten to inform him or her it is just as lucky to die, and I know it.

'Song of Myself' (1855)

Wilde, Oscar (1854–1900)
Irish poet, dramatist, writer, critic and wit

All her bright golden hair
Tarnished with rust,
She that was young and fair
Fallen to dust.

'Requiescat' (1881)

Wright, Judith (1915–)
Australian poet, critic and writer

Death marshals up his armies round us now.
Their footsteps crowd too near.

Lock your warm hand above the chilling heart
and for a time I live without my fear.
Grope in the night to find me and embrace,
for the dark preludes of the drums begin,
and round us, round the company of lovers,
death draws his cordons in.

'The Company of Lovers' (1946)

Yeats, W.B. (1865–1939)
Irish poet, dramatist, editor, writer and senator
Nor dread nor hope attend
A dying animal;
A man awaits his end
Dreading and hoping all.

'Death' (1933)

Young, Edward (1683–1765)
English poet, dramatist, satirist and clergyman
Life is the desert, life the solitude;
Death joins us to the great majority.

The Revenge (1721)

▶▶ AFTERLIFE; EPITAPHS; FUNERALS; GRIEF; LAST
WORDS; MORTALITY; MOURNING; MURDER; SLEEP;
SUICIDE

death: dying

Addison, Joseph (1672–1719)
English essayist, poet, playwright and statesman
See in what peace a Christian can die.

Dying words

Alexander the Great (356–323 BC)
Macedonian king and conquering army commander
I am dying with the help of too many physicians.

Attr.

Allen, Woody (1935–)
US film director, writer, actor and comedian
It's not that I'm afraid to die. I just don't want to
be there when it happens.

Without Feathers (1976)

Alther, Lisa (1944–)
US novelist
Dying was apparently a weaning process; all the
attachments to familiar people and objects have
to be undone.

Kinflicks (1976)

Anouilh, Jean (1910–1987)
French dramatist and screenwriter
Dying is nothing. So start by living. It's less fun
and it lasts longer.

Roméo et Jeannette
(1946)

Bacon, Francis (1561–1626)
English philosopher, essayist, politician and courtier
I do not believe that any man fears to be dead,

but only the stroke of death.

The Remaines of … Lord Verulam (1648)

Barrie, Sir J.M. (1860–1937)
Scottish dramatist and writer
To die will be an awfully big adventure.

Peter Pan (1904)

Betjeman, Sir John (1906–1984)
English poet laureate
There was sun enough for lazing upon beaches,
There was fun enough for far into the night.
But I'm dying now and done for,
What on earth was all the fun for?
For I'm old and ill and terrified and tight.

'Sun and Fun' (1954)

Browne, Sir Thomas (1605–1682)
English physician, author and antiquary
The long habit of living indisposeth us for dying.

Hydriotaphia: Urn Burial (1658)

Butler, Samuel (1835–1902)
English writer, painter, philosopher and scholar
It costs a lot of money to die comfortably.

The Note-Books of Samuel Butler (1912)

Charles II (1630–1685)
King of Great Britain and Ireland
He had been, he said, a most unconscionable
time dying; but he hoped that they would
excuse it.

In Macaulay, The History of England (1849)

Childers, Erskine (1870–1922)
English writer and historian; Irish revolutionary
Writing about his imminent execution
It seems perfectly simple and inevitable, like
lying down after a long day's work.

Prison letter to his wife

Crashaw, Richard (c.1612–1649)
English religious poet
And when life's sweet fable ends,
Soul and body part like friends;
No quarrels, murmurs, no delay;
A kiss, a sigh, and so away.

'Temperance' (1652)

Darrow, Clarence (1857–1938)
US lawyer, reformer and writer
I have never killed a man, but I have read many
obituaries with a lot of pleasure.

Medley

Dickinson, Emily (1830–1886)
US poet
I heard a Fly buzz – when I died …
With Blue – uncertain stumbling Buzz –
Between the light – and me –
And then the Windows failed – and then
I could not see to see.

'I heard a Fly buzz – when I died' (c.1862)

Edwards, Jonathan (1703–1758)
US theologian and philosopher
> The bodies of those that made such a noise and
> tumult when alive, when dead, lie as quietly
> among the graves of their neighbours as any
> others.
>> *Works* (1834)

Farmer, Edward (c.1809–1876)
English poet and writer
> I have no pain, dear mother, now;
> But oh! I am so dry:
> Just moisten poor Jim's lips once more;
> And, mother, do not cry!
>> 'The Collier's Dying Child'

Fielding, Henry (1707–1754)
English writer, dramatist and journalist
> It hath been often said, that it is not death, but
> dying, which is terrible.
>> *Amelia* (1751)

Hall, Rodney (1935–)
US poet and writer
> They're dying just the same in station
> homesteads
> they're dying in Home Beautiful apartments
> in among their lovely Danish furniture
> on and across the furniture they're dying
> spewing blood or stiffening dry and seeming
> never
> to have been alive.
>> *Black Bagatelles* (1978)

Johnson, Samuel (1709–1784)
English lexicographer, poet, critic, conversationalist and
essayist
> It matters not how a man dies, but how he lives.
> The act of dying is not of importance, it lasts so
> short a time.
>> In Boswell, *The Life of Samuel Johnson* (1791)

Maugham, William Somerset (1874–1965)
English writer, dramatist and physician
> Dying is a very dull, dreary affair. And my advice
> to you is to have nothing whatever to do with it.
>> In R. Maugham, *Escape from the Shadows* (1972)

Millay, Edna St Vincent (1892–1950)
US poet and dramatist
> Down, down, down into the darkness of the
> grave
> Gently they go, the beautiful, the tender, the
> kind;
> Quietly they go, the intelligent, the witty, the
> brave.
> I know. But I do not approve. And I am not
> resigned.
>> 'Dirge without Music' (1928)

Mitford, Jessica (1917–1996)
English writer

> Gracious dying is a huge, macabre and
> expensive joke on the American public.
>> *The American Way of Death* (1963)

Pascal, Blaise (1623–1662)
French philosopher and scientist
> *On mourra seul.*
> We shall die alone.
>> *Pensées* (1670

Plath, Sylvia (1932–1963)
US poet, writer and diarist
> Dying
> Is an art, like everything else.
> I do it exceptionally well.
>> 'Lady Lazarus' (1963)

Pope, Alexander (1688–1744)
English poet, translator and editor
> I mount! I fly!
> O Grave! where is thy victory?
> O Death! where is thy sting?
>> 'The Dying Christian to his Soul' (1730)

Shakespeare, William (1564–1616)
English dramatist, poet and actor
> Nothing in his life
> Became him like the leaving it: he died
> As one that had been studied in his death
> To throw away the dearest thing he ow'd
> As 'twere a careless trifle.
>> *Macbeth*, I.iv

> Dar'st thou die?
> The sense of death is most in apprehension;
> And the poor beetle that we tread upon
> In corporal sufferance finds a pang as great
> As when a giant dies.
>> *Measure For Measure*, III.i

Smith, Logan Pearsall (1865–1946)
US-born British epigrammatist, critic and writer
> I cannot forgive my friends for dying; I do not
> find these vanishing acts of theirs at all amusing.
>> *Afterthoughts* (1931)

Swarbrick, Dave (1941–)
English folk musician
On reading his obituary in the *Daily Telegraph*
> It's not the first time I have died in Coventry.
>> *The Times*, 1999

Thomas, Dylan (1914–1953)
Welsh poet, writer and radio dramatist
> Do not go gentle into that good night,
> Old age should burn and rave at close of day;
> Rage, rage against the dying of the light.
>> 'Do Not Go Gentle into that Good Night' (1952)

Twain, Mark (1835–1910)
US humorist, writer, journalist and lecturer
> All say, 'How hard it is to die' – a strange
> complaint to come from the mouths of people

who have had to live.
>   *Pudd'nhead Wilson's Calendar* (1894)

▶▶ AFTERLIFE; EPITAPHS; FUNERALS; GRIEF; LAST
WORDS; MORTALITY; MOURNING; MURDER; SUICIDE

debt

Caesar, Augustus (63 BC–AD 14)
First Roman emperor
Said of those who never pay their debts. The term *Kalends*
was Roman and did not exist in Greek
>   *Ad Kalendas Graecas soluturos.*
>   It will be paid at the Greek Kalends.
>   In Suetonius, *Lives of the Caesars*

Coolidge, Calvin (1872–1933)
US President
Of Allied war debts
>   They hired the money, didn't they?
>   Remark, 1925

Fox, Henry Stephen (1791–1846)
English diplomat
Remark after an illness
>   I am so changed that my oldest creditors would
>   hardly know me.
>   Quoted by Byron in a letter to John Murray, 1817

Franklin, Benjamin (1706–1790)
US statesman, scientist, political critic and printer
>   Creditors have better memories than debtors.
>   *Poor Richard's Almanac* (1758)

Ibsen, Henrik (1828–1906)
Norwegian writer, dramatist and poet
>   Home life ceases to be free and beautiful as
>   soon as it is founded on borrowing and debt.
>   *A Doll's House* (1879)

Mumford, Ethel (1878–1940)
US writer, dramatist and humorist
>   In the midst of life we are in debt.
>   *Altogether New Cynic's Calendar*
>   (1907)

Shakespeare, William (1564–1616)
English dramatist, poet and actor
>   I can get no remedy against this consumption of
>   the purse; borrowing only lingers and lingers it
>   out, but the disease is incurable.
>   *Henry IV Part II*, I.ii

>   He that dies pays all debts.
>   *The Tempest*, III.ii

Sheridan, Richard Brinsley (1751–1816)
Irish dramatist, politician and orator
To his tailor when he requested payment of a debt, or at least
the interest on it
>   It is not my interest to pay the principal, nor my

principle to pay the interest.
>   Attr.

Handing one of his creditors an IOU
>   Thank God, that's settled.
>   In Shriner, *Wit, Wisdom, and Foibles of the Great*
>   (1918)

After being refused a loan of £25 from a friend who asked him
to repay the £500 he had already borrowed
>   My dear fellow, be reasonable; the sum you ask
>   me for is a very considerable one, whereas I only
>   ask you for twenty-five pounds.
>   Attr.

Thackeray, William Makepeace (1811–1863)
Indian-born English writer
>   By paying scarcely anybody people can manage,
>   for a time at least, to make a great show with
>   very little means.
>   *Vanity Fair* (1847–1848)

Ward, Artemus (1834–1867)
US humorist, journalist, editor and lecturer
>   Let us all be happy, and live within our means,
>   even if we have to borrer the money to do it
>   with.
>   'Science and Natural History'

Wilde, Oscar (1854–1900)
Irish poet, dramatist, writer, critic and wit
It is only by not paying one's bills that one can hope
to live in the memory of the commercial classes.
>   *The Chameleon*, 1894

Wodehouse, P.G. (1881–1975)
English humorist and writer
>   I don't owe a penny to a single soul – not
>   counting tradesmen, of course.
>   'Jeeves and the Hard-Boiled Egg' (1919)

▶▶ BORROWING AND LENDING

deception

Aesop (6th century BC)
Legendary Greek writer of fables
>   The lamb that belonged to the sheep whose skin
>   the wolf was wearing began to follow the wolf in
>   the sheep's clothing.
>   'The Wolf in Sheep's Clothing'

Allen, Woody (1935–)
US film director, writer, actor and comedian
>   I was thrown out of NYU my freshman year for
>   cheating in my metaphysics final. I looked into
>   the soul of the boy sitting next to me.
>   *Annie Hall* (film, 1977)

Berkeley, Bishop George (1685–1753)
Irish philosopher and scholar

It is impossible that a man who is false to his friends and neighbours should be true to the public.

Maxims Concerning Patriotism (1750)

Carswell, Catherine (1879–1946)
Scottish writer

It wasn't a woman who betrayed Jesus with a kiss.

The Savage Pilgrimage (1932)

Chaucer, Geoffrey (c.1340–1400)
English poet, public servant and courtier

The carl spak oo thing, but he thoghte another.

The Canterbury Tales (1387)

The smylere with the knyf under the cloke.

The Canterbury Tales (1387)

Colman, the Younger, George (1762–1836)
English dramatist and Examiner of Plays

Says he, 'I am a handsome man, but I'm a gay deceiver.'

Love Laughs at Locksmiths (1808)

Congreve, William (1670–1729)
English dramatist

Man was by Nature Woman's cully made:
We never are, but by ourselves, betrayed.

The Old Bachelor (1693)

Demosthenes (c.384–322 BC)
Athenian statesman and orator

There is a great deal of wishful thinking in such cases; it is the easiest thing of all to deceive one's self.

Olynthiac

Fadiman, Clifton (1904–)
US writer, editor and broadcaster

Experience teaches you that the man who looks you straight in the eye, particularly if he adds a firm handshake, is hiding something.

Enter, Conversing

Gay, John (1685–1732)
English poet, dramatist and librettist

To cheat a man is nothing; but the woman must have fine parts indeed who cheats a woman!

The Beggar's Opera (1728)

Henry, O. (1862–1910)
US short-story writer

It was beautiful and simple as all truly great swindles are.

'The Octopus Marooned' (1908)

Hill, Joe (1879–1914)
Swedish-born US songwriter and workers' organizer

You will eat (You will eat)
Bye and bye (Bye and bye)
In that glorious land above the sky (Way up high)
Work and pray (Work and pray)

Live on hay (Live on hay)
You'll get pie in the sky when you die (That's a lie.).

'The Preacher and the Slave', song, 1911

La Fontaine, Jean de (1621–1695)
French poet and fabulist

C'est double plaisir de tromper le trompeur.
It is a double pleasure to trick the trickster.

'Le coq et le renard'

Lysander (d. 395 BC)
Spartan admiral

Deceive boys with toys, but men with oaths.

In Plutarch, *Parallel Lives*, 'Lysander'

Scott, Sir Walter (1771–1832)
Scottish writer and historian

O what a tangled web we weave,
When first we practise to deceive!

Marmion (1808)

Shakespeare, William (1564–1616)
English dramatist, poet and actor

O villain, villain, smiling, damned villain!
My tables – meet it is I set it down
That one may smile, and smile, and be a villain.

Hamlet, I.v

False face must hide what the false heart doth know.

Macbeth, I.vii

So may the outward shows be least themselves;
The world is still deceiv'd with ornament.

The Merchant of Venice, III.ii

All that glisters is not gold,
Often have you heard that told.

The Merchant of Venice, II.vii

Swift, Jonathan (1667–1745)
Irish satirist, poet, essayist and cleric

This is the sublime and refined point of felicity, called the possession of being well deceived; the serene peaceful state of being a fool among knaves.

A Tale of a Tub (1704

Taylor, Bishop Jeremy (1613–1667)
English divine and writer

In the matter of interest we are wary as serpents, subtle as foxes, vigilant as the birds of the night, rapacious as kites, tenacious as grappling-hooks and the weightiest anchors, and, above all, false and hypocritical as a thin crust of ice spread upon the face of a deep, smooth, and dissembling pit.

XXV Sermons Preached at Golden Grove (1653)

Thurber, James (1894–1961)
US humorist, writer and dramatist

It is not so easy to fool little girls today as it

used to be.

Fables for Our Time (1940)

You can fool too many of the people too much of the time.

The New Yorker, 1939

Virgil (70–19 BC)
Roman poet
> *Quis fallere possit amantem?*
> Who may deceive a lover?

Aeneid

▶▶ APPEARANCE; HYPOCRISY; LIES

decisions

Caesar, Gaius Julius (c.102–44 BC)
Roman statesman, historian and army commander
Remark on crossing the Rubicon
> *Iacta alea est.*
> The die is cast.

In Suetonius, *Lives of the Caesars*

Canetti, Elias (1905–1994)
Bulgarian-born English writer, dramatist and critic
> Every decision is liberating, even if it leads to disaster. Otherwise, why do so many people walk upright and with open eyes into their misfortune?

The Secret Heart of the Clock: Notes, Aphorisms, Fragments 1973-1985 (1991)

Denning, Lord (1899–1999)
English Master of the Rolls
> A wrong decision can make me very miserable. But I have trust in God. If you have this trust you don't have to worry, as you don't have the sole responsibility.

Speech on his retirement, 1982

Hughes, Howard (1905–1976)
US millionaire industrialist, aviator and film producer
> Never make a decision. Let someone else make it and then if it turns out to be the wrong one, you can disclaim it, and if it is the right one you can abide by it.

The Hughes Legacy: Scramble for the Billion (1976)

Parkinson, C. Northcote (1909–1993)
English political scientist and historian
> The man who is denied the opportunity of taking decisions of importance begins to regard as important the decisions he is allowed to take.

Parkinson's Law (1958)

Quarles, Francis (1592–1644)
English poet, writer and royalist
> The road to resolution lies by doubt:
> The next way home's the farthest way about.

Emblems (1643)

Rifkin, Jeremy (c.1860–1930)
US bioethicist
> When the Iroquois made a decision, they said, 'How does it affect seven generations in the future?'.

New York Times Magazine, 1988

defeat

Beauvoir, Simone de (1908–1986)
French writer, feminist critic and philosopher
> If you live long enough, you'll see that every victory turns into a defeat.

All Men are Mortal (1946)

Hemingway, Ernest (1898–1961)
US author
> It is in defeat that we become Christian.

A Farewell to Arms (1929)

Livy (59 BC–AD 17)
Roman historian
> *Vae victis.*
> Woe to the vanquished.

History

Louis XIV (1638–1715)
King of France
On hearing of the French defeat at Malplaquet
> *Dieu, a-t-il donc oublié ce que j'ai fait pour lui?*
> Has God then forgotten what I have done for him?

Attr.

Nixon, Richard (1913–1994)
US Republican politician and President
> Defeat doesn't finish a man – quit does. A man is not finished when he's defeated. He's finished when he quits.

In William Safire, *Before the Fall* (1975)

Stevenson, Adlai (1900–1965)
US lawyer, statesman and United Nations ambassador
Said after losing an election, quoting a story told by Abraham Lincoln
> He said that he was too old to cry, but it hurt too much to laugh.

Speech, 1952

Taft, William Howard (1857–1930)
US Republican politician and President
Referring to his disastrous defeat in the 1912 presidential election
> Well, I have one consolation. No candidate was ever elected ex-president with such a large majority!

Attr.

demagogues

Macaulay, Lord (1800–1859)
English Liberal statesman, essayist and poet
> In every age the vilest specimens of human nature are to be found among demagogues.
> *History of England* (1849)

democracy

Adams, John (1735–1826)
US lawyer, diplomat and President
> Remember, democracy never lasts long. It soon wastes, exhausts, and murders itself. There never was a democracy yet that did not commit suicide.
> *The Works of John Adams* (1856), letter, 1814

Anonymous
> Democracy is mob rule, but with income taxes.

Chinese Student during protests in Tianamen Square, Beijing, 1989
> I don't know exactly what democracy is. But we need more of it.

Attlee, Clement (1883–1967)
English statesman and Prime Minister
> Democracy means government by discussion but it is only effective if you can stop people talking.
> Speech, 1957

Benn, Tony (1925–)
English Labour politician
> We've had our political democracy decapitated in the interests of the worship of money.
> *The Observer*, 1999

Beveridge, William Henry (1879–1963)
British economist and social reformer
> The trouble in modern democracy is that men do not approach to leadership until they have lost the desire to lead anyone.
> *The Observer*, 1934

Cartwright, John (1740–1824)
English political reformer
> One man shall have one vote.
> *The People's Barrier Against Undue Influence* (1780)

Chesterton, G.K. (1874–1936)
English writer, poet and critic
> You can never have a revolution in order to establish a democracy. You must have a democracy in order to have a revolution.
> *Tremendous Trifles*

> Democracy means government by the uneducated, while aristocracy means government by the badly educated.
> *New York Times*, 1931

Churchill, Sir Winston (1874–1965)
English Conservative Prime Minister
> Many forms of government have been tried, and will be tried in this world of sin and woe. No one pretends that democracy is perfect or all-wise. Indeed, it has been said that democracy is the worst form of Government except all those other forms that have been tried from time to time.
> Speech, 1947

Demosthenes (c.384–322 BC)
Athenian statesman and orator
> There is one safeguard, which is an advantage and security for all, but especially to democracies against despots. What is it? Distrust.
> *Philippics*

Flers, Marquis de (1872–1927) and **Caillavet, Armande** (1869–1915)
French playwrights
> *Démocratie est le nom que nous donnons au peuple toutes les fois que nous avons besoin de lui.*
> Democracy is the name we give the people whenever we need them.
> *L'habit vert*

Fo, Dario (1926–)
Italian playwright and actor
> *Giusto! L'ha detto! Lo scandalo è il concime della democrazia.*
> Correct! You said it! Scandal is the manure of democracy.
> *Accidental Death of an Anarchist* (1974)

Forster, E.M. (1879–1970)
English writer, essayist and literary critic
> So Two cheers for Democracy: one because it admits variety and two because it permits criticism. Two cheers are quite enough: there is no occasion to give three. Only Love the Beloved Republic deserves that.
> *Two Cheers for Democracy* (1951)

Ibsen, Henrik (1828–1906)
Norwegian writer, dramatist and poet
> The most dangerous foe to truth and freedom in our midst is the compact majority. Yes, the damned, compact liberal majority.
> *An Enemy of the People* (1882)

Inge, William Ralph (1860–1954)
English divine, writer and teacher
> Democracy is only an experiment in government, and it has the obvious disadvantage of merely counting votes instead of weighing them.
> *Possible Recovery?* (c.1922)

Junius (1769–1772)

Pen-name of anonymous author of letters criticising ministers of George III

> The right of election is the very essence of the constitution.
>
> *Letters* (1769–1771)

Lincoln, Abraham (1809–1865)

US statesman and President

> No man is good enough to govern another man without that other's consent.
>
> Speech, 1854

> The ballot is stronger than the bullet.
>
> Speech, 1856

Lissouba, Pascal

President of Congo Brazzaville

> You don't arrange elections if you are going to lose them.
>
> *The Guardian*, 1999

Macaulay, Lord (1800–1859)

English Liberal statesman, essayist and poet

> Thus our democracy was, from an early period, the most aristocratic, and our aristocracy the most democratic in the world.
>
> *History of England* (1849)

Niebuhr, Reinhold (1892–1971)

US Protestant theologian and writer

> Man's capacity for justice makes democracy possible, but man's inclination to injustice makes democracy necessary.
>
> *The Children of Light and the Children of Darkness* (1944)

Pericles (c.495–429)

Athenian statesman, general, orator and cultural patron

> We enjoy a constitution that does not follow the customs of our neighbours; we are rather an example to them than they to us. Our government is called a democracy because power is in the hands not of the few but of the many.
>
> In Thucydides, *Histories*

Preston, Keith (1884–1927)

US poet, writer and teacher

Of democracy

> An institution in which the whole is equal to the scum of all the parts.
>
> *Pot Shots from Pegasus*

Roosevelt, Franklin Delano (1882–1945)

US Democrat President

> We must be the great arsenal of democracy.
>
> Radio broadcast, 1940

Sand, George (1804–1876)

French writer and dramatist

> *Il faut s'avouer impuissant devant cette fatalité politique d'un nouvel ordre dans l'histoire: le suffrage universel.*
>
> One must admit one is powerless in the face of the political inevitability of this new order in history: universal suffrage.
>
> Letter to Joseph Mazzini, 1848

Sellar, Walter (1898–1951) and **Yeatman, Robert Julian** (1897–1968)

British writers

> Magna Charter was … the cause of Democracy in England, and thus a Good Thing for everyone (except the Common People).
>
> *1066 And All That* (1930)

Shaw, George Bernard (1856–1950)

Irish socialist, writer, dramatist and critic

> Our political experiment of democracy, the last refuge of cheap misgovernment.
>
> *Man and Superman* (1903), Epistle Dedicatory

> Our political experiment of democracy, the last refuge of cheap misgovernment.
>
> *Man and Superman* (1903)

> Democracy substitutes election by the incompetent many for appointment by the corrupt few.
>
> *Man and Superman* (1903)

Tocqueville, Alexis de (1805–1859)

French historian, politician, lawyer and memoirist

> I sought the image of democracy, in order to learn what we have to fear and to hope from its progress.
>
> *De la Démocratie en Amérique* (1840)

Webster, Daniel (1782–1852)

US statesman, orator and lawyer

> The people's government, made for the people, made by the people, and answerable to the people.
>
> Speech, 1830

Wilde, Oscar (1854–1900)

Irish poet, dramatist, writer, critic and wit

Democracy means simply the bludgeoning of the people by the people for the people.

> *The Fortnightly Review*, 1891

Williams, Tennessee (1911–1983)

US dramatist and writer

> Knowledge – Zzzzzp! Money – Zzzzzp! – Power! That's the cycle democracy is built on!
>
> *The Glass Menagerie* (1945)

Wilson, Woodrow (1856–1924)

US Democrat President

> The world must be made safe for democracy.
>
> Speech, 1917

▶▶ CLASS; GOVERNMENT

dentists

Perelman, S.J. (1904–1979)
US humorist, writer and dramatist
> For years I have let dentists ride roughshod over my teeth: I have been sawed, hacked, chopped, whittled, bewitched, bewildered, tattooed, and signed on again; but this is cuspid's last stand.
>> *Crazy Like a Fox* (1944)

Wells, H.G. (1866–1946)
English writer
> He had one peculiar weakness; he had faced death in many forms but he had never faced a dentist. The thought of dentists gave him just the same sick horror as the thought of Socialism.
>> *Bealby* (1915)

Wilde, Oscar (1854–1900)
Irish poet, dramatist, writer, critic and wit
> It is very vulgar to talk like a dentist when one isn't a dentist. It produces a false impression.
>> *The Importance of Being Earnest* (1895)

design

Anonymous
> Design flaws travel in groups.
>> Fifth Law of Design

> Information necessitating a change of design will be conveyed to the designer after and only after the design is complete.
>> 'Now They Tell Us' Law

> The more innocuous the modification appears to be, the further its influence will extend and the more the design will have to be redrawn.
>> Law of Revision I

> If, when completion of a design is imminent, field dimensions are finally supplied as they actually are, instead of as they were meant to be, it is always simpler to start over from scratch.
>> Law of Revision II

Bayley, Stephen
English designer and critic
> Interior design is a travesty of the architectural process and a frightening condemnation of the credulity, helplessness and gullibilty of the most formidable consumers – the rich.
>> *Taste* (1991)

Le Corbusier (1887–1965)
Swiss architect
> I prefer drawing to talking. Drawing is faster,

and allows less room for lies.
>> *Time*, 1961

▶▶ ART; ARCHITECTURE

desire

Blake, William (1757–1827)
English poet, engraver, painter and mystic
> Those who restrain desire, do so because theirs is weak enough to be restrained.
>> *The Marriage of Heaven and Hell* (c.1790–1793)

> Man's desires are limited by his perceptions; none can desire what he has not perceiv'd.
>> *There is No Natural Religion* (c.1788)

> The desire of Man being Infinite the possession is Infinite and himself Infinite.
>> *There is No Natural Religion* (c.1788)

> Abstinence sows sand all over
> The ruddy limbs & flaming hair
> But Desire Gratified
> Plants fruits of life & beauty there.
>> 'Abstinence sows sand all over' (c.1793)

> What is it men in women do require?
> The lineaments of Gratified Desire.
> What is it women do in men require?
> The lineaments of Gratified Desire.
>> 'What is it men in women do require'

Browne, Sir Thomas (1605–1682)
English physician, author and antiquary
> My desires only are, and I shall be happy therein, to be but the last man, and bring up the rear in heaven.
>> *Religio Medici* (1643)

Congreve, William (1670–1729)
English dramatist
> O, she is the antidote to desire.
>> *The Way of the World* (1700)

Drayton, Michael (1563–1631)
English poet
> Thus when we fondly flatter our desires,
> Our best conceits do prove the greatest liars.
>> *The Barrons' Wars* (1603)

Joyce, James (1882–1941)
Irish writer
Commenting on the interruption of a music recital when a moth flew into the singer's mouth
> The desire of the moth for the star.
>> In Ellmann, *James Joyce* (1958)

Kipling, Rudyard (1865–1936)
Indian-born British poet and writer
> The depth and dream of my desire,
> The bitter paths wherein I stray –

Thou knowest Who hast made the Fire,
Thou knowest Who hast made the Clay.

Life's Handicap (1888)

Patten, Brian (1946–)
British poet

Not all that you want and ought not to have is
forbidden to you,
Not all that you want and are allowed to want Is
acceptable.

Vanishing Trick

Proust, Marcel (1871–1922)
French writer and critic

Le désir fleurit, la possession flétrit toutes choses.
Desire makes everything blossom; possession
makes everything wither and fade.

Les Plaisirs et les Jours (1896)

*Il n'y a rien comme le désir pour empêcher les choses
qu'on dit d'avoir aucune ressemblance avec ce qu'on a
dans la pensée.*
There is nothing like desire for preventing the
things one says from bearing any resemblance
to what one has in mind.

Le Côté de Guermantes (1921)

Shaw, George Bernard (1856–1950)
Irish socialist, writer, dramatist and critic

There are two tragedies in life. One is to lose
your heart's desire. The other is to gain it.

Man and Superman (1903)

Swift, Jonathan (1667–1745)
Irish satirist, poet, essayist and cleric

The stoical scheme of supplying our wants, by
lopping off our desires, is like cutting off our
feet when we want shoes.

Thoughts on Various Subjects (1711)

Swinburne, Algernon Charles (1837–1909)
English poet, critic, dramatist and letter writer

The delight that consumes the desire,
The desire that outruns the delight.

'Dolores' (1866)

▶▶ HUNGER

despair

Allen, Woody (1935–)
US film director, writer, actor and comedian

More than any other time in history, mankind
faces a crossroads. One path leads to despair
and utter hopelessness. The other, to total
extinction. Let us pray we have the wisdom to
choose correctly.

Side Effects

Camus, Albert (1913–1960)
Algerian-born French writer

He who despairs over an event is a coward, but
he who holds hopes for the human condition is a
fool.

The Rebel (1951)

Clare, John (1793–1864)
English rural poet; died in an asylum

My life hath been one chain of contradictions,
Madhouses, prisons, whore-shops …

Pale death, the grand physician, cures all pain;
The dead rest well who lived for joys in vain …

Hopeless hope hopes on and meets no end,
Wastes without springs and homes without a
friend.

'Child Harold' (1841)

Fitzgerald, F. Scott (1896–1940)
US writer

In the real dark night of the soul it is always
three o'clock in the morning.

The Crack-Up (1945)

Greene, Graham (1904–1991)
English writer and dramatist

Despair is the price one pays for setting oneself
an impossible aim.

Heart of the Matter (1948)

Harris, Max (1921–1995)
Australian critic, poet and publisher

We know no mithridatum of despair
as drunks, the angry penguins of the night,
straddling the cobbles of the square,
tying a shoelace by fogged lamplight.

The Gift of Blood (1940),
'Progress of Defeat'

Hopkins, Gerard Manley (1844–1889)
English Jesuit priest, poet and classicist

Not, I'll not, carrion comfort, Despair, not feast
on thee;
Not untwist – slack they may be – these last
strands of man
In me or, most weary, cry I can no more. I can;
Can something, hope, wish day come, not
choose not to be.

'Carrion Comfort' (1885)

I wake and feel the fell of dark, not day.
What hours, O what black hours we have spent
This night!

'I wake and Feel the Fell of dark, not day' (c.1885)

No worst, there is none. Pitched past pitch of
grief,
More pangs will, schooled at forepangs, wilder
wring.
Comforter, where, where is your comforting?

'No Worst, there is None' (1885)

Kafka, Franz (1883–1924)
Czech-born German-speaking writer
> Do not despair, not even about the fact that you
> do not despair.
>> *Diary*, 1913

Shakespeare, William (1564–1616)
English dramatist, poet and actor
> I shall despair. There is no creature loves me;
> And if I die no soul will pity me:
> And wherefore should they, since that I myself
> Find in myself no pity to myself?
>> *Richard III*, V.iii

> The worst is not
> So long as we can say 'This is the worst'
>> *King Lear*, IV.i

Shaw, George Bernard (1856–1950)
Irish socialist, writer, dramatist and critic
> He who has never hoped can never despair.
>> *Caesar and Cleopatra*
>> (1901)

St John of the Cross (1542–1591)
> *Noche oscura del alma*
> The dark night of the soul.
>> Title of poem

Thoreau, Henry David (1817–1862)
US essayist, social critic and writer
> The mass of men lead lives of quiet desperation.
>> *Walden* (1854)

Walsh, William (1663–1708)
English critic, poet and politician
> I can endure my own despair,
> But not another's hope.
>> 'Song: Of All the Torments'

▶▶ SUFFERING

destiny

Aeschylus (525–456 BC)
Greek dramatist and poet
> Things are where things are, and, as fate has
> willed,
> So shall they be fulfilled.
>> *Agamemnon*, trans. Browning

Appius Claudius Caecus (4th–3rd century BC)
> *Faber est suae quisque fortunae.*
> Each man is the architect of his own destiny.
>> In Sallust, *Ad Caesarem*

Arnold, Matthew (1822–1888)
English poet, critic, essayist and educationist
> Yet they, believe me, who await
> No gifts from chance, have conquered fate.
>> 'Resignation' (1849)

Aurelius, Marcus (121–180)
Roman emperor and Stoic philosopher
> That 'all that happens, happens as it should', if
> you observe carefully, you will find to be the
> case.
>> *Meditations*

> Whatever may happen to you was prepared for
> you from all eternity; and the thread of causes
> was spinning from eternity both your being and
> this which is happening to you.
>> *Meditations*

> Nothing happens to any thing which that thing is
> not made by nature to bear.
>> *Meditations*

Bacon, Francis (1561–1626)
English philosopher, essayist, politician and courtier
> If a man look sharply, and attentively, he shall
> see Fortune: for though she be blind, yet she is
> not invisible.
>> *Essays* (1625)

Beckett, Samuel (1906–1989)
Irish dramatist, writer and poet
> What do I know of man's destiny? I could tell
> you more about radishes.
>> *Six Residua* (1978)

Bowen, Elizabeth (1899–1973)
Irish writer
> Fate is not an eagle, it creeps like a rat.
>> *The House in Paris* (1935)

Büchner, Georg (1813–1837)
German playwright
> *Puppen sind wir von unbekannten Gewalten am Draht*
> *gezogen; nichts, nichts wir selbst!*
> We are puppets on strings worked by unknown
> forces; we ourselves are nothing, nothing!
>> *Danton's Death* (1835)

Burns, Robert (1759–1796)
Scottish poet and song writer
> The best-laid schemes o' mice an' men
> Gang aft agley,
> An' lea'e us nought but grief an' pain,
> For promis'd joy!
>> 'To a Mouse' (1785)

Churchill, Sir Winston (1874–1965)
English Conservative Prime Minister
> Which brings me to my conclusion upon Free
> Will and Predestination, namely – let the reader
> mark it – that they are identical.
>> *My Early Life* (1930)

> I felt as if I were walking with destiny, and that
> all my past life had been but a preparation for
> this hour and this trial.
>> *The Gathering Storm*

Clive, Lord (1725–1774)

English general, statesman and Indian administrator

Said when his pistol failed to go off twice, in his attempt to commit suicide

> I feel that I am reserved for some end or other.
>
> In Gleig, *The Life of Robert, First Lord Clive* (1848)

Crisp, Quentin (1908–1999)

English writer, publicist and model

> Believe in fate, but lean forward where fate can see you.
>
> Attr.

Defoe, Daniel (c.1661–1731)

English writer and critic

> The best of men cannot suspend their fate:
> The good die early, and the bad die late.
>
> 'Character of the late Dr S. Annesley' (1697)

Delille, Abbé Jacques (1738–1813)

French poet and translator

> *Le sort fait les parents, le choix fait les amis.*
> Relations are made by fate, friends by choice.
>
> *Malheur et pitié* (1803)

Dryden, John (1631–1700)

English poet, satirist, dramatist and critic

Of Fortune

> I can enjoy her while she's kind;
> But when she dances in the wind,
> And shakes the wings, and will not stay,
> I puff the prostitute away.
>
> *Sylvae* (1685)

Eliot, George (1819–1880)

English writer and poet

Of Fortune

> 'Character', says Novalis, in one of his questionable aphorisms – 'character is destiny.'
>
> *The Mill on the Floss* (1860)

Emerson, Ralph Waldo (1803–1882)

US poet, essayist, transcendentalist and teacher

> The bitterest tragic element in life to be derived from an intellectual source is the belief in a brute Fate or Destiny.
>
> *Natural History of Intellect* (1893)

Fitzgerald, Edward (1809–1883)

English poet, translator and letter writer

> 'Tis all a Chequer-board of Nights and Days
> Where Destiny with Men for Pieces plays:
> Hither and thither moves, and mates, and slays,
> And one by one back in the Closet lays.
>
> *The Rubáiyát of Omar Khayyám* (1859)

> The Moving Finger writes; and, having writ,
> Moves on: nor all thy Piety nor Wit
> Shall lure it back to cancel half a Line,
> Nor all thy Tears wash out a Word of it.
>
> *The Rubáiyát of Omar Khayyám* (1859)

Ford, John (c.1586–c.1640)

English dramatist and poet

> Tempt not the stars, young man, thou canst not play
> With the severity of fate.
>
> *The Broken Heart* (1633)

Gay, John (1685–1732)

English poet, dramatist and librettist

> 'Tis a gross error, held in schools,
> That Fortune always favours fools.
>
> *Fables* (1738)

Hare, Maurice Evan (1886–1967)

English limerick writer

> There once was a man who said, 'Damn!
> It is borne in upon me I am
> An engine that moves
> In predestinate grooves,
> I'm not even a bus, I'm a tram.'
>
> 'Limerick', 1905

Hitler, Adolf (1889–1945)

German Nazi dictator, born in Austria

> *Ich gehe mit traumwandlerischer Sicherheit den Weg, den mich die Vorsehung gehen heisst.*
> I go the way that Providence bids me go with the certainty of a sleepwalker.
>
> Speech, Munich, 1936

Horace (65–8 BC)

Roman poet

> *Tu ne quaesieris, scire nefas, quem mihi, quem tibi Finem di dederint.*
> Do not ask – it is forbidden to know – what end the gods have in store for me or for you.
>
> *Odes*

Jonson, Ben (1572–1637)

English dramatist and poet

> Blind Fortune still
> Bestows her gifts on such as cannot use them.
>
> *Every Man out of His Humour* (1599)

Loos, Anita (1893–1981)

US writer and screenwriter

> Fate keeps on happening.
>
> *Gentlemen Prefer Blondes* (1925)

Macaulay, Lord (1800–1859)

English Liberal statesman, essayist and poet

Of Rumbold

> He never would believe that Providence had sent a few men into the world ready booted and spurred to ride, and millions ready saddled and bridled to be ridden.
>
> *History of England* (1849)

Machiavelli (1469–1527)

Florentine statesman, political theorist and historian

> *La fortuna, come donna, è amica de giovani, perché*

sono meno respettivi, più feroci e con più audacia la comandano.
Fortune, like a woman, is friendly to the young, because they show her less respect, they are more daring and command her with audacity.

The Prince (1532)

Mallarmé, Stéphane (1842–1898)
French poet
Un coup de dés jamais n'abolira le hasard.
A throw of the dice will never eliminate chance.

Title of work, 1897

O'Sullivan, John L. (1813–1895)
US editor and diplomat
Our manifest destiny to overspread the continent allotted by Providence for the free development of our yearly multiplying millions.

United States Magazine and Democratic Review, 1837

Popper, Sir Karl (1902–1994)
Austrian-born British philosopher
We may become the makers of our fate when we have ceased to pose as its prophets.

The Observer, 1975

Reade, Charles (1814–1884)
English novelist and dramatist
Sow an act, and you reap a habit. Sow a habit, and you reap a character. Sow a character, and you reap a destiny.

Attr.

Sarraute, Nathalie (1900–1999)
French novelist
Je ne crois pas aux rencontres fortuites.
I don't believe in chance encounters.

Martereau

Schopenhauer, Arthur (1788–1860)
German philosopher
Das Schicksal mischt die Karten und wir spielen.
Fate shuffles the cards and we play.

'Aphorisms for Wisdom' (1851)

Shakespeare, William (1564–1616)
English dramatist, poet and actor
Let us sit and mock the good housewife Fortune from her wheel, that her gifts may henceforth be bestowed equally.

As You Like It, I.ii

Men at some time are masters of their fates:
The fault, dear Brutus, is not in our stars,
But in ourselves, that we are underlings.

Julius Caesar, I.ii

Fortune is merry,
And in this mood will give us any thing.

Julius Caesar, III.ii

There is a tide in the affairs of men
Which, taken at the flood, leads on to fortune;

Omitted, all the voyage of their life
Is bound in shallows and in miseries.

Julius Caesar, IV.iii.

O God! that one might read the book of fate,
And see the revolution of the times
Make mountains level, and the continent,
Weary of solid firmness, melt itself
Into the sea.

Henry IV, Part 2, III.i

Simpson, N.F. (1919–)
English dramatist
Each of us as he receives his private trouncings at the hands of fate is kept in good heart by the moth in his brother's parachute, and the scorpion in his neighbour's underwear.

A Resounding Tinkle (1958)

Singer, Isaac Bashevis (1904–1991)
Polish-born US Yiddish writer
We have to believe in free will. We've got no choice.

The Times, 1982

Steele, Sir Richard (1672–1729)
Irish-born English writer, dramatist and politician
Every Man is the Maker of his own Fortune.

The Tatler, 52, 1709

Temple, Frederick, Archbishop (1821–1902)
'My aunt was suddenly prevented from going a voyage in a ship what went down – would you call that a case of Providential interference?'
'Can't tell: didn't know your aunt.'

In Sandford, Memoirs of Archbishop Temple

Terence (c.190–159 BC)
Carthaginian-born Roman dramatist
Fortis fortuna adiuvat.
Fortune favours the brave.

Phormio

Turgenev, Ivan (1818–1883)
Russian writer and dramatist
Hardly have I succeeded in reaching a definite position or in stopping at a familiar point of view, when fate drags me down from it.

Attr.

Webster, John (c.1580–c.1625)
English dramatist
Fortune's a right whore:
If she give aught, she deals it in small parcels,
That she may take away all at one swoop.

The White Devil (1612)

We are merely the stars' tennis-balls, struck and bandied,
Which way please them.

The Duchess of Malfi (1623)

destruction

Arnold, Matthew (1822–1888)
English poet, critic, essayist and educationist
> He bears the seed of ruin in himself.
>
> *Merope* (1858)

Bakunin, Mikhail (1814–1876)
Russian anarchist and writer
> *Die Lust der Zerstörung ist zugleich eine schaffende Lust!*
> The desire for destruction is, at the same time, a creative desire.
>
> In *Jahrbuch für Wissenschaft und Kunst*, 1842

Betjeman, Sir John (1906–1984)
English poet laureate
> Come, friendly bombs, and fall on Slough
> It isn't fit for humans now,
> There isn't grass to graze a cow
> Swarm over, Death! …
>
> Come, friendly bombs, and fall on Slough
> To get it ready for the plough.
>
> *Continual Dew* (1937)

Chekhov, Anton (1860–1904)
Russian writer, dramatist and doctor
> Human beings have been endowed with reason and a creative power so that they can add to what thay have been given. But until now they have been not creative, but destructive. Forests are disappearing, rivers are drying up, wildlife is becoming extinct, the climate's being ruined and with every passing day the earth is becoming poorer and uglier.
>
> *Uncle Vanya* (1897)

Connolly, Cyril (1903–1974)
English literary editor, writer and critic
> Whom the gods wish to destroy they first call promising.
>
> *Enemies of Promise* (1938)

Euripides (c.485–406 BC)
Greek dramatist and poet
> Those whom God wishes to destroy, he first makes mad.
>
> *Fragment*

details

Doyle, Sir Arthur Conan (1859–1930)
Scottish writer and war correspondent
> You will remember, Watson, how the dreadful business of the Abernetty family was first brought to my notice by the depth which the parsley had sunk into the butter upon a hot day.
>
> *The Return of Sherlock Holmes* (1905),
> 'The Adventure of the Six Napoleons'

Johnson, Samuel (1709–1784)
English lexicographer, poet, critic, conversationalist and essayist
> Particulars are not to be examined till the whole has been surveyed.
>
> *The Plays of William Shakespeare* (1765), Preface

Lewis, Sinclair (1885–1951)
US writer
> She did her work with the thoroughness of a mind that reveres details and never quite understands them.
>
> *Babbit* (1922)

the devil

Anonymous
> During the intervals [between dances] the devil is busy; yes, very busy, as sad experience proves, and on the way home in the small hours of the morning, he is busier still.
>
> Statement on all-night dances, by Irish bishops, quoted in *Irish Catholic*, 1933

Baudelaire, Charles (1821–1867)
French poet, translator and critic
> My dear brothers, never forget when you hear the progress of the Enlightenment praised, that the Devil's cleverest ploy is to persuade you that he doesn't exist.
>
> Attr.

The Bible (King James Version)
> Resist the devil, and he will flee from you.
>
> *James*, 4:7
>
> Be sober, be vigilant; because your adversary the devil, as a roaring lion, walketh about, seeking whom he may devour.
>
> *Peter*, 5:8

Blake, William (1757–1827)
English poet, engraver, painter and mystic
> Truly My Satan thou art but a Dunce
> And dost not know the Garment from the Man.
> Every Harlot was a Virgin once
> Nor canst thou ever change Kate into Nan.
>
> *For the Sexes: The Gates of Paradise* (c.1810)

Browne, Sir Thomas (1605–1682)
English physician, author and antiquary
> Thus the devil played at chess with me, and yielding a pawn, thought to gain a queen of me, taking advantage of my honest endeavours.
>
> *Religio Medici* (1643)

Browning, Elizabeth Barrett (1806–1861)
English poet; wife of Robert Browning

The devil's most devilish when respectable.
Aurora Leigh (1857)

Butler, Samuel (1835–1902)
English writer, painter, philosopher and scholar
An apology for the devil: it must be remembered that we have heard only one side of the case; God has written all the books.
The Note-Books of Samuel Butler (1912)

Carlyle, Thomas (1795–1881)
Scottish historian, biographer, critic, and essayist
Sarcasm I now see to be, in general, the language of the Devil.
Sartor Resartus (1834)

Coleridge, Samuel Taylor (1772–1834)
English poet, philosopher and critic
From his brimstone bed at break of day
A walking the Devil is gone,
To visit his snug little farm the Earth,
And see how his stock goes on …

His jacket was red and his breeches were blue,
And there was a hole where the tail came through …

He saw a Lawyer killing a viper
On a dunghill hard by his own stable;
And the Devil smiled, for it put him in mind
Of Cain and his brother, Abel …

He saw a cottage with a double coach-house,
A cottage of gentility;
And the Devil did grin, for his darling sin
Is pride that apes humility …

As he went through Cold-Bath Fields he saw
A solitary cell;
And the Devil was pleased, for it gave him a hint
For improving his prisons in Hell.
'The Devil's Thoughts' (1799)

Congreve, William (1670–1729)
English dramatist
The Devil watches all opportunities.
The Old Bachelor (1693)

Defoe, Daniel (c.1661–1731)
English writer and critic
Wherever God erects a house of prayer,
The Devil always builds a chapel there;
And 'twill be found, upon examination,
The latter has the largest congregation.
The True-Born Englishman (1701)

Dostoevsky, Fyodor (1821–1881)
Russian writer
I think if the devil doesn't exist, and man has created him, he has created him in his own

image and likeness.
The Brothers Karamazov (1880)

Hill, Rowland (1744–1833)
English preacher and hymn writer
Referring to his writing of hymns
He did not see any reason why the devil should have all the good tunes.
In Broome, *The Rev. Rowland Hill* (1881)

Kraus, Karl (1874–1936)
Austrian scientist, critic and poet
The devil is an optimist if he thinks he can make people worse than they are.
In Thomas Szasz, *Anti-Freud: Karl Kraus's Criticism of Psychoanalysis and Psychiatry* (1976)

Lawrence, D.H. (1885–1930)
English writer, poet and critic
It is no good casting out devils. They belong to us, we must accept them and be at peace with them.
'The Reality of Peace' (1936)

Luther, Martin (1483–1546)
German Protestant theologian and reformer
Der alt böse Feind
Mit Ernst er's itzt meint,
Gross Macht und viel List,
Sein grausam Rüstung ist,
Auf Erd ist nicht seins gleichen.
The ancient prince of hell
Hath risen with purpose fell;
Strong mail of craft and power
He weareth in this hour;
On earth is not his fellow.
Hymn, c.1527–1528; trans. Carlyle

Milton, John (1608–1674)
English poet, libertarian and pamphleteer
Abasht the Devil stood,
And felt how awful goodness is.
Paradise Lost (1667)

Motteux, Peter Anthony (1660–1718)
The devil was sick, the devil a monk would be;
The devil was well, and the devil a monk he'd be.
Translation of Rabelais, *Gargantua and Pantagruel* (1693)

Proverbs
The devil is not so black as he is painted.

The devil looks after his own.

He who sups with the devil should have a long spoon.

Talk of the devil, and he is bound to appear.

Reade, Charles (1814–1884)
English novelist and dramatist
Courage, my friend, the devil is dead.
The Cloister and the Hearth (1861)

Shakespeare, William (1564–1616)
English dramatist, poet and actor

The devil can cite Scripture for his purpose.

The Merchant of Venice, I.iii

Marry, he must have a long spoon that must eat with the devil.

The Comedy of Errors, IV.iii

What, can the devil speak true?

Macbeth, I.iii

Shaw, George Bernard (1856–1950)
Irish socialist, writer, dramatist and critic

Is the devil to have all the passions as well as all the good tunes?

Man and Superman (1903)

Stevenson, Robert Louis (1850–1894)
Scottish writer, poet and essayist

The devil, depend upon it, can sometimes do a very gentlemanly thing.

New Arabian Nights (1882)

Wilde, Oscar (1854–1900)
Irish poet, dramatist, writer, critic and wit

We are each our own devil, and we make
This world our hell.

The Duchess of Padua (1883)

▶▶ HELL

diaries

Bankhead, Tallulah (1903–1968)
US actress

Only good girls keep diaries. Bad girls don't have the time.

Attr.

Minnelli, Liza (1946–)
US actress, singer and dancer

In Hollywood now when people die they don't say, 'Did he leave a will?' but 'Did he leave a diary?'

The Observer, 1989

Terry, Dame Ellen (1847–1928)
English actress, theatrical manager and memoirist

What is a diary as a rule? A document useful to the person who keeps it, dull to the contemporary who reads it, invaluable to the student, centuries afterwards, who treasures it!

The Story of My Life (1933)

Tolstoy, Sophie (1844–1919)
Russian diarist; wife of Leo Tolstoy
Of Tolstoy

He would like to destroy his old diaries and to appear before his children and the public only in his patriarchal robes. His vanity is enormous!

A Diary of Tolstoy's Wife, 1860–1891

dictionaries

Anonymous

Two men wrote a lexicon, Liddell and Scott;
Some parts were clever, but some parts were not.
Hear, all ye learned, and read me this riddle,
How the wrong part wrote Scott, and the right part wrote Liddell.

On Henry Liddell and Robert Scott, co-authors of the *Greek Lexicon* (1843)

Johnson, Samuel (1709–1784)
English lexicographer, poet, critic, conversationalist and essayist

But these were the dreams of a poet doomed at last to wake a lexicographer.

A Dictionary of the English Language (1755), Preface

Dull. 8. To make dictionaries is dull work.

A Dictionary of the English Language (1755)

Lexicographer. A writer of dictionaries, a harmless drudge.

A Dictionary of the English Language (1755)

diet

Cartland, Barbara (1901–2000)
English writer

The right diet directs sexual energy into the parts that matter.

The Observer, 1981

Montagu, Lady Mary Wortley (1689–1762)
English letter writer, poet, traveller and introducer of smallpox inoculation

Be plain in dress, and sober in your diet;
In short, my deary! kiss me, and be quiet.

Summary of Lord Lyttleton's Advice

Smith, Sydney (1771–1845)
English clergyman, essayist, journalist and wit
On his convalescent diet

If you hear of sixteen or eighteen pounds of human flesh, they belong to me. I look as if a curate has been taken out of me.

Letter to Lady Carlisle, 1844

▶▶ COOKERY; DINING; FOOD

dining

Bowra, Sir Maurice (1898–1971)
English scholar
> I'm a man
> More dined against than dining.
>> In Betjeman, *Summoned by Bells* (1960)

Edwards, Oliver (1711–1791)
English lawyer
> For my part now, I consider supper as a turnpike through which one must pass, in order to get to bed.
>> In Boswell, *The Life of Samuel Johnson* (1791)

Evarts, William Maxwell (1818–1901)
US lawyer and statesman
Of a dinner given by US President and temperance advocate Rutherford B. Hayes
> It was a brilliant affair; water flowed like champagne.
>> Attr.

Galsworthy, John (1867–1933)
English writer and dramatist
> He could take nothing for dinner but a partridge, with an imperial pint of champagne.
>> *The Man of Property* (1906)

Gulbenkian, Nubar (1896–1972)
British industrialist, diplomat and philanthropist
> The best number for a dinner party is two: myself and a damn good head waiter.
>> *The Observer*, 1965

Harington, Sir John (1561–1612)
English courtier
> When I make a feast,
> I would my guests should praise it, not the cooks.
>> *Epigrams* (1618)

Johnson, Samuel (1709–1784)
English lexicographer, poet, critic, conversationalist and essayist
> We could not have had a better dinner had there been a Synod of Cooks.
>> In Boswell, *The Life of Samuel Johnson* (1791)

> This was a good dinner enough, to be sure; but it was not a dinner to ask a man to.
>> In Boswell, *The Life of Samuel Johnson* (1791)

> A man seldom thinks with more earnestness of anything than he does of his dinner.
>> In Piozzi, *Anecdotes of the Late Samuel Johnson* (1786)

> A man is in general better pleased when he has a good dinner upon his table, than when his wife talks Greek.
>> In Hawkins, *Life of Samuel Johnson* (1787)

Landor, Walter Savage (1775–1864)
English poet and writer
> I shall dine late; but the dining-room will be well lighted, the guests few and select.
>> *Imaginary Conversations* (1853)

Lane, George Martin (1823–1897)
> The waiter roars it through the hall:
> 'We don't give bread with one fish-ball!'.
>> 'Lay of the Lone Fish-Ball' (1855)

Martial (c.AD 40–c.104)
Spanish-born Latin epigrammatist and poet
> *Caenae fercula nostrae malim convivis quam placuisse cocis.*
> I prefer that the courses at our banquet should give pleasure to the guests rather than to the cooks.
>> *Epigrammata*

Maugham, William Somerset (1874–1965)
English writer, dramatist and physician
> At a dinner party one should eat wisely but not too well, and talk well but not too wisely.
>> *A Writer's Notebook* (1949)

Pepys, Samuel (1633–1703)
English diarist, naval administrator and politician
> Strange to see how a good dinner and feasting reconciles everybody.
>> *Diary*, 1665

Powell, Anthony (1905–2000)
English writer and critic
> Dinner at the Huntercombes' possessed 'only two dramatic features – the wine was a farce and the food a tragedy'.
>> *A Dance to the Music of Time: The Acceptance World* (1955)

Scott, William (1745–1836)
> A dinner lubricates business.
>> In Boswell, *The Life of Samuel Johnson* (1791)

Smith, Sydney (1771–1845)
English clergyman, essayist, journalist and wit
> Most London dinners evaporate in whispers to one's next-door neighbour. I make it a rule never to speak a word to mine, but fire across the table; though I broke it once … I turned suddenly round and said, 'Madam, I have been looking for a person who disliked gravy all my life; let us swear eternal friendship.'
>> In Holland, *A Memoir of the Reverend Sydney Smith* (1855)

From his recipe for salads
> Serenely full, the epicure would say,
> Fate cannot harm me, I have dined today.
>> In Holland, *A Memoir of the Reverend Sydney Smith* (1855)

Swift, Jonathan (1667–1745)
Irish satirist, poet, essayist and cleric

> We were to do more business after dinner; but
> after dinner is after dinner – an old saying and a
> true, 'much drinking, little thinking'.
>
> *Journal to Stella*, 1711

> He showed me his bill of fare to tempt me to
> dine with him; Poh, said I, I value not your bill of
> fare; give me your bill of company.
>
> *Journal to Stella*, 1711

Wilde, Oscar (1854–1900)
Irish poet, dramatist, writer, critic and wit
Said to Frank Harris who was listing the houses he had dined
at

> Dear Frank, we believe you; you have dined in
> every house in London – once.
>
> Attr.

▶▶ FOOD

diplomacy

Cromwell, Oliver (1599–1658)
English general, statesman and Puritan leader

> A man-of-war is the best ambassador.
>
> Attr.

Denning, Lord (1899–1999)
English Master of the Rolls
His views on the difference between a diplomat and a lady

> When a diplomat says yes, he means perhaps.
> When he says perhaps he means no. When he
> says no, he is not a diplomat. When a lady says
> no, she means perhaps. When she says perhaps,
> she means yes. But when she says yes, she is no
> lady.
>
> Speech at meeting of Magistrates Association,
> 14 October 1982

Frost, Robert (1874–1963)
US poet

> A diplomat is a man who always remembers a
> woman's birthday but never remembers her age.
>
> Attr.

Goldberg, Isaac (1887–1938)

> Diplomacy is to do and say
> The nastiest thing in the nicest way.
>
> *The Reflex*, 1927

Grant, Bruce Alexander (1925–)
Australian writer, critic and civil servant

> I recall at least two Australian ambassadors who
> complained to me in the past about the
> constraints which the inherited British style
> placed on Australian diplomacy, but, when their
> time came to resist the invitation of knighthood,
> their resolve buckled under the terrible strain.
>
> *Gods and Politicians* (1982)

Pearson, Lester B. (1897–1972)
Canadian diplomat and politician

> Diplomacy is letting someone else have your
> way.
>
> *The Observer*, 1965

Rogers, Will (1879–1935)
US humorist, actor, rancher, writer and wit

> Diplomacy is the art of saying 'nice doggy' until
> you can find a rock.
>
> Attr.

Ustinov, Sir Peter (1921–)
English actor, director, dramatist, writer and raconteur

> A diplomat these days is nothing but a head-
> waiter who's allowed to sit down occasionally.
>
> *Romanoff and Juliet* (1956)

Wotton, Sir Henry (1568–1639)
English diplomat, traveller and poet

> *Legatus est vir bonus peregre missus ad mentiendum
> rei publicae causa.*
> An ambassador is an honest man sent to lie
> abroad for the good of his country.
>
> Written in an album, 1606

disability

Sassoon, Siegfried (1886–1967)
English poet and writer

> Does it matter? – losing your legs? …
> For people will always be kind,
> And you need not show that you mind
> When others come in after hunting
> To gobble their muffins and eggs.
>
> Does it matter? – losing your sight? …
> There's such splendid work for the blind;
> And people will always be kind,
> As you sit on the terrace remembering
> And turning your face to the light.
>
> 'Does it Matter?' (1917)

disappointment

Eliot, George (1819–1880)
English writer and poet

> Nothing is so good as it seems beforehand.
>
> *Silas Marner* (1861)

Goldsmith, Oliver (c.1728–1774)
Irish dramatist, poet and writer

> As for disappointing them, I should not so much
> mind; but I can't abide to disappoint myself.
>
> *She Stoops to Conquer*
> (1773)

Moore, Thomas (1779–1852)
Irish poet
> Like Dead Sea fruits, that tempt the eye,
> But turn to ashes on the lips!
>> *Lalla Rookh* (1817)

Pope, Alexander (1688–1744)
English poet, translator and editor
> 'Blessed is the man who expects nothing, for he shall never be disappointed, ' was the ninth beatitude which a man of wit (who like a man of wit was a long time in gaol) added to the eighth.
>> Letter to William Fortescue, 1725

discovery

Archimedes (c.287–212 BC)
Greek mathematician
> *Eureka!*
> I've got it!
>> In Vitruvius Pollio, *De Architectura*

Keats, John (1795–1821)
English poet
> Much have I travell'd in the realms of gold,
> And many goodly states and kingdoms seen …
> Then felt I like some watcher of the skies
> When a new planet swims into his ken;
> Or like stout Cortez when with eagle eyes
> He star'd at the Pacific – and all his men
> Look'd at each other with a wild surmise –
> Silent, upon a peak in Darien.
>> 'On First Looking into Chapman's Homer' (1816)

Smiles, Samuel (1812–1904)
> We often discover what will do, by finding out what will not do; and probably he who never made a mistake never made a discovery.
>> *Self-Help* (1859)

Teilhard de Chardin, Pierre (1881–1955)
French Jesuit philosopher and palaeontologist
> *Rien ne vaut la peine d'être trouvé que ce qui n'a jamais existé encore.*
> Nothing is worth discovering except that which has not yet existed.
>> *La Vision du passé*

▶▶ SCIENCE

distance

Campbell, Thomas (1777–1844)
Scottish poet, ballad writer and journalist
> 'Tis distance lends enchantment to the view,
> And robes the mountain in its azure hue.
>> *Pleasures of Hope* (1799)

White, Patrick (1912–1990)
English-born Australian writer and dramatist
> Anyone who stares long enough into the distance is bound to be mistaken for a philosopher or mystic in the end.
>> *Happy Valley* (1939)

Wordsworth, William (1770–1850)
English poet
> Sweetest melodies
> Are those by distance made more sweet.
>> *Personal Talk* (1807)

divorce

Atwood, Margaret (1939–)
Canadian writer, poet and critic
> A divorce is like an amputation; you survive, but there's less of you.
>> *Time*, 1973

Kerr, Jean (1923–)
US writer and dramatist
> A lawyer is never entirely comfortable with a friendly divorce, any more than a good mortician wants to finish his job and then have the patient sit up on the table.
>> *Time*, 1961

Parker, Dorothy (1893–1967)
US writer, poet, critic and wit
Said of her husband on the day their divorce became final
> Oh, don't worry about Alan … Alan will always land on somebody's feet.
>> In J. Keats, *You Might As Well Live* (1970)

Thorndike, Dame Sybil (1882–1976)
English actress
Replying to a query as to whether she had ever considered divorce during her long marriage to Sir Lewis Casson
> Divorce? Never. But murder often!
>> Attr.

West, Dame Rebecca (1892–1983)
English writer, critic and feminist
> If our divorce laws were improved, we could at least say that if marriage does nobody much good it does nobody any harm.
>> *The Clarion*

diy

Anonymous
> Don't force it; get a larger hammer.

> Any tool when dropped, will roll into the least accessible corner of the workshop.
>> Law of the Workshop

On the way to the corner, any dropped tool will first strike your toes.

Corollary to Law of the Workshop

Interchangeable parts won't.

Laws of Assembly

Any product cut to length will be too short.

Klipstein's Observation

If you need four screws for the job, the first three are easy to find.

The N-1 Law

Barry, Dave
US columnist and journalist
In fact, most home projects are impossible, which is why you should do them yourself. There is no point in paying other people to screw things up when you can easily screw them up yourself for far less money.

'The Taming of the Screw'

Proverb
A bad workman always blames his tools.

Zwanzig, Carl
Duct tape is like the force. It has a light side, and a dark side, and it holds the universe together.

Attr.

▶▶ DESIGN

documentation

Anonymous
If it should exist, it doesn't.

Arnold's First Law of Documentation

If it does exist, it's out of date.

Arnold's Second Law of Documentation

dogs

Anonymous
Advertisement for National Canine Defence League
So if you want to know more about neutering and why it's best for you and your dog, give us a call.

The Observer, 2000

Beerbohm, Sir Max (1872–1956)
English satirist, cartoonist, critic and essayist
You will find that the woman who is really kind to dogs is always one who has failed to inspire sympathy in men.

Zuleika Dobson (1911)

Bennett, Alan (1934–)
English dramatist, actor and diarist

It's the one species I wouldn't mind seeing vanish from the face of the earth. I wish they were like the white rhino – six of them left in the Serengeti National Park, and all males.

Attr.

Eliot, George (1819–1880)
English writer and poet
Though, as we know, she was not fond of pets that must be held in the hands or trodden on, she was always attentive to the feelings of dogs, and very polite if she had to decline their advances.

Middlemarch (1872)

Huxley, Aldous (1894–1963)
English writer, poet and critic
To his dog, every man is Napoleon; hence the constant popularity of dogs.

Attr.

Macaulay, Lord (1800–1859)
English Liberal statesman, essayist and poet
We were regaled by a dogfight … How odd that people of sense should find any pleasure in being accompanied by a beast who is always spoiling conversation.

In Trevelyan, Life and Letters of Macaulay (1876)

Muir, Frank (1920–1998)
English writer, humorist and broadcaster
Dogs, like horses, are quadrupeds. That is to say, they have four rupeds, one at each corner, on which they walk.

You Can't Have Your Kayak and Heat It, with Dennis Norden

Nash, Ogden (1902–1971)
US poet
A door is what a dog is perpetually on the wrong side of.

'A Dog's Best Friend Is His Illiteracy' (1952)

Sparrow, John (1906–1992)
English lawyer and writer
That indefatigable and unsavoury engine of pollution, the dog.

Letter to The Times, 1975

Streatfield, Sir Geoffrey Hugh Benbow (1897–1978)
British judge
I loathe people who keep dogs. They are cowards who haven't got the guts to bite people themselves.

A Madman's Diary

▶▶ ANIMALS; CHILDREN

doubt

Austen, Jane (1775–1817)
English writer
Where so many hours have been spent in convincing myself that I am right, is there not some reason to fear I may be wrong?
Sense and Sensibility (1811)

Bacon, Francis (1561–1626)
English philosopher, essayist, politician and courtier
If a man will begin with certainties, he shall end in doubts; but if he will be content to begin with doubts, he shall end in certainties.
The Advancement of Learning (1605)

The Bible (King James Version)
How long halt ye between two opinions?
I Kings, 18: 21
O thou of little faith, wherefore didst thou doubt?
Matthew, 14: 31

Blake, William (1757–1827)
English poet, engraver, painter and mystic
He who Doubts from what he sees
Will neer Believe do what you Please.
If the Sun & Moon should doubt,
Theyd immediately Go out.
'Auguries of Innocence' (c.1803)

Borges, Jorge Luis (1899–1986)
Argentinian writer, poet and librarian
He conocido io que ignoran los griegos: la incertidumbre.
I have known what the Greeks knew not: uncertainty.
The Garden of Paths which Diverge (1941)

Boyd, William (1952–)
Scottish writer
What now? What next? All these questions. All these doubts. So few certainties. But then I have taken new comfort and refuge in the doctrine that advises one not to seek tranquillity in certainty, but in permanently suspended judgement.
Brazzaville Beach (1990)

Browning, Robert (1812–1889)
English poet
All we have gained then by our unbelief
Is a life of doubt diversified by faith,
For one of faith diversified by doubt:
We called the chess-board white, – we call it black.
'Bishop Blougram's Apology' (1855)

Butler, Samuel (1835–1902)
English writer, painter, philosopher and scholar

My Lord, I do not believe. Help thou mine unbelief.
Samuel Butler's Notebooks (1951)

Chesterton, G.K. (1874–1936)
English writer, poet and critic
John Grubby, who was short and stout
And troubled with religious doubt,
Refused about the age of three
To sit upon the curate's knee.
Poems (1915)

Darrow, Clarence (1857–1938)
US lawyer, reformer and writer
Remark during the trial of John Scopes, 1925, for teaching evolution in school
I do not consider it an insult but rather a compliment to be called an agnostic.I do not pretend to know where many ignorant men are sure – that is all that agnosticism means.
Attr.

Dent, Alan (1905–1978)
Scottish writer and critic
This is the tragedy of a man who could not make up his mind.
Introduction to film *Hamlet*, 1948

Emerson, Ralph Waldo (1803–1882)
US poet, essayist, transcendentalist and teacher
I am the doubter and the doubt,
And I the hymn the Brahmin sings.
'Brahma' (1867)

Hardwicke, Philip Yorke, Earl of (1690–1764)
English judge and Lord Chancellor
Referring to Dirleton's *Doubts*
His doubts are better than most people's certainties.
In Boswell, *The Life of Samuel Johnson* (1791)

Huxley, Aldous (1894–1963)
English writer, poet and critic
Defined in psychological terms, a fanatic is a man who consciously overcompensates a secret doubt.
Proper Studies (1927)

Huxley, T.H. (1825–1895)
English biologist, Darwinist and agnostic
I am too much of a sceptic to deny the possibility of anything.
Letter to Herbert Spencer, 1886

Koran
There is no doubt in this book.
Chapter 1

Lichtenberg, Georg (1742–1799)
German physicist, satirist and writer
Zweifle an allem wenigstens einmal, und wäre es auch der Satz: zweimal zwei ist vier.
Doubt everything at least once – even the

proposition that two and two are four.

Miscellaneous Writings

Newman, John Henry, Cardinal (1801–1890)
English Cardinal, theologian and poet
> Ten thousand difficulties do not make one doubt.

Apologia pro Vita Sua (1864)

Pirsig, Robert (1928–)
US author
> You are never dedicated to something you have complete confidence in. No one is fanatically shouting that the sun is going to rise tomorrow. They know it's going to rise tomorrow. When people are fanatically dedicated to political or religious faiths or any other kind of dogmas or goals, it's always because these dogmas or goals are in doubt.

Zen and the Art of Motorcycle Maintenance (1974)

Rushdie, Salman (1947–)
Indian-born English author
> Doubt, it seems to me, is the central condition of a human being in the twentieth century.

The Observer, 1989

Tennyson, Alfred, Lord (1809–1892)
English lyric poet
> There lives more faith in honest doubt,
> Believe me, than in half the creeds.

In Memoriam A. H. H. (1850)

> For nothing worthy proving can be proven,
> Nor yet disproven: wherefore thou be wise,
> Cleave ever to the sunnier side of doubt.

'The Ancient Sage' (1885)

Unamuno, Miguel de (1864–1936)
Spanish philosopher, poet and writer
> *Una fe que no duda es una fe muerta.*
> A faith which does not doubt is a dead faith.

La agonía del cristianismo (1931)

▶▶ UNCERTAINTY

dreams

Bacon, Francis (1561–1626)
English philosopher, essayist, politician and courtier
> Dreams and predictions of astrology … ought to serve but for winter talk by the fireside.

Essays (1625)

Beddoes, Thomas Lovell (1803–1849)
> If there were dreams to sell,
> What would you buy?
> Some cost a passing bell;
> Some a light sigh,
> That shakes from Life's fresh crown
> Only a roseleaf down.

> If there were dreams to sell,
> Merry and sad to tell,
> And the crier rung the bell,
> What would you buy?

'Dream-Pedlary' (1851)

Browne, Sir Thomas (1605–1682)
English physician, author and antiquary
> That children dream not in the first half year, that men dream not in some countries, are to me sick men's dreams, dreams out of the ivory gate, and visions before midnight.

In S. Wilkin (ed.), *Sir Thomas Browne's Works* (1835)

Bunn, Alfred (1796–1860)
English theatrical manager, librettist and poet
> I dreamt that I dwelt in marble halls,
> With vassals and serfs at my side.

The Bohemian Girl (1843)

Calderón de la Barca, Pedro (1600–1681)
Spanish dramatist and poet
> *Aun en sueños*
> *no se pierde el hacer bien.*
> Even in dreams doing good is not wasted.

Life is a Dream (1636)

> *Pues veo estando dormido,*
> *que sueñe estando despierto.*
> For I see, since I am asleep, that I dream while I am awake.

Life is a Dream (1636)

Chuang Tse (c.369–286 BC)
> I do not know whether I was then a man dreaming I was a butterfly, or whether I am now a butterfly dreaming I am a man.

Chuang Tse (1889)

Clarke, Arthur C. (1917–)
English writer
Voice of computer HAL 2000
> Dr Chandra, will I dream?

2001, A Space Odyssey (film, 1969)

Coleridge, Mary (1861–1907)
> Egypt's might is tumbled down
> Down a-down the deeps of thought;
> Greece is fallen and Troy town,
> Glorious Rome hath lost her crown,
> Venice' pride is nought.

> But the dreams their children dreamed
> Fleeting, unsubstantial, vain.
> Shadowy as the shadows seemed
> Airy nothing, as they deemed,
> These remain.

Poems (1894), 'Egypt's Might is Tumbled Down'

Donne, John (1572–1631)
English poet
> So, if I dream I have you, I have you,

For, all our joys are but fantastical.

Elegies (c.1600)

Herrick, Robert (1591–1674)
English poet, royalist and clergyman

> With thousand such enchanting dreams, that meet
> To make sleep not so sound, as sweet.

Hesperides (1648)

Jackson, Jesse (1941–)
US clergyman and civil rights leader

> No one should negotiate their dreams. Dreams must be free to flee and fly high. No government, no legislature, has a right to limit your dreams. You should never agree to surrender your dreams.

In *Playboy*, 1969

Lawrence, T.E. (1888–1935)
British soldier, archaeologist, translator and writer; known as 'Lawrence of Arabia'

> All men dream: but not equally. Those who dream by night in the dusty recesses of their minds wake in the day to find that it was vanity; but the dreamers of the day are dangerous men, for they may act their dream with open eyes, to make it possible.

The Seven Pillars of Wisdom (1926)

Miller, Arthur (1915–)
US dramatist and screenwriter

> Nobody dast blame this man. A salesman is got to dream, boy. It comes with the territory.

Death of a Salesman (1949)

Montaigne, Michel de (1533–1592)
French essayist and moralist

> *Ceux qui ont apparié notre vie à un songe, ont eu de la raison, à l'aventure plus qu'ils ne pensaient … Nous veillons dormants, et veillants dormons.*
> Those who have compared our life to a dream were, by chance, more right than they thought … We are awake while sleeping, and sleeping while awake.

Essais (1580)

Patten, Brian (1946–)
British poet

> Sink then dreamer into what might have been!

'Lethargy'

Poe, Edgar Allan (1809–1849)
US poet, writer and editor

> They who dream by day are cognizant of many things which escape those who dream only by night.

Eleonora (1841)

> All that we see or seem
> Is but a dream within a dream.

'A Dream within a Dream' (1849)

Rossetti, Christina (1830–1894)
English poet

> The hope I dreamed of was a dream,
> Was but a dream; and now I wake,
> Exceeding comfortless, and worn, and old,
> For a dream's sake.

'Mirage' (1862)

Rostand, Edmond (1868–1918)
French poet and dramatist

> *Le seul rêve intéresse,*
> *Vivre sans rêve, qu'est-ce?*
> *Et j'aime la Princesse*
> *Lointaine.*
> Only dreaming is of interest. What is life, without dreams? And I love the Far-away Princess.

La Princesse Lointaine (1895)

Salk, Jonas (1914–1995)
US virologist

> I have had dreams, and I've had nightmares. I overcame the nightmares because of my dreams.

Reader's Digest, 1980

Shakespeare, William (1564–1616)
English dramatist, poet and actor

> To die, to sleep;
> To sleep, perchance to dream. Ay, there's the rub;
> For in that sleep of death what dreams may come,
> When we have shuffled off this mortal coil,
> Must give us pause.

Hamlet, III.i

> O God, I could be bounded in a nutshell and count myself a king of infinite space, were it not that I have bad dreams.

Hamlet, II.ii

> O, I have pass'd a miserable night,
> So full of fearful dreams, of ugly sights,
> That, as I am a Christian faithful man,
> I would not spend another such a night
> Though 'twere to buy a world of happy days –
> So full of dismal terror was the time!

Richard III, I.iv

> We are such stuff
> As dreams are made on; and our little life
> Is rounded with a sleep.

The Tempest, IV.i

> Weary with toil, I haste me to my bed,
> The dear repose for limbs with travel tired;
> But then begins a journey in my head
> To work my mind when body's work's expired.

Sonnet 27

Smith, Alexander (1830–1867)
Scottish poet and writer
> Looking into a dream is like looking into the interior of a watch; you see the processes at work by which results are obtained. A man thus becomes his own eavesdropper, he plays the spy on himself. Hope and fear, and the other passions, are all active; but the activity is uncontrolled by the will, and in remembering dreams one has the somewhat peculiar feeling of being one's own spiritual anatomist.
> > *On Dreams and Dreaming*

Spielberg, Steven (1947–)
US film director and producer
> I dream for a living.
> > *Time*, 1985

Tennyson, Alfred, Lord (1809–1892)
English lyric poet
> Dreams are true while they last, and do we not live in dreams?
> > 'The Higher Pantheism' (1867)

Updike, John (1932–)
US writer, poet and critic
> Dreams come true; without that possibility, nature would not incite us to have them.
> > *Self-Consciousness: Memoirs* (1989)

Virgil (70–19 BC)
Roman poet
> *Sunt geminae Somni portae; quarum altera fertur*
> *Cornea, qua veris facilis datur exitus umbris,*
> *Altera candenti perfecta nitens elephanto,*
> *Sed falsa ad caelum mittunt insomnia Manes.*
> Two gates the silent house of Sleep adorn;
> Of polished ivory this, that of transparent horn:
> True visions through transparent horn arise;
> Through polished ivory pass deluding lies.
> > *Aeneid*

Yeats, W.B. (1865–1939)
Irish poet, dramatist, editor, writer and senator
> In dreams begins responsibility.
> > *Responsibilities* (1914)

▶▶ BED; SLEEP

dress

Adams, Scott (1957–)
US cartoonist
> Your business clothes are naturally attracted to staining liquids. This attraction is strongest just before an important meeting.
> > *Building a Better Life by Stealing Office Supplies: Dogbert's Big Book of Business* (1991)

Aesop (6th century BC)
Legendary Greek writer of fables
> It is not only fine feathers that make fine birds.
> > 'The Jay and the Peacock'

Ashford, Daisy (1881–1972)
English child author
> You look rather rash my dear your colors dont quite match your face.
> > *The Young Visiters* (1919)

Barry, Dave
US columnist and journalist
> Look, in particular, at the people who, like you, are making average incomes for doing average jobs – bank vice presidents, insurance salesman, auditors, secretaries of defense – and you'll realize they all dress the same way, essentially the way the mannequins in the Sears menswear department dress. Now look at the real successes, the people who make a lot more money than you – Elton John, Captain Kangaroo, anybody from Saudi Arabia, Big Bird, and so on. They all dress funny – and they all succeed. Are you catching on?
> > 'How to Dress for Real Success'

Bongay, Amy
President of the Models Guild
Commenting on the fact that the fashion industry had begun to find supermodels too demanding
> It's a terrible sign. It will be the death of this profession if designers start using real people on the catwalks and in their advertising.
> > *Daily Mail*, 1995

Carter, Angela (1940–1992)
English writer
> Clothes are our weapons, our challenges, our visible insults.
> > *Nothing Sacred* (1982)

Chanel, Coco (1883–1971)
French couturier and perfumer
> Fashion is architecture: it is a matter of proportions.
> > In Haedrich, *Coco Chanel, Her Life, Her Secrets* (1971)

On Dior's New Look
> These are clothes by a man who doesn't know women, never had one and dreams of being one.
> > *Scotland on Sunday*, 1995

Clough, Arthur Hugh (1819–1861)
English poet and letter writer
> Petticoats up to the knees, or even, it might be, above them,
> Matching their lily-white legs with the clothes that they trod in the wash-tub!
> > *The Bothie of Tober-na-Vuolich* (1848)

Curie, Marie (1867–1934)
Polish-born French physicist
Referring to a wedding dress
> I have no dress except the one I wear every day. If you are going to be kind enough to give me one, please let it be practical and dark so that I can put it on afterwards to go to the laboratory.
>> *Letter to a friend, 1894*

Darrow, Clarence (1857–1938)
US lawyer, reformer and writer
> I go to a better tailor than any of you and pay more for my clothes. The only difference is that you probably don't sleep in yours.
>> In E. Fuller, *2500 Anecdotes*

Dickens, Charles (1812–1870)
English writer
> Any man may be in good spirits and good temper when he's well drest. There ain't much credit in that.
>> *Martin Chuzzlewit* (1844)

> If you could see my legs when I take my boots off, you'd form some idea of what unrequited affection is.
>> *Dombey and Son* (1848)

Ebner-Eschenbach, Marie von (1830–1916)
Austrian writer
> 'Himmel!', ruft er, 'wenn es Kleider sind, die uns in der Welt möglich machen, wie hoch müssen wir den halten, der sie verfertigt!'
> 'Goodness, ' he cried, 'if it is our clothes which fit us for this world, in what high esteem must we hold those who make them!'.
>> *The Two Countesses*, 'Countess Muschi' (1884)

Edward VII (1841–1910)
King of the United Kingdom
> I thought everyone must know that a short jacket is always worn with a silk hat at a private view in the morning.
>> In Sir P. Magnus, *Edward VII*

Emerson, Ralph Waldo (1803–1882)
US poet, essayist, transcendentalist and teacher
> I have heard with admiring submission the experience of the lady who declared that 'the sense of being well-dressed gives a feeling of inward tranquillity which religion is powerless to bestow.'
>> *Letters and Social Aims* (1875)

Of the English
> They think him the best dressed man, whose dress is so fit for his use that you cannot notice or remember to describe it.
>> *English Traits* (1856)

> The Frenchman invented the ruffle, the Englishman added the shirt.
>> *English Traits* (1856)

> It is only when the mind and character slumber that the dress can be seen.
>> *Letters and Social Aims* (1875)

Farquhar, George (1678–1707)
Irish dramatist
> A lady, if undrest at Church, looks silly,
> One cannot be devout in dishabilly.
>> *The Stage Coach* (1704)

Forbes, Miss C.F. (1817–1911)
English writer
> The sense of being well-dressed gives a feeling of inward tranquillity which religion is powerless to bestow.
>> In Emerson, *Social Aims* (1876)

Gaskell, Elizabeth (1810–1865)
English writer
> The Cranford ladies' dress is very independent of fashion; as they observe, 'What does it signify how we dress here at Cranford, where everybody knows us?' And if they go from home, their reason is equally cogent, 'What does it signify how we dress here, where nobody knows us?'.
>> *Cranford* (1853)

Hazlitt, William (1778–1830)
English writer and critic
> Those who make their dress a principal part of themselves, will, in general, become of no more value than their dress.
>> 'On the Clerical Character'

Herrick, Robert (1591–1674)
English poet, royalist and clergyman
> When as in silks my Julia goes,
> Then, then (me thinks) how sweetly flowes
> That liquefaction of her clothes.
> Next, when I cast mine eyes and see
> That brave Vibration each way free;
> O how that glittering taketh me!
>> *Hesperides* (1648)

> A sweet disorder in the dresse
> Kindles in cloathes a wantonnesse:
> A Lawne about the shoulders thrown
> Into a fine distraction ...

> A winning wave (deserving Note)
> In the tempestuous petticote:
> A carelesse shooe-string, in whose tye
> I see a wilde civility:
> Doe more bewitch me, than when Art
> Is too precise in every part.
>> 'Delight in Disorder' (1648)

Hewett, Dorothy (1923–)
Australian dramatist and poet

Gentlemen may remove any garment consistent with decency.
Ladies may remove any garment consistent with charm.

'Beneath the Arches'

Johnson, Samuel (1709–1784)
English lexicographer, poet, critic, conversationalist and essayist

Fine clothes are good only as they supply the want of other means of procuring respect.

In Boswell, *The Life of Samuel Johnson* (1791)

Jonson, Ben (1572–1637)
English dramatist and poet

Still to be neat, still to be drest,
As you were going to a feast;
Still to be powder'd, still perfum'd,
Lady, it is to be presumed,
Though art's hid causes are not found,
All is not sweet, all is not sound.
Give me a look, give me a face,
That makes simplicity a grace;
Robes loosely flowing, hair as free:
Such sweet neglect more taketh me,
Than all the adulteries of art;
They strike mine eyes, but not my heart.

Epicoene (1609)

Julia (39 BC–AD 14)
On being complimented by her father on the modest dress she was wearing that day

Today I dressed to meet my father's eyes; yesterday it was for my husband's.

In Macrobius, *Saturnalia*

Kaufman, Jean-Claude

The sock is a highly sensitive conjugal object.

The Observer, 1992

Loesser, Frank (1910–1969)
US songwriter and composer

Isn't it grand! Isn't it fine!
Look at the cut, the style, the line!
The suit of clothes is altogether, but altogether it's altogether
The most remarkable suit of clothes that I have ever seen.

'The King's New Clothes' (song, 1952)

Loos, Anita (1893–1981)
US writer and screenwriter

You have got to be a Queen to get away with a hat like that.

Gentlemen Prefer Blondes (1925)

Masters, John (1914–1983)
English writer

Join a Highland regiment, me boy. The kilt is an unrivalled garment for fornication and diarrhoea.

Bugles and a Tiger

Moore, Brian (1921–1999)
Canadian writer

So the years hang like old clothes, forgotten in the wardrobe of our minds. Did I wear that? Who was I then?

No Other Life (1993)

Nash, Ogden (1902–1971)
US poet

There was a young belle of old Natchez
Whose garments were always in patchez.
When comment arose
On the state of her clothes,
She drawled, When Ah itchez, Ah scratchez!

I'm a Stranger Here Myself (1935)

Sure, deck your lower limbs in pants;
Yours are the limbs, my sweeting.
You look divine as you advance –
Have you seen yourself retreating?

'What's the Use?' (1940)

O'Rourke, P.J. (1947–)
US writer

The only really firm rule of taste about cross dressing is that neither sex should ever wear anything they haven't yet figured out how to go to the bathroom in.

Modern Manners (1984)

Parker, Dorothy (1893–1967)
US writer, poet, critic and wit

Where's the man could ease a heart,
Like a satin gown?

'The Satin Dress' (1937)

Brevity is the soul of lingerie.

In Woollcott, *While Rome Burns* (1934)

Parton, Dolly (1946–)
US country and western singer

You'd be surprised how much it costs to look this cheap.

In Carole McKenzie, *Quotable Women* (1992)

Rimbaud, Arthur (1854–1891)
French poet

Je m'en allais, les poings dans mes poches crevées;
Mon paletot aussi devenait idéal.
I was walking along, fists in my torn pockets; my overcoat also was entering the realm of the ideal.

'Ma Bohème' (1870)

Saki (1870–1916)
Burmese-born British writer

His shoes exhaled the right soupçon of harness-room; his socks compelled one's attention without losing one's respect.

The Chronicles of Clovis (1911)

Surtees, R.S. (1805–1864)
English writer

No one knows how ungentlemanly he can look, until he has seen himself in a shocking bad hat.

Mr Facey Romford's Hounds (1865)

Swift, Jonathan (1667–1745)
Irish satirist, poet, essayist and cleric

She wears her clothes, as if they were thrown on with a pitchfork.

Polite Conversation (1738)

Taylor, John (20th century)

The only man who really needs a tail coat is a man with a hole in his trousers.

The Observer, 'Shouts and Murmurs'

Thoreau, Henry David (1817–1862)
US essayist, social critic and writer

Beware of all enterprises that require new clothes.

Walden (1854)

Watts, Isaac (1674–1748)
English hymn-writer, poet and minister

The tulip and the butterfly
Appear in gayer coats than I:
Let me be dressed fine as I will,
Flies, worms, and flowers, exceed me still.

'Against Pride in Clothes' (1715)

West, Mae (1892–1980)
US actress and scriptwriter

You can say what you like about long dresses, but they cover a multitude of shins.

In J. Weintraub, *Peel Me a Grape* (1975)

Whitehorn, Katherine (1926–)
English writer

Hats divide generally into three classes: offensive hats, defensive hats, and shrapnel.

Shouts and Murmurs (1963)

Wilde, Oscar (1854–1900)
Irish poet, dramatist, writer, critic and wit

A well-tied tie is the first serious step in life.

A Woman of No Importance (1893)

The only way to atone for being occasionally a little over-dressed is by being always absolutely over-educated.

The Chameleon, 1894

Wodehouse, P.G. (1881–1975)
English humorist and writer

The Right Hon was a tubby little chap who looked as if he had been poured into his clothes and had forgotten to say 'When!'.

Very Good, Jeeves (1930)

driving

Buchwald, Art (1925–)
US humorist

People are broad-minded. They'll accept the fact that a person can be an alcoholic, a dope fiend, a wife beater and even a newspaperman, but if a man doesn't drive, there's something wrong with him.

Have I Ever Lied to You? (1968)

Keane, Conrad
On 'Road lust'

Some motorists view their cars as the extension to their sexuality and driving develops into a complicated mating ritual.

The Times, 1998

drugs

Anonymous

Reality is a crutch for people who can't handle drugs.

LSD melts your mind, not in your hand.

Bush, George W.
US Republican politician
Reply when asked if he had experimented with drugs

When I was young and irresponsible, I was young and irresponsible.

The Times, 1999

Holiday, Billie (1915–1959)
US singer

If you think dope is for kicks and for thrills, you're out of your mind. There are more kicks to be had in a good case of paralytic polio or by living in an iron lung.

Lady Sings the Blues (1956)

Parker, Charlie (1920–1955)
US jazz musician and composer

Any musician who says he is playing better either on tea, the needle, or when he is juiced, is a plain straight liar … You can miss the most important years of your life, the years of possible creation.

In Nat Shapiro and Nat Hentoff, *Hear Me Talkin' To Ya* (1955)

▶▶ ADDICTION

drunkenness

Byron, Lord (1788–1824)
English poet satirist and traveller

Man, being reasonable, must get drunk;
The best of life is but intoxication:
Glory, the grape, love, gold, in these are sunk
The hopes of all men, and of every nation.

Don Juan (1824)

Chaucer, Geoffrey (c.1340–1400)
English poet, public servant and courtier
> For dronkenesse is verray sepulture
> Of mannes wit and his discrecioun.
>> *The Canterbury Tales* (1387)

Churchill, Randolph (1911–1968)
English journalist and writer
In a letter to a hostess after ruining her dinner party with one of his displays of drunken rudeness
> I should never be allowed out in private.
>> In B. Roberts, *Randolph: a Study of Churchill's Son* (1984)

Churchill, Sir Winston (1874–1965)
English Conservative Prime Minister
To Bessie Braddock MP who told him he was drunk
> And you, madam, are ugly. But I shall be sober in the morning.
>> Attr.

Dickens, Charles (1812–1870)
English writer
> It's my opinion, sir, that this meeting is drunk, sir.
>> *The Pickwick Papers* (1837)

Lightner, Candy (1946–)
US estate agent and founder of MADD (Mothers Against Drunk Driving)
> Death by drunken driving is a socially acceptable form of homicide.
>> *San José Mercury*, April 1981

Franklin, Benjamin (1706–1790)
US statesman, scientist, political critic and printer
> There are more old drunkards than old doctors.
>> Attr.

Halifax, Lord (1633–1695)
English politician, courtier, pamphleteer and epigrammatist
> It is a piece of Arrogance to dare to be drunk, because a Man sheweth himself without a Vail.
>> 'Drunkenness' (1750)

James, William (1842–1910)
US psychologist and philosopher
> If merely 'feeling good' could decide, drunkenness would be the supremely valid human experience.
>> *Varieties of Religious Experience* (1902)

Johnson, Samuel (1709–1784)
English lexicographer, poet, critic, conversationalist and essayist
> A man who exposes himself when he is intoxicated, has not the art of getting drunk.
>> In Boswell, *The Life of Samuel Johnson* (1791)

Junell, Thomas
Host of Finland's seaborne drinking championships
> The Finns have a very different alcohol culture from other European countries. Basically, it's

nothing to do with socialising – it's about getting drunk.
>> *Daily Mail*, 1996

Proverb
> *Qu'il faut à chaque mois,*
> *Du moins s'enivrer une fois.*
> Every month one should get drunk at least once.
>> French proverb

Russell, Bertrand (1872–1970)
English philosopher, mathematician, essayist and social reformer
> Drunkenness is temporary suicide: the happiness that it brings is merely negative, a momentary cessation of unhappiness.
>> *The Conquest of Happiness* (1930)

Seneca (c.4 BC–AD 65)
Roman philosopher, poet, dramatist, essayist, rhetorician and statesman
> Drunkenness doesn't create vices, but it brings them to the fore.
>> *Letters to Lucilius*, 100 AD

Squire, Sir J.C. (1884–1958)
English poet, critic, writer and editor
> But I'm not so think as you drunk I am.
>> 'Ballade of Soporific Absorption' (1931)

Tynan, Kenneth (1927–1980)
English drama critic, producer and essayist
> What, when drunk, one sees in other women, one sees in Garbo sober.
>> *The Sunday Times*, 1963

▶▶ ADDICTION; ALCOHOL

duty

Anonymous
> Straight is the line of Duty
> Curved is the line of Beauty
> Follow the first and thou shallt see
> The second ever following thee.

The Bible (King James Version)
> Fear God, and keep his commandments: for this is the whole duty of man.
>> *Ecclesiastes*, 12:13

Bierce, Ambrose (1842–c.1914)
US writer, verse writer and soldier
> *Duty*: That which sternly impels us in the direction of profit, along the line of desire.
>> *The Enlarged Devil's Dictionary* (1967)

Cobbett, William (1762–1835)
English politician, reformer, writer, farmer and army officer

From a very early age, I had imbibed the opinion, that it was every man's duty to do all that lay in his power to leave his country as good as he had found it.

> *Political Register*, 1832

Corneille, Pierre (1606–1684)
French dramatist, poet and lawyer

> *Faites votre devoir et laissez faire aux dieux.*
> Do your duty, and put yourself into the hands of the gods.
>
> *Horace* (1640)

Eliot, George (1819–1880)
English writer and poet

> She, stirred somewhat beyond her wont, and taking as her text the three words which have been used so often as the inspiring trumpet-calls of men – the words God, Immortality, Duty – pronounced, with terrible earnestness, how inconceivable was the first, how unbelievable the second, and yet how peremptory and absolute the third. Never, perhaps, have the sterner accents affirmed the sovereignty of impersonal and unrecompensing Law.
>
> In F.W.H. Myers, 'George Eliot' (1881)

Emerson, Ralph Waldo (1803–1882)
US poet, essayist, transcendentalist and teacher

> So nigh is grandeur to our dust,
> So near is God to man,
> When Duty whispers low, Thou must,
> The youth replies, I can.
>
> *May-Day* (1867)

Fielding, Henry (1707–1754)
English writer, dramatist and journalist

> When I'm not thank'd at all, I'm thank'd enough,
> I've done my duty, and I've done no more.
>
> *Tom Thumb the Great* (1731)

Fitzgerald, Penelope (1916–2000)
English novelist

> Duty is what no one else will do at the moment.
>
> *Offshore*

Gibbon, Edward (1737–1794)
English historian, politician and memoirist

> Dr Winchester well remembered that he had a salary to receive, and only forgot that he had a duty to perform.
>
> *Memoirs of My Life and Writings* (1796)

Gilbert, W.S. (1836–1911)
English dramatist, humorist and librettist

> The question is, had he not been a thing of beauty,
> Would she be swayed by quite as keen a sense of duty?
>
> *The Pirates of Penzance* (1880)

Goethe (1749–1832)
German poet, writer, dramatist and scientist

> *Du kannst, denn du sollst!*
> You can, for you ought to!
>
> 'An eighth' (1796); written with Schiller

Grant, Ulysses S. (1822–1885)
US President, general and memoirist

> No personal consideration should stand in the way of performing a public duty.
>
> Note on letter, 1875

Hooper, Ellen Sturgis (1816–1841)
US poet and hymn writer

> I slept, and dreamed that life was Beauty;
> I woke, and found that life was Duty.
>
> 'Beauty and Duty' (1840)

Ibsen, Henrik (1828–1906)
Norwegian writer, dramatist and poet

> What's a man's first duty? The answer's brief: To be himself.
>
> *Peer Gynt* (1867)

Johnson, Samuel (1709–1784)
English lexicographer, poet, critic, conversationalist and essayist

> It is our first duty to serve society, and, after we have done that, we may attend wholly to the salvation of our own souls. A youthful passion for abstracted devotion should not be encouraged.
>
> In Boswell, *The Life of Samuel Johnson* (1791)

Lee, Robert E. (1807–1870)
US general

> Duty then is the sublimest word in our language. Do your duty in all things. You cannot do more. You should never wish to do less.
>
> Inscription in the Hall of Fame

Lincoln, Abraham (1809–1865)
US statesman and President

> Let us have faith that right makes might; and in that faith let us to the end, dare to do our duty as we understand it.
>
> Speech, 1860

Milner, Alfred (1854–1925)
British statesman and colonial administrator

> If we believe a thing to be bad, and if we have a right to prevent it, it is our duty to try to prevent it and to damn the consequences.
>
> Speech, 1909

Nelson, Lord (1758–1805)
English admiral
Nelson's last signal at the Battle of Trafalgar, 1805

> England expects every man to do his duty.
>
> In Southey, *The Life of Nelson* (1860)

Peacock, Thomas Love (1785–1866)
English writer and poet

Sir, I have quarrelled with my wife; and a man who has quarrelled with his wife is absolved from all duty to his country.

Nightmare Abbey
(1818)

Salisbury, Lord (1830–1903)
English Conservative Prime Minister

Our first duty is towards the people of this country, to maintain their interests and their rights; our second duty is to all humanity.

Speech, 1896

Shakespeare, William (1564–1616)
English dramatist, poet and actor

Every subject's duty is the King's; but every subject's soul is his own.

Henry V, IV.i

O good old man, how well in thee appears
The constant service of the antique world,
When service sweat for duty, not for meed!
Thou art not for the fashion of these times,
Where none will sweat but for promotion,
And having that do choke their service up
Even with the having.

As You Like It, II.iii

Shaw, George Bernard (1856–1950)
Irish socialist, writer, dramatist and critic

When a stupid man is doing something he is ashamed of, he always declares that it is his duty.

Caesar and Cleopatra (1901)

Stevenson, Robert Louis (1850–1894)
Scottish writer, poet and essayist

There is no duty we so much underrate as the duty of being happy.

Virginibus Puerisque (1881)

Tennyson, Alfred, Lord (1809–1892)
English lyric poet

O hard, when love and duty clash!

The Princess (1847)

Washington, George (1732–1799)
US general, statesman and President

To persevere in one's duty and be silent is the best answer to calumny.

Moral Maxims

Wilde, Oscar (1854–1900)
Irish poet, dramatist, writer, critic and wit

Duty is what one expects of others, it is not what one does oneself.

A Woman of No Importance (1893)

E

economics

Bagehot, Walter (1826–1877)
English economist and political philosopher
> No real English gentleman, in his secret soul, was ever sorry for the death of a political economist.
>> 'The First Edinburgh Reviewers' (1858)

Blair, Tony (1953–)
British Labour Prime Minister
> I want Britain to be a stake-holder economy where everyone has a chance to get on and succeed, where there is a clear sense of national purpose and where we leave behind some of the battles between Left and Right which really are not relevant in the new global economy of today.
>> Speech in Singapore, 1996

Carlyle, Thomas (1795–1881)
Scottish historian, biographer, critic, and essayist
Of Political Economics
> And the Social Science, – not a 'gay science', … no, a dreary, desolate, and indeed quite abject and distressing one; what we might call …the dismal science.
>> Latter-Day Pamphlets (1850)

Douglas-Home, Sir Alec (1903–1995)
Scottish statesman
> When I have to read economic documents I have to have a box of matches and start moving them into position to illustrate and simplify the points to myself.
>> Interview in The Observer, 1962

Eden, Anthony (1897–1977)
English Conservative Prime Minister
> Everybody is always in favour of general economy and particular expenditure.
>> The Observer, 1956

Eisenhower, Dwight D. (1890–1969)
US Republican President and general
> Every gun that is made, every warship launched, every rocket fired signifies, in the final sense, a theft from those who hunger and are not fed, those who are cold and are not clothed. This world in arms is not spending money alone. It is spending the sweat of its labourers, the genius of its scientists, the hopes of its children.
>> Speech, 1953

Friedman, Milton (1912–)
US economist
> There's no such thing as a free lunch.
>> Title of book

Galbraith, J.K. (1908–)
Canadian-born US economist, diplomat and writer
> Economics is extremely useful as a form of employment for economists.
>> Attr.

> If all else fails, immortality can always be assured by spectacular error.
>> Attr.

George, Eddie (1938–)
Governor of the Bank of England
> There are three kinds of economist. Those who can count and those who can't.
>> The Observer Review, 1996

Heller, Walter (1915–)
Definition of an economist
> Someone who can't see something working in practice without asking whether it would work in theory.
>> Attr.

Henderson, Leon (1895–1986)
> Having a little inflation is like being a little pregnant.
>> Attr.

Jones, Barry Owen (1932–)
> Academic economists have about the status and reliability of astrologers or the readers of Tarot cards. If the medical profession was as lacking in resources as the economics we would not have advanced very far beyond the provision of splints for broken arms.
>> In John Wilkes (ed.), The Future of Work

Keynes, John Maynard (1883–1946)
English economist
> But this long run is a misleading guide to current affairs. In the long run we are all dead. Economists set themselves too easy, too useless a task if in tempestuous seasons they can only tell us that when the storm is long past the ocean will be flat again.
>> A Tract on Monetary Reform (1923)

> It is better that a man should tyrannize over his bank balance than over his fellow-citizens.
>> The General Theory of Employment, Interest and Money (1936)

> Practical men, who believe themselves to be quite exempt from any intellectual influences, are usually the slaves of some defunct economist. Madmen in authority, who hear voices in the air, are distilling their frenzy from some academic scribbler of a few years back.
>> The General Theory of Employment, Interest and Money (1936)

Levin, Bernard (1928–)
British writer
> Inflation in the Sixties was a nuisance to be endured, like varicose veins or French foreign policy.
>> *The Pendulum Years* (1970)

Macleod, Iain (1913–1970)
English Conservative politician and writer
> We now have the worst of both worlds – not just inflation on the one side or stagnation on the other side, but both of them together. We have a sort of 'stagflation' situation.
>> Speech, 1965

Malthus, Thomas Robert (1766–1834)
English political economist
> Population, when unchecked, increases in a geometrical ratio. Subsistence only increases in an arithmetical ratio.
>> *Essay on the Principle of Population* (1798)

Mellon, Andrew William (1855–1937)
US, banker, public official and art collector
> A nation is not in danger of financial disaster merely because it owes itself money.
>> Attr.

Roosevelt, Franklin Delano (1882–1945)
US Democrat President
> We have always known that heedless self-interest was bad morals; we know now that it is bad economics.
>> First Inaugural Address, 1933

Rutskoi, Alexander (1947–)
Russian politician
> The dollar is Russia's national currency now, the rouble is just a sweetie paper. We've handed our sword to America.
>> *Newsweek*, 1994

Schumacher, E.F. (1911–1977)
German-born British economist and essayist
> Small is Beautiful. A study of economics as if people mattered.
>> Title of book, 1973

Sellar, Walter (1898–1951) and **Yeatman, Robert Julian** (1897–1968)
British writers
> The National Debt is a very Good Thing and it would be dangerous to pay it off, for fear of Political Economy.
>> *1066 And All That* (1930)

Shaw, George Bernard (1856–1950)
Irish socialist, writer, dramatist and critic
> Whether you think Jesus was God or not, you must admit that he was a first-rate political economist.
>> *Androcles and the Lion* (1915)

> If all economists were laid end to end, they would not reach a conclusion.
>> Attr.

Truman, Harry S. (1884–1972)
US Democrat President
> It's a recession when your neighbour loses his job; it's a depression when you lose your own.
>> *The Observer*, 1958

Wilson, Harold (1916–1995)
English Labour Prime Minister
> It does not mean, of course, that the pound here in Britain, in your pocket or purse or in your bank, has been devalued.
>> Television broadcast, 1967

Yeltsin, Boris (1931–)
Russian President
> I am for the market, not for the bazaar.
>> *The Times*, 1992

editing

Allen, Fred (1894–1956)
US vaudeville performer and comedian
Remark to writers who had heavily edited one of his scripts
> Where were you fellows when the paper was blank?
>> Attr.

Aubrey, John (1626–1697)
English antiquary, folklorist and biographer
> He Shakespeare was wont to say that he 'never blotted out a line of his life'; said Ben Jonson, 'I wish he had blotted out a thousand.'
>> *Brief Lives* (c.1693)

Boileau-Despréaux, Nicolas (1636–1711)
French writer
> *Si j'écris quatre mots, j'en effacerai trois.*
> If I write four words, I shall strike out three.
>> *Satires* (1666)

Chandler, Raymond (1888–1959)
US crime writer
> Would you convey my compliments to the purist who reads your proofs and tell him or her that I write in a sort of broken-down patois which is something like the way a Swiss waiter talks, and that when I split an infinitive, God damn it, I split it so it will stay split.
>> Letter to Edward Weeks, his English publisher, 1947

Cheever, John (1912–1982)
US novelist
> Trust your editor, and you'll sleep on straw.
>> In Susan Cheever, *Home Before Dark* (1984)

Hubbard, Elbert (1856–1915)

US printer, editor, writer and businessman

> *Editor*: a person employed by a newspaper whose business it is to separate the wheat from the chaff and to see that the chaff is printed.
>
> *A Thousand and One Epigrams* (1911)

Johnson, Samuel (1709–1784)

English lexicographer, poet, critic, conversationalist and essayist

> Read over your compositions, and where ever you meet with a passage which you think is particularly fine, strike it out.
>
> In Boswell, *The Life of Samuel Johnson* (1791)

MacKenzie, Kelvin

English editor

On Janet Street-Porter's appointment as editor of *Independent on Sunday*

> She couldn't edit a bus ticket.
>
> Attr.

Mayer, Louis B. (1885–1957)

Russian-born US film executive

Comment to writers who had objected to changes in their work

> The number one book of the ages was written by a committee, and it was called The Bible.
>
> In Halliwell, *The Filmgoer's Book of Quotes* (1973)

Pascal, Blaise (1623–1662)

French philosopher and scientist

> I have made this letter longer only because I have not had time to make it shorter.
>
> *Lettres Provinciales* (1657)

Ross, Harold W. (1892–1951)

US editor

On founding *The New Yorker* in 1925

> *The New Yorker* will not be edited for the old lady from Dubuque.
>
> Remark

Twain, Mark (1835–1910)

US humorist, writer, journalist and lecturer

> As to the Adjective: when in doubt, strike it out.
>
> *Pudd'nhead Wilson's Calendar* (1894)

▶▶ BOOKS; NEWSPAPERS; PUBLISHING

education

Ade, George (1866–1944)

US fabulist and playwright

> 'Whom are you?' said he, for he had been to night school.
>
> Attr.

Amis, Kingsley (1922–1995)

English writer, poet and critic

On 'the delusion' that thousands of young people were capable of benefiting from university but had somehow failed to find their way there

> I wish I could have a little tape-and-loudspeaker arrangement sewn into the binding of this magazine, to be triggered off by the light reflected from the reader's eyes on to this part of the page, and set to bawl out at several bels: MORE WILL MEAN WORSE.
>
> *Encounter*, 1960

Aristotle (384–322 BC)

Greek philosopher

> The roots of education are bitter, but the fruit is sweet.
>
> In Diogenes Laertius, *Lives of Philosophers*

Arnold, Thomas (1795–1842)

English historian and educator

> My object will be, if possible, to form Christian men, for Christian boys I can scarcely hope to make.
>
> Letter, 1828

Ascham, Roger (1515–1568)

English scholar, educationist and archer

> I said ... how, and why, young children were sooner allured by love, than driven by beating, to attain good learning.
>
> *The Scholemaster* (1570)

Bacon, Francis (1561–1626)

English philosopher, essayist, politician and courtier

> Reading maketh a full man; conference a ready man; and writing an exact man.
>
> *Essays* (1625)

Bankhead, Tallulah (1903–1968)

US actress

> I read Shakespeare and the Bible and I can shoot dice. That's what I call a liberal education.
>
> Attr.

Bierce, Ambrose (1842–c.1914)

US writer, verse writer and soldier

> *Education*: That which discloses to the wise and disguises from the foolish their lack of understanding.
>
> *The Cynic's Word Book* (1906)

Blair, Tony (1953–)

British Labour Prime Minister

> Ask me my three main priorities for Government, and I tell you: education, education and education.
>
> Speech at the Labour Party Conference, 1996

Bloom, Allan (1930–1992)

US academic and critic

> The liberally educated person is one who is able to resist the easy and preferred answers, not because he is obstinate but because he knows others worthy of consideration.
>
> *The Closing of the American Mind* (1987)

Brougham, Lord Henry (1778–1868)
Scottish politician, abolitionist and journalist
> Education makes a people easy to lead, but difficult to drive; easy to govern, but impossible to enslave.
>> *Attr.*

Brown, Rita Mae (1944–)
US writer and poet
> Education is a wonderful thing. If you couldn't sign your name you'd have to pay cash.
>> *Starting From Scratch* (1988)

Buchan, John (1875–1940)
Scottish writer, lawyer and Conservative politician
> To live for a time close to great minds is the best kind of education.
>> *Memory Hold the Door*

Carroll, Lewis (1832–1898)
English writer and photographer
> 'Reeling and Writhing, of course, to begin with,' the Mock Turtle replied; 'and then the different branches of Arithmetic – Ambition, Distraction, Uglification, and Derision.'
>> *Alice's Adventures in Wonderland* (1865)

> 'That's the reason they're called lessons, 'the Gryphon remarked: 'because they lessen from day to day.'
>> *Alice's Adventures in Wonderland* (1865)

Chesterton, G.K. (1874–1936)
English writer, poet and critic
> Education is simply the soul of a society as it passes from one generation to another.
>> *The Observer*, 1924

Cody, Henry John (1868–1951)
Anglican churchman
> Education is casting false pearls before real swine.
>> *Attr.*

Cooper, Roger
British hostage in Iran
After five years in an Iranian prison
> I can say that anyone who, like me, has been educated in English public schools and served in the ranks of the British Army is quite at home in a Third World prison.
>> *Newsweek*, 1991

Coward, Sir Noël (1899–1973)
English dramatist, actor, producer and composer
> I've over-educated myself in all the things I shouldn't have known at all.
>> *Mild Oats* (1931)

D'Souza, Dinesh (1961–)
> If education cannot help separate truth from falsehood, beauty from vulgarity, right from wrong, then what can it teach us?
>> *Atlantic Monthly*, 1991

Dickens, Charles (1812–1870)
English writer
> Now, what I want is, Facts. Teach these boys and girls nothing but Facts. Facts alone are wanted in life. Plant nothing else, and root out everything else … Stick to Facts, sir!
>> *Hard Times* (1854)

Diogenes (the Cynic) (c.400–325 BC)
Greek ascetic philosopher
> Education is something that tempers the young and consoles the old, gives wealth to the poor and adorns the rich.
>> In Diogenes Laertius, *Lives of Eminent Philosophers*

Disraeli, Benjamin (1804–1881)
English statesman and writer
> Upon the education of the people of this country the fate of this country depends.
>> Speech, 1874

Dryden, John (1631–1700)
English poet, satirist, dramatist and critic
> By education most have been misled;
> So they believe, because they so were bred.
> The priest continues what the nurse began,
> And thus the child imposes on the man.
>> *The Hind and the Panther* (1687)

Emerson, Ralph Waldo (1803–1882)
US poet, essayist, transcendentalist and teacher
> I pay the schoolmaster, but 'tis the schoolboys that educate my son.
>> *Journals*

Hazlitt, William (1778–1830)
English writer and critic
> It is better to be able neither to read nor write than to be able to do nothing else.
>> *The Edinburgh Magazine*, 1818

Helvétius, Claude Adrien (1715–1771)
French philosopher
> *L'éducation nous faisait ce que nous sommes.*
> Education made us what we are.
>> *De l'esprit* (1758)

Huxley, Aldous (1894–1963)
English writer, poet and critic
> The solemn foolery of scholarship for scholarship's sake.
>> *The Perennial Philosophy* (1945)

Johnson, Samuel (1709–1784)
English lexicographer, poet, critic, conversationalist and essayist

> Example is always more efficacious than precept.
>
> *Rasselas* (1759)

> All intellectual improvement arises from leisure.
>
> In Boswell, *The Life of Samuel Johnson* (1791)

> It is no matter what you teach them [children] first, any more than what leg you shall put into your breeches first.
>
> In Boswell, *The Life of Samuel Johnson* (1791)

Kant, Immanuel (1724–1804)
German idealist philosopher

> *Der Mensch ist das einzige Geschöpf, das erzogen werden muss.*
> Man is the only creature which must be educated.
>
> *On Pedagogy* (1803)

Kraus, Karl (1874–1936)
Austrian scientist, critic and poet

> *Bildung ist das, was die meisten empfangen, viele weitergeben und wenige haben.*
> Education is what most people receive, many pass on and few actually have.
>
> *Pro domo et mundo* (1912)

Lodge, David (1935–)
English writer, satirist and literary critic

> Four times, under our educational rules, the human pack is shuffled and cut – at eleven-plus, sixteen-plus, eighteen-plus and twenty-plus – and happy is he who comes top of the deck on each occasion, but especially the last. This is called Finals, the very name of which implies that nothing of importance can happen after it. The British postgraduate student is a lonely forlorn soul … for whom nothing had been real since the Big Push.
>
> *Changing Places* (1975)

McIver, Charles D. (1860–1906)
US educationist

> When you educate a man you educate an individual; when you educate a woman you educate a whole family.
>
> Address at women's college

Melbourne, Lord (1779–1848)
English statesman
To the Queen

> I don't know, Ma'am, why they make all this fuss about education; none of the Pagets can read or write, and they get on well enough.
>
> Attr.

Milton, John (1608–1674)
English poet, libertarian and pamphleteer

> … the right path of a vertuous and noble Education, laborious indeed at the first ascent, but else so smooth, so green, so full of goodly prospect, and melodious sounds on every side, that the harp of Orpheus was not more charming.
>
> *Of Education: To Master Samuel Hartlib* (1644)

Moravia, Alberto (1907–1990)
Italian writer

> The ratio of literacy to illiteracy is constant, but nowadays the illiterates can read and write.
>
> *The Observer*, 1979

Morrison, Toni (1931–)
US writer

> Bryn Mawr had done what a four-year dose of liberal education was designed to do: unfit her for eighty per cent of useful work of the world.
>
> *Song of Solomon* (1977)

Phillips, Melanie (1951–)
English journalist
Reviewing a book on King Alfred School, a progressive co-educational independent school, described as an experiment in Fabian utopianism

> King Alfred's parents paid for their children to be taught next to nothing. When utopia was nationalized, state-school parents got the same service for free.
>
> *Times Literary Supplement*, 1998

Rogers, Will (1879–1935)
US humorist, actor, rancher, writer and wit

> Instead of giving money to found colleges to promote learning, why don't they pass a constitutional amendment prohibiting anybody from learning anything? If it works as good as the Prohibition one did, why, in five years we would have the smartest race of people on earth.
>
> Attr.

Rousseau, Jean-Jacques (1712–1778)
Swiss-born French philosopher, educationist and essayist

> *On n'est curieux qu'á proportion qu'on est instruit.*
> One is only curious in proportion to one's level of education.
>
> *Émile ou De l'éducation* (1762)

Ruskin, John (1819–1900)
English art critic, philosopher and reformer

> To make your children capable of honesty is the beginning of education.
>
> *Time and Tide by Weare and Tyne* (1867)

Scott, Alexander (1920–)

> I tellt ye
> I tellt ye.
>
> *Scotched*, 'Scotch Education'

Scott, Sir Walter (1771–1832)
Scottish writer and historian
> All men who have turned out worth anything
> have had the chief hand in their own education.
>> *Letter to J.G. Lockhart, 1830*

Seeger, Pete (1919–)
US singer and songwriter
> Education is when you read the fine print.
> Experience is what you get if you don't.
>> Attr.

Sitwell, Sir Osbert (1892–1969)
English writer
> My education takes place during the holidays
> from Eton.
>> *Who's Who* (1929)

Skinner, B.F. (1904–1990)
US psychologist
> Education is what survives when what has been
> learned has been forgotten.
>> *New Scientist*, 1964

> Indeed one of the ultimate advantages of an
> education is simply coming to the end of it.
>> *The Technology of Teaching* (1968)

Smith, Adam (1723–1790)
Scottish economist, philosopher and essayist
> There are no public institutions for the education
> of women, and there is accordingly nothing
> useless, absurd, or fantastical in the common
> course of their education.
>> *Wealth of Nations* (1776)

Spark, Muriel (1918–)
Scottish writer, poet and dramatist
> To me education is a leading out of what is
> already there in the pupil's soul. To Miss Mackay
> it is a putting in of something that is not there,
> and that is not what I call education, I call it
> intrusion.
>> *The Prime of Miss Jean Brodie* (1961)

> Give me a girl at an impressionable age, and she
> is mine for life.
>> *The Prime of Miss Jean Brodie* (1961)

> Art and religion first; then philosophy; lastly
> science. That is the order of the great subjects
> of life, that's their order of importance.
>> *The Prime of Miss Jean Brodie* (1961)

Spencer, Herbert (1820–1903)
English philosopher and journalist
> Education has for its object the formation of
> character.
>> *Social Statics* (1850)

Steele, Sir Richard (1672–1729)
Irish-born English writer, dramatist and politician
> The truth of it is, the first rudiments of

education are given very indiscreetly by most
parents.
>> *The Tatler*, 173

Stocks, Mary, Baroness (1891–1975)
English educationist, broadcaster and biographer
> Today we enjoy a social structure which offers
> equal opportunity in education. It is indeed
> regrettably true that there is no equal
> opportunity to take advantage of the equal
> opportunity.
>> *Still More Commonplace* (1973)

Trevelyan, G.M. (1876–1962)
English historian and writer
> Education … has produced a vast population
> able to read but unable to distinguish what is
> worth reading.
>> *English Social History* (1942)

Updike, John (1932–)
US writer, poet and critic
> The Founding Fathers in their wisdom decided
> that children were an unnatural strain on
> parents. So they provided jails called schools,
> equipped with tortures called an education.
>> *The Centaur* (1963)

Ustinov, Sir Peter (1921–)
English actor, director, dramatist, writer and raconteur
> People at the top of the tree are those without
> qualifications to detain them at the bottom.
>> Attr.

White, Patrick (1912–1990)
English-born Australian writer and dramatist
> 'I dunno,' Arthur said. 'I forget what I was
> taught. I only remember what I've learnt.'
>> *The Solid Mandala* (1966)

Wilde, Oscar (1854–1900)
Irish poet, dramatist, writer, critic and wit
> Education is an admirable thing, but it is well to
> remember from time to time that nothing that is
> worth knowing can be taught.
>> 'The Critic as Artist' (1891)

▶▶ EXAMINATIONS; KNOWLEDGE; LEARNING; SCHOOL;
TEACHERS; UNIVERSITY

efficiency

Edwards, Bob (1864–1922)
> One trouble with being efficient is that it makes
> everybody hate you so.
>> *The Calgary Eye Opener* (1916)

Shaw, George Bernard (1856–1950)
Irish socialist, writer, dramatist and critic
> There are only two qualities in the world:
> efficiency and inefficiency; and only two sorts of

people: the efficient and the inefficient.

John Bull's Other Island
(1907)

egoism

Adler, Alfred (1870–1937)
Austrian psychiatrist and psychologist
On hearing that an egocentric had fallen in love
> Against whom?

Attr.

Alcott, Louisa May (1832–1888)
US writer
> Conceit spoils the finest genius. There is not
> much danger that real talent or goodness will be
> overlooked long; even if it is, the consciousness
> of possessing and using it well should satisfy
> one …

Little Women (1869)

Ali, Muhammad (1942–)
US heavyweight boxer
> I am the greatest.

Catchphrase

> I'm the greatest golfer. I just have not played
> yet.

Attr.

Anonymous
> My name is George Nathaniel Curzon,
> I am a most superior person.

The Masque of Balliol (c.1870)

Bacon, Francis (1561–1626)
English philosopher, essayist, politician and courtier
> It was prettily devised of Aesop, 'The fly sat
> upon the axletree of the chariot-wheel and said,
> what a dust do I raise.'

'Of Vain-Glory' (1625)

Barnes, Peter (1931–)
English dramatist
> I know I am God because when I pray to him I
> find I'm talking to myself.

The Ruling Class (1968)

Beerbohm, Sir Max (1872–1956)
English satirist, cartoonist, critic and essayist
> To give an accurate and exhaustive account of
> that period would need a far less brilliant pen
> than mine.

Attr.

Bierce, Ambrose (1842–c.1914)
US writer, verse writer and soldier
> *Egoist*: A person of low taste, more interested in
> himself than in me.

The Cynic's Word Book (1906)

Bone, Sir David (1874–1959)
Scottish novelist and sailor
> It's 'Damn you, Jack – I'm all right!' with you
> chaps.

The Brassbounder (1910)

Bulmer-Thomas, Ivor (1905–1993)
English writer and politician
Of Harold Wilson
> If ever he went to school without any boots it
> was because he was too big for them.

Remark, 1949

Butler, Samuel (1835–1902)
English writer, painter, philosopher and scholar
> The advantage of doing one's praising for
> oneself is that one can lay it on so thick and
> exactly in the right places.

The Way of All Flesh (1903)

Chamfort, Nicolas (1741–1794)
French writer
> *Quelqu'un disait d'un homme très personnel; il*
> *brûlerait votre maison pour se faire cuire deux oeufs.*
> Someone said of a great egotist: 'He would burn
> your house down to cook himself a couple of
> eggs.'

Caractères et anecdotes

Churchill, Charles (1731–1764)
English poet, political writer and clergyman
Of Thomas Franklin, Professor of Greek, Cambridge
> He sicken'd at all triumphs but his own.

The Rosciad (1761)

Cicero (106–43 BC)
Roman orator, statesman, essayist and letter writer
> *O fortunatam natam me consule Romam!*
> O happy Rome, born when I was consul!

In Juvenal, *Satires*

Disraeli, Benjamin (1804–1881)
English statesman and writer
> Every day when he looked into the glass, and
> gave the last touch to his consummate toilette,
> he offered his grateful thanks to Providence that
> his family was not unworthy of him.

Lothair (1870)

Dulles, John Foster (1888–1959)
US statesman and lawyer
Reply when asked if he had ever been wrong
> Yes, once – many, many years ago. I thought I
> had made a wrong decision. Of course, it
> turned out that I had been right all along.
> But I was wrong to have thought that I was
> wrong.

Attr.

Eliot, George (1819–1880)
English writer and poet
> He was like a cock, who thought the sun had

risen to hear him crow.

Adam Bede (1859)

I've never any pity for conceited people, because I think they carry their comfort about with them.

The Mill on the Floss (1860)

Gorton, John Grey (1911–)
Australian parliamentarian
    I am always prepared to recognize that there can be two points of view – mine, and one that is probably wrong.

In Trengove, *John Grey Gorton*

Hartley, L.P. (1895–1972)
English writer and critic
    'Should I call myself an egoist?' Miss Johnstone mused. 'Others have called me so. They merely meant I did not care for them.'

Simonetta Perkins (1925)

Hawke, Bob (1929–)
Australian Premier
On first entering Parliament, 1979
    Well, I don't want to be any more egotistical than possible. I have total confidence in my ability.

In Thomson and Butel, *The World According to Hawke*

James, Brian (1892–1972)
Australian writer
    A dominant personality doesn't believe in its own will. All it needs is the inability to recognise the existence of anybody else's.

Falling Towards England

Jerome, Jerome K. (1859–1927)
English writer and dramatist
    Conceit is the finest armour a man can wear.

Idle Thoughts of an Idle Fellow (1886)

Keith, Penelope (1940–)
English actress
    Shyness is just egotism out of its depth.

The Observer, 1988

Kournikova, Anna (1981–)
Russian tennis player
    Frankly, I am beautiful, famous and gorgeous.

Scotland on Sunday, 1998

Meredith, George (1828–1909)
English writer, poet and critic
    In … the book of Egoism, it is written, Possession without obligation to the object possessed approaches felicity.

The Egoist (1879)

Roux, Joseph (1834–1886)
French priest and epigrammatist

The egoist does not tolerate egoism.

Meditations of a Parish Priest (1886)

Sitwell, Dame Edith (1887–1964)
English poet, anthologist, critic and biographer
    I have often wished I had time to cultivate modesty … But I am too busy thinking about myself.

The Observer, 1950

Strachey, Lytton (1880–1932)
English biographer and critic
Of Hurrell Froude
    The time was out of joint, and he was only too delighted to have been born to set it right.

Eminent Victorians (1918)

Suzuki, D.T. (1870–1966)
Japanese Buddhist scholar and main interpreter of Zen to the West
    The individual ego asserts itself strongly in the West. In the East, there is no ego. The ego is non-existent and, therefore, there is no ego to be crucified.

Mysticism Christian and Buddhist (1957)

Trollope, Anthony (1815–1882)
English writer, traveller and post office official
    As for conceit, what man will do any good who is not conceited? Nobody holds a good opinion of a man who has a low opinion of himself.

Orley Farm (1862)

Webb, Beatrice (1858–1943)
English writer and reformer
    If I ever felt inclined to be timid as I was going into a room full of people, I would say to myself, 'You're the cleverest member of one of the cleverest families in the cleverest class of the cleverest nation in the world, why should you be frightened?'.

In Russell, *Portraits from Memory* (1956)

Whistler, James McNeill (1834–1903)
US painter, etcher and pamphleteer
Replying to the pointed observation that it was as well that we do not see ourselves as others see us
    Isn't it? I know in my case I would grow intolerably conceited.

In Pearson, *The Man Whistler*

Wilde, Oscar (1854–1900)
Irish poet, dramatist, writer, critic and wit
    I am the only person in the world I should like to know thoroughly.

Lady Windermere's Fan (1892)

▶▶ PRIDE; SELF

empire

Belloc, Hilaire (1870–1953)
English writer of verse, essayist and critic; Liberal MP
> We had intended you to be
> The next Prime Minister but three:
> The stocks were sold; the Press was squared;
> The Middle Class was quite prepared.
> But as it is! –
> My language fails!
> Go out and govern New South Wales!
>> *Cautionary Tales* (1907), 'Lord Lundy'

Chamberlain, Joseph (1836–1914)
English politician
> Learn to think Imperially.
>> Speech, London, 1904

> The day of small nations has long passed away.
> The day of Empires has come.
>> Speech, Birmingham, 1904

Churchill, Sir Winston (1874–1965)
English Conservative Prime Minister
> I have not become the King's First Minister in order to preside over the liquidation of the British Empire.
>> Speech, Mansion House, November 1942

Disraeli, Benjamin (1804–1881)
English statesman and writer
> You are not going, I hope, to leave the destinies of the British Empire to prigs and pedants.
>> Speech, House of Commons, 1863

> Colonies do not cease to be colonies because they are independent.
>> Speech, House of Commons, 1863

Galloway, George (1954–)
Scottish Labour politician
> My father used to say that the reason the sun never set on the British Empire is because God would never trust the British in the dark.
>> *Glasgow Herald*, April 2000

Hawke, Bob (1929–)
Australian Premier
> We are still prisoners of our colonial history.
>> *The Resolution of Conflict* (1979)

Kipling, Rudyard (1865–1936)
Indian-born British poet and writer
> Take up the White Man's burden –
> Send forth the best ye breed –
> Go, bind your sons to exile
> To serve your captives' need;
> To wait in heavy harness
> On fluttered folk and wild –
> Your new-caught, sullen peoples,
> Half devil and half child …

> By all ye cry or whisper,
> By all ye leave or do,
> The silent, sullen peoples
> Shall weigh your Gods and you.
>> 'The White Man's Burden' (1899)

Macaulay, Lord (1800–1859)
English Liberal statesman, essayist and poet
> The reluctant obedience of distant provinces generally costs more than it the territory is worth.
>> *Collected Essays* (1843), 'War of the Succession in Spain'

Mandela, Nelson (1918–)
South African statesman and President
> Through its imperialist system Britain brought about untold suffering of millions of people. And this is an historical fact. To be able to admit this would increase the respect, you know, which we have for British institutions.
>> *The Guardian*, 1990

Mao Tse-Tung (1893–1976)
Chinese Communist leader
> Imperialism is a paper tiger.
>> *Quotations from Chairman Mao Tse-Tung*

Montesquieu, Charles (1689–1755)
French philosopher and jurist
> *Un empire fondé par les armes a besoin de se soutenir par les armes.*
> An empire founded by war has to maintain itself by war.
>> *Considérations sur les causes de la grandeur des Romains et de leur décadence* (1734)

North, Christopher (1785–1854)
Scottish poet, writer, editor and critic
> His Majesty's dominions, on which the sun never sets.
>> *Blackwood's Edinburgh Magazine*, 1829

Richter, Jean Paul Friedrich (1763–1825)
> Providence has given to the French the empire of the land, to the English that of the sea, and to the Germans that of – the air!
>> In Thomas Carlyle, 'Jean Paul Friedrich Richter' (1827)

Rosebery, Earl of (1847–1929)
English statesman
> The Empire is a Commonwealth of Nations.
>> Speech, Adelaide, 1884

> Imperialism, sane Imperialism, as distinguished from what I may call wild-cat Imperialism, is nothing but this – a larger patriotism.
>> Speech at a City Liberal Club dinner, 1899

Smith, Adam (1723–1790)
Scottish economist, philosopher and essayist

To found a great empire for the sole purpose of raising up a people of customers, may at first sight appear a project fit only for a nation of shopkeepers. It is, however, a project altogether unfit for a nation of shopkeepers; but extremely fit for a nation whose government is influenced by shopkeepers.

Wealth of Nations (1776)

▶▶ ENGLAND

endurance

Acheson, Dean (1893–1971)
US Democrat politician
> The manner in which one endures what must be endured is more important than the thing that must be endured.
> *Plain Speaking: An Oral Biography of Harry S. Truman*

Proverb
> What can't be cured, must be endured.

▶▶ COURAGE; SUFFERING

enemies

Bevin, Ernest (1881–1951)
English trade union leader and politicia
When told that another Labourite was 'his own worst enemy'
> Not while I'm alive, he ain't.
> In M. Foot, *Aneurin Bevan 1945–60* (1975)

The Bible (King James Version)
> Love your enemies, bless them that curse you, do good to them that hate you, and pray for them which despitefully use you, and persecute you.
> *Matthew*, 5:44

Breton, Nicholas (c.1545–c.1626)
English writer and poet
> I wish my deadly foe, no worse
> Than want of friends, and empty purse.
> 'A Farewell to Town' (1577)

Burke, Edmund (1729–1797)
Irish-born British statesman and philosopher
> He that wrestles with us strengthens our nerves, and sharpens our skill. Our antagonist is our helper.
> *Reflections on the Revolution in France* (1790)

Callas, Maria (1923–1977)
US opera singer
> When my enemies stop hissing, I shall know I'm slipping.
> In Arianna Stassinopoulos, *Maria Callas* (1981)

Conrad, Joseph (1857–1924)
Polish-born British writer, sailor and explorer
> You shall judge of a man by his foes as well as by his friends.
> *Lord Jim* (1900)

Kissinger, Henry (1923–)
German-born US Secretary of State
> Even a paranoid can have enemies.
> *Time*, 1977

Lesage, Alain-René (1668–1747)
French writer and dramatist
> *On nous réconcilia: nous nous embrassâmes, et depuis ce temps-lá nous sommes ennemis mortels.*
> They made peace between us; we embraced, and since that time we have been mortal enemies.
> *Le Diable boiteux*

Linklater, Eric (1899–1974)
Welsh-born Scottish writer and satirist
> With a heavy step Sir Matthew left the room and spent the morning designing mausoleums for his enemies.
> *Juan in America* (1931)

Montagu, Lady Mary Wortley (1689–1762)
English letter writer, poet, traveller and introducer of smallpox inoculation
> People wish their enemies dead – but I do not; I say give them the gout, give them the stone!
> In a letter from Horace Walpole to the Earl of Harcourt, 1778

Narváez, Ramón María (1800–1868)
Spanish general and politician
On his deathbed, when asked by a priest if he forgave his enemies
> I do not have to forgive my enemies, I have had them all shot.
> Attr.

Puzo, Mario (1920–)
US writer
> Keep your friends close, but your enemies closer.
> *The Godfather, Part II* (film, 1974)

Roosevelt, Franklin Delano (1882–1945)
US Democrat President
> I ask you to judge me by the enemies I have made.
> *The Observer*, 1932

Whitman, Walt (1819–1892)
US poet and writer
> Beautiful that war and all its deeds of carnage must in time be utterly lost,
> That the hands of the sisters Death and Night incessantly softly wash again, and ever again, this soil'd world;

For my enemy is dead, a man as divine as myself is dead,
I look where he lies white-faced and still in the coffin – I draw near,
Bend down and touch lightly with my lips the white face in the coffin.

'Reconciliation' (1865)

Wilde, Oscar (1854–1900)

Irish poet, dramatist, writer, critic and wit

A man cannot be too careful in the choice of his enemies.

The Picture of Dorian Gray (1891)

england

Addison, Joseph (1672–1719)

English essayist, poet, playwright and statesman

The Knight in the triumph of his heart made several reflections on the greatness of the British Nation; as, that one Englishman could beat three Frenchmen; that we cou'd never be in danger of Popery so long as we took care of our fleet; that the Thames was the noblest river in Europe; that London Bridge was a greater piece of work than any of the Seven Wonders of the World; with many other honest prejudices which naturally cleave to the heart of a true Englishman.

The Spectator, May 1712

Agate, James (1877–1947)

English drama critic and writer

The English instinctively admire any man who has no talent and is modest about it.

Attr.

Anonymous

Introduction to a new Lonely Planet British Phrasebook

The English – in England – are among the most tolerant bigots on earth.

The Times, 1999

Bagehot, Walter (1826–1877)

English economist and political philosopher

Of all nations in the world the English are perhaps the least a nation of pure philosophers.

The English Constitution (1867)

Behan, Brendan (1923–1964)

Irish dramatist, writer and Republican

He was born an Englishman and remained one for years.

The Hostage (1958)

Bossuet, Jacques-Bénigne (1627–1704)

L'Angleterre, ah, la perfide Angleterre, que le rempart de ses mers rendoit inaccessible aux Romains, la foi du Sauveur y est abordée.

England, ah, perfidious England, which the bulwarks of the sea rendered inaccessible to the Romans, the faith of the Saviour made landfall even there.

Oeuvres de Bossuet (1816)

Bradbury, Malcolm (1932–)

English writer, critic and academic

I like the English. They have the most rigid code of immorality in the world.

Eating People is Wrong (1954)

Bright, John (1811–1889)

English Liberal politician and social reformer

England is the mother of Parliaments.

Speech, 1865

Brooke, Rupert (1887–1915)

English poet

If I should die, think only this of me:
That there's some corner of a foreign field
That is for ever England.

'The Soldier' (1914)

Browne, Sir Thomas (1605–1682)

English physician, author and antiquary

All places, all airs make unto me one country; I am in England, everywhere, and under any meridian.

Religio Medici (1643)

Browning, Robert (1812–1889)

English poet

Oh, to be in England
Now that April's there,
And whoever wakes in England
Sees, some morning, unaware,
That the lowest boughs and the brushwood sheaf
Round the elm-tree bole are in tiny leaf,
While the chaffinch sings on the orchard bough
In England – now!

'Home Thoughts, from Abroad' (1845)

Butler, Samuel (1835–1902)

English writer, painter, philosopher and scholar

The wish to spread those opinions that we hold conducive to our own welfare is so deeply rooted in the English character that few of us can escape its influence.

Erewhon (1872)

Byron, Lord (1788–1824)

English poet satirist and traveller

The English winter – ending in July,
To recommence in August.

Don Juan (1824)

I am sure my bones would not rest in an English grave, or my clay mix with the earth of that country. I believe the thought would drive me mad on my deathbed, could I suppose that any of my friends would be base enough to convey my carcass back to your soil. I would not even feed your worms if I could help it.

Letter to John Murray, 1819

Carlyle, Thomas (1795–1881)

Scottish historian, biographer, critic, and essayist

When asked what the population of England was

Thirty millions, mostly fools.

Attr.

Carroll, Lewis (1832–1898)

English writer and photographer

He's an Anglo-Saxon Messenger – and those are Anglo-Saxon attitudes.

Through the Looking-Glass (and What Alice Found There) (1872)

Charles, Hughie (1907–)

There'll always be an England
While there's a country lane.

'There'll always be an England' (song, 1939)

Chesterton, G.K. (1874–1936)

English writer, poet and critic

Smile at us, pay us, pass us; but do not quite forget.
For we are the people of England, that never have spoken yet.

Poems (1915), 'The Secret People'

Churchill, Charles (1731–1764)

English poet, political writer and clergyman

Be England what she will,
With all her faults, she is my country still.

'The Farewell' (1764)

Compton-Burnett, Dame Ivy (1884–1969)

English novelist

Well, the English have no family feelings. That is, none of the kind you mean. They have them, and one of them is that relations must cause no expense.

Parents and Children (1941)

Coward, Sir Noël (1899–1973)

English dramatist, actor, producer and composer

Mad dogs and Englishmen go out in the mid-day sun;
The Japanese don't care to, the Chinese wouldn't dare to;
Hindus and Argentines sleep firmly from twelve to one,
But Englishmen detest a
Siesta …

In the mangrove swamps where the python romps
There is peace from twelve till two.
Even caribous lie around and snooze,
For there's nothing else to do.
In Bengal, to move at all

Is seldom, if ever done.

'Mad Dogs and Englishmen', song, 1931

Cowper, William (1731–1800)

English poet, hymn and letter writer

England, with all thy faults, I love thee still –
My country!

The Task (1785)

Cunningham, Peter Miller (1789–1864)

Surgeon-superintendent on convict ships

A young girl, when asked how she would like to go to England, replied with great naïveté, 'I should be afraid to go, from the number of thieves there,' doubtless conceiving England to be a downright hive of such, that threw off its annual swarms to people the wilds of this colony.

Two Years in New South Wales (1827)

Defoe, Daniel (c.1661–1731)

English writer and critic

Your Roman-Saxon-Danish-Norman English.

The True-Born Englishman (1701)

Dickens, Charles (1812–1870)

English writer

'This Island was Blest, Sir, to the Direct Exclusion of such Other Countries as – as there may happen to be. And if we were all Englishmen present, I would say,' added Mr Podsnap … 'that there is in the Englishman a combination of qualities, a modesty, an independence, a responsibility, a repose, combined with an absence of everything calculated to call a blush into the cheek of a young person, which one would seek in vain among the Nations of the Earth.'

Our Mutual Friend (1865)

Dryden, John (1631–1700)

English poet, satirist, dramatist and critic

But 'tis the talent of our English nation,
Still to be plotting some new reformation.

Prologue at Oxford (1680)

Forster, E.M. (1879–1970)

English writer, essayist and literary critic

It is not that the Englishman can't feel – it is that he is afraid to feel. He has been taught at his public school that feeling is bad form. He must not express great joy or sorrow, or even open his mouth too wide when he talks – his pipe might fall out if he did.

Abinger Harvest (1936)

Golding, William (1911–1993)

English writer and poet

We've got to have rules and obey them. After all, we're not savages. We're English; and the English are best at everything. So we've got to do the right things.

Lord of the Flies (1954)

Halsey, Margaret (1910–)
US writer
> The attitude of the English ... toward English history reminds one a good deal of the attitude of a Hollywood director toward love.
>
> *With Malice Toward Some* (1938)

> Living in England, provincial England, must be like being married to a stupid but exquisitely beautiful wife.
>
> *With Malice Toward Some* (1938)

Hazlitt, William (1778–1830)
English writer and critic
> The English (it must be owned) are rather a foul-mouthed nation.
>
> *Table-Talk* (1822)

Herbert, Sir A.P. (1890–1971)
English humorist, writer, dramatist and politician
> The Englishman never enjoys himself except for a noble purpose.
>
> *Uncommon Law* (1935)

Hill, Reginald (1936–)
British writer and playwright
> Nobody has ever lost money by overestimating the superstitious credulity of an English jury.
>
> *Pictures of Perfection* (1994)

Howard, Philip (1933–)
English journalist
> Every time an Englishman opens his mouth, he enables other Englishmen if not to despise him, at any rate to place him in some social and class pigeonhole.
>
> *The Times*, 1992

Howkins, Alun (1947–)
British historian and writer
> The English pub is, we are told from childhood, a unique institution. Nothing 'quite like it' exists anywhere else. That's true. The pub uniquely represents, even in metropolitan England, the precise inequalities of gender, race and class that construct our society. From the inclusive white, male and proletarian 'public' of many northern pubs to the parasitic blazer and cotton dress 'locals' of the home counties, our unique institution divides our society and our social life.
>
> *New Statesman and Society*, 1989

Hugo, Victor (1802–1885)
French poet, writer, dramatist and politician
> England has two books: the Bible and Shakespeare. England made Shakespeare but the Bible made England.
>
> Attr.

Joad, C.E.M. (1891–1953)
English popularizer of philosophy
> It will be said of this generation that it found England a land of beauty and left it a land of beauty spots.
>
> *The Observer*, 1953

Joyce, James (1882–1941)
Irish writer
> We feel in England that we have treated you Irish rather unfairly. It seems history is to blame.
>
> *Ulysses* (1922)

Kingsley, Charles (1819–1875)
English writer, poet, lecturer and clergyman
> 'Tis the hard grey weather
> Breeds hard English men.
>
> 'Ode to the North-East Wind' (1854)

Kipling, Rudyard (1865–1936)
Indian-born British poet and writer
> For Allah created the English mad – the maddest of all mankind!
>
> *The Five Nations* (1903)

Of the English
> For undemocratic reasons and for motives not of State,
> They arrive at their conclusions – largely inarticulate.
> Being void of self-expression they confide their views to none;
> But sometimes in a smoking-room, one learns why things were done.
>
> *Actions and Reactions* (1909)

> The Saxon is not like us Normans. His manners are not so polite.
> But he never means anything serious till he talks about justice and right,
> When he stands like an ox in the furrow with his sullen set eyes on your own,
> And grumbles, 'This isn't fair dealing,' my son, leave the Saxon alone.
>
> C.R.L. Fletcher's *A History of England* (1911)

Lawrence, D.H. (1885–1930)
English writer, poet and critic
> It was one of those places where the spirit of aboriginal England still lingers, the old savage England, whose last blood flows still in a few Englishmen, Welshmen, Cornishmen.
>
> *St Mawr* (1925)

Macaulay, Lord (1800–1859)
English Liberal statesman, essayist and poet
> The history of England is emphatically the history of progress.
>
> 'Sir James Mackintosh' (1843)

MacInnes, Colin (1914–1976)
English writer

England is ... a country infested with people who love to tell us what to do, but who very rarely seem to know what's going on.

England, Half English

Mary, Queen of Scots (1542–1587)
Daughter of James V, mother of James VI and I; executed by Elizabeth I of England
> England is not all the world.
>
> Said at her trial, 1586

Mikes, George (1912–1987)
Hungarian-born British writer
> On the Continent people have good food; in England people have good table manners.
>
> *How to be an Alien* (1946)

> An Englishman, even if he is alone, forms an orderly queue of one.
>
> *How to be an Alien* (1946)

Montesquieu, Charles (1689–1755)
French philosopher and jurist
> *Les Anglais sont occupés; ils n'ont pas le temps d'être polis.*
> The English are busy; they don't have the time to be polite.
>
> *Pensées et fragments inédits* (1899)

Napoleon I (1769–1821)
> *L'Angleterre est une nation de boutiquiers.*
> England is a nation of shopkeepers.
>
> In O'Meara, *Napoleon in Exile* (1822)

Nash, Ogden (1902–1971)
US poet
> Let us pause to consider the English
> Who when they pause to consider themselves they get all reticently thrilled and tinglish.
> Englishmen are distinguished by their traditions and ceremonials,
> And also by their affection for their colonies and their condescension to their colonials.
>
> 'England Expects' (1929)

O'Connell, Daniel (1775–1847)
Irish nationalist politician
> The Englishman has all the qualities of a poker except its occasional warmth.
>
> Attr.

Orwell, George (1903–1950)
English writer and critic
> England is not the jewelled isle of Shakespeare's much-quoted passage, nor is it the inferno depicted by Dr Goebbels. More than either it resembles a family, a rather stuffy Victorian family, with not many black sheep in it but with all its cupboards bursting with skeletons. It has rich relations who have to be kow-towed to and poor relations who are horribly sat upon, and there is a deep conspiracy about the source of the family income. It is a family in which the young are generally thwarted and most of the power is in the hands of irresponsible uncles and bedridden aunts. Still, it is a family ... A family with the wrong members in control.
>
> 'England, Your England' (1941)

Parsons, Tony (1953–)
British journalist and broadcaster
> To be born an Englishman – ah, what an easy conceit that builds in you, what a self-righteous nationalism, a secure xenophobia, what a pride in your ignorance. No other people speak so few languages. No other people – certainly not the Germans, Italians or French, and not even the multi-ethnic Americano – have an expression that is the equivalent of 'greasy foreign muck'. The noble, wisecracking savages depicted everywhere from *Eastenders* to *Boys from the Blackstuff* are exercises in nostalgia who no longer exist.
>
> *Arena*, 1989

Pepys, Samuel (1633–1703)
English diarist, naval administrator and politician
> But Lord! to see the absurd nature of Englishmen, that cannot forbear laughing and jeering at everything that looks strange.
>
> *Diary*, 1662

Pitt, William (1759–1806)
English politician and Prime Minister
> England has saved herself by her exertions, and will, as I trust, save Europe by her example.
>
> Speech, 1805

Rhodes, Cecil (1853–1902)
English imperialist, financier and South African statesman
> Remember that you are an Englishman, and have consequently won first prize in the lottery of life.
>
> In Ustinov, *Dear Me* (1977)

Rousseau, Jean-Jacques (1712–1778)
Swiss-born French philosopher, educationist and essayist
> The English people imagine themselves to be free, but they are wrong: it is only during the election of members of parliament that they are so.
>
> *Du Contrat Social* (1762)

Santayana, George (1863–1952)
Spanish-born US philosopher and writer
> England is the paradise of individuality, eccentricity, heresy, anomalies, hobbies, and humours.
>
> *Soliloquies in England* (1922)

Seeley, Sir John Robert (1834–1895)
English historian, essayist and scholar
> We the English seem as it were to have

conquered and peopled half the world in a fit of absence of mind.

The Expansion of England (1883)

Sellar, Walter (1898–1951) and **Yeatman, Robert Julian** (1897–1968)

British writers

Pope Gregory ... made the memorable joke –'Non Angli, sed Angeli' ('not Angels, but Anglicans').

1066 And All That (1930)

Shakespeare, William (1564–1616)

English dramatist, poet and actor

This royal throne of kings, this scept'red isle,
This earth of majesty, this seat of Mars,
This other Eden, demi-paradise,
This fortress built by Nature for herself
Against infection and the hand of war,
This happy breed of men, this little world,
This precious stone set in the silver sea,
Which serves it in the office of a wall,
Or as a moat defensive to a house,
Against the envy of less happier lands;
This blessed plot, this earth, this realm, this England.

Richard II, II.i

Shaw, George Bernard (1856–1950)

Irish socialist, writer, dramatist and critic

There is nothing so bad or so good that you will not find Englishmen doing it; but you will never find an Englishman in the wrong. He does everything on principle. He fights you on patriotic principles; he robs you on business principles; he enslaves you on imperial principles; he bullies you on manly principles; he supports his king on loyal principles and cuts off his king's head on republican principles.

The Man of Destiny (1898)

How can what an Englishman believes be heresy? It is a contradiction in terms.

Saint Joan (1924)

Smith, Sydney (1771–1845)

English clergyman, essayist, journalist and wit

What a pity it is that we have no amusements in England but vice and religion!

In H. Pearson, The Smith of Smiths (1934)

Steiner, George (1929–)

French-born US writer and critic

This land is blessed with a powerful mediocrity of mind. It has saved you from communism and from fascism.

The Observer, 1998 from a review of Jeremy Paxman's The English

Sully, Duc de (1559–1641)

French statesman and financier

Les Anglais s'amusent tristement, selon l'usage de leur pays.
The English enjoy themselves sadly, according to the custom of their country.

Memoirs (1638)

Tree, Sir Herbert Beerbohm (1853–1917)

English actor and theatre manager

The national sport of England is obstacle-racing. People fill their rooms with useless and cumbersome furniture, and spend the rest of their lives trying to dodge it.

In Hesketh Pearson, Beerbohm Tree (1956)

Twain, Mark (1835–1910)

US humorist, writer, journalist and lecturer

The English are mentioned in the Bible: Blessed are the meek for they shall inherit the earth.

Pudd'nhead Wilson's Calendar (1894)

Voltaire (1694–1778)

French philosopher, dramatist, poet, historian writer and critic

Le sombre Anglais, même dans ses amours,
Veut raisonner toujours.
On est plus raisonner en France.
The gloomy Englishman, even in love, always wants to reason. We are more reasonable in France.

Les Originaux, Entrée des Diverses Nations

Wells, H.G. (1866–1946)

English writer

In England we have come to rely upon a comfortable time-lag of fifty years or a century intervening between the perception that something ought to be done and a serious attempt to do it.

The Work, Wealth and Happiness of Mankind (1931)

Welsh, Irvine (1957–)

Scottish novelist

It's nae good blamin' it oan the English fir colonising us. Ah don't hate the English. They're just wankers. We can't even pick a decent vibrant, healthy culture to be colonised by.

Trainspotting (1994)

Winters, Shelley (1922–)

US actress

I did a picture in England one winter and it was so cold I almost got married.

New York Times, 1956

Wilde, Oscar (1854–1900)

Irish poet, dramatist, writer, critic and wit

Those things which the English public never forgives – youth, power, and enthusiasm.

In R. Ross (ed.), Collected Works of Oscar Wilde (1908)

The English have a miraculous power of turning wine into water.

Attr.

Wordsworth, William (1770–1850)
English poet

I travelled among unknown men
In lands beyond the sea;
Nor, England! did I know till then
What love I bore to thee.

'I travelled among unknown men'
(1807)

Milton! thou shouldst be living at this hour:
England hath need of thee; she is a fen
Of stagnant waters: altar, sword, and pen,
Fireside, the heroic wealth of hall and bower,
Have forfeited their ancient English dower
Of inward happiness.

'Milton! thou shouldst be living at this hour'
(1807)

Yeats, W.B. (1865–1939)
Irish poet, dramatist, editor, writer and senator

The Irish mind has still in country rapscallion or in Bernard Shaw an ancient, cold, explosive, detonating impartiality. The English mind, excited by its newspaper proprietors and its schoolmasters, has turned into a bed-hot harlot.

'Ireland after the Revolution'
(1939)

▶▶ CITIES; PATRIOTISM

environment

Bottomley, Gordon (1874–1948)
English poet and verse dramatist

When you destroy a blade of grass
You poison England at her roots:
Remember no man's foot can pass
Where evermore no green life shoots.

'To Ironfounders and Others' (1912)

Carson, Rachel Louise (1907–1964)
US marine biologist and writer

As man proceeds towards his announced goal of the conquest of nature, he has written a depressing record of destruction, directed not only against the earth he inhabits but against the life that shares it with him.

The Silent Spring (1962)

Over increasingly large areas of the United States, spring now comes unheralded by the return of the birds, and the early mornings are strangely silent where once they were filled with the beauty of bird song.

The Silent Spring (1962)

Under the philosophy that now seems to guide our destinies, nothing must get in the way of the man with the spray gun.

The Silent Spring (1962)

Chekhov, Anton (1860–1904)
Russian writer, dramatist and doctor

Human beings have been endowed with reason and a creative power so that they can add to what thay have been given. But until now they have been not creative, but destructive. Forests are disappearing, rivers are drying up, wildlife is becoming extinct, the climate's being ruined and with every passing day the earth is becoming poorer and uglier.

Uncle Vanya (1897)

Lawrence, D.H. (1885–1930)
English writer, poet and critic

It is the hideous rawness of the world of men, the horrible desolating harshness of the advance of the industrial world upon the world of nature, that is so painful … If only we could learn to take thought for the whole world instead of for merely tiny bits of it.

Twilight in Italy (1916)

McLean, Joyce (1860–1904)
Canadian writer

There's an old saying which goes: Once the last tree is cut and the last river poisoned, you will find you cannot eat your money.

The Globe and Mail, 1989

Mead, Margaret (1901–1978)
US anthropologist, psychologist and writer

We are living beyond our means. As a people we have developed a life-style that is draining the earth of its priceless and irreplaceable resources without regard for the future of our children and people all around the world.

Redbook

Quayle, Dan (1947–)
US Republican politician and Vice President

It isn't pollution that's harming the environment. It's the impurities in our air and water that are doing it.

Attr.

Stretton, Hugh (1924–)
Australian political scientist and historian

People can't change the way they use resources without changing their relations with one another. … How to conserve is usually a harder question than whether, or what, to conserve.

Capitalism, Socialism and the Environment (1976)

▶▶ COUNTRY

envy

Beerbohm, Sir Max (1872–1956)
English satirist, cartoonist, critic and essayist
> The dullard's envy of brilliant men is always
> assuaged by the suspicion that they will come to
> a bad end.
>> *Zuleika Dobson* (1911)

The Bible (King James Version)
> Through envy of the devil came death into the
> world.
>> *Apocrypha, Wisdom of Solomon*, 2:24

Brontë, Charlotte (1816–1855)
English writer
> Had I been in anything inferior to him, he would
> not have hated me so thoroughly, but I knew all
> that he knew, and, what was worse, he
> suspected that I kept the padlock of silence on
> mental wealth in which he was no sharer.
>> *The Professor* (1857)

Churchill, Charles (1731–1764)
English poet, political writer and clergyman
> Who wit with jealous eye surveys,
> And sickens at another's praise.
>> *The Ghost* (1763)

Fielding, Henry (1707–1754)
English writer, dramatist and journalist
> Some folks rail against other folks because other
> folks have what some folks would be glad of.
>> *Joseph Andrews* (1742)

Gay, John (1685–1732)
English poet, dramatist and librettist
> Fools may our scorn, not envy raise,
> For envy is a kind of praise.
>> *Fables* (1727)

Moore, Brian (1921–1999)
Canadian writer
> How many works of the imagination have been
> goaded into life by envy of an untalented
> contemporary's success.
>> *An Answer from Limbo* (1994)

Proverb
> Better be envied than pitied.

Shakespeare, William (1564–1616)
English dramatist, poet and actor
Of Cassius
> Such men as he be never at heart's ease
> Whiles they behold a greater than themselves,
> And therefore are they very dangerous.
>> *Julius Caesar*, I.ii

> The general 's disdain'd
> By him one step below, he by the next,
> That next by him beneath; so every step,

> Exampl'd by the first pace that is sick
> Of his superior, grows to an envious
> fever
> Of pale and bloodless emulation.
>> *Troilus and Cressida*, I.iii

▶▶ DISAPPOINTMENT; JEALOUSY

epitaphs

Anonymous
> All who come my grave to see
> Avoid damp beds and think of me.
>> Epitaph of Lydia Eason, St Michael's, Stoke

On a child dead of snake-bite
> From a subtle serpents Bite he cride
> our RoseBud cut he drup'd his head and died,
> He was his Fathers glorey
> And Mothers pride.
>> Memorial to John Howorth, died 8 October 1804
>> at 11 years, St John's Churchyard, Wilberforce,
>> New South Wales

> God took our flour,
> Our little Nell;
> He thought He too
> Would like a smell.
>> In Thomas Wood, *Cobbers*

> Here lie I and my four daughters,
> Killed by drinking Cheltenham waters.
> Had we but stuck to Epsom salts,
> We wouldn't have been in these here vaults.
>> 'Cheltenham Waters'

> Here lie I by the chancel door;
> They put me here because I was poor.
> The further in, the more you pay,
> But here lie I as snug as they.
>> Epitaph, Devon churchyard

> Here lies a child that took one peep of Life
> And viewed its endless troubles with dismay,
> Gazed with an anguish'd glance upon the strife
> And sickening at the sight flew fast away.
> What though for many the gate of Heaven is
> shut,
> It stands wide open for this little Butt.
>> Epitaph on Allena Butt, who had died when only 6
>> weeks old

> Here lies a man who was killed by lightning;
> He died when his prospects seemed to be
> brightening.
> He might have cut a flash in this world of
> trouble,
> But the flash cut him, and he lies in the stubble.
>> Epitaph, Torrington, Devon

> Here lies a poor woman who always was tired,

For she lived in a place where help wasn't hired.
Her last words on earth were, Dear friends I am
going
Where washing ain't done nor sweeping nor
sewing,
And everything there is exact to my wishes,
For there they don't eat and there's no washing
of dishes …
Don't mourn for me now, don't mourn for me
never,
For I'm going to do nothing for ever and ever.

Epitaph in Bushey churchyard

Here lies Fred,
Who was alive and is dead;
Had it been his father,
I had much rather;
Had it been his brother,
Still better than another;
Had it been his sister,
No one would have missed her;
Had it been the whole generation,
Still better for the nation:
But since 'tis only Fred,
Who was alive and is dead, –
There's no more to be said.

In Horace Walpole, Memoirs of George II (1847)

Here lies my wife,
Here lies she;
Hallelujah!
Hallelujee!

Epitaph, Leeds churchyard

Here lies the body of Mary Ann Lowder,
She burst while drinking a seidlitz powder.
Called from the world to her heavenly rest,
She should have waited till it effervesced.

Epitaph

Here lies the body of Richard Hind,
Who was neither ingenious, sober, nor kind.

Epitaph

Here lies Will Smith – and, what's something
rarish,
He was born, bred, and hanged, all in the same
parish.

Epitaph

Lo, Huddled up, together Lye
Gray Age, Grene youth, White Infancy.
If Death doth Nature's Laws dispence,
And reconciles All Difference
Tis Fit, One Flesh, One House Should have
One Tombe, One Epitaph, One Grave:
And they that Liv'd and Lov'd Either,
Should Dye and Lye and Sleep together.

Good reader, whether go or stay
Thou must not hence be Long Away.

*Epitaph, of William Bartholomew (died 1662), his
wife and some of their children, St John the
Baptist, Burford*

Mary Ann has gone to rest,
Safe at last on Abraham's breast,
Which may be nuts for Mary Ann,
But is certainly rough on Abraham.

Epitaph

My sledge and anvil lie declined
My bellows too have lost their wind
My fire's extinct, my forge decayed,
And in the Dust my Vice is laid
My coals are spent, my iron's gone
My Nails are Drove, My Work is done.

Epitaph in Nettlebed churchyard

Reader, one moment stop and think,
That I am in eternity, and you are on the brink.

Tombstone inscription at Perth, Scotland

Remember man, as thou goes by,
As thou art now so once was I,
As I am now so must thou be,
Remember man that thou must die.

Headstone in Straiton, Ayrshire

Rest in peace – until we meet again.

*Widow's epitaph for husband; in Mitford, The
American Way of Death*

Sacred to the memory of
Captain Anthony Wedgwood
Accidentally shot by his gamekeeper
Whilst out shooting
'Well done thou good and faithful servant'.

Epitaph

Stranger! Approach this spot with gravity!
John Brown is filling his last cavity.

Epitaph of a dentist

That we spent, we had:
That we gave, we have:
That we left, we lost.

Epitaph of the Earl of Devonshire

This is the grave of Mike O'Day
Who died maintaining his right of way.
His right was clear, his will was strong.
But he's just as dead as if he'd been wrong.

Epitaph

Warm summer sun shine kindly here:
Warm summer wind blow softly here:
Green sod above lie light, lie light:
Good-night, Dear Heart: good-night, good-
night.

*Memorial to Clorinda Haywood, St Bartholomew's,
Edgbaston*

Little Willy from his mirror
Licked the mercury right off,

Thinking in his childish error,
It would cure the whooping cough.
At the funeral his mother
Smartly said to Mrs Brown:
'Twas a chilly day for Willie
When the mercury went down'

'Willie's Epitaph'

Of Sir Francis Drake

The Sun himself cannot forget
His fellow traveller.

Wit's Recreations (1640)

Arbuthnot, John (1667–1735)
Scottish physician, pamphleteer and wit

Here continueth to rot the body of Francis
Chartres.

First line of epitaph

Atkinson, Surgeon-Captain E.L. (1882–1929)
English polar explorer, doctor and naval officer

Hereabouts died a very gallant gentleman,
Captain L.E.G. Oates of the Inniskilling
Dragoons. In March 1912, returning from the
Pole, he walked willingly to his death in a
blizzard, to try and save his comrades, beset by
hardships.

Epitaph on a cairn and cross erected in the
Antarctic, November 1912

Auden, W.H. (1907–1973)
English poet, essayist, critic, teacher and dramatist

Perfection, of a kind, was what he was after,
And the poetry he invented was easy to
understand;
He knew human folly like the back of his hand,
And was greatly interested in armies and fleets;
When he laughed, respectable senators burst
with laughter,
And when he cried the little children died in the
streets.

Collected Poems, 1933–1938, 'Epitaph on a Tyrant'

To save your world you asked this man to die:
Would this man, could he see you now, ask why?

'Epitaph for the Unknown Soldier' (1955)

He disappeared in the dead of winter:
The brooks were frozen, the airports almost
deserted,
And snow disfigured the public statues;
The mercury sank in the mouth of the dying day.
What instruments we have agree
The day of his death was a dark cold day …

Collected Poems, 1939–1947, 'In Memory of W.B.
Yeats'

Barham, Rev. Richard Harris (Thomas Ingoldsby)
(1788–1845)
English clergyman and comic poet

Though I've always considered Sir Christopher
Wren,

As an architect, one of the greatest of men;
And, talking of Epitaphs, – much I admire his,
'Circumspice, si Monumentum requiris';
Which an erudite Verger translated to me,
'If you ask for his Monument, Sir-come-spy-see!'.

The Ingoldsby Legends (1840–1847), 'The
Cynotaph'

Barnfield, Richard (1574–1627)
English poet
In memory of Sir John Hawkins

The waters were his winding sheet, the sea was
made his tomb;
Yet for his fame the ocean sea, was not sufficient
room.

The Encomion of Lady Pecunia (1598), 'To the
Gentlemen Readers'

Belloc, Hilaire (1870–1953)
English writer of verse, essayist and critic; Liberal MP

When I am dead, I hope it may be said:
'His sins were scarlet, but his books were read.'

Sonnets and Verse (1923), 'On His Books'

Benchley, Robert (1889–1945)
US essayist, humorist and actor
Suggesting an epitaph for an actress

She sleeps alone at last.

Attr.

Blauveldt, Robert R.
On the cairn dedicated to the memory of the United Empire
Loyalists, Tusket, Yarmouth County, N.S.; words chosen by
Blauveldt who is of U.E.L. descent

They Sacrificed Everything Save Honour.

Inscription, 1964

Bray, John Jefferson (1912–)
Australian lawyer and poet

A hundred canvasses and seven sons
He left, and never got a likeness once.

'Epitaph on a Portrait Painter'

Browne, William (c.1591–1643)
English poet

Underneath this sable hearse
Lies the subject of all verse,
Sidney's sister, Pembroke's mother;
Death! ere thou hast slain another,
Fair and learn'd, and good as she,
Time shall throw a dart at thee.

'Epitaph on the Countess of Pembroke'
(1623)

Burke, Edmund (1729–1797)
Irish-born British statesman and philosopher

His virtues were his arts.

Inscription on the statue of the Marquis of
Rockingham in Wentworth Park

Burns, Robert (1759–1796)
Scottish poet and song writer

Here lie Willie Michie's banes:
O Satan, when ye tak him,
Gie him the schulin' o' your weans,
For clever Deils he'll mak them!

'Epitaph for William Michie. Schoolmaster of Cleish Parish, Fifeshire' (1787)

Byron, Lord (1788–1824)
English poet satirist and traveller

With death doomed to grapple,
Beneath this cold slab, he
Who lied in the chapel
Now lies in the Abbey.

'Epitaph for William Pitt' (1820)

Camden, William (1551–1623)
English scholar, antiquary and historian

My friend, judge not me,
Thou seest I judge not thee.
Betwixt the stirrup and the ground
Mercy I asked, mercy I found.

Remains Concerning Britain (1605), 'Epitaph for a Man Killed by Falling from His Horse'

Carew, Thomas (c.1595–1640)
English poet, musician and dramatist

Here lyes a King, that rul'd, as he thought fit
The Universal Monarchie of wit,
Here lyes two Flamens, and both those, the best,
Apollo's first, at last, the true God's Priest.

'An Elegy upon the death of Doctor Donne' (1640)

So though a Virgin, yet a Bride
To every Grace, she justifi'd
A chaste Poligamie, and dy'd.

'Inscription on Tomb of Lady Mary Wentworth' (1640)

Carlyle, Thomas (1795–1881)
Scottish historian, biographer, critic, and essayist
Epitaph for Jane Welsh Carlyle in Haddington Church

For forty years she was the true and ever-loving helpmate of her husband, and, by act and word, unweariedly forwarded him as none else could, in all of worthy that he did or attempted. She died at London, 21st April 1866, suddenly snatched away from him, and the light of his life as if gone out.

In Hector C. Macpherson, *Thomas Carlyle* (1896)

Cleveland, John (1613–1658)
English poet

Here lies wise and valiant dust,
Huddled up, 'twixt fit and just:
Strafford, who was hurried hence
'Twixt treason and convenience.
He spent his time here in a mist,
A Papist, yet a Calvinist.
His Prince's nearest joy and grief:
He had, yet wanted, all relief:
The Prop and Ruin of the State,

The people's violent love and hate:
One in extremes lov'd and abhor'd.
Riddles lie here, or in a word,
Here lies blood; and let it lie
Speechless till, and never cry.

'Epitaph on the Earl of Strafford' (1647)

Coleridge, Samuel Taylor (1772–1834)
English poet, philosopher and critic

Ere sin could blight or sorrow fade,
Death came with friendly care:
The opening bud to Heaven convey'd
And bade it blossom there.

'Epitaph on an Infant' (1794)

Cornford, Frances Crofts (1886–1960)
English poet and translator

Whoso maintains that I am humbled now
(Who wait the Awful Day) is still a liar;
I hope to meet my Maker brow to brow
And find my own the higher.

'Epitaph for a Reviewer' (1954)

Crashaw, Richard (c.1612–1649)
English religious poet

To these, Whom Death again did wed,
This Grave's the second Marriage-Bed …
Peace, good Reader, doe not weepe;
Peace, the Lovers are asleepe:
They (sweet Turtles) folded lye,
In the last knot that love could tye.

Steps to the Temple (1646), 'An Epitaph upon Husband and Wife, which died, and were buried together'

Day Lewis, C. (1904–1972)
Irish-born British academic, writer and critic

Now we lament one
Who danced on a plume of words,
Sang with a fountain's panache,
Dazzled like slate roofs in sun
After rain, was flighty as birds
And alone as a mountain ash.
The ribald, inspired urchin
Leaning over the lip
Of his world, as over a rock pool
Or a lucky dip,
Found everything brilliant and virgin.

'In Memory of Dylan Thomas'

Douglas, James, Earl of Morton (c.1516–1581)
Regent of Scotland
Said during the burial of John Knox, 1572

Here lies he who neither feared nor flattered any flesh.

Attr.

Dryden, John (1631–1700)
English poet, satirist, dramatist and critic

Here lies my wife: here let her lie!
Now she's at rest, and so am I.

'Epitaph intended for his wife'

Emmet, Robert (1778–1803)
Irish patriot
Before his execution
> When my country takes her place among the
> nations of the earth, then and not till then, let
> my epitaph be written. I have done.
>
> Attr.

Evans, Abel (1679–1737)
English churchman, poet and satirist
> Under this stone, Reader, survey
> Dead Sir John Vanbrugh's house of clay.
> Lie heavy on him, Earth! for he
> Laid many heavy loads on thee!

'Epitaph on Sir John Vanbrugh, Architect of Blenheim Palace'
(died 1726)

Fields, W.C. (1880–1946)
US film actor
> On the whole, I'd rather be in Philadelphia.
>
> His own epitaph

Franklin, Benjamin (1706–1790)
US statesman, scientist, political critic and printer
> The body of
> Benjamin Franklin, printer,
> (Like the cover of an old book,
> Its contents worn out,
> And stript of its lettering and gilding)
> Lies here, food for worms!
> Yet the work itself shall not be lost,
> For it will, as he believed, appear once more
> In a new
> And more beautiful edition,
> Corrected and amended
> By its Author!
>
> Epitaph for himself, 1728

Frost, Robert (1874–1963)
US poet
> I would have written of me on my stone:
> I had a lover's quarrel with the world.
>
> 'The Lesson for Today' (1942)

Garrick, David (1717–1779)
English actor and theatre manager
> Here lies Nolly Goldsmith, for shortness call'd
> Noll,
> Who wrote like an angel, but talk'd like poor
> Poll.
>
> 'Impromptu Epitaph on Goldsmith', 1774

Halleck, Fitz-Greene (1790–1867)
US poet, satirist and banker
> Green be the turf above thee,
> Friend of my better days!
> None knew thee but to love thee,
> Nor named thee but to praise.
>
> 'On the Death of J.R. Drake' (1820)

Hope, Alec (Derwent) (1907–)
Australian poet and critic

An ironic parody of the Greek epitaph commemorating the
Spartans who died at Thermopylae in 480 BC
> Go tell those old men, safe in bed,
> We took their orders and are dead.
>
> 'Inscription for Any War'

Hope, Anthony (1863–1933)
> His foe was folly and his weapon wit.
>
> Inscription on the tablet to W.S. Gilbert, Victoria
> Embankment, London, 1915

Housman, A.E. (1859–1936)
English poet and scholar
> These, in the day when heaven was falling,
> The hour when earth's foundations fled,
> Followed their mercenary calling
> And took their wages and are dead.
>
> Their shoulders held the sky suspended;
> They stood, and earth's foundations stay;
> What God abandoned, these defended,
> And saved the sum of things for pay.
>
> *Last Poems* (1922)

Hume, David (1711–1776)
Scottish philosopher and political economist
> Within this circular idea
> Call'd vulgarly a tomb,
> The ideas and impressions lie
> That constituted Hume.
>
> Epitaph on his monument on Calton Hill,
> Edinburgh

Huxley, Henrietta (1825–1915)
English writer and poet; wife of T.H. Huxley
> And if there be no meeting past the grave,
> If all is darkness, silence, yet 'tis rest.
> Be not afraid ye waiting hearts that weep;
> For still He giveth His beloved sleep,
> And if an endless sleep He wills, so best.
>
> Lines on the grave of her husband, 1895, in
> Deighton, *Huxley, His Life and Work* (1904)

Johnson, Samuel (1709–1784)
English lexicographer, poet, critic, conversationalist and
essayist
> In lapidary inscriptions a man is not upon oath.
>
> In Boswell, *The Life of Samuel Johnson* (1791)

> *Olivarii Goldsmith, Poetae, Physici, Historici, Qui nullum*
> *fere scribendi genus non tetigit, Nullum quod tetigit*
> *non ornavit.*
> To Oliver Goldsmith, A Poet, Naturalist, and
> Historian, who left scarcely any style of writing
> untouched, and touched none that he did not
> adorn.
>
> In Boswell, *The Life of Samuel Johnson* (1791)

On the death of Mr Levett
> Officious, innocent, sincere,
> Of every friendless name the friend.
> Yet still he fills affection's eye,

Obscurely wise, and coarsely kind.

> In Boswell, *The Life of Samuel Johnson* (1791)

Jonson, Ben (1572–1637)

English dramatist and poet

> Weep with me, all you that read
> This little story:
> And know for whom a tear you shed
> Death's self is sorry.
> 'Twas a child that so did thrive
> In grace and feature,
> As Heaven and Nature seem'd to strive
> Which own'd the creature.
> Years he number'd scarce thirteen
> When Fates turn'd cruel,
> Yet three fill'd Zodiacs had he been
> The stage's jewel;
> And did act, what now we moan,
> Old men so duly,
> As sooth the Parcae thought him one,
> He play'd so truly.
> So, by error, to his fate
> They all consented;
> But viewing him since, alas, too late!
> They have repented;
> And have sought (to give new birth)
> In baths to steep him;
> But being so much too good for earth,
> Heaven vows to keep him.

> *Epigrams* (1616), 'An Epitaph on Salomon Pavy, a
> Child of Queen Elizabeth's Chapel'

> Rest in soft peace, and, ask'd say here doth lye
> Ben Jonson his best piece of poetrie.

> *Epigrams* (1616), 'On My First Son'

> O rare Ben Jonson.

> Epitaph in Westminster
> Abbey

Kaufman, George S. (1889–1961)

US scriptwriter, librettist and journalist

Suggestion for his own epitaph

> Over my dead body!

> Attr.

Keats, John (1795–1821)

English poet

> Here lies one whose name was writ in water.

> Epitaph for himself

Kipling, Rudyard (1865–1936)

Indian-born British poet and writer

> A Soldier of the Great War Known unto God.

> Inscription on the graves of unidentified soldiers,
> 1919

> I could not look on Death, which being known,
> Men led me to him, blindfold and alone.

> *The Years Between* (1919), 'Epitaphs – The
> Coward'

Knox, John (1505–1572)

Scottish religious reformer

> *Un homme avec Dieu est toujours dans la majorité.*
> A man with God is always in the majority.

> Inscription on the Reformation Monument,
> Geneva, Switzerland

Lee, Henry (1756–1818)

US soldier and statesman

Of Washington

> A citizen, first in war, first in peace, and first in
> the hearts of his countrymen.

> Resolution adopted by Congress on the death of
> George Washington, 1799

Lockhart, John Gibson (1794–1854)

Scottish writer, critic, and translator

> Here lies that peerless peer Lord Peter,
> Who broke the laws of God and man and metre.

> Epitaph for Patrick ('Peter'), Lord Robertson, 1890

Macaulay, Lord (1800–1859)

English Liberal statesman, essayist and poet

> To my true king I offer'd free from stain
> Courage and faith; vain faith, and courage vain …

> By those white cliffs I never more must see,
> By that dear language which I spake like thee,
> Forget all feuds, and shed one English tear
> O'er English dust. A broken heart lies here.

> 'A Jacobite's Epitaph' (1845)

MacDonald, George (1824–1905)

Scottish writer, poet and preacher

> Here lie I, Martin Elginbrodde:
> Hae mercy o' my soul, Lord God;
> As I wad do, were I Lord God,
> And you were Martin Elginbrodde.

> *David Elginbrod* (1863)

Marvell, Andrew (1621–1678)

English poet and satirist

> Who can foretell for what high cause
> This Darling of the Gods was born! …

> Gather the flowers, but spare the buds.

> 'The Picture of Little T.C. in a Prospect of Flowers' (1681)

Mencken, H.L. (1880–1956)

US writer, critic, philologist and satirist

> If, after I depart this vale, you ever remember
> me and have thought to please my ghost,
> forgive some sinner and wink your eye at some
> homely girl.

> *Smart Set*, 1921, Epitaph

Mill, John Stuart (1806–1873)

English philosopher, economist and reformer

> Were there but a few hearts and intellects like
> hers this earth would already become the
> hoped-for heaven.

> Epitaph for his wife, Harriet, 1859

Moore, George (1852–1933)
Irish writer, dramatist and critic
What he would like on his tombstone
> Here lies George Moore, who looked upon
> corrections as the one morality.
>> Conversation with Geraint Goodwin

Newcastle, Margaret, Duchess of (c.1624–1674)
English poet, dramatist and woman of letters
> Her name was Margaret Lucas youngest
> daughter of Lord Lucas, earl of Colchester, a
> noble family, for all the brothers were valiant,
> and all the sisters virtuous.
>> Epitaph in Westminster Abbey; quoted by Joseph
>> Addison

Parker, Dorothy (1893–1967)
US writer, poet, critic and wit
> He lies below, correct in cypress wood,
> And entertains the most exclusive worms.
>> *Not So Deep as a Well* (1937), 'Epitaph for a Very
>> Rich Man'

Suggesting words for tombstone
> This is on me.
>> In J. Keats, *You Might As Well Live* (1970)

Her own epitaph
> Excuse my dust.
>> In Alexander Woollcott, *While Rome Burns* (1934)

Peacock, Thomas Love (1785–1866)
English writer and poet
> Long night succeeds thy little day
> Oh blighted blossom! can it be,
> That this gray stone and grassy clay
> Have closed our anxious care of thee?
>> In Henry Cole (ed.), *Works of Peacock* (1875)

Pope, Alexander (1688–1744)
English poet, translator and editor
> Nature, and Nature's laws lay hid in night:
> God said, Let Newton be! and all was light.
>> 'Epitaph for Sir Isaac Newton' (1730)

> Of manners gentle, of affections mild;
> In wit, a man; simplicity, a child:
> With native humour temp'ring virtuous rage,
> Formed to delight at once and lash the age.
>> 'Epitaph: On Mr. Gay in Westminster Abbey', 1733

Prior, Matthew (1664–1721)
English poet
> Nobles and heralds, by your leave,
> Here lies what once was Matthew Prior;
> The son of Adam and of Eve,
> Can Bourbon or Nassau go higher?
>> 'Epitaph' (1702)

Rochester, Earl of (1647–1680)
English poet, satirist, courtier and libertine
> Here lies our sovereign lord the King
> Whose word no man relies on,
> Who never said a foolish thing,
> Nor ever did a wise one.
>> Epitaph written for Charles II (1706)

Rossetti, Christina (1830–1894)
English poet
> O Earth, lie heavily upon her eyes;
> Seal her sweet eyes weary of watching.
>> 'Rest' (1862)

Sassoon, Siegfried (1886–1967)
English poet and writer
> Here sleeps the Silurist; the loved physician;
> The face that left no portraiture behind;
> The skull that housed white angels and had
> vision
> Of daybreak through the gateways of the mind.
>> *The Heart's Journey* (1928)

Scott, Sir Walter (1771–1832)
Scottish writer and historian
> Here lies one who might be trusted with untold
> gold, but not with unmeasured whisky.
>> Epitaph for his favourite servant, Tom Purdie

Shakespeare, William (1564–1616)
English dramatist, poet and actor
Epitaph on his tomb
> Good friend, for Jesu's sake forbear,
> To dig the dust enclosed here.
> Blest be the man that spares these stones,
> And curst be he that moves my bones.
>> Attr.

Simonides (c.556–468 BC)
Greek poet and epigrammatist
Epitaph for the three hundred Spartans under Leonidas who
died at Thermopylae in 480
> Go, tell the Spartans, thou who passest by,
> That here, obedient to their laws, we lie.
>> In Herodotus, *Histories*

Smith, Joseph (1805–1844)
Founder of the Mormon Church
> No man knows my history.
>> Funeral sermon, written by himself

Stevenson, Robert Louis (1850–1894)
Scottish writer, poet and essayist
> Under the wide and starry sky
> Dig the grave and let me lie.
> Glad did I live and gladly die,
> And I laid me down with a will.
> This be the verse you grave for me:
> 'Here he lies where he longed to be;
> Home is the sailor, home from sea,
> And the hunter home from the hill.'
>> *Underwoods* (1887), 'Requiem'

Sturges, Preston (1898–1959)
US film director and scriptwriter
Suggested epitaph for himself

Now I've laid me down to die
I pray my neighbours not to pry
Too deeply into sins that I
Not only cannot here deny
But much enjoyed as time flew by.

> In Halliwell, *The Filmgoer's Book of Quotes* (1973)

Surrey, Henry Howard, Earl of (c.1517–1547)
English poet, courtier and soldier
But to the heavens that simple soule is fled:
Which left with such, as covet Christ to know,
Witnesse of faith, that never shall be ded:
Sent for our helth, but not received so.
Thus, for our gilte, this jewel have we lost:
The earth his bones, the heavens possesse his
gost.

> 'Of the death of Sir T.W. Thomas Wyatt'

Swift, Jonathan (1667–1745)
Irish satirist, poet, essayist and cleric
Poor Pope will grieve a month, and Gay
A week, and Arbuthnot a day.
St John himself will scarce forbear
To bite his pen, and drop a tear.
The rest will give a shrug, and cry,
'I'm sorry – but we all must die!' …

Yet malice never was his aim;
He lash'd the vice, but spared the name;
No individual could resent,
Where thousands equally were meant …

He gave the little wealth he had
To build a house for fools and mad;
And show'd, by one satiric touch,
No nation wanted it so much.
That kingdom he hath left a debtor,
I wish it soon may have a better.

> 'Verses on the Death of Dr. Swift' (1731)

Where fierce indignation can no longer tear his
heart.

> Epitaph

Turgot, A.-R.-J. (1727–1781)
French economist and statesman
Inscription for a bust of Benjamin Franklin, who invented the
lightning conductor
Eripuit coelo fulmen, sceptrumque tyrannis.
He snatched the lightning shaft from heaven,
and the sceptre from tyrants.

> In A.N. de Condorcet, *Vie de Turgot*

Walton, Izaak (1593–1683)
English writer
An excellent angler, and now with God.

> *The Compleat Angler* (1653)

Wilde, Oscar (1854–1900)
Irish poet, dramatist, writer, critic and wit
All her bright golden hair

Tarnished with rust,
She that was young and fair
Fallen to dust.

> 'Requiescat' (1881)

Wordsworth, William (1770–1850)
English poet
Three years she grew in sun and shower,
Then Nature said, 'A lovelier flower
On earth was never sown;
This child I to myself will take;
She shall be mine, and I will make
A Lady of my own'.

> 'Three years she grew' (1800)

Wotton, Sir Henry (1568–1639)
English diplomat, traveller and poet
He first deceased; she for a little tried
To live without him: liked it not, and died.

> 'Death of Sir Albertus Moreton's Wife' (c.1610)

Wren, Sir Christopher (1632–1723)
English architect and mathematician and astronomer
Si monumentum requiris, circumspice.
If you are looking for his memorial, look around
you.

> Inscription written by his son, in St Paul's Cathedral, London

Yeats, W.B. (1865–1939)
Irish poet, dramatist, editor, writer and senator
Swift has sailed into his rest;
Savage indignation there
Cannot lacerate his breast.
Imitate him if you dare,
World-besotted traveller; he
Served human liberty.

> In the *Dublin Magazine*, 1931, 'Swift's Epitaph'

Under bare Ben Bulben's head
In Drumcliff churchyard Yeats is laid …
On limestone quarried near the spot
By his command these words are cut:
Cast a cold eye
On life, on death.
Horseman, pass by!

> In *The Irish Times*, *Irish Independent*, and *Irish Press*,
> 1939 (Yeats' epitaph)

equality

Anthony, Susan B. (1820–1906)
US reformer, feminist and abolitionist
There never will be complete equality until
women themselves help to make laws and elect
lawmakers.

> *The Arena*, 1897

Aristotle (384–322 BC)
Greek philosopher
Inferiors agitate in order that they may be equal

and equals that they may be superior. Such is
the state of mind which creates party strife.

Politics

Bakunin, Mikhail (1814–1876)
Russian anarchist and writer
Anarchist declaration, Lyon, 1870
We wish, in a word, equality – equality in fact as
corollary, or rather, as primordial condition of
liberty. From each according to his faculties, to
each according to his needs; that is what we
wish sincerely and energetically.

In J. Morrison Davidson, *The Old Order and the New*
(1890)

Balzac, Honoré de (1799–1850)
French writer
Equality may perhaps be a right, but no power
on earth can ever turn it into a fact.

La Duchesse de Langeais (1834)

Barrie, Sir J.M. (1860–1937)
Scottish dramatist and writer
His Lordship may compel us to be equal
upstairs, but there will never be equality in the
servants' hall.

The Admirable Crichton (1902)

Burns, Robert (1759–1796)
Scottish poet and song writer
The rank is but the guinea's stamp,
The man's the gowd for a' that …

For a' that, an' a' that,
It's comin yet for a' that,
That man to man the world o'er
Shall brithers be for a' that.

'A Man's a Man for a' that' (1795)

Emerson, Ralph Waldo (1803–1882)
US poet, essayist, transcendentalist and teacher
There is a little formula, couched in pure Saxon,
which you may hear in the corners of the streets
and in the yard of the dame's school, from very
little republicans: 'I'm as good as you be,' which
contains the essence of the Massachusetts Bill of
Rights and
of the American Declaration of Independence.

Natural History of Intellect (1893)

Forster, E.M. (1879–1970)
English writer, essayist and literary critic
All men are equal – all men, that is to say, who
possess umbrellas.

Howard's End (1910)

Gilbert, W.S. (1836–1911)
English dramatist, humorist and librettist
They all shall equal be!
The Earl, the Marquis, and the Dook,
The Groom, the Butler, and the Cook,
The Aristocrat who banks with Coutts,

The Aristocrat who cleans the boots.

The Gondoliers (1889)

Huxley, Aldous (1894–1963)
English writer, poet and critic
That all men are equal is a proposition to which,
at ordinary times, no sane human being has ever
given his assent.

Proper Studies (1927)

Johnson, Samuel (1709–1784)
English lexicographer, poet, critic, conversationalist and
essayist
Your levellers wish to level down as far as
themselves; but they cannot bear levelling up to
themselves.

In Boswell, *The Life of Samuel Johnson* (1791)

It is better that some should be unhappy than
that none should be happy, which would be the
case in a general state of equality.

In Boswell, *The Life of Samuel Johnson* (1791)

King, Martin Luther (1929–1968)
US civil rights leader and Baptist minister
Now, I say to you today my friends, even though
we face the difficulties of today and tomorrow, I
still have a dream. It is a dream deeply rooted in
the American dream. I have a dream that one
day this nation will rise up and live out the true
meaning of its creed: – 'We hold these truths to
be self-evident, that all men are created equal'.

Speech at Civil Rights March on Washington,
August 28, 1963

Mandela, Nelson (1918–)
South African statesman and President
I have fought against white domination, and I have
fought against black domination. I have cherished
the ideal of a democratic and free society in which
all persons will live together in harmony and with
equal opportunities. It is an ideal which I hope to
live for and achieve. But, if needs be, it is an ideal
for which I am prepared to die.

Statement in the dock, 1964

Mill, John Stuart (1806–1873)
English philosopher, economist and reformer
The principle which regulates the existing social
relations between the two sexes – the legal
subordination of one sex to the other – is wrong
in itself, and now one of the chief hindrances to
human improvement; and … it ought to be
replaced by a principle of perfect equality,
admitting no power or privilege on the one side,
nor disability on the other.

The Subjection of Women (1869)

Murdoch, Iris (1919–1999)
Irish-born British writer, philosopher and dramatist
The cry of equality pulls everyone down.

The Observer, 1987

Orwell, George (1903–1950)
English writer and critic
> All animals are equal, but some animals are more
> equal than others.
>> *Animal Farm* (1945)

Proverb
> The beak of the goose is no longer than that of
> the gander.

Rainborowe, Thomas (d. 1648)
English parliamentarian and soldier
> The poorest he that is in England hath a life to
> live as the greatest he.
>> Speech in Army debates, 1647

Ruskin, John (1819–1900)
English art critic, philosopher and reformer
> It ought to be quite as natural and straight-
> forward a matter for a labourer to take his
> pension from his parish, because he has
> deserved well of his parish, as for a man in
> higher rank to take his pension from his country,
> because he has deserved well of his country.
>> *Unto this Last* (1862), Preface

Wedgwood, Josiah (1730–1795)
English potter, manufacturer and pamphleteer
> Am I not a man and a brother?
>> Motto adopted by Anti-Slavery Society

Willkie, Wendell (1892–1944)
> The Constitution does not provide for first and
> second class citizens.
>> *An American Program* (1944)

Wilson, Harold (1916–1995)
English Labour Prime Minister
> Everybody should have an equal chance – but
> they shouldn't have a flying start.
>> *The Observer*, 1963

▶▶ CLASS; FEMINISM

error

Aeschylus (525–456 BC)
Greek dramatist and poet
> Even he who is wiser than the wise may
> err.
>> *Fragments*

Anonymous
> If anything can go wrong, it will.
> 'Murphy's Law', probably dating from the US in the 1940s.
> A Captain E. Murphy of the California Northrop aviation
> firm may have formulated it

> Once a job is fouled up, anything done to
> improve it only makes it worse.
>> Finagle's Fourth Law

Banville, Théodore Faullain de (1823–1891)
French poet, lyricist and dramatist
> *Et ceux qui ne font rien ne se trompent jamais.*
> Those who do nothing are never wrong.
>> *Odes funambulesques*

Bidault, Georges (1899–1983)
French statesman
> The weak have one weapon: the errors of those
> who think they are strong.
>> *The Observer*, 1962

Bolingbroke, Henry (1678–1751)
English statesman, historian and actor
> Truth lies within a little and certain compass, but
> error is immense.
>> *Reflections upon Exile* (1716)

Browne, Sir Thomas (1605–1682)
English physician, author and antiquary
> Many … have too rashly charged the troops of
> error, and remain as trophies unto the enemies
> of truth.
>> *Religio Medici* (1643)

Destouches, Philippe Néricault (1680–1754)
French dramatist
> *Les absents ont toujours tort.*
> The absent are always in the wrong.
>> *L'Obstacle Imprévu* (1717)

Dryden, John (1631–1700)
English poet, satirist, dramatist and critic
> Errors, like straws, upon the surface flow;
> He who would search for pearls must dive
> below.
>> *All for Love* (1678)

Eliot, George (1819–1880)
English writer and poet
> Errors look so very ugly in persons of small
> means – one feels they are taking quite a liberty
> in going astray; whereas people of fortune may
> naturally indulge in a few delinquencies.
>> *Scenes of Clerical Life* (1858)

Goethe (1749–1832)
German poet, writer, dramatist and scientist
> *Es irrt der Mensch, solang' er strebt.*
> Man errs as long as he strives.
>> *Faust* (1808)

Locke, John (1632–1704)
English philosopher
> It is one thing to show a man that he is in an
> error, and another to put him in possession of
> truth.
>> *Essay concerning Human Understanding* (1690)

> All men are liable to error; and most men are, in
> many points, by passion or interest, under
> temptation to it.
>> *Essay concerning Human Understanding* (1690)

Malesherbes, Chrétien Guillaume de Lamoignonde (1721–1794)
French statesman
> A new maxim is often a brilliant error.
>> *Pensées et maximes*

Markham, Beryl (1902–1986)
English aviator and writer
> Who thinks it just to be judged by a single error?
>> *West with the Night* (1942)

Metternich, Prince Clement (1773–1859)
Austrian statesman
> *L'erreur n'a jamais approché de mon esprit.*
> Error has never even come close to my mind.
>> Remark, 1848

Oppenheimer, J. Robert (1904–1967)
US nuclear physicist
Of Albert Einstein
> A man whose errors take ten years to correct is quite a man.
>> Attr.

Pope, Alexander (1688–1744)
English poet, translator and editor
> A man should never be ashamed to own he has been in the wrong, which is but saying, in other words, that he is wiser today than he was yesterday.
>> *Miscellanies* (1727)

Proverb
> To err is human.

Schopenhauer, Arthur (1788–1860)
German philosopher
> *Es gibt nur einen angeborenen Irrtum, und es ist der, dass wir dasind, um glücklich zu sein.*
> There is only one innate error, and that is that we are here in order to be happy.
>> *The World as Will and Idea* (1859)

Shakespeare, William (1564–1616)
English dramatist, poet and actor
> O hateful error, melancholy's child,
> Why dost thou show to the apt thoughts of men
> The things that are not?
>> *Julius Caesar*, V.iii

Shirley, James (1596–1666)
English poet and dramatist
> I presume you're mortal, and may err.
>> *The Lady of Pleasure* (1637)

Teller, Edward (1908–)
Hungarian-born US physicist
> An expert is a man who has made all the mistakes which can be made in a very narrow field.
>> Remark, 1972

West, Mae (1892–1980)
US actress and scriptwriter
> To err is human, but it feels divine.
>> In Simon Rose, *Classic Film Guide* (1995)

▶▶ MISTAKES; TRUTH

estate agents

Wells, H.G. (1866–1946)
English writer
> Everybody hates house-agents because they have everybody at a disadvantage. All other callings have a certain amount of give and take; the house-agent simply takes.
>> *Kipps: the Story of a Simple Soul* (1905)

eternity

Aurelius, Marcus (121–180)
Roman emperor and Stoic philosopher
> All things from eternity are of similar forms and come round in a circle.
>> *Meditations*

Blake, William (1757–1827)
English poet, engraver, painter and mystic
> To see a World in a Grain of Sand
> And a Heaven in a Wild Flower
> Hold Infinity in the palm of your hand
> And Eternity in an hour.
>> 'Auguries of Innocence' (c.1803)

Browne, Sir Thomas (1605–1682)
English physician, author and antiquary
> Who can speak of eternity without a solecism, or think thereof without an ecstasy? Time we may comprehend, 'tis but five days elder than ourselves.
>> *Religio Medici* (1643)

Congreve, William (1670–1729)
English dramatist
> Eternity was in that moment.
>> *The Old Bachelor* (1693)

Crisp, Quentin (1908–1999)
English writer, publicist and model
> It may be true that preoccupation with time has been the downfall of Western man, but it can also be argued that conjecture about eternity is a waste of time.
>> In Guy Kettlehack (ed.), *The Wit and Wisdom of Quentin Crisp*

Dickinson, Emily (1830–1886)
US poet
> Our journey had advanced –

Our feet were almost come
To that odd Fork in Being's Road –
Eternity – by term.

'Our Journey had Advanced' (c.1862)

Dostoevsky, Fyodor (1821–1881)
Russian writer

We keep imagining eternity as an idea that can't be understood, as something enormous ... instead of all that there will just be one little room, somewhat like a country bath-house, with spiders in all the corners – that's eternity.

Crime and Punishment (1865)

Servetus, Michael (1511–1553)
Spanish theologian
Comment to the judges of the Inquisition after being condemned to be burned at the stake

I will burn, but this is a mere incident. We shall continue our discussion in eternity.

Attr.

Shakespeare, William (1564–1616)
English dramatist, poet and actor

Eternity was in our lips and eyes,
Bliss in our brows' bent.

Antony and Cleopatra, I.iii

Thoreau, Henry David (1817–1862)
US essayist, social critic and writer

As if you could kill time, without injuring eternity.

Walden (1854)

▶▶ TIME

europe

Ascherson, Neal (1932–)
Scottish journalist

Europe and the United States together invented representative democracy and human rights. But Europe invented fascism and communism all by itself.

The Observer, June 1998

Baldwin, James (1924–1987)
US writer, dramatist, poet and civil rights activist

Europe has what we do not have yet, a sense of the mysterious and inexorable limits of life, a sense, in a word, of tragedy. And we have what they sorely need: a sense of life's possibilities.

Attr.

Baldwin, Stanley (1867–1947)
English Conservative statesman and Prime Minister

When you think of the defence of England you no longer think of the chalk cliffs of Dover. You think of the Rhine. That is where our frontier lies today.

Speech, 1934

Benes, Eduard (1884–1948)
Czechoslovak statesman

To make peace in Europe possible, the last representative of the pre-war generation must die and take his pre-war mentality into the grave with him.

Interview, 1929

Bevin, Ernest (1881–1951)
English trade union leader and politician
On the Council of Europe

If you open that Pandora's Box you never know what Trojan 'orses will jump out.

In Sir Roderick Barclay, *Ernest Bevin and the Foreign Office* (1975)

Chase, Ilka (1905–1978)
US writer, broadcaster and actress

That is what is so marvellous about Europe; the people long ago learned that space and beauty and quiet refuges in a great city, where children may play and old people sit in the sun, are of far more value to the inhabitants than real estate taxes and contractors' greed.

Fresh From the Laundry (1967)

Churchill, Sir Winston (1874–1965)
English Conservative Prime Minister

We must build a kind of United States of Europe.

Speech, Zurich, September 1946

Cohn-Bendit, Daniel (1945–)

Europa soll aus Bosnien ein neues Westberlin machen.
Europe should make a new West-Berlin out of Bosnia.

Interview in *Süddeutsche Zeitung*, 1994

Delors, Jacques (1925–)
French politician

Europe is not just about material results, it is about spirit. Europe is a state of mind.

The Independent, May 1994

The hardest thing is to convince European citizens that even the most powerful nation is no longer able to act alone.

The Independent, May 1994

Fanon, Frantz (1925–1961)
West Indian psychoanalyst and philosopher

When I search for man in the technique and style of Europe, I see only a succession of negations of man, and an avalanche of murders.

The Wretched of the Earth (1961)

Fisher, H.A.L. (1856–1940)
English historian

Purity of race does not exist. Europe is a continent of energetic mongrels.

History of Europe (1935)

Gladstone, William (1809–1898)
English statesman and reformer
> We are part of the community of Europe, and we must do our duty as such.
>> Speech, 1888

Goldsmith, James (1933–1997)
British business magnate and MEP
> Brussels is madness. I will fight it from within.
>> *The Times*, June 1994

Goldsmith, Oliver (c.1728–1774)
Irish dramatist, poet and writer
> On whatever side we regard the history of Europe, we shall perceive it to be a tissue of crimes, follies, and misfortunes.
>> *The Citizen of the World* (1762)

Hazzard, Shirley (1931–)
Australian writer
> Going to Europe, someone had written, was about as final as going to heaven. A mystical passage to another life, from which no one returned the same.
>> *The Transit of Venus* (1980)

Healey, Denis (1917–)
English Labour politician
Of Conservatives
> Their Europeanism is nothing but imperialism with an inferiority complex.
>> *The Observer*, 1962

Heath, Sir Edward (1916–)
English Conservative Prime Minister
> Nor would it be in the interests of the European Community that its enlargement should take place except with the full-hearted consent of the Parliament and people of the new member countries.
>> Speech to the Franco-British Chamber of Commerce, Paris, 1970

Hugo, Victor (1802–1885)
French poet, writer, dramatist and politician
> I represent a party which does not yet exist: the party of revolution, civilisation. This party will make the twentieth century. There will issue from it first the United States of Europe, then the United States of the World.
>> Written on the wall of the room in which Hugo died, Paris, 1885

Kohl, Helmut (1930–)
German Chancellor
On plans for a single currency
> economic and political union … is the next step toward a United States of Europe.
>> Comment, 1990

McCarthy, Mary (1912–1989)
US writer and critic
> When an American heiress wants to buy a man, she at once crosses the Atlantic. The only really materialistic people I have ever met have been Europeans.
>> *On the Contrary* (1961)

> The immense popularity of American movies abroad demonstrates that Europe is the unfinished negative of which America is the proof.
>> *On the Contrary* (1961)

Nicholson, Sir Bryan (1932–)
British businessman
On the government's non-cooperation with Europe over the ban on exporting British beef
> In this pungent atmosphere of romantic nationalism and churlish xenophobia, I sometimes wonder if there are some among us who have failed to notice that the war with Germany has ended.
>> *The Observer*, May 1996

Pitt, William (1759–1806)
English politician and Prime Minister
Commenting on the map of Europe, after the Battle of Austerlitz, 1805
> Roll up that map; it will not be wanted these ten years.
>> In Lord Stanhope, *Life of the Rt. Hon. William Pitt*, (1862)

Salisbury, Lord (1830–1903)
English Conservative Prime Minister
> We are part of the community of Europe and we must do our duty as such.
>> Speech, 1888

Scanlon, Hugh, Baron (1913–)
British trade union leader
> Referring to his union's attitude to the Common Market
> Here we are again with both feet firmly planted in the air.
>> *The Observer*, 1973

Sherman, Alfred (1919–)
British journalist
> Britain does not wish to be ruled by a conglomerate in Europe which includes Third World nations such as the Greeks and Irish, nor for that matter the Italians and French, whose standards of political morality are not ours, and never will be.
>> *The Independent*, August 1990

Soames, Nicholas (1948–)
English Conservative politician
Comment during a Commons debate, the topics of which included positive discrimination for women in the armed forces and a European Union directive on equality
> All that EC nonsense is beyond me.
>> The *Mail on Sunday*, 1996

Thatcher, Margaret (1925–)
English Conservative Prime Minister

Historians will one day look back and think it a curious folly that just as the Soviet Union was forced to recognize reality by dispersing power to its separate states and by limiting the powers of its central government, some people in Europe were trying to create a new artificial state by taking powers from national states and concentrating them at the centre.

Speech, 1994

Victoria, Queen (1819–1901)
Queen of the United Kingdom

I am sick of all this horrid business of politics, and Europe in general, and I think you will hear of me going with the children to live in Australia, and to think of Europe as the Moon!

Letter to her daughter, the Princess Royal, 1859

▶▶ BRITAIN; ENGLAND; FRANCE; GERMANY; IRELAND; ITALY; RUSSIA; SCOTLAND; SWITZERLAND; WALES

evil

Anonymous

Honi soit qui mal y pense.
Evil be to him who evil thinks.

Motto of the Order of the Garter

Whenever God prepares evil for a man, He first damages his mind.

Scholiast on Sophocles

Arendt, Hannah (1906–1975)
German-born US theorist
Of Eichmann

It was as though in those last minutes he was summing up the lessons that this long course in human wickedness had taught us – the lesson of the fearsome, word-and-thought-defying banality of evil.

Eichmann in Jerusalem (1963)

The Bible (King James Version)

The heart is deceitful above all things, and desperately wicked.

Jeremiah, 17:9

I have seen the wicked in great power, and spreading himself like a green bay tree.

Psalms, 37:35

There is no peace, saith the Lord, unto the wicked.

Isaiah, 48:22

Boileau-Despréaux, Nicolas (1636–1711)
French writer

Souvent la peur d'un mal nous conduit dans un pire.

The fear of one evil often leads us into a greater one.

L'Art Poétique (1674)

Brecht, Bertolt (1898–1956)
German dramatist

Die Gemeinheit der Welt ist gross, und man muss sich die Beine ablaufen, damit sie einem nicht gestohlen werden.
The wickedness of the world is so great that you have to run your legs off so you don't get them stolen from you.

The Threepenny Opera (1928)

Burke, Edmund (1729–1797)
Irish-born British statesman and philosopher

The only thing necessary for the triumph of evil is for good men to do nothing.

Attr.

Conrad, Joseph (1857–1924)
Polish-born British writer, sailor and explorer

The belief in a supernatural source of evil is not necessary; men alone are quite capable of every wickedness.

Under Western Eyes (1911)

Crisp, Quentin (1908–1999)
English writer, publicist and model

Vice is its own reward.

The Naked Civil Servant (1968)

Delbanco, Andrew (1952–)
Writer and academic

The idea of evil is something on which the health of society depends. We have an obligation to name evil and oppose it in ourselves as well as in others.

The Guardian, 1995

Goldsmith, Oliver (c.1728–1774)
Irish dramatist, poet and writer

Don't let us make imaginary evils, when you know we have so many real ones to encounter.

The Good Natur'd Man (1768)

Hattersley, Roy (1932–)
British Labour politician and writer

Familiarity with evil breeds not contempt but acceptance.

The Guardian, 1993

Hazlitt, William (1778–1830)
English writer and critic

Wrong dressed out in pride, pomp, and circumstance, has more attraction than abstract right.

Characters of Shakespeare's Plays (1817)

To great evils we submit, we resent little provocations.

Table-Talk (1822)

Hood, Thomas (1799–1845)
English poet, editor and humorist
> But evil is wrought by want of Thought,
> As well as want of Heart!
>> 'The Lady's Dream' (1844)

Kempis, Thomas à (c.1380–1471)
German mystic, monk and writer
> *De duobus malis minus est semper eligendum.*
> Of two evils the lesser is always to be chosen.
>> *De Imitatione Christi* (1892)

La Rochefoucauld (1613–1680)
French writer
> *Il n'y a guère d'homme assez habile pour connaître tout le mal qu'il fait.*
> There is scarcely a single man clever enough to know all the evil he does.
>> *Maximes* (1678)

McCarthy, Mary (1912–1989)
US writer and critic
> If someone tells you he is going to make 'a realistic decision', you immediately understand that he has resolved to do something bad.
>> *On the Contrary* (1961)

Newman, John Henry, Cardinal (1801–1890)
English Cardinal, theologian and poet
> Whatever is the first time persons hear evil, it is quite certain that good has been beforehand with them, and they have a something within them which tells them it is evil.
>> *Parochial and Plain Sermons*

Nietzsche, Friedrich Wilhelm (1844–1900)
German philosopher, critic and poet
> *Wer mit Ungeheurn kämpft, mag zusehn, dass er nicht dabei zum Ungeheuer wird. Und wenn du lange in einen Abgrund blickst, blickt der Abgrund auch in dich hinein.*
> Whoever struggles with monsters might watch that he does not thereby become a monster. When you stare into an abyss for a long time, the abyss also stares into you.
>> *Beyond Good and Evil* (1886)

Pope, Alexander (1688–1744)
English poet, translator and editor
> Vice is a monster of so frightful mien,
> As, to be hated, needs but to be seen;
> Yet soon too oft, familiar with her face,
> We first endure, then pity, then embrace.
>> *An Essay on Man* (1733)

Roosevelt, Theodore (1858–1919)
US Republican President
> No man is justified in doing evil on the ground of expediency.
>> *The Strenuous Life* (1900)

Sartre, Jean-Paul (1905–1980)
French philosopher, writer, dramatist and critic
> *On ne peut vaincre un mal que par un autre mal.*
> One can only overcome an evil by means of another evil.
>> *Les Mouches* (1943)

Shakespeare, William (1564–1616)
English dramatist, poet and actor
> How oft the sight of means to do ill deeds
> Make deeds ill done!
>> *King John*, IV.ii

> Through tatter'd clothes small vices do appear;
> Robed and furr'd gowns hide all.
>> *King Lear*, IV.vi

> Oftentimes to win us to our harm,
> The instruments of darkness tell us truths,
> Win us with honest trifles, to betray's
> In deepest consequence.
>> *Macbeth*, I.iii

> An evil soul producing holy witness
> Is like a villain with a smiling cheek,
> A goodly apple rotten at the heart.
> O, what a goodly outside falsehood hath!
>> *The Merchant of Venice*, I.iii

Socrates (469–399 BC)
Athenian philosopher
> No evil can befall a good man either in life or death.
>> Attr. in Plato, *Apology*

Vega, Garcilaso de la (c.1501–1536)
Spanish poet
> *Aquéste es de los hombres el oficio:*
> *tentar el mal, y si es malo el suceso,*
> *pedir con humildad perdón del vicio.*
> This is man's rôle:
> to try evil, and if the outcome be evil,
> to ask humbly for forgiveness for the act of depravity.
>> *Second Eclogue*

West, Mae (1892–1980)
US actress and scriptwriter
> Whenever I'm caught between two evils, I take the one I've never tried.
>> *Klondike Annie* (film, 1936)

Wilde, Oscar (1854–1900)
Irish poet, dramatist, writer, critic and wit
> Wickedness is a myth invented by good people to account for the curious attractiveness of others.
>> *The Chameleon*, 1894

Wollstonecraft, Mary (1759–1797)
English feminist, writer and teacher
> No man chooses evil because it is evil; he only

mistakes it for happiness, the good he seeks.

A Vindication of the Rights of Men (1790)

▶▶ GOOD AND EVIL; SIN

evolution

Blackwell, Antoinette Brown (1825–1921)
US writer

Mr Darwin ... has failed to hold definitely before his mind the principle that the difference of sex, whatever it may consist in, must itself be subject to natural selection and to evolution.

The Sexes Throughout Nature (1875)

Congreve, William (1670–1729)
English dramatist

I confess freely to you, I could never look long upon a monkey, without very mortifying reflections.

Letter to Mr Dennis, 1695

Darwin, Charles (1809–1882)
English naturalist

The expression often used by Mr Herbert Spencer of the Survival of the Fittest is more accurate, and is sometimes equally convenient.

The Origin of Species (1859)

We will now discuss in a little more detail the struggle for existence.

The Origin of Species (1859)

It is interesting to contemplate an entangled bank, clothed with many plants of many kinds, with birds singing on the bushes, with various insects flitting about, and with worms crawling through the damp earth, and to reflect that these elaborately constructed forms, so different from each other, and dependent upon each other in so complex a manner, have all been produced by laws acting around us ... Growth with Reproduction; Inheritance ... Variability ... a Ratio of Increase so high as to lead to a Struggle for Life, and as a consequence to Natural Selection, entailing Divergence of Character and the Extinction of less-improved forms.

The Origin of Species (1859)

I have called this principle, by which each slight variation, if useful, is preserved, by the term of Natural Selection.

The Origin of Species (1859)

We must, however, acknowledge, as it seems to me, that man with all his noble qualities ... still bears in his bodily frame the indelible stamp of his lowly origin.

The Descent of Man (1871)

Believing as I do that man in the distant future will be a far more perfect creature than he now is, it is an intolerable thought that he and all other sentient beings are doomed to complete annihilation after such long-continued slow progress. To those who fully admit the immortality of the human soul, the destruction of our world will not appear so dreadful.

Life and Letters (1973)

Darwin, Charles Galton (1887–1962)
English physicist; grandson of Charles Darwin

The evolution of the human race will not be accomplished in the ten thousand years of tame animals, but in the million years of wild animals, because man is and will always be a wild animal.

The Next Ten Million Years

Disraeli, Benjamin (1804–1881)
English statesman and writer

Is man an ape or an angel? Now I am on the side of the angels.

Speech, 1864

Huxley, T.H. (1825–1895)
English biologist, Darwinist and agnostic
Reply to Bishop Wilberforce during debate on Darwin's theory of evolution

I asserted – and I repeat – that a man has no reason to be ashamed of having an ape for his grandfather. If there were an ancestor whom I should feel shame in recalling it would rather be a man – a man of restless and versatile intellect – who, not content with an equivocal success in his own sphere of activity, plunges into scientific questions with which he has no real acquaintance, only to obscure them by an aimless rhetoric, and distract the attention of his hearers from the real point at issue by eloquent digressions and skilled appeals to religious prejudice.

Speech, Oxford, 1860

Rogers, Will (1879–1935)
US humorist, actor, rancher, writer and wit

Coolidge is a better example of evolution than either Bryan or Darrow, for he knows when not to talk, which is the biggest asset the monkey possesses over the human.

Saturday Review, 'A Rogers Thesaurus', 1962

Smith, Langdon (1858–1918)

When you were a tadpole, and I was a fish,
In the Palaezoic time,
And side by side in the ebbing tide
We sprawled through the ooze and slime.

'A Toast to a Lady' (1906)

Spencer, Herbert (1820–1903)
English philosopher and journalist

Evolution ... is – a change from an indefinite, incoherent homogeneity, to a definite coherent heterogeneity.

First Principles (1862)

It cannot but happen … that those will survive whose functions happen to be most nearly in equilibrium with the modified aggregate of external forces … This survival of the fittest implies multiplication of the fittest.

The Principles of Biology (1864)

Vonnegut, Kurt (1922–)

US author and journalist

I was taught that the human brain was the crowning glory of evolution so far, but I think it's a very poor scheme for survival.

The Observer, 1987

Wilberforce, Bishop Samuel (1805–1873)

English divine and writer

To T.H. Huxley

And, in conclusion, I would like to ask the gentleman … whether the ape from which he is descended was on his grandmother's or his grandfather's side of the family.

Speech at Oxford, 1860

▶▶ SURVIVAL

examinations

Colton, Charles Caleb (c.1780–1832)

English clergyman and satirist

Examinations are formidable even to the best prepared, for the greatest fool may ask more than the wisest man can answer.

Lacon (1820)

Saintsbury, George (1845–1933)

English critic and historian

From an examination paper

Without remarking that the thing became a trumpet in his hands, say something relevant about Milton's sonnets.

In Stephen Potter, The Muse in Chains (1937)

Sellar, Walter (1898–1951) and **Yeatman, Robert Julian** (1897–1968)

British writers

Do not on any account attempt to write on both sides of the paper at once.

1066 And All That (1930)

Wilde, Oscar (1854–1900)

Irish poet, dramatist, writer, critic and wit

In examinations the foolish ask questions that the wise cannot answer.

The Chameleon, 1894

▶▶ EDUCATION

excess

Best, George (1946–)

English footballer

I spent a lot of money on booze, birds and fast cars. The rest I just squandered.

Attr.

Blake, William (1757–1827)

English poet, engraver, painter and mystic

The road of excess leads to the palace of Wisdom.

'Proverbs of Hell' (1793)

Churchill, Charles (1731–1764)

English poet, political writer and clergyman

The best things carried to excess are wrong.

The Rosciad (1761)

Goldwater, Barry (1909–1998)

US presidential candidate and writer

I would remind you that extremism in the defence of liberty is no vice. And let me remind you also that moderation in the pursuit of justice is no virtue!

Speech, 1964

Letterman, David (1947–)

US talk show host

Sometimes something worth doing is worth overdoing.

CBS Late Show, 1994

Wilde, Oscar (1854–1900)

Irish poet, dramatist, writer, critic and wit

Moderation is a fatal thing, Lady Hunstanton. Nothing succeeds like excess.

A Woman of No Importance (1893)

▶▶ MODERATION

excuses

Lincoln, Abraham (1809–1865)

US statesman and President

He reminds me of the man who murdered both his parents, and then, when sentence was about to be pronounced, pleaded for mercy on the grounds that he was an orphan.

In Gross, Lincoln's Own Stories

Shakespeare, William (1564–1616)

English dramatist, poet and actor

Thou knowest in the state of innocency Adam fell; and what should poor Jack Falstaff do in the days of villainy? Thou seest I have more flesh than another man, and therefore more frailty.

Henry IV, Part 1, III.iii

Wilde, Oscar (1854–1900)
Irish poet, dramatist, writer, critic and wit

> I have invented an invaluable permanent invalid
> called Bunbury, in order that I may be able to go
> down into the country whenever I choose.
>> *The Importance of Being Earnest* (1895)

> I must decline your invitation owing to a
> subsequent engagement.
>> Attr.

execution

Aubrey, John (1626–1697)
English antiquary, folklorist and biographer

> The parliament intended to have hanged him;
> and he expected no less, but resolved to be
> hanged with the Bible under one arm and
> Magna Carta under the other.
>> *Brief Lives* (c.1693), 'David Jenkins'

Dryden, John (1631–1700)
English poet, satirist, dramatist and critic
Sarcastic reference to Jack Ketch, executioner, 1663–1686,
who was notorious for his barbarity

> A man may be capable, as Jack Ketch's wife said
> of his servant, of a plain piece of work, a bare
> hanging; but to make a malefactor die sweetly
> was only belonging to her husband.
>> *Of Satire* (1693)

Johnson, Samuel (1709–1784)
English lexicographer, poet, critic, conversationalist and
essayist

> Sir, executions are intended to draw spectators.
> If they do not draw spectators, they don't
> answer their purpose.
>> In *The Economist*, 1993

Sartre, Jean-Paul (1905–1980)
French philosopher, writer, dramatist and critic

> *Je déteste les victimes quand elles respectent leurs
> bourreaux.*
> I hate victims who respect their executioners.
>> *Les Séquestrés d'Altona* (1960)

Twain, Mark (1835–1910)
US humorist, writer, journalist and lecturer

> I admire him [Cecil Rhodes], I frankly confess it;
> and when his time comes I shall buy a piece of
> the rope for a keepsake.
>> *Following the Equator* (1897)

exercise

Cartland, Barbara (1901–2000)
English writer

> The two best exercises in the world are making
> love and dancing. But a simple one is to stand
> on tiptoe.
>> *The Guardian*, 2000

Dryden, John (1631–1700)
English poet, satirist, dramatist and critic

> Better to hunt in fields, for health unbought,
> Than fee the doctor for a nauseous draught.
> The wise, for cure, on exercise depend;
> God never made his work, for man to mend.
>> *Epistles* (1700)

Ford, Henry (1863–1947)
US car manufacturer

> Exercise is bunk. If you are healthy, you don't
> need it: if you are sick you shouldn't take it.
>> Attr.

Hutchins, Robert M. (1899–1977)

> Whenever I feel like exercise, I lie down until the
> feeling passes.
>> In Jarman, *The Guinness Dictionary of Sports
>> Quotations* (1990)

O'Toole, Peter (1932–)
English actor

> The only exercise I get these days is from
> walking behind the coffins of friends who took
> too much exercise.
>> *The Observer*, 'Sayings of the Year', 1998

Skelton, Red (1913–1997)
US comedian

> I get plenty of exercise carrying the coffins of
> my friends who exercise.
>> Attr.

▶▶ HEALTH

exile

Aytoun, W.E. (1813–1865)
Scottish poet, ballad writer and satirist

> They bore within their breasts the grief
> That fame can never heal –
> The deep, unutterable woe
> Which none save exiles feel.
>> 'The Island of the Scots' (1849)

> The earth is all the home I have,
> The heavens my wide roof-tree.
>> 'The Wandering Jew' (1867)

The Bible (King James Version)

> I have been a stranger in a strange land.
>> *Exodus*, 2:22

Bierce, Ambrose (1842–c.1914)
US writer, verse writer and soldier

> *Exile*: One who serves his country by residing

abroad, yet is not an ambassador.
The Enlarged Devil's Dictionary (1967)

Brown, Ford Madox (1821–1893)
French-born English painter and designer
The last of England! O'er the sea, my dear,
Our homes to seek amid Australian fields.
Us, not our million-acred island yields
The space to dwell in. Thrust out, forced to hear
Low ribaldry from sots, and share rough cheer
From rudely nurtured men.
'Sonnet'

Galt, John (1779–1839)
Scottish writer and Canadian pioneer
From the lone shieling of the misty island
Mountains divide us, and the waste of seas –
Yet still the blood is strong, the heart is
Highland,
And we in dreams behold the Hebrides!
Fair these broad meads, these hoary woods are
grand;
But we are exiles from our fathers' land.
Attr. in *Blackwoods Edinburgh Magazine*, 1829

Gregory VII (c.1020–1085)
Last words
I have loved righteousness and hated iniquity:
therefore I die in exile.
In Bowden, *The Life and Pontificate of Gregory VII*
(1840)

Santayana, George (1863–1952)
Spanish-born US philosopher and writer
People who feel themselves to be exiles in this
world are mightily inclined to believe themselves
citizens of another.
Attr.

Scott, Sir Walter (1771–1832)
Scottish writer and historian
From the lone shieling of the misty island
Mountains divide us and the waste of the seas –
Yet still the blood is strong, the heart is
Highland,
And we in dreams behold the Hebrides!
'Canadian Boat Song' (1829)

Spark, Muriel (1918–)
Scottish writer, poet and dramatist
It was Edinburgh that bred within me the
conditions of exiledom; and what have I been
doing since then but moving from exile to exile?
It has ceased to be a fate, it has become a
calling.
'What Images Return'

Stevenson, Robert Louis (1850–1894)
Scottish writer, poet and essayist
Blows the wind today, and the sun and the rain
are flying,
Blows the wind on the moors today and now,

Where about the graves of the martyrs the
whaups are crying,
My heart remembers how! …

Be it granted to me to behold you again in
dying,
Hills of home! and to hear again the call;
Hear about the graves of the martyrs the
peewees crying,
And hear no more at all.
Songs of Travel (1896)

existence

Hawking, Stephen (1942–)
English theoretical physicist
On the reason for the existence of the universe
If we find the answer to that, it would be the
ultimate triumph of human reason – for then we
would know the mind of God.
A Brief History of Time (1988)

experience

Ali, Muhammad (1942–)
US heavyweight boxer
The man who views the world at fifty the same
as he did at twenty has wasted thirty years of his
life.
Playboy, 1975

Anonymous
Experience is the comb that nature gives us
when we are bald.

Antrim, Minna (1861–1950)
US writer
Experience is a good teacher, but she sends in
terrific bills.
Naked Truth and Veiled Allusions (1902)

Bax, Sir Arnold (1883–1953)
English composer
You should make a point of trying every
experience once, excepting incest and folk-
dancing.
Farewell My Youth (1943)

Beerbohm, Sir Max (1872–1956)
English satirist, cartoonist, critic and essayist
You will think me lamentably crude: my
experience of life has been drawn from life itself.
Zuleika Dobson (1911)

Blake, William (1757–1827)
English poet, engraver, painter and mystic
What is the price of Experience? do

men buy it for a song?
Or wisdom for a dance in the street?
No, it is bought with the price
Of all that a man hath, his house, his
wife, his children.
Wisdom is sold in the desolate market
where none come to buy,
And in the wither'd field where the
farmer plows for bread in vain.

Vala, or the Four Zoas

Bowen, Elizabeth (1899–1973)
Irish writer
Experience isn't interesting till it begins to
repeat itself – in fact, till it does that, it hardly is
experience.

The Death of the Heart (1938)

Congreve, William (1670–1729)
English dramatist
Ay, ay, I have experience: I have a wife, and so
forth.

The Way of the World (1700)

Disraeli, Benjamin (1804–1881)
English statesman and writer
Experience is the child of Thought, and Thought
is the child of Action. We cannot learn men from
books.

Vivian Grey (1826)

Emerson, Ralph Waldo (1803–1882)
US poet, essayist, transcendentalist and teacher
The years teach much which the days never
know.

'Experience' (1844)

Fadiman, Clifton (1904–)
US writer, editor and broadcaster
Experience teaches you that the man who looks
you straight in the eye, particularly if he adds a
firm handshake, is hiding something.

Enter, Conversing

Froude, James Anthony (1818–1894)
English historian and scholar
Experience teaches slowly, and at the cost of
mistakes.

Short Studies on Great Subjects (1877)

Halifax, Lord (1633–1695)
English politician, courtier, pamphleteer and
epigrammatist
The best way to suppose what may come, is to
remember what is past.

*Political, Moral and Miscellaneous Thoughts and
Reflections* (1750)

Hegel, Georg Wilhelm (1770–1831)
German philosopher
*Was die Erfahrung aber und die Geschichte lehren, ist
dieses, dass Völker und Regierungen niemals etwas aus
der Geschichte gelernt haben.*
What experience and history teach us, however,
is this, that peoples and governments have
never learned anything from history.

Lectures on the Philosophy of History (1837)

Holmes, Oliver Wendell (1809–1894)
US physician, poet, writer and scientist
A moment's insight is sometimes worth a life's
experience.

The Professor at the Breakfast-Table (1860)

Huxley, Aldous (1894–1963)
English writer, poet and critic
experience is not what happens to a man. It is
what a man does with what happens to him.

Attr.

James, Henry (1843–1916)
US-born British writer, critic and letter writer
Experience is never limited, and it is never
complete; it is an immense sensibility, a kind of
huge spider-web of the finest silken threads
suspended in the chamber of consciousness, and
catching every air-borne particle in its tissue.

Partial Portraits (1888)

Keats, John (1795–1821)
English poet
Nothing ever becomes real till it is experienced
– Even a Proverb is no proverb to you till your
Life has illustrated it.

Letter to George and Georgiana Keats, 1819

MacCaig, Norman (1910–1996)
Scottish lecturer and poet
Experience teaches
that it doesn't.

A World of Difference (1983)

Meredith, George (1828–1909)
English writer, poet and critic
We spend our lives in learning pilotage,
And grow good steersmen when the vessel's
crank!

'The Wisdom of Eld'

Pomfret, John (1667–1702)
English poet and clergyman
We live and learn, but not the wiser grow.

'Reason' (1700)

Proverbs
Experience is the mother of wisdom.

Experience is the best teacher.

Waller, Edmund (1606–1687)
English poet and politician
The soul's dark cottage, batter'd and decay'd
Lets in new light through chinks that time has
made;
Stronger by weakness, wiser men become,

As they draw nearer to their eternal home.
Leaving the old, both worlds at once they view,
That stand upon the threshold of the new.

'Of the Last Verses in the Book' (1685)

Wilde, Oscar (1854–1900)
Irish poet, dramatist, writer, critic and wit
Dumby: Experience is the name every one gives
to their mistakes.
Cecil Graham: One shouldn't commit any.
Dumby: Life would be very dull without them.

Lady Windermere's Fan (1892)

Experience is the name every one gives to their
mistakes.

Lady Windermere's Fan (1892)

▶▶ HISTORY; PAST

experts

Bohr, Niels Henrik David (1885–1962)
Danish nuclear physicist
An expert is a man who has made all the
mistakes which can be made in a very narrow
field.

Attr.

Doyle, Sir Arthur Conan (1859–1930)
Scottish writer and war correspondent
All other men are specialists, but his specialism
is omniscience.

His Last Bow (1917)

Heisenberg, Werner (1901–1976)
German theoretical physicist
An expert is a man who knows some of the
worst errors that can be made in the subject in
question and who therefore understands how to
avoid them.

The Part and the Whole (1969)

Mayo, William James (1861–1939)
Specialist – A man who knows more and more
about less and less.

Attr.

Morgan, Elaine (1920–)
The trouble with specialists is that they tend to
think in grooves.

The Descent of Woman

explanations

Barrie, Sir J.M. (1860–1937)
Scottish dramatist and writer
I do loathe explanations.

My Lady Nicotine (1890)

Carroll, Lewis (1832–1898)
English writer and photographer
'Why,' said the Dodo, 'the best way to explain it
is to do it.'

Alice's Adventures in Wonderland
(1865)

'I can't explain myself, I'm afraid, sir,' said Alice,
'because I'm not myself, you see.' 'I don't see,'
said the Caterpillar.

Alice's Adventures in Wonderland (1865)

I can explain all the poems that ever were
invented – and a good many that haven't been
invented just yet.

*Through the Looking-Glass (and What Alice Found
There)* (1872)

Grayson, Victor (1881–c.1920)
British Labour politician
Never explain: your friends don't need it and
your enemies won't believe it.

Attr.

Marx, Chico (1886–1961)
US comedian
Explanation given when his wife caught him kissing a chorus
girl
But I wasn't kissing her. I was whispering in her
mouth.

In G. Marx and R. Anobile, *The Marx Brothers
Scrapbook* (1974)

eyes

Arnold, Matthew (1822–1888)
English poet, critic, essayist and educationist
Let beam upon my inward view
Those eyes of deep, soft, lucent hue –
Eyes too expressive to be blue,
Too lovely to be grey.

'Faded Leaves' (1852)

Bagehot, Walter (1826–1877)
English economist and political philosopher
There is a glare in some men's eyes which seems
to say, 'Beware, I am dangerous; *Noli me
tangere.*' Lord Brougham's face has this. A
mischievous excitability is the most obvious
expression of it. If he were a horse, nobody
would buy him; with that eye no one could
answer for his temper.

Historical Essays

Beerbohm, Sir Max (1872–1956)
English satirist, cartoonist, critic and essayist
It needs no dictionary of quotations to remind
me that the eyes are the windows of the soul.

Zuleika Dobson (1911)

The Bible (King James Version)
> If thine eye offend thee, pluck it out.
>> *Matthew, 18:9*

Coborn, Charles (1852–1945)
English comedian and singer
> Two lovely black eyes,
> Oh, what a surprise!
> Only for telling a man he was wrong.
> Two lovely black eyes!
>> 'Two Lovely Black Eyes' (song, 1886)

Colette (1873–1954)
French writer
> When she raises her eyelids she seems to be
> taking her clothes off at the same time.
>> *Claudine Goes Away* (1903)

Crashaw, Richard (c.1612–1649)
English religious poet
> Two walking baths; two weeping motions;
> Portable, and compendious oceans.
>> 'Saint Mary Magdalene, or The Weeper' (1652)

Dickens, Charles (1812–1870)
English writer
> 'Yes, I have a pair of eyes,' replied Sam, 'and
> that's just it. If they wos a pair o' patent double
> million magnifyin' gas microscopes of hextra
> power, p'raps I might be able to see through a
> flight o' stairs and a deal door; but bein' only
> eyes, you see my wision's limited.'
>> *The Pickwick Papers* (1837)

Fletcher, Phineas (1582–1650)
English poet and clergyman
> Love's tongue is in the eyes.
>> 'Piscatory Eclogues' (1633)

Herrick, Robert (1591–1674)
English poet, royalist and clergyman
> Sweet, be not proud of those two eyes,
> Which Star-like sparkle in their skies …
>
> That Rubie which you weare,
> Sunk from the tip of your soft eare,
> Will last to be a precious Stone,
> When all your world of Beautie's gone.
>> *Hesperides* (1648)

Hodges, Mike (1932–)
English film director
> *Carter*: So you're doing all right then, Eric.
> You're making good … Do you know, I'd almost
> forgotten what your eyes looked like. They're
> still the same. Piss holes in the snow.
>> *Get Carter* (film, 1971)

John, Elton (1947–)
English singer
> So excuse me forgetting, but these things I do
> You see I've forgotten, if they're green or
> they're blue
> Anyway, the thing is, what I really mean
> Yours are the sweetest eyes, I've ever seen.
>> 'Your Song' (1971)

Mercer, Johnny (1909–1976)
US lyricist and composer
> Jeepers Creepers – where'd you get them
> peepers?
>> 'Jeepers Creepers' (song, 1938)

Pope, Alexander (1688–1744)
English poet, translator and editor
> Bright as the sun, her eyes the gazers strike,
> And, like the sun, they shine on all alike.
>> *The Rape of the Lock* (1714)
>
> Why has not Man a microscopic eye?
> For this plain reason, Man is not a fly.
> Say what the use, were finer optics giv'n,
> T' inspect a mite, not comprehend the heav'n?
>> *An Essay on Man* (1733)

Pound, Ezra (1885–1972)
US poet
> Free us, for we perish
> In this ever-flowing monotony
> Of ugly print marks, black
> Upon white parchment.
>> 'The Eyes' (1908)

Shakespeare, William (1564–1616)
English dramatist, poet and actor
> For where is any author in the world
> Teaches such beauty as a woman's eye?
>> *Love's Labour Lost*, IV.iii
>
> Men's eyes were made to look, and let them
> gaze;
> I will not budge for no man's pleasure, I.
>> *Romeo and Juliet*, III.i

Spark, Muriel (1918–)
Scottish writer, poet and dramatist
> But I did not remove my glasses, for I had not
> asked for her company in the first place, and
> there is a limit to what one can listen to with the
> naked eye.
>> *Voices at Play* (1961)

Sterne, Laurence (1713–1768)
Irish-born English writer and clergyman
> 'I am half distracted, Captain Shandy,' said Mrs
> Wadman, … 'a mote – or sand – or something –
> I know not what, has got into this eye of mine –
> do look in to it.'… In saying which, Mrs Wadman
> edged herself close in beside my uncle Toby, …
> 'Do look into it,' – said she …
> If thou lookest, uncle Toby, in search of this
> mote one moment longer – thou art undone.

Tristram Shandy (1759–1767)

An eye full of gentle salutations – and soft responses – ... whispering soft – like the last low accents of an expiring saint ... It did my uncle Toby's business.

Tristram Shandy (1759–1767)

Zola, Emile (1840–1902)
French writer

Stop looking at me like that, or you'll wear your eyes out.

La Bête Humaine (1889–1890)

▶▶ APPEARANCE; CRYING

F

facts

Agassiz, Louis (1807–1873)
Swiss-born US naturalist
> Facts are stupid until brought into connection with some general law.
>> In Laurence J. Peter, *Peter's Quotations* (1977)

Barrie, Sir J.M. (1860–1937)
Scottish dramatist and writer
> Facts were never pleasing to him. He acquired them with reluctance and got rid of them with relief. He was never on terms with them until he had stood them on their heads.
>> *The Greenwood Hat* (1937)

Burns, Robert (1759–1796)
Scottish poet and song writer
> But facts are chiels that winna ding,
> And downa be disputed.
>> 'A Dream' (1786)

Doyle, Sir Arthur Conan (1859–1930)
Scottish writer and war correspondent
> 'I should have more faith,' he said; 'I ought to know by this time that when a fact appears opposed to a long train of deductions it invariably proves to be capable of bearing some other interpretation.'
>> *A Study in Scarlet* (1887)

Huxley, Aldous (1894–1963)
English writer, poet and critic
> Facts do not cease to exist because they are ignored.
>> *Proper Studies* (1927)

James, Henry (1843–1916)
US-born British writer, critic and letter writer
> The fatal futility of Fact.
>> *Prefaces* (1897)

Jerrold, Douglas William (1803–1857)
English dramatist, writer and wit
> Talk to him of Jacob's ladder, and he would ask the number of the steps.
>> *Wit and Opinions of Douglas Jerrold* (1859)

Ryle, Gilbert (1900–1976)
English philosopher
> A myth is, of course, not a fairy story. It is the presentation of facts belonging to one category in the idioms appropriate to another. To explode a myth is accordingly not to deny the facts but to re-allocate them.
>> *The Concept of Mind* (1949)

Tindal, Matthew (1657–1733)
English deist and writer
> Matters of fact, which as Mr Budgell somewhere observes, are very stubborn things.
>> *The Will of Matthew Tindal* (1733)

▶▶ TRUTH

failure

Barrie, Sir J. M. (1860–1937)
Scottish dramatist and writer
> We are all failures – at least, the best of us are.
>> Rectorial address at St Andrew's University, 3 May 1922

Beckett, Samuel (1906–1989)
Irish dramatist, writer and poet
> Ever tried. Ever failed. No matter. Try Again. Fail again. Fail better.
>> *Worstward Ho* (1984)

Ciano, Count Galeazzo (1903–1944)
Italian politician
> As always, victory finds a hundred fathers, but defeat is an orphan.
>> *Diary*, 1942

Coward, Sir Noël (1899–1973)
English dramatist, actor, producer and composer
On Randolph Churchill
> Dear Randolph, utterly unspoiled by failure.
>> Attr.

Dylan, Bob (1941–)
US singer and songwriter
> She knows there's no success like failure
> And that failure's no success at all.
>> 'Love Minus Zero/No Limit' (song, 1965)

Hare, Augustus (1792–1834)
English clergyman and writer
> Half the failures in life arise from pulling in one's horse as he is leaping.
>> *Guesses at Truth* (1827)

Healey, Denis (1917–)
English Labour politician
> Examining one's entrails while fighting a battle is a recipe for certain defeat.
>> *The Observer*, 1983

Heller, Joseph (1923–1999)
US writer
> He was a self-made man who owed his lack of success to nobody.
>> *Catch-22* (1961)

Hemingway, Ernest (1898–1961)
US author
> But man is not made for defeat … A man can be

destroyed but not defeated.

The Old Man and the Sea (1952)

Keats, John (1795–1821)
English poet
> I would sooner fail than not be among the greatest.

Letter to James Hessey, 1818

Newman, Paul (1925–)
US actor
> Show me a good loser and I'll show you a loser.

The Observer, 1982

Renard, Jules (1864–1910)
French writer and dramatist
> Failure is not the only punishment for laziness: there is also the success of others.

Journal, 1898

Rockne, Knut (1888–1931)
US football coach
> Show me a good and gracious loser and I'll show you a failure.

Attr.

Shakespeare, William (1564–1616)
English dramatist, poet and actor
> Macbeth: If we should fail?
> Lady Macbeth: We fail!
> But screw your courage to the sticking place,
> And we'll not fail.

Macbeth, I.vii

Stevenson, Robert Louis (1850–1894)
Scottish writer, poet and essayist
> Here lies one who meant well, tried a little, failed much: – surely that may be his epitaph, of which he need not be ashamed.

Across the Plains (1892)

Victoria, Queen (1819–1901)
Queen of the United Kingdom
Said of the Boer War in 'Black Week', 1899
> We are not interested in the possibilities of defeat; they do not exist.

In Cecil, Life of Robert, Marquis of Salisbury (1931)

Voltaire (1694–1778)
French philosopher, dramatist, poet, historian writer and critic
> Never having been able to succeed in the world, he took his revenge by speaking ill of it.

Zadig, or Fate (1747)

Welles, Orson (1915–1985)
US actor, director and producer
> When you are down and out something always turns up – and it is usually the noses of your friends.

New York Times, 1962

Wilde, Oscar (1854–1900)
Irish poet, dramatist, writer, critic and wit
> We women adore failures. They lean on us.

A Woman of No Importance (1893)

▶▶ SUCCESS

fairness

Alda, Alan (1936–)
US actor and director
> Here's my Golden Rule for a tarnished age: Be fair with others, but keep after them until they're fair with you.

Connecticut College News, 1980

faith

Alcuin (735–804)
English theologian, scholar and educationist
> Men can be attracted but not forced to the faith. You may drive people to baptism, (but) you won't move them one step further in religion.

In Frank S. Mead, 12,000 Religious Quotations (1989)

Arnold, Matthew (1822–1888)
English poet, critic, essayist and educationist
> The Sea of Faith
> Was once, too, at the full, and round earth's shore
> Lay like the folds of a bright girdle furl'd.
> But now I only hear
> Its melancholy, long, withdrawing roar,
> Retreating, to the breath
> Of the night-wind, down the vast edges drear
> And naked shingles of the world.

'Dover Beach' (1867)

Benn, Tony (1925–)
English Labour politician
> A faith is something you die for; a doctrine is something you kill for: there is all the difference in the world.

The Observer, 1989

The Bible (King James Version)
> Faith is the substance of things hoped for, the evidence of things not seen.

Hebrews, 11: 1

> Faith without works is dead.

James, 2: 20

Browne, Sir Thomas (1605–1682)
English physician, author and antiquary
> To believe only possibilities, is not faith, but mere Philosophy.

Religio Medici (1643)

Buck, Pearl S. (1892–1973)
US writer and dramatist
> I feel no need for any other faith than my faith in human beings.
>> *I Believe* (1939)

Chesterton, G.K. (1874–1936)
English writer, poet and critic
> Reason is itself a matter of faith. It is an act of faith to assert that our thoughts have any relation to reality at all.
>> *Orthodoxy* (1908)

Coward, Sir Noël (1899–1973)
English dramatist, actor, producer and composer
> Life without faith is an arid business.
>> *Blithe Spirit* (1941)

Melville, Herman (1819–1891)
US writer and poet
> Faith, like a Jackal, feeds among the tombs, and even from these dead doubts she gathers her most vital hope.
>> Attr.

Mencken, H.L. (1880–1956)
US writer, critic, philologist and satirist
> Faith may be defined briefly as an illogical belief in the occurrence of the improbable.
>> *Prejudices* (1927)

Stevenson, Robert Louis (1850–1894)
Scottish writer, poet and essayist
> Life is not all Beer and Skittles. The inherent tragedy of things works itself out from white to black and blacker, and the poor things of a day look ruefully on. Does it shake my cast iron faith? I cannot say it does. I believe in an ultimate decency of things; ay, and if I woke in hell, should still believe it!
>> Letter to Sidney Colvin, 1893

Storr, Dr Anthony (1920–)
British writer and psychiatrist
> One man's faith is another man's delusion.
>> *Feet of Clay* (1996)

Voltaire (1694–1778)
French philosopher, dramatist, poet, historian writer and critic
> Faith consists in believing what reason does not believe … It is not enough that a thing may be possible for it to be believed.
>> *Questions sur l'Encyclopédie* (1770–1772)

▶▶ BELIEF; RELIGION

fame

Alcott, Louisa May (1832–1888)
US writer

> Fame is a pearl many dive for and only a few bring up. Even when they do, it is not perfect, and they sigh for more, and lose better things in struggling for them.
>> *Jo's Boys* (1886)

Anonymous
> Fame is a mask that eats the face.

Bennett, Alan (1934–)
English dramatist, actor and diarist
> My claim to literary fame is that I used to deliver meat to a woman who became T.S. Eliot's mother-in-law.
>> *The Observer*, 'Sayings of the Year', 1992

Berners, Lord (1883–1950)
Of T.E. Lawrence
> He's always backing into the limelight.
>> Attr.

Boorstin, Daniel (1914–)
US librarian, historian, lawyer and writer
> The celebrity is a person who is known for his well-knownness.
>> *The Image* (1962)

Bridges, Robert (1844–1930)
English poet, dramatist, essayist and doctor
> Rejoice ye dead, where'er your spirits dwell,
> Rejoice that yet on earth your fame is bright,
> And that your names, remembered day and night,
> Live on the lips of those who love you well.
>> 'Ode to Music' (1896)

Burke, Edmund (1729–1797)
Irish-born British statesman and philosopher
> Passion for fame; a passion which is the instinct of all great souls.
>> *Speech on American Taxation* (1774)

Byron, Lord (1788–1824)
English poet satirist and traveller
Remark on the instantaneous success of Childe Harold
> I awoke one morning and found myself famous.
>> In Moore, *Letters and Journals of Lord Byron* (1830)

Calderón de la Barca, Pedro (1600–1681)
Spanish dramatist and poet
> Fame, like water, bears up the lighter things, and lets the weighty sink.
>> Attr.

Carew, Thomas (c.1595–1640)
English poet, musician and dramatist
> Know, Celia (since thou art so proud,)
> 'Twas I that gave thee thy renowne:
> Thou had'st in the forgotten crowd
> Of common beauties, liv'd unknowne,
> Had not my verse exhal'd thy name,
> And with it imped the wings of fame.
>> 'Ingratefull Beauty Threatened' (1640)

Cato the Elder (234–149 BC)
Roman statesman
> I would much rather have men ask why I have no statue than why I have one.
>> In Plutarch, *Lives*

Dante Alighieri (1265–1321)
Italian poet
> *Ché, seggendo in piuma,*
> *In fama non si vien, né sotto coltre.*
> For fame is not achieved by sitting on feather cushions or lying in bed.
>> *Divina Commedia* (1307)

Danton, Georges (1759–1794)
French revolutionary leader
Response to formal questions during his trial in Paris, 2 April 1794
> My address will soon be Annihilation. As for my name you will find it in the Pantheon of History.
>> Attr.

Davis Jnr., Sammy (1925–1990)
US actor, singer and dancer
> Fame creates its own standard. A guy who twitches his lips is just another guy with a lip twitch – unless he's Humphrey Bogart.
>> *Yes I Can* (1965)

Dobson, Henry Austin (1840–1921)
English poet, essayist and biographer
> Fame is a food that dead men eat, –
> I have no stomach for such meat.
>> 'Fame is a Food' (1906)

Farber, Barry (1859–1930)
> I was the only one there I never heard of.
>> In Lieberman, *3,500 Good Quotes for Speakers* (1983)

Goethe (1749–1832)
German poet, writer, dramatist and scientist
> *Die Tat ist alles, nichts der Ruhm.*
> The deed is all, the glory is naught.
>> *Faust* (1832)

Grainger, James (c.1721–1766)
Scottish poet, army surgeon and editor
> What is fame? an empty bubble;
> Gold? a transient, shining trouble.
>> 'Solitude' (1755)

Greene, Graham (1904–1991)
English writer and dramatist
> Fame is a powerful aphrodisiac.
>> *Radio Times*, 1964

Hepburn, Katharine (1909–)
US actress
> I don't care what is written about me as long as it isn't true.
>> In Cooper and Hartman, *Violets and Vinegar* (1980)

Hillel, 'The Elder' (c.60 BC–c.10 AD)
> A name made great is a name destroyed.
>> In Taylor (ed.), *Sayings of the Jewish Fathers* (1877)

Hugo, Victor (1802–1885)
French poet, writer, dramatist and politician
> *La popularité? c'est la gloire en gros sous.*
> Fame? It's glory in small change.
>> *Ruy Blas* (1838)

Huxley, Aldous (1894–1963)
English writer, poet and critic
> I'm afraid of losing my obscurity. Genuineness only thrives in the dark. Like celery.
>> *Those Barren Leaves* (1925)

Huxley, T.H. (1825–1895)
English biologist, Darwinist and agnostic
Remark to George Howell
> Posthumous fame is not particularly attractive to me, but, if I am to be remembered at all, I would rather it should be as 'a man who did his best to help the people' than by any other title.
>> In L. Huxley, *Life and Letters of Thomas Henry Huxley* (1900)

Keats, John (1795–1821)
English poet
> Fame, like a wayward girl, will still be coy
> To those who woo her with too slavish knees.
>> 'On Fame (1)' (1819)

Lebowitz, Fran (1946–)
US writer
> The best fame is a writer's fame: it's enough to get a table at a good restaurant, but not enough that you get interrupted when you eat.
>> *The Observer*, 1993

Melba, Dame Nellie (1861–1931)
Australian opera singer
To the editor of the Argus
> I don't care what you say, for me or against me, but for heaven's sake say something about me.
>> In Thompson, *On Lips of Living Men*

Montaigne, Michel de (1533–1592)
French essayist and moralist
> *La gloire et le repos sont choses qui ne peuvent loger en même gîte.*
> Fame and tranquillity cannot dwell under the same roof.
>> *Essais* (1580)

Murdoch, Iris (1919–1999)
Irish-born British writer, philosopher and dramatist
> 'What are you famous for?'
> 'For nothing. I am just famous.'
>> *The Flight from the Enchanter* (1955)

Peck, Gregory (1916–)
US actor
On the fact that no-one in a crowded restaurant recognized him

If you have to tell them who you are, you aren't anybody.

In S. Harris, Pieces of Eight

Pericles (c.495–429)
Athenian statesman, general, orator and cultural patron
For the whole earth is the supulchre of famous men.

In Thucydides, Histories

Pindar, Peter (John Wolcot) (1738–1819)
English satirical poet
What rage for fame attends both great and small!
Better be damned than mentioned not at all!

'To the Royal Academicians' (1782–1785)

Pope, Alexander (1688–1744)
English poet, translator and editor
Then teach me, Heav'n! to scorn the guilty bays,
Drive from my breast that wretched lust of praise,
Unblemished let me live, or die unknown;
Oh grant an honest fame, or grant me none!

The Temple of Fame (1715)

Roosevelt, Theodore (1858–1919)
US Republican President
It is better to be faithful than famous.

In Riis, Theodore Roosevelt, the Citizen

Salinger, J.D. (1919–)
US writer
They didn't act like people and they didn't act like actors. It's hard to explain. They acted more like they knew they were celebrities and all. I mean they were good, but they were too good.

The Catcher in the Rye (1951)

Sitwell, Dame Edith (1887–1964)
English poet, anthologist, critic and biographer
A pompous woman of his acquaintance, complaining that the head-waiter of a restaurant had not shown her and her husband immediately to a table, said 'We had to tell him who we were.' Gerald, interested, enquired, 'And who were you?'.

Taken Care Of (1965)

Spenser, Edmund (c.1522–1599)
English poet
One day I wrote her name upon the strand,
But came the waves and washed it away:
Agayne I wrote it with a second hand,
But came the tyde, and made my paynes his pray.
Vayne man, sayd she, that doest in vaine assay,
A mortall thing so to immortalize,
For I my selfe shall lyke to this decay,
And eek my name bee wyped out lykewize.
Not so, (quod I) let baser things devize
To dy in dust, but you shall live by fame:

My verse your vertues rare shall eternize,
And in the hevens wryte your glorious name.
Where whenas death shall all the world subdew,
Our love shall live, and later life renew.

Amoretti, and Epithalamion (1595)

Tacitus (AD c.56–c.120)
Roman historian
The desire for fame is the last thing to be put aside, even by the wise.

Histories

Warhol, Andy (c.1926–1987)
US painter, graphic designer and filmmaker
In the future everyone will be world famous for fifteen minutes.

Catalogue for an exhibition, 1968

Webster, John (c.1580–c.1625)
English dramatist
Vain the ambition of kings
Who seek by trophies and dead things,
To leave a living name behind,
And weave but nets to catch the wind.

The Devil's Law-Case (1623)

Wilde, Oscar (1854–1900)
Irish poet, dramatist, writer, critic and wit
There is only one thing in the world worse than being talked about, and that is not being talked about.

The Picture of Dorian Gray (1891)

▶▶ CELEBRITY; POPULARITY; REPUTATION

familiarity

Stein, Gertrude (1874–1946)
US writer, dramatist, poet and critic
I like familiarity. In me it does not breed contempt. Only more familiarity.

Dale Carnegie's Scrapbook

Proverb
Familiarity breeds contempt.

families

Beerbohm, Sir Max (1872–1956)
English satirist, cartoonist, critic and essayist
They were a tense and peculiar family, the Oedipuses, weren't they?

Attr.

Belloc, Hilaire (1870–1953)
English writer of verse, essayist and critic; Liberal MP
Mothers of large families (who claim to common sense)

Will find a Tiger well repays the trouble and
expense.

The Bad Child's Book of Beasts (1896)

Browne, Sir Thomas (1605–1682)
English physician, author and antiquary
Generations pass while some tree stands, and
old families last not three oaks.

Hydriotaphia: Urn Burial (1658)

Butler, Samuel (1835–1902)
English writer, painter, philosopher and scholar
I believe that more unhappiness comes from this
source than from any other – I mean from the
attempt to prolong family connection unduly
and to make people hang together artificially
who would never naturally do so. The mischief
among the lower classes is not so great, but
among the middle and upper classes it is killing
a large number daily. And the old people do not
really like it much better than the young.

The Note-Books of Samuel Butler (1912)

Congreve, William (1670–1729)
English dramatist
A branch of one of your antediluvian families,
fellows that the flood could not wash away.

Love for Love (1695)

Dickens, Charles (1812–1870)
English writer
It is a melancholy truth that even great men
have their poor relations.

Bleak House (1853)

Accidents will occur in the best-regulated
families.

David Copperfield (1850)

Elizabeth II (1926–)
Queen of the United Kingdom
Like all the best families, we have our share of
eccentricities, of impetuous and wayward
youngsters and of family disagreements.

Daily Mail, 1989

Forster, E.M. (1879–1970)
English writer, essayist and literary critic
I felt for a moment that the whole Wilcox family
was a fraud, just a wall of newspapers and
motor-cars and golf-clubs, and that if it fell I
should find nothing behind it but panic and
emptiness.

Howard's End (1910)

Frazer, Sir James (1854–1941)
Scottish anthropologist and writer
The awe and dread with which the untutored
savage contemplates his mother-in-law
are amongst the most familiar facts of
anthropology.

The Golden Bough (1900)

Freud, Sigmund (1856–1939)
Austrian physicist; founder of psychoanalysis
Philosophers and politicians have agreed that
the bonding together in family groups is both
instinctive and necessary to human welfare – and
therefore essential to the health of a society.
The family is the microcosm.

Attr. in *The Times*, May 1996

Goldsmith, Oliver (c.1728–1774)
Irish dramatist, poet and writer
I was ever of opinion, that the honest man who
married and brought up a large family, did more
service than he who continued single, and only
talked of population.

The Vicar of Wakefield (1766)

Hazlitt, William (1778–1830)
English writer and critic
A person may be indebted for a nose or an eye,
for a graceful carriage or a voluble discourse, to
a great-aunt or uncle, whose existence he has
scarcely heard of.

London Magazine, 1821

Hope, Anthony (1863–1933)
English writer, dramatist and lawyer
Good families are generally worse than any others.

The Prisoner of Zenda (1894)

John Paul II (1920–)
Polish pope
Treasure your families – the future of humanity
passes by way of the family.

Speech, 1982

Jackson, Shirley (1919–1965)
US novelist
It has long been my belief that in times of great
stress, such as a 4-day vacation, the thin veneer
of family wears off almost at once, and we are
revealed in our true personalities.

Raising Demons (1956)

John Paul II (1920–)
Polish pope
As the family goes, so goes the nation and so
goes the whole world in which we live.

The Observer, 1986

Juvenal (c.60–130)
Roman verse satirist and Stoic
Desperanda tibi salva concordia socru.
Despair of peace as long as your mother-in-law
is alive.

Satires

Lamb, Charles (1775–1834)
English essayist, critic and letter writer
A poor relation – is the most irrelevant thing in
nature.

Last Essays of Elia (1833)

Leach, Sir Edmund (1910–1989)
English social anthropologist
>Far from being the basis of the good society, the family, with its narrow privacy and tawdry secrets, is the source of all our discontents.
>>*BBC Reith Lecture, 1967*

Lennon, John (1940–1980)
English rock musician
>She's leaving home after living alone for so many years.
>>'She's Leaving Home', song, 1967, with Paul McCartney

Lincoln, Abraham (1809–1865)
US statesman and President
>I don't know who my grandfather was; I am much more concerned to know what his grandson will be.
>>In Gross, *Lincoln's Own Stories*

Macaulay, Dame Rose (1881–1958)
English writer
>A group of closely related persons living under one roof; it is a convenience, often a necessity, sometimes a pleasure, sometimes the reverse; but who first exalted it as admirable, an almost religious ideal?
>>*The World My Wilderness* (1950)

Marx, Groucho (1895–1977)
US comedian
>You're a disgrace to our family name of Wagstaff, if such a thing is possible.
>>*Horse Feathers* (film, 1932)

Mitchell, Julian (1935–)
English writer
>The sink is the great symbol of the bloodiness of family life. All life is bad, but family life is worse.
>>*As Far as You Can Go* (1963)

Montaigne, Michel de (1533–1592)
French essayist and moralist
>*Il n'y a guère moins de tourment au gouvernement d'une famille que d'un état entier ... et, pour être les occupations domestiques moins importantes, elles n'en sont pas moins importunes.*
>There is scarcely any less trouble in running a family than in governing an entire state ... and domestic matters are no less importunate for being less important.
>>*Essais* (1580)

Mooney, Bel (1946–)
British writer
On the need for family life
>I find myself surprised at how its realism actually unites morality with – yes – romance. It is that need that draws us to nest in rows, separated by thin walls, hoping to be tolerated and loved forever – and to go on reproducing ourselves in family patterns, handing on some misery (perhaps), but untold happiness too.
>>*The Times*, 1996

Nash, Ogden (1902–1971)
US poet
>One would be in less danger
>From the wiles of a stranger
>If one's own kin and kith
>Were more fun to be with.
>>'Family Court' (1931)

Pound, Ezra (1885–1972)
US poet
>Oh how hideous it is
>To see three generations of one house gathered together!
>It is like an old tree with shoots,
>And with some branches rotted and falling.
>>'Commission' (1916)

Proverb
>Every family has a skeleton in the cupboard.

Rossetti, Christina (1830–1894)
English poet
>For there is no friend like a sister
>In calm or stormy weather;
>To cheer one on the tedious way,
>To fetch one if one goes astray,
>To lift one if one totters down,
>To strengthen whilst one stands.
>>'Goblin Market' (1862)

Shakespeare, William (1564–1616)
English dramatist, poet and actor
>A little more than kin, and less than kind.
>>*Hamlet*, I.ii

Thackeray, William Makepeace (1811–1863)
Indian-born English writer
>If a man's character is to be abused, say what you will, there's nobody like a relation to do the business.
>>*Vanity Fair* (1848)

Tolstoy, Leo (1828–1910)
Russian writer, essayist, philosopher and moralist
>All happy families resemble one another, but every unhappy family is unhappy in its own way.
>>*Anna Karenina* (1877)

Wodehouse, P.G. (1881–1975)
English humorist and writer
>It is no use telling me that there are bad aunts and good aunts. At the core they are all alike. Sooner or later, out pops the cloven hoof.
>>*The Code of the Woosters* (1938)

▶▶ ANCESTORS; BABIES; BIRTH; CHILDREN; FATHERS; MARRIAGE; MOTHERS; PREGNANCY

fantasy

Ibsen, Henrik (1828–1906)
Norwegian writer, dramatist and poet
> Castles in the air – they're so easy to take
> refuge in. So easy to build, too.
>> *The Master Builder* (1892)

Monroe, Marilyn (1926–1962)
US film actress and model
> I guess I am a fantasy.
>> In Steinem, *Outrageous Acts and Everyday
>> Rebellions* (1984)

Yeats, W.B. (1865–1939)
Irish poet, dramatist, editor, writer and senator
> We had fed the heart on fantasies,
> The heart's grown brutal from the fare.
>> 'Meditations in Time of Civil War' (1928)

fascism

Bevan, Aneurin (1897–1960)
Welsh Labour politician, miner and orator
> Fascism is not in itself a new order of society. It
> is the future refusing to be born.
>> Attr.

Castellani, Maria (fl 1930s)
Italian educator and writer
> Fascism recognises women as part of the life
> force of the country, laying down a division of
> duties between the two sexes, without putting
> obstacles in the way of those women who by
> their intellectual gifts reach the highest
> positions.
>> *Italian Women, Past and Present* (1937)

Ibárruri, Dolores ('La Pasionaria') (1895–1989)
Basque Communist leader
> Wherever they pass, they the fascists sow death
> and desolation.
>> *Speeches and Articles* (1938)

McKenney, Ruth (1911–1972)
US writer
> If modern civilisation had any meaning it was
> displayed in the fight against Fascism.
>> In Seldes, *The Great Quotations* (1960)

Mosley, Sir Oswald (1896–1980)
British founder of the British Union of Fascists
> Before the organization of the Blackshirt
> movement free speech did not exist in this
> country.
>> In *New Statesman, This England*

Mussolini, Benito (1883–1945)
Italian fascist dictator

On Hitler's seizing power
> Fascism is a religion; the twentieth century will
> be known in history as the century of Fascism.
>> In Seldes, *Sawdust Caesar*

> *Per noi fascisti le frontiere, tutte le frontiere, sono
> sacre. Non si discutono: si defendono.*
> For us fascists, frontiers, all frontiers, are sacred.
> We do not dispute them: we defend them.
>> Speech to the Lower House, 1938

> Fascism is not an article for export.
>> Article in the German press, 1932

Plath, Sylvia (1932–1963)
US poet, writer and diarist
> Every woman adores a Fascist,
> The boot in the face, the brute
> Brute heart of a brute like you.
>> 'Daddy' (1963)

Strachey, John St Loe (1901–1963)
English politician
> Fascism means war.
>> Slogan, 1930s

fashion

Austen, Jane (1775–1817)
English writer
> A person and face, of strong, natural, sterling
> insignificance, though adorned in the first style
> of fashion.
>> *Sense and Sensibility* (1811)

Bailey, David (1938–)
English photographer
> I never cared for fashion much, amusing little
> seams and witty little pleats: it was the girls I
> liked.
>> *The Independent*, 1990

Beaton, Cecil (1904–1980)
English photographer
On the miniskirt
> Never in the history of fashion has so little
> material been raised so high to reveal so much
> that needs to be covered so badly.
>> Attr.

Cassini, Oleg (1913–)
> Fashion anticipates, and elegance is a state of mind.
>> *In My Own Fashion* (1987)

Chanel, Coco (1883–1971)
French couturier and perfumer
Remark at a press conference, 1967
> Fashion is reduced to a question of hem lengths.
> Haute couture is finished because it's in the
> hands of men who don't like women.
>> In Madsen, *Coco Chanel* (1990)

A fashion for the young? That is a pleonasm: there is no fashion for the old.

> In Haedrich, *Coco Chanel, Her Life, Her Secrets* (1971)

Churchill, Charles (1731–1764)
English poet, political writer and clergyman
> Fashion – a word which knaves and fools may use,
> Their knavery and folly to excuse.

> *The Rosciad* (1761)

Cibber, Colley (1671–1757)
English actor, dramatist and poet
> One had as good be out of the world, as out of the fashion.

> *Love's Last Shift* (1696)

Goldsmith, Oliver (c.1728–1774)
Irish dramatist, poet and writer
> And, even while fashion's brightest arts decoy,
> The heart distrusting asks, if this be joy.

> *The Deserted Village* (1770)

Radner, Gilda (1946–1989)
US actress and comedian
> I base most of my fashion taste on what doesn't itch.

> *It's Always Something* (1989)

Steele, Sir Richard (1672–1729)
Irish-born English writer, dramatist and politician
> Fashion, the arbiter, and rule of right.

> *The Spectator*, 478

Walpole, Horace (1717–1797)
English writer and politician
> It is charming to totter into vogue.

> Letter to George Selwyn, 1765

▶▶ APPEARANCE; STYLE

fathers

Aubrey, John (1626–1697)
English antiquary, folklorist and biographer
Of Sir Walter Raleigh
> Sir Walter, being strangely surprised and put out of his countenance at so great a table, gives his son a damned blow over the face. His son, as rude as he was, would not strike his father, but strikes over the face the gentleman that sat next to him and said 'Box about: 'twill come to my father anon.'

> *Brief Lives* (c.1693)

The Bible (King James Version)
> The fathers have eaten sour grapes, and the children's teeth are set on edge.

> *Ezekiel*, 18:2

Burton, Robert (1577–1640)
English clergyman and writer
> Diogenes struck the father when the son swore.

> *Anatomy of Melancholy* (1621)

Chesterfield, Lord (1694–1773)
English politician and letter writer
> As fathers commonly go, it is seldom a misfortune to be fatherless; and considering the general run of sons, as seldom a misfortune to be childless.

> Attr.

Code Napoléon
> *La recherche de la paternité est interdite.*
> Investigations into paternity are forbidden.

> Article 340

Colman, the Younger, George (1762–1836)
English dramatist and Examiner of Plays
> My father was an eminent button maker – but I had a soul above buttons – I panted for a liberal profession.

> *Sylvester Daggerwood: or New Hay at the Old Market* (1795)

Harrison, Tony (1937–)
English poet
> When the chilled dough of his flesh went in an oven
> not unlike those he fuelled all his life,
> I thought of his cataracts ablaze with Heaven
> and radiant with the sight of his dead wife,
> light streaming from his mouth to shape her name,
> 'not Florence and not Flo but always Florrie'.

> *Continuous* (1981)

Holmes, Oliver Wendell, Jr (1841–1935)
US jurist and judge
In response to Andrew Lang's enquiring if he were the son of the celebrated Oliver Wendell Holmes
> No, he was my father.

> In C. Bowen, *Yankee from Olympus* (1945)

McAuley, James Philip (1917–1976)
Australian poet and critic
> Small things can pit the memory like a cyst:
> Having seen other fathers greet their sons,
> I put my childish face up to be kissed
> After an absence. The rebuff still stuns
> My blood. The poor man's embarrassment
> At such a delicate proffer of affection
> Cut like a saw. But home the lesson went:
> My tenderness thenceforth escaped detection.

> *Collected Poems* (1971)

Russell, Bertrand (1872–1970)
English philosopher, mathematician, essayist and social reformer
> The fundamental defect of fathers is that they want their children to be a credit to them.

> Attr.

Shakespeare, William (1564–1616)
English dramatist, poet and actor
> It is a wise father that knows his own child.
>> *The Merchant of Venice*, II.ii

Tennyson, Alfred, Lord (1809–1892)
English lyric poet
> How many a father have I seen,
> A sober man, among his boys,
> Whose youth was full of foolish noise.
>> *In Memoriam A. H. H.* (1850)

Turnbull, Margaret (fl. 1920s–1942)
Scottish-born US writer and dramatist
> No man is responsible for his father. That is entirely his mother's affair.
>> *Alabaster Lamps* (1925)

Twain, Mark (1835–1910)
US humorist, writer, journalist and lecturer
> When I was a boy of 14 my father was so ignorant I could hardly stand to have the old man around. But when I got to be 21, I was astonished at how much he had learned in seven years.
>> In Mackay, *The Harvest of a Quiet Eye* (1977)

▶▶ BABIES; CHILDREN; FAMILIES; MOTHERS

faults

Belloc, Hilaire (1870–1953)
English writer of verse, essayist and critic; Liberal MP
> The Chief Defect of Henry King
> Was chewing little bits of String.
>> *Cautionary Tales* (1907), 'Henry King'

Berenson, Bernard (1865–1959)
Lithuanian-born US art critic
> Life has taught me that it is not for our faults that we are disliked and even hated but for our qualities.
>> *The Passionate Sightseer* (1960)

Carlyle, Thomas (1795–1881)
Scottish historian, biographer, critic, and essayist
> The greatest of faults, I should say, is to be conscious of none.
>> *On Heroes, Hero-Worship, and the Heroic in History*

Coleridge, Samuel Taylor (1772–1834)
English poet, philosopher and critic
> The faults of great authors are generally excellences carried to an excess.
>> *Miscellanies*

Confucius (c.550–c.478 BC)
Chinese philosopher and teacher of ethics
> When you have faults, do not fear to abandon them.
>> *Analects*

Goldsmith, Oliver (c.1728–1774)
Irish dramatist, poet and writer
> All his faults are such that one loves him still the better for them.
>> *The Good Natur'd Man* (1768)

La Rochefoucauld (1613–1680)
French writer
> *Si nous n'avions point de défauts, nous ne prendrions pas tant de plaisir à en remarquer dans les autres.*
> If we had no faults of our own, we should not take so much pleasure in noticing them in others.
>> *Maximes* (1678)

> *Nous n'avouons de petits défauts que pour persuader que nous n'en avons pas de grands.*
> We only admit our little faults to persuade others that we have no great ones.
>> *Maximes* (1678)

Proust, Marcel (1871–1922)
French writer and critic
> People often say that, by pointing out to a man the faults of his mistress, you succeed only in strengthening his attachment to her, because he does not believe you; yet how much more so if he does!
>> *Du côté de chez Swann* (1913)

Shakespeare, William (1564–1616)
English dramatist, poet and actor
> Condemn the fault and not the actor of it!
>> *Measure For Measure*, II.ii

> They say best men are moulded out of faults;
> And, for the most, become much more the better
> For being a little bad.
>> *Measure For Measure*, V.i

> Roses have thorns, and silver fountains mud;
> Clouds and eclipses stain both moon and sun,
> And loathsome canker lives in sweetest bud.
> All men make faults.
>> Sonnet 35

▶▶ ERROR; MISTAKES

fear

Adler, Renata
US film critic and writer
> Fear … is forward. No one is afraid of yesterday.
>> In Melissa Stein, *The Wit & Wisdom of Women* (1993)

Aeschylus (525–456 BC)
Greek dramatist and poet
> There are times when fear is good. It must keep its watchful place.
>> *Eumenides*

Allen, Woody (1935–)
US film director, writer, actor and comedian
> I'm really a timid person – I was beaten up by
> Quakers.
>> *Sleeper* (film, 1973)

Atwood, Margaret (1939–)
Canadian writer, poet and critic
> The truly fearless think of themselves as normal.
>> *Bluebeard's Egg* (1986)

Bacon, Sir Francis (1561–1626)
English philosopher, essayist, politician and courtier
> To suffering there is a limit; to fearing, none.
>> *Essays* (1625)

Bowen, Elizabeth (1899–1973)
Irish writer
> Proust has pointed out that the predisposition
> to love creates its own objects: is this not true of
> fear?
>> *Collected Impressions* (1950)

Boyd, Martin a'Beckett (1893–1972)
Australian novelist
> The only effect the atomic age has had on man
> had been to give him an underlying sense of
> nervous apprehension, which must also have
> been felt during the Black Death, and by the
> Christians under Diocletian.
>> *Day of My Delight* (1965)

Burke, Edmund (1729–1797)
Irish-born British statesman and philosopher
> No passion so effectually robs the mind of all its
> powers of acting and reasoning as fear.
>> *A Philosophical Enquiry into the Origin of our Ideas*
>> *of the Sublime and Beautiful* (1757)

> The concessions of the weak are the concessions
> of fear.
>> *Speech on Conciliation with America*
>> (1775)

Burton, Robert (1577–1640)
English clergyman and writer
> The fear of some divine and supreme powers,
> keeps men in obedience.
>> *Anatomy of Melancholy* (1621)

Cervantes, Miguel de (1547–1616)
Spanish writer and dramatist
> *Tiene el miedo muchos ojos, y vee las cosas debajo de*
> *tierra.*
> Fear has many eyes and can see things which
> are underground.
>> *Don Quixote* I (1605)

Churchill, Sir Winston (1874–1965)
English Conservative Prime Minister
> When I look back on all these worries I
> remember the story of the old man who said on
> his deathbed that he had had a lot of trouble in
> his life, most of which had never happened.
>> *Their Finest Hour*

Clough, Arthur Hugh (1819–1861)
English poet and letter writer
> If hopes were dupes, fears may be liars.
>> 'Say Not the Struggle Naught Availeth' (1855)

Cowper, William (1731–1800)
English poet, hymn and letter writer
> He has no hope who never had a fear.
>> 'Truth' (1782)

Curie, Marie (1867–1934)
Polish-born French physicist
> Nothing in life is to be feared, it is only to be
> understood. Now is the time to understand
> more, so that we may fear less.
>> Attr.

Delaney, Shelagh (1939–)
English dramatist, screenwriter and writer
> I'm not frightened of the darkness outside. It's
> the darkness inside houses I don't like.
>> *A Taste of Honey* (1959)

Dryden, John (1631–1700)
English poet, satirist, dramatist and critic
> I am devilishly afraid, that's certain; but ... I'll
> sing, that I may seem valiant.
>> *Amphitryon* (1690)

Emerson, Ralph Waldo (1803–1882)
US poet, essayist, transcendentalist and teacher
> Fear is an instructor of great sagacity, and the
> herald of all revolutions.
>> *Essays, First Series* (1841)

Foch, Ferdinand (1851–1929)
French marshal
> None but a coward dares to boast that he has
> never known fear.
>> Attr.

Froude, James Anthony (1818–1894)
English historian and scholar
> Fear is the parent of cruelty.
>> *Short Studies on Great Subjects* (1877)

Jonson, Ben (1572–1637)
English dramatist and poet
> Tell proud Jove,
> Between his power and thine there is no odds:
> 'Twas only fear first in the world made gods.
>> *Sejanus* (1603)

Kierkegaard, Søren (1813–1855)
Danish philosopher
> Dread is a sympathetic antipathy and an
> antipathetic sympathy.
>> In W.H. Auden, *Kierkegaard*

Mtshali, Oswald (1940–)
South African poet

Man is
a great wall builder …
but the wall
most impregnable
has a moat
flowing with fright
around his heart.

Sounds of a Cowhide Drum (1971)

Parris, Matthew (1949–)
British Conservative politician and journalist
Terror of discovery and fear of reproval slip into our unconscious minds during infancy and remain there forever, always potent, usually unacknowledged.

The Spectator, 1996

Plato (c.429–347 BC)
Greek philosopher
Nothing in the affairs of men is worthy of great anxiety.

Republic

Roosevelt, Franklin Delano (1882–1945)
US Democrat President
The only thing we have to fear is fear itself.

First Inaugural Address, 1933

Shakespeare, William (1564–1616)
English dramatist, poet and actor
I have almost forgot the taste of fears.
The time has been my senses would have cool'd
To hear a night-shriek, and my fell of hair
Would at a dismal treatise rouse and stir
As life were in't. I have supp'd full with horrors;
Direness, familiar to my slaughterous thoughts,
Cannot once start me.

Macbeth, V.v

Shaw, George Bernard (1856–1950)
Irish socialist, writer, dramatist and critic
There is only one universal passion: fear.

The Man of Destiny (1898)

Spenser, Edmund (c.1522–1599)
English poet
Still as he fled, his eye was backward cast,
As if his feare still followed him behind.

The Faerie Queene (1596)

Stephens, James (1882–1950)
Irish poet and writer
Curiosity will conquer fear even more than bravery will.

The Crock of Gold (1912)

Thomas, Lewis (1913–)
US pathologist and university administrator
Worrying is the most natural and spontaneous of all human functions. It is time to acknowledge this, perhaps even to learn to do it better.

More Notes of a Biology Watcher

Voltaire (1694–1778)
French philosopher, dramatist, poet, historian writer and critic
La crainte suit le crime, et c'est son châtiment.
Fear follows crime, and is its punishment.

Sémiramis (1748)

▶▶ DEATH

feelings

Austen, Jane (1775–1817)
English writer
It was too pathetic for the feelings of Sophia and myself – we fainted Alternately on a Sofa.

Love and Freindship (1791)

Harris, Max (1921–1995)
Australian critic, poet and publisher
In an atmosphere of reciprocal banter or rubbishing Australians can express mutual affection without running into risk of indecently exposing states of feeling.

In Keith Dunstan, *Knockers* (1972)

Ridding, Bishop George (1828–1904)
I feel a feeling which I feel you all feel.

Sermon, 1885

feminism

Anthony, Susan B. (1820–1906)
US reformer, feminist and abolitionist
Men their rights and nothing more; women their rights and nothing less.

Motto of The Revolution, 1868

Atkinson, Ti-Grace (c.1938–)
US feminist
Feminism is the theory: lesbianism is the practice.

Attr. in *Amazons, Bluestockings and Crones: A Feminist Dictionary*

Brown, Arnold
Scottish comedian
Uncle Harry was an early feminist … Our family would often recount how, at a race-meeting in Ayr, he threw himself under a suffragette.

Are You Looking at Me, Jimmy?

Burchill, Julie (1960–)
English writer
The freedom that women were supposed to have found in the Sixties largely boiled down to easy contraception and abortion; things to make life easier for men, in fact.

Born again Cows (1986)

A good part – and definitely the most fun part – of being a feminist is about frightening men.

Time Out, 1989

Dworkin, Andrea (1946–)
US writer and feminist

We imagined, in our ignorance, that we might be novelists and philosophers... We did not know that our professors had a system of beliefs and convictions that designated us as an inferior gender class, and that that system of beliefs and convictions was virtually universal – the cherished assumption of most of the writers, philosophers, and historians we were so ardently studying.

Our Blood: Prophecies and Discourses on Sexual Politics (1976)

Fairbairn, Sir Nicholas (1933–1995)
Scottish Conservative MP and barrister
On feminism

It's a cover for lesbian homosexuality.

Daily Mail, 1993

Faludi, Susan (1959–)
US writer and feminist

The "feminine" woman is forever static and childlike. She is like the ballerina in an old-fashioned music box, her unchanging features tiny and girlish, her voice tinkly, her body stuck on a pin, rotating in a spiral that will never grow.

Backlash: The Undeclared War Against American Women (1991)

Faust, Beatrice Eileen (1939–)
Australian writer and feminist

If the women's movement can be summed up in a single phrase, it is 'the right to choose'.

Women, Sex and Pornography (1980)

Fourier, François Charles Marie (1772–1837)
French social theorist

L'extension des privilèges des femmes est le principe général de tous progrès sociaux.
The extension of women's privileges is the basic principle of all social progress.

Théorie des Quatre Mouvements (1808)

Friedan, Betty (1921–)
US feminist leader and writer

I hope there will come a day when you, daughter mine, or your daughter, can truly afford to say 'I'm not a feminist. I'm a person' – and a day, not too far away, I hope, when I can stop fighting for women and get onto other matters that interest me now.

Letter to her daughter, in Cosmopolitan, 1978

Greer, Germaine (1939–)
Australian feminist, critic, English scholar and writer

If women understand by emancipation the

adoption of the masculine role then we are lost indeed.

The Female Eunuch (1970)

Johnston, Jill (1929–)
English-born US dancer, critic and feminist

Until all women are lesbians there will be no true political revolution.

Lesbian Nation: The Feminist Solution (1973)

Feminists who still sleep with men are delivering their most vital energies to the oppressor.

Lesbian Nation: The Feminist Solution (1973)

No one should have to dance backwards all their life.

In Miles, The Women's History of the World (1988)

Key, Ellen (1849–1926)
Swedish feminist, writer and lecturer

The emancipation of women is practically the greatest egoistic movement of the nineteenth century, and the most intense affirmation of the right of the self that history has yet seen.

The Century of the Child (1909)

Lewis, Wyndham (1882–1957)
US-born British painter, critic and writer

I believe that (in one form or another) castration may be the solution. And the feminization of the white European and American is already far advanced, coming in the wake of the war.

The Art of Being Ruled (1926)

Livermore, Mary Ashton (c.1820–1905)
US writer

Above the titles of wife and mother, which, although dear, are transitory and accidental, there is the title human being, which precedes and out-ranks every other.

What Shall We Do with Our Daughters

Loos, Anita (1893–1981)
US writer and screenwriter

I'm furious about the Women's Liberationists. They keep getting up on soapboxes and proclaiming that women are brighter than men. That's true, but it should be kept very quiet or it ruins the whole racket.

The Observer, 1973

Martineau, Harriet (1802–1876)
English writer

Is it to be understood that the principles of the Declaration of Independence bear no relation to half of the human race?

Society in America (1837)

Mill, John Stuart (1806–1873)
English philosopher, economist and reformer

The most important thing women have to do is to stir up the zeal of women themselves.

Letter to Alexander Bain, 1869

O'Brien, Edna (1936–)
Irish writer and dramatist
> The vote, I thought, means nothing to women.
> We should be armed.
>> In Erica Jong, *Fear of Flying* (1973)

Orbach, Susie (1946–)
US psychotherapist
> Fat is a Feminist Issue.
>> Title of book, 1978

Paglia, Camille (1947–)
US academic
> Women and children first is an unscientific
> sentimentality which must be opposed.
>> *The Observer*, 1998

Pankhurst, Dame Christabel (1880–1958)
English suffragette
> We are here to claim our right as women, not
> only to be free, but to fight for freedom. It is
> our privilege, as well as our pride and our joy, to
> take some part in this militant movement, which,
> as we believe, means the regeneration of all
> humanity.
>> Speech, 1911

Pankhurst, Emmeline (1858–1928)
English suffragette
> We have taken this action, because as women …
> we realize that the condition of our sex is so
> deplorable that it is our duty even to break the
> law in order to call attention to the reasons why
> we do so.
>> Speech in court, 1908

Parton, Dolly (1946–)
US country and western singer
> When women's lib started I was the first to burn
> my bra and it took three days to put out the fire.
>> In Simon Rose, *Essential Film Guide* (1993)

Rilke, Rainer Maria (1875–1926)
Austrian poet, born in Prague
> *Eines … Tages wird das Mädchen da sein und die Frau,*
> *deren Name nicht mehr nur einen Gegensatz zum*
> *Männlichen bedeuten wird, sondern etwas für sich,*
> *etwas, wobei man an keine Ergänzung und Grenze*
> *denkt, nur an Leben und Dasein, – der weibliche*
> *Mensch. Dieser Fortschritt wird das Liebe-Erleben … zu*
> *einer Beziehung umbilden, die von Mensch zu Mensch*
> *gemeint ist, nicht mehr von Mann und Weib. Und diese*
> *menschlichere Liebe … wird jener ähneln, … die darin*
> *besteht, dass zwei Einsamkeiten einander schützen,*
> *grenzen und grüssen.*
> One day … there will be the girl and the woman,
> whose name will no longer signify merely a
> contrast to masculinity, but something of value
> in itself, something in respect of which one
> thinks not of a complement and a limitation, but
> only of life and existence: the female person.

> This progress will make the experience of love
> … become a relationship which is one of person
> to person, no longer one of man and wife. And
> this more human love … will resemble one …
> which consists in this, that two solitary people
> protect and limit and greet each other.
>> *Letters to a Young Poet* (1929)

Robertson, Pat (1930–)
US fundamentalist Christian broadcaster and politician
> It is about a socialist, anti-family movement that
> encourages women to leave their husbands, kill
> their children, practice witchcraft and become
> lesbians.
>> *The World Almanac and Book of Facts*, 1993

Shaw, George Bernard (1856–1950)
Irish socialist, writer, dramatist and critic
> Give women the vote, and in five years there will
> be a crushing tax on bachelors.
>> *Man and Superman* (1903)

Solanas, Valerie (1940–1998)
US artist
SCUM (Society for Cutting Up Men), manifesto, 1968
> Every man, deep down, knows he's a worthless
> piece of shit.
>> In Bassnett, *Feminist Experiences: The Women's*
>> *Movement in Four Cultures* (1986)

Stanton, Elizabeth Cady (1815–1902)
US suffragist, abolitionist, feminist, editor and writer
On Genesis
> As to woman's subjection, on which both the
> canon and the civil law delight to dwell, it is
> important to note that equal dominion is given
> to woman over every living thing, but not one
> word is said giving man dominion over woman.
>> *The Woman's Bible* (1895)

> Womanhood is the great fact in her life;
> wifehood and motherhood are but incidental
> relations.
>> In Anthony and Gage (eds), *History of Woman*
>> *Suffrage* (1881)

> … we still wonder at the stolid incapacity of all
> men to understand that woman feels the
> invidious distinctions of sex exactly as the black
> man does those of color, or the white man the
> more transient distinctions of wealth, family,
> position, place, and power; that she feels as
> keenly as man the injustice of disfranchisement.
>> In Anthony and Gage (eds), *History of Woman*
>> *Suffrage* (1881)

> We hold these truths to be self-evident, that all
> men and women are created equal.
>> 'Declaration of Sentiments', 1848

Stead, Christina (1902–1983)
Australian writer

I don't believe in segregation of any kind, and I think men and women should unite to fight the battle. All the men I've known have been in favour of women's success.

Interview with Rodney Wetherell, first broadcast by Australian Broadcasting Commission, 1980

Steinem, Gloria (1934–)
US writer and feminist activist
Some of us have become the men we wanted to marry.

The Observer, 1982

Tweedie, Jill (1936–1993)
English journalist
I blame the women's movement for ten years in a boiler suit.

Attr.

Victoria, Queen (1819–1901)
Queen of the United Kingdom
The Queen is most anxious to enlist every one who can speak or write to join in checking this mad, wicked folly of 'Women's Rights', with all its attendant horrors, on which her poor feeble sex is bent, forgetting every sense of womanly feeling and propriety … It is a subject which makes the Queen so furious that she cannot contain herself. God created men and women different – then let them remain each in their own position.

Letter to Sir Theodore Martin, 1870

Watson, James Dewey (1928–)
US biologist
The thought could not be avoided that the best home for a feminist was in another person's lab.

The Double Helix (1968)

Weldon, Fay (1931–)
British writer
There has to be a halt in the gender war and feminism must extend its remit to include the rights of men.

The Observer debate on feminism, 1998

West, Dame Rebecca (1892–1983)
English writer, critic and feminist
People call me a feminist whenever I express sentiments that differentiate me from a doormat or a prostitute.

In Anne Stibbs (ed.), *Hell Hath No Fury*

Whittlesey, Faith
Remember, Ginger Rogers did everything Fred Astaire did, but she did it backwards and in high heels.

Attr.

Wollstonecraft, Mary (1759–1797)
English feminist, writer and teacher
The divine right of husbands, like the divine right

of kings, may, it is hoped, in this enlightened age, be contested without danger.

A Vindication of the Rights of Woman (1792)

Of women
I do not wish them to have power over men; but over themselves.

A Vindication of the Rights of Woman (1792)

▶▶ EQUALITY; MEN AND WOMEN; WOMEN

fiction

Adams, Franklin P. (1881–1960)
US writer, poet, translator and editor
The best part of the fiction in many novels is the notice that the characters are purely imaginary.

In Jonathan Green, *The Cynic's Lexicon* (1984)

Albee, Edward (1928–)
US dramatist
A play is fiction and fiction is fact distilled into truth.

New York Times, 1966

Aldiss, Brian (1925–)
English writer
Science fiction is no more written for scientists than ghost stories are written for ghosts.

Penguin Science Fiction (1961)

Auden, W.H. (1907–1973)
English poet, essayist, critic, teacher and dramatist
Political history is far too criminal and pathological to be a fit subject of study for the young. All teachers know this. In consequence, they bowdlerize, but to bowdlerize political history is not to simplify but to falsify it. Children should acquire their heroes and villains from fiction.

A Certain World (1970)

Austen, Jane (1775–1817)
English writer
'And what are you reading, Miss —?' 'Oh! it is only a novel!' replies the young lady; while she lays down her book with affected indifference, or momentary shame. It is only *Cecilia*, or *Camilla*, or *Belinda*; or, in short, only some work in which the greatest powers of the mind are displayed, in which the most thorough knowledge of human nature, the happiest delineation of its varieties, the liveliest effusions of wit and humour, are conveyed to the world in the best chosen language.

Northanger Abbey (1818)

Barth, John (1930–)
US writer
If you are a novelist of a certain type of

temperament, then what you really want to do is re-invent the world. God wasn't too bad a novelist, except he was a Realist.

Attr.

Cecil, Lord David (1902–1986)
English critic and writer
It does not matter that Dickens' world is not lifelike: it is alive.

Early Victorian Novelists (1934)

Chandler, Raymond (1888–1959)
US crime writer
When I started out to write fiction I had the great disadvantage of having absolutely no talent for it … If more than two people were on scene I couldn't keep one of them alive.

Letter to Paul Brooks, 1949

Cheever, John (1912–1982)
US novelist
The novel remains for me one of the few forms where we can record man's complexity and the strength and decency of his longings.

Accepting the National Book Award, 1958

Chesterton, G.K. (1874–1936)
English writer, poet and critic
It is the art in which the conquests of woman are quite beyond controversy … The novel of the nineteenth century was female.

The Victorian Age in Literature (1913)

A good novel tells us the truth about its hero; but a bad novel tells us the truth about its author.

Heretics (1905)

Davison, Frank Dalby (1893–1970)
Australian writer
You need a skin as thin as a cigarette paper to write a novel and the hide of an elephant to publish it.

Meanjin, 1982

Disraeli, Benjamin (1804–1881)
English statesman and writer
When I want to read a novel I write one.

Attr.

Emerson, Ralph Waldo (1803–1882)
US poet, essayist, transcendentalist and teacher
Novels are as useful as Bibles, if they teach you the secret, that the best of life is conversation, and the greatest success is confidence.

Conduct of Life (1860)

Forster, E.M. (1879–1970)
English writer, essayist and literary critic
Yes – oh dear, yes – the novel tells a story.

Aspects of the Novel (1927)

That the story is the highest factor common to all novels, and I wish that it was not so, that it could be something different – melody, or perception of the truth, not this low atavistic form.

Aspects of the Novel (1927)

Fowles, John (1926–)
English writer
There are many reasons why novelists write, but they all have one thing in common – a need to create an alternative world.

The Sunday Times Magazine, 1977

García Márquez, Gabriel (1928–)
Colombian author
El periodismo es un género literario, muy parecido a la novela, y tiene la gran ventaja de que el reportero puede inventar cosas. Y eso el novelista lo tiene totalmente prohibido.
Journalism is a literary genre very similar to that of the novel, and has the great advantage that the reporter can invent things. And that is completely forbidden to the novelist.

Speech, April 1994, reported in El País

Gibbon, Edward (1737–1794)
English historian, politician and memoirist
The romance of Tom Jones, that exquisite picture of human manners, will outlive the palace of the Escurial and the imperial eagle of the house of Austria.

Memoirs of My Life and Writings (1796)

Goncourt, Edmond de (1822–1896)
French novelist
Les historiens sont des raconteurs du passé, les romanciers des raconteurs du présent.
Historians tell stories of the past, novelists stories of the present.

Journal

James, Henry (1843–1916)
US-born British writer, critic and letter writer
The only obligation to which in advance we may hold a novel, without incurring the accusation of being arbitrary, is that it be interesting.

Partial Portraits (1888)

I remember once saying to Henry James, in reference to a novel of the type that used euphemistically to be called 'unpleasant': 'You know, I was rather disappointed; that book wasn't nearly as bad as I expected'; to which he replied, with his incomparable twinkle: 'Ah, my dear, the abysses are all so shallow.'

In Edith Wharton, The House of Mirth (1936)

Larkin, Philip (1922–1985)
English poet, writer and librarian
Referring to modern novels
Far too many relied on the classic formula of a

beginning, a muddle, and an end.

New Fiction, 1978

Lawrence, D.H. (1885–1930)
English writer, poet and critic
> I am a man, and alive … For this reason I am a novelist. And being a novelist, I consider myself superior to the saint, the scientist, the philosopher, and the poet, who are all great masters of different bits of man alive, but never get the whole hog.

Phoenix (1936)

> The novel is the one bright book of life.

Phoenix (1936)

McCarthy, Mary (1912–1989)
US writer and critic
> The suspense of a novel is not only in the reader, but in the novelist, who is intensely curious about what will happen to the hero.

Attr.

Nabokov, Vladimir (1899–1977)
Russian-born US writer, poet, translator and critic
> A novelist is, like all mortals, more fully at home on the surface of the present than in the ooze of the past.

Strong Opinions (1973)

Powell, Anthony (1905–2000)
English writer and critic
> People think that because a novel's invented, it isn't true. Exactly the reverse is the case. Biography and memoirs can never be wholly true, since they cannot include every conceivable circumstance of what happened. The novel can do that.

Hearing Secret Harmonies (1975)

Reade, Charles (1814–1884)
English novelist and dramatist
Programme for a serial novel
> Make 'em laugh; make 'em cry; make 'em wait.

Attr.

Sayers, Dorothy L. (1893–1957)
English writer, dramatist and translator
> My impression is that I was thinking about writing a detective story, and that he walked in, complete with spats.

Harcourt Brace News, 1936, 'How I came to Invent the Character of Lord Peter'

On *Whose Body?*, 1923, her first book
> One cannot write a novel unless one has something to say about life, and I had nothing to say about it, because I knew nothing.

In Hone, *Dorothy L. Sayers: A Literary Biography* (1979)

Scott, Sir Walter (1771–1832)
Scottish writer and historian
> But I must say to the Muse of fiction, as the Earl

of Pembroke said to the ejected nun of Wilton, 'Go spin, you jade, go spin!'.

Journal, 1826

Shaw, George Bernard (1856–1950)
Irish socialist, writer, dramatist and critic
> It is clear that a novel cannot be too bad to be worth publishing … It certainly is possible for a novel to be too good to be worth publishing.

Plays Pleasant and Unpleasant (1898)

Sheridan, Richard Brinsley (1751–1816)
Irish dramatist, politician and orator
> I hate Novels, and love Romances. The Praise of the best of the former, their being natural, as it is called, is to me their greatest Demerit.

Letter, 1772

Stendhal (1783–1842)
French writer, critic and soldier
> A novel is a mirror walking along a wide road.

Le Rouge et le Noir (1830)

Theroux, Paul (1941–)
US writer
> Fiction gives us a second chance that life denies us.

New York Times, 1976

Tynan, Kenneth (1927–1980)
English drama critic, producer and essayist
> A novel is a static thing that one moves through; a play is a dynamic thing that moves past one.

Curtains (1961)

Waugh, Auberon (1939–)
English writer and critic
> It is a sad feature of modern life that only women for the most part have time to write novels, and they seldom have much to write about.

The Observer, 1981

Wilde, Oscar (1854–1900)
Irish poet, dramatist, writer, critic and wit
> The good ended happily, and the bad unhappily. That is what Fiction means.

The Importance of Being Earnest (1895)

Woolf, Virginia (1882–1941)
English writer and critic
> A woman must have money and a room of her own if she is to write fiction.

A Room of One's Own (1929)

▶▶ BOOKS; LITERATURE; WRITERS; WRITING

fire

Brennan, Christopher (1870–1932)
Australian poet

Fire in the heavens, and fire along the hills,
and fire made solid in the flinty stone,
thick-mass'd or scatter'd pebble, fire that fills
the breathless hour that lives in fire alone.

Poems (1914)

Frost, Robert (1874–1963)
US poet
> Some say the world will end in fire,
> Some say in ice.
> From what I've tasted of desire,
> I hold with those who favour fire,
> But if it had to perish twice,
> I think I know enough of hate
> To say that for destruction ice
> Is also great
> And would suffice.

'Fire and Ice' (1923)

Graham, Harry (1874–1936)
English writer
> Billy, in one of his nice new sashes,
> Fell in the fire and was burnt to ashes;
> Now, although the room grows chilly,
> I haven't the heart to poke poor Billy.

Ruthless Rhymes for Heartless Homes (1899)

Greville, Fulke (1554–1628)
English poet, dramatist, biographer, courtier and politician
> Fire and people do in this agree,
> They both good servants, both ill masters be.

'An Inquisition upon Fame and Honour' (1633)

St Francis de Sales (1567–1622)
French bishop and theologian
> *Ce sont les grans feux qui s'enflamment au vent, mays les petitz s'esteignent si on ne les y porte a couvert.*
> Great fires flare up in the wind, but little ones are blown out if they are not sheltered.

Introduction à la vie dévote (1609)

Shakespeare, William (1564–1616)
English dramatist, poet and actor
> A little fire is quickly trodden out,
> Which, being suffer'd, rivers cannot quench.

Henry VI, Part 3, IV.viii

Sheridan, Richard Brinsley (1751–1816)
Irish dramatist, politician and orator
At a coffee house, during the fire which destroyed his Drury Lane theatre, 1809
> A man may surely be allowed to take a glass of wine by his own fireside.

In Moore, *Memoirs of the Life of Sheridan* (1825)

Sitwell, Dame Edith (1887–1964)
English poet, anthologist, critic and biographer
> The fire was furry as a bear.

'Dark Song' (1922)

flattery

Austen, Jane (1775–1817)
English writer
> It is happy for you that you possess the talent of flattering with delicacy. May I ask whether these pleasing attentions proceed from the impulse of the moment, or are the result of previous study?

Pride and Prejudice (1813)

Bierce, Ambrose (1842–c.1914)
US writer, verse writer and soldier
> *Flatter*: To impress another with a sense of one's own merit.

The Enlarged Devil's Dictionary (1961)

Colton, Charles Caleb (c.1780–1832)
English clergyman and satirist
> Imitation is the sincerest form of flattery.

Lacon (1820)

Congreve, William (1670–1729)
English dramatist
> She lays it on with a trowel.

The Double Dealer (1694)

Disraeli, Benjamin (1804–1881)
English statesman and writer
To Queen Victoria
> We authors, Ma'am.

Attr.

Dunbar, William (c.1460–c.1525)
Scottish poet, satirist and courtier
> Flattery wearis ane furrit gown,
> And falsett with the lord does roun,
> And truth stands barrit at the dure.

'Into this World May None Assure' (1834 edition)

Halifax, Lord (1633–1695)
English politician, courtier, pamphleteer and epigrammatist
> It is flattering some Men to endure them.

'Of Company' (1750)

Johnson, Samuel (1709–1784)
English lexicographer, poet, critic, conversationalist and essayist
Remark to Hannah More
> Madam, before you flatter a man so grossly to his face, you should consider whether or not your flattery is worth his having.

Diary and Letters of Madame d'Arblay (1842)

La Fontaine, Jean de (1621–1695)
French poet and fabulist
> *Mon bon Monsieur,*
> *Apprenez que tout flatteur*
> *Vit au dépens de celui qui l'écoute.*
> My dear Monsieur, know that every flatterer

lives at the expense of the one who listens to him.

'Le corbeau et le renard'

Proverbs

Fine words butter no parsnips.

Imitation is the sincerest form of flattery.

Rhodes, Cecil (1853–1902)

English imperialist, financier and South African statesman

Replying to Queen Victoria who remarked that she disliked women

How can I possibly dislike a sex to which Your Majesty belongs?

Attr.

Scott, Sir Walter (1771–1832)

Scottish writer and historian

For ne'er
Was flattery lost on poet's ear:
A simple race! they waste their toil
For the vain tribute of a smile.

The Lay of the Last Minstrel (1805), IV

Shakespeare, William (1564–1616)

English dramatist, poet and actor

He that loves to be flattered is worthy o' th' flatterer.

Timon of Athens, I.i

Shaw, George Bernard (1856–1950)

Irish socialist, writer, dramatist and critic

What really flatters a man is that you think him worth flattering.

John Bull's Other Island (1907)

Stevenson, Adlai (1900–1965)

US lawyer, statesman and United Nations ambassador

I suppose flattery hurts no one – that is, if he doesn't inhale.

Meet the Press, TV broadcast, 1952

Twain, Mark (1835–1910)

US humorist, writer, journalist and lecturer

I can live for two months on a good compliment.

Attr.

▶▶ PRAISE

flirtation

Chesterfield, Lord (1694–1773)

English politician and letter writer

I assisted at the birth of that most significant word flirtation, which dropped from the most beautiful mouth in the world.

The World, 1754

Smith, Sydney (1771–1845)

English clergyman, essayist, journalist and wit

How can a bishop marry? How can he flirt? The most he can say is, 'I will see you in the vestry after service.'

In Holland, *A Memoir of the Reverend Sydney Smith* (1855)

Sterne, Laurence (1713–1768)

Irish-born English writer and clergyman

Vive l'amour! et vive la bagatelle!
Long live love! Long live philandering!

A Sentimental Journey (1768)

Wilde, Oscar (1854–1900)

Irish poet, dramatist, writer, critic and wit

The amount of women in London who flirt with their own husbands is perfectly scandalous. It looks so bad. It is simply washing one's clean linen in public.

The Importance of Being Earnest (1895)

flowers

Fletcher, John (1579–1625)

English dramatist

Daisies smell-less, yet most quaint,
And sweet thyme true,
Primrose first born child of Ver,
Merry Springtime's Harbinger.

Two Noble Kinsmen (with Shakespeare, 1634)

Kawabata, Yasunari (1899–1972)

Japanese novelist

A single flower could impress you with more gorgeousness than one hundred such.

'Japan the Beautiful and I' (1968)

Keats, John (1795–1821)

English poet

I cannot see what flowers are at my feet,
Nor what soft incense hangs upon the boughs,
But, in embalmed darkness, guess each sweet
Wherewith the seasonable month endows
The grass, the thicket, and the fruit-tree wild –
White hawthorn, and the pastoral eglantine;
Fast fading violets cover'd up in leaves;
And mid-May's eldest child,
The coming musk-rose, full of dewy wine,
The murmurous haunt of flies on summer eves.

'Ode to a Nightingale' (1819)

Moore, Thomas (1779–1852)

Irish poet

'Tis the last rose of summer
Left blooming alone;
All her lovely companions
Are faded and gone.

Irish Melodies (1807), 'Tis the Last Rose'

O'Keeffe, Georgia (1887–1986)

US artist

When you take a flower in your hand and really look at it, it's your world for the moment.

New York Post, 1946

I hate flowers – I paint them because they're cheaper than models and they don't move.

New York Herald Tribune, 1954

Seeger, Pete (1919–)
US folksinger and songwriter
Where have all the flowers gone?
The girls have picked them every one.
Oh, when will you ever learn?

'Where Have All the Flowers Gone?', song, 1961

Shakespeare, William (1564–1616)
English dramatist, poet and actor
There's rosemary, that's for remembrance; pray you, love, remember. And there is pansies, that's for thoughts.

Hamlet, IV.v

Here's flow'rs for you:
Hot lavender, mints, savory, marjoram;
The marigold, that goes to bed wi' th' sun,
And with him rises weeping.

The Winter's Tale, IV.iv

Skelton, John (c.1460–1529)
English poet and clergyman
She is the vyolet,
The daysy delectable,
The columbyn commendable
This jelofer amyable;
For this most goodly floure,
This blossom of fressh colour,
So Jupiter me succour,
She florysheth new and new
In beautie and vertew.

'Phyllyp Sparowe: The Commendacions'

Spenser, Edmund (c.1522–1599)
English poet
Bring hether the Pincke and purple Cullambine,
With Gelliflowres:
Bring Coronations, and Sops in wine,
Worne of Paramoures.
Strowe me the ground with Daffadowndillies,
And Cowslips, and Kingcups, and loved Lillies:
The pretie Pawnce,
And the Chevisaunce,
Shall match with the fayre flowre Delice.

The Shepheardes Calender (1579)

▶▶ GARDENS

flying

Earhart, Amelia (1898–1937)
US aviator

Flying might not be all plain sailing, but the fun of it is worth the price.

The Fun of It (1932)

Elizabeth, the Queen Mother (1900–)
Queen of the United Kingdom and mother of Elizabeth II
On her love of helicopters
The chopper has changed my life as conclusively as that of Anne Boleyn.

Quoted in *The Guardian*, 2000

Welles, Orson (1915–1985)
US actor, director and producer
There are only two emotions in a plane: boredom and terror.

The Times, 1985

Wright, Orville (1871–1948)
US airplane pioneer
Explaining the principles of powered flight
The airplane stays up because it doesn't have the time to fall.

Attr.

food

Ade, George (1866–1944)
US fabulist and playwright
One man's poison ivy is another man's spinach.

Attr

Atwood, Margaret (1939–)
Canadian writer, poet and critic
Eating is our earliest metaphor, preceding our consciousness of gender difference, race, nationality, and language. We eat before we talk.

The CanLit Foodbook: From Pen to Palate – A Collection of Tasty Literary Fare (1987

Bareham, Lindsey (1948–)
Food critic and writer
Good mashed potato is one of the great luxuries of life and I don't blame Elvis for eating it every night for the last year of his life.

In Praise of the Potato (1989)

Beard, James (1903–1985)
US chef and author
Food is our common ground, a universal experience.

Beard on Food (1974)

The Bible (King James Version)
Better is a dinner of herbs where love is, than a stalled ox and hatred therewith.

Proverbs, 15:17

Bradley, Chris
Scottish chef
My cooking is modern Scottish – if you complain

you get headbutted.

The Times, 1999

Brillat-Savarin, Anthelme (1755–1826)

French jurist and gastronome

Dis-moi ce que tu manges, je te dirai ce que tu es.
Tell me what you eat and I will tell you what you are.

Physiologie du Goût (1825)

Carroll, Lewis (1832–1898)

English writer and photographer

Beautiful Soup, so rich and green,
Waiting in a hot tureen!
Who for such dainties would not stoop?
Soup of the evening, beautiful Soup!

Alice's Adventures in Wonderland (1865)

Cartland, Barbara (1901–2000)

English writer

Soup is usually the only course served by the butler.

In *The Guardian*, 2000

Cervantes, Miguel de (1547–1616)

Spanish writer and dramatist

La mejor salsa del mundo es la hambre.
Hunger is the best sauce in the world.

Don Quixote (1615)

Dahl, Roald (1916–1990)

British writer

Do you know what breakfast cereal is made of? It's made of all those little curly wooden shavings you find in pencil sharpeners!

Charlie and the Chocolate Factory (1964)

David, Elizabeth (1913–1992)

British cookery writer

To eat figs off the tree in the very early morning, when they have been barely touched by the sun, is one of the exquisite pleasures of the Mediterranean.

Italian Food (1954)

Davies, David (1742–1819)

Welsh cleric

Though the potato is an excellent root, deserving to be brought into general use, yet it seems not likely that the use of it should ever be normal in the country.

The Case of the Labourers in Husbandry (1795)

De La Mare, Walter (1873–1956)

English poet

It's a very odd thing –
As odd as can be –
That whatever Miss T eats
Turns into Miss T.

'Miss T' (1913)

De Vries, Peter (1910–1993)

US novelist

Gluttony is an emotional escape, a sign something is eating us.

Comfort me with Apples (1956)

Durrell, Lawrence (1912–1990)

Indian-born British poet and writer

The whole Mediterranean, the sculpture, the palms, the gold beads, the bearded heroes, the wine, the ideas, the ships, the moonlight, the winged gorgons, the bronze men, the philosophers – all of it seems to rise in the sour, pungent taste of these black olives between the teeth. A taste older than meat, older than wine. A taste as old as cold water.

Prospero's Cell (1945)

Fadiman, Clifton (1904–)

US writer, editor and broadcaster

Cheese – milk's leap toward immortality.

Any Number Can Play (1957)

Feuerbach, Ludwig (1804–1872)

German philosopher

Man is what he eats.

In Moleschott, *Lehre der Nahrungsmittel: Für das Volk* (1850)

Fincher, David (1963–)

US film director

Actor Edward Norton (the anonymous narrator) on the character Tyler Durden, played by Brad Pitt.

He was the guerilla terrorist for the food service industry. Apart from seasoning the lobster bisque, he farted on the meringue, sneezed on braised endive, and as for the cream of mushroom soup, well …

Fight Club (film, 1999)

Franklin, Benjamin (1706–1790)

US statesman, scientist, political critic and printer

To lengthen thy life, lessen thy meals.

Poor Richard's Almanac (1733)

Fuller, Thomas (1608–1661)

English churchman and antiquary

He was a very valiant man who first ventured on eating of oysters.

The History of the Worthies of England (1662)

Garfield, James A. (1831–1881)

US President

Man cannot live by bread alone; he must have peanut butter.

Inaugural address, 1881

Groening, Matt

US cartoonist

Groundskeeper Willie: Get yer haggis right here! Chopped heart and lungs, boiled in a wee sheep's stomach! Tastes as good as it sounds!

The Simpsons, TV cartoon series

Herbert, George (1593–1633)
English poet and priest
>   A cheerful look makes a dish a feast.
>> *Jacula Prudentum* (1640)

Herbert, Sir A.P. (1890–1971)
English humorist, writer, dramatist and politician
>   Bring porridge, bring sausage, bring fish, for a
>   start,
>   Bring kidneys, and mushrooms, and partridges'
>   legs,
>   But let the foundation be bacon and eggs.
>> In Catherine Brown, *Scottish Cookery* (1985)

Holmes, Oliver Wendell (1809–1894)
US physician, poet, writer and scientist
>   That most wonderful object of domestic art
>   called trifle – with its charming confusion of
>   cream and cake and almonds and jam and jelly
>   and wine and cinnamon and froth.
>> *Elsie Venner* (1861)

Johnson, Samuel (1709–1784)
English lexicographer, poet, critic, conversationalist and
essayist
>   A cucumber should be well sliced, and dressed
>   with pepper and vinegar, and then thrown out,
>   as good for nothing.
>> In Boswell, *Journal of a Tour to the Hebrides* (1785)

>   I look upon it, that he who does not mind his
>   belly will hardly mind anything else.
>> In Boswell, *The Life of Samuel Johnson* (1791)

Lamb, Charles (1775–1834)
English essayist, critic and letter writer
Of food
>   I hate a man who swallows it, affecting not to
>   know what he is eating. I suspect his taste in
>   higher matters.
>> *Essays of Elia* (1823)

Lebowitz, Fran (1946–)
US writer
>   Food is an important part of a balanced diet.
>> *Metropolitan Life* (1978)

Llewellyn, Richard (1907–1983)
Welsh novelist
>   And there is good fresh trout for supper. My
>   mother used to put them on a hot stone over
>   the fire, wrapped in breadcrumbs, butter,
>   parsley and lemon rind, all bound about with the
>   fresh leaves of leeks. If there is better food in
>   heaven, I am in a hurry to be there.
>> *How Green Was My Valley* (1939)

Lutyens, Sir Edwin Landseer (1869–1944)
English architect
Comment made in a restaurant
>   This piece of cod passes all understanding.
>> In Robert Lutyens, *Sir Edwin Lutyens* (1942)

Molière (1622–1673)
French dramatist, actor and director
>> *Il faut manger pour vivre et non pas vivre pour manger.*
>   One should eat to live, not live to eat.
>> *L'Avare* (1669)

Monroe, Marilyn (1926–1962)
US film actress and model
>> On having matzo balls for supper at Arthur Miller's parents
>   Isn't there another part of the matzo you can
>   eat?
>> Attr.

Newman, Paul (1925–)
US actor
On his salad dressing company
>   The embarrassing thing is that the salad
>   dressing is out-grossing my films.
>> Attr.

Orwell, George (1903–1950)
English writer and critic
>   We may find in the long run that tinned food is a
>   deadlier weapon than the machine-gun.
>> *The Road to Wigan Pier* (1937)

Paltrow, Gwyneth (1973–)
US actress
On British cuisine
>   The food is so bad I couldn't wait to get home.
>> *The Times* 1998

Peter, Laurence J. (1919–1990)
Canadian educationist and writer
>   The noblest of all dogs is the hot-dog; it feeds
>   the hand that bites it.
>> *Quotations for Our Time* (1977)

Piggy, Miss
Character from *The Muppets*
>   Never eat anything at one sitting that you can't
>   lift.
>> *Woman's Hour*, 1992

Poole, Shona Crawford (1943–)
Cookery writer
>   Ice cream is the most evocative of puddings. It
>   brings back summer holidays and the bicycle
>   bell call of the hokey-cokey man with his tricycle
>   cart, and rushing down the garden path with
>   grandpa's big mug to have it filled for the ice
>   cream sodas which were invariably constructed
>   in tall sundae glasses.
>> *The New Times Cookbook*

Pope, Alexander (1688–1744)
English poet, translator and editor
>   Fame is at best an unperforming cheat;
>   But 'tis substantial happiness, to eat.
>> 'Prologue for Mr D'Urfey's Last Play' (1727)

Portland, Sixth Duke of (1857–1943)
British aristocrat

On being told to reduce his expenses by dispensing with one of his two Italian pastry cooks

> What! Can't a fellow even enjoy a biscuit any more?

In Winchester, Their Noble Lordships

Prior, Matthew (1664–1721)
English poet

> Salads, and eggs, and lighter fare,
> Tune the Italian spark's guitar.
> And, if I take Dan Congreve right,
> Pudding and beef make Britons fight.

Alma (1718)

Proverbs

> A meal without flesh is like feeding on grass.

> An apple pie without some cheese is like a kiss without a squeeze.

> Bread is the staff of life.

> The nearer the bone the sweeter the flesh.

> There is much meat in God's storehouse.

Danish proverb

Rabelais, François (c.1494–c.1553)
French monk, physician, satirist and humanist

> *L'appétit vient en mangeant, … la soif s'en va en beuvant.*
> Appetite comes with eating … thirst goes with drinking.

Gargantua (1534)

Raleigh, Sir Walter A. (1861–1922)
English scholar, critic and essayist

> We would not lead a pleasant life,
> And 'twould be finished soon,
> If peas were eaten with the knife,
> And gravy with the spoon.
> Eat slowly: only men in rags
> And gluttons old in sin
> Mistake themselves for carpet bags
> And tumble victuals in.

'Stans puer ad mensam' (1923)

Ramsay, Allan (1686–1758)
Scottish poet and dramatist

> … bannocks and a share of cheese
> Will make a breakfast that a laird might please.

'The Gentle Shepherd' (1725)

Raphael, Frederic (1931–)
English author

> Great restaurants are, of course, nothing but mouth-brothels. There is no point in going to them if one intends to keep one's belt buckled.

The Sunday Times Magazine, 1977

Rousseau, Émile
Agent-General in London for Saskatchewan

> *Les grands mangeurs de viande sont en général cruels et féroces plus que les autres hommes … La barbarie anglaise est connue.*
> Great eaters of meat are in general more cruel and ferocious than other men. The English are known for their cruelty.

Attr.

Runyon, Damon (1884–1946)
US writer

> These citizens are always willing to bet that what Nicely-Nicely dies of will be over-feeding and never anything small like pneumonia, for Nicely-Nicely is known far and wide as a character who dearly loves to commit eating.

Take it Easy (1938)

Saki (1870–1916)
Burmese-born British writer

> Oysters are more beautiful than any religion … There's nothing in Christianity or Buddhism that quite matches the sympathetic unselfishness of an oyster.

The Chronicles of Clovis (1911)

> I believe I once considerably scandalized her by declaring that clear soup was a more important factor in life than a clear conscience.

Beasts and Super-Beasts (1914)

Secombe, Sir Harry (1921–)
Welsh comedian, actor and singer

> My advice if you insist on slimming: Eat as much as you like – just don't swallow it.

Daily Herald, 1962

Shakespeare, William (1564–1616)
English dramatist, poet and actor

> Methinks sometimes I have no more wit than a Christian or an ordinary man has; but I am a great eater of beef, and I believe that does harm to my wit.

Twelfth Night, I.iii

Shaw, George Bernard (1856–1950)
Irish socialist, writer, dramatist and critic

> There is no love sincerer than the love of food.

Man and Superman (1903)

Shelley, Percy Bysshe (1792–1822)
English poet, dramatist and essayist

> There are two Italies – the one is the most sublime and lovely contemplation that can be conceived by the imagination of man; the other is the most degraded, disgusting and odious. What do you think? Young women of rank actually eat – you will never guess what – garlick!

Attr.

Smith, Delia (1941–)
English food writer

> A perfect chip should be (i) crisp on the outside, (ii) soft, almost melting, in the middle, and (iii)

dry, which is to say not greasy, oily or soggy. It is relatively easy to cook soggy chips, but far more difficult to produce a beautifully dry, crisp and melting chip.

Complete Illustrated Cookery Course

St Leger, Warham (1850–c.1915)
Irish aristocrat
There is a fine stuffed chavender,
A chavender, or chub,
That decks the rural pavender,
The pavender, or pub,
Wherein I eat my gravender,
My gravender, or grub.

'The Chavender, or Chub'

Stevenson, Robert Louis (1850–1894)
Scottish writer, poet and essayist
Many's the long night I Ben Gunn have dreamed of cheese – toasted mostly, and woke up again and here I were … You might not happen to have a piece of cheese about you now?

Treasure Island (1883)

Trollope, Joanna
English novelist
What makes food such a tyranny for women? A man may in times of crisis hit the bottle (or another person), but he rarely hits the fridge.

The Times, 1998

Voltaire (1694–1778)
French philosopher, dramatist, poet, historian writer and critic
On learning that coffee was considered a slow poison
I think it must be so, for I have been drinking it for sixty-five years and I am not dead yet.

Attr.

Webster, John (c.1580–c.1625)
English dramatist
I saw him even now going the way of all flesh, that is to say towards the kitchen.

Westward Hoe (1607)

Wodehouse, P.G. (1881–1975)
English humorist and writer
The lunches of fifty-seven years had caused his chest to slip down to the mezzanine floor.

The Heart of a Goof (1926)

▶▶ COOKERY; DINING; VEGETARIANISM

foolishness

Anonymous
When I was a little boy, I had but a little wit,
'Tis a long time ago, and I have no more yet;
Nor ever ever shall, until that I die,
For the longer I live the more fool am I.

In *Wit and Mirth, an Antidote against Melancholy* (1684)

Antrim, Minna (1861–1950)
US writer
A fool bolts pleasure, then complains of moral indigestion.

Naked Truth and Veiled Allusions (1902)

Barnum, Phineas T. (1810–1891)
US showman and writer
There's a sucker born every minute.

Attr.

Beecher, Henry Ward (1813–1887)
US clergyman, lecturer, editor and writer
On receiving a note containing only one word: 'Fool'
I have known many an instance of a man writing a letter and forgetting to sign his name, but this is the only instance I have ever known of a man signing his name and forgetting to write the letter.

Attr.

The Bible (King James Version)
As a dog returneth to his vomit, so a fool returneth to his folly.

Proverbs 26:11

Blake, William (1757–1827)
English poet, engraver, painter and mystic
If the fool would persist in his folly he would become wise.

'Proverbs of Hell' (1793)

Boileau-Despréaux, Nicolas (1636–1711)
French writer
Un sot trouve toujours un plus sot qui l'admire.
A fool will always find a greater fool to admire him.

L'Art Poétique (1674)

Burns, Robert (1759–1796)
Scottish poet and song writer
That's a' your jargon o' your Schools,
Your Latin names for horns an' stools?
If honest Nature made you fools,
What sairs your grammers.

'First Epistle to Lapraik' (1785)

Cervantes, Miguel de (1547–1616)
Spanish writer and dramatist
…I es un entreverado loco, lleno de lúcidos intervalos.
He's an intermittent fool, full of lucid intervals.

Don Quixote (1615)

Christina of Sweden (1626–1689)
Queen of Sweden
Fools are more to be feared than the wicked.

Pensées de Christine, reine de Suede (1825)

Cowper, William (1731–1800)
English poet, hymn and letter writer

A fool must now and then be right, by chance.

'Conversation' (1782)

Darwin, Erasmus (1731–1802)
Dutch scholar and humanist
A fool … is a man who never tried an experiment in his life.

In a letter from Maria Edgeworth to Sophy Ruxton, 1792

Eliot, T.S. (1888–1965)
US-born British poet, verse dramatist and critic
When lovely woman stoops to folly and
Paces about her room again, alone,
She smoothes her hair with automatic hand,
And puts a record on the gramophone.

The Waste Land (1922)

Fielding, Henry (1707–1754)
English writer, dramatist and journalist
One fool at least in every married couple.

Amelia (1751)

Franklin, Benjamin (1706–1790)
US statesman, scientist, political critic and printer
Experience keeps a dear school, but fools will learn in no other.

Poor Richard's Almanac (1743)

Goldsmith, Oliver (c.1728–1774)
Irish dramatist, poet and writer
In my time, the follies of the town crept slowly among us, but now they travel faster than a stage-coach.

She Stoops to Conquer (1773)

Gracián, Baltasar (1601–1658)
Spanish writer
No es necio el que hace la necedad, sino el que, hecha, no la sabe encubrir.
It is not the one who commits an act of foolishness who is foolish, but the one who, once such an act has been committed, does not know how to cover it up.

Handbook-Oracle and the Art of Prudence, 1647

Horace (65–8 BC)
Roman poet
Misce stultitiam consiliis brevem:
Dulce est desipere in loco.
Mix a little folly with your plans: it is sweet to be silly at the right moment.

Odes

Ibsen, Henrik (1828–1906)
Norwegian writer, dramatist and poet
Fools are in a terrible, overwhelming majority, all the wide world over.

An Enemy of the People (1882)

Molière (1622–1673)
French dramatist, actor and director
C'est une folie à nulle autre seconde,

De vouloir se mêler à corriger le monde.
The greatest folly of all is wanting to busy oneself in setting the world to rights.

Le Misanthrope (1666)

Un sot savant est sot plus qu'un sot ignorant.
A knowledgeable fool is more foolish than an ignorant fool.

Les Femmes savantes (1672)

Pope, Alexander (1688–1744)
English poet, translator and editor
For Fools rush in where Angels fear to tread.

An Essay on Criticism (1711)

Proverbs
A fool at forty is a fool indeed.

Better be a fool than a knave.

Empty vessels make the greatest sound.

Fools build houses, and wise men buy them.

There's no fool like an old fool.

Rowland, Helen (1875–1950)
US writer
The follies which a man regrets most in his life are those which he didn't commit when he had the opportunity.

A Guide to Men (1922)

Schiller, Johann Christoph Friedrich (1759–1805)
German writer, dramatist, poet and historian
Mit der Dummheit kämpfen Götter selbst vergebens.
Gods themselves struggle in vain with stupidity.

The Maid of Orleans (1801)

Shadwell, Thomas (c.1642–1692)
The haste of a Fool is the slowest thing in the World.

A True Widow (1679), III

Shakespeare, William (1564–1616)
English dramatist, poet and actor
He uses his folly like a stalking-horse, and under the presentation of that he shoots his wit.

As You Like It, V.iv

Shenstone, William (1714–1763)
English poet, essayist and letter writer
A fool and his words are soon parted; a man of genius and his money.

Essays on Men and Manners

Spencer, Herbert (1820–1903)
English philosopher and journalist
The ultimate result of shielding men from the effects of folly, is to fill the world with fools.

Essays (1891)

Stevenson, Robert Louis (1850–1894)
Scottish writer, poet and essayist

It is better to be a fool than to be dead.

Virginibus Puerisque (1881),

For God's sake give me the young man who has brains enough to make a fool of himself!

Virginibus Puerisque (1881)

Swift, Jonathan (1667–1745)
Irish satirist, poet, essayist and cleric
Hated by fools, and fools to hate,
Be that my motto and my fate.

'To Mr Delany' (1718)

The Bible (King James Version)
Answer a fool according to his folly.

Proverbs, 26:5

Thoreau, Henry David (1817–1862)
US essayist, social critic and writer
Any fool can make a rule and every fool will mind it.

Attr.

Tusser, Thomas (c.1524–1580)
English writer, poet and musician
A fool and his money be soon at debate.

Five Hundred Points of Good Husbandry (1557)

Whately, Richard (1787–1863)
English philosopher, theologian, educationist and writer
It is a folly to expect men to do all that they may reasonably be expected to do.

Apophthegms (1854)

Young, Edward (1683–1765)
English poet, dramatist, satirist and clergyman
Be wise with speed;
A fool at forty is a fool indeed.

Love of Fame, the Universal Passion (1728)

▶▶ IGNORANCE; STUPIDITY

football

Allison, Malcolm
English footballer and coach
Professional football is no longer a game. It's a war. And it brings out the same primitive instincts that go back thousands of years.

The Observer, 1973

Atkinson, Ron (1939–)
English football coach and commentator
I would not say he [David Ginola] is the best left winger in the Premiership, but there are none better.

Sky Sports

He dribbles a lot and the opposition don't like it – you can see it over their faces.

Sky Sports

I never comment on referees and I'm not going to break the habit of a lifetime for that prat.

Sky Sports

An inch or two either side of the post and that would have been a goal.

Sky Sports

Ball, Alan
English footballer and coach
After making a substitution which enabled his team to win a key relegation battle
I thought if we were going to lose it, we might as well lose it by trying to win it.

Daily Mail, 1996

Blanchflower, Danny (1926–1993)
English footballer
The great fallacy is that the game is first and last about winning. It is nothing of the kind. The game is about glory, it is about doing things in style and with a flourish, about going out and beating the lot, not waiting for them to die of boredom.

Attr.

Clark, Alan (1928–1999)
English Conservative politican, historian and diarist
On football hooligans
A compliment to the English martial spirit.

The Times, 1998

Crooks, Garth (1958–)
English footballer
Football is football; if that weren't the case, it wouldn't be the game it is.

In Fantoni, *Private Eye's Colemanballs (2)* (1984)

Duffy, Jim
Scottish football pundit
Of goalkeeper Andy Murdoch
He has an answerphone installed on his six-yard line and the message says: 'Sorry, I'm not in just now, but if you'd like to leave the ball in the back of the net, I'll get back to you as soon as I can.'

In *Umbro Book of Football Quotations* (1993)

Greer, Germaine (1939–)
Australian feminist, critic, English scholar and writer
Football is an art more central to our culture than anything the Arts Council deigns to recognize.

Independent, 1996

Hickson, Paul
English sports subeditor
Headline describing Celtic's 3-1 defeat by Inverness Caledonian Thistle
Super Caley Go Ballistic, Celtic Are Atrocious.

The Sun, 2000

Keegan, Kevin (1951–)
English footballer and coach
> Gary always weighed up his options, especially when he had no choice.
>> *Radio 5 live*

> Ardiles strokes the ball like it is part of his own anatomy.
>> RTE

> England have the best fans in the world and Scotland's fans are second to none.
>> Attr.

> The game has gone rather scrappy as both sides realise they could win this match or lose it or draw it even.
>> Attr.

> Chile have three options – they could win or they could lose. It's up to them, the tide is in their court now.
>> Attr.

> Argentina are the second-best team in the world, and there's no higher praise than that.
>> Attr.

Lebowitz, Fran (1946–)
US writer
> Being a woman is of special interest only to aspiring male transsexuals. To actual women, it is merely a good excuse not to play football.
>> *Metropolitan Life* (1978)

Lineker, Gary (1960–)
English footballer and sports presenter
> The nice aspect about football is that, if things go wrong, it's the manager who gets the blame.
>> *Independent*, 1990

Maradona, Diego (1960–)
Argentinian footballer
On his controversial goal against England in the 1986 World Cup
> The goal was scored a little bit by the hand of God, another bit by the head of Maradona.
>> *The Guardian*, 1986

McGregor, Jimmie (1932–)
Scottish folk singer
> Oh, he's football crazy, he's football mad
> And the football it has robbed him o' the wee bit sense he had.
> And it would take a dozen skivvies, his clothes to wash and scrub,
> Since our Jock became a member of that terrible football club.
>> 'Football Crazy' (song, 1960)

Osgood, Peter (1947–)
English footballer

> Women are around all the time but World Cups come only every four years.
>> *The Times*, 1998

Parris, Matthew (1949–)
British Conservative politician and journalist
> And now the worst news of all. Gay men are getting interested in football … What a catastrophe. One became homosexual to get away from this sort of thing.
>> *The Times*, 1998

Paxman, Jeremy (1950–)
English journalist, writer and broadcaster
> Internationally, football has become a substitute for war.
>> *The Sunday Times*, 2000

Pelé (1940–)
Brazilian footballer
> Football? It's the beautiful game.
>> Attr.

Rider, Steve
BBC sports commentator
> The match will be shown on *Match of the Day*. If you don't want to know the result, look away now as we show you Tony Adams lifting the cup for Arsenal.
>> BBC announcement, 1998

Robson, Bobby (1933–)
British football coach
> The first ninety minutes are the most important.
>> Quoted as the title of a TV documentary, 1983

Shankly, Bill (1914–1981)
Scottish football player and manager
> Some people think football is a matter of life and death. I don't like that attitude. I can assure them it is much more serious than that.
>> Remark on BBC TV, 1981

Smith, Delia (1941–)
English food writer
On her appointment as a director of Norwich City football club
> Football and cookery are the two most important subjects in the country.
>> *The Observer*, 1997

Souness, Graeme (1953–)
Scottish footballer and coach
> How could I carry out a policy where I won't sign a Catholic but I'll go home and live with one?
>> In Kenny MacDonald, *Scottish Football Quotations* (1994)

Stubbes, Philip (c.1555–1610)
English Puritan pamphleteer and writer
> Football … causeth fighting, brawling, contention, quarrel picking, murder, homicide and great effusion of blood, as daily experience

teacheth.

Anatomy of Abuses (1583)

Viera, Ondina
Uruguayan football manager
Other nations have history. We have football.

The Spectator, 1996

▶▶ SPORT AND GAMES

force

Asimov, Isaac (1920–1992)
Russian-born US scientist, academic and writer
Violence is the last refuge of the incompetent.

Foundation (1951)

Brien, Alan (1925–)
English writer
Violence is the repartee of the illiterate.

Punch, 1973

Bright, John (1811–1889)
English Liberal politician and social reformer
Force is not a remedy.

Speech, 1880

Bronowski, Jacob (1908–1974)
British scientist, writer and TV presenter
The wish to hurt, the momentary intoxication
with pain, is the loophole through which the
pervert climbs into the minds of ordinary men.

The Face of Violence (1954)

Burke, Edmund (1729–1797)
Irish-born British statesman and philosopher
The use of force alone is but temporary. It may
subdue for a moment; but it does not remove
the necessity of subduing again: and a nation is
not governed, which is perpetually to be
conquered.

'Speech on Conciliation with
America' (1775)

Horace (65–8 BC)
Roman poet
Vis consili expers mole ruit sua.
Brute force without judgement collapses under
its own weight.

Odes

Inge, William Ralph (1860–1954)
English divine, writer and teacher
A man may build himself a throne of bayonets,
but he cannot sit upon it.

Philosophy of Plotinus (1923)

King, Martin Luther (1929–1968)
US civil rights leader and Baptist minister
A riot is at bottom the language of the unheard.

Chaos or Community (1967)

Koran
Let there be no violence in religion.

Chapter 2

La Fontaine, Jean de (1621–1695)
French poet and fabulist
La raison du plus fort est toujours la meilleure.
The reason of the strongest is always the best.

'Le loup et l'agneau'

MacKenzie, Sir Compton (1883–1972)
Scottish writer and broadcaster
There is little to choose morally between
beating up a man physically and beating him up
mentally.

On Moral Courage (1962)

Milton, John (1608–1674)
English poet, libertarian and pamphleteer
… who overcomes
By force, hath overcome but half his foe.

Paradise Lost (1667)

Roosevelt, Theodore (1858–1919)
US Republican President
There is a homely old adage which runs, 'Speak
softly and carry a big stick; you will go far.'

Speech, 1903

Saint-Pierre, Bernardin de (1737–1814)
Women are false in countries where men are
tyrants. Violence everywhere leads to deception.

Paul et Virginie (1788)

Trotsky, Leon (1879–1940)
Russian revolutionary and Communist theorist
Where force is necessary, one should make use
of it boldly, resolutely, and right to the end. But
it is as well to know the limitations of force; to
know where to combine force with manoeuvre,
assault with conciliation.

What Next? (1932)

Unamuno, Miguel de (1864–1936)
Spanish philosopher, poet and writer
Of Franco's supporters
Vencer no es convencer.
To conquer is not to convince.

Speech, 1936

▶▶ POWER; VIOLENCE

foreigners

Bradbury, Malcolm (1932–)
English writer, critic and academic
Sympathy – for all these people, for being
foreigners – lay over the gathering like a woolly
blanket; and no one was enjoying it at all.

Eating People is Wrong (1954)

Botham, Ian (1955–)
English cricketer
On Pakistan
> The sort of place everyone should send his mother-in-law for a month, all expenses paid.
> > *BBC Radio 2 interview, March 1984*

Boycott, Geoffrey (1940–)
English cricketer
During his trial in Grasse, France
> Everybody's talking French. I don't understand.
> > *The Times, 1998*

Browne, Sir Thomas (1605–1682) ·
English physician, author and antiquary
> I feel not in myself those common antipathies that I can discover in others; those national repugnances do not touch me, nor do I behold with prejudice the French, Italian, Spaniard, or Dutch; but where I find their actions in balance with my countrymen's, I honour, love and embrace them in the same degree.
> > *Religio Medici (1643)*

Crisp, Quentin (1908–1999)
English writer, publicist and model
> I don't hold with abroad and think that foreigners speak English when our backs are turned.
> > *The Naked Civil Servant (1968)*

Du Belloy, P.-L.B. (1727–1775)
French poet
> *Plus je vis d'étrangers, plus j'aimai ma patrie.*
> The more foreigners I saw, the more I loved my native land.
> > *Le Siège de Calais (1765)*

Erasmus (c.1466–1536)
Dutch scholar and humanist
> Is not the Turk a man and a brother?
> > *Querela Pacis*

Goldsmith, Oliver (c.1728–1774)
Irish dramatist, poet and writer
> The Scotch may be compared to a tulip planted in dung, but I never see a Dutchman in his own house, but I think of a magnificent Egyptian Temple dedicated to an ox.
> > *Letter from Leyden to Rev. Thomas Contarine, 1754*

Meynell, Hugo (1727–1780)
Frequenter of London society, acquaintance of Dr Johnson
> For anything I see, foreigners are fools.
> > *In Boswell, The Life of Samuel Johnson (1791)*

Mitford, Nancy (1904–1973)
English writer
> I loathe abroad, nothing would induce me to live there … and, as for foreigners, they are all the same, and they all make me sick.
> > *The Pursuit of Love (1945)*

> Abroad is unutterably bloody and foreigners are fiends.
> > *The Pursuit of Love (1945)*

Trollope, Anthony (1815–1882)
English writer, traveller and post office official
> We cannot bring ourselves to believe it possible that a foreigner should in any respect be wiser than ourselves. If any such point out to us our follies, we at once claim those follies as the special evidences of our wisdom.
> > *Orley Farm (1862)*

Twain, Mark (1835–1910)
US humorist, writer, journalist and lecturer
> They spell it Vinci and pronounce it Vinchy; foreigners always spell better than they pronounce.
> > *The Innocents Abroad (1869)*

▶▶ TRAVEL

forgetting

Browne, Sir Thomas (1605–1682)
English physician, author and antiquary
> But the iniquity of oblivion blindly scattereth her poppy, and deals with the memory of men without distinction to merit of perpetuity.
> > *Hydriotaphia: Urn Burial (1658)*

> Oblivion is a kind of Annihilation.
> > *Christian Morals (1716)*

Calverley, C.S. (1831–1884)
English poet, parodist, scholar and lawyer
> I cannot sing the old songs now!
> It is not that I deem them low;
> 'Tis that I can't remember how
> They go.
> > *'Changed' (1872)*

Carroll, Lewis (1832–1898)
English writer and photographer
> 'The horror of that moment,' the King went on, 'I shall never, never forget!'
> 'You will, though,' the Queen said, 'if you don't make a memorandum of it.'
> > *Through the Looking-Glass (and What Alice Found There) (1872)*

Disraeli, Benjamin (1804–1881)
English statesman and writer
> Nobody is forgotten when it is convenient to remember him.
> > *Attr.*

> When I meet a man whose name I can't

remember, I give myself two minutes; then, if it is a hopeless case, I always say, And how is the old complaint?

Attr.

Fenton, James (1949–)
English poet

How comforting it is, once or twice a year
To get together and forget the old times.

The Memory of War. Poems 1968–1982 (1983)

Johnson, Samuel (1709–1784)
English lexicographer, poet, critic, conversationalist and essayist

Men more frequently require to be reminded than informed.

The Rambler (1750–1752)

Marx, Groucho (1895–1977)
US comedian

I never forget a face, but I'll make an exception in your case.

The Guardian, 1965

Saki (1870–1916)
Burmese-born British writer

Women and elephants never forget an injury.

Reginald (1904)

Sheridan, Richard Brinsley (1751–1816)
Irish dramatist, politician and orator

Illiterate him, I say, quite from your memory.

The Rivals (1775)

Stevenson, Robert Louis (1850–1894)
Scottish writer, poet and essayist

I've a grand memory for forgetting, David.

Kidnapped (1886)

Svevo, Italo (1861–1928)
Italian writer

There are three things I always forget. Names, faces and – the third I can't remember.

Attr.

▶▶ MEMORY

forgiveness

Austen, Jane (1775–1817)
English writer

You ought certainly to forgive them as a Christian, but never to admit them in your sight, or allow their names to be mentioned in your hearing.

Pride and Prejudice (1813)

The Bible (King James Version)

Father, forgive them; for they know not what they do.

Luke, 23:34

Browning, Robert (1812–1889)
English poet

Good, to forgive;
Best, to forget!
Living, we fret;
Dying, we live.

La Saisiaz (1878)

Catherine the Great (1729–1796)
Empress of Russia

Moi, je serai autocrate: c'est mon métier. Et le bon Dieu me pardonnera: c'est son métier.
I shall be an autocrat: that's my job. And the good Lord will forgive me: that's his job.

Attr.

Churchill, Sir Winston (1874–1965)
English Conservative Prime Minister

Men will forgive a man anything except bad prose.

Election speech, Manchester, 1906

Dietrich, Marlene (1901–1992)
German-born US actress and singer

Once a woman has forgiven her man, she must not reheat his sins for breakfast.

Marlene Dietrich's ABC (1962)

Dryden, John (1631–1700)
English poet, satirist, dramatist and critic

Forgiveness to the injured does belong;
But they ne'er pardon, who have done the wrong.

The Conquest of Granada (1670)

Frost, Robert (1874–1963)
US poet

Forgive, O Lord, my little jokes on Thee
And I'll forgive Thy great big one on me.

'Cluster of Faith' (1962)

Gay, John (1685–1732)
English poet, dramatist and librettist

Well, Polly; as far as one woman can forgive another, I forgive thee.

The Beggar's Opera (1728)

Heine, Heinrich (1797–1856)
German lyric poet, essayist and journalist

We should forgive our enemies, but only after they have been hanged first.

Attr.

Kennedy, Robert F. (1925–1968)
US Attorney General and Democrat politician

Always forgive your enemies – but never forget their names.

Attr.

Proverbs

To err is human; to forgive divine.

Forgive and forget.

Yeats, W.B. (1865–1939)
Irish poet, dramatist, editor, writer and senator
> Only the dead can be forgiven;
> But when I think of that my tongue's a stone.
>> 'A Dialogue of Self and Soul'
>> (1933)

france

Anonymous
Paris Chamber of Commerce spokesman commenting on the results of a tourist survey
> The overall impression from the British and the Germans is that they love France itself but would rather that the French didn't live there.

Arnold, Matthew (1822–1888)
English poet, critic, essayist and educationist
> France, famed in all great arts, in none supreme.
>> 'To a Republican Friend' (1849)

Caesar, Gaius Julius (c.102–44 BC)
Roman statesman, historian and army commander
> *Gallia est omnis divisa in partes tres.*
> The whole territory of Gaul is divided into three parts.
>> *De Bello Gallico*

Carlyle, Thomas (1795–1881)
Scottish historian, biographer, critic, and essayist
> France was long a despotism tempered by epigrams.
>> *History of the French Revolution* (1837)

Churchill, Sir Winston (1874–1965)
English Conservative Prime Minister
> The Almighty in His infinite wisdom did not see fit to create Frenchmen in the image of Englishmen.
>> Speech, House of Commons, December 1942

Coward, Sir Noël (1899–1973)
English dramatist, actor, producer and composer
> There's always something fishy about the French.
>> *Conversation Piece* (1934)

De Gaulle, Charles (1890–1970)
French general and statesman
> One can only unite the French under the threat of danger. One cannot simply bring together a nation that produces 265 kinds of cheese.
>> Speech, 1951

> When I want to know what France thinks, I ask myself.
>> Attr.

Du Bellay, Joachim (1522–1560)
French poet
> *France, mère des arts, des armes et des lois.*

> France, mother of arts, of arms, and of laws.
>> *Les Regrets* (1558)

Gallico, Paul (1897–1976)
US author and scriptwriter
> The words Liberté, Egalité, Fraternité rimming their coins might well be replaced by the slogan 'It can be arranged'.
>> *The Zoo Gang* (1971)

Graham, Harry (1874–1936)
English writer
> Weep not for little Léonie
> Abducted by a French Marquis!
> Though loss of honour was a wrench
> Just think how it's improved her French.
>> *More Ruthless Rhymes for Heartless Homes* (1930)

Joan of Arc (c.1412–1431)
French patriot and martyr
> You think when you have slain me you will conquer France, but that you will never do. Though there were a hundred thousand God-dammees more in France than there are, they will never conquer that kingdom.
>> Attr.

Johnson, Samuel (1709–1784)
English lexicographer, poet, critic, conversationalist and essayist
> A Frenchman must be always talking, whether he knows anything of the matter or not; an Englishman is content to say nothing, when he has nothing to say.
>> In Boswell, *The Life of Samuel Johnson* (1791)

> What I gained by being in France was learning to be better satisfied with my own country.
>> In Boswell, *The Life of Samuel Johnson* (1791)

Napoleon I (1769–1821)
French emperor
> France has more need of me than I have need of France.
>> Speech, 1813

Novello, Ivor (1893–1951)
Welsh actor, composer, songwriter and dramatist
> There's something Vichy about the French.
>> In Marsh, *Ambrosia and Small Beer*

Rivarol, Antoine de (1753–1801)
French writer and wit
> *Ce qui n'est pas clair n'est pas français.*
> What is not clear is not French.
>> *Discours sur l'Universalité de la Langue Française* (1784)

Sidney, Sir Philip (1554–1586)
English poet, critic, soldier, courtier and diplomat
> That sweet enemy, France.
>> *Astrophel and Stella* (1591)

Spencer, Herbert (1820–1903)

English philosopher and journalist

> French art, if not sanguinary, is usually obscene.
>
> In *Home Life with Herbert Spencer* (1906)

Sterne, Laurence (1713–1768)

Irish-born English writer and clergyman

Of the French

> They are a loyal, a gallant, a generous, an ingenious, and good tempered people as is under heaven – if they have a fault, they are too serious.
>
> *A Sentimental Journey* (1768)

Tocqueville, Alexis de (1805–1859)

French historian, politician, lawyer and memoirist

> *L'esprit français est de ne pas vouloir de supérieur. L'esprit anglais de vouloir des inférieurs. Le Français lève les yeux sans cesse au-dessus de lui avec inquiétude. L'Anglais les baisse au-dessous de lui avec complaisance. C'est de part et d'autre de l'orgueil, mais entendu de manière différente.*
>
> The French want no-one to be their superior. The English want inferiors. The Frenchman constantly looks above him with anxiety. The Englishman looks beneath him with complacency. On either side it is pride, but understood in a different manner.
>
> *Voyage en Angleterre et en Irlande de 1835* (1835)

Walpole, Horace (1717–1797)

English writer and politician

> I do not dislike the French from the vulgar antipathy between neighbouring nations, but for their insolent and unfounded airs of superiority.
>
> Letter, 1787

Wilder, Billy (1906–)

Austrian-born US fllm director, producer and screenwriter

> France is a country where the money falls apart in your hands and you can't tear the toilet paper.
>
> In Halliwell, *Filmgoer's Book of Quotes* (1973)

freedom

Addison, Joseph (1672–1719)

English essayist, poet, playwright and statesman

> A day, an hour of virtuous liberty
> Is worth a whole eternity in bondage.
>
> *Cato* (1713)

Anonymous

> As a general rule, the freedom of any people can be judged by the volume of their laughter.

Declaration sent to Pope John XXII by the Scottish barons

> For so long as but a hundred of us remain alive, we will in no way yield ourselves to the dominion of the English. For it is not for glory, nor riches, nor honour that we fight, but for Freedom only, which no good man lays down but with his life.
>
> Declaration of Arbroath, 1320

Aristotle (384–322 BC)

Greek philosopher

> Where we are free to act, we are also free not to act, and where we are able to say No, we are also able to say Yes.
>
> *Nicomachean Ethics*

Aurelius, Marcus (121–180)

Roman emperor and Stoic philosopher

> Remember that to change your mind and follow someone who puts you right is to be none the less free than you were before.
>
> *Meditations*

Baldwin, Stanley (1867–1947)

English Conservative statesman and Prime Minister

> There is a wind of nationalism and freedom blowing round the world, and blowing as strongly in Asia as elsewhere.
>
> Speech, London, 4 December 1934

Barbour, John (c.1316–1395)

Scottish poet, churchman and scholar

> A! fredome is a noble thing!
> Fredome mayss man to haiff liking;
> Fredome all solace to man giffio:
> He levys at ess that frely levys!
>
> *The Bruce* (1375)

Bell, Clive (1881–1964)

English art critic

> Only reason can convince us of those three fundamental truths without a recognition of which there can be no effective liberty: that what we believe is not necessarily true; that what we like is not necessarily good; and that all questions are open.
>
> *Civilisation* (1928)

Berlin, Isaiah (1909–1997)

English philosopher

> Liberty is liberty, not equality or fairness or justice or culture, or human happiness or a quiet conscience.
>
> *Four Essays on Liberty* (1969)

> Rousseau asks why it is that man, who was born free, is nevertheless everywhere in chains; one might as well ask, says Maistre, why it is that sheep, who are born carnivorous, nevertheless everywhere nibble grass. Men are not born for freedom, nor for peace.
>
> 'The Counter-Enlightenment'

Burke, Edmund (1729–1797)

Irish-born British statesman and philosopher

> Abstract liberty, like other mere abstractions, is

not to be found.

Speech on Conciliation with America (1775)

Freedom and not servitude is the cure of anarchy; as religion, and not atheism, is the true remedy for superstition.

Speech on Conciliation with America (1775)

Liberty, too, must be limited in order to be possessed.

Letter to the Sheriffs of Bristol on the Affairs of America (1777)

The only liberty I mean, is a liberty connected with order; that not only exists along with order and virtue, but which cannot exist at all without them.

Speech, 1774

Burns, Robert (1759–1796)
Scottish poet and song writer

Scots, wha hae wi' Wallace bled,
Scots, wham Bruce has aften led,
Welcome to your gory bed
Or to victorie! …

Lay the proud usurpers low!
Tyrants fall in ev'ry foe!
Liberty's in every blow!
Let us do, or die!

'Scots, Wha Hae' (1793)

Byron, Lord (1788–1824)
English poet satirist and traveller

Yet, Freedom! yet thy banner, torn, but flying,
Streams like the thunder-storm against the wind.

Childe Harold's Pilgrimage (1812–18)

Coleridge, Hartley (1796–1849)
English poet and writer

But what is Freedom? Rightly understood,
A universal licence to be good.

'Liberty' (1833)

Coleridge, Samuel Taylor (1772–1834)
English poet, philosopher and critic

With what deep worship I have still adored
The spirit of divinest Liberty.

'France' (1798)

For what is freedom, but the unfettered use
Of all the powers which God for use had given?

'The Destiny of Nations'

Collingwood, R.G. (1889–1943)
English philosopher and archaeologist

Perfect freedom is reserved for the man who lives by his own work and in that work does what he wants to do.

Speculum Mentis (1924)

Columbanus, Saint (c.543–615)
Irish missionary and abbot

To the Pope

Liberty was ever the tradition of my fathers, and, among us, no person avails, but rather reason.

In Brendan Lehane, *Early Celtic Christianity* (1994)

Connolly, James (1868–1916)
Irish labour leader

Apostles of Freedom are ever idolised when dead, but crucified when alive.

Workers Republic, 1898

Cowper, William (1731–1800)
English poet, hymn and letter writer

Freedom has a thousand charms to show,
That slaves, howe'er contented, never know.

Table Talk (1782)

Curran, John Philpot (1750–1817)
Irish judge, orator, politician and reformer

The condition upon which God hath given liberty to man is eternal vigilance; which condition if he break, servitude is at once the consequence of his crime, and the punishment of his guilt.

Speech, 1790

Debs, Eugene Victor (1855–1926)
US radical politician and trade union leader

While there is a lower class, I am in it. While there is a criminal class I am of it. While there is a soul in prison, I am not free.

Remark made during his trial for sedition, 1918

Diderot, Denis (1713–1784)
French philosopher, encyclopaedist, writer and dramatist

Men will never be free until the last king is strangled with the entrails of the last priest.

Dithyrambe sur la Fête des Rois

Engels, Friedrich (1820–1895)
German socialist and political philosopher

Freedom is the recognition of necessity.

In Mackay, *The Harvest of a Quiet Eye* (1977)

Ewer, William Norman (1885–1976)
English journalist

I gave my life for freedom – This I know:
For those who bade me fight had told me so.

'The Souls' (1917)

Ford, John (c.1586–c.1640)
English dramatist and poet

Whilst we strive
To live most free,
we're caught in our own toils.

The Lover's Melancholy (1629)

George, Dan (1899–1982)
Canadian Indian chief

O Freedom, what liberties are taken in thy name!

In Sagittarius and D. George, *Perpetual Pessimist* (1963)

Gibbon, Edward (1737–1794)
English historian, politician and memoirist
> Corruption, the most infallible symptom of
> constitutional liberty.
>> *Decline and Fall of the Roman Empire* (1776–88)

Halifax, Lord (1633–1695)
English politician, courtier, pamphleteer and
epigrammatist
> Power is so apt to be insolent and Liberty to be
> saucy, that they are very seldom upon good
> Terms.
>> *Political, Moral and Miscellaneous Thoughts and*
>> *Reflections* (1750)

> When the people contend for their Liberty, they
> seldom get any thing by their Victory but new
> Masters.
>> *Political, Moral and Miscellaneous Thoughts and*
>> *Reflections* (1750)

Hattersley, Roy (1932–)
British Labour politician and writer
> The proposition that Muslims are welcome in
> Britain if, and only if, they stop behaving like
> Muslims is incompatible with the principles of a
> free society.
>> *The Independent*, 1995

Hazlitt, William (1778–1830)
English writer and critic
> The love of liberty is the love of others; the love
> of power is the love of ourselves.
>> *Political Essays* (1819)

Henry, Patrick (1736–1799)
US lawyer, orator and statesman
> Give me liberty, or give me death!
>> Speech, 1775

Hill, Christopher (1912–)
English historian
> Only very slowly and late have men come to
> realize that unless freedom is universal it is only
> extended privilege.
>> *Century of Revolution* (1961)

Hoffer, Eric (1902–1983)
US writer, philosopher and longshoreman
> When people are free to do as they please, they
> usually imitate each other.
>> *The Passionate State of Mind* (1955)

Horace (65–8 BC)
Roman poet
> *Quisnam igitur liber? Sapiens qui sibi imperiosus,*
> *Quem neque pauperies neque mors neque vincula*
> *terrent. Responsare cupidinibus, contemnere honores*
> *Fortis, et in se ipso totus, teres, atque rotundus.*
> Who then is free? The wise man who commands
> himself, whom neither poverty nor death nor
> chains can terrify, who is strong enough to defy

his passions and to despise distinctions, a man
who is complete in himself, polished and well-
rounded.
>> *Satires*

Huxley, Aldous (1894–1963)
English writer, poet and critic
> As political and economic freedom diminish,
> sexual freedom tends compensatingly to
> increase.
>> *Brave New World* (1932)

James I of Scotland (1394–1437)
King of Scotland
> The bird, the beast, the fish eke in the sea,
> They live in freedom everich in his kind;
> And I a man, and lackith liberty.
>> *The Kingis Quair*

Jefferson, Thomas (1743–1826)
US Democrat statesman and President
> The tree of liberty must be refreshed from time
> to time with the blood of patriots and tyrants. It
> is its natural manure.
>> Letter to W.S. Smith, 1787

Kafka, Franz (1883–1924)
Czech-born German-speaking writer
> *Es ist oft besser, in Ketten, als frei zu sein.*
> It's often better to be in chains than to be free.
>> *The Trial* (1925)

Kierkegaard, Søren (1813–1855)
Danish philosopher
> People hardly ever make use of the freedom
> they have, for example, the freedom of thought;
> instead they demand freedom of speech as a
> compensation.
>> In *The Faber Book of Aphorisms* (1962)

King, Martin Luther (1929–1968)
US civil rights leader and Baptist minister
> Free at last, free at last, thank God Almighty, we
> are free at last!
>> Speech, 1963

Kristofferson, Kris (1936–)
US singer and film actor
> Freedom's just another word for nothing left to
> lose.
>> 'Me and Bobby McGee', song,
>> 1969

Lenin, V.I. (1870–1924)
Russian revolutionary, Marxist theoretician and first
leader of the USSR
> It is true that liberty is precious – so precious
> that it must be rationed.
>> In Sidney and Beatrice Webb, *Soviet Communism*
>> (1936)

Lincoln, Abraham (1809–1865)
US statesman and President

I leave you, hoping that the lamp of liberty will burn in your bosoms, until there shall no longer be a doubt that all men are created free and equal.

Speech, 1858

Those who deny freedom to others, deserve it not for themselves.

Speech, 1856

Luxemburg, Rosa (1871–1919)
German revolutionary
> Freedom is always and exclusively freedom for the one who thinks differently.
> *The Russian Revolution* (1922, trans. 1961)

Macaulay, Lord (1800–1859)
English Liberal statesman, essayist and poet
> There is only one cure for the evils which newly acquired freedom produces; and that is freedom.
> *Collected Essays* (1843)

> Many politicians of our time are in the habit of laying it down as a self-evident proposition, that no people ought to be free till they are fit to use their freedom. The maxim is worthy of the fool in the old story, who resolved not to go into the water till he had learnt to swim. If men are to wait for liberty till they become wise and good in slavery, they may indeed wait for ever.
> *Collected Essays* (1843)

Malcolm X (1925–1965)
US black leader
> You can't separate peace from freedom because no one can be at peace unless he has his freedom.
> *Malcolm X Speaks*, 1965

Mandela, Nelson (1918–)
South African statesman and President
> I cannot and will not give any undertaking at a time when I, and you, the people, are not free. Your freedom and mine cannot be separated.
> Message to a rally in Soweto, 1985

> A sudden access of psychological freedom often turns from sheer excitement to deep panic.
> *The Man Who Dreamed of Tomorrow* (1980)

Mill, John Stuart (1806–1873)
English philosopher, economist and reformer
> The liberty of the individual must be thus far limited; he must not make himself a nuisance to other people.
> *On Liberty* (1859)

> Liberty consists in doing what one desires.
> *On Liberty* (1859)

> The sole end for which mankind are warranted, individually or collectively, in interfering with the liberty of action of any of their number, is self-protection.
> *On Liberty* (1859)

Milton, John (1608–1674)
English poet, libertarian and pamphleteer
> Give me the liberty to know, to utter, and to argue freely according to conscience, above all liberties.
> *Areopagitica* (1644)

> None can love freedom heartilie, but good men; the rest love not freedom, but licence.
> *The Tenure of Kings and Magistrates* (1649)

Montesquieu, Charles (1689–1755)
French philosopher and jurist
> *La liberté est le droit de faire tout ce que les lois permettent.*
> Freedom is the right to do whatever the laws permit.
> *De l'esprit des lois* (1748)

Mussolini, Benito (1883–1945)
Italian fascist dictator
> *Ci sono le libertá; la libertá non è mai esistita.*
> There are freedoms; freedom has never existed.
> Speech, 1923

Orwell, George (1903–1950)
English writer and critic
> I sometimes think that the price of liberty is not so much eternal vigilance as eternal dirt.
> *The Road to Wigan Pier* (1937)

Pankhurst, Dame Christabel (1880–1958)
English suffragette
> What we suffragettes aspire to be when we are enfranchised is ambassadors of freedom to women in other parts of the world, who are not so free as we are.
> Speech, 1915

Pitt, William (1759–1806)
English politician and Prime Minister
> Necessity is the plea for every infringement of human freedom. It is the argument of tyrants; it is the creed of slaves.
> Speech, 1783

Popper, Sir Karl (1902–1994)
Austrian-born British philosopher
> We must plan for freedom, and not only for security, if for no other reason than that only freedom can make security secure.
> *The Open Society and its Enemies* (1945)

Rand, Ayn (1905–1982)
Russian-born US writer
> Intellectual freedom cannot exist without political freedom; political freedom cannot exist without economic freedom; a free mind and a

free market are corollaries.

For The New Intellectual

Roland, Madame (1754–1793)
French revolutionary and writer
Remark on mounting the scaffold
> *O liberté! O liberté! que de crimes on commet en ton nom!*
> O liberty! O liberty! how many crimes are committed in your name!

In Lamartine, *Histoire des Girondins* (1847)

Roosevelt, Franklin Delano (1882–1945)
US Democrat President
> In the future days, which we seek to make secure, we look forward to a world founded upon four essential human freedoms. The first is freedom of speech and expression – everywhere in the world. The second is freedom of every person to worship God in his own way – everywhere in the world. The third is freedom from want … The fourth is freedom from fear.

Address, 1941

Rousseau, Jean-Jacques (1712–1778)
Swiss-born French philosopher, educationist and essayist
> Man was born free, and everywhere he is in chains.

Du Contrat Social (1762)

Sartre, Jean-Paul (1905–1980)
French philosopher, writer, dramatist and critic
> Once freedom has exploded in the soul of a man, the gods have no more power over him.

The Flies (1943)

> Man is condemned to be free.

Existentialism and Humanism

Shakespeare, William (1564–1616)
English dramatist, poet and actor
> I must have liberty
> Withal, as large a charter as the wind,
> To blow on whom I please.

As You Like It, II.vii

Shaw, George Bernard (1856–1950)
Irish socialist, writer, dramatist and critic
> Liberty means responsibility. That is why most men dread it.

Man and Superman (1903)

Smith, Sydney (1771–1845)
English clergyman, essayist, journalist and wit
> I love liberty, but hope that it can be so managed that I shall have soft beds, good dinners, fine linen, etc., for the rest of my life. I am too old to fight or to suffer.

Letter to J.A. Murray, Jan. 3rd, 1830

Solzhenitsyn, Alexander (1918–)
Russian writer, dramatist and historian
> You took my freedom away long ago and you

can't give it back to me because you haven't got it yourself.

The First Circle (1968)

> You only have power over people as long as you don't take everything away from them. But when you've robbed a man of everything he's no longer in your power – he's free again.

The First Circle (1968)

Stevenson, Adlai (1900–1965)
US lawyer, statesman and United Nations ambassador
> My definition of a free society is a society where it is safe to be unpopular.

Speech, Detroit, 1952

Turner, Tina (1938–)
US singer
> Sometimes you've got to let everything go … purge yourself. If you are unhappy with anything … whatever is bringing you down, get rid of it. Because you'll find that when you're free, your true creativity, your true self comes out.

I, Tina (1986)

Twain, Mark (1835–1910)
US humorist, writer, journalist and lecturer
> It is by the goodness of God that in our country we have those three unspeakably precious things: freedom of speech, freedom of conscience, and the prudence never to practise either of them.

Following the Equator (1897)

Voltaire (1694–1778)
French philosopher, dramatist, poet, historian writer and critic
> *La Liberté est née en Angleterre des querelles des tyrans.*
> Liberty was born in England from the quarrels of tyrants.

Lettres philosophiques (1734)

Washington, George (1732–1799)
US general, statesman and President
> Liberty, when it begins to take root, is a plant of rapid growth.

Letter, 1788

Willkie, Wendell (1892–1944)
US lawyer, industrialist and Republican politician
> Freedom is an indivisible word. If we want to enjoy it, and fight for it, we must be prepared to extend it to everyone, whether they are rich or poor, whether they agree with us or not, no matter what their race or the colour of their skin.

One World (1943)

Wilson, Woodrow (1856–1924)
US Democrat President
> The history of liberty is a history of resistance.

Speech, 1912

free speech

Broun, Heywood (1888–1939)
US journalist

> Everybody favours free speech in the slack moments when no axes are being ground.
>> *New York World,* 1926

friendship

Adams, Henry (1838–1918)
US historian and memoirist

> A friend in power is a friend lost.
>> *The Education of Henry Adams* (1918)

> One friend in a lifetime is much; two are many; three are hardly possible. Friendship needs a certain parallelism of life, a community of thought, a rivalry of aim.
>> *The Education of Henry Adams* (1918)

Adams, Victoria (1974–)
English pop singer, member of the Spice Girls
On her marriage to footballer David Beckham

> David and I haven't got that many friends. We could have our wedding in a postbox.
>> *The Observer,* 1999

Addison, Joseph (1672–1719)
English essayist, poet, playwright and statesman

> Friendships, in general, are suddenly contracted; and therefore it is no wonder they are easily dissolved.
>> *Interesting Anecdotes, Memoirs, Allegories, Essays, and Poetical Fragments* (1794)

Anonymous

> A friend is someone who will help you move. A real friend is someone who will help you move a body.

Aristotle (384–322 BC)
Greek philosopher

> On being asked what is a friend, he said 'A single soul dwelling in two bodies.'
>> In Diogenes Laertius, *Lives of Philosophers*

Aubrey, John (1626–1697)
English antiquary, folklorist and biographer
Of Francis Beaumont

> There was a wonderful consimility of phansey between him and Mr John Fletcher, which caused that dearness of friendship between them … They lived together on the Bank side, not far from the Playhouse, both bachelors; lay together; had one wench in the house between them, which they did so admire; the same clothes and cloak, &c.; between them.
>> *Brief Lives* (c.1693)

Bacon, Francis (1561–1626)
English philosopher, essayist, politician and courtier

> A false friend is more dangerous than an open enemy.
>> *A Letter of Advice … to the Duke of Buckingham* (1616)

> It is the worst solitude, to have no true friendships.
>> *The Advancement of Learning* (1605)

> This communicating of a man's self to his friend works two contrary effects; for it redoubleth joys, and cutteth griefs in halves.
>> *Essays* (1625)

Belloc, Hilaire (1870–1953)
English writer of verse, essayist and critic; Liberal MP

> From quiet homes and first beginning,
> Out to the undiscovered ends,
> There's nothing worth the wear of winning,
> But laughter and the love of friends.
>> *Verses* (1910)

The Bible (King James Version)

> A faithful friend is a sturdy shelter: he that has found one has found a treasure. There is nothing so precious as a faithful friend, and no scales can measure his excellence.
>> *Apocrypha, Ecclesiasticus*

> Forsake not an old friend; for the new is not comparable to him; a new friend is as new wine; when it is old, thou shalt drink it with pleasure.
>> *Apocrypha, Ecclesiasticus*

Bierce, Ambrose (1842–c.1914)
US writer, verse writer and soldier

> *Antipathy:* The sentiment inspired by one's friend's friend.
>> *The Enlarged Devil's Dictionary* (1961)

Bradbury, Malcolm (1932–)
English writer, critic and academic

> I've noticed your hostility towards him … I ought to have guessed you were friends.
>> *The History Man* (1975)

Brecht, Bertolt (1898–1956)
German dramatist

> *Ich trau ihm nicht, wir sind befreundet.*
> I'm wary of him. We're friends.
>> *Mother Courage and her Children* (1941)

Brontë, Emily (1818–1848)
English poet and writer

> Love is like the wild rose-briar,
> Friendship like the holly-tree,
> The holly is dark when the rose-briar blooms
> But which will bloom most constantly?
>> 'Love and Friendship'

Bulwer-Lytton, Edward (1803–1873)
English novelist and politician
> There is no man so friendless but what he can find a friend sincere enough to tell him disagreeable truths.
>> *What Will He Do With It?* (1857)

Byron, Lord (1788–1824)
English poet satirist and traveller
> Friendship is Love without his wings.
>> 'L'amitié est l'amour sans ailes' (1806)

Canning, George (1770–1827)
English Prime Minister, orator and poet
> Give me the avowed, erect and manly foe;
> Firm I can meet, perhaps return the blow;
> But of all plagues, good Heaven, thy wrath can send,
> Save me, oh, save me, from the candid friend.
>> 'New Morality' (1821)

Catherwood, Mary (1847–1901)
> Two may talk together under the same roof for many years, yet never really meet; and two others at first speech are old friends.
>> *Mackinac and Lake Stories*, 'Marianson'

Christina of Sweden (1626–1689)
Queen of Sweden
> Life becomes useless and insipid when we have no longer either friends or enemies.
>> *Pensées de Christine, reine de Suede* (1825)

Churchill, Charles (1731–1764)
English poet, political writer and clergyman
> Greatly his foes he dreads, but more his friends;
> He hurts me most who lavishly commends.
>> 'The Apology, addressed to the Critical Reviewers' (1761)

Colette (1873–1954)
French writer
> My true friends have always given me that supreme proof of devotion, a spontaneous aversion for the man I loved.
>> *Break of Day* (1928)

Colton, Charles Caleb (c.1780–1832)
English clergyman and satirist
> Friendship often ends in love; but love in friendship – never.
>> *Lacon* (1820)

Confucius (c.550–c.478 BC)
Chinese philosopher and teacher of ethics
> Have no friends not equal to yourself.
>> *Analects*

Congreve, William (1670–1729)
English dramatist
> O the pious friendships of the female sex!
>> *The Way of the World* (1700)

Cowley, Abraham (1618–1667)
English poet and dramatist
> Acquaintance I would have, but when't depends
> Not on the number, but the choice of friends.
>> *Essays in Verse and Prose* (1668)

De Gaulle, Charles (1890–1970)
French general and statesman
Replying to Jacques Soustelle's complaint that he was being attacked by his own friends
> *Changez vos amis.*
> Change your friends.
>> Attr.

Eliot, George (1819–1880)
English writer and poet
> Friendships begin with liking or gratitude – roots that can be pulled up.
>> *Daniel Deronda* (1876)

Emerson, Ralph Waldo (1803–1882)
US poet, essayist, transcendentalist and teacher
> Let the soul be assured that somewhere in the universe it should rejoin its friend, and it would be content and cheerful alone for a thousand years.
>> 'Friendship' (1841)

> A friend is a person with whom I may be sincere. Before him I may think aloud.
>> 'Friendship' (1841)

> A friend may well be reckoned the masterpiece of Nature.
>> 'Friendship' (1841)

> The only reward of virtue is virtue; the only way to have a friend is to be one.
>> 'Friendship' (1841)

Epicurus (341–270 BC)
Greek philosopher and teacher
> It is not so much our friends' help that helps us as the confident knowledge that they will help us.
>> Attr.

Frostrup, Mariella
English TV presenter
> A friend in need is an acquaintance.
>> In *The Observer*, 1998

García Márquez, Gabriel (1928–)
Colombian author
> *Un solo minuto de reconciliación tiene más mérito que toda una vida de amistad.*
> One single minute of reconciliation is worth more than an entire life of friendship.
>> *One Hundred Years of Solitude* (1968)

Gay, John (1685–1732)
English poet, dramatist and librettist
> A woman's friendship ever ends in love.
>> *Dione* (1720)

Goldsmith, Oliver (c.1728–1774)
Irish dramatist, poet and writer
> Friendship is a disinterested commerce between equals; love, an abject intercourse between tyrants and slaves.
>> *The Good Natur'd Man* (1768)

Harding, Warren G. (1865–1923)
US statesman and Republican President
> I have no trouble with my enemies. I can take care of my enemies all right. But my damn friends … They're the ones that keep me walking the floor nights!
>> *Autobiography* (1946)

Herbert, George (1593–1633)
English poet and priest
> But love is lost, the way of friendship's gone, Though David had his Jonathan, Christ his John.
>> *The Temple* (1633), 'The Church-Porch'

Humphries, Barry (1934–)
Australian entertainer
> Friendship is tested in the thick years of success rather than in the thin years of struggle.
>> In Green, *A Dictionary of Contemporary Quotations* (1982)

Johnson, Samuel (1709–1784)
English lexicographer, poet, critic, conversationalist and essayist
> The endearing elegance of female friendship.
>> *Rasselas* (1759)

> If a man does not make new acquaintance as he advances through life, he will soon find himself left alone. A man, Sir, should keep his friendship in constant repair.
>> In Boswell, *The Life of Samuel Johnson* (1791)

> How few of his friends' houses would a man choose to be at when he is sick.
>> In Boswell, *The Life of Samuel Johnson* (1791)

> Friendship is not always the sequel of obligation.
>> *The Lives of the Most Eminent English Poets* (1779–1781)

Kingsmill, Hugh (1889–1949)
English critic and writer
> Friends are God's apology for relations.
>> In Ingrams, *God's Apology* (1977)

La Rochefoucauld (1613–1680)
French writer
> *Dans l'adversité de nos meilleurs amis, nous trouvons toujours quelque chose qui ne nous déplaît pas.*
> In the misfortunes of our closest friends, we always find something which is not displeasing to us.
>> *Maximes* (1665)

> *Il est plus honteux de se défier de ses amis que d'en être trompé.*
> There is more shame in distrusting one's friends than in being deceived by them.
>> *Maximes* (1678)

Lewis, C.S. (1898–1963)
Irish-born English academic, writer and critic
> Friendship is unnecessary, like philosophy, like art. … It has no survival value; rather it is one of those things that give value to survival.
>> *The Four Loves* (c.1936)

Machiavelli (1469–1527)
Florentine statesman, political theorist and historian
> Friendships that are acquired with money, and not through greatness and nobility of character, are paid for but not secured, and prove unreliable just when they are needed.
>> *The Prince*

Medici, Cosimo de' (1389–1464)
Member of Medici family, rulers of Tuscany and Florence
> We read that we ought to forgive our enemies; but we do not read that we ought to forgive our friends.
>> In Bacon, *Apophthegms* (1625)

Montaigne, Michel de (1533–1592)
French essayist and moralist
> Of his friend Étienne de la Boétie
> *Si on me presse de dire pourquoi je l'aimais, je sens que cela ne se peut s'exprimer, qu'en répondant: 'Parce que c'était lui; parce que c'était moi.'*
> If I am pressed to say why I loved him, I feel it can only be explained by replying: 'Because it was he; because it was me.'
>> *Essais* (1580)

Pope, Alexander (1688–1744)
English poet, translator and editor
> True friendship's laws are by this rule express'd, Welcome the coming, speed the parting guest.
>> *The Odyssey* (1726)

> How often are we to die before we go quite off this stage? In every friend we lose a part of ourselves, and the best part.
>> Letter to Swift, 1732

Proverbs
> A friend in need is a friend indeed.

> A hedge between keeps friendship green.

> One who looks for a friend without faults will have none.

> The road to a friend's house is never long.
>> Danish Proverb

Pythagoras (6th century BC)
Greek philosopher and mathematician

Friends share all things.
> In Diogenes Laertius, *Lives of Eminent Philosophers*

Sallust (86–c.34 BC)
Roman historian and statesman
> *Idem velle atque idem nolle, ea demum firma amicitia est.*
> To like and dislike the same things, this in the end is the basis of true friendship.
> *Catiline*

Selden, John (1584–1654)
English historian, jurist and politician
> Old friends are best. King James used to call for his old shoes; they were easiest for his feet.
> *Table Talk* (1689)

Shakespeare, William (1564–1616)
English dramatist, poet and actor
> Friendship is constant in all other things
> Save in the office and affairs of love.
> *Much Ado About Nothing*, II.i

> I count myself in nothing else so happy
> As in a soul rememb'ring my good friends.
> *Richard II*, II.iii

Smith, Logan Pearsall (1865–1946)
US-born British epigrammatist, critic and writer
> I might give my life for my friend, but he had better not ask me to do up a parcel.
> *Afterthoughts* (1931)

> I cannot forgive my friends for dying; I do not find these vanishing acts of theirs at all amusing.
> *Afterthoughts* (1931)

Swift, Jonathan (1667–1745)
Irish satirist, poet, essayist and cleric
> In all distresses of our friends,
> We first consult our private ends;
> While nature, kindly bent to ease us,
> Points out some circumstance to please us –
> Some great misfortune to portend,
> No enemy can match a friend.
> 'Verses on the Death of Dr. Swift' (1731)

Thoreau, Henry David (1817–1862)
US essayist, social critic and writer
> Enemies publish themselves. They declare war. The friend never declares his love.
> *Journal*, 1856

Twain, Mark (1835–1910)
US humorist, writer, journalist and lecturer
> The holy passion of Friendship is of so sweet and steady and loyal and enduring a nature that it will last through a whole lifetime, if not asked to lend money.
> *Pudd'nhead Wilson's Calendar* (1894)

> The proper office of a friend is to side with you when you are in the wrong. Nearly anybody will side with you when you are in the right.
> Attr.

Vidal, Gore (1925–)
US writer, critic and poet
> Whenever a friend succeeds, a little something in me dies.
> *The Sunday Times Magazine*, 1973

Washington, George (1732–1799)
US general, statesman and President
> Be courteous to all, but intimate with few, and let those few be well tried before you give them your confidence. True friendship is a plant of slow growth, and must undergo and withstand the shocks of adversity before it is entitled to the appellation.
> Letter, 1783

Waugh, Evelyn (1903–1966)
English writer and diarist
> We cherish our friends not for their ability to amuse us, but for our ability to amuse them.
> Attr.

Whitman, Walt (1819–1892)
US poet and writer
> I no doubt deserved my enemies, but I don't believe I deserved my friends.
> In Bradford, *Biography and the Human Heart*

Woolf, Virginia (1882–1941)
English writer and critic
> I have lost friends, some by death … others through sheer inability to cross the street.
> *The Waves* (1931)

Yeats, W.B. (1865–1939)
Irish poet, dramatist, editor, writer and senator
> Always we'd have the new friend meet the old
> And we are hurt if either friend seem cold.
> In the *English Review*, 1918

> Think where man's glory most begins and ends,
> And say my glory was I had such friends.
> 'The Municipal Gallery Revisited' (1937)

▶▶ ENEMIES

fun

Sayers, Dorothy L. (1893–1957)
English writer, dramatist and translator
> I admit it is better fun to punt than to be punted, and that a desire to have all the fun is nine-tenths of the law of chivalry.
> *Gaudy Night* (1935)

Victoria, Queen (1819–1901)
Queen of the United Kingdom
> No pudding and no fun!
> Attr.

funerals

Browne, Sir Thomas (1605–1682)
English physician, author and antiquary
> With rich flames, and hired tears, they
> solemnized their obsequies.
>> *Hydriotaphia: Urn Burial* (1658)

> They carried them out of the world with their
> feet forward.
>> *Hydriotaphia: Urn Burial* (1658)

Catullus (84–c.54 BC)
Roman poet
> *Multas per gentes et multa per aequora vectus*
> *Advenio has miseras, frater, ad inferias,*
> *Ut te postremo donarem munere mortis*
> *Et mutam nequiquam alloquerer cinerem.*
> *Quandoquidem fortuna mihi tete abstulit ipsum,*
> *Heu miser indigne frater adempte mihi,*
> *Nunc tamen interea haec, prisco quae more parentum*
> *Tradita sunt tristi munere ad inferias,*
> *Accipe fraterno multum manantia fletu,*
> *Atque in perpetuum, frater, ave atque vale.*
> Having journeyed through many peoples and
> over many a sea I come, my brother, for these
> sad funeral rites, that I may present to you a last
> gift in death and vainly address your dumb
> ashes, since fortune has taken you from me –
> alas, poor brother cruelly snatched from me –
> but now accept these offerings which by our
> parents' custom have been handed down as a
> funeral gift, bedewed with many fraternal tears,
> and for all time, my brother, hail and farewell.
>> *Carmina*

Day, Clarence Shepard (1874–1935)
US essayist and humorist
> 'If you don't go to other men's funerals,' he told
> Father stiffly, 'they won't go to yours.'
>> *Life with Father* (1935),
>> 'Father plans'

Mann, Thomas (1875–1955)
German writer and critic
> *Man sollte, statt in die Kirche, zu einem Begräbnis*
> *gehen, wenn man sich ein bisschen erbauen will. Die*
> *Leute haben gutes schwarzes Zeug an und nehmen die*
> *Hüte ab und sehen auf den Sarg und halten sich ernst*
> *und andächtig, und niemand darf faule Witze machen.*
> Instead of going to church you should go to a
> funeral when you wish to be uplifted. The
> people have got good black clothes on, they
> take their hats off, look at the coffin and are
> serious and reverent, and no-one dares make
> bad jokes.
>> *The Magic Mountain* (1924)

Miller, Arthur (1915–)
US dramatist and screenwriter

When asked if he would attend Marilyn Monroe's funeral
> Why should I go? She won't be there.
>> Attr.

Mitford, Jessica (1917–1996)
English writer
> I have nothing against undertakers personally.
> It's just that I wouldn't want one to bury my
> sister.
>> Attr. in *Saturday Review*, 1964

Mountbatten of Burma, First Earl (1900–1979)
English admiral and statesman
> I can't think of a more wonderful thanksgiving
> for the life I have had than that everyone should
> be jolly at my funeral.
>> TV interview, shown after his death in August 1979

Pitts, William (1900–1980)
English chief constable
> It is the overtakers who keep the undertakers
> busy.
>> *The Observer*, 1963

the future

Abernathy, Ralph (1926–1990)
US religious and civil rights leader
> I don't know what the future may hold, but I
> know who holds the future.
>> In Andrew Young, *A Way Out of No Way* (1994)

Acheson, Dean (1893–1971)
US Democrat politician
> Always remember that the future comes one day
> at a time.
>> *Sketches From Life*

Addison, Joseph (1672–1719)
English essayist, poet, playwright and statesman
> 'We are always doing,' says he, 'something for
> Posterity, but I would fain see Posterity do
> something for us.'
>> *The Spectator*, August 1714

Bacon, Francis (1561–1626)
English philosopher, essayist, politician and courtier
> Men must pursue things which are just in
> present, and leave the future to the divine
> Providence.
>> *The Advancement of Learning* (1605)

Baldwin, James (1924–1987)
US writer, dramatist, poet and civil rights activist
> The future is … black.
>> *The Observer*, 1963

Balfour, A.J. (1848–1930)
British Conservative Prime Minister
> The energies of our system will decay, the glory
> of the sun will be dimmed, and the earth,

tideless and inert, will no longer tolerate the race which has for a moment disturbed its solitude. Man will go down into the pit, and all his thoughts will perish.

The Foundations of Belief (1895)

Benjamin, Walter (1892–1940)
German writer, philosopher and critic
He who asks fortune-tellers the future unwittingly forfeits an inner intimation of coming events that is a thousand times more exact than anything they may say.

One-Way Street (1928)

Bennett, Arnold (1867–1931)
English writer, dramatist and journalist
The people who live in the past must yield to the people who live in the future. Otherwise the world would begin to turn the other way round.

Attr.

Berra, Yogi (1925–)
US baseball player
The future ain't what it used to be.

Attr.

Bierce, Ambrose (1842–c.1914)
US writer, verse writer and soldier
Future: That period of time in which our affairs prosper, our friends are true and our happiness is assured.

The Cynic's Word Book (1906)

Burke, Edmund (1729–1797)
Irish-born British statesman and philosopher
People will not look forward to posterity, who never look backward to their ancestors.

Reflections on the Revolution in France (1790)

You can never plan the future by the past.

Letter to a Member of the National Assembly (1791)

Camus, Albert (1913–1960)
Algerian-born French writer
The future is the only kind of property that the masters willingly concede to slaves.

The Rebel (1951)

Churchill, Sir Winston (1874–1965)
English Conservative Prime Minister
The empires of the future are empires of the mind.

Speech,1943

Clark, Lord Kenneth (1903–1983)
English art historian
One may be optimistic, but one can't exactly be joyful at the prospect before us.

End of TV series, *Civilization*

Coleridge, Samuel Taylor (1772–1834)
English poet, philosopher and critic
Often do the spirits

Of great events stride on before the events,
And in to-day already walks to-morrow.

'Death of Wallenstein' (1800)

Confucius (c.550–c.478 BC)
Chinese philosopher and teacher of ethics
Study the past, if you would divine the future.

Analects

Coward, Sir Noël (1899–1973)
English dramatist, actor, producer and composer
I don't give a hoot about posterity. Why should I worry about what people think of me when I'm dead as a doornail anyway?

Present Laughter (1943)

Crisp, Quentin (1908–1999)
English writer, publicist and model
I still lived in the future – a habit which is the death of happiness.

The Naked Civil Servant (1968)

Disraeli, Benjamin (1804–1881)
English statesman and writer
He seems to think that posterity is a pack-horse, always ready to be loaded.

Speech, House of Commons, 1862

What we anticipate seldom occurs; what we least expected generally happens.

Henrietta Temple (1837)

Dix, Dorothy (1870–1951)
US writer
I have learned to live each day as it comes, and not to borrow trouble by dreading tomorrow. It is the dark menace of the future that makes cowards of us.

Dorothy Dix, Her Book (1926)

Einstein, Albert (1879–1955)
German-born US mathematical physicist
I never think of the future. It comes soon enough.

Interview, 1930

Hill, Reginald (1936–)
British writer and playwright
I have seen the future and it sucks.

Pictures of Perfection (1994)

Hugo, Victor (1802–1885)
French poet, writer, dramatist and politician
In the twentieth century, war will be dead, the scaffold will be dead, hatred will be dead, frontier boundaries will be dead, dogmas will be dead; man will live. He will possess something higher than all these – a great country, the whole earth, and a great hope, the whole heaven.

The Future of Man

Johnson, Samuel (1709–1784)
English lexicographer, poet, critic, conversationalist and essayist
> The future is purchased by the present.
>> Attr.

Lewis, C.S. (1898–1963)
Irish-born English academic, writer and critic
> The Future is something which everyone reaches at the rate of sixty minutes an hour, whatever he does, whoever he is.
>> *The Screwtape Letters* (1942)

Mitchell, Margaret (1900–1949)
US author
> After all, tomorrow is another day.
>> *Gone with the Wind* (1936)

Ortega y Gasset, José (1883–1955)
Spanish philosopher
> You don't fight hand-to-hand with the past. The future conquers it because it swallows it. If it leaves part of it outside, it is lost.
>> *The Rebellion of the Masses* (1930)

Orwell, George (1903–1950)
English writer and critic
> If you want a picture of the future, imagine a boot stamping on a human face – for ever.
>> *Nineteen Eighty-Four* (1949)

Popcorn, Faith (1947–)
US management consultant
> The future bears a resemblance to the past, only more so.
>> *The Popcorn Report* (1991)

Proust, Marcel (1871–1922)
French writer and critic
> *Nous appelons notre avenir l'ombre de lui-même que notre passé projette devant nous.*
> What we call our future is the shadow which our past throws in front of us.
>> *A l'ombre des jeunes filles en fleurs* (1918)

Quayle, Dan (1947–)
US Republican politician and Vice President
> The future will be better tomorrow.
>> Attr

Roche, Sir Boyle (1743–1807)
Irish politician
> What has posterity done for us?
>> Speech, 1780

Snow, C.P. (1905–1980)
English writer, critic, physicist and public administrator
On industrialisation
> Common men can show astonishing fortitude in chasing jam tomorrow. Jam today, and men aren't at their most exciting: jam tomorrow, and one often sees them at their noblest.
>> *The Two Cultures and the Scientific Revolution* (1959)

Steffens, Lincoln (1866–1936)
US political analyst and writer
Remark after visiting Russia in 1919
> I have seen the future; and it works.
>> Letter to Marie Howe, 1919

Weil, Simone (1909–1943)
French philosopher, essayist and mystic
> The future is made of the same stuff as the present.
>> *On Science, Necessity, and the Love of God*

Wells, H.G. (1866–1946)
English writer
> One thousand years more. That's all *Homo sapiens* has before him.
>> In H. Nicolson, *Diary*

Williams, Tennessee (1911–1983)
US dramatist and writer
> The future is called 'perhaps', which is the only possible thing to call the future. And the important thing is not to allow that to scare you.
>> Attr.

▶▶ PAST; PRESENT; TIME

G

gambling

Adams, Joey (b. 1911)
US comedian and author
> The difference between playing the stock market and the horses is that one of the horses must win.
>> *Reader's Digest*, 1985

Gilbert, Fred (1850–1903)
British songwriter
> As I walk along the Bois Bou-long,
> With an independent air,
> You can hear the girls declare,
> 'He must be a millionaire',
> You can hear them sigh and wish to die,
> You can see them wink the other eye
> At the man who broke the bank at Monte Carlo.
>> 'The Man who Broke the Bank at Monte Carlo', 1892

Herbert, Sir A.P. (1890–1971)
English humorist, writer, dramatist and politician
> Don't let's go to the dogs tonight
> For mother will be there.
>> *She-Shanties* (1926), 'Don't Let's Go to the Dogs Tonight'

Taylor, A.J.P. (1906–1990)
English historian, writer, broadcaster and lecturer
> A racing tipster who only reached Hitler's level of accuracy would not do well for his clients.
>> *The Origins of the Second World War* (1961)

Twain, Mark (1835–1910)
US humorist, writer, journalist and lecturer
> If there was two birds sitting on a fence, he would bet you which one would fly first.
>> *The Celebrated Jumping Frog* (1867)

gardens

Addison, Joseph (1672–1719)
English essayist, poet, playwright and statesman
> I value my garden more for being full of blackbirds than of cherries, and very frankly give them fruit for their songs.
>> *The Spectator*, 1712

Atwood, Margaret (1939–)
Canadian writer, poet and critic
> Gardening is not a rational act.
>> *Bluebeard's Egg* (1986)

Bacon, Francis (1561–1626)
English philosopher, essayist, politician and courtier
> God Almighty first planted a garden. And indeed, it is the purest of human pleasures. It is the greatest refreshment to the spirits of man; without which, buildings and palaces are but gross handiworks.
>> 'Of Gardens' (1625)

Brown, Thomas Edward (1830–1897)
Manx poet, teacher and curate
> A garden is a lovesome thing, God wot!
>> 'My Garden' (1893)

Cowley, Abraham (1618–1667)
English poet and dramatist
> God the first garden made, and the first city Cain.
>> 'The Garden' (1668)

Emerson, Ralph Waldo (1803–1882)
US poet, essayist, transcendentalist and teacher
> What is a weed? A plant whose virtues have not yet been discovered.
>> *Fortune of the Republic* (1878)

Gardiner, Richard (b. c.1533)
English writer
> Sowe Carrets in your Gardens, and humbly praise God for them, as for a singular and great blessing.
>> *Profitable Instructions for the Manuring, Sowing and Planting of Kitchen Gardens*

Gurney, Dorothy (1858–1932)
English poet
> The kiss of the sun for pardon,
> The song of the birds for mirth,
> One is nearer God's Heart in a garden
> Than anywhere else on earth.
>> 'God's Garden' (1913)

Kipling, Rudyard (1865–1936)
Indian-born British poet and writer
> Oh, Adam was a gardener, and God who made him sees
> That half a proper gardener's work is done upon his knees,
> So when your work is finished, you can wash your hands and pray
> For the Glory of the Garden, that it may not pass away!
> And the Glory of the Garden it shall never pass away!
>> Songs written for C.R.L. Fletcher's *A History of England* (1911)

Marvell, Andrew (1621–1678)
English poet and satirist
> I have a garden of my own,
> But so with roses overgrown,
> And lilies, that you would it guess

To be a little wilderness.

'The Nymph Complaining for the Death of her Fawn' (1681)

Here at the fountain's sliding foot,
Or at some fruit-tree's mossy root,
Casting the body's vest aside,
My soul into the boughs does glide.

'The Garden' (1681)

Milton, John (1608–1674)
English poet, libertarian and pamphleteer
And add to these retired leisure,
That in trim gardens takes his pleasure.

'Il Penseroso' (1645)

Russell, Bertrand (1872–1970)
English philosopher, mathematician, essayist and social reformer
Every time I talk to a savant I feel quite sure that happiness is no longer a possibility. Yet when I talk to my gardener, I'm convinced of the opposite.

Attr.

Shakespeare, William (1564–1616)
English dramatist, poet and actor
'Tis in ourselves that we are thus or thus. Our bodies are our gardens to the which our wills are gardeners.

Othello, I.iii

Sheridan, Richard Brinsley (1751–1816)
Irish dramatist, politician and orator
Won't you come into the garden? I would like my roses to see you.

Attr.

Simmons, John (1937–)
A weed is simply a plant that you don't want.

The Observer, 1983

Tennyson, Alfred, Lord (1809–1892)
English lyric poet
Come into the garden, Maud,
For the black bat, night, has flown,
Come into the garden, Maud,
I am here at the gate alone;
And the woodbine spices are wafted abroad,
And the musk of the rose is blown.

Maud (1855)

Thomas, Dylan (1914–1953)
Welsh poet, writer and radio dramatist
Nothing grows in our garden, only washing.
And babies.

Under Milk Wood (1954)

Voltaire (1694–1778)
French philosopher, dramatist, poet, historian writer and critic
Cela est bien dit, répondit Candide, mais il faut cultiver notre jardin.

'That is well said,' replied Candide, 'but we must cultivate our garden.'

Candide (1759)

▶▶ FLOWERS

generalization

Blake, William (1757–1827)
English poet, engraver, painter and mystic
To generalize is to be an idiot.

In Gilchrist, Life of Blake

Macaulay, Lord (1800–1859)
English Liberal statesman, essayist and poet
Nothing is so useless as a general maxim.

Collected Essays (1843), 'Machiavelli'

generations

Agnew, Spiro T. (1918–1996)
US Vice President
The lessons of the past are ignored and obliterated in a contemporary antagonism known as the generation gap.

New York Times, 1969

Orwell, George (1903–1950)
English writer and critic
Each generation imagines itself to be more intelligent than the one that went before it, and wiser than the one that comes after it.

Attr.

Stein, Gertrude (1874–1946)
US writer, dramatist, poet and critic
Remark made in the 1920s
That's what you are. That's what you all are. All of you young people who served in the war. You are a lost generation.

In Hemingway, A Moveable Feast (1964)

▶▶ AGE

generosity

Barrie, Sir J.M. (1860–1937)
Scottish dramatist and writer
Never ascribe to an opponent motives meaner than your own.

Address, St Andrews University, 1922

The Bible (King James Version)
It is more blessed to give than to receive.

Acts of the Apostles, 20:35

God loveth a cheerful giver.

II Corinthians, 9:7

Whosoever shall compel thee to go a mile, go with him twain.

Matthew, 5:41

Burns, Robert (1759–1796)
Scottish poet and song writer

To be overtopped in anything else, I can bear: but in the tests of generous love, I defy all mankind!

Letter to Clarinda, 1788

Corneille, Pierre (1606–1684)
French dramatist, poet and lawyer

Le façon de donner vaut mieux que ce qu'on donne.
The manner of giving is worth more than the gift.

Le Menteur (1643)

Gibbs, Sir Philip (1877–1962)
British journalist

It is better to give than to lend, and it costs about the same.

Attr.

La Bruyère, Jean de (1645–1696)
French satirist

La liberalité consiste moins à donner beaucoup qu'à donner à propos.
Liberality consists less in giving a great deal than in gifts well timed.

Les caractères ou les moeurs de ce siècle (1688)

Loyola, St Ignatius (1491–1556)
Spanish soldier and founder of the Jesuits

Teach us, good Lord, to serve Thee as Thou deservest:
To give and not to count the cost;
To fight and not to heed the wounds;
To toil and not to seek for rest;
To labour and not to ask for any reward
Save that of knowing that we do Thy will.

'Prayer for Generosity'

Muir, Edwin (1887–1959)
Scottish poet, critic, translator and writer

I think it possible that all Scots are illegitimate, Scotsmen being so mean and Scotswomen so generous.

Scottish Journey (1935)

Talleyrand, Charles-Maurice de (1754–1838)
French statesman, memoirist and prelate

Méfiez-vous du premier mouvement; il est toujours généreux.
Don't trust first impulses; they are always generous.

Attr.

▶▶ BENEFACTORS; CHARITY

genetically modified food

Charles, Prince of Wales (1948–)
Son and heir of Elizabeth II and Prince Philip
On genetically modified food crops

I happen to believe that this kind of genetic modification takes mankind into the realms that belong to God, and to God alone ... do we have the right to experiment with, and commercialise, the building blocks of life?

Daily Telegraph, 1998

Are we going to allow the industrialisation of Life itself, redesigning the natural world for the sake of convenience and embarking on an Orwellian future? – Or should we be adopting a gentler, more considered approach, seeking always to work with the grain of Nature in making better, more sustainable use of what we have, for the long-term benefit of mankind as a whole?

Daily Mail, 1999

Since bees and wind don't obey any sort of rules, we shall soon have an unprecedented and unethical situation in which one farmer's crop will contaminate another's against his will.

The Times, 1999

May, Sir Robert
British scientist; Chief Scientific Adviser to the UK government

Properly handled, GM crops have the potential to be more wildlife-friendly than the ones we have now.

The Scotsman, May 1999

Wood, Paul
Caption to cartoon

American to Briton: You say tomato and I say genetically modified tomato.

Private Eye

genius

Adams, Joey (b. 1911)
US comedian and author

A genius is one who can do anything except make a living.

Attr.

Alcott, Louisa May (1832–1888)
US writer

It takes people a long time to learn the difference between talent and genius, especially ambitious young men and women.

Little Women (1869)

Talent isn't genius and no amount of energy can

make it so. I want to be great, or nothing. I won't be a commonplace dauber, so I don't intend to try any more.

Little Women (1869)

Anonymous
The difference between genius and stupidity is that genius has its limits.

No amount of genius can overcome a preoccupation with detail.

Levy's Eighth Law

Arnold, Matthew (1822–1888)
English poet, critic, essayist and educationist
So we have the Philistine of genius in religion – Luther; the Philistine of genius in politics – Cromwell; the Philistine of genius in literature – Bunyan.

Mixed Essays (1879)

Beerbohm, Sir Max (1872–1956)
English satirist, cartoonist, critic and essayist
I have known no man of genius who had not to pay, in some affliction or defect either physical or spiritual, for what the gods had given him.

And Even Now (1920)

Browning, Elizabeth Barrett (1806–1861)
English poet; wife of Robert Browning
Since when was genius found respectable?

Aurora Leigh (1857)

Buckminster Fuller, Richard (1895–1983)
US architect and engineer
Everyone is born a genius, but the process of living de-geniuses them.

New York Post, 1968

Buffon, Comte de (1707–1788)
French naturalist
Le génie n'est qu'une plus grande aptitude à la patience.
Genius is merely a greater aptitude for patience.

In *Hérault de Séchelles, Voyage à Montbar* (1803)

Butler, Samuel (1835–1902)
English writer, painter, philosopher and scholar
Genius ... has been defined as a supreme capacity for taking trouble ... It might be more fitly described as a supreme capacity for getting its possessors into pains of all kinds, and keeping them therein so long as the genius remains.

The Note-Books of Samuel Butler (1912)

Carlyle, Thomas (1795–1881)
Scottish historian, biographer, critic, and essayist
'Genius' (which means transcendent capacity of taking trouble, first of all).

History of Frederick the Great (1858–1865)

Churchill, Charles (1731–1764)
English poet, political writer and clergyman
Genius is of no country.

The Rosciad (1761)

Dali, Salvador (1904–1989)
Spanish painter and writer
I'm going to live forever. Geniuses don't die.

The Observer, 1986

Doyle, Sir Arthur Conan (1859–1930)
Scottish writer and war correspondent
Mediocrity knows nothing higher than itself, but talent instantly recognizes genius.

The Valley of Fear (1914)

Edison, Thomas Alva (1847–1931)
US inventor and industrialist
Genius is one per cent inspiration and ninety-nine per cent perspiration.

Life, 1932

Emerson, Ralph Waldo (1803–1882)
US poet, essayist, transcendentalist and teacher
To believe your own thought, to believe that what is true for you in your private heart is true for all men, – that is genius.

Essays, First Series (1841)

When Nature has work to be done, she creates a genius to do it.

Lecture, 1841, 'Method of Nature'

Goldsmith, Oliver (c.1728–1774)
Irish dramatist, poet and writer
True Genius walks along a line, and, perhaps, our greatest pleasure is in seeing it so often near falling, without being ever actually down.

The Bee (1759)

Hazlitt, William (1778–1830)
English writer and critic
Rules and models destroy genius and art.

'Thoughts on Taste' (1818)

Hope, Anthony (1863–1933)
English writer, dramatist and lawyer
Unless one is a genius, it is best to aim at being intelligible.

The Dolly Dialogues (1894)

Hopkins, Jane Ellice (1836–1904)
English social reformer and writer
Gift, like genius, I often think, only means an infinite capacity for taking pains.

Work amongst Working Men, 1870

Hubbard, Elbert (1856–1915)
US printer, editor, writer and businessman
One machine can do the work of fifty ordinary men. No machine can do the work of one extraordinary man.

A Thousand and One Epigrams (1911)

James, Henry (1843–1916)
US-born British writer, critic and letter writer
Of Thoreau
> Whatever question there may be of his talent,
> there can be none, I think, of his genius. It was a
> slim and crooked one; but it was eminently
> personal. He was imperfect, unfinished,
> inartistic; he was worse than provincial – he was
> parochial.
>> *Hawthorne* (1879)

Johnson, Samuel (1709–1784)
English lexicographer, poet, critic, conversationalist and essayist
> The true genius is a mind of large general
> powers, accidentally determined to some
> particular direction.
>> *The Lives of the Most Eminent English Poets* (1779–1781)

Joyce, James (1882–1941)
Irish writer
> A man of genius makes no mistakes. His errors
> are volitional and are the portals of discovery.
>> *Ulysses* (1922)

Keats, John (1795–1821)
English poet
> So I do believe … that works of genius are the
> first things in this world.
>> Letter to George and Tom Keats,
>> 13 January 1818

Kennedy, John F. (1917–1963)
US Democrat President
> At a dinner held at the White House for Nobel prizewinners
> … probably the greatest concentration of talent
> and genius in this house, except for perhaps
> those times when Thomas Jefferson ate alone.
>> *New York Times*, 1962

Meredith, Owen (1831–1891)
English statesman and poet
> Genius does what it must, and Talent does what
> it can.
>> 'Last Words of a Sensitive Second-Rate Poet' (1868)

Stephen, Sir James Fitzjames (1829–1894)
English judge and essayist
> The way in which the man of genius rules is by
> persuading an efficient minority to coerce an
> indifferent and self-indulgent majority.
>> *Liberty, Equality and Fraternity* (1873)

Swift, Jonathan (1667–1745)
Irish satirist, poet, essayist and cleric
> When a true genius appears in the world, you
> may know him by this sign, that the dunces are
> all in confederacy against him.
>> *Thoughts on Various Subjects* (1711)

Of *A Tale of a Tub*
> Good God! what a genius I had when I wrote

that book.
>> In Sir Walter Scott, *Works of Swift* (1824)

Vidal, Gore (1925–)
US writer, critic and poet
Of Andy Warhol
> A genius with the IQ of a moron.
>> *The Observer*, 1989

Welles, Orson (1915–1985)
US actor, director and producer
> Everybody denies I am a genius – but nobody
> ever called me one!
>> In Halliwell *Filmgoer's Companion* (1984)

Whistler, James McNeill (1834–1903)
US painter, etcher and pamphleteer
Replying to a lady inquiring whether he thought genius hereditary
> I cannot tell you that, madam. Heaven has
> granted me no offspring.
>> In Seitz, *Whistler Stories* (1913)

Wilde, Oscar (1854–1900)
Irish poet, dramatist, writer, critic and wit
Spoken to André Gide
> *Voulez-vous savoir le grand drame de ma vie? C'est
> que j'ai mis mon génie dans ma vie; je n'ai mis que
> mon talent dans mes oeuvres.*
> Do you want to know the great tragedy of my
> life? I have put all of my genius into my life; all
> I've put into my works is my talent.
>> In Gide, *Oscar Wilde* (1910)

At the New York Customs
> I have nothing to declare except my genius.
>> In Harris, *Oscar Wilde* (1918)

▶▶ TALENT

genteel behaviour

Betjeman, Sir John (1906–1984)
English poet laureate
> Phone for the fish-knives, Norman
> As Cook is a little unnerved;
> You kiddies have crumpled the serviettes
> And I must have things daintily served …
>
> I know what I wanted to ask you;
> Is trifle sufficient for sweet? …
>
> Milk and then just as it comes dear?
> I'm afraid the preserve's full of stones;
> Beg pardon, I'm soiling the doileys
> With afternoon tea-cakes and scones.
>> *A Few Late Chrysanthemums* (1954)

Boswell, James (1740–1795)
Scottish lawyer and writer

A man, indeed, is not genteel when he gets drunk; but most vices may be committed very genteelly: a man may debauch his friend's wife genteelly: he may cheat at cards genteelly.

The Life of Samuel Johnson (1791)

Dickinson, Emily (1830–1886)

US poet

What Soft – Cherubic Creatures –
These Gentlewomen are –
One would as soon assault a Plush –
Or violate a Star –
Such Dimity Convictions –
A Horror so refined
Of freckled Human Nature –
Of Deity – ashamed.

'What Soft – Cherubic Creatures'
(c.1862)

Ridge, William Pett (c.1860–1930)

English writer

'How did you think I managed at dinner, Clarence?' 'Capitally!' 'I had a knife and two forks left at the end,' she said regretfully.

Love at Paddington Green

Saki (1870–1916)

Burmese-born British writer

I think she must have been very strictly brought up, she's so desperately anxious to do the wrong thing correctly.

Reginald (1904)

Shaw, George Bernard (1856–1950)

Irish socialist, writer, dramatist and critic

I am a woman of the world, Hector; and I can assure you that if you will only take the trouble always to do the perfectly correct thing, and to say the perfectly correct thing, you can do just what you like.

Heartbreak House (1919)

Smith, Stevie (1902–1971)

English poet and writer

This Englishwoman is so refined
She has no bosom and no behind.

'This Englishwoman' (1937)

Thirkell, Angela Margaret (1890–1961)

English novelist

Major Bowen narrating

'I don't mind if I do,' said I.
Mrs Jerry turned round to the girl and said:
'That means Major Bowen thanks me very much and is delighted to accept.'
I didn't tumble to what she meant, but I supposed it was all right.

Trooper to the Southern Cross

Williams, Tennessee (1911–1983)

US dramatist and writer

I can't stand a naked light bulb, any more than I can a rude remark or a vulgar action.

A Streetcar Named Desire (1947)

gentlemen

Allen, Fred (1894–1956)

US vaudeville performer and comedian

A gentleman is any man who wouldn't hit a woman with his hat on.

Attr.

Anonymous

When Adam delved, and Eve span,
Who was then a gentleman?

Attr. John Ball, 1381

Ashford, Daisy (1881–1972)

English child author

I do hope I shall enjoy myself with you … I am parshial to ladies if they are nice I suppose it is my nature. I am not quite a gentleman but you would hardly notice it.

The Young Visiters (1919)

Benchley, Robert (1889–1945)

US essayist, humorist and actor

Even nowadays a man can't step up and kill a woman without feeling just a bit unchivalrous.

Attr.

Brome, Richard (c.1590–1652)

English dramatist

I am a gentleman, though spoiled i' the breeding. The Buzzards are all gentlemen. We came in with the Conqueror.

English Moor (1637)

Burke, Edmund (1729–1797)

Irish-born British statesman and philosopher

It is therefore our business carefully to cultivate in our minds, to rear to the most perfect vigour and maturity, every sort of generous and honest feeling that belongs to our nature. To bring the dispositions that are lovely in private life into the service and conduct of the commonwealth; so to be patriots, as not to forget we are gentlemen.

Thoughts on the Cause of the Present Discontents (1770)

Somebody has said, that a king may make a nobleman but he cannot make a Gentleman.

Letter to William Smith, 1795

Chifley, Joseph Benedict (1885–1951)

My experience of gentlemen's agreements is that, when it comes to the pinch, there are rarely enough bloody gentlemen about.

In Crisp, *Ben Chifley* (1960)

Curzon, Lord (1859–1925)

English statesman and scholar

Gentlemen do not take soup at luncheon.

In Woodward, Short Journey (1942)

Emerson, Ralph Waldo (1803–1882)
US poet, essayist, transcendentalist and teacher

Living blood and a passion of kindness does at last distinguish God's gentlemen from Fashion's.

'Manners' (1844)

Furphy, Joseph (1843–1912)
Australian writer and poet

For there is no such thing as a democratic gentleman; the adjective and the noun are hyphenated by a drawn sword.

Such is Life (1903)

Linton, W.J. (1812–1897)
English wood engraver, editor and printer

For he is one of Nature's Gentlemen, the best of every time.

Nature's Gentleman

Matthews, Brander (1852–1929)
US critic, lecturer, dramatist and writer

A gentleman need not know Latin, but he should at least have forgotten it.

Attr.

Nelson, Lord (1758–1805)
English admiral
To his midshipmen

Recollect that you must be a seaman to be an officer; and also, that you cannot be a good officer without being a gentleman.

In Southey, The Life of Nelson (1860)

Newman, John Henry, Cardinal (1801–1890)
English Cardinal, theologian and poet

It is almost a definition of a gentleman to say that he is one who never inflicts pain.

'Knowledge and Religious Duty' (1852)

Shaw, George Bernard (1856–1950)
Irish socialist, writer, dramatist and critic

I am a gentleman: I live by robbing the poor.

Man and Superman (1903)

Stevenson, Robert Louis (1850–1894)
Scottish writer, poet and essayist

Between the possibility of being hanged in all innocence, and the certainty of a public and merited disgrace, no gentleman of spirit could long hesitate.

The Wrong Box (1889)

Surtees, R.S. (1805–1864)
English writer

He was a gentleman who was generally spoken of as having nothing a-year, paid quarterly.

Mr Sponge's Sporting Tour (1853)

The only infallible rule we know is, that the man

who is always talking about being a gentleman never is one.

Ask Mamma (1858)

Waugh, Evelyn (1903–1966)
English writer and diarist

For generations the British bourgeoisie have spoken of themselves as gentlemen, and by that they have meant, among other things, a self-respecting scorn of irregular perquisites. It is the quality that distinguishes the gentleman from both the artist and the aristocrat.

Decline and Fall (1928)

germany

Bismarck, Prince Otto von (1815–1898)
First Chancellor of the German Reich
Describing Germany's role in peace negotiations

Ich denke mir die Macht des Deutschen Reiches … mehr die eines ehrlichen Maklers.

I consider the power of the German Empire …to be more than that of an honest broker.

Speech, Reichstag, 1878

Legt eine möglichst starke militärische Kraft, mit anderen Worten möglichst viel Blut und Eisen in die Hand des Königs von Preussen, dann wird er die Politik machen können, die Ihr wünscht; mit Reden und Schützenfesten und Liedern macht sie sich nicht, sie macht sich nur durch 'Blut und Eisen'!

Put the strongest possible military power, in other words as much blood and iron as possible, in the hands of the King of Prussia, and then he will be able to carry out the policy you want; this cannot be achieved with speeches and shooting-matches and songs; it can only be achieved by 'blood and iron'!

Speech, Prussian House of Deputies, 1886

Fischer, Joschka
German politician
Commenting on the war in Serbia

For the first time in its history, Germany is fighting on the right side.

The Times, June 1999

Hölderlin, Friedrich (1770–1843)
German poet

Denn, ihr Deutschen, auch ihr seid Tatenarm und gedankenvoll.

For, you Germans, you too are Poor in deed and rich in thoughts.

'To the Germans' (1798)

Huxley, Aldous (1894–1963)
English writer, poet and critic

How appallingly thorough these Germans always managed to be, how emphatic! In sex no less than in war – in scholarship, in science. Diving deeper than anyone else and coming up muddier.

Time Must Have a Stop (1944)

Kraus, Karl (1874–1936)
Austrian scientist, critic and poet

> *Die deutsche Sprache ist die tiefste, die deutsche Rede die seichteste.*
> The German language is the most profound one, German speech the most shallow.

By Night (1919)

Lawrence, D.H. (1885–1930)
English writer, poet and critic

> It is as if the life had retreated eastwards. As if the Germanic life were slowly ebbing away from contact with western Europe, ebbing to the deserts of the east.

A Letter from Germany (1924)

Lichtenberg, Georg (1742–1799)
German physicist, satirist and writer

> *Sagt, ist noch ein Land ausser Deutschland, wo man die Nase eher rümpfen lernt als putzen?*
> Tell me, is there a country besides Germany where you learn to turn up your nose rather than wipe it?

Aphorisms (Scrawlings) (1775–1776)

Schopenhauer, Arthur (1788–1860)
German philosopher

> *Ein eigentümlicher Fehler der Deutschen ist, dass sie, was vor ihren Füssen liegt, in den Wolken suchen.*
> It is a curious failing in the German people that they search in the clouds for what lies at their feet.

Parerga und Paralipomena (1851)

Tucholsky, Kurt (1890–1935)
German satirist and writer

> There is an old saying: 'When a German falls over, he doesn't stand up, but looks about to see who is liable to pay him compensation.'

Scraps (1973)

▶▶ EUROPE; WAR

ghosts

Betjeman, Sir John (1906–1984)
English poet laureate

> The gas was on in the Institute,
> The flare was up in the gym,
> A man was running a mineral line,
> A lass was singing a hymn,
> When Captain Webb the Dawley man,
> Captain Webb from Dawley,
> Came swimming along the old canal
> That carried the bricks to Lawley …

We saw the ghost of Captain Webb,
Webb in a water sheeting,
Come dripping along in a bathing dress
To the Saturday evening meeting.
Dripping along –
Dripping along –
To the Congregational Hall;
Dripping and still he rose over the sill and faded away in a wall.

Old Lights for New Chancels (1940)

Shenstone, William (1714–1763)
English poet, essayist and letter writer

> Beneath a church-yard yew
> Decay'd and worn with age,
> At dusk of eve methought I spy'd
> Poor Slender's ghost, that whimpering cry'd
> O sweet, O sweet Anne Page!

'Slender's Ghost'

Thomas, Dylan (1914–1953)
Welsh poet, writer and radio dramatist

> I, born of flesh and ghost, was neither
> A ghost nor man, but mortal ghost.
> And I was struck down by death's feather.

'Before I knocked' (1933)

gifts

Browning, Elizabeth Barrett (1806–1861)
English poet; wife of Robert Browning

> God's gifts put man's best gifts to shame.

Sonnets from the Portuguese (1850)

Carroll, Lewis (1832–1898)
English writer and photographer

> They gave it me … for an un-birthday present.

Through the Looking-Glass (and What Alice Found There) (1872)

Conrad, Joseph (1857–1924)
Polish-born British writer, sailor and explorer

> The fatal imperfection of all the gifts of life, which makes of them a delusion and a snare.

Victory (1915)

Lamb, Charles (1775–1834)
English essayist, critic and letter writer

> 'Presents,' I often say 'endear Absents.'

Essays of Elia (1823)

Reed, Henry (1914–1986)
English poet, radio dramatist and translator

> If one doesn't get birthday presents it can remobilize very painfully the persecutory anxiety which usually follows birth.

The Primal Scene, as it were (1958)

Sophocles (496–406 BC)
Greek dramatist

Gifts from enemies are no gifts, and bring no good.

Ajax, line 665

▶▶ CHARITY; GENEROSITY; KINDNESS

girls

Crompton, Richmal (1890–1969)
English writer and teacher
'I don't play little girls' games, ' [William] said scathingly. But Violet Elizabeth did not appear to be scathed. 'Don't you know any little girlth?' she said pityingly. 'I'll teach you little girlth gameth, ' she added pleasantly. 'I don't want to, ' said William. 'I don't like them. I don't like little girls' games. I don't want to know 'em.'
The Just William Collection (1991), 'The Sweet Little Girl in White'

cummings, e. e. (1894–1962)
US poet, noted for his typography, and painter
a pretty girl who naked is
is worth a million statues.
Collected Poems, 133

Hudson, Bob (1946–)
Girls in our town leave school at fifteen
Work at the counter or behind the machine
Spend all their money on making the scene
And plan on going to England …

Girls in our town are too good for the Pill
But if you keep asking they probably will
Perhaps 'cause they like you, or else for the thrill
And explain it away in the morning.
'Girls in our Town', song

Huxley, Aldous (1894–1963)
English writer, poet and critic
Oh, she's a splendid girl. Wonderfully pneumatic.
Brave New World (1932)

Longfellow, Henry Wadsworth (1807–1882)
US poet and writer
Written for his second daughter when she was a baby
There was a little girl
Who had a little curl
Right in the middle of her forehead,
When she was good
She was very, very good,
But when she was bad she was horrid.
'There was a Little Girl' (1882)

Salinger, J.D. (1919–)
US writer
I was about half in love with her by the time we sat down. That's the thing about girls. Every time they do something pretty, even if they're not much to look at, or even if they're sort of

stupid, you fall half in love with them, and then you never know where you are.
The Catcher in the Rye (1951)

▶▶ BOYS; CHILDREN

glory

Anonymous
Sic transit gloria mundi.
Thus passes the glory of the world.
Spoken during the coronation of a new Pope

Bacon, Francis (1561–1626)
English philosopher, essayist, politician and courtier
Knowledge is a rich storehouse for the glory of the Creator and the relief of man's estate.
The Advancement of Learning (1605)

Blake, William (1757–1827)
English poet, engraver, painter and mystic
The pride of the peacock is the glory of God.
'Proverbs of Hell' (c.1793)

Byron, Lord (1788–1824)
English poet satirist and traveller
Glory, like the phoenix 'midst her fires,
Exhales her odours, blazes, and expires.
English Bards and Scotch Reviewers (1809)

Oh, talk not to me of a name great in story;
The days of our youth are the days of our glory;
And the myrtle and ivy of sweet two-and-twenty
Are worth all your laurels, though ever so plenty.
'Stanzas Written on the Road between Florence and Pisa, November 1821'

Campbell, Thomas (1777–1844)
Scottish poet, ballad writer and journalist
The combat deepens. On, ye brave,
Who rush to glory, or the grave!
'Hohenlinden'

Drake, Sir Francis (c.1540–1596)
English navigator
There must be a beginning of any great matter, but the continuing unto the end until it be thoroughly finished yields the true glory.
Dispatch to Sir Francis Walsingham, 1587

Gray, Thomas (1716–1771)
English poet and scholar
The boast of heraldry, the pomp of pow'r,
And all that beauty, all that wealth e'er gave,
Awaits alike th' inevitable hour,
The paths of glory lead but to the grave … .
'Elegy Written in a Country Churchyard' (1751)

Kempis, Thomas à (c.1380–1471)
German mystic, monk and writer
O quam cito transit gloria mundi.

Oh, how quickly the glory in this world passes away.

De Imitatione Christi (1892)

La Fontaine, Jean de (1621–1695)
French poet and fabulist
Aucun chemin de fleurs ne conduit à la gloire.
No flowery path leads to glory.

'Les deux aventuriers et le talisman'

Mordaunt, Thomas Osbert (1730–1809)
British soldier
Sound, sound the clarion, fill the fife,
Throughout the sensual world proclaim,
One crowded hour of glorious life
Is worth an age without a name.

'Verses written during the War, 1756–1763' (1791)

Propertius, Sextus Aurelius (c.50–c.15 BC)
Roman poet
Magnum iter ascendo, sed dat mihi gloria vires.
Great is the height that I must scale, but the prospect of glory gives me strength.

Elegies

Rossetti, Christina (1830–1894)
English poet
'Come cheer up, my lads, 'tis to glory we steer!'
As the soldier remarked whose post lay in the rear.

Untitled couplet (c.1845)

Rouget de Lisle, Claude-Joseph (1760–1836)
Allons, enfants de la patrie,
Le jour de gloire est arrivé!
Let us go, children of this land, the day of glory has arrived!

'La Marseillaise', 1792

Shakespeare, William (1564–1616)
English dramatist, poet and actor
Like madness is the glory of this life.

Timon of Athens, I.ii

O the fierce wretchedness that glory brings us!
Timon of Athens, IV.ii

Webster, John (c.1580–c.1625)
English dramatist
Glories, like glow-worms, afar off shine bright,
But, looked too near, have neither heat nor light.

The Duchess of Malfi (1623)

Wordsworth, William (1770–1850)
English poet
Not in entire forgetfulness,
And not in utter nakedness,
But trailing clouds of glory do we come
From God, who is our home:
Heaven lies about us in our infancy!

'Ode: Intimations of Immortality'
(1807)

Yeats, W.B. (1865–1939)
Irish poet, dramatist, editor, writer and senator
Think where man's glory most begins and ends,
And say my glory was I had such friends.

A Speech and Two Poems (1937)

goals

Berlin, Isaiah (1909–1997)
English philosopher
Injustice, poverty, slavery, ignorance – these may be cured by reform or revolution. But men do not live only by fighting evils. They live by positive goals, individual and collective, a vast variety of them, seldom predictable, at times incompatible.

'Political Ideas in the Twentieth Century' (1969)

Kafka, Franz (1883–1924)
Czech-born German-speaking writer
There is a goal but no way of reaching it; what we call the way is hesitation.

Reflections on Sin, Sorrow, Hope and the True Way

Longfellow, Henry Wadsworth (1807–1882)
US poet and writer
If you would hit the mark, you must aim a little above it;
Every arrow that flies feels the attraction of earth.

'Elegiac Verse' (1880)

Santayana, George (1863–1952)
Spanish-born US philosopher and writer
Fanaticism consists in redoubling your effort when you have forgotten your aim.

The Life of Reason (1906)

Sidney, Sir Philip (1554–1586)
English poet, critic, soldier, courtier and diplomat
Who shoots at the midday sun, though he be sure he shall never hit the mark, yet as sure is he he shall shoot higher than who aims but at a bush.

New Arcadia (1590)

Smith, Logan Pearsall (1865–1946)
US-born British epigrammatist, critic and writer
When people come and talk to you of their aspirations, before they leave you had better count your spoons.

Afterthoughts (1931)

Stevenson, Robert Louis (1850–1894)
Scottish writer, poet and essayist
To be honest, to be kind – to earn a little and to spend a little less, to make upon the whole a family happier for his presence, to renounce when that shall be necessary and not be embittered, to keep a few friends, but these

without capitulation – above all, on the same grim condition, to keep friends with himself – here is a task for all that a man has of fortitude and delicacy.

Across the Plains (1892)

An aspiration is a joy forever.

Virginibus Puerisque (1881)

Thatcher, Margaret (1925–)
English Conservative Prime Minister

If you are going from A to B you do not always necessarily go in a straight line.

The Observer, 1980

White, Patrick (1912–1990)
English-born Australian writer and dramatist

That is men all over … They will aim too low. And achieve what they expect.

Voss (1957)

Young, Edward (1683–1765)
English poet, dramatist, satirist and clergyman

At thirty man suspects himself a Fool;
Knows it at forty, and reforms his Plan;
At fifty chides his infamous Delay,
Pushes his prudent Purpose to Resolve;
In all the magnanimity of Thought
Resolves; and re-resolves; then dies the same.

Night-Thoughts on Life, Death and Immortality (1742–1746)

▶▶ AMBITION

god

Agathon (c.445–400 BC)
Athenian poet

Even God is deprived of this one thing only: the power to undo what has been done.

In Aristotle, *Nicomachean Ethics*

Agee, James (1909–1955)
US novelist and poet

God doesn't believe in the easy way.

Attr.

Ainger, A.C. (1841–1919)
English writer, lecturer and preacher

God is working His purpose out as year succeeds to year,
God is working His purpose out and the time is drawing near;
Nearer and nearer draws the time, the time that shall surely be,
When the earth shall be filled with the glory of God as the waters cover the sea.

Hymn

Alcuin (735–804)
English theologian, scholar and educationist

Man thinks, God directs.

Epistles

Allen, Woody (1935–)
US film director, writer, actor and comedian

Not only is there no God, but try getting a plumber on weekends.

Getting Even (1971)

Of God

The worst that can be said is that he's an under-achiever.

Love and Death (film, 1976)

If only God would give me some clear sign! Like making a large deposit in my name at a Swiss bank.

Without Feathers (1976)

Andrewes, Bishop Lancelot (1555–1626)
English churchman

What gets God by nobiscum? Nothing He. What get we?

Sermon 9, Of the Nativity (c.1614)

Anonymous

Dear Sir,
Your astonishment's odd:
I am always about in the Quad.
And that's why the tree
Will continue to be,
Since observed by Yours faithfully, God.

Reply to Ronald Knox, 'There was once a man'

Anouilh, Jean (1910–1987)
French dramatist and screenwriter

Dieu est avec tout le monde … Et, en fin de compte, il est toujours avec ceux qui ont beaucoup d'argent, et de grosses armées.
God is on everyone's side … And, in the final analysis, he is on the side of those who have plenty of money and large armies.

The Lark (1953)

Asturias, Miguel Angel (1899–1974)
Guatemalan writer and poet

Para un pueblo hambriento e inactivo la sola forma en que Dios puede aparecer es en la de trabajo y comida.
For people who are hungry and inactive, God can only appear in the form of work and food.

The Little Rich Boy (1961)

Augustine, Saint (354–430)
Numidian-born Christian theologian and philosopher

Fecisti nos ad te, et inquietum est cor nostrum donec requiescat in te.
Thou hast created us for Thyself, and our heart is restless till it finds rest in Thee.

Confessions (397–398)

Baldwin, James (1924–1987)
US writer, dramatist, poet and civil rights activist

If the concept of God has any validity or any

use, it can only be to make us larger, freer, and more loving. If God cannot do this, then it is time we got rid of Him.

The Fire Next Time (1963)

Baxter, Richard (1615–1691)
English Nonconformist clergyman
Suppose you saw the Lord in glory continually before you; When you are hearing, praying, talking, jesting, eating, drinking, and when you are tempted to wilful sin: Suppose you saw the Lord stand over you, as verily as you see a man! Would you be godly or ungodly after it? As sure as you live, and see one another, God always seeth you.

'The Life of Faith' (1660)

The Bible (King James Version)
In the beginning God created the heaven and the earth.
And the earth was without form, and void; and darkness was upon the face of the deep. And the Spirit of God moved upon the face of the waters.
And God said, Let there be light: and there was light.

Genesis, 1:1–3

For the Lord seeth not as man seeth: for man looketh on the outward appearance, but the Lord looketh on the heart.

I Samuel, 16:7

God is a Spirit: and they that worship him must worship him in spirit and in truth.

John, 4:24

God is our refuge and strength, a very present help in trouble.
Therefore will not we fear, though the earth be removed, and though the mountains be carried into the midst of the sea.

Psalms, 46:1–2

Bonhoeffer, Dietrich (1906–1945)
German theologian, executed by the Nazis
Ein Gott, der sich von uns beweisen liesse, wäre ein Götze.
A God who allowed us to prove his existence would be an idol.

'If you believe it, you have it' (1931)

Der Mensch hat gelernt, in allen wichtigen Fragen mit sich selbst fertig zu werden ohne Zuhilfenahme der 'Arbeitshypothese: Gott.'
In all important questions, man has learned to cope without recourse to God as a working hypothesis.

Letter to a friend, 1944

Brooke, Rupert (1887–1915)
English poet

Because God put His adamantine fate
Between my sullen heart and its desire,
I swore that I would burst the Iron Gate,
Rise up, and curse Him on His throne of fire.

'Failure' (1905–1908)

Browne, Sir Thomas (1605–1682)
English physician, author and antiquary
God is like a skilful Geometrician.

Religio Medici (1643)

Browning, Elizabeth Barrett (1806–1861)
English poet; wife of Robert Browning
God answers sharp and sudden on some prayers,
And thrusts the thing we have prayed for in our face,
A gauntlet with a gift in't.

Aurora Leigh (1857)

Clough, Arthur Hugh (1819–1861)
English poet and letter writer
'There is no God,' the wicked saith,
'And truly it's a blessing,
For what he might have done with us
It's better only guessing.' ...

But country folks who live beneath
The shadow of the steeple;
The parson and the parson's wife,
And mostly married people;

Youths green and happy in first love,
So thankful for illusion;
And men caught out in what the world
Calls guilt, in first confusion;

And almost every one when age,
Disease, or sorrows strike him,
Inclines to think there is a God,
Or something very like Him.

Dipsychus (1865)

Cowper, William (1731–1800)
English poet, hymn and letter writer
God moves in a mysterious way
His wonders to perform;
He plants his footsteps in the sea,
And rides upon the storm.

Olney Hymns (1779)

De Vries, Peter (1910–1993)
US novelist
It is the final proof of God's omnipotence that he need not exist in order to save us.

The Mackerel Plaza (1958)

Donne, John (1572–1631)
English poet
Batter my heart, three person'd God; for, you

As yet but knock, breathe, shine, and seek to
mend –
I, like an usurpt town, to another due,
Labour to admit you, but Oh, to no end –
Take me to you, imprison me, for I
Except you enthrall me, never shall be free,
Nor ever chaste, except you ravish me.
Holy Sonnets (1609–1617)

Dostoevsky, Fyodor (1821–1881)
Russian writer
It's not God that I don't accept, Alyosha, only I
most respectfully return the ticket to Him.
The Brothers Karamazov (1879–1880)

Duhamel, Georges (1884–1966)
French writer, poet, dramatist and physician
*Je respecte trop l'idée de Dieu pour la rendre
responsable d'un monde aussi absurde.*
I have too much respect for the idea of God to
make it responsible for such an absurd world.
Chronique des Pasquier (1948)

Dumas, Alexandre (**Fils**) (1824–1895)
French dramatist, novelist and critic
*Si Dieu pouvait tout à coup être condamné à vivre de la
vie qu'il inflige à l'homme, il se tuerait.*
If God were suddenly condemned to live the life
which he had inflicted on men, He would kill
Himself.
Pensées d'album (1847)

Dürrenmatt, Friedrich (1921–1990)
Swiss dramatist and writer
Gott ist ein unmenschlicher Begriff.
God is an inhuman concept.
The Marriage of Mr Mississippi (1951)

Einstein, Albert (1879–1955)
German-born US mathematical physicist
Raffiniert ist der Herrgott, aber bashaft ist er nicht.
The Lord God is crafty but he is not spiteful.
Inscription in the Mathematical Institute at Princeton

Gott würfelt nicht.
God does not play dice.
Attr.

Before God we are all equally wise – equally
foolish.
Address, Sorbonne, Paris

Ellis, Havelock (1859–1939)
English sexologist and essayist
God is an unutterable Sigh in the Human Heart,
said the old German mystic. And therewith said
the last word.
*Impressions and Comments
(1914)*

Empedocles (c.490–c.430 BC)
Greek philosopher and poet
God is a circle whose centre is everywhere and

whose circumference is nowhere.
Attr.

Freud, Sigmund (1856–1939)
Austrian physicist; founder of psychoanalysis
At bottom God is nothing more than an exalted
father.
Totem and Taboo (1919)

Fuller, Richard Buckminster (1895–1983)
US architect and engineer
God, to me, it seems,
is a verb
not a noun,
proper or improper.
No More Secondhand God (1963)

Galilei, Galileo (1564–1642)
Italian scientist
I do not feel obliged to believe that the same
God who has endowed us with sense, reason,
and intellect has intended us to forgo their use.
Attr.

Gallup, George (1901–1984)
US statistician and market research pioneer
I could prove God statistically.
Attr.

Greene, Graham (1904–1991)
English writer and dramatist
Those who marry God … can become
domesticated too – it's just as hum-drum a
marriage as all the others.
A Burnt-Out Case (1961)

Gypsy Rose Lee (1914–1970)
US stripper, actress and author
God is love, but get it in writing.
Attr

Haldane, J.B.S. (1892–1964)
British biochemist, geneticist and popularizer of science
Reply when asked what inferences could be drawn about the
nature of God from a study of his works
The Creator … has a special preference for
beetles.
Lecture, 1951

Heine, Heinrich (1797–1856)
German lyric poet, essayist and journalist
Last words
Dieu me pardonnera, c'est son métier.
God will forgive me. It is his profession.
In Meissner, *H H Erinnerungen (1856)*

Hooker, Richard (c.1554–1600)
English theologian and churchman
The earth may shake, the pillars of the world
may tremble under us, the countenance of the
heaven may be appalled, the sun may lose his
light, the moon her beauty, the stars their glory;
but concerning the man that trusteth in God …

what is there in the world that shall change his heart, overthrow his faith, alter his affection towards God, or the affection of God to him?

Of the Laws of Ecclesiasticall Politie (1593)

Hughes, Sean (1966–)

Irish comedian

I'd like to thank God for fucking up my life and at the same time not existing, quite a special skill.

The Independent, 1993

Hughes, Ted (1930–1998)

English poet

God is a good fellow, but His mother's against him.

Wodwo (1967)

Huxley, Sir Julian Sorell (1887–1975)

English biologist and Director-General of UNESCO

Operationally, God is beginning to resemble not a ruler but the last fading smile of a cosmic Cheshire cat.

Religion without Revelation (1957)

Inge, William Ralph (1860–1954)

English divine, writer and teacher

Many people believe that they are attracted by God, or by Nature, when they are only repelled by man.

More Lay Thoughts of a Dean (1931)

Jowett, Benjamin (1817–1893)

English scholar, translator, essayist and priest

Responding to a conceited young student's assertion that he could find no evidence for a God

If you don't find a God by five o'clock this afternoon you must leave the college.

Attr.

Kempis, Thomas à (c.1380–1471)

German mystic, monk and writer

Nam homo proponit, sed Deus disponit.
For man proposes, but God disposes.

De Imitatione Christi (1892)

Knox, Ronald (1888–1957)

English Catholic priest and biblical translator

There was once a man who said 'God
Must think it exceedingly odd
If he finds that this tree
Continues to be
When there's no one about in the Quad.'

Attr.

O God, for as much as without Thee
We are not enabled to doubt Thee,
Help us all by Thy grace
To convince the whole race
It knows nothing whatever about Thee.

Attr.

Koestler, Arthur (1905–1983)

British writer, essayist and political refugee

God seems to have left the receiver off the hook, and time is running out.

The Ghost in the Machine (1961)

La Fontaine, Jean de (1621–1695)

French poet and fabulist

Dieu fait bien ce qu'il fait.
What God does, He does well.

Fables, 'Le gland et la citrouille'

Laplace, Pierre-Simon, Marquis de (1749–1827)

French mathematician and astronomer

Reply when asked by Napoleon why he had made no reference to God in his book about the universe, *Mécanique céleste*

I have no need of that hypothesis.

In E. Bell, *Men of Mathematics*

Logau, Friedrich von (1605–1655)

German epigrammatist

Gottes Mühlen mahlen langsam, mahlen aber trefflich klein;
Ob aus Langmut er sich säumet, bringt mit Schärf' er alles ein.
Though the mills of God grind slowly, yet they grind extremely small;
Though his patience makes him tarry, with exactness grinds He all.

Epigrams (1653), no. 638

Luther, Martin (1483–1546)

German Protestant theologian and reformer

Worauf du nun … dein Herz hängt und verlässt, das ist eigentlich dein Gott.
Whatever your heart clings to and relies upon, that is really your God.

Large Catechism (1529)

Ein feste Burg ist unser Gott,
Ein gute Wehr und Waffen.
A strong castle is our God,
A good defence and weapon.

Hymn, first extant version, *Rauscher's Hymnal* (1531)

Mallock, William Hurrell (1849–1923)

English poet and theological writer

Whatever may be God's future, we cannot forget His past.

Is Life Worth Living?

Mencken, H.L. (1880–1956)

US writer, critic, philologist and satirist

God is the immemorial refuge of the incompetent, the helpless, the miserable. They find not only sanctuary in His arms, but also a kind of superiority, soothing to their macerated egos; He will set them above their betters.

Notebooks (1956)

It takes a long while for a naturally trustful

person to reconcile himself to the idea that after all God will not help him.

Notebooks (1956)

Montesquieu, Charles (1689–1755)
French philosopher and jurist
If triangles created a god, they would give him three sides.

Lettres persanes (1721)

Nerval, Gérard de (1808–1855)
French poet and writer
Dieu est mort! le ciel est vide –
Pleurez! enfants, vous n'avez plus de père.
God is dead! Heaven is empty – Weep, children, you no longer have a father.

'Le Christ aux Oliviers'

Nietzsche, Friedrich Wilhelm (1844–1900)
German philosopher, critic and poet
Gott ist tot: aber so wie die Art der Menschen ist, wird es vielleicht noch jahrtausendelang Höhlen geben, in denen man seinen Schatten zeigt.
God is dead: but men's natures are such that for thousands of years yet there will perhaps be caves in which his shadow will be seen.

The Gay Science (1887)

Owen, John (c.1560–1622)
Welsh epigrammatist and teacher
God and the doctor we alike adore
But only when in danger, not before;
The danger o'er, both are alike requited,
God is forgotten, and the Doctor slighted.

Epigrams

Pascal, Blaise (1623–1662)
French philosopher and scientist
Je ne puis pardonner à Descartes: il aurait bien voulu, dans toute sa philosophie, pouvoir se passer de Dieu; mais il n'a pu s'empêcher de lui faire donner une chiquenaude, pour mettre le monde en mouvement; après celà, il n'a plus eu que faire de Dieu.
I cannot forgive Descartes; in all his philosophy he did his best to dispense with God. But he could not avoid making Him set the world in motion with a flick of His finger; after that he had no more use for God.

Pensées (1670)

Phillips, Wendell (1811–1884)
US reformer
One, on God's side, is a majority.

Lecture, 1859

Picasso, Pablo (1881–1973)
Spanish painter, sculptor and graphic artist
God is really only another artist. He invented the giraffe, the elephant, and the cat. He has no real style. He just goes on trying other things.

In Françoise Gilot and Carlton Lake, *Life with Picasso* (1964)

Pope, Alexander (1688–1744)
English poet, translator and editor
Nor God alone in the still calm we find,
He mounts the storm, and walks upon the wind.

An Essay on Man (1733)

All are but parts of one stupendous whole,
Whose body Nature is, and God the soul.

An Essay on Man, I (1733

Prévert, Jacques (1900–1977)
French poet and screenwriter
Notre Père qui êtes aux cieux
Restez-y
Et nous nous resterons sur la terre.
Our Father which art in heaven, stay there; and as for us, we shall stay on earth.

Paroles (1946)

Priestley, J.B. (1894–1984)
English writer, dramatist and critic
God can stand being told by Professor Ayer and Marghanita Laski that He doesn't exist.

The Listener, 1965

Sartre, Jean-Paul (1905–1980)
French philosopher, writer, dramatist and critic
L'absence c'est Dieu. Dieu, c'est la solitude des hommes.
God is absence. God is the solitude of man.

Le Diable et le Bon Dieu (1951)

Shakespeare, William (1564–1616)
English dramatist, poet and actor
There's a divinity that shapes our ends,
Rough-hew them how we will.

Hamlet, V.ii

As flies to wanton boys are we to th' gods –
They kill us for their sport.

King Lear, IV.i

Shaw, George Bernard (1856–1950)
Irish socialist, writer, dramatist and critic
Beware of the man whose god is in the skies.

Man and Superman (1903)

Squire, Sir J.C. (1884–1958)
English poet, critic, writer and editor
God heard the embattled nations sing and shout
'Gott strafe England!' and 'God save the King!'
God this, God that, and God the other thing –
'Good God!' said God, 'I've got my work cut out.'

The Survival of the Fittest (1916)

Strachey, Lytton (1880–1932)
English biographer and critic
Yet her conception of God was certainly not orthodox. She felt towards Him as she might have felt towards a glorified sanitary engineer; and in some of her speculations she seems

hardly to distinguish between the Deity and the Drains.

'Florence Nightingale' (1918)

Thomson, James (1834–1882)

Scottish poet and dramatist

> The vilest thing must be less vile than Thou
> From whom it had its being, God and Lord!

The City of Dreadful Night (1880)

Thoreau, Henry David (1817–1862)

US essayist, social critic and writer

On being urged to make his peace with God

> I did not know that we had ever quarrelled.

Attr.

Tillich, Paul (1886–1965)

> He who knows about depth knows about God.

The Shaking of the Foundations (1962 edition)

Vaughan, Henry (1622–1695)

Welsh poet and physician

> There is in God (some say)
> A deep, but dazzling darkness; as men here
> Say it is late and dusky, because they
> See not all clear;
> O for that night! where I in him
> Might live invisible and dim.

Silex Scintillans (1650–1655)

Vigny, Alfred de (1797–1863)

French writer

> *Le vrai Dieu, le Dieu fort, est le Dieu des idées.*
> The true God, the mighty God, is the God of ideas.

'The Bottle in the Sea', 1847

Voltaire (1694–1778)

French philosopher, dramatist, poet, historian writer and critic

> *Dieu n'est pas pour les gros bataillons, mais pour ceux qui tirent le mieux.*
> God is not on the side of the big batallions, but of the best marksmen.

'The Piccini Notebooks' (c.1735–1750)

> *Si Dieu n'existait pas, il faudrait l'inventer.*
> If God did not exist, it would be necessary to invent him.

Epîtres, 'A l'auteur du livre des trois imposteurs'

Walker, Alice (1944–)

US writer and poet

> I think it pisses God off if you walk by the color purple in a field somewhere and don't notice it.

The Color Purple (film, 1985)

Weldon, Fay (1931–)

British writer

> Even God has become female. God is no longer the bearded patriarch in the sky. He has had a sex change and turned into Mother Nature.

The Times, 1998

Wiesel, Elie (1928–)

Romanian-born US writer

Replying to the question 'Why did God allow the Holocaust to happen?'

> If you'll forgive me, that's an immoral question!

Debate, Oxford Union

Wolsey, Thomas, Cardinal (c.1475–1530)

English Cardinal and statesman

Remark to Sir William Kingston

> Had I but served God as diligently as I have served the King, he would not have given me over in my grey hairs.

In Cavendish, *Negotiations of Thomas Wolsey* (1641)

Xenophanes (c.570–480 BC)

Greek philosopher and poet

> Ethiopians say that their gods are snub-nosed and black, Thracians that theirs have light blue eyes and red hair.

In J.H. Lesher, *Xenophanes of Colophon* (1992)

Young, Edward (1683–1765)

English poet, dramatist, satirist and clergyman

> A God All mercy, is a God unjust.

Night-Thoughts on Life, Death and Immortality (1742–1745)

▶▶ ATHEISM; BELIEF

golf

Aaron, Hank (1934–)

> It took me seventeen years to get three thousand hits in baseball. I did it in one afternoon on the golf course.

In Lee Green, *Sportswit* (1984)

James, Mark

US golfer

When asked how his sport could be improved

> I always feel that the ball is too small.

The Times, 1998

Lang, Andrew (1844–1912)

Scottish poet, writer, mythologist and anthropologist

> Golf is a thoroughly national game. It is as Scotch as haggis, cockie-leekie, high cheekbones, or rowanberry jam.

In W. Pett Ridge (ed.), *Daily News, Lost Leaders,*1889

Leacock, Stephen (1869–1944)

English-born Canadian humorist, writer and economist

> Golf may be played on Sunday, not being a game within the view of the law, but being a form of moral effort.

Over the Footlights (1923)

MacDonald, Charles Blair (1855–1939)

Remark by a caddy at St Andrews to a professor who was having difficulty learning the game

When ye come to play golf ye maun hae a heid!
Scotland's Gift – Golf (1928)

Palmer, Arnold (1929–)
US golfer
Replying to an onlooker who observed that he was playing so
well he must have plenty of luck on his side
The more I practise the luckier I get.
Attr.

Twain, Mark (1835–1910)
US humorist, writer, journalist and lecturer
Golf is a good walk spoiled.
Attr.

▶▶ SPORT AND GAMES

good and evil

Anonymous
There is so much good in the worst of us,
And so much bad in the best of us,
That it hardly becomes any of us
To talk about the rest of us.
Variously attr.

The Bible (King James Version)
Ye shall be as gods, knowing good and evil.
Genesis, 3:5

The wicked flee when no man pursueth: but the
righteous are bold as a lion.
Proverbs, 28:1

Woe unto them that call evil good, and good
evil.
Isaiah, 5:20

Brecht, Bertolt (1898–1956)
German dramatist
Something must be wrong with your world. Why
Is a price set on wickedness, and why is the
good man
Attended by such harsh punishments?
Good Woman of Setzuan
(1943)

Burns, Robert (1759–1796)
Scottish poet and song writer
Whatever mitigates the woes or increases the
happiness of others, this is my criterion of
goodness; and whatever injures society at large,
or any individual in it, this is my measure of
iniquity.
Attr.

Dana, Charles Anderson (1819–1897)
US newspaper editor and reformer
All the goodness of a good egg cannot make up
for the badness of a bad one.
The Making of a Newspaper Man

Goldsmith, Oliver (c.1728–1774)
Irish dramatist, poet and writer
We must touch his weaknesses with a delicate
hand. There are some faults so nearly allied to
excellence, that we can scarce weed out the vice
without eradicating the virtue.
The Good Natur'd Man (1768)

Halifax, Lord (1633–1695)
English politician, courtier, pamphleteer and
epigrammatist
Our Vices and Virtues couple with one another,
and get Children that resemble both their
Parents.
'Of the World' (1750)

Hamsun, Knut (1859–1952)
Norwegian novelist
When good befalls a man he calls it Providence,
when evil fate.
Vagabonds (1909)

King, Martin Luther (1929–1968)
US civil rights leader and Baptist minister
I believe that unarmed truth and unconditional
love will have the final word in reality. That is
why right, temporarily defeated, is stronger than
evil triumphant.
Speech at Civil Rights March on Washington,
August 28, 1963

Lermontov, Mikhail (1814–1841)
Russian poet and writer
What is the greatest good and evil? – two ends
of an invisible chain which come closer together
the further they move apart.
Vadim (1834)

Proverb
Better be a fool than a knave.

Shakespeare, William (1564–1616)
English dramatist, poet and actor
Men's evil manners live in brass: their virtues
We write in water.
Henry VIII, IV.ii

The evil that men do lives after them;
The good is oft interred with their bones.
Julius Caesar, III.ii

Some rise by sin, and some by virtue fall.
Measure for Measure, II.i

Virtue that transgresses is but patch'd with sin,
and sin that amends is but patch'd with virtue.
Twelfth Night, I.v

Spinoza, Baruch (1632–1677)
Dutch philosopher and theologian
*Nam una eadem res potest eodem tempore bona et
mala, e.g. Musica bona est Melancholico, mala Lugenti;
Surdo autem neque bona neque mala.*

One and the same thing can at the same time be good and bad, for example, music is good to the melancholy, bad to the mourner, and neither good nor bad to the deaf.

Ethics (1677)

Surtees, R.S. (1805–1864)
English writer
> More people are flattered into virtue than bullied out of vice.

The Analysis of the Hunting Field (1846)

Vanbrugh, Sir John (1664–1726)
English dramatist and baroque architect
> *Belinda*: Ay, but you know we must return good for evil.
> *Lady Brute*: That may be a mistake in the translation.

The Provok'd Wife (1697)

▶▶ GOODNESS

goodness

Addison, Joseph (1672–1719)
English essayist, poet, playwright and statesman
> Content thyself to be obscurely good.
> When vice prevails, and impious men bear sway,
> The post of honour is a private station.

Cato (1713)

Aristotle (384–322 BC)
Greek philosopher
> The good has been well said to be that at which all things aim.

Nicomachean Ethics

> In all things the middle state is to be praised. But it is sometimes necessary to incline towards overshooting and sometimes to shooting short of the mark, since this is the easiest way of hitting the mean and the right course.

Nicomachean Ethics

Bacon, Francis (1561–1626)
English philosopher, essayist, politician and courtier
> The inclination to goodness is imprinted deeply in the nature of man: insomuch, that if it issue not towards men, it will take unto other living creatures.

'Of Goodness, and Goodness of Nature' (1625)

Bagehot, Walter (1826–1877)
English economist and political philosopher
> The most melancholy of human reflections, perhaps, is that, on the whole, it is a question whether the benevolence of mankind does most good or harm.

Physics and Politics (1872)

Barth, Karl (1886–1968)
Swiss Protestant theologian
> Men have never been good, they are not good, they never will be good.

Time, 1954

Blake, William (1757–1827)
English poet, engraver, painter and mystic
> He who would do good to another must do it in Minute Particulars.
> General Good is the plea of the Scoundrel hypocrite & flatterer.

Jerusalem (1804–1820)

Buddha (c.563–483 BC)
Indian religious teacher; founder of Buddhism
> This Ayrian Eightfold Path, that is to say: Right view, right aim, right speech, right action, right living, right effort, right mindfulness, right contemplation.

In Woodward, *Some Sayings of the Buddha*

Burke, Edmund (1729–1797)
Irish-born British statesman and philosopher
> When bad men combine, the good must associate; else they will fall, one by one, an unpitied sacrifice in a contemptible struggle.

Thoughts on the Cause of the Present Discontents (1770)

> Good order is the foundation of all good things.

Reflections on the Revolution in France (1790)

Butler, Samuel (1835–1902)
English writer, painter, philosopher and scholar
> Virtue and vice are like life and death or mind and matter: things which cannot exist without being qualified by their opposite.

The Way of All Flesh (1903)

> When the righteous man turneth away from his righteousness that he hath committed and doeth that which is neither quite lawful nor quite right, he will generally be found to have gained in amiability what he has lost in holiness.

The Note-Books of Samuel Butler (1912)

Campion, Thomas (1567–1620)
> The man of life upright,
> Whose guiltlesse hart is free
> From all dishonest deedes
> Or thought of vanitie …
>
> Good thoughts his onely friendes,
> His wealth a well-spent age,
> The earth his sober Inne
> And quiet Pilgrimage.

A Booke of Ayres (1601)

Compton-Burnett, Dame Ivy (1884–1969)
English novelist
> At any time you might act for my good. When people do that, it kills something precious

between them.

Manservant and Maidservant (1947)

Confucius (c.550–c.478 BC)

Chinese philosopher and teacher of ethics

True goodness springs from a man's own heart.
All men are born good.

Analects

Crabbe, George (1754–1832)

English poet, clergyman, surgeon and botanist

He tried the luxury of doing good.

Tales of the Hall (1819)

Creighton, Mandell (1843–1901)

English churchman, historian and biographer

No people do so much harm as those who go
about doing good.

The Life and Letters of Mandell Creighton (1904)

Gracián, Baltasar (1601–1658)

Spanish writer

Lo bueno, si breve, dos veces bueno.

Good things, if they are short, are twice as
good.

Attr.

Grellet, Stephen (1773–1855)

French missionary

I expect to pass through this world but once;
any good thing therefore that I can do, or any
kindness that I can show to any fellow-creature,
let me do it now; let me not defer or neglect it,
for I shall not pass this way again.

Attr.

Hardy, Thomas (1840–1928)

English writer and poet

Good, but not religious-good.

Under the Greenwood Tree (1872)

Hutcheson, Francis (1694–1746)

Scottish philosopher

That action is best, which procures the greatest
happiness for the greatest numbers.

*An Inquiry into the Original of our Ideas of Beauty
and Virtue* (1725)

Kingsley, Charles (1819–1875)

English writer, poet, lecturer and clergyman

Be good, sweet maid, and let who can be clever;
Do lovely things, not dream them, all day long;
And so make Life, and Death, and that For Ever,
One grand sweet song.

'A Farewell. To C.E.G.' (1856)

Landor, Walter Savage (1775–1864)

English poet and writer

Goodness does not more certainly make men
happy than happiness makes them good.

Imaginary Conversations
(1853)

Machiavelli (1469–1527)

Florentine statesman, political theorist and historian

Men never do anything good except out of
necessity.

Discourse

Meredith, George (1828–1909)

English writer, poet and critic

Much benevolence of the passive order may be
traced to a disinclination to inflict pain upon
oneself.

Vittoria (1866)

Plato (c.429–347 BC)

Greek philosopher

The good is the beautiful.

Lysis

Proverbs

The good die young.

If you can't be good, be careful.

One good turn deserves another.

Sallust (86–c.34 BC)

Roman historian and statesman

Of Cato

Esse quam videri bonus malebat.

He preferred to be rather than to seem good.

Catiline

Shakespeare, William (1564–1616)

English dramatist, poet and actor

How far that little candle throws his beams!
So shines a good deed in a naughty world.

The Merchant of Venice, V.i

Tolstoy, Leo (1828–1910)

Russian writer, essayist, philosopher and moralist

But my life now, my whole life, independently of
anything that can happen to me, every minute of
it is no longer meaningless as it was before, but
has a positive meaning of goodness with which I
have the power to invest it.

Anna Karenina (1875–7)

Voltaire (1694–1778)

French philosopher, dramatist, poet, historian writer and
critic

Le mieux est l'ennemi du bien.

The best is the enemy of the good.

'Art dramatique' (1770)

Wells, H.G. (1866–1946)

English writer

He was quite sure that he had been wronged.
Not to be wronged is to forgo the first privilege
of goodness.

Bealby (1915)

Wesley, John (1703–1791)

English theologian and preacher

Do all the good you can,

By all the means you can,
In all the ways you can,
In all the places you can,
At all the times you can,
To all the people you can,
As long as ever you can.

Letters (1915)

West, Mae (1892–1980)
US actress and scriptwriter
When I'm good I'm very good, but when I'm bad I'm better.

I'm No Angel (film, 1933)

Wilde, Oscar (1854–1900)
Irish poet, dramatist, writer, critic and wit
It is better to be beautiful than to be good. But … it is better to be good than to be ugly.

The Picture of Dorian Gray (1891)

Wordsworth, Dame Elizabeth (1840–1932)
English educationist and writer
If all the good people were clever,
And all clever people were good,
The world would be nicer than ever
We thought that it possibly could.
But somehow, 'tis seldom or never
The two hit it off as they should;
The good are so harsh to the clever,
The clever so rude to the good.

'The Clever and the Good' (1890)

▶▶ BEAUTY; BENEFACTORS; GOOD AND EVIL; MORALITY; VIRTUE

gossip

Bierce, Ambrose (1842–c.1914)
US writer, verse writer and soldier
Backbite: To speak of a man as you find him when he can't find you.

The Enlarged Devil's Dictionary (1961)

Chesterfield, Lord (1694–1773)
English politician and letter writer
In the case of scandal, as in that of robbery, the receiver is always thought as bad as the thief.

Letter to his son, 1748

Congreve, William (1670–1729)
English dramatist
Retired to their tea and scandal, according to their ancient custom.

The Double Dealer (1694)

They come together like the Coroner's Inquest, to sit upon the murdered reputations of the week.

The Way of the World (1700)

Eliot, George (1819–1880)
English writer and poet
Gossip is a sort of smoke that comes from the dirty tobacco-pipes of those who diffuse it: it proves nothing but the bad taste of the smoker.

Daniel Deronda (1876)

Farquhar, George (1678–1707)
Irish dramatist
I believe they talked of me, for they laughed consumedly.

The Beaux' Stratagem (1707)

Longworth, Alice Roosevelt (1884–1980)
US writer
Embroidered on a cushion at her home in Washington
If you haven't anything nice to say about anyone, come and sit by me.

New York Times, 1980

Ouida (1839–1908)
English writer and critic
A cruel story runs on wheels, and every hand oils the wheels as they run.

Wisdom, Wit and Pathos, 'Moths'

Pope, Alexander (1688–1744)
English poet, translator and editor
At ev'ry word a reputation dies.

The Rape of the Lock (1714)

Proverbs
A tale never loses in the telling.

Believe nothing of what you hear, and only half of what you see.

Don't wash your dirty linen in public.

There's no smoke without fire.

Throw dirt enough, and some will stick.

Walls have ears.

Rogers, Will (1879–1935)
US humorist, actor, rancher, writer and wit
So live that you wouldn't be ashamed to sell the family parrot to the town gossip.

Attr.

Russell, Bertrand (1872–1970)
English philosopher, mathematician, essayist and social reformer
No one gossips about other people's secret virtues.

On Education, especially in early childhood (1926)

Shakespeare, William (1564–1616)
English dramatist, poet and actor
Rumour is a pipe
Blown by surmises, jealousies, conjectures,
And of so easy and so plain a stop
That the blunt monster with uncounted heads,

The still-discordant wav'ring multitude,
Can play upon it.

Henry IV, Part 2, Induction

Sheridan, Richard Brinsley (1751–1816)
Irish dramatist, politician and orator
Tale-bearers are as bad as the tale-makers.

The School for Scandal (1777)

Here is the whole set! a character dead at every word.

The School for Scandal (1777)

▶▶ SECRETS

government

Acton, Lord (1834–1902)
English historian and moralist
The danger is not that a particular class is unfit to govern. Every class is unfit to govern.

Letter to Mary Gladstone, 1881

Anonymous
Anarchy may not be the best form of government, but it's better than no government at all.

Government expands to absorb revenue and then some.

Wiker's Law

Bagehot, Walter (1826–1877)
English economist and political philosopher
The Crown is, according to the saying, the 'fountain of honour'; but the Treasury is the spring of business.

The English Constitution (1867)

It has been said that England invented the phrase, 'Her Majesty's Opposition'; that it was the first Government which made a criticism of administration as much a part of the polity as administration itself. This critical opposition is the consequence of Cabinet government.

The English Constitution (1867)

Royalty is a government in which the attention of the nation is concentrated on one person doing interesting actions. A Republic is a government in which that attention is divided between many, who are all doing uninteresting actions. Accordingly, so long as the human heart is strong and the human reason weak, royalty will be strong because it appeals to diffused feeling, and Republics weak because they appeal to the understanding.

The English Constitution (1867)

A severe though not unfriendly critic of our institutions said that 'the cure for admiring the

House of Lords was to go and look at it.'

The English Constitution (1867)

Bentham, Jeremy (1748–1832)
English writer and philosopher
It is with government as with medicine, its only business is the choice of evils. Every law is an evil, for every law is an infraction of liberty.

An Introduction to the Principles of Morals and Legislation (1789)

Beveridge, William Henry (1879–1963)
British economist and social reformer
The object of government in peace and in war is not the glory of rulers or of races, but the happiness of the common man.

Report on Social Insurance and Allied Services (1942)

Burke, Edmund (1729–1797)
Irish-born British statesman and philosopher
All government, indeed every human benefit and enjoyment, every virtue, and every prudent act, is founded on compromise and barter.

Speech on Conciliation with America (1775)

In all forms of Government the people is the true legislator.

Tracts on the Popery Laws (1812)

Campbell-Bannerman, Sir Henry (1836–1908)
Scottish Liberal statesman
Good government could never be a substitute for government by the people themselves.

Speech, 1905

Carter, Jimmy (1924–)
US Democrat President
Visiting Egypt in 1979, when told that it took only twenty years to build the Great Pyramid
I'm surprised that a government organization could do it that quickly.

In *Time*, March 1979

Churchill, Lord Randolph (1849–1894)
English Conservative politician
The duty of an opposition is to oppose.

In W.S. Churchill, *Lord Randolph Churchill* (1906)

Clay, Henry (1777–1852)
US statesman
Government is a trust, and the officers of the government are trustees. And both the trust and the trustees are created for the benefit of the people.

Speech, 1829

Confucius (c.550–c.478 BC)
Chinese philosopher and teacher of ethics
An oppressive government is more to be feared than a tiger.

Analects

Coolidge, Calvin (1872–1933)
US President

> The governments of the past could fairly be characterized as devices for maintaining in perpetuity the place and position of certain privileged classes ... The Government of the United States is a device for maintaining in perpetuity the rights of the people, with the ultimate extinction of all privileged classes.
>
> Speech, 1924

Derby, Earl of (1799–1869)
English politician; Conservative Prime Minister

> When I first came into Parliament, Mr Tierney, a great Whig authority, used always to say that the duty of an Opposition was very simple – it was, to oppose everything, and propose nothing.
>
> Speech, House of Commons, 1841

Disraeli, Benjamin (1804–1881)
English statesman and writer

> No Government can be long secure without a formidable opposition.
>
> *Coningsby* (1844)

> I believe that without party Parliamentary government is impossible.
>
> Speech, Manchester, 1872

Ford, Gerald R. (1913–)
US Republican politician and President

> If the Government is big enough to give you everything you want, it is big enough to take away everything you have.
>
> J. F. Parker *If Elected* (1960)

Friedman, Milton (1912–)
US economist

> Governments never learn. Only people learn.
>
> *The Observer*, 1996

Gibbon, Edward (1737–1794)
English historian, politician and memoirist

> The principles of a free constitution are irrecoverably lost, when the legislative power is nominated by the executive.
>
> *Decline and Fall of the Roman Empire* (1776–88)

Goldwater, Barry (1909–1998)
US presidential candidate and writer

> A government that is big enough to give you all you want is big enough to take it all away.
>
> Bachman's *Book of Freedom Quotations*

Gordimer, Nadine (1923–)
South African writer

> I don't think any writers since the generation of Jean-Paul Sartre and Camus in France have influenced a government.
>
> Interview, *The Observer*, 1998

Herbert, Sir A.P. (1890–1971)
English humorist, writer, dramatist and politician

> Well, fancy giving money to the Government!
> Might as well have put it down the drain.
> Fancy giving money to the Government!
> Nobody will see the stuff again.
> Well, they've no idea what money's for –
> Ten to one they'll start another war.
> I've heard a lot of silly things, but, Lor'!
> Fancy giving money to the Government!
>
> 'Too Much!'

Hobbes, Thomas (1588–1679)
English political philosopher

> The only way to erect such a common power, as may be able to defend them from the invasion of foreigners, and the injuries of one another ... is, to confer all their power and strength upon one man, or upon one assembly of men, that may reduce all their wills, by plurality of voices, unto one will ... This is the generation of that great Leviathan, or rather, to speak more reverently, of that mortal god, to which we owe under the immortal God, our peace and defence.
>
> *Leviathan* (1651)

> They that are discontented under monarchy, call it tyranny; and they that are displeased with aristocracy, call it oligarchy: so also, they which find themselves grieved under a democracy, call it anarchy, which signifies want of government; and yet I think no man believes, that want of government, is any new kind of government.
>
> *Leviathan* (1651)

Hume, David (1711–1776)
Scottish philosopher and political economist

> Nothing appears more surprising to those, who consider human affairs with a philosophical eye, than the easiness with which the many are governed by the few; and the implicit submission, with which men resign their own sentiments and passions to those of their rulers.
>
> *Essays, Moral, Political, and Literary* (1742)

James VI of Scotland and I of England (1566–1625)
King of Scotland from 1567 and of England from 1603

> I will govern according to the common weal, but not according to the common will.
>
> Remark, 1621

Johnson, Samuel (1709–1784)
English lexicographer, poet, critic, conversationalist and essayist

> I would not give half a guinea to live under one form of government rather than another. It is of no moment to the happiness of an individual.
>
> In Boswell, *The Life of Samuel Johnson* (1791)

Keynes, John Maynard (1883–1946)
English economist
> The important thing for government is not to do things which individuals are doing already, and to do them a little better or a little worse; but to do those things which at present are not done at all.
>> 'The End of Laissez-Faire' (1926)

Lévis, Duc de (1764–1830)
French writer and soldier
> *Gouverner, c'est choisir.*
> To govern is to make choices.
>> *Maximes et réflexions* (1812)

Mackintosh, Sir James (1765–1832)
Scottish philosopher, historian, lawyer and politician
> The Commons, faithful to their system, remained in a wise and masterly inactivity.
>> *Vindiciae Gallicae* (1791)

Maistre, Joseph de (1753–1821)
French diplomat and political philosopher
> *Toute nation a le gouvernement qu'elle mérite.*
> Each country has the government it deserves.
>> Letter, 1811

Mencken, H.L. (1880–1956)
US writer, critic, philologist and satirist
> The worst government is the most moral. One composed of cynics is often very tolerant and human. But when fanatics are on top there is no limit to oppression.
>> *Notebooks* (1956)

Moynihan, Daniel (1927–)
US academic and politician
> The single most exciting thing you encounter in government is competence, because it's so rare.
>> *New York Times*, 1976

O'Rourke, P.J. (1947–)
US writer
> Feeling good about government is like looking on the bright side of any catastrophe. When you quit looking on the bright side, the catastrophe is still there.
>> *Parliament of Whores* (1991)

O'Sullivan, John L. (1813–1895)
US editor and diplomat
> Understood as a central consolidated power, managing and directing the various general interests of the society, all government is evil, and the parent of evil ... The best government is that which governs least.
>> *United States Magazine and Democratic Review*, 1837, Introduction

Paine, Thomas (1737–1809)
English-born US political theorist and pamphleteer
> Government, even in its best state, is but a necessary evil; in its worst state, an intolerable one. Government, like dress, is the badge of lost innocence; the palaces of kings are built upon the ruins of the bowers of paradise.
>> *Common Sense* (1776)

> As to religion, I hold it to be the indispensable duty of government to protect all conscientious professors thereof, and I know of no other business which government hath to do therewith.
>> *Common Sense* (1776)

> Man is not the enemy of Man, but through the medium of a false system of government.
>> *The Rights of Man* (1791)

Passmore, John Arthur (1914–)
Australian philosopher and academic
> Never trust governments absolutely, and always do what you can to prevent them from doing too much harm.
>> *The Limits of Government*

Pembroke, Second Earl of (c.1534–1601)
Welsh courtier
> A parliament can do any thing but make a man a woman, and a woman a man.
>> Quoted in speech made by his son, the 4th Earl, 1648

Rippon, Geoffrey (1924–1997)
English Conservative politician
> Governments don't retreat, they simply advance in another direction.
>> *The Observer*, 1981

Robertson, George (1946–)
Scottish Labour statesman; Secretary General of NATO
On John Major's government
> If this government was an individual, it would be locked up in the interests of public safety.
>> Speech, Labour Party Conference, 1993

Rogers, Will (1879–1935)
US humorist, actor, rancher, writer and wit
> I don't make jokes – I just watch the government and report the facts.
>> Attr.

Ruskin, John (1819–1900)
English art critic, philosopher and reformer
> Government and cooperation are in all things the laws of life; anarchy and competition, the laws of death.
>> *Unto this Last* (1862)

Spencer, Herbert (1820–1903)
English philosopher and journalist
> The Republican form of government is the highest form of government; but because of this it requires the highest type of human nature – a type nowhere at present existing.
>> *Essays* (1891)

Stevenson, Adlai (1900–1965)
US lawyer, statesman and United Nations ambassador
> Government by postponement is bad enough, but it is far better than government by desperation.
>> *The Observer*, 1953

Thoreau, Henry David (1817–1862)
US essayist, social critic and writer
> I heartily accept the motto, 'That government is best which governs least'; and I should like to see it acted up to more rapidly and systematically. Carried out, it finally amounts to this, which I also believe, – 'That government is best which governs not at all.'
>> *Civil Disobedience* (1849)

Trollope, Anthony (1815–1882)
English writer, traveller and post office official
> A fainéant government is not the worst government that England can have. It has been the great fault of our politicians that they have all wanted to do something.
>> *Phineas Finn* (1869)

Voltaire (1694–1778)
French philosopher, dramatist, poet, historian writer and critic
> *Il faut, dans le gouvernement, des bergers et des bouchers.*
> In governments there must be both shepherds and butchers.
>> 'The Piccini Notebooks'

Washington, George (1732–1799)
US general, statesman and President
> Mankind, when left to themselves, are unfit for their own government.
>> Letter, 1786

▶▶ CAPITALISM; DEMOCRACY; MONARCHY AND ROYALTY; POLITICIANS; POLITICS

gratitude

Blake, William (1757–1827)
English poet, engraver, painter and mystic
> To Mercy, Pity, Peace and Love
> All pray in their distress,
> And to these virtues of delight
> Return their thankfulness.
>> *Songs of Innocence* (1789)

Catullus (84–c.54 BC)
Roman poet
> *Desine de quoquam quicquam bene velle mereri,*
> *Aut aliquem fieri posse putare pium.*
> Stop wishing to merit anyone's gratitude or thinking that anyone can become grateful.
>> *Carmina*

La Rochefoucauld (1613–1680)
French writer
> *La reconnaissance de la plupart des hommes n'est qu'une secrète envie de recevoir de plus grands bienfaits.*
> In most of mankind gratitude is merely a secret hope for greater favours.
>> *Maximes* (1678)

greatness

Amiel, Henri-Frédéric (1821–1881)
Swiss philosopher and writer
> The age of great men is going; the epoch of the ant-hill, of life in multiplicity, is beginning.
>> *Journal*, 1851

Asquith, Margot (1864–1945)
Scottish political hostess and writer
> Mrs Asquith remarked indiscreetly that if Kitchener was not a great man, he was, at least, a great poster.
>> In Sir Philip Magnus, *Kitchener: Portrait of an Imperialist* (1958)

Bacon, Francis (1561–1626)
English philosopher, essayist, politician and courtier
> All rising to great place is by a winding stair.
>> 'Of Great Place' (1625)

Beerbohm, Sir Max (1872–1956)
English satirist, cartoonist, critic and essayist
> Great men are but life-sized. Most of them, indeed, are rather short.
>> Attr.

Burke, Edmund (1729–1797)
Irish-born British statesman and philosopher
> Great men are the guide-posts and landmarks in the state.
>> *Speech on American Taxation* (1774)

Campbell, Thomas (1777–1844)
Scottish poet, ballad writer and journalist
> What millions died – that Caesar might be great!
>> *Pleasures of Hope* (1799)

Carlyle, Thomas (1795–1881)
Scottish historian, biographer, critic, and essayist
> No sadder proof can be given by a man of his own littleness than disbelief in great men.
>> *On Heroes, Hero-Worship, and the Heroic in History*

> No great man lives in vain. The History of the world is but the Biography of great men.
>> 'The Hero as Divinity' (1841)

Chapman, George (c.1559–c.1634)
English poet, dramatist and translator
> They're only truly great who are truly good.
>> *Revenge for Honour* (1654)

Defoe, Daniel (c.1661–1731)
English writer and critic

> True greatness consists in being master of one's
> self.
>
> *The Life and Adventures of Robinson Crusoe* (1719)

Emerson, Ralph Waldo (1803–1882)
US poet, essayist, transcendentalist and teacher

> It is easy in the world to live after the world's
> opinion; it is easy in solitude after our own; but
> the great man is he who, in the midst of the
> crowd, keeps with perfect sweetness the
> independence of solitude.
>
> *Essays, First Series* (1841)

> Nothing great was ever achieved without
> enthusiasm.
>
> *Essays, First Series* (1841)

> A foolish consistency is the hobgoblin of little
> minds, adored by little statesmen and
> philosophers and divines. With consistency a
> great soul has simply nothing to do.
>
> *Essays, First Series* (1841)

> Is it so bad, then, to be misunderstood?
> Pythagoras was misunderstood, and Socrates,
> and Jesus, and Luther, and Copernicus, and
> Galileo, and Newton, and every pure and wise
> spirit that ever took flesh. To be great is to be
> misunderstood.
>
> *Essays, First Series* (1841)

Fielding, Henry (1707–1754)
English writer, dramatist and journalist

> Greatness consists in bringing all manner of
> mischief on mankind, and goodness in removing
> it from them.
>
> *Jonathan Wild* (1743)

Frazer, Sir James (1854–1941)
Scottish anthropologist and writer

> The world cannot live at the level of its great
> men.
>
> *The Golden Bough* (1900)

La Rochefoucauld (1613–1680)
French writer

> *La gloire des grands hommes se doit toujours mesurer*
> *aux moyens dont ils se sont servis pour l'acquérir.*
> The glory of great men must always be
> measured by the means they have used to
> obtain it.
>
> *Maximes* (1678)

Longfellow, Henry Wadsworth (1807–1882)
US poet and writer

> Lives of great men all remind us
> We can make our lives sublime,
> And, departing, leave behind us
> Footprints on the sands of time.
>
> 'A Psalm of Life' (1838)

> The heights by great men reached and kept
> Were not attained by sudden flight,
> But they, while their companions slept,
> Were toiling upward in the night.
>
> 'The Ladder of Saint Augustine' (1850)

Pasternak, Boris (1890–1960)
Russian poet and novelist

> Only real greatness can be so misplaced and so
> untimely.
>
> *Doctor Zhivago* (1958)

Proverb

> From small beginnings come great things.

Shakespeare, William (1564–1616)
English dramatist, poet and actor

> Be not afraid of greatness. Some are born great,
> some achieve greatness, and some have
> greatness thrust upon 'em.
>
> *Twelfth Night*, II.v

> The soul and body rive not more in parting
> Than greatness going off.
>
> *Antony and Cleopatra*, IV.xiii

> His legs bestrid the ocean; his rear'd arm
> Crested the world. His voice was propertied
> As all the tuned spheres, and that to friends;
> But when he meant to quail and shake the orb,
> He was as rattling thunder. For his bounty,
> There was no winter in't; an autumn 'twas
> That grew the more by reaping. His delights
> Were dolphin-like: they show'd his back above
> The element they liv'd in. In his livery
> Walk'd crowns and crownets; realms and islands
> were
> As plates dropp'd from his pocket.
>
> *Antony and Cleopatra*, V.ii

Spender, Sir Stephen (1909–1995)
English poet, editor, translator and diarist

> I think continually of those who were truly great.
> The names of those who in their lives fought for
> life
> Who wore at their hearts the fire's centre.
> Born of the sun they travelled a short while
> towards the sun,
> And left the vivid air signed with their honour.
>
> 'I think continually of those who were truly great'
> (1933)

Twain, Mark (1835–1910)
US humorist, writer, journalist and lecturer

> Keep away from people who try to belittle your
> ambitions. Small people always do that, but the
> really great make you feel that you, too, can
> become great.
>
> Attr.

Walpole, Horace (1717–1797)
English writer and politician

They who cannot perform great things
themselves may yet have a satisfaction in doing
justice to those who can.

Attr.

greed

Aesop (6th century BC)
Legendary Greek writer of fables
> Thinking to get all the gold that the goose could
> give in one go, he killed it, and opened it only to
> find – nothing.
>
> 'The Goose with the Golden Eggs'

Douglas, Michael (1944–)
US film actor
As Gordon Gheko, unscrupulous Wall Street financier
> Greed, for lack of a better word, is good! Greed
> is right! Greed works! Greed clarifies, cuts
> through, and captures the essence of the
> evolutionary spirit. Greed, in all of its forms.
>
> Wall Street (film, 1987)

Proverb
> The eye is bigger than the belly.

Sellers, Peter (1925–1980)
English actor and comedian
> People will swim through shit if you put a few
> bob in it.
>
> In Halliwell, The Filmgoer's and Video Viewer's Companion

Virgil (70–19 BC)
Roman poet
> *Quid non mortalia pectora cogis,*
> *Auri sacra fames!*
> O sacred hunger of pernicious gold!
> What bands of faith can impious lucre hold?
>
> Aeneid

 FOOD

grief

Arnold, Matthew (1822–1888)
English poet, critic, essayist and educationist
> Strew on her roses, roses,
> And never a spray of yew.
> In quiet she reposes:
> Ah! would that I did too.
>
> 'Requiescat' (1853)

Austen, Jane (1775–1817)
English writer
> We met … Dr Hall in such very deep mourning
> that either his mother, his wife, or himself must
> be dead.
>
> Letter to Cassandra Austen, 1799

Baillie, Joanna (1762–1851)
Scottish dramatist and poet
> But woman's grief is like a summer storm,
> Short as it violent is.
>
> Plays on the Passions (1798)

Brenan, Gerald (1894–1987)
English writer
> When we attend the funerals of our friends we
> grieve for them, but when we go to those of
> other people it is chiefly our own deaths that we
> mourn for.
>
> Thoughts in a Dry Season
> (1978)

Brontë, Emily (1818–1848)
English poet and writer
> Cold in the earth – and fifteen wild Decembers,
> From those brown hills, have melted into
> spring …
>
> Sweet Love of youth, forgive if I forget thee
> While the World's tide is bearing me along:
> Sterner desires and darker hopes beset me,
> Hopes which obscure but cannot do thee
> wrong! …
>
> But when the days of golden dreams had
> perished,
> And even Despair was powerless to destroy,
> Then did I learn how existence could be
> cherished,
> Strengthened, and fed without the aid of joy …
>
> Once drinking deep of that divinest anguish,
> How could I seek the empty world again?
>
> 'Remembrance' (1845)

Browning, Elizabeth Barrett (1806–1861)
English poet; wife of Robert Browning
> I tell you, hopeless grief is passionless.
>
> Sonnets, 'Grief' (1844)

Byron, Lord (1788–1824)
English poet satirist and traveller
A cypress
> Dark tree, still sad when others' grief is fled,
> The only constant mourner o'er the dead!
>
> 'The Giaour' (1813)

Cowper, William (1731–1800)
English poet, hymn and letter writer
> Grief is itself a med'cine.
>
> 'Charity' (1782)

Dickens, Charles (1812–1870)
English writer
> Grief never mended no broken bones, and as
> good people's wery scarce, what I says is, make
> the most on 'em.
>
> Sketches by Boz (1836)

Dickinson, Emily (1830–1886)
US poet
> After great pain, a formal feeling comes –
> The Nerves sit ceremonious, like Tombs –
> The stiff Heart questions was it He, that bore,
> And Yesterday, or Centuries before? …
>
> This is the Hour of Lead –
> Remembered, if outlived,
> As Freezing persons, recollect the Snow –
> First – Chill – then Stupor – then the letting go.
>> 'After great pain, a formal feeling comes' (c.1862)

> The Bustle in a House
> The Morning after Death
> Is solemnest of industries
> Enacted upon Earth –
>
> The Sweeping up the Heart
> And putting Love away
> We shall not want to use again
> Until Eternity.
>> 'The Bustle in a House' (c.1866)

Elliot, Jean (1727–1805)
Scottish lyricist
> I've heard them lilting, at our yowe-milking,
> Lasses a' lilting before the dawn o' day;
> But now they are moaning on ilka green loaning –
> The Flowers of the Forest are a' wede away.
>> 'The Flowers of the Forest' (1756

Emerson, Ralph Waldo (1803–1882)
US poet, essayist, transcendentalist and teacher
> There are people who have an appetite for grief;
> pleasure is not strong enough and they crave
> pain.
>> In *The Faber Book of Aphorisms* (1962)

Ford, John (c.1586–c.1640)
English dramatist and poet
> They are the silent griefs which cut the heart-
> strings.
>> *The Broken Heart* (1633)

Gaskell, Elizabeth (1810–1865)
English writer
> Bombazine would have shown a deeper sense of
> her loss.
>> *Cranford* (1853)

Graves, Robert (1895–1985)
English poet, writer, critic, translator and mythologist
> His eyes are quickened so with grief,
> He can watch a grass or leaf
> Every instant grow …
>
> Across two counties he can hear
> And catch your words before you speak.
> The woodlouse or the maggot's weak
> Clamour rings in his sad ear,

And noise so slight it would surpass
Credence.
>> 'Lost Love' (1921)

Henryson, Robert (c.1425–1505)
Scottish poet
> Thar was na solace mycht his sobbing ces,
> Bot cryit ay, with caris cald and kene,
> 'Quhar art thow gane, my luf Erudices?'.
>> 'Orpheus and Eurydice' (1508)

Hume, David (1711–1776)
Scottish philosopher and political economist
> Grief and disappointment give rise to anger,
> anger to envy, envy to malice, and malice to
> grief again, until the whole circle be completed.
>> *A Treatise of Human Nature* (1739)

Johnson, Samuel (1709–1784)
English lexicographer, poet, critic, conversationalist and essayist
> Grief is a species of idleness.
>> Letter to Mrs. Thrale, 1773

Lowell, James Russell (1819–1891)
US poet, editor, abolitionist and diplomat
> Sorrow, the great idealizer.
>> Attr

MacDiarmid, Hugh (1892–1978)
Scottish poet
> I met ayont the cairney
> A lass wi' tousie hair
> Singin' till a bairnie
> That was nae langer there.
>
> Wund wi' warlds to swing
> Dinna sing sae sweet,
> The licht that bends owre a' thing
> Is less ta'en up wi't.
>> 'Empty Vessel' (1926)

Mann, Thomas (1875–1955)
German writer and critic
> *Was wir Trauer nennen, ist vielleicht nicht sowohl der Schmerz über die Unmöglichkeit, unsere Toten ins Leben kehren zu sehen, als darüber, dies gar nicht wünschen zu können.*
> What we call mourning is perhaps not so much grief that it is impossible to see our dead return to life as grief that we are quite unable to wish to do so.
>> *The Magic Mountain* (1924)

Melville, Herman (1819–1891)
US writer and poet
> In these flashing revelations of grief's wonderful fire, we see all things as they are; and though when the electric element is gone, the shadows once more descend, and the false outlines of objects again return; yet not with their former

power to deceive.

In Lewis Wolpert, Malignant Sadness (1999)

Milton, John (1608–1674)
English poet, libertarian and pamphleteer
> Methought I saw my late espoused Saint
> Brought to me like Alcestis from the grave ...
>
> But O as to embrace me she enclin'd,
> I wak'd, she fled, and day brought back my
> night.

'Methought I saw my late espoused Saint' (1658)

Proust, Marcel (1871–1922)
French writer and critic
> *Le bonheur seul est salutaire pour le corps, mais c'est le chagrin qui développe les forces de l'esprit.*
> Happiness alone is beneficial for the body, but it is grief that develops the powers of the mind.

Le Temps retrouvé (1926)

Rossetti, Dante Gabriel (1828–1882)
English poet, painter, translator and letter-writer
> From perfect grief there need not be
> Wisdom or even memory:
> One thing then learnt remains to me, –
> The woodspurge has a cup of three.

'The Woodspurge' (1870)

Seneca (c.4 BC–AD 65)
Roman philosopher, poet, dramatist, essayist, rhetorician and statesman
> Nothing becomes so offensive so quickly as grief. When fresh it finds someone to console it, but when it becomes chronic, it is ridiculed, and rightly.

Attr.

Shakespeare, William (1564–1616)
English dramatist, poet and actor
> Grief fills the room up of my absent child,
> Lies in his bed, walks up and down with me,
> Puts on his pretty looks, repeats his words,
> Remembers me of all his gracious parts,
> Stuffs out his vacant garments with his form;
> Then have I reason to be fond of grief.

King John, III.iv

> Howl, howl, howl, howl! O, you are men of stones!
> Had I your tongues and eyes, I'd use them so
> That heaven's vault should crack. She's gone for ever.

King Lear, V.iii

> What, man! Ne'er pull your hat upon your brows;
> Give sorrow words. The grief that does not speak
> Whispers the o'erfraught heart and bids it break.

Macbeth, IV.iii

> Every one can master a grief but he that has it.

Much Ado About Nothing, III.ii

> What's gone and what's past help
> Should be past grief.

The Winter's Tale, III.ii

> Great griefs, I see, med'cine the less.

Cymbeline, IV.ii

> But to persever
> In obstinate condolement is a course
> Of impious stubbornness; 'tis unmanly grief;
> It shows a will most incorrect to heaven,
> A heart unfortified, a mind impatient.

Hamlet I.ii

Shelley, Percy Bysshe (1792–1822)
English poet, dramatist and essayist
> Ah, woe is me! Winter is come and gone,
> But grief returns with the revolving year.

Adonais (1821)

Smith, Sydney (1771–1845)
English clergyman, essayist, journalist and wit
Written in response to the death of one of Lady Holland's children
> The World is full of all sorts of sorrows and miseries – and I think it is better never to have been born – but when evils have happened turn away your mind from them as soon as you can to everything of good which remains. Most people grieve as if grief were a duty or a pleasure, but all who can control it should control it – and remember that these renovations of sorrows are almost the charter and condition under which life is held.

Letter to Lady Holland,
November 1819

Stowe, Harriet Beecher (1811–1896)
US writer and reformer
> The bitterest tears shed over graves are for words left unsaid and deeds left undone.

Little Foxes (1866)

Tennyson, Alfred, Lord (1809–1892)
English lyric poet
> I sometimes hold it half a sin
> To put in words the grief I feel;
> For words, like Nature, half reveal
> And half conceal the Soul within.
>
> But, for the unquiet heart and brain,
> A use in measured language lies;
> The sad mechanic exercise,
> Like dull narcotics, numbing pain.

In Memoriam A. H. H. (1850)

> Death has made
> His darkness beautiful with thee.

In Memoriam A. H. H. (1850)

Twain, Mark (1835–1910)
US humorist, writer, journalist and lecturer
On receiving news of the death of a loved one
> It is one of the mysteries of our nature that man, all unprepared, can receive a thunder-stroke like that and live. There is but one reasonable explanation of it. The intellect is stunned by the shock and but gropingly gathers the meaning of the words. The power to realize their full import is mercifully lacking.
>
> *Autobiography*

Whitman, Walt (1819–1892)
US poet and writer
> When lilacs last in the dooryard bloom'd,
> And the great stars early droop'd in the western sky in the night,
> I mourn'd, and yet shall mourn with ever-returning spring.
>
> 'When lilacs last in the dooryard bloom'd' (1865)

Wordsworth, William (1770–1850)
English poet
> Surprised by joy – impatient as the Wind
> I turned to share the transport – Oh! with whom
> But thee, deep buried in the silent tomb.
>
> 'Surprised by joy' (1815)

guilt

Arendt, Hannah (1906–1975)
German-born US theorist
> It is quite gratifying to feel guilty if you haven't done anything wrong: how noble! Whereas it is rather hard and certainly depressing to admit guilt and to repent.
>
> *Eichmann in Jerusalem: A Report on the Banality of Evil* (1963)

Barker, George (1913–1991)
English poet and writer
> My tall dead wives with knives in their breasts
> Gaze at me, I am guilty, as they roll
> Like derelicts in my tempests.
>
> *Eros in Dogma* (1944)

Goethe (1749–1832)
German poet, writer, dramatist and scientist
> *Denn alle Schuld rächt sich auf Erden.*
> For all guilt is avenged on earth.
>
> *Wilhelm Meister's Apprentice Years* (1796)

Goldsmith, Oliver (c.1728–1774)
Irish dramatist, poet and writer
> When lovely woman stoops to folly
> And finds too late that men betray,
> What charm can soothe her melancholy,
> What art can wash her guilt away?
>
> The only art her guilt to cover,

> To hide her shame from every eye,
> To give repentance to her lover
> And wring his bosom – is to die.
>
> *The Vicar of Wakefield* (1766)

Horace (65–8 BC)
Roman poet
> *Hic murus aeneus esto,*
> *Nil conscire sibi, nulla pallescere culpa.*
> This be your wall of brass, to have nothing on your conscience, no reason to grow pale with guilt.
>
> *Epistles*

Kafka, Franz (1883–1924)
Czech-born German-speaking writer
> *'Ich bin aber nicht schuldig', sagte K., 'es ist ein Irrtum. Wie kann denn ein Mensch überhaupt schuldig sein.'*
> 'But I'm not guilty,' said K., 'there's been a mistake. How can a man be guilty anyway.'
>
> *The Trial* (1925)

Kennedy, A.L. (1965–)
Scottish novelist
> Guilt is of course not an emotion in the Celtic countries, it is simply a way of life – a kind of gleefully painful social anaesthetic.
>
> *So I am Glad* (1995)

McGough, Roger (1937–)
English poet and teacher
> You will put on a dress of guilt
> and shoes with broken high ideals.
>
> 'Comeclose and Sleepnow' (1967)

Orwell, George (1903–1950)
English writer and critic
> Saints should always be judged guilty until they are proved innocent.
>
> *Shooting an Elephant* (1950)

Ruskin, John (1819–1900)
English art critic, philosopher and reformer
> Life without industry is guilt.
>
> 'The Relation of Art to Morals' (1870)

Shakespeare, William (1564–1616)
English dramatist, poet and actor
> Suspicion always haunts the guilty mind:
> The thief doth fear each bush an officer.
>
> *Henry VI, Part 3*, V.vi

> And then it started like a guilty thing
> Upon a fearful summons.
>
> *Macbeth*, I.i

> Will all great Neptune's ocean wash this blood
> Clean from my hand? No; this my hand will rather
> The multitudinous seas incarnadine,
> Making the green one red.
>
> *Macbeth*, II.ii

Out, damned spot! out, I say! One, two; why then 'tis time to do't. Hell is murky. Fie, my lord, fie! a soldier, and afeard? What need we fear who knows it, when none can call our pow'r to account? Yet who would have thought the old man to have had so much blood in him?

Macbeth, V.i

Here's the smell of the blood still. All the perfumes of Arabia will not sweeten this little hand. Oh, oh, oh!

Macbeth, V.i

Stevenson, Robert Louis (1850–1894)
Scottish writer, poet and essayist

What hangs people ... is the unfortunate circumstance of guilt.

The Wrong Box (1889)

▶▶ CONSCIENCE; REGRET

gypsies

Havel, Vaclav (1936–)
Czech President

The Gypsies are a litmus test not of democracy but of civil society.

Attr.

H

habit

Beckett, Samuel (1906–1989)
Irish dramatist, writer and poet
> The air is full of our cries. But habit is a great deadener.
>> *Waiting for Godot* (1955)

Christie, Agatha (1890–1976)
English crime writer and playwright
> Curious things, habits. People themselves never knew they had them.
>> *Witness for the Prosecution* (1953)

Proverb
> Old habits die hard.

▶▶ CUSTOM

happiness

Adams, Scott (1957–)
US cartoonist
> Smile, it confuses people.
>> *The Dilbert Principle*

Addison, Joseph (1672–1719)
English essayist, poet, playwright and statesman
> The important question is not, what will yield to man a few scattered pleasures, but what will render his life happy on the whole amount.
>> *Interesting Anecdotes, Memoirs, Allegories, Essays, and Poetical Fragments* (1794)

Aristotle (384–322 BC)
Greek philosopher
> One swallow does not make a summer, neither does one fine day; similarly one day or brief time of happiness does not make a person entirely happy.
>> *Nicomachean Ethics*

Austen, Jane (1775–1817)
English writer
> Perfect happiness, even in memory, is not common.
>> *Emma* (1816)

> Why not seize the pleasure at once? How often is happiness destroyed by preparation, foolish preparation!
>> *Emma* (1816)

Bentham, Jeremy (1748–1832)
English writer and philosopher
Quoting Francis Hutcheson
> … this sacred truth – that the greatest happiness of the greatest number is the foundation of morals and legislation.
>> *Works*

Bergman, Ingrid (1915–1982)
Swedish actress
> Happiness is good health – and a bad memory.
>> In Simon Rose, *Classic Film Guide* (1995)

The Bible (Vulgate)
> *Beatus vir, qui timet Dominum, in mandatis eius cupit nimis!*
> Happy is the man who fears the Lord, who is only too willing to follow his orders.
>> *Psalms*, 111:1

Boethius (c.475–524)
Roman statesman, scholar and philosopher
> *Nihil est miserum nisi cum putes; contraque beata sors omnis est aequanimitate tolerantis.*
> Nothing is miserable unless you think it so; conversely, every lot is happy to one who is content with it.
>> *De Consolatione Philosophiae*

Bradley, F.H. (1846–1924)
English philosopher
> The secret of happiness is to admire without desiring. And that is not happiness.
>> *Aphorisms* (1930)

Browne, Sir Thomas (1605–1682)
English physician, author and antiquary
> Certainly there is no happiness within this circle of flesh, nor is it in the optics of these eyes to behold felicity; the first day of our Jubilee is death.
>> *Religio Medici* (1643)

Campbell, Thomas (1777–1844)
Scottish poet, ballad writer and journalist
> One moment may with bliss repay
> Unnumber'd hours of pain.
>> 'The Ritter Bann'

Chesterton, G.K. (1874–1936)
English writer, poet and critic
> Happiness is a mystery like religion, and should never be rationalized.
>> *Heretics* (1905)

Coleridge, Samuel Taylor (1772–1834)
English poet, philosopher and critic
> We ne'er can be
> Made happy by compulsion.
>> 'The Three Graves' (1809)

Colton, Charles Caleb (c.1780–1832)
English clergyman and satirist
> True contentment depends not on what we

have; a tub was large enough for Diogenes, but a world was too little for Alexander.

Lacon (1820)

Cowper, William (1731–1800)
English poet, hymn and letter writer
Domestic happiness, thou only bliss
Of Paradise that has surviv'd the fall!

The Task (1785)

Crist, Judith (1922–)
Happiness is too many things these days for anyone to wish it on anyone lightly. So let's just wish each other a bileless New Year and leave it at that.

The Private Eye, the Cowboy and the Very Naked Girl (1968)

Dryden, John (1631–1700)
English poet, satirist, dramatist and critic
For all the happiness mankind can gain
Is not in pleasure, but in rest from pain.

The Indian Emperor (1665)

Happy the man, and happy he alone,
He, who can call to-day his own:
He who, secure within, can say,
Tomorrow do thy worst, for I have lived to-day.

Sylvae (1685)

Eliot, George (1819–1880)
English writer and poet
The happiest women, like the happiest nations, have no history.

The Mill on the Floss (1860)

Emerson, Ralph Waldo (1803–1882)
US poet, essayist, transcendentalist and teacher
To fill the hour, – that is happiness.

Essays, Second Series (1844)

Frank, Anne (1929–1945)
Jewish diarist; died in Nazi concentration camp
Whoever is happy will make others happy, too.

The Diary of Anne Frank (1947)

Franklin, Benjamin (1706–1790)
US statesman, scientist, political critic and printer
Be in general virtuous, and you will be happy.

'On Early Marriages'

Heller, Joseph (1923–1999)
US writer
The idea of always being at peace, always being blissfully happy, is scary. Anyone in a placid state is just going to vegetate.

In *The Observer*, 1999

Horace (65–8 BC)
Roman poet
Non possidentem multa vocaveris
Recte beatum: rectius occupat
Nomen beati, qui deorum
Muneribus sapienter uti
Duramque callet pauperiem pati
Peiusque leto flagitium timet.
You would not rightly call the man who has many possessions happy; he more rightly deserves to be called happy who knows how to use the gifts of the gods wisely, and can endure the hardship of poverty, and who fears dishonour more than death.

Odes

Hugo, Victor (1802–1885)
French poet, writer, dramatist and politician
The supreme happiness in life is the conviction that we are loved.

Attr.

Huxley, Aldous (1894–1963)
English writer, poet and critic
Happiness is like coke – something you get as a by-product in the process of making something else.

Point Counter Point (1928)

Stability isn't nearly so spectacular as instability. And being contented has none of the glamour of a good fight against misfortune, none of the picturesqueness of a struggle with temptation, or a fatal overthrow by passion or doubt. Happiness is never grand.

Brave New World (1932)

Jerome, Jerome K. (1859–1927)
English writer and dramatist
If you are foolish enough to be contented, don't show it, but grumble with the rest.

Idle Thoughts of an Idle Fellow (1886)

Johnson, Samuel (1709–1784)
English lexicographer, poet, critic, conversationalist and essayist
That all who are happy, are equally happy, is not true. A peasant and a philosopher may be equally satisfied, but not equally happy. Happiness consists in the multiplicity of agreeable consciousness.

In Boswell, *The Life of Samuel Johnson* (1791)

There is nothing which has yet been contrived by man, by which so much happiness is produced as by a good tavern or inn.

In Boswell, *The Life of Samuel Johnson* (1791)

Kant, Immanuel (1724–1804)
German idealist philosopher
... weil Glückseligkeit nicht ein Ideal der Vernunft, sondern der Einbildungskraft ist.
... because bliss is not an ideal of reason, but of the powers of imagination.

Outline of the Metaphysics of Morals (1785)

Tue das, wodurch du würdig wirst, glücklich zu sein.

Act in such a way that you will be worthy of being happy.

Critique of Pure Reason (1787)

Keats, John (1795–1821)
English poet
It is a flaw
In happiness, to see beyond our bourn, –
It forces us in summer skies to mourn:
It spoils the singing of the nightingale.

'To J. H. Reynolds, Esq.' (1818)

Lindsay, Sir David (c.1490–1555)
Scottish poet and satirist
What vails your kingdome, and your rent,
And all your great treasure;
Without ye haif ane mirrie lyfe,
And cast aside all sturt, and stryfe.

Satyre of the Thrie Estaitis

Marmion, Shackerley (1603–1639)
English dramatist and poet
Great joys, like griefs, are silent.

Holland's Leaguer (1632)

Mencken, H.L. (1880–1956)
US writer, critic, philologist and satirist
The only really happy people are married women and single men.

Attr.

Mill, John Stuart (1806–1873)
English philosopher, economist and reformer
Ask yourself whether you are happy, and you cease to be so.

Autobiography (1873)

Paine, Thomas (1737–1809)
English-born US political theorist and pamphleteer
It is necessary to the happiness of man that he be mentally faithful to himself. Infidelity does not consist in believing, or in disbelieving, it consists in professing to believe what one does not believe.

The Age of Reason (1794)

Palacio Valdés, Armando (1853–1938)
Si quieres ser feliz, aparenta ser desgraciado.
If you want to be happy, pretend to be miserable.

Doctor Angélico's Papers (1911)

Pope, Alexander (1688–1744)
English poet, translator and editor
Oh Happiness! our being's end and aim!

Essay on Man (1734)

Rooney, Mickey (1920–)
US film actor
Had I been brighter, the ladies been gentler, the Scotch been weaker, had the gods been kinder, had the dice been hotter, this could have been a one-sentence story: Once upon a time I lived

happily ever after.

Attr.

Rousseau, Jean-Jacques (1712–1778)
Swiss-born French philosopher, educationist and essayist
Happiness: a good bank account, a good cook, and a good digestion.

Treasury of Humorous Quotations

Sagan, Françoise (1935–)
French writer
Quel mur s'impose donc toujours entre les êtres humains et leur désir le plus intime, leur effroyable volonté de bonheur? … Est-ce une nostalgie cultivée depuis l'enfance?
What is that wall that always rises up between human beings and their most intimate desire, their frightening will to be happy? … Is it a nostalgia nurtured from childhood?

Le Garde du coeur (1968)

Saint-Exupéry, Antoine de (1900–1944)
French author and aviator
Si tu veux comprendre le mot de bonheur, il faut l'entendre comme récompense et non comme but.
If you want to understand the meaning of happiness, you must see it as a reward and not as a goal.

Carnets

Sand, George (1804–1876)
French writer and dramatist
One is happy as a result of one's own efforts, once one knows the necessary ingredients of happiness - simple tastes, a certain degree of courage, self denial to a point, love of work, and, above all, a clear conscience. Happiness is no vague dream, of that I now feel certain.

Correspondence

Santayana, George (1863–1952)
Spanish-born US philosopher and writer
Happiness is the only sanction of life; where happiness fails, existence remains a mean and lamentable experience.

The Life of Reason (1905–1906)

Shakespeare, William (1564–1616)
English dramatist, poet and actor
O, how bitter a thing it is to look into happiness through another man's eyes!

As You Like It, V.ii

I swear 'tis better to be lowly born
And range with humble livers in content
Than to be perk'd up in a glist'ring grief
And wear a golden sorrow.

Henry VIII, II.iii

Shaw, George Bernard (1856–1950)
Irish socialist, writer, dramatist and critic
We have no more right to consume happiness

without producing it than to consume wealth without producing it.

Candida (1898)

A lifetime of happiness! No man alive could bear it: it would be hell on earth.

Man and Superman (1903)

Smith, Sydney (1771–1845)
English clergyman, essayist, journalist and wit
This great spectacle of human happiness.

Essays (1877)

Mankind are always happy for having been happy, so that if you make them happy now, you make them happy twenty years hence by the memory of it.

Sketches of Moral Philosophy (1849)

Solon (c.638–c.559 BC)
Athenian statesman, reformer and poet
Until a man dies, be careful to call him not happy but lucky.

In Herodotus, *Histories*

Spenser, Edmund (c.1522–1599)
English poet
What more felicitie can fall to creature,
Than to enjoy delight with libertie.

Complaints (1591)

Surrey, Henry Howard, Earl of (c.1517–1547)
English poet, courtier and soldier
Martial, the things for to attain
The happy life be these, I find:
The riches left, not got with pain;
The fruitful ground, the quiet mind;
The equal friend; no grudge nor strife;
No charge or rule nor governance;
Without disease the healthful life;
The household of continuance.

The chaste wife wise, without debate;
Such sleeps as may beguile the night;
Content thyself with thine estate;
Neither wish death, nor fear his might.

'The Happy Life' (1547)

Szasz, Thomas (1920–)
Hungarian-born US psychiatrist and writer
Happiness is an imaginary condition, formerly often attributed by the living to the dead, now usually attributed by adults to children, and by children to adults.

The Second Sin (1973)

Tolstoy, Leo (1828–1910)
Russian writer, essayist, philosopher and moralist
If you want to be happy, be.

Attr.

Waugh, Evelyn (1903–1966)
English writer and diarist

I can't quite explain it, but I don't believe one can ever be unhappy for long provided one does just exactly what one wants to and when one wants to.

Decline and Fall (1928)

Weldon, Fay (1931–)
British writer
I don't believe in happiness: why should we expect to be happy? In such a world as this, depression is rational, rage reasonable.

The Observer, 1995

Whately, Richard (1787–1863)
English philosopher, theologian, educationist and writer
Happiness is no laughing matter.

Apophthegms (1854)

Wordsworth, William (1770–1850)
English poet
Happy is he, who, caring not for Pope,
Consul, or King, can sound himself to know
The destiny of Man, and live in hope.

Sonnets Dedicated to Liberty and Order (1807)

Yevtushenko, Yevgeny (1933–)
Russian poet
The hell with it. Who never knew
the price of happiness will not be happy.

'Lies' (1955)

▶▶ LAUGHTER; PLEASURE

haste

Emerson, Ralph Waldo (1803–1882)
US poet, essayist, transcendentalist and teacher
In skating over thin ice, our safety is in our speed.

Essays (1860)

Pope, Alexander (1688–1744)
English poet, translator and editor
For fools rush in where angels fear to tread.

An Essay on Criticism (1711)

Proverbs
Don't throw the baby out with the bathwater.

Haste makes waste.

More haste, less speed.

Shakespeare, William (1564–1616)
English dramatist, poet and actor
Wisely and slow; they stumble that run fast.

Romeo and Juliet, II:iii

Stravinsky, Igor (1882–1971)
Russian composer and conductor
Responding to his publisher's request that he hurry his completion of a composition

Hurry! I never hurry. I have no time to hurry.

Attr.

Wesley, John (1703–1791)

English theologian and preacher

Though I am always in haste, I am never in a hurry.

Letter to Miss March, 1777

hatred

Accius, Lucius (170–86 BC)

Roman poet

Oderint dum metuant.

Let them hate provided that they fear.

Atreus

Anonymous

Hatred is toxic waste in the river of life.

Bacon, Francis (1561–1626)

English philosopher, essayist, politician and courtier

Severity breedeth fear, but roughness breedeth hate. Even reproofs from authority ought to be grave, and not taunting.

'Of Great Place' (1625)

Butler, Samuel (1835–1902)

English writer, painter, philosopher and scholar

It does not matter much what a man hates provided that he hates something.

Notebooks

Byron, Lord (1788–1824)

English poet satirist and traveller

Now hatred is by far the longest pleasure;
Men love in haste, but they detest at leisure.

Don Juan (1824)

Cather, Willa (1876–1947)

US writer

I tell you there is such a thing as creative hate.

The Song of the Lark (1915)

De Vries, Peter (1910–1993)

US novelist

Everybody hates me because I'm so universally liked.

The Vale of Laughter (1967)

Farquhar, George (1678–1707)

Irish dramatist

I hate all that don't love me, and slight all that do.

The Constant Couple (1699)

Fields, W.C. (1880–1946)

US film actor

I am free of all prejudice. I hate everyone equally.

Attr.

Gabor, Zsa-Zsa (1919–)

Hungarian-born US actress

I never hated a man enough to give him his diamonds back.

The Observer, 1957

Hazlitt, William (1778–1830)

English writer and critic

Violent antipathies are always suspicious, and betray a secret affinity.

Table-Talk (1822)

The dupe of friendship, and the fool of love; have I not reason to hate and to despise myself? Indeed I do; and chiefly for not having hated and despised the world enough.

The Plain Speaker (1826)

Violent antipathies are always suspicious, and betray a secret affinity.

Table-Talk (1822)

We can scarcely hate any one that we know.

Table-Talk (1825)

Hesse, Hermann (1877–1962)

German novelist and poet

Wenn wir einen Menschen hassen, so hassen wir in seinem Bild etwas, was in uns selber sitzt. Was nicht in uns selber ist, das regt uns nicht auf.

If we hate a person, we hate something in our image of him that lies within ourselves. What is not within ourselves doesn't upset us.

Demian (1919)

Hoffer, Eric (1902–1983)

US writer, philosopher and longshoreman

Passionate hatred can give meaning and purpose to an empty life.

Attr.

Jung Chang (1952–)

Chinese author

He Mao Zedong was, it seemed to me, really a restless fight promoter by nature and good at it. He understood ugly human instincts such as envy and resentment, and knew how to mobilize them for his ends. He ruled by getting people to hate each other.

Wild Swans (1991)

Nash, Ogden (1902–1971)

US poet

Any kiddie in school can love like a fool,
But hating, my boy, is an art.

Happy Days (1933)

Nixon, Richard (1913–1994)

US Republican politician and President

Always give your best, never get discouraged, never be petty. Always remember, others may hate you, but those who hate you don't win unless you hate them, and then you destroy yourself.

Farewell speech to his staff, 1974

O'Casey, Sean (1880–1964)
Irish dramatist

Sacred Heart of the Crucified Jesus, take away our hearts o' stone … an' give us hearts o' flesh! … Take away this murdherin' hate … an' give us Thine own eternal love!

Juno and the Paycock (1924)

Renault, Mary (1905–1983)
English novelist

In hatred as in love, we grow like the thing we brood upon. What we loathe, we graft into our very soul.

The Mask of Apollo (1966)

Rosten, Leo (1908–1997)
Polish-born US social scientist, writer and humorist
Of W.C. Fields; often attributed to him

Any man who hates dogs and babies can't be all bad.

Speech, 1939

Russell, Bertrand (1872–1970)
English philosopher, mathematician, essayist and social reformer

Few people can be happy unless they hate some other person, nation or creed.

Attr.

Scott, Sir Walter (1771–1832)
Scottish writer and historian

I never saw a richer company or to speak my mind a finer people. The worst of them is the bitter and envenomed dislike which they have to each other; their factions have been so long envenomed and have so little ground to fight their battle in that they are like people fighting with daggers in a hogshead.

Letter to Joanna Baillie, 1825

Swift, Jonathan (1667–1745)
Irish satirist, poet, essayist and cleric

I have ever hated all nations, professions and communities, and all my love is towards individuals … But principally I hate and detest that animal called man; although I heartily love John, Peter, Thomas, and so forth.

Letter to Pope, 1725

Tacitus (AD c.56–c.120)
Roman historian

Proprium humani ingenii est odisse quem laeseris.
It is part of human nature to hate those whom you have injured.

Agricola

Thoreau, Henry David (1817–1862)
US essayist, social critic and writer

It were treason to our love
And a sin to God above
One iota to abate
Of a pure impartial hate.

'Indeed, Indeed I Cannot Tell' (1852)

▶▶ LOVE

health

Ashford, Daisy (1881–1972)
English child author

I am very pale owing to the drains in this house.

The Young Visiters (1919)

Butler, Samuel (1835–1902)
English writer, painter, philosopher and scholar

The healthy stomach is nothing if not conservative. Few radicals have good digestions.

The Note-Books of Samuel Butler (1912)

Davis, Adelle (1904–1974)
US nutritionist and author

Thousands upon thousands of persons have studied disease. Almost no one has studied health.

Let's Eat Right to Keep Fit (1954)

Dryden, John (1631–1700)
English poet, satirist, dramatist and critic

Better to hunt in fields, for health unbought,
Than fee the doctor for a nauseous draught.
The wise, for cure, on exercise depend;
God never made his work, for man to mend.

'To John Driden of Chesterton' (1700)

Jay, Douglas (1907–)
British economist and writer

For in the case of nutrition and health, just as in the case of education, the gentleman in Whitehall really does know better what is good for people than the people know themselves.

The Socialist Case (1947)

Juvenal (c.60–130)
Roman verse satirist and Stoic

Orandum est ut sit mens sana in corpore sano.
Your prayers should be for a healthy mind in a healthy body.

Satires

Martial (c.AD 40–c.104)
Spanish-born Latin epigrammatist and poet

Non est vivere, sed valere vita est.
It is not to live but to be healthy that makes a life.

Epigrammata

Ménage, Gilles (1613–1692)
French lexicographer
Part of a conversation with Jean-Louis Guez de Balzac

Comme nous nous entretenions de ce qui pouvait rendre heureux, je lui dis; Sanitas sanitatum, et omnia sanitas.

While we were talking about what could make one happy, I said to him: *Sanitas sanitatum et omnia sanitas.*

In Ménagiana (1693)

Proverbs

Health is better than wealth.

The health of the salmon to you.

Irish toast

Smith, Sydney (1771–1845)

English clergyman, essayist, journalist and wit

I am convinced digestion is the great secret of life.

Letter to Arthur Kinglake, 1837

Swift, Jonathan (1667–1745)

Irish satirist, poet, essayist and cleric

I row after health like a waterman, and ride after it like a postboy, and find little success.

Attr.

Tolstoy, Leo (1828–1910)

Russian writer, essayist, philosopher and moralist

Our body is a machine for living. It is geared towards it, it is its nature. Let life go on in it unhindered and let it defend itself, it will be more effective than if you paralyse it by encumbering it with remedies.

War and Peace (1869)

Tusser, Thomas (c.1524–1580)

English writer, poet and musician

Make hunger thy sauce, as a medicine for health.

Five Hundred Points of Good Husbandry (1557)

Walton, Izaak (1593–1683)

English writer

Look to your health; and if you have it, praise God, and value it next to a good conscience; for health is the second blessing that we mortals are capable of; a blessing money cannot buy.

The Compleat Angler (1653)

▶▶ ILLNESS; MEDICINE

heart

Beddoes, Thomas Lovell (1803–1849)

English poet and dramatist

If thou wilt ease thine heart
Of love and all its smart,
Then sleep, dear, sleep …

But wilt thou cure thine heart
Of love and all its smart,

Then die, dear, die.

Death's Jest Book (1850)

The Bible (King James Version)

A merry heart doeth good like a medicine.

Proverbs, 17:22

Where your treasure is, there will your heart be also.

Matthew, 6:21

Bridges, Robert (1844–1930)

English poet, dramatist, essayist and doctor

Awake, my heart, to be loved, awake, awake!

'Awake, My Heart, To be Loved' (1890)

Bridie, James (1888–1951)

Scottish dramatist, writer and physician

The Heart of Man, we are told, is deceitful and desperately wicked. However that may be, it consists of four chambers, the right ventricle, the left ventricle, the left auricle, the right auricle.

The Anatomist (1931)

Burns, Robert (1759–1796)

Scottish poet and song writer

He'll hae misfortunes great an' sma',
But ay a heart aboon them a'.

'There was a Lad' (1785)

The heart ay's the part ay
That makes us right or wrang.

'Epistle to Davie, a Brother Poet' (1785)

Campbell, Thomas (1777–1844)

Scottish poet, ballad writer and journalist

The proud, the cold untroubled heart of stone,
That never mused on sorrow but its own.

Pleasures of Hope (1799)

Davidson, John (1857–1909)

Scottish writer

'In shuttered rooms let others grieve,
And coffin thought in speech of lead;
I'll tie my heart upon my sleeve:
It is the Badge of Men,' he said.

'The Badge of Men' (1891)

Diana, Princess of Wales (1961–1997)

I want to be the queen of people's hearts.

BBC Panorama interview, 1996

Dickens, Charles (1812–1870)

English writer

There are strings … in the human heart that had better not be wibrated.

Barnaby Rudge (1841), 22

Donne, John (1572–1631)

English poet

A naked thinking heart, that makes no show,
Is to a woman, but a kind of ghost.

Songs and Sonnets (1611)

Granville, George (1666–1735)
English poet, dramatist and politician
> I'll be this abject thing no more;
> Love, give me back my heart again.
>> 'Adieu l'Amour'

Longfellow, Henry Wadsworth (1807–1882)
US poet and writer
> The secret anniversaries of the heart.
>> *Sonnets* (1877)

MacLeod, Fiona (William Sharp) (1855–1905)
Scottish poet, novelist and dramatist
> My heart is a lonely hunter that hunts on a lonely hill.
>> 'The Lonely Hunter' (1896)

Meynell, Alice (1847–1922)
English poet
> My heart shall be thy garden.
>> 'The Garden' (1875)

Muir, Edwin (1887–1959)
Scottish poet, critic, translator and writer
> The heart could never speak
> But that the Word was spoken.
> We hear the heart break
> Here with hearts unbroken.
> Time, teach us the art
> That breaks and heals the heart.
>> 'The heart could never speak' (1960)

Newman, John Henry, Cardinal (1801–1890)
English Cardinal, theologian and poet
> *Cor ad cor loquitur.*
> Heart speaks to heart.
>> Motto adopted for his coat-of-arms as cardinal, 1879

Proverb
> Cold hands, warm heart.

Quarles, Francis (1592–1644)
English poet, writer and royalist
> The heart is a small thing, but desireth great matters.
> It is not sufficient for a kite's dinner, yet the whole world is not sufficient for it.
>> *Emblems* (1635)

Raleigh, Sir Walter (c.1552–1618)
English courtier, explorer, military commander, poet, historian and essayist
Reply when asked which way he would like to lay his head on the block
> So the heart be right, it is no matter which way the head lies.
>> In W. Stebbing, *Sir Walter Raleigh* (1891)

Rossetti, Christina (1830–1894)
English poet
> My heart is like a singing bird
> Whose nest is in a watered shoot;
> My heart is like an apple-tree
> Whose boughs are bent with thickset fruit;
> My heart is like a rainbow shell
> That paddles in a halcyon sea;
> My heart is gladder than all these
> Because my love is come to me.
>> 'A Birthday' (1862)

Scott, Sir Walter (1771–1832)
Scottish writer and historian
> We shall never learn to feel and respect our real calling and destiny, unless we have taught ourselves to consider every thing as moonshine, compared with the education of the heart.
>> Letter to J.G. Lockhart, 1825

Shakespeare, William (1564–1616)
English dramatist, poet and actor
> I would not have such a heart in my bosom for the dignity of the whole body.
>> *Macbeth*, V.i

Sidney, Sir Philip (1554–1586)
English poet, critic, soldier, courtier and diplomat
> My true Love hathe my harte and I have his,
> By just exchaunge one for the other given,
> I holde his deare, and myne hee can not misse,
> There never was a better Bargayne driven.
>> *Old Arcadia* (1581)

Spenser, Edmund (c.1522–1599)
English poet
> The noble hart, that harbours vertuous thought,
> And is with child of glorious great intent,
> Can never rest, untill it forth have brought
> Th' eternall brood of glorie excellent.
>> *The Faerie Queene* (1596)

Suckling, Sir John (1609–1642)
English poet and dramatist
> I prithee send me back my heart,
> Since I cannot have thine
> For if from yours you will not part,
> Why then shouldst thou have mine?
>> 'Song'

Thomas, Dylan (1914–1953)
Welsh poet, writer and radio dramatist
> Light breaks where no sun shines;
> Where no sea runs, the waters of the heart
> Push in their tides.
>> 'Light breaks where no sun shines' (1934)

Yeats, W.B. (1865–1939)
Irish poet, dramatist, editor, writer and senator
> Out-worn heart, in a time out-worn,
> Come clear of the nets of wrong and right;
> Laugh, heart, again in the grey twilight,
> Sigh, heart, again in the dew of the morn.
>> In the *National Observer*, 1893, 'Into the Twilight'

▶▶ LOVE

heaven

Borges, Jorge Luis (1899–1986)
Argentinian writer, poet and librarian
> *Que el cielo exista, aunque mi lugar sea el infierno.*
> Let heaven exist, even if my place be hell.
> > 'The Library of Babel' (1941)

Brown, Helen Gurley (1922–)
US writer and editor
Promotional line for *Cosmopolitan* magazine
> Good girls go to heaven, bad girls go everywhere.
> > Attr.

Browning, Robert (1812–1889)
English poet
> On the earth the broken arcs; in the heaven, a perfect round.
> > 'Abt Vogler' (1864)

Carlyle, Jane Welsh (1801–1866)
Scottish letter writer, literary hostess and poet
> They must be comfortable people who have leisure to think about going to heaven! My most constant and pressing anxiety is to keep out of bedlam, that's all …
> > *Letters and Memorials of Jane Welsh Carlyle* (1883)

Coleridge, Samuel Taylor (1772–1834)
English poet, philosopher and critic
> If a man could pass through Paradise in a dream, and have a flower presented to him as a pledge that his soul had really been there, and if he found that flower in his hand when he awoke – Aye, and what then?
> > *Anima Poetae* (1816)

De Quincey, Thomas (1785–1859)
English writer
> Thou hast the keys of Paradise, oh just, subtle, and mighty opium!
> > *Confessions of an English Opium Eater* (1822)

Fitzgerald, Edward (1809–1883)
English poet, translator and letter writer
> Here with a Loaf of Bread beneath the Bough,
> A Flask of Wine, a Book of Verse – and Thou
> Beside me singing in the Wilderness –
> And Wilderness is Paradise enow.
> > *The Rubáiyát of Omar Khayyám* (1859)

Lichtenberg, Georg (1742–1799)
German physicist, satirist and writer
> Probably no invention came more easily to man than Heaven.
> > *Aphorisms*

Milton, John (1608–1674)
English poet, libertarian and pamphleteer
> Heav'n is for thee too high

> To know what passes there; be lowlie wise:
> Think onely what concerns thee and thy being.
> > *Paradise Lost* (1667)

Proust, Marcel (1871–1922)
French writer and critic
> *Les vrais paradis sont les paradis qu'on a perdus.*
> The true paradises are the paradises we have lost.
> > *Le Temps retrouvé* (1926)

Sedgwick, Catharine Maria (1789–1867)
US writer and feminist
Comparing heaven with her home town of Stockbridge, Massachussetts
> I expect no very violent transition.
> > Attr.

Shakespeare, William (1564–1616)
English dramatist, poet and actor
> Heaven is above all yet: there sits a Judge
> That no king can corrupt.
> > *Henry VIII*, III.i

Shaw, George Bernard (1856–1950)
Irish socialist, writer, dramatist and critic
> In heaven an angel is nobody in particular.
> > *Man and Superman* (1903)

> Heaven, as conventionally conceived, is a place so inane, so dull, so useless, so miserable, that nobody has ever ventured to describe a whole day in heaven, though plenty of people have described a day at the seaside.
> > *Misalliance* (1914)

Smith, Sydney (1771–1845)
English clergyman, essayist, journalist and wit
> My idea of heaven is, eating pâté de foie gras to the sound of trumpets.
> > In H. Pearson, *The Smith of Smiths* (1934)

Swift, Jonathan (1667–1745)
Irish satirist, poet, essayist and cleric
> What they do in heaven we are ignorant of; what they do not we are told expressly, that they neither marry, nor are given in marriage.
> > *Thoughts on Various Subjects* (1711)

Tintoretto (1518–1594)
Venetian painter
Arguing that he be allowed to paint the Paradiso at the Doge's palace in Venice, despite his advanced age
> Grant me paradise in this world; I'm not so sure I'll reach it in the next.
> > Attr.

Waddell, Helen Jane (1889–1965)
Irish scholar and writer
> Would you think Heaven could be so small a thing
> As a lit window on the hills at night.
> > 'I Shall Not Go To Heaven'

Williams, William Carlos (1883–1963)
US poet, writer and paediatrician
> Is it any better in Heaven, my friend Ford,
> Than you found it in Provence?
>> 'To Ford Madox Ford in Heaven' (1944)

▶▶ AFTERLIFE

hell

Beckford, William (1760–1844)
English writer, collector and politician
> He did not think with the Caliph Omar Ben
> Adalaziz, that it was necessary to make a hell of
> this world to enjoy paradise in the next.
>> *Vathek* (1787)

Bernanos, Georges (1888–1948)
French novelist and essayist
> *L'enfer, madame, c'est de ne plus aimer.*
> Hell, madam, is to love no longer.
>> *The Diary of a Country Priest* (1936)

Betjeman, Sir John (1906–1984)
English poet laureate
> Maud was my hateful nurse who smelt of soap …
> She rubbed my face in messes I had made
> And was the first to tell me about Hell,
> Admitting she was going there herself.
>> *Summoned by Bells* (1960)

Bunyan, John (1628–1688)
English preacher, pastor and writer
> Then I saw there was a way to Hell, even from
> the gates of heaven.
>> *The Pilgrim's Progress* (1678)

Burton, Robert (1577–1640)
English clergyman and writer
> If there is a hell upon earth, it is to be found in a
> melancholy man's heart.
>> *Anatomy of Melancholy* (1621)

Clare, Dr Anthony (1942–)
Irish professor, psychiatrist and broadcaster
> Hell is when you get what you think you want.
>> *The Observer*, 1983

Dante Alighieri (1265–1321)
Italian poet
> *PER ME SI VA NELLA CITTA' DOLENTE,*
> *PER ME SI VA NELL'ETERNO DOLORE,*
> *PER ME SI VA TRA LA PERDUTA GENTE …*
> *LASCIATE OGNI SPERANZA VOI CH'ENTRATE!*
> Through me one goes to the sorrowful city.
> Through me one goes to eternal suffering.
> Through me one goes among lost people …
> Abandon all hope, you who enter!
>> *Divina Commedia* (1307)

Questi non hanno speranza di morte,

E la lor cieca vita è tanto bassa,
Che invidiosi son d'ogni altra sorte.
> There is no hope of death for these souls, and
> their lost life is so low, that they are envious of
> any other kind.
>> *Divina Commedia* (1307)

Eliot, T.S. (1888–1965)
US-born British poet, verse dramatist and critic
> Hell is oneself;
> Hell is alone, the other figures in it
> Merely projections. There is nothing to escape
> from
> And nothing to escape to. One is always alone.
>> *The Cocktail Party* (1950)

Johnson, Samuel (1709–1784)
English lexicographer, poet, critic, conversationalist and
essayist
> *Johnson*: As I cannot be sure that I have fulfilled
> the conditions on which salvation is granted, I
> am afraid I may be one of those who shall be
> damned (*looking dismally*).
> *Dr Adams*: What do you mean by damned?
> *Johnson (passionately and loudly)*: Sent to Hell,
> Sir, and punished everlastingly.
>> In Boswell, *The Life of Samuel Johnson* (1791)

Of a Jamaican gentleman, then lately dead
> He will not, whither he is now gone, find much
> difference, I believe, either in the climate or the
> company.
>> In Piozzi, *Anecdotes of the Late Samuel Johnson* (1786)

Lewis, C.S. (1898–1963)
Irish-born English academic, writer and critic
> There is wishful thinking in Hell as well as on
> earth.
>> *The Screwtape Letters* (1942)

Marlowe, Christopher (1564–1593)
English poet and dramatist
> Hell hath no limits nor is circumscrib'd
> In one self place, where we are is Hell,
> And where Hell is, there must we ever be.
> And to be short, when all the world dissolves,
> And every creature shall be purified,
> All places shall be hell that are not heaven.
>> *Doctor Faustus* (1604)

Milton, John (1608–1674)
English poet, libertarian and pamphleteer
> Here we may reign secure, and in my choice
> To reign is worth ambition though in Hell:
> Better to reign in Hell, then serve in Heav'n.
>> *Paradise Lost* (1667)

> Long is the way
> And hard, that out of Hell leads up to Light.
>> *Paradise Lost* (1667)

Proverb
> The road to hell is paved with good intentions.

Sade, Marquis de (1740–1814)
French soldier and writer
> *Il n'y a d'autre enfer pour l'homme que la bêtise ou la*
> *méchanceté de ses semblables.*
> There is no other hell for man than the stupidity
> and wickedness of his own kind.
>> *Histoire de Juliette* (1797)

Sartre, Jean-Paul (1905–1980)
French philosopher, writer, dramatist and critic
> *Alors, c'est ça l'enfer. Je n'aurais jamais cru … Vous*
> *vous rappelez: le soufre, le bûcher, le gril … Ah! quelle*
> *plaisanterie. Pas besoin de gril, l'enfer, c'est les Autres.*
> So that's what Hell is. I'd never have believed it
> … Do you remember, brimstone, the stake, the
> gridiron? … What a joke! No need of a gridiron,
> Hell is other people.
>> *In Camera* (1944)

Shakespeare, William (1564–1616)
English dramatist, poet and actor
> The flow'ry way that leads to the broad gate
> and the great fire.
>> *All's Well That Ends Well*, IV.v

Shaw, George Bernard (1856–1950)
Irish socialist, writer, dramatist and critic
> A perpetual holiday is a good working definition
> of hell.
>> Attr.

Teilhard de Chardin, Pierre (1881–1955)
French Jesuit philosopher and palaeontologist
> *Vous m'avez dit, mon Dieu, de croire à l'enfer. Mais*
> *vous m'avez interdit de penser, avec absolue certitude,*
> *d'un seul homme, qu'il était damné.*
> You have told me, O God, to believe in hell. But
> you have forbidden me to think, with absolute
> certainty, of any man as damned.
>> *Le Milieu divin*

Virgil (70–19 BC)
Roman poet
> *Facilis descensus Averno:*
> *Noctes atque dies patet atri ianua Ditis;*
> *Sed revocare gradum superasque evadere ad auras,*
> *Hoc opus, hic labor est.*
> The gates of Hell are open night and day;
> Smooth the descent, and easy is the way:
> But to return, and view the cheerful skies,
> In this the task and mighty labour lies.
>> *Aeneid*

Watts, Isaac (1674–1748)
English hymn-writer, poet and minister
> There is a dreadful Hell,
> And everlasting pains;
> There sinners must with devils dwell
> In darkness, fire and chains.
>> *Divine Songs for Children*
>> (1715)

Wilde, Oscar (1854–1900)
Irish poet, dramatist, writer, critic and wit
> We are each our own devil, and we make
> This world our hell.
>> *The Duchess of Padua* (1883)

▶▶ DEVIL

heroes

Brecht, Bertolt (1898–1956)
German dramatist
> *Andrea: Unglücklich das Land, das keine Helden hat! …*
> *Galileo: Nein. Unglücklich das Land, das Helden nötig*
> *hat.*
> Andrea: Unhappy the country that has no
> heroes! Galileo: No. Unhappy the country that
> needs heroes.
>> *Life of Galileo* (1938–1939)

Carlyle, Thomas (1795–1881)
Scottish historian, biographer, critic, and essayist
> The Hero can be Poet, Prophet, King, Priest or
> what you will, according to the kind of world he
> finds himself born into.
>> 'The Hero as Poet' (1841)

Cornuel, Madame Anne-Marie Bigot de
(1605–1694)
French society hostess
> *Il n'y a point de grand homme pour son valet de*
> *chambre.*
> No man is a hero to his valet.
>> In *Lettres de Mlle Aïssé à Madame C* (1787)

Gambetta, Léon (1838–1882)
French statesman and Prime Minister
> *Les temps héroïques sont passés.*
> Heroic times have passed away.
>> Saying

Harris, Max (1921–1995)
Australian critic, poet and publisher
> The Australian world is peopled with good
> blokes and bastards, but not heroes.
>> In Coleman (ed.), *Australian Civilization*

Henderson, Hamish (1919–)
Scottish folklorist, composer, translator and poet
> There were our own, there were the others.
> Their deaths were like their lives, human and
> animal.
> There were no gods and precious few heroes.
>> *Elegies for the Dead in Cyrenaica* (1948)

Landor, Walter Savage (1775–1864)
English poet and writer
> Hail, ye indomitable heroes, hail!
> Despite of all your generals ye prevail.
>> 'The Crimean Heroes'

Mackenzie, Sir Compton (1883–1972)
Scottish writer and broadcaster
> Ever since the first World War there has been an inclination to denigrate the heroic aspect of man.
>> *On Moral Courage* (1962)

Morell, Thomas (1703–1784)
English scholar, librettist, editor and clergyman
> See, the conquering hero comes!
> Sound the trumpets, beat the drums!
>> *Joshua* (1748)

Orwell, George (1903–1950)
English writer and critic
> The high sentiments always win in the end, leaders who offer blood, toil, tears and sweat always get more out of their followers than those who offer safety and a good time. When it comes to the pinch, human beings are heroic.
>> *Horizon*, 1941

Rilke, Rainer Maria (1875–1926)
Austrian poet, born in Prague
> *Wunderlich nah ist der Held doch den jugendlichen Toten.*
> Wondrous close is the hero to those who die young.
>> *Duino Elegies* (1923)

Rogers, Will (1879–1935)
US humorist, actor, rancher, writer and wit
> Heroing is one of the shortest-lived professions there is.
>> In Grove, *The Will Rogers Book* (1961)

▶▶ COURAGE; PATRIOTISM; WAR

history

Adenauer, Konrad (1876–1967)
German Chancellor
> History is the sum total of things that could have been avoided.
>> Attr.

Angelou, Maya (1928–)
US writer, poet and dramatist
> History, faced with courage, need not be lived again.
> Speech at the Inauguration of President William Clinton, 1993

Anonymous
> Every time history repeats itself the price goes up.

Austen, Jane (1775–1817)
English writer
> N.B. There will be very few Dates in this History.
>> *The History of England* (1791)

> History tells me nothing that does not either vex or weary me; the men are all so good for nothing, and hardly any women at all.
>> Letter

> Real solemn history, I cannot be interested in … The quarrels of popes and kings, with wars or pestilences, in every page; the men all so good for nothing, and hardly any women at all, it is very tiresome.
>> *Northanger Abbey* (1818)

Balfour, A.J. (1848–1930)
British Conservative Prime Minister
> History does not repeat itself. Historians repeat each other.
>> Attr.

Beecham, Sir Thomas (1879–1961)
English conductor and impresario
> When the history of the first half of this century comes to be written – properly written – it will be acknowledged the most stupid and brutal in the history of civilisation.
>> Attr.

Birrell, Augustine (1850–1933)
> That great dust-heap called 'history'.
>> *Obiter Dicta* (1884–1887)

Bolingbroke, Henry (1678–1751)
English statesman, historian and actor
> I have read somewhere or other – in Dionysius of Halicarnassus, I think – that History is Philosophy teaching by examples.
>> *Letters on Study and Use of History* (1752)

Of Thucydides and Xenophon
> They maintained the dignity of history.
>> *Letters on Study and Use of History* (1752)

Brown, George MacKay (1921–1996)
Scottish novelist, poet and playwright
> History can show few benign mergings of people with people. Flame and blood is always the cement.
>> 'The View from Orkney'

Butler, Samuel (1835–1902)
English writer, painter, philosopher and scholar
> It has been said that though God cannot alter the past, historians can; it is perhaps because they can be useful to Him in this respect that He tolerates their existence.
>> *Erewhon Revisited* (1901)

Carlyle, Thomas (1795–1881)
Scottish historian, biographer, critic, and essayist
> History a distillation of rumour.
>> *History of the French Revolution* (1837)

> For, as I take it, Universal History, the history of what man has accomplished in this world, is at

bottom the History of the Great Men who have worked here.

On Heroes, Hero-Worship, and the Heroic in History

History is the essence of innumerable biographies.

'On History' (1839)

Happy the people whose annals are blank in history-books!

History of Frederick the Great (1865)

Cather, Willa (1876–1947)
US writer
The history of every country begins in the heart of a man or a woman.

O Pioneers! (1913)

Cicero (106–43 BC)
Roman orator, statesman, essayist and letter writer
History is the witness that testifies to the passing of time; it illumines reality, vitalizes memory, provides guidance in daily life, and brings us tidings of antiquity.

Pro Publio Sestio

Coleridge, Samuel Taylor (1772–1834)
English poet, philosopher and critic
If men could learn from history, what lessons it might teach us! But passion and party blind our eyes, and the light which experience gives is a lantern on the stern, which shines only on the waves behind us!

Table Talk (1835)

Dionysius of Halicarnassus (fl. 30–7 BC)
Greek historian
History is philosophy teaching from examples.

Ars Rhetorica

Durrell, Lawrence (1912–1990)
Indian-born British poet and writer
History is an endless repetition of the wrong way of living.

The Listener, 1978

Eban, Abba (1915–)
South African-born Israeli statesman and writer
History teaches us that men and nations behave wisely once they have exhausted all other alternatives.

Speech, 1970

Fisher, H.A.L. (1856–1940)
English historian
One intellectual excitement has, however, been denied me. Men wiser and more learned than I have discerned in history a plot, a rhythm, a predetermined pattern. These harmonies are concealed from me. I can see only one emergency following upon another as wave follows upon wave, only one great fact with respect to which, since it is unique, there can be

no generalizations, only one safe rule for the historian: that he should recognize in the development of human destinies the play of the contingent and the unforeseen.

History of Europe (1935)

Ford, Henry (1863–1947)
US car manufacturer
Popularly remembered as 'History is bunk'
History is more or less bunk. It's tradition. We don't want tradition. We want to live in the present and the only history that is worth a tinker's damn is the history we make today.

Chicago Tribune, 1916

Forster, E.M. (1879–1970)
English writer, essayist and literary critic
The historian must have ... some conception of how men who are not historians behave. Otherwise he will move in a world of the dead.

Abinger Harvest (1936)

Gibbon, Edward (1737–1794)
English historian, politician and memoirist
If a man were called to fix the period in the history of the world during which the condition of the human race was most happy and prosperous, he would, without hesitation, name that which elapsed from the death of Domitian to the accession of Commodus.

Decline and Fall of the Roman Empire (1776–88)

History ... is, indeed, little more than the register of the crimes, follies, and misfortunes of mankind.

Decline and Fall of the Roman Empire (1776–88)

James, Henry (1843–1916)
US-born British writer, critic and letter writer
It takes a great deal of history to produce a little literature.

Hawthorne (1879)

Johnson, Samuel (1709–1784)
English lexicographer, poet, critic, conversationalist and essayist
Great abilities are not requisite for an Historian ... Imagination is not required in any high degree.

In Boswell, *The Life of Samuel Johnson* (1791)

Joyce, James (1882–1941)
Irish writer
History is a nightmare from which I am trying to awake.

Ulysses (1922)

Khrushchev, Nikita (1894–1971)
Russian statesman and Premier of the USSR
Whether you like it or not, history is on our side.

Speech to Western ambassadors, 1956

Koestler, Arthur (1905–1983)

British writer, essayist and political refugee

> The most persistent sound which reverberates through men's history is the beating of war drums.
>
> *Janus: A Summing Up* (1978)

Lang, Ian (1940–)

Scottish Conservative politician

> History is littered with dead opinion polls.
>
> *The Independent*, 1994

Macaulay, Lord (1800–1859)

English Liberal statesman, essayist and poet

> Every schoolboy knows who imprisoned Montezuma, and who strangled Atahualpa.
>
> *Collected Essays* (1843), 'Lord Clive'

MacLeod, Iain (1913–1970)

English Conservative politician and writer

> History is too serious to be left to historians.
>
> *The Observer*, 1961

McLuhan, Marshall (1911–1980)

Canadian communications theorist

> The hydrogen bomb is history's exclamation point. It ends an age-long sentence of manifest violence.
>
> Attr.

Marx, Karl (1818–1883)

German political philosopher and economist; founder of Communism

> Hegel says somewhere that all great events and personalities in world history reappear in one way or another. He forgot to add: the first time as tragedy, the second as farce.
>
> *The Eighteenth Brumaire of Louis Napoleon* (1852)

Ortega y Gasset, José (1883–1955)

Spanish philosopher

> We need all of history in order to see if we can manage to escape from it and not fall back into it.
>
> *The Rebellion of the Masses* (1930)

Orwell, George (1903–1950)

English writer and critic

> To a surprising extent the war-lords in shining armour, the apostles of the martial virtues, tend not to die fighting when the time comes. History is full of ignominious getaways by the great and famous.
>
> 'Who are the War Criminals?' (1941)

Pasternak, Boris (1890–1960)

Russian poet and novelist

> But what is history? It is the setting up, through the ages, of works which are consistently devoted to solving death and to overcoming it in the future.
>
> *Doctor Zhivago* (1958)

Patten, Brian (1946–)

British poet

> History's full of absurd mistakes.
> King Arthur if he ever existed
> would only have farted and excused himself
> from the Round Table in a hurry.
>
> *Grinning Jack* (1990)

Péguy, Charles (1873–1914)

French Catholic socialist, poet and writer

> It is impossible to write ancient history because we do not have enough sources, and impossible to write modern history because we have far too many.
>
> *Clio*

Popper, Sir Karl (1902–1994)

Austrian-born British philosopher

> There is no history of mankind, there are only many histories of all kinds of aspects of human life. And one of these is the history of political power. This is elevated into the history of the world.
>
> *The Open Society and its Enemies* (1945)

Proverb

> History repeats itself.

Saki (1870–1916)

Burmese-born British writer

> The people of Crete unfortunately make more history than they can consume locally.
>
> *The Chronicles of Clovis* (1911)

Samuel, Lord (1870–1963)

English Liberal statesman, philosopher and administrator

> Hansard is history's ear, already listening.
>
> *The Observer*, 1949

Schiller, Johann Christoph Friedrich (1759–1805)

German writer, dramatist, poet and historian

> *Die Weltgeschichte ist das Weltgericht.*
> The history of the world is its judgement.
>
> 'Resignation' (1786)

Schlegel, Friedrich von (1772–1829)

German critic and philosopher

> *Anfang und Ende der Geschichte ist prophetisch, kein Objekt mehr der reinen Historie.*
> The beginning and end of history are prophetic, they are no longer the object of pure history.
>
> *Fragments on Literature and Poetry*

> *Der Historiker ist ein rückwärts gekehrter Prophet.*
> A historian is a prophet in reverse.
>
> *Athenäum – Fragmente*

Seeley, Sir John Robert (1834–1895)

English historian, essayist and scholar

Quoting E.A. Freeman

> History is past politics, and politics present history.
>
> *The Growth of British Policy* (1895)

Sellar, Walter (1898–1951) and **Yeatman, Robert Julian** (1897–1968)
British writers

> A Bad Thing: America was thus clearly top nation, and History came to a .
>> *1066 And All That* (1930)

> The Cavaliers (Wrong but Wromantic) and the Roundheads (Right but Repulsive).
>> *1066 And All That* (1930)

Stalin, Joseph (1879–1953)
Soviet Communist leader

> History shows that there are no invincible armies.
>> Speech on the declaration of war on Germany, 1941

Taylor, A.J.P. (1906–1990)
English historian, writer, broadcaster and lecturer

> History gets thicker as it approaches recent times.
>> *English History, 1914–1945* (1965)

Of Napoleon III

> He was what I often think is a dangerous thing for a statesman to be – a student of history; and like most of those who study history, he learned from the mistakes of the past how to make new ones.
>> *The Listener*, 1963

Tebbitt, Norman (1931–)
English Conservative politician

> Youngsters of all races born here should be taught that British history is their history, or they will forever be foreigners holding British passports, and this kingdom will become a Yugoslavia.
>> Speech, Conservative Party Conference, 1997

Tolstoy, Leo (1828–1910)
Russian writer, essayist, philosopher and moralist

> History would be an excellent thing if only it were true.
>> Attr.

> Historians are like deaf people who go on answering questions that no one has asked them.
>> Attr.

Ustinov, Sir Peter (1921–)
English actor, director, dramatist, writer and raconteur

> … the great thing about history is that it is adaptable.
>> *Romanoff and Juliet* (1956)

Voltaire (1694–1778)
French philosopher, dramatist, poet, historian writer and critic

> Indeed, history is nothing but a tableau of crimes and misfortunes.
>> *L'Ingénu* (1767)

Walpole, Robert (1676–1745)
British statesman and first British Prime Minister
On being asked whether he would like to be read to

> Anything but history, for history must be false.
>> Attr.

Wedgwood, Cicely Veronica (1910–1997)
English historian

> … truth can neither be apprehended nor communicated … history is an art like all other sciences.
>> *Truth and Opinion* (1960)

Wells, H.G. (1866–1946)
English writer

> Human history becomes more and more a race between education and catastrophe.
>> *The Outline of History* (1920)

Wilde, Oscar (1854–1900)
Irish poet, dramatist, writer, critic and wit

> To give an accurate description of what has never occurred is not merely the proper occupation of the historian, but the inalienable privilege of any man of parts and culture.
>> *Intentions* (1891), 'The Critic as Artist'

Yeltsin, Boris (1931–)
Russian statesman and President
Said after the failure of the communist coup

> History will record that the twentieth century essentially ended on 19–21 August 1991.
>> Article in *Newsweek*, 1994

▶▶ EXPERIENCE; PAST

holidays

Priestley, J.B. (1894–1984)
English writer, dramatist and critic

> A good holiday is one spent among people whose notions of time are vaguer than yours.
>> Attr.

Shakespeare, William (1564–1616)
English dramatist, poet and actor

> If all the year were playing holidays,
> To sport would be as tedious as to work;
> But when they seldom come, they wish'd-for come.
>> *Henry IV, Part 1*, I.ii

hollywood

Chandler, Raymond (1888–1959)
US crime writer

> If my books had been any worse I should not have been invited to Hollywood, and if they had

been any better I should not have come.

Letter, 1945, to *Atlantic Monthly* editor,
Charles W. Morton

Grant, Cary (1904–1986)
English-born US actor
> We have our factory, which is called a stage. We make a product, we color it, we title it and we ship it out in cans.

Newsweek, 1969

Hawn, Goldie (1945–)
US film actress
> There are only three ages for women in Hollywood – Babe, District Attorney, and Driving Miss Daisy.

Attr.

Holland, Agnieska
> In Hollywood they don't feel guilt.

Attr.

Hopper, Hedda (1890–1966)
US actress and writer
> In Hollywood gratitude is Public Enemy Number One.

From Under My Hat (1952)

Jong, Erica (1942–)
US writer
> Where is Hollywood located? Chiefly between the ears. In that part of the American brain lately vacated by God.

How To Save Your Own Life (1977)

Levant, Oscar (1906–1972)
US pianist and autobiographer
> Strip the phoney tinsel off Hollywood and you'll find the real tinsel underneath.

Attr.

Lucas, George (1944–)
US film director
Advice to Steven Spielberg
> If the boy and girl walk off into the sunset hand-in-hand in the last scene, it adds 10 million to the box office.

Attr.

Mature, Victor (1915–)
US film actor
> Hollywood: Where the stars twinkle until they wrinkle.

Attr.

Mizner, Wilson (1876–1933)
US writer, wit and dramatist
> A trip through a sewer in a glass-bottomed boat.

Attr.

Monroe, Marilyn (1926–1962)
US film actress and model

Hollywood is a place where they'll pay you $50,000 for a kiss and 50 cents for your soul.

Attr.

Reed, Rex (1938–)
US film and music critic and columnist
> In Hollywood, if you don't have happiness, you send out for it.

In Colombo *Colombo's Hollywood*

Rogers, Will (1879–1935)
US humorist, actor, rancher, writer and wit
> In Hollywood the woods are full of people that learned to write but evidently can't read; if they could read their stuff, they'd stop writing.

The Autobiography of Will Rogers (1949)

Rowland, Richard (c.1881–1947)
US film executive
When United Artists was established in 1919 by Mary Pickford, Douglas Fairbanks, Charlie Chaplin and D.W. Griffith
> The lunatics have taken over the asylum.

Attr.

Stallings, Laurence (1894–1968)
> Hollywood – a place where the inmates are in charge of the asylum.

Attr.

▶▶ CINEMA; SHOWBUSINESS

home

Ace, Jane (1905–1974)
US comedian and radio personality
> Home wasn't built in a day.

In G. Ace, *The Fine Art of Hypochondria* (1966)

Anonymous
Graffiti in Notting Hill
> Dwelling unit sweet dwelling unit.

In Nigel Rees, *Graffiti Lives, OK* (1979)

> Be it ever so humble there's no place like home for sending one slowly
> crackers.

> There's no place like home, after the other places close.

Baker, Russell (1925–)
> What the New Yorker calls home would seem like a couple of closets to most Americans, yet he manages not only to live there but also to grow trees and cockroaches right on the premises.

New York Times, 1978

Beauvoir, Simone de (1908–1986)
French writer, feminist critic and philosopher
> The ideal of happiness has always taken material form in the house, whether cottage or castle; it

stands for permanence and separation from the world.

The Second Sex (1949)

Beeton, Isabella (1836–1865)
British cookery writer
It ought … to enter into the domestic policy of any parent, to make her children feel that home is the happiest place in the world.

Mrs Beeton's Household Management (1861)

Cicero (106–43 BC)
Roman orator, statesman, essayist and letter writer
What is more agreeable than one's home?

Ad Familiares

Clarke, John (fl. 1639)
English scholar
Home is home, though it be never so homely.

Paraemiologia Anglo-Latina (1639)

Coke, Sir Edward (1552–1634)
English judge, writer and politician
The house of everyone is to him as his castle and fortress, as well for his defence against injury and violence, as for his repose.

Semayne's Case

De Wolfe, Elsie (1865–1950)
US interior designer
It is the personality of the mistress that the home expresses. Men are forever guests in our homes, no matter how much happiness they may find there.

The House in Good Taste (1920)

Douglas, Norman (1868–1952)
Austrian-born Scottish writer
Many a man who thinks to found a home discovers that he has merely opened a tavern for his friends.

South Wind (1917)

Fletcher, John (1579–1625)
English dramatist
Charity and beating begins at home.

Wit Without Money (c.1614)

Ford, Lena (1870–1916)
US verse writer
Keep the home fires burning while your hearts are yearning,
Though your lads are far away, they dream of home.
There's a silver lining through the dark cloud shining:
Turn the dark cloud inside out, till the boys come home.

'Keep the Home Fires Burning' (1914)

Frost, Robert (1874–1963)
US poet

'Home is the place where, when you have to go there,
They have to take you in.'
'I should have called it
Something you somehow haven't to deserve.'

'The Death of the Hired Man' (1914)

Fuller, Margaret
A house is no home unless it contain food and fire for the mind as well as for the body.

Woman in the Nineteenth Century (1845)

Grossmith, George (1847–1912) and **Grossmith, Weedon** (1854–1919)
English singer and comedian/English writer, painter and actor
What's the good of a home, if you are never in it?

Diary of a Nobody (1894)

Higley, Brewster (19th century)
US songwriter
Oh give me a home where the buffalo roam,
Where the deer and the antelope play,
Where seldom is heard a discouraging word
And the skies are not cloudy all day.

'Home on the Range' (song, c.1873)

Jerome, Jerome K. (1859–1927)
English writer and dramatist
I want a house that has got over all of its troubles; I don't want to spend the rest of my life bringing up a young and inexperienced house.

Attr.

Kaufman, Sue (1926–)
In violent and chaotic times such as these, our only chance for survival lies in creating our own little islands of sanity and order, in making little havens of our homes.

Falling Bodies (1974)

Luce, Clare Boothe (1903–1987)
US diplomat, politician and writer
A man's home may seem to be his castle on the outside; inside, it is more often his nursery.

Attr.

Meyer, Agnes (1887–c.1970)
US writer and social worker
What the nation must realise is that the home, when both parents work, is non-existent. Once we have honestly faced the fact, we must act accordingly.

Washington Post, 1943

More, Hannah (1745–1833)
English poet, dramatist and religious writer
The sober comfort, all the peace which springs
From the large aggregate of little things;
On these small cares of daughter, wife, or friend,

The almost sacred joys of home depend.

'Sensibility' (1782)

Morris, William (1834–1896)
English poet, designer, craftsman, artist and socialist
> If you want a golden rule that will fit everybody, this is it: Have nothing in your houses that you do not know to be useful, or believe to be beautiful.

Hopes and Fears for Art (1882)

Parker, Dorothy (1893–1967)
US writer, poet, critic and wit
On her requirements for an apartment
> [Enough space] to lay a hat (and a few friends).

In J. Keats, You Might As Well Live (1970)

Payne, J.H. (1791–1852)
US dramatist, poet and actor
> Mid pleasures and palaces though we may roam,
> Be it ever so humble, there's no place like home;
> A charm from the skies seems to hallow us there,
> Which, seek through the world, is ne'er met with elsewhere.
> Home, home, sweet, sweet home!
> There's no place like home! there's no place like home!

'Home, Sweet Home', song, 1823

Pitt, William (1708–1778)
English politician and Prime Minister
> The poorest man may in his cottage bid defiance to all the forces of the Crown. It may be frail – its roof may shake – the wind may blow through it – the rain may enter – but the King of England cannot enter – all his force dares not cross the threshold of the ruined tenement!

Speech, c.1763

Proverbs
> East, west, home's best.

> Home is where the heart is.

Rowland, Helen (1875–1950)
US writer
> 'Home' is any four walls that enclose the right person.

Reflections of a Bachelor Girl (1909)

Shaw, George Bernard (1856–1950)
Irish socialist, writer, dramatist and critic
> Home is the girl's prison and the woman's workhouse.

Man and Superman (1903)

> The great advantage of a hotel is that it's a refuge from home life.

You Never Can Tell (1898)

Sitwell, Dame Edith (1887–1964)
English poet, anthologist, critic and biographer

One's own surroundings mean so much to one, when one is feeling miserable.

Selected Letters (1970)

Stowe, Harriet Beecher (1811–1896)
US writer and reformer
> Home is a place not only of strong affections, but of entire unreserve; it is life's undress rehearsal, its backroom, its dressing room, from which we go forth to more careful and guarded intercourse, leaving behind us much debris of cast-off and everyday clothing.

Little Foxes (1866)

Thatcher, Margaret (1925–)
English Conservative Prime Minister
> Home is where you come to when you have nothing better to do.

Vanity Fair, 1991

Thoreau, Henry David (1817–1862)
US essayist, social critic and writer
> I had three chairs in my house; one for solitude, two for friendship, three for society.

Walden (1854)

Tusser, Thomas (c.1524–1580)
English writer, poet and musician
> Seek home for rest,
> For home is best.

Five Hundred Points of Good Husbandry (1557)

▶▶ TRAVEL

homosexuality

Bryant, Anita (1940–)
Australian feminist writer
> If homosexuality were the normal way, God would have made Adam and Bruce.

New York Times, 1977

Crisp, Quentin (1908–1999)
English writer, publicist and model
> I became one of the stately homos of England.

The Naked Civil Servant (1968)

Dixson, Miriam Joyce (1930–)
> Mateship is an informal male-bonding institution involving powerful subliminal homosexuality. Indeed some of its most ardent intellectual celebrants are slowly coming to see that mateship is deeply antipathetic to women.

The Real Matilda … (1976)

Dunstan, Keith (1925–)
Australian journalist
On the opinion that Ned Kelly and his gang were homosexuals, expressed by Sidney Baker in *The Australian Language*, 1966
> It is all very well to call him a white-livered cur, a

bully, a coward, a liar and a psychotic murderer but to actually name him as a queer is going too far.

Knockers (1972)

Frye, Marilyn (1934–)
US feminist and writer
Gay men generally are in significant ways, perhaps in all important ways, more loyal to masculinity and male-supremacy than other men. The gay rights movement may be the fundamentalism of the global religion which is patriarchy.

In Julie Burchill, *Sex and Sensibility*

Hall, Radclyffe (1883–1943)
English writer and poet
Acknowledge us, oh God, before the whole world. Give us also the right to our existence!

The Well of Loneliness (1928)

Lewis, Wyndham (1882–1957)
US-born British painter, critic and writer
The 'homo' is the legitimate child of the 'suffragette'.

The Art of Being Ruled (1926)

Marx, Groucho (1895–1977)
US comedian
Many years ago I chased a woman for almost two years, only to discover her tastes were exactly like mine: we were both crazy about girls.

Attr.

▶▶ SEX

honesty

Auden, W.H. (1907–1973)
English poet, essayist, critic, teacher and dramatist
Only God can tell the saintly from the suburban,
Counterfeit values always resemble the true;
Neither in Life nor Art is honesty bohemian,
The free behave much as the respectable do.

'New Year Letter' (1941)

Blake, William (1757–1827)
English poet, engraver, painter and mystic
Always be ready to speak your mind, and a base man will avoid you.

Attr.

Browne, Sir Thomas (1605–1682)
English physician, author and antiquary
I have tried if I could reach that great resolution … to be honest without a thought of Heaven or Hell.

Religio Medici (1643)

Burns, Robert (1759–1796)
Scottish poet and song writer
From scenes like these, old Scotia's grandeur springs
That makes her lov'd at home, rever'd abroad:
Princes and lords are but the breath of kings,
'An honest man's the noblest work of God.'

'The Cotter's Saturday Night' (1785)

Carlyle, Thomas (1795–1881)
Scottish historian, biographer, critic, and essayist
Make yourself an honest man and then you may be sure there is one rascal less in the world.

Attr.

Cromwell, Oliver (1599–1658)
English general, statesman and Puritan leader
A few honest men are better than numbers.

Letter to Sir William Spring, 1643

Defoe, Daniel (c.1661–1731)
English writer and critic
Necessity makes an honest man a knave.

Serious Reflections of Robinson Crusoe (1720)

Fitzgerald, F. Scott (1896–1940)
US writer
I am one of the few honest people that I have ever known.

The Great Gatsby (1926)

Juvenal (c.60–130)
Roman verse satirist and Stoic
Probitas laudatur et alget.
Honesty is praised and is left out in the cold.

Satires

Marquis, Don (1878–1937)
US columnist, satirist and poet
honesty is a good
thing but
it is not profitable to
its possessor
unless it is
kept under control.

'archygrams' (1933)

Proverb
Honesty is the best policy.

Ruskin, John (1819–1900)
English art critic, philosopher and reformer
Your honesty is not to be based either on religion or policy. Both your religion and policy must be based on it. Your honesty must be based, as the sun is, in vacant heaven; poised, as the lights in the firmament, which have rule over the day and over the night.

Time and Tide by Weare and Tyne (1867)

Shakespeare, William (1564–1616)
English dramatist, poet and actor
O wretched fool,

That liv'st to make thine honesty a vice!
O monstrous world! Take note, take note, O world,
To be direct and honest is not safe.

Othello, III.iii

Though I am not naturally honest, I am so sometimes by chance.

The Winter's Tale, IV.iv

Whately, Richard (1787–1863)
English philosopher, theologian, educationist and writer
Honesty is the best policy, but he who is governed by that maxim is not an honest man.

Apophthegms (1854)

▶▶ TRUTH

honour

Bulgakov, Mikhail (1891–1940)
Russian writer and dramatist
No man should break his word of honour.

The White Guard (1925)

Emerson, Ralph Waldo (1803–1882)
US poet, essayist, transcendentalist and teacher
The louder he talked of his honor, the faster we counted our spoons.

Conduct of Life (1860)

Hare, Augustus (1792–1834)
English clergyman and writer
Purity is the feminine, Truth the masculine, of Honour.

Guesses at Truth (1827)

Lovelace, Richard (1618–1658)
English poet
True; a new mistress now I chase,
The first foe in the field;
And with a stronger faith embrace
A sword, a horse, a shield.

Yet this inconstancy is such,
As you too shall adore;
I could not love thee (Dear) so much,
Lov'd I not honour more.

'To Lucasta, Going to the Wars'
(1649)

Mandeville, Bernard (1670–1733)
Dutch-born British doctor and satirist
The only thing of weight that can be said against modern honour is that it is directly opposite to religion. The one bids you bear injuries with patience, the other tells you if you don't resent them, you are not fit to live.

The Fable of the Bees
(1714)

Marx, Groucho (1895–1977)
US comedian
Remember, men, we're fighting for this woman's honour; which is probably more than she ever did.

Duck Soup (film, 1933)

Proverb
There is honour among thieves.

Racine, Jean (1639–1699)
French tragedian and poet
Sans argent l'honneur n'est qu'une maladie.
Without money, honour is no more than a disease.

Les Plaideurs (1668)

Shakespeare, William (1564–1616)
English dramatist, poet and actor

By heaven, methinks it were an easy leap
To pluck bright honour from the pale-fac'd moon;
Or dive into the bottom of the deep,
Where fathom-line could never touch the ground,
And pluck up drowned honour by the locks.

Henry IV, Part 1, I.iii

Honour pricks me on. Yea, but how if honour prick me off when I come on? How then? Can honour set to a leg? No. Or an arm? No. Or take away the grief of a wound? No. Honour hath no skill in surgery, then? No. What is honour? A word. What is in that word? Honour. What is that honour? Air. A trim reckoning! Who hath it? He that died o' Wednesday. Doth he feel it? No. Doth he hear it? No. 'Tis insensible, then? Yea, to the dead. But will it not live with the living? No. Why? Detraction will not suffer it. Therefore I'll none of it. Honour is a mere scutcheon. And so ends my catechism.

Henry IV, Part 1, V.i

Rightly to be great
Is not to stir without great argument,
But greatly to find quarrel in a straw,
When honour's at the stake.

Hamlet, IV.iv

Stevenson, Robert Louis (1850–1894)
Scottish writer, poet and essayist
Still obscurely fighting the lost fight of virtue, still clinging, in the brothel or on the scaffold, to some rag of honour, the poor jewel of their souls!

Across the Plains (1892)

hooligans

Saki (1870–1916)
Burmese-born British writer
> Even the Hooligan was probably invented in China centuries before we thought of him.
>> *Reginald* (1904)

hope

Alcott, Louisa May (1832–1888)
US writer
> Far away there in the sunshine are my highest aspirations. I may not reach them, but I can look up and see their beauty, believe in them, and follow where they lead.
>> *Little Women* (1869)

Arnold, Matthew (1822–1888)
English poet, critic, essayist and educationist
> And the pale master on his spar-
> strewn deck
> With anguish'd face and flying hair
> Grasping the rudder hard,
> Still bent to make some port he knows
> not where,
> Still standing for some false,
> impossible shore.
>> 'A Summer Night' (1852)

> Still nursing the unconquerable hope,
> Still clutching the inviolable shade.
>> 'The Scholar-Gipsy' (1853)

> The foot less prompt to meet the morning dew,
> The heart less bounding at emotion new,
> And hope, once crushed, less quick to spring again.
>> 'Thyrsis' (1866)

Bacon, Francis (1561–1626)
English philosopher, essayist, politician and courtier
> Hope is a good breakfast, but it is a bad supper.
>> 'Apophthegms'

Burke, Edmund (1729–1797)
Irish-born British statesman and philosopher
> Those who have much to hope and nothing to lose will always be dangerous.
>> Letter, 1777

Chesterton, G.K. (1874–1936)
English writer, poet and critic
> Hope is the power of being cheerful in circumstances which we know to be desperate.
>> *Heretics* (1905)

Clare, John (1793–1864)
English rural poet; died in an asylum
> Hopeless hope hopes on and meets no end,
> Wastes without springs and homes without a friend.
>> 'Child Harold' (1841)

Coleridge, Samuel Taylor (1772–1834)
English poet, philosopher and critic
> Work without hope draws nectar in a sieve,
> And hope without an object cannot live.
>> 'Work Without Hope' (1828)

Franklin, Benjamin (1706–1790)
US statesman, scientist, political critic and printer
> He that lives upon hope will die fasting.
>> *Poor Richard's Almanac* (1758)

Herbert, George (1593–1633)
English poet and priest
> He that lives in hope danceth without music.
>> *Jacula Prudentum* (1640)

Illich, Ivan (1926–)
Austrian-born US educator, sociologist, writer and priest
> We must rediscover the distinction between hope and expectation.
>> *Deschooling Society* (1971)

Kerr, Jean (1923–)
US writer and dramatist
> Hope is the feeling you have that the feeling you have isn't permanent.
>> *Finishing Touches* (1973)

Osborne, John (1929–1994)
English dramatist and actor
A notice in his bathroom
> Since I gave up hope I feel so much better.
>> *The Independent*, 1994

Pope, Alexander (1688–1744)
English poet, translator and editor
> Hope springs eternal in the human breast;
> Man never Is, but always To be blest.
>> *An Essay on Man* (1733)

Prior, Matthew (1664–1721)
English poet
> For hope is but a dream of those that wake.
>> Solomon (1718)

Proverb
> Every cloud has a silver lining.

Shakespeare, William (1564–1616)
English dramatist, poet and actor
> True hope is swift and flies with swallow's wings;
> Kings it makes gods, and meaner creatures kings.
>> *Richard III*, V.ii

Terence (c.190–159 BC)
Carthaginian-born Roman dramatist
> *Modo liceat vivere, est spes.*

Where there's life, there's hope.

Heauton Timoroumenos

▶▶ AMBITION; DESIRE; OPTIMISM

hosts and guests

Coleridge, Samuel Taylor (1772–1834)
English poet, philosopher and critic
Like some poor nigh-related guest,
That may not rudely be dismist;
Yet hath outstay'd his welcome while,
And tells the jest without the smile.

'Youth and Age' (1834)

Davis, Thomas (1814–1845)
Irish poet
Come in the evening, or come in the morning,
Come when you're looked for, or come without
warning.

'The Welcome' (1846)

Fitzgerald, F. Scott (1896–1940)
US writer
I was one of the few guests who had actually
been invited. People were not invited – they
went there.

The Great Gatsby (1925)

I entertained on a cruising trip that was so much
fun that I had to sink my yacht to make my
guests go home.

The Crack-Up (1945)

Homer (fl. c.8th century BC)
Greek epic poet
Alike he thwarts the hospitable end
Who drives the free or stays the hasty friend;
True friendship's laws are by this rule express'd,
Welcome the coming, speed the parting guest.

Odyssey

Kennedy, A.L. (1965–)
Scottish novelist
On book promotion tours
You are put up in Five-Star-Hotel land, when you
come from One-Star-Hotel land – you can't even
afford to go out of the door. So you go to the
bookshop, you drink sour wine, you talk to
people who don't want to talk to you, and you
go back to your hotel room with a club sandwich,
and watch a documentary on East Timor …

Sunday Herald, 1999

Leacock, Stephen (1869–1944)
English-born Canadian humorist, writer and economist
The landlady of a boarding-house is a parallelogram
– that is, an oblong angular figure, which cannot be
described, but which is equal to anything.

Literary Lapses (1910)

Pope, Alexander (1688–1744)
English poet, translator and editor
True friendship's laws are by this rule express'd,
Welcome the coming, speed the parting guest.

The Odyssey

Proverb
A guest always brings pleasure: if not the arrival,
the departure.

Portuguese proverb

The first day a guest, the second day a guest,
the third day a calamity.

Runyon, Damon (1884–1946)
US writer
A free-loader is a confirmed guest. He is the
man who is always willing to come to dinner.

Short Takes (1946)

Saki (1870–1916)
Burmese-born British writer
By insisting on having your bottle pointing to the
north when the cork is being drawn, and calling
the waiter Max, you may induce an impression on
your guests which hours of laboured boasting
might be powerless to achieve. For this purpose,
however, the guests must be chosen as carefully
as the wine.

The Chronicles of Clovis (1911)

Sickert, Walter (1860–1942)
German-born British painter and writer
To Denton Welch
Come again when you can't stay so long.

In D. Welch, 'Sickert at St Peter's', *Horizon*, 1942

Smith, Sydney (1771–1845)
English clergyman, essayist, journalist and wit
Tory and Whig in turns shall be my host,
I taste no politics in boil'd and roast.

Letters, To John Murray, 1834

Smollett, Tobias (1721–1771)
Scottish writer, satirist, historian, traveller and physician
The painful ceremony of receiving and returning
visits.

The Adventures of Peregrine Pickle
(1751)

hotels

Tyler, Anne (1941–)
I've always thought a hotel ought to offer
optional small animals… I mean a cat to sleep on
your bed at night, or a dog of some kind to act
pleased when you come in. You ever notice how
a hotel room feels so lifeless?

The Accidental Tourist (1985)

house of lords

Anonymous
Catering manager of the House of Lords on what happened when the macaroons ran out.

I was summoned to see Lord Orr-Ewing and told that this was a most grave matter and must never be repeated.

The Times, 1999

Bagehot, Walter (1826–1877)
English economist and political philosopher

The House of Peers has never been a House where the most important peers were most important.

The English Constitution (1867)

A severe though not unfriendly critic of our institutions said that 'the cure for admiring the House of Lords was to go and look at it'.

The English Constitution (1867)

Charles II (1630–1685)
King of Great Britain and Ireland
On the Debates in the House of Lords on Lord Ross's Divorce Bill, 1670

Better than going to a play.

In A. Bryant, *King Charles II* (1931)

Cranborne, Robert Cecil, Lord (1946–)
English critic and writer
Member of the Cecil family, represented in the House of Lords since 1603

Thanks to Mr Blair, my family and I will be leaving British politics after a limited period of involvement.

The Observer, 1998

Disraeli, Benjamin (1804–1881)
English statesman and writer
Said to a fellow peer when moving on to the House of Lords

I am dead: dead, but in the Elysian fields.

In Monypenny and Buckle, *Life of Disraeli* (1920)

Hailsham, Quintin Hogg, Baron (1907–)
English Conservative politician and Lord Chancellor

When I'm sitting on the Woolsack in the House of Lords I amuse myself by saying 'Bollocks' sotto voce to the bishops.

The Observer, 1985

Healey, Denis (1917–)
English Labour politician

A statesman is a dead politician. I'm in the home of the living dead – the House of Lords.

The Sunday Times, 2000

Jay, Margaret, Baroness
English Labour politician; leader of the House of Lords
On her fellow members of the House of Lords

We haven't said they're all hopeless, but quite a few of them are.

The Times 1998

When I gave my big speech on the Lords, the longest letter I received was from a lady who wanted to know where I had bought my blouse.

The Times, 1999

Lloyd George, David (1863–1945)
British Liberal statesman

The House of Lords is not the watchdog of the constitution: it is Mr Balfour's poodle.

Speech, 1908

Every man has a House of Lords in his own head. Fears, prejudices, misconceptions – those are the peers, and they are hereditary.

Speech, Cambridge, 1927

Norfolk, Lord (1746–1815)
English Whig politician

I cannot be a good Catholic; I cannot go to heaven; and if a man is to go to the devil, he may as well go thither from the House of Lords as from any other place on earth.

In Henry Best, *Personal and Literary Memorials* (1829)

Onslow, Lord (1938–)
English Conservative politician
Opposing plans to reform the House of Lords

I will be sad, if I look up or down after my death and don't see my son asleep on the same benches on which I slept.

The Observer, 1998

Parris, Matthew (1949–)
British Conservative politician and journalist
On the House of Lords

Bishops are the unguided missiles of the Upper Chamber – unguided by human agency, anyway: you can never know what a bishop is about to say because all too often he does not know himself.

The Times, 1998

▶▶ ARISTOCRACY; GOVERNMENT; POLITICS

housework

Alcott, Louisa May (1832–1888)
US writer

Housekeeping ain't no joke.

Little Women (1868)

Beauvoir, Simone de (1908–1986)
French writer, feminist critic and philosopher

Few tasks are more like the torture of Sisyphus than housework, with its endless repetition ... The housewife wears herself out marking time:

she makes nothing, simply perpetuates the present.

The Second Sex (1949)

Binchy, Maeve (1940–)
Irish novelist
> I don't want to hear about ironing. I don't want to smell the iron. Why? I regard it as a badge of servitude.

The Times, 1998

Crisp, Quentin (1908–1999)
English writer, publicist and model
> There was no need to do any housework at all. After the first four years the dirt doesn't get any worse.

The Naked Civil Servant (1968)

Diller, Phyllis (1917–1974)
US comedian
> Cleaning your house while your kids are growing Is like shoveling the walk before it stops snowing.

Phyllis Diller's Housekeeping Hints

Gibbons, Stella (1902–1989)
English poet and novelist
> There's nothing like a thorn twig for cletterin' dishes.

Cold Comfort Farm (1932)

Gregory, Lady Isabella Augusta (1852–1932)
Irish dramatist, writer and translator
> I am so tired of housekeeping I dreamed I was being served up for my guests and awoke only when the knife was at my throat.

In Mary-Lou Kohfeldt, *Lady Gregory (1985)*

Oakley, Ann (1944–)
British sociologist
> Housework is work directly opposed to the possibility of human self-actualization.

Woman's Work: The Housewife, Past and Present (1974)

Thurber, James (1894–1961)
US humorist, writer and dramatist
> I was seized by the stern hand of Compulsion, that dark, unreasonable Urge that impels women to clean house in the middle of the night.

Alarms and Diversions

White, Patrick (1912–1990)
English-born Australian writer and dramatist
> The tragedy of domesticity, that avalanche of overcoats and boots.

The Aunt's Story (1948)

▶▶ FEMINISM; WOMEN

humanity and human nature

Auden, W.H. (1907–1973)
English poet, essayist, critic, teacher and dramatist
> Man is a history-making creature who can neither repeat his past nor leave it behind.

The Dyer's Hand (1963)

> Alone, alone, about a dreadful wood
> Of conscious evil runs a lost mankind,
> Dreading to find its Father.

'For the Time Being' (1945)

Austen, Jane (1775–1817)
English writer
> Human nature is so well disposed towards those who are in interesting situations, that a young person, who either marries or dies, is sure of being kindly spoken of.

Emma (1816)

Bacon, Francis (1561–1626)
English philosopher, essayist, politician and courtier
> There is in human nature generally more of the fool than of the wise.

Essays (1625)

> Nature is often hidden; sometimes overcome; seldom extinguished.

Essays (1625)

Beaumarchais (1732–1799)
French dramatist
> *Boire sans soif et faire l'amour en tout temps, madame, il n'y a que ça qui nous distingue des autres bêtes.*
> Drinking when we're not thirsty and making love all the time, madam, that is all there is to distinguish us from other animals.

Le Barbier de Seville (1775)

Beerbohm, Sir Max (1872–1956)
English satirist, cartoonist, critic and essayist
> Mankind is divisible into two great classes: hosts and guests.

Attr.

The Bible (King James Version)
> And God said, Let us make man in our image, after our likeness.

Genesis, 1:26

> Man that is born of a woman is of few days, and full of trouble.

Job, 14:1

> Man is born unto trouble, as the sparks fly upward.

Job, 5:7

> As for man, his days are as grass: as a flower of the field, so he flourisheth.

Psalms, 103:15

Blackstone, Sir William (1723–1780)
English judge, historian and politician
> Man was formed for society.
>> *Commentaries on the Laws of England* (1765–1769)

Borrow, George (1803–1881)
English writer and linguist
> My favourite, I might say, my only study, is man.
>> *The Bible in Spain* (1843)

Bradley, F.H. (1846–1924)
English philosopher
> It is good to know what a man is, and also what the world takes him for. But you do not understand him until you have learnt how he understands himself.
>> *Aphorisms* (1930)

Browne, Sir Thomas (1605–1682)
English physician, author and antiquary
> There is surely a piece of divinity in us, something that was before the elements, and owes no homage unto the sun.
>> *Religio Medici* (1643)

Bronowski, Jacob (1908–1974)
British scientist, writer and TV presenter
> Every animal leaves traces of what it was; man alone leaves traces of what he created.
>> *The Ascent of Man* (1973)

Brontë, Anne (1820–1849)
English writer and poet
> The human heart is like Indian rubber: a little swells it, but a great deal will not burst it.
>> *Agnes Grey* (1847)

Browne, Sir Thomas (1605–1682)
English physician, author and antiquary
> Man is a noble animal, splendid in ashes, and pompous in the grave.
>> *Hydriotaphia: Urn Burial* (1658)

Büchner, Georg (1813–1837)
German playwright
> *Puppen sind wir von unbekannten Gewalten am Draht gezogen; nichts, nichts wir selbst!*
> We are puppets on strings worked by unknown forces; we ourselves are nothing, nothing!
>> *Danton's Death* (1835)

Burns, Robert (1759–1796)
Scottish poet and song writer
> Man's inhumanity to man
> Makes countless thousands mourn!
>> 'Man was made to Mourn, a Dirge' (1784)

Butler, Samuel (1835–1902)
English writer, painter, philosopher and scholar
> 'Man wants but little here below' but likes that little good – and not too long in coming.
>> *Further Extracts from the Note-Books of Samuel Butler* (1934)

> Man is the only animal that can remain on friendly terms with the victims he intends to eat until he eats them.
>> *Samuel Butler's Notebooks* (1951)

Caine, Michael (1933–)
English actor
> The basic rule of human nature is that powerful people speak slowly and subservient people quickly – because if they don't speak fast nobody will listen to them.
>> *The Times*, 1992

Campbell, Roy (1901–1957)
South African poet and journalist
> I hate 'Humanity' and all such abstracts: but I love people. Lovers of 'Humanity' generally hate people and children, and keep parrots or puppy dogs.
>> *Light on a Dark Horse* (1951)

Camus, Albert (1913–1960)
Algerian-born French writer
> A single sentence will suffice for modern man: he fornicated and read the papers.
>> *The Fall* (1956)

Canning, George (1770–1827)
English Prime Minister, orator and poet
> Man, only – rash, refined, presumptuous man,
> Starts from his rank, and mars creation's plan.
>> 'Progress of Man' (1799)

Carlyle, Thomas (1795–1881)
Scottish historian, biographer, critic, and essayist
> Man is a Tool-using Animal … feeblest of bipeds! … Without Tools he is nothing, with Tools he is all.
>> *Sartor Resartus* (1834)

Catechism
The Shorter Catechism, approved 1648 by the General Assembly of the Church of Scotland
> Man's chief end is to glorify God, and to enjoy him forever.
>> Question 1

> All mankind by their fall lost communion with God, are under his wrath and curse, and so made liable to all the miseries in this life, to death itself, and to the pains of hell for ever.
>> Question 19

> No mere man since the fall is able in this life perfectly to keep the commandments of God, but doth daily break them in thought, word, and deed.
>> Question 82

Cervantes, Miguel de (1547–1616)
Spanish writer and dramatist
> *Cada uno es como Dios le hizo, y aun peor muchas veces.*

Every man is as God made him, and often even worse.

Don Quixote (1615)

Charron, Pierre (1541–1603)
French theologian and philosopher

> *La vraye science et la vray estude de l'homme, c'est l'homme.*
>
> The true science and the true study of man is man.
>
> *De la Sagesse* (1601)

Chesterton, G.K. (1874–1936)
English writer, poet and critic

> The human race, to which so many of my readers belong, has been playing at children's games from the beginning, and will probably do it till the end, which is a nuisance for the few people who grow up.
>
> *The Napoleon of Notting Hill* (1904)

> Individually, men may present a more or less rational appearance, eating, sleeping and scheming. But humanity as a whole is changeful, mystical, fickle and delightful. Men are men, but Man is a woman.
>
> *The Napoleon of Notting Hill* (1904)

Cleaver, Eldridge (1935–1998)

> You don't have to teach people to be human. You have to teach them how to stop being inhuman.
>
> *Conversations with Eldridge Cleaver* (1970)

Coleridge, Samuel Taylor (1772–1834)
English poet, philosopher and critic

> A Fall of some sort or other – the creation as it were, of the non-absolute – is the fundamental postulate of the moral history of man. Without this hypothesis, man is unintelligible; with it, every phenomenon is explicable.
>
> *Table-Talk* (1835)

Colton, Charles Caleb (c.1780–1832)
English clergyman and satirist

> Man is an embodied paradox, a bundle of contradictions.
>
> *Lacon* (1820)

Confucius (c.550–c.478 BC)
Chinese philosopher and teacher of ethics

> Men's natures are alike; it is their habits that carry them far apart.
>
> *Analects*

Dante Alighieri (1265–1321)
Italian poet

> Consider your origins: you were not made to live as brutes, but to pursue virtue and knowledge.
>
> *Divina Commedia* (1307), 'Inferno'

Disraeli, Benjamin (1804–1881)
English statesman and writer

Addressed to Bishop Wilberforce

> Man, my Lord, is a being born to believe.
>
> Speech, Meeting of Society for Increasing Endowments of Small Livings in the Diocese of Oxford, 1864

> Man is only truly great when he acts from the passions.
>
> *Coningsby* (1844)

Donleavy, J.P. (1926–)
US-born Irish writer and dramatist

> I got disappointed in human nature as well and gave it up because I found it too much like my own.
>
> *Fairy Tales of New York* (1961)

Donne, John (1572–1631)
English poet

> No man is an Island, entire of it self; every man is a piece of Continent, a part of the main; if a clod be washed away by the sea, Europe is the less, as well as if a promontory were, as well as if a manor of thy friends or of thine own were; any man's death diminishes me, because I am involved in Mankind;
>
> And therefore never send to know for whom the bell tolls; it tolls for thee.
>
> *Devotions upon Emergent Occasions* (1624)

Eliot, George (1819–1880)
English writer and poet

> There is a great deal of unmapped country within us which would have to be taken into account in an explanation of our gusts and storms.
>
> *Daniel Deronda* (1876)

Eliot, T.S. (1888–1965)
US-born British poet, verse dramatist and critic

> Human kind
> Cannot bear very much reality.
>
> *Four Quartets* (1944)

Franklin, Benjamin (1706–1790)
US statesman, scientist, political critic and printer

> Man is a tool-making animal.
>
> In Boswell, *The Life of Samuel Johnson* (1791)

Froude, James Anthony (1818–1894)
English historian and scholar

> Wild animals never kill for sport. Man is the only one to whom the torture and death of his fellow creatures is amusing in itself.
>
> *Oceana, or England and her Colonies* (1886)

Fry, Christopher (1907–)
English verse dramatist, theatre director and translator

> Over all the world
> Men move unhoming, and eternally

Concerned: a swarm of bees who have lost their queen.

Venus Unobserved (1950)

Goldsmith, Oliver (c.1728–1774)
Irish dramatist, poet and writer

Man wants but little here below,
Nor wants that little long.

The Vicar of Wakefield (1766)

Gorky, Maxim (1868–1936)
Russian writer, dramatist and revolutionary

Man and man alone is, I believe, the creator of all things and all ideas.

Attr.

Greville, Fulke (1554–1628)
English poet, dramatist, biographer, courtier and politician

Oh wearisome Condition of Humanity!
Borne under one Law, to another, bound:
Vainely begot, and yet forbidden vanity,
Created sicke, commanded to be sound.

Mustapha (1609)

Hazlitt, William (1778–1830)
English writer and critic

Man is an intellectual animal, and therefore an everlasting contradiction to himself. His senses centre in himself, his ideas reach to the ends of the universe; so that he is torn in pieces between the two, without a possibility of its ever being otherwise.

Characteristics (1823)

Herbert, George (1593–1633)
English poet and priest

Man is God's image, but a poore man is Christ's stamp to boot.

The Temple (1633)

Johnson, Samuel (1709–1784)
English lexicographer, poet, critic, conversationalist and essayist

Sir, are you so grossly ignorant of human nature, as not to know that a man may be very sincere in good principles without having good practice?

In Boswell, *Journal of a Tour to the Hebrides* (1785)

Jung, Carl Gustav (1875–1961)
Swiss psychiatrist and pupil of Freud

We need more understanding of human nature, because the only real danger that exists is man himself … We know nothing of man, far too little. His psyche should be studied because we are the origin of all coming evil.

BBC television interview, 1959

Kant, Immanuel (1724–1804)
German idealist philosopher

Aus so krummen Holze, als woraus der Mensch gemacht ist, kann nichts ganz Gerades gezimmert werden.
No straight thing can ever be formed from timber as crooked as that from which humanity is made.

Idea for a General History with a Cosmopolitan purpose (1784)

Ob … der Mensch nun von Natur moralisch gut oder böse ist? Keines von beiden, denn er ist von Natur gar kein moralisches Wesen; er wird dieses nur, wenn seine Vernunft sich bis zu den Begriffen der Pflicht und des Gesetzes erhebt.
Is man by nature morally good or evil? Neither, for he is by nature not a moral being; he only becomes such when his reason is raised to the concepts of duty and law.

On Pedagogy (1803)

Keats, John (1795–1821)
English poet

Scenery is fine – but human nature is finer.

Letter to Benjamin Bailey, 13 March 1818

Upon the whole I dislike Mankind: whatever people on the other side of the question may advance they cannot deny that they are always surprised at hearing of a good action and never of a bad one.

Letter to Georgiana Keats, 13–28 January, 1820

Kingsmill, Hugh (1889–1949)
English critic and writer

It is difficult to love mankind unless one has a reasonable private income and when one has a reasonable private income one has better things to do than loving mankind.

In R. Ingrams, *God's Apology* (1977)

La Bruyère, Jean de (1645–1696)
French satirist

La plupart des hommes emploient la meilleure partie de leur vie à rendre l'autre misérable.
Most men spend the best part of their lives in making their remaining years unhappy.

Les caractères ou les moeurs de ce siècle (1688)

Lawrence, D.H. (1885–1930)
English writer, poet and critic

Ideal mankind would abolish death, multiply itself million upon million, rear up city upon city, save every parasite alive, until the accumulation of mere existence is swollen to a horror.

St Mawr (1925)

Lee, Nathaniel (c.1653–1692)
English dramatist

Man, false man, smiling, destructive man.

Theodosius (1680)

Longfellow, Henry Wadsworth (1807–1882)
US poet and writer

Ships that pass in the night, and speak each
other in passing;
Only a signal shown and a distant voice in the
darkness;
So on the ocean of life we pass and speak one
another,
Only a look and a voice; then darkness again
and a silence.

Tales of a Wayside Inn (1863–1874)

Machiavelli (1469–1527)
Florentine statesman, political theorist and historian
Dio fa gli uomini, è' s'appaiono.
God creates men, but they choose each other.
The Mandrake (1518)

Men sooner forget the death of their father than
the loss of their possessions.
The Prince, 1532

Maugham, William Somerset (1874–1965)
English writer, dramatist and physician
I'll give you my opinion of the human race. …
Their heart's in the right place, but their head is
a thoroughly inefficient organ.
The Summing Up (1938)

Millay, Edna St Vincent (1892–1950)
US poet and dramatist
Man has never been the same since God died.
He has taken it very hard. Why, you'd think it
was only yesterday,
The way he takes it.
Not that he says much, but he laughs much
louder than he used to,
And he can't bear to be left alone even for a
minute, and he can't
Sit still.
Conversation at Midnight
(1937)

Monash, Sir John (1865–1931)
Australian military commander
Nothing man does to the animal creation is
equal to the cruelties he commits on his own
kind.
The Seals

Montaigne, Michel de (1533–1592)
French essayist and moralist
*L'homme est bien insensé. Il ne saurait forger un ciron,
et forge des Dieux à douzaines.*
Man is quite insane. He wouldn't know how to
create a maggot, yet he creates Gods by the
dozen.
Essais (1580)

Nietzsche, Friedrich Wilhelm (1844–1900)
German philosopher, critic and poet
*Wie? ist der Mensch nur ein Fehlgriff Gottes? Oder
Gott nur ein Fehlgriff des Meschen?*
What? is man only a mistake made by God, or

God only a mistake made by man?
Twilight of the Idols (1889)

O'Brien, Flann (1911–1966)
Irish novelist and journalist
The pocket was the first instinct of humanity and
was used long years before the human race had
a trousers between them – the quiver for arrows
is one example and the pocket of the kangaroo
is another.
At Swim-Two-Birds (1939)

Orwell, George (1903–1950)
English writer and critic
The high sentiments always win in the end,
leaders who offer blood, toil, tears and sweat
always get more out of their followers than
those who offer safety and a good time. When it
comes to the pinch, human beings are heroic.
Horizon, 1941

Man is the only creature that consumes without
producing.
Animal Farm (1945)

Pascal, Blaise (1623–1662)
French philosopher and scientist
*L'homme n'est qu'un roseau, le plus faible de la nature;
mais c'est un roseau pensant.*
Man is only a reed, the feeblest thing in nature;
but he is a thinking reed.
Pensées (1670)

Plautus, Titus Maccius (c.254–184 BC)
Roman comic dramatist
Lupus est homo homini.
Man is a wolf to man.
Asinaria

Pope, Alexander (1688–1744)
English poet, translator and editor
Know then thyself, presume not God to scan;
The proper study of Mankind is Man.
Plac'd on this isthmus of a middle state,
A being darkly wise, and rudely great:
With too much knowledge for the Sceptic side,
With too much weakness for the Stoic's pride,
He hangs between; in doubt to act or rest,
In doubt to deem himself a God, or Beast;
In doubt his Mind or Body to prefer,
Born but to die, and reas'ning but to err;
Alike in ignorance, his reason such,
Whether he thinks too little or too
much.
An Essay on Man (1733)

Created half to rise, and half to fall;
Great lord of all things, yet a prey to all;
Sole judge of truth, in endless error hurl'd:
The glory, jest, and riddle of the world!
An Essay on Man (1733)

Pound, Ezra (1885–1972)
US poet
> When I carefully consider the curious habits of
> dogs
> I am compelled to conclude
> That man is the superior animal.
>
> When I consider the curious habits of man
> I confess, my friend, I am puzzled.
>> 'Meditatio' (1916)

Protagoras (c.485–c.410 BC)
> Man is the measure of all things.
>> In Plato, *Theaetetus*

Quarles, Francis (1592–1644)
English poet, writer and royalist
> No man is born unto himself alone;
> Who lives unto himself, he lives to none.
>> 'Esther' (1621)
>
> Man is Heaven's masterpiece.
>> *Emblems* (1635)
>
> Man is man's A.B.C. There is none that can
> Read God aright, unless he first spell Man.
>> *Hieroglyphics of the Life of Man* (1638)

Raleigh, Sir Walter A. (1861–1922)
English scholar, critic and essayist
> I wish I loved the Human Race;
> I wish I loved its silly face;
> I wish I liked the way it walks;
> I wish I liked the way it talks;
> And when I'm introduced to one,
> I wish I thought What Jolly Fun!
>> 'Wishes of an Elderly Man' (1923)

Rousseau, Jean-Jacques (1712–1778)
Swiss-born French philosopher, educationist and essayist
> *La nature a fait l'homme heureux et bon, mais … la
> société le déprave et le rend misérable.*
> Nature made man happy and good, but …
> society corrupts him and makes him miserable.
>> *Rousseau juge de Jean-Jacques*

Ruskin, John (1819–1900)
English art critic, philosopher and reformer
> No human being, however great, or powerful,
> was ever so free as a fish.
>> *The Two Paths* (1859)

Sartre, Jean-Paul (1905–1980)
French philosopher, writer, dramatist and critic
> *Ainsi, il n'y a pas de nature humaine, puisqu'il n'y a pas
> de Dieu pour la concevoir.*
> So there is no human nature, since there is no
> God to conceive it.
>> *Existentialism and Humanism* (1946)

Schiller, Johann Christoph Friedrich (1759–1805)
German writer, dramatist, poet and historian
> *Der zahlreichere Teil der Menschen wird durch den*

> *Kampf mit der Not viel zu sehr ermüdet und
> abgespannt, als dass er sich zu einem neuen und
> härtern Kampf mit dem Irrtum aufraffen sollte.*
> The greater part of humanity is far too weary
> and worn down by the struggle with want to
> rouse itself for a new and harder struggle with
> error.
>> *On the Aesthetic Education of Man* (1793–1795)
>
> *Das Herz und nicht die Meinung ehrt den Mann.*
> Man is honoured by his heart and not by his
> opinions.
>> *Wallensteins Tod* (1801)

Shakespeare, William (1564–1616)
English dramatist, poet and actor
> What a piece of work is a man! How noble in
> reason! how infinite in faculties! in form and
> moving, how express and admirable! in action,
> how like an angel! in apprehension, how like a
> god! the beauty of the world! the paragon of
> animals!
>> *Hamlet*, II.ii
>
> Roses have thorns, and silver fountains mud;
> Clouds and eclipses stain both moon and sun,
> And loathsome canker lives in sweetest bud.
> All men make faults.
>> Sonnet 35

Shaw, George Bernard (1856–1950)
Irish socialist, writer, dramatist and critic
> Man can climb to the highest summits; but he
> cannot dwell there long.
>> *Candida* (1898)

Solzhenitsyn, Alexander (1918–)
Russian writer, dramatist and historian
> The salvation of mankind lies only in making
> everything the concern of everyone.
>> Nobel Lecture, 1970

Sophocles (496–406 BC)
Greek dramatist
> Of wonders there are many, but none more
> wonderful than man.
>> *Antigone*

Taine, Hippolyte Adolphe (1828–1893)
French writer and philosopher
> *On peut considérer l'homme comme un animal
> d'espèce supérieure qui produit des philosophies et
> des poèmes à peu près comme les vers à soie font
> leurs cocons et comme les abeilles font leurs ruches.*
> Man can be considered as a superior animal who
> produces philosophies and poems much as
> silkworms construct their cocoons and bees their
> hives.
>> *La Fontaine and his Fables*, 1860

Temple, William (1881–1944)
Anglican prelate, social reformer and writer

It is not the ape, nor the tiger in man that I fear, it is the donkey.

Attr.

Terence (c.190–159 BC)
Carthaginian-born Roman dramatist

Homo sum; humani nil a me alienum puto.
I am a man, I count nothing human indifferent to me.

Heauton Timoroumenos

Tertz, Abram (1925–1997)
Russian writer and dissident

Man is always both much worse and much better than is expected of him. The fields of good are just as limitless as the wastelands of evil.

A Voice From the Chorus (1973)

Thoreau, Henry David (1817–1862)
US essayist, social critic and writer

The finest qualities of our nature, like the bloom on fruits, can be preserved only by the most delicate handling. Yet we do not treat ourselves nor one another delicately.

Walden (1854)

Twain, Mark (1835–1910)
US humorist, writer, journalist and lecturer

Adam was but human – this explains it all. He did not want the apple for the apple's sake, he wanted it only because it was forbidden.

Pudd'nhead Wilson (1894)

Man is the Only Animal that Blushes. Or needs to.

Following the Equator (1897)

Unamuno, Miguel de (1864–1936)
Spanish philosopher, poet and writer

El hombre, por ser hombre, por tener conciencia, es ya, respecto al burro o a un cangrejo, un animal enfermo. La conciencia es una enfermedad.
Man, because he is man, because he is conscious, is, in relation to the ass or to a crab, already a diseased animal. Consciousness is a disease.

The Tragic Sense of Life (1913)

Valéry, Paul (1871–1945)
French poet, mathematician and philosopher

A man is infinitely more complicated than his thoughts.

In Auden, *A Certain World*

Vaughan, Henry (1622–1695)
Welsh poet and physician

Man is the shuttle, to whose winding quest
And passage through these looms
God order'd motion, but ordain'd no rest.

Silex Scintillans (1650–1655)

Voltaire (1694–1778)
French philosopher, dramatist, poet, historian writer and critic

Si Dieu nous a fait à son image, nous le lui avons bien rendu.
If God has created us in his image, we have repaid him well.

Le Sottisier (c.1778)

Wachowski, Andy and **Wachowski, Larry**
US film directors and screenwriters
Agent Smith to Morpheus

I'd like to share a revelation that I've had during my time here. It came to me when I tried to classify your species. I realized that you're not actually mammals. Every mammal on this planet instinctively develops a natural equilibrium with the surrounding environment, but you humans do not. You move to an area, and you multiply, and multiply, until every natural resource is consumed. The only way you can survive is to spread to another area. There is another organism on this planet that follows the same pattern. A virus. Human beings are a disease, a cancer of this planet, you are a plague, and we are the cure.

The Matrix (film, 1999)

Waugh, Evelyn (1903–1966)
English writer and diarist

Instead of this absurd division into sexes they ought to class people as static and dynamic.

Decline and Fall (1928)

Wilde, Oscar (1854–1900)
Irish poet, dramatist, writer, critic and wit

It is absurd to divide people into good and bad. People are either charming or tedious.

Lady Windermere's Fan (1892)

Williams, Tennessee (1911–1983)
US dramatist and writer

We're all of us guinea pigs in the laboratory of God. Humanity is just a work in progress.

Camino Real (1953)

Yevtushenko, Yevgeny (1933–)
Russian poet

In the final analysis, humanity has only two ways out – either universal destruction or universal brotherhood.

'The Spirit of Elbe' (1966)

▶▶ LIFE

humility

Dickens, Charles (1812–1870)
English writer

I am well aware that I am the umblest person

going … My mother is likewise a very umble person. We live in a numble abode.

David Copperfield (1850)

Longford, Lord (1905–)
English politician, social reformer and biographer
In 1969 I published a small book on Humility. It was a pioneering work which has not, to my knowledge, been superseded.

Tablet, 1994

Stillingfleet, Edward (1635–1699)
'My Lord,' a certain nobleman is said to have observed, after sitting next to Richard Bentley at dinner, 'that chaplain of yours is a very extraordinary man.' Stillingfleet agreed, adding, 'Had he but the gift of humility, he would be the most extraordinary man in Europe.'

In R.J. White, *Dr Bentley*

Trollope, Anthony (1815–1882)
English writer, traveller and post office official
Not only humble but umble, which I look upon to be the comparative, or, indeed, superlative degree.

Doctor Thorne (1858)

humour

Addison, Joseph (1672–1719)
English essayist, poet, playwright and statesman
If we may believe our logicians, man is distinguished from all other creatures by the faculty of laughter.

The Spectator, 1712

Ayckbourn, Alan (1939–)
English dramatist and theatre director
Few women care to be laughed at and men not at all, except for large sums of money.

The Norman Conquests (1975)

Barker, Ronnie (1929–)
English comedian
The marvellous thing about a joke with a double meaning is that it can only mean one thing.

Attr.

Beaumarchais (1732–1799)
French dramatist
Je me presse de rire de tout, de peur d'être obligé d'en pleurer.
I make myself laugh at everything, for fear of having to cry.

Le Barbier de Seville (1775)

Berlin, Irving (1888–1989)
Russian-born US musical and songwriter
Telegram message to Groucho Marx on his seventy-first birthday

The world would not be in such a snarl, had Marx been Groucho instead of Karl.

Attr.

Bono, Edward De (1933–)
British physician and writer
Humour is by far the most significant activity of the human brain.

Daily Mail, 1990

Borge, Victor (1909–)
Danish-born US entertainer and pianist
Humour [is] something that thrives between man's aspirations and his limitations. There is more logic in humour than in anything else. Because, you see, humour is truth.

The Times, 1984

Bracken, Brendan, First Viscount (1901–1958)
Irish journalist and Conservative politician
It's a good deed to forget a poor joke.

The Observer, 1943

Brown, Rita Mae (1944–)
US writer and poet
Humour comes from self-confidence. There's an aggressive element to wit.

Starting From Scratch (1988)

Brown, Thomas Edward (1830–1897)
Manx poet, teacher and curate
A rich man's joke is always funny.

'The Doctor' (1887)

Butler, Samuel (1835–1902)
English writer, painter, philosopher and scholar
The most perfect humour and irony is generally quite unconscious.

Life and Habit (1877)

Carlyle, Thomas (1795–1881)
Scottish historian, biographer, critic, and essayist
No man who has once heartily and wholly laughed can be altogether irreclaimably bad.

Sartor Resartus (1834)

Chamfort, Nicolas (1741–1794)
French writer
La plus perdue de toutes les journées est celle où l'on n'a pas ri.
The most wasted of all days is the day one did not laugh.

Maximes et pensées (1796

Chesterfield, Lord (1694–1773)
English politician and letter writer
In my mind, there is nothing so illiberal and so ill-bred, as audible laughter … I am neither of a melancholy, nor a cynical disposition; and am as willing, and as apt, to be pleased as anybody; but I am sure that, since I have had the full use of my reason, nobody has ever heard me laugh.

Letter to his son, 1748

Churchill, Charles (1731–1764)
English poet, political writer and clergyman
> A joke's a very serious thing.
>> *The Ghost* (1763)

Colby, Frank Moore (1865–1925)
US editor, historian and economist
> Men will confess to treason, murder, arson, false teeth, or a wig. How many of them will own up to a lack of humour?
>> *Essays*

Colette (1873–1954)
French writer
> *Une totale absence d'humour rend la vie impossible.*
> A total absence of humour makes life impossible.
>> *Chance Acquaintances*

Congreve, William (1670–1729)
English dramatist
> It is the business of a comic poet to paint the vices and follies of human kind.
> There is nothing more unbecoming a man of quality than to laugh; Jesu, 'tis such a vulgar expression of the passion!
>> *The Double Dealer* (1694)

Cook, Peter (1937–1995)
English comedian and writer
> There's terrific merit in having no sense of humour, no sense of irony, practically no sense of anything at all. If you're born with these so-called defects you have a very good chance of getting to the top.
>> In Ronald Bergan, *Beyond the Fringe...and Beyond* (1989)

Dennis, John (1657–1734)
English critic and dramatist
> A man who could make so vile a pun would not scruple to pick a pocket.
>> *The Gentleman's Magazine*, 1781

Dodd, Ken (1931–)
English comedian, singer, entertainer and actor
Commenting on Freud's theory that a good joke will lead to great relief and elation
> The trouble with Freud is that he never played the Glasgow Empire Saturday night after Rangers and Celtic had both lost.
>> TV interview, 1965

Eliot, George (1819–1880)
English writer and poet
> A difference of taste in jokes is a great strain on the affections.
>> *Daniel Deronda* (1876)

Griffiths, Trevor (1935–)
English dramatist
> Comedy is medicine.
>> *The Comedians* (1979)

Hobbes, Thomas (1588–1679)
Political philosopher
> Laughter is nothing else but sudden glory arising from some sudden conception of some eminency in ourselves, by comparison with infirmity of others, or with our own formerly.
>> *Human Nature* (1650)

Humphries, Barry (1934–)
Australian entertainer
> The only people really keeping the spirit of irony alive in Australia are taxi-drivers and homosexuals.
>> *Australian Women's Weekly*, 1983

La Bruyère, Jean de (1645–1696)
French satirist
> *Il faut rire avant que d'être heureux, de peur de mourir sans avoir ri.*
> One must laugh before one is happy, for fear of dying without ever having laughed at all.
>> *Les caractères ou les moeurs de ce siècle* (1688)

Lamb, Charles (1775–1834)
English essayist, critic and letter writer
Referring to the nature of a pun
> It is a pistol let off at the ear; not a feather to tickle the intellect.
>> *Last Essays of Elia* (1833)

Lewis, C.S. (1898–1963)
Irish-born English academic, writer and critic
> The coarse joke proclaims that we have here an animal which finds its own animality either objectionable or funny.
>> *Miracles* (c.1936)

Lichtenberg, Georg (1742–1799)
German physicist, satirist and writer
> A person reveals his character by nothing so clearly as the joke he resents.
>> Attr.

Lorenz, Konrad (1903–1989)
Austrian zoologist and psychologist
> Humour and knowledge are the two great hopes of our culture.
>> *Reader's Digest*, 1978

Muggeridge, Malcolm (1903–1990)
English writer
> It is not for nothing that, in the English language alone, to accuse someone of trying to be funny is highly abusive.
>> *Tread Softly* (1966)

> Good taste and humour ... are a contradiction in terms, like a chaste whore.
>> *Time*, 1953

Orwell, George (1903–1950)
English writer and critic
> Whatever is funny is subversive, every joke is

ultimately a custard pie ... A dirty joke is not ...
a serious attack upon morality, but it is a sort of
mental rebellion, a momentary wish that things
were otherwise.

'The Art of Donald McGill'
(1941)

Owen, Roderic (1921–)
English playwright and novelist
> The important thing is to know when to laugh,
> or since laughing is somewhat undignified, to
> smile.

The Golden Bubble

Priestley, J.B. (1894–1984)
English writer, dramatist and critic
> Comedy, we may say, is society protecting itself
> – with a smile.

George Meredith (1926)

Renard, Jules (1864–1910)
French writer and dramatist
> *L'ironie est la pudeur de l'humanité.*
> Irony is humanity's sense of propriety.

Journal, 1892

Rogers, Will (1879–1935)
US humorist, actor, rancher, writer and wit
> Everything is funny as long as it is happening to
> someone else.

The Illiterate Digest (1924)

Runcie, Robert (1921–2000)
Archbishop of Canterbury 1980–91
> People who have not got a sense of humour
> shoudn't ever be put in charge.

In *The Guardian*, 2000

Shakespeare, William (1564–1616)
English dramatist, poet and actor
> A jest's prosperity lies in the ear
> Of him that hears it, never in the tongue
> Of him that makes it.

Love's Labour Lost, V.ii

Shaw, George Bernard (1856–1950)
Irish socialist, writer, dramatist and critic
> My way of joking is to tell the truth. It's the
> funniest joke in the world.

John Bull's Other Island
(1907)

Sterne, Laurence (1713–1768)
Irish-born English writer and clergyman
> 'Tis no extravagant arithmetic to say, that for
> every ten jokes, – thou hast got a hundred
> enemies.

Tristram Shandy

> I live in a constant endeavour to fence against
> the infirmities of ill health, and other evils of life,
> by mirth; being firmly persuaded that every time
> a man smiles, – but much more so, when he

laughs, it adds something to this Fragment of
Life.

Tristram Shandy

Stevenson, Robert Louis (1850–1894)
Scottish writer, poet and essayist
> Nothing like a little judicious levity.

The Wrong Box (1889)

Swift, Jonathan (1667–1745)
Irish satirist, poet, essayist and cleric
> Humour is odd, grotesque, and wild,
> Only by affectation spoil'd;
> 'Tis never by invention got,
> Men have it when they know it not.

'To Mr Delany' (1718)

Thurber, James (1894–1961)
US humorist, writer and dramatist
> Humour is emotional chaos remembered in
> tranquillity.

Attr.

Tucholsky, Kurt (1890–1935)
German satirist and writer
> *Humor ist ein Element, das dem deutschen Menschen*
> *abhanden gekommen ist.*
> Humour is an element which the German man
> has lost.

'What may Satire do –?' (1973)

Walton, Izaak (1593–1683)
English writer
> I love such mirth as does not make friends
> ashamed to look upon one another next
> morning.

The Compleat Angler (1653)

Wilcox, Ella Wheeler (1850–1919)
US poet and writer
> Laugh and the world laughs with you;
> Weep, and you weep alone;
> For the sad old earth must borrow its mirth,
> But has trouble enough of its own.

'Solitude' (1917)

Wodehouse, P.G. (1881–1975)
English humorist and writer
> She had a penetrating sort of laugh. Rather like
> a train going into a tunnel.

The Inimitable Jeeves (1923)

hunger

Aristophanes (c.445–385 BC)
Greek playwright
> Hunger knows no friend but its feeder.

The Wasps

Henry, Matthew (1662–1714)
English Nonconformist minister

Those that die by famine die by inches.

An Exposition of the Old and New Testament (1706)

Kennedy, John F. (1917–1963)
US Democrat President

The war against hunger is truly mankind's war of liberation.

Speech, 4 June 1963

La Fontaine, Jean de (1621–1695)
French poet and fabulist

A hungry stomach will not listen.

Fables, 'Le milan et le rossignol'

Marie-Antoinette (1755–1793)
Queen of France

On being told the people had no bread to eat

Let them eat cake.

Attr.

Proverbs

The full man doesn't understand the wants of the hungry.

Hunger finds no fault with the cookery.

Hunger is the best sauce.

Stevenson, Adlai (1900–1965)
US lawyer, statesman and United Nations ambassador

A hungry man is not a free man.

Speech, 1962

Wilson, Woodrow (1856–1924)
US Democrat President

No one can worship God or love his neighbour on an empty stomach.

Speech, 1912

▶▶ DESIRE; FOOD

hunting

Cowper, William (1731–1800)
English poet, hymn and letter writer

Of hunting

Detested sport,
That owes its pleasures to another's pain.

The Task (1785)

Muir, Edwin (1887–1959)
Scottish poet, critic, translator and writer

On hunting trophies

To find these abominations on the walls of Highland hotels, among people of such delicacy in other things, is peculiarly revolting.

Scottish Journey

Pepys, Samuel (1633–1703)
English diarist, naval administrator and politician

Most of their discourse was about hunting, in a

dialect I understand very little.

Diary, November 1663

Seal, Christopher (1880–1954)
British churchman

Hunting people tend to be churchgoers on a higher level than ordinary folk. One has a religious experience in the field.

The Times, 1993

Surtees, R.S. (1805–1864)
English writer

'Unting is all that's worth living for – all time is lost wot is not spent in 'unting – it is like the hair we breathe – if we have it not we die – it's the sport of kings, the image of war without its guilt, and only five-and-twenty per cent of its danger.

Handley Cross (1843)

Tell me a man's a fox-hunter, and I loves him at once.

Handley Cross (1843)

Wilde, Oscar (1854–1900)
Irish poet, dramatist, writer, critic and wit

The English country gentleman galloping after a fox – the unspeakable in full pursuit of the uneatable.

A Woman of No Importance (1893)

hypocrisy

Bacon, Francis (1561–1626)
English philosopher, essayist, politician and courtier

It is the wisdom of the crocodiles, that shed tears when they would devour.

'Of Wisdom for a Man's Self' (1625)

Even innocence itself has many a wile,
And will not dare to trust itself with truth,
And love is taught hypocrisy from youth.

Don Juan (1824)

Burns, Robert (1759–1796)
Scottish poet and song writer

Their sighin, cantin, grace-proud faces,
Their three-mile prayers, an' hauf-mile graces.

'To the Rev. John M'Math' (1785)

Chaucer, Geoffrey (c.1340–1400)
English poet, public servant and courtier

The smylere with the knyf under the cloke.

The Canterbury Tales (1387)

Chesterton, G.K. (1874–1936)
English writer, poet and critic

We ought to see far enough into a hypocrite to see even his sincerity.

Heretics (1905)

Churchill, Charles (1731–1764)
English poet, political writer and clergyman
Keep up appearances; there lies the test;
The world will give thee credit for the rest.
Outward be fair, however foul within;
Sin if thou wilt, but then in secret sin.

'Night' (1761)

Dickens, Charles (1812–1870)
English writer
With affection beaming in one eye, and
calculation shining out of the other.

Martin Chuzzlewit (1844)

Emerson, Ralph Waldo (1803–1882)
US poet, essayist, transcendentalist and teacher
The book written against fame and learning has
the author's name on the title-page.

Journals

Gay, John (1685–1732)
English poet, dramatist and librettist
An open foe may prove a curse,
But a pretended friend is worse.

Fables (1727)

Hawthorne, Nathaniel (1804–1864)
US allegorical writer
I have laughed in bitterness and agony of heart,
at the contrast between what I seem and what I
am!

The Scarlet Letter (1850)

Kerr, Jean (1923–)
US writer and dramatist
Man is the only animal that learns by being
hypocritical. He pretends to be polite and then,
eventually, he becomes polite.

Finishing Touches
(1973)

La Rochefoucauld (1613–1680)
French writer
*L'hypocrisie est un hommage que le vice rend à la
vertu.*
Hypocrisy is a homage that vice pays to virtue.

Maximes (1678)

Maugham, William Somerset (1874–1965)
English writer, dramatist and physician
Hypocrisy is the most difficult and nerve-racking
vice that any man can pursue; it needs an
unceasing vigilance and a rare detachment of
spirit. It cannot, like adultery or gluttony, be
practised at spare moments; it is a whole-time job.

Cakes and Ale (1930)

Milton, John (1608–1674)
English poet, libertarian and pamphleteer
For neither Man nor Angel can discern
Hypocrisie, the onely evil that walks
Invisible, except to God alone.

Paradise Lost (1667)

Tolstoy, Leo (1828–1910)
Russian writer, essayist, philosopher and moralist
Hypocrisy in anything whatever may deceive the
cleverest and most penetrating man, but the
least wide-awake of children recognizes it, and is
revolted by it, however ingeniously it may be
disguised.

Attr.

Wilde, Oscar (1854–1900)
Irish poet, dramatist, writer, critic and wit
I hope that you have not been leading a double
life, pretending to be wicked and being really
good all the time. That would be hypocrisy.

The Importance of Being Earnest (1895)

▶▶ DECEPTION

I

idealism

Bellow, Saul (1915–)
Canadian-born US Jewish writer
> The great enemy of progressive ideals is not the Establishment but the limitless dullness of those who take them up.
>> *To Jerusalem and Back: A Personal Account* (1976)

Dalai Lama (1935–)
Spiritual and temporal leader of Tibet
> History shows that most of the positive or beneficial developments in human society have occurred as the result of care and compassion. Consider, for example, the abolition of the slave trade – ideals are the engine of progress.
>> *The Times*, June 1999

King, Martin Luther (1929–1968)
US civil rights leader and Baptist minister
> I submit to you that if a man hasn't discovered something he will die for, he isn't fit to live.
>> Speech in Detroit, June 23, 1963

Lawrence, D.H. (1885–1930)
English writer, poet and critic
> Away with all ideals. Let each individual act spontaneously from the for ever incalculable prompting of the creative wellhead within him. There is no universal law.
>> *Phoenix* (1936)

McCartney, Paul (1942–)
English rock musician
> The issues are the same. We wanted peace on earth, love, and understanding between everyone around the world. We have learned that change comes slowly.
>> *The Observer*, 1987

Tarkington, Booth (1869–1946)
US writer and dramatist
> An ideal wife is any woman who has an ideal husband.
>> Attr.

Thatcher, Margaret (1925–)
English Conservative Prime Minister
> If a woman like Eva Peron with no ideals can get that far, think how far I can go with all the ideals that I have.
>> *The Sunday Times*, 1980

ideas

Alain (Emile-Auguste Chartier) (1868–1951)
French philosopher, teacher and essayist
> *Rien n'est plus dangereux qu'une idée, quand on n'a qu'une idée.*
> Nothing is more dangerous than an idea, when you only have one idea.
>> *Remarks on Religion* (1938)

> There are only two kinds of scholars; those who love ideas and those who hate them.
>> In Alan L. Mackay, *The Harvest of a Quiet Eye* (1977)

Bagehot, Walter (1826–1877)
English economist and political philosopher
> One of the greatest pains to human nature is the pain of a new idea.
>> *Physics and Politics* (1872)

Bowen, Elizabeth (1899–1973)
Irish writer
> One can live in the shadow of an idea without grasping it.
>> *The Heat of the Day* (1949)

Emerson, Ralph Waldo (1803–1882)
US poet, essayist, transcendentalist and teacher
> It is a lesson which all history teaches wise men, to put trust in ideas, and not in circumstances.
>> *Miscellanies* (1856

Geddes, Patrick (1854–1932)
Scottish biologist and sociologist
> When an idea is dead it is embalmed in a textbook.
>> In Boardman, *The Worlds of Patrick Geddes* (1978)

Holmes, Oliver Wendell, Jr (1841–1935)
US jurist and judge
> Many ideas grow better when transplanted into another mind than in the one where they sprang up.
>> In Bowen, *Yankee from Olympus* (1945)

Hugo, Victor (1802–1885)
French poet, writer, dramatist and politician
> *On résiste à l'invasion des armées; on ne résiste pas à l'invasion des idées.*
> One can resist the invasion of an army; but one cannot resist the invasion of ideas.
>> *Histoire d'un Crime* (1852)

Jarrell, Randall (1914–1965)
US poet, critic and translator
> It is better to entertain an idea than to take it home to live with you for the rest of your life.
>> *Pictures from an Institution* (1954)

Keynes, John Maynard (1883–1946)
English economist
> The difficulty lies, not in the new ideas, but in escaping the old ones, which ramify, for those brought up as most of us have been, into every corner of our minds.
>
> In K. Eric Drexler *Engines of Creation*, 1987

> The power of vested interests is vastly exaggerated compared with the gradual encroachment of ideas. Not, indeed, immediately … But, soon or late, it is ideas, not vested interests, which are dangerous for good or evil.
>
> *The General Theory of Employment, Interest and Money* (1936)

Lewis, Wyndham (1882–1957)
US-born British painter, critic and writer
> 'Dying for an idea,' again, sounds well enough, but why not let the idea die instead of you?
>
> *The Art of Being Ruled* (1926)

Lorenz, Konrad (1903–1989)
Austrian zoologist and psychologist
> *Überhaupt ist es für den Forscher ein guter Morgensport, täglich vor dem Frühstück eine Lieblingshypothese einzustampfen – das erhält jung.*
> In general it is a good morning exercise for a researcher to destroy a favourite hypothesis every day before breakfast – it keeps him young.
>
> *On Aggression* (1963)

MacDonald, Ramsay (1866–1937)
Scottish Labour politician, Prime Minister
> Society goes on and on and on. It is the same with ideas.
>
> Speech, 1935

Marquis, Don (1878–1937)
US columnist, satirist and poet
> An idea isn't responsible for the people who believe in it.
>
> *New York Sun*

Medawar, Sir Peter (1915–1987)
British zoologist and immunologist
> The human mind treats a new idea the way the body treats a strange protein – it rejects it.
>
> Attr.

Montagu, Lady Mary Wortley (1689–1762)
English letter writer, poet, traveller and introducer of smallpox inoculation
> General notions are generally wrong.
>
> Letter to her husband, Edward Wortley Montagu, 1710

Paxman, Jeremy (1950–)
English journalist, writer and broadcaster
> The English way with ideas is not to kill them but to let them die of neglect.
>
> *The Observer*, 'Sayings of the Year', 1998

Santayana, George (1863–1952)
Spanish-born US philosopher and writer
> For an idea ever to be fashionable is ominous, since it must afterwards be always old-fashioned.
>
> *Winds of Doctrine* (1913)

Shaw, George Bernard (1856–1950)
Irish socialist, writer, dramatist and critic
> This creature Man, who in his own selfish affairs is a coward to the backbone, will fight for an idea like a hero.
>
> *Man and Superman* (1903)

Steinbeck, John (1902–1968)
US writer
> Ideas are like rabbits. You get a couple and learn how to handle them, and pretty soon you have a dozen.
>
> Attr.

Sterne, Laurence (1713–1768)
Irish-born English writer and clergyman
> It is the nature of an hypothesis, when once a man has conceived it, that it assimilates every thing to itself as proper nourishment; and, from the first moment of your begetting it, it generally grows the stronger by every thing you see, hear, read, or understand. This is of great use.
>
> *Tristram Shandy* (1759–1767)

Swift, Jonathan (1667–1745)
Irish satirist, poet, essayist and cleric
> A nice man is a man of nasty ideas.
>
> *Thoughts on Various Subjects* (1711)

Unamuno, Miguel de (1864–1936)
Spanish philosopher, poet and writer
> *No suelen ser nuestras ideas las que nos hacen optimistas o pesimistas, sino que es nuestro optimismo o nuestro pesimismo, de origen fisiológico o patalógico quizás … el que hace nuestras ideas.*
> It is not normally our ideas which make us optimists or pessimists, but it is our optimism or our pessimism, which is perhaps of a physiological or pathological origin … which makes our ideas.
>
> *The Tragic Sense of Life* (1913)

▶▶ MIND; OPINIONS; THOUGHT

identity

Wilde, Oscar (1854–1900)
Irish poet, dramatist, writer, critic and wit
> Most people are other people. Their thoughts are someone else's opinions, their lives a mimicry, their passions a quotation.
>
> *De Profundis* (1897)

idleness and unemployment

Adams, Scott (1957–)
US cartoonist

> Of course I don't look busy, I did it right the first time.

The Dilbert Principle

Anonymous

> Doing nothing gets pretty tiresome because you can't stop and rest.

Boileau-Despréaux, Nicolas (1636–1711)
French writer

> *Le pénible fardeau de n'avoir rien à faire!*
> What a terrible burden it is to have nothing to do!

Epitres (c.1690)

Brasch, Charles Orwell (1909–1973)
New Zealand poet and editor
On walking on a week-day in Dunedin, 1938, when he was unemployed

> It is not only an offence against society to be seen in the streets flaunting the fact that one does not work like everyone else; it challenges the settled order of things, a threat that no right thinking New Zealander could tolerate. It makes one an object of suspicion, and more, an enemy.

Indirections: A Memoir 1909–1947 (1980)

Brummel, Beau (1778–1840)
English dandy and wit

> I always like to have the morning well-aired before I get up.

In Macfarlane, *Reminiscences of a Literary Life* (1917)

Chesterfield, Lord (1694–1773)
English politician and letter writer

> Idleness is only the refuge of weak minds, and the holiday of fools.

Letter to his son, 1749

Christie, Agatha (1890–1976)
English crime writer and playwright

> We owe most of our great inventions and most of the achievements of genius to idleness – either enforced or voluntary.

The Moving Finger (1942)

Cicero (106–43 BC)
Roman orator, statesman, essayist and letter writer

> *Numquam se minus otiosum esse quam cum otiosus, nec minus solum quam cum solus esset.*
> Never less idle than when free from work, nor less lonely than when completely alone.

De Officiis

Conran, Shirley (1932–)
English writer

> I make no secret of the fact that I would rather lie on a sofa than sweep beneath it. But you have to be efficient if you're going to be lazy.

Superwoman (1975)

Cowper, William (1731–1800)
English poet, hymn and letter writer

> How various his employments, whom the world
> Calls idle.

The Task (1785)

Defoe, Daniel (c.1661–1731)
English writer and critic

> A state of idleness is the very dregs of life.

The Life and Adventures of Robinson Crusoe (1719)

Eliot, George (1819–1880)
English writer and poet

> There's many a one would be idle if hunger didn't pinch him; but the stomach sets us to work.

Felix Holt (1866)

Ewart, Gavin (1916–1995)
English poet

> After Cambridge – unemployment. No one wanted much to know.
> Good degrees are good for nothing in the business world below.

'The Sentimental Education'

Farquhar, George (1678–1707)
Irish dramatist

> Says little, thinks less, and does – nothing at all, faith.

The Beaux' Stratagem (1707)

Fitzgerald, F. Scott (1896–1940)
US writer

> 'What'll we do with ourselves this afternoon?' cried Daisy, 'and the day after that, and the next thirty years?'.

The Great Gatsby (1925)

Furphy, Joseph (1843–1912)
Australian writer and poet

> Unemployed at last!

Such is Life (1903)

Hewett, Dorothy (1923–)
Australian dramatist and poet

> For dole bread is bitter bread
> Bitter bread and sour
> There's grief in the taste of it
> There's weevils in the flour.

'Weevils in the Flour'

Hoover, Herbert Clark (1874–1964)
US Republican President

> When a great many people are unable to find work, unemployment results.

In Boller, *Presidential Anecdotes* (1981)

Jerome, Jerome K. (1859–1927)
English writer and dramatist
> It is impossible to enjoy idling thoroughly unless one has plenty of work to do.
>> *Idle Thoughts of an Idle Fellow* (1886)

> George goes to sleep at a bank from ten to four each day, except Saturdays, when they wake him up and put him outside at two.
>> *Three Men in a Boat* (1889)

Johnson, Samuel (1709–1784)
English lexicographer, poet, critic, conversationalist and essayist
> Every man is, or hopes to be, an idler.
>> *The Idler* (1758–1760)

> If you are idle, be not solitary; if you are solitary, be not idle.
>> Letter to Boswell, 1779

Joseph, Jenny
British poet
> I was raised to feel that doing nothing was a sin. I had to learn to do nothing.
>> *The Observer*, 1998

Jowett, Benjamin (1817–1893)
English scholar, translator, essayist and priest
> Research! A mere excuse for idleness; it has never achieved, and will never achieve any results of the slightest value.
>> In Logan Pearsall Smith, *Unforgotten Years*

Kempis, Thomas à (c.1380–1471)
German mystic, monk and writer
> Never be completely idle, but be either reading, or writing, or praying, or meditating, or working at something useful for the community.
>> *De Imitatione Christi* (1892)

Lynes, J. Russel (1910–1991)
> Wasting time is negative, but there is something positive about idleness.
>> Attr.

Madan, Geoffrey (1895–1947)
English bibliophile
> The devil finds mischief still for hands that have not learnt how to be idle.
>> *Livre sans nom: Twelve Reflections* (1934)

Marx, Karl (1818–1883)
German political philosopher and economist; founder of Communism
> Without doubt machinery has greatly increased the number of well-to-do idlers.
>> *Das Kapital* (1867)

Maugham, William Somerset (1874–1965)
English writer, dramatist and physician
> It was such a lovely day I thought it was a pity to get up.
>> *Our Betters* (1923)

Nash, Ogden (1902–1971)
US poet
> I would live my life in nonchalance and insouciance
> Were it not for making a living, which is rather a nouciance.
>> 'Introspective Reflection' (1940)

Pope, Alexander (1688–1744)
English poet, translator and editor
> She marked thee there,
> Stretch'd on the rack of a too easy chair,
> And heard thy everlasting yawn confess
> The Pains and Penalties of idleness.
>> *The Dunciad* (1742)

Proverb
> The devil finds work for idle hands to do.

Samuel, Lord (1870–1963)
English Liberal statesman, philosopher and administrator
> To help the unemployed is not the same thing as dealing with unemployment.
>> *The Observer*, 1933

Sheridan, Richard Brinsley (1751–1816)
Irish dramatist, politician and orator
On a notice fixed to his door when he was a Secretary to the Treasury
> No applications can be received here on Sundays, nor any business done during the remainder of the week.
>> Attr. in Morwood, *The Life and Works of Sheridan* (1985)

Steele, Sir Richard (1672–1729)
Irish-born English writer, dramatist and politician
> The insupportable Labour of doing nothing.
>> *The Spectator*, 54, 1711

Stevenson, Robert Louis (1850–1894)
Scottish writer, poet and essayist
> Extreme busyness, whether at school or college, kirk or market, is a symptom of deficient vitality; and a faculty for idleness implies a catholic appetite and a strong sense of personal identity.
>> *Virginibus Puerisque* (1881)

Thurber, James (1894–1961)
US humorist, writer and dramatist
> It is better to have loafed and lost than never to have loafed at all.
>> *Fables for Our Time* (1940)

Ward, Artemus (1834–1867)
US humorist, journalist, editor and lecturer
> I am happiest when I am idle. I could live for months without performing any kind of labour, and at the expiration of that time I should feel fresh and vigorous enough to go right on in the

same way for numerous more months.

Artemus Ward in London (1867)

Watts, Isaac (1674–1748)
English hymn-writer, poet and minister

In works of labour, or of skill,
I would be busy too;
For Satan finds some mischief still
For idle hands to do.

Divine Songs for Children (1715)

▶▶ BED

ignorance

Anonymous

If ignorance is bliss, why aren't more people happy?

What you don't know will always hurt you.

First Law of Blissful Ignorance

A little ignorance can go a long way.

Gerrold's Law

Beveridge, William Henry (1879–1963)
British economist and social reformer

Ignorance is an evil weed, which dictators may cultivate among their dupes, but which no democracy can afford among its citizens.

Full Employment in a Full Society (1944)

Disraeli, Benjamin (1804–1881)
English statesman and writer

Mr Kremlin himself was distinguished for ignorance, for he had only one idea, – and that was wrong.

Sybil (1845)

Durrell, Sir Gerald (1925–1995)
English writer and naturalist

I said I liked being half-educated; you were so much more surprised at everything when you were ignorant.

My Family and Other Animals (1956)

Gray, Thomas (1716–1771)
English poet and scholar

Where ignorance is bliss,
'Tis folly to be wise.

'Ode on a Distant Prospect of Eton College' (1742)

Hope, Anthony (1863–1933)
English writer, dramatist and lawyer

I wish you would read a little poetry sometimes. Your ignorance cramps my conversation.

The Dolly Dialogues (1894)

King, Martin Luther (1929–1968)
US civil rights leader and Baptist minister

Nothing in all the world is more dangerous than

sincere ignorance and conscientious stupidity.

Strength to Love, 1963

Lombroso, Cesare (1853–1909)
Italian criminologist

L'uomo ignorante ama ciò che non capisce.
The ignorant man always loves that which he cannot understand.

The Man of Genius (1894)

Marlowe, Christopher (1564–1593)
English poet and dramatist

I count religion but a childish toy,
And hold there is no sin but ignorance.

The Jew of Malta (c.1592)

Monsarrat, Nicholas (1910–1979)
English novelist

You English … think we know damn nothing but I tell you we know damn all.

The Cruel Sea (1951)

Proverb

What you don't know can't hurt you.

Smith, Sydney (1771–1845)
English clergyman, essayist, journalist and wit

What you don't know would make a great book.

In Lady Holland, *Memoir* (1855)

Tolstoy, Leo (1828–1910)
Russian writer, essayist, philosopher and moralist

The most powerful weapon of ignorance – the diffusion of printed material.

War and Peace (1868–1869)

Wilde, Oscar (1854–1900)
Irish poet, dramatist, writer, critic and wit

Ignorance is like a delicate exotic fruit; touch it, and the bloom is gone.

The Importance of Being Earnest (1895)

▶▶ FOOLISHNESS; STUPIDITY

illness

Adair, Gilbert
English author and critic

We 'need' cancer because, by the very fact of its insurability, it makes all other diseases, however virulent, not cancer.

Myths and Memories (1986)

Aubrey, John (1626–1697)
English antiquary, folklorist and biographer

Sciatica: he cured it, by boiling his buttock.

Brief Lives (c.1693)

Augustine, Saint (354–430)
Numidian-born Christian theologian and philosopher

All diseases of Christians are to be ascribed to demons; chiefly do they torment freshly-baptized Christians, yea, even the guiltless new-born infants.

Attr.

Austin, Alfred (1835–1913)
English poet and journalist
On the illness of the Prince of Wales
> Across the wires the electric message came:
> 'He is no better, he is much the same.'

Attr.

Bacon, Francis (1561–1626)
English philosopher, essayist, politician and courtier
> The remedy is worse than the disease.

'Of Seditions and Troubles' (1625)

Bennett, Arnold (1867–1931)
English writer, dramatist and journalist
> 'Ye can call it influenza if ye like,' said Mrs Machin. 'There was no influenza in my young days. We called a cold a cold.'

The Card (1911)

Browne, Sir Thomas (1605–1682)
English physician, author and antiquary
> We all labour against our own cure, for death is the cure of all diseases.

Religio Medici (1643)

Butler, Samuel (1835–1902)
English writer, painter, philosopher and scholar
> I reckon being ill as one of the great pleasures of life, provided one is not too ill and is not obliged to work till one is better.

The Way of the Flesh (1903)

Chekhov, Anton (1860–1904)
Russian writer, dramatist and doctor
> If many remedies are suggested for a disease, that means the disease is incurable.

The Cherry Orchard (1904)

Davies, Robertson (1913–1995)
Canadian playwright, writer and critic
> Not to be healthy ... is one of the few sins that modern society is willing to recognise and condemn.

The Cunning Man (1994)

Emerson, Ralph Waldo (1803–1882)
US poet, essayist, transcendentalist and teacher
> A person seldom falls sick, but the bystanders are animated with a faint hope that he will die.

Conduct of Life (1860)

Fox, Michael (1961–)
US actor
Joking about the tremors caused by Parkinson's Disease
> I can mix a Margarita in five seconds.

The Times, 1998

Galbraith, J.K. (1908–)
Canadian-born US economist, diplomat and writer

Much of the world's work, it has been said, is done by men who do not feel quite well. Marx is a case in point.

The Age of Uncertainty

Heller, Joseph (1923–1999)
US writer
> Hungry Joe collected lists of fatal diseases and arranged them in alphabetical order so that he could put his finger without delay on any one he wanted to worry about.

Catch-22 (1961)

Hippocrates (c.460–357 BC)
Greek physician
> For extreme illnesses extreme remedies are most fitting.

Aphorisms

Hood, Thomas (1799–1845)
English poet, editor and humorist
> For that old enemy the gout
> Had taken him in toe!

Comic Melodies (1830)

Keegan, Kevin (1951–)
English footballer and manager
> In some ways, cramp is worse than having a broken leg. But leukaemia is worse still. Probably.

Attr.

Kerr, Jean (1923–)
US writer and dramatist
> One of the most difficult things to contend with in a hospital is the assumption on the part of the staff that because you have lost your gall bladder you have also lost your mind.

Please Don't Eat the Daisies (1957)

Lamb, Charles (1775–1834)
English essayist, critic and letter writer
> How sickness enlarges the dimensions of a man's self to himself!

Last Essays of Elia (1833)

Lawrence, D.H. (1885–1930)
English writer, poet and critic
> I am only half there when I am ill, and so there is only half a man to suffer. To suffer in one's whole self is so great a violation, that it is not to be endured.

Letter to Catherine Carswell, 1916

Leonard, Hugh (1926–)
Irish dramatist and screenwriter
> *Drumm*: I asked him if he had the results of the x-rays. He took me into his surgery ... He gave me one of those looks of his, redolent of the cemetery, and said that I should buy day-returns from now on instead of season tickets.

A Life (1986)

McAuley, James Philip (1917–1976)
Australian poet and critic
After his first cancer operation; to a friend
> Well, better a semi-colon than a full stop!
>> *In Coleman*, The Heart of James McAuley (1980)

Moore, Dudley (1935–)
English comedian and actor
On his brain disease, said to affect only one in 10, 000 people
> I think it is considerate of me to have taken on the disease, thus protecting the remaining 99,999 Screen Actors' Guild members from this fate.
>> The Times, 1999

Nash, Ogden (1902–1971)
US poet
> A cough is something that you yourself can't help, but everybody else does on purpose just to torment you.
>> You Can't Get There From Here (1957)

Paterson, Jennifer (1928–1999)
Request from her hospital bed
> No flowers, please, just caviare.
>> The Times, 1999

Perelman, S.J. (1904–1979)
US humorist, writer and dramatist
> I've got Bright's disease and he's got mine.
>> Attr.

Persius Flaccus, Aulus (AD 34–62)
Roman satirical poet
> *Venienti occurrite morbo.*
> Confront disease at its onset.
>> Satires

Philip, Sir Robert (1857–1939)
> Mankind is responsible for tuberculosis. What an ignorant civilisation has introduced, an educated civilisation can remove.
>> Attr.

Proust, Marcel (1871–1922)
French writer and critic
> As soon as he ceased to be mad he became merely stupid. There are maladies we must not seek to cure because they alone protect us from others that are more serious.
>> Le Côté de Guermantes (1921)

Proverbs
> Sickness comes on horseback and departs on foot.
>> Dutch Proverb

> Show him death, and he'll be content with fever.
>> Russian Proverb

Shakespeare, William (1564–1616)
English dramatist, poet and actor
> Diseases desperate grown

> By desperate appliance are reliev'd,
> Or not at all.
>> Hamlet, IV.iii

Sontag, Susan (1933–)
US critic and writer
> Illness is the night-side of life, a more onerous citizenship. Everyone who is born holds dual citizenship, in the kingdom of the well and in the kingdom of the sick. Although we all prefer to use only the good passport, sooner or later each of us is obliged, at least for a spell, to identify ourselves as citizens of that other place.
>> Illness as Metaphor (1978)

Stacpoole, H. de Vere (1863–1951)
Irish writer and physician
> In home-sickness you must keep moving – it is the only disease that does not require rest.
>> The Bourgeois (1901)

Stevenson, Robert Louis (1850–1894)
Scottish writer, poet and essayist
> Even if the doctor does not give you a year, even if he hesitates about a month, make one brave push and see what can be accomplished in a week.
>> Virginibus Puerisque (1881)

Swift, Jonathan (1667–1745)
Irish satirist, poet, essayist and cleric
> We are so fond of one another, because our ailments are the same.
>> Journal to Stella, 1711

Williams, Richard D'Alton (1822–1862)
Irish poet
> They brought her to the city
> And she faded slowly there –
> Consumption has no pity
> For blue eyes and golden hair.
>> 'The Dying Girl'

Wolfe, Thomas (1900–1938)
US novelist and dramatist
> Most of the time we think we're sick, it's all in the mind.
>> Look Homeward, Angel (1929)

▶▶ AIDS; HEALTH; MEDICINE

imagination

Austen, Jane (1775–1817)
English writer
> A lady's imagination is very rapid; it jumps from admiration to love, from love to matrimony, in a moment.
>> Pride and Prejudice (1813)

Bacall, Lauren (1924–)
US actress
> Imagination is the highest kite that one can fly.
>> *Lauren Bacall, By Myself*

The Bible (King James Version)
> For the imagination of man's heart is evil from his youth.
>> *Genesis, 8:21*

Blake, William (1757–1827)
English poet, engraver, painter and mystic
> What is now proved was once only imagin'd.
>> 'Proverbs of Hell' (c.1793)

Cervantes, Miguel de (1547–1616)
Spanish writer and dramatist
Don Quixote of his lady, Dulcinea del Toboso
> I imagine that everything is as I say it is, neither more or less, and I paint her in my imagination the way I want her to be.
>> *Don Quixote* (1605)

Chase, Alexander (1926–)
US journalist and author
> The most imaginative people are the most credulous, for them everything is possible.
>> *Perspectives* (1966)

Coleridge, Samuel Taylor (1772–1834)
English poet, philosopher and critic
> The primary imagination I hold to be the living power and prime agent of all human perception, and as a repetition in the finite mind of the eternal act of creation in the infinite I AM. The secondary imagination … dissolves, diffuses, dissipates, in order to recreate; or where this process is rendered impossible, yet still at all events it struggles to idealize and to unify.
>> *Biographia Literaria* (1817)

> Fancy, on the contrary, has no other counters to play with, but fixities and definites. The fancy is indeed no other than a mode of memory emancipated from the order of time and space.
>> *Biographia Literaria* (1817)

Einstein, Albert (1879–1955)
German-born US mathematical physicist
> Imagination is more important than knowledge.
>> *On Science*

Eliot, George (1819–1880)
English writer and poet
> He said he should prefer not to know the sources of the Nile, and that there should be some unknown regions preserved as hunting-grounds for the poetic imagination.
>> *Middlemarch* (1872)

Johnson, Samuel (1709–1784)
English lexicographer, poet, critic, conversationalist and essayist

> Were it not for imagination, Sir, a man would be as happy in the arms of a chambermaid as of a Duchess.
>> In Boswell, *The Life of Samuel Johnson* (1791)

Joubert, Joseph (1754–1824)
French essayist
> Imagination is the eye of the soul.
>> Attr.

Keats, John (1795–1821)
English poet
> The Imagination may be compared to Adam's dream – he awoke and found it truth.
>> Letter to Benjamin Bailey, 22 November 1817

> I am certain of nothing but of the holiness of the Heart's affections and the truth of Imagination – What the imagination seizes as Beauty must be truth – whether it existed before or not.
>> Letter to Benjamin Bailey, 22 November 1817

Macaulay, Lord (1800–1859)
English Liberal statesman, essayist and poet
> His imagination resembled the wings of an ostrich. It enabled him to run, though not to soar.
>> 'John Dryden' (1843)

Poe, Edgar Allan (1809–1849)
US poet, writer and editor
> It will be found, in fact, that the ingenious are always fanciful, and the truly imaginative never otherwise than analytic.
>> *The Murders in the Rue Morgue* (1841)

Robinson, Roland Edward (1912–1992)
Irish-born Australian poet
> Where does imagination start
> but from primeval images
> in man's barbaric heart?
>> 'Mopoke'

Stead, Christina (1902–1983)
Australian writer
> I don't know what imagination is, if not an unpruned, tangled kind of memory.
>> *Letty Fox: Her Luck* (1946)

Vidal, Gore (1925–)
US writer, critic and poet
> It is the spirit of the age to believe that any fact, no matter how suspect, is superior to any imaginative exercise, no matter how true.
>> *French Letters: Theories of the New Novel*

immortality

Allen, Woody (1935–)
US film director, writer, actor and comedian
> I don't want to achieve immortality through my

work ... I want to achieve it by not dying.

Attr.

Beckett, Samuel (1906–1989)
Irish dramatist, writer and poet
> *Clov*: Do you believe in the life to come?
> *Hamm*: Mine was always that.

Endgame (1958)

Butler, Bishop Joseph (1692–1752)
English philosopher and divine
> That which is the foundation of all our hopes
> and of all our fears; all our hopes and fears
> which are of any consideration: I mean a Future
> Life.

The Analogy of Religion (1736)

Dostoevsky, Fyodor (1821–1881)
Russian writer
> If you were to destroy in mankind the belief in
> immortality, not only love but every living force
> maintaining the life of the world would at once
> dry up. Moreover, nothing then would be
> immoral, everything would be lawful, even
> cannibalism.

The Brothers Karamazov (1879–1880)

Emerson, Ralph Waldo (1803–1882)
US poet, essayist, transcendentalist and teacher
> Other world! There is no other world! Here or
> nowhere is the whole fact.

'Natural Religion'

Ertz, Susan (1894–1985)
English writer
> Someone has somewhere commented on the
> fact that millions long for immortality who don't
> know what to do with themselves on a rainy
> Sunday afternoon.

Anger in the Sky (1943)

Hazlitt, William (1778–1830)
English writer and critic
> No young man believes he shall ever die.

'On the Feeling of Immortality in Youth' (1827)

Heller, Joseph (1923–1999)
US writer
> He had decided to live forever or die in the
> attempt.

Catch-22 (1961)

Keats, John (1795–1821)
English poet
> There is an awful warmth about my heart like a
> load of Immortality.

Letter to J.H. Reynolds, 22 September 1818

> I long to believe in immortality ... If I am
> destined to be happy with you here – how short
> is the longest Life. I wish to believe in
> immortality – I wish to live with you for ever.

Letter to Fanny Brawne, July 1820

Kraus, Karl (1874–1936)
Austrian scientist, critic and poet
> *Die Unsterblichkeit ist das einzige, was keinen Aufschub
> verträgt.*
> Immortality is the only thing which doesn't
> tolerate being postponed.

Sayings and Contradictions (1909)

Pindar (518–438 BC)
Greek lyric poet
> Strive not, my soul, for an immortal life, but
> make the most of what is possible.

Pythian Odes

Plato (c.429–347 BC)
Greek philosopher
> Let us be persuaded ... to consider that the soul
> is immortal and capable of enduring all evil and
> all good, and so we shall always hold to the
> upward way and pursue justice with wisdom.

Republic

Shakespeare, William (1564–1616)
English dramatist, poet and actor
> Your monument shall be my gentle verse,
> Which eyes not yet created shall o'er-read;
> And tongues to be your being shall rehearse,
> When all the breathers of this world are dead.
> You still shall live, such virtue hath my pen,
> Where breath most breathes, even in the
> mouths of men.

Sonnet 81

Spinoza, Baruch (1632–1677)
Dutch philosopher and theologian
> *Sentimus experimurque, nos aeternos esse.*
> We feel and know by experience that we are
> eternal.

Ethics (1677)

Stassinopoulos, Arianna (1950–)
Greek writer
> Our current obsession with creativity is the
> result of our continued striving for immortality in
> an era when most people no longer believe in an
> afterlife.

The Female Woman (1973)

Thoreau, Henry David (1817–1862)
US essayist, social critic and writer
On being asked his opinion of the hereafter
> One world at a time.

Attr.

Upanishads (c.800–300 BC)
> When all desires that dwell within the human
> heart are cast away, then a mortal becomes
> immortal and here he attaineth to Brahman.

Katha Upanishad

Vaughan, Henry (1622–1695)
Welsh poet and physician

My Soul, there is a countrie
Far beyond the stars,
Where stands a winged Sentry
All skilfull in the wars;
There above noise and danger,
Sweet peace sits crown'd with smiles,
And one born in a Manger
Commands the Beauteous files.

Silex Scintillans (1655)

▶▶ ETERNITY; MORTALITY

importance and unimportance

Carroll, Lewis (1832–1898)
English writer and photographer
'Unimportant, of course, I meant, ' the King
hastily said, and went on to himself in an
undertone, 'important – unimportant –
unimportant – important –' as if he were trying
which word sounded best.

Alice's Adventures in Wonderland (1865)

impossibility

Anonymous
Difficult things take a long time; the impossible
takes a little longer.

Sometimes attributed to Nansen, and others

Aristophanes (c.445–385 BC)
Greek playwright
You will never make a crab walk straight.

Peace

Aristotle (384–322 BC)
Greek philosopher
Probable impossibilities are always to be
preferred to improbable possibilities.

Poetics

Calonne, Charles Alexandre de (1734–1802)
French statesman
*Madame, si c'est possible, c'est fait; impossible? cela se
fera.*
Madam, if it is possible, it has been done;
impossible? It will be done.

In J. Michelet, *Histoire de la Révolution Française* (1847)

Carroll, Lewis (1832–1898)
English writer and photographer
'There's no use trying,' she said: 'one can't
believe impossible things.'
'I dare say you haven't had much practice,' said
the Queen. 'When I was your age, I always did it
for half an hour a day. Why, sometimes I've
believed as many as six impossible things before

breakfast.'

*Through the Looking-Glass (and What Alice Found
There)* (1872)

Grainger, Percy (1882–1961)
Australian composer and pianist
Why be difficult when with a little extra effort
you can make yourself impossible?

Anecdotes, Index Part I, Grainger Collection

Twain, Mark (1835–1910)
US humorist, writer, journalist and lecturer
There ain't no way to find out why a snorer can't
hear himself snore.

Tom Sawyer Abroad (1894)

income

Austen, Jane (1775–1817)
English writer
An annuity is a very serious business; it comes
over and over every year, and there is no getting
rid of it.

Sense and Sensibility (1811)

A large income is the best recipe for happiness I
ever heard of. It certainly may secure all the
myrtle and turkey part of it.

Mansfield Park (1814)

Butler, Samuel (1835–1902)
English writer, painter, philosopher and scholar
All progress is based upon a universal innate
desire on the part of every organism to live
beyond its income.

The Note-Books of Samuel Butler (1912)

Dickens, Charles (1812–1870)
English writer
Annual income twenty pounds, annual
expenditure nineteen nineteen six, result
happiness. Annual income twenty pounds,
annual expenditure twenty pounds ought and
six, result misery.

David Copperfield (1850)

Flynn, Errol (1909–1959)
US actor
My difficulty is trying to reconcile my gross
habits with my net income.

Attr.

Lambton, John, First Earl of Durham (1792–1840)
English statesman
He said he considered £40,000 a year a
moderate income – such a one as a man might
jog on with.

In *The Creevey Papers* (1903)

Morley, John David (1812–1870)
British writer

For the average European a job was an income, for the average Japanese it was a home.

Pictures From the Water Trade – An Englishman in Japan

Nash, Ogden (1902–1971)

US poet

He who is ridden by a conscience
Worries about a lot of nonscience;
He without benefit of scruples
His fun and income soon quadruples.

'Reflection on the Fallibility of Nemesis' (1940)

Parkinson, C. Northcote (1909–1993)

English political scientist and historian

Expenditure rises to meet income.

Attr.

Saki (1870–1916)

Burmese-born British writer

I'm living so far beyond my income that we might almost be said to be living apart.

Attr.

All decent people live beyond their incomes nowadays, and those who aren't respectable live beyond other people's. A few gifted individuals manage to do both.

The Chronicles of Clovis (1911)

Saunders, Ernest (1935–)

English businessman

I was on a basic £100,000 a year. You don't make many savings on that.

The Observer, 1987

Shakespeare, William (1564–1616)

English dramatist, poet and actor

Remuneration! O, that's the Latin word for three farthings.

Love's Labour Lost, III.i

Smith, Logan Pearsall (1865–1946)

US-born British epigrammatist, critic and writer

There are few sorrows, however poignant, in which a good income is of no avail.

Afterthoughts (1931)

▶▶ MONEY AND WEALTH

indecision

Asquith, Margot (1864–1945)

Scottish political hostess and writer

Of Sir Stafford Cripps

He has a brilliant mind until he makes it up.

In *The Wit of the Asquiths*

Bevan, Aneurin (1897–1960)

Welsh Labour politician, miner and orator

We know what happens to people who stay in the middle of the road. They get run over.

The Observer, 1953

The Bible (King James Version)

How long halt ye between two opinions?

I Kings, 18:21

Brooks, Mel (1926–)

US film actor and director

He who hesitates is poor.

The Producers (film, 1968)

Dickens, Charles (1812–1870)

English writer

On a performance of *Hamlet*

Whenever that undecided Prince had to ask a question or state a doubt, the public helped him out with it – on the question whether 'twas nobler in the mind to suffer, some roared yes, and some no, and some inclining to both opinions said 'toss up for it'.

Great Expectations (1861)

James, William (1842–1910)

US psychologist and philosopher

There is no more miserable human being than one in whom nothing is habitual but indecision.

Principles of Psychology (1890)

Nash, Ogden (1902–1971)

US poet

If I could but spot a conclusion, I should race to it.

'All, All Are Gone, The Old Familiar Quotations' (1952)

Smith, Sir Cyril (1928–)

English politician

If the fence is strong enough I'll sit on it.

The Observer, 1974

Twain, Mark (1835–1910)

US humorist, writer, journalist and lecturer

I must have a prodigious quantity of mind; it takes me as much as a week, sometimes, to make it up.

The Innocents Abroad (1869)

▶▶ UNCERTAINTY

independence

Aesop (6th century BC)

Legendary Greek writer of fables

The gods help those who help themselves.

'Hercules and the Waggoner'

Brancusi, Constantin (1876–1957)

Romanian sculptor

Refusing Rodin's invitation to work in his studio

Nothing grows well in the shade of a big tree.

Attr.

Emerson, Ralph Waldo (1803–1882)
US poet, essayist, transcendentalist and teacher
> It is easy in the world to live after the world's opinion; it is easy in solitude after our own; but the great man is he who, in the midst of the crowd, keeps with perfect sweetness the independence of solitude.
> > 'Self-Reliance' (1841)

Gibbon, Edward (1737–1794)
English historian, politician and memoirist
> The first of earthly blessings, independence.
> > *Memoirs of My Life and Writings* (1796)

Ibsen, Henrik (1828–1906)
Norwegian writer, dramatist and poet
> The strongest man in the world is the man who stands alone.
> > *An Enemy of the People* (1882)

La Fontaine, Jean de (1621–1695)
French poet and fabulist
> *Aide-toi, le ciel t'aidera.*
> Help yourself, and heaven will help you.
> > *Fables*, 'Le Chartier embourbé'

Marryat, Frederick (1792–1848)
English naval officer and writer
> I think it much better that … every man paddle his own canoe.
> > *Settlers in Canada* (1844)

Scott, Sir Walter (1771–1832)
Scottish writer and historian
Refusing offers of help following his bankruptcy in 1826
> No! this right hand shall work it all off!
> > In Cockburn, *Memorials of His Time* (1856)

Shakespeare, William (1564–1616)
English dramatist, poet and actor
> I earn that I eat, get that I wear; owe no man hate, envy no man's happiness; glad of other men's good, content with my harm.
> > *As You Like It*, III.ii

Thoreau, Henry David (1817–1862)
US essayist, social critic and writer
> I would rather sit on a pumpkin and have it all to myself than be crowded on a velvet cushion.
> > *Walden* (1854)

individuality

Ariosto, Ludovico (1474–1533)
Italian poet
> *Natura il fece, e poi roppe la stampa.*
> Nature first made him, and then smashed the mould.
> > *Orlando furioso* (1516)

Blake, William (1757–1827)
English poet, engraver, painter and mystic
> O why was I born with a different face?
> Why was I not born like the rest of my race?
> > 'Letter to Thomas Butts' (1803)

Browne, Sir Thomas (1605–1682)
English physician, author and antiquary
> It is the common wonder of all men, how among so many millions of faces, there should be none alike.
> > *Religio Medici* (1643)

Huxley, T.H. (1825–1895)
English biologist, Darwinist and agnostic
> One of the unpardonable sins, in the eyes of most people, is for a man to go about unlabelled. The world regards such a person as the police do an unmuzzled dog, not under proper control.
> > *Evolution and Ethics* (1893)

Mill, John Stuart (1806–1873)
English philosopher, economist and reformer
> Whatever crushes individuality is despotism, by whatever name it may be called.
> > *On Liberty* (1859)

Schopenhauer, Arthur (1788–1860)
German philosopher
> *Aus seiner Individualität kann Keiner heraus.*
> No-one can escape from his individuality.
> > *Parerga und Paralipomena* (1851)

Wilde, Oscar (1854–1900)
Irish poet, dramatist, writer, critic and wit
> Most people are other people. Their thoughts are someone else's opinions, their life a mimicry, their passions a quotation.
> > Letter to Lord Alfred Douglas

▶▶ OPINIONS; TASTE

industrial relations

Anonymous
> In his chamber, weak and dying,
> While the Norman Baron lay,
> Loud, without, his men were crying,
> 'Shorter hours and better pay.'
> > 'A Strike among the Poets'

Castle, Ted (1907–1979)
> In Place of Strife.
> > Title of White Paper on industrial relations legislation, 1969

Cook, A.J. (1885–1931)
English miners' leader
> Not a penny off the pay, not a minute on the day.
> > Speech, 1926

Coolidge, Calvin (1872–1933)
US President
Of the Boston police strike
> There is no right to strike against the public safety by anybody, anywhere, any time.
>> Telegram to the President of the American Federation of Labour, 1919

Feather, Vic, Baron (1906–1976)
English trade unionist
> Industrial relations are like sexual relations. It's better between two consenting parties.
>> *Guardian Weekly*, 1976

Keynes, John Maynard (1883–1946)
English economist
> There are the Trade Unionists, once the oppressed, now the tyrants, whose selfish and sectional pretensions need to be bravely opposed.
>> 'Liberalism and Labour' (1926)

Macmillan, Harold (1894–1986)
British Conservative Prime Minister
Referring to privatization of profitable nationalized industries
> Selling the family silver.
>> Speech, House of Lords, 1986

Muir, Frank (1920–1998)
English writer, humorist and broadcaster
> Another fact of life that will not have escaped you is that, in this country, the twenty-four-hour strike is like the twenty-four-hour flu. You have to reckon on it lasting at least five days.
>> *You Can't Have Your Kayak and Heat It*, 'Great Expectations', with Dennis Norden

Shinwell, Emanuel (1884–1986)
British Labour politician
> We know that you, the organized workers of the country, are our friends … As for the rest, they do not matter a tinker's curse.
>> Speech at the Electrical Trades Union Conference, Margate, 1947

Speight, Johnny (1920–1998)
English screenwriter
> Have you noticed, the last four strikes we've had, it's pissed down? It wouldn't be a bad idea to check the weather reports before they pull us out next time.
>> *Till Death Do Us Part*, television programme

Wilson, Harold (1916–1995)
English Labour Prime Minister
> We are redefining and we are restating our socialism in terms of the scientific revolution … the Britain that is going to be forged in the white heat of this revolution will be no place for restrictive practices or out-dated methods on either side of industry.
>> Speech, 1963

> One man's wage rise is another man's price increase.
>> *The Observer*, 1970

▶▶ DIPLOMACY

inequality

Alexander, Cecil Frances (1818–1895)
Irish poet and hymn writer
> The rich man in his castle,
> The poor man at his gate,
> God made them, high or lowly,
> And order'd their estate.
>> *Hymn*, 1848

Bellow, Saul (1915–)
Canadian-born US Jewish writer
> One part of mankind is in prison; another is starving to death; and those of us who are free and fed are not awake. What will it take to rouse us?
>> *Critical Enquiry*, 1975, 'A World Too Much With Us'

Brecht, Bertolt (1898–1956)
German dramatist
> *Der Sieg und Niederlagen der Grosskopfigen oben und der von unten fallen nämlich nicht immer zusammen.*
> Victories and defeats for the bigshots at the top aren't always victories and defeats for those at the bottom.
>> *Mother Courage and her Children* (1941)

Froude, James Anthony (1818–1894)
English historian and scholar
> Men are made by nature unequal. It is vain, therefore, to treat them as if they were equal.
>> *Short Studies on Great Subjects* (1877)

Goldsmith, Oliver (c.1728–1774)
Irish dramatist, poet and writer
> Ye friends to truth, ye statesmen, who survey
> The rich man's joys increase, the poor's decay,
> 'Tis yours to judge, how wide the limits stand
> Between a splendid and a happy land.
>> *The Deserted Village* (1770)

Johnson, Samuel (1709–1784)
English lexicographer, poet, critic, conversationalist and essayist
> Subordination tends greatly to human happiness. Were we all upon an equality, we should have no other enjoyment than mere animal pleasure.
>> In Boswell, *The Life of Samuel Johnson* (1791)

Penn, William (1644–1718)
English Quaker, founder of state of Pennsylvania
> It is a reproach to religion and government to

suffer so much poverty and excess.
>   *Some Fruits of Solitude, in Reflections and Maxims*
>   *relating to the Conduct of Humane Life* (1693)

Shelley, Percy Bysshe (1792–1822)
English poet, dramatist and essayist
> Many faint with toil,
> That few may know the cares and woe of sloth.
>   *Queen Mab* (1813)

Watson, Sir William (1858–1936)
English poet
> Too long, that some may rest,
> Tired millions toil unblest.
>   'New National Anthem'

▶▶ CLASS; FEMINISM

influence

Carnegie, Dale (1888–1955)
> How to Win Friends and Influence People.
>   Book title

Einstein, Albert (1879–1955)
German-born US mathematical physicist
> Setting an example is not the main means of
> influencing others, it is the only means.
>   Attr.

Naisbitt, John (1929–)
> The new source of power is not money in the
> hands of a few but information in the hands of
> many.
>   *Megatrends*

Wilde, Oscar (1854–1900)
Irish poet, dramatist, writer, critic and wit
> The man who can dominate a London
> dinnertable can dominate the world.
>   Attr.

▶▶ INSPIRATION; POWER

ingratitude

Chillingworth, William (1602–1644)
English theologian and scholar
> I once knew a man out of courtesy help a lame
> dog over a stile, and he for requital bit his
> fingers.
>   *The Religion of Protestants* (1637)

García Márquez, Gabriel (1928–)
Colombian author
> *La ingratitud humana no tiene limites.*
> There are no limits to human ingratitude.
>   *No-one Writes to the Colonel* (1961)

Huxley, Aldous (1894–1963)
English writer, poet and critic
> Most human beings have an almost infinite
> capacity for taking things for granted.
>   *Themes and Variations* (1950)

La Rochefoucauld (1613–1680)
French writer
> Over-great haste to repay an obligation is a form
> of ingratitude.
>   *Maximes* (1678)

Louis XIV (1638–1715)
King of France
> *Toutes les fois que je donne une place vacante, je fais*
> *cent mécontents et un ingrat.*
> Every time I make an appointment, I make a
> hundred men discontented and one ungrateful.
>   In Voltaire, *Siècle de Louis XIV*

Shakespeare, William (1564–1616)
English dramatist, poet and actor
> Blow, blow, thou winter wind,
> Thou art not so unkind
> As man's ingratitude …
> Thy tooth is not so keen,
>
> Freeze, freeze, thou bitter sky,
> That dost not bite so nigh
> As benefits forgot.
>   *As You Like It*, II.vii
>
> How sharper than a serpent's tooth it is
> To have a thankless child.
>   *King Lear*, I.iv
> Time hath, my lord, a wallet at his back,
> Wherein he puts alms for oblivion,
> A great-siz'd monster of ingratitudes.
> Those scraps are good deeds past, which are
> devour'd
> As fast as they are made, forgot as soon
> As done.
>   *Troilus and Cressida*, III.iii
>
> I hate ingratitude more in a man
> Than lying, vainness, babbling drunkenness,
> Or any taint of vice whose strong
> corruptionInhabits our frail blood.
>   *Twelfth Night*, III.iv

Twain, Mark (1835–1910)
US humorist, writer, journalist and lecturer
> There's plenty of boys that will come hankering
> and gruvvelling around when you've got an
> apple, and beg the core off you; but when
> they've got one, and you beg for the core and
> remind them how you give them a core one
> time, they make a mouth at you and say thank
> you 'most to death, but there ain't-a-going to be
> no core.
>   *The Adventures of Tom Sawyer* (1876)

innocence

Bowen, Elizabeth (1899–1973)

Irish writer

No, it is not only our fate but our business to lose innocence, and once we have lost that, it is futile to attempt a picnic in Eden.

In R. Lehmann and others (eds.), Orion III (1946)

Bradbury, Malcolm (1932–)

English writer, critic and academic

Only the old are innocent. That is what the Victorians understood, and the Christians. Original sin is a property of the young. The old grow beyond corruption very quickly.

Stepping Westward (1965)

Golding, William (1911–1993)

English writer and poet

Ralph wept for the end of innocence, the darkness of man's heart, and the fall through the air of the true, wise friend called Piggy.

Lord of the Flies (1954)

Greene, Graham (1904–1991)

English writer and dramatist

Innocence always calls mutely for protection, when we would be so much wiser to guard ourselves against it: innocence is like a dumb leper who has lost his bell, wandering the world meaning no harm.

The Quiet American (1955)

Proverb

Every one is innocent until he is proved guilty.

Racine, Jean (1639–1699)

French tragedian and poet

My innocence is at last becoming a burden to me.

Andromaque (1667)

Yeats, W.B. (1865–1939)

Irish poet, dramatist, editor, writer and senator

The innocent and the beautiful
Have no enemy but time.

The Winding Stair and Other Poems (1933)

▶▶ IGNORANCE

innovation

Anonymous

Every revolutionary idea – in science, politics, art, or whatever – evokes three stages of reaction in a hearer:

- It is completely impossible – don't waste my time.
- It is possible, but it is not worth doing.
- I said it was a good idea all along.

Bacon, Francis (1561–1626)

English philosopher, essayist, politician and courtier

He that will not apply new remedies must expect new evils; for time is the greatest innovator.

Essays (1625)

▶▶ CONSERVATISM; ORIGINALITY; PROGRESS

inspiration

Colette (1873–1954)

French writer

On ne fait bien que ce qu'on aime. Ni la science, ni la conscience ne modèlent un grand cuisinier. De quoi sert l'application où il faut l'inspiration?

One only does well what one loves doing. Neither science nor conscience makes a great cook. What use is application where inspiration is what's needed?

Prisons et paradis (1932)

Markham, Beryl (1902–1986)

English aviator and writer

I could never tell where inspiration begins and impulse leaves off. I suppose the answer is in the outcome. If your hunch proves a good one, you were inspired; if it proves bad, you are guilty of yielding to thoughtless impulse.

West With the Night (1941)

Millais, Sir John Everett (1829–1896)

English painter

One day the inspiration comes, and then it goes. It's all stomach.

Attr.

Porter, Cole (1891–1964)

US composer and lyricist

My sole inspiration is a telephone call from a director.

Press interview, 1955

Proverb

Ninety per cent of inspiration is perspiration.

insults

Allen, Dave (1936–)

Irish comedian and television personality

If I had a head like yours, I'd have it circumcised.

In Gus Smith, God's Own Comedian

Austen, Jane (1775–1817)

English writer

You have delighted us long enough.

Pride and Prejudice (1813)

Baker, Josephine (1906–1975)
French dancer, singer and entertainer
I like Frenchmen very much, because even when they insult you they do it so nicely.

Attr.

Ball, Alan (1957–)
US screenwriter
Lester Burnham's response to criticism by his wife
You're one to talk, you bloodless, money-grubbing freak.

American Beauty (film, 1999)

Bevan, Aneurin (1897–1960)
Welsh Labour politician, miner and orator
Wishing to address Harold Macmillan, the Prime Minister, rather than Selwyn Lloyd, the Foreign Secretary, in the post-Suez debate
I am not going to spend any time whatsoever in attacking the Foreign Secretary. Quite honestly I am beginning to feel extremely sorry for him. If we complain about the tune, there is no reason to attack the monkey when the organ grinder is present.

Speech, House of Commons, 1957

Brahms, Johannes (1833–1897)
German composer, pianist and conductor
Said on leaving a gathering of friends
If there is anyone here whom I have not insulted, I beg his pardon.

Attr.

Brummel, Beau (1778–1840)
English dandy and wit
Said of the Prince of Wales, 1813
Who's your fat friend?

In Gronow, *Reminiscences* (1862)

Chesterfield, Lord (1694–1773)
English politician and letter writer
An injury is much sooner forgotten than an insult.

Letter to his son, 1746

Corneille, Pierre (1606–1684)
French dramatist, poet and lawyer
He who allows himself to be insulted, deserves to be.

Héraclius (1646)

Disraeli, Benjamin (1804–1881)
English statesman and writer
Speaking to Lord Palmerston
Your dexterity seems a happy compound of the smartness of an attorney's clerk and the intrigue of a Greek of the lower empire.

Attr.

If a traveller were informed that such a man Lord

John Russell was leader of the House of Commons, he may well begin to comprehend how the Egyptians worshipped an insect.

Attr.

Gilbert, W.S. (1836–1911)
English dramatist, humorist and librettist
I shouldn't be sufficiently degraded in my own estimation unless I was insulted with a very considerable bribe.

The Mikado (1885)

Grossmith, George (1847–1912) and **Grossmith, Weedon** (1854–1919)
English singer and comedian/English writer, painter and actor
I am a poor man, but I would gladly give ten shillings to find out who sent me the insulting Christmas card I received this morning.

Diary of a Nobody (1894)

Johnson, Samuel (1709–1784)
English lexicographer, poet, critic, conversationalist and essayist
A fellow who makes no figure in company, and has a mind as narrow as the neck of a vinegar cruet.

In Boswell, *Journal of a Tour to the Hebrides* (1785)

To an abusive Thames waterman
Sir, your wife, under pretence of keeping a bawdy-house, is a receiver of stolen goods.

In Boswell, *The Life of Samuel Johnson* (1791)

Lloyd George, David (1863–1945)
Of Sir Douglas Haig
He was brilliant to the top of his army boots.

Attr.

Parker, Dorothy (1893–1967)
US writer, poet, critic and wit
Reply to the comment, 'Anyway, she's always very nice to her inferiors'
Where does she find them?

In Lyttelton Hart-Davis, *Letters*

Sayers, Dorothy L. (1893–1957)
English writer, dramatist and translator
I can't see that she could have found anything nastier to say if she'd thought it out with both hands for a fortnight.

Busman's Honeymoon (1937)

Sheridan, Richard Brinsley (1751–1816)
Irish dramatist, politician and orator
If it is abuse, – why one is always sure to hear of it from one damned good-natured friend or another!

The Critic (1779)

Sitwell, Dame Edith (1887–1964)
English poet, anthologist, critic and biographer
On novelist Ethel Mannin

I do not want Miss Mannin's feelings to be hurt by the fact that I have never heard of her ... At the moment I am debarred from the pleasure of putting her in her place by the fact that she has not got one.

> In J. Pearson, *Façades* (1978)

Smith, F.E. (1872–1930)
English politician and Lord Chancellor
Judge Willis: You are extremely offensive, young man.
F.E. Smith: As a matter of fact, we both are, and the only difference between us is that I am trying to be, and you can't help it.

> In Birkenhead, *Frederick Elwin, Earl of Birkenhead* (1933)

Smith, Sydney (1771–1845)
English clergyman, essayist, journalist and wit
Let the Dean and Canons lay their heads together and the thing will be done. (It being proposed to surround St Paul's with a wooden pavement.).

> In H. Pearson, *The Smith of Smiths* (1934)

Thompson, William Hepworth (1810–1886)
English Greek scholar
Of Sir Richard Jebb, Professor of Greek at Cambridge
What time he can spare from the adornment of his person he devotes to the neglect of his duties.

> In M.R. Bobbit, *With Dearest Love to All* (1960)

Thurber, James (1894–1961)
US humorist, writer and dramatist
A man should not insult his wife publicly, at parties. He should insult her in the privacy of the home.

> *Thurber Country* (1953)

Wilder, Billy (1906–)
Austrian-born US film director, producer and screenwriter
Said to Cliff Osmond
You have Van Gogh's ear for music.

> Attr.

Wilkes, John (1727–1797)
Reply to Lord Sandwich, who had told him that he would die either on the gallows or of the pox
That must depend on whether I embrace your lordship's principles or your mistress.

> Attr. in Sir Charles Petrie, *The Four Georges* (1935)

▶▶ ACTORS; CRITICISM; POLITICIANS

intellectuals

Ade, George (1866–1944)
US fabulist and playwright

She was short on intellect, but long on shape.

> Attr.

Agnew, Spiro T. (1918–1996)
US Vice President
A spirit of national masochism prevails, encouraged by an effete corps of impudent snobs who characterize themselves as intellectuals.

> *New York Times*, 1969

An intellectual is a man who doesn't know how to park a bike.

> Attr.

Auden, W.H. (1907–1973)
English poet, essayist, critic, teacher and dramatist
To the man-in-the-street, who, I'm sorry to say,
Is a keen observer of life,
The word intellectual suggests straight away
A man who's untrue to his wife.

> *Collected Poems*, 1939–1947

Bankhead, Tallulah (1903–1968)
US actress
I've been called many things, but never an intellectual.

> *Tallulah* (1952)

Barzun, Jacques (1907–)
French-born US historian, teacher and author
The intellectuals' chief cause of anguish are one another's works.

> *The House of Intellect* (1959)

Blake, William (1757–1827)
English poet, engraver, painter and mystic
I care not whether a Man is Good or Evil; all that I care
Is whether he is a Wise Man or a Fool. Go! put off Holiness
And put on Intellect.

> *Jerusalem* (1804–1820)

Camus, Albert (1913–1960)
Algerian-born French writer
Intellectuel? Oui. Et ne jamais renier. Intellectuel = celui qui se dédouble. Ça me plaît. Je suis content d'être les deux.
An intellectual? Yes. And never deny it. An intellectual = one who splits himself in two. I like that. I am happy to be both halves.

> *Carnets, 1935–1942* (1962)

Schweitzer, Albert (1875–1965)
French Protestant theologian, physician and musician
'Heda, Kamerad', rufe ich, 'willst du uns nicht ein wenig helfen?' 'Ich bin ein Intellektueller und trage kein Holz', lautete die Antwort. 'Hast du Glück', erwiderte ich; 'auch ich wollte ein Intellektueller werden, aber es ist mir nicht gelungen.'
'Hello, friend,' I shout, 'Won't you help us?' 'I am

an intellectual and don't carry wood around,'
came the answer. 'You're lucky,' I replied. 'I too
wanted to become an intellectual, but I didn't
manage it.'

> *Mitteilungen aus Lambarene* (1928)

Shortis, Gregory Brien (1945–)
I'm observing the golden mean and living
frugally
In the country without plumbing and only
A smoky, open fire, and things would be perfect
If my wife wasn't an intellectual.

> 'To Malcolm from an Unemployed Youth'

Stevenson, Adlai (1900–1965)
US lawyer, statesman and United Nations ambassador
Eggheads of the world unite; you have nothing
to lose but your yolks.

> Attr.

▶▶ INTELLIGENCE; MIND; THOUGHT

intelligence

Allen, Woody (1935–)
US film director, writer, actor and comedian
My brain: it's my second favourite organ.

> *Sleeper* (film, 1973)

Asquith, Margot (1864–1945)
Scottish political hostess and writer
On F.E. Smith
He's very clever, but sometimes his brains go to
his head.

> Quoted by Baroness Asquith in TV programme, *As
> I Remember*, 30 April 1967

Baldwin, Stanley (1867–1947)
English Conservative statesman and Prime Minister
The intelligent are to the intelligentsia what a
gentleman is to a gent.

> Attr.

Bogarde, Dirk (1921–1999)
British actor and writer
I'm not very clever, but I'm quite intelligent.

> Attr.

Brenan, Gerald (1894–1987)
English writer
Intellectuals are people who believe that ideas
are of more importance than values. That is to
say, their own ideas and other people's values.

> *Thoughts in a Dry Season* (1978)

Christie, Agatha (1890–1976)
English crime writer and playwright
Hercule Poirot tapped his forehead. 'These little
gray cells, it is 'up to them' – as you say over
here.'

> *The Mysterious Affair at Styles* (1920)

Cowper, William (1731–1800)
English poet, hymn and letter writer
His wit invites you by his looks to come,
But when you knock it is never at home.

> 'Conversation' (1782)

De Vries, Peter (1910–1993)
US novelist
We know the human brain is a device to keep
the ears from grating on one another.

> *Comfort me with Apples* (1956)

Diderot, Denis (1713–1784)
French philosopher, encyclopaedist, writer and dramatist
A retort which comes to mind too late
L'esprit de l'escalier.
Staircase wit.

> *Paradoxe sur le Comédien* (c.1778)

Doyle, Sir Arthur Conan (1859–1930)
Scottish writer and war correspondent
I am a brain, Watson. The rest of me is a mere
appendix.

> *The Case Book of Sherlock Holmes* (1927)

Freud, Sigmund (1856–1939)
Austrian physicist; founder of psychoanalysis
The voice of the intellect is a soft one, but it
does not rest till it has gained a hearing.

> *The Future of an Illusion*

Frisch, Max (1911–1991)
Swiss dramatist, writer and architect
*Wieso haben die Intellektuellen, wenn sie scharenweise
zusammenkommen, unweigerlich etwas Komisches?*
Why is there invariably something comic about
intellectuals when they meet together in
crowds?

> *Diary*, 1948

Goulburn, Edward, Dean of Norwich (1818–1897)
English divine and teacher
Let the scintillations of your wit be like the
coruscations of summer lightning, lambent but
innocuous.

> *Sermon at Rugby*

Herbert, George (1593–1633)
English poet and priest
Wit's an unruly engine, wildly striking
Sometimes a friend, sometimes the engineer.

> *The Temple* (1633

Keats, John (1795–1821)
English poet
The only means of strengthening one's intellect
is to make up one's mind about nothing – to let
the mind be a thoroughfare for all thoughts. Not
a select party.

> Letter to George and Georgiana Keats, 1819

La Rochefoucauld (1613–1680)
French writer

On peut être plus fin qu'un autre, mais non pas plus fin que tous les autres.
One can be more astute than another, but not more astute than all the others.

Maximes (1678)

C'est une grande habileté que de savoir cacher son habileté.
The height of cleverness is to be able to conceal it.

Maximes (1678)

Macaulay, Lord (1800–1859)
English Liberal statesman, essayist and poet
The highest intellects, like the tops of mountains, are the first to catch and to reflect the dawn.

'Sir James Mackintosh' (1843)

Mann, Thomas (1875–1955)
German writer and critic
Every intellectual attitude is latently political.

The Observer, 1974

Nietzsche, Friedrich Wilhelm (1844–1900)
German philosopher, critic and poet
Der Witz ist das Epigramm auf dem Tod eines Gefühls.
Wit is the epigram for the death of an emotion.

Human, All too Human (1886)

Pascal, Blaise (1623–1662)
French philosopher and scientist
A mesure qu'on a plus d'esprit, on trouve qu'il y a plus d'hommes originaux. Les gens du commun ne trouvent point de différence entre les hommes.
The more intelligence one has the more people one finds original. Commonplace people see no difference between men.

Pensées (1670)

Schopenhauer, Arthur (1788–1860)
German philosopher
Intellect is invisible to the man who has none.

Aphorismen zur Lebensweisheit

Shakespeare, William (1564–1616)
English dramatist, poet and actor
Brevity is the soul of wit.

Hamlet, II.ii

Look, he's winding up the watch of his wit; by and by it will strike.

The Tempest, II.i

This fellow is wise enough to play the fool;
And to do that well craves a kind of wit.

Twelfth Night, III.i

Su Tung-P'o (**Su Shih**) (1036–1101)
Chinese poet, painter and public official
Families, when a child is born
Want it to be intelligent.
I, through intelligence,

Having wrecked my whole life,
Only hope the baby will prove
Ignorant and stupid.
Then he will crown a tranquil life
By becoming a Cabinet Minister.

In Waley, *170 Chinese Poems*

Whitehead, A.N. (1861–1947)
English mathematician and philosopher
Intelligence is quickness to apprehend as distinct from ability, which is capacity to act wisely on the thing apprehended.

Dialogues (1954)

▶▶ INTELLECTUALS; KNOWLEDGE; MIND; PERCEPTION; THOUGHT; WISDOM

the internet

Anonymous
The Internet is like a vault with a screen door on the back. I don't need jackhammers and an atom bomb to get in when I can walk through the door.

Chomsky, Noam (1928–)
US linguist and political critic
The Internet is an élite organisation; most of the population of the world has never even made a phone call.

The Observer Review, 1996

Dench, Dame Judi (1934–)
English actress
When asked whether she uses e-mail
I am afraid it is a non-starter. I cannot even use a bicycle pump.

The Times, 1999

Fasulo, Tom
US entomologist and writer
Surfing on the Internet is like sex; everyone boasts about doing more than they actually do. But in the case of the Internet, it's a lot more.

Attr.

Gerstner, Lou
US business executive; Chairman of IBM
The killer application will not be a shrink-wrapped program that sells in millions. The killer app will be a Web site that touches millions of people and helps them to do what they want to do.

Attr.

Gibson, William (1948–)
US writer
Cyberspace: A consensual hallucination experienced daily by billions of legitimate

operators, in every nation.

Neuromancer (1984)

Nicholson, Jack (1937–)
US actor
Explaining why he disconnected his home computer from the Internet

There's so much darn porn out there, I never got out of the house.

The Times, 1999

Siriam, M.G.

Looking at the proliferation of personal web pages on the net, it looks like very soon everyone on earth will have 15 Megabytes of fame.

Attr.

Wilensky, Robert (1951–)

We've all heard that a million monkeys banging on a million typewriters will eventually reproduce the entire works of Shakespeare. Now, thanks to the Internet, we know this is not true.

Mail on Sunday, 1997

▶▶ ARTIFICIAL INTELLIGENCE; COMPUTERS; MEDIA; TECHNOLOGY

invention

Bierce, Ambrose (1842–c.1914)
US writer, verse writer and soldier

An inventor is a person who makes an ingenious arrangement of wheels, levers and springs, and believes it civilization.

The Devil's Dictionary,
1958

Buckminster Fuller, Richard (1895–1983)
US architect and engineer
On geodesic domes

I just invent, then wait until man comes around to needing what I've invented.

Time, 1964

Carlyle, Thomas (1795–1881)
Scottish historian, biographer, critic, and essayist

He who first shortened the labour of Copyists by device of Movable Types was disbanding hired Armies, and cashiering most Kings and Senates, and creating a whole new Democratic world: he had invented the Art of Printing.

Sartor Resartus (1834)

Edison, Thomas Alva (1847–1931)
US inventor and industrialist

To invent, you need a good imagination and a pile of junk.

Attr.

Emerson, Ralph Waldo (1803–1882)
US poet, essayist, transcendentalist and teacher

Invention breeds invention.

Society and Solitude (1870)

Flaubert, Gustave (1821–1880)
French writer

Tout ce qu'on invente est vrai, sois-en sûre. La poésie est une chose aussi précise que la géométrie.
Everything one invents is true, you can be sure of that. Poetry is as exact a science as geometry.

Letter to Louise Colet, 1853

Franklin, Benjamin (1706–1790)
US statesman, scientist, political critic and printer
On being asked the use of a new invention

What is the use of a new-born child?

In Parton, *Life and Times of Benjamin Franklin* (1864)

Grass, Günter (1927–)
German writer

Only a real lazybones can produce labour-saving inventions.

The Tin Drum (1959)

Piozzi, Hester Lynch (Mrs Henry Thrale)
(1741–1821)
English writer
Of a balloonist exhibiting in London

Monsieur Garnevin goes up again tomorrow with an Umbrella Thing to hinder his Fall, he calls it for that Reason a Parachute. We shall see how it answers – taking so much money at such a Risk of breaking all his bones.

Letter to Lady Williams, 2 July 1802

Proverb

Necessity is the mother of invention.

Swift, Jonathan (1667–1745)
Irish satirist, poet, essayist and cleric

He had been eight years upon a project for extracting sun-beams out of cucumbers, which were to be put into vials hermetically sealed, and let out to warm the air in raw inclement summers.

Gulliver's Travels (1726)

Voltaire (1694–1778)
French philosopher, dramatist, poet, historian writer and critic

The most amazing and effective inventions are not those which do most honour to the human genius.

Lettres philosophiques (1734)

▶▶ INNOVATION; SCIENCE

investments

Buffett, Warren (1930–)
US billionaire investment expert

Put all your eggs in one basket, and then pay very close attention to that basket.

Attr.

Keillor, Garrison (1942–)
US writer and broadcaster

Where I'm from we don't trust paper. Wealth is what's here on the premises. If I open a cupboard and see, say, 30 cans of tomato sauce and a five-pound bag of rice, I get a little thrill of well-being – much more so than if I take a look at the quarterly dividend report from my mutual fund.

Attr.

▶▶ MONEY AND WEALTH

ireland

Allen, Dave (1936–)
Irish comedian and television personality

The foreman says, 'You must have an intelligence test'. The Irishman says, 'All right.' So the foreman says, 'What is the difference between joist and girder?' And the Irishman says, 'Joyce wrote *Ulysses* and Goethe wrote *Faust*.'

Retelling the only Irish joke he really liked, quoted in Gus Smith, *God's Own Comedian*

Allingham, William (1824–1889)
Irish poet and diarist

Not men and women in an Irish street
But Catholics and Protestants you meet.

Attr.

Anonymous

Ah well, they say it's not as bad as they say it is.

An Irish woman's view on the situation in Ulster

Anyone who isn't confused here doesn't really understand what's going on.

Belfast citizen, 1970

Ascherson, Neal (1932–)
Scottish journalist

Peace in Northern Ireland has to built on its divisions, not on a fiction of unity which does not yet exist.

The Observer, 1998

Bates, Daisy May (1863–1951)
Irish-born journalist, anthropologist and reformer

There are a few fortunate races that have been endowed with cheerfulness as their main characteristic, the Australian Aborigine and the Irish being among these.

The Passing of the Aborigines … (1938)

Behan, Brendan (1923–1964)
Irish dramatist, writer and Republican

Pat: He was an Anglo-Irishman.

Meg: In the blessed name of God, what's that?
Pat: A Protestant with a horse.

The Hostage (1958)

The English and Americans dislike only some Irish – the same Irish that the Irish themselves detest, Irish writers – the ones that think.

Richard's Cork Leg (1972)

Other people have a nationality. The Irish and the Jews have a psychosis.

Richard's Cork Leg (1972)

Blackwood, Helen Selina (1807–1867)
English poet

And the red was on your lip, Mary,
The love-light in your eye …

I'm sitting on the stile, Mary,
Where we sat, side by side …

They say there's bread and work for all,
And the sun shines always there:
But I'll not forget old Ireland,
Were it fifty times as fair.

'Lament of the Irish Emigrant' (1845)

Chesterton, G.K. (1874–1936)
English writer, poet and critic

For the great Gaels of Ireland
Are the men that God made mad,
For all their wars are merry,
And all their songs are sad.

Ballad of the White Horse (1911)

Child, Lydia M. (1802–1880)
US writer, abolitionist and suffragist

Not in vain is Ireland pouring itself all over the earth … The Irish, with their glowing hearts and reverent credulity, are needed in this cold age of intellect and skepticism.

Letters from New York (1842)

Clare, Dr Anthony (1942–)
Irish professor, psychiatrist and broadcaster

The whole notion of holding a referendum on women's access to information is such a profound disgrace for a nation such as this that I … apologise to Irish women on behalf of what has been predominantly a male-dominated, male-driven male disgrace.

The Irish Times, 1993

Clinton, William ('Bill') (1946–)
US Democrat President
On the IRA, shortly after they resumed their campaign of violence in February 1996

We must not let the men of the past ruin the future of the children of Northern Ireland.

Daily Mail, 1996

Collins, Michael (1890–1922)
Irish revolutionary leader
Said on signing the agreement with Great Britain, 1921, that established the Irish Free State; he was assassinated some months later

> Think – what have I got for Ireland? Something which she has wanted these past seven hundred years. Will anyone be satisfied at the bargain? Will anyone? I tell you this – early this morning I signed my death warrant. I thought at the time how odd, how ridiculous – a bullet may just as well have done the job five years ago.
>
> *Letter to John O'Kane, 1921*

De Valera, Eamon (1882–1975)
Irish statesman

> Whenever I wanted to know what the Irish people wanted, I had only to examine my own heart and it told me straight off what the Irish people wanted.
>
> *Dáil Éireann, 1922*

> ... a land whose countryside would be bright with cosy homesteads, whose fields and villages would be joyous with the sounds of industry, with the romping of sturdy children, the contests of athletic youths and the laughter of comely maidens, whose firesides would be forums for the wisdom of serene old age.
>
> *Radio broadcast, St Patrick's Day, 1943*

Disraeli, Benjamin (1804–1881)
English statesman and writer

> A starving population, an absentee aristocracy, and an alien Church, and in addition the weakest executive in the world. That is the Irish question.
>
> *Speech, 1844*

Doyle, Roddy (1958–)
Irish writer

> The Irish are the niggers of Europe ... An' Dubliners are the niggers of Ireland ... An' the northside Dubliners are the niggers o' Dublin – Say it loud. I'm black an' I'm proud.
>
> *The Commitments (1987)*

Emmet, Robert (1778–1803)
Irish patriot
Before his execution

> When my country takes her place among the nations of the earth, then and not till then, let my epitaph be written. I have done.
>
> Attr.

Gallant, Mavis (1922–)
Canadian writer

> The Irish were not English. God had sent them to Canada to keep people from marrying Protestants.
>
> *Across the Bridge (1993)*

Gogarty, Oliver St John (1878–1957)
Irish poet, dramatist, writer, politician and surgeon

> Politics is the chloroform of the Irish people, or rather the hashish.
>
> *As I Was Going Down Sackville Street (1937)*

Hewitt, John (1907–1987)
Irish poet and museum and art gallery director

> The names of a land show the heart of the race;
> They move on the tongue like the lilt of a song.
> You say the name and I see the place –
> Drumbo, Dungannon, or Annalong.
> Barony, townland, we cannot go wrong.
>
> 'Ulster Names'

Johnson, Samuel (1709–1784)
English lexicographer, poet, critic, conversationalist and essayist

> The Irish are a fair people; – they never speak well of one another.
>
> *In Boswell, The Life of Samuel Johnson (1791)*

Joyce, James (1882–1941)
Irish writer

> Ireland is the old sow that eats her farrow.
>
> *A Portrait of the Artist as a Young Man (1916)*

> My intention was to write a chapter of the moral history of my country and I chose Dublin for the scene because that city seemed to me the centre of paralysis.
>
> *Letter to Grant Richards, 1905*

Leonard, Hugh (1926–)
Irish dramatist and screenwriter

> The problem with Ireland is that it's a country full of genius, but with absolutely no talent.
>
> *Interview in The Times, 1977*

Major, John (1943–)
English Conservative Prime Minister
On the search for peace in Northern Ireland after the end of the IRA ceasefire in February 1996

> If we are pushed back, we will start again. If we are pushed back, we will start again. If we are pushed back a third time we will start again.
>
> *The Observer Review, 1996*

Morrison, Danny (1950–)
Irish Republican activist

> Who here really believes that we can win the war through the ballot box? But will anyone here object if with a ballot box in this hand and an Armalite in this hand we take power in Ireland.
>
> *Provisional Sinn Féin Conference, 1981*

O'Faolain, Sean (1900–1991)

> An Irish Quaker is a fellow who prefers women to drink.
>
> *Attr. on Nigel Rees' BBC programme, Quote Unquote, 1999*

O'Leary, Father Joseph

On the IRA, during the search for the bodies of the 'disappeared'

How could we tolerate for all those years the deeds of a fascist organisation dedicated to torture and murder? What cowardice or connivance prevented us from speaking out against these atrocities? Were we any better than the denizens of Buchenwald who couldn't smell the smoke from the crematoria?

Letter to The Irish Times, *June 1999*

Robinson, Mary (1944–)

President of Ireland 1990–1997

As the elected choice of the people of this part of our island I want to extend the hand of friendship and of love to both communities in the other part.

Inaugural speech as President, 1991

Shaw, George Bernard (1856–1950)

Irish socialist, writer, dramatist and critic

An Irishman's heart is nothing but his imagination.

John Bull's Other Island (1907)

If you want to bore an Irishman, play him an Irish melody, or introduce him to another Irishman.

In Holroyd, Shaw *(1989)*

Smith, Adam (1723–1790)

Scottish economist, philosopher and essayist

Without a union with Great Britain, the inhabitants of Ireland are not likely for many ages to consider themselves as one people.

Wealth of Nations (1776)

Smith, Sydney (1771–1845)

English clergyman, essayist, journalist and wit

The moment the very name of Ireland is mentioned, the English seem to bid adieu to common feeling, common prudence, and to common sense, and to act with the barbarity of tyrants, and the fatuity of idiots.

Letters of Peter Plymley (1807)

Watson, Sir William (1858–1936)

Of Ireland

The lovely and lonely bride,
Whom we have wedded but never won.

'Ode on the Coronation of Edward VII' (1902)

Yeats, W.B. (1865–1939)

Irish poet, dramatist, editor, writer and senator
Of Ireland

This blind bitter land.

The Green Helmet and Other Poems (1912)

Behind Ireland fierce and militant, is Ireland poetic, passionate, remembering, idyllic, fanciful, and always patriotic.

'Popular Ballad Poetry of Ireland', 1889

From Yeats's speech on divorce, in which he stressed the contribution made by the Protestant minority to the literary and political life of Ireland

We against whom you have done this thing are no petty people. We are one of the great stocks of Europe. We are the people of Burke; we are the people of Grattan; we are the people of Swift, the people of Emmett, the people of Parnell. We have created the most of the modern literature of this country. We have created the best of its political intelligence.

Speech to the Senate, June 1925

italy

Biagi, Enzo (1920–)

Italian writer
On the Italians

Allora siamo i più disonesti? Credo proprio di no: ma probabilmente i più indifferenti.

Are we then the most dishonest people? I don't really think so: but probably we are the most indifferent ones.

The Good and the Bad, 1989)

After the kidnapping and subsequent murder of Aldo Moro, Christian Democrat Premier, May 1978

All'annuncio del rapimento l'Italia è come messa al tappeto da un colpo basso: non riesce a capire che cosa sta succedendo, le pare impossibile che il terrorismo sia cos' forte.

At the announcement of Moro's kidnapping, Italy looked as if she had been knocked out by a blow below the belt: she doesn't understand what's happening; it seems impossible to her that terrorism could be so powerful.

We Terrorists, 1985)

Di Pietro, Antonio (1947–)

Speaking of 'Mani pulite'

L'Italia si sta tirando fuori il suo dente; che ciascuno degli altri Paesi provi a cavare il suo di dente.

Italy is pulling out her own rotten tooth, let all other Countries pull out their own.

Speech in Toronto, Canada, November 1993, reported in the magazine, EPOCA, 1994

Jotti, Nilde (1920–)

Quali difetti attribuisce al maschio italiano: Primo è prepotente. Secondo una vittima, un prodotto che non sa badare a se stesso.

Which faults do you attribute to the Italian male: First he's a bully. Second a victim, a product that cannot look after himself.

In E. Biagi, La Geografia di Italia *(1975)*

Lampedusa, Giuseppe Tomasi di (1896–1957)

Italian novelist

L'Italia era nata in quell'accigliata sera a Donnafugata, nata proprio lì in quel paese dimenticato.
Una fata cattiva però della quale non si conosceva il nome doveva essere stata presente.

Italy was born on that sombre evening at Donnafugata, she was indeed born in that forgotten village.
A bad fairy, however, whose name no one knew must have been there.

The Leopard (1958)

Metternich, Prince Clement (1773–1859)
Austrian statesman
> *Italien ist ein geographischer Begriff.*
> Italy is a geographical concept.

Letter, 1849

Rush, Ian
English footballer
> I couldn't settle in Italy – it was like living in a foreign country.

Attr.

J

japan

Hodson, Peregrine
British author

... Japan is like a quicksand – the more one tries to get out of it, the more it sucks one in – or a maze without a centre – a sphinx without a riddle – or like Peer Gynt's onion, peel away the layers one after another and in the end all there is left is mush and tears.

A Circle Round The Sun – A Foreigner in Japan

Hyde, Robin (1906–1939)
New Zealand writer

The Japanese are described as 'the most nostalgic people on earth,' but I think possibly the remark applies to all island people, who have the spirit of adventure, but also the feeling of being secure on a small place among the waters.

Mirror, 1938

Morishima, Michio

The ability of the Japanese to assimilate Western technology and science with astonishing rapidity after the Meiji Restoration was due, at least in part, to their education under Confucianism; Western rationalist thinking was not entirely foreign.

'Why Has Japan Succeeded?, quoted in *Created in Japan*

Morita, Akio (1921–1999)
Japanese businessman, chief executive of Sony

Whereas Americans and Europeans often develop complex, large-scale solutions to problems, the Japanese constantly pare down and reduce the complexity of products and ideas to the barest minimum. They streamline the design, reduce the number of parts, and simplify the inner workings and moving parts. The influence of Zen and haiku poetry are often evident in the simplicity and utility of Japanese designs.

Made in Japan (1986)

Rauch, Jonathan
US journalist

... Japan's social and economic systems conspire, not against foreigners, but against newcomers.

Business Magazine, 1992

To enter any Japanese social system you must first get past the sign on the front door, which invariably says, 'By introduction only'. If you want to know how the business climate is for outsiders in Japan, meet Kochan the master sushi-chef. He hides his fish so that he can refuse service to strangers. When a customer walks in without the proper introduction, Kochan shakes his head and claims, absurdly, that he is fresh out of everything.

Business Magazine, 1992

Theroux, Paul (1941–)
US writer

Outside the Nichigeki Music Hall, the Japanese men who had watched with fastidious languor and then so enthusiastically applauded the savage eroticism that could enjoy no encore – baring their teeth as they did so – these men, as I say, bowed deeply to one another, murmured polite farewells to their friends, linked arms with their wives with the gentleness of old-fashioned lovers, and, in the harsh lights of the street, smiled, looking positively cherubic.

The Great Railway Bazaar (1975)

It is with a kind of perverse pride that the Japanese point out how expensive their country has become. But this is as much a measure of wealth as of inflation.

The Great Railway Bazaar (1975)

jealousy

Herbert, Sir A.P. (1890–1971)
English humorist, writer, dramatist and politician

I'm not a jealous woman, but I can't see what he sees in her.

'I Can't Think What He Sees in Her'

Jong, Erica (1942–)
US writer

Jealousy is all the fun you think they had.

Fear of Flying (1973)

Milton, John (1608–1674)
English poet, libertarian and pamphleteer

Nor jealousie
Was understood, the injur'd Lover's Hell.

Paradise Lost (1667)

Sagan, Françoise (1935–)
French writer

To jealousy nothing is more frightful than laughter.

Attr.

Shakespeare, William (1564–1616)
English dramatist, poet and actor

O, beware, my lord, of jealousy;

It is the green-ey'd monster which doth mock
The meat it feeds on.

Othello, III.iii

Trifles light as air
Are to the jealous confirmations strong
As proofs of holy writ.

Othello, III.iii

Jealous souls will not be answer'd so;
They are not ever jealous for the cause,
But jealous for they are jealous.

Othello, III.iv

The venom clamours of a jealous woman
Poisons more deadly than a mad dog's tooth.

The Comedy of Errors, V.i

Vanbrugh, Sir John (1664–1726)
English dramatist and baroque architect
Jealousy's a city passion; 'tis a thing unknown amongst people of quality.

The Confederacy (1705)

Wells, H.G. (1866–1946)
English writer
Moral indignation is jealousy with a halo.

The Wife of Sir Isaac Harman (1914)

▶▶ ENVY

jewellery

Dickens, Charles (1812–1870)
English writer
It was not a bosom to repose upon, but it was a capital bosom to hang jewels upon.

Little Dorrit (1857)

Lennon, John (1940–1980)
English rock musician
Those in the cheaper seats clap. The rest of you rattle your jewellery.

Remark, Royal Variety Performance, 15 November 1963

Loos, Anita (1893–1981)
US writer and screenwriter
Any girl who was a lady would not even think of having such a good time that she did not remember to hang on to her jewelry.

Gentlemen Prefer Blondes (1925)

Reade, Charles (1814–1884)
English novelist and dramatist
She wrenched from her brow a diamond and eyed it with contempt, took from her pocket a sausage and contemplated it with respect and affection.

Peg Woffington (1852)

Robin, Leo (1899–)
US songwriter

Diamonds Are A Girl's Best Friend.

Song title, 1949

Stevenson, Adlai (1900–1965)
US lawyer, statesman and United Nations ambassador
As the girl said, 'A kiss on the wrist feels good, but a diamond bracelet lasts forever.'

Address to Chicago Council on Foreign Relations

West, Mae (1892–1980)
US actress and scriptwriter
'Goodness, what beautiful diamonds!'
'Goodness had nothing to do with it!'.

Night After Night (film, 1932)

jews

Balfour, A.J. (1848–1930)
British Conservative Prime Minister
His Majesty's Government views with favour the establishment in Palestine of a national home for the Jewish people.

'The Balfour Declaration', 1917

Blue, Rabbi Lionel (1930–)
English lecturer, writer and broadcaster
There is always a danger in Judaism of seeing history as a sort of poker game played between Jews and God, in which the presence of others is noted but not given much importance.

The Observer, 1982

Browne, Cecil (1932–)
US businessman
But not so odd
As those who choose
A Jewish God,
But spurn the Jews.

Reply to William Norman Ewer: *How odd/Of God/To choose/The Jews*

Dryden, John (1631–1700)
English poet, satirist, dramatist and critic
The Jews, a headstrong, moody, murmuring race
As ever tried the extent and stretch of grace,
God's pampered people, whom, debauched with ease,
No king could govern nor no God could please.
Gods they had tried of every shape and size
That godsmiths could produce or priests devise.

Absalom and Achitophel (1681)

Heine, Heinrich (1797–1856)
German lyric poet, essayist and journalist
When people talk about a wealthy man of my creed, they call him an Israelite; but if he is poor they call him a Jew.

MS. Papers

It is extremely difficult for a Jew to be converted, for how can he bring himself to believe in the divinity of – another Jew?

Attr.

Johnson, Paul (1928–)
British editor and writer

For me this is a vital litmus test: no intellectual society can flourish where a Jew feels even slightly uneasy.

The Sunday Times Magazine, 1977

Lawrence, D.H. (1885–1930)
English writer, poet and critic

The very best that is in the Jewish blood: a faculty for pure disinterestedness, and warm, physically warm love, that seems to make the corpuscles of the blood glow.

Kangaroo (1923)

Marx, Groucho (1895–1977)
US comedian

When excluded, on racial grounds, from a beach club

Since my daughter is only half-Jewish, could she go into the water up to her knees?

The Observer, 1977

Miller, Jonathan (1934–)
English writer, director, producer and physician

I'm not really a Jew; just Jew-ish, not the whole hog.

Beyond the Fringe (1961)

Milligan, Spike (1918–)
Irish comedian and writer

Q. Are you Jewish?
A. No, a tree fell on me.

Private Eye, 1973

Peres, Shimon (1923–)
Israeli statesman and Prime Minister

Leading the Jewish people is not easy – we are a divided, obstinate, highly individualistic people who have cultivated faith, sharp wittedness and polemics to a very high level.

New York Times, 1986

Richler, Mordecai (1931–)
Canadian novelist

And furthermore did you know that behind the discovery of America there was a Jewish financier?

Cocksure (1968)

Roden, Claudia
Egyptian-born British cookery writer

The real crystallisation of Jewish cuisine took place in the 16th century, when the Jews were confined to ghettos by edict. It may seem surprising that interest in food should blossom in a ghetto, especially one devoted to religious worship; but people focused on their home life

as an antidote to the misery and degradation outside. Hospitality became a means of survival and the celebration of religious festivals ... made it possible to remain indifferent to the world outside the gates.

The Good Food Guide, 1985

Roth, Philip (1933–)
US writer

A Jewish man with parents alive is a fifteen-year-old boy, and will remain a fifteen-year-old boy until they die.

Portnoy's Complaint (1969)

Doctor, my doctor, what do you say – let's put the id back in yid!

Portnoy's Complaint (1969)

Shakespeare, William (1564–1616)
English dramatist, poet and actor

Hath not a Jew eyes? Hath not a Jew hands, organs, dimensions, senses, affections, passions, fed with the same food, hurt with the same weapons, subject to the same diseases, healed by the same means, warmed and cooled by the same winter and summer, as a Christian is? If you prick us, do we not bleed? If you tickle us, do we not laugh? If you poison us, do we not die? And if you wrong us, shall we not revenge? If we are like you in the rest, we will resemble you in that.

The Merchant of Venice, III.i

Stein, Gertrude (1874–1946)
US writer, dramatist, poet and critic

The Jews have produced only three originative geniuses: Christ, Spinoza, and myself.

In Mellow, *Charmed Circle* (1974)

Ustinov, Sir Peter (1921–)
English actor, director, dramatist, writer and raconteur

I believe that the Jews have made a contribution to the human condition out of all proportion to their numbers: I believe them to be an immense people. Not only have they supplied the world with two leaders of the stature of Jesus Christ and Karl Marx, but they have even indulged in the luxury of following neither one nor the other.

Dear Me (1977)

Zangwill, Israel (1864–1926)
English writer and Jewish spokesman

No Jew was ever fool enough to turn Christian unless he was a clever man.

Children of the Ghetto (1892)

▶▶ PREJUDICE; RACE; RELIGION

journalism

Balfour, A.J. (1848–1930)
British Conservative Prime Minister
> Frank Harris ... said ...: 'The fact is, Mr Balfour, all the faults of the age come from Christianity and journalism.' To which Arthur replied ... 'Christianity, of course ... but why journalism?'.
>> In Margot Asquith, *Autobiography* (1920)

Bennett, Arnold (1867–1931)
English writer, dramatist and journalist
> Journalists say a thing that they know isn't true, in the hope that if they keep on saying it long enough it will be true.
>> *The Title* (1918)

Bennett, James Gordon (1795–1872)
Scottish-born US editor
Advice to journalists
> Remember, son, many a good story has been ruined by over-verification.
>> Attr.

Bentley, Nicolas (1907–1978)
English publisher and artist
> No news is good news; no journalists is even better.
>> Attr.

Bernstein, Carl (1944–)
US journalist
> The lowest form of popular culture – lack of information, misinformation, disinformation, and a contempt for the truth or the reality of most people's lives – has overrun real journalism. Today, ordinary Americans are being stuffed with garbage.
>> *The Guardian*, 1992

> The failures of the press have contributed immensely to the emergence of a talk-show nation, in which public discourse is reduced to ranting and raving and posturing.
>> *The Guardian*, 1992

Bishop, Jim (1907–1987)
US author and journalist
> The reporter is the daily prisoner of clocked facts... On all working days, he is expected to do his best in one swift swipe at each story.
>> *A Bishop's Confession* (1981)

Curzon, Lord (1859–1925)
English statesman and scholar
> I hesitate to say what the functions of the modern journalist may be; but I imagine that they do not exclude the intelligent anticipation of facts even before they occur.
>> Speech, 1898

Duras, Marguerite (1914–1996)
French author and film-maker
> Journalism without a moral position is impossible. Every journalist is a moralist. It's absolutely unavoidable.
>> *Outside: Selected Writings* (1984)

Eldershaw, M. Barnard (1897–1987)
Australian writer, critic and librarian
> Journalists are people who take in one another's washing and then sell it.
>> *Plaque with Laurel* (1937)

García Márquez, Gabriel (1928–)
Colombian author
> *El periodismo es un género literario, muy parecido a la novela, y tiene la gran ventaja de que el reportero puede inventar cosas. Y eso el novelista lo tiene totalmente prohibido.*
> Journalism is a literary genre very similar to that of the novel, and has the great advantage that the reporter can invent things. And that is completely forbidden to the novelist.
>> Speech, 1994

> Destructive journalism fosters the belief that politicians routinely evade the truth and break their promises. It creates a climate in which trust in society as a whole dissolves; in which difficulties are magnified beyond all proportion; in which no one is believed to act except for the most self-centred of motives.
>> *The Spectator*, May 1996

Graham, Katherine (1917–)
US newspaper propietor; owner of the *Washington Post*
On Watergate coverage
> If we had failed to pursue the facts as far as they led, we would have denied the public any knowledge of an unprecedented scheme of political surveillance and sabotage.
>> *Washington Post*, 1973

Hepworth, John (1921–)
Australian writer
> Most journalists of my generation died early, succumbing to one or other of the two great killers in the craft – cirrhosis or terminal alimony.
>> *National Review*, 1974

Kraus, Karl (1874–1936)
Austrian scientist, critic and poet
> *Keinen Gedanken haben und ihn ausdrücken können – das macht den Journalisten.*
> To have no thoughts and be able to express them – that's what makes a journalist.
>> *Pro domo et mundo* (1912)

> Journalist: a person without any ideas but with an ability to express them; a writer whose skill is improved by a deadline: the more time he has,

the worse he writes.

> In Thomas Szasz, *Anti-Freud: Karl Kraus's Criticism of Psychoanalysis and Psychiatry* (1976)

Lewis, Willmott (1877–1950)
English journalist

I think it well to remember that, when writing for the newspapers, we are writing for an elderly lady in Hastings who has two cats of which she is passionately fond. Unless our stuff can successfully compete for her interest with those cats, it is no good.

> In Claud Cockburn, *In Time of Trouble* (1957)

Luce, Henry R. (1898–1967)
US publisher and editor

I became a journalist to come as close as possible to the heart of the world.

> *Esquire*, 1983

MacCarthy, Sir Desmond (1878–1952)
English critic

Journalists are more attentive to the minute hand of history than to the hour hand.

> In Tynan, *Curtains* (1961)

Tomalin, Nicholas (1931–1973)
English journalist

The only qualities essential for real success in journalism are rat-like cunning, a plausible manner, and a little literary ability.

> *The Sunday Times Magazine*, 1969

Wilde, Oscar (1854–1900)
Irish poet, dramatist, writer, critic and wit

As for modern journalism, it is not my business to defend it. It justifies its own existence by the great Darwinian principle of the survival of the vulgarest.

> *Intentions* (1891)

There is much to be said in favour of modern journalism. By giving us the opinions of the uneducated, it keeps us in touch with the ignorance of the community.

> 'The Critic as Artist' (1891)

Zappa, Frank (1940–1993)
US rock musician, songwriter and record producer

Rock journalism is people who can't write interviewing people who can't talk for people who can't read.

> In Linda Botts, *Loose Talk* (1980)

▶▶ NEWS AND NEWSPAPERS

joy

Blake, William (1757–1827)
English poet, engraver, painter and mystic

… I have no name

I am but two days old – '
What shall I call thee?
… I happy am,
Joy is my name, – '
Sweet joy befall thee!

> *Songs of Innocence* (1789)

Joys impregnate. Sorrows bring forth.

> *The Marriage of Heaven and Hell* (c.1790–1793)

He who binds to himself a joy
Does the winged life destroy;
But he who kisses the joy as it flies
Lives in eternity's sun rise.

> 'Eternity' (c.1793), from 'The Rossetti Manuscript'

Lang, Andrew (1844–1912)
Scottish poet, writer, mythologist and anthropologist

There's a joy without canker or cark,
There's a pleasure eternally new,
'Tis to gloat on the glaze and the mark
Of China that's ancient and blue.

> 'Ballade of Blue China'

Reid, Bill

Joy is a well-made object.

> *Maclean's*, 1989

Schiller, Johann Christoph Friedrich (1759–1805)
German writer, dramatist, poet and historian

Freude, schöner Götterfunken,
Tochter aus Elysium,
Wir betreten feuertrunken
Himmlische, dein Heiligtum.
Deine Zauber binden wieder,
Was die Mode streng geteilt,
Alle Menschen werden Brüder,
Wo dein sanfter Flügel weilt.
Joy, fair ray of the gods,
Daughter of Elysium,
Dazzled we enter,
Heavenly one, thy shrine.
Against thy charms join together
What custom has harshly divided,
All men become brothers,
Under thy gentle wing.

> 'To Joy' (revised 1803); set to music by Beethoven in the last movement of his Ninth Symphony

▶▶ HAPPINESS; LAUGHTER; PLEASURE

judgement

Addison, Joseph (1672–1719)
English essayist, poet, playwright and statesman

Sir Roger told them, with the air of a man who would not give his judgement rashly, that much might be said on both sides.

> *The Spectator*, July 1711

Augustine, Saint (354–430)

Numidian-born Christian theologian and philosopher

The judgement of the world is sure.

Contra Epistolam Parmeniani

Bentley, Edmund Clerihew (1875–1956)

English writer

Between what matters and what seems to matter, how should the world we know judge wisely?

Trent's Last Case (1913)

His judgement of persons was penetrating, but its process was internal; no-one felt on good behaviour with a man who seemed always to be enjoying himself.

Trent's Last Case (1913)

The Bible (King James Version)

Judge not, that ye be not judged.

Matthew, 7:1

By their fruits ye shall know them.

Matthew, 7:20

He that is without sin among you, let him first cast a stone at her.

Luke, 8:7

Browning, Elizabeth Barrett (1806–1861)

English poet; wife of Robert Browning

Let no one till his death
Be called unhappy. Measure not the work,
Until the day's out and the labour done.

Aurora Leigh (1857)

Bruno, Giordano (1548–1600)

Italian philosopher

Said to the cardinals who excommunicated him

Perhaps your fear in passing judgement is greater than mine in receiving it.

Attr.

Camus, Albert (1913–1960)

Algerian-born French writer

N'attendez pas le jugement dernier. Il a lieu tous les jours.
Don't wait for the Last Judgement. It is taking place every day.

The Fall (1956)

Celano, Thomas de (c.1190–c.1260)

Italian disciple and biographer of St Francis of Assisi

Tuba mirum sparget sonum
Per sepulchra regionum,
Coget omnes ante thronum.

Mors stupebit et natura,
Cum resurget creatura
Iudicanti responsura.

Liber scriptus proferetur,
In quo totum continetur

Unde mundus iudicetur.
The trumpet will fling out a stupendous sound through the tombs of all regions, it will drive everyone before the throne. Death will be amazed and so will nature, when creation rises again to make answer to the judge. The written book will be brought forward, in which everything is contained whereby the world will be judged.

Dies irae

Compton-Burnett, Dame Ivy (1884–1969)

English novelist

Appearances are not held to be a clue to the truth. But we seem to have no other.

Manservant and Maidservant (1947)

Cowper, William (1731–1800)

English poet, hymn and letter writer

Judgment drunk, and brib'd to lose his way,
Winks hard, and talks of darkness at noon-day.

'The Progress of Error' (1782)

Edgeworth, Maria (1767–1849)

English-born Irish writer

We cannot judge either of the feelings or of the characters of men with perfect accuracy, from their actions or their appearance in public; it is from their careless conversations, their half-finished sentences, that we may hope with the greatest probability of success to discover their real character.

Castle Rackrent (1800)

Euripides (c.485–406 BC)

Greek dramatist and poet

The wisest men follow their own direction
And listen to no prophet guiding them.
None but the fools believe in oracles,
Forsaking their own judgement. Those who know,
Know that such men can only come to grief.

Iphigenia in Tauris

Kafka, Franz (1883–1924)

Czech-born German-speaking writer

Dann erinnere ich Sie an den alten Rechtsspruch: für den Verdächtigen ist Bewegung besser als Ruhe, denn der, welcher ruht, kann immer, ohne es zu wissen, auf einer Waagschale sein und mit seinen Sünden gewogen werden.
Then I shall remind you of the old verdict: the person under suspicion is better to be moving than at rest, for at rest one can, without knowing it, be in the balance being weighed together with one's sins.

The Trial (1914)

Maurois, André (1885–1967)
French writer

> *Aucun de nous ne vit à chaque instant toutes ses idées; mais il faut juger les êtres plus par leurs dépassements que par leurs défaillances.*
> None of us lives out, at every moment, all of our ideas; but one should judge human beings more by their excellence than by their weaknesses.
> *Lélia ou la vie de George Sand* (1952)

Montaigne, Michel de (1533–1592)
French essayist and moralist

> It is a dangerous and serious presumption, and argues an absurd temerity, to condemn what we do not understand.
> *Essais* (1580)

Pliny the Elder (AD 23–79)
Roman scholar

> *Ne supra crepidam sutor iudicaret.*
> The cobbler should not judge beyond his last.
> *Historia Naturalis*

Pope, Alexander (1688–1744)
English poet, translator and editor

> 'Tis with our judgements as our watches, none
> Go just alike, yet each believes his own.
> *An Essay on Criticism* (1711)

Proverb

> A judge knows nothing unless it has been explained to him three times.

Shakespeare, William (1564–1616)
English dramatist, poet and actor

> What judgment shall I dread, doing no wrong?
> *The Merchant of Venice*, IV.i

justice and injustice

Bennett, Arnold (1867–1931)
English writer, dramatist and journalist

> The price of justice is eternal publicity.
> *Things That Have Interested Me*

Bingham, Sir Thomas (1933–)
English Master of the Rolls
Discussing the rising costs of going to law

> We cannot for ever be content to acknowledge that in England justice is open to all – like the Ritz Hotel.
> *Independent on Sunday*, 1994

Bird, Rose Elizabeth (1936–)
US Supreme Court judge

> It is easy to be popular. It is not easy to be just.
> *Boston Globe*, 1982

Blackstone, Sir William (1723–1780)
English judge, historian and politician

> It is better that ten guilty persons escape than one innocent suffer.
> *Commentaries on the Laws of England* (1765–1769)

Bowen, Lord (1835–1894)
English judge and scholar

> The rain it raineth on the just
> And also on the unjust fella:
> But chiefly on the just, because
> The unjust steals the just's umbrella.
> In Sichel, *Sands of Time* (1923)

Burroughs, William S. (1914–1999)
US writer

> If you can't be just, be arbitrary.
> *Naked Lunch* (1959)

Cardozo, Benjamin (1870–1938)
US Supreme Court judge

> Justice is not to be taken by storm. She is to be wooed by slow advances.
> *The Growth of the Law* (1924)

Carlyle, Jane Welsh (1801–1866)
Scottish letter writer, literary hostess and poet

> When one has been threatened with a great injustice, one accepts a smaller as a favour.
> *Journal*, 1855

Carroll, Lewis (1832–1898)
English writer and photographer

> 'I'll be judge, I'll be jury,' said cunning old Fury: 'I'll try the whole cause, and condemn you to death.'
> *Alice's Adventures in Wonderland* (1865)

> 'No! No!' said the Queen. 'Sentence first – verdict afterwards'.
> *Alice's Adventures in Wonderland* (1865)

Confucius (c.550–c.478 BC)
Chinese philosopher and teacher of ethics

> Recompense injury with justice, and recompense kindness with kindness.
> *Analects*

Denman, Lord (1779–1854)
English politician and Lord Chief Justice

> Trial by jury itself, instead of being a security to persons who are accused, will be a delusion, a mockery, and a snare.
> Speech in the House of Lords, 1844

Disraeli, Benjamin (1804–1881)
English statesman and writer

> Justice is truth in action.
> Speech, House of Commons, 1851

Dürrenmatt, Friedrich (1921–1990)
Swiss dramatist and writer

> *Die Gerechtigkeit ist etwas Fürchterliches.*
> Justice is something terrible.
> *Romulus the Great* (1964)

> *Die Gerechtigkeit ist nicht eine Hackmaschine, sondern*

ein Abkommen.
Justice is not a mincer but an agreement.
The Marriage of Mr Mississippi (1951)

Ferdinand I, Emperor (1503–1564)
Fiat justitia, et pereat mundus.
Let there be justice though the world perish.

Fielding, Henry (1707–1754)
English writer, dramatist and journalist
Thwackum was for doing justice, and leaving mercy to Heaven.
Tom Jones (1749)

France, Anatole (1844–1924)
French writer and critic
Désarmer les forts et armer les faibles ce serait changer l'ordre social que j'ai mission de conserver. La justice est la sanction des injustices établies.
To disarm the strong and arm the weak would be to change a social order which I have been commissioned to preserve. Justice is the means whereby established injustices are sanctioned.
Crainquebille (1904)

Hardy, Thomas (1840–1928)
English writer and poet
'Justice' was done, and the President of the Immortals, in Aeschylean phrase, had ended his sport with Tess.
Tess of the D'Urbervilles (1891

Hewart, Gordon (1870–1943)
English Liberal politician and Lord Chief Justice
It is not merely of some importance but is of fundamental importance that justice should not only be done, but should manifestly and undoubtedly be seen to be done.
Rex v. Sussex Justices, 1923

Junius (1769–1772)
Pen-name of anonymous author of letters criticising ministers of George III
The injustice done to an individual is sometimes of service to the public.
Letters (1769–1771)

Justinian, Emperor (c.482–565)
Byzantine emperor
Justitia est constans et perpetua voluntas ius suum cuique tribuens.
Justice is the constant and perpetual wish to give to every one his due.
Institutes

Kafka, Franz (1883–1924)
Czech-born German-speaking writer
Sie können einwenden, dass es ja überhaupt kein Verfahren ist, Sie haben sehr recht, denn es ist ja nur ein Verfahren, wenn ich als solches anerkenne.
You may raise the objection that it really is not a trial at all; you are quite right, for it is only a trial

if I recognise it as such.
The Trial (1925)

Kelly, Ned (1855–1880)
Australian outlaw folk hero
There never was such a thing as justice in the English laws but any amount of injustice to be had.
In *Overland*, 1981

King, Martin Luther (1929–1968)
US civil rights leader and Baptist minister
Injustice anywhere is a threat to justice everywhere.
Letter from Birmingham Jail, April 16, 1963

La Rochefoucauld (1613–1680)
French writer
L'amour de la justice n'est, en la plupart des hommes, que la crainte de souffrir l'injustice.
The love of justice in most men is no more than the fear of suffering injustice.
Maximes (1678)

Lincoln, Abraham (1809–1865)
US statesman and President
The probability that we may fail in the struggle ought not to deter us from the support of a cause we believe to be just.
Speech, 1859

Magna Carta (1215)
Nulli vendemus, nulli negabimus aut differemus, rectum aut justitiam.
To no one will we sell, to no one will we deny, or delay, right or justice.
Clause 40

Mansfield, William Murray, Earl of (1705–1793)
Scottish judge
Advice given to a new colonial governor
Consider what you think justice requires, and decide accordingly. But never give your reasons; for your judgement will probably be right, but your reasons will certainly be wrong.
In Campbell, *Lives of the Chief Justices* (1849)

Mencken, H.L. (1880–1956)
US writer, critic, philologist and satirist
Injustice is relatively easy to bear: what stings is justice.
Attr.

Milton, John (1608–1674)
English poet, libertarian and pamphleteer
Yet I shall temper so
Justice with Mercie.
Paradise Lost (1667)

Molière (1622–1673)
French dramatist, actor and director
Ils commencent ici par faire pendre un homme et puis ils lui font son procès.

Here they have a man hanged, and then proceed to try him.

Monsieur de Pourceaugnac
(1670)

Osborne, John (1929–1994)
English dramatist and actor

The injustice of it is almost perfect! The wrong people going hungry, the wrong people being loved, the wrong people dying!

Look Back in Anger (1956)

Peters, Ellis (1913–1995)
English writer

'It may well be,' said Cadfael, 'that our justice sees as in a mirror image, left where right should be, evil reflected back as good, good as evil, your angel as her devil. But God's justice, if it makes no haste, makes no mistakes.'

The Potter's Field (1989)

Pope, Alexander (1688–1744)
English poet, translator and editor

The hungry Judges soon the sentence sign,
And wretches hang that jury-men may dine.

The Rape of the Lock (1714)

Publilius, Syrus (1st century BC)
Roman writer

Iudex damnatur ubi nocens absolvitur.
The judge is condemned when the guilty party is acquitted.

Sententiae

Pulteney, William, Earl of Bath (1684–1764)
English politician

Since twelve honest men have decided the cause,
And were judges of fact, though not judges of laws.

'The Honest Jury' (1729)

Richelieu, Cardinal (1585–1642)
Prime Minister to Louis XIII, 1624–1642

If you give me six lines written by the most honest man, I will find something in them to hang him.

Attr.

Roux, Joseph (1834–1886)
French priest and epigrammatist

We love justice greatly, and just men but little.

Meditations of a Parish Priest (1886)

Shakespeare, William (1564–1616)
English dramatist, poet and actor

What stronger breastplate than a heart untainted?
Thrice is he arm'd that hath his quarrel just;
And he but naked, though lock'd up in steel,
Whose conscience with injustice is corrupted.

Henry VI, Part 2, III.ii

Shirley, James (1596–1666)
English poet and dramatist

Only the actions of the just
Smell sweet, and blossom in their dust.

The Contention of Ajax and Ulysses (1659)

Stoppard, Tom (1937–)
British dramatist

This is a British murder inquiry and some degree of justice must be seen to be more or less done.

Jumpers (1972)

Vergniaud, Pierre (1753–1793)
French politician and revolutionary

When justice has spoken, humanity must have its turn.

Speech, 1793

Wilde, Oscar (1854–1900)
Irish poet, dramatist, writer, critic and wit

For Man's grim Justice goes its way,
And will not swerve aside:
It slays the weak, it slays the strong,
It has a deadly stride.

The Ballad of Reading Gaol (1898)

▶▶ JUDGEMENT; LAW

K

karma

Hoddle, Glen
English footballer and coach
> You and I have been physically given two hands and two legs and half-decent brains. Some people have not been born like that for a reason. The karma is working from another lifetime. I have nothing to hide about that. It is not only people with disabilities. What you sow, you have to reap.
> > *The Times*, 1999

kindness

Anonymous
> Be kind to unkind people – they need it the most.

Camus, Albert (1913–1960)
Algerian-born French writer
> *Ils savaient maintenant que s'il est une chose qu'on puisse désirer toujours et obtenir quelquefois, c'est la tendresse humaine.*
> They now knew that if there is one thing which can always be desired and sometimes obtained, it is human tenderness.
> > *The Plague* (1947)

Confucius (c.550–c.478 BC)
Chinese philosopher and teacher of ethics
> Recompense injury with justice, and recompense kindness with kindness.
> > *Analects*

Davies, William Henry (1871–1940)
Welsh poet, writer and tramp
> I love thee for a heart that's kind –
> Not for the knowledge in thy mind.
> > 'Sweet Stay-at-Home' (1913)

Gide, André (1869–1951)
French writer, critic, dramatist and poet
> True kindness presupposes the faculty of imagining as one's own the suffering and joy of others.
> > Attr.

Jackson, F.J. Foakes (1855–1941)
English divine and church historian
Advice given to a new don at Jesus College, Cambridge
> It's no use trying to be clever – we are all clever here; just try to be kind – a little kind.
> > In *Benson's Commonplace Book*

Johnson, Samuel (1709–1784)
English lexicographer, poet, critic, conversationalist and essayist
> Always, Sir, set a high value on spontaneous kindness. He whose inclination prompts him to cultivate your friendship of his own accord, will love you more than one whom you have been at pains to attach to you.
> > In Boswell, *The Life of Samuel Johnson* (1791)

Marshall, Alan John (1911–1968)
Australian zoologist and explorer
> Beware of people you've been kind to.
> > Remark to John Morrison

Shakespeare, William (1564–1616)
English dramatist, poet and actor
> I must be cruel, only to be kind.
> > *Hamlet*, III.iv

Wilcox, Ella Wheeler (1850–1919)
US poet and writer
> So many gods, so many creeds,
> So many paths that wind and wind,
> While just the art of being kind
> Is all the sad world needs.
> > 'The World's Need' (1917)

Williams, Tennessee (1911–1983)
US dramatist and writer
> I have always depended on the kindness of strangers.
> > *A Streetcar Named Desire* (1947)

Wordsworth, William (1770–1850)
English poet
> On that best portion of a good man's life;
> His little, nameless, unremembered acts
> Of kindness and of love.
> > 'Lines composed a few miles above Tintern Abbey' (1798)

▶▶ CHARITY

kissing

Adams, Joey (b. 1911)
US comedian and author
> Never let a fool kiss you, or a kiss fool you.
> > Attr.

Fletcher, John (1579–1625)
English dramatist
> Kiss till the cow comes home.
> > *The Scornful Lady* (produced 1610, published 1616)

Kipling, Rudyard (1865–1936)
Indian-born British poet and writer

Being kissed – by a man who didn't wax his moustache was – like eating an egg without salt.

The Story of the Gadsbys (1888), 'Poor Dear Mamma'

Marx, Groucho (1895–1977)
US comedian

Whoever named it necking was a poor judge of anatomy.

Attr.

Shakespeare, William (1564–1616)
English dramatist, poet and actor

O, a kiss
Long as my exile, sweet as my revenge!
Now, by the jealous queen of heaven, that kiss
I carried from thee, dear, and my true lip
Hath virgin'd it e'er since.

The Comedy of Errors, V.iii

Present mirth hath present laughter;
What's to come is still unsure.
In delay there lies no plenty,
Then come kiss me, sweet and twenty;
Youth's a stuff will not endure.

Twelfth Night, II.iii

Thomas, Dylan (1914–1953)
Welsh poet, writer and radio dramatist

Gomer Owen who kissed her once by the pig-sty when she wasn't looking and never kissed her again although she was looking all the time.

Under Milk Wood (1954)

knowledge

Adams, Henry (1838–1918)
US historian and memoirist

They know enough who know how to learn.

The Education of Henry Adams (1918)

Adler, Freda (1934–)
US educator and writer

The passionate controversies of one era are viewed as sterile preoccupations by another, for knowledge alters what we seek as well as what we find.

Sisters in Crime (1975)

Aeschylus (525–456 BC)
Greek dramatist and poet

Old men are always young enough to learn with profit.

Agamemnon

Alexander the Great (356–323 BC)
Macedonian king and conquering army commander

I would rather excel in the knowledge of what is excellent, than in the extent of my power.

In Plutarch, *Lives*

Anonymous

An expert is someone who knows more and more about less and less, until eventually he knows everything about nothing.

Aristotle (384–322 BC)
Greek philosopher

All men naturally desire knowledge.

Metaphysics

Bacon, Francis (1561–1626)
English philosopher, essayist, politician and courtier

Knowledge itself is power.

'Of Heresies' (1597)

Beeching, Rev. H.C. (1859–1919)
English theologian, poet and essayist

First come I; my name is Jowett.
There's no knowledge but I know it.
I am Master of this college:
What I don't know isn't knowledge.

'The Masque of Balliol' (late 1870s)

Behn, Aphra (1640–1689)
English dramatist, writer, poet, translator and spy

Of all that writ, he was the wisest bard, who spoke this mighty truth –
He that knew all that ever learning writ,
Knew only this – that he knew nothing yet.

The Emperor of the Moon (1687)

The Bible (King James Version)

He that increaseth knowledge increaseth sorrow.

Ecclesiastes, 1:18

Carlyle, Thomas (1795–1881)
Scottish historian, biographer, critic, and essayist

What is all knowledge too but recorded experience, and a product of history; of which, therefore, reasoning and belief, no less than action and passion, are essential materials?

Critical and Miscellaneous Essays (1839)

Chesterfield, Lord (1694–1773)
English politician and letter writer

The knowledge of the world is only to be acquired in the world, and not in a closet.

Letter to his son, 1746

Cicero (106–43 BC)
Roman orator, statesman, essayist and letter writer

I prefer tongue-tied knowledge to ignorant loquacity.

De Oratore

Clough, Arthur Hugh (1819–1861)
English poet and letter writer

Grace is given of God, but knowledge is bought in the market.

The Bothie of Tober-na-Vuolich (1848)

Cowper, William (1731–1800)
English poet, hymn and letter writer

Knowledge is proud that he has learn'd so much;
Wisdom is humble that he knows no more.

The Task (1785)

Doyle, Sir Arthur Conan (1859–1930)
Scottish writer and war correspondent
A man should keep his little brain attic stocked with all the furniture that he is likely to use, and the rest he can put away in the lumber-room of his library, where he can get it if he wants it.

The Adventures of Sherlock Holmes (1892)

Emerson, Ralph Waldo (1803–1882)
US poet, essayist, transcendentalist and teacher
There is no knowledge that is not power.

Society and Solitude (1870)

Hegel, Georg Wilhelm (1770–1831)
German philosopher
We do not need to be shoemakers to know if our shoes fit, and just as little have we any need to be professionals to acquire knowledge of matters of universal interest.

The Philosophy of Right (1821)

Holmes, Oliver Wendell (1809–1894)
US physician, poet, writer and scientist
It is the province of knowledge to speak and it is the privilege of wisdom to listen.

The Poet at the Breakfast-Table (1872)

Huxley, T.H. (1825–1895)
English biologist, Darwinist and agnostic
The saying that a little knowledge is a dangerous thing is, to my mind, a very dangerous adage. If knowledge is real and genuine, I do not believe that it is other than a very valuable possession however infinitesimal its quantity may be. Indeed, if a little knowledge is dangerous, where is the man who has so much as to be out of danger?

Science and Culture (1877)

Inge, William Ralph (1860–1954)
English divine, writer and teacher
The fruit of the tree of knowledge always drives man from some para-dise or other.

Attr.

Joad, C.E.M. (1891–1953)
English popularizer of philosophy
There was never an age in which useless knowledge was more important than in ours.

The Observer, 1951

Johnson, Samuel (1709–1784)
English lexicographer, poet, critic, conversationalist and essayist
In my early years I read very hard. It is a sad reflection, but a true one, that I knew almost as much at eighteen as I do now.

In Boswell, *The Life of Samuel Johnson* (1791)

Integrity without knowledge is weak and useless, and knowledge without integrity is dangerous and dreadful.

Rasselas (1759)

If it rained knowledge, I'd hold out my hand; but I would not give myself the trouble to go in quest of it.

In Boswell, *The Life of Samuel Johnson* (1791)

Keats, John (1795–1821)
English poet
Knowledge enormous makes a God of me.

'Hyperion. A Fragment (1818)'

La Fontaine, Jean de (1621–1695)
French poet and fabulist
Il connaît l'univers et ne se connaît pas.
He knows the world and does not know himself.

Fables

Linklater, Eric (1899–1974)
Welsh-born Scottish writer and satirist
For the scientific acquisition of knowledge is almost as tedious as a routine acquisition of wealth.

White Man's Saga

Locke, John (1632–1704)
English philosopher
No man's knowledge here can go beyond his experience.

Essay concerning Human Understanding (1690)

Macaulay, Lord (1800–1859)
English Liberal statesman, essayist and poet
Knowledge advances by steps, and not by leaps.

'History' (1828)

Menéndez y Pelayo, Marcelino (1856–1912)
Desde luego, es más cómodo saber poco que saber mucho.
Of course, knowing a little is more agreeable than knowing a lot.

Spanish Literature Programme (1934)

Milton, John (1608–1674)
English poet, libertarian and pamphleteer
The first and wisest of them all professd
To know this onely, that he nothing knew.

Paradise Regained (1671)

Molière (1622–1673)
French dramatist, actor and director
Ah, la belle chose que de savoir quelque chose.
Ah, what a fine thing it is, to know something.

Le Bourgeois Gentilhomme (1671)

Mumford, Ethel (1878–1940)
US writer, dramatist and humorist
Knowledge is power if you know it about the right person.

In Cowan, *The Wit of Women*

Popper, Sir Karl (1902–1994)

Austrian-born British philosopher

> Our knowledge can only be finite, while our ignorance must necessarily be infinite.
>
> *Conjectures and Refutations* (1963)

Proverb

> Knowledge is power.

Renan, J. Ernest (1823–1892)

French philologist, writer and historian

> *'Savoir c'est pouvoir' est le plus beau mot qu'on ait dit.* 'Knowledge is power' is the finest idea ever put into words.
>
> *Dialogues et fragments philosophiques* (1876)

Sharpe, Tom (1928–)

English writer

> His had been an intellectual decision founded on his conviction that if a little knowledge was a dangerous thing, a lot was lethal.
>
> *Porterhouse Blue* (1974)

Sheridan, Richard Brinsley (1751–1816)

Irish dramatist, politician and orator

> Madam, a circulating library in a town is an evergreen tree of diabolical knowledge! – It blossoms through the year! – And depend on it, Mrs Malaprop, that they who are so fond of handling the leaves, will long for the fruit at last.
>
> *The Rivals* (1775)

Sterne, Laurence (1713–1768)

Irish-born English writer and clergyman

> The desire of knowledge, like the thirst of riches, increases ever with the acquisition of it.
>
> *Tristram Shandy* (1767)

▶▶ EDUCATION; LEARNING; WISDOM

L

land

Frost, Robert (1874–1963)
US poet
> The land was ours before we were the land's.
>> 'The Gift Outright'
>> (1942)

Gibbon, Lewis Grassic (1901–1935)
> Nothing endured at all, nothing but the land …
> The land was forever, it moved and changed
> below you, but was forever.
>> *Sunset Song* (1932)

Rowse, A.L. (1903–1997)
English historian, writer and poet
> What is there in a Cornish hedge
> The broken herring-bone pattern of stones,
> The gorse, the ragged rick,
> The way the little elms are,
> Sea-bent, sea-shorn
> That so affects the heart?
>> 'Cornish Landscape'

Trollope, Anthony (1815–1882)
English writer, traveller and post office official
> It is a comfortable feeling to know that you
> stand on your own ground. Land is about the
> only thing that can't fly away.
>> *The Last Chronicle of Barset* (1867)

language

Auden, W.H. (1907–1973)
English poet, essayist, critic, teacher and dramatist
> Time that is intolerant
> Of the brave and innocent,
> And indifferent in a week
> To a beautiful physique,
>
> Worships language and forgives
> Everyone by whom it lives.
>> *Collected Poems, 1939–1947*

Churchill, Sir Winston (1874–1965)
English Conservative Prime Minister
Marginal comment on a document
> This is the sort of English up with which I will not
> put.
>> In Gowers, *Plain Words*
>> (1948)
>
> Everybody has a right to pronounce foreign
> names as he chooses.
>> *The Observer*, 1951

Daly, Mary (1928–)
US feminist and theologian
> The liberation of language is rooted in the
> liberation of ourselves.
>> *Beyond God The Father, Toward a Philosophy of*
>> *Women's Liberation* (1973)

Day, Clarence Shepard (1874–1935)
US essayist and humorist
> Imagine the Lord talking French! Aside from a
> few odd words in Hebrew, I took it completely
> for granted that God had never spoken anything
> but the most dignified English.
>> *Life with Father* (1935)

Dickens, Charles (1812–1870)
English writer
> There was no light nonsense about Miss Blimber
> … She was dry and sandy with working in the
> graves of deceased languages. None of your live
> languages for Miss Blimber. They must be dead
> – stone dead – and then Miss Blimber dug them
> up like a Ghoul.
>> *Dombey and Son* (1848)

Dobbs, Kildare (1923–)
Canadian writer
> My country is the English language.
>> In Galt (ed.), *The Saturday Night Traveller* (1990)

Duppa, Richard (1770–1831)
English artist and writer
> In language, the ignorant have prescribed laws
> to the learned.
>> *Maxims* (1830)

Eliot, George (1819–1880)
English writer and poet
> Correct English is the slang of prigs who write
> history and essays.
>> *Middlemarch* (1872)

Emerson, Ralph Waldo (1803–1882)
US poet, essayist, transcendentalist and teacher
> Language is fossil poetry.
>> 'The Poet' (1844)

Franklin, Benjamin (1706–1790)
US statesman, scientist, political critic and printer
> Write with the learned, pronounce with the
> vulgar.
>> *Poor Richard's Almanac* (1738)

Goethe (1749–1832)
German poet, writer, dramatist and scientist
> *Wer fremde Sprachen nicht kennt, weiss nichts von*
> *seiner eigenen.*
> Whoever is not acquainted with foreign
> languages knows nothing of his own.
>> *On Art and Antiquity* (1827)

Goldsmith, Oliver (c.1728–1774)
Irish dramatist, poet and writer
> The true use of speech is not so much to
> express our wants as to conceal them.
>> *The Bee* (1759)

Goldwyn, Samuel (1882–1974)
Polish-born US film producer
> Let's have some new clichés.
>> *The Observer*, 1948

Housman, A.E. (1859–1936)
English poet and scholar
> If one cannot discriminate between grammar
> and solecism, sequence and incoherency, sense
> and nonsense, one has no protection against
> falsehood, and believes all the lies one is told.
>> *M. Manilii Astronomicon* (1903)

Hyde, Douglas (1860–1949)
> In order to de-Anglicise ourselves we must at
> once arrest the decay of the language.
>> 'The Necessity for de-Anglicising Ireland' (1892)

Jespersen, Otto (1860–1943)
Danish philologist
> In his whole life man achieves nothing so great
> and so wonderful as what he achieved when he
> learned to talk.
>> *Language* (1904)

Johnson, Samuel (1709–1784)
English lexicographer, poet, critic, conversationalist and
essayist
> I have laboured to refine our language to
> grammatical purity, and to clear it from
> colloquial barbarisms, licentious idioms, and
> irregular combinations.
>> *The Rambler* (1750–1752)

> I am not yet so lost in lexicography, as to forget
> that words are the daughters of the earth, and
> that things are the sons of heaven. Language is
> only the instrument of science, and words are
> but the signs of ideas: I wish, however, that the
> instrument might be less apt to decay, and that
> signs might be permanent, like the things which
> they denote.
>> *A Dictionary of the English Language* (1755)

> Language is only the instrument of science, and
> words are but the signs of ideas: I wish,
> however, that the instrument might be less apt
> to decay, and that signs might be permanent,
> like the things which they denote.
>> *A Dictionary of the English Language* (1755)

> Language is the dress of thought.
>> *The Lives of the Most Eminent English Poets* (1781)

> I am always sorry when any language is lost,
> because languages are the pedigree of nations.
>> In Boswell, *Journal of a Tour to the Hebrides* (1785)

Langland, William (c.1330–c.1400)
English poet
> Grammere, that grounde is of alle.
>> *The Vision of William Concerning Piers the Plowman*

Lévi-Strauss, Claude (1908–)
French anthropologist
> *La langue est une raison humaine qui a ses raisons, et
> que l'homme ne connaît pas.*
> Language is a kind of human reason, which has
> its own internal logic of which man knows
> nothing.
>> *The Savage Mind* (1962)

Lively, Penelope (1933–)
English novelist
> Language tethers us to the world; without it we
> spin like atoms.
>> *Moon Tiger* (1987)

Macaulay, Lord (1800–1859)
English Liberal statesman, essayist and poet
> The English Bible, a book which, if everything
> else in our language should perish, would alone
> suffice to show the whole extent of its beauty
> and power.
>> 'John Dryden' (1843)

Milne, A.A. (1882–1956)
English writer, dramatist and poet
> If the English language had been properly
> organized … then there would be a word which
> meant both 'he' and 'she', and I could write, 'If
> John or Mary comes heesh will want to play
> tennis,' which would save a lot of trouble.
>> *The Christopher Robin Birthday Book*

Murrow, Edward R. (1908–1965)
US reporter and war correspondent
Of Churchill
> He mobilized the English language and sent it
> into battle to steady his fellow countrymen and
> hearten those Europeans upon whom the long
> dark night of tyranny had descended.
>> Broadcast, 1954

Narayan, R. K. (1907–)
Indian writer and translator
> English is a very adaptable language. And it's so
> transparent it can take on the tint of any
> country.
>> Radio conversation, 1968

O'Connor, Mark (1945–)
Australian poet and dramatist
> Yet all world languages die at last:
> Greek of grammar and factions; Latin
> of clotted syntax and Renaissance purism;
> French of bad admirals and over-subtle vowels;
> English and Chinese of their written forms;
> Russian of subject people's hate.
>> 'Lingua Romana'

Parker, Dorothy (1893–1967)
US writer, poet, critic and wit
Of an acquaintance
> You know, she speaks eighteen languages. And she can't say 'No' in any of them.
>> In J. Keats, *You Might As Well Live* (1970)

Paz, Octavio (1914–)
Mexican poet and critic
> *Las diferencias entre el idioma hablado o escrito y los otros – plásticos o musicales – son muy profundas, pero no tanto que nos hagan olvidar que todos son, esencialmente, lenguaje: sistemas expresivos dotados de poder significativo.*
> The differences between the spoken or written language and the other ones – plastic or musical – are very profound, but not to such an extent that they make us forget that essentially they are all language: expressive systems which possess a significative power.
>> *The Bow and the Lyre* (1956)

Philip, Prince, Duke of Edinburgh (1921–)
Greek-born consort of Queen Elizabeth II
> I include 'pidgin-English' … even though I am referred to in that splendid language as 'Fella belong Mrs Queen'.
>> Speech, English-Speaking Union Conference, Ottawa, 1958

Porson, Richard (1759–1808)
English scholar
> Life is too short to learn German.
>> In Thomas Love Peacock, *Gryll Grange* (1861

Ross, Alan S.C. (1907–1980)
British linguistics scholar
> U and Non-U. An Essay in Sociological Linguistics.
>> In Nancy Mitford (ed.), *Noblesse Oblige* (1956)

Shaw, George Bernard (1856–1950)
Irish socialist, writer, dramatist and critic
> The English have no respect for their language, and will not teach their children to speak it … It is impossible for an Englishman to open his mouth without making some other Englishman hate or despise him.
>> *Pygmalion* (1916)

> England and America are two countries separated by the same language.
>> *Reader's Digest*, 1942

Sheridan, Richard Brinsley (1751–1816)
Irish dramatist, politician and orator
> An aspersion upon my parts of speech! … If I reprehend anything in this world, it is the use of my oracular tongue, and a nice derangement of epitaphs!
>> *The Rivals* (1775)

Sigismund (1368–1437)
King of Hungary, Bohemia and Holy Roman Emperor
Responding to criticism of his Latin
> I am the Roman Emperor, and am above grammar.
>> Attr.

Smith, F.E. (1872–1930)
English politician and Lord Chancellor
When the Labour MP J.H. Thomas complained he "ad a 'eadache'
> Try taking a couple of aspirates.
>> Attr.

Spenser, Edmund (c.1522–1599)
English poet
> So now they have made our English tongue, a gallimaufray or hodgepodge of al other speches.
>> *The Shepheardes Calender* (1579)

Sprat, Thomas (1635–1713)
English bishop and writer
Of the Royal Society
> They have exacted from all their members a close, naked, natural way of speaking; positive expressions; clear senses; a native easiness: bringing all things as near the mathematical plainness, as they can; and preferring the language of artizans, countrymen, and merchants, before that of wits or scholars.
>> *The History of the Royal Society* (1667)

Sullivan, Annie (1866–1936)
US lecturer, writer and teacher
> Language grows out of life, out of its needs and experiences … Language and knowledge are indissolubly connected; they are interdependent. Good work in language presupposes and depends on a real knowledge of things.
>> Speech, 1894

Swift, Jonathan (1667–1745)
Irish satirist, poet, essayist and cleric
> Nor do they trust their tongue alone,
> But speak a language of their own;
> Can read a nod, a shrug, a look,
> Far better than a printed book;
> Convey a libel in a frown,
> And wink a reputation down.
>> 'The Journal of a Modern Lady' (1729)

Tomlin, Lily (1939–)
US actress
> Man invented language in order to satisfy his deep need to complain.
>> In Pinker, *The Language Instinct* (1994)

Tucholsky, Kurt (1890–1935)
German satirist and writer
> *Das Englische ist eine einfache, aber schwere Sprache. Es besteht aus lauter Fremdwörtern die falsch*

ausgesprochen werden.

English is a simple, yet hard language. It consists entirely of foreign words pronounced wrongly.

Scraps (1973)

Twain, Mark (1835–1910)

US humorist, writer, journalist and lecturer

A verb has a hard time enough of it in this world when it's all together. It's downright inhuman to split it up. But that's just what those Germans do. They take part of a verb and put it down here, like a stake, and they take the other part of it and put it away over yonder like another stake, and between these two limits they just shovel in German.

Address, 1900

Voltaire (1694–1778)

French philosopher, dramatist, poet, historian writer and critic

Je ne suis pas comme une dame de la cour de Versailles, qui disait: c'est bien dommage que l'aventure de la tour de Babel ait produit la confusion des langues; sans cela tout le monde aurait toujours parlé français.

I am not like a lady at the court of Versailles, who said: 'What a great pity it is that the adventure at the tower of Babel should have produced the confusion of languages; if it weren't for that, everyone would always have spoken French.'

Letter to Catherine the Great, 1767

A language is a dialect that has an army and a navy.

In Rosten, *The Joys of Yiddish* (1968)

Whitman, Walt (1819–1892)

US poet and writer

Language ... is not an abstract construction of the learned, or of dictionary-makers, but is something arising out of the work, needs, ties, joys, affections, tastes, of long generations of humanity, and has its bases broad and low, close to the ground.

November Boughs (1888)

Whorf, Benjamin (1897–1941)

US anthropological linguist and engineer

We dissect nature along lines laid down by our native language ... Language is not simply a reporting device for experience but a defining framework for it.

In Hoyer (ed.), *New Directions in the Study of Language* (1964)

Woollcott, Alexander (1887–1943)

US writer, drama critic and anthologist

Subjunctive to the last, he preferred to ask, 'And that, sir, would be the Hippodrome?'.

While Rome Burns (1934), 'Our Mrs Parker'

▶▶ CLASS; STYLE; WORDS; WRITING

last words

Addison, Joseph (1672–1719)

English essayist, poet, playwright and statesman

See in what peace a Christian can die.

Dying words

Alexander the Great (356–323 BC)

Macedonian king and conquering army commander

I am dying with the help of too many physicians.

Attr.

Appel, George (d.1928)

Executed in electric chair in New York.

Well, gentlemen, you are about to see a baked Appel.

Attr.

Bailly, Jean Sylvain (1736–1793)

French astronomer and politician

Reflection on the evening before his execution

It's time for me to enjoy another pinch of snuff. Tomorrow my hands will be bound, so as to make it impossible.

Attr.

Bankhead, Tallulah (1903–1968)

US actress

Codeine ... bourbon.

Attr.

Barnum, Phineas T. (1810–1891)

US showman and writer

How were the receipts today at Madison Square Garden?

Attr.

Barrie, Sir J.M. (1860–1937)

Scottish dramatist and writer

I can't sleep.

Attr.

Barrymore, Ethel (1879–1959)

Is everybody happy? I want everybody to be happy. I know I'm happy.

Attr.

Beecher, Henry Ward (1813–1887)

US clergyman, lecturer, editor and writer

Now comes the mystery.

Attr.

Beethoven, Ludwig van (1770–1827)

German composer

Friends applaud, the comedy is finished.

Attr.

Behan, Brendan (1923–1964)

Irish dramatist, writer and Republican

Remark from his deathbed to a nun who was nursing him

> Thank you, sister. May you be the mother of a bishop!

Attr.

Bell, Alexander Graham (1847–1922)
Scottish-born US inventor and educator of the deaf
> So little done. So much to do.

Attr.

Bismarck, Prince Otto von (1815–1898)
First Chancellor of the German Reich
Remark made just before he died
> If there is ever another war in Europe, it will come out of some damned silly thing in the Balkans.

Attr.

Bogart, Humphrey (1899–1957)
US film actor
> I should never have changed from scotch to martinis.

In Simon Rose, *Classic Film Guide* (1995)

Crockett, Davy (1786–1836)
> Pop, pop, pop!
> Bom, bom, bom!
> Throughout the day
> no time for memorandums now.
> Go ahead!
> Liberty and independence forever.

Last entry in his journal at the Alamo, 5 March 1836

Danton, Georges (1759–1794)
French revolutionary leader
Said as he mounted the scaffold, 5 April 1794
> Thou wilt show my head to the people: it is worth showing.

In Carlyle, *French Revolution*

Gandhi, Indira (1917–1984)
Indian statesman and Prime Minister
Said 24 hours before she was assassinated
> Even if I die in the service of this nation, I would be proud of it. Every drop of my blood, I am sure, will contribute to the growth of this nation and make it strong and dynamic.

Attr.

George V (1865–1936)
King of the United Kingdom
To Lord Wigram, his secretary; sometimes quoted as his last words
> How is the Empire?

Attr.

Gillmore, Gary (d.1977)
Executed by firing squad, Utah.
> Let's do it!

Attr.

Goethe (1749–1832)
German poet, writer, dramatist and scientist
> *Mehr Licht!*
> More light!

Attr.

Graham, James, Marquis of Montrose (1612–1650)
Scottish Covenanter, soldier, poet and Royalist
> May God have mercy upon this afflicted Kingdom.

Attr.

Gregory VII (c.1020–1085)
Italian pope
> *Dilexi justitiam et odivi iniquitatem: propterea morior in exilio.*
> I have loved righteousness and hated iniquity: therefore I die in exile.

In Bowden, *The Life and Pontificate of Gregory VII* (1840)

Gwenn, Edmund (1875–1959)
English actor
Reply on his deathbed, when someone said to him, 'It must be very hard'
> It is. But not as hard as farce.

Time, 1984

Hale, Nathan (1755–1776)
US soldier and revolutionary
Speech before he was executed by the British
> I only regret that I have but one life to lose for my country.

In Johnston, *Nathan Hale* (1974)

Hazlitt, William (1778–1830)
English writer and critic
> Well, I've had a happy life.

In W.C. Hazlitt, *Memoirs of William Hazlitt* (1867)

Hegel, Georg Wilhelm (1770–1831)
German philosopher
Said on his deathbed
> Only one man ever understood me. ... And he didn't understand me.

In B. Conrad, *Famous Last Words* (1962)

Heine, Heinrich (1797–1856)
German lyric poet, essayist and journalist
> *Dieu me pardonnera, c'est son métier.*
> God will forgive me. It is his profession.

In Meissner, *H H Erinnerungen* (1856)

Henry, O. (1862–1910)
US short-story writer
Attr. last words, quoting the song 'I'm Afraid to Go Home in the Dark'
> Don't turn down the light, I'm afraid to go home in the dark.

In Leacock, 'The Amazing Genius of O. Henry', 1916

Hobbes, Thomas (1588–1679)
Political philosopher
> I am about to take my last voyage, a great leap

in the dark.

In Watkins, Anecdotes of Men of Learning (1808)

Hokusai (1760–1849)

Japanese artist

Said on his deathbed

> If heaven had granted me five more years, I could have become a real painter.

In B. Conrad, Famous Last Words (1962)

Holland, First Lord (**Henry Fox**) (1705–1774)

Said during his last illness

> If Mr Selwyn calls, let him in: if I am alive I shall be very glad to see him, and if I am dead he will be very glad to see me.

Attr.

Holt, Harold Edward (1908–1967)

Australian statesman and Prime Minister

> I know this beach like the back of my hand.

Sydney Morning Herald, 1967

Hubbock, Chris (d.1970)

US newsreader before shooting herself during a broadcast.

> And now, in keeping with Channel 40's policy of always bringing you the latest in blood and guts, in living color, you're about to see another first – an attempted suicide.

Attr.

Hume, David (1711–1776)

Scottish philosopher and political economist

> I am dying as fast as my enemies, if I have any, could wish, and as cheerfully as my best friends could desire.

Attr.

Huss, Jan (c.1370–1415)

Bohemian religious reformer, preacher and martyr

At the stake, on seeing a peasant bringing wood

> *O sancta simplicitas!*
> O holy simplicity!

In Zincgreff and Weidner, Apothegmata (1653)

Ibsen, Henrik (1828–1906)

Norwegian writer, dramatist and poet

Ibsen's last words; his nurse had just remarked that he was feeling a little better

> On the contrary!

Attr.

Jackson, Thomas (Stonewall) (1824–1863)

US general

Last words before being mistakenly shot by his own men

> Let us cross over the river and rest in the shade.

Attr.

John XXIII (1881–1963)

Italian pope

Remark made two days before he died

> I am able to follow my own death step by step. Now I move softly towards the end.

The Guardian,1963

Johnson, Samuel (1709–1784)

English lexicographer, poet, critic, conversationalist and essayist

On his deathbed

> I will be conquered; I will not capitulate.

In Boswell, The Life of Samuel Johnson (1791)

Keats, John (1795–1821)

English poet

> I shall soon be laid in the quiet grave – thank God for the quiet grave – O! I can feel the cold earth upon me – the daisies growing over me – O for this quiet – it will be my first.

Attr.

Kelly, Ned (1855–1880)

Australian outlaw folk hero

On the scaffold, 11 November 1880

> Ah well, I suppose it has come to this! ... Such is life!

Attr.

Latimer, Bishop Hugh (c.1485–1555)

English Protestant churchman

Said shortly before being put to death

> Be of good comfort, Master Ridley, and play the man. We shall this day light such a candle by God's grace in England, as (I trust) shall never be put out.

In Foxe, Actes and Monuments (1562–1563)

Lawrence, James (1781–1813)

US naval officer

> Don't give up the ship.

Last words, during naval battle

Le Mesurier, John (1912–1983)

English actor

> It's all been rather lovely.

In The Times, 1983

Louis XIV (1638–1715)

King of France

Noticing as he lay on his deathbed that his attendants were crying

> Why are you weeping? Did you imagine that I was immortal?

Attr.

Marco Polo (c.1254–1324)

Venetian traveller

> I have not told half of what I saw.

In W. Durant, The Story of Civilization, I

McAlpine, Sir Alfred (1881–1944)

Scottish building contractor

> Keep Paddy behind the big mixer.

Attr.

Monmouth, Duke of (1649–1685)

Illegitimate son of Charles II

Words to his executioner

Do not hack me as you did my Lord Russell.

> In Macaulay, *History of England* (1849)

Moore, General Sir John (1761–1809)
Scottish soldier
> I hope the people of England will be satisfied. I hope my country will do me justice.

> Attr.

More, Sir Thomas (1478–1535)
English statesman and humanist
> After his head was upon the block, he lift it up again, and gently drew his beard aside, and said, This hath not offended the king.

> In Francis Bacon, *Apophthegms New and Old* (1625)

Morris, William (1834–1896)
English poet, designer, craftsman, artist and socialist
> I want to get Mumbo-Jumbo out of the world.

> Attr.

Nelson, Lord (1758–1805)
English admiral
Last words at the Battle of Trafalgar, 1805
> Thank God, I have done my duty.

> In Robert Southey, *The Life of Nelson* (1860)

Nero (37–68)
Roman emperor
> *Qualis artifex pereo!*
> What a great artist dies with me!

> In Suetonius, *Lives of the Caesars*, 'Nero'

O'Neill, Eugene (1888–1953)
US dramatist
> I knew it. I knew it. Born in a hotel room – and God damn it – died in a hotel room.

> Attr.

Oates, Captain Lawrence (1880–1912)
English Antarctic explorer
> I am just going outside, and may be some time.

> In Captain Scott's diary

Palmerston, Lord (1784–1865)
British Prime Minister
> Die, my dear Doctor, that's the last thing I shall do!

> Attr.

Pavlova, Anna (1881–1931)
Russian ballet dancer
> Get my swan costume ready.

> Attr.

Perelman, S.J. (1904–1979)
US humorist, writer and dramatist
Giving his reasons for refusing to see a priest as he lay dying
> I am curious to see what happens in the next world to one who dies unshriven.

> Attr.

Pheidippides (d. 490 BC)
His last words, after he had run to Athens with news of the

Battle of Marathon
> Greetings, we have won.

> In Lucian, 'Pro Lapsu inter salutandum'

Picasso, Pablo (1881–1973)
Spanish painter, sculptor and graphic artist
> Drink to me.

> Attr.

Pitt, William (1759–1806)
English politician and Prime Minister
> I think I could eat one of Bellamy's veal pies.

> Attr.

Pope, Alexander (1688–1744)
English poet, translator and editor
> Here am I, dying of a hundred good symptoms.

> In Spence, *Anecdotes*

Rabelais, François (c.1494–c.1553)
French monk, physician, satirist and humanist
> *Je vais quérir un grand peut-être … Tirez le rideau, la farce est jouée.*
> I am going to seek a great perhaps …Bring down the curtain, the farce is played out.

> Attr.

Raleigh, Sir Walter (c.1552–1618)
English courtier, explorer, military commander, poet, historian and essayist
On feeling the edge of the axe before his execution
> 'Tis a sharp remedy, but a sure one for all ills.

> Attr.

Reynolds, Sir Joshua (1723–1792)
English portrait painter
> I should desire that the last words which I should pronounce in this Academy, and from this place, might be the name of – Michael Angelo.

> *Discourses on Art*, XV (1790)

Rhodes, Cecil (1853–1902)
English imperialist, financier and South African statesman
> So little done, so much to do!

> In Lewis Mitchell, *Life of Rhodes* (1910)

Saki (1870–1916)
Burmese-born British writer
Last words, said by Corporal Munro to one of his men who had lit up; he was killed by a German sniper
> Put that bloody cigarette out!

> In A. J. Langguth, *Life of Saki*

Sanders, George (1906–1972)
Russian-born British film actor
> Dear World, I am leaving you because I am bored. I feel I have lived long enough. I am leaving you with your worries in this sweet cesspool – good luck.

> Suicide note

Saro-Wiwa, Ken (1941–1995)
> Lord take my soul, but the struggle continues.
>> *The Observer*, 1995

Saroyan, William (1908–1981)
US writer and dramatist
> Everybody has got to die, but I have always believed an exception would be made in my case. Now what?
>> *Time*, 1984

Scarron, Paul (1610–1660)
French dramatist, writer and poet
As he lay dying
> At last I am going to be well!
>> Attr.

Scott, Robert Falcon (1868–1912)
English naval officer and Antarctic explorer
> For God's sake look after our people.
>> *Journal*, 25 March 1912

> Had we lived, I should have had a tale to tell of the hardihood, endurance, and courage of my companions which would have stirred the heart of every Englishman. These rough notes and our dead bodies must tell the tale.
>> Message to the Public, 1912

Sedgwick, John (1813–1864)
His last words, in response to a suggestion that he should not show himself over the parapet during the Battle of the Wilderness
> Nonsense, they couldn't hit an elephant at this dist –.
>> Attr.

Sidney, Sir Philip (1554–1586)
English poet, critic, soldier, courtier and diplomat
Offering his water-bottle, despite his own injuries, to a dying soldier on the battlefield near Zutphen, 1586
> Thy necessity is yet greater than mine.
>> In Sir Fulke Greville, *Life of Sir Philip Sidney* (1652)

Sinatra, Frank (1915–1998)
US singer and actor
> I'm losing.
>> *The Times*, 1998

Smith, Adam (1723–1790)
Scottish economist, philosopher and essayist
> I believe we must adjourn this meeting to some other place.
>> Attr.

Smith, Joseph (1805–1844)
Founder of the Mormon Church
> No man knows my history.
>> Funeral sermon, written by himself

Socrates (469–399 BC)
Athenian philosopher
> Crito, we owe a cock to Asclepius. Pay it and do

not neglect it.
>> Attr. in Plato, *Phaedo*

Spencer, Sir Stanley (1891–1959)
English painter
Thanking the nurse who had given him his nightly injection, just before he died
> Beautifully done.
>> In Collis, *Stanley Spencer* (1962)

Spenkelink, John (d.1979)
Executed in electric chair, Florida.
> Capital punishment: them without the capital get the punishment.
>> Attr.

Stein, Gertrude (1874–1946)
US writer, dramatist, poet and critic
> Just before she Stein died she asked, 'What is the answer?' No answer came. She laughed and said, 'In that case, what is the question?' Then she died.
>> In Sutherland, *Gertrude Stein* (1951)

Strachey, Lytton (1880–1932)
English biographer and critic
> If this is dying, then I don't think much of it.
>> In Michael Holroyd, *Lytton Strachey: A Critical Biography* (1968)

Swift, Jonathan (1667–1745)
Irish satirist, poet, essayist and cleric
Learning of the arrival of Handel: Swift's last words
> Ah, a German and a genius! a prodigy, admit him!
>> Attr.

Thurber, James (1894–1961)
US humorist, writer and dramatist
> God bless … God damn.
>> Attr.

Tichborne, Chidiock (c.1558–1586)
English Catholic conspirator against Elizabeth I
> My prime of youth is but a frost of cares;
> My feast of joy is but a dish of pain;
> My crop of corn is but a field of tares;
> And all my good is but vain hope of gain.
> The day is past, and yet I saw no sun;
> And now I live, and now my life is done.
>> 'Elegy', written in the Tower of London before his execution

Tolstoy, Leo (1828–1910)
Russian writer, essayist, philosopher and moralist
Refusing to reconcile himself with the Russian Orthodox Church as he lay dying
> Even in the valley of the shadow of death, two and two do not make six.
>> Attr.

Vega Carpio, Félix Lope de (1562–1635)
Spanish dramatis and poet
On learning that he was about to die

All right, then, I'll say it: Dante makes me sick.

Attr.

Vespasian (AD 9–79)
Roman emperor
> *Vae, puto deus fio.*
> Woe is me, I think I am becoming a god.

In Suetonius, *Lives of the Caesars*

Wilde, Oscar (1854–1900)
Irish poet, dramatist, writer, critic and wit
Last words, as he lay dying in a drab Paris bedroom
> Either that wallpaper goes, or I do.

Time, 16 January 1984

Wilhelm I, Kaiser (1797–1888)
King of Prusssia and first Emperor of Germany
Said during his last illness
> I haven't got time to be tired.

Attr.

Wolfe, James (1727–1759)
English major-general
Dying words
> Now God be praised, I will die in peace.

In J. Knox, *Historical Journal of Campaigns* (1914 edition)

laughter

Adams, Scott (1957–)
US cartoonist
> The amount of energy spent laughing at a joke should be directly proportional to the hierarchical status of the joke teller.

Building a Better Life by Stealing Office Supplies: Dogbert's Big Book of Business (1991)

Addison, Joseph (1672–1719)
English essayist, poet, playwright and statesman
> Mirth is like a flash of lightning that breaks through a gloom of clouds and glitters for a moment.

The Spectator, 1712

> If we may believe our logicians, man is distinguished from all other creatures by the faculty of laughter. He has a heart capable of mirth, and naturally disposed to it.

The Spectator, 1712

The Bible (King James Version)
> I said of laughter, It is mad: and of mirth, What doeth it?

Ecclesiastes, 2:2

Peacock, Thomas Love (1785–1866)
English writer and poet
> Laughter is pleasant, but the exertion is too much for me.

Nightmare Abbey (1818)

Proverbs
> Laugh and grow fat.

> Laugh before breakfast, you'll cry before supper.

> Laughter is brightest where food is best.

> Laughter is the best medicine.

Racine, Jean (1639–1699)
French tragedian and poet
> He who laughs on Friday will cry on Sunday.

Les Plaideurs (1668)

Wilcox, Ella Wheeler (1850–1919)
US poet and writer
> Laugh, and the world laughs with you;
> Weep, and you weep alone,
> For the sad old earth must borrow its mirth,
> But has trouble enough of its own.

'Solitude' (1917)

▶▶ HAPPINESS; HUMOUR

law

Adams, Richard (1846–1908)
Irish journalist, barrister and judge
> You have been acquitted by a Limerick jury and you may now leave the dock without any other stain on your character.

In Healy, *The Old Munster Circuit*

Adler, Freda (1934–)
US educator and writer
> That man is a creature who needs order yet yearns for change is the creative contradiction at the heart of the laws which structure his conformity and define his deviancy.

Sisters in Crime (1975)

Adler, Renata
US film critic and writer
> In the strange heat all litigation brings to bear on things, the very process of litigation fosters the most profound misunderstandings in the world.

Reckless Disregard (1986)

Anonymous
> The law doth punish man or woman
> That steals the goose from off the common,
> But lets the greater felon loose,
> That steals the common from the goose.

On enclosures, 18th Century

> A gentleman haranguing on the perfection of our law, and that it was equally open to the poor and the rich, was answered by another, 'So is the London Tavern'.

Tom Paine's Jests (1794)

Arbuthnot, John (1667–1735)
Scottish physician, pamphleteer and wit
> Law is a bottomless pit.
>
> *The History of John Bull* (c.1712)

Bacon, Francis (1561–1626)
English philosopher, essayist, politician and courtier
> One of the Seven was wont to say: 'That laws
> were like cobwebs; where the small flies were
> caught, and the great brake through.'
>
> *Apophthegms New and Old* (1624)

Bentham, Jeremy (1748–1832)
English writer and philosopher
> Lawyers are the only persons in whom ignorance
> of the law is not punished.
>
> Attr.

Bierce, Ambrose (1842–c.1914)
US writer, verse writer and soldier
> *Lawsuit:* A machine which you go into as a pig
> and come out as a sausage.
>
> *The Cynic's Word Book* (1906)

Bismarck, Prince Otto von (1815–1898)
First Chancellor of the German Reich
> Laws are like sausages. It's better not to see
> them being made.
>
> Attr.

Braxfield, Lord (1722–1799)
Scottish judge
> Let them bring me prisoners, and I'll find them
> law.
>
> Attr. by Cockburn

Burke, Edmund (1729–1797)
Irish-born British statesman and philosopher
> Laws, like houses, lean on one another.
>
> *Tracts on the Popery Laws* (1812)

> People crushed by law have no hopes but from
> power. If laws are their enemies, they will be
> enemies to laws; and those who have much to
> hope and nothing to lose will always be
> dangerous more or less.
>
> Letter to Charles James Fox, 1777

> There is but one law for all, namely, that law
> which governs all law – the law of our Creator,
> the law of humanity, justice, equity, the law of
> nature, and of nations.
>
> Speech, 1794

Carroll, Lewis (1832–1898)
English writer and photographer
> 'I'll be judge, I'll be jury,' said cunning
>   old Fury:
> 'I'll try the whole cause, and condemn
>   you to death.'
>
> *Alice's Adventures in Wonderland*
> (1865)

Chapman, George (c.1559–c.1634)
English poet, dramatist and translator
> I'me asham'd the law is such an Ass.
>
> *Revenge for Honour* (1654)

Coetzee, J.M. (1940–)
South African writer
> All we can do is to uphold the laws, all of us,
> without allowing the memory of justice to fade.
>
> *Waiting for the Barbarians* (1980)

Colton, Charles Caleb (c.1780–1832)
English clergyman and satirist
> Law and equity are two things which God hath
> joined, but which man hath put asunder.
>
> *Lacon* (1820)

Darling, Charles (1849–1936)
English judge and Conservative politician
> The Law of England is a very strange one; it
> cannot compel anyone to tell the truth … But
> what the Law can do is to give you seven years
> for not telling the truth.
>
> In Walker-Smith, *Lord Darling*

Denning, Lord (1899–1999)
English Master of the Rolls
> To every subject of this land, however powerful,
> I would use Thomas Fuller's words over three
> hundred years ago, 'Be ye never so high, the law
> is above you'.
>
> High Court ruling against the Attorney-General, 1977

Dobson, Frank
English Labour politician
On growing litigation in the NHS
> As far as I am concerned the only proper place
> for lawyers in the NHS is on the operating table.
>
> In *The Observer*, 1999

Emerson, Ralph Waldo (1803–1882)
US poet, essayist, transcendentalist and teacher
> Good men must not obey the laws too well.
>
> 'Politics' (1844)

France, Anatole (1844–1924)
French writer and critic
> *La majestueuse égalité des lois, qui interdit au riche*
> *comme au pauvre de coucher sous les ponts, de*
> *mendier dans les rues et de voler du pain.*
> The law, in its majestic equality, forbids the rich
> as well as the poor to sleep under bridges, to
> beg in the streets, and to steal bread.
>
> *Le Lys Rouge* (1894)

Giraudoux, Jean (1882–1944)
French dramatist, poet, writer and satirist
> *Nous savons tous ici que le droit est la plus puissante*
> *des écoles de l'imagination. Jamais poète n'a*
> *interprété la nature aussi librement qu'un juriste la*
> *réalité.*
> All of us here know that there is no better way

of exercising the imagination than the study of law. No poet has ever interpreted nature as freely as a lawyer interprets reality.

La Guerre de Troie n'aura pas lieu (1935)

Goethe (1749–1832)
German poet, writer, dramatist and scientist
Wenn man alle Gesetze studieren sollte, so hätte man gar keine Zeit, sie zu übertreten.
If one were to study all the laws, one would have absolutely no time to break them.
'Experience and Life'

Goldsmith, Oliver (c.1728–1774)
Irish dramatist, poet and writer
Laws grind the poor, and rich men rule the law.
'The Traveller' (1764)

Grant, Ulysses S. (1822–1885)
US President, Civil War general and memoirist
I know no method to secure the repeal of bad or obnoxious laws so effective as their stringent execution.
Inaugural Address, 1869

Herbert, Sir A.P. (1890–1971)
English humorist, writer, dramatist and politician
The Common Law of England has been laboriously built about a mythical figure – the figure of 'The Reasonable Man'.
Uncommon Law (1935)

Holmes, Hugh (**Lord Justice Holmes**) (1840–1916)
Irish judge
An elderly pensioner on being sentenced to fifteen years' penal servitude cried 'Ah! my Lord, I'm a very old man, and I'll never do that sentence.' The judge replied 'Well try to do as much of it as you can'.
In Healy, *The Old Munster Circuit* (1939)

Horsley, Bishop Samuel (1733–1806)
English bishop
In this country, my Lords, ... the individual subject ... 'has nothing to do with the laws but to obey them'.
Speech, House of Lords, 1795

Ingham, Sir Bernard (1932–)
Chief Press Secretary to Margaret Thatcher
Comment after being bound over to keep the peace by Croydon magistrates
I have considered myself bound to observe the law for the whole of my 66 years.
The Times, 1999

Ingrams, Richard (1937–)
British journalist and editor of *Private Eye*
I have come to regard the law courts not as a cathedral but rather as a casino.
The Guardian, 1977

Johnson, Samuel (1709–1784)
English lexicographer, poet, critic, conversationalist and essayist
Johnson observed, that 'he did not care to speak ill of any man behind his back, but he believed the gentleman was an attorney.'
In Boswell, *The Life of Samuel Johnson* (1791)

Knox, Philander Chase (1853–1921)
US lawyer and Republican politician
Reply when Theodore Roosevelt requested legal justification for US acquisition of the Panama Canal Zone
Oh, Mr President, do not let so great an achievement suffer from any taint of legality.
Attr.

Locke, John (1632–1704)
English philosopher
Wherever Law ends, Tyranny begins.
Second Treatise of Civil Government (1690)

Machiavelli (1469–1527)
Florentine statesman, political theorist and historian
Li buoni esempi nascano dalla buona educazione; la buona educazione dalle buone leggi: e le buone leggi, da quei tumulti che molti inconsideratamente dannano.
Good examples are borne out of good education, which is the outcome of good legislation; and good legislation is borne out of those uprisings which are unduly damned by so many people.
Discourse

Maynard, Sir John (1602–1690)
English judge, politician and royalist
Reply to Judge Jeffreys' suggestion that he was so old he had forgotten the law
I have forgotten more law than you ever knew, but allow me to say, I have not forgotten much.
Attr.

Mortimer, John (1923–)
English lawyer, dramatist and writer
No brilliance is needed in the law. Nothing but common sense, and relatively clean finger nails.
A Voyage Round My Father (1971)

North, Christopher (1785–1854)
Scottish poet, writer, editor and critic
Laws were made to be broken.
Blackwood's Edinburgh Magazine, 1830

Parker, Hubert Lister (1900–1972)
English Lord Chief Justice
A judge is not supposed to know anything about the facts of life until they have been presented in evidence and explained to him at least three times.
The Observer, 1961

Proverbs

> With a Scotsman or a priest, don't begin a lawsuit.

> Possession is nine points of the law.

Puzo, Mario (1920–)

US writer

> A lawyer with his briefcase can steal more than a thousand men with guns.

> *The Godfather* (1969)

Richelieu, Cardinal (1585–1642)

Prime Minister to Louis XIII

> *Faire une loi et ne pas la faire exécuter, c'est autoriser la chose qu'on veut défendre.*

> To pass a law and not have it enforced is to authorize the very thing you wish to prohibit.

> *Mémoires*

Robespierre, Maximilien (1758–1794)

French revolutionary

> *Toute loi qui viole les droits imprescriptibles de l'homme, est essentiellement injuste et tyrannique; elle n'est point une loi.*

> Any law which violates the indefeasible rights of man is in essence unjust and tyrannical; it is no law.

> *Déclaration des Droits de l'homme* (1793)

Rousseau, Jean-Jacques (1712–1778)

Swiss-born French philosopher, educationist and essayist

> *Les lois sont toujours utiles à ceux qui possèdent et nuisibles à ceux qui n'ont rien.*

> Laws are always useful to those who have possessions, and harmful to those who have nothing.

> *Du Contrat Social* (1762)

Scott, Sir Walter (1771–1832)

Scottish writer and historian

> *Mrs Bertram*: That sounds like nonsense, my dear.
> *Mr Bertram*: May be so, my dear; but it may be very good law for all that.

> *Guy Mannering* (1815)

Selden, John (1584–1654)

English historian, jurist and politician

> Every law is a contract between the king and the people and therefore to be kept.

> *Table Talk* (1689)

> Ignorance of the law excuses no man; not that all men know the law, but because 'tis an excuse every man will plead, and no man can tell how to confute him.

> *Table Talk* (1689)

Seward, William (1801–1872)

US statesman

> There is a higher law than the Constitution.

> Speech against Fugitive Slave Law, 1850

Shakespeare, William (1564–1616)

English dramatist, poet and actor

> We must not make a scarecrow of the law,
> Setting it up to fear the birds of prey,
> And let it keep one shape till custom make it
> Their perch, and not their terror.

> *Measure for Measure*, II.i

> The law hath not been dead, though it hath slept.

> *Measure For Measure*, II.ii

> Still you keep o' th' windy side of the law.

> *Twelfth Night*, III.iv

Shenstone, William (1714–1763)

English poet, essayist and letter writer

> Laws are generally found to be nets of such a texture, as the little creep through, the great break through, and the middle-sized are alone entangled in.

> *Works in Verse and Prose* (1764)

Smith, F.E. (1872–1930)

English politician and Lord Chancellor

> *Judge Willis*: What do you suppose I am on the Bench for, Mr Smith?
> *F.E. Smith*: It is not for me to attempt to fathom the inscrutable workings of Providence.

> In Birkenhead, *Frederick Elwin, Earl of Birkenhead* (1933)

To a judge who complained that he was no wiser at the end than at the start of one of Smith's cases

> Possibly not, My Lord, but far better informed.

> In Birkenhead, *Life of F.E. Smith* (1959)

Solon (c.638–c.559 BC)

Athenian statesman, reformer and poet

> Laws are like spider's webs, which hold firm when any light, yielding object falls upon them, while a larger thing breaks through them and escapes.

> In Diogenes Laertius, *Lives of the Eminent Philosophers*

Swift, Jonathan (1667–1745)

Irish satirist, poet, essayist and cleric

> Laws are like cobwebs, which may catch small flies, but let wasps and hornets break through.

> *A Critical Essay upon the Faculties of the Mind* (1709)

▶▶ CRIME; JUSTICE

leadership

Anonymous

> If it weren't for the last minute, nothing would ever get done.

> Some leaders are born women.

> T-shirt slogan

Baruch, Bernard (1870–1965)
US financier, government advisor and writer
> A political leader must keep looking over his shoulder all the time to see if the boys are still there. If they aren't still there, he's no longer a political leader.
>> *New York Times*, 1965

Beveridge, William Henry (1879–1963)
British economist and social reformer
> The trouble in modern democracy is that men do not approach to leadership until they have lost the desire to lead anyone.
>> *The Observer*, 1934

Byron, Lord (1788–1824)
English poet satirist and traveller
> And when we think we lead, we are most led.
>> *The Two Foscari* (1821)

Canning, George (1770–1827)
English Prime Minister, orator and poet
Of Pitt
> Here's to the Pilot that weathered the storm.
>> 'The Pilot', song for the inauguration of the Pitt Club, 1802

Compton-Burnett, Dame Ivy (1884–1969)
English novelist
> 'She still seems to me in her own way a person born to command,' said Luce …
> 'I wonder if anyone is born to obey,' said Isabel. 'That may be why people command rather badly, that they have no suitable material to work on.'
>> *Parents and Children* (1941)

Hitler, Adolf (1889–1945)
German Nazi dictator, born in Austria
> The art of leadership… consists in consolidating the attention of the people against a single adversary and taking care that nothing will split up that attention.
>> *Mein Kampf* (1925)

Keating, Paul (1944–)
Australian Labor statesman and Prime Minister
> Leadership is not about being nice. It's about being right and being strong.
>> *Time*, 1995

Law, Bonar (1858–1923)
Canadian-born British statesman and Conservative MP
> I must follow them; I am their leader.
>> In E.T. Raymond, *Mr Balfour*

Ledru-Rollin, Alexandre Auguste (1807–1874)
French lawyer and politician
Trying to force his way through a mob during the 1848 revolution, of which he was one of the chief instigators
> *Eh! je suis leur chef, il fallait bien les suivre.*
> Ah well! I am their leader, I really should be

following them!
>> In E. de Mirecourt, *Histoire Contemporaine* (1857)

Lippmann, Walter (1889–1974)
Canadian sociologist
> The final test of a leader is that he leaves behind him in other men the conviction and the will to carry on.
>> *New York Herald Tribune*, 1945

Massinger, Philip (1583–1640)
English dramatist and poet
> He that would govern others, first should be The master of himself.
>> *The Bondman: an Antient Story* (1624)

Monty Python
Addressing King Arthur
> *Peasant*: Look, you can't expect to wield supreme executive power just because some watery tart threw a sword at you!
>> *Monty Python and the Holy Grail* (1974)

Murray, Les A. (1938–)
Australian poet and writer
> Never trust a lean meritocracy
> nor the leader who has been lean;
> only the lifelong big have the knack of wedding greatness with balance.
>
> Never wholly trust the fat man
> who lurks in the lean achiever
> and the defeated, yearning to get out.
>> 'Quintets for Robert Morley'

Sartre, Jean-Paul (1905–1980)
French philosopher, writer, dramatist and critic
> *Il est toujours facile d'obéir, si l'on rêve de commander.*
> It is always easy to obey, if one dreams of being in command.
>> *Situations*

Shakespeare, William (1564–1616)
English dramatist, poet and actor
> We were not born to sue, but to command.
>> *Richard II*, I.i

Tacitus (AD c.56–c.120)
Roman historian
Of the Emperor Galba
> *Omnium consensu capax imperii nisi imperasset.*
> No one would have doubted his ability to rule had he never been emperor.
>> *Histories*

learning

Addison, Joseph (1672–1719)
English essayist, poet, playwright and statesman
> The truth of it is, learning … makes a silly man

ten thousand times more insufferable, by supplying variety of matter to his impertinence, and giving him an opportunity of abounding in absurdities.

The Man of the Town

Aristotle (384–322 BC)
Greek philosopher
> What we have to learn to do, we learn by doing.
>> *Nicomachean Ethics*

Armstrong, Dr John (1709–1779)
Scottish physician, poet and writer
> Much had he read,
> Much more had seen; he studied from the life,
> And in th' original perus'd mankind.
>> *The Art of Preserving Health* (1744)

Ascham, Roger (1515–1568)
English scholar, educationist and archer
> There is no such whetstone, to sharpen a good wit and encourage a will to learning, as is praise.
>> *The Scholemaster* (1570)

Bacon, Francis (1561–1626)
English philosopher, essayist, politician and courtier
> Studies serve for delight, for ornament, and for ability.
>> 'Of Studies' (1625)

> Crafty men contemn studies; simple men admire them; and wise men use them.
>> 'Of Studies' (1625)

Bierce, Ambrose (1842–c.1914)
American writer, verse writer and soldier
> *Learning*: The kind of ignorance distinguishing the studious.
>> *The Devil's Dictionary* (1911)

Chesterfield, Lord (1694–1773)
English politician and letter writer
> Wear your learning, like your watch, in a private pocket; and do not merely pull it out and strike it merely to show you have one. If you are asked what o'clock it is, tell it; but do not proclaim it hourly and unasked like the watchman.
>> Letter to his son, 1748

Confucius (c.550–c.478 BC)
Chinese philosopher and teacher of ethics
> Learning without thought is labour lost; thought without learning is perilous.
>> *Analects*

Foote, Samuel (1720–1777)
English actor, dramatist and wit
> For as the old saying is,
> When house and land are gone and spent
> Then learning is most excellent.
>> *Taste* (1752)

Gregory, Lady Isabella Augusta (1852–1932)
Irish dramatist, writer and translator
> There's more learning than is taught in books.
>> *The Jester*

Huxley, T.H. (1825–1895)
English biologist, Darwinist and agnostic
> Try to learn something about everything and everything about something.
>> Memorial stone

Knox, Vicesimus (1752–1821)
English churchman and writer
> That learning belongs not to the female character, and that the female mind is not capable of a degree of improvement equal to that of the other sex, are narrow and unphilosophical prejudices.
>> *Essays, Moral and Literary* (1782)

Lessing, Doris (1919–)
British writer, brought up in Zimbabwe
> … that is what learning is. You suddenly understand something you've understood all your life, but in a new way.
>> *The Four-Gated City* (1969)

Mill, John Stuart (1806–1873)
English philosopher, economist and reformer
> As often as a study is cultivated by narrow minds, they will draw from it narrow conclusions.
>> *Auguste Comte and Positivism* (1865)

Milton, John (1608–1674)
English poet, libertarian and pamphleteer
> Where there is much desire to learn, there of necessity will be much arguing, much writing, many opinions; for opinion in good men is but knowledge in the making.
>> *Areopagitica* (1644)

Ovid (43 BC–AD 18)
Roman poet
> *Adde quod ingenuas didicisse fideliter artes*
> *Emollit mores nec sinit esse feros.*
> Add the fact that to have diligently studied the liberal arts refines behaviour and does not allow it to be savage.
>> *Epistulae Ex Ponto*

Pope, Alexander (1688–1744)
English poet, translator and editor
> A little learning is a dangerous thing;
> Drink deep, or taste not the Pierian spring:
> There shallow draughts intoxicate the brain,
> And drinking largely sobers us again.
>> *An Essay on Criticism* (1711)

White, Patrick (1912–1990)
English-born Australian writer and dramatist
> 'I dunno,' Arthur said. 'I forget what I was

taught. I only remember what I've learnt.'

The Solid Mandala (1966)

▶▶ EDUCATION; KNOWLEDGE; SCHOOL; UNIVERSITY

letters

Adams, Abigail (1744–1818)
US letter writer and wife of President John Adams
Of letter-writing
> ... a habit the pleasure of which increases with practice, but becomes more irksome with neglect.

Letter to her daughter, 1808

Auden, W.H. (1907–1973)
English poet, essayist, critic, teacher and dramatist
> This is the Night Mail crossing the Border,
> Bringing the cheque and the postal order,
>
> Letters for the rich, letters for the poor,
> The shop at the corner, the girl next door.
>
> Pulling up Beattock, a steady climb:
> The gradient's against her, but she's on time.
>
> Past cotton-grass and moorland border,
> Shovelling white steam over her shoulder ...
>
> Letters of thanks, letters from banks,
> Letters of joy from girl and boy,
> Receipted bills and invitations
> To inspect new stock or to visit relations,
> And applications for situations,
> And timid lovers' declarations,
> And gossip, gossip from all the nations.

Collected Poems, 1933–1938,
'Night Mail'

Donne, John (1572–1631)
English poet
> Sir, more than kisses, letters mingle souls.

'To Sir Henry Wotton' (1597–1598)

Johnson, Samuel (1709–1784)
English lexicographer, poet, critic, conversationalist and essayist
> An odd thought strikes me: – we shall receive no letters in the grave.

In Boswell, *The Life of Samuel Johnson* (1791)

> In a man's letter his soul lies naked.

Quoted in *The Times*

Morley, John, 1st Viscount Morley (1838–1923)
British journalist, critic and statesman
Of letter-writing
> That most delightful way of wasting time.

Critical Miscellanies (1886), 'Life of George Eliot'

Osborne, Dorothy (**Lady Temple**) (1627–1695)
English letter writer
> All letters, methinks, should be as free and easy as one's discourse, not studied as an oration, nor made up of hard words like a charm.

Letter to Sir William Temple, 1653

Prior, Matthew (1664–1721)
English poet
> And oft the pangs of absence to remove
> By letters, soft interpreters of love.

'Henry and Emma' (1708)

Steele, Sir Richard (1672–1729)
Irish-born English writer, dramatist and politician
> I have heard Will Honeycomb say, A Woman seldom Writes her Mind but in her Postscript.

The Spectator, 79, 1711

liberals

Frayn, Michael (1933–)
English dramatist and writer
> To be absolutely honest, what I feel really bad about is that I don't feel worse. There's the ineffectual liberal's problem in a nutshell.

The Observer, 1965

O'Rourke, P.J. (1947–)
American writer
> Liberals have invented whole college majors – psychology, sociology, women's studies – to prove that nothing is anybody's fault.

Give War a Chance (1992)

Paton, Alan (1903–1988)
South African writer
> By liberalism I don't mean the creed of any party or any century. I mean a generosity of spirit, a tolerance of others, an attempt to comprehend otherness, a commitment to the rule of law, a high ideal of the worth and dignity of man, a repugnance for authoritarianism and a love of freedom.

Lecture on South Africa at Yale University, 1973

libraries

Greer, Germaine (1939–)
Australian feminist, critic, English scholar and writer
> Libraries are reservoirs of strength, grace and wit, reminders of order, calm and continuity, lakes of mental energy, neither warm nor cold, light nor dark. The pleasure they give is steady, unorgiastic, reliable, deep and long-lasting.

Daddy, We Hardly Knew You (1989)

Housman, A.E. (1859–1936)
English poet and scholar

> The arsenals of divine vengeance, if I may so describe the Bodleian library.
>
> *D. Iunii Iuvenalis Saturae* (1905), Preface

Ruskin, John (1819–1900)
English art critic, philosopher and reformer

> We call ourselves a rich nation, and we are filthy and foolish enough to thumb each other's books out of circulating libraries!
>
> *Sesame and Lilies* (1865), 'Of Kings' Treasuries'

Shakespeare, William (1564–1616)
English dramatist, poet and actor

> My library
> Was dukedom large enough.
>
> *The Tempest*, I.ii

> Come and take choice of all my library,
> And so beguile thy sorrow.
>
> *Titus Andronicus*, IV.i

Stoppard, Tom (1937–)
British dramatist

> It is a librarian's duty to distinguish between poetry and a sort of belle-litter.
>
> *Travesties* (1975)

▶▶ BOOKS; EDUCATION; KNOWLEDGE; SCHOOL; UNIVERSITY

lies

Adler, Alfred (1870–1937)
Austrian psychiatrist and psychologist

> It is the patriotic duty of every man to lie for his country.
>
> Attr.

Anonymous

> An abomination unto the Lord, but a very present help in time of trouble.
>
> Definition of a lie

> He lies like an eyewitness.
>
> Russian saying

> We Catholics may lie and say we are Protestants when we are among the Protestants or we may lie when we are among the Huguenots and say we are Huguenots; and if we wish we can stoop so low as to say we are Jews when we are among the Jews if our lying would benefit the Catholic Church.
>
> Jesuit oath

Armstrong, Sir Robert (1927–)
English civil servant
Replying to an allegation in court that a letter he had written on behalf of the British Government had contained a lie

> It contains a misleading impression, not a lie. It was being economical with the truth.
>
> *The Observer*, 1986

Asquith, Margot (1864–1945)
Scottish political hostess and writer
Of Lady Desborough

> She tells enough white lies to ice a wedding cake.
>
> Quoted by Lady Violet Bonham Carter in *The Listener*
> 1953

Bacon, Francis (1561–1626)
English philosopher, essayist, politician and courtier

> But it is not the lie that passeth through the mind, but the lie that sinketh in, and settleth in it, that doth the hurt.
>
> 'Of Truth' (1625)

Belloc, Hilaire (1870–1953)
English writer of verse, essayist and critic; Liberal MP

> Matilda told such Dreadful Lies,
> It made one Gasp and Stretch one's Eyes;
> Her Aunt, who, from her Earliest Youth,
> Had kept a Strict Regard for Truth,
> Attempted to Believe Matilda:
> The effort very nearly killed her.
>
> 'Matilda' (1907)

Benét, Stephen Vincent (1898–1943)
US poet

> … the lounging mirth of cracker-barrel men,
> Snowed in by winter, spitting at the fire,
> And telling the disreputable truth
> With the sad eye that marks the perfect liar.
>
> 'Poem'

The Bible (King James Version)

> God is not a man, that he should lie.
>
> *Numbers*, 23:19

Burke, Edmund (1729–1797)
Irish-born British statesman and philosopher

> Falsehood has a perennial spring.
>
> *Speech on American Taxation* (1774)

Butler, Samuel (1835–1902)
English writer, painter, philosopher and scholar

> Any fool can tell the truth, but it requires a man of some sense to know how to lie well.
>
> *The Note-Books of Samuel Butler* (1912)

Byron, Lord (1788–1824)
English poet satirist and traveller

> And, after all, what is a lie? 'Tis but
> The truth in masquerade.
>
> *Don Juan* (1824)

Callaghan, James (1912–)
English Labour statesman and Prime Minister

> A lie can be half-way round the world before the

truth has got its boots on.

Speech, 1976

Corneille, Pierre (1606–1684)
French dramatist, poet and lawyer
> *Il faut bonne mémoire après qu'on a menti.*
> One needs a good memory after telling lies.
>> *Le Menteur* (1643)

Davies, Robertson (1913–1995)
Canadian playwright, writer and critic
> Better a noble lie than a miserable truth.
>> In Twigg, *Conversations with Twenty-four Canadian Writers* (1981)

Evans, Harold (1928–)
English journalist and newspaper editor
> The camera cannot lie. But it can be an accessory to untruth.
>> Attr.

Goldsmith, Oliver (c.1728–1774)
Irish dramatist, poet and writer
> As ten millions of circles can never make a square, so the united voice of myriads cannot lend the smallest foundation to falsehood.
>> *The Vicar of Wakefield* (1766), 27

Hampton, Christopher (1946–)
English dramatist
> You see, I always divide people into two groups. Those who live by what they know to be a lie, and those who live by what they believe, falsely, to be the truth.
>> *The Philanthropist* (1970)

Herbert, George (1593–1633)
English poet and priest
> The stormie working soul spits lies and froth.
> Dare to be true. Nothing can need a ly.
> A fault which needs it most grows two thereby.
>> *The Temple* (1633)

Hervey, Lord (1696–1743)
English politican and memoirist
> Whoever would lie usefully should lie seldom.
>> In Croker, *Memoirs of the Reign of George II* (1848)

Hitler, Adolf (1889–1945)
German Nazi dictator, born in Austria
> The broad mass of a nation … will more easily fall victim to a big lie than to a small one.
>> *Mein Kampf* (1925)

Household, Geoffrey (1900–1988)
English writer
> It's easy to make a man confess the lies he tells to himself; it's far harder to make him confess the truth.
>> *Rogue Male* (1939)

Ibsen, Henrik (1828–1906)
Norwegian writer, dramatist and poet

Take the saving lie from the average man and you take his happiness away, too.
>> *The Wild Duck* (1884)

Jowett, Benjamin (1817–1893)
English scholar, translator, essayist and priest
> The lie in the Soul is a true lie.
>> From the introduction to his translation (1871) of Plato's *Republic*

Luce, Clare Boothe (1903–1987)
US diplomat, politician and writer
> Lying increases the creative faculties… It is only in lies, wholeheartedly and bravely told, that human nature attains through words and speech the forbearance, the nobility, the romance, the idealism, that it falls so short of in fact and in deeds.
>> *Vanity Fair*, 1930

Maugham, William Somerset (1874–1965)
English writer, dramatist and physician
> She's too crafty a woman to invent a new lie when an old one will serve.
>> *The Constant Wife* (1927)

Murdoch, Iris (1919–1999)
Irish-born British writer, philosopher and dramatist
> He led a double life. Did that make him a liar? He did not feel a liar. He was a man of two truths.
>> *The Sacred and Profane Love Machine* (1974)

Nietzsche, Friedrich Wilhelm (1844–1900)
German philosopher, critic and poet
> *Wir haben die Lüge nötig, … um zu leben.*
> We need lies … in order to live.
>> *Fragments* (1880–1889)

Proust, Marcel (1871–1922)
French writer and critic
> *Une de ces dépêches dont M. de Guermantes avait spirituellement fixé le modèle: 'Impossible venir, mensonge suit'.*
> One of those telegrams of which M. de Guermantes had wittily fixed the formula: 'Cannot come, lie follows'.
>> *Le Temps retrouvé* (1926)

Proverbs
> Better a lie that heals than a truth that wounds.

> A liar is worse than a thief.

Quintilian (c.35–c.100)
Roman rhetorician
> *Mendacem memorem esse oportere.*
> A liar must have a good memory.
>> *Institutio Oratoria*, IV, 2, 91

Rossetti, Dante Gabriel (1828–1882)
English poet, painter, translator and letter-writer
> Was it a friend or foe that spread these lies?

Nay, who but infants question in such wise?
'Twas one of my most intimate enemies.

'Fragment'

Russell, Bertrand (1872–1970)

English philosopher, mathematician, essayist and social reformer

I have never but once succeeded in making George Moore tell a lie, that was by a subterfuge. 'Moore,' I said, 'do you always speak the truth?' 'No,' he replied. I believe this to be the only lie he had ever told.

The Autobiography of Bertrand Russell (1967–1969)

Saki (1870–1916)

Burmese-born British writer

A little inaccuracy sometimes saves tons of explanation.

The Square Egg (1924)

Salmon, George (1819–1904)

Provost of Trinity College, Dublin

Remark at the unveiling of a portrait of a colleague

Excellent, excellent, you can just hear the lies trickling out of his mouth.

Attr.

Shakespeare, William (1564–1616)

English dramatist, poet and actor

A very honest woman, but something given to lie.

Antony and Cleopatra, V.ii

For my part, if a lie may do thee grace,
I'll gild it with the happiest terms I have.

Henry IV, Part 1, V.iv

Lord, Lord, how subject we old men are to this vice of lying!

Henry IV, Part 2, III.ii

Solzhenitsyn, Alexander (1918–)

Russian writer, dramatist and historian

In our country the lie has become not just a moral category but a pillar of the State. In recoiling from the lie we are performing a moral act, not a political act.

Interview in Time magazine, 1974

This universal, compulsory, force-feeding with lies is now the most agonizing aspect of existence in our country – worse than all our material miseries, worse than any lack of civil liberties.

Letter to Soviet Leaders (1974)

Stead, Christina (1902–1983)

Australian writer

A lie is real; it aims at success. A liar is a realist.

Letty Fox: Her Luck (1946)

Stevenson, Adlai (1900–1965)

US lawyer, statesman and United Nations ambassador

A lie is an abomination unto the Lord, and a very present help in trouble.

Speech, Springfield, Illinois, 1951

Stevenson, Robert Louis (1850–1894)

Scottish writer, poet and essayist

The cruellest lies are often told in silence.

Virginibus Puerisque (1881)

Swift, Jonathan (1667–1745)

Irish satirist, poet, essayist and cleric

He replied that I must needs be mistaken, or that I said the thing which was not. (For they have no word in their language to express lying or falsehood.).

Gulliver's Travels (1726)

I mean, you lie – under a mistake.

Polite Conversation (1738)

Tennyson, Alfred, Lord (1809–1892)

English lyric poet

A lie which is all a lie may be met and fought with outright,
But a lie which is part a truth is a harder matter to fight.

'The Grandmother' (1859)

Twain, Mark (1835–1910)

US humorist, writer, journalist and lecturer

An experienced, industrious, ambitious, and often quite picturesque liar.

Private History of a Campaign that Failed (1885)

Washington, George (1732–1799)

US general, statesman and President

On being accused of cutting down a cherry tree

Father, I cannot tell a lie; I did it with my little hatchet.

Attr., probably apocryphal

Wells, H.G. (1866–1946)

English writer

The Social Contract is nothing more or less than a vast conspiracy of human beings to lie to and humbug themselves and one another for the general Good. Lies are the mortar that bind the savage individual man into the social masonry.

Love and Mr Lewisham (1900)

Wilde, Oscar (1854–1900)

Irish poet, dramatist, writer, critic and wit

The final revelation is that Lying, the telling of beautiful untrue things, is the proper aim of Art.

'The Decay of Lying' (1889)

▶▶ ART; DECEPTION; HONESTY; TRUTH

life

Ackerman, Diane (1948–)
US poet

It began in mystery, and it will end in mystery, but what a savage and beautiful country lies in between.

A Natural History of the Senses (1990)

Adams, Douglas (1952–)
English writer

The Answer to the Great Question Of ... Life, the Universe and Everything ... Is ... Forty-two.

The Hitch Hiker's Guide to the Galaxy (1979)

Adams, Henry (1838–1918)
US historian and memoirist

Chaos often breeds life, when order breeds habit.

The Education of Henry Adams (1918)

Adams, Scott (1957–)
US cartoonist

Accept that some days you're the pigeon, and some days you're the statue.

The Dilbert Principle

On the keyboard of life, always keep one finger on the escape key.

The Dilbert Principle

Adler, Polly (1900–1962)
US brothel keeper

I am one of those people who just can't help getting a kick out of life – even when it's a kick in the teeth.

A House Is Not a Home (1953)

Ambrose, Saint (c.340–397)
French-born churchman; writer of music and hymns

Si fueris Romae, Romano vivito more;
Si fueris alibi, vivito sicut ibi.
If you are in Rome, live in the Roman fashion; if you are elsewhere, live as they do there.

In Taylor, *Ductor Dubitantium* (1660)

Amiel, Henri-Frédéric (1821–1881)
Swiss philosopher and writer

Every life is a profession of faith, and exercises an inevitable and silent influence.

Journal, 1852

Anka, Paul (1941–)
US pop singer and songwriter

And now the end is near
And so I face the final curtain,
My friends, I'll say it clear,
I'll state my case of which I'm certain.
I've lived a life that's full, I've travelled each and evr'y high-way

And more, much more than this, I did it my way.

'My Way', song, 1969

Anonymous

Live well. It is the greatest revenge.

The Talmud

The reverse side also has a reverse side.

Japanese Proverb

Almost anything is easier to get into than out of.

Allen's Law

Hot glass looks the same as cold glass.

Dominic Cirino's Law of Burnt Fingers

When you need to knock on wood is when you realize that the world is composed of vinyl, naugahyde and aluminum.

Flugg's Law

If you knew what you were doing, you'd probably be bored.

Fresco's Law

It ain't necessarily so.

Gershwin's Law

Be happy while y'er leevin,
For y'er a lang time deid.

Scottish motto

Aristotle (384–322 BC)
Greek philosopher

Just as at the Olympic games it is not the handsomest or strongest men who are crowned with victory but the successful competitors, so in life it is those who act rightly who carry off all the prizes and rewards.

Nicomachean Ethics

Arnold, Matthew (1822–1888)
English poet, critic, essayist and educationist

For most men in a brazen prison live,
Where, in the sun's hot eye,
With heads bent o'er their toil, they languidly
Their lives to some unmeaning taskwork give,
Dreaming of nought beyond their prison-wall.

'A Summer Night' (1852)

Is it so small a thing
To have enjoy'd the sun,
To have liv'd light in the spring,
To have lov'd, to have thought, to have done?

'Empedocles on Etna' (1852)

When we are asked further, what is conduct? – let us answer: Three fourths of life.

Literature and Dogma (1873)

Aurelius, Marcus (121–180)
Roman emperor and Stoic philosopher

Remember that no one loses any other life than this which he now lives, nor lives any other than this which he now loses.

Meditations

Bacon, Francis (1561–1626)

English philosopher, essayist, politician and courtier

But men must know, that in this theatre of man's life it is reserved only for God and angels to be lookers on.

The Advancement of Learning (1605)

Balfour, A.J. (1848–1930)

British Conservative Prime Minister

Nothing matters very much, and very few things matter at all.

Attr.

Barrie, Sir J.M. (1860–1937)

Scottish dramatist and writer

The life of every man is a diary in which he means to write one story, and writes another; and his humblest hour is when he compares the volume as it is with what he vowed to make it.

Attr.

Beckett, Samuel (1906–1989)

Irish dramatist, writer and poet

We always find something, eh, Didi, to give us the impression that we exist?

Waiting for Godot (1955)

Bede, The Venerable (673–735)

English monk, historian and scholar

When we compare the present life of man with that time of which we have no knowledge, it seems to me like the swift flight of a lone sparrow through the banqueting-hall where you sit in the winter months … This sparrow flies swiftly in through one door of the hall, and out through another … Similarly, man appears on earth for a little while, but we know nothing of what went on before this life, and what follows.

Ecclesiastical History

Behan, Beatrice (1931–1993)

Wife of Brendan Behan

I wonder why dreams must be broken, idylls lost and love forgotten? The transience of life has always exasperated me.

My Life with Brendan Behan (1973)

Bennett, Alan (1934–)

English dramatist, actor and diarist

You know life … it's rather like opening a tin of sardines. We are all of us looking for the key.

Beyond the Fringe (1962)

Bentley, Nicolas (1907–1978)

English publisher and artist

One should not exaggerate the importance of trifles. Life, for instance, is much too short to be taken seriously.

Attr.

Berryman, John (1914–1972)

US poet and author

Life, friends, is boring. We must not say so.

Dream Songs (1964)

Blake, William (1757–1827)

English poet, engraver, painter and mystic

For every thing that lives is holy, life delights in life.

America: a Prophecy (1793)

Brenan, Gerald (1894–1987)

English writer

We should live as if we were going to live forever, yet at the back of our minds remember that our time is short.

Thoughts in a Dry Season (1978)

Brontë, Charlotte (1816–1855)

English writer

Life, believe, is not a dream,
So dark as sages say;
Oft a little morning rain
Foretells a pleasant day!

'Life' (1846)

Browne, Sir Thomas (1605–1682)

English physician, author and antiquary

Life itself is but the shadow of death, and souls but the shadows of the living. All things fall under this name. The sun itself is but the dark *simulacrum*, and light but the shadow of God.

The Garden of Cyrus (1658)

The long habit of living indisposeth us for dying.

Hydriotaphia: Urn Burial (1658)

Buchan, John (1875–1940)

Scottish writer, lawyer and Conservative politician

It's a great life if you don't weaken.

Mr Standfast (1919)

Butler, Samuel (1835–1902)

English writer, painter, philosopher and scholar

Life is one long process of getting tired.

The Note-Books of Samuel Butler (1912)

To live is like love, all reason is against it, and all healthy instinct for it.

The Note-Books of Samuel Butler (1912)

Chamfort, Nicolas (1741–1794)

French writer

Vivre est une maladie dont le sommeil nous soulage toutes les 16 heures. C'est un palliatif. La mort est le remède.

Living is an illness to which sleep provides relief every sixteen hours.
It's a palliative. Death is the remedy.

Maximes et pensées (1796)

Chaplin, Charlie (1889–1977)

English comedian, film actor, director and satirist

Life is a tragedy when seen in close-up, but a comedy in long-shot.

> In *The Guardian*, Obituary, 1977

Christie, Agatha (1890–1976)
English crime writer and playwright

I like living. I have sometimes been wildly, despairingly, acutely miserable, racked with sorrow, but through it all I still know quite certainty that just to be alive is a grand thing.

> *An Autobiography* (1977)

Clare, John (1793–1864)
English rural poet; died in an asylum

And what is Life? – an hour glass on
   the run
A mist retreating from the morning
   sun
A busy bustling still repeated dream
Its length? – A moment's pause, a
   moment's thought
And happiness? A Bubble on the
   stream
That in the act of seizing shrinks to
   nought.

> 'What is Life?' (1820)

If life had a second edition, how I would correct the proofs.

> Letter to a friend

Cocteau, Jean (1889–1963)
French dramatist, poet, film writer and director

Vivre est une chute horizontale.
Life is falling sideways.

> *Opium* (1930)

Compton-Burnett, Dame Ivy (1884–1969)
English novelist

As regards plots I find real life no help at all. Real life seems to have no plots.

> In R. Lehmann et al., *Orion I* (1945)

Conran, Shirley (1932–)
English writer

Life is too short to stuff a mushroom.

> *Superwoman* (1975)

Cook, Peter (1937–1995)
English comedian and writer

Life is a matter of passing the time enjoyably. There may be other things in life, but I've been too busy passing my time enjoyably to think very deeply about them.

> *The Guardian*, 1994

Cory, William (1823–1892)
English poet, teacher and writer

You promise heavens free from strife,
Pure truth, and perfect change of will;
But sweet, sweet is this human life,
So sweet, I fain would breathe it still;

Your chilly stars I can forgo,
This warm kind world is all I know …
All beauteous things for which we live
By laws of space and time decay.
But Oh, the very reason why
I clasp them, is because they die.

> 'Mimnermus in Church' (1858)

Coubertin, Pierre de (1863–1937)
French educationist and sportsman

L'important dans la vie ce n'est point le triomphe mais le combat; l'essentiel ce n'est pas d'avoir vaincu mais de s'être bien battu.
The most important thing in life is not the winning but the taking part; the essential thing is not conquering but fighting well.

> Speech, 1908

Cowper, William (1731–1800)
English poet, hymn and letter writer

Variety's the very spice of life,
That gives all its flavour.

> *The Task* (1785)

Crowfoot (1821–1890)
Blackfoot warrior

What is life? It is the flash of a firefly in the night. It is the breath of a buffalo in the wintertime. It is the little shadow which runs across the grass and loses itself in the sunset.

> Last words

Davies, William Henry (1871–1940)
Welsh poet, writer and tramp

What is this life if, full of care,
We have no time to stand and stare?

> *Songs of Joy* (1911)

Dawkins, Richard (1941–)
English biologist and author

The essence of life is statistical improbability on a colossal scale.

> *The Blind Watchmaker* (1986)

Dickens, Charles (1812–1870)
English writer

'I am ruminating,' said Mr Pickwick, 'on the strange mutability of human affairs.'
'Ah, I see – in at the palace door one day, out at the window the next. Philosopher, sir?'
'An observer of human nature, sir,' said Mr Pickwick.

> *The Pickwick Papers* (1837)

Disraeli, Benjamin (1804–1881)
English statesman and writer

Next to knowing when to seize an opportunity, the most important thing in life is to know when to forego an advantage.

> Attr.

Duncan, Isadora (1878–1927)
US modern dance pioneer
> People do not live nowadays – they get about ten percent out of life.
>> *This Quarter Autumn, 'Memoirs'*

Einstein, Albert (1879–1955)
German-born US mathematical physicist
> Only a life lived for others is a life worthwhile.
>> *'Defining Success'*

Emerson, Ralph Waldo (1803–1882)
US poet, essayist, transcendentalist and teacher
> Life is good only when it is magical and musical, a perfect timing and consent, and when we do not anatomize it. You must treat the days respectfully, you must be a day yourself, and not interrogate it like a college professor ... You must hear the bird's song without attempting to render it into nouns and verbs.
>> *Society and Solitude* (1870)

Fincher, David (1963–)
US film director
> This is your life and it's ending one minute at a time.
>> *Fight Club* (film, 1999)

Franklin, Benjamin (1706–1790)
US statesman, scientist, political critic and printer
> Dost thou love life? Then do not squander time, for that's the stuff life is made of.
>> *Poor Richard's Almanac* (1746)

Fry, Christopher (1907–)
English verse dramatist, theatre director and translator
> What a minefield
> Life is! One minute you're taking a stroll in the sun,
> The next your legs and arms are all over the hedge.
> There's no dignity in it.
>> *A Yard of Sun* (1970)

Gay, John (1685–1732)
English poet, dramatist and librettist
> Life is a jest; and all things show it.
> I thought so once; but now I know it.
>> *'My Own Epitaph'* (1720)

Gibbons, Orlando (1583–1625)
English organist and composer of church music
> What is our life? a play of passion,
> Our mirth the music of derision,
> Our mothers' wombs the tiring houses be,
> Where we are dressed for this short comedy ...
> Only we die in earnest, that's no jest.
>> *The First Set of Madrigals and Motets of Five Parts* (1612)

Goethe (1749–1832)
German poet, writer, dramatist and scientist
> *Grau, teuer Freund, ist alle Theorie,*
> *Und grün des Lebens goldner Baum.*
> Grey, dear friend, is all theory,
> And green the golden tree of life.
>> *Faust* (1808)

Gordon, Adam Lindsay (1833–1870)
Australian poet and ballad writer
> Life is mostly froth and bubble,
> Two things stand like stone,
> Kindness in another's trouble,
> Courage in your own.
>> *Ye Wearie Wayfarer* (1866)

> A little season of love and laughter,
> Of light and life, and pleasure and pain,
> And a horror of outer darkness after,
> And dust returneth to dust again.
>> *'The Swimmer'* (1903)

Hardy, Thomas (1840–1928)
English writer and poet
> 'What do you think of it, Moon,
> As you go?
> Is Life much, or no?'
> 'O, I think of it, often think of it
> As a show
> God ought surely to shut up soon,
> As I go.'
>> *'To the Moon'* (1917)

Hawthorne, Nathaniel (1804–1864)
US allegorical writer
> Life is made up of marble and mud.
>> *The House of the Seven Gables* (1851)

Henry, O. (1862–1910)
US short-story writer
> Life is made up of sobs, sniffles, and smiles, with sniffles predominating.
>> *The Four Million* (1906)

Henshaw, Bishop Joseph (1603–1679)
English churchman and writer
> One doth but breakfast here, another dines, he that liveth longest doth but sup; we must all go to bed in another world.
>> *Horae Succisivae* (1631)

Hobbes, Thomas (1588–1679)
Political philosopher
> No arts; no letters; no society; and which is worst of all, continual fear, and danger of violent death; and the life of man, solitary, poor, nasty, brutish, and short.
>> *Leviathan* (1651)

Hodson, Peregrine
British author
> It shows hunger for life, like the Zen parable of a man holding on to a tree root over the edge of a cliff: below him rocks, above him a tiger, and a

black and white mouse nibbling at the root: the man notices a strawberry beside him and picks it.

A Circle Round The Sun – A Foreigner in Japan

Hubbard, Elbert (1856–1915)
US printer, editor, writer and businessman
Life is just one damned thing after another.

Philistine, 1909

Huxley, Aldous (1894–1963)
English writer, poet and critic
Living is an art; and to practise it well, men need, not only acquired skill, but also a native tact and taste.

Texts and Pretexts (1932)

Most of one's life ... is one prolonged effort to prevent oneself thinking.

Mortal Coils (1922)

Huxley, T.H. (1825–1895)
English biologist, Darwinist and agnostic
The chess-board is the world; the pieces are the phenomena of the universe; the rules of the game are what we call the laws of Nature. The player on the other side is hidden from us. We know that his play is always fair, just, and patient. But we also know, to our cost, that he never overlooks a mistake, or makes the smallest allowance for ignorance.

Macmillan's Magazine, 1868

James, Henry (1843–1916)
US-born British writer, critic and letter writer
Live all you can; it's a mistake not to. It doesn't so much matter what you do in particular, so long as you have your life. If you haven't had that then what have you had?

The Ambassadors (1903)

Jeans, Sir James Hopwood (1877–1946)
English mathematician, physicist and astronomer
Life exists in the universe only because the carbon atom possesses certain exceptional properties.

The Mysterious Universe (1930)

Johnson, Samuel (1709–1784)
English lexicographer, poet, critic, conversationalist and essayist
Life is a pill which none of us can bear to swallow without gilding.

In Hester Lynch Piozzi, *Anecdotes of the Late Samuel Johnson* (1786)

Human life is everywhere a state in which much is to be endured, and little to be enjoyed.

Rasselas (1759)

Jung, Carl Gustav (1875–1961)
Swiss psychiatrist and pupil of Freud
Soweit wir zu erkennen vermögen, ist es der einzige Sinn der menschlichen Existenz, ein Licht anzuzünden in der Finsternis des blossen Seins.
As far as we are able to understand, the only aim of human existence is to kindle a light in the darkness of mere being.

Memories, Dreams, Thoughts (1962)

Keats, John (1795–1821)
English poet
But this is human life: the war, the deeds,
The disappointment, the anxiety,
Imagination's struggles, far and nigh,
All human.

'Endymion' (1818)

I compare human life to a large Mansion of Many Apartments, two of which I can only describe, the doors of the rest being as yet shut upon me.

Letter to J.H. Reynolds, 3 May 1818

A Man's life of any worth is a continual allegory.

Letter to George and Georgiana Keats, 1819

Kierkegaard, Søren (1813–1855)
Danish philosopher
Life can only be understood backwards; but it must be lived forwards.

Life

La Bruyère, Jean de (1645–1696)
French satirist
Il n'y a pour l'homme que trois événements: naître, vivre, et mourir. Il ne se sent pas naître, il souffre à mourir, et il oublie de vivre.
There are only three events in a man's life; birth, life, and death; he is not aware of being born, he dies in suffering, and he forgets to live.

Les caractères ou les moeurs de ce siècle (1688)

Laforgue, Jules (1860–1887)
Ah! que la vie est quotidienne!
Oh, what an everyday affair life is!

Les complaintes (1885)

Leary, Timothy (1920–1996)
US writer and psychologist
If you take the game of life seriously, if you take your nervous system seriously, if you take your sense organs seriously, if you take the energy process seriously, you must turn on, tune in, and drop out.

Politics of Ecstasy (1968)

Lehrer, Tom (1928–)
US academic and songwriter
Life is like a sewer. What you get out of it depends on what you put in.

Record album, *An Evening Wasted with Tom Lehrer* (1953)

Lennon, John (1940–1980)
English rock musician
Life is what happens to you when you're busy

making other plans.

'Beautiful Boy', song, 1980

Leonardo da Vinci (1452–1519)

While I thought that I was learning how to live, I have been learning how to die.

Selections from the Notebooks of Leonardo da Vinci (1952 edition)

Lessing, Gotthold Ephraim (1729–1781)
German dramatist, critic and theologian

Gestern liebt' ich,
Heute leid' ich,
Morgen sterb' ich.
Dennoch denk' ich
Heut und morgen
Gern an gestern.

Yesterday I loved, today I suffer, tomorrow I shall die. Nonetheless I still think with pleasure, today and tomorrow, of yesterday.

'Song taken from the Spanish'

Lewis, C.S. (1898–1963)
Irish-born English academic, writer and critic

Term, holidays, term, holidays, till we leave school, and then work, work, work till we die.

Surprised by Joy (1955)

Lewis, Sir George Cornewall (1806–1863)
English Liberal politician and writer

Life would be tolerable but for its amusements.

In *Dictionary of National Biography*

Longfellow, Henry Wadsworth (1807–1882)
US poet and writer

Lives of great men all remind us
We can make our lives sublime,
And, departing, leave behind us
Footprints on the sands of time …

'A Psalm of Life' (1838)

Our ingress into the world
Was naked and bare;
Our progress through the world
Is trouble and care.

Tales of a Wayside Inn (1863–1874), 'The Student's Tale'

Lucretius (c.95–55 BC)
Roman philosopher

Vitaque mancipio, nulli datur, omnibus usu.
For life is not confined to him or thee;
'Tis given to all for use, to none for property.

De Rerum Natura

Malamud, Bernard (1914–1986)
US writer

Life is a tragedy full of joy.

New York Times, 1979

Mann, Thomas (1875–1955)
German writer and critic

Der Mensch lebt nicht nur sein persönliches Leben als Einzelwesen, sondern, bewusst oder unbewusst, auch das seiner Epoche und Zeitgenossenschaft.
Man does not only live his personal life as an individual, but also, consciously or unconsciously, the life of his era and of his contemporaries.

The Magic Mountain (1924)

Martial (c.AD 40–c.104)
Spanish-born Latin epigrammatist and poet

Non est, crede mihi, sapientis dicere 'Vivam':
Sera nimis vita est crastina: vive hodie.
Believe me, 'I shall live' is not the saying of a wise man. Tomorrow's life is too late: live today.

Epigrammata

Maugham, William Somerset (1874–1965)
English writer, dramatist and physician

Life is too short to do anything for oneself that one can pay others to do for one.

The Summing Up (1938)

Mitchell, Joni (1943–)
US singer and songwriter

I've looked at life from both sides now
From win and lose and still somehow
It's life's illusions I recall
I really don't know life at all.

'Both Sides Now', song, 1968

Montaigne, Michel de (1533–1592)
French essayist and moralist

L'utilité de vivre n'est pas en l'espace, elle est en l'usage … Il gît en votre volonté, non au nombre des ans, que vous ayez assez vécu.
The value of life does not lie in the number of years but in the use you make of them… Whether you have lived enough depends on your will, not on the number of your years.

Essais (1580)

Mon métier et mon art, c'est vivre.
Living is both my job and my art.

Essais (1580)

Nash, Ogden (1902–1971)
US poet

When I consider how my life is spent,
I hardly ever repent.

'Reminiscent Reflection' (1931)

Nietzsche, Friedrich Wilhelm (1844–1900)
German philosopher, critic and poet

Glaubt es mir! – das Geheimnis, um die grösste Fruchtbarkeit und den grössten Genuss vom Dasein einzuernten, heisst: gefährlich leben!
Believe me! – the secret of gathering in the greatest fruitfulness and the greatest enjoyment from existence is living dangerously!

The Gay Science (1887)

O'Casey, Sean (1880–1964)
Irish dramatist

I am going where life is more like life than it is here.

Cock-a-Doodle Dandy (1949)

O'Keeffe, Georgia (1887–1986)
US artist

My feeling about life is a curious kind of triumphant feeling about seeing it bleak, knowing it is so, and walking into it fearlessly because one has no choice.

Attr.

Olivier, Sir Laurence (1907–1989)
English actor and director

Living is strife and torment, disappointment and love and sacrifice, golden sunsets and black storms. I said that some time ago, and today I do not think I would add one word.

Los Angeles Times, 1978

O'Neill, Eugene (1888–1953)
US dramatist

Our lives are merely strange dark interludes in the electric display of God the Father!

Strange Interlude (1928)

Ortega y Gasset, José (1883–1955)
Spanish philosopher

Poca cosa es la vida si no piafa en ella un afán formidable de ampliar sus fronteras. Se vive en la proporción en que se ans'a vivir más.
Life is a petty thing unless there is pounding within it an enormous desire to extend its boundaries. We live in proportion to the extent to which we yearn to live more.

The Dehumanization of Art (1925)

Pascal, Blaise (1623–1662)
French philosopher and scientist

Le dernier acte est sanglant, quelque belle que soit la comédie en tout le reste.
The last act is bloody, however delightful the rest of the play may be.

Pensées (1670)

Proust, Marcel (1871–1922)
French writer and critic

Good-bye, I've barely said a word to you, it is always like that at parties, we never see the people, we never say the things we should like to say, but it is the same everywhere in this life. Let us hope that when we are dead things will be better arranged.

A la recherche du temps perdu, Sodome et Gomorrhe (1922)

Proverbs

Life begins at forty.

All's well that ends well.

The best things in life are free.

Life is just a bowl of cherries.

Life is sweet.

He that lives long suffers much.

Rabelais, François (c.1494–c.1553)
French monk, physician, satirist and humanist

Man never found the deities so kindly
As to assure him that he'd live tomorrow.

Pantagruel (1532)

Renard, Jules (1864–1910)
French writer and dramatist

Il faut dompter la vie par la douceur.
Life should be tamed with tenderness.

Journal, 1892

Russell, Bertrand (1872–1970)
English philosopher, mathematician, essayist and social reformer

Brief and powerless is Man's life; on him and all his race the slow, sure doom falls pitiless and dark.

Mysticism and Logic (1918)

Santayana, George (1863–1952)
Spanish-born US philosopher and writer

There is no cure for birth and death save to enjoy the interval.

Soliloquies in England (1922)

Life is not a spectacle or a feast; it is a predicament.

In Sagittarius and George, *The Perpetual Pessimist*

Seneca (c.4 BC–AD 65)
Roman philosopher, poet, dramatist, essayist, rhetorician and statesman

Nil melius aeterna lex fecit, quam quod unum introitum nobis ad vitam dedit, exitus multos.
Eternal law has arranged nothing better than this, that it has given us one way in to life, but many ways out.

Epistulae Morales

Live among men as if God beheld you; speak to God as if men were listening.

Epistles

Shakespeare, William (1564–1616)
English dramatist, poet and actor

All the world's a stage,
And all the men and women merely players;
They have their exits and their entrances;
And one man in his time plays many parts.

As You Like It, II.vii

O gentlemen, the time of life is short!
To spend that shortness basely were too long.

Henry IV, Part 1, V.ii

To-morrow, and to-morrow, and to-morrow,
Creeps in this petty pace from day to day

To the last syllable of recorded time,
And all our yesterdays have lighted fools
The way to dusty death. Out, out, brief candle!
Life's but a walking shadow, a poor player,
That struts and frets his hour upon the stage,
And then is heard no more; it is a tale
Told by an idiot, full of sound and fury,
Signifying nothing.

Macbeth, V.v

Shelley, Percy Bysshe (1792–1822)
English poet, dramatist and essayist
Lift not the painted veil which those who live
Call Life.

'Sonnet' (1818)

Smith, Logan Pearsall (1865–1946)
US-born British epigrammatist, critic and writer
There are two things to aim at in life: first, to get
what you want; and, after that, to enjoy it. Only
the wisest of mankind achieve the second.

Afterthoughts (1931)

Smollett, Tobias (1721–1771)
Scottish writer, satirist, historian, traveller and physician
What is life but a veil of affliction?

The Expedition of Humphry Clinker (1771)

Socrates (469–399 BC)
Athenian philosopher
The unexamined life is not a life worth living for
a human being.

Attr. in Plato, Apology

But now it is time to depart, for me to die and
for you to go on living; but which of us has the
better lot, is unknown to anyone but God.

Attr. in Plato, Apology

Southey, Robert (1774–1843)
English poet, essayist, historian and letterwriter
Live as long as you may, the first twenty years
are the longest half of your life.

The Doctor (1812)

Steiner, Rudolf (1861–1925)
Austrian philosopher and founder of anthroposophy
The history of our spiritual life is a continuing
search for the unity between ourselves and the
world.

The Philosophy of Freedom (1964)

Stevenson, Robert Louis (1850–1894)
Scottish writer, poet and essayist
To love playthings well as a child, to lead an
adventurous and honourable youth, and to settle
when the time arrives, into a green and smiling
age, is to be a good artist in life and deserve
well of yourself and your neighbour.

Virginibus Puerisque (1881)

Stoppard, Tom (1937–)
British dramatist

Life is a gamble, at terrible odds – if it was a
bet, you wouldn't take it.

Rosencrantz and Guildenstern Are Dead (1967)

Taylor, Bishop Jeremy (1613–1667)
English divine and writer
As our life is very short, so it is very miserable,
and therefore it is well it is short.

The Rule and Exercise of Holy Dying (1651)

Temple, Sir William (1628–1699)
English diplomat and writer
When all is done, human life is, at the greatest
and the best, but like a forward child, that must
be play'd with and humoured a little to keep it
quiet till it falls asleep, and then the care is over.

Miscellanea, The Second Part (1690)

Terence (c.190–159 BC)
Carthaginian-born Roman dramatist
Modo liceat vivere, est spes.
Where there's life, there's hope.

Heauton Timoroumenos

Thales (c.624–547 BC)
Ionian philosopher, mathematician and astronomer
His reply when asked why he chose to carry on living after
saying there was no difference between life and death
Because there is no difference.

In Durant, The Story of Civilization

Thomas, Dylan (1914–1953)
Welsh poet, writer and radio dramatist
Oh, isn't life a terrible thing, thank God?

Under Milk Wood (1954)

Thoreau, Henry David (1817–1862)
US essayist, social critic and writer
I wanted to live deep and suck out all the
marrow of life … to drive life into a corner, and
reduce it to its lowest terms, and, if it proved to
be mean, why then to get the whole and
genuine meanness of it, and publish its
meanness to the world; or if it were sublime, to
know it by experience, and be able to give a
true account of it in my next excursion.

Walden (1854)

Our life is frittered away by detail … Simplify,
simplify.

Walden (1854)

Tucker, Sophie (1884–1966)
Russian-born US vaudeville singer
Life begins at forty.

Attr.

Twain, Mark (1835–1910)
US humorist, writer, journalist and lecturer
All say, 'How hard it is to die' – a strange
complaint to come from the mouths of people
who have had to live.

Pudd'nhead Wilson's Calendar (1894)

Vauvenargues, Marquis de (1715–1747)
French soldier and moralist

> *Pour exécuter de grandes choses, il faut vivre comme si on ne devait jamais mourir.*
> In order to achieve great things we must live as though we were never going to die.
>> *Réflexions et Maximes* (1746)

Villiers de L'Isle-Adam, Philippe-Auguste (1838–1889)
French poet and writer

> *Vivre? Les serviteurs feront cela pour nous.*
> Live? The servants will do that for us.
>> *Axel* (1890)

Wells, H.G. (1866–1946)
English writer

> I tell you, we're in a blessed drainpipe, and we've got to crawl along it till we die.
>> *Kipps: the Story of a Simple Soul* (1905)

Whitehead, A.N. (1861–1947)
English mathematician and philosopher

> It is the essence of life that it exists for its own sake.
>> *Nature and Life* (1934)

Wilde, Oscar (1854–1900)
Irish poet, dramatist, writer, critic and wit

> *Lord Illingworth*: The soul is born old but grows young. That is the comedy of life.
> *Mrs Allonby*: And the body is born young and grows old. That is life's tragedy.
>> *A Woman of No Importance* (1893)

> One can live for years sometimes without living at all, and then all life comes crowding into one single hour.
>> *Vera, or The Nihilist* (1880)

> One's real life is so often the life that one does not lead.
>> 'L'Envoi to Rose-Leaf and Apple-Leaf'

Wodehouse, P.G. (1881–1975)
English humorist and writer

> I spent the afternoon musing on Life. If you come to think of it, what a queer thing Life is! So unlike anything else, don't you know, if you see what I mean.
>> *My Man Jeeves* (1919)

Xerxes (c.519–465 BC)
King of Persia
On surveying his army

> I was thinking, and I was moved to pity that the whole of human life is so short – not one of this great number will be alive a hundred years from now.
>> In Herodotus, *Histories*

Yeats, W.B. (1865–1939)
Irish poet, dramatist, editor, writer and senator

> When I think of all the books I have read, and of the wise words I have heard spoken, and of the anxiety I have given to parents and grandparents, and of the hopes that I have had, all life weighed in the scales of my own life seems to me preparation for something that never happens.
>> *Autobiographies* (1955)

Zola, Emile (1840–1902)
French novelist

> *Le seul intérêt à vivre est de croire à la vie, de l'aimer et de mettre toutes les forces de son intelligence à la mieux connaître.*
> The only interest in living comes from believing in life, from loving life and using all the power of your intelligence to know it better.
>> *Le Docteur Pascal* (1893)

▶▶ AFTERLIFE; HUMANITY AND HUMAN NATURE; MORTALITY; PURPOSE; TIME

light

The Bible (King James Version)

> And God said, Let there be light: and there was light.
>> *Genesis*, I:3

> The people that walked in darkness have seen a great light: they that dwell in the shadow of death, upon them hath the light shined.
>> *Isaiah*, 9:2

> The light shineth in darkness; and the darkness comprehended it not.
>> *John*, 1:5

Dickinson, Emily (1830–1886)
US poet

> There's a certain Slant of light,
> Winter Afternoons –
> That oppresses, like the Heft
> Of Cathedral Tunes –
> Heavenly Hurt, it gives us –
> We can find no scar,
> But internal difference,
> Where the Meanings, are.
>> 'There's a certain Slant of light' (c.1861)

Keats, John (1795–1821)
English poet

> Ay, on the shores of darkness there is light,
> And precipices show untrodden green;
> There is a budding morrow in midnight;
> There is a triple sight in blindness keen.
>> 'To Homer' (1818)

Keller, Helen (1880–1968)
US writer and educator of the blind and deaf

How reconcile this world of fact with the bright world of my imagining? My darkness has been filled with the light of intelligence, and behold, the outer day-light world was stumbling and groping in social blindness.

> In Upton Sinclair (ed.), *The Cry for Justice* (1963)

Patten, Brian (1946–)
British poet
> We pass –
> And lit briefly by one another's light
> Think the way we go is right.

> 'One another's light'

Shakespeare, William (1564–1616)
English dramatist, poet and actor
> How far that little candle throws his beams!
> So shines a good deed in a naughty world.

> *The Merchant of Venice*, V.i

liking

Austen, Jane (1775–1817)
English writer
> I do not want people to be very agreeable, as it saves me the trouble of liking them a great deal.

> Letter, 1798

Halifax, Lord (1633–1695)
English politician, courtier, pamphleteer and epigrammatist
> It is a general Mistake to think the Men we like are good for every thing, and those we do not, good for nothing.

> *Political, Moral and Miscellaneous Thoughts and Reflections* (1750)

Martial (c.AD 40–c.104)
Spanish-born Latin epigrammatist and poet
> I do not like you, Sabidius, and I cannot say why; all I can say is this: I do not like you.

> *Epigrammata*

Maugham, William Somerset (1874–1965)
English writer, dramatist and physician
> I've always been interested in people, but I've never liked them.

> *The Observer*, 'Sayings of the Week', 1949

Spencer, Sir Stanley (1891–1959)
English painter
> I no more like people personally than I like dogs. When I meet them I am only apprehensive whether they will bite me, which is reasonable and sensible.

> In Collis, *Stanley Spencer* (1962)

Taylor, A.J.P. (1906–1990)
English historian, writer, broadcaster and lecturer

They say that men become attached even to Widnes.

> *The Observer*, 1963

Twain, Mark (1835–1910)
American humorist, writer, journalist and lecturer
Of Thomas Carlyle and Americans
> At bottom he was probably fond of them, but he was always able to conceal it.

> *My First Lie*

listening

Kundera, Milan (1929–)
Czech writer and critic
> All man's life among men is nothing more than a battle for the ears of others.

> *The Book of Laughter and Forgetting* (1981)

Whitehorn, Katherine (1926–)
English writer
> A good listener is not someone who has nothing to say. A good listener is a good talker with a sore throat.

> Attr.

Wilder, Thornton (1897–1975)
US author and playwright
> There's nothing like eavesdropping to show you that the world outside your head is different from the world inside your head.

> *The Matchmaker* (1954)

literature

Brenan, Gerald (1894–1987)
English writer
> The cliché is dead poetry. English, being the language of an imaginative race, abounds in clichés, so that English literature is always in danger of being poisoned by its own secretions.

> *Thoughts in a Dry Season* (1978)

Brookner, Anita (1928–)
English writer
> Dr Weiss, at forty, knew that her life had been ruined by literature.

> *A Start in Life* (1981)

Cheever, John (1912–1982)
US novelist
Speech on receiving the National Medal for Literature
> Literature has been the salvation of the damned, literature has inspired and guided lovers, routed despair and can perhaps in this case save the world.

> Susan Cheever, *Home before Dark* (1984)

Connolly, Cyril (1903–1974)
English literary editor, writer and critic
> Literature is the art of writing something that will be read twice; journalism what will be grasped at once.
>
> *Enemies of Promise* (1938)

Flaubert, Gustave (1821–1880)
French writer
> Ulysses is the strongest character in the whole of ancient literature, Hamlet the strongest character in the whole of modern literature.
>
> *Letter to Louise Colet, 1853*

Gaisford, Rev. Thomas (1779–1855)
Dean of Christ Church, Oxford
> Nor can I do better, in conclusion, than impress upon you the study of Greek literature, which not only elevates above the vulgar herd, but leads not infrequently to positions of considerable emolument.
>
> *Christmas Day Sermon, Oxford Cathedral*

Goethe (1749–1832)
German poet, writer, dramatist and scientist
> *Nationalliteratur will jetzt nicht viel sagen, die Epoche der Weltliteratur ist an der Zeit.*
> National literature does not now have much significance, it is time for the era of world literature.
>
> *Gespräche mit Eckermann, 1827*

Heller, Joseph (1923–1999)
US writer
> He knew everything about literature except how to enjoy it.
>
> *Catch-22* (1961)

Horace (65–8 BC)
Roman lyric poet and satirist
> *Inceptis gravibus plerumque et magna professis Purpureus, late qui splendeat, unus et alter Adsuitur pannus.*
> In serious works and ones that promise great things, one or two purple patches are often stitched in, to glitter far and wide.
>
> *Ars Poetica*

Inge, William Ralph (1860–1954)
English divine, writer and teacher
> Literature flourishes best when it is half a trade and half an art.
>
> 'The Victorian Age' (1922)

Lewis, Sinclair (1885–1951)
US writer
> Our American professors like their literature clear, cold, pure, and very dead.
>
> *Address to Swedish Academy, 1930*

Lodge, David (1935–)
English writer, satirist and literary critic
> Literature is mostly about having sex and not much about having children; life is the other way round.
>
> *The British Museum is Falling Down* (1965)

Lover, Samuel (1797–1868)
Irish songwriter, painter, writer and dramatist
> When once the itch of literature comes over a man, nothing can cure it but the scratching of a pen.
>
> *Handy Andy* (1842)

Nabokov, Vladimir (1899–1977)
Russian-born US writer, poet, translator and critic
> Literature and butterflies are the two sweetest passions known to man.
>
> *Radio Times, 1962*

Palmer, Nettie (1885–1964)
Australian literary critic
> But is there, I wonder, any such thing as 'pure' literature? Isn't it just a conception of people who look on writing as an escape from the living world? Perhaps a painter, or musician, can cut himself off, in his work, from what's going on around him, but a writer can't.
>
> *Fourteen Years …, Journal entry, 1939*

Pound, Ezra (1885–1972)
US poet
> Great Literature is simply language charged with meaning to the utmost possible degree.
>
> *How to Read* (1931)

> Literature is news that STAYS news.
>
> *ABC of Reading* (1934)

Quiller-Couch, Sir Arthur ('Q') (1863–1944)
English man of letters
> Does it or does it not strike you as queer that the people who set you 'courses of study' in English Literature never include the Authorised Version, which not only intrinsically but historically is out and away the greatest book of English Prose? Perhaps they pay you the compliment of supposing that you are perfectly acquainted with it? … I wonder.
>
> *On the Art of Writing* (1916)

Rushdie, Salman (1947–)
Indian-born English author
> Literature is where I go to explore the highest and lowest places in human society and in the human spirit, where I hope to find not absolute truth but the truth of the tale, of the imagination and of the heart.
>
> *The Observer, 1989*

Southey, Robert (1774–1843)
English poet, essayist, historian and letterwriter
> Your true lover of literature is never fastidious.
>
> *The Doctor* (1812)

Stein, Gertrude (1874–1946)
US writer, dramatist, poet and critic
Speaking to a friend she considered knew little about literature

> Besides Shakespeare and me, who do you think there is?

In Mellow, *Charmed Circle* (1974)

Stendhal (1783–1842)
French writer, critic and soldier

> *Le romantisme est l'art de présenter aux peuples les oeuvres littéraires qui, dans l'état actuel de leurs habitudes et de leurs croyances, sont susceptibles de leur donner le plus de plaisir possible. Le classicisme, au contraire, leur présente la littérature qui donnait le plus grand plaisir possible à leurs arrière-grand-pères.*
> Romanticism is the art of presenting people with the literary works which are capable of giving them the greatest possible pleasure, in the present state of their customs and beliefs. Classicism, on the other hand, presents them with the literature that gave the greatest possible pleasure to their great-grandfathers.

Racine et Shakespeare (1823)

Tolstoya, Tatyana

> Literature is written according to certain rules, but which rules?

Interview, Waterstones, Glasgow

Twain, Mark (1835–1910)
US humorist, writer, journalist and lecturer
Definition of a classic

> Something that everybody wants to have read and nobody wants to read.

'The Disappearance of Literature'

Wilde, Oscar (1854–1900)
Irish poet, dramatist, writer, critic and wit

> Movement, that problem of the visible arts, can be truly realized by Literature alone. It is Literature that shows us the body in its swiftness and the soul in its unrest.

'The Critic as Artist' (1891)

Wilder, Thornton (1897–1975)
US author and playwright

> Literature is the orchestration of platitudes.

Time, 1953

Woolf, Virginia (1882–1941)
English writer and critic

> Literature is strewn with the wreckage of men who have minded beyond reason the opinions of others.

A Room of One's Own (1929)

Yeats, W.B. (1865–1939)
Irish poet, dramatist, editor, writer and senator

> All folk literature, and all literature that keeps the folk tradition, delights in unbounded and

immortal things.

'The Celtic Element in Literature' (1902)

> We have no longer in any country a literature as great as the literature of the old world, and that is because the newspapers, all kinds of second-rate books, the preoccupation of men with all kinds of practical changes, have driven the living imagination out of this world.

'First Principles' (1904)

▶▶ ART; BOOKS; CRITICISM; FICTION; POETRY; POETS; READING; WRITERS; WRITING

logic

Anonymous

> Logic is a systematic method of coming to the wrong conclusion with confidence.

Manley's Maxim

Chesterton, G.K. (1874–1936)
English writer, poet and critic

> You can only find truth with logic if you have already found truth without it.

The Man who was Orthodox

Huxley, T.H. (1825–1895)
English biologist, Darwinist and agnostic

> Logical consequences are the scarecrows of fools and the beacons of wise men.

Nature, 1874, 'On the Hypothesis that Animals are Automata and its History'

Wittgenstein, Ludwig (1889–1951)
Austrian philosopher

> Logic must look after itself.

Tractatus Logico-Philosophicus (1922)

▶▶ PHILOSOPHY

loneliness

Arnold, Matthew (1822–1888)
English poet, critic, essayist and educationist

> Yes! in the sea of life enisled,
> With echoing straits between us thrown,
> Dotting the shoreless watery wild,
> We mortal millions live alone.

'To Marguerite – Continued' (1852)

> This truth – to prove, and make thine own:
> 'Thou hast been, shalt be, art, alone.'

'Isolation. To Marguerite' (1857)

Conrad, Joseph (1857–1924)
Polish-born British writer, sailor and explorer

> Who knows what true loneliness is – not the conventional word but the naked terror? To the

lonely themselves it wears a mask.

Attr.

Hammarskjöld, Dag (1905–1961)
Swedish statesman, Secretary-General of the United Nations
> Pray that your loneliness may spur you into finding something to live for, great enough to die for.

Diaries, 1951

Hubbard, Elbert (1856–1915)
US printer, editor, writer and businessman
> Loneliness is to endure the presence of one who does not understand.

Attr.

Lennon, John (1940–1980)
English rock musician
> Waits at the window, wearing the face that she keeps in a jar by the door
> Who is it for? All the lonely people, where do they all come from?
> All the lonely people, where do they all belong?

'Eleanor Rigby', 1966, with Paul McCartney

O'Brien, Edna (1936–)
Irish writer and dramatist
> I often get lonely for unrealistic things: for something absolute.

The Observer, 1992

Sarton, May (1912–1995)
US poet and writer
> Loneliness is the poverty of self; solitude is the richness of self.

Mrs Stevens Hears the Mermaids Singing (1993)

Williams, Hank (1923–1953)
US country music singer
> Hear that lonesome whippoorwill?
> He sounds too blue to fly.
> The midnight train is whining low,
> I'm so lonesome I could cry.

'I'm So Lonesome I Could Cry', 1942

▶▶ SOLITUDE

lottery

Jones, Roger
> I guess I think of lotteries as a tax on the mathematically challenged.

Attr.

Monkhouse, Bob (1928–)
English comedian
> Statistically you stand just as good a chance of winning the lottery if you don't buy a ticket.

The Times, 1998

Wood, Victoria (1953–)
English comedian
> Please Lord, let me prove to you that winning the lottery won't spoil me.

The Sunday Times, 2000

love

Anonymous
> My lover looked like an eagle from the distance, but alas
> When he came nearer I saw that he was nothing but a buzzard.

In John Robert Colombo (ed.), Songs of the Great Land, 'Song of a Maiden Disappointed in Love', Blackfoot poem

> Roseberry to his lady says,
> 'My hinny and my succour,
> O shall we do the thing you ken,
> Or shall we take our supper?'
> Wi' modest face, sae fu' o' grace,
> Replied the bonny lady;
> 'My noble lord do as you please,
> But supper is na ready.'

'Supper is na Ready'; collected by Burns and included in The Merry Muses of Caledonia (c.1800)

> Let those love now, who never loved before;
> Let those who always loved, now love the more.

Pervigilium Veneris

> Western wind, when wilt thou blow,
> The small rain down can rain?
> Christ, if my love were in my arms
> And I in my bed again!

New Oxford Book of 16th-Century Verse (1991)

Anouilh, Jean (1910–1987)
French dramatist and screenwriter
> Vous savez bien que l'amour, c'est avant tout le don de soi!
> Love is, above all else, the gift of oneself.

Ardèle ou la Marguerite (1949)

Auden, W.H. (1907–1973)
English poet, essayist, critic, teacher and dramatist
> When it comes, will it come without warning
> Just as I'm picking my nose?
> Will it knock on my door in the morning,
> Or tread in the bus on my toes?
> Will it come like a change in the weather?
> Will its greeting be courteous or rough?
> Will it alter my life altogether?
> O tell me the truth about love.

'Twelve Songs'

> Stop all the clocks, cut off the telephone,
> Prevent the dog from barking with a juicy bone,
> Silence the pianos and with muffled drum
> Bring out the coffin, let the mourners come.

He was my North, my South, my East and West,
My working week and my Sunday rest,
My noon, my midnight, my talk, my song;
I thought that love would last for ever: I was
wrong.

'Twelve Songs'

Reindeer are coming to drive you away
Over the snow on an ebony sleigh,
Over the mountains and over the sea
You shall go happy and handsome and free.

Auden and Isherwood, *The Ascent of F.6*
(1936)

Lay your sleeping head, my love,
Human on my faithless arm;
Time and fevers burn away
Individual beauty from
Thoughtful children, and the grave
Proves the child ephemeral:
But in my arms till break of day
Let the living creature lie,
Mortal, guilty, but to me
The entirely beautiful.

Collected Poems, 1933–1938, 'Lullaby'

In an upper room at midnight
See us gathered on behalf
Of love according to the gospel
Of the radio-phonograph.

Nones (1951), 'The Love Feast'

Augustine, Saint (354–430)
Numidian-born Christian theologian and philosopher
I came to Carthage where a whole frying pan full
of abominable loves crackled about me on every
side. I was not in love yet, yet I loved to be in
love … I was looking for something to love, in
love with love itself.

Confessions (397–398)

Austen, Jane (1775–1817)
English writer
All the privilege I claim for my own sex … is that
of loving longest, when existence or when hope
is gone.

Persuasion (1818)

Bacon, Francis (1561–1626)
English philosopher, essayist, politician and courtier
They do best who, if they cannot but admit love,
yet make it keep quarter; and sever it wholly
from their serious affairs and actions of life: for if
it check once with business, it troubleth men's
fortunes, and maketh men, that they can no
ways be true to their own ends.

'Of Love' (1625)

Balzac, Honoré de (1799–1850)
French writer
It is easier to be a lover than a husband, for the
same reason that it is more difficult to show a

ready wit all day long than to produce an
occasional bon mot.

Attr.

Barnfield, Richard (1574–1627)
English poet
My flocks feed not, my ewes breed not,
My rams speed not, all is amiss:
Love is denying, Faith is defying,
Heart's renying, causer of this.

In Nicholas Ling (ed.), *England's Helicon* (1600)

Behn, Aphra (1640–1689)
English dramatist, writer, poet, translator and spy
Oh, what a dear ravishing thing is the beginning
of an Amour!

The Emperor of the Moon (1687)

Betjeman, Sir John (1906–1984)
English poet laureate
'Let us not speak, for the love we bear one
another –
Let us hold hands and look.'
She, such a very ordinary little woman;
He, such a thumping crook;
But both, for a moment, little lower than the
angels
In the teashop's ingle-nook.

New Bats in Old Belfries (1945)

The Bible (King James Version)
And Jacob served seven years for Rachel; and
they seemed unto him but a few days, for the
love he had to her.

Genesis, 29:20

Intreat me not to leave thee, or to return from
following after thee: for whither thou goest, I
will go; and where thou lodgest, I will lodge: thy
people shall be my people, and thy God my
God.

Ruth, 1:16–17

Greater love hath no man than this, that a man
lay down his life for his friends.

John, 15:13

He that loveth not knoweth not God; for God is
love.

I John, 4:8

Perfect love casteth out fear.

I John, 4:18

Bickerstaffe, Isaac (c.1733–c.1808)
Irish dramatist and author of ballad operas
Perhaps it was right to dissemble your love,
But – why did you kick me downstairs?

'An Expostulation' (1789)

Blake, William (1757–1827)
English poet, engraver, painter and mystic
Love seeketh not Itself to please,

Nor for itself hath any care;
But for another gives its ease,
And builds a Heaven in Hells despair.

'The Clod & the Pebble' (1794)

Children of the future Age,
Reading this indignant page:
Know that in a former time,
Love! sweet Love! was thought a crime.

'A Little Girl Lost' (1794)

Blanch, Lesley (1907–)
British biographer and travel writer
Of Jane Digby who was successively Lady Ellenborough,
Baroness Venningen, Countess Theotoky and the wife of Sheik
Abdul Medjuel El Mezrab
She was an Amazon. Her whole life was spent
riding at breakneck speed towards the wilder
shores of love.

The Wilder Shores of Love (1954)

Boethius (c.475–524)
Roman statesman, scholar and philosopher
Quis legem dat amantibus? Major lex amor est sibi.
Who can give a law to lovers? Love is a greater
law unto itself.

De Consolatione Philosophiae (c.522–524)

Brennan, Christopher (1870–1932)
Australian poet
My heart was wandering in the sands,
a restless thing, a scorn apart;
Love set his fire in my hands,
I clasped the flame into my heart.

Poems (1914)

Brice, Fanny (1891–1951)
US singer and comedian
I never liked the men I loved, and never loved
the men I liked.

In Norman Katkov, *The Fabulous Fanny* (1952)

Bridges, Robert (1844–1930)
English poet, dramatist, essayist and doctor
When first we met we did not guess
That Love would prove so hard a master.

'Triolet' (1890)

Brooke, Rupert (1887–1915)
English poet
I thought when love for you died, I
should die.
It's dead. Alone, mostly strangely, I live on.

'The Life Beyond' (1910)

Browning, Elizabeth Barrett (1806–1861)
English poet; wife of Robert Browning
How do I love thee? Let me count the ways.

Sonnets from the Portuguese (1850)

Burns, Robert (1759–1796)
Scottish poet and song writer
Ae fond kiss, and then we sever!

Ae fareweel, and then forever! …
But to see her was to love her,
Love but her, and love for ever.
Had we never lov'd sae kindly,
Had we never lov'd sae blindly,
Never met – or never parted –
We had ne'er been broken-hearted.

'Ae Fond Kiss' (1791)

O Luve will venture in where it daur na weel be
seen!

'The Posie' (1792)

O, my luve's like a red, red, rose
That's newly sprung in June.
O, my luve's like the melodie,
That's sweetly play'd in tune.

'A Red Red Rose' (1794)

Burton, Robert (1577–1640)
English clergyman and writer
No chord, nor cable can so forcibly draw, or hold
so fast, as love can do with a twined thread.

Anatomy of Melancholy (1621)

Butler, Samuel (1612–1680)
English poet
For money has a power above
The stars and fate, to manage love.

Hudibras (1678)

All love at first, like generous wine,
Ferments and frets until 'tis fine;
But when 'tis settled on the lee,
And from th' impurer matter free,
Becomes the richer still the older,
And proves the pleasanter the colder.

Miscellaneous Thoughts

Butler, Samuel (1835–1902)
English writer, painter, philosopher and scholar
'Tis better to have loved and lost than never to
have lost at all.

The Way of All Flesh (1903)

God is Love, I dare say. But what a mischievous
devil Love is.

The Note-Books of Samuel Butler (1912)

Byron, Lord (1788–1824)
English poet satirist and traveller
In her first passion woman loves her
lover,
In all the others all she loves is love.

Don Juan (1824)

Chagall, Marc (1887–1985)
Russian-born French painter
In our life there is a single colour, as on an
artist's palette, which provides the meaning of
life and art. It is the colour of love.

Newsweek, 1985

Chamfort, Nicolas (1741–1794)

French writer

*L'amour, tel qu'il existe dans la société, n'est que
l'échange de deux fantaisies et le contact de deux
épidermes.*

Love, as it exists in society, is nothing more than
the exchange of two fantasies and the contact
of two skins.

Maximes et pensées (1796)

Cher (1946–)

US singer and actress

If grass can grow through cement, love can find
you at every time in your life.

The Times, 1998

Chevalier, Maurice (1888–1972)

French singer and actor

Many a man has fallen in love with a girl in a
light so dim he would not have chosen a suit by
it.

Attr.

Clare, John (1793–1864)

English rural poet; died in an asylum

Language has not the power to speak
  what love indites:
The soul lies buried in the ink that
  writes.

Attr.

Colman, the Elder, George (1732–1794)

English dramatist and theatrical manager

Love and a cottage! Eh, Fanny! Ah, give me
indifference and a coach and six!

The Clandestine Marriage (1766)

Congreve, William (1670–1729)

English dramatist

In my conscience I believe the baggage loves
me, for she never speaks well of me her self, nor
suffers any body else to rail me.

The Old Bachelor (1693)

Cope, Wendy (1945–)

English poet

2 cures for love
1. Don't see him. Don't phone or write a letter.
2. The easy way: get to know him better.

Attr.

Diderot, Denis (1713–1784)

French philosopher, encyclopaedist, writer and dramatist

*On a dit que l'amour qui ôtait l'esprit à ceux qui en
avaient en donnait à ceux qui n'en avaient pas.*

They say that love takes wit away from those
who have it, and gives it to those who have
none.

Paradoxe sur le Comédien

Dietrich, Marlene (1901–1992)

German-born US actress and singer

Latins are tenderly enthusiastic. In Brazil they
throw flowers at you. In Argentina they throw
themselves.

Newsweek, 1959

Donne, John (1572–1631)

English poet

Love built on beauty, soon as beauty dies.

Elegies (c.1595)

Who ever loves, if he do not propose
The right true end of love, he's one
  that goes
To sea for nothing but to make him sick.

Elegies (c.1600)

Chang'd loves are but chang'd sorts of
  meat,
And when he hath the kernel eat,
Who doth not fling away the shell?

Songs and Sonnets (1611)

I wonder by my troth, what thou, and I
Did, till we lov'd?

Songs and Sonnets (1611)

Just such disparity
As is 'twixt Air and Angels' purity,
'Twixt women's love and men's will ever be.

Songs and Sonnets (1611)

Douglas, Lord Alfred (1870–1945)

English poet; intimate of Oscar Wilde

I am the Love that dare not speak its name.

'Two Loves' (1896)

Dryden, John (1631–1700)

English poet, satirist, dramatist and critic

Pains of love be sweeter far
Than all other pleasures are.

Tyrannic Love (1669)

For, Heaven be thanked, we live in
  such an age,
When no man dies for love, but on the
  stage.

Mithridates (1678)

Ellis, Havelock (1859–1939)

English sexologist and essayist

Love is friendship plus sex.

Attr.

Etherege, Sir George (c.1635–1691)

English dramatist

When love grows diseased, the best thing we
can do is put it to a violent death; I cannot
endure the torture of a lingering and
consumptive passion.

*The Man of Mode
(1676)*

Farquhar, George (1678–1707)

Irish dramatist

Money is the sinews of love, as of war.

Love and a Bottle (1698)

Farrell, J.G. (1935–1979)
English novelist
Vera, who had carefully educated herself in the arts of love, did not believe that this sacred art, whose purpose was to unite her not only with her lover but with the earth and the firmament, too, should take place in the Western manner which to her resembled nothing so much as a pair of drunken rickshaw coolies colliding briefly at some foggy crossroads at the dead of night.

The Singapore Grip (1979)

Fielding, Henry (1707–1754)
English writer, dramatist and journalist
Love and scandal are the best sweeteners of tea.

Love in Several Masques (1728)

What is commonly called love, namely the desire of satisfying a voracious appetite with a certain quantity of delicate white human flesh.

Tom Jones (1749)

Fletcher, Phineas (1582–1650)
English poet and clergyman
Love is like linen often chang'd, the sweeter.

Sicelides (1614)

Florian, Jean-Pierre Claris de (1755–1794)
French writer
Plaisir d'amour ne dure qu'un moment,
Chagrin d'amour dure toute la vie.
Love's pleasure only lasts a moment; love's sorrow lasts one's whole life long.

'Célestine' (1784)

Forster, E.M. (1879–1970)
English writer, essayist and literary critic
Only connect! That was the whole of her sermon. Only connect the prose and the passion, and both will be exalted, and human love will be seen at its highest.

Howard's End (1910)

Franklin, Benjamin (1706–1790)
US statesman, scientist, political critic and printer
The having made a young girl miserable may give you frequent bitter reflection; none of which can attend the making of an old woman happy.

On the Choice of a Mistress

Fry, Christopher (1907–)
English verse dramatist, theatre director and translator
Oh, the unholy mantrap of love!

The Lady's not for Burning (1949)

Try thinking of love, or something.
Amor vincit insomnia.

A Sleep of Prisoners (1951)

Gay, John (1685–1732)
English poet, dramatist and librettist
Then nature rul'd, and love, devoid of art,
Spoke the consenting language of the heart.

Dione (1720)

She who has never lov'd, has never liv'd.

The Captives (1724)

Pretty Polly, say,
When I was away,
Did your fancy never stray
To some newer lover?

The Beggar's Opera (1728)

How happy could I be with either,
Were t'other dear charmer away!

The Beggar's Opera (1728)

Gibran, Kahlil (1883–1931)
Lebanese poet, mystic and painter
Love has no other desire but to fulfil itself.
But if you love and must needs have desires, let these be your desires:
To melt and be like the running brook that sings its melody to the night.
To know the pain of too much tenderness.
To be wounded by your own understanding of love;
And to bleed willingly and joyfully.
To wake at dawn with a winged heart and give thanks for another day of loving;
To rest at the noon hour and meditate love's ecstasy;
To return home at eventide with gratitude;
And then to sleep with a prayer for the beloved in your heart and a song of praise upon your lips …

Love one another, but make not a bond of love:
Let it be rather a moving sea between the shores of your souls …

Let each one of you be alone,
Even as the strings of the lute are alone though they quiver with the same music …

Stand together yet not too near together:
For the pillars of the temple stand apart,
And the oak tree and the cypress grow not in each other's shadow.

The Prophet (1923)

Gogarty, Oliver St John (1878–1957)
Irish poet, dramatist, writer, politician and surgeon
Only the Lion and the Cock;
As Galen says, withstand Love's shock.
So, dearest, do not think me rude
If I yield now to lassitude,
But sympathize with me. I know

You would not have me roar, or crow.
Collected Poems (1951)

Goldsmith, Oliver (c.1728–1774)
Irish dramatist, poet and writer
It seemed to me pretty plain, that they had
more of love than matrimony in them.
The Vicar of Wakefield (1766)

Gorky, Maxim (1868–1936)
Russian writer, dramatist and revolutionary
Love is always a bit deceitful,
Truth always struggles with it,
We wait long for a woman worthy of it,
And we wait in vain.
In *Samara Gazette*, 1895

Gower, John (c.1330–1408)
English poet
It hath and schal ben evermor
That love is maister wher he wile.
'Confessio Amantis' (1390)

Granville, George (1666–1735)
English poet, dramatist and politician
O Love! thou bane of the most generous souls!
Thou doubtful pleasure, and thou certain pain.
'Heroic Love'

Graves, Robert (1895–1985)
English poet, writer, critic, translator and mythologist
Down, wanton, down! Have you no shame
That at the whisper of Love's name,
Or Beauty's, presto! up you raise
Your angry head and stand at gaze?
'Down, Wanton, Down'

In love as in sport, the amateur status must be
strictly maintained.
Occupation: Writer

Greer, Germaine (1939–)
Australian feminist, critic, English scholar and writer
Love, love, love – all the wretched cant of it,
masking egotism, lust, masochism, fantasy under
a mythology of sentimental postures, a welter of
self induced miseries and joys, blinding and
masking the essential personalities in the frozen
gestures of courtship, in the kissing and the
dating and the desire, the compliments and the
quarrels which vivify its barrenness.
The Female Eunuch (1970)

Groening, Matt
US cartoonist
Love is a snowmobile racing across the tundra
and then suddenly it flips over, pinning you
underneath. At night, the ice weasels come.
Attr.

Halm, Friedrich (1806–1871)
*Mein Herz, ich will dich fragen:
Was ist denn Liebe? Sag'! –*

*'Zwei Seelen und ein Gedanke,
Zwei Herzen und ein Schlag!"*
'My heart, I want to ask you:
What is love? Tell me!' –
'Two souls with just one thought,
Two hearts with just one beat.'
The Son of the Wilderness, 1842

Hardy, Thomas (1840–1928)
English writer and poet
Love is lame at fifty years.
'The Revisitation' (1904)

A lover without indiscretion is no lover at all.
The Hand of Ethelberta (1876)

Hartley, L.P. (1895–1972)
English writer and critic
Once she had loved her fellow human beings;
she did not love them now, she had seen them
do too many unpleasant things.
Facial Justice (1960)

Hazzard, Shirley (1931–)
Australian writer
When we are young, she thought, we worship
romantic love for the wrong reasons … and,
because of that, subsequently repudiate it. Only
later, and for quite other reasons, we discover
its true importance. And by then it has become
tiring even to observe.
The Evening of a Holiday (1966)

Heaney, Seamus (1939–)
Irish poet
And in that dream I dreamt – how like you
this? –
Our first night years ago in that hotel
When you came with your deliberate kiss
To raise us towards the lovely and painful
Covenants of flesh; our separateness;
The respite in our dewy dreaming faces.
Field Work (1979)

Hemingway, Ernest (1898–1961)
US author
Love is just another dirty lie. … I know about
love. Love always hangs up behind the bathroom door. It smells like lysol. To hell with love.
To Have and Have Not
(1937)

Herbert, Edward (1583–1648)
English statesman, poet and philosopher
O that our love might take no end,
Or never had beginning took! …

For where God doth admit the fair,
Think you that he excludeth Love?
'An Ode upon a Question moved, Whether Love
should continue for ever?' (1665)

Herbert, George (1593–1633)
English poet and priest

> Love bade me welcome; yet my soul drew back,
> Guiltie of dust and sinne.
> But quick-ey'd Love, observing me grow slack
> From my first entrance in,
> Drew nearer to me, sweetly questioning
> If I lack'd any thing …
>
> Love took my hand, and smiling did reply,
> Who made the eyes but I? …
>
> You must sit down, sayes Love, and taste my meat:
> So I did sit and eat.

The Temple (1633)

Herbert, Sir A.P. (1890–1971)
English humorist, writer, dramatist and politician

> I wouldn't be too ladylike in love if I were you.

'I Wouldn't be Too Ladylike'

Herrick, Robert (1591–1674)
English poet, royalist and clergyman

> Love is a circle that doth restlesse move
> In the same sweet eternity of love.

Hesperides (1648)

> Give me a kiss, add to that kiss a score;
> Then to that twenty, adde an hundred more:
> A thousand to that hundred: so kiss on,
> To make that thousand up a million.
> Treble that million, and when that is done,
> Let's kiss afresh, as when we first begun.

Hesperides (1648)

> You say, to me-wards your affection's strong;
> Pray love me little, so you love me long.

Hesperides (1648)

> Thou art my life, my love, my heart,
> The very eyes of me:
> And hast command of every part,
> To live and die for thee.

Hesperides (1648)

Hewett, Dorothy (1923–)
Australian dramatist and poet

> My body turns to you as the earth turns.
> O for such bitter need you've taken me,
> To dub me lover, friend and enemy,
> Take neither one can set the other free.
> But still there is a loveliness that burns
> That burns between us two so tenderly.

'There is a Loveliness that Burns'

Hogg, James (1770–1835)
Scottish poet, ballad writer and writer

> O, love, love, love!
> Love is like a dizziness;
> It winna let a poor body

> Gang about his biziness!

'Love is Like a Dizziness'

Hudson, Louise (1958–)
English poet and editor

> Now I go to films alone
> watch a silent telephone
> send myself a valentine
> whisper softly 'I am mine'.

'Men, Who Needs Them'

James I of Scotland (1394–1437)
King of Scotland

> So far I fallen was in loves dance,
> That suddenly my wit, my countenance,
> My heart, my will, my nature, and my mind
> Was changit right clean in another kind.

The Kingis Quair

Jerome, Jerome K. (1859–1927)
English writer and dramatist

> Love is like the measles; we all have to go through it.

Idle Thoughts of an Idle Fellow (1886)

Jerrold, Douglas William (1803–1857)
English dramatist, writer and wit

> Love's like the measles – all the worse when it comes late in life.

Wit and Opinions of Douglas Jerrold (1859)

Jonson, Ben (1572–1637)
English dramatist and poet

> Drink to me only with thine eyes,
> And I will pledge with mine;
> Or leave a kiss upon the cup,
> And I'll not look for wine.
> The thirst that from the soul doth rise
> Doth ask a drink divine;
> But might I of Jove's nectar sup,
> I would not change for thine.
> I sent thee late a rosy wreath,
> Not so much honouring thee,
> As giving it a hope that there
> It could not wither'd be.

The Forest (1616)

Juliana of Norwich (c.1343–c.1429)
English mystic

> Wouldest thou wit thy Lord's meaning in this thing? Wit it well: Love was his meaning. Who shewed it thee? Love. What shewed He thee? Love. Wherefore shewed it He? for Love … Thus was I learned that Love is our Lord's meaning.

Revelations of Divine Love (1393)

Kafka, Franz (1883–1924)
Czech-born German-speaking writer

> *Liebe ist, dass Du mir das Messer bist, mit dem ich in mir wühle.*
> Love is, that you are the knife which I plunge

into myself.

> Letter to Milena Jesenká, 1920

Keats, John (1795–1821)
English poet
> I never was in love – yet the voice and the shape of a Woman has haunted me these two days.
>> Letter to J.H. Reynolds, 22 September 1818

Key, Ellen (1849–1926)
Swedish feminist, writer and lecturer
> Love is moral even without legal marriage, but marriage is immoral without love.
>> 'The Morality of Women' (1911)

Kidman, Nicole (1967–)
Australian actress
> I'm past the seven-year itch. When you're loved for your flaws, that's when you feel really safe.
>> The Observer, 1998

King, Bishop Henry (1592–1669)
English royal chaplain; poet and sermonist
> Sleep on, my Love, in thy cold bed,
> Never to be disquieted!
> My last good night! Thou wilt not wake
> Till I thy fate shall overtake:
> Till age, or grief, or sickness must
> Marry my body to that dust
> It so much loves; and fill the room
> My heart keeps empty in thy tomb.
> Stay for me there; I will not fail
> To meet thee in that hollow vale …
>
> But hark! My pulse like a soft drum
> Beats my approach, tells thee I come.
>> 'Exequy upon his Wife' (1651)

La Rochefoucauld (1613–1680)
French writer
> *Si on juge de l'amour par la plupart de ses effets, il ressemble plus à la haine qu'á l'amitié.*
> If love is to be judged by most of its effects, it looks more like hatred than like friendship.
>> Maximes (1678)

> *Il n'y a guère de gens qui ne soient honteux de s'être aimés quand ils ne s'aiment plus.*
> There are very few people who are not ashamed of having loved one another once they have fallen out of love.
>> Maximes (1678)

Lamartine, Alphonse de (1790–1869)
French poet, historian, royalist and statesman
> *Un seul être vous manque, et tout est dépeuplé.*
> Only one being is missing, and your whole world is bereft of people.
>> Premières Méditations poétiques (1820)

Larkin, Philip (1922–1985)
English poet, writer and librarian

What will survive of us is love.

> 'An Arundel Tomb' (1964)

Lauder, Sir Harry (1870–1950)
Scottish music-hall entertainer
> I love a lassie, a bonnie, bonnie lassie,
> She's as pure as a lily in the dell.
> She's as sweet as the heather,
> The bonnie, bloomn' heather,
> Mary, my Scotch Blue-bell.
>> Song, 'I Love a Lassie'

Lawrence, D.H. (1885–1930)
English writer, poet and critic
> I'm not sure if a mental relation with a woman doesn't make it impossible to love her. To know the mind of a woman is to end in hating her. Love means the pre-cognitive flow … it is the honest state before the apple.
>> Letter to Dr Trigant Burrow, 1927

Lawrence, T.E. (1888–1935)
British soldier, archaeologist, translator and writer; known as 'Lawrence of Arabia'
> I loved you, so I drew these tides of men into my hands
> and wrote my will across the sky in stars
> To earn you Freedom, the seven pillared worthy house,
> that your eyes might be shining for me
> When we came.
>> The Seven Pillars of Wisdom (1926)

Lewis, Wyndham (1882–1957)
US-born British painter, critic and writer
> To give up another person's love is a mild suicide.
>> Tarr (1918)

Lindsay, Norman (1879–1969)
Australian artist and writer
> The best love affairs are those we never had.
>> Bohemians of the Bulletin (1965)

Lodge, Thomas (1558–1625)
English poet
> Love, in my bosom, like a bee,
> Doth suck his sweet.
>> 'Love, In My Bosom' (1590)

Lovelace, Richard (1618–1658)
English poet
> When Love with unconfined wings
> Hovers within my gates;
> And my divine Althea brings
> To whisper at the grates:
> When I lie tangled in her hair,
> And fettered to her eye;
> The Gods, that wanton in the air,
> Know no such liberty.
>> 'To Althea, From Prison' (1649)

Lovell, Maria (1803–1877)
English actress and playwright
> Two souls with but a single thought,
> Two hearts that beat as one.
>> *Ingomar the Barbarian*

Lowry, Malcolm (1909–1957)
English writer and poet
> How alike are the groans of love to those of the
> dying.
>> *Under the Volcano* (1947)

Lydgate, John (c.1370–c.1451)
English monk, poet and translator
> Love is mor than gold or gret richesse.
>> 'The Story of Thebes' (c.1420)

MacDiarmid, Hugh (1892–1978)
Scottish poet
> It is very rarely that a man loves
> And when he does it is nearly always fatal.
>> 'The International Brigade' (1957)

Marlowe, Christopher (1564–1593)
English poet and dramatist
> Where both deliberate, the love is slight;
> Who ever loved that loved not at first sight?
>> *Hero and Leander* (1598), First Sestiad

> Come live with me, and be my love,
> And we will all the pleasures prove.
>> 'The Passionate Shepherd to his Love'

Marvell, Andrew (1621–1678)
English poet and satirist
> Therefore the love which us doth bind,
> But Fate so enviously debars,
> Is the conjunction of the mind,
> And opposition of the stars.
>> 'The Definition of Love' (1681)

McCuaig, Ronald (1908–1990)
Australian journalist and poet
> Love me, and never leave me,
> Love, nor ever deceive me,
> And I shall always bless you
> If I may undress you:
> This I heard a lover say
> To his sweetheart where they lay.

> He, though he did undress her,
> Did not always bless her;
> She, though she would not leave him,
> Often did deceive him;
> Yet they loved, and when they died
> They were buried side by side.
>> 'Love Me and Never Leave Me' (1930)

Millay, Edna St Vincent (1892–1950)
US poet and dramatist
> This have I known always: Love is no more
> Than the wide blossom which the wind assails,

> Than the great tide that treads the shifting
> shore,
> Strewing fresh wreckage gathered in the gales:
> Pity me that the heart is slow to learn
> What the swift mind beholds at every turn.
>> *The Harp-Weaver and Other Poems* (1923)

Mitford, Nancy (1904–1973)
English writer
> Like all the very young we took it for granted
> that making love is child's play.
>> *The Pursuit of Love* (1945)

Molière (1622–1673)
French dramatist, actor and director
> *On est aisément dupé par ce qu'on aime.*
> One is easily taken in by what one loves.
>> *Tartuffe* (1664)

Moore, Thomas (1779–1852)
Irish poet
> No, there's nothing half so sweet in life
> As love's young dream.
>> *Irish Melodies* (1807)

Morris, William (1834–1896)
English poet, designer, craftsman, artist and socialist
> Love is enough: though the world be a-waning,
> And the woods have no voice but the voice of
> complaining.
>> 'Love is Enough' (1872)

Nietzsche, Friedrich Wilhelm (1844–1900)
German philosopher, critic and poet
> There is always some madness in love. But there
> is also always some reason in madness.
>> *On Reading and Writing*

> So that love is possible, God must be a person –
> In love, one endures more than at other times,
> one tolerates everything.
>> *Der Antichrist* (1888)

O'Brien, Edna (1936–)
Irish writer and dramatist
> Oh, shadows of love, inebriations of love,
> foretastes of love, trickles of love, but never yet
> the one true love.
>> *Night* (1972)

Ovid (43 BC–AD 18)
Roman poet
> *Qui finem quaeris amoris,*
> *Cedet amor rebus; res age, tutus eris.*
> You who seek an end to love, love will yield to
> business: be busy, and you will be safe.
>> *Remedia Amoris*

Parker, Dorothy (1893–1967)
US writer, poet, critic and wit
> By the time you swear you're his,
> Shivering and sighing,
> And he vows his passion is

Infinite, undying –
Lady, make a note of this:
One of you is lying.

> 'Unfortunate Coincidence' (1937)

Oh, life is a glorious cycle of song,
A medley of extemporanea;
And love is a thing that can never go wrong,
And I am Marie of Roumania.

> Not So Deep as a Well (1937)

Parnell, Anna (1852–1911)
Irish politician

Two children playing by a stream
Two lovers walking in a dream
A married pair whose dream is o'er,
Two old folks who are quite a bore.

> 'Love's Four Ages'

Patten, Brian (1946–)
British poet

Love, smeared across his face, like a road
accident.

> Grinning Jack (1990), 'Schoolboy'

Patterson, Johnny (1840–1889)

Have you ever been in love, me boys
Oh! have you felt the pain,
I'd rather be in jail, I would,
Than be in love again.

> 'The Garden where the Praties Grow'

Peele, George (c.1558–c.1597)
English dramatist and poet

What thing is love for (well I wot) love is a thing.
It is a prick, it is a sting,
It is a pretty, pretty thing;
It is a fire, it is a coal
Whose flame creeps in at every hole.

> 'The Hunting of Cupid' (c.1591)

Pound, Ezra (1885–1972)
US poet

And we knew all that stream,
And our two horses had traced out the valleys;
Knew the low flooded lands squared out with
poplars,
In the young days when the deep sky
befriended.
And great wings beat above us in the twilight,
And the great wheels in heaven
Bore us together … surging … and apart …
Believing we should meet with lips and hands,
High, high and sure … and then the counter-
thrust:
'Why do you love me? Will you always love me?
But I am like the grass, I cannot love you.'

> 'Near Perigord' (1915)

Proulx, E. Annie (1935–)
US writer

Water may be older than light, diamonds crack
in hot goat's blood, mountaintops give off cold
fire, forests appear in mid-ocean, it may happen
that a crab is caught with the shadow of a hand
on its back, that the wind be imprisoned in a bit
of knotted string. And it may be that love
sometimes occurs without pain or misery.

> The Shipping News (1993

Proust, Marcel (1871–1922)
French writer and critic

There can be no peace of mind in love, since the
advantage one has secured is never anything
but a fresh starting-point for further desires.

> A l'ombre des jeunes filles en fleurs (1918)

Une dame prétentieuse: Que pensez-vous de l'amour?
Mme Leroi: L'amour? Je le fais souvent, mais je n'en
parle jamais.
A pretentious lady: What are your views on
love?
Mme Leroi: I often make love but I never talk
about it.

> Le Côté de Guermantes (1921)

On a tort de parler en amour de mauvais choix,
puisque dès qu'il y a choix il ne peut être que mauvais.
It is wrong to speak of making a bad choice in
love, since as soon as there is choice, it can only
be bad.

> La Fugitive (1923)

Proverbs

All is fair in love and war.

All the world loves a lover.

In love, there is always one who kisses, and one
who offers his cheek.

Love conquers all.

Love is blind.

Love laughs at locksmiths.

Love me, love my dog.

Lucky at cards, unlucky in love.

No love like the first love.

True love never grows cold.

Racine, Jean (1639–1699)
French tragedian and poet

Je t'aimais inconstant, qu'aurais-je fait fidèle?
I loved you inconstant; what would I have done
had you been faithful?

> Andromaque (1667)

Ah! je l'ai trop aimé pour ne le point haïr!
Ah, I have loved him too much not to hate him!

> Andromaque (1667)

Raleigh, Sir Walter (c.1552–1618)
English courtier, explorer, military commander, poet,

historian and essayist

> Now what is love? I pray thee, tell.
> It is that fountain and that well,
> Where pleasure and repentance dwell.
> It is perhaps that saucing bell,
> That tolls all in to heaven or hell:
> And this is love, as I hear tell.
>
> *'A Description of Love'*

Rochester, Earl of (1647–1680)

English poet, satirist, courtier and libertine

> That cordial drop heaven in our cup has thrown
> To make the nauseous draught of life go down.
>
> *'A letter from Artemisa in the Town to Chloe in the Country' (1679)*

Rogers, Samuel (1763–1855)

English poet

> Oh! she was good as she was fair.
> None – none on earth above her!
> As pure in thought as angels are,
> To know her was to love her.
>
> *Jacqueline (1814)*

> But there are moments which he calls his own,
> Then, never less alone than when alone,
> Those whom he loved so long and sees no more,
> Loved and still loves – not dead – but gone before,
> He gathers round him.
>
> *'Human Life' (1819)*

Russell, Bertrand (1872–1970)

English philosopher, mathematician, essayist and social reformer

> Of all forms of caution, caution in love is perhaps the most fatal to true happiness.
>
> *Marriage and Morals (1929)*

Sagan, Françoise (1935–)

French writer

> Every little girl knows about love. It is only her capacity to suffer because of it that increases.
>
> *Daily Express*

Saint-Exupéry, Antoine de (1900–1944)

French author and aviator

> *L'expérience nous montre qu'aimer ce n'est point nous regarder l'un l'autre mais regarder ensemble dans la même direction.*
> Experience shows us that love is not looking into one another's eyes but looking together in the same direction.
>
> *Wind, Sand and Stars (1939)*

Saki (1870–1916)

Burmese-born British writer

> Romance at short notice was her speciality.
>
> *Beasts and Super-Beasts (1914)*

Sand, George (1804–1876)

French writer and dramatist

> Liszt said to me today that God alone deserves to be loved. It may be true, but when one has loved a man it is very different to love God.
>
> *Intimate Journal*

Scott, Alexander (c.1525–c.1584)

Scottish poet

> Luve is ane fervent fire,
> Kendillit without desire;
> Short pleisure, lang displeisure,
> Repentence is the hire;
> Ane puir treisure without meisure.
> Luve is ane fervent fire.
>
> *'A Rondel of Luve' (c.1568)*

Scott, Sir Walter (1771–1832)

Scottish writer and historian

> In peace, Love tunes the shepherd's reed;
> In war, he mounts the warrior's steed;
> In halls, in gay attire is seen;
> In hamlets, dances on the green.
> Love rules the court, the camp, the grove,
> And men below, and saints above;
> For love is heaven, and heaven is love.
>
> *The Lay of the Last Minstrel (1805)*

> True love's the gift which God has given
> To man alone beneath the heaven:
> It is the secret sympathy,
> The silver link, the silken tie,
> Which heart to heart, and mind to mind,
> In body and in soul can bind.
>
> *The Lay of the Last Minstrel (1805)*

Sedley, Sir Charles (c.1639–1701)

English poet

> Love still has something of the Sea
> From whence his Mother rose.
>
> *'Song: Love still has Something'*

> Not, Celia, that I juster am
> Or better than the rest,
> For I would change each hour like them,
> Were not my heart at rest ...

> Why then should I seek farther store,
> And still make love anew;
> When change itself can give no more,
> 'Tis easy to be true.
>
> *'To Celia'*

Segal, Erich (1937–)

US writer

> Love means never having to say you're sorry.
>
> *Love Story (1970)*

Shakespeare, William (1564–1616)

English dramatist, poet and actor

> *Cleopatra*: If it be love indeed, tell me how much.

Antony: There's beggary in the love that can be reckon'd.
Cleopatra: I'll set a bourn how far to be belov'd.
Antony: Then must thou needs find out new heaven, new earth.

Antony and Cleopatra, I.i

We that are true lovers run into strange capers.

As You Like It, II.iv

Men have died from time to time, and worms have eaten them, but not for love.

As You Like It, IV.i

It is as easy to count atomies as to resolve the propositions of a lover.

As You Like It, III.ii

Doubt thou the stars are fire;
Doubt that the sun doth move;
Doubt truth to be a liar;
But never doubt I love.

Hamlet, II.ii

Ay me! for aught that I could ever read,
Could ever hear by tale or history,
The course of true love never did run smooth.

A Midsummer Night's Dream, I.i

Love looks not with the eyes, but with the mind;
And therefore is wing'd Cupid painted blind.

A Midsummer Night's Dream, I.i

I thank God, and my cold blood, I am of your humour for that: I had rather hear my dog bark at a crow than a man swear he loves me.

Much Ado About Nothing, I.i

My bounty is as boundless as the sea,
My love as deep: the more I give to thee,
The more I have, for both are infinite.

Romeo and Juliet, II.ii

If music be the food of love, play on,
Give me excess of it, that, surfeiting,
The appetite may sicken and so die.
That strain again! It had a dying fall;
O, it came o'er my ear like the sweet sound
That breathes upon a bank of violets,
Stealing and giving odour! Enough,
no more;
'Tis not so sweet now as it was before.

Twelfth Night, I.i

She never told her love,
But let concealment, like a worm i' th' bud,
Feed on her damask cheek. She pin'd in thought;
And with a green and yellow melancholy
She sat like Patience on a monument,
Smiling at grief. Was not this love indeed?
We men may say more, swear more, but indeed
Our shows are more than will; for still we prove

Much in our vows, but little in our love.

Twelfth Night, II.iv

Love sought is good, but given unsought is better.

Twelfth Night, III.i

Fie, fie, how wayward is this foolish love,
That like a testy babe will scratch the nurse,
And presently, all humbled, kiss the rod!

Two Gentlemen of Verona, I.ii

Love is blind, and lovers cannot see
The pretty follies that themselves commit.

The Merchant of Venice, II.vi

Love goes toward love as school-boys from their books;
But love from love, toward school with heavy looks.

Romeo and Juliet, II.ii

This is the monstruosity in love, lady, that the will is infinite, and the execution confin'd; that the desire is boundless, and the act a slave to limit.

Troilus and Cressida, III.ii

To be wise and love
Exceeds man's might.

Troilus and Cressida, III.ii

Love's fire heats water, water cools not love.

Sonnet 154

Let me not to the marriage of true minds
Admit impediments. Love is not love
Which alters when it alteration finds,
Or bends with the remover to remove.

Sonnet 116

When my love swears that she is made of truth,
I do believe her, though I know she lies.

Sonnet 138

Shaw, George Bernard (1856–1950)
Irish socialist, writer, dramatist and critic
The fickleness of the women I love is only equalled by the infernal constancy of the women who love me.

The Philanderer (1898)

Shelley, Percy Bysshe (1792–1822)
English poet, dramatist and essayist
Familiar acts are beautiful through love.

Prometheus Unbound (1820)

Sidney, Sir Philip (1554–1586)
English poet, critic, soldier, courtier and diplomat
They love indeede who dare not say they love.

Astrophel and Stella (1591)

Smollett, Tobias (1721–1771)
Scottish writer, satirist, historian, traveller and physician
On being tongue-tied when alone with one's object of desire

'Tis very surprising that love should act so inconsistent with itself, as to deprive its votaries of the use of their faculties, when they have most occasion for them.

The Adventures of Roderick Random (1748)

Spenser, Edmund (c.1522–1599)
English poet
> To be wise and eke to love,
> Is graunted scarce to God above.

The Shepheardes Calender (1579), 'March'

> So let us love, deare love, lyke as we ought,
> Love is the lesson which the Lord us taught.

Amoretti, and Epithalamion (1595), Sonnet 68

Stead, Christina (1902–1983)
Australian writer
> When women are free, we'll see other emotions, no love. Love is a slave emotion, like a dog's.

For Love Alone (1944)

Sterne, Laurence (1713–1768)
Irish-born English writer and clergyman
> Love, an' please your honour, is exactly like war, in this; that a soldier, though he has escaped three weeks complete o' Saturday night, – may nevertheless be shot through his heart on Sunday morning.

Tristram Shandy

Stoddard, Elizabeth Drew (1823–1902)
US novelist and poet
> A woman despises a man for loving her, unless she returns his love.

Attr.

Stow, Randolph (1935–)
Australian poet and novelist
> The love of man is a weed of the waste places. One may think of it as the spinifex of dry souls.

'The Land's Meaning' (1969)

Suckling, Sir John (1609–1642)
English poet and dramatist
> Out upon it, I have loved
> Three whole days together;
> And am like to love three more
> If it prove fair weather.

> Time shall moult away his wings,
> Ere he shall discover
> In the whole wide world again
> Such a constant lover …

> Had it any been but she,
> And that very face,
> There had been at least ere this
> A dozen dozen in her place.

'A Poem with the Answer' (1659)

> But love is such a mystery,
> I cannot find it out:

> For when I think I'm best resolv'd.
> I then am in most doubt.

'Song'

Swinburne, Algernon Charles (1837–1909)
English poet, critic, dramatist and letter writer
> If love were what the rose is,
> And I were like the leaf,
> Our lives would grow together
> In sad or singing weather,
> Blown fields or flowerful closes,
> Green pleasure or grey grief.

'A Match' (1866)

Symons, Michael Brooke (1945–)
Australian journalist
> Love is what makes the world go around – that and clichés.

Sydney Morning Herald, 1970

Tennyson, Alfred, Lord (1809–1892)
English lyric poet
> In the Spring a young man's fancy lightly turns to thoughts of love.

'Locksley Hall' (1838)

> I hold it true, whate'er befall;
> I feel it, when I sorrow most;
> 'Tis better to have loved and lost
> Than never to have loved at all.

In Memoriam A. H. H. (1850)

> To love one maiden only, cleave to her,
> And worship her by years of noble deeds,
> Until they won her; for indeed I knew
> Of no more subtle master under heaven
> Than is the maiden passion for a maid,
> Not only to keep down the base in man,
> But teach high thought, and amiable words
> And courtliness, and the desire of fame,
> And love of truth, and all that makes a man.

The Idylls of the King

Terence (c.190–159 BC)
Carthaginian-born Roman dramatist
> *Amantium irae amoris integratio est.*
> Lovers' quarrels are the renewal of love.

Andria

Thackeray, William Makepeace (1811–1863)
Indian-born English writer
> Some cynical Frenchman has said that there are two parties to a love transaction; the one who loves and the other who condescends to be so treated.

Vanity Fair (1847–1848)

> We love being in love, that's the truth on't.

The History of Henry Esmond (1852)

> Werther had a love for Charlotte
> Such as words could never utter;
> Would you know how first he met her?

She was cutting bread and butter.
Charlotte was a married lady,
And a moral man was Werther,
And for all the wealth of Indies,
Would do nothing for to hurt her.
So he sighed and pined and ogled,
And his passion boiled and bubbled,
Till he blew his silly brains out
And no more was by it troubled.
Charlotte, having seen his body
Borne before her on a shutter,
Like a well-conducted person,
Went on cutting bread and butter.

'Sorrows of Werther' (1855)

Tibullus (c.54–19 BC)
Roman poet

Te spectem, suprema mihi cum venerit hora,
Et teneam moriens deficiente manu.
May I be looking at you when my last hour has
come, and as I die may I hold you with my
weakening hand.

Elegies

Tolstoy, Leo (1828–1910)
Russian writer, essayist, philosopher and moralist

All, everything that I understand, I understand
only because I love.

War and Peace (1869)

Love is God, and when I die it means that I, a
particle of love, shall return to the general and
eternal source.

War and Peace (1869)

Tomlin, Lily (1939–)
US actress

If love is the answer, could you rephrase the
question?

Attr.

Trollope, Anthony (1815–1882)
English writer, traveller and post office official

Love is like any other luxury. You have no right
to it unless you can afford it.

The Way We Live Now (1875)

Virgil (70–19 BC)
Roman poet

Omnia vincit Amor: et nos cedamus Amori.
Love conquers all: let us also yield to love.

Eclogues

Wax, Ruby (1953–)
US comedian

This 'relationship' business is one big waste of
time. It is just Mother Nature urging you to
breed, breed, breed. Learn from nature. Learn
from our friend the spider. Just mate once and
then kill him.

Spectator, 1994

Webster, John (c.1580–c.1625)
English dramatist

Is not old wine wholesomest, old pippins
toothsomest? Does not old wood burn
brightest, old linen wash whitest? Old soldiers,
sweethearts, are surest, and old lovers are
soundest.

Westward Hoe (1607)

Wesley, John (1703–1791)
English theologian and preacher

Beware you be not swallowed up in books! An
ounce of love is worth a pound of knowledge.

In Southey, *Life of Wesley*
(1820)

Wilcox, Ella Wheeler (1850–1919)
US poet and writer

We flatter those we scarcely know,
We please the fleeting guest,
And deal full many a thoughtless blow
To those who love us best.

'Life's Scars' (1917)

Wilde, Oscar (1854–1900)
Irish poet, dramatist, writer, critic and wit

Yet each man kills the thing he loves,
By each let this be heard,
Some do it with a bitter look,
Some with a flattering word,
The coward does it with a kiss,
The brave man with a sword!

The Ballad of Reading Gaol
(1898)

When one is in love one begins by deceiving
oneself. And one ends by deceiving others.

A Woman of No Importance
(1893)

Wycherley, William (c.1640–1716)
English dramatist and poet

A mistress should be like a little country retreat
near the town, not to dwell in constantly, but
only for a night and away.

The Country Wife (1675)

Yeats, W.B. (1865–1939)
Irish poet, dramatist, editor, writer and senator

A pity beyond all telling
Is hid in the heart of love.

'The Pity of Love' (1892)

It seems to me that true love is a discipline, and
it needs so much wisdom that the love of
Solomon and Sheba must have lasted, for all the
silence of the Scriptures.

Estrangement: Being some fifty Thoughts from a
Diary kept in the year nineteen hundred and
nine (1926)

▶▶ PASSION; SEX

loyalty

Johnson, Lyndon Baines (1908–1973)
US Democrat President
> I want loyalty. I want him to kiss my ass in Macy's window at high noon and tell me it smells like roses. I want his pecker in my pocket.
> *In D. Halberstam, The Best and the Brightest (1972)*

Nairne, Carolina, Baroness (1766–1845)
Referring to Bonnie Prince Charlie
> Better lo'ed ye canna be,
> Will ye no come back again?
> *Lays from Strathearn (1846), 'Bonnie Charlie's now awa!'*

Shakespeare, William (1564–1616)
English dramatist, poet and actor
> This above all – to thine own self be true,
> And it must follow, as the night the day,
> Thou canst not then be false to any man.
> *Hamlet, I.iii*

Ustinov, Sir Peter (1921–)
English actor, director, dramatist, writer and raconteur
> I can take no allegiance to a flag if I don't know who's holding it.
> *Dear Me (1977)*

White, E.B. (1899–1985)
US humorist and writer
> It is easier for a man to be loyal to his club than to his planet: the by-laws are shorter and he is personally acquainted with the other members.
> *One Man's Meat*

▶▶ BETRAYAL; PATRIOTISM

luck

Anonymous
> Today, we were unlucky, but remember, we only have to be lucky once – you will have to be lucky always.
> *IRA statement after the bombing of Conservative Party Conference in Brighton, October 1984*

Eastwood, Clint (1930–)
American actor and film director
Said by Eastwood to a wounded bank robber reaching for his shotgun
> I know what you're thinking, did he fire six shots or only five? To tell the truth in all this confusion I forgot myself. Now being that this is a .44 magnum the most powerful handgun in the world and can take your head clean off, you have to ask yourself a question, do I feel lucky? Well do ya, punk?
> *Dirty Harry (film 1971)*

Jerrold, Douglas William (1803–1857)
English dramatist, writer and wit
> Some people are so fond of ill-luck that they run half-way to meet it.
> *Wit and Opinions of Douglas Jerrold (1859)*

Merrill, Bob (1921–1977)
> People who need people are the luckiest people in the world.
> *'People Who Need People' (song, 1964)*

Napoleon I (1769–1821)
French emperor
Question of potential officers
> Has he luck?
> *Attr.*

Proverb
> It is better to be born lucky than rich.

Stead, Christina (1902–1983)
Australian writer
> A self-made man is one who believes in luck and sends his son to Oxford.
> *House of All Nations (1938)*

Tyler, Anne (1941–)
US novelist
> People always call it luck when you've acted more sensibly than they have.
> *Celestial Navigation (1974)*

Webster, John (c.1580–c.1625)
English dramatist
> And of all axioms this shall win the prize, –
> 'Tis better to be fortunate than wise.
> *The White Devil (1612)*

Whitman, Walt (1819–1892)
US poet and writer
> Has anyone supposed it lucky to be born?
> I hasten to inform him or her it is just as lucky to die, and I know it.
> *'Song of Myself' (1855)*

▶▶ CHANCE; SUPERSTITION

luxury

Ashford, Daisy (1881–1972)
English child author
> It was a sumpshous spot all done up in gold with plenty of looking glasses.
> *The Young Visiters (1919)*

Chaplin, Charlie (1889–1977)
English comedian, actor, director and satirist
> The saddest thing I can imagine is to get used to luxury.
> *My Autobiography (1964)*

Gay, John (1685–1732)
English poet, dramatist and librettist
> Whether we can afford it or no, we must have superfluities.
>
> *Polly* (1729)

Keats, John (1795–1821)
English poet
> I have two luxuries to brood over in my walks, your Loveliness and the hour of my death. O that I could have possession of them both in the same minute.
>
> Letter to Fanny Brawne, 25 July 1819

Motley, John Lothrop (1814–1877)
US diplomat and historian
> Give us the luxuries of life, and we will dispense with its necessities.
>
> In Oliver Wendell Holmes, *Autocrat of the Breakfast Table* (1857–1858)

Orton, Joe (1933–1967)
English dramatist and writer
> Every luxury was lavished on you – atheism, breast-feeding, circumcision. I had to make my own way.
>
> *Loot* (1967)

Shakespeare, William (1564–1616)
English dramatist, poet and actor
> They are as sick that surfeit with too much as they that starve with nothing. It is no mean happiness, therefore, to be seated in the mean: superfluity comes sooner by white hairs, but competency lives longer.
>
> *The Merchant of Venice*, I.ii

Wright, Frank Lloyd (1869–1959)
US architect and writer
> Give me the luxuries of life and I will willingly do without the necessities.
>
> Quoted in his obituary, April 9, 1959

▶▶ MONEY AND WEALTH

M

machines

O'Brien, Flann (1911–1966)
Irish novelist and journalist

People who spend most of their natural lives riding iron bicycles over the rocky roadsteads of this parish get their personalities mixed up with the personalities of their bicycles as a result of the interchanging of the atoms of each of them and you would be surprised at the number of people in these parts who nearly are half people and half bicycles.

The Third Policeman (1967)

Patten, Brian (1946–)
British poet

I can imagine the night when waking from a nervous sleep
you find the telephone has dragged itself up the stairs one at a time
and sits mewing,
the electronic pet waiting for its bowl of words.

'I studied telephones constantly'

Russell, Bertrand (1872–1970)
English philosopher, mathematician, essayist and social reformer

Machines are worshipped because they are beautiful, and valued because they confer power; they are hated because they are hideous, and loathed because they impose slavery.

Sceptical Essays (1928)

Slezak, Leo (1873–1946)
Austrian-born US tenor
When the mechanical swan left the stage without him during a performance of Lohengrin

What time is the next swan?

In W. Slezak, *What Time's the Next Swan?* (1962)

Spender, Sir Stephen (1909–1995)
English poet, editor, translator and diarist

After the first powerful plain manifesto
The black statement of pistons, without more fuss
But gliding like a queen, she leaves the station.

'The Express' (1933)

Swift, Jonathan (1667–1745)
Irish satirist, poet, essayist and cleric
Describing a watch

He put this engine to our ears, which made an incessant noise like that of a water-mill; and we conjecture it is either some unknown animal, or the god that he worships; but we are more inclined to the latter opinion.

Gulliver's Travels (1726)

Wellington, Duke of (1769–1852)
Irish-born British military commander and statesman
Referring to steam locomotives

I see no reason to suppose that these machines will ever force themselves into general use.

In J. Gere, *Geoffrey Madan's Notebooks*

▶▶ TECHNOLOGY

madness

Beckett, Samuel (1906–1989)
Irish dramatist, writer and poet

We are all born mad. Some remain so.

Waiting for Godot (1955)

Beerbohm, Sir Max (1872–1956)
English satirist, cartoonist, critic and essayist

Only the insane take themselves quite seriously.

Attr.

Chesterton, G.K. (1874–1936)
English writer, poet and critic

The madman is not the man who has lost his reason. The madman is the man who has lost everything except his reason.

Orthodoxy (1908)

Clare, John (1793–1864)
English rural poet; died in an asylum

Dear Sir, – I am in a Madhouse and quite forget your name or who you are.

Letter, 1860

Dali, Salvador (1904–1989)
Spanish painter and writer

There is only one difference between a madman and me. I am not mad.

The American, 1956

Davies, Scrope Berdmore (c.1783–1852)
English conversationalist

Babylon in all its desolation is a sight not so awful as that of the human mind in ruins.

Letter to Thomas Raikes, 1835

Dryden, John (1631–1700)
English poet, satirist, dramatist and critic

Great wits are sure to madness near alli'd,
And thin partitions do their bounds divide.

Absalom and Achitophel (1681)

Euripides (c.485–406 BC)
Greek dramatist and poet

Whom God wishes to destroy, he first makes mad.

Fragment

George II (1683–1760)
King of Great Britain and Ireland
Reply to the Duke of Newcastle who complained that General Wolfe was a madman
> Mad, is he? Then I hope he will *bite* some of my other generals.
>> In Wilson, *The Life and Letters of James Wolfe* (1909)

Ginsberg, Allen (1926–1997)
US poet
> I saw the best minds of my generation destroyed by madness, starving hysterical naked.
>> *Howl* (1956)

Grant, Cary (1904–1986)
English-born US actor
> Insanity runs in my family. It practically gallops.
>> *Arsenic and Old Lace* (film, 1944)

Greene, Graham (1904–1991)
English writer and dramatist
> Innocence is a kind of insanity.
>> *The Quiet American* (1955)

Harris, Thomas (1940–)
US thriller writer
> *Wil Graham*: I know that I'm not smarter than you.
> *Dr Hannibal Lector*: Then how did you catch me?
> *Wil Graham*: You had disadvantages.
> *Dr Hannibal Lector*: What disadvantages?
> *Wil Graham*: You're insane.
>> *Manhunter* (film, 1986)

Heller, Joseph (1923–1999)
US writer
> Orr was crazy and could be grounded. All he had to do was ask; and as soon as he did, he would no longer be crazy and would have to fly more missions … Yossarian was moved very deeply by the absolute simplicity of this clause of Catch-22 and let out a respectful whistle.
>> *Catch-22* (1961)

Johnson, Samuel (1709–1784)
English lexicographer, poet, critic, conversationalist and essayist
> I inherited a vile melancholy from my father, which has made me mad all my life, at least not sober.
>> In Boswell, *Journal of a Tour to the Hebrides* (1785)

> If a madman were to come into this room with a stick in his hand, no doubt we should pity the state of his mind; but our primary consideration would be to take care of ourselves. We should

knock him down first, and pity him afterwards.
>> In Boswell, *The Life of Samuel Johnson* (1791)

Jung, Carl Gustav (1875–1961)
Swiss psychiatrist and pupil of Freud
> Show me a sane man and I will cure him for you.
>> *The Observer*, 1975

Kipling, Rudyard (1865–1936)
Indian-born British poet and writer
> Every one is more or less mad on one point.
>> *Plain Tales from the Hills* (1888)'

> The mad all are in God's keeping.
>> *Kim* (1901)

Kyd, Thomas (1558–1594)
English dramatist and poet
> I am never better than when I am mad. Then methinks I am a brave fellow; then I do wonders. But reason abuseth me, and there's the torment, there's the hell.
>> *The Spanish Tragedy* (1592)

Laing, R.D. (1927–1989)
Scottish psychiatrist, psychoanalyst and poet
> Madness need not be all breakdown. It may also be break-through. It is potential liberation and renewal as well as enslavement and existential death.
>> *The Politics of Experience* (1967)

> The statesmen of the world who boast and threaten that they have Doomsday weapons are far more dangerous, and far more estranged from 'reality', than many of the people on whom the label 'psychotic' is affixed.
>> *The Divided Self* (1960)

> Schizophrenia cannot be understood without understanding despair.
>> *The Divided Self* (1960)

Lamb, Charles (1775–1834)
English essayist, critic and letter writer
> The six weeks that finished last year and begun this, your very humble servant spent very agreeably in a madhouse at Hoxton. I am got somewhat rational now, and don't bite anyone.
>> Letter to Coleridge, 1796

Lee, Nathaniel (c.1653–1692)
English dramatist
Objecting to being confined in Bedlam
> They called me mad, and I called them mad, and damn them, they outvoted me.
>> In Porter, *A Social History of Madness*

Newton, Sir Isaac (1642–1727)
English scientist and philosopher
> I can calculate the motion of heavenly bodies but not the madness of people.
>> *Attr.*

Plath, Sylvia (1932–1963)
US poet, writer and diarist

> If neurotic is wanting two mutually exclusive things at one and the same time, then I'm neurotic as hell. I'll be flying back and forth between one mutually exclusive thing and another for the rest of my days.
>
> *The Bell Jar* (1963)

Poe, Edgar Allan (1809–1849)
US poet, writer and editor

> Men have called me mad; but the question is not yet settled, whether madness is or is not the loftiest intelligence – whether much that is glorious – whether all that is profound – does not spring from disease of thought – from moods of mind exalted at the expense of the general intellect.
>
> *Eleonora* (1841)

Proust, Marcel (1871–1922)
French writer and critic

> *Tout ce que nous connaissons de grand nous vient des nerveux. Ce sont eux et non pas d'autres qui ont fondé les religions et composé les chefs-d'œuvre.*
>
> Everything great in the world is done by neurotics; they alone founded our religions and composed our masterpieces.
>
> *Le Côté de Guermantes* (1921)

> Neurosis has an absolute genius for malingering. There is no illness which it cannot counterfeit perfectly … If it is capable of deceiving the doctor, how should it fail to deceive the patient?
>
> *Le Côté de Guermantes* (1921)

Renoir, Pierre Auguste (1841–1919)
French painter
Of the men of the French Commune

> *C'étaient des fous, mais ils avaient cette petite flamme qui ne s'éteint pas.*
>
> They were madmen; but they had in them that little flame which does not go out.
>
> In Jean Renoir, *Renoir, My Father* (1962)

Shakespeare, William (1564–1616)
English dramatist, poet and actor

> To define true madness,
> What is't but to be nothing else but mad?
>
> *Hamlet*, II.ii

> And he repelled, a short tale to make,
> Fell into a sadness, then into a fast,
> Thence to a watch, thence into a weakness,
> Thence to a lightness, and, by this declension,
> Into the madness wherein now he raves
> And all we mourn for.
>
> *Hamlet*, II.ii

> O, what a noble mind is here o'erthrown!
> The courtier's, soldier's, scholar's, eye, tongue, sword;

> Th' expectancy and rose of the fair state,
> The glass of fashion and the mould of form,
> Th' observ'd of all observers – quite, quite down!
>
> *Hamlet*, III.i

> O, let me not be mad, not mad, sweet heaven!
> Keep me in temper; I would not be mad!
>
> *King Lear*, I.v

> Canst thou not minister to a mind diseas'd,
> Pluck from the memory a rooted sorrow,
> Raze out the written troubles of the brain,
> And with some sweet oblivious antidote
> Cleanse the stuff'd bosom of that perilous stuff
> Which weighs upon the heart?
>
> *Macbeth*, V.iii

> It is the very error of the moon;
> She comes more nearer earth than she was wont,
> And makes men mad.
>
> *Othello*, V.ii

Sheridan, Richard Brinsley (1751–1816)
Irish dramatist, politician and orator

> O Lord, sir, when a heroine goes mad she always goes into white satin.
>
> *The Critic* (1779)

Smollett, Tobias (1721–1771)
Scottish writer, satirist, historian, traveller and physician

> I think for my part one half of the nation is mad – and the other not very sound.
>
> *The Adventures of Sir Launcelot Greaves* (1762)

Szasz, Thomas (1920–)
Hungarian-born US psychiatrist and writer

> If you talk to God, you are praying; if God talks to you, you have schizophrenia. If the dead talk to you, you are a spiritualist; if God talks to you, you are a schizophrenic.
>
> *The Second Sin* (1973)

> Psychiatrists classify a person as neurotic if he suffers from his problems in living, and a psychotic if he makes others suffer.
>
> *The Second Sin* (1973)

Tillich, Paul (1886–1965)
German-born US philosopher and theologian

> Neurosis is the way of avoiding non-being by avoiding being.
>
> *The Courage to Be* (1952)

Voltaire (1694–1778)
French philosopher, dramatist, poet, historian writer and critic

> Men will always be mad and those who think they can cure them are the maddest of all.
>
> Letter, 1762

▶▶ PSYCHIATRY

magic

Shakespeare, William (1564–1616)
English dramatist, poet and actor
Eye of newt, and toe of frog,
Wool of bat, and tongue of dog,
Adder's fork, and blind-worm's sting,
Lizard's leg, and howlet's wing –
For a charm of pow'rful trouble,
Like a hell-broth boil and bubble.

Macbeth, IV.i

This rough magic
I here abjure – I'll break my staff,
Bury it certain fathoms in the earth,
And, deeper than did ever plummet sound
I'll drown my book.

The Tempest, V.i

malice

Spiel, Hilde (1911–1990)
Malice is like a game of poker or tennis; you don't play it with anyone who is manifestly inferior to you.

The Darkened Room

manners

Belloc, Hilaire (1870–1953)
English writer of verse, essayist and critic; Liberal MP
A manner rude and wild
Is common at your age …

Who take their manners from the Ape,
Their habits from the Bear,
Indulge the loud unseemly jape,
And never brush their hair.

The Bad Child's Book of Beasts (1896)

Bogart, Humphrey (1899–1957)
US actor
I don't mind if you don't like my manners. I don't like them myself. They're pretty bad. I grieve over them on long winter evenings.

The Big Sleep (film, 1946)

Bradbury, Malcolm (1932–)
English writer, critic and academic
The English are polite by telling lies. The Americans are polite by telling the truth.

Stepping Westward (1965)

Coward, Sir Noël (1899–1973)
English dramatist, actor, producer and composer
Comedies of manners swiftly become obsolete when there are no longer any manners.

Relative Values (1951)

Eastman, Max (1883–1969)
US writer, editor and critic
On chivalry
It is but the courteous exterior of a bigot.

Woman Suffrage and Sentiment

Emerson, Ralph Waldo (1803–1882)
US poet, essayist, transcendentalist and teacher
Good manners are made up of petty sacrifices.

'Social Aims' (1875)

Jarrell, Randall (1914–1965)
US poet, critic and translator
To Americans English manners are far more frightening than none at all.

Pictures from an Institution (1954)

Kerr, Jean (1923–)
US writer and dramatist
Man is the only animal that learns by being hypocritical. He pretends to be polite and then, eventually, he becomes polite.

Finishing Touches (1973)

Louis XVIII (1755–1824)
King of France
L'exactitude est la politesse des rois.
Punctuality is the politeness of kings.

Attr.

Mankiewicz, Herman J. (1897–1953)
US journalist and screenwriter
After being sick at the table of a fastidious host
It's all right, Arthur. The white wine came up with the fish.

Attr.

Montagu, Lady Mary Wortley (1689–1762)
English letter writer, poet, traveller and introducer of smallpox inoculation
Civility costs nothing and buys everything.

Letter to the Countess of Bute, 1756

Sheridan, Richard Brinsley (1751–1816)
Irish dramatist, politician and orator
He is the very pine-apple of politeness!

The Rivals (1775)

Smith, Sydney (1771–1845)
English clergyman, essayist, journalist and wit
Where etiquette prevents me from doing things disagreeable to myself, I am a perfect martinet.

Letters, To Lady Holland

Spenser, Edmund (c.1522–1599)
English poet
The gentle minde by gentle deeds is knowne.
For a man by nothing is so well bewrayd,
As by his manners.

The Faerie Queene (1596)

Sterne, Laurence (1713–1768)
Irish-born English writer and clergyman
> Hail ye small sweet courtesies of life.
>> *A Sentimental Journey* (1768)

Theroux, Paul (1941–)
US writer
> The Japanese have perfected good manners and made them indistinguishable from rudeness.
>> *The Great Railway Bazaar* (1975)

Twain, Mark (1835–1910)
US humorist, writer, journalist and lecturer
> Good breeding consists in concealing how much we think of ourselves and how little we think of other persons.
>> *Notebooks* (1935)

Waugh, Evelyn (1903–1966)
English writer and diarist
> Manners are especially the need of the plain. The pretty can get away with anything.
>> *The Observer*, 1962

William of Wykeham (1324–1404)
> Manners maketh man.
>> Motto of Winchester College and New College, Oxford

▶▶ COURTESY; GENTEEL BEHAVIOUR; RESPECT

marriage

Albert, Prince Consort (1819–1861)
German-born husband of Queen Victoria
> Tomorrow our marriage will be 21 years old! How many a storm has swept over it and still it continues green and fresh and throws out vigorous roots.
>> *Attr.*

Allen, Woody (1935–)
US film director, writer, actor and comedian
> It was partially my fault that we got divorced … I tended to place my wife under a pedestal.
>> At a nightclub in Chicago, 1964

Amin, Idi (1925–)
Ugandan dictator
Public message to Lord Snowdon, when his marriage to Princess Margaret broke up
> Your experience will be a lesson to all of us men to be careful not to marry ladies in very high positions.
>> In A. Barrow, *International Gossip* (1983)

Asquith, Margot (1864–1945)
Scottish political hostess and writer
> To marry a man out of pity is folly; and, if you think you are going to influence the kind of fellow who has 'never had a chance, poor devil,' you are profoundly mistaken. One can only influence the strong characters in life, not the weak; and it is the height of vanity to suppose that you can make an honest man of anyone.
>> *The Autobiography of Margot Asquith* (1920)

Astor, Nancy, Viscountess (1879–1964)
US-born British Conservative politician and hostess
> I married beneath me – all women do.
>> *Dictionary of National Biography*

Atwood, Margaret (1939–)
Canadian writer, poet and critic
> Marriage is not
> a house or even a tent
> it is before that, and colder:
> the edge of the forest, the edge
> of the desert …
> the edge of the receding glacier
> where painfully and with wonder
> at having survived even
> this far
> we are learning to make fire.
>> *Procedures for Underground* (1970)

Aubrey, John (1626–1697)
English antiquary, folklorist and biographer
> Sir Thomas More's daughters were then both together abed … asleep. He carries Sir William Roper, who wished to marry one of More's daughters into the chamber and takes the sheet by the corner and suddenly whips it off. They lay on their backs and their smocks up as high as their armpits. This awakened them, and immediately they turned on their bellies. Quoth Roper, I have seen both sides, and so gave a pat on her buttock he made choice of, saying 'Thou art mine.' Here was all the trouble of the wooing.
>> *Brief Lives* (c.1693)

Austen, Jane (1775–1817)
English writer
> It is a truth universally acknowledged, that a single man in possession of a good fortune, must be in want of a wife.
>> *Pride and Prejudice* (1813)

> Happiness in marriage is entirely a matter of chance.
>> *Pride and Prejudice* (1813)

> Matrimony, as the origin of change, was always disagreeable.
>> *Emma* (1816)

Bacon, Francis (1561–1626)
English philosopher, essayist, politician and courtier
> He that hath wife and children, hath given hostages to fortune; for they are impediments to great enterprises, either of virtue or mischief.
>> 'Of Marriage and Single Life' (1625)

But the most ordinary cause of a single life, is liberty; especially in certain self-pleasing and humorous minds, which are so sensible of every restraint as they will go near to think their girdles and garters to be bonds and shackles.

'Of Marriage and Single Life' (1625)

Wives are young men's mistresses, companions for middle age, and old men's nurses.

'Of Marriage and Single Life' (1625)

What is it then to have or have no wife,
But single thraldom, or a double strife?

The World (1629)

Balzac, Honoré de (1799–1850)
French writer

Le sort d'un mariage dépend de la première nuit.
The fate of a marriage depends on the first night.

La Physiologie du mariage (1826)

Barnard, Lady Ann (1750–1825)
Scottish poet

My father argued sair – my mother didna speak,
But she looked in my face till my heart was like to break;
They gied him my hand but my heart was in the sea;
And so auld Robin Gray, he was gudeman to me.

'Auld Robin Gray' (1771)

Bennett, Arnold (1867–1931)
English writer, dramatist and journalist

Being a husband is a whole-time job. That is why so many husbands fail. They cannot give their entire attention to it.

The Title (1918)

Bernard, Jessie (1932–)
US sociologist and writer

Women at marriage move from the status of female to that of neuter being.

The Future of Marriage

The Bible (King James Version)

Therefore shall a man leave his father and his mother, and shall cleave unto his wife: and they shall be one flesh.

Genesis, 2:24

It is better to marry than to burn.

I Corinthians, 7:9

Bennet, Jill (1931–1990)
English actress

Never marry a man who hates his mother, because he'll end up hating you.

The Observer, 1982

Blackstone, Sir William (1723–1780)
English judge, historian and politician

Husband and wife are one, and that one is the husband.

In Miles, The Women's History of the World (1988)

Burton, Robert (1577–1640)
English clergyman and writer

One was never married, and that's his hell; another is, and that's his plague.

Anatomy of Melancholy (1621)

Byron, Lord (1788–1824)
English poet satirist and traveller

Though women are angels, yet wed-lock's the devil.

'To Eliza' (1806)

Romances paint at full length people's wooings,
But only give a bust of marriages:
For no one cares for matrimonial cooings.
There's nothing wrong in a connubial kiss:
Think you, if Laura had been Petrarch's wife,
He would have written sonnets all his life?

Don Juan (1824)

Chaucer, Geoffrey (c.1340–1400)
English poet, public servant and courtier

Experience, though noon auctoritee
Were in this world, is right ynogh for me
To speke of wo that is in mariage.

The Canterbury Tales (1387)

Christina of Sweden (1626–1689)
Queen of Sweden

Nuns and married women are equally unhappy, if in different ways.

Pensées de Christine, reine de Suede (1825)

Coleridge, Samuel Taylor (1772–1834)
English poet, philosopher and critic

The most happy marriage I can picture or imagine to myself would be union of a deaf man to a blind woman.

In Allsop, Recollections (1836)

De Vries, Peter (1910–1993)
US novelist

The value of marriage is not that adults produce children but that children produce adults.

The Tunnel of Love (1954)

Diana, Princess of Wales (1961–1997)
Referring to the Prince of Wales' relationship with Camilla Parker-Bowles

There were three of us in this marriage, so it was a bit crowded.

BBC television interview, 1995

Disraeli, Benjamin (1804–1881)
English statesman and writer

I have always thought that every woman should marry – and no man.

Lothair (1870)

Marriage is the greatest earthly happiness when founded on complete sympathy.

Letter to Gladstone

Eastwood, Clint (1930–)
US actor and film director

There's only one way to have a happy marriage and as soon as I learn what it is I'll get married again.

Attr.

Eliot, George (1819–1880)
English writer and poet

A woman dictates before marriage in order that she may have an appetite for submission afterwards.

Middlemarch (1872)

Farquhar, George (1678–1707)
Irish dramatist

It is a maxim that man and wife should never have it in their power to hang one another.

The Beaux' Stratagem (1707)

Gabor, Zsa-Zsa (1919–)
Hungarian-born US actress

Husbands are like fires. They go out when unattended.

Newsweek, 1960

Her answer to the question 'How many husbands have you had?'

You mean apart from my own?

Attr.

A man in love is incomplete until he has married. Then he's finished.

Newsweek, 1960

Gay, John (1685–1732)
English poet, dramatist and librettist

Do you think your mother and I should have liv'd comfortably so long together, if ever we had been married?

The Beggar's Opera (1728)

Polly: Then all my sorrows are at an end.
Mrs Peachum: A mighty likely speech in troth, for a wench who is just married!

The Beggar's Opera (1728)

I am ready, my dear Lucy, to give you satisfaction – if you think there is any in marriage.

The Beggar's Opera (1728)

One wife is too much for most husbands to hear,
But two at a time there's no mortal can bear.

This way, and that way, and which way I will,
What would comfort the one, t'other wife would take ill.

The Beggar's Opera (1728)

Gibbons, Stella (1902–1989)
English poet and novelist

Mr Mybug said that, by God, D.H. Lawrence was right when he had said there must be a dumb, dark, dull, bitter belly-tension between a man and a woman, and how else could this be achieved save in the long monotony of marriage?

Cold Comfort Farm (1932)

Goldsmith, Oliver (c.1728–1774)
Irish dramatist, poet and writer

I … chose my wife as she did her wedding gown, not for a fine glossy surface, but such qualities as would wear well.

The Vicar of Wakefield (1766)

Guitry, Sacha (1885–1957)
Russian-born French actor, dramatist and film director

There are women whose infidelity is the only thing that still links them to their husbands.

Elles et toi (1948)

Hardy, Rev. E.J. (1849–1920)
Irish army chaplain and writer

How To Be Happy Though Married.

Title of book, 1885

Hume, David (1711–1776)
Scottish philosopher and political economist

I shall tell the women what it is our sex complains of in the married state; and if they be disposed to satisfy us in this particular, all the other difficulties will easily be accommodated. If I be not mistaken, 'tis their love of dominion.

Essays, Moral, Political and Literary (1742)

Johnson, Samuel (1709–1784)
English lexicographer, poet, critic, conversationalist and essayist

Supposing … a wife to be of a studious or argumentative turn, it would be very troublesome: for instance, – if a woman should continually dwell upon the subject of the Arian heresy.

In Boswell, *The Life of Samuel Johnson* (1791)

Marriage has many pains, but celibacy has no pleasures.

Rasselas (1759)

A gentleman who had been very unhappy in marriage married immediately after his wife died. Dr Johnson said, it was the triumph of hope over experience.

In Boswell, *The Life of Samuel Johnson* (1791)

It is so far from being natural for a man and

woman to live in a state of marriage that we find all the motives which they have for remaining in that connection, and the restraints which civilized society imposes to prevent separation, are hardly sufficient to keep them together.

In Boswell, The Life of Samuel Johnson (1791)

Marriages would in general be as happy, and often more so, if they were all made by the Lord Chancellor ... without the parties having any choice in the matter.

In Boswell, The Life of Samuel Johnson (1791)

Keats, John (1795–1821)
English poet

The roaring of the wind is my wife and the Stars through the window pane are my Children. The mighty abstract Idea I have of Beauty in all things stifles the more divided and minute domestic happiness ... the opinion I have of the generality of women – who appear to me as children to whom I would rather give a Sugar Plum than my time, forms a barrier against Matrimony which I rejoice in.

Letter to George and Georgiana Keats, 1818

La Rochefoucauld (1613–1680)
French writer

Il y a de bons mariages, mais il n'y en a point de délicieux.

There are good marriages, but no delightful ones.

Maximes (1678)

Lamb, Charles (1775–1834)
English essayist, critic and letter writer

Nothing to me is more distasteful than that entire complacency and satisfaction which beam in the countenance of a new-married couple.

Essays of Elia (1823)

Longfellow, Henry Wadsworth (1807–1882)
US poet and writer

The men that women marry,
And why they marry them, will always be
A marvel and a mystery to the world.

Michael Angelo (1883)

Lovett, Lyle (1956–)
US singer
On marrying actress Julia Roberts, 1994

It's true that I did get the girl, but then my grandfather always said, 'Even a blind chicken finds a few grains of corn now and then.'

Attr.

MacNeice, Louis (1907–1963)
Belfast-born poet, writer, radio producer, translator and critic

So they were married – to be the more together –
And found they were never again so much together,
Divided by the morning tea,
By the evening paper,
By children and tradesmen's bills.

'Les Sylphides' (1941)

Madonna (1958–)
US singer and actress

I'm anal retentive. I'm a workaholic. I have insomnia. And I'm a control freak. That's why I'm not married. Who could stand me?

In Christopher Andersen, Madonna Unauthorized (1991)

Martineau, Harriet (1802–1876)
English writer

Any one must see at a glance that if men and women marry those whom they do not love, they must love those whom they do not marry.

Society in America (1837)

I am in truth very thankful for not having married at all.

Harriet Martineau's Autobiography (1877)

Mill, John Stuart (1806–1873)
English philosopher, economist and reformer

The moral regeneration of mankind will only really commence, when the most fundamental of the social relations marriage is placed under the rule of equal justice, and when human beings learn to cultivate their strongest sympathy with an equal in rights and cultivation.

The Subjection of Women (1869)

Milton, John (1608–1674)
English poet, libertarian and pamphleteer

Flesh of Flesh,
Bone of my Bone thou art, and from thy State
Mine never shall be parted, weal or woe.

Paradise Lost (1667)

Molière (1622–1673)
French dramatist, actor and director

Le mariage, Agnès, n'est pas un badinage.
Marriage, Agnès, is not a joke.

L'Ecole des Femmes (1662)

Mooney, Bel (1946–)
English writer

Far from going together like a horse and carriage, love and marriage have been in opposition for years.

The Times, 1998

Moore, Thomas (1779–1852)
Irish poet

'Come, come', said Tom's father, 'at your time of life,
There's no longer excuse for thus playing the rake –
It is time you should think, boy, of taking a wife' –

'Why, so it is, father – whose wife shall I take?'.

Miscellaneous Poems (1840), 'A Joke Versified'

Murray, Jenni (1950–)

English journalist and broadcaster

Marriage is an insult and women should not touch it.

Attr.

Newman, Andrea (1938–)

English author

Women will only leave a marriage if it's unbearable, whereas men will split if they get a better offer.

The Observer, 1999

'What is the difference between marriage and prison?'

'In prison somebody else does the cooking.'

Love Hurts (film, 1990)

Peacock, Thomas Love (1785–1866)

English writer and poet

Marriage may often be a stormy lake, but celibacy is almost always a muddy horse-pond.

Melincourt (1817)

Pepys, Samuel (1633–1703)

English diarist, naval administrator and politician

Strange to say what delight we married people have to see these poor fools decoyed into our condition.

Diary, December 1665

Pope, Alexander (1688–1744)

English poet, translator and editor

She who ne'er answers till a Husband cools,
Or, if she rules him, never shows she rules;
Charms by accepting, by submitting sways,
Yet has her humour most, when she obeys.

'Epistle to a Lady' (1735)

Proverbs

Marry in haste, and repent at leisure.

Marriages are made in heaven.

Punch

Advice to persons about to marry – 'Don't!'

1845

Ramsay, Allan (1686–1758)

Scottish poet and dramatist

Ane canna wive an' thrive baith in ae year.

A Collection of Scots Proverbs (1737)

Rogers, Samuel (1763–1855)

English poet

It doesn't much signify whom one marries, for one is sure to find next morning that it was someone else.

Recollections of the Table-Talk of Samuel Rogers (1856)

Rooney, Mickey (1920–)

US film actor

On his frequent marriages

It's confusing. I've had so many wives and so many children I don't know which house to go to first on Christmas.

New York Post, 1960

Rostand, Jean (1894–1977)

French biologist

Never feel remorse for what you have thought about your wife; she has thought much worse things about you.

Le Mariage

Rowland, Helen (1875–1950)

US writer

Before marriage, a man will lie awake thinking about something you said; after marriage, he'll fall asleep before you finish saying it.

In Cowan, *The Wit of Women*

Saikaku, Ihara (1642–1693)

Japanese writer and poet

Marrying off your daughter is a piece of business you may expect to do only once in a lifetime, and, bearing in mind that none of the losses are recoverable later, you should approach the matter with extreme caution.

The Japanese Family Storehouse (1688)

And why do people wilfully exhaust their strength in promiscuous living, when their wives are on hand from bridal night till old age – to be taken when required, like fish from a private pond.

The Japanese Family Storehouse (1688)

Saki (1870–1916)

Burmese-born British writer

A woman who takes her husband about with her everywhere is like a cat that goes on playing with a mouse long after she's killed it.

Attr.

The Western custom of one wife and hardly any mistresses.

Reginald in Russia (1910)

Samuel, Lord (1870–1963)

English Liberal statesman, philosopher and administrator

It takes two to make a marriage a success and only one a failure.

A Book of Quotations (1947)

Selden, John (1584–1654)

English historian, jurist and politician

Marriage is nothing but a civil contract.

Table Talk (1689)

Seth, Vikram (1952–)

Indian author

'You will marry a boy I choose,' said Mrs Rupa

Mehra firmly to her younger daughter.

A Suitable Boy (1993)

Shakespeare, William (1564–1616)

English dramatist, poet and actor

A young man married is a man that's marr'd.

All's Well That Ends Well, II.iii

Men are April when they woo, December when they wed: maids are May when they are maids, but the sky changes when they are wives.

As You Like It, IV.i

Let me give light, but let me not be light,
For a light wife doth make a heavy husband.

The Merchant of Venice, V.i

Thy husband is thy lord, thy life, thy keeper,
Thy head, thy sovereign; one that cares for thee,
And for thy maintenance commits his body
To painful labour both by sea and land.

The Taming of the Shrew, V.ii

Let still the woman take
An elder than herself; so wears she to him,
So sways she level in her husband's heart.
For, boy, however we do praise ourselves,
Our fancies are more giddy and unfirm,
More longing, wavering, sooner lost and won,
Than women's are.

Twelfth Night, II.iv

Shaw, George Bernard (1856–1950)

Irish socialist, writer, dramatist and critic

It is a woman's business to get married as soon as possible, and a man's to keep unmarried as long as he can.

Man and Superman (1903)

Marriage is popular because it combines the maximum of temptation with the maximum of opportunity.

Man and Superman (1903)

Those who talk most about the blessings of marriage and the constancy of its vows are the very people who declare that if the chain were broken and the prisoners left free to choose, the whole social fabric would fly asunder. You cannot have the argument both ways. If the prisoner is happy, why lock him in? If he is not, why pretend that he is?

Man and Superman (1903)

Sheridan, Richard Brinsley (1751–1816)

Irish dramatist, politician and orator

'Tis safest in matrimony to begin with a little aversion.

The Rivals (1775)

You had no taste when you married me.

The School for Scandal (1777)

Simpson, Ronald Albert (1929–)

Australian poet

She cannot say just when
The cooking first began within her mind –
But here she knows … like cakes or bread, a wife
Must lie content as if within a hand
And feel the teeth of time upon her life.

'Wife'

Smith, Bessie (1894–1937)

US singer

No time to marry, no time to settle down;
I'm a young woman, and I ain't done runnin' around.

'Young Woman's Blues' (song, 1927)

Smith, Logan Pearsall (1865–1946)

US-born British epigrammatist, critic and writer

Married women are kept women, and they are beginning to find it out.

Afterthoughts (1931)

Smith, Sydney (1771–1845)

English clergyman, essayist, journalist and wit

On marriage

It resembles a pair of shears, so joined that they cannot be separated; often moving in opposite directions, yet always punishing anyone who comes between them.

In Holland, *A Memoir of the Reverend Sydney Smith* (1855)

Stevenson, Robert Louis (1850–1894)

Scottish writer, poet and essayist

In marriage, a man becomes slack and selfish, and undergoes a fatty degeneration of his moral being.

Virginibus Puerisque (1881)

Lastly (and this is, perhaps, the golden rule), no woman should marry a teetotaller, or a man who does not smoke.

Virginibus Puerisque (1881)

Marriage is like life in this – that it is a field of battle and not a bed of roses.

Virginibus Puerisque (1881)

To marry is to domesticate the Recording Angel. Once you are married, there is nothing left for you, not even suicide, but to be good.

Virginibus Puerisque (1881)

Even if we take matrimony at its lowest, even if we regard it as no more than a sort of friendship recognized by the police.

Virginibus Puerisque (1881)

Marriage is a step so grave and decisive that it attracts light-headed, variable men by its very awfulness.

Virginibus Puerisque (1881)

Times are changed with him who marries; there are no more by-path meadows, where you may innocently linger, but the road lies long and straight and dusty to the grave.

Virginibus Puerisque (1881)

Trusty, dusky, vivid, true,
With eyes of gold and bramble-dew,
Steel-true and blade-straight,
The great artificer
Made my mate.

'My Wife' (1896)

Swift, Jonathan (1667–1745)
Irish satirist, poet, essayist and cleric
The reason why so few marriages are happy, is, because young ladies spend their time in making nets, not in making cages.

Thoughts on Various Subjects (1711)

Taylor, Bishop Jeremy (1613–1667)
English divine and writer
He that loves not his wife and children, feeds a lioness at home and broods a nest of sorrows.

XXV Sermons Preached at Golden Grove (1653)

Thackeray, William Makepeace (1811–1863)
Indian-born English writer
And this I set down as a positive truth. A woman with fair opportunities, and without an absolute hump may marry whom she likes.

Vanity Fair (1847–1848)

Remember, it is as easy to marry a rich woman as a poor woman.

Pendennis (1848–1850)

Thatcher, Denis (1915–)
Replying to the question 'Who wears the pants in this house?'
I do, and I also wash and iron them.

Times (Los Angeles), 1981

Thomas, Irene (1920–)
English writer and broadcaster
It should be a very happy marriage – they are both so much in love with him.

Attr.

Tooke, John Horne (1736–1812)
British radical politician
Replying to the suggestion that he take a wife
With all my heart. Whose wife shall it be?

Attr.

Vanbrugh, Sir John (1664–1726)
English dramatist and baroque architect
No man worth having is true to his wife, or can be true to his wife, or ever was, or ever will be so.

The Relapse, or Virtue in Danger (1696)

Ward, Artemus (1834–1867)
US humorist, journalist, editor and lecturer

If you mean gettin hitched, I'M IN!

Artemus Ward, His Book (1862), 'The Showman's Courtship'

He is dreadfully married. He's the most married man I ever saw in my life.

Artemus Ward's Lecture (1869)

Webb, Sidney (1859–1947)
English reformer, historian and socialist
Marriage is the waste-paper basket of the emotions.

In Bertrand Russell, *Autobiography* (1967)

Weldon, Fay (1931–)
British writer
… the great wonderful construct which is marriage – a construct made up of a hundred little kindnesses, a thousand little bitings back of spite, tens of thousands of minor actions of good intent – this must not, as an institution, be brought down in ruins.

Splitting (1995)

Werb, Mike
US screenwriter
Most of the men in this town think monogamy is some kind of wood.

The Mask (film, 1994)

Wilde, Oscar (1854–1900)
Irish poet, dramatist, writer, critic and wit
There's nothing in the world like the devotion of a married woman. It's a thing no married man knows anything about.

Lady Windermere's Fan (1893)

You don't seem to realise, that in married life three is company and two is none.

The Importance of Being Earnest (1895)

The real drawback to marriage is that it makes one unselfish. And unselfish people are colourless.

The Picture of Dorian Gray (1891)

Twenty years of romance make a woman look like a ruin; but twenty years of marriage make her something like a public building.

A Woman of No Importance (1893)

The amount of women in London who flirt with their own husbands is perfectly scandalous. It looks so bad. It is simply washing one's clean linen in public.

The Importance of Being Earnest (1895)

I am not in favour of long engagements. They give people the opportunity of finding out each other's character before marriage, which I think is never advisable.

The Importance of Being Earnest (1895)

Wilder, Thornton (1897–1975)
US author and playwright

The best part of married life is the fights. The rest is merely so-so.

The Matchmaker (1954)

Wodehouse, P.G. (1881–1975)
English humorist and writer

All the unhappy marriages come from the husbands having brains. What good are brains to a man? They only unsettle him.

The Adventures of Sally (1920)

Like so many substantial Americans, he had married young and kept on marrying, springing from blonde to blonde like the chamois of the Alps leaping from crag to crag.

In Usborne, *Wodehouse at Work to the End* (1976)

Wylie, Betty Jane (1931–)
Canadian writer

A marriage is really a nonstop conversation.

All in the Family: A Survival Guide for Living and Loving in a Changing World

▶▶ ADULTERY; FAMILY

martyrdom

Boleyn, Anne (1507–1536)
Wife of Henry VIII and mother of Elizabeth I
Said on hearing that she was to be executed for adultery

The king has been very good to me. He promoted me from a simple maid to be a marchioness. Then he raised me to be a queen. Now he will raise me to be a martyr.

Attr.

Browne, Sir Thomas (1605–1682)
English physician, author and antiquary

Were the happiness of the next world as closely apprehended as the felicities of this, it were a martyrdom to live.

Hydriotaphia: Urn Burial (1658)

Dryden, John (1631–1700)
English poet, satirist, dramatist and critic

For all have not the gift of martyrdom.

The Hind and the Panther (1687)

Ibárruri, Dolores ('La Pasionaria') (1895–1989)
Basque Communist leader

Il vaut mieux mourir debout que vivre à genoux!
It is better to die on your feet than to live on your knees.

Speech, Paris, 1936

Kierkegaard, Søren (1813–1855)
Danish philosopher

The tyrant dies and his rule is over; the martyr dies and his rule begins.

Attr.

Lewis, C.S. (1898–1963)
Irish-born English academic, writer and critic

She's the sort of woman who lives for others – you can tell the others by their hunted expression.

The Screwtape Letters (1942)

Smith, Sydney (1771–1845)
English clergyman, essayist, journalist and wit

The only way to deal with such a man as O'Connell is to hang him up and erect a statue to him under the gallows.

In H. Pearson, *The Smith of Smiths* (1934)

Tertullian (c.AD 160–c.225)
Carthaginian theologian

Plures efficimur quoties metimur a vobis, semen est sanguis Christianorum.
As often as we are mown down by you, the more we grow in numbers; the blood of Christians is the seed.

Apologeticus

Voltaire (1694–1778)
French philosopher, dramatist, poet, historian writer and critic

I am very fond of truth, but not at all of martyrdom.

Letter to d'Alembert, 1776

Wilde, Oscar (1854–1900)
Irish poet, dramatist, writer, critic and wit

A thing is not necessarily true because a man dies for it.

Sebastian Melmoth (1904)

mathematics

Abel, Niels Henrik (1809–1829)
Norwegian mathematician
Explaining how he had become a great mathematician at such a young age

By studying the masters – not their pupils.

In E.T. Bell, *Men of Mathematics* (1937)

Anonymous

Multiplication is vexation,
Division is as bad;
The rule of three doth puzzle me,
And practice drives me mad.

Elizabethan rhyme

Augustine, Saint (354–430)
Numidian-born Christian theologian and philosopher

The good Christian should beware of mathematicians and all those who make empty prophecies. The danger already exists that mathematicians have made a covenant with the devil to darken the spirit and confine man in the bonds of Hell.

Attr.

Barrie, Sir J.M. (1860–1937)
Scottish dramatist and writer
> What is algebra exactly; is it those three-cornered things?

Quality Street (1901)

Browne, Sir Thomas (1605–1682)
English physician, author and antiquary
> I have often admired the mystical way of Pythagoras, and the secret magic of numbers.

Religio Medici (1643)

Carlyle, Thomas (1795–1881)
Scottish historian, biographer, critic, and essayist
> It is a mathematical fact that the casting of this pebble from my hand alters the centre of gravity of the Universe.

Sartor Resartus (1834)

Einstein, Albert (1879–1955)
German-born US mathematical physicist
> As far as the laws of mathematics refer to reality, they are not certain, and as far as they are certain, they do not refer to reality.

In Capra, *The Tao of Physics* (1975)

Euclid (fl. c.300 bc)
Greek mathematician
> A line is length without breadth.

Elements

To Ptolemy I
> There is no royal road to geometry.

In Proclus, *Commentaria in Euclidem*

Fleming, Marjory (1803–1811)
Scottish child diarist
> The most devilish thing is 8 times 8 and 7 times 7 it is what nature itselfe cant endure.

In Esdaile, *Journals, Letters and Verses* (1934)

Galilei, Galileo (1564–1642)
Italian scientist
> This grand book, the universe, is written in the language of mathematics.

Quoted by Melvyn Bragg, BBC radio, 1999

Hobbes, Thomas (1588–1679)
Political philosopher
> Geometry … is the only science that it hath pleased God hitherto to bestow on mankind.

Leviathan (1651)

Milligan, Spike (1918–)
Irish comedian and writer
> Moriarty: How are you at Mathematics?
> Harry Secombe: I speak it like a native.

The Goon Show

Plato (c.429–347 BC)
Greek philosopher

Inscription written over the entrance to the Academy
> Let no one ignorant of mathematics enter here.

Attr.

Ramanujan, Srinivasa (1887–1920)
Indian mathematician
Reply to the mathematician, G.H. Hardy, who remarked that a cab's number –1729 – was dull
> No, it is a very interesting number; it is the smallest number expressible as a sum of two cubes in two different ways.

Proceedings of the London Mathematical Society (1921); the two ways are 13 + 123, and 93 + 103

Russell, Bertrand (1872–1970)
English philosopher, mathematician, essayist and social reformer
> Mathematics may be defined as the subject in which we never know what we are talking about, nor whether what we are saying is true.

Mysticism and Logic (1918)

> Mathematics, rightly viewed, possesses not only truth, but supreme beauty – a beauty cold and austere, like that of sculpture.

Mysticism and Logic (1918)

> Pure mathematics consists entirely of assertions to the effect that, if such and such a proposition is true of anything, then such and such another proposition is true of that thing. It is essential not to discuss whether the first proposition is really true, and not to mention what the anything is, of which is is supposed to be true.

Mysticism and Logic (1918)

Smith, Sydney (1771–1845)
English clergyman, essayist, journalist and wit
> What would life be without arithmetic, but a scene of horrors.

Letters, To Miss – , 1835

Weil, Simone (1909–1943)
French philosopher, essayist and mystic
> Algebra and money are essentially levellers; the first intellectually, the second effectively.

Attr.

meaning

Jung, Carl Gustav (1875–1961)
Swiss psychiatrist and pupil of Freud
> The least of things with a meaning is worth more in life than the greatest of things without it.

Modern Man in Search of a Soul

Smith, Logan Pearsall (1865–1946)
US-born British epigrammatist, critic and writer
Contemplating whether life has any meaning, shortly before his death

Yes, there is a meaning, at least for me, there is one thing that matters – to set a chime of words tinkling in the minds of a few fastidious people.

New Statesman, 1946

Wallas, Graham (1858–1932)
English political scientist
The little girl had the makings of a poet in her who, being told to be sure of her meaning before she spoke, said: 'How can I know what I think till I see what I say?'.

The Art of Thought (1926)

▶▶ PURPOSE; WORDS

media

Bakewell, Joan (1933–)
British journalist and television presenter
The BBC is full of men appointing men who remind them of themselves when young, so you get the same backgrounds, the same education, and the same programmes.

The Observer, 1993

Bjelke-Petersen, Sir Johannes (1911–)
Australian politician, Premier of Queensland
The greatest thing that could happen to the state and the nation is when we can get rid of all the media. Then we could live in peace and tranquillity, and no one would know anything.

The Spectator, 1987

Hoffman, Abbie (1936–1989)
US political activist
The idea that media is there to educate us, or to inform us, is ridiculous because that's about tenth or eleventh on their list.

Speech, 1987

Howard, Philip (1933–)
English journalist
The proliferation of radio and television channels has produced a wilderness of cave-dwellers instead of the promised global village.

The Times, 1992

Jackson, Robert (1946–)
English Conservative politician and writer
To have open government you need mature media. It is more difficult for people to discuss complex issues than it used to be because of the destructive power of the tabloids. The TV sound bite also makes it impossible to communicate complex arguments. It is all black and white, cut and dried, yaa-boo.

Independent on Sunday, 1994

Kavanau, Ted
CNN news editor
Statement of CNN editorial policy

If it bleeds, it leads.

The Guardian, 1999

McLuhan, Marshall (1911–1980)
Canadian communications theorist
The medium is the message. This is merely to say that the personal and social consequences of any medium … result from the new scale that is introduced into our affairs by each extension of ourselves or by any new technology.

Understanding Media (1964)

Murdoch, Rupert (1931–)
Australian-born publisher and international businessman
Monopoly is a terrible thing, till you have it.

The New Yorker, 1979

In reply to Ted Turner (*see below*)
It is true that I am a low mean snake. But you could walk beneath me wearing a top hat.

The Guardian, 1999

Reith, Lord (1889–1971)
Scottish wartime minister, administrator, diarist and Director-General of the BBC
It was in fact the combination of public service motive, sense of moral obligation, assured finance and the brute force of monopoly which enabled the BBC to make of broadcasting what no other country has made of it.

Into the Wind (1949)

Shelley, Sir James
As Director of Broadcasting
There was once a wicked lady called Circe, who was reputed to turn human beings into swine. The object of broadcasting should be the exact opposite.

In Hamish Keith and William Main (eds), New Zealand Yesterdays: A Look at Our Recent Past

Stevenson, Adlai (1900–1965)
US lawyer, statesman and United Nations ambassador
The trouble with this country is that it has a two-party system and a one-party press.

Speech, 1952

Stoppard, Tom (1937–)
British dramatist
The media. It sounds like a convention of spiritualists.

Night and Day (1978)

Turner, Ted (1938–)
US media tycoon
CNN Launch speech, 1980
See we're gonna take the news and put it on satellite and then we're gonna beam it down to Russia, and we're gonna bring world peace and we're gonna get rich in the process!

The Guardian, 1999

After launch of Rupert Murdoch's Fox news in 1996
> Murdoch's a schlockmeister. We're gonna squish Rupert like a bug.
>> *The Guardian*, 1999

Whitlam, Gough (1916–)
Australian Labor statesman and Prime Minister
> Quite small and ineffectual demonstrations can be made to look like the beginnings of a revolution if the cameraman is in the right place at the right time.
>> *A Dictionary of Contemporary Quotations* (1982)

▶▶ INTERNET; MONEY AND WEALTH; NEWS; NEWSPAPERS; TELEVISION

medicine

Arnold, Matthew (1822–1888)
English poet, critic, essayist and educationist
> Nor bring, to see me cease to live,
> Some doctor full of phrase and fame,
> To shake his sapient head and give
> The ill he cannot cure a name.
>> 'A Wish' (1867)

Asquith, Margot (1864–1945)
Scottish political hostess and writer
> The King told me he would never have died if it had not been for that fool Dawson of Penn.
>> In K. Rose, *King George V* (1983)

Belloc, Hilaire (1870–1953)
English writer of verse, essayist and critic; Liberal MP
> Physicians of the Utmost Fame
> Were called at once; but when they came
> They answered, as they took their Fees,
> 'There is no Cure for this Disease.'
>> *Cautionary Tales* (1907)

The Bible (King James Version)
> Physician, heal thyself.
>> *Luke*, 4:23

Chekhov, Anton (1860–1904)
Russian writer, dramatist and doctor
> Medicine is my lawful wife but literature is my mistress. When I'm bored with one, I spend the night with the other.
>> Letter to Suvorin, 1888

Fletcher, John (1579–1625)
English dramatist
> I find the medicine worse than the malady.
>> *The Lover's Progress* (1623)

Franklin, Benjamin (1706–1790)
US statesman, scientist, political critic and printer
> He's the best physician that knows the worthlessness of the most medicines.
>> *Poor Richard's Almanac* (1733)

Goldsmith, Oliver (c.1728–1774)
Irish dramatist, poet and writer
> The doctor found, when she was dead, –
> Her last disorder mortal.
>> 'Elegy on Mrs Mary Blaize' (1759)

Goldwyn, Samuel (1882–1974)
Polish-born US film producer
> Any man who goes to a psychiatrist should have his head examined.
>> In Zierold, *Moguls* (1969)

Hahnemann, C.F.S. (1755–1843)
German physician and founder of homeopathy
> *Similia similibus curantur.*
> Like cures like.
>> Motto of homeopathic medicine

Hippocrates (c.460–357 BC)
Greek physician
Of medicine
> Life is short, science is so long to learn, opportunity is elusive, experience is dangerous, judgement is difficult.
>> *Aphorisms* (c.415 bc)

James, Alice (1848–1892)
US diarist
> I suppose one has a greater sense of intellectual degradation after an interview with a doctor than from any human experience.
>> In Leon Edel (ed.), *The Diary of Alice James*, 1890

Johnson, Samuel (1709–1784)
English lexicographer, poet, critic, conversationalist and essayist
> It is incident to physicians, I am afraid, beyond all other men, to mistake subsequence for consequence.
>> In Boswell, *The Life of Samuel Johnson* (1791)

Kaufman, George S. (1889–1961)
US scriptwriter, librettist and journalist
> The kind of doctor I want is one who when he's not examining me is home studying medicine.
>> In Howard Teichmann, *George S. Kaufman: An Intimate Portrait* (1972)

La Bruyère, Jean de (1645–1696)
French satirist
> *Les médecins laissent mourir, les charlatans tuent.*
> Doctors allow us to die; charlatans kill us.
>> *Les caractères ou les moeurs de ce siècle* (1688)

Loos, Anita (1893–1981)
US writer and screenwriter
> So then Dr Froyd said that all I needed was to cultivate a few inhibitions and get some sleep.
>> *Gentlemen Prefer Blondes* (1925)

McLuhan, Marshall (1911–1980)
Canadian communications theorist
> If the nineteenth century was the age of the

editorial chair, ours is the century of the psychiatrist's couch.

Understanding Media (1964)

Molière (1622–1673)

French dramatist, actor and director

> *C'est un homme expéditif, qui aime à dépêcher ses malades; et quand on a à mourir, cela se fait avec lui le plus vite du monde.*
>
> He's an expeditious man, who likes to hurry his patients along; and when you have to die, he gets it over with quicker than anyone else.

Monsieur de Pourceaugnac (1670)

Proverb

> Prevention is better than cure.

Quarles, Francis (1592–1644)

English poet, writer and royalist

> Physicians of all men are most happy; what good success soever they have, the world proclaimeth, and what faults they commit, the earth covereth.

Hieroglyphics of the Life of Man (1638)

Rolleston, Sir Humphrey (1862–1944)

English physician

Of physicians

> First they get on, then they get honour, then they get honest.

In David Ogilvy, *Confessions of an Advertising Man* (1963)

Shaw, George Bernard (1856–1950)

Irish socialist, writer, dramatist and critic

> If you are going to have doctors you had better have doctors well off; just as if you are going to have a landlord you had better have a rich landlord. Taking all the round of professions and occupations, you will find that every man is the worse for being poor; and the doctor is a specially dangerous man when poor.

The Socialist Criticism of the Medical Profession (1909)

> Optimistic lies have such immense therapeutic value that a doctor who cannot tell them convincingly has mistaken his profession.

Misalliance (1914)

Webster, John (c.1580–c.1625)

English dramatist

> Physicians are like kings – they brook no contradiction.

The Duchess of Malfi (1623)

Williams, Tennessee (1911–1983)

US dramatist and writer

Explaining why he had stopped seeing his psychoanalyst

> He was meddling too much in my private life.

Attr.

▶▶ HEALTH; ILLNESS; PSYCHIATRY

mediocrity

Beerbohm, Sir Max (1872–1956)

English satirist, cartoonist, critic and essayist

> Only mediocrity can be trusted to be always at its best.

In S.N. Behrman, *Conversations with Max*

Heller, Joseph (1923–1999)

US writer

> Some men are born mediocre, some men achieve mediocrity, and some men have mediocrity thrust upon them. With Major Major it had been all three.

Catch-22 (1961)

Molière (1622–1673)

French dramatist, actor and director

> Man is, I admit it, a mediocre creature.

Tartuffe (1664)

melancholy

Burton, Robert (1577–1640)

English clergyman and writer

> If there is a hell upon earth, it is to be found in a melancholy man's heart.

Anatomy of Melancholy (1621)

Lamb, Charles (1775–1834)

English essayist, critic and letter writer

> The man must have a rare recipe for melancholy, who can be dull in Fleet Street.

Letter to Thomas Manning, 1802

Rogers, Samuel (1763–1855)

English poet

> Go – you may call it madness, folly;
> You shall not chase my gloom away.
> There's such a charm in melancholy,
> I would not, if I could, be gay.

'To –, 1814'

▶▶ DESPAIR

memory

Adams, Franklin P. (1881–1960)

US writer, poet, translator and editor

> Nothing is more responsible for the good old days than a bad memory.

In William Cole and Louis Phillips, *Treasury of Humorous Quotations* (1996)

Aeschylus (525–456 BC)

Greek dramatist and poet

Memory is the mother of all wisdom.

Prometheus Bound

Allingham, William (1824–1889)
Irish poet and diarist
> Four ducks on a pond,
> A grass-bank beyond,
> A blue sky of spring,
> White clouds on the wing:
> What a little thing
> To remember for years –
> To remember with tears.

'A Memory' (1888)

Apollinaire, Guillaume (1880–1918)
French poet and writer
> *Les souvenirs sont cors de chasse*
> *Dont meurt le bruit parmi le vent.*
> Memories are hunting horns whose sound dies away in the wind.

'Cors de Chasse' (1913)

Arnold, Matthew (1822–1888)
English poet, critic, essayist and educationist
> Ere the parting hour go by,
> Quick, thy tablets, Memory!

'A Memory Picture' (1849)

> And we forget because we must
> And not because we will.

'Absence' (1852)

Austen, Jane (1775–1817)
English writer
> There seems something more speakingly incomprehensible in the powers, the failures, the inequalities of memory, than in any other of our intelligences.

Mansfield Park (1814)

Barrie, Sir J.M. (1860–1937)
Scottish dramatist and writer
> A safe but sometimes chilly way of recalling the past is to force open a crammed drawer. If you are searching for anything in particular you don't find it, but something falls out at the back that is often more interesting.

'To the Five – A Dedication' in *Peter Pan* (1902)

Baudelaire, Charles (1821–1867)
French poet, translator and critic
> *J'ai plus de souvenirs que si j'avais mille ans.*
> I have more memories than if I had lived for a thousand years.

Les Fleurs du mal (1857)

Betti, Ugo (1892–1953)
Italian playwright
> Memories are like stones, time and distance erode them like acid.

Goat Island (1946)

Bridges, Robert (1844–1930)
English poet, dramatist, essayist and doctor
> Rejoice ye dead, where'er your spirits dwell,
> Rejoice that yet on earth your fame is bright,
> And that your names, remembered day and night,
> Live on the lips of those who love you well.

'Ode to Music' (1896)

Brodsky, Joseph (1940–1996)
Russian poet, essayist, critic and exile
> What memory has in common with art is the knack for selection, the taste for detail … More than anything, memory resembles a library in alphabetical disorder, and with no collected works by anyone.

'In a Room and a Half' (1986)

Campbell, Thomas (1777–1844)
Scottish poet, ballad writer and journalist
> To live in hearts we leave behind
> Is not to die.

'Hallowed Ground'

Dali, Salvador (1904–1989)
Spanish painter and writer
> The difference between false memories and true ones is the same as for jewels: it is always the false ones that look the most real, the most brilliant.

The Secret Life of Salvador Dali (1948)

Dickens, Charles (1812–1870)
English writer
> All human memory is fraught with sorrow and trouble.

A Christmas Carol (1843)

Disraeli, Benjamin (1804–1881)
English statesman and writer
> Nobody is forgotten when it is convenient to remember him.

Attr.

Lang, Andrew (1844–1912)
Scottish poet, writer, mythologist and anthropologist
> A mist of memory broods and floats,
> The border waters flow;
> The air is full of ballad notes
> Borne out of long ago.

'Twilight on Tweed' (1905)

La Rochefoucauld (1613–1680)
French writer
> *Tout le monde se plaint de sa mémoire, et personne ne se plaint de son jugement.*
> Everyone complains of his memory; nobody of his judgment.

Maximes (1678)

Lavin, Mary (1912–)
Irish novelist
> What did they know about memory? What was it but another name for dry love and barren longing?
>> *In the Middle of the Fields* (1967)

Levi, Primo (1919–1987)
Italian writer, poet and chemist; survivor of Auschwitz
> Human memory is a marvellous but fallacious instrument … The memories which lie within us are not carved in stone; not only do they tend to become erased as the years go by, but often they change, or even increase by incorporating extraneous features.
>> *The Drowned and the Saved* (1988)

Proust, Marcel (1871–1922)
French writer and critic
> *Et tout d'un coup le souvenir m'est apparu. Ce goût c'était celui du petit morceau de madeleine que le dimanche matin à Combray … ma tante Léonie m'offrait après l'avoir trempé dans son infusion de thé ou de tilleul.*
>
> And suddenly the memory came back to me. The taste was that of the little piece of madeleine which on Sunday mornings at Combray … my aunt Léonie used to give me, after dipping it first in her cup of tea or tisane.
>> *Du côté de chez Swann* (1913)

Proverb
> I hate a man with a memory at a drinking bout.
>> Greek proverb

Rossetti, Christina (1830–1894)
English poet
> Come to me in the silence of the night;
> Come in the speaking silence of a dream;
> Come with soft rounded cheeks and eyes as bright
> As sunlight on a stream;
> Come back in tears,
> O memory, hope, love of finished years.
>> 'Echo' (1862)
>
> Remember me when I am gone away,
> Gone far away into the silent land.
>> 'Remember'

Schopenhauer, Arthur (1788–1860)
German philosopher
> To expect a man to retain everything that he has ever read is like expecting him to carry about in his body everything that he has ever eaten.
>> *Parerga and Paralipomena* (1851)

Shakespeare, William (1564–1616)
English dramatist, poet and actor
> Praising what is lost
> Makes the remembrance dear.
>> *All's Well That Ends Well*, V.iii
>
> I can suck melancholy out of a song, as a weasel sucks eggs.
>> *As You Like It*, II.v
>
> In sooth I know not why I am so sad.
> It wearies me; you say it wearies you;
> But how I caught it, found it, or came by it,
> What stuff 'tis made of, whereof it is born,
> I am to learn;
> And such a want-wit sadness makes of me
> That I have much ado to know myself.
>> *The Merchant of Venice*, I.i

Shaw, George Bernard (1856–1950)
Irish socialist, writer, dramatist and critic
> Reminiscences make one feel so deliciously aged and sad.
>> *The Irrational Knot* (1905)

▶▶ NOSTALIGIA; PAST

men

Barrie, Sir J.M. (1860–1937)
Scottish dramatist and writer
> I have always found that the man whose second thoughts are good is worth watching.
>> *What Every Woman Knows* (1908)

Beauvoir, Simone de (1908–1986)
French writer, feminist critic and philosopher
> A man would never get the notion of writing a book on the peculiar situation of the human male.
>> *The Second Sex* (1953)

Bly, Robert (1926–)
US writer
> Every modern male has, lying at the bottom of his psyche, a large, primitive being covered with hair down to his feet. Making contact with this Wild Man is the step the Eighties male or the Nineties male has yet to take.
>> *Iron John* (1990)

Bombeck, Erma (1927–1996)
US humorist and writer
> What's wrong with you men? Would hair stop growing on your chest if you asked directions somewhere?
>> *When You Look Like Your Passport Photo, It's Time to Go Home* (1991)

Christina of Sweden (1626–1689)
Queen of Sweden
> I love men, not because they are men, but because they are not women.
>> *Pensées de Christine, reine de Suede* (1825)

Collins, Joan (1933–)
English actress and author
>I've never yet met a man who could look after me. I don't need a husband. What I need is a wife.
>
>> *The Sunday Times*, 1987

Diana, Princess of Wales (1961–1997)
>If men had to have babies, they would only ever have one each.
>
>> *The Observer*, 1984

Duras, Marguerite (1914–1996)
French author and film-maker
>Before they're plumbers or writers or taxi drivers or unemployed or journalists, men are men. Whether heterosexual or homosexual. The only difference is that some of them remind you of it as soon as you meet them, and others wait for a little while.
>
>> *Practicalities* (1987)

>You have to be very fond of men. Very, very fond. You have to be very fond of them to love them. Otherwise they're simply unbearable.
>
>> *Practicalities* (1987)

Dworkin, Andrea (1946–)
US writer and feminist
>Men love death. In everything they make, they hollow out a central place for death … Men especially love murder. In art they celebrate it. In life, they commit it.
>
>> *The Independent*, 1992

Emerson, Ralph Waldo (1803–1882)
US poet, essayist, transcendentalist and teacher
>Men are what their mothers made them.
>
>> *The Conduct of Life* (1860)

Ford, Anna (1943–)
English television newscaster and reporter
>It is men who face the biggest problems in the future, adjusting to their new and complicated role.
>
>> Attr.

Franklin, Miles (1879–1954)
Australian writer
>Men are clumsy, stupid creatures regarding little things, but in their right place they are wonderful animals.
>
>> *My Brilliant Career* (1901)

Gaskell, Elizabeth (1810–1865)
English writer
>A man … is so in the way in the house!
>
>> *Cranford* (1853)

Hammerstein II, Oscar (1895–1960)
US lyricist
>I'm Gonna Wash That Man Right Out of My Hair.
>
>> Title song from the musical *South Pacific*

Keillor, Garrison (1942–)
US writer and broadcaster
>Years ago, manhood was an opportunity for achievement, and now it is a problem to be overcome.
>
>> *The Book of Guys* (1994)

Kennedy, Florynce R. (1916–)
US lawyer, feminist and civil rights activist
>If men could get pregnant, abortion would be a sacrament.
>
>> In Steinem, *The Verbal Karate of Florynce R. Kennedy, Esq.* (1973)

Maugham, William Somerset (1874–1965)
English writer, dramatist and physician
>Men have an extraordinarily erroneous opinion of their position in nature; and the error is ineradicable.
>
>> *A Writer's Notebook* (1949)

Rochester, Earl of (1647–1680)
English poet, satirist, courtier and libertine
>What vain, unnecessary things are men!
>How well we do without 'em!
>
>> 'Fragment' (published 1953)

Sévigné, Marquise de (1626–1696)
French letter writer
>The more I see of men the more I admire dogs.
>
>> Attr.

West, Dame Rebecca (1892–1983)
English writer, critic and feminist
>There is, of course, no reason for the existence of the male sex except that sometimes one needs help with moving the piano.
>
>> *The Sunday Telegraph*, 1970

Whitehorn, Katherine (1926–)
English writer
>No nice men are good at getting taxis.
>
>> *The Observer*, 1977

Williams, Robin (1952–)
US comedian and actor
>God gave all men a penis and a brain, but only enough blood to run one at a time.
>
>> Attr.

men and women

Adams, Scott (1957–)
US cartoonist
>Needing someone is like needing a parachute. If he isn't there the first time you need him, chances are you won't be needing him again.
>
>> *The Dilbert Principle*

Austen, Jane (1775–1817)
English writer

There certainly are not so many men of large fortune in the world as there are pretty women to deserve them.

Mansfield Park (1814)

The Bible (King James Version)

It is not good that the man should be alone; I will make him an help meet for him.

Genesis, 2:18

Burchill, Julie (1960–)
English writer

Men have charisma; women have vital statistics.

Sex and Sensibility (1992)

Byron, Lord (1788–1824)
English poet satirist and traveller

Man's love is of man's life a thing
 apart,
'Tis woman's whole existence.

Don Juan (1824)

The more I see of men, the less I like them. If I could but say so of women too, all would be well.

Journal, 1814

Chesterfield, Lord (1694–1773)
English politician and letter writer

Have you found out that every woman is infallibly to be gained by every sort of flattery, and every man by one sort or other?

Letter to his son, 1752

Coleridge, Samuel Taylor (1772–1834)
English poet, philosopher and critic

The man's desire is for the woman; but the woman's desire is rarely other than for the desire of the man.

Table Talk (1835)

Connolly, Cyril (1903–1974)
English literary editor, writer and critic

The true index of a man's character is the health of his wife.

The Unquiet Grave (1944)

Cope, Wendy (1945–)
English poet

There are so many kinds of awful
 men –
One can't avoid them all. She often said
She'd never make the same mistake again:
She always made a new mistake instead.

'Rondeau Redoublé' (1986)

Cosby, Bill (1937–)
US comedian, actor and author

Men and women belong to different species,

and communication between them is a science still in its infancy.

Love and Marriage (1989)

Davies, Robertson (1913–1995)
Canadian playwright, writer and critic

Women tell men things that men are not very likely to find out for themselves.

In J. Madison Davis, *Conversations with Robertson Davies* (1989)

Dickinson, Angie (1931–)
US actress

Men should be the ones who succeed. It makes me feel comfortable if men are the ones in control.

Daily Mail, 1995

Dietrich, Marlene (1901–1992)
German-born US actress and singer

The average man is more interested in a woman who is interested in him than he is in a woman – any woman – with beautiful legs.

News item, 1954

Most women set out to try to change a man, and when they have changed him they do not like him.

Attr.

Dryden, John (1631–1700)
English poet, satirist, dramatist and critic

Men are but children of a larger
 growth;
Our appetites as apt to change as theirs,
And full as craving too, and full as vain.

All for Love (1678)

Ebner-Eschenbach, Marie von (1830–1916)
Austrian writer

Eine gescheite Frau hat Millionen geborener Feinde – alle dummen Männer.
A clever woman has millions of born enemies – all stupid men.

Aphorisms (1880)

Eliot, George (1819–1880)
English writer and poet

I'm not denyin' the women are foolish: God Almighty made 'em to match the men.

Adam Bede (1859)

A man is seldom ashamed of feeling that he cannot love a woman so well when he sees a certain greatness in her: nature having intended greatness for men.

Middlemarch (1872)

Evans, Dame Edith (1888–1976)
English actress

When a woman behaves like a man, why doesn't

she behave like a nice man?

The Observer, 1956

Fairbairn, Lady Sam
Wife of Conservative MP, Sir Nicholas Fairbairn
Behind every great man is an exhausted woman.

The Independent, 1994

Fisher, Carrie (1956–)
US actress and writer
Here's how men think. Sex, work– and those are
reversible, depending on age– sex, work, food,
sports and 1astly, begrudgingly, relationships.
And here's how women think. Relationships,
relationships, relationships, work, sex, shopping,
weight, food.

Surrender the Pink (1990)

Francis, Clare (1946–)
English yachtswoman and writer
I think men are intimidated by my independence
and wonder what they have to offer me when I
already have a house in Kensington and a career.
Men of my generation still need to feel needed.

Daily Mail, 1995

French, Marilyn (1929–)
US writer and critic
Whatever they may be in public life, whatever
their relations with men, in their relations with
women, all men are rapists, and that's all they
are. They rape us with their eyes, their laws and
their codes.

The Women's Room (1977)

Friedan, Betty (1921–)
US feminist leader and writer
Men weren't really the enemy – they were fellow
victims suffering from an outmoded masculine
mystique that made them feel unnecessarily
inadequate when there were no bears to kill.

Christian Science Monitor,
1974

Gabor, Zsa-Zsa (1919–)
Hungarian-born US actress
Never despise what it says in the women's
magazines: it may not be subtle but neither are
men.

The Observer, 1976

Gay, John (1685–1732)
English poet, dramatist and librettist
Man may escape from rope and gun;
Nay, some have out-liv'd the doctor's pill:
Who takes a woman must be undone,
That basilisk is sure to kill.
The fly that sips treacle is lost in the sweets,
So he that tastes woman, woman, woman,
He that tastes woman, ruin meets.

The Beggar's Opera (1728)

Greer, Germaine (1939–)
Australian feminist, critic, English scholar and writer
Probably the only place where a man can feel
really secure is in a maximum security prison,
except for the imminent threat of release.

The Female Eunuch (1970)

A woman becomes the extension of a man's ego
like his horse or his car.

The Female Eunuch (1970)

Women have very little idea of how much men
hate them.

The Female Eunuch (1970)

A man who is slovenly and untidy is considered
normal. The woman who is either is a slut or a
sloven or a slag.

The Times, 1999

Hall, Jerry (1956–)
US fashion model and actress
My mother said it was simple to keep a man,
you must be a maid in the living room, a cook in
the kitchen and a whore in the bedroom. I said
I'd hire the other two and take care of the
bedroom bit.

The Observer, 1985

Harlow, Jean (1911–1937)
US film actress
I like to wake up feeling a new man.

In Simon Rose, *Classic Film Guide* (1995)

Henry, O. (1862–1910)
US short-story writer
If men knew how women pass the time when
they are alone they'd never marry.

'Memoirs of a Yellow Dog' (1906)

Hill, Reginald (1936–)
British writer and playwright
He created a man who was hard of head, blunt
of speech, knew which side his bread was
buttered on, and above all took no notice of
women. Then God sent him forth to multiply in
Yorkshire.

Pictures of Perfection (1994)

Holmes, Oliver Wendell (1809–1894)
US physician, poet, writer and scientist
Man has his will, – but woman has her way.

The Autocrat of the Breakfast-Table (1858)

Jong, Erica (1942–)
US writer
Men and women, women and men. It will never
work.

Attr.

Kipling, Rudyard (1865–1936)
Indian-born British poet and writer
Take my word for it, the silliest woman can

manage a clever man; but it needs a very clever woman to manage a fool.

Plain Tales from the Hills (1888)

For a man he must go with a woman, which women don't understand –
Or the sort that say they can see it, they aren't the marrying brand.

'The Mary Gloster' (1894)

Open and obvious devotion from any sort of man is always pleasant to any sort of woman.

Plain Tales from the Hills (1888)

Laver, James (1899–1975)
English art, costume and design historian
Man in every age has created woman in the image of his own desire.

In Neustater, *Hyenas in Petticoats: a Look at 20 Years of Feminism* (1989)

Lawrence, D.H. (1885–1930)
English writer, poet and critic
There is no comradeship between men and women, none whatsoever, but rather a condition of battle, reserve, hostility.

Twilight in Italy (1916)

One realizes with horror, that the race of men is almost extinct in Europe. Only Christ-like heroes and woman-worshipping Don Juans, and rabid equality-mongrels.

Sea and Sardinia (1921)

Lerner, Alan Jay (1918–1986)
US lyricist and screenwriter
Why can't a woman be more like a man?
Men are so honest, so thoroughly square;
Eternally noble, historically fair.

My Fair Lady (1956)

Longfellow, Henry Wadsworth (1807–1882)
US poet and writer
As unto the bow the cord is,
So unto the man is woman;
Though she bends him, she obeys him,
Though she draws him, yet she follows;
Useless each without the other!

The Song of Hiawatha (1855)

MacDonald, Sir John A. (1815–1891)
Exchange between an irate suffragette and Sir John A. MacDonald when he was Prime Minister
Q. What is the difference between the Prime Minister and myself?
A. Madame, I cannot conceive.

Attr.

Marx, Groucho (1895–1977)
US comedian
A man is only as old as the woman he feels.

Attr.

Mead, Margaret (1901–1978)
US anthropologist, psychologist and writer
Women want mediocre men, and men are working to be as mediocre as possible.

Quote Magazine, 1958

Mencken, H.L. (1880–1956)
US writer, critic, philologist and satirist
Every normal man must be tempted, at times, to spit on his hands, hoist the black flag, and begin slitting throats.

Prejudices (1922)

Women hate revolutions and revolutionists. They like men who are docile, and well-regarded at the bank, and never late at meals.

Prejudices (1922)

Men have a much better time of it than women. For one thing, they marry later. For another thing, they die earlier.

A Mencken Chrestomathy (1949)

Meredith, George (1828–1909)
English writer, poet and critic
I expect that Woman will be the last thing civilized by Man.

The Ordeal of Richard Feverel (1859)

Norris, Kathleen (1880–1966)
US writer, pacifist and activist
There are men I could spend eternity with. But not this life.

The Middle of the World (1981)

O'Brien, Conan
A study in the *Washington Post* says that women have better verbal skills than men. I just want to say to the authors of that study: *Duh.*

Attr.

Palacio Valdés, Armando (1853–1938)
Cuando un hombre deja de ser un dios para su esposa, puede tener la seguridad de que ya es menos que un hombre.
When a man stops being a god for his wife, he can be sure that he's now less than a man.

Doctor Angélico's Papers (1911)

Parker, Dorothy (1893–1967)
US writer, poet, critic and wit
Men seldom make passes
At girls who wear glasses.

Not So Deep as a Well (1937)

Patmore, Coventry (1823–1896)
English poet
A woman is a foreign land,
Of which, though there he settle young,
A man will ne'er quite understand
The customs, politics, and tongue.

The Angel in the House (1854–1862)

Pizzey, Erin (1939–)
English writer and activist

> Men are gentle, honest and straightforward.
> Women are convoluted, deceptive and
> dangerous.
>
> *Attr. in The Observer, 1996*

Pope, Alexander (1688–1744)
English poet, translator and editor

> Men, some to business, some to pleasure take;
> But every Woman is at heart a rake:
> Men, some to quiet, some to public strife;
> But every lady would be queen for life.
>
> *'Epistle to a Lady' (1735)*

Ramey, Estelle (1917–)
US physiologist, educator and feminist

> More and more it appears that, biologically, men
> are designed for short, brutal lives and women
> for long miserable ones.
>
> *The Observer, 1985*

Rhondda, Viscountess (1883–1958)
English magazine editor and suffragette

> Women must come off the pedestal. Men put us
> up there to get us out of the way.
>
> *The Observer, 1920*

Rowland, Helen (1875–1950)
US writer

> Never trust a husband too far, nor a bachelor
> too near.
>
> *The Rubaiyat of a Bachelor (1925)*

Sainte-Beuve, Charles-Augustin (1804–1869)
French writer and critic

> One of the greatest satisfactions for a man is
> when the woman he passionately desired and
> who obstinately refused to give herself to him
> ceases to be beautiful.
>
> *Notebooks (1834–1847)*

Schreiner, Olive (1855–1920)
South African writer

> It is delightful to be a woman; but every man
> thanks the Lord devoutly that he isn't one.
>
> *The Story of an African Farm (1884)*

Shakespeare, William (1564–1616)
English dramatist, poet and actor

> O heaven, were man
> But constant he were perfect!
>
> *The Two Gentlemen of Verona, V.iv*

Shaw, George Bernard (1856–1950)
Irish socialist, writer, dramatist and critic

> A man who has no office to go to – I don't care
> who he is – is a trial of which you can have no
> conception.
>
> *The Irrational Knot (1905)*

Spark, Muriel (1918–)
Scottish writer, poet and dramatist

> Do you think it pleases a man when he looks
> into a woman's eyes and sees a reflection of the
> British Museum Reading Room?
>
> *In Cowan, The Wit of Women (1969)*

Stanton, Elizabeth Cady (1815–1902)
US suffragist, abolitionist, feminist, editor and writer

> Men are uniformly more attentive to women of
> rank, family, and fortune, who least need their
> care, than to any other class.
>
> *In Anthony and Gage (eds), History of Woman
> Suffrage (1881)*

Steinem, Gloria (1934–)
US writer and feminist activist

> A woman needs a man like a fish needs a
> bicycle.
>
> *Attr.*

Tennyson, Alfred, Lord (1809–1892)
English lyric poet

> Man is the hunter; woman is his game:
> The sleek and shining creatures of the chase,
> We hunt them for the beauty of their skins;
> They love us for it, and we ride them down.
>
> *The Princess (1847)*

> Man for the field and woman for the hearth:
> Man for the sword and for the needle she:
> Man with the head and woman with the heart:
> Man to command and woman to obey;
> All else confusion.
>
> *The Princess (1847)*

Thackeray, William Makepeace (1811–1863)
Indian-born English writer

> 'Tis strange what a man may do, and a woman
> yet think him an angel.
>
> *The History of Henry Esmond (1852)*

Thatcher, Margaret (1925–)
English Conservative Prime Minister

> I always say that if you want a speech made you
> should ask a man, but if you want something
> done you should ask a woman.
>
> *Speech to a townswomen's
> guild, 1982*

Trollope, Anthony (1815–1882)
English writer, traveller and post office official

> How I did respect you when you dared to speak
> the truth to me! Men don't know women, or
> they would be harder to them.
>
> *The Claverings (1867)*

> Men are so seldom really good. They are so little
> sympathetic. What man thinks of changing
> himself so as to suit his wife? And yet men
> expect that women shall put on altogether new
> characters when they are married, and girls think
> that they can do so.
>
> *Phineas Redux (1874)*

Tucholsky, Kurt (1890–1935)
German satirist and writer

> *Die Frauen haben es ja von Zeit zu auch nicht leicht.*
> *Wir Männern aber müssen uns rasieren.*
> Women from time to time don't have it easy
> either. But we men have to shave.
>
> *Scraps (1973))*

Turnbull, Margaret (fl. 1920s–1942)
Scottish-born US writer and dramatist

> When a man confronts catastrophe on the road,
> he looks in his purse – but a woman looks in her
> mirror.
>
> *The Left Lady (1926)*

Twain, Mark (1835–1910)
US humorist, writer, journalist and lecturer
Responding to the question 'In a world without women what
would men become?'

> Scarce, sir. Mighty scarce.
>
> Attr.

Vail, Amanda (1921–1966)
US writer

> Sometimes I think if there was a third sex men
> wouldn't get so much as a glance from me.
>
> *Love Me Little (1957)*

West, Dame Rebecca (1892–1983)
English writer, critic and feminist
Defining an anti-feminist

> The man who is convinced that his mother was a
> fool.
>
> *The Clarion*

West, Mae (1892–1980)
US actress and scriptwriter

> A man in the house is worth two in the street.
>
> *Belle of the Nineties (film, 1934)*

> When women go wrong, men go right after
> them.
>
> In Weintraub, *The Wit and Wisdom of Mae*
> *West (1967)*

Whitton, Charlotte (1896–1975)
Canadian writer

> Whatever women do they must do twice as well
> as men to be thought half as good. Luckily, this
> is not difficult.
>
> *Canada Month, 1963*

Wilde, Oscar (1854–1900)
Irish poet, dramatist, writer, critic and wit

> Women represent the triumph of matter over
> mind, just as men represent the triumph of mind
> over morals.
>
> *The Picture of Dorian Gray (1891)*

> Men can be analysed, women … merely adored.
>
> *An Ideal Husband (1895)*

> All women become like their mothers. That is

their tragedy. No man does. That's his.

> *The Importance of Being Earnest (1895)*

> Men play the game; women know the score.
>
> *The Observer, 1982*

Woolf, Virginia (1882–1941)
English writer and critic

> It is the masculine values that prevail. Speaking
> crudely, football and sport are 'important'; the
> worship of fashion, the buying of clothes
> 'trivial'… This is an important book, the critic
> assumes, because it deals with war. This is an
> insignificant book because it deals with feelings
> of women in a drawing-room … everywhere and
> much more subtly the difference of values
> persists.
>
> *A Room of One's Own (1929)*

> Why are women … so much more interesting to
> men than men are to women?
>
> *A Room of One's Own (1929)*

▶▶ FEMINISM; HOMOSEXUALS; HUMANITY AND
HUMAN NATURE; MARRIAGE; WOMEN

merit

Benny, Jack (1894–1974)
US comedian
Said on receiving an award

> I don't deserve this, but I have arthritis, and I
> don't deserve that either.
>
> Attr.

Melbourne, Lord (1779–1848)
English statesman
On the Order of the Garter

> I like the Garter; there is no damned merit in it.
>
> In H. Dunckley, *Lord Melbourne (1890)*

Pope, Alexander (1688–1744)
English poet, translator and editor

> Good-humour can prevail,
> When airs, and flights, and screams, and
> scolding fail.
> Beauties in vain their pretty eyes may roll;
> Charms strike the sight, but merit wins the soul.
>
> *The Rape of the Lock (1714)*

Richardson, Samuel (1689–1761)
English novelist

> Desert and reward, I can assure her, seldom
> keep company.
>
> *Clarissa (1747–1748)*

Thatcher, Margaret (1925–)
English Conservative Prime Minister
Said after receiving school prize, aged nine

> I wasn't lucky. I deserved it.
>
> Attr.

Westmorland, John Fane, Tenth Earl of
(1759–1841)

> Merit, indeed! … We are come to a pretty pass if they talk of merit for a bishopric.
>> In C. Oman, *The Gascoyne Heiress* (1968)

millennium

Hume, Basil (1923–1999)
English Cardinal, Archbishop of Westminster
On millennium jamborees

> The crib will always be more important than the Dome.
>> *The Times*, 1999

James, P.D. (1920–)
English crime writer
Comment on the Millennium Dome

> O dome gigantic, dome immense;
> Built in defiance of common sense.
>> In *The Observer*, 1999

Sutch, Dom Antony
English Benedictine monk and headmaster
Comment on his plans for the millennium

> I will either take a large sleeping tablet and sleep through the whole thing, or become a waiter for the night. After all, monks are born to serve.
>> *The Times*, 1999

Waugh, Auberon (1939–)
English writer and critic

> All the signs are that the millennium is going to be one of the greatest flops of British social history.
>> *The Observer*, 1999

mind

Berkeley, Bishop George (1685–1753)
Irish philosopher and scholar

> All the choir of heaven and furniture of earth – in a word, all those bodies which compose the mighty frame of the world – have not any subsistence without a mind.
>> *A Treatise Concerning the Principles of Human Knowledge* (1710)

Bethell, Richard (1800–1873)
English judge

> His Lordship says he will turn it over in what he is pleased to call his mind.
>> In Nash, *Life of Westbury*

Bradley, F.H. (1846–1924)
English philosopher

> His mind is open; yes, it is so open that nothing is retained; ideas simply pass through him.
>> Attr.

Burke, Edmund (1729–1797)
Irish-born British statesman and philosopher

> The march of the human mind is slow.
>> *Speech on Conciliation with America* (1775)

Chesterton, G.K. (1874–1936)
English writer, poet and critic

> There is a road from the eye to the heart that does not go through the intellect.
>> *The Defendant* (1901)

Day Lewis, C. (1904–1972)
Irish-born British academic, writer and critic

> Those Himalayas of the mind
> Are not so easily possessed:
> There's more than precipice and storm
> Between you and your Everest.
>> *Transitional Poem* (1924), 'Those Himalayas of the Mind'

Dostoevsky, Fyodor (1821–1881)
Russian writer

> The mind is a tool, a machine, moved by spiritual fire.
>> Letter to his brother, 1838

Dyer, Sir Edward (c.1540–1607)
English poet and courtier

> My mind to me a kingdom is,
> Such present joys therein I find,
> That it excels all other bliss
> That earth affords or grows by kind.
> Though much I want which most
> would have,
> Yet still my mind forbids to crave.
>> 'In praise of a contented mind' (1588). Attr.

Gay, John (1685–1732)
English poet, dramatist and librettist

> Give me, kind heav'n, a private station,
> A mind serene for contemplation.
>> *Fables* (1738)

Hamilton, Sir William (1788–1856)
Scottish metaphysical philosopher
Quoting Phavorinus

> On earth there is nothing great but man; in man there is nothing great but mind.
>> *Lectures on Metaphysics and Logic* (1859)

Hopkins, Gerard Manley (1844–1889)
English Jesuit priest, poet and classicist

> O the mind, mind has mountains; cliffs of fall
> Frightful, sheer, no-man-fathomed.
>> 'No Worst, there is None' (1885)

Hubbard, Elbert (1856–1915)
US printer, editor, writer and businessman

> Little minds are interested in the extraordinary;

great minds in the commonplace.
> *A Thousand and One Epigrams* (1911)

Jung, Carl Gustav (1875–1961)
Swiss psychiatrist and pupil of Freud
> *Das geistige Pendel schwingt zwischen Sin und Unsinn und nicht zwischen richtig und unrichtig.*
> The pendulum of the mind swings between sense and nonsense, and not between what is right and what is wrong.
> *Memories, Dreams, Thoughts* (1962)'

La Rochefoucauld (1613–1680)
French writer
> *L'esprit est toujours la dupe du coeur.*
> The mind is always fooled by the heart.
> *Maximes* (1678)

Pirsig, Robert (1928–)
US author
> That's the classical mind at work, runs fine inside but looks dingy on the surface.
> *Zen and the Art of Motorcycle Maintenance* (1974)

Prior, Matthew (1664–1721)
English poet
> Be to her virtues very kind;
> Be to her faults a little blind;
> Let all her ways be unconfin'd;
> And clap your padlock – on her mind.
> 'An English Padlock' (1705)

Punch
> What is Matter? – Never mind.
> What is Mind? – No matter.
> 1855

Radcliffe-Brown, Alfred Reginald (1881–1935)
British social anthropologist
On the anthropologist and reformer, Daisy Bates
> The contents of her mind … were somewhat similar to the contents of a well-stored sewing-basket after half a dozen kittens had been playing there undisturbed for a few days.
> In E.L. Grant Watson, *But to What Purpose*

Ryle, Gilbert (1900–1976)
English philosopher
> The dogma of the Ghost in the Machine.
> *The Concept of Mind* (1949)

Sallust (86–c.34 BC)
Roman historian and statesman
> *Dux atque imperator vitae mortalium animus est.*
> The mind is the guide and ruler of men's lives.
> *Jugurtha*

Shakespeare, William (1564–1616)
English dramatist, poet and actor
> In nature there's no blemish but the mind:
> None can be call'd deform'd but the unkind.
> *Twelfth Night*, III.iv

Shaw, George Bernard (1856–1950)
Irish socialist, writer, dramatist and critic
> One man that has a mind and knows it can always beat ten men who haven't and don't.
> *The Apple Cart* (1930)

Sherrington, Sir Charles Scott (1857–1952)
> If it is for mind that we are searching the brain, then we are supposing the brain to be much more than a telephone-exchange. We are supposing it a telephone-exchange along with the subscribers as well.
> *Man on his Nature*

Smith, Sydney (1771–1845)
English clergyman, essayist, journalist and wit
> Not body enough to cover his mind decently with; his intellect is improperly exposed.
> In Holland, *A Memoir of the Reverend Sydney Smith* (1855)

Snyder, Gary (1930–)
US mystical poet
> A clear, attentive mind
> Has no meaning but that
> Which sees is truly seen.
> *Riprap* (1959)

Spark, Muriel (1918–)
Scottish writer, poet and dramatist
> A short neck denotes a good mind … You see, the messages go quicker to the brain because they've shorter to go.
> *The Ballad of Peckham Rye* (1960)

Walpole, Horace (1717–1797)
English writer and politician
> When people will not weed their own minds, they are apt to be overrun with nettles.
> Letter to the Countess of Ailesbury, 1779

Welch, Raquel (1940–)
US actress
> The mind can also be an erogenous zone.
> Attr.

Williams, William Carlos (1883–1963)
US poet, writer and paediatrician
> Minds like beds always made up,
> (more stony than a shore)
> unwilling or unable.
> *Paterson* (1958)

▶▶ IDEAS; INTELLIGENCE; THOUGHT

mistakes

Anonymous
> No one is listening until you make a mistake.

> In any collection of data, the figure most

obviously correct, beyond all need of checking, is the mistake.

Finagle's Third Law

Boulay de la Meurthe, Antoine (1761–1840)
On the execution of the Duc d'Enghien, 1804
> *C'est pire qu'un crime, c'est une faute.*
> It is worse than a crime; it is a mistake.

Attr.

Cromwell, Oliver (1599–1658)
English general, statesman and Puritan leader
> I beseech you, in the bowels of Christ, think it possible you may be mistaken.

Letter to the General Assembly of the Church of Scotland, 1650

Doyle, Sir Arthur Conan (1859–1930)
Scottish writer and war correspondent
> It is a capital mistake to theorize before one has data.

The Adventures of Sherlock Holmes (1892)

Eliot, George (1819–1880)
English writer and poet

> Among all forms of mistake, prophecy is the most gratuitous.

Middlemarch (1872)

Halifax, Lord (1633–1695)
English politician, courtier, pamphleteer and epigrammatist
> It is a general Mistake to think the Men we like are good for every thing, and those we do not, good for nothing.

Political, Moral and Miscellaneous Thoughts and Reflections (1750)

Hubbard, Elbert (1856–1915)
US printer, editor, writer and businessman
> The greatest mistake you can make in life is to be continually fearing you will make one.

Johnson, Samuel (1709–1784)
English lexicographer, poet, critic, conversationalist and essayist
Asked the reason for a mistake in his Dictionary
> Ignorance, madam, sheer ignorance.

In Boswell, *The Life of Samuel Johnson* (1791)

Kissinger, Henry (1923–)
German-born US Secretary of State
On the second volume of his memoirs, *Years of Upheaval*
> I am being frank about myself in this book. I tell of my first mistake on page 850.

The Observer, 1983

Phelps, E.J. (1822–1900)
US lawyer and diplomat
> The man who makes no mistakes does not usually make anything.

Speech, 1899

Reagan, Ronald (1911–)
US President
> You know, by the time you reach my age, you've made plenty of mistakes if you've lived your life properly.

The Observer, 1987

Sagan, Carl (1934–1996)
US astrophysicist
> In science it often happens that scientists say, 'You know that's a really good argument; my position is mistaken, ' and then they would actually change their minds and you never hear that old view from them again. They really do it. It doesn't happen as often as it should, because scientists are human and change is sometimes painful. But it happens every day. I cannot recall the last time something like that happened in politics or religion.

Lecture, 1987

Smiles, Samuel (1812–1904)
English writer
> We often discover what will do, by finding out what will not do; and probably he who never made a mistake never made a discovery.

Self-Help (1859)

Straw, Jack (1946–)
English Labour politician and Home Secretary
> The only people who never make mistakes are those who have never taken a decision.

The Observer, May 1999

Valéry, Paul (1871–1945)
French poet, mathematician and philosopher
> The able man is the one who makes mistakes according to the rules.

Bad Thoughts and Not So Bad

▶▶ ERROR; TRUTH

miracles

Agnelli, Giovanni (1921–)
Italian industrialist
> *I miracoli si possono fare, ma con il sudore.*
> Miracles can be made, but only by sweating.

Corriere della Sera, 1994

Arnold, Matthew (1822–1888)
English poet, critic, essayist and educationist
> Miracles do not happen.

Literature and Dogma (1883 edition)

Hume, David (1711–1776)
Scottish philosopher and political economist
> The Christian religion not only was at first attended with miracles, but even at this day cannot be believed by any reasonable person

without one. Mere reason is insufficient to convince us of its veracity: and whoever is moved by Faith to assent to it, is conscious of a continued miracle in his own person, which subverts all the principles of his understanding, and gives him a determination to believe what is most contrary to custom and experience.

Philosophical Essays Concerning Human Understanding (1748)

No testimony is sufficient to establish a miracle, unless the testimony be of such a kind that its falsehood would be more miraculous than the fact which it endeavours to establish.

Philosophical Essays Concerning Human Understanding (1748)

Rice, Tim (1944–)
English songwriter
Herod to Christ
> Prove to me that you're no fool,
> Walk across my swimming pool.
'King Herod's Song', 1970, from *Jesus Christ Superstar!*

moderation

Aristotle (384–322 BC)
Greek philosopher
> Blessed is the state in which those in power have moderate and sufficient means since where some are immoderately wealthy and others have nothing, the result will be extreme democracy or absolute oligarchy, or a tyranny may result from either of these extremes.

Politics

Augustine, Saint (354–430)
Numidian-born Christian theologian and philosopher
> *Multi quidem facilius se abstinent ut non utantur, quam temperent ut bene utantur.*
> Many find it easier to abstain totally than to use moderation.

On the Good of Marriage

Bankhead, Tallulah (1903–1968)
US actress
> Let's not quibble! I'm the foe of moderation, the champion of excess. If I may lift a line from a die-hard whose identity is lost in the shuffle, 'I'd rather be strongly wrong than weakly right'.

Tallulah (1952)

Proverb
> Moderation in all things.

Terence (c.190–159 BC)
Carthaginian-born Roman dramatist
> *Id arbitror*
> *Adprime in vita esse utile, ut nequid nimis.*
> My view is that the golden rule in life is never to

have too much of anything.

Andria

Wilde, Oscar (1854–1900)
Irish poet, dramatist, writer, critic and wit
> Moderation is a fatal thing, Lady Hunstanton. Nothing succeeds like excess.

A Woman of No Importance (1893)

▶▶ EXCESS

modesty

Barrie, Sir J.M. (1860–1937)
Scottish dramatist and writer
> I'm a second eleven sort of chap.

The Admirable Crichton (1902)

Buchanan, Robert Williams (1841–1901)
British poet, writer and dramatist
> She just wore
> Enough for modesty – no more.

'White Rose and Red' (1873)

Churchill, Sir Winston (1874–1965)
English Conservative Prime Minister
Of Clement Attlee
> He is a modest man who has a good deal to be modest about.

In *Chicago Sunday Tribune Magazine of Books*, 1954

Congreve, William (1670–1729)
English dramatist
> Ah! Madam, … you know every thing in the world but your perfections, and you only know not those, because 'tis the top of perfection not to know them.

Incognita (1692)

Gilbert, W.S. (1836–1911)
English dramatist, humorist and librettist
> Wherever valour true is found,
> True modesty will there abound.

The Yeoman of the Guard (1888)

Russell, Bertrand (1872–1970)
English philosopher, mathematician, essayist and social reformer
> … the nuns who never take a bath without wearing a bathrobe all the time. When asked why, since no man can see them, the reply 'Oh, but you forget the good God.'

The Basic Writings of Bertrand Russell (1961)

Steele, Sir Richard (1672–1729)
Irish-born English writer, dramatist and politician
> These Ladies of irresistible Modesty are those who make Virtue unamiable.

The Tatler, 1710

monarchy and royalty

Abelard, Peter (1079–1142)
French theologian and philosopher
> *Quis rex, quae curia, quale palatium,*
> *Quae pax, quae requies, quod illud gaudium.*
> What a king, what a court, how fine a palace,
> what peace, what repose, what joy is there!
> > *Hymnus Paraclitensis*

Altrincham, Lord (John Grigg) (1924–)
English columnist and writer
On Queen Elizabeth II's style when speaking in public
> The personality conveyed by the utterances
> which are put into her mouth is that of a
> priggish schoolgirl, captain of the hockey team,
> a prefect, and a recent candidate for
> confirmation. It is not thus that she will be able
> to come into her own as an independent and
> distinctive character.
> > *National and English Review*, August 1958

Ames, Fisher (1758–1808)
US statesman and essayist
> A monarchy is a merchantman which sails well,
> but will sometimes strike on a rock, and go to
> the bottom; a republic is a raft which will never
> sink, but then your feet are always in the water.
> > Attr.

Andrews, Elizabeth
Said when an intruder was found in Queen Elizabeth II's
bedroom
> Bloody hell, Ma'am, what's he doing here?
> > *Daily Mail*, 1982

Anonymous
> Hark the herald angels sing
> Mrs Simpson's pinched our king.
> > Quoted by Clement Attlee in a letter of 26 December 1938

> Most Gracious Queen, we thee implore
> To go away and sin no more,
> But if that effort be too great,
> To go away at any rate.
> > Epigram on Queen Caroline, quoted in Lord Colchester's
> > Diary, 1820

Archer, Lord Jeffrey (1940–)
English Conservative politician and novelist
> An entire family of divorcees, and they're head
> of the Church of England. It's going to make the
> person out there wonder if it's all worth it.
> > Comment on the Royal Family, 1992

Bagehot, Walter (1826–1877)
English economist and political philosopher
> The Monarchy gives now a vast strength to the
> entire Constitution, by enlisting on its behalf the
> credulous obedience of enormous masses.
> > *The English Constitution* (1867)

> The sovereign has, under a constitutional
> monarchy such as ours, three rights – the right
> to be consulted, the right to encourage, the
> right to warn.
> > *The English Constitution* (1867)

> The mystic reverence, the religious allegiance,
> which are essential to a true monarchy, are
> imaginative sentiments that no legislature can
> manufacture in any people.
> > *The English Constitution* (1867)

> The best reason why Monarchy is a strong
> government is, that it is an intelligible
> government. The mass of mankind understand
> it, and they hardly anywhere in the world
> understand any other.
> > *The English Constitution* (1867)

> It has been said, not truly, but with a possible
> approximation to truth, 'that in 1802 every
> hereditary monarch was insane.'
> > *The English Constitution* (1867)

Beaverbrook, Lord (1879–1964)
Canadian-born British newspaper owner
Remark to Winston Churchill during the abdication crisis, 1936
> Our cock won't fight.
> > In Frances Donaldson, *Edward VIII* (1974)

Bentley, Edmund Clerihew (1875–1956)
English writer
> George the Third
> Ought never to have occurred.
> One can only wonder
> At so grotesque a blunder.
> > *More Biography* (1929)

Blackstone, Sir William (1723–1780)
English judge, historian and politician
> That the king can do no wrong, is a necessary
> and fundamental principle of the English
> constitution.
> > *Commentaries on the Laws of England* (1765–1769)

> The king never dies.
> > *Commentaries on the Laws of England* (1765–1769)

Blair, Tony (1953–)
British Labour Prime Minister
On hearing of the death of Diana, Princess of Wales,
31 August 1997
> She was the People's Princess, and that is how
> she will stay … in our hearts and in our
> memories forever.
> > *The Times*, 1997

Burchill, Julie (1960–)
English writer
Of Princess Diana of Wales
> She is Madonna crossed with Mother Theresa –
> a glorious totem of Western ideals.
> > *Sex and Sensibility* (1992)

Campbell, David (1915–1979)
Australian poet, rugby player and wartime pilot
> 'Hop in,' said the Queen Mother. In I piled
> Between them to lie like a stick of wood.
> I couldn't find a thing to say. My blood
> Beat, but like rollers at the ebb of tide.
> 'I hope Your Majesties sleep well,' I lied.
> A hand touched mine and the Queen said, 'I am
> Most grateful to you, Jock. Please call me
> Ma'am.'
>> 'The Australian Dream' (c.1965)

Carnegie, Andrew (1835–1919)
Scottish-born US millionaire and philanthropist
> A king is an insult to every other man in the
> land.
>> Letter, 1887

Charles Francis Joseph, Emperor of Austria (1887–1922)
On hearing of his accession to emperor
> What should I do? I think the best thing is to
> order a new stamp to be made with my face on it.
>> In H. Hoffmeister, *Anekdotenschatz*

Charles X (1757–1836)
King of France
> I would rather hew wood than be a king under
> the conditions of the King of England.
>> Attr.

Corneille, Pierre (1606–1684)
French dramatist, poet and lawyer
> *Et enfin la clémence est la plus belle marque*
> *Qui fasse à l'univers connaître un vrai monarque.*
> For in the end, mercy is the greatest sign by
> which the world may recognise a true king.
>> *Cinna* (1641)

Coward, Sir Noël (1899–1973)
English dramatist, actor, producer and composer
Coward had been asked, while watching the 1953 Coronation on TV, who the man was riding in a carriage with the portly Queen of Tonga
> Her lunch.
>> Attr.

Cunningham, Allan (1784–1842)
Scottish poet, reporter and biographer
> Wha the deil hae we got for a King,
> But a wee, wee German lairdie!
>> 'The Wee, Wee German Lairdie' (1825)

Disraeli, Benjamin (1804–1881)
English statesman and writer
To Queen Victoria
> Your Majesty is the head of the literary
> profession.
>> Attr.

In answer to Gladstone's taunt that Disraeli could make a joke of any subject, including Queen Victoria

> Her Majesty is not a subject.
>> Attr.

Asked if Queen Victoria should visit him during his last illness
> No, it is better not. She would only ask me to
> take a message to Albert.
>> Attr.

To Matthew Arnold
> Everyone likes flattery; and when you come to
> Royalty you should lay it on with a trowel.
>> Attr.

Edward VIII (later Duke of Windsor) (1894–1972)
King of the United Kingdom; abdicated 11 December 1936
On receiving a large bill from a luxury hotel
> Now what do I do with this?
>> Attr.

> I have found it impossible to carry the heavy
> burden of responsibility and to discharge my
> duties as King as I would wish to do without the
> help and support of the woman I love.
>> Abdication speech, 1936

Elizabeth I (1533–1603)
Queen of England
> I am your anointed Queen. I will never be by
> violence constrained to do anything. I thank God
> I am endued with such qualities that if I were
> turned out of the Realm in my petticoat I were
> able to live in any place in Christome.
>> Attr. Speech, 1566

> The queen of Scots is lighter of a fair son, and I
> am but a barren stock.
>> In F. Chamberlin, *The Sayings of Queen Elizabeth* (1923)

Of Mary Queen of Scots
> The daughter of debate, that eke discord doth
> sow.
>> In F. Chamberlin, *The Sayings of Queen Elizabeth* (1923)

Of the approaching Armada
> I know I have the body of a weak and feeble
> woman, but I have the heart and stomach of a
> king, and of a king of England too; and think
> foul scorn that Parma or Spain, or any prince of
> Europe, should dare to invade the borders of my
> realm.
>> Speech, 1588

> Though God hath raised me high, yet this I
> count the glory of my crown: that I have reigned
> with your loves.
>> The Golden Speech, 1601

Elizabeth II (1926–)
Queen of the United Kingdom
Comment about Princess Michael of Kent

She's more royal than we are.

> Attr., in *Sunday* magazine, 1985

Elizabeth, the Queen Mother (1900–)

Queen of the United Kingdom and mother of Elizabeth II

On whether, after the bombing of Buckingham Palace, her children would leave England

> The children will not leave unless I do. I shall not leave unless their father does, and the King will not leave the country in any circumstances whatever.
>
> Attr.

On hearing the National Anthem on TV

> Do turn it off. So embarrassing unless one is there. Like hearing the Lord's Prayer when playing canasta.
>
> *The Guardian*, 2000

Fabyan, Robert (d.1513)

English chronicler

> King Henry I being in Normandy, after some writers, fell from or with his horse, whereof he caught his death; but Ranulphe says he took a surfeit by eating of a lamprey, and thereof died.
>
> *The New Chronicles of England and France* (1516)

Farouk I (1920–1965)

Last king of Egypt

Remark made to Lord Boyd-Orr, 1948

> There will soon be only five kings left – the Kings of England, Diamonds, Hearts, Spades and Clubs.
>
> Attr.

Ferdinand I, Emperor of Austria (1793–1875)

> I am the emperor, and I want dumplings.
>
> In E. Crankshaw, *The Fall of the House of Habsburg* (1963)

Frederick the Great (1712–1786)

King of Prussia

> *Une couronne n'est qu'un chapeau qui laisse passer la pluie.*
> A crown is merely a hat that lets the rain in.
>
> Remark on declining a formal coronation, 1740

George III (1738–1820)

King of Great Britain and Ireland

> Born and educated in this country I glory in the name of Briton.
>
> Speech, 1760

George V (1865–1936)

King of the United Kingdom

Having just asked Ramsay MacDonald to form the first Labour Government

> Today, 23 years ago, dear Grandmama died. I wonder what she would have thought of a Labour Government.
>
> Diary, 22 January 1924

George VI (1895–1952)

King of the United Kingdom

> We're not a family; we're a firm.
>
> Attr. in Lane, *Our Future King*

Gilmour, Sir Ian (1926–)

Scottish Conservative politician

> The monarch is a person and a symbol. He makes power and state both intelligible and mysterious.
>
> *The Times*, 1992

Hamilton, William (Willie) (1917–)

British politician, teacher and antiroyalist

> The tourists who come to our island take in the Monarchy along with feeding the pigeons in Trafalgar Square.
>
> *My Queen and I* (1975)

Hanover, Ernst August, Elector of (1629–1698)

On seeing Louis XIV's stables at Versailles

> The king of France's horses are better housed than I am.
>
> Attr.

Hardie, Keir (1856–1915)

English Labour politician

> From his childhood onward this boy the future Edward VIII will be surrounded by sycophants and flatterers by the score – Cries of 'Oh, oh!' – and will be taught to believe himself as of a superior creation. Cries of 'Oh, oh!' A line will be drawn between him and the people whom he is to be called upon some day to reign over. In due course, following the precedent which has already been set, he will be sent on a tour round the world, and probably rumours of a morganatic alliance will follow – Loud cries of 'Oh, oh!' and 'Order!' – and the end of it all will be that the country will be called upon to pay the bill. – Cries of 'Divide!'.
>
> Speech, House of Commons, 1894

Hattersley, Roy (1932–)

British Labour politician and writer

> The institution of monarchy is inherently silly.
>
> *The Times*, 1998

Henri IV (1553–1610)

King of France

> *Je veux qu'il n'y ait si pauvre paysan en mon royaume qu'il n'ait tous les dimanches sa poule au pot.*
> It is my wish that in my kingdom there should be no peasant so poor that he cannot have a chicken in his pot every Sunday.
>
> In Hardouin de Péréfixe, *Histoire du Roy Henry le Grand* (1681)

Of James VI and I

> The wisest fool in Christendom.
>
> Attr.; also attributed to Sully

James V of Scotland (1512–1542)
King of Scotland
On the rule of the Stuart dynasty in Scotland
> It cam' wi' a lass, and it'll gang wi' a lass.
>> Remark, 1542

Jefferson, Thomas (1743–1826)
US Democrat statesman and President
> There is not a single crowned head in Europe whose talents or merit would entitle him to to be elected a vestryman by the people of any parish in America.
>> Attr.

Johnson, Lionel (1867–1902)
English poet and critic
> The saddest of all Kings
> Crown'd, and again discrown'd ...
> Alone he rides, alone,
> The fair and fatal king.
>> 'By the Statue of King Charles I at Charing Cross' (1895)

Jonson, Ben (1572–1637)
English dramatist and poet
> They say princes learn no art truly, but the art of horsemanship. The reason is, the brave beast is no flatterer. He will throw a prince as soon as his groom.
>> Timber, or Discoveries made upon Men and Matter (1641)

Kipling, Rudyard (1865–1936)
Indian-born British poet and writer
> He wrote that monarchs were divine,
> And left a son who – proved they weren't!
>> Songs written for C.R.L. Fletcher's A History of England (1911), 'James I'

Landor, Walter Savage (1775–1864)
English poet and writer
> George the First was always reckoned
> Vile, but viler George the Second;
> And what mortal ever heard
> Any good of George the Third?
> When from earth the Fourth descended
> God be praised, the Georges ended!
>> The Atlas, 1855

Lawson, Henry (1867–1922)
Australian writer and poet
> The Queen has lived for seventy years, for seventy years and three;
> And few have lived a flatter life, more useless life than she;
> She never said a clever thing or wrote a clever line,
> She never did a noble deed, in coming times to shine;
> And yet we read, and still we read, in every magazine,
> The praises of that woman whom the English call 'the Queen',
> Whom the English call 'the Queen',
> Whom the English call 'the Queen' –
> That dull and brainless woman whom the English call 'the Queen'.
>> 'The English Queen: A Birthday Ode'

Leopold II (1835–1909)
King of the Belgians
Instructing Prince Albert, the heir apparent, to pick up some papers from the floor
> A constitutional king must learn to stoop.
>> In Kelen, The Mistress

Louis XIV (1638–1715)
King of France
> *J'ai failli attendre.*
> I almost had to wait.
>> Attr.

Machiavelli (1469–1527)
Florentine statesman, political theorist and historian
> *Debbe, pertanto, uno principe non si curare della infamia di crudele, per tenere li sudditi suoi uniti e in fede.*
> In order to keep his people united and faithful, a prince must not be concerned with being reputed as a cruel man.
>> The Prince (1532)

Marvell, Andrew (1621–1678)
English poet and satirist
Of Charles II
> For though the whole world cannot shew such another,
> Yet we'd better by far have him than his brother.
>> 'The Statue in Stocks-Market' (1689)

Melbourne, Lord (1779–1848)
English statesman
Advising Queen Victoria against granting Prince Albert the title of King Consort
> For God's sake, ma'am, let's have no more of that. If you get the English people into the way of making kings, you'll get them into the way of unmaking them.
>> In Lord David Cecil, Lord M. (1954)

Pegler, Westbrook (1894–1969)
US journalist
On the abdication of Edward VIII
> He will go from resort to resort getting more tanned and more tired.
>> In Alistair Cooke, Six Men

Plato (c.429–347 BC)
Greek philosopher
> *Debbe, pertanto, uno principe non si curare della infamia di crudele, per tenere li sudditi suoi uniti e in fede.*
> Every king springs from a race of slaves, and

every slave has had kings among his ancestors.

Theaetetus

Prior, Matthew (1664–1721)
English poet
What is a King? – a man condemn'd to bear
The public burden of the nation's care.

Solomon (1718)

Rochester, Earl of (1647–1680)
English poet, satirist, courtier and libertine
A merry monarch, scandalous and poor.

'A Satire on King Charles II' (1697)

Here lies our sovereign lord the King
Whose word no man relies on,
Who never said a foolish thing,
Nor ever did a wise one.

Epitaph written for Charles II
(1706)

Roosevelt, Theodore (1858–1919)
US Republican President
Kings and such like are just as funny as
politicians.

In John Dos Passos, *Mr Wilson's War* (1963)

Schiller, Johann Christoph Friedrich (1759–1805)
German writer, dramatist, poet and historian
Die Könige sind nur Sklaven ihres Standes,
Dem eignen Herzen dürfen sie nicht folgen.
Kings are but slaves of their rank,
They may not follow their own heart.

Maria Stuart (1800)

Selden, John (1584–1654)
English historian, jurist and politician
A king is a thing men have made for their own
sakes, for quietness' sake. Just as in a family one
man is appointed to buy the meat.

Table Talk (1689)

Sellar, Walter (1898–1951) and **Yeatman, Robert Julian** (1897–1968)
British writers
Charles II was always very merry and was
therefore not so much a king as a Monarch.

1066 And All That (1930)

Shakespeare, William (1564–1616)
English dramatist, poet and actor
Uneasy lies the head that wears a crown.

Henry IV, Part 2, III.i

I think the King is but a man as I am: the violet
smells to him as it doth to me.

Henry V, IV.i

For God's sake let us sit upon the ground
And tell sad stories of the death of kings:
How some have been depos'd, some
slain in war,
Some haunted by the ghosts they have depos'd,

Some poison'd by their wives, some
sleeping kill'd,
All murder'd – for within the hollow
crown
That rounds the mortal temples of a
king
Keeps Death his court.

Richard II, III.ii

Thiers, Louis Adolphe (1797–1877)
French statesman and historian
The king reigns, and the people govern
themselves.

Le National, 1830

Thompson, William Hale 'Big Bill' (1867–1944)
US politician
If ever King George V were to set foot in
Chicago I'd punch him in the snoot.

Attr.

Twain, Mark (1835–1910)
US humorist, writer, journalist and lecturer
All kings is mostly rapscallions.

The Adventures of Huckleberry Finn (1884)

The institution of monarchy in any form is an
insult to the human race.

Notebook, 1888

Victoria, Queen (1819–1901)
Queen of the United Kingdom
We are not amused.

Attr. in Holland, *Notebooks of a Spinster Lady* (1919)

Wilson, Harold (1916–1995)
English Labour Prime Minister
The monarchy is a labour-intensive industry.

The Observer, 1977

Worsthorne, Sir Peregrine (1923–)
English journalist
A little more willingness to bore, and much less
eagerness to entertain, would do the monarchy
no end of good in 1993.

The Sunday Telegraph, 1993

Dull men do make the best kings.

Comment on BBC programme, *George VI – The
Reluctant King*, 1999

Zamoyski, Jan (1541–1605)
Polish Chancellor and army leader
The king reigns, but does not govern.

Speech, Polish Parliament, 1605

▶▶ GOVERNMENT

money and wealth

Adams, Franklin P. (1881–1960)
US writer, poet, translator and editor

The rich man has his motor car,
His country and his town estate.
He smokes a fifty-cent cigar
And jeers at Fate ...
Yet though my lamp burns low and dim,
Though I must slave for livelihood –
Think you that I would change with him?
You bet I would!

'The Rich Man'

Aesop (6th century BC)
Legendary Greek writer of fables
Wealth unused might as well not exist.

Attr

Agassiz, Louis (1807–1873)
Swiss naturalist
On lecturing for fees
I can't afford to waste my time making money.

Attr.

Alcott, Louisa May (1832–1888)
US writer
People don't have fortunes left them in that
style nowadays; men have to work and women
to marry for money. It's a dreadfully unjust
world.

Little Women (1869)

Allainval, Abbé d' (c.1700–1753)
French dramatist
L'Embarras des Richesses.
The embarrassment of riches.

Title of play, 1725

Anonymous
Money talks ... but all mine ever says is good-
bye.

Money no longer talks. It just goes without
saying.

In Lieberman, *3,500 Good Quotes for Speakers* (1983)

The almighty dollar is the only object of worship.

Philadelphia Public Ledger, 1860

You pays your money and you takes your choice.

Punch, 1846

Archer, Lord Jeffrey (1940–)
English Conservative politician and novelist
Reply to a journalist who asked whether it he had any regrets
in life
It's me sitting in this house with £50m in the
bank, not you.

The Times, 1998

Asquith, Margot (1864–1945)
Scottish political hostess and writer
Rich men's houses are seldom beautiful, rarely
comfortable, and never original. It is a constant
source of surprise to people of moderate means
to observe how little a big fortune contributes
to Beauty.

The Autobiography of Margot Asquith (1920)

Astor, John Jacob (1763–1848)
German-born US fur-trader and financier
A man who has a million dollars is as well off as
if he were rich.

Attr.

Bacon, Francis (1561–1626)
English philosopher, essayist, politician and courtier
Riches are a good handmaid, but the worst
mistress.

The Dignity and Advancement of Learning (1623)

And money is like muck, not good except it be
spread.

'Of Seditions and Troubles' (1625)

Baldwin, James (1924–1987)
US writer, dramatist, poet and civil rights activist
Money, it turned out, was exactly like sex, you
thought of nothing else if you didn't have it and
thought of other things if you did.

Nobody Knows My Name (1961)

Baring, Maurice (1874–1945)
English diplomat and writer
If you would know what the Lord God thinks of
money, you have only to look at those to whom
He gives it.

Attr.

Behn, Aphra (1640–1689)
English dramatist, writer, poet, translator and spy
Money speaks sense in a language all nations
understand.

The Rover (1677)

Belloc, Hilaire (1870–1953)
English writer of verse, essayist and critic; Liberal MP
Lord Finchley tried to mend the Electric Light
Himself. It struck him dead: And serve him right!
It is the business of the wealthy man
To give employment to the artisan.

More Peers (1911)

I'm tired of Love: I'm still more tired of Rhyme.
But Money gives me pleasure all the time.

Sonnets and Verse (1923)

Benchley, Robert (1889–1945)
US essayist, humorist and actor
Comment on being told his request for a loan had been
granted
I don't trust a bank that would lend money to
such a poor risk.

Attr.

Betjeman, Sir John (1906–1984)
English poet laureate
I've to prostitute myself to live comfortably and I
see no point in money except to buy off anxiety.

I don't want to be rich. I want to be unanxious.
Interview with Graham Lord, Sunday Express, 1974

The Bible (King James Version)
The love of money is the root of all evil.
I Timothy, 6:10

No man can serve two masters: – Ye cannot serve God and mammon.
Matthew, 6:24

The Bible (The New Testament in Scots)
Nae man can sair two maisters: aither he will ill-will the tane an luve the tither, or he will grip til the tane an lichtlifie the tither. Ye canna sair God an Gowd baith.
Matthew, 6:24

Brenan, Gerald (1894–1987)
English writer
Those who have some means think that the most important thing in the world is love. The poor know that it is money.
Thoughts in a Dry Season (1978)

Burke, Edmund (1729–1797)
Irish-born British statesman and philosopher
If we command our wealth, we shall be rich and free: if our wealth commands us, we are poor indeed.
Two Letters on the Proposals for Peace with the Regicide Directory of France

Butler, Samuel (1835–1902)
English writer, painter, philosopher and scholar
It has been said that the love of money is the root of all evil. The want of money is so quite as truly.
Erewhon (1872)

Carnegie, Andrew (1835–1919)
Scottish-born US millionaire and philanthropist
Surplus wealth is a sacred trust which its possessor is bound to administer in his lifetime for the good of the com-munity.
The Gospel of Wealth

Dennis, Nigel (1912–1989)
English writer, dramatist and critic
But then one is always excited by descriptions of money changing hands. It's much more fundamental than sex.
Cards of Identity (1955)

Dylan, Bob (1941–)
US singer and songwriter
Money doesn't talk, it swears.
'It's Alright, Ma (I'm Only Bleeding)' (song, 1965)

France, Anatole (1844–1924)
French writer and critic
Dans tout État policé, la richesse est chose sacrée; dans les démocraties elle est la seule chose sacrée.

In every well-governed state, wealth is a sacred thing; in democracies it is the only sacred thing.
Penguin Island (1908)

Galbraith, J.K. (1908–)
Canadian-born US economist, diplomat and writer
Wealth has never been a sufficient source of honor in itself. It must be advertised, and the normal medium is obtrusively expensive goods.
The Affluent Society (1958)

Wealth is not without its advantages, and the case to the contrary, although it has often been made, has never proved widely persuasive.
The Affluent Society (1958)

Money differs from an automobile, a mistress or cancer in being equally important to those who have it and those who do not.
Attr.

Getty, J. Paul (1892–1976)
US oil billionaire and art collector
The meek shall inherit the earth, but not the mineral rights.
Attr.

If you can actually count your money you are not really a rich man.
In A. Barrow, Gossip

Goldsmith, Oliver (c.1728–1774)
Irish dramatist, poet and writer
Ill fares the land, to hastening ills a prey,
Where wealth accumulates, and men decay;.
The Deserted Village (1770)

Gregory, Lady Isabella Augusta (1852–1932)
Irish dramatist, writer and translator
It's a good thing to be able to take up your money in your hand and to think no more of it when it slips away from you than you would of a trout that would slip back into the stream.
Twenty-Five

Healey, Denis (1917–)
English Labour politician
I warn you there are going to be howls of anguish from the 80,000 people who are rich enough to pay over 75% on the last slice of their income.
Speech, Labour Party Conference, 1 October 1973

Hoogstraten, Nicholas van
English property developer
Banning ramblers who claimed their was a public right of way across his land
The only purpose in creating wealth like mine is to separate oneself from the riff-raff.
The Observer, 1998

Horace (65–8 BC)
Roman lyric poet and satirist

Rem facias, rem si possis recte, si non, quocumque modo rem.
Make money: make it honestly if possible; if not, make it by any means.

Epistles

Hughes, Howard (1905–1976)
US millionaire industrialist, aviator and film producer
Response when called a 'paranoid, deranged millionaire' by a newspaper

Goddammit, I'm a billionaire.

Attr.

Huxley, Sir Julian Sorell (1887–1975)
English biologist and Director-General of UNESCO

We all know how the size of sums of money appears to vary in a remarkable way according as they are being paid in or paid out.

Essays of a Biologist

Illich, Ivan (1926–)
Austrian-born US educator, sociologist, writer and priest

Man must choose whether to be rich in things or in the freedom to use them.

Deschooling Society (1971)

Irving, Washington (1783–1859)
US writer and diplomat

The almighty dollar, that great object of universal devotion throughout our land.

Wolfert's Roost (1855)

Johnson, Samuel (1709–1784)
English lexicographer, poet, critic, conversationalist and essayist

Sir, the insolence of wealth will creep out.

In Boswell, *The Life of Samuel Johnson* (1791)

You never find people labouring to convince you that you may live very happily upon a plentiful fortune.

In Boswell, *The Life of Samuel Johnson* (1791)

There are few ways in which a man can be more innocently employed than in getting money.

In Boswell, *The Life of Samuel Johnson* (1791)

Kennedy, Joseph P. (1888–1969)
US businessman and diplomat

If you want to make money, go where the money is.

In A.M. Schlesinger Jr, *Robert Kennedy and his Times* (1978)

La Bruyère, Jean de (1645–1696)
French satirist

If we did not see it with our own eyes, could we ever imagine the extraordinary disproportion created between men by a larger or smaller degree of wealth?

Les caractères ou les moeurs de ce siècle (1688)

Lawrence, D.H. (1885–1930)
English writer, poet and critic

Money is our madness, our vast collective madness.

'Money-Madness' (1929)

Lennon, John (1940–1980)
English rock musician

For I don't care too much for money,
For money can't buy me love.

'Can't Buy Me Love', song, 1964, with Paul McCartney

Livingstone, Ken (1945–)
English Labour politician and Mayor of London

The working classes are never embarrassed about money – only the absence of it.

Comment, 1987

Lower, Lennie (1903–1947)
Australian journalist

The best way to tell gold is to pass the nugget around a crowded bar, and ask them if it's gold. If it comes back, it's not gold.

Here's Another (1932)

Luther, Martin (1483–1546)
German Protestant theologian and reformer

Darum gibt unser Herr Gott gemeiniglich Reichtum den groben Eseln, denen er sonst nichts gönnt.
For that reason our Lord God commonly gives wealth to those coarse asses to whom he grants nothing else.

Table Talk (1531–1546)

Macaulay, Lord (1800–1859)
English Liberal statesman, essayist and poet

We have heard it said that five per cent is the natural interest of money.

Collected Essays (1843)

MacNeice, Louis (1907–1963)
Belfast-born poet, writer, radio producer, translator and critic

Better authentic mammon than a bogus god.

Autumn Journal (1939)

It is particularly vulgar to talk about one's money – whether one has lots of it, and boasts about it, or is broke, and says so. Now I myself cannot see why a man should not talk about his money. Everybody is interested in everybody else's finances, and it seems hypocrisy to hush the subject up in the drawing room – as if bank balances were found under gooseberry bushes.

'In Defence of Vulgarity' (1937)

Mason, Jackie (1934–)
US comedian

I have enough money to last me the rest of my life, unless I buy something.

Jackie Mason's America

Maugham, William Somerset (1874–1965)
English writer, dramatist and physician

Money is like a sixth sense without which you

cannot make a complete use of the other five.
Of Human Bondage (1915)

Milligan, Spike (1918–)
Irish comedian and writer
> Money can't buy friends, but you can get a better class of enemy.
Puckoon (1963)

Milne, A.A. (1882–1956)
English writer, dramatist and poet
> For one person who dreams of making fifty thousand pounds, a hundred people dream of being left fifty thousand pounds.
If I May

Moravia, Alberto (1907–1990)
Italian writer
> *Ma è morto come potrebbe domani morire tanta gente come lui: correndo dietro al denaro e illudendosi che non ci sia che il denaro; e poi, improvvisamente, restando agghiacciato dalla paura alla vista di ciò che sta dietro il denaro.*
> But he died as many people like him could die tomorrow, running after money, and believing that there is nothing but money; then he was suddenly frozen by the fear of seeing what lies behind money.
Two Women (1957)

More, Sir Thomas (1478–1535)
English statesman and humanist
> Everyone knows that if money were abolished, fraud, theft, robbery, quarrels, brawls, seditions, murders, treasons poisonings and a whole set of crimes which are avenged but not prevented by the hangman would at once die out. If money disappeared, so would fear, anxiety, worry, toil and sleepless nights. Even poverty, which seems to need money more than anything else, would vanish if money were entirely done away with.
Utopia (1516)

Nicholson, Jack (1937–)
US film actor
> I am in an age group where it is rude to discuss money, and now it is all anyone cares about.
The Observer, 1999

Parsons, Tony (1953–)
British journalist and author
> There are few things in this world more reassuring than an unhappy Lottery winner.
The Observer, 1998

Pepys, Samuel (1633–1703)
English diarist, naval administrator and politician
> I bless God I do find that I am worth more than ever I yet was, which is £6,200, for which the Holy Name of God be praised!
Diary, October 1666

But it is pretty to see what money will do.
Diary, March 1667

Pindar (518–438 BC)
Greek lyric poet
> Water is best, but gold like fire blazing in the night shines more brightly than all other lordly wealth.
Olympian Odes

Porter, Cole (1891–1964)
US songwriter
> Who Wants to Be a Millionaire? I don't.
Title song, 1956, from *Who Wants to be a Millionaire?*

Porter, Sylvia (1913–1991)
US financial journalist
> Money never remains just coins and pieces of paper. Money can be translated into the beauty of living, a support in misfortune, an education, or future security. It also can be translated into a source of bitterness.
Sylvia Porter's Money Book (1975)

Price, Richard (1949–)
US screenwriter, actor and producer
> Money won is twice as sweet as money earned.
The Color of Money (film, 1986)

Proverbs
> A fool and his money are soon parted.
>
> Take care of the pence, and the pounds will take care of themselves.

Quant, Mary (1934–)
English fashion designer
> Having money is rather like being a blond. It is more fun but not vital.
The Observer, 1986

Reinhardt, Gottfried (1911–)
Austrian film producer
> Money is good for bribing yourself through the inconveniences of life.
In L. Ross, *Picture*

Rivers, Joan (1937–)
US comedian
> People say that money is not the key to happiness, but I always figured if you have enough money, you can have a key made.
Enter Talking (1986)

Runyon, Damon (1884–1946)
US writer
> Always try to rub up against money, for if you rub up against money long enough, some of it may rub off on you.
Furthermore (1938)

Ruskin, John (1819–1900)
English art critic, philosopher and reformer

There is no wealth but life.

Unto this Last (1862)

Whereas it has long been known and declared that the poor have no right to the property of the rich, I wish it also to be known and declared that the rich have no right to the property of the poor.

Unto this Last (1862)

Schopenhauer, Arthur (1788–1860)
German philosopher
Wealth is like sea-water; the more we drink, the thirstier we become; and the same is true of fame.

Parerga and Paralipomena (1851)

Scott, William (1745–1836)
The elegant simplicity of the three per cents.

In Campbell, *Lives of the Lord Chancellors*

Shakespeare, William (1564–1616)
English dramatist, poet and actor
Well, whiles I am a beggar, I will rail
And say there is no sin but to be rich;
And being rich, my virtue then shall be
To say there is no vice but beggary.

King John, II.i

If thou art rich, thou'rt poor;
For, like an ass whose back with ingots bows,
Thou bear'st thy heavy riches but a journey,
And Death unloads thee.

Measure For Measure, III.i

Shaw, George Bernard (1856–1950)
Irish socialist, writer, dramatist and critic
Money is indeed the most important thing in the world; and all sound and successful personal and national morality should have this fact for its basis.

The Irrational Knot (1905)

The universal regard for money is the one hopeful fact in our civilization, the one sound spot in our social conscience. Money is the most important thing in the world. It represents health, strength, honour, generosity and beauty as conspicuously and undeniably as the want of it represents illness, weakness, disgrace, meanness and ugliness.

Major Barbara (1907)

Sheridan, Tom (1775–1817)
To his father, after learning that he was to be cut out of his will with a shilling
I'm sorry to hear that, sir, you don't happen to have the shilling about you now, do you?

In L. Harris, *The Fine Art of Political Wit* (1965)

Sickert, Walter (1860–1942)
German-born British painter and writer
Nothing knits man to man ... like the frequent

passage from hand to hand of cash.

'The Language of Art'

Smith, Adam (1723–1790)
Scottish economist, philosopher and essayist
With the greater part of rich people, the chief enjoyment of riches consists in the parade of riches, which in their eyes is never so complete as when they appear to possess those decisive marks of opulence which nobody can possess but themselves.

Wealth of Nations (1776)'

Smith, Logan Pearsall (1865–1946)
US-born British epigrammatist, critic and writer
I love money; just to be in the room with a millionaire makes me less forlorn.

Afterthoughts (1931)

To suppose, as we all suppose, that we could be rich and not behave as the rich behave, is like supposing that we could drink all day and keep absolutely sober.

Afterthoughts (1931)

Socrates (469–399 BC)
Athenian philosopher
I see that you are indifferent about money, which is a characteristic rather of those who have inherited their fortunes than of those who have acquired them; the makers of fortunes have a second love of money as a creation of their own, resembling the affection of authors for their own poems, or of parents for their children, besides that natural love of it for the sake of use and profit which is common to them and all men. And hence they are very bad company, for they can talk about nothing but the praises of wealth.

In Plato's *Republic*

Stoppard, Tom (1937–)
British dramatist
I have always treated money as the stuff with which one purchases time.

Attr.

Swift, Jonathan (1667–1745)
Irish satirist, poet, essayist and cleric
If heaven had looked upon riches to be a valuable thing, it would not have given them to such a scoundrel.

Letter to Miss Vanhomrigh, 1720

Swinson, Antonia
British novelist
I am always fascinated by wealth makeovers for, like the 'before and after' style makeovers in women's magazines, I usually feel the subjects were better off before the advice was given.

Scotland on Sunday, 1999

Thatcher, Margaret (1925–)
English Conservative Prime Minister
> Pennies do not come from heaven. They have to be earned here on earth.
>> *The Sunday Telegraph*, 1982

Tucker, Sophie (1884–1966)
Russian-born US vaudeville singer
> From birth to eighteen, a girl needs good parents. From eighteen to thirty-five, she needs good looks. From thirty-five to fifty-five, she needs a good personality. From fifty-five on, she needs good cash.
>> In Freedland, *Sophie* (1978)

> I've been poor and I've been rich. Rich is better.
>> In Cowan, *The Wit of Women*

Twain, Mark (1835–1910)
US humorist, writer, journalist and lecturer
Agreeing with a friend's comment that the money of a particular rich industrialist was 'tainted'
> That's right. 'Taint yours, and 'taint mine.
>> Attr.

> A banker is a person who lends you his umbrella when the sun is shining and wants it back the minute it rains.
>> Attr.

Vanderbilt, William H. (1821–1885)
US financier and railway magnate
> I have had no real gratification or enjoyment of any sort more than my neighbor on the next block who is worth only half a million.
>> In B. Conrad, *Famous Last Words* (1961)

Vespasian (AD 9–79)
Roman emperor
> *Pecunia non olet.*
> Money does not smell.
>> In Suetonius, *Lives of the Caesars*

Wells, H.G. (1866–1946)
English writer
> I don't 'old with Wealth. What is Wealth? Labour robbed out of the poor.
>> *Kipps: the Story of a Simple Soul* (1905)

Williams, Tennessee (1911–1983)
US dramatist and writer
> You can be young without money but you can't be old without it.
>> *Cat on a Hot Tin Roof* (1955)

Youngman, Henry
US comedian
> I've got all the money I'll ever need – just so long as I die by four o'clock.
>> Attr.

▶▶ CAPITALISM; EXCESS; GREED; CONSUMER SOCIETY; INCOME

morality

Alcott, Louisa May (1832–1888)
US writer
> People want to be amused, not preached at, you know. Morals don't sell nowadays.
>> *Little Women* (1869)

Ayer, A.J. (1910–1989)
English philosopher
> No morality can be founded on authority, even if the authority were divine.
>> *Essay on Humanism*

Greene, Graham (1904–1991)
English writer and dramatist
> Morality comes with sad wisdom of age. When the sense of curiosity has withered.
>> Attr. in *The Observer*, 1996

Hardy, Thomas (1840–1928)
English writer and poet
> I like a story with a bad moral … all true stories have a coarse touch or a bad moral, depend upon't. If the story-tellers could ha' got decency and good morals from true stories, who'd have troubled to invent parables?
>> *Under the Greenwood Tree* (1872)

Hawthorne, Nathaniel (1804–1864)
US allegorical writer
> Dr Johnson's morality was as English an article as a beefsteak.
>> *Our Old Home* (1863)

Huxley, Aldous (1894–1963)
English writer, poet and critic
> The quality of moral behaviour varies in inverse ratio to the number of human beings involved.
>> *Grey Eminence* (1941)

Johnson, Samuel (1709–1784)
English lexicographer, poet, critic, conversationalist and essayist
> We are perpetually moralists, but we are geometricians only by chance. Our intercourse with intellectual nature is necessary; our speculations upon matter are voluntary, and at leisure.
>> 'Milton'

Jong, Erica (1942–)
US writer
> Your morals are like roads through the Alps. They make these hairpin turns all the time.
>> *Fear of Flying* (1973)

Kant, Immanuel (1724–1804)
German idealist philosopher
> *Endlich gibt es einen Imperativ, der, ohne irgend eine andere durch ein gewisses Verhalten zu erreichende*

Absicht als Bedingung zum Grunde zu legen, dieses Verhalten unmittelbar gebietet. Dieser Imperativ ist kategorisch … Dieser Imperativ mag der der Sittlichkeit heissen.

Finally, there is an imperative which immediately dictates a certain mode of behaviour, without having as its condition any other purpose to be achieved by means of that behaviour. This imperative is categorical … This imperative may be called that of morality.

Outline of the Metaphysics of Morals (1785)

Handle so, dass du die Menschheit, sowohl in deiner Person, als in der Person eines jeden andern, jederzeit zugleich als Zweck, niemals bloss als Mittel brauchest.

Act in such a way that you treat humanity, both in your own person as well as in that of any other, at any time as an end withal, never merely as a means.

Outline of the Metaphysics of Morals (1785)

Kraus, Karl (1874–1936)

Austrian scientist, critic and poet

Moral ist die Tendenz, das Bad mit dem Kinde auszuschütten.

Morality is the tendency to throw out the bath along with the baby.

Pro domo et mundo (1912)

Lawrence, D.H. (1885–1930)

English writer, poet and critic

Morality which is based on ideas, or on an ideal, is an unmitigated evil.

Fantasia of the Unconscious (1922)

Macaulay, Lord (1800–1859)

English Liberal statesman, essayist and poet

We know of no spectacle so ridiculous as the British public in one of its periodical fits of morality.

'Moore's Life of Byron' (1843)

Nietzsche, Friedrich Wilhelm (1844–1900)

German philosopher, critic and poet

Es gibt Herren-Moral und Sklaven-Moral.

There is master-morality and slave-morality.

Beyond Good and Evil (1886)

Moralität ist Herden-Instinkt im Einzelnen.

Morality is the herd-instinct in the individual.

The Gay Science (1887)

Pankhurst, Emmeline (1858–1928)

English suffragette

Men made the moral code and they expect women to accept it.

Speech, 1913

Proust, Marcel (1871–1922)

French writer and critic

On devient moral dès qu'on est malheureux.

One becomes moral as soon as one is unhappy.

A l'ombre des jeunes filles en fleurs (1918)

Russell, Bertrand (1872–1970)

English philosopher, mathematician, essayist and social reformer

We have, in fact, two kinds of morality side by side: one which we preach but do not practise, and another which we practise but seldom preach.

Sceptical Essays (1928)

Samuel, Lord (1870–1963)

English Liberal statesman, philosopher and administrator

Without doubt the greatest injury of all was done by basing morals on myth. For, sooner or later, myth is recognized for what it is, and disappears. Then morality loses the foundation on which it has been built.

Romanes Lecture, 1947

Shaw, George Bernard (1856–1950)

Irish socialist, writer, dramatist and critic

I'm one of the undeserving poor: that's what I am. Think of what that means to a man. It means that he's up agen middle class morality all the time … What is middle class morality? Just an excuse for never giving me anything.

Pygmalion (1916)

An Englishman thinks he is moral when he is only uncomfortable.

Man and Superman (1903)

Spencer, Herbert (1820–1903)

English philosopher and journalist

Absolute morality is the regulation of conduct in such a way that pain shall not be inflicted.

'Prison Ethics' (1891)

Stevenson, Robert Louis (1850–1894)

Scottish writer, poet and essayist

If your morals make you dreary, depend upon it, they are wrong.

Across the Plains (1892)

Wilde, Oscar (1854–1900)

Irish poet, dramatist, writer, critic and wit

The moral life of man forms part of the subject matter of the artist, but the morality of art consists in the perfect use of an imperfect medium.

The Picture of Dorian Gray (1891)

Morality is simply the attitude we adopt towards people whom we personally dislike.

An Ideal Husband (1895)

Wittgenstein, Ludwig (1889–1951)

Austrian philosopher

Ethics does not treat of the world. Ethics must be a condition of the world, like logic.

In Auden, *A Certain World*

▶▶ GOOD AND EVIL; GOODNESS; PRINCIPLES; VIRTUE

mortality

Anonymous

> *Gaudeamus igitur,*
> *Juvenes dum sumus*
> *Post jucundam juventutem,*
> *Post molestam senectutem,*
> *Nos habebit humus.*

Let us be happy while we are young, for after carefree youth and careworn age, the earth will hold us also.

'Gaudeamus Igitur', 13th century

Aurelius, Marcus (121–180)

Roman emperor and Stoic philosopher

> And you will give yourself peace if you perform each act as if it were your last.

Meditations

> Everything is ephemeral, both that which remembers and that which is remembered.

Meditations

Behn, Aphra (1640–1689)

English dramatist, writer, poet, translator and spy

> Faith, Sir, we are here today and gone tomorrow.

The Lucky Chance (1687)

The Bible (King James Version)

> All flesh is grass, and all the goodliness thereof is as the flower of the field.

Isaiah, 40:6

Dowson, Ernest (1867–1900)

English poet

> They are not long, the weeping and
> the laughter,
> Love and desire and hate:
> I think they have no portion in us after
> We pass the gate.
> They are not long, the days of wine
> and roses;
> Out of a misty dream
> Our path emerges for a while, then
> closes
> Within a dream.

'Vitae Summa Brevis Spem Nos Vetat Incohare Longam' (1896)

Herrick, Robert (1591–1674)

English poet, royalist and clergyman

> Gather ye Rose-buds while ye may,
> Old Time is still aflying:
> And this same flower that smiles today,
> Tomorrow will be dying.

Hesperides (1648)

> Faire Daffadills, we weep to see
> You haste away so soone:
> As yet the early-rising Sun
> Has not attain'd his Noone.
> Stay, stay,
> Untill the hasting day
> Has run
> But to the Even-song;
> And, having pray'd together, we
> Will goe with you along.
>
> We have short time to stay, as you,
> We have as short a Spring;
> As quick a growth to meet Decay,
> As you, or any thing.

Hesperides (1648)

Homer (fl. c.8th century BC)

Greek epic poet

> Like Leaves on Trees the Race of Man is found,
> Now green in Youth, now with'ring on the Ground,
> Another Race the following Spring supplies,
> They fall successive, and successive rise.

Iliad

Horace (65–8 BC)

Roman lyric poet and satirist

> *Omnem crede diem tibi diluxisse supremum.*
> Believe every day that has dawned is your last.

Epistles

Leacock, Stephen (1869–1944)

English-born Canadian humorist, writer and economist

> I detest life-insurance agents; they always argue that I shall someday die, which is not so.

Literary Lapses (1910)

Martial (c.AD 40–c.104)

Spanish-born Latin epigrammatist and poet

> *Bonosque*
> *Soles effugere atque abire sentit,*
> *Qui nobis pereunt et imputantur.*
> Each of us feels the good days hasten and depart, our days that perish and are counted against us.

Epigrammata

Marvell, Andrew (1621–1678)

English poet and satirist

> But at my back I always hear
> Time's wingèd chariot hurrying near.
> And yonder all before us lie
> Deserts of vast eternity.
> Thy beauty shall no more be found;
> Nor, in thy marble vault, shall sound
> My echoing song: then worms shall try
> That long preserved virginity:
> And your quaint honour turn to dust;
> And into ashes all my lust.

The grave's a fine and private place,
But none I think do there embrace.

'To His Coy Mistress' (1681)

Millay, Edna St Vincent (1892–1950)
US poet and dramatist

Death devours all lovely things:
Lesbia with her sparrow
Shares the darkness, – presently
Every bed is narrow ...

After all, my erstwhile dear,
My no longer cherished,
Need we say it was not love,
Just because it perished?

'Passer Mortuus Est' (1921)

Montaigne, Michel de (1533–1592)
French essayist and moralist

Il faut être toujours botté et prêt à partir.
One should always have one's boots on and be
ready to leave.

Essais (1580)

Moore, Thomas (1779–1852)
Irish poet

Oh! ever thus, from childhood's hour,
I've seen my fondest hopes decay;
I never lov'd a tree or flow'r,
But 'twas the first to fade away.
I never nurs'd a dear gazelle,
To glad me with its soft black eye,
But when it came to know me well,
And love me, it was sure to die!

Lalla Rookh (1817)

Shakespeare, William (1564–1616)
English dramatist, poet and actor

Since brass, nor stone, nor earth, nor boundless
sea,
But sad mortality o'erswears their power,
How with this rage shall beauty hold a plea,
Whose action is no stronger than a flower?

Sonnet 65

Spenser, Edmund (c.1522–1599)
English poet

So passeth, in the passing of a day,
Of mortall life the leafe, the bud, the flowre,
Ne more doth flourish after first decay,
That earst was sought to decke both bed and
bowre,
Of many a Ladie, and many a Paramowre:
Gather therefore the Rose, whilest yet is prime,
For soone comes age, that will her pride
deflowre:
Gather the Rose of love, whilest yet is time,
Whilest loving thou mayst loved be with equall
crime.

The Faerie Queene (1596)

Stevenson, Robert Louis (1850–1894)
Scottish writer, poet and essayist

Old and young, we are all on our last cruise.

Virginibus Puerisque (1881)

Thomas, Dylan (1914–1953)
Welsh poet, writer and radio dramatist

The force that through the green fuse drives the
flower
Drives my green age; that blasts the roots of
trees
Is my destroyer.
And I am dumb to tell the crooked rose
My youth is bent by the same wintry fever.

'The force that through the green fuse drives the
flower' (1934)

Young, Edward (1683–1765)
English poet, dramatist, satirist and clergyman

All men think all men Mortal, but themselves.

Night-Thoughts on Life, Death and Immortality
(1742–1746)

▶▶ DEATH; IMMORTALITY; LIFE; TIME

mothers

Achebe, Chinua (1930–)
Nigerian writer, poet and critic

It's true that a child belongs to its father. But
when a father beats his child, it seeks sympathy
in its mother's hut. A man belongs to his
fatherland when times are good and life is
sweet. But when there is sorrow and bitterness
he finds refuge in his motherland. Your mother is
there to protect you. She is buried there. And
that is why we say that mother is supreme.

Things Fall Apart (1958)

Alcott, Louisa May (1832–1888)
US writer

What do girls do who haven't any mothers to
help them through their troubles?

Little Women (1868)

Anonymous

You can fool all of the people some of the time,
and some of the people all of the time, but you
Can't Fool Mom.

Captain Penny's Law

Ballantyne, Sheila (1936–)
US writer

I acknowledge the cold truth of her death for
perhaps the first time. She is truly gone, forever
out of reach, and I have become my own judge.

Imaginary Crimes (1982)

Barker, George (1913–1991)
English poet and writer

Seismic with laughter,
Gin and chicken helpless in her Irish hand,
Irresistible as Rabelais, but most tender for
The lame dogs and hurt birds that surround her.

'Sonnet: To My Mother' (1944)

Barzan, Gerald

Mother always said that honesty was the best policy, and money isn't everything. She was wrong about other things too.

Attr.

Behan, Brendan (1923–1964)
Irish dramatist, writer and Republican

Never throw stones at your mother,
You'll be sorry for it when she's dead,
Never throw stones at your mother,
Throw bricks at your father instead.

The Hostage (1958)

Bombeck, Erma (1927–1996)
US humorist and writer

My mother phones daily to ask, 'Did you just try to reach me?' When I reply, 'No', she adds, 'So, if you're not too busy, call me while I'm still alive,' and hangs up.

The 1992 Erma Bombeck Calendar

Campbell, David (1915–1979)
Australian poet, rugby player and wartime pilot

The cruel girls we loved
Are over forty,
Their subtle daughters
Have stolen their beauty;
And with a blue stare
Of cool surprise
They mock their anxious mothers
With their mothers' eyes.

'Mothers and Daughters' (c.1965)

Dawe, (Donald) Bruce (1930–)
Australian poet

Mum, you would have loved the way you went!
one moment, at a barbecue in the garden
– the next, falling out of your chair,
hamburger in one hand,
and a grandson yelling.

'Going' (1970)

Edgeworth, Maria (1767–1849)
English-born Irish writer

My mother took too much, a great deal too much, care of me; she over-educated, over-instructed, over-dosed me with premature lessons of prudence: she was so afraid that I should ever do a foolish thing, or not say a wise one, that she prompted my every word, and guided my eyes, hearing with her ears, and judging with her understanding, till, at length, it was found out that

I had no eyes, or understanding of my own.

Vivian (1812)

Ellis, Alice Thomas (1932–)
British writer

Claudia … remembered that when she'd had her first baby she had realised with astonishment that the perfect couple consisted of a mother and child and not, as she had always supposed, a man and woman.

The Other Side of the Fire

Fisher, Dorothy Canfield (1879–1958)
US writer

A mother is not a person to lean on but a person to make leaning unnecessary.

Her Son's Wife (1926)

Freud, Sigmund (1856–1939)
Austrian physicist; founder of psychoanalysis

A mother is only brought unlimited satisfaction by her relation to a son; this is altogether the most perfect, the most free from ambivalence of all human relationships.

Freud on Women (1990)

Friday, Nancy (1937–)
US writer

Blaming mother is just a negative way of clinging to her still.

My Mother/My Self (1977)

Gay, John (1685–1732)
English poet, dramatist and librettist

Where yet was ever found a mother,
Who'd give her booby for another?

Fables (1727)

Greer, Germaine (1939–)
Australian feminist, critic, English scholar and writer

Mother is the dead heart of the family, spending father's earnings on consumer goods to enhance the environment in which he eats, sleeps and watches the television.

The Female Eunuch (1970)

Hubbard, Kin (1868–1930)
US humorist and journalist

The old-time mother who used to wonder where her boy was now has a grandson who wonders where his mother is.

Attr.

Proverb

God could not be everywhere, so therefore he made mothers.

Jewish proverb

Key, Ellen (1849–1926)
Swedish feminist, writer and lecturer

The mother is the most precious possession of the nation, so precious that society advances its highest wellbeing when it protects the functions of the mother.

The Century of the Child (1909)

Lawrence, D.H. (1885–1930)
English writer, poet and critic
On his relationship with his mother

> We have loved each other, almost with a husband and wife love, as well as filial and maternal … It has been rather terrible and has made me, in some respects, abnormal.

Attr.

Lazarre, Jane (1943–)
US journalist

> At her best, she is … quietly receptive and intelligent in only a moderate, concrete way; she is of even temperament, almost always in control of her emotions. She loves her children completely and unambivalently. Most of us are not like her.

The Mother Knot (1976)

Lindbergh, Anne Morrow (1906–)
US aviator, poet and writer

> By and large, mothers and housewives are the only workers who do not have regular time off. They are the great vacationless class.

Gift From the Sea (1955)

Masefield, John (1878–1967)
English poet, writer and critic

> In the dark womb where I began
> My mother's life made me a man.
> Through all the months of human birth
> Her beauty fed my common earth.
> I cannot see, nor breathe, nor stir,
> But through the death of some of her.

'C.L.M.' (1910)

Maugham, William Somerset (1874–1965)
English writer, dramatist and physician

> Few misfortunes can befall a boy which bring worse consequences than to have a really affectionate mother.

A Writer's Notebook (1949)

Olsen, Tillie (1913–)
US writer

> More than in any other human relationship, overwhelmingly more, motherhood means being instantly interruptible, responsive, responsible.

Silences: When Writers Don't Write (1965)

Paglia, Camille (1947–)
US academic and writer

> Every man must define his identity against his mother. If he does not, he just falls back into her and is swallowed up.

Sex, Art, and American Culture (1992)

Rayner, Claire (1931–)
English journalist

> Motherhood is a dead-end job. You've no sooner learned the skills than you are redundant.

Weekend Guardian, 1960

Riley, Janet Mary
US lawyer, educator and civil rights activist

> The role of mother is probably the most important career a woman can have.

The Times-Picayune, 1986

Scott-Maxwell, Florida (1884–1979)

> No matter how old a mother is, she watches her middle-aged children for signs of improvement.

The Measure of My Days (1968)

Shakespeare, William (1564–1616)
English dramatist, poet and actor

> *Paris*: Younger than she are happy mothers made.
> *Capulet*: And too soon marr'd are those so early made.

Romeo and Juliet, I.ii

> Thou art thy mother's glass, and she in thee
> Calls back the lovely April of her prime.

Sonnet 3

Stanton, Elizabeth Cady (1815–1902)
US suffragist, abolitionist, feminist, editor and writer

> … mothers of the race, the most important actors in the grand drama of human progress.

History of Woman Suffrage (1881)

Stead, Christina (1902–1983)
Australian writer

> A mother! What are we really? They all grow up whether you look after them or not.

The Man Who Loved Children (1940)

Stefano, Joseph (1922–)
US screenwriter

> A boy's best friend is his mother.

Psycho, screenplay, 1960

Taylor, Jane (1783–1824)

> Who ran to help me when I fell,
> And would some pretty story tell,
> Or kiss the place to make it well?
> My Mother.

Original Poems for Infant Minds (1804)

Wallace, William Ross (c.1819–1881)
US lawyer and poet

> The hand that rocks the cradle
> Is the hand that rules the world.

'What Rules the World' (c.1865)

Whistler, James McNeill (1834–1903)
US painter, etcher and pamphleteer
Explaining to a snobbish lady why he had been born in such an unfashionable place as Lowell, Massachusetts

The explanation is quite simple. I wished to be near my mother.

Attr.

Wilde, Oscar (1854–1900)
Irish poet, dramatist, writer, critic and wit
All women become like their mothers. That is their tragedy. No man does. That's his.

The Importance of Being Earnest (1895)

Wood, Mrs Henry (1814–1887)
English writer and editor
Dead! and … never called me mother.

East Lynne (stage adaptation, 1874)

▶▶ BABIES; BIRTH; CHILDREN; FAMILY; FATHERS; PREGNANCY

mountains

Auden, W.H. (1907–1973)
English poet, essayist, critic, teacher and dramatist
Five minutes on even the nicest mountain Is awfully long.

Mountains

Canetti, Elias (1905–1994)
Bulgarian-born English writer, dramatist and critic
You mountains, you mountains, you see it all and still you have not fallen on top of us.

The Human Province. Notes from 1942 to 1972 (1973)

Hillary, Sir Edmund (1919–)
New Zealand mountaineer, explorer and apiarist
Mount Everest is now littered with junk from bottom to top.

The Observer, 1982

Remark after first ascent of Mount Everest, 1953
Well, we knocked the bastard off!

Nothing Venture, Nothing Win (1975)

Lamb, Charles (1775–1834)
English essayist, critic and letter writer
Separate from the pleasure of your company, I don't much care if I never see another mountain in my life.

Letter to William Wordsworth, 1801

Mallory, George Leigh (1886–1924)
Asked why he wished to climb Mt Everest
Because it is there.

New York Times, 1923

Pope, Alexander (1688–1744)
English poet, translator and editor
Hills peep o'er hills, and Alps on Alps arise!

An Essay on Criticism (1711)

Ruskin, John (1819–1900)
English art critic, philosopher and reformer
Mountains are the beginning and the end of all natural scenery.

Modern Painters (1856)

Wordsworth, William (1770–1850)
English poet
A huge peak, black and huge, As if with voluntary power instinct Upreared its head.

The Prelude (1850)

mourning

Proust, Marcel (1871–1922)
French writer and critic
On l'enterra, mais toute la nuit funèbre, aux vitrines éclairées, ses livres disposés trois par trois veillaient comme des anges aux ailes éployées et semblaient, pour celui qui n'était plus, le symbole de sa résurrection.
They buried him, but all through the night of mourning, in lighted windows, his books arranged three by three kept watch like angels with outspread wings and seemed, for him who was no more, the symbol of his resurrection.

La Prisonnière (1923)

Rossetti, Christina (1830–1894)
English poet
When I am dead, my dearest, Sing no sad songs for me; Plant thou no roses at my head, Nor shady cypress tree: Be the green grass above me With showers and dewdrops wet; And if thou wilt, remember, And if thou wilt, forget.

'Song: When I am Dead' (1862)

Sitwell, Dame Edith (1887–1964)
English poet, anthologist, critic and biographer
A lady asked me why, on most occasions, I wore black. 'Are you in mourning?'
'Yes.'
'For whom are you in mourning?'
'For the world.'

Taken Care Of (1965)

Shakespeare, William (1564–1616)
English dramatist, poet and actor
No longer mourn for me when I am dead Than you shall hear the surly sullen bell Give warning to the world that I am fled From this vile world, with vilest worms to dwell.

Sonnet 71

▶▶ DEATH; REGRET

moustaches

Marx, Groucho (1895–1977)
US comedian

> There's a man outside with a big black
> moustache.
> – Tell him I've got one.
>
> *Horse Feathers* (film, 1932)

murder

James, Henry (1843–1916)
US-born British writer, critic and letter writer

> To kill a human being is, after all, the least injury
> you can do him.
>
> *Complete Tales* (1867)

Marx, Groucho (1895–1977)
US comedian

> My husband is dead.
> – I'll bet he's just using that as an excuse.
> I was with him to the end.
> – No wonder he passed away.
> I held him in my arms and kissed him.
> – So it was murder!
>
> *Duck Soup* (film, 1933)

Mortimer, John (1923–)
English lawyer, dramatist and writer

> Murderers are really very agreeable clients. I do
> think murderers get a very bad press.
>
> *The Observer*, 1999

Porteus, Beilby (1731–1808)
English religious writer

> One murder made a villain,
> Millions a hero.
>
> 'Death' (1759)

Saki (1870–1916)
Burmese-born British writer

> 'The man is a common murderer.'
> 'A common murderer, possibly, but a very
> uncommon cook.'
>
> *Beasts and Super-Beasts*
> (1914)

Sexby, Edward (d.1658)
English soldier and conspirator

> Killing noe Murder. Briefly Discourst in three
> quaestions.
>
> Title of pamphlet, 1657

Shakespeare, William (1564–1616)
English dramatist, poet and actor

> Murder most foul, as in the best it is;
> But this most foul, strange, and unnatural.
>
> *Hamlet*, I.v

Wainewright, Thomas Griffiths (1794–1847)
On being asked by a caller at Newgate prison how he could
have the barbarity to poison such a 'fair, innocent and trusting
creature' as his sister-in-law Helen Abercromby

> Upon my soul, I don't know, unless it was
> because she had such thick legs.
>
> In W.C. Hazlitt, *Wainewright's Essays* (1880)

Webster, John (c.1580–c.1625)
English dramatist

> Other sins only speak; murder shrieks out.
>
> *The Duchess of Malfi* (1623)

Whiteing, Richard (1840–1928)
English journalist and novelist

> 'Did you hear that fearful cry?'
> 'Ah! I 'eerd somethink.'
> 'There's murder going on – a woman, I think.'
> 'Dessay. It's Sat'dy night.'
>
> *No 5 John Street* (1899)

▶▶ CRIME

music

Addison, Joseph (1672–1719)
English essayist, poet, playwright and statesman

> Music, the greatest good that mortals know,
> And all of heaven we have below.
>
> 'Song for St Cecilia's Day' (1694)

Ade, George (1866–1944)
US fabulist and playwright

> The music teacher came twice a week to bridge
> the awful gap between Dorothy and Chopin.
>
> Attr.

Allen, Woody (1935–)
US film director, writer, actor and comedian

> I can't listen to that much Wagner. I start getting
> the urge to conquer Poland.
>
> *Manhattan Murder Mystery* (film. 1993)

Andersen, Hans Christian (1805–1875)
Danish writer and dramatist
Of the music to be played at his funeral

> Most of the people who walk after me will be
> children; make the beat keep time with little
> steps.
>
> In R. Godden, *Hans Christian Andersen* (1955)

Armstrong, Louis (1900–1971)
US jazz trumpeter, singer and bandleader

> When asked how he felt about people copying his style
> A lotta cats copy the Mona Lisa, but people still
> line up to see the original.
>
> Attr.

Beecham, Sir Thomas (1879–1961)
English conductor and impresario
On Elgar's A Flat Symphony

The musical equivalent of the towers of St Pancras station – neo-Gothic, you know.

> In N. Cardus, *Sir Thomas Beecham* (1961)

The English may not like music – but they absolutely love the noise it makes.

> In L. Ayre, *The Wit of Music* (1966)

On Beethoven's 7th Symphony

What can you do with it? – it's like a lot of yaks jumping about.

> In H. Atkins and A. Newman, *Beecham Stories: Anecdotes, Sayings and Impressions of Sir Thomas Beecham* (1978)

On Herbert von Karajan

He's a kind of musical Malcolm Sargent.

> In H. Atkins and A. Newman, *Beecham Stories: Anecdotes, Sayings and Impressions of Sir Thomas Beecham* (1978)

A musicologist is a man who can read music but can't hear it.

> Attr.

Of Bruckner's 7th Symphony

In the first movement alone, I took note of six pregnancies and at least four miscarriages.

> Attr.

At a dinner given in honour of his seventieth birthday, when messages of congratulation from great musicians all over the world were being read out, he was heard to murmur, 'What, nothing from Mozart?'.

> In Patricia Young, *Great Performers*

There are two golden rules for an orchestra: start together and finish together. The public doesn't give a damn what goes on in between.

> In Atkins and Newman, *Beecham Stories* (1978)

Of Bach

Too much counterpoint; what is worse, Protestant counterpoint.

> *The Guardian*, 1971

The sound of the harpsichord resembles that of a bird-cage played with toasting-forks.

> Attr.

Brass bands are all very well in their place – outdoors and several miles away.

> Attr.

Beethoven, Ludwig Van (1770–1827)
German composer
Said to a violinist complaining that a passage was unplayable

When I composed that, I was conscious of being inspired by God Almighty. Do you think I can consider your puny little fiddle when He speaks to me?

> Attr.

Belloc, Hilaire (1870–1953)
English writer of verse, essayist and critic; Liberal MP

It is the best of all trades, to make songs, and the second best to sing them.

> *On Everything* (1909)

Bernstein, Leonard (1918–1990)
US composer and conductor

I'm not interested in having an orchestra sound like itself. I want it to sound like the composer.

> *New York Times*, 1985

Birtwistle, Harrison (1934–)
English composer

I get someone to write the programme notes. Then I know what the piece is about.

> *The Observer*, 1996

You can't stop. Composing's not voluntary, you know. There's no choice, you're not free. You're landed with an idea and you have responsibility to that idea.

> *The Observer*, 1996

Browne, Sir Thomas (1605–1682)
English physician, author and antiquary

For there is a music wherever there is a harmony, order or proportion; and thus far we may maintain the music of the spheres; for those well ordered motions, and regular paces, though they give no sound unto the ear, yet to the understanding they strike a note most full of harmony.

> *Religio Medici* (1643)

Burney, Fanny (1752–1840)
English diarist

All the delusive seduction of martial music.

> *Diary*, 1802

Butler, Samuel (1835–1902)
English writer, painter, philosopher and scholar

How thankful we ought to feel that Wordsworth was only a poet and not a musician. Fancy a symphony by Wordsworth! Fancy having to sit it out! And fancy what it would have been if he had written fugues!

> *The Note-Books of Samuel Butler* (1912)

Carter, Betty (1929–1998)
US singer

If it wasn't for [pimps, prostitutes, hustlers, gangsters, and gamblers] there wouldn't be no jazz! They supported the club owners who bought the music. It wasn't the middle-class people who said 'Let's go hear Charlie Parker tonight.'

> *Jazz Forum*, 1979

Coltrane, John (1926–1967)
US jazz musician

All a musician can do is to get closer to the

sources of nature, and so feel that he is in communion with the natural laws.

Interview, 1962

Congreve, William (1670–1729)
English dramatist
Music has charms to soothe a savage breast.
The Mourning Bride (1697)

Coward, Sir Noël (1899–1973)
English dramatist, actor, producer and composer
Extraordinary how potent cheap music is.
Private Lives (1930)

Davis, Miles (1926–1991)
US jazz musician
I never thought that the music called 'jazz' was ever meant to reach just a small group of people, or become a museum thing locked under glass like all other dead things that were once considered artistic.
Miles (1989)

Debussy, Claude (1862–1918)
French composer and critic
Music is the arithmetic of sounds as optics is the geometry of light.
Attr.

Dryden, John (1631–1700)
English poet, satirist, dramatist and critic
What passion cannot Music raise and quell?
'A Song for St. Cecilia's Day' (1687)

Forster, E.M. (1879–1970)
English writer, essayist and literary critic
Beethoven's Fifth Symphony is the most sublime noise that ever penetrated into the ear of man.
Howard's End (1910)

Gaskell, Elizabeth (1810–1865)
English writer
We were none of us musical, though Miss Jenkyns beat time, out of time, by way of appearing to be so.
Cranford (1853)

Geldof, Bob (1954–)
Irish rock musician
I'm into pop because I want to get rich, get famous and get laid.
Attr.

Hendrix, Jimi (1942–1970)
US rock singer, songwriter and guitarist
Blues is easy to play, but hard to feel.
In Charles Shaar Murray, Crosstown Traffic (1989)

Herbert, George (1593–1633)
English poet and priest
Music helps not the tooth-ache.
Jacula Prudentum; or Outlandish Proverbs, Sentences &c. (1640)

Holiday, Billie (1915–1959)
US singer
You can't copy anybody and end with anything. If you copy, it means you're working without any real feeling. No two people on earth are alike, and it's got to be that way in music or it isn't music.
Lady Sings the Blues (1956)

I can't stand to sing the same song the same way two nights in succession, let alone two years or ten years. If you can, then it ain't music, it's close-order drill or exercise or yodeling or something, not music.
Lady Sings the Blues (1956)

Holst, Gustav (1874–1934)
English composer
Never compose anything unless the not composing of it becomes a positive nuisance to you.
Letter to W.G. Whittaker

Huxley, Aldous (1894–1963)
English writer, poet and critic
Since Mozart's day composers have learned the art of making music throatily and palpitatingly sexual.
Along the Road (1925)

Jagger, Mick (1943–)
English rock musician
On audiences that want songs the Rolling Stones sang 30 years ago.
The more I think about it the more awful it is.
The Times, 1998

Jennings, Paul (1918–1989)
British humorous writer
Of all musicians, flautists are most obviously the ones who know something we don't know.
The Jenguin Pennings, 'Flautists Flaunt Afflatus'

John, Elton (1947–)
English singer
The great thing about rock and roll is that someone like me can be a star.
The New York Times, 1992

Johnson, Samuel (1709–1784)
English lexicographer, poet, critic, conversationalist and essayist
Of music Dr Johnson used to say that it was the only sensual pleasure without vice.
In European Magazine, 1795

Jonson, Ben (1572–1637)
English dramatist and poet
Slow, slow, fresh fount, keep time with my salt tears:
Yet, slower, yet; O faintly, gentle springs:
List to the heavy part the music bears,

Woe weeps out her division, when she sings.

Cynthia's Revels (1600)

Lamb, Charles (1775–1834)
English essayist, critic and letter writer

I even think that sentimentally I am disposed to harmony. But organically I am incapable of a tune.

Essays of Elia (1823), 'A Chapter on Ears'

Landowska, Wanda (1877–1959)
Polish-born US harpsichordist
Remark to a fellow musician

Oh, well, you play Bach your way. I'll play him his.

Attr.

Lehrer, Tom (1928–)
US academic and songwriter

It is sobering to consider that when Mozart was my age he had already been dead for a year.

In N. Shapiro, *An Encyclopedia of Quotations about Music*

Lenin, V.I. (1870–1924)
Russian revolutionary, Marxist theoretician and first leader of the USSR
Remark made to Gorky, while listening to Beethoven

I can't listen to music too often. It affects your nerves; you want to say nice, stupid things and stroke the heads of people who could create such beauty while living in this vile hell. And now you must not stroke anyone's head – you might get your hand bitten off. You have to hit them on the head, without any mercy.

In Lev Trotsky, trans. M. Eastman, *The History of the Russian Revolution* (1933)

McLean, Don (1945–)
US singer
On the death of Buddy Holly

Something touched me deep inside
The day the music died.

'American Pie' (song, 1972)

Morrison, Van (1945–)
Irish singer

Music is spiritual. The music business is not.

The Times, 1990

Parker, Charlie (1920–1955)
US jazz musician and composer

Music is your own experience, your thoughts, your wisdom. If you don't live it, it won't come out of your horn.

In Shapiro and Hentoff, *Hear Me Talkin' to Ya* (1955)

They teach you there's a boundary line to music. But, man, there's no boundary line to art.

In Shapiro and Hentoff, *Hear Me Talkin' To Ya* (1955))

Parker, Henry Taylor (1867–1934)
US music critic

Rebuking some talkative members of an audience, near whom he was sitting

Those people on the stage are making such a noise I can't hear a word you're saying.

In L. Humphrey, *The Humor of Music*

Pavarotti, Luciano (1935–)
Italian opera singer

Learning music by reading about it is like making love by mail.

Reader's Digest, 1988

You don't need any brains to listen to music.

Attr.

Pepys, Samuel (1633–1703)
English diarist, naval administrator and politician

Went to hear Mrs Turner's daughter … play on the harpsichon; but, Lord! it was enough to make any man sick to hear her; yet was I forced to commend her highly.

Diary, May 1663

Music and women I cannot but give way to, whatever my business is.

Diary, 1666

Pound, Ezra (1885–1972)
US poet

Music begins to atrophy when it departs too far from the dance; … poetry begins to atrophy when it gets too far from music.

ABC of Reading (1934)

Previn, André (1929–)
German-born US conductor and composer

The basic difference between classical music and jazz is that in the former the music is always greater than its performance – whereas the way jazz is performed is always more important than what is being played.

In Shapiro, *An Encyclopedia of Quotations about Music*

Proverb

Music is the food of love.

Reddington, Helen
Lecturer in commercial music

The Beatles are a Shakespeare for the 20th century.

The Times, 1999

Rimsky-Korsakov, Nikolai (1844–1908)
Russian composer
Of Debussy's music

I have already heard it. I had better not go: I will start to get accustomed to it and finally like it.

In Robert Craft and Igor Stavinsky, *Conversations with Stravinsky* (1959)

Rossini, Gioacchino (1792–1868)
Italian composer

Monsieur Wagner a de beaux moments, mais de mauvais quart d'heures.

Wagner has beautiful moments but awful quarters of an hour.

In E. Naumann, Italienische Tondichter (1883)

Give me a laundry-list and I will set it to music.

Attr.

Santayana, George (1863–1952)
Spanish-born US philosopher and writer
> Music is essentially useless, as life is: but both have an ideal extension which lends utility to its conditions.
>
> The Life of Reason (1905–1906)

Sarasate (y Navascués), Pablo (1844–1908)
On being hailed as a genius by a critic
> A genius! For thirty-seven years I've practised fourteen hours a day, and now they call me a genius!
>
> Attr.

Sargent, Sir Malcolm (1895–1967)
English conductor
Rehearsing a female chorus in 'For Unto Us a Child is Born' from Handel's Messiah
> Just a little more reverence, please, and not so much astonishment.
>
> Attr.

Satie, Erik (1866–1925)
French composer
Direction on one of his piano pieces
> To be played with both hands in the pocket.
>
> Attr.

> The musician is perhaps the most modest of animals, but he is also the proudest. It is he who invented the sublime art of ruining poetry.
>
> In Pierre-Daniel Templier, Erik Satie

Schnabel, Artur (1882–1951)
Austrian pianist and composer
> I know two kinds of audience only – one coughing and one not coughing.
>
> My Life and Music (1961)

> The sonatas of Mozart are unique; they are too easy for children, and too difficult for artists.
>
> In Nat Shapiro (ed.), An Encyclopaedia of Quotations about Music (1978)

Advice given to the pianist Vladimir Horowitz
> When a piece gets difficult make faces.
>
> Attr.

> The notes I handle no better than many pianists. But the pauses between the notes – ah, that is where the art resides.
>
> Chicago Daily News, 1958

Schubert, Franz (1797–1828)
Austrian composer

> My compositions spring from my sorrows. Those that give the world the greatest delight were born of my deepest griefs.
>
> Diary, 1824

Shakespeare, William (1564–1616)
English dramatist, poet and actor
> In sweet music is such art,
> Killing care and grief of heart
> Fall asleep or hearing die.
>
> Henry VIII, III.i

> Music oft hath such a charm
> To make bad good and good provoke to harm.
>
> Measure For Measure, IV.i

> The man that hath no music in himself,
> Nor is not mov'd with concord of sweet sounds,
> Is fit for treasons, stratagems, and spoils;
> The motions of his spirit are dull as night,
> And his affections dark as Erebus.
> Let no such man be trusted.
>
> The Merchant of Venice, V.i

> How sour sweet music is
> When time is broke and no proportion kept!
> So is it in the music of men's lives.
>
> Richard II, V.v

> I have a reasonable good ear in music. Let's have the tongs and the bones.
>
> A Midsummer Night's Dream, IV.i

> Now, divine air! now is his soul ravish'd. Is it not strange that sheeps' guts should hale souls out of men's bodies?
>
> Much Ado About Nothing, II.iii

Shaw, George Bernard (1856–1950)
Irish socialist, writer, dramatist and critic
> At every one of those concerts in England you will find rows of weary people who are there, not because they really like classical music, but because they think they ought to like it.
>
> Man and Superman (1903)

> Hell is full of musical amateurs: music is the brandy of the damned.
>
> Man and Superman (1903)

Stevens, Wallace (1879–1955)
US poet, essayist, dramatist and lawyer
> Just as my fingers on these keys
> Make music, so the self-same sounds
> On my spirit make a music, too.

> Music is feeling, then, not sound.
> And thus it is what I feel,
> Here in this room, desiring you.

> Thinking of your blue-shadowed silk,
> Is music.
>
> 'Peter Quince at the Clavier' (1923)

Stravinsky, Igor (1882–1971)
Russian composer and conductor
> Rachmaninov's immortalizing totality was his
> scowl. He was a six-and-a-half-foot-tall scowl.
>> In Igor Stravinsky and Robert Craft, *Conversations
>> with Igor Stravinsky* (1958)

On Rachmaninov
> He was the only pianist I have ever seen who did
> not grimace. That is a great deal.
>> In Igor Stravinsky and Robert Craft, *Conversations
>> with Igor Stravinsky* (1958)

> My music is best understood by children and
> animals.
>> *The Observer*, 1961

Tennyson, Alfred, Lord (1809–1892)
English lyric poet
> Music that gentlier on the spirit
> lies,
> Than tir'd eyelids upon tir'd
> eyes.
>> 'The Lotos-Eaters'
>> (1832)

Thomas, Irene (1920–)
English writer and broadcaster
> The cello is not one of my favourite instruments.
> It has such a lugubrious sound, like someone
> reading a will.
>> Attr.

Toscanini, Arturo (1867–1957)
Italian conductor
Rebuking an incompetent woman cellist
> Madame, there you sit with that magnificent
> instrument between your legs, and all you can
> do is scratch it!
>> Attr.

Twain, Mark (1835–1910)
US humorist, writer, journalist and lecturer
> I have been told that Wagner's music is better
> than it sounds.
>> *Autobiography* (1959 edition)

Vaughan Williams, Ralph (1872–1958)
Asked what he thought about music
> It's a Rum Go!
>> Attr.

Vicious, Sid (1957–1979)
English punk singer
> You just pick a chord, go twang, and you've got
> music.
>> Attr.

Williamson, Malcolm (1931–)
Master of the Queen's Music
> Lloyd Webber's music is everywhere, but so is
> Aids.
>> Attr.

Zappa, Frank (1940–1993)
US rock musician, songwriter and record producer
> Most people wouldn't know music if it came up
> and bit them on the ass.
>> Attr.

> A composer? What the fuck do they do? All the
> good music's already been written by people
> with wigs and stuff.
>> Attr.

▶▶ CRITICISM; OPERA; SONGS AND SINGERS

N

names

Benét, Stephen Vincent (1898–1943)
US poet
> I have fallen in love with American names,
> The sharp gaunt names that never get fat,
> The snakeskin-titles of mining-claims,
> The plumed war-bonnet of Medicine Hat,
> Tucson and Deadwood and Lost Mule Flat.
>> 'American Names' (1927)

Fawsley, Lord St John of
British Conservative politician and constitutional expert
> Name-dropping is so vulgar, as I was telling the Queen last week.
>> In *The Observer*, 1999

Hazlitt, William (1778–1830)
English writer and critic
> A nickname is the heaviest stone that the devil can throw at a man.
>> *Edinburgh Magazine*, 1818'

Hewitt, John (1907–1987)
Irish poet and museum and art gallery director
> The names of a land show the heart of the race;
> They move on the tongue like the lilt of a song.
> You say the name and I see the place –
> Drumbo, Dungannon, or Annalong.
> Barony, townland, we cannot go wrong.
>> 'Ulster Names'

Huxley, Aldous (1894–1963)
English writer, poet and critic
> It's like the question of the authorship of the Iliad … The author of that poem is either Homer or, if not Homer, somebody else of the same name.
>> *Those Barren Leaves* (1925)

Joyce, James (1882–1941)
Irish writer
> I am afraid I am more interested, Mr Connolly, in the Dublin street names than in the riddle of the universe.
>> Remark to Cyril Connolly

Laurence, Margaret (1926–1987)
Canadian novelist
> Women have no surnames of their own. Their names are literally sirnames. Women only have one name that is ours, our first or given name.
>> *Dance on the Earth: A Memoir* (1989)

Marx, Groucho (1895–1977)
US comedian
> No, Groucho is not my real name. I'm breaking it in for a friend.
>> Attr.

Reid, Sir George Houstoun (1845–1918)
On being asked at a meeting, apropos of his stomach, 'What are you going to call it, George?'
> If it's a boy, I'll call it after myself. If it's a girl I'll call it Victoria after our Queen. But if, as I strongly suspect, it's nothing but piss and wind, I'll call it after you.
>> In Humphrey McQueen, *Social Sketches of Australia*

Shakespeare, William (1564–1616)
English dramatist, poet and actor
> What's in a name? That which we call a rose
> By any other name would smell as sweet.
>> *Romeo and Juliet*, II.ii

Sitwell, Dame Edith (1887–1964)
English poet, anthologist, critic and biographer
> Would you please substitute Dame Edith for Dr Sitwell. The Queen has honoured my poetry by making me a Dame, so that is now my name.
>> Letter to G. Singleton, 1955

Spooner, William (1844–1930)
English churchman and university warden
> I remember your name perfectly, but I just can't think of your face.
>> Attr.

Stein, Gertrude (1874–1946)
US writer, dramatist, poet and critic
> Rose is a rose is a rose is a rose, is a rose.
>> *Sacred Emily* (1913)

Vanzetti, Bartolomeo (1888–1927)
Italian-born US political radical
On his co-accused; a statement disallowed at his trial with Sacco for alleged armed robbery
> Sacco's name will live in the hearts of the people and in their gratitude when Katzmann's and yours bones will be dispersed by time, when your name, his name, your laws, institutions, and your false god are but a deem rememoring of a cursed past in which man was wolf to the man.
>> In Frankfurter and Jackson, *Letters of Sacco and Vanzetti* (1928)

nations

Bolingbroke, Henry (1678–1751)
English statesman, historian and actor
> Nations, like men, have their infancy.
>> *Letters on Study and Use of History* (1752)

Inge, William Ralph (1860–1954)

English divine, writer and teacher

A nation is a society united by a delusion about its ancestry and by a common hatred of its neighbours.

In Sagittarius and George, The Perpetual Pessimist

Kubrick, Stanley (1928–1999)

US screenwriter, producer and director

The great nations have always acted like gangsters, and the small nations like prostitutes.

The Guardian, 1963

McMillan, Joyce (1952–)

Scottish critic

… recognition of the suffering inflicted on peoples by their own leaders is undermining the idea of absolute national sovereignty, just as recognition of the unacceptability of domestic violence undermined the idea of absolute patriarchal rights in the family.

Scotland on Sunday, 1992

Parnell, Charles Stewart (1846–1891)

Irish nationalist politician

No man has a right to fix the boundary of the march of a nation: no man has a right to say to his country – thus far shalt thou go and no further.

Speech, 1885

Wilson, Woodrow (1856–1924)

US Democrat President

No nation is fit to sit in judgement upon any other nation.

Speech, 1915

nature

Addison, Joseph (1672–1719)

English essayist, poet, playwright and statesman

Should the whole frame of nature round him break,
In ruin and confusion hurled,
He, unconcerned, would hear the mighty crack,
And stand secure amidst a falling world.

Translation of Horace, Odes

Agassiz, Louis (1807–1873)

Swiss-born US naturalist

The study of Nature is intercourse with the Highest Mind. You should never trifle with Nature.

In Shulman and Asimov, Isaac Asimov's Book of Science and Nature Quotations (1988)

Akenside, Mark (1721–1770)

English poet

O ye Northumbrian Shades, which overlook
The rocky pavement and the mossy falls
Of solitary Wensbeck's limpid streams;
How gladly I recall your well-known seats
Beloved of old, and that delightful time
When all alone, for many a summer's day,
I wandered through your calm recesses, led
In silence by some powerful hand unseen.

The Pleasures of Imagination (1744)

Baudelaire, Charles (1821–1867)

French poet, translator and critic

La nature est un temple où de vivants piliers
Laissent parfois sortir de confuses paroles;
L'homme y passe à travers des forêts de symboles
Qui l'observent avec des regards familiers.

Nature is a temple in which living columns sometimes utter confused words. Man walks through it among forests of symbols, which watch him with knowing eyes.

Les Fleurs du mal (1857)

The Bible (King James Version)

While the earth remaineth, seedtime and harvest, and cold and heat, and summer and winter, and day and night shall not cease.

Genesis, 8:22

Bridges, Robert (1844–1930)

English poet, dramatist, essayist and doctor

Man masters nature not by force but by understanding.

Attr.

Browne, Sir Thomas (1605–1682)

English physician, author and antiquary

All things are artificial, for nature is the art of God.

Religio Medici (1643)

Burns, Robert (1759–1796)

Scottish poet and song writer

Gie me ae spark o' Nature's fire,
That's a' the learning I desire.

'First Epistle to Lapraik' (1785)

Byron, Lord (1788–1824)

English poet satirist and traveller

There is a pleasure in the pathless woods,
There is a rapture on the lonely shore,
There is society, where none intrudes,
By the deep Sea, and music in its roar:
I love not Man the less, but Nature more,
From these our interviews, in which I steal
From all I may be, or have been before,
To mingle with the Universe, and feel
What I can ne'er express, yet cannot all conceal.

Childe Harold's Pilgrimage (1818)

Chesterton, G.K. (1874–1936)

English writer, poet and critic

Is ditchwater dull? Naturalists with microscopes

have told me that it teems with quiet fun.

The Listener, 1936

Churchill, Charles (1731–1764)
English poet, political writer and clergyman
> It can't be Nature, for it is not sense.

'The Farewell' (1764)

Clarke, Marcus (1846–1881)
English-born Australian writer
> In Australia alone is to be found the Grotesque, the Weird, the strange scribblings of nature learning how to write.

Preface to A.L. Gordon, *Sea Spray and Smoke Drift* (1867)

Cowper, William (1731–1800)
English poet, hymn and letter writer
> Nature is but a name for an effect,
> Whose cause is God.

The Task (1785)

Curie, Marie (1867–1934)
Polish-born French physicist
> All my life through, the new sights of Nature made me rejoice like a child.

Pierre Curie

Darwin, Charles (1809–1882)
English naturalist
> What a book a devil's chaplain might write on the clumsy, wasteful, blundering, low, and horribly cruel works of nature!

Letter to J.D. Hooker, 1856

Donne, John (1572–1631)
English poet
> There is nothing that God hath established in a constant course of nature, and which therefore is done every day, but would seem a Miracle, and exercise our admiration, if it were done but once.

LXXX Sermons (1640)

Dylan, Bob (1941–)
US singer and songwriter
> I am against nature. I don't dig nature at all. I think nature is very unnatural. I think the truly natural things are dreams, which nature can't touch with decay.

In Robert Shelton, *No Direction Home* (1986)

Emerson, Ralph Waldo (1803–1882)
US poet, essayist, transcendentalist and teacher
> Nature is full of freaks, and now puts an old head on young shoulders, and then a young heart beating under fourscore winters.

Society and Solitude (1870)

Fielding, Henry (1707–1754)
English writer, dramatist and journalist
> All Nature wears one universal grin.

Tom Thumb the Great (1731)

Frank, Anne (1929–1945)
Jewish diarist; died in Nazi concentration camp
> The best remedy for those who are afraid, lonely or unhappy is to go outside, somewhere where they can be quiet, alone with the heavens, nature and God. Because only then does one feel that all is as it should be …

The Diary of Anne Frank (1947)

Gracián, Baltasar (1601–1658)
> *No es menester arte donde basta la Naturaleza.*
> Art is not essential where Nature is sufficient.

The Hero (1637)

Grey Owl (1888–1938)
English-born Canadian Indian imposter
> Civilisation says, 'Nature belongs to man.' The Indian says, 'No, man belongs to nature.'

Address at Norwich

Hawking, Stephen (1942–)
English theoretical physicist
> There are grounds for cautious optimism that we may now be near the end of the search for the ultimate laws of nature.

A Brief History of Time: From the Big Bang to Black Holes (1988)

Hepburn, Katharine (1909–)
US actress
As Rose Sayer to Humphrey Bogart's Charlie Allnut
> Nature, Mr Allnut, is what we are put in this world to rise above.

The African Queen (film, 1951)

Horace (65–8 BC)
Roman lyric poet and satirist
> *Naturam expelles furca, tamen usque recurret.*
> You may drive out Nature with a pitchfork, but she always comes hurrying back.

Epistles

Housman, A.E. (1859–1936)
English poet and scholar
> The cuckoo shouts all day at nothing
> In leafy dells alone –
> For nature, heartless, witless nature,
> Will neither care nor know
> What stranger's feet may find the meadow
> And trespass there and go,
> Nor ask amid the dews of morning
> If they are mine or no.

Last Poems (1922)

Hugo, Victor (1802–1885)
French poet, writer, dramatist and politician
> *La nature est impitoyable; elle ne consent pas à retirer ses fleurs, ses musiques, ses parfums et ses rayons devant l'abomination humaine.*
> Nature is unforgiving; she will not agree to withdraw her flowers, her music, her scents or

her rays of light before the abominations of man.

Ninety-three (1874)

Ingersoll, Robert G. (1833–1899)
US lawyer, soldier and writer

In nature there are neither rewards nor punishments – there are consequences.

Some Reasons Why (1881)

Linnaeus, Carl (1707–1778)
Swedish botanist

Natura non facit saltus.
Nature does not make progress by leaps and bounds.

Philosophia Botanica

Locke, John (1632–1704)
English philosopher

Nature never makes excellent things for mean or no uses.

Essay concerning Human Understanding (1690)

Milton, John (1608–1674)
English poet, libertarian and pamphleteer

In those vernal seasons of the yeer, when the air is calm and pleasant, it were an injury and sullennesse against nature not to go out, and see her riches, and partake in her rejoycing with heaven and earth.

Of Education: To Master Samuel Hartlib (1644)

Newton, Sir Isaac (1642–1727)
English scientist and philosopher

Nature is very consonant and conformable to her self.

Opticks (1730)

Whence is it that nature doth nothing in vain; and whence arises all that Order and Beauty which we see in the World?

Opticks (1730)

Pope, Alexander (1688–1744)
English poet, translator and editor

All Nature is but Art, unknown to thee;
All Chance, Direction which thou canst not see;
All Discord, Harmony, not understood;
All partial Evil, universal Good;
And, spite of Pride, in erring
Reason's spite,
One truth is clear, 'Whatever is, is right.'

An Essay on Man, I (1733)

Rabelais, François (c.1494–c.1553)
French monk, physician, satirist and humanist

Natura abhorret vacuum.
Nature abhors a vacuum.

Gargantua (1534)

Schiller, Johann Christoph Friedrich (1759–1805)
German writer, dramatist, poet and historian
Remark to Goethe

When Nature conquers, Art must then give way.

Es gibt Augenblicke in unserm Leben, wo wir der Natur in Pflanzen, Mineralen, Tieren, Landschaften sowie der menschliche Natur in Kindern, in den Sitten des Landvolks und der Urwelt, nicht weil sie unsern Sinnen wohltut, auch nicht weil sie unsern Verstand oder Geschmack befriedigt … sondern bloss weil sie Natur ist, eine Art von Liebe und von rührender Achtung widmen.
There are moments in our life when we accord a kind of love and touching respect to nature in plants, minerals, the countryside, as well as human nature in children, in the customs of country folk and the primitive world, not because it is beneficial for our senses, and not because it satisfies our understanding or taste either … but simply because it is nature.

'On Naive and Sentimental Poetry', 1795–1796)

Shakespeare, William (1564–1616)
English dramatist, poet and actor

In nature's infinite book of secrecy
A little I can read.

Antony and Cleopatra, I.ii

This is an art
Which does mend nature – change it rather; but
The art itself is nature.

The Winter's Tale, IV.iv

Smith, Alexander (1830–1867)
Scottish poet and writer

Nature, who makes the perfect rose and bird,
Has never made the full and perfect man.

City Poems (1857)

Snyder, Gary (1930–)
US mystical poet

My political position is to be a spokesman for wild nature. I take that as a primary constituency.

The Real Work, Interviews and Talks 1964–1979 (1980)

Tennyson, Alfred, Lord (1809–1892)
English lyric poet

So careful of the type she seems,
So careless of the single life …

Who trusted God was love indeed
And love Creation's final law –
Tho' Nature, red in tooth and claw
With ravine, shrieked against his creed.

In Memoriam A. H. H. (1850)

Thomas, R.S. (1913–)
Welsh poet

We will listen instead to the wind's text
Blown through the roof, or the thrush's song
In the thick bush that proved him wrong,
Wrong from the start, for nature's truth

Is primary and her changing seasons
Correct out of a vaster reason
The vague errors of the flesh.

Song at the Year's Turning (1955)

Thoreau, Henry David (1817–1862)
US essayist, social critic and writer
> I frequently tramped eight or ten miles through the deepest snow to keep an appointment with a beech-tree, or a yellow birch, or an old acquaintance among the pines.

Walden (1854)

Uvavnuk
Inuit singer and shaman
> The arch of sky and mightiness of storms
> Have moved the spirit within me,
> Till I am carried away
> Trembling with joy.

In Rasmussen, *Intellectual Culture of the Igulik Eskimos* (1929)

Vachell, Horace Annesley (1861–1955)
> In nature there are no rewards or punishments; there are consequences.

The Face of Clay (1906), 10

Voltaire (1694–1778)
French philosopher, dramatist, poet, historian writer and critic
> *Sachez que le secret des arts*
> *Est de corriger la nature.*
> Know that the secret of the arts is to correct nature.

Epîtres

Whistler, James McNeill (1834–1903)
US painter, etcher and pamphleteer
> Nature is usually wrong.

Mr Whistler's 'Ten O'Clock' (1885)

Whitman, Walt (1819–1892)
US poet and writer
> After you have exhausted what there is in business, politics, conviviality, and so on – have found that none of these finally satisfy, or permanently wear – what remains? Nature remains.

Specimen Days and Collect (1882)

Wordsworth, William (1770–1850)
English poet
> I have learned
> To look on nature, not as in the hour
> Of thoughtless youth; but hearing often-times
> The still, sad music of humanity.

'Lines composed a few miles above Tintern Abbey' (1798)

> Nature never did betray
> The heart that loved her.

'Lines composed a few miles above Tintern Abbey' (1798)

> One impulse from a vernal wood
> May teach you more of man,
> Of moral evil and of good,
> Than all the sages can …

> Sweet is the lore which Nature brings;
> Our meddling intellect
> Misshapes the beauteous forms of things:
> We murder to dissect.

'The Tables Turned' (1798)

▶▶ ANIMALS; BIRDS; HUMANITY AND HUMAN NATURE; FLOWERS; SCIENCE

the navy

Berlin, Irving (1888–1989)
Russian-born US musical and songwriter
> We joined the Navy to see the world,
> And what did we see? We saw the sea.

'We Saw the Sea', song, 1936; in film *Follow the Fleet*

Blackstone, Sir William (1723–1780)
English judge, historian and politician
> The royal navy of England hath ever been its greatest defence and ornament; it is its ancient and natural strength; the floating bulwark of the island.

Commentaries on the Laws of England (1765–1769)

Campbell, Thomas (1777–1844)
Scottish poet, ballad writer and journalist
> Britannia needs no bulwarks,
> No towers along the steep;
> Her march is o'er the mountain waves,
> Her home is on the deep.
> With thunders from her native oak
> She quells the floods below.

'Ye Mariners of England' (1801)

Charles II (1630–1685)
King of Great Britain and Ireland
> It is upon the Navy under the good Providence of God that the safety, honour, and welfare of this Realm do chiefly depend.

Preamble to Articles of War, 1652, in Callender, *The Naval Side of British History* (1924)

Churchill, Sir Winston (1874–1965)
English Conservative Prime Minister
> Don't talk to me about naval tradition. It's nothing but rum, sodomy and the lash.

In Gretton, *Former Naval Person* (1968)

Coventry, Thomas (1578–1640)
English Attorney-General and politician
> The dominion of the sea, as it is an ancient and undoubted right of the crown of England, so it is the best security of the land. The wooden walls

are the best walls of this kingdom.

Speech in Star Chamber, 1635

Drake, Sir Francis (c.1540–1596)
English navigator
I must have the gentleman to haul and draw with the mariner, and the mariner with the gentleman … I would know him, that would refuse to set his hand to a rope, but I know there is not any such here.

In Corbett, Drake and the Tudor Navy (1898)

Fisher, John Arbuthnot (1841–1920)
British admiral
On the ruinous cost of the Fleet and those responsible for it
You must be ruthless, relentless, and remorseless! Sack the lot!

Letter, The Times, 1919

The British navy always travels first class.

In W. Churchill, The Second World War (1948–1954)

Garrick, David (1717–1779)
English actor and theatre manager
Come cheer up, my lads! 'tis to glory we steer,
To add something more to this wonderful year;
To honour we call you, not press you like slaves,
For who are so free as the sons of the waves?
Heart of oak are our ships,
Heart of oak are our men:
We always are ready;
Steady, boys, steady;
We'll fight and we'll conquer again and again.

'Heart of Oak' (1759)

Glover, Denis (1912–1980)
New Zealand poet and printer
On overcrowding in Royal Navy ships
With five or six faces in front of a mirror it sometimes becomes a problem just which one to shave.

In Lehmann, I Am My Brother (1960)

Halsey, Admiral W.F. ('Bull') (1882–1959)
US naval commander
Our ships have been salvaged and are retiring at high speed toward the Japanese fleet.

Radio message, 1944, following claims by the Japanese that most of the American Third Fleet had been sunk or were retiring

Johnson, Samuel (1709–1784)
English lexicographer, poet, critic, conversationalist and essayist
No man will be a sailor who has contrivance enough to get himself into a jail; for being in a ship is being in a jail, with the chance of being drowned … A man in a jail has more room, better food, and commonly better company.

In Boswell, The Life of Samuel Johnson (1791)

Macaulay, Lord (1800–1859)
English Liberal statesman, essayist and poet
There were gentlemen and there were seamen in the navy of Charles the Second. But the seamen were not gentlemen; and the gentlemen were not seamen.

History of England (1849)

Mountbatten of Burma, First Earl (1900–1979)
English admiral and statesman
In my experience, I have always found that you cannot have an efficient ship unless you have a happy ship, and you cannot have a happy ship unless you have an efficient ship. That is the way I intend to start this commission, and that is the way I intend to go on – with a happy and an efficient ship.

Address to crew of HMS Kelly, 1939

Voltaire (1694–1778)
French philosopher, dramatist, poet, historian writer and critic
Referring to the execution of the British Admiral Byng for refusing to attack a French fleet
Dans ce pays-ci il est bon de tuer de temps en temps un amiral pour encourager les autres.
In this country it is considered a good idea to kill an admiral from time to time, to encourage the others.

Candide (1759)

▶▶ SEA; WAR

necessity

Cromwell, Oliver (1599–1658)
English general, statesman and Puritan leader
Necessity hath no law. Feigned necessities, imaginary necessities … are the greatest cozenage that men can put upon the Providence of God, and make pretences to break known rules by.

Speech to Parliament, 1654

Franklin, Benjamin (1706–1790)
US statesman, scientist, political critic and printer
Necessity never made a good bargain.

Poor Richard's Almanac (1735)

Proverb
Necessity is the mother of invention.

Publilius, Syrus (1st century BC)
Roman writer
Necessitas dat legem non ipsa accipit.
Necessity gives the law without itself recognizing any.

Sententiae

Necessitas non habet legem.

Necessity has no law.

Attr. proverb

Shakespeare, William (1564–1616)
English dramatist, poet and actor
> The art of our necessities is strange
> That can make vile things precious.

King Lear, III.ii

Thomson, James (1834–1882)
Scottish poet and dramatist
> I find no hint throughout the universe
> Of good or ill, of blessing or of curse;
> I find alone Necessity Supreme.

The City of Dreadful Night (1880)

Voltaire (1694–1778)
French philosopher, dramatist, poet, historian writer and critic
> *Le superflu, chose très nécessaire.*
> The superfluous, a very necessary thing.

Le Mondain (1736)

neglect

Franklin, Benjamin (1706–1790)
US statesman, scientist, political critic and printer
> A little neglect may breed mischief – for want of a nail, the shoe was lost; for want of a shoe, the horse was lost; and for want of a horse the rider was lost.

Poor Richard's Almanac (1758)

Johnson, Samuel (1709–1784)
English lexicographer, poet, critic, conversationalist and essayist
> I had done all I could; and no man is well pleased to have his all neglected, be it ever so little.

In Boswell, *The Life of Samuel Johnson* (1791)

Shakespeare, William (1564–1616)
English dramatist, poet and actor
> He was but as the cuckoo is in June,
> Heard, not regarded.

Henry IV, Part 1, III.ii

neighbours

Austen, Jane (1775–1817)
English writer
> For what do we live, but to make sport for our neighbours, and laugh at them in our turn?

Pride and Prejudice (1813)

The Bible (King James Version)
> Thou shalt love thy neighbour as thyself.

Leviticus, 19:18

Bradley, F.H. (1846–1924)
English philosopher
> The propriety of some persons seems to consist in having improper thoughts about their neighbours.

Aphorisms (1930)

Carlyle, Jane Welsh (1801–1866)
Scottish letter writer, literary hostess and poet
> Some new neighbours, that came a month or two ago, brought with them an accumulation of all the things to be guarded against in a London neighbourhood, viz, a pianoforte, a lap-dog, and a parrot.

Letter to Mrs Carlyle, 1839

Chesterton, G.K. (1874–1936)
English writer, poet and critic
> We make our friends, we make our enemies; but God makes our next-door neighbour.

Heretics (1905)

Cleese, John (1939–)
British comedian, actor and writer
> Loving your neighbour as much as yourself is practically bloody impossible … You might as well have a Commandment that states, 'Thou shalt fly'.

The Times, 1993

Frost, Robert (1874–1963)
US poet
> Something there is that doesn't love a wall –
> My apple trees will never get across
> And eat the cones under his pines, I tell him.
> He only says, 'Good fences make good neighbours.'

'Mending Wall' (1914)

Holmes, Oliver Wendell (1809–1894)
US physician, poet, writer and scientist
> But when our neighbours do wrong, we sometimes feel the fitness of making them smart for it, whether they have repented or not.

The Common Law (1881)

Horace (65–8 BC)
Roman lyric poet and satirist
> *Nam tua res agitur, paries cum proximus ardet.*
> For your own safety is at stake, when your neighbour's wall catches fire.

Epistles

Proverbs
> Good fences make good neighbours.
> Love your neighbour, but don't pull down the fence.

new zealand

Adams, Phillip (1939–)
On attitudes to New Zealanders
> And while we don't exactly hate New Zealanders, we're not exactly fond of each other. While they regard us as vulgar yobboes, almost Yank-like, we think of them as second-hand, recycled Poms.
>> *Age*, 1977

Allen, Dave (1936–)
Irish comedian and television personality
> New Zealanders are the most balanced people in the world – they have a chip on each shoulder.
>> A regular joke during his New Zealand tour, 1978

Anonymous
> The aircraft is now approaching New Zealand. Please move your watches forward two hours – and back 20 years.
>> Heard from a steward on a QANTAS flight from Sydney to Auckland, 1970

Of New Zealand; usually attributed to an American visitor
> Where do you go when the tide comes in?

Davison, Sir Ronald Keith (1920–)
New Zealand judge
Giving judgement in the trial of Alain Mafart and Dominique Prieur, two French agents charged with manslaughter and wilful damage over the bombing of the Greenpeace vessel *Rainbow Warrior*
> People who come to this country and commit terrorist activities cannot expect to have a short holiday at the expense of our government and return home as heroes.
>> In Michael King, *Death of the Rainbow Warrior* (1986)

Freud, Clement (1924–)
British Liberal politician, broadcaster and writer
On being asked his opinion of New Zealand
> I find it hard to say, because when I was there it seemed to be shut.
>> BBC radio, 1978

news and newspapers

Agnew, Spiro T. (1918–1996)
US Vice President
> Some newspapers are fit only to line the bottom of bird cages.
>> Attr.

Anonymous
> *The Times* is a tribal noticeboard.
>> Remark by a candidate for the editorship of the paper's Woman's Page in the 1960s

Arnold, Harry
British journalist
Commenting on the news that the Queen had started to refer privately to Royal reporters as 'scum'
> At least we're la crème de la scum.
>> *The Observer*, 1995

Arnold, Matthew (1822–1888)
English poet, critic, essayist and educationist
> The magnificent roaring of the young lions of the Daily Telegraph.
>> *Essays in Criticism* (1865)

Austen, Jane (1775–1817)
English writer
> Lady Middleton … exerted herself to ask Mr Palmer if there was any news in the paper. 'No, none at all,' he replied, and read on.
>> *Sense and Sensibility* (1811)

Baldwin, Stanley (1867–1947)
English Conservative statesman and Prime Minister
> What the proprietorship of these papers is aiming at is power, and power without responsibility – the prerogative of the harlot through the ages.
>> Speech at an election rally, 1931

Bennett, James Gordon (1841–1918)
Scottish-born US editor
> Deleted by French censor.
>> Used to fill empty spaces in his papers during World War I when news was scarce

Bevan, Aneurin (1897–1960)
Welsh Labour politician, miner and orator
> I read the newspapers avidly. It is my one form of continuous fiction.
>> *The Observer*, 1960

Bishop, Jim (1907–1987)
US author and journalist
> A newspaper is lumber made malleable. It is ink made into words and pictures. It is conceived, born, grows up and dies of old age in a day.
>> *Quill*, 1963

Beaverbrook, Lord (1879–1964)
Canadian-born British newspaper owner
> I ran the paper [*Daily Express*] purely for propaganda, and with no other purpose.
>> In A.J.P. Taylor, *Beaverbrook* (1972)

Bone, James (1872–1962)
Scottish journalist
Referring to C.P. Scott, former editor of *The Manchester Guardian*
> He made righteousness readable.
>> Attr.

Bradbury, Malcolm (1932–)
English writer, critic and academic
> Reading someone else's newspaper is like

sleeping with someone else's wife. Nothing seems to be precisely in the right place, and when you find what you are looking for, it is not clear then how to respond to it.

Stepping Westward (1965)

Cantona, Eric (1966–)
French footballer
Commenting on the interest taken by the press in the outcome of his court case

When the seagulls follow the trawler, it is because they think sardines will be thrown into the sea.

The Observer, 1995

Carlyle, Thomas (1795–1881)
Scottish historian, biographer, critic, and essayist
Burke said there were Three Estates in Parliament; but, in the Reporters' Gallery yonder, there sat a Fourth Estate more important far than they all.

'The Hero as Man of Letters' (1841)

Chesterton, G.K. (1874–1936)
English writer, poet and critic
It's not the world that's got so much worse but the news coverage that's got so much better.

Attr.

Cowper, William (1731–1800)
English poet, hymn and letter writer
Thou god of our idolatry, the press …
Thou fountain, at which drink the good and wise;
Thou ever-bubbling spring of endless lies;
Like Eden's dread probationary tree,
Knowledge of good and evil is from thee.

'The Progress of Error' (1782)

Crabbe, George (1754–1832)
English poet, clergyman, surgeon and botanist
A master-passion is the love of news.

The Newspaper (1785)

Dana, Charles Anderson (1819–1897)
US newspaper editor and reformer
When a dog bites a man that is not news, but when a man bites a dog that is news.

New York Sun, 1882

Devonshire, Duke of (1895–1950)
English politician
Referring to Stanley Baldwin's attack on newspaper proprietors

Good God, that's done it. He's lost us the tarts' vote.

Attr.

Drayton, Michael (1563–1631)
English poet
Ill news hath wings, and with the wind doth go,

Comfort's a cripple and comes ever slow.

The Barrons' Wars (1603)

Fairburn, A.R.D. (1904–1957)
New Zealand poet
The press: slow dripping of water on mud; thought's daily bagwash, ironing out opinion, scarifying the edges of ideas.

Collected Poems (1966)

Fielding, Henry (1707–1754)
English writer, dramatist and journalist
A newspaper, which consists of just the same number of words, whether there be news in it or not … may, likewise, be compared to a stagecoach, which performs constantly the same course, empty as well as full.

Tom Jones (1749)

Flaubert, Gustave (1821–1880)
French writer
Je regarde comme un des bonheurs de ma vie de ne pas écrire dans les journaux. Il en coûte ma bourse – mais ma conscience s'en trouve bien.
I regard the fact that I don't write for the newspapers as a source of happiness in my life. My purse suffers – but my conscience is glad of it.

Letter, 1866

Hearst, William Randolph (1863–1951)
US newspaper proprietor
Instruction to artist Frederic Remington, who wished to return from peaceful Havana in spring 1898

Please remain. You furnish the pictures and I'll furnish the war.

Attr. in Winkler, W.R. Hearst (1928)

Ignatieff, Michael (1947–)
Canadian writer and media personality
News is a genre as much as fiction or drama: it is a regime of visual authority, a coercive organization of images according to a stopwatch.

Daedalus, 1988

Kipling, Rudyard (1865–1936)
Indian-born British poet and writer
Of newspaper barons

Power without responsibility – the prerogative of the harlot throughout the ages.

Remark, quoted by Baldwin in 1931

Lamb, Charles (1775–1834)
English essayist, critic and letter writer
Newspapers always excite curiosity. No one ever lays one down without a feeling of disappointment.

Last Essays of Elia (1833)

Lincoln, Abraham (1809–1865)
US statesman and President

The London *Times* is one of the greatest powers in the world. In fact, I don't know anything which has much more power, except perhaps the Mississippi.

> Remark to *Times* correspondent William Howard Russell, 1861

Longford, Lord (1905–)
English politician, social reformer and biographer
> On the whole I would not say that our Press is obscene. I would say that it trembles on the brink of obscenity.
>
> *The Observer*, 1963

Macaulay, Lord (1800–1859)
English Liberal statesman, essayist and poet
> The gallery in which the reporters sit has become a fourth estate of the realm.
>
> *Collected Essays* (1843)

Mailer, Norman (1923–)
US writer
> Once a newspaper touches a story, the facts are lost forever, even to the protagonists.
>
> *The Presidential Papers* (1976)

Mankiewicz, Herman J. (1897–1953)
US journalist and screenwriter
> I run a couple of newspapers. What do you do?
>
> *Citizen Kane*, film (1941)

Marquis, Don (1878–1937)
US columnist, satirist and poet
> The art of newspaper paragraphing is to stroke a platitude until it purrs like an epigram.
>
> In Anthony, *O Rare Don Marquis* (1962)

Miller, Arthur (1915–)
US dramatist and screenwriter
> A good newspaper, I suppose, is a nation talking to itself.
>
> *The Observer*, 1961

Murdoch, Rupert (1931–)
Australian-born publisher and international businessman
On the publication of the *Kinsey Report*, a survey of human sexual behaviour
> Family newspapers like ourselves gain great kudos leaving this muck alone.
>
> Telegram sent to the *Adelaide News*, 1953

> I think the important thing is that there be plenty of newspapers with plenty of people controlling them so there can be choice.
>
> Film interview, 1967

Murray, David (1888–1962)
British writer
> A reporter is a man who has renounced everything in life but the world, the flesh, and the devil.
>
> *The Observer*, 1931

Ochs, Adolph S. (1858–1935)
US newspaper publisher and editor
> All the news that's fit to print.
>
> Motto of the *New York Times*

Phillips, Wendell (1811–1884)
US reformer
> We live under a government of men and morning newspapers.
>
> *Address: The Press*

Proverbs
> Bad news travels fast.

> No news is good news.

Salisbury, Lord (1830–1903)
English Conservative Prime Minister
Of the *Daily Mail*
> By office boys for office boys.
>
> In Fyfe, *Northcliffe, an Intimate Biography* (1930)

Scott, C.P. (1846–1932)
English newspaper editor and Liberal politician
> Comment is free, but facts are sacred.
>
> *Manchester Guardian*, 1921

Shakespeare, William (1564–1616)
English dramatist, poet and actor
> The nature of bad news infects the teller.
>
> *Antony and Cleopatra*, I.ii

> Though it be honest, it is never good
> To bring bad news. Give to a gracious message
> An host of tongues; but let ill tidings tell
> Themselves when they be felt.
>
> *Antony and Cleopatra*, II.v

Sheridan, Richard Brinsley (1751–1816)
Irish dramatist, politician and orator
> The newspapers! Sir, they are the most villainous – licentious – abominable – infernal – Not that I ever read them – No – I make it a rule never to look into a newspaper.
>
> *The Critic* (1779)

Stoppard, Tom (1937–)
British dramatist
> *Milne*: No matter now imperfect things are, if you've got a free press everything is correctable, and without it everything is conceivable.
> *Ruth*: I'm with you on the free press. It's the newspapers I can't stand.
>
> *Night and Day* (1978)

Referring to foreign correspondents
> He's someone who flies around from hotel to hotel and thinks the most interesting thing about any story is the fact that he has arrived to cover it.
>
> *Night and Day* (1978)

Swaffer, Hannen (1879–1962)
English writer

Freedom of the press in Britain is freedom to print such of the proprietor's prejudices as the advertisers don't object to.

In Driberg, Swaff (1974)

Waugh, Evelyn (1903–1966)
English writer and diarist

News is what a chap who doesn't care much about anything wants to read. And it's only news until he's read it. After that it's dead.

Scoop (1938)

Wellington, Duke of (1769–1852)
Irish-born British military commander and statesman

Possible? Is anything impossible? Read the newspapers.

In Fraser, Words on Wellington (1889)

Wolfe, Humbert (1886–1940)
Italian-born British poet, critic and civil servant

You cannot hope
To bribe or twist,
thank God! the
British journalist.
But, seeing what
the man will do
unbribed, there's
no occasion to.

'Over the Fire' (1930)

▶▶ JOURNALISM; MEDIA; TELEVISION

night

Blixen, Karen (1885–1962)
Danish novelist

The tropical night has the companionability of a Roman Catholic cathedral compared to the Protestant churches of the north, which let you in on business only.

Out of Africa (1937)

Dutton, Geoffrey (1922–)

Hunters and lovers see best in the dark.

'Night Fishing'

Frost, Robert (1874–1963)
US poet

I have been one acquainted with the night.
I have walked out in rain – and back in rain.
I have outwalked the furthest city light.
I have looked down the saddest city lane.
I have passed by the watchman on his beat
And dropped my eyes, unwilling to explain.

'Acquainted with the Night' (1928)

Fuller, Thomas (1608–1661)
English churchman and antiquary

It is always darkest just before the day dawneth.

Pisgah Sight (1650)

Herrick, Robert (1591–1674)
English poet, royalist and clergyman

Night makes no difference 'twixt the Priest and Clark;
Jone as my Lady is as good i' th' dark.

Hesperides (1648), 'No Difference i' th' Dark'

Johnson, Samuel (1709–1784)
English lexicographer, poet, critic, conversationalist and essayist

In the description of night in Macbeth, the beetle and the bat detract from the general idea of darkness, – inspissated gloom.

In Boswell, The Life of Samuel Johnson (1791)

Lyly, John (c.1554–1606)
English dramatist and politician

Night hath a thousand eyes.

Love's Metamorphosis (1601)

Milton, John (1608–1674)
English poet, libertarian and pamphleteer

Sable-vested Night, eldest of things.

Paradise Lost (1667)

Shakespeare, William (1564–1616)
English dramatist, poet and actor

Let's have one other gaudy night. Call to me
All my sad captains; fill our bowls once more;
Let's mock the midnight bell.

Antony and Cleopatra, III.xiii

Night's swift dragons cut the clouds full fast;
And yonder shines Aurora's harbinger,
At whose approach ghosts, wand'ring here and there,
Troop home to churchyards.

A Midsummer Night's Dream, III.ii

Come, night; come, Romeo; come, thou day in night;
For thou wilt lie upon the wings of night
Whiter than new snow on a raven's back.
Come, gentle night, come, loving, black-brow'd night,
Give me my Romeo; and, when he shall die,
Take him and cut him out in little stars,
And he will make the face of heaven so fine
That all the world will be in love with night,
And pay no worship to the garish sun.

Romeo and Juliet, III.ii

Southey, Robert (1774–1843)
English poet, essayist, historian and letterwriter

How beautiful is the night!
A dewy freshness fills the silent air;
No mist obscures, nor cloud, nor speck, nor stain,
Breaks the serene of heaven.

Thalaba the Destroyer

Thomas, Dylan (1914–1953)
Welsh poet, writer and radio dramatist
> To begin at the beginning: It is spring, moonless night in the small town, starless and bible-black, the cobblestreets silent and the hunched, courters'-and-rabbits' wood limping invisible down to the sloe-black, slow, black, crowblack, fishingboat-bobbing sea.
>> *Under Milk Wood* (1954)

Vaughan, Henry (1622–1695)
Welsh poet and physician
> Dear night! this world's defeat;
> The stop to busie fools; care's check and curb;
> The day of Spirits; my soul's calm retreat
> Which none disturb!
>> *Silex Scintillans* (1650–1655), 'The Night'

Young, Edward (1683–1765)
English poet, dramatist, satirist and clergyman
> Night, sable Goddess! from her Ebon throne,
> In rayless Majesty, now stretches forth
> Her leaden Scepter o'er a slumbering world.
>> *Night-Thoughts on Life, Death and Immortality* (1742–1746)

nostalgia

Adams, Scott (1957–)
US cartoonist
> Someday we'll look back on this and plow into a parked car.
>> *The Dilbert Principle*

Augier, Emile (1820–1889)
French dramatist and poet
> *La nostalgie de la boue.*
> Homesickness for the gutter.
>> *Le Mariage d'Olympe* (1855)

Byron, Lord (1788–1824)
English poet satirist and traveller
> Ah! happy years! once more who would not be a boy?
>> *Childe Harold's Pilgrimage* (1818)

> The 'good old times' – all times when old are good –
> Are gone.
>> 'The Age of Bronze' (1823)

Carr, J.L. (1912–1994)
English writer and publisher
> We can ask and ask but we can't have again what once seemed ours forever – the way things looked, that church alone in the fields, a bed on a belfry floor, a loved face … They'd gone, and you could only wait for the pain to pass.
>> *A Month in the Country* (1980)

Fitzgerald, Penelope (1916–2000)
English author
Her hopes for the New Year
> Conductors should be back on the buses, packets of salt back in the crisps, clockwork back in clocks and levers back in pens.
>> *The Observer*, 1998

Housman, A.E. (1859–1936)
English poet and scholar
> Into my heart an air that kills
> From yon far country blows:
> What are those blue remembered hills,
> What spires, what farms are those?
>
> That is the land of lost content,
> I see it shining plain,
> The happy highways where I went
> And cannot come again.
>> *A Shropshire Lad* (1896)

Lamb, Charles (1775–1834)
English essayist, critic and letter writer
> All, all are gone, the old familiar faces.
>> 'The Old Familiar Faces'

Orwell, George (1903–1950)
English writer and critic
> Before the war, and especially before the Boer War, it was summer all the year round.
>> *Coming Up for Air* (1939)

Steinbeck, John (1902–1968)
US writer
> Cannery Row in Monterey in California is a poem, a stink, a grating noise, a quality of light, a tone, a habit, a nostalgia, a dream.
>> *Cannery Row* (1939)

Tennyson, Alfred, Lord (1809–1892)
English lyric poet
> Tears, idle tears, I know not what they mean,
> Tears from the depth of some divine despair
> Rise in the heart, and gather to the eyes,
> In looking on the happy Autumn-fields,
> And thinking of the days that are no more.
>> *The Princess* (1847)

Thomas, Dylan (1914–1953)
Welsh poet, writer and radio dramatist
> Years and years and years ago, when I was a boy, when there were wolves in Wales, and birds the colour of red-flannel petticoats whisked past the harp-shaped hills … when we rode the daft and happy hills bareback, it snowed and it snowed.
>> *A Child's Christmas in Wales* (1954)

Ustinov, sir Peter (1921–)
English actor, director, dramatist, writer and raconteur
> The English have an enormous nostalgia for school. There is no other country in the world

where you see elderly gentleman dressed like schoolboys.

The Observer, 1998

Villon, François (1431–1485)
French poet

Mais où sont les neiges d'antan?
But where are the snows of yesteryear?

Le Grand Testament (1461)

Yeats, W.B. (1865–1939)
Irish poet, dramatist, editor, writer and senator

In the Junes that were warmer than these are, the waves were more gay,
When I was a boy with never a crack in my heart.

'The Meditation of the Old Fisherman' (1886)

▶▶ MEMORY; PAST; REGRET

novelty

Hood, Thomas (1799–1845)
English poet, editor and humorist

There are three things which the public will always clamour for, sooner or later: namely, Novelty, novelty, novelty.

Announcement of *The Comic Annual* for 1836

Voltaire (1694–1778)
French philosopher, dramatist, poet, historian writer and critic

If we do not find anything pleasant, we shall at least find something new.

Candide (1759)

nuclear weapons

Anonymous

The best defence against the atom bomb is not to be there when it goes off.

The British Army Journal, quoted in *The Observer*, 1949

Einstein, Albert (1879–1955)
German-born US mathematical physicist
Of his part in the development of the atom bomb

If only I had known, I should have become a watchmaker.

New Statesman, 1965

Foot, Michael (1913–)
British Labour politician

Saddam Hussein is not fit to have a finger on the nuclear trigger. And once we stop to think, nor is anyone else.

The Times, 1999

Lange, David Russell (1942–)
New Zealand Prime Minister
A statement released during the investigations into the bombing of the Greenpeace vessel, *Rainbow Warrior*, in 1985

We are an enemy of the nuclear threat and we are an enemy of testing nuclear weapons in the South Pacific. New Zealand did not buy into this fight. France put agents into New Zealand. France put spies into New Zealand. France lets off bombs in the Pacific. France puts its President in the Pacific to crow about it.

In Michael King, *Death of the Rainbow Warrior* (1986)

Laurence, William L. (1888–1977)
US scientific journalist
Referring to the explosion of the first atomic bomb, over Hiroshima, 6 August 1945

At first it was a giant column that soon took the shape of a supramundane mushroom.

New York Times, 1945

King, Martin Luther (1929–1968)
US civil rights leader and Baptist minister

Our scientific power has outrun our spiritual power. We have guided missiles and misguided men.

Strength to Love, 1963

Le Blanc, Jacques
Describing France's nuclear testing, 1995

I do not like this word bomb. It is not a bomb; it is a device which is exploding.

Attr.

McLuhan, Marshall (1911–1980)
Canadian communications theorist

The hydrogen bomb is history's exclamation point. It ends an age-long sentence of manifest violence.

Attr.

Oppenheimer, J. Robert (1904–1967)
US nuclear physicist
On the consequences of the first atomic test

We knew the world would not be the same.

In Giovanitti and Freed, *The Decision to Drop the Bomb* (1965)

Owen, Dr David (1938–)
English politician

It was on this issue, the nuclear defence of Britain, on which I left the Labour Party, and on this issue I am prepared to stake my entire political career.

The Observer, 1986

Russell, Bertrand (1872–1970)
English philosopher, mathematician, essayist and social reformer
On the possibility of nuclear war between the USA and the USSR

You may reasonably expect a man to walk a

tightrope safely for ten minutes; it would be unreasonable to do so without accident for two hundred years.

> In Desmond Bagley, *The Tightrope Men* (1973)

Rutherford, Ernest (1871–1937)
English physicist
Joking about the atom's enormous potential energy
> Some fool in a laboratory might blow up the universe unawares.

> In Mark Oliphant, *Rutherford Recollections of the Cambridge Days* (1972)

Schroeder, Patricia (1940–)
US politician
> We've got the kind of President who thinks arms control means some kind of deodorant.

> *The Observer*, 1987

Stevenson, Adlai (1900–1965)
US lawyer, statesman and United Nations ambassador
> There is no evil in the atom; only in men's souls.

> Speech, Hartford, Connecticut, 1952

Tibbet, Paul W. (20th century)
Description of atomic bomb explosion
> A mushroom of boiling dust up to 20,000 feet.

> Attr.

Toynbee, Arnold (1889–1975)
British historian
Urging the need for a greater British influence in the United Nations Organisation, 1947
> No annihilation without representation.

> Attr.

White, Patrick (1912–1990)
English-born Australian writer and dramatist
> Today when science has perfected the techniques of destruction, nuclear warfare could mean the immediate annihilation of what we know as civilisation, followed by a slow infection of those who inhabit the less directly involved surface of this globe – as it revolves in space – swathed in its contaminated shroud.

> Speech to public meeting on nuclear disarmament, Melbourne, 1981

Wigg, George Edward Cecil, Baron (1900–1983)
English politician
> For Hon. Members opposite the deterrent is a phallic symbol. It convinces them that they are men.

> *The Observer*, 1964

▶▶ WAR

nursery rhymes

(For sources, the reader is referred to the authoritative *Oxford Dictionary of Nursery Rhymes*)

As I was going to St Ives,
I met a man with seven wives.
Each wife had seven sacks,
Each sack had seven cats,
Each cat had seven kits:
Kits, cats, sacks, and wives,
How many were going to St Ives?
One or none.

Baa, baa, black sheep,
Have you any wool?
Yes, sir, yes, sir,
Three bags full;
One for the master,
And one for the dame,
And one for the little boy who lives down the lane.

Bobby Shafto's gone to sea,
Silver buckles on his knee;
He'll come back and marry me,
Bonny Bobby Shafto!

Boys and girls come out to play,
The moon doth shine as bright as day.
Bye, baby bunting,
Daddy's gone a-hunting,
Gone to get a rabbit skin
To wrap the baby bunting in.

Cock a doodle doo!
My dame has lost her shoe,
My master's lost his fiddling stick,
And doesn't know what to do.

Come, let's to bed
Says Sleepy-head;
Tarry a while, says Slow;
Put on the pan;
Says Greedy Nan,
Let's sup before we go.

Curly locks, Curly locks,
Wilt thou be mine?
Thou shalt not wash dishes
Nor yet feed the swine;
But sit on a cushion
And sew a fine seam,
And feed upon strawberries,
Sugar and cream.

Ding, dong, bell,
Pussy's in the well.
Who put her in?
Little Johnny Green.
Who pulled her out?
Little Timmy Stout.

Doctor Foster went to Gloucester
In a shower of rain;
He stepped in a puddle,
Right up to his middle,
And never went there again.

Fee, fi, fo, fum,
I smell the blood of an Englishman;
Be he alive or be he dead,
I'll grind his bones to make my bread.

A frog he would a-wooing go,
Heigh ho! says Rowley,
Whether his mother would let him or no.
With a rowley, powley, gammon and spinach,
Heigh ho! says Anthony Rowley.

Georgie Porgie, pudding and pie,
Kissed the girls and made them cry;
When the boys came out to play,
Georgie Porgie ran away.

Goosey, goosey gander,
Whither shall I wander?
Upstairs and downstairs
And in my lady's chamber.
There I met an old man
Who wouldn't say his prayers,
I took him by the left leg
And threw him down the stairs.

Here is the church, and here is the steeple;
Open the door and here are the people.

Hey diddle diddle,
The cat and the fiddle,
The cow jumped over the moon;
The little dog laughed
To see such sport,
And the dish ran away with the spoon.

Hickory, dickory, dock,
The mouse ran up the clock.
The clock struck one,
The mouse ran down,
Hickory, dickory, dock.

Hot cross buns!
Hot cross buns!
One a penny, two a penny,
Hot cross buns!

How many miles to Babylon?
Three score miles and ten.
Can I get there by candle-light?
Yes, and back again.

Humpty Dumpty sat on a wall,

Humpty Dumpty had a great fall.
All the king's horses,
And all the king's men,
Couldn't put Humpty together again.

I had a little nut tree,
Nothing would it bear
But a silver nutmeg
And a golden pear;
The King of Spain's daughter
Came to visit me,
And all for the sake
Of my little nut tree.

I had a little pony,
His name was Dapple Grey;
I lent him to a lady
To ride a mile away.
She whipped him, she lashed him,
She rode him though the mire;
I would not lend my pony now,
For all the lady's hire.

I love little pussy,
Her coat is so warm,
And if I don't hurt her,
She'll do me no harm.

I love sixpence, jolly little sixpence,
I love sixpence better than my life;
I spent a penny of it, I lent a penny of it,
And I took fourpence home to my wife.

I'm the king of the castle,
Get down, you dirty rascal!

I see the moon,
And the moon sees me;
God bless the moon,
And God bless me.

Jack and Jill went up the hill
To fetch a pail of water;
Jack fell down and broke his crown,
And Jill came tumbling after.

Jack Sprat could eat no fat,
His wife could eat no lean,
And so between them both, you see,
They licked the platter clean.

Ladybird, ladybird,
Fly away home,
Your house is on fire
And your children are gone.
All except one
And that's little Ann

And she has crept under
The warming pan.

Lavender's blue, dilly dilly,
Lavender's green;
When I am king, dilly dilly,
You shall be queen.

The lion and the unicorn
Were fighting for the crown;
The lion beat the unicorn
All around the town.

Little boy blue, come blow your horn,
The sheep's in the meadow, the cow's in the corn.

Little Jack Horner
Sat in the corner,
Eating a Christmas pie;
He put in his thumb,
And pulled out a plum,
And said, What a good boy am I!

Little Miss Muffet
Sat on a tuffet,
Eating her curds and whey;
There came a big spider,
Who sat down beside her
And frightened Miss Muffet away.

Little Polly Flinders
Sat among the cinders,
Warming her pretty little toes;
Her mother came and caught her,
And whipped her little daughter
For spoiling her nice new clothes.

Little Tommy Tucker,
Sings for his supper:
What shall we give him?
White bread and butter
How shall he cut it
Without a knife?
How will he be married
Without a wife?

London Bridge is falling down,
My fair lady.

Mary had a little lamb,
Its fleece was white as snow;
And everywhere that Mary went
The lamb was sure to go.
It followed her to school one day,
That was against the rule;
It made the children laugh and play
To see a lamb at school.

Mary, Mary, quite contrary,
How does your garden grow?
With silver bells and cockle shells,
And pretty maids all in a row.

Monday's child is fair of face,
Tuesday's child is full of grace,
Wednesday's child is full of woe,
Thursday's child has far to go,
Friday's child is loving and giving,
Saturday's child works hard for a living,
And the child that is born on the Sabbath day
Is bonny and blithe, and good and gay.

My mother said that I never should
Play with the gypsies in the wood;
If I did, she would say,
Naughty girl to disobey.

The north wind doth blow,
And we shall have snow,
And what will poor robin do then?
Poor thing.

O dear, what can the matter be?
Dear, dear, what can the matter be,
Oh, dear, what can the matter be?
Johnny's so long at the fair.
He promised he'd buy me a fairing should
please me,
And then for a kiss, oh! he vowed he would
tease me,
He promised he'd buy me a bunch of blue
ribbons
To tie up my bonny brown hair.

Oh! the grand old Duke of York
He had ten thousand men;
He marched them up to the top of the hill,
And he marched them down again.
And when they were up they were up,
And when they were down they were down,
And when they were only half way up.
They were neither up nor down.

Old King Cole
Was a merry old soul,
And a merry old soul was he;
He called for his pipe,
And he called for his bowl,
And he called for his fiddlers three.

Old Mother Hubbard
Went to the cupboard,
To fetch her poor dog a bone;
But when she came there
The cupboard was bare
And so the poor dog had none.

One, two, buckle my shoe;
Three, four, knock at the door;
Five, six, pick up sticks;
Seven, eight, lay them straight;
Nine, ten, big fat hen;
Eleven, twelve, dig and delve;
Thirteen, fourteen, maids a-courting;
Fifteen, sixteen, maids in the kitchen,
Seventeen, eighteen, maids in waiting;
Nineteen, twenty, my plate's empty!

Oranges and lemons,
Say the bells of St Clement's …

You owe me five farthings,
Say the bells of St Martin's.

When will you pay me?
Say the bells of Old Bailey.

When I grow rich
Say the bells of Shoreditch.

Pray, when will that be?
Say the bells of Stepney.

I'm sure I don't know
Says the great bell at Bow.

Here comes a candle to light you to bed,
Here comes a chopper to chop off your head!

Pat-a-cake, pat-a-cake, baker's man,
Bake me a cake as fast as you can;
Pat it and prick it, and mark it with B,
Put it in the oven for baby and me.

Peter, Peter, pumpkin eater,
Had a wife and couldn't keep her;
He put her in a pumpkin shell
And there he kept her very well.

Peter Piper picked a peck of pickled pepper.
A peck of pickled pepper Peter Piper picked.
If Peter Piper picked a peck of pickled pepper,
Where's the peck of pickled pepper Peter Piper
picked?

Please to remember
The Fifth of November,
Gunpowder, treason and plot;
We know no reason
Why gunpowder treason
Should ever be forgot.

Polly put the kettle on,
Polly put the kettle on,
Polly put the kettle on,

We'll all have tea.
Sukey take it off again,
Sukey take it off again,
Sukey take it off again,
They've all gone away.

Pussy cat, pussy cat,
Where have you been?
I've been to London
To look at the queen.
Pussy cat, pussy cat,
What did you there?
I frightened a little mouse
Under her chair.

The Queen of Hearts
She made some tarts,
All on a summer's day;
The Knave of Hearts
He stole the tarts,
And took them clean away.

Rain, rain, go away,
Come again another day.

Ride a cock-horse to Banbury Cross,
To see a fine lady upon a white horse;
Rings on her fingers and bells on her toes,
She shall have music wherever she goes.

Ring-a-ring o' roses,
A pocket full of posies,
A-tishoo! A-tishoo!
We all fall down.

Rock-a-bye, baby, on the tree top,
When the wind blows the cradle will rock;
When the bough breaks the cradle will fall,
Down will come baby, cradle, and all.

Round and round the garden
Like a teddy bear;
One step, two step,
Tickle you under there!

Round and round the rugged rock
The ragged rascal ran.

Rub-a-dub-dub,
Three men in a tub,
And how do you think they got there?
The butcher, the baker,
The candlestick-maker.
They all jumped out of a rotten potato,
'Twas enough to make a man stare.

See-saw, Margery Daw,
Jacky shall have a new master;

Jacky shall have but a penny a day,
Because he can't work any faster.

Simple Simon met a pieman,
Going to the fair;
Says Simple Simon to the pieman,
Let me taste your ware.

Sing a song of sixpence,
A pocket full of rye;
Four and twenty blackbirds,
Baked in a pie.
When the pie was opened,
The birds began to sing;
Wasn't that a dainty dish,
To set before the king?
The king was in his counting-house,
Counting out his money;
The queen was in the parlour,
Eating bread and honey.
The maid was in the garden,
Hanging out the clothes,
When down came a blackbird
And pecked off her nose!

Solomon Grundy,
Born on Monday
Christened on Tuesday
Married on Wednesday
Took ill on Thursday
Worse on Friday
Died on Saturday
Buried on Sunday.
This is the end of Solomon Grundy.

Taffy was a Welshman, Taffy was a thief,
Taffy came to my house and stole a piece of beef.

Tell tale, tit!
Your tongue shall be split,
And all the dogs in town
Shall have a little bit.

There was a crooked man, and he walked a
crooked mile,
He found a crooked sixpence against a crooked
stile;
He bought a crooked cat, which caught a
crooked mouse,
And they all lived together in a little crooked
house.

There was an old woman who lived in a shoe,
She had so many children she didn't know what
to do.
She gave them some broth without any bread,
She whipped them all soundly and put them to
bed.

Thirty days hath September,
April, June and November;
All the rest have thirty-one,
Excepting February alone
And that has twenty-eight days clear
And twenty-nine in each leap year.

This is the horse and the hound and the horn
That belonged to the farmer sowing his corn,
That kept the cock that crowed in the morn,
That waked the priest all shaven and shorn,
That married the man all tattered and torn,
That kissed the maiden all forlorn,
That milked the cow with the crumpled horn,
That tossed the dog,
That worried the cat,
That killed the rat,
That ate the corn,
That lay in the house that Jack built.

This little pig went to market,
This little pig stayed at home,
This little pig had roast beef,
This little pig had none,
And this little pig cried, Wee-wee-wee-wee-wee,
I can't find my way home.

Three blind mice, see how they run!
They all ran after the farmer's wife,
She cut off their tails with a carving knife,
Did ever you see such a thing in your life,
As three blind mice?

Three little kittens they lost their mittens,
And they began to cry.
Oh mother dear, we sadly fear
Our mittens we have lost.
What! lost your mittens,
You naughty kittens!
Then you shall have no pie.

Tinker,
Tailor,
Soldier,
Sailor,
Rich man,
Poor man,
Beggarman,
Thief.

Tom, he was a piper's son,
He learnt to play when he was young,
And all the tune that he could play
Was 'Over the hills and far away'.

Tom, Tom, the piper's son,
Stole a pig and away he run.
The pig was eat,

And Tom was beat,
And Tom went howling down the street.

The twelfth day of Christmas,
My true love sent to me
Twelve lords a-leaping,
Eleven ladies dancing,
Ten pipers piping,
Nine drummers drumming,
Eight maids a-milking,
Seven swans a-swimming,
Six geese a-laying,
Five gold rings,
Four calling birds,
Three French hens,
Two turtle doves, and
A partridge in a pear
tree.

Two little dicky birds,
Sitting on a wall;
One named Peter,
The other named Paul,
Fly away, Peter!
Fly away, Paul!
Come back, Peter!
Come back, Paul!

Wee Willie Winkie runs through the town
Upstairs and downstairs and in his nightgown,
Rapping at the window, crying through the lock,
Are the children all in bed? It's past eight
o'clock.

What are little boys made of?
Frogs and snails
And puppy-dogs' tails,
That's what little boys are made of.
What are little girls made of?

Sugar and spice
And all things nice,
That's what little girls are made of.

What are young men made of ?
Sighs and leers,
And crocodile tears,
That's what young men are made of.

What are young women made of?
Ribbons and laces,
And sweet, pretty faces,
That's what young women are made
of.

Where are you going to, my pretty maid?
I'm going a-milking, sir, she said.
What is your fortune, my pretty maid?
My face is my fortune, sir, she said.

Who killed Cock Robin?
I, said the Sparrow,
With my bow and arrow,
I killed Cock Robin.

Who saw him die?
I, said the Fly,
With my little eye,
I saw him die.

And all the birds of the air
Fell to sighing and sobbing,
When they heard the bell toll
For poor Cock Robin.

A wise old owl lived in an oak;
The more he saw the less he spoke;
The less he spoke the more he heard.
Why can't we all be like that wise old bird?

O

obedience

The Bible (King James Version)
> To obey is better than sacrifice, and to hearken than the fat of rams.
>> *I Samuel*, 15:22

Edgeworth, Maria (1767–1849)
English-born Irish writer
> Come when you're call'd;
> And do as you're bid;
> Shut the door after you;
> And you'll never be chid.
>> *Popular Tales* (1804), 'The Contrast'

Gibbon, Edward (1737–1794)
English historian, politician and memoirist
> I sighed as a lover, I obeyed as a son.
>> *Memoirs of My Life and Writings* (1796)

Plato (c.429–347 BC)
Greek philosopher
> Through obedience learn to command.
>> *Leges*

Schiller, Johann Christoph Friedrich (1759–1805)
German writer, dramatist, poet and historian
> Obedience is woman's earthly duty,
> Harsh suffering is her sorry fate.
>> *The Maid of Orleans* (1801)

Storr, Dr Anthony (1920–)
British writer and psychiatrist
> I myself believe that the tendency towards obedience is one of the most sinister of human traits.
>> *Feet of Clay* (1996)

obstinacy

Aristotle (384–322 BC)
Greek philosopher
> Obstinate people may be subdivided into the opinionated, the ignorant, and the boorish.
>> *Nicomachean Ethics*

Browne, Sir Thomas (1605–1682)
English physician, author and antiquary
> Obstinacy in a bad cause, is but constancy in a good.
>> *Religio Medici* (1643)

MacNeice, Louis (1907–1963)
Belfast-born poet, writer, radio producer, translator and critic

> One must not dislike people ... because they are intransigent. For that could be only playing their own game.
>> *Zoo* (1938)

Maugham, William Somerset (1874–1965)
English writer, dramatist and physician
> Like all weak men he laid an exaggerated stress on not changing one's mind.
>> *Of Human Bondage* (1915)

Proverb
> None so deaf as those who will not hear.

Sheridan, Richard Brinsley (1751–1816)
Irish dramatist, politician and orator
> She's as headstrong as an allegory on the banks of the Nile.
>> *The Rivals* (1775)

Sterne, Laurence (1713–1768)
Irish-born English writer and clergyman
> 'Tis known by the name of perseverance in a good cause, – and of obstinacy in a bad one.
>> *Tristram Shandy* (1759–67)

opera

Appleton, Sir Edward Victor (1892–1965)
English physicist
> I do not mind what language an opera is sung in so long as it is a language I don't understand.
>> *The Observer*, 1955

Bing, Rudolf (1902–)
Director of the New York Metropolitan Opera
> The opera always loses money. That's as it should be. Opera has no business making money.
>> *New York Times*, 1959

Gershwin, George (1898–1937)
On his opera *Porgy and Bess*
> I think the music is so marvelous – I really can't believe I wrote it.
>> Quoted by E. Jablonski in sleeve notes to the RCA Victor recording

Melba, Dame Nellie (1861–1931)
Australian opera singer
> The first rule in opera is the first rule in life: see to everything yourself.
>> *Melodies and Memories* (1925)

Mencken, H.L. (1880–1956)
US writer, critic, philologist and satirist
> Opera in English is, in the main, just about as

sensible as baseball in Italian.

Attr.

More, Hannah (1745–1833)
English poet, dramatist and religious writer
> Going to the opera, like getting drunk, is a sin
> that carries its own punishment with it.
>
> *The Letters of Hannah More* (1925)

Newman, Ernest (1868–1959)
English music critic and writer
> I sometimes wonder which would be nicer – an
> opera without an interval, or an interval without
> an opera.
>
> In Heyworth (ed.), *Berlioz, Romantic and Classic*

Pavarotti, Luciano (1935–)
Italian tenor
> In opera, as with any performing art, to be in
> great demand and to command high fees you
> must be good of course, but you must also be
> famous. The two are different things.
>
> *Autobiography*

Randolph, David (1914–)
On Parsifal
> The kind of opera that starts at six o'clock and
> after it has been going three hours, you look at
> your watch and it says 6.20.
>
> In *The Frank Muir Book* (1976)

Wharton, Edith (1862–1937)
US writer
> An unalterable and unquestioned law of the
> musical world required that the German text of
> French operas sung by Swedish artists should be
> translated into Italian for the clearer
> understanding of English speaking audiences.
>
> *The Age of Innocence* (1920)

▶▶ MUSIC

opinions

Baez, Joan (1941–)
US folksinger and songwriter
> I've never had a humble opinion. If you've got
> an opinion, why be humble about it.
>
> *Scotland on Sunday*, 1992

Browne, Sir Thomas (1605–1682)
English physician, author and antiquary
> I could never divide my self from any man upon
> the difference of an opinion, or be angry with his
> judgment for not agreeing with me in that, from
> which perhaps within a few days I should dissent
> my self.
>
> *Religio Medici* (1643)

Chesterton, G.K. (1874–1936)
English writer, poet and critic

Bigotry may be roughly defined as the anger of
men who have no opinions

Heretics (1905)

Congreve, William (1670–1729)
English dramatist
> I am always of the opinion with the learned, if
> they speak first.
>
> *Incognita* (1692)

Emerson, Ralph Waldo (1803–1882)
US poet, essayist, transcendentalist and teacher
> Tomorrow a stranger will say with masterly good
> sense precisely what we have thought and felt
> all the time, and we shall be forced to take with
> shame our own opinion from another.
>
> 'Self-Reliance' (1841)

Halsey, Margaret (1910–)
US writer
> … the English think of an opinion as something
> which a decent person, if he has the misfortune
> to have one, does all he can to hide.
>
> *With Malice Toward Some* (1938)

Hobbes, Thomas (1588–1679)
Political philosopher
> They that approve a private opinion, call it
> opinion; but they that mislike it, heresy: and yet
> heresy signifies no more than private opinion.
>
> *Leviathan* (1651)

James, Henry (1843–1916)
US-born British writer, critic and letter writer
> The superiority of one man's opinion over
> another's is never so great as when the opinion
> is about a woman.
>
> *The Tragic Muse* (1890)

Jefferson, Thomas (1743–1826)
US Democrat statesman and President
> Error of opinion may be tolerated where reason
> is left free to combat it.
>
> First inaugural address, 1801

Locke, John (1632–1704)
English philosopher
> New opinions are always suspected, and usually
> opposed, without any reason but because they
> are not already common.
>
> *Essay concerning Human Understanding* (1690)

Mackintosh, Sir James (1765–1832)
Scottish philosopher, historian, lawyer and politician
> Men are never so good or so bad as their
> opinions.
>
> 'Jeremy Bentham' (1830)

Maistre, Joseph de (1753–1821)
French diplomat and political philosopher
> *Les fausses opinions ressemblent à la fausse monnaie
> qui est frappée d'abord par de grands coupables, et
> dépensée ensuite par d'honnêtes gens qui perpétuent*

le crime sans savoir ce qu'ils font.
Wrong opinions are like counterfeit coins, which are first minted by great wrongdoers, then spent by decent people who perpetuate the crime without knowing what they are doing.

Les soirées de Saint-Pétersbourg

Mill, John Stuart (1806–1873)
English philosopher, economist and reformer
If all mankind minus one, were of one opinion, and only one person were of the contrary opinion, mankind would be no more justified in silencing that one person, than he, if he had the power, would be justified in silencing mankind.

On Liberty (1859)

Palmerston, Lord (1784–1865)
British Prime Minister
What is merit? The opinion one man entertains of another.

In Carlyle, 'Shooting Niagara and After?' (1837)

Persius Flaccus, Aulus (AD 34–62)
Roman satirical poet
Nec te quaesiveris extra.
Do not look for opinions beyond your own.

Satires

Shakespeare, William (1564–1616)
English dramatist, poet and actor
You are now sail'd into the north of my lady's opinion; where you will hang like an icicle on a Dutchman's beard.

Twelfth Night, III.ii

Spencer, Herbert (1820–1903)
English philosopher and journalist
Opinion is ultimately determined by the feelings, and not by the intellect.

Social Statics (1850)

Stevenson, Robert Louis (1850–1894)
Scottish writer, poet and essayist
All opinions, properly so called, are stages on the road to truth.

Virginibus Puerisque, 'Crabbed Age and Youth'

Terence (c.190–159 BC)
Carthaginian-born Roman dramatist
Quot homines tot sententiae: suos quoique mos.
There are as many opinions as there are people: each has his own point of view.

Phormio

Turgenev, Ivan (1818–1883)
Russian writer and dramatist
I submit to no man's opinion; I have opinions of my own.

Fathers and Sons (1862), 13

Twain, Mark (1835–1910)
US humorist, writer, journalist and lecturer
You tell me whar a man gets his corn pone, en I'll tell you what his 'pinions is.

'Corn Pone Opinions'

It is difference of opinion that makes horse races.

Pudd'nhead Wilson's Calendar (1894)

Webster, Daniel (1782–1852)
US statesman, orator and lawyer
Inconsistencies of opinion, arising from changes of circumstances, are often justifiable.

Speech, 1846

Wenders, Wim (1945–)
German film director
The more opinions you have, the less you see.

Attr.

▶▶ IDEAS

opportunity

Anonymous
Opportunity may knock only once, but temptation leans on the doorbell.

Opportunity always knocks at the least opportune moment.

Ducharme's Precept

Bacon, Francis (1561–1626)
English philosopher, essayist, politician and courtier
A wise man will make more opportunities than he finds.

Essays

Bell, Alexander Graham (1847–1922)
Scottish-born US inventor and educator of the deaf
When one door closes another door opens; but we often look so long and so regretfully upon the closed door that we do not see the ones which open for us.

Attr.

Henryson, Robert (c.1425–1505)
Scottish poet
The man that will nocht quhen he may
Sall haif nocht quhen he wald.

'Robene and Makyne' (c.1560)

Proverbs
A bird in the hand is worth two in the bush.

The early bird catches the worm.

God helps them that help themselves.

Opportunity seldom knocks twice.

▶▶ CHANCE

opposition

Roosevelt, Eleanor (1884–1962)
US writer and lecturer
> I have spent many years of my life in opposition
> and I rather like the role.
>> *Letter to Bernard Baruch, 1952*

Rusk, Dean (1909–1994)
US politician and diplomat
Of the Cuban missile crisis
> We're eye-ball to eye-ball and the other fellow
> just blinked.
>> *Remark, 1962*

Stevens, Wallace (1879–1955)
US poet, essayist, dramatist and lawyer
> Two things of opposite natures seem to depend
> On one another, as a man depends
> On a woman, day on night, the imagined
> On the real.
>> *'Notes Toward a Supreme Fiction' (1948)*

▶▶ GOVERNMENT; POLITICS

optimism

Ball, Lucille (1911–1989)
US actress and comedian
> One of the things I learned the hard way was
> that it doesn't pay to get discouraged. Keeping
> busy and making optimism a way of life can
> restore your faith in yourself.
>> *In Eleanor Harris, The Real Story of Lucille Ball (1954)*

Cabell, James Branch (1879–1958)
US writer, poet, genealogist and historian
> The optimist proclaims that we live in the best of
> all possible worlds; and the pessimist fears this
> is true.
>> *The Silver Stallion (1926)*

Eliot, George (1819–1880)
English writer and poet
> I am not an optimist but a meliorist.
>> *In L. Housman, A.E.H. (1937)*

Ellis, Havelock (1859–1939)
English sexologist and essayist
> The place where optimism most flourishes is the
> lunatic asylum.
>> *The Dance of Life*

Mailer, Norman (1923–)
US writer
> Being married six times shows a degree of
> optimism over wisdom, but I am incorrigibly
> optimistic.
>> *The Observer, 1988*

Marquis, Don (1878–1937)
US columnist, satirist and poet
> an optimist is a guy
> that has never had
> much experience.
>> *archy and mehitabel (1927)*

O'Casey, Sean (1880–1964)
Irish dramatist
> A lament in one ear, maybe; but always a song in
> the other. And to me life is simply an invitation
> to live.
>> *In Eileen O'Casey, Eileen*

Shorter, Clement King (1857–1926)
English writer and critic
> The latest definition of an optimist is one who
> fills up his crossword puzzle in ink.
>> *The Observer, 1925*

Ustinov, Sir Peter (1921–)
English actor, director, dramatist, writer and raconteur
> I am an optimist, unrepentant and militant. After
> all, in order not to be a fool an optimist must
> know how sad a place the world can be. It is
> only the pessimist who finds this out anew every
> day.
>> *Dear Me (1977)*

Voltaire (1694–1778)
French philosopher, dramatist, poet, historian writer and critic
> *Tout est pour le mieux dans le meilleur des mondes possibles.*
> Everything is for the best in the best of all
> possible worlds.
>> *Candide (1759)*

▶▶ HOPE; PESSIMISM

order

Browne, Sir Thomas (1605–1682)
English physician, author and antiquary
> All things began in order, so shall they end, and
> so shall they begin again; according to the
> ordainer of order and mystical mathematics of
> the city of heaven.
>> *The Garden of Cyrus (1658)*

Pope, Alexander (1688–1744)
English poet, translator and editor
> Order is Heav'n's first law.
>> *Essay on Man (1734)*

Shakespeare, William (1564–1616)
English dramatist, poet and actor
> The heavens themselves, the planets, and this
> centre,
> Observe degree, priority, and place,

Insisture, course, proportion, season, form,
Office, and custom, in all line of order.

Troilus and Cressida, I.iii

Smiles, Samuel (1812–1904)
English writer
A place for everything, and everything in its
place. Order is wealth.

Thrift (1875)

Stevens, Wallace (1879–1955)
US poet, essayist, dramatist and lawyer
Oh! Blessed rage for order, pale Ramon.
The maker's rage to order words of the sea,
Words of the fragrant portals, dimly-starred,
And of ourselves and of our origins,
In ghostlier demarcations, keener sounds.

'The Idea of Order at Key West' (1936)

orgies

Voltaire (1694–1778)
French philosopher, dramatist, poet, historian writer and
critic
Turning down an invitation to an orgy, having attended one
the previous night for the first time
Once: a philosopher; twice: a pervert!

Attr.

originality

Mill, John Stuart (1806–1873)
English philosopher, economist and reformer
All good things which exist are the fruits of
originality.

On Liberty (1859)

Nishimura, Yoshifumi
Japanese chemist

In conversation with Stephen Kreider Yoder, former Tokyo
correspondent of the *Wall Street Journal*
There's no environment where you can do wacky
things that end up being creative … If you're
different, you're a minus … That nips originality
in the bud.

In *Created in Japan*

Beauvoir, Simone de (1908–1986)
French writer, feminist critic and philosopher
The writer of originality, unless dead, is always
shocking, scandalous; novelty disturbs and
repels.

The Second Sex (1953)

Twain, Mark (1835–1910)
US humorist, writer, journalist and lecturer
What a good thing Adam had. When he said a
good thing he knew nobody had said it before.

Notebooks

Wordsworth, William (1770–1850)
English poet
Never forget what I believe was observed to
you by Coleridge, that every great and original
writer, in proportion as he is great and original,
must himself create the taste by which he is to
be relished.

Letter to Lady Beaumont, 1807

outdoors

Macaulay, Dame Rose (1881–1958)
English writer
Gentlemen know that fresh air should be kept in
its proper place – out of doors – and that, God
having given us indoors and out-of-doors, we
should not attempt to do away with this
distinction.

Crewe Train (1926)

P

painting

Blake, William (1757–1827)
English poet, engraver, painter and mystic
> When Sr Joshua Reynolds died
> All Nature was degraded:
> The King dropd a tear into the Queens Ear:
> And all his Pictures Faded.
>> *Annotations to Sir Joshua Reynolds' Works* (c. 1808)

Bray, John Jefferson (1912–)
Australian lawyer and poet
> A hundred canvasses and seven sons
> He left, and never got a likeness once.
>> 'Epitaph on a Portrait Painter'

Cervantes, Miguel de (1547–1616)
Spanish writer and dramatist
> *Digo que los buenos pintores imitaban a naturaleza;*
> *pero que los malos la vomitaban.*
> I say that good painters imitated nature; but
> that bad ones vomited it.
>> *Exemplary Novels*, 1613

Chagall, Marc (1887–1985)
Russian-born French painter
> When I'm finishing a picture I hold some God-
> made object up to it – a rock, a flower, or a tree
> branch – as a final test. If the painting stands up
> beside a thing man cannot make, the painting is
> authentic. If there's a clash, it's bad art.
>> *Saturday Evening Post* 2 December 1962

Constable, John (1776–1837)
English painter
Description of Watteau's 'Plaisirs du Bal'
> As if painted in honey.
>> In *The Times Literary Supplement*, 1993

> In Claude's landscape all is lovely – all amiable –
> all is amenity and repose; – the calm sunshine of
> the heart.
>> In C.R. Leslie, *Memoirs of the Life of John Constable*
>> (1843)

> The amiable but eccentric Blake ... said of a
> beautiful drawing of an avenue of fir trees ...
> 'Why, this is not drawing, but inspiration.' ...
> Constable replied, 'I never knew it before; I
> meant it for drawing'.
>> In C.R. Leslie, *Memoirs of the Life of John Constable*
>> (1843)

> The sound of water escaping from mill-dams,
> etc, willows, old rotten planks, slimy posts, and
> brickwork, I love such things ... those scenes
> made me a painter and I am grateful.
>> Letter to John Fisher, 1821

Cromwell, Oliver (1599–1658)
English general, statesman and Puritan leader
> Mr Lely, I desire you would use all your skill to
> paint my picture freely like me, and not flatter
> me at all; but remark all these roughnesses,
> pimples, warts, and everything as you see me,
> otherwise I will never pay a farthing for it.
>> In Horace Walpole, *Anecdotes of Painting in*
>> *England* (1763)

Landseer, Sir Edwin Henry (1802–1873)
English painter, engraver and sculptor
> If people only knew as much about painting as I
> do, they would never buy my pictures.
>> In Campbell Lennie, *Landseer the Victorian*
>> *Paragon*

Matisse, Henri (1869–1954)
French artist and author
> There is nothing more difficult for a truly
> creative painter than to paint a rose, because
> before he can do so he has first to forget all the
> roses that were ever painted.
>> Attr.

Moses, Grandma (1860–1961)
US painter
Of painting
> I don't advise any one to take it up as a business
> proposition, unless they really have talent, and
> are crippled so as to deprive them of physical
> labor.
>> Attr.

> If I didn't start painting, I would have raised
> chickens.
>> In Aotto Kallir (ed.), *Grandma Moses, My*
>> *Life's History*

Palmer, Samuel (1805–1881)
English landscape painter
> A picture has been said to be something
> between a thing and a thought.
>> In Arthur Symons, *Life of Blake*

Picasso, Pablo (1881–1973)
Spanish painter, sculptor and graphic artist
> Painting is a blind man's profession. He paints
> not what he sees, but what he feels, what he
> tells himself about what he has seen.
>> In Jean Cocteau, *Journals* (1929), 'Childhood'

Explaining why a Renoir in his apartment was hung crooked
> It's better like that, if you want to kill a picture
> all you have to do is to hang it beautifully on a
> nail and soon you will see nothing of it but the
> frame. When it's out of place you see it better.
>> In Roland Penrose, *Picasso: His Life and Work*
>> (1958)

There's no such thing as a bad Picasso, but some are less good than others.

> In A. Whitman, *Come to Judgement*

Remark made at an exhibition of children's drawings

When I was their age, I could draw like Raphael, but it took me a lifetime to learn to draw like them.

> In Penrose, *Picasso: His Life and Work* (1958)

Renoir, Pierre Auguste (1841–1919)
French painter
Of the lifelike flesh tones of his nudes

I just keep painting till I feel like pinching. Then I know it's right.

> Attr.

On why he still painted although he had arthritis of his hands

The pain passes, but the beauty remains.

> Attr.

Reynolds, Sir Joshua (1723–1792)
English portrait painter

A mere copier of nature can never produce anything great.

> *Discourses on Art* (1770)

Ross, Harold W. (1892–1951)
US editor

I've never been in there the Louvre … but there are only three things to see, and I've seen colour reproductions of all of them.

> In Ernest Hemingway, *A Farewell to Arms* (1929)

Ruskin, John (1819–1900)
English art critic, philosopher and reformer
Of one of Whistler's works

I have seen, and heard, much of Cockney impudence before now; but never expected to hear a coxcomb ask two hundred guineas for flinging a pot of paint in the public's face.

> *Fors Clavigera*, Letter 79, 1877

Sargent, John Singer (1856–1925)
Amencan painter

Every time I paint a portrait I lose a friend.

> In Bentley and Esar, *Treasury of Humorous Quotations* (1951)

Shahn, Ben (1898–1969)
Lithuanian-born US painter and muralist
Outlining the difference between professional and amateur painters

An amateur is an artist who supports himself with outside jobs which enable him to paint. A professional is someone whose wife works to enable him to paint.

> Attr.

Stevenson, Robert Louis (1850–1894)
Scottish writer, poet and essayist

A little amateur painting in water-colours shows the innocent and quiet mind.

> *Virginibus Puerisque* (1881)

Turner, Joseph Mallord William (1775–1851)
Responding to a criticism of the fact that he had painted no portholes on the ships in a view of Plymouth

My business is to paint not what I know, but what I see.

> In E. Chubb, *Sketches of Great Painters*

His customary remark following the sale of one of his paintings

I've lost one of my children this week.

> In E. Chubb, *Sketches of Great Painters*

Whistler, James McNeill (1834–1903)
US painter, etcher and pamphleteer
To a lady who told him a landscape reminded her of his work

Yes, madam, Nature is creeping up.

> In D.C. Seitz, *Whistler Stories* (1913)

▶▶ ART

parents

Allen, Woody (1935–)
US film director, writer, actor and comedian

My parents were very old world. They come from Brooklyn which is the heart of the old world. Their values in life are God, and carpeting.

> In Adler and Feinman, *Woody Allen: Clown Prince of American Humor*

And my parents finally realize that I'm kidnapped and they snap into action immediately: they rent out my room.

> In Eric Lax, *Woody Allen* (1991)

Bacon, Francis (1561–1626)
English philosopher, essayist, politician and courtier

The joys of parents are secret, and so are their griefs and fears.

> 'Of Parents and Children' (1625)

Beauvoir, Simone de (1908–1986)
French writer, feminist critic and philosopher

It's frightening to think that you mark your children merely by being yourself. It seems unfair. You can't assume the responsibility for everything you do – or don't do.

> *Les Belles Images* (1966)

Butler, Samuel (1835–1902)
English writer, painter, philosopher and scholar

Parents are the last people on earth who ought to have children.

> Attr.

Compton-Burnett, Dame Ivy (1884–1969)
English novelist

Don't be too hard on parents. You may find yourself in their place.

> *Elders and Betters* (1944)

Cosby, Bill (1937–)
US comedian, actor and author
> The truth is that parents are not really interested in justice. They just want quiet.
>> *Fatherhood* (1986)

De Vries, Peter (1910–1993)
US novelist
> There are times when parenthood seems nothing but feeding the mouth that bites you.
>> *The Tunnel of Love*

Emerson, Ralph Waldo (1803–1882)
US poet, essayist, transcendentalist and teacher
> Respect the child. Be not too much his parent. Trespass not on his solitude.
>> Attr.

Fukuyama, Francis (1952–)
US historian
> It takes a great deal of effort to separate a mother from her infant, and a fair amount to get a father to be involved with his.
>> *The Great Disruption* (1999)

Jennings, Elizabeth (1926–)
English poet
> Lying apart now, each in a separate bed,
> He with a book, keeping the light on late,
> She like a girl dreaming of childhood,
> All men elsewhere – it is as if they wait
> Some new event: the book he holds unread,
> Her eyes fixed on the shadows overhead.
>
> Tossed up like flotsam from a former passion,
> How cool they lie. They hardly ever touch,
> Or if they do it is like a confession
> Of having little feeling – or too much.
> Chastity faces them, a destination
> For which their whole lives were a preparation.
>
> Strangely apart, yet strangely close together,
> Silence between them like a thread to hold
> And not wind in. And time itself's a feather
> Touching them gently. Do they know they're old,
> These two who are my father and my mother
> Whose fire from which I came, has now grown cold?
>> *The Mind has Mountains* (1966)

Larkin, Philip (1922–1985)
English poet, writer and librarian
> They fuck you up, your mum and dad.
> They may not mean to, but they do.
> They fill you with the faults they had
> And add some extra, just for you.
>> 'This be the Verse' (1974)

Leacock, Stephen (1869–1944)
English-born Canadian humorist, writer and economist
> The parent who could see his boy as he really is,

would shake his head and say: 'Willie is no good: I'll sell him.'
>> *Essays and Literary Studies* (1916)

Nash, Ogden (1902–1971)
US poet
> Children aren't happy with nothing to ignore,
> And that's what parents were created for.
>> *Happy Days* (1933)

Onassis, Jacqueline Kennedy (1929–1994)
US First Lady
> If you bungle raising your children, I don't think whatever else you do well matters very much.
>> In Theodore C. Sorenson, *Kennedy* (1965)

Powell, Anthony (1905–2000)
English writer and critic
> All the same, you know parents – especially step-parents – are sometimes a bit of a disappointment to their children. They don't fulfil the promise of their early years.
>> *A Buyer's Market*

Schmich, Mary
US writer
> Get to know your parents. You never know when they'll be gone for good.
>> 'Everybody's Free (To Wear Sunscreen)' (speech and song, 1997)

Shaw, George Bernard (1856–1950)
Irish socialist, writer, dramatist and critic
> Parentage is a very important profession; but no test of fitness for it is ever imposed in the interest of the children.
>> *Everybody's Political What's What* (1944)

Spark, Muriel (1918–)
Scottish writer, poet and dramatist
> Parents learn a lot from their children about coping with life.
>> *The Comforters* (1957)

Spock, Dr Benjamin (1903–1998)
US pediatrician and psychiatrist
> In automobile terms, the child supplies the power but the parents have to do the steering.
>> *Common Sense Book of Baby and Child Care* (1946)

Sterne, Laurence (1713–1768)
Irish-born English writer and clergyman
> I wish either my father or my mother, or indeed both of them, as they were in duty both equally bound to it, had minded what they were about when they begot me.
>> *Tristram Shandy* (1759–1767)

Ustinov, Sir Peter (1921–)
English actor, director, dramatist, writer and raconteur
> The young need old men. They need men who are not ashamed of age, not pathetic imitations of themselves … Parents are the bones on which

children sharpen their teeth.

Dear Me (1977)

Wilde, Oscar (1854–1900)

Irish poet, dramatist, writer, critic and wit

To lose one parent may be regarded as a misfortune … to lose both seems like carelessness.

The Importance of Being Earnest (1895)

▶▶ CHILDREN; FAMILIES; FATHERS; MOTHERS

parties

Austen, Jane (1775–1817)

English writer

The sooner every party breaks up the better.

Emma (1816)

Porter, Cole (1891–1964)

He: Have you heard it's in the stars
Next July we collide with Mars?
She: Well, did you evah! What a swell party this is.

'Well, Did you Evah!', song, 1956, from *High Society*

Whitehorn, Katherine (1926–)

English writer

The Life and Soul, the man who will never go home while there is one man, woman or glass of anything not yet drunk.

Sunday Best (1976)

▶▶ SOCIETY

passion

Chapman, George (c.1559–c.1634)

English poet, dramatist and translator

For one heate (all know) doth drive out another,
One passion doth expell another still.

Monsieur D'Olive (1606)

Connolly, Cyril (1903–1974)

English literary editor, writer and critic

The man who is master of his passions is Reason's slave.

In V.S. Pritchett (ed.), *Turnstile One*

Dryden, John (1631–1700)

English poet, satirist, dramatist and critic

A man is to be cheated into passion, but to be reasoned into truth.

Religio Laici (1682)

Hume, David (1711–1776)

Scottish philosopher and political economist

We never remark any passion or principle in others, of which, in some degree or other, we

may not find a parallel in ourselves.

A Treatise of Human Nature (1739)

Jung, Carl Gustav (1875–1961)

Swiss psychiatrist and pupil of Freud

Ein Mensch, der nicht durch die Hölle seiner Leidenschaften gegangen ist, hat sie auch nie überwunden.

A man who has not gone through the hell of his passions has never overcome them either.

Memories, Dreams, Thoughts (1962)

Kempis, Thomas à (c.1380–1471)

German mystic, monk and writer

We are sometimes moved by passion and think it zeal.

De Imitatione Christi (1892)

L'Estrange, Sir Roger (1616–1704)

English writer, royalist, translator and politician

It is with our passions as it is with fire and water, they are good servants, but bad masters.

Translation of *Aesop's Fables*

Meredith, George (1828–1909)

English writer, poet and critic

In tragic life, God wot,
No villain need be! Passions spin the plot:
We are betrayed by what is false within.

Modern Love (1862)

Pope, Alexander (1688–1744)

English poet, translator and editor

The ruling Passion, be it what it will,
The ruling Passion conquers Reason still.

'Epistle to Lord Bathurst' (1733)

In Men, we various Ruling Passions find,
In Women, two almost divide the kind;
Those, only fix'd, they first or last obey,
The Love of Pleasure, and the Love of Sway.

'Epistle to a Lady' (1735)

Pound, Ezra (1885–1972)

US poet

As a bathtub lined with white porcelain,
When the hot water gives out or goes tepid,
So is the slow cooling of our chivalrous passion,
O my much praised but-not-altogether-satisfactory lady.

'The Bath Tub' (1916)

Racine, Jean (1639–1699)

French tragedian and poet

*Ce n'est plus une ardeur dans mes veines cachée:
C'est Vénus tout entière à sa proie attachée.*

It is no longer an ardour hidden in my veins: it's Venus in all her power fastening on her prey.

Phèdre (1677)

Russell, Bertrand (1872–1970)

English philosopher, mathematician, essayist and social reformer

Three passions, simple but overwhelmingly strong, have governed my life: the longing for love, the search for knowledge, and unbearable pity for the suffering of mankind.

The Autobiography of Bertrand Russell (1967–1969)

Shaffer, Peter (1926–)
English dramatist
Passion, you see, can be destroyed by a doctor. It cannot be created.

Equus (1973)

Shakespeare, William (1564–1616)
English dramatist, poet and actor
A man that Fortune's buffets and rewards
Hast ta'en with equal thanks; and blest are those
Whose blood and judgment are so well comeddled
That they are not a pipe for Fortune's finger
To sound what stop she please. Give me that man
That is not passion's slave, and I will wear him
In my heart's core, ay, in my heart of heart,
As I do thee.

Hamlet, III.ii

Steele, Sir Richard (1672–1729)
Irish-born English writer, dramatist and politician
Women dissemble their Passions better than Men, but ... Men subdue their Passions better than Women.

The Lover (1714)

Sterne, Laurence (1713–1768)
Irish-born English writer and clergyman
Having been in love, with one princess or other, almost all my life, and I hope I shall go on so till I die, being firmly persuaded, that if ever I do a mean action, it must be in some interval betwixt one passion and another.

A Sentimental Journey (1768)

Stevenson, Robert Louis (1850–1894)
Scottish writer, poet and essayist
You have only to look these happy couples in the face, to see they have never been in love, or in hate, or in any other high passion all their days.

Virginibus Puerisque (1881)

Thackeray, William Makepeace (1811–1863)
Indian-born English writer
Yes, I am a fatal man, Madame Fribsbi. To inspire hopeless passion is my destiny.

Pendennis (1848–50)

▶▶ FEELINGS; LOVE

the past

Beerbohm, Sir Max (1872–1956)
English satirist, cartoonist, critic and essayist
There is always something rather absurd about the past.

Attr.

Colette (1873–1954)
French writer
But the past, the beautiful past striped with sunshine, grey with mist, childish, blooming with hidden joy, bruised with sweet sorrow. ... Ah! if only I could resurrect one hour of that time, one alone – but which one?

Paysages et portraits (1958)

Congreve, William (1670–1729)
English dramatist
In hours of bliss we oft have met;
They could not always last;
And though the present I regret
I'm grateful for the past.

'False though she be'

Fitzgerald, F. Scott (1896–1940)
US writer
So we beat on, boats against the current, borne back ceaselessly into the past.

The Great Gatsby (1925)

Hartley, L.P. (1895–1972)
English writer and critic
The past is a foreign country: they do things differently there.

The Go-Between (1953)

Remark just before he died
I seem to have become part of my past.

In Wright, *Foreign Country: The Life of L.P. Hartley*

Huxley, Aldous (1894–1963)
English writer, poet and critic
One of the evil results of the political subjection of one people by another is that it tends to make the subject nation unnecessarily and excessively conscious of its past ... It is to the past – the gorgeous imaginary past of those whose present is inglorious, sordid, and humiliating – it is to the delightful founded-on-fact romances of history that subject peoples invariably turn.

Jesting Pilate (1926)

Lawrence, D.H. (1885–1930)
English writer, poet and critic
So now it is vain for the singer to burst into clamour
With the great black piano appassionato. The glamour
Of childish days is upon me, my manhood is cast

Down in the flood of remembrance, I weep like a child for the past.

New Poems (1918), 'Piano'

Ondaatje, Michael (1943–)
Canadian writer

The past is still, for us, a place that is not yet safely settled.

The Faber Book of Contemporary Canadian Short Stories (1990)

Santayana, George (1863–1952)
Spanish-born US philosopher and writer

Those who cannot remember the past are condemned to repeat it.

The Life of Reason (1906)

Tertz, Abram (1925–1997)
Russian writer and dissident

In the past, people did not cling to life quite as much, and it was easier to breathe.

A Voice From the Chorus (1973)

Thomas, Edward (1878–1917)
English poet

The past is the only dead thing that smells sweet.

'Early One Morning' (1917

Wain, John (1925–1994)
English poet, writer and critic

Keep off your thoughts from things
  that are past and done;
For thinking of the past wakes regret
  and pain.

Resignation, translated from the Chinese of Po-Chü-I

Webster, Daniel (1782–1852)
US statesman, orator and lawyer

The past, at least, is secure.

Speech, 1830

Whitelaw, William (1918–)
English Conservative politician

I do not intend to prejudge the past.

The Times, 1973

▶▶ EXPERIENCE; FUTURE; HISTORY; MEMORY; NOSTALGIA; PRESENT; REGRET; TIME

patience

Arnold, Matthew (1822–1888)
English poet, critic, essayist and educationist

With close-lipped patience for our only friend,
Sad patience, too near neighbour to despair.

'The Scholar-Gipsy' (1853)

Beauvoir, Simone de (1908–1986)
French writer, feminist critic and philosopher

Patience is one of those 'feminine' qualities which have their origin in our oppression but should be preserved after our liberation.

Marie-Claire, 1976

Bierce, Ambrose (1842–c.1914)
US writer, verse writer and soldier

Patience: A minor form of despair, disguised as a virtue.

The Cynic's Word Book (1906)

Campbell, Roy (1901–1957)
South African poet and journalist

The timeless, surly patience of the serf
That moves the nearest to the naked earth
And ploughs down palaces, and thrones, and towers.

Adamastor (1930), 'The Serf'

Cervantes, Miguel de (1547–1616)
Spanish writer and dramatist

I say have patience, and shuffle the cards.

Don Quixote (1615)

La Fontaine, Jean de (1621–1695)
French poet and fabulist

Patience et longueur de temps
Font plus que force ni que rage.
Patience and time do more than force and rage.

Fables

Massinger, Philip (1583–1640)
English dramatist and poet

Patience, the beggar's virtue.

A New Way to Pay Old Debts (1633)

Proverbs

Everything comes to him who waits.
Patience is a virtue.

Shakespeare, William (1564–1616)
English dramatist, poet and actor

Though patience be a tired mare, yet she will plod.

Henry V, II.i

How poor are they that have not patience!
What wound did ever heal but by degrees?

Othello, II.iii

Taylor, Elizabeth (1912–1975)
English writer

It is very strange … that the years teach us patience; that the shorter our time, the greater our capacity for waiting.

A Wreath of Roses (1950)

Thatcher, Margaret (1925–)
English Conservative Prime Minister

I'm extraordinarily patient provided I get my own way in the end.

The Observer, 1983

▶▶ PERSISTENCE

patriotism

Addison, Joseph (1672–1719)
English essayist, poet, playwright and statesman
> What pity is it
> That we can die but once to serve our country!
>> *Cato* (1713)

Barrington, George (1755–c.1835)
Irish pickpocket and writer; transported to Australia
Of convicts transported to Botany Bay
> From distant climes, o'er widespread seas we come,
> Though not with much éclat or beat of drum;
> True patriots we; for be it understood,
> We left our country for our country's good.
> No private views disgraced our generous zeal,
> What urged our travels was our country's weal;
> And none will doubt but that our emigration
> Has proved most useful to the British nation.
>> 'Prologue' for the opening of the Playhouse, Sydney, 1796

Cavell, Edith (1865–1915)
English nurse, executed by the Germans
Said on the eve of her execution
> Standing, as I do, in view of God and eternity I realize that patriotism is not enough. I must have no hatred or bitterness towards anyone.
>> *The Times*, 1915

Chesterton, G.K. (1874–1936)
English writer, poet and critic
> They died to save their country and they only saved the world.
>> *The Ballad of Saint Barbara and Other Verses* (1922)

Decatur, Stephen (1779–1820)
US naval commander
Toast during a banquet, 1815
> Our country! In her intercourse with foreign nations, may she always be in the right; but our country, right or wrong.
>> In Mackenzie, *Life of Decatur* (1846)

Dryden, John (1631–1700)
English poet, satirist, dramatist and critic
> Never was patriot yet, but was a fool.
>> *Absalom and Achitophel* (1681)

Farquhar, George (1678–1707)
Irish dramatist
> 'Twas for the good of my country that I should be abroad. – Anything for the good of one's country – I'm a Roman for that.
>> *The Beaux' Stratagem* (1707)

Forster, E.M. (1879–1970)
English writer, essayist and literary critic
> I hate the idea of causes, and if I had to choose between betraying my country and betraying my friend, I hope I should have the guts to betray my country.
>> *Two Cheers for Democracy* (1951)

Garibaldi, Giuseppe (1807–1882)
Italian soldier and patriot
> *Soldati, io esco da Roma. Chi vuole continuare la guerra contro lo straniero venga con me. Non posso offrirgli né onori né stipendi; gli offro fame, sete, marcie forzate, battaglie e morte. Chi ama la patria mi segua.*
> Men, I am leaving Rome. If you want to carry on fighting the invader, come with me. I cannot promise you either honours or wages; I can only offer you hunger, thirst, forced marches, battles and death. If you love your country, follow me.
>> In Guerzoni, *Garibaldi* (1929)

Gaskell, Elizabeth (1810–1865)
English writer
> That kind of patriotism which consists in hating all other nations.
>> *Sylvia's Lovers* (1863)

Goldsmith, Oliver (c.1728–1774)
Irish dramatist, poet and writer
> Such is the patriot's boast, where'er we roam,
> His first best country ever is at home.
>> 'The Traveller' (1764)

Hale, Nathan (1755–1776)
US soldier and revolutionary
Speech before he was executed by the British
> I only regret that I have but one life to lose for my country.
>> In Johnston, *Nathan Hale* (1974)

Homer (fl. c.8th century BC)
Greek epic poet
Hector rejects ill omens
> Without a sign, his Sword the brave Man draws,
> And asks no Omen but his Country's Cause.
>> *Iliad* (trans. Pope)

Horace (65–8 BC)
Roman lyric poet and satirist
> *Dulce et decorum est pro patria mori.*
> It is sweet and honourable to die for one's country.
>> *Odes*

Hunt, G.W. (1829–1904)
British song-writer and painter
> We don't want to fight, but, by jingo if we do,
> We've got the ships, we've got the men, we've got the money too.
>> Music hall song, 1878

Johnson, Samuel (1709–1784)
English lexicographer, poet, critic, conversationalist and essayist
> Patriotism is the last refuge of a scoundrel.
>> In Boswell, *The Life of Samuel Johnson* (1791)

Kinnock, Neil (1942–)
Welsh Labour politician
Of nuclear disarmament
> I would die for my country but I could never let my country die for me.
>> Speech, 1987

La Rochefoucauld (1613–1680)
French writer
> The accent of one's native country remains in the mind and the heart, as it does in one's speech.
>> *Réflexions ou Sentences et Maximes Morales* (1678)

Owen, Wilfred (1893–1918)
English poet
> If you could hear, at every jolt, the blood
> Come gargling from the froth-corrupted lungs,
> Obscene as cancer, bitter as the cud
> Of vile, incurable sores on innocent tongues, –
> My friend, you would not tell with such high zest
> To children ardent for some desperate glory,
> The old Lie: Dulce et decorum est
> Pro patria mori.
>> 'Dulce et decorum est' (1917)

Paine, Thomas (1737–1809)
English-born US political theorist and pamphleteer
> These are the times that try men's souls. The summer soldier and the sunshine patriot will, in this crisis, shrink from the service of their country; but he that stands it now, deserves the love and thanks of men and women.
>> *The Crisis* (1776)

> My country is the world, and my religion is to do good.
>> *The Rights of Man* (1791)

Plomer, William (1903–1973)
South African-born British writer and editor
> Patriotism is the last refuge of the sculptor.
>> Attr.

Russell, Bertrand (1872–1970)
English philosopher, mathematician, essayist and social reformer
> Patriots always talk of dying for their country, and never of killing for their country.
>> Attr.

Schurz, Carl (1829–1906)
German-born US lawyer, soldier, Republican politician and writer
> Our country, right or wrong! When right, to be kept right; when wrong, to be put right!
>> Speech, 1872

Scott, Sir Walter (1771–1832)
Scottish writer and historian
> Breathes there the man, with soul so dead,
> Who never to himself hath said,
> This is my own, my native land!

> Whose heart hath ne'er within him burned,
> As home his footsteps he hath turned,
> From wandering on a foreign strand!
>> *The Lay of the Last Minstrel* (1805)

Smollett, Tobias (1721–1771)
Scottish writer, satirist, historian, traveller and physician
> True Patriotism is of no Party.
>> *The Adventures of Sir Launcelot Greaves* (1762)

Spring-Rice, Cecil Arthur (1859–1918)
English diplomat and hymn writer
> I vow to thee, my country – all earthly things above –
> Entire and whole and perfect, the service of my love.
>> 'I Vow to Thee, My Country' (1918)

Trotsky, Leon (1879–1940)
Russian revolutionary and Communist theorist
> Patriotism to the Soviet State is a revolutionary duty, whereas patriotism to a bourgeois State is treachery.
>> In Fitzroy Maclean, *Disputed Barricade*

Whittier, John Greenleaf (1807–1892)
US poet, abolitionist and journalist
> 'Shoot if you must, this old grey head,
> But spare your country's flag,' she said.
>> 'Barbara Frietchie' (1863)

Wilde, Oscar (1854–1900)
Irish poet, dramatist, writer, critic and wit
> Patriotism is the virtue of the vicious.
>> Attr.

▶▶ WAR

peace

Anonymous
> Since wars begin in the minds of men, it is in the minds of men that the defences of peace must be constructed.
>> Constitution of UNESCO

Belloc, Hilaire (1870–1953)
English writer of verse, essayist and critic; Liberal MP
> Pale Ebenezer thought it wrong to fight,
> But Roaring Bill (who killed him) thought it right.
>> 'The Pacifist' (1938)

The Bible (King James Version)
> The peace of God, which passeth all understanding.
>> *Philippians*, 4:7

> They shall beat their swords into plowshares, and their spears into pruninghooks: nation shall not lift up sword against nation, neither shall

they learn war any more.

Isaiah, 2:4

Bierce, Ambrose (1842–c.1914)
US writer, verse writer and soldier

Peace: In international affairs, a period of cheating between two periods of fighting.

The Cynic's Word Book (1906)

Brecht, Bertolt (1898–1956)
German dramatist

Sagen sie mir nicht, dass Friede ausgebrochen ist.
Don't tell me that peace has broken out.

Mother Courage (1939)

Chamberlain, Neville (1869–1940)
English Conservative Prime Minister

This is the second time in our history that there has come back from Germany to Downing Street peace with honour. I believe it is peace for our time.

Speech, Downing Street, after Munich Agreement, 1938, in Feiling, *The Life of Neville Chamberlain* (1946)

Cicero (106–43 BC)
Roman orator, statesman, essayist and letter writer

Id quod est praestantissimum maximeque optabile omnibus sanis et bonis et beatis, cum dignitate otium.
The thing which is by far the best and most desirable for all who are sane and good and fortunate is 'peace with honour'.

Pro Sestio, 98

Cromwell, Oliver (1599–1658)
English general, statesman and Puritan leader

It's a maxim not to be despised, 'Though peace be made, yet it's interest that keeps peace.'

Speech, 1654

Disraeli, Benjamin (1804–1881)
English statesman and writer

Lord Salisbury and myself have brought you back peace – but peace, I hope, with honour.

Speech, 1878

Einstein, Albert (1879–1955)
German-born US mathematical physicist

Peace cannot be kept by force. It can only be achieved by understanding.

Notes on Pacifism

I am an absolute pacifist … It is an instinctive feeling. It is a feeling that possesses me, because the murder of men is disgusting.

Interview, 1929

Eisenhower, Dwight D. (1890–1969)
US President and general

The peace we seek, founded upon decent trust and co-operative effort among nations, can be fortified, not by weapons of war but by wheat and by cotton, by milk and by wool, by meat and by timber and by rice. These are words that translate into every language on earth. These are needs that challenge this world in arms.

Speech, 1953

I think that people want peace so much that one of these days governments had better get out of the way and let them have it.

Broadcast discussion, 1959

Gandhi (1869–1948)
Indian political leader

I wanted to avoid violence. Non-violence is the first article of my faith. It is also the last article of my creed.

Speech, 1922

George V (1865–1936)
King of the United Kingdom
On the battlefield cemeteries in Flanders, 1922

I have many times asked myself whether there can be more potent advocates of peace upon earth through the years to come than this massed multitude of silent witnesses to the desolation of war.

Attr.

Hardy, Thomas (1840–1928)
English writer and poet

'Peace upon earth!' was said. We sing it,
And pay a million priests to bring it.
After two thousand years of mass
We've got as far as poison-gas.

'Christmas: 1924' (1928)

Izetbegovic, Alija (1865–1936)
President of Bosnia
On signing the Balkan peace accord in Paris, December 1995

I feel like a man who is drinking a bitter but useful medicine.

The Observer Review, 1995

Jerrold, Douglas William (1803–1857)
English dramatist, writer and wit

We love peace, as we abhor pusillanimity; but not peace at any price.

'Peace' (1859)

Lie, Trygve (1896–1968)
Norwegian politician and Secretary-General of the UN

Now we are in a period which I can characterize as a period of cold peace.

The Observer, 1949

Litvinov, Maxim (1876–1951)
Soviet politician and diplomat

Peace is indivisible.

Speech to League of Nations, 1936

Mayhew, Christopher (1915–1997)
British parliamentarian and writer
On the Munich Agreement

The peace that passeth all understanding.

Speech, 1938

Milton, John (1608–1674)
English poet, libertarian and pamphleteer
Peace hath her victories
No less renowned than war.

'To the Lord General Cromwell' (1652)

Rendall, Montague John (1862–1950)
English schoolmaster
Nation shall speak peace unto nation.

Motto of BBC

Roosevelt, Franklin Delano (1882–1945)
US Democrat President
When peace has been broken anywhere, the
peace of all countries everywhere is in danger.

Radio broadcast, 1939

Russell, Lord John (1792–1878)
English Liberal Prime Minister and writer
If peace cannot be maintained with honour, it is
no longer peace.

Speech, 1853

Shakespeare, William (1564–1616)
English dramatist, poet and actor
A peace above all earthly dignities,
A still and quiet conscience.

Henry VIII, III.ii

Tacitus (AD c.56–c.120)
Roman historian
Ubi solitudinem faciunt pacem appellant.
They create a desert, and call it peace.

Agricola

Walpole, Horace (1717–1797)
English writer and politician
When will the world know that peace and
propagation are the two most delightful things
in it?

Letter to Sir Horace Mann, 1778

Wilson, Woodrow (1856–1924)
US Democrat President
There is a price which is too great to pay for
peace, and that price can be put in one word.
One cannot pay the price of self-respect.

Speech, 1916

It must be a peace without victory … only a
peace between equals can last.

Speech, 1917

▶▶ WAR; WAR AND PEACE

the people

Alcuin (735–804)
English theologian, scholar and educationist

*Nec audiendi qui solent dicere, Vox populi, vox Dei,
quum tumultuositas vulgi semper insaniae proxima sit.*
Nor should those be heeded who are wont to
say 'The voice of the people is the voice of
God', since popular uproar is always akin to
madness.

Letter to Charlemagne

Browne, Sir Thomas (1605–1682)
English physician, author and antiquary
If there be any among those common objects of
hatred I do contemn and laugh at, it is that great
enemy of reason, virtue, and religion, the
multitude; that numerous piece of monstrosity,
which, taken asunder, seem men, and the
reasonable creatures of God, but, confused
together, make but one great beast, and a
monstrosity more prodigious than Hydra.

Religio Medici (1643)

Burke, Edmund (1729–1797)
Irish-born British statesman and philosopher
It is a general popular error to imagine the
loudest complainers for the public to be the
most anxious for its welfare.

Observations on 'The Present State of the Nation' (1769)

The people never give up their liberties but
under some delusion.

Speech, 1784

Burns, Robert (1759–1796)
Scottish poet and song writer
Who will not sing God save the King
Shall hang as high's the steeple;
But while we sing God save the King,
We'll ne'er forget the People!

'Does Haughty Gaul Invasion Threat?' (1795)

Carlyle, Thomas (1795–1881)
Scottish historian, biographer, critic, and essayist
The Public is an old woman. Let her maunder
and mumble.

Attr.

Chaplin, Charlie (1889–1977)
English comedian, film actor, director and satirist
I am for people. I can't help it.

The Observer, 1952

Cicero (106–43 BC)
Roman orator, statesman, essayist and letter writer
Salus populi suprema est lex.
The good of the people is the chief law.

De Legibus

Cocteau, Jean (1889–1963)
French dramatist, poet, film writer and director
If the crowd has to choose someone to crucify, it
will always save Barabbas.

*Le Coq et l'Arlequin
(1918)*

Confucius (c.550–c.478 BC)
Chinese philosopher and teacher of ethics

> The people may be made to follow a course of
> action, but they may not be made to understand
> it.
>
> *Analects*

Cromwell, Oliver (1599–1658)
English general, statesman and Puritan leader
Referring to a cheering crowd

> The people would be just as noisy if they were
> going to see me hanged.
>
> Attr.

De Mille, Cecil B. (1881–1959)

> The public is always right.
>
> In Colombo, *Wit and Wisdom of the Moviemakers*

Dickens, Charles (1812–1870)
English writer

> 'But suppose there are two mobs?' suggested
> Mr Snodgrass. 'Shout with the largest,' replied
> Mr Pickwick.
>
> *The Pickwick Papers* (1837)

Dryden, John (1631–1700)
English poet, satirist, dramatist and critic

> Nor is the people's judgement always true:
> The most may err as grossly as the few.
>
> *Absalom and Achitophel* (1681)

> If by the people you understand the multitude,
> the hoi polloi 'tis no matter what they think; they
> are sometimes in the right, sometimes in the
> wrong: their judgement is a mere lottery.
>
> *Essay of Dramatic Poesy* (1668)

Elliott, Ebenezer (1781–1849)
English poet and merchant

> When wilt thou save the people?
> Oh, God of Mercy! when?
> The people, Lord, the people!
> Not thrones and crowns, but men!
>
> 'The People's Anthem'
> (1850)

Gladstone, William (1809–1898)
English statesman and reformer

> All the world over, I will back the masses against
> the classes.
>
> Speech, Liverpool, 1886

Hazlitt, William (1778–1830)
English writer and critic

> There is not a more mean, stupid, dastardly,
> pitiful, selfish, spiteful, envious, ungrateful
> animal than the Public. It is the greatest of
> cowards, for it is afraid of itself.
>
> *Table-Talk* (1822)

Hitler, Adolf (1889–1945)
German Nazi dictator, born in Austria

> *Die breite Masse eines Volkes ... fällt einer grossen*
> *Lüge leichter zum Opfer als einer kleinen.*
> The broad mass of a people ... falls victim to a
> big lie more easily than to a small one.
>
> *Mein Kampf* (1925)

Hooker, Richard (c.1554–1600)
English theologian and churchman

> He that goeth about to persuade a multitude,
> that they are not so well governed as they ought
> to be, shall never want attentive and favourable
> hearers.
>
> *Of the Laws of Ecclesiasticall Politie* (1593)

Ibsen, Henrik (1828–1906)
Norwegian writer, dramatist and poet

> The majority has the might – more's the pity –
> but it hasn't right ... The minority is always right.
>
> *An Enemy of the People* (1882)

Juvenal (c.60–130)
Roman verse satirist and Stoic

> *Duas tantum res anxius optat,*
> *Panem et circenses.*
> Two things only the people anxiously desire:
> bread and circuses.
>
> *Satires*

Kennedy, Robert F. (1925–1968)
US Attorney General and Democrat politician

> One fifth of the people are against everything all
> the time.
>
> *The Observer*, 1964

La Bruyère, Jean de (1645–1696)
French satirist

> *Le peuple n'a guère d'esprit et les grands n'ont point*
> *d'âme ... faut-il opter, je ne balance pas, je veux être*
> *peuple.*
> The people have little intelligence, the great no
> heart ... if I had to choose I should not hesitate:
> I would be of the people.
>
> *Les caractères ou les moeurs de ce siècle* (1688)

Lincoln, Abraham (1809–1865)
US statesman and President

> You can fool some of the people all of the time,
> and all of the people some of the time, but you
> cannot fool all of the people all the time.
>
> Attr.

Montesquieu, Charles (1689–1755)
French philosopher and jurist

> *Les grands seigneurs ont des plaisirs, le peuple a de la*
> *joie.*
> Great lords have pleasures, but the people have
> fun.
>
> *Pensées et fragments inédits* (1899)

Morris, William (1834–1896)
English poet, designer, craftsman, artist and socialist

> What is this, the sound and rumour? What is this
> that all men hear,

Like the wind in hollow valleys when the storm is drawing near,
Like the rolling on of ocean in the eventide of fear?
'Tis the people marching on.
Chants for Socialists (1885), 'The March of the Workers'

Northcliffe, Lord (1865–1922)
Irish-born British newspaper proprietor
Rumoured to have been a notice to remind his staff of his opinion of the mental age of the general public
They are only ten.
Attr.

Papprill, Ross F. (1908–1975)
There are two kinds of people in the world: those who believe there are two kinds of people in the world, and those who don't.
Attr.

Parkman, Francis (1823–1893)
US historian
The public demands elocution rather than reason of those who address it … On matters of the greatest interest it craves to be excited or amused.
The Tale of the Ripe Scholar

Pope, Alexander (1688–1744)
English poet, translator and editor
The People's Voice is odd,
It is, and it is not, the voice of God.
Imitations of Horace (1737–1738)

Roscommon, Fourth Earl of (1633–1685)
Irish translator and poet
The multitude is always in the wrong.
An Essay on Translated Verse (1684)

Sandburg, Carl (1878–1967)
US poet, writer and song collector
The people will live on.
The learning and blundering people will live on.
The People, Yes (1936)

Schulz, Charles (1922–2000)
US cartoonist
I love mankind – it's people I can't stand.
Go Fly a Kite, Charlie Brown

Sitwell, Dame Edith (1887–1964)
English poet, anthologist, critic and biographer
During the writing … of this book, I realized that the public will believe anything – so long as it is not founded on truth.
Taken Care Of (1965)

Vanderbilt, William H. (1821–1885)
US financier and railway magnate
When asked whether the public should be consulted about luxury trains

The public be damned! I'm working for my stockholders.
Remark, 1883

Walpole, Horace (1717–1797)
English writer and politician
Our supreme governors, the mob.
Letter to Sir Horace Mann, 1743

Wellington, Duke of (1769–1852)
Irish-born British military commander and statesman
You must build your House of Parliament upon the river: so … that the populace cannot exact their demands by sitting down round you.
In Fraser, *Words on Wellington* (1889)

▶▶ HUMANITY AND HUMAN NATURE

perception

Blake, William (1757–1827)
English poet, engraver, painter and mystic
Mans desires are limited by his perceptions; none can desire what he has not perceiv'd.
There is No Natural Religion (c.1788)

If the doors of perception were cleansed every thing would appear to man as it is, infinite.
The Marriage of Heaven and Hell (c.1790–1793)

Langbridge, Frederick (1849–1923)
English religious writer
Two men look out through the same bars:
One sees the mud, and one the stars.
'A Cluster of Quiet Thoughts' (1896)

Ruskin, John (1819–1900)
English art critic, philosopher and reformer
Not only is there but one way of doing things rightly, but there is only one way of seeing them, and that is, seeing the whole of them.
The Two Paths (1859)

Trumbull, John (1750–1831)
English dramatist
But optics sharp it needs I ween,
To see what is not to be seen.
McFingal

perfection and imperfection

Dali, Salvador (1904–1989)
Spanish painter and writer
Have no fear of perfection – you'll never reach it.
Attr.

De Quincey, Thomas (1785–1859)
English writer

Even imperfection itself may have its ideal or perfect state.

'Murder Considered as One of the Fine Arts' (1839)

Hall, Joseph (1574–1656)
English bishop and writer

Perfection is the child of Time.

Works (1625)

Mill, John Stuart (1806–1873)
English philosopher, economist and reformer

The great majority of those who speak of perfectibility as a dream, do so because they feel that it is one which would afford them no pleasure if it were realized.

Speech on Perfectibility (1828)

Pope, Alexander (1688–1744)
English poet, translator and editor

Whoever thinks a faultless piece to see,
Thinks what ne'er was, nor is, nor e'er shall be.

An Essay on Criticism (1711)

Then say not man's imperfect, Heav'n in fault;
Say rather, Man's as perfect as he ought.

An Essay on Man (1733)

Pound, Ezra (1885–1972)
US poet

Come, my songs, let us speak of perfection –
We shall get ourselves rather disliked.

'Salvationists' (1916)

Roydon, Matthew (fl. 1580–1622)

Was never eye, did see that face,
Was never ear, did hear that tongue,
Was never mind, did mind his grace,
That ever thought the travel long –
But eyes, and ears, and ev'ry thought,
Were with his sweet perfections caught.

'An Elegy, or Friend's Passion, for his Astrophill' (1593)

Smith, Robert (1634–1716)

Powers act but weakly and irregularly, till they are heightened and perfected by their habits. A well radicated habit, in a lively, vegete faculty, is like an apple of gold in a picture of silver; it is perfection upon perfection, it is a coat of mail upon our armour, and, in a word, it is the raising the soul at least one story higher: for take off but these wheels and the powers of all their operations will drive but heavily.

Sermon, 30 April 1668

Stephens, James (1882–1950)
Irish poet and writer

Finality is death. Perfection is finality. Nothing is perfect. There are lumps in it.

The Crock of Gold (1912)

perseverance

Churchill, Sir Winston (1874–1965)
English Conservative Prime Minister
Remark, December 1941

We must just KBO ('Keep Buggering On').

In M. Gilbert, *Finest Hour*

Hickson, William Edward (1803–1870)
English educationist

'Tis a lesson you should heed,
Try, try again.
If at first you don't succeed,
Try, try again.

'Try and Try Again'

Latimer, Bishop Hugh (c.1485–1555)
English Protestant churchman

Gutta cavat lapidem, non vi sed saepe cadendo.
The drop of rain maketh a hole in the stone, not by violence, but by oft falling.

Sermon preached before Edward VI, 1549

Stevenson, Robert Louis (1850–1894)
Scottish writer, poet and essayist

Surely we should find it both touching and inspiriting, that in a field from which success is banished, our race should not cease to labour.

Across the Plains (1892)

▶▶ PATIENCE

pessimism

Bennett, Arnold (1867–1931)
English writer, dramatist and journalist

Pessimism, when you get used to it, is just as agreeable as optimism.

Things That Have Interested Me

Beveridge, William Henry (1879–1963)
British economist and social reformer

Scratch a pessimist, and you find often a defender of privilege.

The Observer, 1943

Cohen, Leonard (1934–)
Canadian singer

I don't consider myself a pessimist. I think of a pessimist as someone who is waiting for it to rain. And I feel soaked to the skin.

The Observer, 1993

King, Benjamin (1857–1894)
US humorist

Nothing to do but work,
Nothing to eat but food,
Nothing to wear but clothes
To keep one from going nude.

Nothing to breathe but air,
Quick as a flash 'tis gone;
Nowhere to fall but off,
Nowhere to stand but on!

'The Pessimist'

Lowell, Robert (1917–1977)
US poet and writer
If we see light at the end of the tunnel,
It's the light of the oncoming train.

'Since 1939' (1977)

Mallet, Robert (1915–)
French university rector, poet and writer
How many pessimists end up by desiring the
things they fear, in order to prove that they are
right.

Apostilles

Meir, Golda (1898–1978)
Russian-born Israeli stateswoman and Prime Minister
Pessimism is a luxury that a Jew can never allow
himself.

The Observer, 1974

Peter, Laurence J. (1919–1990)
Canadian educationist and writer
A pessimist is a man who looks both ways
before crossing a one-way street.

Attr.

▶▶ OPTIMISM

philosophy

Adams, Henry (1838–1918)
US historian and memoirist
Philosophy: unintelligible answers to insoluble
problems.

In Bert Leston Taylor, *The So-Called Human Race*
(1922)

Addison, Joseph (1672–1719)
English essayist, poet, playwright and statesman
It was said of Socrates that he brought
philosophy down from heaven to inhabit among
men; and I shall be ambitious to have it said of
me that I have brought philosophy out of closets
and libraries, schools and colleges, to dwell in
clubs and assemblies, at tea-tables and in
coffee-houses.

The Spectator, March 1711

Ayer, A.J. (1910–1989)
English philosopher
The principles of logic and metaphysics are true
simply because we never allow them to be
anything else.

Language, Truth and Logic
(1936)

Bacon, Francis (1561–1626)
English philosopher, essayist, politician and courtier
All good moral philosophy … is but an handmaid
to religion.

The Advancement of Learning (1605)

Bowen, Lord (1835–1894)
English judge and scholar
On a metaphysician: A blind man in a dark room
– looking for a black hat – which isn't there.

Attr.

Bradley, F.H. (1846–1924)
English philosopher
Metaphysics is the finding of bad reasons for
what we believe upon instinct; but to find these
reasons is no less an instinct.

Appearance and Reality (1893)

Canetti, Elias (1905–1994)
Bulgarian-born English writer, dramatist and critic
The profoundest thoughts of the philosophers
have something tricklike about them. A lot
disappears in order for something to suddenly
appear in the palm of the hand.

The Secret Heart of the Clock: Notes, Aphorisms,
Fragments 1973-1985 (1991)

Chamfort, Nicolas (1741–1794)
French writer
*Je dirais volontiers des métaphysiciens ce que Scalinger
disait des Basques, on dit qu'ils s'entendent, mais je
n'en crois rien.*
I am tempted to say about metaphysicians what
Scalinger would say about the Basques: they are
said to understand one another, but I don't
believe a word of it.

Maximes et Pensées (1796)

Cicero (106–43 BC)
Roman orator, statesman, essayist and letter writer
*Sed nescio quo modo nihil tam absurde dici potest
quod non dicatur ab aliquo philosophorum.*
But somehow there is nothing so absurd that
some philosopher has not said it.

De Divinatione

Edwards, Oliver (1711–1791)
English lawyer
I have tried too in my time to be a philosopher;
but, I don't know how, cheerfulness was always
breaking in.

In Boswell, *The Life of Samuel Johnson*
(1791)

Ford, John (c.1586–c.1640)
English dramatist and poet
Nice philosophy
May tolerate unlikely arguments,
But heaven admits no jest.

'Tis Pity She's a Whore (1633)

Goldsmith, Oliver (c.1728–1774)
Irish dramatist, poet and writer

> To a philosopher, no circumstance, however trifling, is too minute.
>
> *The Citizen of the World* (1762

> This same philosophy is a good horse in the stable, but an errant jade on a journey.
>
> *The Good Natur'd Man* (1768)

Hume, David (1711–1776)
Scottish philosopher and political economist

> Philosophers never balance between profit and honesty, because their decisions are general, and neither their passions nor imaginations are interested in the objects.
>
> *A Treatise of Human Nature* (1739)

Huxley, Aldous (1894–1963)
English writer, poet and critic

> Finding bad reasons for what one believes for other bad reasons – that's philosophy.
>
> *Brave New World* (1932)

Huxley, T.H. (1825–1895)
English biologist, Darwinist and agnostic

> I doubt if the philosopher lives, or has ever lived, who could know himself to be heartily despised by a street boy without some irritation.
>
> *Evolution and Ethics* (1893)

James, William (1842–1910)
US psychologist and philosopher

> There is only one thing a philosopher can be relied on to do, and that is to contradict other philosophers.
>
> Attr.

Johnson, Samuel (1709–1784)
English lexicographer, poet, critic, conversationalist and essayist
Kicking a stone in order to disprove Berkeley's theory of the non-existence of matter

> I refute it thus.
>
> In Boswell, *The Life of Samuel Johnson* (1791)

Kafka, Franz (1883–1924)
Czech-born German-speaking writer

> *Metaphysisches Bedürfnis ist nur Todesbedürfnis.*
> A metaphysical need is only a need for death.
>
> *Diary* (1912)

Keats, John (1795–1821)
English poet

> Do not all charms fly
> At the mere touch of cold philosophy?
> There was an awful rainbow once in heaven:
> We know her woof, her texture; she is given
> In the dull catalogue of common things.
> Philosophy will clip an Angel's wings.
>
> 'Lamia' (1819)

Lao-Tzu (c.604–531 BC)
Chinese philosopher

> Acting without design, occupying oneself without making a business of it, finding the great in what is small and the many in the few, repaying injury with kindness, effecting difficult things while they are easy, and managing great things in their beginnings: this is the method of Tao.
>
> *Tao Te Ching*

Leary, Timothy (1920–1996)
US writer and psychologist

> In the information age, you don't teach philosophy as they did after feudalism. You perform it. If Aristotle were alive today he'd have a talk show.
>
> *Evening Standard*, 1989

MacNeice, Louis (1907–1963)
Belfast-born poet, writer, radio producer, translator and critic

> Good-bye now, Plato and Hegel,
> The shop is closing down;
> They don't want any philosopher-kings in England,
> There ain't no universals in this man's town.
>
> *Autumn Journal* (1939)

Nietzsche, Friedrich Wilhelm (1844–1900)
German philosopher, critic and poet

> *Wie ich den Philosophen verstehe, als einen furchtbaren Explosionsstoff, vor dem Alles in Gefahr ist.*
> What I understand philosophers to be: a terrible explosive, in the presence of which everything is in danger.
>
> *Ecce Homo* (1888)

Ortega y Gasset, José (1883–1955)
Spanish philosopher

> *El placer sexual parece consistir en una súbita descarga de energ'a nerviosa. La fruic'on estética es una súbita descarga de emociones alusivas. Análogamente es la filosofia como una súbita descarga de intelección.*
> Sexual pleasure seems to consist in a sudden discharge of nervous energy. Aesthetic enjoyment is a sudden discharge of allusive emotions. Similarly, philosophy is like a sudden discharge of intellectual activity.
>
> *Meditations on Quijote* (1914)

Pascal, Blaise (1623–1662)
French philosopher and scientist

> *Se moquer de la philosophie, c'est vraiment philosopher.*
> To ridicule philosophy is truly to philosophize.
>
> *Pensées* (1670)

Peabody, Elizabeth (1804–1894)
US teacher and writer
Giving a Transcendentalist explanation for her accidentally

walking into a tree
> I saw it, but I did not realize it.
>> In L. Tharp, *The Peabody Sisters of Salem*

Plato (c.429–347 BC)
Greek philosopher
> Unless either philosophers become kings in our states, or those who are now called kings and rulers become to a serious and sufficient degree philosophers ... there will be no fewer ills afflicting our states or indeed the whole of the human race.
>> *Republic*

Russell, Bertrand (1872–1970)
English philosopher, mathematician, essayist and social reformer
> Matter ... a convenient formula for describing what happens where it isn't.
>> *An Outline of Philosophy* (1927)

> Organic life, we are told, has developed gradually from the protozoon to the philosopher, and this development, we are assured, is indubitably an advance. Unfortunately it is the philosopher, not the protozoon, who gives us this assurance.
>> *Mysticism and Logic* (1918)

Ryle, Gilbert (1900–1976)
English philosopher
> Philosophy is the replacement of category-habits by category-disciplines.
>> *The Concept of Mind* (1949)

Santayana, George (1863–1952)
Spanish-born US philosopher and writer
> It is a great advantage for a system of philosophy to be substantially true.
>> *The Unknowable* (1923)

Selden, John (1584–1654)
English historian, jurist and politician
> Philosophy is nothing but discretion.
>> *Table Talk* (1689)

Shakespeare, William (1564–1616)
English dramatist, poet and actor
> There are more things in heaven and earth, Horatio,
> Than are dreamt of in your philosophy.
>> *Hamlet*, I.v

> Adversity's sweet milk, philosophy.
>> *Romeo and Juliet*, III.iii

Swift, Jonathan (1667–1745)
Irish satirist, poet, essayist and cleric
> Philosophy! the lumber of the schools.
>> 'Ode to Sir W. Temple' (1692)

Thoreau, Henry David (1817–1862)
US essayist, social critic and writer

> There are now-a-days professors of philosophy but not philosophers.
>> *Walden* (1854)

Voltaire (1694–1778)
French philosopher, dramatist, poet, historian writer and critic
> *En philosophie, il faut se défier de ce qu'on croit entendre trop trop aisément, aussi bien que des choses qu'on n'entend pas.*
> In philosophy, we must distrust the things we understand too easily as well as the things we don't understand.
>> *Lettres philosophiques* (1734)

> *La superstition met le monde entier en flammes; la philosophie les éteint.*
> Superstition sets the whole world on fire; philosophy quenches the flames.
>> *Dictionnaire philosophique* (1764)

Whitehead, A.N. (1861–1947)
English mathematician and philosopher
> The safest general characterization of the European philosophical tradition is that it consists of a series of footnotes to Plato.
>> *Process and Reality* (1929)

> The systematic thought of ancient writers is now nearly worthless; but their detached insights are priceless.
>> Attr.

> Philosophy is the product of wonder.
>> *Nature and Life* (1934)

Wittgenstein, Ludwig (1889–1951)
Austrian philosopher
> Philosophy is not a theory but an activity.
>> *Tractatus Logico-Philosophicus* (1922)

> Philosophy is a struggle against the bewitching of our minds by means of language.
>> *Philosophical Investigations* (1953)

▶▶ LOGIC; THOUGHT

photography

Abbott, Berenice (1898–1991)
US photographer
> Photography can never grow up if it imitates some other medium. It has to walk alone; it has to be itself.
>> *Infinity*, 1951

Adams, Ansel (1902–1984)
US photographer
> Sometimes I do get to places just when God's ready to have somebody click the shutter.
>> *American Way* (1974)

There are always two people in every picture: the photographer and the viewer.

Playboy, 1983

Arbus, Diane (1923–1971)
US photographer
> A photograph is a secret about a secret. The more it tells you the less you know.
>
> In Patricia Bosworth, *Diane Arbus: a Biography* (1985)

Astor, Nancy, Viscountess (1879–1964)
US-born British Conservative politician and hostess
Refusing to pose for a close-up photograph
> Take a close-up of a woman past sixty! You might as well use a picture of a relief map of Ireland!
>
> Attr.

Benn, Tony (1925–)
English Labour politician
> Most things in life are moments of pleasure and a lifetime of embarrassment; photography is a moment of embarrassment and a lifetime of pleasure.
>
> *The Independent*, 1989

Hillary, Sir Edmund (1919–)
Referring to Tenzing Norgay, his companion on the conquest of Mt Everest, 1953
> As far as I knew, he had never taken a photograph before, and the summit of Everest was hardly the place to show him how.
>
> *High Adventure*

Hockney, David (1937–)
English artist
On the death of photography
> Once you can manipulate pictures on a computer you can't believe them any more. There will be no more Cartier-Bressons.
>
> Interview, *The Observer*, May 1999

Lawrence, D.H. (1885–1930)
English writer, poet and critic
> The modern pantheist not only sees the god in everything, he takes photographs of it.
>
> *St Mawr* (1925)

Reagan, Ronald (1911–)
US actor, Republican statesman and President
> I like photographers, you don't ask questions.
>
> Speech to White House News Photographers Association, 1983

Sontag, Susan (1933–)
US critic and writer
> A photograph is not only an image (as a painting is an image), an interpretation of the real; it is also a trace, something directly stencilled off the real, like a footprint or a death mask.
>
> *New York Review of Books*, 1977

Social misery has inspired the comfortably-off with the urge to take pictures, the gentlest of predations, in order to document a hidden reality, that is, a reality hidden from them.

New York Review of Books, 1977

Vidal, Gore (1925–)
US writer, critic and poet
> As much of an art form as interior decorating.
>
> Attr.

plagiarism

Bayley, Stephen
English designer and critic
> 'Where do architects and designers get their ideas?' The answer, of course, is mainly from other architects and designers, so is it mere casuistry to distinguish between tradition and plagiarism?
>
> *Commerce and Culture* (1989)

Bierce, Ambrose (1842–c.1914)
US writer, verse writer and soldier
> *Plagiarize:* To take the thought or style of another writer whom one has never, never read.
>
> *The Enlarged Devil's Dictionary* (1961)

Lehrer, Tom (1928–)
US humorist
> Plagiarize! Let no one else's work evade your eyes,
> Remember why the good Lord made your eyes.
>
> 'Lobachevski' (song, 1953)

Mizner, Wilson (1876–1933)
US writer, wit and dramatist
> When you steal from one author, it's plagiarism; if you steal from many, it's research.
>
> Attr.

Montaigne, Michel de (1533–1592)
French essayist and moralist
> *Quelqu'un pourrait dire de moi que j'ai seulement fait ici un amas de fleurs étrangères, n'y ayant fourni du mien que le filet à les lier.*
> One could say of me that in this book I have only made up a bunch of other men's flowers, providing of my own only the string to tie them together.
>
> *Essais* (1580)

More, Hannah (1745–1833)
English poet, dramatist and religious writer
> He lik'd those literary cooks
> Who skim the cream of others' books;
> And ruin half an author's graces
> By plucking bon-mots from their places.
>
> Attr.

Sheridan, Richard Brinsley (1751–1816)
Irish dramatist, politician and orator

All that can be said is, that two people
happened to hit on the same thought – and
Shakespeare made use of it first, that's all.

The Critic (1779)

Stevenson, Robert Louis (1850–1894)
Scottish writer, poet and essayist

Of all my verse, like not a single line;
But like my title, for it is not mine,
That title from a better man I stole;
Ah, how much better, had I stol'n the whole!

Underwoods (1887)

Stravinsky, Igor (1882–1971)
Russian composer and conductor

A good composer does not imitate; he steals.

In Yates, *Twentieth Century Music* (1967)

Sullivan, Sir Arthur (1842–1900)
English composer, particularly of operettas
Accused of plagiarism

We all have the same eight notes to work with.

Attr.

plans

Bierce, Ambrose (1842–c.1914)
US writer, verse writer and soldier

Plan: To bother about the best method of
accomplishing an accidental result.

The Enlarged Devil's Dictionary (1961)

Brecht, Bertolt (1898–1956)
German dramatist

*Die schönsten Plän sind schon zuschanden geworden
durch die Kleinlichkeit von denen, wo sie ausführen
sollten.*

The best plans have always been wrecked by the
narrow-mindedness of those who should carry
them out.

Mother Courage and her Children
(1941)

Burns, Robert (1759–1796)
Scottish poet and song writer

The best-laid schemes o' mice an' men
Gang aft agley,
An' lea'e us nought but grief an' pain,
For promis'd joy!

'To a Mouse' (1785)

Canetti, Elias (1905–1994)
Bulgarian-born English writer, dramatist and critic

It is important what you still have planned at the
end. It shows the extent of injustice in your
death.

The Human Province (1973)

Dryden, John (1631–1700)
English poet, satirist, dramatist and critic

Plots, true or false, are necessary
things,
To raise up commonwealths and ruin
kings.

Absalom and Achitophel (1681)

Gilman, Charlotte Perkins (1860–1935)
US writer, social reformer and feminist

Where young boys plan for what they will achieve
and attain, young girls plan for whom they will
achieve and attain.

Women and Economics (1898)

Osler, Sir William (1849–1919)
Canadian physician

When schemes are laid in advance, it is
surprising how often the circumstances fit in
with them.

Attr.

Young, Edward (1683–1765)
English poet, dramatist, satirist and clergyman

For her own breakfast she'll project a scheme,
Nor take her tea without a stratagem.

Love of Fame, the Universal Passion (1725–1728)

pleasure

Alcott, Bronson (1799–1888)
US educator, reformer and transcendentalist

A sip is the most that mortals are permitted
from any goblet of delight.

Table Talk (1877)

Austen, Jane (1775–1817)
English writer

'I am afraid,' replied Elinor, 'that the
pleasantness of an employment does not always
evince its propriety.'

Sense and Sensibility (1811)

One half of the world cannot understand the
pleasures of the other.

Emma (1816)

Bataille, Georges (1897–1962)
French writer

Pleasure only starts once the worm has got into
the fruit, to become delightful happiness must
be tainted with poison.

My Mother (1966)

Behn, Aphra (1640–1689)
English dramatist, writer, poet, translator and spy

Variety is the soul of pleasure.

The Rover (1677)

Bierce, Ambrose (1842–c.1914)
US writer, verse writer and soldier

Debauchee: One who has so earnestly pursued pleasure that he has had the misfortune to overtake it.

The Cynic's Word Book (1906)

Burke, Edmund (1729–1797)
Irish-born British statesman and philosopher
> I am convinced that we have a degree of delight, and that no small one, in the real misfortunes and pains of others.
>
> *A Philosophical Enquiry into the Origin of our Ideas of the Sublime and Beautiful* (1757)

Burns, Robert (1759–1796)
Scottish poet and song writer
> But pleasures are like poppies spread:
> You seize the flow'r, its bloom is shed;
> Or like the snow falls in the river,
> A moment white – then melts for ever.
>
> 'Tam o' Shanter' (1790)

Byron, Lord (1788–1824)
English poet satirist and traveller
> There's not a joy the world can give like that it takes away.
>
> 'Stanzas for Music' (1815)

> Pleasure's a sin, and sometimes sin's a pleasure.
>
> *Don Juan* (1824)

> Though sages may pour out their wisdom's treasure,
> There is no sterner moralist than Pleasure.
>
> *Don Juan* (1824)

Cabell, James Branch (1879–1958)
US writer, poet, genealogist and historian
> A man possesses nothing certainly save a brief loan of his own body: and yet the body of man is capable of much curious pleasure.
>
> *Jurgen* (1919)

Camus, Albert (1913–1960)
Algerian-born French writer
> *Il semblait être l'ami de tous les plaisirs normaux, sans en être l'esclave.*
> He seemed to indulge in all the usual pleasures without being a slave to any of them.
>
> *The Plague*, 1947)

Clare, John (1793–1864)
English rural poet; died in an asylum
> Summer's pleasures they are gone like to visions every one
> And the cloudy days of autumn and of winter cometh on
> I tried to call them back but unbidden they are gone
> Far away from heart and eye and for ever far away.
>
> 'Remembrances' (1908)

Clark, Manning (1915–1991)
Australian historian
Of the Australian writer, Henry Lawson
> He said later that the greatest pleasure he ever knew in the world was when his eyes met the eyes of a mate over the top of two foaming glasses of beer.
>
> *In Search of Henry Lawson* (1987)

Clough, Arthur Hugh (1819–1861)
English poet and letter writer
> The horrible pleasure of pleasing inferior people.
>
> *Amours de Voyage* (1858)

Cowper, William (1731–1800)
English poet, hymn and letter writer
> Remorse, the fatal egg by pleasure laid.
>
> 'The Progress of Error' (1782)

David, Elizabeth (1913–1992)
British cookery writer
> To eat figs off the tree in the very early morning, when they have been barely touched by the sun, is one of the exquisite pleasures of the Mediterranean.
>
> *Italian Food* (1954)

Dryden, John (1631–1700)
English poet, satirist, dramatist and critic
> For present joys are more to flesh and blood
> Than a dull prospect of a distant good.
>
> *The Hind and the Panther* (1687)

Gay, John (1685–1732)
English poet, dramatist and librettist
> A miss for pleasure, and a wife for breed.
>
> 'The Toilette' (1716)

Hazlitt, William (1778–1830)
English writer and critic
> The art of pleasing consists in being pleased.
>
> *The Round Table* (1817)

Herbert, George (1593–1633)
English poet and priest
> Look not on pleasures as they come, but go.
>
> *The Temple* (1633)

Herbert, Sir A.P. (1890–1971)
English humorist, writer, dramatist and politician
> People must not do things for fun. We are not here for fun. There is no reference to fun in any Act of Parliament.
>
> *Uncommon Law* (1935)

Hunt, Leigh (1784–1859)
English writer, poet and literary editor
> A pleasure so exquisite as almost to amount to pain.
>
> Letter to Alexander Ireland, 1848

Johnson, Samuel (1709–1784)
English lexicographer, poet, critic, conversationalist and essayist
> Pleasure is very seldom found where it is sought; our brightest blazes of gladness are commonly kindled by unexpected sparks.
>> *The Idler* (1758–1760)

> The great source of pleasure is variety.
>> *The Lives of the Most Eminent English Poets* (1779–1781)

> If I had no duties, and no reference to futurity, I would spend my life in driving briskly in a post-chaise with a pretty woman.
>> In Boswell, *The Life of Samuel Johnson* (1791)

> No man is a hypocrite in his pleasures.
>> In Boswell, *The Life of Samuel Johnson* (1791)

Keats, John (1795–1821)
English poet
> Ever let the Fancy roam,
> Pleasure never is at home.
>> 'Fancy' (1819)

Lamb, Charles (1775–1834)
English essayist, critic and letter writer
> The greatest pleasure I know, is to do a good action by stealth, and to have it found out by accident.
>> 'Table Talk by the Late Elia'

Loos, Anita (1893–1981)
US writer and screenwriter
> Fun is fun but no girl wants to laugh all of the time.
>> *Gentlemen Prefer Blondes* (1925)

Lucretius (c.95–55 BC)
Roman philosopher
> From the midst of the fountain of delights rises something bitter that is a torment even among the flowers.
>> *De Rerum Natura*

Luther, Martin (1483–1546)
German Protestant theologian and reformer
> *Wer nicht liebt Wein, Weib und Gesang,*
> *Der bleibt ein Narr sein Leben lang.*
> Whoever does not love wine, woman and song,
> Remains a fool his whole life long.
>> Attr

Marvell, Andrew (1621–1678)
English poet and satirist
> Let us roll our strength and all
> Our sweetness up into one ball,
> And tear our pleasures with rough strife
> Thorough the iron gates of life:
> Thus, though we cannot make our sun
> Stand still, yet we will make him run.
>> 'To His Coy Mistress' (1681)

Molière (1622–1673)
French dramatist, actor and director
> *Le ciel défend, de vrai, certains contentements*
> *Mais on trouve avec lui des accommodements.*
> Heaven forbids certain pleasures, it is true, but one can arrive at certain compromises.
>> *Tartuffe* (1664)

Moore, Thomas (1779–1852)
Irish poet
> Then awake! the heavens look bright, my dear;
> 'Tis never too late for delight, my dear;
> And the best of all ways
> To lengthen our days
> Is to steal a few hours from the night, my dear!
>> *Irish Melodies* (1807), 'The Young May Moon'

O'Rourke, P.J. (1947–)
US writer
> After all, what is your hosts' purpose in having a party? Surely not for you to enjoy yourself; if that were their sole purpose, they'd have simply sent champagne and women over to your place by taxi.
>> Attr.

Pope, Alexander (1688–1744)
English poet, translator and editor
> Pleasures are ever in our hands or eyes,
> And when in act they cease, in prospect rise;
> Present to grasp, and future still to find,
> The whole employ of body and of mind.
>> *An Essay on Man* (1733)

Rochester, Earl of (1647–1680)
English poet, satirist, courtier and libertine
> 'Is there then no more?'
> She cries. 'All this to love and rapture's due;
> Must we not pay a debt to pleasure too?'.
>> 'The Imperfect Enjoyment' (1680)

Selden, John (1584–1654)
English historian, jurist and politician
> Pleasure is nothing else but the intermission of pain, the enjoyment of something I am in great trouble for till I have it.
>> *Table Talk* (1689)

Shadbolt, Tim (1932–)
New Zealand novelist
On teenage pleasures, c.1960
> I used to love sitting in the gutter with barefeet, a chrome-studded chair-covered leather jacket and filthy jeans. Eatin' chips. People look at you with such disgust and hate. It was terrific.
>> *Bullshit & Jellybeans* (1971)

Shakespeare, William (1564–1616)
English dramatist, poet and actor
> These violent delights have violent ends.
>> *Romeo and Juliet*, II.vi

No profit grows where is no pleasure ta'en;
In brief, sir, study what you most affect.

The Taming of the Shrew, I.i

Smollett, Tobias (1721–1771)
Scottish writer, satirist, historian, traveller and physician
I consider the world as made for me, not me for the world: it is my maxim therefore to enjoy it while I can, and let futurity shift for itself.

The Adventures of Roderick Random (1748)

Spenser, Edmund (c.1522–1599)
English poet
And painefull pleasure turnes to pleasing paine.

The Faerie Queene (1596)

Virgil (70–19 BC)
Roman poet
Trahit sua quemque voluptas.
Each one's pleasure draws him on.

Eclogues

Woollcott, Alexander (1887–1943)
US writer, drama critic and anthologist
All the things I really like to do are either immoral, illegal, or fattening.

In Drennan, *Wit's End* (1973)

▶▶ HAPPINESS

poetry

Ackerman, Diane (1948–)
US poet
A poem records emotions and moods that lie beyond normal language, that can only be patched together and hinted at metaphorically.

In Janet Sternburg, *The Writer on Her Work* (1991)

Addison, Joseph (1672–1719)
English essayist, poet, playwright and statesman
Of The Georgics
The most complete, elaborate, and finisht piece of all antiquity.

Essay on Virgil's Georgics (1697)

Nothing which is a phrase or saying in common talk, should be admitted into a serious poem.

Essay on Virgil's Georgics (1697)

Aristotle (384–322 BC)
Greek philosopher
The task of the poet is not to describe what actually happened, but the kind of thing that might happen according to probability or necessity … For this reason poetry is something more philosophical and more worthy of serious attention than history.

Poetics, IX

Arnold, Matthew (1822–1888)
English poet, critic, essayist and educationist
Of poetry
A criticism of life under the conditions fixed for such a criticism by the laws of poetic truth and poetic beauty.

Essays in Criticism (1888)

Ashbery, John (1927–)
English poet
I like poems you can tack all over with a hammer and there are no hollow places.

The Times, 1984

There is the view that poetry should improve your life. I think people confuse it with the Salvation Army.

International Herald Tribune, 1989

Bacon, Francis (1561–1626)
English philosopher, essayist, politician and courtier
Poesy was ever thought to have some participation of divineness, because it doth raise and erect the mind, by submitting the shows of things to the desires of the mind; whereas reason doth buckle and bow the mind unto the nature of things.

The Advancement of Learning (1605)

Banville, Théodore Faullain de (1823–1891)
French poet, lyricist and dramatist
Licences poétiques. Il n'y en a pas.
Poetic licence. There's no such thing.

Petit traité de poésie française

Barrow, Isaac (1630–1677)
English divine
Poetry is a kind of ingenious nonsense.

In Spence, *Anecdotes*

Bentley, Richard (1662–1742)
English scholar
It is a pretty poem, Mr Pope, but you must not call it Homer.

In John Hawkins (ed.), *The Works of Samuel Johnson* (1787)

Betjeman, Sir John (1906–1984)
English poet laureate
Too many people in the modern world view poetry as a luxury, not a necessity like petrol. But to me it's the oil of life.

The Observer, 1974

Boileau-Despréaux, Nicolas (1636–1711)
French writer
Quelque sujet qu'on traite, ou plaisant, ou sublime,
Que toujours le bon sens s'accorde avec la rime.
Be the subject lighthearted or sublime, sense always should agree with rhyme.

L'Art Poétique (1674)

Boland, Eavan (1944–)
Irish poet and critic

Poetry is defined by its energies and its eloquence, not by the passport of the poet or the editor; or the name of the nationality. That way lie all the categories, the separations, the censorships that poetry exists to dispel.

Review of Seamus Heaney's *An Open Letter, The Irish Times*, 1983

Bradstreet, Anne (c.1612–1672)
English-born US poet

I am obnoxious to each carping tongue,
Who says my hand a needle better fits,
A Poet's Pen, all scorne, I should thus wrong;
For such despight they cast on female wits:
If what I doe prove well, it won't advance,
They'll say it's stolne, or else, it was by chance …

Let Greeks be Greeks, and Women what they are,
Men have precedency, and still excell …

This meane and unrefined stuffe of mine,
Will make your glistering gold but more to shine.

'The Prologue' (1650)

Brontë, Charlotte (1816–1855)
English novelist

One day, in the autumn of 1845, I accidentally lighted on a MS volume of verse in my sister Emily's handwriting … I looked it over, and something more than surprise seized me, – a deep conviction that these were not common effusions, nor at all like the poetry women generally write. I thought them condensed and terse, vigorous and genuine. To my ear, they had also a peculiar music – wild, melancholy, and elevating.

Biographical notice

Byron, Lord (1788–1824)
English poet satirist and traveller

Nothing so difficult as a beginning
In poesy, unless perhaps the end.

Don Juan (1819–1824)

What is poetry? – The feeling of a Former world and Future.

Journal, 1821

Cage, John (1912–1992)
US composer and writer

I have nothing to say, I am saying it, and that is poetry.

Silence (1961)

Carroll, Lewis (1832–1898)
English writer and photographer

'I can repeat poetry as well as other folk if it comes to that –'
'Oh, it needn't come to that!' Alice hastily said.

Through the Looking-Glass (and What Alice Found There) (1872)

Chapman, George (c.1559–c.1634)
English poet, dramatist and translator

A Poeme, whose subject is not truth, but things like truth.

Revenge of Bussy D'Ambois (1613)

Coleridge, Samuel Taylor (1772–1834)
English poet, philosopher and critic

In the hexameter rises the fountain's silvery column;
In the pentameter aye falling in melody back.

'Ovidian Elegiac Metre' (1799

Trochee trips from long to short;
From long to long in solemn sort
Slow Spondee stalks; strong foot! yet ill able
Ever to come up with Dactyl trisyllable.
Iambics march from short to long; –
With a leap and a bound the swift Anapaests throng.

'Metrical Feet' (1806)

That willing suspension of disbelief for the moment, which constitutes poetic faith.

Biographia Literaria (1817)

Poetry is not the proper antithesis to prose, but to science. Poetry is opposed to science, and prose to metre.

Lectures and Notes of 1818

I wish our clever young poets would remember my homely definitions of prose and poetry; that is prose = words in their best order; poetry = the best words in the best order.

Table Talk (1835)

Poetry is certainly something more than good sense, but it must be good sense at all events; just as a palace is more than a house, but it must be a house, at least.

Table Talk (1835)

Cope, Wendy (1945–)
English poet

I hardly ever tire of love or rhyme –
That's why I'm poor and have a rotten time.

'Variation on Belloc's 'Fatigue'

Cowper, William (1731–1800)
English poet, hymn and letter writer

There is a pleasure in poetic pains
Which only poets know.

The Task (1785)

Eliot, T.S. (1888–1965)
US-born British poet, verse dramatist and critic

After the erection of the Chinese Wall of Milton, blank verse has suffered not only arrest but retrogression.

'Christopher Marlowe' (1919)

In the seventeenth century a dissociation of sensibility set in, from which we have never recovered.

'The Metaphysical Poets' (1921)

Poetry is not a turning loose of emotion, but an escape from emotion; it is not the expression of personality, but an escape from personality.

'Tradition and the Individual Talent' (1919)

Elizabeth, the Queen Mother (1900–)
Queen of the United Kingdom and mother of Elizabeth II
On a private reading by TS Eliot of *The Waste Land*

We had this rather lugubrious man in a suit, and he read a poem – I think it was called *The Desert* – and first the girls got the giggles, and then I did, and then even the King. Such a gloomy man. Looked as though he worked in a bank, and we didn't understand a word.

Quoted in *The Guardian*, 2000

Emerson, Ralph Waldo (1803–1882)
US poet, essayist, transcendentalist and teacher

It is not metres, but a metre-making argument, that makes a poem.

Essays, Second Series (1844)

Ewart, Gavin (1916–1995)
English poet

Good light verse is better than bad heavy verse any day of the week.

Penultimate Poems (1989)

Farquhar, George (1678–1707)
Irish dramatist

Poetry's a mere drug, Sir.

Love and a Bottle (1698)

Frost, Robert (1874–1963)
US poet

A poem may be worked over once it is in being, but may not be worried into being.

Collected Poems
(1939)

Poetry is a way of taking life by the throat.

In Sergeant, *Robert Frost: the Trial by Existence*
(1960)

Granville-Barker, Harley (1877–1946)
English actor and playwright

Rightly thought of there is poetry in peaches … even when they are canned.

The Madras House

Hardy, Thomas (1840–1928)
English writer and poet

If Galileo had said in verse that the world

moved, the Inquisition might have let him alone.

In F.E. Hardy, *The Later Years of Thomas Hardy* (1930)

Hopkins, Gerard Manley (1844–1889)
English Jesuit priest, poet and classicist

The poetical language of an age should be the current language heightened.

Letter to Robert Bridges, 1879

Housman, A.E. (1859–1936)
English poet and scholar

Experience has taught me, when I am shaving of a morning, to keep watch over my thoughts, because, if a line of poetry strays into my memory, my skin bristles so that the razor ceases to act.

'The Name and Nature of Poetry' (1933)

Even when poetry has a meaning, as it usually has, it may be inadvisable to draw it out … perfect understanding will sometimes almost extinguish pleasure.

'The Name and Nature of Poetry' (1933)

James VI of Scotland and I of England (1566–1625)
King of Scotland from 1567 and of England from 1603

Dr Donne's verses are like the peace of God; they pass all understanding.

Attr.

Jarrell, Randall (1914–1965)
US poet, critic and translator

Some poetry seems to have been written on typewriters by other typewriters.

Attr.

Keats, John (1795–1821)
English poet

Poetry should surprise by a fine excess and not by Singularity – it should strike the Reader as a wording of his own highest thoughts, and appear almost a Remembrance … Its touches of Beauty should never be half way, thereby making the reader breathless instead of content: the rise, the progress, the setting of imagery should, like the Sun, come naturally to him.

Letter to John Taylor, 27 February 1818

A long Poem is a test of Invention which I take to be the Polar Star of Poetry, as Fancy is the Sails, and Imagination the Rudder.

Letter to Benjamin Bailey, 1817

We hate poetry that has a palpable design upon us – and if we do not agree, seems to put its hand in its breeches pocket. Poetry should be great and unobtrusive, a thing which enters into one's soul, and does not startle it or amaze it with itself, but with its subject.

Letter to J.H. Reynolds, 1818

If Poetry comes not as naturally as Leaves to a

tree it had better not come at all.

Letter to John Taylor, 1818

Kennedy, John F. (1917–1963)
US Democrat President

> When power narrows the areas of man's concern, poetry reminds him of the richness and diversity of his existence.

Speech, 1963

Klopstock, Friedrich (1724–1803)
German poet
Of one of his poems

> God and I both knew what it meant once; now God alone knows.

Attr.

Landor, Walter Savage (1775–1864)
English poet and writer

> Past ruin'd Ilion Helen lives,
> Alcestis rises from the shades;
> Verse calls them forth; 'tis verse that gives
> Immortal youth to mortal maids.

'To Ianthe' (1831)

> Prose on certain occasions can bear a great deal of poetry: on the other hand, poetry sinks and swoons under a moderate weight of prose.

Imaginary Conversations (1853)

Larkin, Philip (1922–1985)
English poet, writer and librarian

> I rather think poetry has given me up, which is a great sorrow to me, but not an enormous, crushing sorrow. It's rather like going bald.

The Observer, 1984

> I can't understand these chaps who go round American universities explaining how they write poems: it's like going round explaining how you sleep with your wife.

New York Times, 1986

Macaulay, Dame Rose (1881–1958)
English writer

> Poem me no poems.

Poetry Review, 1963

Macaulay, Lord (1800–1859)
English Liberal statesman, essayist and poet

> As civilization advances, poetry almost necessarily declines.

Collected Essays (1843)

MacDiarmid, Hugh (1892–1978)
Scottish poet

> Poetry like politics maun cut
> The cackle and pursue real ends,
> Unerringly as Lenin, and to that
> Its nature better tends.

'Second Hymn to Lenin' (1935)

MacLeish, Archibald (1892–1982)
US poet and librarian

> A Poem should be palpable and mute
> As a globed fruit,
>
> Dumb
> As old medallions to the thumb,
>
> Silent as the sleeve-worn stone
> Of casement ledges where the moss has grown –
>
> A poem should be wordless
> As the flight of birds …
>
> A poem should not mean
> But be.

'Ars poetica' (1926)

Mencken, H.L. (1880–1956)
US writer, critic, philologist and satirist

> Poetry is a comforting piece of fiction set to more or less lascivious music.

Prejudices (1919–1927)

Monroe, Harriet (1860–1936)
US poet and editor

> … poetry, 'The Cinderella of the Arts.'

In Hope Stoddard, *Famous American Women*, 'Harriet Monroe'

Nemerov, Howard (1920–1991)
US poet, novelist and critic

> I've never read a political poem that's accomplished anything. Poetry makes things happen, but rarely what the poet wants.

International Herald Tribune, 1988

Patten, Brian (1946–)
British poet

> When in public poetry should take off its clothes and wave to the nearest person in sight; it should be seen in the company of thieves and lovers rather than that of journalists and publishers.

'Prose poem towards a definition of itself'

> It should guide all those who are safe into the middle of busy roads and leave them there.

'Prose poem towards a definition of itself'

Paz, Octavio (1914–)
Mexican poet and critic

> *La poesía no es nada sino tiempo, ritmo perpetuamente creador.*
> Poetry is nothing but time, ceaselessly creative rhythm.

The Bow and the Lyre (1956)

Pound, Ezra (1885–1972)
US poet

> And give up verse, my boy,

There's nothing in it.

Hugh Selwyn Mauberley (1920)

Preston, Keith (1884–1927)
US poet, writer and teacher
Of all the literary scenes
Saddest this sight to me:
The graves of little magazines
Who died to make verse free.

'The Liberators'

Reich, Wilhelm (1897–1957)
Austrian-born US psychiatrist
The few bad poems which occasionally are
created during abstinence are of no great
interest.

The Sexual Revolution

Richards, I.A. (1893–1979)
English critic, linguist, poet and teacher
Of poetry
It is a perfectly possible means of overcoming
chaos.

Science and Poetry (1926)

Rossetti, Dante Gabriel (1828–1882)
English poet, painter, translator and letter-writer
A sonnet is a moment's monument, –
Memorial from the Soul's eternity
To one dead deathless hour.

The House of Life (1881)

Shelley, Percy Bysshe (1792–1822)
English poet, dramatist and essayist
Poetry lifts the veil from the hidden beauty of
the world, and makes familiar objects be as if
they were not familiar.

A Defence of Poetry (1821)

Sitwell, Dame Edith (1887–1964)
English poet, anthologist, critic and biographer
My poems are hymns of praise to the glory of
Life.

Selected Poems (1952)

Sitwell, Sir Osbert (1892–1969)
English writer
Poetry is like fish: if it's fresh, it's good; if it's
stale, it's bad; and if you're not certain, try it on
the cat.

Attr.

Sprat, Thomas (1635–1713)
English bishop and writer
Poetry is the mother of superstition.

The History of the Royal Society
(1667)

Stevens, Wallace (1879–1955)
US poet, essayist, dramatist and lawyer
Poetry is the supreme fiction, madame.

'A High-Toned old Christian Woman' (1923)

Thomas, Dylan (1914–1953)
Welsh poet, writer and radio dramatist
These poems, with all their crudities, doubts,
and confusions, are written for the love of Man
and in praise of God, and I'd be a damn' fool if
they weren't.

Collected Poems (1952)

Thoreau, Henry David (1817–1862)
US essayist, social critic and writer
Poetry is nothing but healthy speech.

Journal, 1841

I do not perceive the poetic and dramatic
capabilities of an anecdote or story which is told
me, its significance, till some time afterwards …
We do not enjoy poetry unless we know it to be
poetry.

Journal, 1856

Valéry, Paul (1871–1945)
French poet, mathematician and philosopher
Mes vers ont le sens qu'on leur prête.
My poems mean what people take them to
mean.

Variety (1924)

A poem is never finished, only abandoned.

In Auden, *A Certain World*

Wain, John (1925–1994)
English poet, writer and critic
Poetry is to prose as dancing is to walking.

BBC broadcast, 1976

Wilde, Oscar (1854–1900)
Irish poet, dramatist, writer, critic and wit
There seems to be some curious connection
between piety and poor rhymes.

In Lucas, *A Critic in Pall Mall* (1919)

Wordsworth, William (1770–1850)
English poet
I have said that poetry is the spontaneous
overflow of powerful feelings: it takes its origin
from emotion recollected in tranquillity: the
emotion is contemplated till, by a species of
reaction, the tranquillity gradually disappears,
and an emotion, kindred to that which was
before the subject of contemplation, is gradually
produced, and does itself actually exist in the
mind.

Lyrical Ballads (1802)

Yeats, W.B. (1865–1939)
Irish poet, dramatist, editor, writer and senator
We make out of the quarrel with others,
rhetoric; but of the quarrel with ourselves,
poetry.

'Anima Hominis' (1917)

Zephaniah, Benjamin (1958–)
English poet

I think poetry should be alive. You should be able to dance it.

The Sunday Times, 1987

▶▶ CRITICISM; INSPIRATION; LITERATURE; POETS; WRITING

poets

Addison, Joseph (1672–1719)
English essayist, poet, playwright and statesman
Of Virgil

He delivers the meanest of his precepts with a kind of grandeur, he breaks the clods and tosses the dung about with an air of gracefulness.

Essay on Virgil's Georgics (1697)

Of Milton

Our language sunk under him, and was unequal to that greatness of soul which furnished him with such glorious conceptions.

The Spectator, February 1712, 297

Remark made of the poet Cowley

He more had pleas'd us, had he pleas'd us less.

Attr.

Arnold, Matthew (1822–1888)
English poet, critic, essayist and educationist
Of Wordsworth

He spoke, and loosed our heart in tears.
He laid us as we lay at birth
On the cool flowery lap of earth.

'Memorial Verses' (1850)

Wordsworth says somewhere that wherever Virgil seems to have composed 'with his eye on the object', Dryden fails to render him. Homer invariably composes 'with his eye on the object', whether the object be a moral or a material one: Pope composes with his eye on his style, into which he translates his object, whatever it is.

On Translating Homer (1861)

Of Wordsworth

His expression may often be called bald … but it is bald as the bare mountain tops are bald, with a baldness full of grandeur.

Essays in Criticism (1888)

Quoting his own writing on Shelley

In poetry, no less than in life, he is 'a beautiful and ineffectual angel, beating in the void his luminous wings in vain'.

Essays in Criticism (1888)

Aubrey, John (1626–1697)
English antiquary, folklorist and biographer
Of Milton

He was so fair that they called him the lady of Christ's College.

Brief Lives (c.1693)

Auden, W.H. (1907–1973)
English poet, essayist, critic, teacher and dramatist

A poet's hope: to be,
like some valley cheese,
local, but prized elsewhere.

'Shorts II'

It is a sad fact about our culture that a poet can earn much more money writing or talking about his art than he can by practising it.

The Dyer's Hand (1963)

Baudelaire, Charles (1821–1867)
French poet, translator and critic

Le poète est semblable au prince des nuées
Qui hante la tempête et se rit de l'archer;
Exilé sur le sol, au milieu des huées,
Ses ailes de géant l'empêchent de marcher.
The poet is like the prince of the clouds, who haunts the tempest and mocks at the archer. Exiled to the ground, an object of derision, his giant wings prevent him from walking.

Les Fleurs du mal (1857)

Beer, Thomas (1889–1940)
US writer

I agree with one of your reputable critics that a taste for drawing-rooms has spoiled more poets than ever did a taste for gutters.

The Mauve Decade (1926)

Blake, William (1757–1827)
English poet, engraver, painter and mystic

The reason Milton wrote in fetters when he wrote of Angels & God, and at liberty when of Devils & Hell, is because he was a true Poet and of the Devil's party without knowing it.

'The Voice of the Devil'

Boileau-Despréaux, Nicolas (1636–1711)
French writer

Enfin Malherbe vint, et, le premier en France,
Fit sentir dans les vers une juste cadence.
At last came Malherbe, and, the first in France, gave poetry a proper rhythm.

L'Art Poétique (1674)

Burns, Robert (1759–1796)
Scottish poet and song writer

I never had the least thought or inclination of turning Poet till I once got heartily in love, and then rhyme and song were, in a manner, the spontaneous language of my head.

Attr.

Carlyle, Jane Welsh (1801–1866)
Scottish letter writer, literary hostess and poet

If they had said the sun and the moon was gone

out of the heavens it could not have struck me with the idea of a more awful and dreary blank in the creation than the words: Byron is dead.

Letter to Thomas Carlyle, May 1824

Carlyle, Thomas (1795–1881)
Scottish historian, biographer, critic, and essayist
The excellence of Burns is, indeed, among the rarest, … but … it is plain and easily recognised: his Sincerity, his indisputable air of Truth.

Critical and Miscellaneous Essays (1839)

A poet without love were a physical and metaphysical impossibility.

Critical and Miscellaneous Essays (1839)

Robert Burns never had the smallest chance to get into Parliament, much as Robert Burns deserved, for all our sakes, to have been found there.

Latter-Day Pamphlets (1850)

Catullus (84–c.54 BC)
Roman poet
Nam castum esse decet pium poetam
Ipsum, versiculos nihil necesse est.
For the sacred poet ought to be chaste himself, but it is not necessary that his verses should be so.

Carmina

Cocteau, Jean (1889–1963)
French dramatist, poet, film writer and director
Un vrai poète se soucie peu de poésie. De même un horticulteur ne parfume pas ses roses.
A true poet scarcely worries about poetry, just as a gardener does not scent his roses.

Professional Secrets (1922)

Coleridge, Samuel Taylor (1772–1834)
English poet, philosopher and critic
With Donne, whose muse on dromedary trots,
Wreathe iron pokers into true-love knots;
Rhyme's sturdy cripple, fancy's maze and clue,
Wit's forge and fire-blast, meaning's press and screw.

'On Donne's Poetry' (1818)

To read Dryden, Pope, etc., you need only count syllables; but to read Donne you must measure time, and discover the time of each word by the sense of passion.

The Friend (1818)

No man was ever yet a great poet, without being at the same time a profound philosopher.

Biographia Literaria (1817)

Congreve, William (1670–1729)
English dramatist
It is the business of a comic poet to paint the vices and follies of human kind.

The Double Dealer (1694

Cope, Wendy (1945–)
English poet
I used to think all poets were Byronic –
Mad, bad and dangerous to know.
And then I met a few. Yes it's ironic –
I used to think all poets were Byronic.
They're mostly wicked as a ginless tonic
And wild as pension plans. Not long ago
I used to think all poets were Byronic –
Mad, bad and dangerous to know.

Making Cocoa for Kingsley Amis (1986)

Cornford, Frances Crofts (1886–1960)
English poet and translator
Of Rupert Brooke
A young Apollo, golden-haired,
Stands dreaming on the verge of strife,
Magnificently unprepared
For the long littleness of life.

'Youth' (1910)

Cowper, William (1731–1800)
English poet, hymn and letter writer
Of Pope
But he (his musical finesse was such,
So nice his ear, so delicate his touch)
Made poetry a mere mechanic art;
And ev'ry warbler has his tune by heart.

Table Talk (1782)

Eliot, T.S. (1888–1965)
US-born British poet, verse dramatist and critic
Tennyson and Browning are poets, and they think; but they do not feel their thought as immediately as the odour of a rose. A thought to Donne was an experience; it modified his sensibility.

'The Metaphysical Poets' (1921)

The business of the poet is not to find new emotions, but to use the ordinary ones and, in working them up into poetry, to express feelings which are not in actual emotions at all.

'Tradition and the Individual Talent' (1919)

Goethe (1749–1832)
German poet, writer, dramatist and scientist
Aber Lord Byron ist nur gross, wenn er dichtet; sobald er reflektiert, ist er ein Kind.
Lord Byron is only great as a poet; as soon as he reflects, he is a child.

Gespräche mit Eckermann, 1825

Graves, Robert (1895–1985)
English poet, writer, critic, translator and mythologist
To be a poet is a condition rather than a profession.

Questionnaire in Horizon

Haldane, J.B.S. (1892–1964)
British biochemist, geneticist and popularizer of science
Shelley and Keats were the last British poets

who were at all up-to-date in their chemical knowledge.

Daedalus or Science and the Future (1924)

Hardy, Thomas (1840–1928)
English writer and poet

> Of course poets have morals and manners of their own, and custom is no argument with them.
>
> *The Hand of Ethelberta* (1876)

Hazlitt, William (1778–1830)
English writer and critic
Of Coleridge

> He talked on for ever; and you wished him to talk on for ever.
>
> *Lectures on the English Poets* (1818)

Heaney, Seamus (1939–)
Irish poet

> To forge a poem is one thing, to forge the uncreated conscience of the race, as Stephen Dedalus put it, is quite another and places daunting pressures and responsibilities on anyone who would risk the name of poet.
>
> *Preoccupations, Selected Prose 1968–1978*

Johnson, Samuel (1709–1784)
English lexicographer, poet, critic, conversationalist and essayist

> The business of a poet, said Imlac, is to examine, not the individual but the species ... he does not number the streaks of the tulip, or describe the different shades in the verdure of the forest.
>
> *Rasselas* (1759)

> He [the poet] must write as the interpreter of nature, and the legislator of mankind, and consider himself as presiding over the thoughts and manners of future generations; as a being superior to time and place.
>
> *Rasselas* (1759)

Joyce, James (1882–1941)
Irish writer

> Lawn Tennyson, gentleman poet.
>
> *Ulysses* (1922)

Keats, John (1795–1821)
English poet

> I think I shall be among the British Poets after my death.
>
> Letter to George and Georgiana Keats, 1818

> A Poet is the most unpoetical of anything in existence; because he has no Identity – he is continually informing and filling some other Body.
>
> Letter to Richard Woodhouse, 1818

Lamb, Charles (1775–1834)
English essayist, critic and letter writer

> Milton almost requires a solemn service of music to be played before you enter upon him.
>
> *Last Essays of Elia* (1833)

Larkin, Philip (1922–1985)
English poet, writer and librarian

> Deprivation is for me what daffodils were for Wordsworth.
>
> *The Observer*, 1979

Leavis, F.R. (1895–1978)
English critic, lecturer and writer

> The Sitwells belong to the history of publicity rather than of poetry.
>
> *New Bearings in English Poetry* (1932)

Of Rupert Brooke

> His verse exhibits ... something that is rather like Keats' vulgarity with a Public School accent.
>
> *New Bearings in English Poetry* (1932)

Leonardo da Vinci (1452–1519)
Italian artist

> The poet ranks far below the painter in the representation of visible things, and far below the musician in that of invisible things.
>
> *Selections from the Notebooks of Leonardo da Vinci* (1952)

Lockhart, John Gibson (1794–1854)
Scottish writer, critic, and translator

> It is a better and a wiser thing to be a starved apothecary than a starved poet; so back to the shop Mr John, back to 'plasters, pills, and ointment boxes'.
>
> *Blackwood's Magazine*, 1818, Review of Keats's *Endymion*

Lodge, David (1935–)
English writer, satirist and literary critic

> Walt Whitman who laid end to end words never seen in each other's company before outside of a dictionary.
>
> *Changing Places* (1975)

Lorca, Federico García (1899–1936)
Spanish poet and dramatist

> *Ni un solo momento, viejo hermoso Walt Whitman, he dejado de ver tu barba llena de mariposas.*
> Not even for a moment, beautiful old Walt Whitman, have I stopped seeing your beard full of butterflies.
>
> *Poeta en Nueva York* (1929–30)

Macaulay, Lord (1800–1859)
English Liberal statesman, essayist and poet

> Perhaps no person can be a poet, or can even enjoy poetry, without a certain unsoundness of mind.
>
> *Collected Essays* (1843)

Owen, Wilfred (1893–1918)
English poet

> All the poet can do today is to warn.

That is why the true Poets must be truthful.

Quoted in Poems (1963)

Pessoa, Fernando (1888–1935)
Portuguese poet

> *Ser poeta não é uma ambição minha.*
> *… a minha maneira de estar sozinho.*
> Being a poet is not an ambition of mine.
> It is my way of being alone.

The Guardian of Flocks (1914)

Plato (c.429–347 BC)
Greek philosopher

> Poets utter great and wise things which they do not themselves understand.

Republic

Pope, Alexander (1688–1744)
English poet, translator and editor

> Poets, like painters, thus, unskill'd to trace
> The naked nature and the living grace,
> With gold and jewels cover ev'ry part,
> And hide with ornaments their want of art.

An Essay on Criticism (1711)

> Sir, I admit your gen'ral Rule
> That every Poet is a Fool;
> But you yourself may serve to show it,
> That every Fool is not a Poet.

'Epigram from the French' (1732)

Shelley, Percy Bysshe (1792–1822)
English poet, dramatist and essayist

> Poets are … the trumpets which sing to battle and feel not what they inspire … Poets are the unacknowledged legislators of the world.

A Defence of Poetry (1821)

Sidney, Sir Philip (1554–1586)
English poet, critic, soldier, courtier and diplomat

> Nature never set foorth the earth inso rich Tapistry as diverse Poets have done … her world is brasen, the Poets only deliver a golden.

The Defence of Poesie (1595)

> There have been many most excellent poets that have never versified, and now swarm many versifiers that need never answer to the name of poets.

The Defence of Poesie (1595)

Spender, Sir Stephen (1909–1995)
English poet, editor, translator and diarist

> People sometimes divide others into those you laugh at and those you laugh with. The young Auden was someone you could laugh-at-with.

Address at W.H. Auden's memorial service, Oxford, 1973

Squire, Sir J.C. (1884–1958)
English poet, critic, writer and editor

> But Shelley had a hyper-thyroid face.

'Ballade of the Glandular Hypothesis'

Stevenson, Robert Louis (1850–1894)
Scottish writer, poet and essayist

> Whitman, like a large shaggy dog, just unchained, scouring the beaches of the world and baying at the moon.

Familiar Studies of Men and Books (1882)

Swift, Jonathan (1667–1745)
Irish satirist, poet, essayist and cleric

> Say, Britain, could you ever boast, –
> Three poets in an age at most?
> Our chilling climate hardly bears
> A sprig of bays in fifty years.

'On Poetry' (1733)

Waller, Edmund (1606–1687)
English poet and politician

> Poets lose half the praise they should have got,
> Could it be known what they discreetly blot.

'On Roscommon's Translation of Horace'

Waterhouse, Keith (1929–)
English journalist and author

> Why do we need a Poet Laureate at all? We might as well still retain a Court Jester or a Royal Food Taster.

Comment following the death of Poet Laureate Ted Hughes, November 1998

Wellington, Duke of (1769–1852)
Irish-born British military commander and statesman

> I hate the whole race … There is no believing a word they say – your professional poets, I mean – there never existed a more worthless set than Byron and his friends for example.

Attr.

Wilde, Oscar (1854–1900)
Irish poet, dramatist, writer, critic and wit
Of Wordsworth

> He found in stones the sermons he had already hidden there.

The Nineteenth Century, 1889

Woolf, Virginia (1882–1941)
English writer and critic

> I would venture to guess that Anon, who wrote so many poems without signing them, was often a woman.

A Room of One's Own (1929)

Wordsworth, William (1770–1850)
English poet

> The Poet writes under one restriction only, namely, that of the necessity of giving pleasure to a human Being possessed of that information which may be expected from him, not as a lawyer, a physician, a mariner, an astronomer or a natural philosopher, but as a Man.

Lyrical Ballads (1802)

> Milton! thou shouldst be living at this hour:

England hath need of thee; she is a fen
Of stagnant waters: altar, sword, and pen,
Fireside, the heroic wealth of hall and bower,
Have forfeited their ancient English dower
Of inward happiness …

Thy soul was like a star, and dwelt apart.

'Milton! thou shouldst be living at this hour' (1807)

Yeats, W.B. (1865–1939)

Irish poet, dramatist, editor, writer and senator

The poet finds and makes his mask in disappointment, the hero in defeat.

'Anima Hominis'

Of Keats

I see a schoolboy when I think of him,
With face and nose pressed to a sweet-shop window,
For certainly he sank into his grave
His senses and his heart unsatisfied,
And made – being poor, ailing and ignorant,
Shut out from all the luxury of the world,
The coarse-bred son of a livery-stable keeper –
Luxuriant song.

The Wild Swans at Coole, Other Verses and a Play (1917)

Referring to Wilfred Owen

He is all blood, dirt and sucked sugar stick.

In D. Wellesley (ed.), *Letters on Poetry from W.B. Yeats to Dorothy Wellesley* (1940)

▶▶ CRITICISM; POETRY; SHAKESPEARE; WRITERS

police

Conrad, Joseph (1857–1924)

Polish-born British writer, sailor and explorer

The terrorist and the policeman both come from the same basket.

The Secret Agent (1907)

Daley, Richard J. (1902–1976)

US politician and Mayor of Chicago

To the press, concerning riots during Democratic Convention, 1968

Gentlemen, get the thing straight once and for all. The policeman isn't there to create disorder, the policeman is there to preserve disorder.

Attr.

Hicks, Sir Seymour (1871–1949)

English actor-manager

You will recognize, my boy, the first sign of old age: it is when you go out into the streets of London and realize for the first time how young the policemen look.

In Pulling, *They Were Singing* (1952)

Lloyd, Marie (1870–1922)

English music-hall singer

You can't trust the 'specials' like the old time 'coppers'
When you can't find your way home.

'Don't Dilly-Dally on the Way' (song, 1919)

Milligan, Spike (1918–)

Irish comedian and writer

Policemen are numbered in case they get lost.

The Last Goon Show of All

Newton, Huey P. (1942–1989)

US political activist

We felt that the police needed a label, a label other than that fear image that they carried in the community. So we used the pig as the rather low-lifed animal in order to identify the police. And it worked.

In Henry Hampton, *Voices of Freedom* (1990)

O'Brien, Flann (1911–1966)

Irish novelist and journalist

Commenting on the fact that policemen always seem to look young

A thing of duty is a boy for ever.

Attr.

O'Casey, Sean (1880–1964)

Irish dramatist

The Polis as Polis, in this city, is Null an' Void!

Juno and the Paycock (1924)

Orwell, George (1903–1950)

English writer and critic

Only the Thought Police mattered.

Nineteen Eighty-Four (1949)

Peel, Arthur Wellesley, First Viscount (1829–1912)

Son of Sir Robert Peel

Protesting against his arrest by the police, recently established by his father

My father didn't create you to arrest me.

Attr.

Philippe, Charles-Louis (1874–1909)

On a toujours l'air de mentir quand on parle à des gendarmes.

One always seems to be lying when one speaks to the police.

Les Chroniques du canard sauvage

Rogers, E.W. (1864–1913)

Ev'ry member of the force
Has a watch and chain, of course;
If you want to know the time,
Ask a P'liceman!

'Ask a P'liceman' (song, 1889)

Sharpe, Tom (1928–)

English writer

The South African Police would leave no stone

unturned to see that nothing disturbed the even tenor of their lives.

Indecent Exposure (1973)

political correctness

Lehrer, Tom (1928–)
US humorist

In my youth there were words you couldn't say in front of a girl; now you can't say 'girl'.

Sunday Telegraph, 1996

political slogans

A bayonet is a weapon with a worker at each end.

Pacifist movement, 1940

All power to the Soviets.

Petrograd workers, 1917

All the way with LBJ.

US Democratic Presidential campaign, 1960

Are we downhearted? No!

World War I, based on remark of Joseph Chamberlain

Ban the bomb.

Current from 1953 onwards

Better red than dead.

British nuclear disarmament movement

Black is beautiful.

US civil rights movement, 1966

Careless talk costs lives.

British Ministry of Information, World War II

Compassionate Conservatism.

George W. Bush Presidential campaign, 2000

Dig for victory.

Ministry of Agriculture, 1939

England Expects – Scotland's Oil.

Scottish National Party, 1973

The family that prays together stays together.

Devised by Al Scalpone for the Roman Catholic Family Rosary Crusade, 1947

Flower Power.

Hippy slogan, 1960s

Hey, hey LBJ, how many kids did you kill today?

Anti-Vietnam War slogan, 1960s

I like Ike.

US button badge, first used in 1947, to support Eisenhower

In your heart you know he's right.

Goldwater Presidential campaign, 1964

Is your journey really necessary?

World War II

It's morning again in America.

Ronald Reagan's 1984 Presidential election campaign

Keep Britain tidy.

British government, 1950s

With a poster showing a long queue outside an unemployment office

Labour isn't working.

Conservative Party slogan, 1978–79

Liberté! Egalité! Fraternité!
Liberty! Equality! Brotherhood!

French Revolution, 1793

Make love, not war.

Common in the mid-1960s

New Labour, new danger.

Conservative Party slogan, 1996

No taxation without representation.

In use before the American War of Independence, 1775–1783

Ein Reich, Ein Volk, Ein Führer
One realm, one people, one leader.

Nazi Party, 1934

Out of the closets and into the streets.

Gay Liberation movement, US c.1969

Power to the People.

Black Panther movement, 1969

Kraft durch Freude
Strength through joy.

German Labour Front, 1933

Ulster will fight, and Ulster will be right.

Ulster Volunteers opposed to Irish Home Rule, 1913–1914, from a letter by Lord Randolph Churchill, 1886

Votes for Women.

Suffragette Movement, 1905, in Emmeline Pankhurst, *My Own Story* (1914)

Would you buy a used car from this man?

Campaign slogan directed against Richard Nixon, 1968

Your King and Country need you.

World War I

politicians

Adams, Franklin P. (1881–1960)
US writer, poet, translator and editor

The trouble with this country is that there are too many politicians who believe, with a conviction based on experience, that you can fool all of the people all of the time.

Nods and Becks (1944)

Allen, Dave (1936–)
Irish comedian and television personality
> If John Major was drowning, his whole life would pass in front of him and he wouldn't be in it.

On stage, 1991

Anonymous
> MPs, ministers or otherwise, do not resign because of their integrity. They do so because they have been found out.

Letter to *The Times*, 1999

> An MP, convicted of making a false election expenses return, has been ordered to to community service. Isn't that what MPs are supposed to do?

The Times, 1999

Comment on Robin Cook in a letter to *The Times*
> It would have been nice if the Foreign Secretary had had an ethical domestic policy as well.

The Times, 1999

Asquith, Herbert (1852–1928)
English Liberal statesman and Prime Minister
On Bonar Law
> It is fitting that we should have buried the Unknown Prime Minister by the side of the Unknown Soldier.

Remark supposedly made at Bonar Law's funeral, November 1923

Asquith, Margot (1864–1945)
Scottish political hostess and writer
Of Lloyd George
> He couldn't see a belt without hitting below it.

As I Remember, 1967

> He a politician always has his arm round your waist and his eye on the clock.

As I Remember, 1967

Bagehot, Walter (1826–1877)
English economist and political philosopher
Of Sir Robert Peel
> No man has come so near our definition of a constitutional statesman – the powers of a first-rate man and the creed of a second-rate man.

Historical Essays, The Character of Sir Robert Peel' (1856)

> A constitutional statesman is in general a man of common opinions and uncommon abilities.

Historical Essays, The Character of Sir Robert Peel' (1856)

Baldwin, Stanley (1867–1947)
English Conservative statesman and Prime Minister
On becoming Prime Minister

> I met Curzon in Downing Street, from whom I got the sort of greeting a corpse would give to an undertaker.

Remark, 1933

On Churchill
> Then comes Winston with his hundred-horse-power mind and what can I do?

In G.M. Young, *Stanley Baldwin* (1952)

Of the House of Commons, 1918
> A lot of hard-faced men who look as if they had done very well out of the war.

Attr.

Balfour, A.J. (1848–1930)
British Conservative Prime Minister
Comment on Winston Churchill in 1899
> I thought he was a young man of promise; but it appears he is a young man of promises.

In Winston Churchill, *My Early Life* (1930)

Barnard, Robert (1936–)
English writer
> Early on in his stint as a junior minister a newspaper had called him 'the thinking man's Tory', and the label had stuck, possibly because there was so little competition.

Political Suicide (1986)

Belloch, Juan Alberto (1950–)
> *Los jueces se rigen por la legalidad; los políticos por la oportunidad.*
> Judges are guided by the law; politicians by expediency.

El país, 1994

Bennett, Arnold (1867–1931)
English writer, dramatist and journalist
> Mr Lloyd George spoke for a hundred and seventeen minutes, in which period he was detected only once in the use of an argument.

Things That Have Interested Me (1921–1925)

Bevan, Aneurin (1897–1960)
Welsh Labour politician, miner and orator
> Listening to a speech by Chamberlain is like paying a visit to Woolworths; everything in its place and nothing over sixpence.

In *Tribune*, 1937

Wishing to address the Prime Minister rather than the Foreign Secretary, in the House of Commons
> If we complain about the tune, there is no reason to attack the monkey when the organ grinder is present.

Speech, 1957

On Churchill
> He is a man suffering from petrified adolescence.

In Brome, *Aneurin Bevan*

Bright, John (1811–1889)
English Liberal politician and social reformer

> The right hon Gentleman … has retired into what may be called his political Cave of Adullam – and he has called about him every one that was in distress and every one that was discontented.
>
> > Speech, House of Commons, 1866

Of Disraeli

> He is a self-made man, and worships his creator.
>
> > Remark, c.1868

Brown, George (1914–1985)
English Conservative politician

> Most British statesmen have either drunk too much or womanized too much. I never fell into the second category.
>
> > *The Observer*, 1974

Brown, Tina (1953–)
English journalist and editor
Of Richard Crossman

> He has the jovial garrulity and air of witty indiscretion that shows he intends to give nothing away.
>
> > *Loose Talk* (1979)

Buchwald, Art (1925–)
US humorist
Of Richard Nixon

> I worship the quicksand he walks in.
>
> > Attr.

Butler, R.A. (1902–1982)
Indian-born British Conservative politician
On Sir Anthony Eden, who had been described as the offspring of a mad baronet and a beautiful woman

> That's Anthony for you – half mad baronet, half beautiful woman.
>
> > Attr.

Cameron, Simon (1799–1889)
US statesman and newspaper editor

> An honest politician is one who, when he is bought, will stay bought.
>
> > Remark

Campbell, Menzies (1941–)
Scottish politician, lawyer and athlete
Of John Smith, leader of the Labour Party

> He had all the virtues of a Scottish Presbyterian, but none of the vices.
>
> > *The Guardian*, 1994

Canning, George (1770–1827)
English Prime Minister, orator and poet

> Pitt is to Addington
> As London is to Paddington.
>
> > 'The Oracle' (c.1803)

Chaplin, Charlie (1889–1977)
English comedian, actor, director and satirist

> I remain just one thing, and one thing only – and that is a clown. It places me on a far higher plane than any politician.
>
> > *The Observer*, 1960

Charmley, John (1955–)
English historian

> What would the man of 1938 have said of the Prime Minister of 1944?
>
> > *Churchill: The End of Glory* (1993)

Churchill, Lord Randolph (1849–1894)
English Conservative politician
Of Gladstone

> For the purposes of recreation he has selected the felling of trees, and we may usefully remark that his amusements, like his politics, are essentially destructive … The forest laments in order that Mr Gladstone may perspire.
>
> > Speech, 1884

Of Gladstone

> An old man in a hurry.
>
> > Speech, 1886

Churchill, Sir Winston (1874–1965)
English Conservative Prime Minister
Of Lord Charles Beresford

> He is one of those orators of whom it was well said, 'Before they get up they do not know what they are going to say; when they are speaking, they do not know what they are saying; and when they sit down, they do not know what they have said'.
>
> > Speech, House of Commons, December 1912

Of Ramsey MacDonald

> I remember, when I was a child, being taken to the celebrated Barnum's circus, which contained an exhibition of freaks and monstrosities, but the exhibit … which I most desired to see was the one described as 'The Boneless Wonder'. My parents judged that that spectacle would be too revolting and demoralising for my youthful eyes, and I have waited 50 years to see the boneless wonder sitting on the Treasury Bench.
>
> > Speech, House of Commons, January 1931

> I have never accepted what many people have kindly said, namely that I inspired the nation. It was the nation and the race dwelling all round the globe that had the lion's heart. I had the luck to be called upon to give the roar.
>
> > Speech at the Palace of Westminster, 1954, on his eightieth birthday

> So they told me how Mr Gladstone read Homer for fun, which I thought served him right.
>
> > *My Early Life* (1930)

> On the night of the tenth of May 1940, at the outset of this mighty battle, I acquired the chief

power in the State, which henceforth I wielded in ever-growing measure for five years and three months of world war, at the end of which time, all our enemies having surrendered unconditionally or being about to do so, I was immediately dismissed by the British electorate from all further conduct of their affairs.

The Second World War (1948–1954)

Referring to the Soviet statesman Molotov
I have never seen a human being who more perfectly represented the modern conception of a robot.

The Second World War (1948–1954)

Of Clement Attlee
He is a modest man who has a good deal to be modest about.

In *Chicago Sunday Tribune Magazine of Books*, 1954

Clemenceau, Georges (1841–1929)
French Prime Minister and journalist
Politique intérieure: je fais la guerre; politique étrangère: je fais la guerre. Je fais toujours la guerre!
My home policy? I wage war. My foreign policy? I wage war. Always, everywhere, I wage war!

Speech to the Chamber of Deputies, 8 March 1918

Clinton, Hillary (1947–)
US Democrat politician
Introducing her husband President Clinton at a gun-control rally
Part of growing up is learning how to control your impulses.

The Times, 1999

Clinton, William ('Bill') (1946–)
Democrat President of the USA
Any President that lies to the American people should resign.

Speech as Governor of Arkasnas, 1974

Cook, Peter (1937–1995)
English comedian and writer
Giving an impersonation of Harold Macmillan
We exchanged many frank words in our respective languages.

Beyond the Fringe,1961

Critchley, Julian (1930–)
English writer, broadcaster, journalist and politician
The only safe pleasure for a parliamentarian is a bag of boiled sweets.

Listener, 1982

cummings, e. e. (1894–1962)
US poet, noted for his typography, and painter
a politician is an arse upon
which everyone has sat except a man.

1 x 1 (1944), no. 10

Curran, John Philpot (1750–1817)
Irish judge, orator, politician and reformer

Of Sir Robert Peel's smile
… like the silver plate on a coffin.

Quoted by Daniel O'Connell, *Hansard*, 1835

Curtin, John (1885–1945)
Australian Prime Minister
Of R.G. Menzies
Ah, poor Bob. It's very sad; he would rather make a point than make a friend.

In Howard Beale, *This Inch of Time* …

Curzon, Lord (1859–1925)
English statesman and scholar
Referring to Stanley Baldwin on his appointment as Prime Minister
Not even a public figure. A man of no experience. And of the utmost insignificance.

In Harold Nicolson, *Curzon: The Last Phase*

Davis, Angela (1944–)
US political activist, revolutionary and author
What this country needs is more unemployed politicians.

Speech, 1967

De Gaulle, Charles (1890–1970)
French general and statesman
Comme un homme politique ne croit jamais ce qu'il dit, il est tout étonné quand il est cru sur parole.
Since a politician never believes what he says, he is quite surprised to be taken at his word.

Attr.

In order to become the master, the politician poses as the servant.

Attr.

Devonshire, Duke of (1895–1950)
English politician
I dreamt that I was making a speech in the House. I woke up, and by Jove I was!

In Churchill, *Thought and Adventures*

Disraeli, Benjamin (1804–1881)
English statesman and writer
Though I sit down now, the time will come when you will hear me.

Maiden Speech in the House of Commons, 1837
Of Gladstone

A sophistical rhetorician, inebriated with the exuberance of his own verbosity.

Speech, 1878

Douglas-Home, Lady Caroline (1937–)
Daughter of Sir Alec Douglas-Home; Lady-in-Waiting
Referring to her father's suitability for his new role as prime minister
He is used to dealing with estate workers. I cannot see how anyone can say he is out of touch.

Daily Herald, 1963

Douglas-Home, Sir Alec (1903–1995)
Scottish statesman
> There are two problems in my life. The political ones are insoluble and the economic ones are incomprehensible.
>> *Speech, 1964*

Fairbairn, Sir Nicholas (1933–1995)
Scottish Conservative MP and barrister
On women MPs
> I can't say I've ever got visually, artistically or sexually excited by any of them. They all look as though they're from the Fifth Kiev Stalinist machine-gun parade.
>> *Daily Mail, 1993*

Foley, Rae (1900–1978)
US writer
> He had the misleading air of open-hearted simplicity that people have come to demand of their politicians.
>> *The Hundredth Door (1950)*

Ford, Gerald R. (1913–)
US Republican President
On taking the vice-presidential oath
> I am a Ford, not a Lincoln. My addresses will never be as eloquent as Lincoln's. But I will do my best to equal his brevity and plain speaking.
>> Speech, published in *Washington Post*, 1973

Referring to his own appointment as President
> I guess it proves that in America anyone can be President.
>> In Reeves, *A Ford Not a Lincoln*

Garel-Jones, Tristan (1941–)
English Conservative politician
> My profession does not allow me to go swanning around buying pints of milk. I wouldn't be of sufficient service to my constituents if I went into shops.
>> *The Independent, 1994*

Gingrich, Newt (1943–)
US Republican politician
> I think one of the great problems we have in the Republican Party is that we don't encourage you to be nasty. We encourage you to be neat, obedient, loyal and faithful and all those Boy Scout words, which would be great around a campfire but are lousy in politics.
>> *Attr.*

Goodhart, Sir Philip (1925–)
On Conservative politician Nicholas Ridley
> I have nothing against Nick's wife or his family but I think it is time he spent more time with them.
>> *Sunday Telegraph, 1990*

Guinan, Texas (1884–1933)
Canadian actress
> A politician is a fellow who will lay down your life for his country.
>> *Attr.*

Haig, Alexander (1924–)
US army officer and politician
Statement after an assassination attempt on President Reagan
> As of now, I am in charge at the White House.
>> *The Times, 1981*

Haig, Douglas (1861–1928)
Scottish military commander
Of Lord Derby
> A very weak-minded fellow, I'm afraid, and, like the feather pillow, bears the marks of the last person who has sat on him!
>> *Letter to his wife, 14 January 1918*

Hague, William (1961–)
English politician; leader of the Conservative Party
Commenting on Peter Mandelson's new appointment in Northern Ireland
> If Roland Rat were appointed to Northern Ireland, I would tell people to work with him. But I would still point out that he is a rat.
>> In *The Observer, 1999*

Harrington, James (1611–1677)
> No man can be a politician, except he be first a historian or a traveller; for except he can see what must be, or what may be, he is no politician.
>> *The Commonwealth of Oceana (1656)*

Hayden, Bill (1933–)
Australian statesman
> Gough Whitlam had many geniuses and one of them was that when he decided we were going to embark on one of the great national disasters, it was done with flair.
>> *Sydney Morning Herald, 1988*

Healey, Denis (1917–)
English Labour politician
On Geoffrey Howe's attack on his Budget proposals
> Like being savaged by a dead sheep.
>> *Speech, 1978*

Of Mrs Thatcher
> For the past few months she has been charging about like some bargain basement Boadicea.
>> *The Observer, 1982*

Heath, Sir Edward (1916–)
At a photocall when Baroness Thatcher said to him, 'You should be on my right.'
> That would be difficult.
>> *The Times, 1999*

Helps, Sir Arthur (1813–1875)
English historian and writer

There is one statesman of the present day, of whom I always say, that he would have escaped making the blunders that he has made if he had only ridden more in omnibuses.

Friends in Council (New Series, 1859)

Hoggart, Simon (1946–)
British journalist

Reagan was probably the first modern president to treat the post as a part-time job, one way of helping to fill the otherwise blank days of retirement.

America 1990

Peter Mandelson is someone who can skulk in broad daylight.

The Observer, 1998

Horne, Donald Richmond (1921–)
Australian novelist

Politicians cannot help being clowns. Political activity is essentially absurd. The hopes held for it can be high, the results tragic, but the political art itself must lack dignity: it can never match our ideals of how such things should be done.

The Legend of King O'Malley

Howar, Barbara (1934–)
US television correspondent and writer

There are no such things as good politicians and bad politicians. There are only politicians, which is to say, they all have personal axes to grind, and all too rarely are they honed for the public good.

Laughing All the Way (1973)

Jackson, Glenda (1936–)
English actress and Labour politician
On career aspirations, 1997

My only political ambition is to be re-elected.

Attr.

Jarrell, Randall (1914–1965)
US poet, critic and translator

President Robbins was so well adjusted to his environment that sometimes you could not tell which was the environment and which was President Robbins.

Pictures from an Institution (1954)

Johnson, Lyndon Baines (1908–1973)
US Democrat President
Correct version of the frequently-misquoted: 'He couldn't walk and chew gum at the same time'

Gerry Ford is so dumb that he can't fart and chew gum at the same time.

In R. Reeves, *A Ford, Not a Lincoln* (1975)

Keating, Paul (1944–)
Australian Premier
On Andrew Peacock's ambitions to become leader of the Liberal Party following the 1987 elections

Can a soufflé rise twice?

ABC television, 1987

Keynes, John Maynard (1883–1946)
English economist
Of Lloyd George

This goat-footed bard, this half-human visitor to our age from the hag-ridden magic and enchanted woods of Celtic antiquity.

Essays and Sketches in Biography (1933)

When asked what happened when Lloyd George was alone in a room

When he's alone in a room, there's nobody there.

As I Remember, 1967

Khrushchev, Nikita (1894–1971)
Russian statesman and Premier of the USSR

Politicians are the same everywhere. They promise to build a bridge even when there's no river.

Remark to journalists in the USA, 1960

Labouchere, Henry (1831–1912)

He [Labouchere] did not object, he once said, to Gladstone's always having the ace of trumps up his sleeve, but only to his pretence that God had put it there.

In Curzon, *Modern Parliamentary Eloquence* (1913)

Lardner, Ring (1885–1933)
US humorist and writer
Referring to W.H. Taft, US President 1909–1913

He looked at me as if I was a side dish he hadn't ordered.

In A.K. Adams, *The Home Book of Humorous Quotations*

Le Guin, Ursula (1929–)
US author

He had grown up in a country run by politicians who sent the pilots to man the bombers to kill the babies to make the world safe for children to grow up in.

The Lathe of Heaven (1971)

Livingstone, Ken (1945–)
British Labour politician and Mayor of London

Being an MP is not really a job for grown-ups – you are wandering around looking for and making trouble.

The Guardian, 2000

Lloyd George, David (1863–1945)
British Liberal statesman
Of Neville Chamberlain

He saw foreign policy through the wrong end of a municipal drainpipe.

In Harris, *The Fine Art of Political Wit*

When they circumcised Herbert Samuel they threw away the wrong bit.

Attr. in *The Listener*, 1978

Speech in Parliament, of Sir John Simon

> The Right Honourable gentleman has sat so long on the fence that the iron has entered his soul.
>
> Attr.

Of Neville Chamberlain

> A good mayor of Birmingham in an off-year.
>
> Attr.; also attributed to Lord Hugh Cecil

Longworth, Alice Roosevelt (1884–1980)
US writer
Of John Calvin Coolidge, US President 1923–1929

> He looks as if he had been weaned on a pickle.
>
> *Crowded Hours* (1933)

Lynne, Liz (1948–)
English politician
On the behaviour of MPs

> It was like a bunch of 11-year-olds at their first secondary school.
>
> *The Independent*, 1992

Lytton, Lady Constance (1869–1923)
British suffragette and writer

> The first time you meet Winston Churchill you see all his faults and the rest of your life you spend in discovering his virtues.
>
> In Christopher Hassall, *Edward Marsh*

MacLennan, Robert (1936–)
Scottish politician

> Tony Blair has pushed moderation to extremes.
>
> *The Observer*, 1996

Macmillan, Harold (1894–1986)
British Conservative Prime Minister
Of Aneurin Bevan

> He enjoys prophesying the imminent fall of the capitalist system, and is prepared to play a part, any part, in its burial, except that of mute.
>
> Speech, House of Commons, 1934

> When you're abroad you're a statesman: when you're at home you're just a politician.
>
> Speech, South African Parliament, 1958

> If people want a sense of purpose they should get it from their archbishop. They should certainly not get it from their politicians.
>
> In Fairlie, *The Life of Politics* (1968)

Major, John (1943–)
English Conservative Prime Minister

> People with vision usually do more harm than good.
>
> *The Economist*, 1993

Maxton, James (1885–1946)
Scottish Labour leader
Said to Ramsay MacDonald when he made his last speech in Parliament

> Sit down, man. You're a bloody tragedy.
>
> Attr.

Mencken, H.L. (1880–1956)
US writer, critic, philologist and satirist
On President Calvin Coolidge

> Here, indeed, was his one really notable talent. He slept more than any other President, whether by day or by night ... Nero fiddled, but Coolidge only snored ... He had no ideas, and he was not a nuisance.
>
> *American Mercury*, 1933

Menzies, Sir Robert (1894–1978)
Australian statesman
In answer to a woman shouting, 'I wouldn't vote for you if you were the Archangel Gabriel'

> If I were the Archangel Gabriel, madam, I'm afraid you would not be in my constituency.
>
> In Robinson, *The Wit of Sir Robert Menzies* (1966)

Mosley, Sir Oswald (1896–1980)
British founder of the British Union of Fascists

> I am not, and never have been, a man of the right. My position was on the left and is now in the centre of politics.
>
> Letter to *The Times*, 1968

Muggeridge, Malcolm (1903–1990)
English writer
Of Anthony Eden

> He was not only a bore; he bored for England.
>
> *Tread Softly For You Tread on My Jokes* (1966)

> Macmillan seemed, in his very person, to embody the national decay he supposed himself to be confuting. He exuded a flavour of mothballs.
>
> *Tread Softly For You Tread on My Jokes* (1966)

Nixon, Richard (1913–1994)
US Republican politician and President

> There can be no whitewash at the White House.
>
> *The Observer*, 1973

> When the President does it, that means it is not illegal.
>
> TV interview with David Frost, May 1977

O'Brien, Conor Cruise (1917–)
Irish journalist

> If I saw Mr Haughey buried at midnight at a cross-roads, with a stake driven through his heart – politically speaking – I should continue to wear a clove of garlic round my neck, just in case.
>
> *The Observer*, 1982

Parker, Dorothy (1893–1967)
US writer, poet, critic and wit
Response to news that President Calvin Coolidge had died

> How could they tell?
>
> In Keats, *You Might As Well Live* (1970)

Pompidou, Georges (1911–1974)
French statesman, Premier and President

A statesman is a politician who places himself at the service of a nation. A politician is a statesman who places the nation at his service.

The Observer, 1973

Prescott, John (1938–)
English Labour politician
Reply when asked why he had taken a chauffeur-driven car on a 300-yard trip to the Labour Party Conference

There were security reasons and my wife does not like to have her hair blown about. Any more stupid questions?

In *The Times*, 1999

Priestley, J.B. (1894–1984)
English writer, dramatist and critic
Of politicians

A number of anxious dwarfs trying to grill a whale.

Outcries and Asides

Reagan, Ronald (1911–)
US actor, Republican statesman and President
To the surgeons about to operate on him after he was wounded in an assassination attempt

Please assure me that you are all Republicans!

In Boller, *Presidential Anecdotes* (1981)

When told by an aide that the Government was running normally, after an attempt to assassinate him

What makes you think I'd be happy about that?

Time, 1981

Roosevelt, Franklin Delano (1882–1945)
US Democrat President

A radical is a man with both feet firmly planted in the air.

Radio broadcast, 1939

Roosevelt, Theodore (1858–1919)
US Republican President

The most successful politician is he who says what everybody is thinking most often and in the loudest voice.

In Andrews, *Treasury of Humorous Quotations*

Russell, Bertrand (1872–1970)
English philosopher, mathematician, essayist and social reformer
Of Anthony Eden

Not a gentleman; dresses too well.

In Alistair Cooke, *Six Men* (1977)

Sahl, Mort (1927–)
Canadian-born US comedian

Washington could not tell a lie; Nixon could not tell the truth; Reagan cannot tell the difference.

The Observer, 1987

Of President Nixon

Would you buy a second-hand car from this man?

Attr.

Salisbury, Fifth Marquess of (1893–1972)

The present Colonial Secretary Iain Macleod has been too clever by half. I believe he is a very fine bridge player. It is not considered immoral, or even bad form to outwit one's opponent at bridge. It almost seems to me as if the Colonial Secretary, when he abandoned the sphere of bridge for the sphere of politics, brought his bridge technique with him.

Speech, House of Lords, 1961

Sheridan, Richard Brinsley (1751–1816)
Irish dramatist, politician and orator
Reply to Mr Dundas

The Right Honourable Gentleman is indebted to his memory for his jests, and to his imagination for his facts.

Speech, House of Commons

Shorten, Caroline
British Social and Liberal Democrat politician

Most Conservatives believe that a creche is something that happens between two Range Rovers in Tunbridge Wells.

The Independent, September 1993

Simon, Guy (1944–)

Jimmy Carter had the air of a man who had never taken any decisions in his life. They had always taken him.

The Sunday Times, 1978

Smith, F.E. (1872–1930)
English politician and Lord Chancellor

Winston Churchill has devoted the best years of his life to preparing his impromptu speeches.

Attr.

Stevenson, Adlai (1900–1965)
US lawyer, statesman and United Nations ambassador

A politician is a statesman who approaches every question with an open mouth.

In Harris, *The Fine Art of Political Wit*

Tebbitt, Norman (1931–)
English Conservative politician

I hope Mrs Thatcher will go until the turn of the century looking like Queen Victoria.

The Observer, 1987

Thatcher, Carol (1953–)
English writer and broadcaster; daughter of Margaret Thatcher
Of her mother, Margaret Thatcher

Reality hasn't really intervened in my mother's life since the seventies.

Daily Mail, 1996

Thatcher, Margaret (1925–)
English Conservative Prime Minister

U-turn if you want to. The lady's not for turning.

Speech, 1980

I don't mind how much my Ministers talk – as long as they do what I say.

The Observer, 1980

I think I have become a bit of an institution – you know, the sort of thing people expect to see around the place.

The Observer, 1987

We have become a grandmother.

The Observer, 1989

Thomas, Norman M. (1884–1968)

US Presbyterian minister and writer

Referring to his lack of success in presidential campaigns

While I'd rather be right than president, at any time I'm ready to be both.

In A. Whitman, *Come to Judgment*

Trollope, Anthony (1815–1882)

English writer, traveller and post office official

It has been the great fault of our politicians that they have all wanted to do something.

Phineas Finn (1869)

Truman, Harry S. (1884–1972)

US Democrat President

A statesman is a politician who's been dead ten or fifteen years.

Attr.

The President spends most of his time kissing people on the cheek in order to get them to do what they ought to do without getting kissed.

The Observer, 1949

Referring to Vice-President Nixon's nomination for President

You don't set a fox to watching the chickens just because he has a lot of experience in the hen house.

Speech, 1960

Twain, Mark (1835–1910)

US humorist, writer, journalist and lecturer

The radical invents the views. When he has worn them out, the conservative adopts them.

Notebooks (1935)

Ustinov, Sir Peter (1921–)

English actor, director, dramatist, writer and raconteur

When Mrs Thatcher says she has a nostalgia for Victorian values I don't think she realises that 90 per cent of her nostalgia would be satisfied in the Soviet Union.

The Observer, 1987

Victoria, Queen (1819–1901)

Queen of the United Kingdom

On Gladstone's last appointment as Prime Minister

The danger to the country, to Europe, to her vast Empire, which is involved in having all these great interests entrusted to the shaking hand of an old, wild, and incomprehensible man of 82, is

very great!

Letter to Lord Lansdowne, 1892

Of Gladstone

He speaks to Me as if I was a public meeting.

In G.W.E. Russell, *Collections and Recollections* (1898)

Walden, George (1939–)

British Conservative politician and diplomat

On the Ron Davies affair

I suspect there is a link between the indiscretions of politicians and the nature of their work.

The Observer, 1998

Walpole, Robert (1676–1745)

British statesman and first British Prime Minister

Of fellow-parliamentarians

All those men have their price.

In Coxe, *Memoirs of Sir Robert Walpole* (1798)

Wark, Kirsty

Scottish journalist and broadcaster

It's very hard to be in awe of politicians.

The Times, 1998

Waterhouse, Keith (1929–)

English journalist and author

If John Prescott remains in office much longer, cars will have to be preceded by a man walking in front of them singing the Red Flag.

In *The Observer*, 1999

Waugh, Evelyn (1903–1966)

English writer and diarist

Of Winston Churchill

Simply a radio personality who outlived his prime.

In Christopher Sykes, *Evelyn Waugh*

Welch, Joseph

US attorney

Denouncing Senator Joseph McCarthy during the Army-McCarthy Congressional Hearings

Until this moment, Senator, I think I never really gauged your cruelty or your recklessness ... Have you no sense of decency, sir, at long last? Have you left no sense of decency?

New York Times, 1954

West, Dame Rebecca (1892–1983)

English writer, critic and feminist

Margaret Thatcher's great strength seems to be the better people know her, the better they like her. But, of course, she has one great disadvantage – she is a daughter of the people and looks trim, as the daughters of the people desire to be. Shirley Williams has such an advantage over her because she's a member of the upper-middle class and can achieve that kitchen-sink-revolutionary look that one cannot

get unless one has been to a really good school.
Interview, The Sunday Times, 1976

Whitehorn, Katherine (1926–)
English writer
It is a pity, as my husband says, that more politicians are not bastards by birth instead of vocation.
The Observer, 1964

Whitelaw, William (1918–)
English Conservative politician
I am not prepared to go about the country stirring up apathy.
Attr.

Widdecombe, Ann (l947–)
English Conservative politician
Of Michael Howard as candidate for the Conservatlve leadership
He has something of the night in him.
The Sunday Times, 1997

Wilson, Harold (1916–1995)
English Labour Prime Minister
Hence the practised performances of latter-day politicians in the game of musical daggers: never be left holding the dagger when the music stops.
The Governance of Britain

Of Tony Benn
He immatures with age.
Attr., BBC programme, 1995

▶▶ GOVERNMENT; HOUSE OF LORDS; INSULTS; POLITICS

politics

Abbott, Diane (1953–)
British Labour politician
Being an MP is the sort of job all working-class parents want for their children – clean, indoors and no heavy lifting.
The Observer, 1994

Acheson, Dean (1893–1971)
US Democrat politician
On retiring to private life
I will undoubtedly have to seek what is happily known as gainful employment, which I am glad to say does not describe holding public office.
Time, 1952

Adams, Douglas (1952–)
English writer
Anyone who is capable of getting themselves made President should on no account be allowed to do the job.
The Hitch Hiker's Guide to the Galaxy (1979)

Adams, Gerry (1948–)
President of Sinn Fein
Comment after the referendum on the Good Friday peace proposals
If no one votes for us, then we'll disappear.
The Observer, 1998

We have to work to make the Omagh bombing the last violent incident in our country. The violence we have seen must be a thing of the past, over, done with and gone.
The Times, 1998

Adams, Franklin P. (1881–1960)
US writer, poet, translator and editor
Elections are won by men and women chiefly because most people vote against somebody rather than for somebody.
In Colin Jarman, *The Guinness Book of Poisonous Quotes*

Adams, Henry (1838–1918)
US historian and memoirist
Politics, as a practice, whatever its professions, has always been the systematic organization of hatreds.
The Education of Henry Adams (1918)

Practical politics consists in ignoring facts.
The Education of Henry Adams (1918)

Adenauer, Konrad (1876–1967)
German Chancellor
The art of politics consists in knowing precisely when it is necessary to hit an opponent slightly below the belt.
Attr.

Agnew, Spiro T. (1918–1996)
US Vice President
To some extent, if you've seen one city slum you've seen them all.
Election speech, Detroit, October 1968

Amery, Leo (1873–1955)
English statesman
Speak for England, Arthur!
Interjection in House of Commons, 1939

To Neville Chamberlain, quoting Cromwell's words when he dismissed the Rump of the Long Parliament in 1653
You have sat too long here for any good you have been doing. Depart, I say, and let us have done with you. In the name of God, go!
Speech, House of Commons, May 1940

Ancram, Michael (1945–)
English Conservative politician
The Liberal Democrats are now so firmly in bed with the Labour Party that they have become little more than a shapeless lump under the Government's duvet.
The Observer, May 1999

Anderson, Bruce (1838–1918)
British journalist
Of Tony Blair's New Labour
> The Labour Party has decided to renounce its
> principles, its policies and its past.
>> *The Spectator*, May 1996

Anonymous
> *Child*: Mamma, are Tories born wicked, or do
> they grow wicked afterwards?
> *Mother*: They are born wicked, and grow worse.
>> In G.W.E. Russell, *Collections and Recollections* (1898)

> Don't tell my mother I'm in politics – she thinks I
> play the piano in a whorehouse.
>> American saying from the Depression

Pensioner's response to Juliet Peck when she introduced
herself as the local Conservative candidate
> Oh, my dear, I know just how you feel. I'm a
> Jehovah's Witness.
>> *The Observer*, 1998

> The personal is political.

> There'll be no need for wind farms once the
> Welsh Assembly gets going. There will be
> enough hot air to keep the principality lit up
> night and day.
>> *The Times*, 1998

Arbuthnot, John (1667–1735)
Scottish physician, pamphleteer and wit
> He warns the heads of parties against believing
> their own lies.
>> *The Art of Political Lying* (1712)

Arendt, Hannah (1906–1975)
German-born US theorist
> Truthfulness has never been counted among the
> political virtues, and lies have always been
> regarded as justifiable tools in political dealings.
>> *Crises of the Republic*
>> (1972)

Aristotle (384–322 BC)
Greek philosopher
> Man is by nature a political animal.
>> *Politics*

Ashdown, Paddy (1941–)
Former leader of the UK Social and Liberal Democrat
Party
> Anybody who thinks that the Liberal Democrats
> are a racist party are staring the facts in the
> face.
>> ITV news, 1993

On Labour's 1999 Budget
> It is extremely frustrating to hear someone else
> singing snatches of our song but doing it so
> completely out of tune.
>> *The Times*, 1999

Astor, Nancy, Viscountess (1879–1964)
US-born British Conservative politician and hostess
> Women are young at politics, but they are old at
> suffering; soon they will learn that through
> politics they can prevent some kinds of
> suffering.
>> *My Two Countries*
>> (1923)

Baldwin, Stanley (1867–1947)
English Conservative statesman and Prime Minister
> You will find in politics that you are much
> exposed to the attribution of false motives.
> Never complain and never explain.
>> To Harold Nicolson, 21 July 1943, quoting Disraeli

> There are three groups that no British Prime
> Minister should provoke: the Vatican, the
> Treasury and the miners.
>> Attr.

Barnes, Julian (1946–)
English author
> One of these days a British Prime Minister will
> have the guts to call an election with the cry
> 'This is a comparatively unimportant time in our
> nation's history.'
>> *The New Yorker*, 1992

Barzan, Gerald
> You don't have to fool all the people all of the
> time; you just have to fool enough to get
> elected.
>> In Lieberman, *3,500 Good Quotes for Speakers* (1983)

Benn, Tony (1925–)
English Labour politician
> When I think of Cool Britannia, I think of old
> people dying of hypothermia.
>> *The Observer*, 1998

Bevan, Aneurin (1897–1960)
Welsh Labour politician, miner and orator
> This island is almost made of coal and
> surrounded by fish. Only an organizing genius
> could produce a shortage of coal and fish at the
> same time.
>> Speech, Blackpool, 1945

> No amount of cajolery, and no attempts at
> ethical or social seduction, can eradicate from
> my heart a deep burning hatred for the Tory
> Party … So far as I am concerned they are lower
> than vermin.
>> Speech, 1948

Opposing unilateral nuclear disarmament
> If you carry this resolution and follow out all its
> implications and do not run away from it you will
> send a Foreign Secretary, whoever he may be,
> naked into the conference chamber.
>> Speech, 1957

Bevin, Ernest (1881–1951)
On foreign policy
> My policy is to be able to take a ticket at Victoria Station and go anywhere I damn well please.
>> *Spectator*, 1951

Bierce, Ambrose (1842–c.1914)
US writer, verse writer and soldier
> *Nepotism*: Appointing your grandfather to office for the good of the party.
>> *The Enlarged Devil's Dictionary* (1961)

Birch, Nigel (1906–1981)
British financier and Conservative politician
> For the second time the Prime Minister has got rid of a Chancellor of the Exchequer who tried to get expenditure under control. Once is more than enough.
>> Letter to *The Times*, 1962

Bismarck, Prince Otto von (1815–1898)
First Chancellor of the German Reich
> *Die Politik ist keine exakte Wissenschaft.*
> Politics is not a precise science.
>> Speech, Prussian House of Deputies, 1863

> *Die Politik ist keine Wissenschaft ... sie ist eben eine Kunst.*
> Politics is not a science ... but an art.
>> Speech, Reichstag, 1884

> *Die Politik ist die Lehre vom Möglichen.*
> Politics is the art of the possible.
>> Remark, 1863

Blair, Cherie (1954–)
English barrister
Comment on her reasons for joining the Labour Party
> Our motives were more social than political as it was a good way to meet boys.
>> *The Times*, 1999

Blair, Tony (1953–)
British Labour Prime Minister
> If we walk away from Kosovo ... it would be a betrayal of everything this nation stands for.
>> *The Independent*, March 1999

On the war in the Balkans
> This is not a battle for territory, this is a battle for humanity.
>> Speech to Kosovan refugees, May 1999

On his plan to reform the welfare state
> It marks the end of a something-for-nothing welfare state.
>> *The Times*, 1999

> When I became leader of the Labour Party, I was determined to put Labour's relations with business on a new footing.
>> *Inside Labour*

Bright, John (1811–1889)
English Liberal politician and social reformer
> This party of two is like the Scotch terrier that was so covered with hair that you could not tell which was the head and which was the tail.
>> Speech, House of Commons, 1866

Brittain, Vera (1893–1970)
English writer and pacifist
> Politics are usually the executive expression of human immaturity.
>> *The Rebel Passion* (1964)

Buckland, Chris
> Mr Blair cannot take a joke – or deliver one. He is, after all, leading a Government that is to humour what Lucretia Borgia was to cordon-bleu cooking.
>> *The Times*, 2000

Burchill, Julie (1960–)
English writer
> Green politics, in the final analysis, is so popular with the rich because it contains no race or class analysis at all; politics with everything but the glow of involvement taken out.
>> *Sex and Sensibility* (1992)

Burgess, Anthony (1917–1993)
English writer, linguist and composer
> The US presidency is a Tudor monarchy plus telephones.
>> In Plimpton (ed.), *Writers at Work* (1977)

Burke, Edmund (1729–1797)
Irish-born British statesman and philosopher
> The conduct of a losing party never appears right: at least it never can possess the only infallible criterion of wisdom to vulgar judgments – success.
>> Letter to a Member of the National Assembly (1791)

> Your representative owes you, not his industry only, but his judgement; and he betrays, instead of serving you, if he sacrifices it to your opinion.
>> Speech to the Electors of Bristol, 1774

Callaghan, James (1912–)
English Labour statesman and Prime Minister
> Either back us or sack us.
>> Speech, Labour Party Conference, 1977

Calwell, Arthur Augustus (1894–1973)
Australian Labour politician
To Arthur Fadden, in the House of Representatives
> I well recall the time when, for forty days and forty nights, you held the destiny of Australia in the hollow of your head.
>> In Fred Daly, *The Politician who Laughed*

Camus, Albert (1913–1960)
Algerian-born French writer
> *La politique et le sort des hommes sont formés par des*

hommes sans idéal et sans grandeur. Ceux qui ont une grandeur ne font pas de politique.
Politics and the fate of mankind are shaped by men without ideals and without greatness. Men who have greatness within them don't concern themselves with politics.

Notebooks, 1935–1942

Champion, Henry Hyde (1859–1928)
Australian politician
On the Labour Party of his day
An army of lions led by asses.

In R.H. Croll, I Recall …

Christopher, Warren (1925–)
US statesman
Sometimes you have to learn how to give the right answer to the wrong question.

Remark, 1994

Clark, Alan (1928–1999)
British Conservative politician, historian and diarist
There are no true friends in politics. We are all sharks circling and waiting, for traces of blood to appear in the water.

Diary, 1990

Clinton, William ('Bill') (1946–)
US Democrat President
What we believe in is what works.

The Times, 1999

Coleridge, Samuel Taylor (1772–1834)
English poet, philosopher and critic
In politics, what begins in fear usually ends in folly.

Table Talk (1835)

Colson, Charles (1931–)
US political aide
To campaign staff, 1972
I would walk over my grandmother if necessary to get Nixon re-elected!

Born Again (1976)

Crewe, Ivor (1945–)
British political scientist
Testimony at the Nolon inquiry into standards in public life.
The British public has always displayed a healthy cynicism of MPs. They have taken it for granted that MPs are selfserving impostors and hypocrites who put party before country and self before party.

The Guardian, 1995

Croker, John Wilson (1780–1857)
Irish politician and dramatist
First use of the phrase 'the Conservative Party'
We now are, as we always have been, decidedly and conscientiously attached to what is called the Tory, and which might with more propriety be called the Conservative, party.

Quarterly Review, 1830

Darrow, Clarence (1857–1938)
US lawyer, reformer and writer
When I was a boy I was told that anybody could become President. I'm beginning to believe it.

In Irving Stone, Clarence Darrow for the Defence (1941)

De Gaulle, Charles (1890–1970)
French general and statesman
I have come to the conclusion that politics are too serious a matter to be left to the politicians.

Attr.

Derby, Earl of (1799–1869)
English politician; Conservative Prime Minister
The Conservatives are the weakest among the intellectual classes: as is natural.

Letter to Disraeli

Dewar, Donald
Scottish Labour politician; First Minister of Scotland
Claiming that an SNP government would hold referendum after referendum if elected to power
It would mean a Scottish neverendum.

The Times, 1999

Comment on the SNP's election manifesto
This must be the first time in history that a separatist party has deliberately tried to conceal its sole purpose for existing from the electorate.

The Times, 1999

Description of the likely intake of Labour MSPs
A very talented group. Well, some of them very talented, some of them not so talented, as you'd expect.

Comment during election campaign, 1999

Disraeli, Benjamin (1804–1881)
English statesman and writer
A man may speak very well in the House of Commons, and fail very completely in the House of Lords. There are two distinct styles requisite: I intend, in the course of my career, if I have time, to give a specimen of both.

The Young Duke (1831)

The practice of politics in the East may be defined by one word – dissimulation.

Contarini Fleming (1832)

A majority is always the best repartee.

Tancred (1847)

Party is organized opinion.

Speech, Meeting of Society for Increasing Endowments of Small Livings in the Diocese of Oxford, 1864

England does not love coalitions.

Speech, 1852

Finality is not the language of politics.

Speech, 1859

Damn your principles! Stick to your party.

Attr.

Einstein, Albert (1879–1955)
German-born US mathematical physicist
An empty stomach is not a good political adviser.

Cosmic Religion (1931)

Eisenhower, Dwight D. (1890–1969)
US Republican President and general
There is one thing about being President – nobody can tell you when to sit down.

The Observer, 1953

Ewing, Winnie (1929–)
Scottish Nationalist politician
On entering Westminster after winning a 1967 by-election for the SNP
As I took my seat it was said by political pundits that 'a chill ran along the Labour back benches looking for a spine to run up'.

Attr.

The Scottish Parliament, adjourned on 25th March 1707, is hereby reconvened.

Speech at the opening of the new Scottish Parliament on 12th May 1999

Fields, W.C. (1880–1946)
US film actor
Hell, I never vote for anybody. I always vote against.

In Taylor, W. C. Fields: His Follies and Fortunes (1950)

Fisher, H.A.L. (1856–1940)
English historian
Politics is the art of human happiness.

History of Europe (1935)

Foucault, Michel (1926–1984)
French philosopher
In 1966, when *Les Mots et les choses* appeared, he was attacked for this remark
Marxism exists in nineteenth-century thought in the same way as a fish exists in water; that is, it stops breathing anywhere else.

In Eribon, Michel Foucault (1989)

Frost, Robert (1874–1963)
US poet
I never dared be radical when young
For fear it would make me conservative when old.

'Precaution' (1936)

A liberal is a man too broadminded to take his own side in a quarrel.

Attr.

Gaitskell, Hugh (1906–1963)
English Labour politician
All terrorists, at the invitation of the

Government, end up with drinks at the Dorchester.

Letter to The Guardian, 1977

Galbraith, J.K. (1908–)
Canadian-born US economist, diplomat and writer
Politics is not the art of the possible. It consists in choosing between the disastrous and the unpalatable.

Ambassador's Journal (1969

Few things are as immutable as the addiction of political groups to the ideas by which they have once won office.

The Affluent Society (1958)

There are times in politics when you must be on the right side and lose.

The Observer, 1968

Garner, John Nance (1868–1937)
US politician
The Vice-Presidency isn't worth a pitcher of warm piss.

Attr.

Goebbels, Joseph (1897–1945)
Nazi politician
Whoever can conquer the street will one day conquer the state, for every form of power politics and any dictatorship-run state has its roots in the street.

Speech to Nazi party congress, Nuremburg, Germany, 1927

Goldberg, Whoopi (1949–)
US actress
You've got to vote for someone. It's a shame, but it's got to be done.

Detroit News, 1988

Hague, William (1961–)
English politician; leader of the Conservative Party
After listing the Labour councillors found guilty of crimes such as fraud
Isn't it the case that these are the only people left in the Labour Party with genuine convictions?

The Times, 1999

Hailsham, Quintin Hogg, Baron (1907–)
English Conservative politician and Lord Chancellor
On the Profumo affair
A great party is not to be brought down because of a squalid affair between a woman of easy virtue and a proved liar.

Interview, BBC TV, 1963

Hattersley, Roy (1932–)
British Labour politician and writer
If the Labour Party does not aspire to reduce class disparities in life expectation, it is hard to

describe the purpose of its existence.

The Observer, 1999

Havel, Václav (1936–)
Czech President

Ideology is a special way of relating to the world. It offers human beings the illusion of an identity, of dignity, and of morality, while making it easier for them to part with it.

Living in Truth (1987)

Hayes, Jerry
English conservative politician

Conservative party policy is not unlike a Wagner opera. It is not always as bad as it sounds.

The Observer, 'Sayings of the Year', December 1998

Healey, Denis (1917–)
English Labour politician

It is a good thing to follow the first law of holes; if you are in one, stop digging.

The Observer, 1988

Hellman, Lillian (1907–1984)
US dramatist and screenwriter

I cannot and will not cut my conscience to fit this year's fashions, even though I long ago came to the conclusion that I was not a political person and could have no comfortable place in any political group.

Letter to the US House of Representatives Committee on Un-American Activities, 1952

Hightower, Jim (1933–)
Texan agriculture commissioner

Only things in the middle of the road are yellow lines and dead armadillos.

Attr.

Hitler, Adolf (1889–1945)
German Nazi dictator, born in Austria

Wesentlich ist die politische Willensbildung der gesamten Nation, sie ist der Ausgangspunkt für politische Aktionen.

What is essential is the formation of the political will of the entire nation: that is the starting point for political actions.

Speech, 1932

Horne, Donald Richmond (1921–)
Australian novelist

Politics is both fraud and vision.

The Legend of King O'Malley

Ickes, Harold L. (1874–1952)
US politician

On his resignation as Secretary of the Interior after a dispute with President Truman

I am against government by crony.

Remark, 1946

Jackson, Glenda (1936–)
English actress and Labour politician

Describing her first impressions of being the new MP for Hampstead and Highgate

People have said to me that your first week in the Commons is like your first week at school. My school was never like this. People told you what to do, they were less friendly, and there were more girls.

The List, 1992

Jeffe, Sherry Bebitch
US political analyst

A definition of the street-car theory of American politics

To win, a candidate must be standing on the right street corner at the right time when a street-car is going in the right direction, and must have the right amount of change in their pockets.

The Independent on Sunday, 1992

Jenkins, Roy (1920–)
Welsh politician and writer

Used in connection with the SDP, established in 1981

Breaking the mould of British politics.

Attr.

Johnson, Lyndon Baines (1908–1973)
US Democrat President

If you're in politics and you can't tell when you walk into a room who's for you and who's against you, then you're in the wrong line of work.

In B. Mooney, *The Lyndon Johnson Story* (1956)

Johnson, Samuel (1709–1784)
English lexicographer, poet, critic, conversationalist and essayist

Why, Sir, most schemes of political improvement are very laughable things.

In Boswell, *The Life of Samuel Johnson* (1791)

Politics are now nothing more than a means of rising in the world.

In Boswell, *The Life of Samuel Johnson* (1791)

Joseph, Sir Keith (1918–1994)
English Conservative politician

We spend more on welfare without achieving well-being, while creating dangerous levels of dependency.

Speech to Oxford Union, 1975

Junius (1769–1772)
Pen-name of anonymous author of letters criticising ministers of George III

There is a holy mistaken zeal in politics as well as in religion. By persuading others, we convince ourselves.

Letters (1769–1771)

Kennedy, Charles (1959–)
Leader of the UK Social and Liberal Democrat Party
> Voting Tory is like being in trouble with the
> police. You'd rather the neighbours didn't know.
>> Speech, Liberal Democrat Conference, 1994

> Paddy Ashdown is the only party leader to be a
> trained killer. Although, to be fair, Mrs Thatcher
> was self-taught.
>> The Observer, 1998

Kinnock, Neil (1942–)
Welsh Labour politician
Attacking militant members in Liverpool
> The grotesque chaos of a Labour council – a
> Labour council – hiring taxis to scuttle around a
> city handing out redundancy notices to its own
> workers.
>> Speech, Labour Party Conference, Bournemouth, 1985

Kissinger, Henry (1923–)
German-born US Secretary of State
> Foreign policy should not be confused with
> missionary work.
>> London Review of Books, 1992

La Bruyère, Jean de (1645–1696)
French satirist
> *L'esprit de parti abaisse les plus grands hommes*
> *jusques aux petitesses du peuple.*
> Party loyalty brings the greatest of men down to
> the petty level of the masses.
>> Les caractères ou les moeurs de ce siècle (1688)

Livingstone, Ken (1945–)
British Labour politician and Mayor of London
> Politics is a marathon, not a sprint.
>> New Statesman, 1997

Macmillan, Harold (1894–1986)
British Conservative Prime Minister
> Let's be frank about it; most of our people have
> never had it so good.
>> Speech, 1957

On the life of a Foreign Secretary
> Forever poised between a cliché and an
> indiscretion.
>> Newsweek, 1956

> As usual the Liberals offer a mixture of sound
> and original ideas. Unfortunately none of the
> sound ideas is original and none of the original
> ideas is sound.
>> The Observer, 1961

> I have never found in a long experience of
> politics that criticism is ever inhibited by
> ignorance.
>> Attr.

Major, John (1943–)
English Conservative Prime Minister
Commenting on his party's disastrous results in local
government elections
> For those people who may suggest that at the
> moment the Conservative Party has its back to
> the wall, I would simply say we will do precisely
> what the British nation has done all through its
> history when it had its back to the wall: turn
> round and fight for the things it believes.
>> The Observer, 1996

Mandela, Nelson (1918–)
South African statesman and President
> The struggle is my life.
>> Letter from underground, 1961

Mandelson, Peter (1953–)
English Labour politican
On the difference between New Labour and the Conservatives
> When was the last time you heard of a Tory
> Minister resigning to spend more time with his
> mortgage?
>> The Observer, 1999

Mao Tse-Tung (1893–1976)
Chinese Communist leader
> All reactionaries are paper tigers.
>> Quotations from Chairman Mao Tse-Tung

Marr, Andrew
Scottish journalist
On political apathy under New Labour
> Today's ministers are a bit like actors in a huge,
> dark theatre, initially delighted at the absence of
> heckling or booing, but beginning uneasily to
> ask themselves whether anyone is still watching.
>> The Observer, 1999

Maxton, James (1885–1946)
Scottish Labour leader
On a man proposing that the ILP should no longer be
affiliated to the Labour Party
> If my friend cannot ride two horses – what's he
> doing in the bloody circus?
>> In G. McAllister, James Maxton: the Portrait of a
>> Rebel (1935)

Mayhew, Christopher (1915–1997)
British parliamentarian and writer
On the Munich Agreement
> A policy of *reculer pour mieux reculer*.
>> Speech, Oxford Union, 1938

McCarthy, Eugene (1916–)
US politician, lecturer and writer
> Being in politics is like being a football coach.
> You have to be smart enough to understand the
> game and dumb enough to think it's important.
>> Interview, 1968

Menzies, Sir Robert (1894–1978)
Australian statesman
> A Prime Minister exercises his greatest public
> influence by creating a public impression of

himself, hoping all the time that the people will be generous rather than just.

> In Mayer and Nelson, *Australian Politics: A Third Reader*

Mill, John Stuart (1806–1873)
English philosopher, economist and reformer
> The Conservatives ... being by the law of their existence the stupidest party.
>> *Considerations on Representative Government* (1861)

> A party of order or stability, and a party of progress or reform, are both necessary elements of a healthy state of political life.
>> *On Liberty* (1859)

Milligan, Spike (1918–)
Irish comedian and writer
Remark made about a pre-election poll
> One day the don't-knows will get in, and then where will we be?
>> Attr.

Mitchell, Austin
English Labour politician
Description of New Labour
> A children's crusade led by the early middle-aged.
>> *The Observer*, 1998

Moore, Patrick (1923–)
British astronomer, writer and broadcaster
On the Monster Raving Loony Party
> They had one advantage over all the other parties. They knew they were loonies.
>> In *The Observer*, 1999

Morton, Rogers (1914–1979)
US government official
Refusing to make any last-ditch attempts to rescue President Ford's re-election campaign, 1976
> I'm not going to re-arrange the furniture on the deck of the Titanic.
>> Attr.

Napoleon I (1769–1821)
To Josephine in 1809, on divorcing her for reasons of state
> I still love you, but in politics there is no heart, only head.
>> Attr.

Orwell, George (1903–1950)
English writer and critic
> No book is genuinely free from political bias. The opinion that art should have nothing to do with politics is itself a political attitude.
>> 'Why I Write' (1946)

> In our time, political speech and writing are largely the defence of the indefensible.
>> *Shooting an Elephant* (1950)

Pankhurst, Dame Christabel (1880–1958)
English suffragette
> Never lose your temper with the Press or the public is a major rule of political life.
>> *Unshackled* (1959)

Pankhurst, Emmeline (1858–1928)
English suffragette
> The argument of the broken pane of glass is the most valuable argument in modern politics.
>> Attr.

Parkinson, C. Northcote (1909–1993)
English political scientist and historian
> The British, being brought up on team games, enter their House of Commons in the spirit of those who would rather be doing something else. If they cannot be playing golf or tennis, they can at least pretend that politics is a game with very similar rules.
>> *Parkinson's Law* (1958)

> It is now known ... that men enter local politics solely as a result of being unhappily married.
>> *Parkinson's Law* (1958)

Parris, Matthew (1949–)
British Conservative politician and journalist
> Being an MP feeds your vanity and starves your self-respect.
>> *The Times*, 1994

On a particularly sycophantic question to Prime Minister Tony Blair from John Hatton MP
> To call it toadying would be to invite a group libel action from toads.
>> *The Times*, 1998

Paxman, Jeremy (1950–)
English journalist, writer and broadcaster
Interview with Henry Kissinger
> Didn't you feel a fraud accepting the Nobel Peace Prize?
>> BBC radio programme *Start the Week*, 1999

Peacock, Thomas Love (1785–1866)
English writer and poet
> A Sympathizer would seem to imply a certain degree of benevolent feeling. Nothing of the kind. It signifies a ready-made accomplice in any species of political villainy.
>> *Gryll Grange* (1861)

Pope, Alexander (1688–1744)
English poet, translator and editor
> Party-spirit, which at best is but the madness of many for the gain of a few.
>> Letter to Edward Blount, 1714

Powell, Enoch (1912–1998)
English politician and scholar
> Above any other position of eminence, that of

Prime Minister is filled by fluke.

The Observer, 1987

Prescott, John (1938–)
English Labour politician
During a debate between Prescott, Tony Blair and Margaret Beckett at the time of the contest for the Labour leadership
We're in danger of loving ourselves to death.

The Observer, 1994

The Green Belt is a Labour achievement, and we intend to build on it.

The Observer, 'Sayings of the Year', 1998

Rawnsley, Andrew
British broadcaster and journalist
A British Prime Minister in command of a parliamentary majority is an elected dictator with vastly more domestic power than an American President.

The Observer, 1999

Reagan, Ronald (1911–)
US actor, Republican statesman and President
Politics is supposed to be the second oldest profession. I have come to understand that it bears a very close resemblance to the first.

Remark at a conference, 1977

Politics is not a bad profession. If you succeed there are many rewards, if you disgrace yourself you can always write a book.

Attr.

Rogers, Will (1879–1935)
US humorist, actor, rancher, writer and wit
The more you read … about this Politics thing, you got to admit that each party is worse than the other.

Autobiography of Will Rogers (1949)

England elects a Labour Government. When a man goes in for politics over here, he has no time to labour, and any man that labours has no time to fool with politics. Over there politics is an obligation; over here it's a business.

Autobiography of Will Rogers (1949)

Rusk, Dean (1909–1994)
US politician and diplomat
Of the Cuban missile crisis
We're eye-ball to eye-ball and I think the other fellow just blinked.

Remark, 1962

Shaw, George Bernard (1856–1950)
Irish socialist, writer, dramatist and critic
He knows nothing; and he thinks he knows everything. That points clearly to a political career.

Major Barbara (1907)

Shawcross, Lord (1902–)
English Labour politician
We are the masters at the moment, and not only at the moment, but for a very long time to come.

Speech, House of Commons, 1946; usually quoted as 'We are the masters now.'

Sheridan, Richard Brinsley (1751–1816)
Irish dramatist, politician and orator
On being asked to apologize for calling a fellow MP a liar
Mr Speaker, I said the honourable member was a liar it is true and I am sorry for it. The honourable member may place the punctuation where he pleases.

Attr.

Sherman, William Tecumseh (1820–1891)
US Civil War general
I would not for a million dollars subject myself and family to the ordeal of a political canvass and afterwards to a four years' service in the White House.

Letter to his brother, 1884

Skelton, Noel (1880–1935)
… to state as clearly as may be what means lie ready to develop a property-owning democracy, to bring the industrial and economic status of the wage-earner abreast of his political and education, to make democracy stable and four-square.

Article in the *Spectator*, 1923

Smith, Sir Cyril (1928–)
New Zealand-born British forensic scientist and writer
English politician
On the House of Commons
The longest running farce in the West End.

Remark to foreign press, 1973

Somoza, Anastasio (1925–1980)
President of Nicaragua
You won the elections. But I won the count.

The Guardian, 1977

Soper, Donald (1903–1998)
Methodist churchman and writer
On the quality of debate in the House of Lords
It is, I think, good evidence of life after death.

The Listener, 1978

Speight, Johnny (1920–1998)
English screenwriter
If Her Majesty stood for Parliament – if the Tory Party had any sense and made Her its leader instead of that grammar school twit Heath – us Tories, mate, would win every election we went in for.

Till Death Do Us Part, television programme

Steel, Sir David (1938–)
English politician

> Go back to your constituencies and prepare for government!
>
> > Speech to party conference, 1981

> I sense that the British electorate is now itching to break out once and for all from the discredited straight-jacket of the past.
>
> > The Times, 1987

Stevenson, Adlai (1900–1965)
US lawyer, statesman and United Nations ambassador
Of the Republican Party

> Needs to be dragged kicking and screaming into the twentieth century.
>
> > In K. Tynan, Curtains (1961)

> I will make a bargain with the Republicans. If they will stop telling lies about Democrats, we will stop telling lies about them.
>
> > Speech, 1952

> We hear the Secretary of State boasting of his brinkmanship – the art of bringing us to the edge of the abyss.
>
> > Speech, Hartford, Connecticut, 1956

Stevenson, Robert Louis (1850–1894)
Scottish writer, poet and essayist

> Politics is perhaps the only profession for which no preparation is thought necessary.
>
> > Familiar Studies of Men and Books (1882)

> These are my politics: to change what we can; to better what we can; but still to bear in mind that man is but a devil weakly fettered by some generous beliefs and impositions; and for no word however sounding, and no cause however just and pious, to relax the stricture of these bonds.
>
> > The Dynamiter (1885)

Stoppard, Tom (1937–)
British dramatist

> The House of Lords, an illusion to which I have never been able to subscribe – reponsibility without power, the prerogative of the eunuch throughout the ages.
>
> > Lord Malquist and Mr Moon (1966)

Thatcher, Margaret (1925–)
English Conservative Prime Minister

> I don't understand Cool Britannia. I believe in Rule Britannia.
>
> > The Observer, 1998

> Let our children grow tall, and some taller than others if they have it in them to do so.
>
> > Speech, US tour, 1975

> Britain is no longer in the politics of the

pendulum, but of the ratchet.

> > Speech, 1977

> Victorian values … were the values when our country became great.
>
> > Television interview, 1982

> No one would have remembered the Good Samaritan if he'd only had good intentions. He had money as well.
>
> > The Observer, 1980

Thorpe, Jeremy (1929–)
English Liberal politician
Remark on Macmillan's Cabinet purge, 1962

> Greater love hath no man than this, that he lay down his friends for his life.
>
> > Speech, 1962

Tocqueville, Alexis de (1805–1859)
French historian, politician, lawyer and memoirist

> *Il faut une science politique nouvelle à un monde tout nouveau.*
> A new world demands a new political science.
>
> > De la démocratie en Amérique (1835–1840)

Toner, Pauline Therese (1935–1989)
Australian politician
The credo of the first woman Minister in the history of the Victorian Parliament

> Why join a women's group to lobby government ministers when you can become a minister yourself?
>
> > Australian Women's Weekly, 1982

Trollope, Anthony (1815–1882)
English writer, traveller and post office official

> It is the necessary nature of a political party in this country to avoid, as long as it can be avoided, the consideration of any question which involves a great change … The best carriage horses are those which can most steadily hold back against the coach as it trundles down the hill.
>
> > Phineas Redux (1874)

Truman, Harry S. (1884–1972)
US Democrat President

> If you can't stand the heat, get out of the kitchen.
>
> > Mr Citizen (1960)

Ustinov, sir Peter (1921–)
English actor, director, dramatist, writer and raconteur

> I could never bear to be a politician. I couldn't bear to be right all the time.
>
> > The Observer, 1998

Valéry, Paul (1871–1945)
French poet, mathematician and philosopher

> *La politique est l'art d'empêcher les gens de se mêler de ce qui les regarde.*
> Politics is the art of preventing people from

becoming involved in affairs which concern them.

As Such 2 (1943)

Vidal, Gore (1925–)
US writer, critic and poet
> Any American who is prepared to run for President should automatically, by definition, be disqualified from ever doing so.

Attr.

Walden, George (1939–)
British Conservative politician and diplomat
On John Major's policy of non-cooperation with Europe over the export ban on British beef
> Patriots are not supposed to make fools of their own people.

The Times, 1996

Waten, Judah Leon (1911–1985)
Australian novelist
> The art of politics is to make more friends than enemies.

Remark to S. Murray-Smith

Waterhouse, Keith (1929–)
English journalist and author
> A newspaper poll found that fewer than one in twenty people could explain the government's third way. Some thought it was a religious cult, others a sexual position, and one man asked if it were a plan to widen the M25.

The Observer, 1998

Wellington, Duke of (1769–1852)
Irish-born British military commander and statesman
On seeing the first Reformed Parliament
> I never saw so many shocking bad hats in my life.

In Fraser, *Words on Wellington* (1889)

Wilson, Harold (1916–1995)
English Labour Prime Minister
> A week is a long time in politics.

Remark, 1964

> The Labour Party is like a stage-coach. If you rattle along at great speed everybody inside is too exhilarated or too seasick to cause any trouble. But if you stop everybody gets out and argues about where to go next.

In L. Smith, *Harold Wilson, The Authentic Portrait*

Zappa, Frank (1940–1993)
US rock musician, songwriter and record producer
> Politics is the entertainment branch of industry.

Attr.

▶▶ COMMUNISM; DEMOCRACY; DIPLOMACY; FASCISM; GOVERNMENT; HOUSE OF LORDS; LIBERALS; MONARCHY AND ROYALTY; OPPOSITION; POLITICIANS; SOCIALISM

popularity

Bennett, Tony (1926–)
US singer
> I think one of the reasons I'm popular again is because I'm wearing a tie. You have to be different.

Halifax, Lord (1633–1695)
English politician, courtier, pamphleteer and epigrammatist
> Popularity is a Crime from the Moment it is sought; it is only a Virtue where Men have it whether they will or no.

Political, Moral and Miscellaneous Thoughts and Reflections (1750)

Kennedy, John F. (1917–1963)
US Democrat President
Of his popularity after the failure of the US invasion of Cuba
> The worse I do, the more popular I get.

Attr.

Lamb, Charles (1775–1834)
English essayist, critic and letter writer
> How I like to be liked, and what I do to be liked!

Letter to D. Wordsworth, 1821

Miller, Arthur (1915–)
US dramatist and screenwriter
> He's liked, but he's not well liked.

Death of a Salesman (1949)

▶▶ CELEBRITY; FAME

pornography

Allbeury, Ted (1917–)
English crime writer
> The real stuff's inside. Whether you want your porn in black and white, full-colour litho, on film or on gramophone records and in any one of five languages, this is Stockholm's place for connoisseurs. There are no pictures of old slags and tattooed sailors here. The girls in the pictures are young and pretty and even the Great Danes are registered at the Swedish Kennel Club.

Snowball (1976)

Allen, Woody (1935–)
US film director, writer, actor and comedian
> *Fielding Mellish*: I once stole a pornographic book that was printed in braille. I used to rub the dirty parts.

Bananas (film, 1971)

Crisp, Quentin (1908–1999)
English writer, publicist and model

What is wrong with pornography is that it is a successful attempt to sell sex for more than it is worth.

> In Kettlehack (ed.), *The Wit and Wisdom of Quentin Crisp*

Ferman, James
Former director of the British Board of Film Classification
> A little of what people want is OK as long as it's on the harmless end of the spectrum. The more you try to ban it the more it will grow.

> *The Times*, 1998

Huxley, Aldous (1894–1963)
English writer, poet and critic
> Real orgies are never so exciting as pornographic books.

> *Point Counter Point* (1928)

Lawrence, D.H. (1885–1930)
English writer, poet and critic
> Pornography is the attempt to insult sex, to do dirt on it.

> *Phoenix* (1936)

Russell, Bertrand (1872–1970)
English philosopher, mathematician, essayist and social reformer
> Obscenity is what happens to shock some elderly and ignorant magistrate.

> *Look* magazine

Speight, Johnny (1920–1998)
English screenwriter
> Don't be daft. You don't get any pornography on there, not on the telly. Get filth, that's all. The only place you get pornography is in yer Sunday papers.

> *Till Death Do Us Part*, TV sitcom

Wolfe, Tom (1931–)
US author and journalist
> Pornography was the great vice of the seventies; plutography – the graphic depiction of the acts of the rich – is the great vice of the eighties.

> *The Sunday Times Magazine*, 1988

▶▶ CENSORSHIP; SEX

poverty

Anouilh, Jean (1910–1987)
French dramatist and screenwriter
> *Moi j'adorerais être pauvre! Seulement, je voudrais être vraiment pauvre. Tout ce qui est excessif m'enchante.*
> I should love to be poor, as long as I was excessively poor! Anything in excess is quite delightful.

> *Ring Round the Moon* (1948)

Bagehot, Walter (1826–1877)
English economist and political philosopher
> Poverty is an anomaly to rich people. It is very difficult to make out why people who want dinner do not ring the bell.

> *Literary Studies* (1879)

Baker, Kenneth, Lord
English Conservative politician
> Now that the Social Security Secretary has defined poverty by reference to 32 factors, what word will we use for a serious lack of money?

> In *The Observer*, 1999

Behn, Aphra (1640–1689)
English dramatist, writer, poet, translator and spy
> Come away; poverty's catching.

> *The Rover* (1677)

The Bible (King James Version)
> The poor always ye have with you.

> *John*, 12:8

Blake, William (1757–1827)
English poet, engraver, painter and mystic
> Is this a holy thing to see,
> In a rich and fruitful land,
> Babes reducd to misery,
> Fed with cold and usurous hand?

> 'Holy Thursday' (1794)

Blunden, Edmund (1896–1974)
English poet
> All things they have in common being so poor,
> And their one fear, Death's shadow at the door.
> Each sundown makes them mournful, each sunrise
> Brings back the brightness in their failing eyes.

> *The Waggoner and Other Poems* (1920)

Booth, General William (1829–1912)
English founder of the Salvation Army
> This Submerged Tenth – is it, then, beyond the reach of the nine-tenths in the midst of whom they live?

> In *Darkest England* (1890)

Chamfort, Nicolas (1741–1794)
French writer
> *Les pauvres sont les nègres de l'Europe.*
> The poor are the negroes of Europe.

> *Maximes et Pensées* (1796)

Cobbett, William (1762–1835)
English politician, reformer, writer, farmer and army officer
> To be poor and independent is very nearly an impossibility.

> *Advice to Young Men* (1829)

Cowper, William (1731–1800)
English poet, hymn and letter writer
Of a burglar

He found it inconvenient to be poor.

'Charity' (1782)

Crabbe, George (1754–1832)
English poet, clergyman, surgeon and botanist
The murmuring poor, who will not fast in peace.

The Newspaper (1785)

Farquhar, George (1678–1707)
Irish dramatist
'Tis still my maxim, that there is no scandal like rags, nor any crime so shameful as poverty.

The Beaux' Stratagem (1707)

France, Anatole (1844–1924)
French writer and critic
It is only the poor who pay cash, and that not from virtue, but because they are refused credit.

In J.R. Solly, *A Cynic's Breviary*

Gay, John (1685–1732)
English poet, dramatist and librettist
No, Sir, tho' I was born and bred in England, I can dare to be poor, which is the only thing now-a-days men are asham'd of.

Polly (1729)

Geldof, Bob (1954–)
Irish rock musician
I'm not interested in the bloody system! Why has he no food? Why is he starving to death?

In Care, *Sayings of the Eighties* (1989)

Hardy, Frank (1917–)
Only the poor will help the poor.

Legends from Benson's Valley (1963)

Harrington, Michael (1928–1989)
US writer
Clothes make the poor invisible … America has the best-dressed poverty the world has ever known.

The Other America (1962)

Horváth, Ödön von (1901–1938)
German-Hungarian writer
Wer arm ist, darf sich was vorlügen – das ist sein Recht. Vielleicht sein einziges Recht.
Whoever is poor may lie to himself – that is his right.
Perhaps his only right.

A Child of our Time (1938)

Jerome, Jerome K. (1859–1927)
English writer and dramatist
It is easy enough to say that poverty is no crime. No; if it were men wouldn't be ashamed of it. It is a blunder, though, and is punished as such. A poor man is despised the whole world over.

Idle Thoughts of an Idle Fellow (1886)

Johnson, Samuel (1709–1784)
English lexicographer, poet, critic, conversationalist and essayist
This mournful truth is ev'rywhere confess'd,
Slow rises worth by poverty depress'd.

London: A Poem (1738)

A man, doubtful of his dinner, or trembling at a creditor, is not much disposed to abstracted meditation, or remote enquiries.

The Lives of the Most Eminent English Poets (1781)

Resolve not to be poor: whatever you have, spend less. Poverty is a great enemy to human happiness; it certainly destroys liberty, and it makes some virtues impracticable and others extremely difficult.

Letter to Boswell, 1782

Juvenal (c.60–130)
Roman verse satirist and Stoic
*Nil habet infelix paupertas durius in se
Quam quod ridiculos homines facit.*
Nothing is harder to bear about luckless poverty than the way it exposes men to ridicule.

Satires

Cantabit vacuus coram latrone viator.
The poure man when he goth by the weye
Bifore the thieves he may synge and playe.

Satires

*Haud facile emergunt quorum virtutibus obstat
Res angusta domi.*
Rarely they rise by virtue's aid, who lie
Plung'd in the depths of helpless poverty.

Satires

Landon, Letitia Elizabeth (1802–1838)
English poet
Few, save the poor, feel for the poor.

'The Poor'

Marx, Groucho (1895–1977)
US comedian
Look at me: I worked my way up from nothing to a state of extreme poverty.

Monkey Business (film, 1931)

Meudell, George Dick (1860–1936)
Australian writer, traveller and social commentator
Until we partially abolish poverty at home we have no right to burden ourselves with millions of paupers from abroad. What we have, we hold. AUSTRALIA FOR THE AUSTRALIANS.

The Pleasant Career of a Spendthrift in London (1929)

Peacock, Thomas Love (1785–1866)
English writer and poet
Respectable means rich, and decent means poor. I should die if I heard my family called decent.

Crotchet Castle (1831)

Proverb

> When poverty comes in at the door, love flies out of the window.

Roosevelt, Franklin Delano (1882–1945)

US Democrat President

> ... the forgotten man at the bottom of the economic pyramid.
>
> > Radio broadcast, 1932

> I see one-third of a nation ill-housed, ill-clad, ill-nourished.
>
> > Second Inaugural Address, 1937

Runcie, Robert (1921–2000)

Archbishop of Canterbury 1980–91

> We don't have to look as far as Ethiopia to find the darkness of disease, death and disaster. It is on our doorsteps.
>
> > Quoted in *The Guardian*, 2000

Saki (1870–1916)

Burmese-born British writer

> 'No one has ever said it,' observed Lady Caroline, 'but how painfully true it is that the poor have us always with them!'
>
> > Attr.

Shaw, George Bernard (1856–1950)

Irish socialist, writer, dramatist and critic

> *Cusins*: Do you call poverty a crime?
> *Undershaft*: The worst of crimes. All the other crimes are virtues beside it: all the other dishonours are chivalry itself by comparison.
>
> > *Major Barbara* (1907)

> The greatest of our evils and the worst of our crimes is poverty.
>
> > *Major Barbara* (1907)

Shuter, Edward (1728–1776)

English actor and wit

Explaining why he did not mend his stocking

> A hole is the accident of a day, but a darn is premeditated poverty.
>
> > *Dictionary of National Biography* (1897)

Smith, Adam (1723–1790)

Scottish economist, philosopher and essayist

> Poverty, though it does not prevent the generation, is extremely unfavourable to the rearing of children. The tender plant is produced, but in so cold a soil and so severe a climate, soon withers and dies.
>
> > *Wealth of Nations* (1776

Smith, Sydney (1771–1845)

English clergyman, essayist, journalist and wit

> Poverty is no disgrace to a man, but it is confoundedly inconvenient.
>
> > In J. Potter Briscoe (ed.), *Sydney Smith* (1900)

Smollett, Tobias (1721–1771)

Scottish writer, satirist, historian, traveller and physician

> Hark ye, Clinker, you are a most notorious offender. You stand convicted of sickness, hunger, wretchedness, and want.
>
> > *The Expedition of Humphry Clinker* (1771)

Teresa, Mother (1910–1997)

Catholic missionary in India

> ... the poor are our brothers and sisters ... people in the world who need love, who need care, who have to be wanted.
>
> > *Time*, 1975

> I think it is very beautiful for the poor to accept their lot, to share it with the passion of Christ. I think the world is being much helped by the suffering of the poor people.
>
> > Attr.

Tracy, Spencer (1900–1967)

US film actor

Of leaner times in his life

> There were times my pants were so thin I could sit on a dime and tell if it was heads or tails.
>
> > In Swindell, *Spencer Tracy*

Wilde, Oscar (1854–1900)

Irish poet, dramatist, writer, critic and wit

> We are often told that the poor are grateful for charity. Some of them are, no doubt, but the best amongst the poor are never grateful. They are ungrateful, discontented, disobedient, and rebellious. They are quite right to be so.
>
> > 'The Soul of Man under Socialism' (1891)

▶▶ HUNGER; MONEY AND WEALTH

power

Acton, Lord (1834–1902)

English historian and moralist

> Power tends to corrupt, and absolute power corrupts absolutely. Great men are almost always bad men ... There is no worse heresy than that the office sanctifies the holder of it.
>
> > Letter to Bishop Mandell Creighton, 1887

Adams, Abigail (1744–1818)

US letter writer and wife of President John Adams

> I am more and more convinced that man is a dangerous creature and that power, whether vested in many or a few, is ever grasping, and like the grave, cries 'Give, give.'
>
> > Letter to John Adams, 1775

Adams, John (1735–1826)

US lawyer, diplomat and President

> Power always thinks it has a great soul and vast

views beyond the comprehension of the weak.

The Works of John Adams (1856), letter to his wife Abigail Adams, 1780

Amis, Kingsley (1922–1995)

English writer, poet and critic

Generally, nobody behaves decently when they have power.

Radio Times, 1992

Andreotti, Giulio (1919–)

Italian statesman and Prime Minister

Il potere logora chi non ce l'ha.

Power wears down the man who doesn't have it.

In Biagi, *The Good and the Bad* (1989

Aung San Suu Kyi, Daw (1945–)

Burmese political leader

Concepts such as truth, justice, compassion are often the only bulwarks which stand against ruthless power.

Index on Censorship, 1994

Bacon, Francis (1561–1626)

English philosopher, essayist, politician and courtier

Men in great place are thrice servants: servants of the sovereign or state, servants of fame, and servants of business ... It is a strange desire to seek power and to lose liberty.

'Of Great Place' (1625)

Beaverbrook, Lord (1879–1964)

Canadian-born British newspaper owner

Of Lloyd George

He did not care in which direction the car was travelling, so long as he remained in the driver's seat.

New Statesman, 1963

Burke, Edmund (1729–1797)

Irish-born British statesman and philosopher

Those who have been once intoxicated with power, and have derived any kind of emolument from it, even though but for one year, never can willingly abandon it.

Letter to a Member of the National Assembly (1791)

Clare, Dr Anthony (1942–)

Irish professor, psychiatrist and broadcaster

Apart from the occasional saint, it is difficult for people who have the smallest amount of power to be nice.

In Care, *Sayings of the Eighties* (1989)

Crisp, Quentin (1908–1999)

English writer, publicist and model

I expect that rape and murder, either separately or mixed together, fill the fantasies of most men and all stylists. They are the supreme acts of ascendancy over others; they yield the only moments when a man is certain beyond all doubt that his message has been received. Of

the few who live out these dreams, some preface rape with murder so as to avoid embracing a partner who might criticize their technique.

In Guy Kettlehack (ed.), *The Wit and Wisdom of Quentin Crisp*

Disraeli, Benjamin (1804–1881)

English statesman and writer

I repeat ... that all power is a trust – that we are accountable for its exercise – that, from the people, and for the people, all springs, and all must exist.

Vivian Grey (1826)

Eisenhower, Dwight D. (1890–1969)

US President and general

In the councils of government, we must guard against the acquisition of unwarranted influence, whether sought or unsought, by the military-industrial complex. The potential for the disastrous rise of misplaced power exists and will persist.

Farewell address, 17 January 1961

Fairlie, Henry (1924–1990)

English journalist

I have several times suggested that what I call the 'Establishment' in this country is today more powerful than ever before. By the 'Establishment' I do not mean only the centres of official power – though they are certainly part of it – but rather the whole matrix of official and social relations within which power is exercised ... the 'Establishment' can be seen at work in the activities of, not only the Prime Minister, the Archbishop of Canterbury and the Earl Marshall, but of such lesser mortals as the Chairman of the Arts Council, the Director-General of the BBC, and even the editor of the Times Literary Supplement, not to mention dignitaries like Lady Violet Bonham-Carter.

Spectator, 1955

Faust, Beatrice Eileen (1939–)

Australian writer and feminist

Women's Liberationists are both right and wrong when they say that rape is not about sex but about power: for men, sex is power, unless culture corrects biology.

Women, Sex and Pornography (1980)

Gielgud, Sir John (1904–2000)

English actor

I have never been interested in any power except my own power in the theatre, which I love.

The Independent, 1994

Goering, Hermann (1893–1946)

Nazi leader and military commander

Guns will make us powerful; butter will only make us fat.

Broadcast, 1936

Halifax, Lord (1633–1695)

English politician, courtier, pamphleteer and epigrammatist

There is … no other Fundamental, but that every Supream Power must be Arbitrary.

Political, Moral and Miscellaneous Thoughts and Reflections (1750)

Hitler, Adolf (1889–1945)

German Nazi dictator, born in Austria

Deutschland wird entweder Weltmacht oder überhaupt nicht sein.

Germany will either be a world power or will not exist at all.

Mein Kampf (1927)

Jones, Sir William (1746–1794)

English orientalist, translator and jurist

My opinion is, that power should always be distrusted, in whatever hands it is placed.

In Teignmouth, *Life of Sir W. Jones* (1835)

Kissinger, Henry (1923–)

German-born US Secretary of State

Power is the ultimate aphrodisiac.

Attr.

Kundera, Milan (1929–)

Czech writer and critic

The struggle of man against power is the struggle of memory against forgetting.

Attr.

Long, Huey (1893–1935)

US populist politician

I looked around at the little fishes present and said, 'I'm the Kingfish.'

In A. Schlesinger Jr, *The Politics of Upheaval* (1961)

Malcolm X (1925–1965)

US black leader

Power never takes a back step – only in the face of more power.

Malcolm X Speaks, 1965

Mao Tse-Tung (1893–1976)

Chinese Communist leader

Every Communist must grasp the truth. Political power grows out of the barrel of a gun.

Speech, 1938

Mill, John Stuart (1806–1873)

English philosopher, economist and reformer

The only purpose for which power can be rightfully exercised over any member of a civilized community, against his will, is to prevent harm to others. His own good, either physical or moral, is not sufficient warrant.

On Liberty (1859)

Pitt, William (1708–1778)

English politician and Prime Minister

Unlimited power is apt to corrupt the minds of those who possess it.

Speech, House of Commons, 1770

Renan, J. Ernest (1823–1892)

French philologist, writer and historian

'Savoir c'est pouvoir' est le plus beau mot qu'on ait dit.

'Knowledge is power' is the finest idea ever put into words.

Dialogues et fragments philosophiques (1876)

Russell, Bertrand (1872–1970)

English philosopher, mathematician, essayist and social reformer

The megalomaniac differs from the narcissist by the fact that he wishes to be powerful rather than charming, and seeks to be feared rather than loved. To this type belong many lunatics and most of the great men of history.

The Conquest of Happiness (1930)

Schiller, Johann Christoph Friedrich (1759–1805)

German writer, dramatist, poet and historian

Said by Philip II

Die Sonne geht in meinem Staat nicht unter.

The sun does not set in my dominions.

Don Carlos (1787)

Stevenson, Adlai (1900–1965)

US lawyer, statesman and United Nations ambassador

Power corrupts, but lack of power corrupts absolutely.

The Observer, 1963

Taylor, A.J.P. (1906–1990)

English historian, writer, broadcaster and lecturer

Of Lord Northcliffe

He aspired to power instead of influence, and as a result forfeited both.

English History, 1914-1945 (1965)

Thatcher, Margaret (1925–)

English Conservative Prime Minister

I love being at the centre of things.

Reader's Digest, 1984

Themistocles (c.528–462 BC)

Athenian soldier and statesman

Explaining his remark that his young son ruled all Greece

Athens holds sway over all Greece; I dominate Athens; my wife dominates me; our newborn son dominates her.

Attr.

Turenne, Henri, Vicomte (1611–1675)

French marshal

Dieu est toujours pour les gros bataillons.

God is always on the side of the big battalions.

Attr.

▶▶ INFLUENCE; LEADERSHIP; RESPONSIBILITY

praise

Bacon, Francis (1561–1626)
English philosopher, essayist, politician and courtier
> For as it is said of calumny, 'calumniate boldly, for some of it will stick' so it may be said of ostentation (except it be in a ridiculous degree of deformity), 'boldly sound your own praises, and some of them will stick.'
> > *Of the Dignity and Advancement of Learning* (1623)

The Bible (King James Version)
> Let us now praise famous men, and our fathers that begat us.
> > *Apocrypha, Ecclesiasticus, 44:1*

Bierce, Ambrose (1842–c.1914)
US writer, verse writer and soldier
> *Eulogy*: Praise of a person who has either the advantages of wealth and power, or the consideration to be dead.
> > *The Enlarged Devil's Dictionary* (1961)

Churchill, Charles (1731–1764)
English poet, political writer and clergyman
> Greatly his foes he dreads, but more his friends;
> He hurts me most who lavishly commends.
> > 'The Apology, addressed to the Critical Reviewers' (1761)

Gay, John (1685–1732)
English poet, dramatist and librettist
> Praising all alike, is praising none.
> > 'A Letter to a Lady' (1714)

Johnson, Samuel (1709–1784)
English lexicographer, poet, critic, conversationalist and essayist
> He who praises everybody praises nobody.
> > In Boswell, *The Life of Samuel Johnson* (1791)

> All censure of a man's self is oblique praise. It is in order to shew how much he can spare.
> > In Boswell, *The Life of Samuel Johnson* (1791)

> The applause of a single human being is of great consequence.
> > In Boswell, *The Life of Samuel Johnson* (1791)

Kipling, Rudyard (1865–1936)
Indian-born British poet and writer
> Never praise a sister to a sister, in the hope of your compliments reaching the proper ears … Sisters are women first, and sisters afterward; and you will find that you do yourself harm.
> > *Plain Tales from the Hills* (1888)

La Rochefoucauld (1613–1680)
French writer
> *Le refus des louanges est un désir d'être loué deux fois.*
> Refusal of praise reveals a desire to be praised twice over.
> > *Maximes* (1678)

Martial (c.AD 40–c.104)
Spanish-born Latin epigrammatist and poet
> *Laudant illa sed ista legunt.*
> They praise those works but they read something else.
> > *Epigrammata*

Pope, Alexander (1688–1744)
English poet, translator and editor
> Fondly we think we honour merit then,
> When we but praise ourselves in other men.
> > *An Essay on Criticism* (1711), line 454

Proverb
> Self-praise is no recommendation.

Shakespeare, William (1564–1616)
English dramatist, poet and actor
> I will praise any man that will praise me.
> > *Antony and Cleopatra*, II.vi

Sheridan, Richard Brinsley (1751–1816)
Irish dramatist, politician and orator
> Yes, sir, puffing is of various sorts; the principal are, the puff direct, the puff preliminary, the puff collateral, the puff collusive, and the puff oblique, or puff by implication.
> > *The Critic* (1779)

Smith, Sydney (1771–1845)
English clergyman, essayist, journalist and wit
> Praise is the best diet for us, after all.
> > In Holland, *A Memoir of the Reverend Sydney Smith* (1855)

Voltaire (1694–1778)
French philosopher, dramatist, poet, historian writer and critic
Giving a funeral oration
> He was a great patriot, a humanitarian, a loyal friend – provided, of course, that he really is dead.
> > *Attr.*

Wodehouse, P.G. (1881–1975)
English humorist and writer
> I can honestly say that I always look on Pauline as one of the nicest girls I was ever engaged to.
> > *Thank You Jeeves* (1934)

▶▶ FLATTERY

prayer

Anonymous
> God be in my head,
> And in my understanding;
> God be in my eyes,
> And in my looking;
> God be in my mouth,
> And in my speaking;

God be in my heart,
And in my thinking;
God be at my end,
And at my departing.

Sarum Missal

Prayer of a common soldier before the Battle of Blenheim
O God, if there be a God, save my soul, if I have
a soul!

Astley, Sir Jacob (1579–1652)
English soldier and Royalist
O Lord! thou knowest how busy I must be this
day; if I forget thee, do not thou forget me.

Prayer before the Battle of Edgehill, 1642

Baylis, Lilian (1874–1937)
English theatrical manager
O God, send me some good actors – cheap.

The Guardian, 1976

Beckett, Samuel (1906–1989)
Irish dramatist, writer and poet
Let us pray to God ... the bastard! He doesn't
exist.

Endgame (1958)

Betjeman, Sir John (1906–1984)
English poet laureate
Gracious Lord, oh bomb the Germans.
Spare their women for Thy Sake,
And if that is not too easy
We will pardon Thy Mistake.
But, gracious Lord, whate'er shall be,
Don't let anyone bomb me.

Old Lights for New Chancels (1940)

Browne, Sir Thomas (1605–1682)
English physician, author and antiquary
Lord, deliver me from myself.

Religio Medici (1643)

Browning, Elizabeth Barrett (1806–1861)
English poet; wife of Robert Browning
God answers sharp and sudden on some
prayers,
And thrusts the thing we have prayed for in our
face,
A gauntlet with a gift in't.

Aurora Leigh (1857)

Churchill, Charles (1731–1764)
English poet, political writer and clergyman
Stay out all night, but take especial care
That Prudence bring thee back to early prayer
As one with watching and with study faint,
Reel in a drunkard, and reel out a saint.

'Night' (1761)

Coleridge, Samuel Taylor (1772–1834)
English poet, philosopher and critic
He prayeth best, who loveth best
All things both great and small;

For the dear God who loveth us,
He made and loveth all.

'The Rime of the Ancient Mariner' (1798), VII

Cowper, William (1731–1800)
English poet, hymn and letter writer
Prayer makes the Christian's armour bright;
And Satan trembles when he sees
The weakest saint upon his knees.

Olney Hymns (1779), 29

Dutton, Geoffrey (1922–)
Australian poet and writer
Those who mumble do not pray.
Prayers grow like windless trees from silence.

'Twelve Sheep'

Hale, Edward Everett (1822–1909)
Chaplain to the US Senate
'Do you pray for the senators, Dr Hale?' 'No, I
look at the senators and I pray for the country.'

In Van Wyck Brooks, *New England Indian Summer* (1940)

Herrick, Robert (1591–1674)
English poet, royalist and clergyman
In Prayer the Lips ne're act the winning part,
Without the sweet concurrence of the Heart.

Noble Numbers (1647)

Lamb, Charles (1775–1834)
English essayist, critic and letter writer
Why have we none i.e. no grace for books,
those spiritual repasts – a grace before Milton –
a grace before Shakespeare – a devotional
exercise proper to be said before reading the
Faerie Queene?

Essays of Elia (1823)

Lessing, Gotthold Ephraim (1729–1781)
German dramatist, critic and theologian
*Ein einziger dankbarer Gedanke gen Himmel ist das
vollkommenste Gebet!*
A single grateful thought raised to heaven is the
most perfect prayer.

Minna von Barnhelm (1767)

More, Hannah (1745–1833)
English poet, dramatist and religious writer
Did not God
Sometimes withhold in mercy what we ask,
We should be ruined at our own request.

Moses in the Bulrushes (1782)

Niebuhr, Reinhold (1892–1971)
US Protestant theologian and writer
God grant me the serenity to accept the things I
cannot change, the courage to change the
things I can, and the wisdom to distinguish the
one from the other.

Prayer adopted by Alcoholics Anonymous,
attributed to but not accepted by
Niebuhr

Otway, Thomas (1652–1685)
English dramatist and poet
> No praying, it spoils business.
>> *Venice Preserv'd* (1682)

Pope, Alexander (1688–1744)
English poet, translator and editor
> Teach me to feel another's Woe,
> To hide the Fault I see;
> That Mercy I to others show,
> That Mercy show to me.
>> 'The Universal Prayer' (1738)

Pound, Ezra (1885–1972)
US poet
> So many thousand beauties are gone down to
> Avernus,
> Ye might let one remain above with us.
>> 'Prayer for his Lady's Life' (1908)

Renan, J. Ernest (1823–1892)
French philologist, writer and historian
> O Lord, if there is a Lord, save my soul, if I have
> a soul.
>> 'A Sceptic's Prayer'

Rolfe, Frederick William (1860–1913)
> Pray for the repose of His soul. He was so tired.
>> *Hadrian VII* (1904)

Shakespeare, William (1564–1616)
English dramatist, poet and actor
> My words fly up, my thoughts remain below.
> Words without thoughts never to heaven go.
>> *Hamlet*, III.iii

> He prays but faintly and would be denied.
>> *Richard II*, V.iii

Smith, Sydney (1771–1845)
English clergyman, essayist, journalist and wit
To Monkton Milnes
> I am just going to pray for you at St Paul's, but
> with no very lively hope of success.
>> In H. Pearson, *The Smith of Smiths*
>> (1934)

Spyri, Johanna (1827–1901)
Swiss writer
> Oh, I wish that God had not given me what I
> prayed for! It was not so good as I thought.
>> *Heidi* (1880–1881)

Tolstoy, Leo (1828–1910)
Russian writer, essayist, philosopher and moralist
> Let me lie down like a stone, O Lord, and rise up
> like new bread.
>> *War and Peace* (1868–1869)

Turgenev, Ivan (1818–1883)
Russian writer and dramatist
> Whatever a man prays for, he prays for a
> miracle. Every prayer reduces itself to this:

> 'Great God, grant that twice two be not four.'
>> 'Prayer' (1881)

▶▶ CHRISTIANITY; GOD; RELIGION

pregnancy

Anne, the Princess Royal (1950–)
> It's a very boring time. I am not particularly
> maternal – it's an occupational hazard of being a
> wife.
>> TV interview, quoted in the *Daily Express*, 1981

Gibbons, Stella (1902–1989)
English poet and novelist
> Every year, in the fulness o' summer, when the
> sukebind hangs heavy from the wains … 'tes the
> same. And when the spring comes her hour is
> upon her again. 'Tes the hand of Nature, and we
> women cannot escape it.
>> *Cold Comfort Farm* (1932)

Lette, Kathy (1959–)
English novelist
> I used to rush to the mirror every morning to
> see if I had bloomed, but all I did was swell. My
> ankles looked like flesh-coloured flares and my
> breasts were so huge they needed their own
> postcode.
>> *The Daily Telegraph*, May 1999

Nicholls, Peter (1927–)
English dramatist
> 'One advantage of being pregnant,' says a wife
> in one of my television plays, 'you don't have to
> worry about getting pregnant.'
>> *Feeling You're Behind* (1984)

Parker, Dorothy (1893–1967)
US writer, poet, critic and wit
Telegram sent to Mary Sherwood after her much-publicised
pregnancy
> Dear Mary, We all knew you had it in you.
>> In J. Keats, *You Might As Well Live* (1970)

Said on going into hospital for an abortion
> It serves me right for putting all my eggs in one
> bastard.
>> Attr. in J. Keats, *You Might As Well Live* (1970)

▶▶ BABIES; BIRTH; MOTHERS

prejudice

Belloc, Hilaire (1870–1953)
English writer of verse, essayist and critic; Liberal MP
> I am a Catholic. As far as possible I go to Mass
> every day. As far as possible I kneel down and

tell these beads every day. If you reject me on account of my religion, I shall thank God that he has spared me the indignity of being your representative.

Speech, 1906

The Anti-Semite is a man so absorbed in his subject that he loses interest in any matter unless he can give it some association with his delusion, for delusion it is.
The Jew cannot help feeling superior, but he can help the expression of that superiority – at any rate he can modify such expression.

'The Jews' (1922)

Fields, W.C. (1880–1946)
US film actor
I am free of all prejudice. I hate everyone equally.

Attr.

Lamb, Charles (1775–1834)
English essayist, critic and letter writer
I am, in plainer words, a bundle of prejudices – made up of likings and dislikings.

Essays of Elia (1823), 'Imperfect Sympathies'

Niemöller, Martin (1892–1984)
German Lutheran theologian
In Germany they first came for the Communists, and I didn't speak up because I wasn't a Communist. Then they came for the Jews, and I didn't speak up because I wasn't a Jew. Then they came for the trade unionists, and I didn't speak up because I wasn't a trade unionist. Then they came for the Catholics, and I didn't speak up because I was a Protestant. Then they came for me – and by that time no one was left to speak up.

Concise Dictionary of Religious Quotations

Russell, Bertrand (1872–1970)
English philosopher, mathematician, essayist and social reformer
The collection of prejudices which is called political philosophy is useful provided that it is not called philosophy.

The Observer, 1962

Sagan, Carl (1934–1996)
US astrophysicist
Prejudice is making a judgment before you have looked at the facts. Postjudice is making a judgment afterwards. Prejudice is terrible, in the sense that you commit injustices and you make serious mistakes. Postjudice is not terrible. You can't be perfect of course; you may make mistakes also. But it is permissible to make a judgment after you have examined the evidence. In some circles it is even encouraged.

'Skeptical Enquirer' Vol. 12

Sterne, Laurence (1713–1768)
Irish-born English writer and clergyman
Prejudice of education, he would say, is the devil, – and the multitudes of them which we suck in with our mother's milk – are the devil and all. – We are haunted with them, brother Toby, in all our lucubrations and researches; and was a man fool enough to submit tamely to what they obtruded upon him, – what would his book be? … nothing but a farrago of the clack of nurses, and of the nonsense of the old women (of both sexes) throughout the kingdom.

Tristram Shandy (1759–1767)

Victoria, Queen (1819–1901)
Queen of the United Kingdom
… I too well know its truth, from experience, that whenever any poor Gipsies are encamped anywhere and crimes and robberies &c. occur, it is invariably laid to their account, which is shocking; and if they are always looked upon as vagabonds, how can they become good people?

Journal, 1836

▶▶ EQUALITY; FEMINISM; JEWS; RACE; RELIGION

the present

Arnold, Matthew (1822–1888)
English poet, critic, essayist and educationist
This strange disease of modern life.

'The Scholar-Gipsy' (1853)

The Bible (King James Version)
Take therefore no thought for the morrow: for the morrow shall take thought for the things of itself. Sufficient unto the day is the evil thereof.

Matthew, 6:34

Burke, Edmund (1729–1797)
Irish-born British statesman and philosopher
To complain of the age we live in, to murmur at the present possessors of power, to lament the past, to conceive extravagant hopes of the future, are the common dispositions of the greatest part of mankind.

Thoughts on the Cause of the Present Discontents (1770)

Clare, John (1793–1864)
English rural poet; died in an asylum
The present is the funeral of the past,
And man the living sepulchre of life.

'The Past' (1845)

Emerson, Ralph Waldo (1803–1882)
US poet, essayist, transcendentalist and teacher
Write it on your heart that every day is the best day in the year. No man has learned anything

rightly until he knows that every day is Doomsday.

Society and Solitude (1870)

Fitzgerald, Edward (1809–1883)
English poet, translator and letter writer
Ah, fill the Cup: – what boots it to repeat
How Time is slipping underneath our Feet:
Unborn TOMORROW and dead YESTERDAY,
Why fret about them if TO-DAY be sweet!

The Rubáiyát of Omar Khayyám (1859)

Franklin, Benjamin (1706–1790)
US statesman, scientist, political critic and printer
The golden age never was the present age.

Poor Richard's Almanac (1750)

Hammarskjöld, Dag (1905–1961)
Swedish statesman, Secretary-General of the United Nations
Do not look back. And do not dream about the future, either. It will neither give you back the past, nor satisfy your other daydreams. Your duty, your reward – your destiny – are here and now.

Markings (1965)

Horace (65–8 BC)
Roman lyric poet and satirist
Carpe diem.
Seize the day.

Odes

McLuhan, Marshall (1911–1980)
Canadian communications theorist
The present cannot be revealed to people until it has become yesterday.

In Marchand, *Marshall McLuhan* (1989)

Mallarmé, Stéphane (1842–1898)
French poet
Le vierge, le vivace et le bel aujourd'hui.
That virgin, vital, beautiful day: today.

Plusieurs sonnets (1881)

Shakespeare, William (1564–1616)
English dramatist, poet and actor
Past and to come seems best; things present, worst.

Henry IV, Part 2, I.iii

▶▶ FUTURE; OPPORTUNITY; PAST; TIME

pride

Addison, Joseph (1672–1719)
English essayist, poet, playwright and statesman
'Tis pride, rank pride, and haughtiness of soul;
I think the Romans call it stoicism.

Cato (1713)

The Bible (King James Version)
Pride goeth before destruction, and an haughty spirit before a fall.

Proverbs, 16:18

Bradshaw, Henry (d.1513)
Monk and theologian
Proude as a pecocke.

The Life of Saint Werburge (1521)

Coleridge, Samuel Taylor (1772–1834)
English poet, philosopher and critic
And the Devil did grin, for his darling sin
Is pride that apes humility.

'The Devil's Thoughts' (1799)

Davies, Sir John (1569–1626)
English poet and politician
I know my life's a pain and but a span,
I know my sense is mock'd in every thing;
And to conclude, I know myself a man,
Which is a proud and yet a wretched thing.

Nosce Teipsum (1599)

Dobrée, Bonamy (1891–1974)
English academic, critic and editor
It is difficult to be humble. Even if you aim at humility, there is no guarantee that when you have attained the state you will not be proud of the feat.

John Wesley

Landor, Walter Savage (1775–1864)
English poet and writer
I know not whether I am proud,
But this I know, I hate the crowd.

'With an Album'

MacNeice, Louis (1907–1963)
Belfast-born poet, writer, radio producer, translator and critic
Pride in your history is pride
In living what your fathers died,
Is pride in taking your own pulse
And counting in you someone else.

'Suite for recorders' (1966)

Pope, Alexander (1688–1744)
English poet, translator and editor
Pride, the never-failing vice of fools.

An Essay on Criticism (1711)

Renard, Jules (1864–1910)
French writer and dramatist
Be modest! It is the kind of pride least likely to offend.

Journal

There is false modesty, but there is no false pride.

Journal

Shakespeare, William (1564–1616)
English dramatist, poet and actor
> O world, how apt the poor are to be proud!
>> *Twelfth Night*, III.i

Shelley, Percy Bysshe (1792–1822)
English poet, dramatist and essayist
> But human pride
> Is skilful to invent most serious names
> To hide its ignorance.
>> *Queen Mab* (1813)

▶▶ EGOISM; SELF; VANITY

principles

Adler, Alfred (1870–1937)
Austrian psychiatrist and psychologist
> It is always easier to fight for one's principles than to live up to them.
>> In Phyllis Bottome, *Alfred Adler: Apostle of Freedom* (1939)

Baldwin, Stanley (1867–1947)
English Conservative statesman and Prime Minister
> I would rather be an opportunist and float than go to the bottom with my principles round my neck.
>> Attr.

Ebner-Eschenbach, Marie von (1830–1916)
Austrian writer
> *Wenn zwei brave Menschen über Grundsätze streiten, haben immer beide recht.*
> Whenever two good people argue over principles, both are always right.
>> *Aphorisms* (1880)

Hattersley, Roy (1932–)
British Labour politician and writer
> Politicians are entitled to change their minds. But when they adjust their principles some explanation is necessary.
>> *The Observer*, March 1999

Long, Huey (1893–1935)
US populist politician
> The time has come for all good men to rise above principle.
>> Attr.

MacKenzie, Sir Compton (1883–1972)
Scottish writer and broadcaster
> I don't believe in principles. Principles are only excuses for what we want to think or what we want to do.
>> *The Adventures of Sylvia Scarlett* (1918)

Mansfield, Katherine (1888–1923)
New Zealand writer
To a magazine editor
> You ask for some details as to myself. I am poor – obscure – just eighteen years of age – with a rapacious appetite for everything and principles as light as my purse.
>> In O'Sullivan and Scott (eds), *The Collected Letters of Katherine Mansfield 1903–1917* (1984)

Maugham, William Somerset (1874–1965)
English writer, dramatist and physician
> You can't learn too soon that the most useful thing about a principle is that it can always be sacrificed to expediency.
>> *The Circle* (1921)

Melbourne, Lord (1779–1848)
English statesman
> Nobody ever did anything very foolish except from some strong principle.
>> Attr.

Roosevelt, Franklin Delano (1882–1945)
US Democrat President
> To stand upon the ramparts and die for our principles is heroic, but to sally forth to battle and win for our principles is something more than heroic.
>> Speech, 1928

Sade, Marquis de (1740–1814)
French soldier and writer
> All universal moral principles are idle fancies.
>> *The 120 Days of Sodom* (1784)

Todd, Ron (1927–)
British Trade Union leader
> You don't have power if you surrender all your principles – you have office.
>> Attr.

▶▶ MORALITY; VIRTUE

prison

Blake, William (1757–1827)
English poet, engraver, painter and mystic
> Prisons are built with stones of Law, Brothels with bricks of Religion.
>> *The Marriage of Heaven and Hell* (c.1790–1793)

Bottomley, Horatio William (1860–1933)
English journalist, politician and bankrupt
When spotted sewing mailbags during his imprisonment for misappropriation of funds
> *Visitor*: Ah, Bottomley, sewing?
> *Bottomley*: No, reaping.
>> Attr.

Brontë, Emily (1818–1848)
English novelist
> Oh dreadful is the check – intense the agony –
> When the ear begins to hear and the eye begins to see;

When the pulse begins to throb, the brain to
think again;
The soul to feel the flesh and the flesh to feel
the chain!

'The Prisoner' (1846)

Dowling, Basil Cairns (1777–1834)
New Zealand poet and pacifist
On prisons

Prisoners and warders – we are all of one blood.
They're much alike, except for a different coat
And a different hat;
And they all seem decent, kindly fellows enough
As they work and chat:
How can it be that men like this have been
hanged
By men like that?

In O.E. Burton, *In Prison* (1945)

Frank, Otto (1889–1980)
Dutch concentration camp survivor and father of Anne
Frank

When you have survived life in a concentration
camp you have ceased to count yourself as a
member of the human race. You will forever be
outside the experience of the rest of mankind.

In the *Daily Mail*, 1996

Hawthorne, Nathaniel (1804–1864)
US allegorical writer

The black flower of civilized society, a prison.

The Scarlet Letter (1850)

What other dungeon is so dark as one's own
heart! What jailer so inexorable as one's self!

The House of the Seven Gables (1851)

Ingrams, Richard (1937–)
British journalist and editor of *Private Eye*
On the prospect of going to gaol, 1976

The only thing I really mind about going to
prison is the thought of Lord Longford coming
to visit me.

Attr.

Keenan, Brian (1950–)
Irish journalist and hostage in Lebanon

I would be the voyeur of myself. This strategy I
employed for the rest of my captivity. I allowed
myself to do and be and say and think and feel
all the things that were in me, but at the same
time could stand outside observing and
attempting to understand.

An Evil Cradling

Léon, Fray Luis de (c.1527–1591)
Spanish Augustinian monk, poet and translator
Resuming a lecture after five years' imprisonment

Dicebamus hesterno die.
As we were saying the other day.

Attr.

Levi, Primo (1919–1987)
Italian writer, poet and chemist; survivor of Auschwitz
Of the Nazi concentration camps

The worst survived – that is, the fittest; the best
all died.

The Drowned and the Saved (1988)

Lovelace, Richard (1618–1658)
English poet

Stone walls do not a prison make
Nor iron bars a cage;
Minds innocent and quiet take
That for an hermitage;
If I have freedom in my love,
And in my soul am free;
Angels alone, that soar above,
Enjoy such liberty.

'To Althea, From Prison' (1649)

Raleigh, Sir Walter (c.1552–1618)
English courtier, explorer, military commander, poet,
historian and essayist

But now close kept, as captives wonted are:
That food, that heat, that light I find no more;
Despair bolts up my doors, and I alone
Speak to dead walls, but those hear not my
moan.

Untitled poem

Said after his trial for treason, 1603

The world itself is but a large prison, out of
which some are daily led to execution.

Attr.

Ramos, Graciliano (1892–1953)
Brazilian writer

*Então mete-se um homem na cadeia porque ele não
sabe falar direito?*
So you put a man in jail because he can't talk
properly?

Vidas secas (*Dry Lives*, 1938)

Solzhenitsyn, Alexander (1918–)
Russian writer, dramatist and historian

Forget the outside world. Life has different laws
in here. This is Campland, an invisible country.
It's not in the geography books, or the
psychology books or the history books. This is
the famous country where ninety-nine men weep
while one laughs.

The Love-Girl and the Innocent

Thoreau, Henry David (1817–1862)
US essayist, social critic and writer

Under a government which imprisons any
unjustly, the true place for a just man is also a
prison.

Civil Disobedience (1849)

Waugh, Evelyn (1903–1966)
English writer and diarist

Anyone who has been to an English public

school will always feel comparatively at home in prison.

Decline and Fall (1928)

Wilde, Oscar (1854–1900)
Irish poet, dramatist, writer, critic and wit
> I know not whether Laws be right,
> Or whether Laws be wrong;
> All that we know who lie in gaol
> Is that the wall is strong;
> And that each day is like a year,
> A year whose days are long –
> The vilest deeds like poison-weeds
> Bloom well in prison-air;
> It is only what is good in Man
> That wastes and withers there:
> Pale Anguish keeps the heavy gate
> And the warder is Despair.

The Ballad of Reading Gaol (1898)

Complaining at having to wait in the rain for transport to take him to prison
> If this is the way Queen Victoria treats her prisoners, she doesn't deserve to have any.

Attr.

▶▶ CRIME; PUNISHMENT

privacy

Auden, W.H. (1907–1973)
English poet, essayist, critic, teacher and dramatist
> Private faces in public places
> Are wiser and nicer
> Than public faces in private places.

The Orators (1932)

Dickinson, Emily (1830–1886)
US poet
> I'm Nobody! Who are you?
> Are you – Nobody – Too?
> Then there's a pair of us?
> Don't tell! they'd advertise – you know!
>
> How dreary – to be – Somebody!
> How public – like a Frog –
> To tell one's name – the livelong June –
> To an admiring Bog!

'I'm Nobody! Who are you?' (c.1861)

Parker, Dorothy (1893–1967)
US writer, poet, critic and wit
Pressing a button marked NURSE during a stay in hospital
> That should assure us of at least forty-five minutes of undisturbed privacy.

In James R. Gaines, *Days and Nights of the Algonquin Round Table* (1977)

Ustinov, Sir Peter (1921–)
English actor, director, dramatist, writer and raconteur

> This is a free country, madam. We have a right to share your privacy in a public place.

Romanoff and Juliet (1956)

privilege

Levi, Primo (1919–1987)
Italian writer, poet and chemist; survivor of Auschwitz
> The ascent of the privileged, not only in the Lager but in all human coexistence, is an anguishing but unfailing phenomenon: only in Utopias are they absent. It is the duty of righteous men to make war on all undeserved privilege, but one must not forget that this is a war without end.

The Drowned and the Saved (1988)

▶▶ ARISTOCRACY; MONEY AND WEALTH

problems

Adams, Scott (1957–)
US cartoonist
> There are very few personal problems that cannot be solved through a suitable application of high explosives.

The Dilbert Principle

Anonymous
> All easy problems have already been solved. Inside every small problem is a large problem struggling to get out.

Second Law of Blissful Ignorance

Cleaver, Eldridge (1935–1998)
US black leader and activist
> If you're not part of the solution, you're part of the problem.

Attr.

Dickens, Charles (1812–1870)
English writer
> Mr Podsnap settled that whatever he put behind him he put out of existence … Mr Podsnap had even acquired a peculiar flourish of his right arm in often clearing the world of its most difficult problems, by sweeping them behind him.

Our Mutual Friend (1865)

Doyle, Sir Arthur Conan (1859–1930)
Scottish writer and war correspondent
> It is quite a three-pipe problem, and I beg that you won't speak to me for fifty minutes.

The Adventures of Sherlock Holmes (1892)

John XXIII (1881–1963)
Italian pope
> It often happens that I wake at night and begin

to think about a serious problem and decide I must tell the Pope about it. Then I wake up completely and remember I am the Pope.

Attr.

Lovell, James (1928–)
US astronaut
After the explosion on board Apollo XIII, which put the crew in serious danger

OK, Houston, we have had a problem here … Houston, we have a problem.

Radio message, 11 April 1970

Marx, Karl (1818–1883)
German political philosopher and economist; founder of Communism

Mankind always sets itself only those problems it can solve; since, looking at the matter more closely, one will always find that the task itself arises only when the material conditions for its solution already exist or are at least in the process of formation.

A Contribution to the Critique of Political Economy (1859)

Palmerston, Lord (1784–1865)
British Prime Minister
Of the Schleswig-Holstein question

There are only three men who have ever understood it: one was Prince Albert, who is dead; the second was a German professor, who became mad. I am the third – and I have forgotten all about it.

Attr. in Palmer, Quotations in History

Wittgenstein, Ludwig (1889–1951)
Austrian philosopher

The solution of the problem of life is seen in the vanishing of the problem.

Tractatus Logico-Philosophicus (1922)

Zeffirelli, Franco (1923–)
Italian film director

All the problems of the world are caused by people who do not listen.

The Observer, 1998

procrastination

Anonymous

Spend sufficient time confirming the need and the need will disappear.

Boyd, William (1952–)
Scottish writer

She felt weary and careworn, in the way one often does before the big job of work is tackled; that sense of premature or projected exhaustion that is the breeding-ground of all procrastination.

Brazzaville Beach (1990)

Proverbs

Never put off till tomorrow what you can do today.

Put off the evil hour as long as you can.

Young, Edward (1683–1765)
English poet, dramatist, satirist and clergyman
Procrastination is the thief of time.

Night-Thoughts on Life, Death and Immortality (1742–1746)

production

Anonymous

The Six Stages of Production:
• Wild Enthusiasm
• Total Confusion
• Utter Despair
• The Search for the Guilty
• The Persecution of the Innocent
• The Promotion of the Incompetent.

No project was ever completed on time and within budget.

Cheops Law

progress

Adler, Freda (1934–)
US educator and writer

It is not only by the questions we have answered that progress may be measured, but also by those we are still asking.

Sisters in Crime (1975)

Anonymous

We've made great medical progress in the last generation. What used to be merely an itch is now an allergy.

Benn, Tony (1925–)
English Labour politician

It's the same each time with progress. First they ignore you, then they say you're mad, then dangerous, then there's a pause and then you can't find anyone who disagrees with you.

The Observer, 1991

Blake, William (1757–1827)
English poet, engraver, painter and mystic

Without Contraries is no progression. Attraction and Repulsion, Reason and Energy, Love and Hate, are necessary to Human existence.

The Marriage of Heaven and Hell (c.1793)

Borges, Jorge Luis (1899–1986)
Argentinian writer, poet and librarian

We have stopped believing in progress. What progress that is!

Ibarra, *Borges et Borges*

Buchanan, Robert Williams (1841–1901)
British poet, writer and dramatist
> A race that binds
> Its body in chains and calls them Liberty,
> And calls each fresh link Progress.

'Titan and Avatar'

Butler, Samuel (1835–1902)
English writer, painter, philosopher and scholar
> All progress is based upon a universal innate desire on the part of every organism to live beyond its income.

The Note-Books of Samuel Butler (1912)

Carlyle, Thomas (1795–1881)
Scottish historian, biographer, critic, and essayist
> The progress of human society consists ... in ... the better and better apportioning of wages to work.

Past and Present (1843)

Clifford, William Kingdon (1845–1879)
English mathematician
> ... scientific thought is not an accompaniement or condition of human progress, but human progress itself.

Aims and Instruments of Scientific Thought (1872)

Comte, Auguste (1798–1857)
French philosopher and mathematician
> *L'Amour pour principe, l'Ordre pour base, et le Progrès pour but.*
> Love our principle, order our foundation, progress our goal.

Système de politique positive

cummings, e. e. (1894–1962)
US poet, noted for his typography, and painter
> pity this busy monster, manunkind,
> not. Progress is a comfortable disease.

1 x 1 (1944), no. 14

De Klerk, F.W. (1936–)
South African politician and President
> A man of destiny knows that beyond this hill lies another and another. The journey is never complete.

The Observer, 1994

Douglass, Frederick (c.1818–1895)
US anti-slavery activist
> If there is no struggle, there is no progress.

Attr.

Du Bois, William (1868–1963)
US academic and author
> Believe in life! Always human beings will live and progress to greater, broader, and fuller life.

Last message to the world, read at his funeral

Eliot, Charles W. (1834–1926)
President of Harvard University
> In the modern world the intelligence of public opinion is the one indispensable condition of social progress.

Speech, 1869

Ellis, Havelock (1859–1939)
English sexologist and essayist
> What we call 'Progress' is the exchange of one nuisance for another nuisance.

Impressions and Comments (1914)

Freud, Sigmund (1856–1939)
Austrian physicist; founder of psychoanalysis
> What progress we are making. In the Middle Ages they would have burned me. Now they are content with burning my books.

Letter, 1933

Gibbon, Edward (1737–1794)
English historian, politician and memoirist
> All that is human must retrograde if it does not advance.

Decline and Fall of the Roman Empire (1776–88)

Hegel, Georg Wilhelm (1770–1831)
German philosopher
> The history of the world is none other than the progress of the consciousness of freedom.

Philosophy of History

Hubbard, Elbert (1856–1915)
US printer, editor, writer and businessman
> The world is moving so fast these days that the man who says it can't be done is generally interrupted by someone doing it.

Attr.

John XXIII (1881–1963)
Italian pope
> The social progress, order, security and peace of each country are necessarily connected with the social progress, order, security and peace of all other countries.

Encyclical letter, April 1963

Lec, Stanislaw (1909–1966)
Polish writer
> Is it progress if a cannibal uses knife and fork?

Unkempt Thoughts (1962)

Lenin, V.I. (1870–1924)
Russian revolutionary, Marxist theoretician and first leader of the USSR
> One step forward, two steps back ... It happens in the lives of individuals, and it happens in the history of nations and in the development of parties.

One Step Forward, Two Steps Back (1904)

Lindbergh, Anne Morrow (1906–)
US aviator, poet and writer

Why do progress and beauty have to be so opposed?

Hour of Gold, Hour of Lead (1973)

Saint-Exupéry, Antoine de (1900–1944)
French author and aviator
Man's 'progress' is but a gradual discovery that his questions have no meaning.

The Wisdom of the Sands

Santayana, George (1863–1952)
Spanish-born US philosopher and writer
Progress, far from consisting in change, depends on retentiveness. Those who cannot temember the past are condemned to repeat it.

The Life of Reason (1906)

Shaw, George Bernard (1856–1950)
Irish socialist, writer, dramatist and critic
The reasonable man adapts himself to the world: the unreasonable one persists in trying to adapt the world to himself. Therefore all progress depends on the unreasonable man.

Man and Superman (1903)

Spencer, Herbert (1820–1903)
English philosopher and journalist
Progress, therefore, is not an accident, but a necessity ... it is a part of nature.

Social Statics (1850)

Stephen, Sir James Fitzjames (1829–1894)
English judge and essayist
Progress has its drawbacks, and they are great and serious; but whatever its value may be, unity in religious belief would further it.

Liberty, Equality and Fraternity (1873)

Thurber, James (1894–1961)
US humorist, writer and dramatist
Progress was all right; only it went on too long.

Attr.

Vigneaud, Vincent de (1901–1978)
Canadian biochemist
Nothing holds up the progress of science so much as the right idea at the wrong time.

Most Secret War (1978)

Walker, Alice (1944–)
US writer and poet
People tend to think that life really does progress for everyone eventually, that people progress, but actually only some people progress. The rest of the people don't.

In C. Tate (ed.), B*lack Women Writers at Work* (1983)

▶▶ CHANGE; CONSERVATISM; TECHNOLOGY

promiscuity

Hall, Jerry (1956–)
US fashion model
On her recent divorce from Mick Jagger
I feel sorry for Mick. Y'know sexual promiscuity just leads to chaos.

The Sunday Times, 2000

Wesley, Mary (1912–)
English novelist
In my day. I would only have sex with a man if I found him extremely attractive. These days, girls seem to choose them in much the same way as they might choose to suck on a boiled sweet.

Independent, 1997

▶▶ ADULTERY; SEX

promises

Eliot, George (1819–1880)
English writer and poet
An election is coming. Universal peace is declared, and the foxes have a sincere interest in prolonging the lives of the poultry.

Felix Holt (1866)

Frost, Robert (1874–1963)
US poet
The woods are lovely, dark and deep,
But I have promises to keep,
And miles to go before I sleep,
And miles to go before I sleep.

'Stopping by Woods on a Snowy Evening' (1923)

King, Martin Luther (1929–1968)
US civil rights leader and Baptist minister
Speech given the day before King was assassinated
... And I've looked over, and I've seen the promised land. I may not get there with you, but I want you to know tonight that we as a people will get to the promised land. So I'm happy tonight. I'm not worried about anything. I'm not fearing any man.

Speech in Memphis, 1968

Service, Robert W. (1874–1958)
Canadian poet
A promise made is a debt unpaid.

'The Cremation of Sam McGee' (1907)

Swift, Jonathan (1667–1745)
Irish satirist, poet, essayist and cleric
Promises and pie-crusts are made to be broken, they say.

Polite Conversation (1738)

Twain, Mark (1835–1910)
US humorist, writer, journalist and lecturer

> To promise not to do a thing is the surest way in the world to make a body want to go and do that very thing.
>
> *The Adventures of Tom Sawyer* (1876)

promotion

Arnold, Matthew (1822–1888)
English poet, critic, essayist and educationist

> Tired of knocking at preferment's door …
>
> 'The Scholar-Gipsy' (1853)

Knopf, Edwin H. (b. 1899)
Said when Louis B. Mayer promoted his daughter's husband (David O. Selznick), c.1933

> The son-in-law also rises.
>
> In Colombo, *Wit and Wisdom of the Moviemakers*

propaganda

Hitler, Adolf (1889–1945)
German Nazi dictator, born in Austria

> All propaganda has to be popular and has to accommodate itself to the comprehension of the least intelligent of those whom it seeks to reach.
>
> *Mein Kampf* (1925)

property

Dickens, Charles (1812–1870)
English writer

> Get hold of portable property.
>
> *Great Expectations* (1861)

Drummond, Thomas (1797–1840)
Scottish statesman and engineer

> Property has its duties as well as its rights.
>
> Letter to the Earl of Donoughmore, 1838

Edgeworth, Maria (1767–1849)
English-born Irish writer

> Well! some people talk of morality, and some of religion, but give me a little snug property.
>
> *The Absentee* (1812)

Emerson, Ralph Waldo (1803–1882)
US poet, essayist, transcendentalist and teacher

> A man builds a fine house; and now he has a master, and a task for life; he is to furnish, watch, show it, and keep it in repair, the rest of his days.
>
> *Society and Solitude* (1870)

Ingersoll, Robert G. (1833–1899)
US lawyer, soldier and writer

> Few rich men own their own property. The property owns them.
>
> Address, 1896

James, Henry (1843–1916)
US-born British writer, critic and letter writer

> The black and merciless things that are behind the great possessions.
>
> *The Ivory Tower* (1917)

Loos, Anita (1893–1981)
US writer and screenwriter

> Kissing your hand may make you feel very very good but a diamond and safire bracelet lasts forever.
>
> *Gentlemen Prefer Blondes* (1925)

Machiavelli (1469–1527)
Florentine statesman, political theorist and historian

> *Gli uomini sdimenticano più presto la morte del padre che la perdita del patrimonio.*
> Men sooner forget the death of their father than the loss of their possessions.
>
> *The Prince* (1532)

Patten, Brian (1946–)
British poet

> Every time a thing is won,
> Every time a thing is owned,
> Every time a thing is possessed,
> It vanishes.
>
> *Love Poems*, 'Tristan, waking in his wood, panics'

Proudhon, Pierre-Joseph (1809–1865)
French social reformer, anarchist and writer

> *Si j'avais à répondre à la question suivante: qu'est-ce que l'esclavage? et que d'un seul mot je répondisse: c'est l'assassinat, ma pensée serait aussitôt comprise … Pourquoi donc à cette autre demande: qu'est-ce que la propriété? ne puis-je répondre de même: c'est le vol!*
> If I were asked to answer the following question: 'What is slavery?' and I replied in one word, 'Murder!' my meaning would be understood at once … Why, then, to this other question: 'What is property?' may I not likewise answer 'Theft'?
>
> *Qu'est-ce que la propriété?* (1840)

Rajneesh, Bhagwan Shree (1931–1990)
Indian guru and teacher

> The more things accumulate the more life is wasted because they have to be purchased at the cost of life.
>
> *The Mustard Seed: Reflections on the Sayings of Jesus* (1978)

Vanbrugh, Sir John (1664–1726)
English dramatist and baroque architect

> The want of a thing is perplexing enough, but the possession of it is intolerable.
>
> *The Confederacy* (1705)

Wilde, Oscar (1854–1900)
Irish poet, dramatist, writer, critic and wit
> If property had simply pleasures, we could stand it; but its duties make it unbearable. In the interest of the rich we must get rid of it.
>> *The Fortnightly Review*, 1891

▶▶ CAPITALISM; MONEY AND WEALTH

prosperity

Bacon, Francis (1561–1626)
English philosopher, essayist, politician and courtier
> Prosperity doth best discover vice, but adversity doth best discover virtue.
>> *Essays* (1625), 'Of Adversity'

Herbert, Xavier (1901–1984)
Australian writer, poet and social critic
> Prosperity is like the tide, being able to flood one shore only by ebbing from another.
>> *Capricornia* (1938), 16

Webster, John (c.1580–c.1625)
English dramatist
> Prosperity doth bewitch men, seeming clear; As seas do laugh, show white, when rocks are near.
>> *The White Devil* (1612)

▶▶ CONSUMER SOCIETY; MONEY AND WEALTH

prophecy

The Bible (King James Version)
> I will pour out my spirit upon all flesh; and your sons and your daughters shall prophesy, your old men shall dream dreams, your young men shall see visions.
>> *Joel*, 2:28

> Beware of false prophets, which come to you in sheep's clothing, but inwardly they are ravening wolves.
>> *Matthew*, 7:15

> A prophet is not without honour, save in his own country, and in his own house.
>> *Matthew*, 13:57

Ionesco, Eugene (1912–1994)
Romanian-born French dramatist
> You can only predict things after they've happened.
>> *Rhinoceros* (1959)

Kipling, Rudyard (1865–1936)
Indian-born British poet and writer
> I'm the Prophet of the Utterly Absurd,

Of the Patently Impossible and Vain.
>> 'The Song of the Banjo' (1894)

Machiavelli (1469–1527)
Florentine statesman, political theorist and historian
> And that is why all the armed prophets were victorious, whilst all the unarmed perished.
>> *The Prince* (1532)

Melbourne, Lord (1779–1848)
English statesman
Of Catholic Emancipation
> What all the wise men promised has not happened, and what all the d—d fools said would happen has come to pass.
>> In H. Dunckley, *Lord Melbourne* (1890)

Shakespeare, William (1564–1616)
English dramatist, poet and actor
> If you can look into the seeds of time
> And say which grain will grow and which will not,
> Speak then to me, who neither beg nor fear
> Your favours nor your hate.
>> *Macbeth*, I.iii

> Methinks I am a prophet new inspir'd,
> And thus expiring do foretell of him:
> His rash fierce blaze of riot cannot last,
> For violent fires soon burn out themselves;
> Small showers last long, but sudden storms are short;
> He tires betimes that spurs too fast betimes.
>> *Richard II*, II.i

Trollope, Anthony (1815–1882)
English writer, traveller and post office official
> Mr Turnbull had predicted evil consequences – and was now doing the best in his power to bring about the verification of his own prophecies.
>> *Phineas Finn* (1869)

Walpole, Horace (1717–1797)
English writer and politician
> The wisest prophets make sure of the event first.
>> Letter to Thomas Walpole, 1785

Wilhelm II, Kaiser (1859–1941)
German emperor
> You will be home before the leaves have fallen from the trees.
>> Remark to troops leaving for the Front, August 1914

prostitution

Adler, Polly (1900–1962)
US brothel keeper
> A House Is Not a Home.
>> Title of memoirs, 1954

Gwyn, Nell (1650–1687)
English actress and mistress of Charles II
On prostitution

> As for me, it is my profession, I do not pretend to anything better.
>
> In Miles, *The Women's History of the World* (1988)

Heller, Joseph (1923–1999)
US writer

> Prostitution gives her an opportunity to meet people. It provides fresh air and wholesome exercise, and it keeps her out of trouble.
>
> *Catch-22* (1961)

Hardy, Thomas (1840–1928)
English writer and poet

> 'You left us in tatters, without shoes or socks,
> Tired of digging potatoes, and spudding up docks;
> And now you've gay bracelets and bright feathers three!'–
> 'Yes: that's how we dress when we're ruined,' said she.
>
> 'The Ruined Maid' (1866)

Parker, Dorothy (1893–1967)
US writer, poet, critic and wit
When challenged to compose a sentence using the word 'horticulture'

> You can lead a horticulture but you can't make her think.
>
> In J. Keats, *You Might As Well Live* (1970)

Philip, Prince, Duke of Edinburgh (1921–)
Greek-born consort of Queen Elizabeth II

> I don't think a prostitute is more moral than a wife, but they are doing the same thing.
>
> *The Observer*, 1988

Scott, Valerie
Canadian prostitute and feminist

> We don't sell our bodies. Housewives do that. What we do is rent our bodies for sexual services.
>
> *The Toronto Star*, 1989

▶▶ SEX

psychiatry

Adams, Joey (b. 1911)
US comedian and author

> A psychiatrist is a fellow who asks you a lot of expensive questions your wife asks for nothing.
>
> Attr.

Anonymous
Definition of a psychoanalyst

> A Jewish doctor who hates the sight of blood.
>
> In Leo Rosten, *The Joys of Yiddish* (1968)

Auden, W.H. (1907–1973)
English poet, essayist, critic, teacher and dramatist

> To us he is no more a person
> Now but a climate of opinion.
>
> *In Memory of Sigmund Freud*

Chase, Alexander (1926–)
US journalist and author

> Psychiatry's chief contribution to philosophy is the discovery that the toilet is the seat of the soul.
>
> *Perspectives* (1966)

Goldwyn, Samuel (1882–1974)
Polish-born US film producer

> Any man who goes to a psychiatrist should have his head examined.
>
> In Zierold, *Moguls* (1969)

Stockwood, Mervyn (1913–)
English Anglican churchman

> A psychiatrist is a man who goes to the Folies-Bergère and looks at the audience.
>
> *The Observer*, 1961

Szasz, Thomas (1920–)
Hungarian-born US psychiatrist and writer

> Psychiatrists classify a person as neurotic if he suffers from his problems in living, and a psychotic if he makes others suffer.
>
> *The Second Sin* (1973)

▶▶ MADNESS

publicity

Hand, Learned (1872–1961)
US judge

> The art of publicity is a black art; but it has come to stay, and every year adds to its potency.
>
> Speech, 1951

Proverb

> Any publicity is good publicity.

Simple, Peter (Michael Wharton) (1913–)
British writer and journalist

> Rentacrowd Ltd, the enterprising firm which supplies crowds for all occasions and has done so much to keep progressive causes in the public eye.
>
> *Daily Telegraph*, 1962

Whitlam, Gough (1916–)
Australian Labor statesman and Prime Minister

> Quite small and ineffectual demonstrations can be made to look like the beginnings of a revolution if the cameraman is in the right place at the right time.
>
> In Jonathon Green (ed.), *A Dictionary of Contemporary Quotations* (1982)

▶▶ CELEBRITY; FAME; MEDIA; POPULARITY

public safety slogans

Be all you can be.
Scottish Health Education Council, 1980s

Choose Life, Not Drugs.
Scottish Health Education Council, 1980s

Clunk, Click, every trip.
Road safety campaign promoting the use of seat belts, 1971

Coughs and sneezes spread diseases.
Ministry of Health, c.1942

Don't Die of Ignorance.
Department of Health AIDS campaign, 1987

publishing

Ayer, A.J. (1910–1989)
English philosopher
If I had been someone not very clever, I would have done an easier job like publishing. That's the easiest job I can think of.
Attr.

Campbell, Thomas (1777–1844)
Scottish poet, ballad writer and journalist
Now Barabbas was a publisher.
Attr. in Samuel Smiles, A Publisher and his Friends (1891)

Connolly, Cyril (1903–1974)
English literary editor, writer and critic
As repressed sadists are supposed to become policemen or butchers so those with irrational fear of life become publishers.
Enemies of Promise (1938)

Cooper, Jilly (1937–)
English novelist
Explaining why she was leaving her literary agent Desmond Elliott for Curtis Brown
I love Desmond. He's a darling. We'll be friends for ever and ever and ever. But I've thought about this for a long time and I just feel I need more people.
Publishing News, 1999

Cornford, F.M. (1874–1943)
English Platonic scholar
University printing presses exist for the purpose of producing books which no one can read, and they are true to their high calling.
Attr.

Ingrams, Richard (1937–)
British journalist and editor of *Private Eye*
Referring to his editorship of *Private Eye*

My own motto is publish and be sued.
BBC radio broadcast, 1977

Slessor, Kenneth (1901–1971)
Australian poet and journalist
… the principal benefit of publication is that it clears work out of the mind finally, and provides an impulse for new work.
Letter to Norman Lindsay, 1944

Wellington, Duke of (1769–1852)
Irish-born British military commander and statesman
Reply to a threat of blackmail by Harriette Wilson
Publish and be damned.
Attr.

Wilde, Oscar (1854–1900)
Irish poet, dramatist, writer, critic and wit
No publisher should ever express an opinion of the value of what he publishes. That is a matter entirely for the literary critic to decide … A publisher is simply a useful middle-man. It is not for him to anticipate the verdict of criticism.
Letter in St James's Gazette, 1890

▶▶ BOOKS; EDITING

punctuality

Mitford, Nancy (1904–1973)
English writer
'Twenty-three and a quarter minutes past,' Uncle Matthew was saying furiously, 'in precisely six and three-quarter minutes the damned fella will be late.'
Love in a Cold Climate (1949)

Proverb
Punctuality is the politeness of princes.

▶▶ TIME

punishment

Arendt, Hannah (1906–1975)
German-born US theorist
No punishment has ever possessed enough power of deterrence to prevent the commission of crimes.
Eichmann in Jerusalem: A Report on the Banality of Evil (1963)

Bentham, Jeremy (1748–1832)
English writer and philosopher
All punishment is mischief: all punishment in itself is evil.
An Introduction to the Principles of Morals and Legislation (1789)

The Bible (King James Version)
>He that spareth his rod hateth his son.
>
>*Proverbs*, 13:24

>Whom the Lord loveth he chasteneth.
>
>*Hebrews*, 12:6

Braxfield, Lord (1722–1799)
Scottish judge
To an eloquent culprit at the bar
>Ye're a vera clever chiel, man, but ye wad be nane the waur o' a hanging.
>
>In Lockhart, *Life of Scott*

Dostoevsky, Fyodor (1821–1881)
Russian writer
>Juridical punishment for crime scares a criminal far less than law-makers think, partly because the criminal himself requires it morally.
>
>Letter to Katkov, 1865

Fisher, Geoffrey (1887–1972)
>The long and distressing controversy over capital punishment is very unfair to anyone meditating murder.
>
>*The Sunday Times*, 1957

Gilbert, W.S. (1836–1911)
English dramatist, humorist and librettist
>My object all sublime
>I shall achieve in time –
>To let the punishment fit the crime –
>The punishment fit the crime.
>
>*The Mikado* (1885)

Halifax, Lord (1633–1695)
English politician, courtier, pamphleteer and epigrammatist
>Men are not hang'd for stealing Horses, but that Horses may not be stolen.
>
>'Of Punishment' (1750)

Hubbard, Elbert (1856–1915)
US printer, editor, writer and businessman
>Men are not punished for their sins, but by them.
>
>*A Thousand and One Epigrams* (1911)

Johnson, Samuel (1709–1784)
English lexicographer, poet, critic, conversationalist and essayist
>The power of punishment is to silence, not to confute.
>
>*Sermons* (1788)

>The rod produces an effect which terminates in itself. A child is afraid of being whipped, and gets his task, and there's an end on't; whereas, by exciting emulation and comparisons of superiority, you lay the foundation of lasting mischief; you make brothers and sisters hate each other.
>
>In Boswell, *The Life of Samuel Johnson* (1791)

>Depend upon it, Sir, when a man knows he is to be hanged in a fortnight, it concentrates his mind wonderfully.
>
>In Boswell, *The Life of Samuel Johnson* (1791)

>There is now less flogging in our great schools than formerly, but then less is learned there; so that what the boys get at one end they lose at the other.
>
>In Boswell, *The Life of Samuel Johnson* (1791)

Juvenal (c.60–130)
Roman verse satirist and Stoic
>*Prima est haec ultio, quod se*
>*Iudice nemo nocens absolvitur.*
>The chief punishment is this: that no guilty man is acquitted in his own judgement.
>
>*Satires*

Karr, Alphonse (1808–1890)
French writer and editor
>If we want to abolish the death penalty, let our friends the murderers take the first step.
>
>*Les Guêpes* (1849)

Key, Ellen (1849–1926)
Swedish feminist, writer and lecturer
>Corporal punishment is as humiliating for him who gives it as for him who receives it; it is ineffective besides. Neither shame nor physical pain have any other effect than a hardening one.
>
>*The Century of the Child* (1909)

Mann, Horace (1796–1859)
US educationist, politician and writer
Roman lyric poet and satirist
>The object of punishment is prevention from evil; it never can be made impulsive to good.
>
>*Lectures and Reports on Education* (1845)

Paine, Thomas (1737–1809)
English-born US political theorist and pamphleteer
>Lay then the axe to the root, and teach governments humanity. It is their sanguinary punishments which corrupt mankind.
>
>*The Rights of Man* (1791)

Pepys, Samuel (1633–1703)
English diarist, naval administrator and politician
>I went out to Charing Cross, to see Major-General Harrison hanged, drawn and quartered; which was done there, he looking as cheerful as any man could do in that condition.
>
>*Diary*, 1660

Russell, Lord John (1792–1878)
English Liberal Prime Minister and writer
When asked to describe a suitable punishment for bigamy
>Two mothers-in-law.
>
>Attr.

Salmon, George (1819–1904)
Provost of Trinity College, Dublin

On hearing a colleague claiming to have been caned only once in his life, and that, for telling the truth

> Well, it certainly cured you, Mahaffy.
>
> Attr.

Shakespeare, William (1564–1616)
English dramatist, poet and actor

> Use every man after his desert, and who shall scape whipping?
>
> *Hamlet*, II.ii

> Now, as fond fathers,
> Having bound up the threat'ning twigs of birch,
> Only to stick it in their children's sight
> For terror, not to use, in time the rod
> Becomes more mock'd than fear'd; so our decrees,
> Dead to infliction, to themselves are dead;
> And liberty plucks justice by the nose;
> The baby beats the nurse, and quite athwart
> Goes all decorum.
>
> *Measure For Measure*, I.iii

Shaw, George Bernard (1856–1950)
Irish socialist, writer, dramatist and critic

> There is no satisfaction in hanging a man who does not object to it.
>
> *The Man of Destiny* (1898)

> If you strike a child, take care that you strike it in anger, even at the risk of maiming it for life. A blow in cold blood neither can nor should be forgiven.
>
> *Man and Superman* (1903)'

Shephard, Gillian
Britisah Conservative politician

> My own personal view is that corporal punishment can be a useful deterrent.
>
> BBC radio interview, 1996

Stowe, Harriet Beecher (1811–1896)
US writer and reformer

> Whipping and abuse are like laudanum; you have to double the dose as the sensibilities decline.
>
> *Uncle Tom's Cabin* (1852)

Toscanini, Arturo (1867–1957)
Italian conductor
Rebuking an incompetent orchestra

> After I die, I shall return to earth as a gatekeeper of a bordello and I won't let any of you – not a one of you – enter!
>
> In Howard Taubman, *The Maestro: The Life of Arturo Toscanini* (1951)

Trollope, Anthony (1815–1882)
English writer, traveller and post office official
Of his headmaster

> He must have known me had he seen me as he was wont to see me, for he was in the habit of flogging me constantly. Perhaps he did not recognize me by my face.
>
> *Autobiography* (1883)

Vidal, Gore (1925–)
US writer, critic and poet
When asked for his views about corporal punishment

> I'm all for bringing back the birch, but only between consenting adults.
>
> TV interview with David Frost

Wilde, Oscar (1854–1900)
Irish poet, dramatist, writer, critic and wit

> A community is infinitely more brutalised by the habitual employment of punishment than it is by the occasional occurrence of crime.
>
> 'The Soul of Man under Socialism' (1891)

▶▶ CRIME; EDUCATION; EXECUTION; RETALIATION

puritans

Brathwaite, Richard (c.1588–1673)
English poet and satirist

> To Banbury came I, O profane one!
> Where I saw a Puritane-one
> Hanging of his cat on Monday
> For killing of a mouse on Sunday.
>
> *Barnabee's Journal* (1638)

Lawrence, D.H. (1885–1930)
English writer, poet and critic

> To the Puritan all things are impure, as somebody says.
>
> *Etruscan Places* (1932), 'Cerveteri'

Macaulay, Lord (1800–1859)
English Liberal statesman, essayist and poet
Of the Puritans

> On the rich and the eloquent, on nobles and priests, they looked down with contempt: for they esteemed themselves rich in a more precious treasure, and eloquent in a more sublime language, nobles by the right of an earlier creation, and priests by the imposition of a mightier hand.
>
> *Collected Essays* (1843)

Of Puritans and Calvinists

> Persecution produced its natural effect on them. It found them a sect; it made them a faction.
>
> *History of England* (1849)

> The Puritan hated bear-baiting, not because it gave pain to the bear, but because it gave pleasure to the spectators.
>
> *History of England* (1849)

Mencken, H.L. (1880–1956)
US writer, critic, philologist and satirist

> Puritanism – The haunting fear that someone, somewhere, may be happy.
>
> *A Mencken Chrestomathy* (1949)

Q

qualifications

Bono, Sonny (1935–1997)
US singer-songwriter, businessman and politician
> What is qualified? What have I been qualified for in my life? I haven't been qualified to be a mayor. I'm not qualified to be a songwriter. I'm not qualified to be a TV producer. I'm not qualified to be a successful businessman. And so, I don't know what qualified means. And I think people get too hung up on that in a way, you know?
>
> *Attr.*

questions

Carroll, Lewis (1832–1898)
English writer and photographer
> 'I have answered three questions, and that is enough, '
> Said his father; 'don't give yourself airs!
> Do you think I can listen all day to such stuff?
> Be off, or I'll kick you downstairs!'.
>
> *Alice's Adventures in Wonderland* (1865)

Darling, Charles (1849–1936)
English judge and Conservative politician
> A timid question will always receive a confident answer.
>
> *Scintillae Juris* (1877)

Johnson, Samuel (1709–1784)
English lexicographer, poet, critic, conversationalist and essayist
> There are innumerable questions to which the inquisitive mind can in this state receive no answer: Why do you and I exist? Why was this world created? Since it was to be created, why was it not created sooner?
>
> *In Boswell*, The Life of Samuel Johnson (1791)

MacLeish, Archibald (1892–1982)
US poet and librarian
> We have learned the answers, all the answers:
> It is the question that we do not know.
>
> *The Hamlet of A. Macleish* (1935)

McLuhan, Marshall (1911–1980)
Canadian communications theorist
Favourite conversational gambit
> For your information, let me ask you a question.
>
> In Philip Marchand, *Marshall McLuhan: The Medium and the Messenger* (1989)

Thurber, James (1894–1961)
US humorist, writer and dramatist

> Well, if I called the wrong number, why did you answer the phone?
>
> Cartoon caption in *The New Yorker*, 1937

Wilcox, Ella Wheeler (1850–1919)
US poet and writer
> No question is ever settled
> Until it is settled right.
>
> 'Settle the Question Right' (1917)

Wilde, Oscar (1854–1900)
Irish poet, dramatist, writer, critic and wit
> Questions are never indiscreet. Answers sometimes are.
>
> *An Ideal Husband* (1895)

quotations

Churchill, Sir Winston (1874–1965)
English Conservative Prime Minister
> It is a good thing for an uneducated man to read books of quotations.
>
> *My Early Life* (1930)

Dunn, Douglas (1942–)
Scottish poet
> And, from an open window, Mozart's strings
> Encourage echoed songs,
> Thrush-throats,
> Thrush-wings.
> Alluded nature, quoting from a quote,
> Returns the symphony
> To its wood-note.
>
> *Northlight* (1988)

Emerson, Ralph Waldo (1803–1882)
US poet, essayist, transcendentalist and teacher
> I hate quotations.
>
> *Journals*, 1849

> Every man is a borrower and a mimic, life is theatrical and literature a quotation.
>
> *Society and Solitude* (1870)

> By necessity, by proclivity, – and by delight, we all quote.
>
> *Letters and Social Aims* (1875)

> Next to the originator of a good sentence is the first quoter of it.
>
> *Letters and Social Aims* (1875)

Fadiman, Clifton (1904–)
US writer, editor and broadcaster
> We prefer to believe that the absence of inverted commas guarantees the originality of a thought, whereas it may be merely that the

utterer has forgotten its source.

Any Number Can Play (1957)

Johnson, Samuel (1709–1784)

English lexicographer, poet, critic, conversationalist and essayist

Of citations of usage in a dictionary

Every quotation contributes something to the stability or enlargement of the language.

A Dictionary of the English Language (1755)

Classical quotation is the parole of literary men all over the world.

In Boswell, *The Life of Samuel Johnson* (1791)

He that tries to recommend him by select quotations, will succeed like the pedant in Hierocles, who, when he offered his house to sale, carried a brick in his pocket as a specimen.

The Plays of William Shakespeare (1765)

Kaufman, George S. (1889–1961)

US scriptwriter, librettist and journalist

Everything I've ever said will be credited to Dorothy Parker.

Attr.

Mikes, George (1912–1987)

Hungarian-born British writer

In England only uneducated people show off their knowledge; nobody quotes Latin or Greek authors in the course of conversation, unless he has never read them.

How to be an Alien (1946)

Montague, C.E. (1867–1928)

English writer and critic

To be amused at what you read – that is the great spring of happy quotation.

A Writer's Notes on his Trade (1930)

Parker, Dorothy (1893–1967)

US writer, poet, critic and wit

How do people go to sleep? I'm afraid I've lost the knack. I might try busting myself smartly over the temple with the nightlight. I might repeat to myself, slowly and soothingly, a list of quotations beautiful from minds profound; if I can remember any of the damned things.

Here Lies (1939)

Peacock, Thomas Love (1785–1866)

English writer and poet

A book that furnishes no quotations is, me judice, no book – it is a plaything.

Crotchet Castle (1831)

Pearson, Hesketh (1887–1964)

English biographer

A widely-read man never quotes accurately … Misquotation is the pride and privilege of the learned.

Common Misquotations (1937)

Misquotations are the only quotations that are never misquoted.

Common Misquotations (1937)

Prior, Matthew (1664–1721)

English poet

He rang'd his tropes, and preach'd up patience;
Back'd his opinion with quotations.

'Paulo Purganti and his Wife' (1709)

Ribblesdale, Lord (1854–1925)

British army officer and courtier

It is gentlemanly to get one's quotations very slightly wrong. In that way one unprigs oneself and allows the company to correct one.

In Cooper, *The Light of Common Day* (1959)

Shaw, George Bernard (1856–1950)

Irish socialist, writer, dramatist and critic

I often quote myself. It adds spice to the conversation.

Reader's Digest, 1943

Stoppard, Tom (1937–)

British dramatist

It's better to be quotable than to be honest.

The Guardian

Strunsky, Simeon (1879–1948)

Famous remarks are seldom quoted correctly.

No Mean City (1944)

Waugh, Evelyn (1903–1966)

English writer and diarist

In the dying world I come from quotation is a national vice. It used to be the classics, now it's lyric verse.

The Loved One (1948)

Williams, Kenneth (1926–1988)

English actor and comedian

The nicest thing about quotes is that they give us a nodding acquaintance with the originator which is often socially impressive.

Acid Drops (1980)

Young, Edward (1683–1765)

English poet, dramatist, satirist and clergyman

Some, for renown, on scraps of learning dote,
And think they grow immortal as they quote.

Love of Fame, the Universal Passion (1725–1728)

R

racism

Abernathy, Ralph (1926–1990)
US religious and civil rights leader

> I'm sick and tired of black and white people of good intent giving aspirin to a society that is dying of a cancerous disease.
>
> *And the Walls Came Tumbling Down* (1989)

> Bring on your tear gas, bring on your grenades, your new supplies of Mace, your state troopers and even your national guards. But let the record show we ain't going to be turned around.
>
> *And the Walls Came Tumbling Down* (1989)

Biko, Steve (1946–1977)
Black South African civil rights leader; murdered in police custody

> We wanted to remove him the white man from our table, strip the table of all the trappings put on it by him, decorate it in true African style, settle down and then ask him to join us if he liked.
>
> Speech, 1971

Bjelke-Petersen, Florence Isabel (1920–)
On her husband, Premier of Queensland

> People who criticise Joh unfairly make me angry. They call him 'a racist pig' in Canberra. Joh's not a racist. Why, he's had Aborigines working for him.
>
> *Woman's Day*, 1975

Bosman, Herman Charles (1905–1951)
South African writer

> Kafirs? (said Oom Schalk Lourens), Yes, I know them. And they're all the same. I fear the Almighty, and I respect His works, but I could never understand why He made the kafir and the rinderpest.
>
> *Mafeking Road* (1947)

Brodsky, Joseph (1940–1996)
Russian poet, essayist, critic and exile

> Racism? But isn't it only a form of misanthropy?
>
> *Less Than One* (1986)

Calwell, Arthur Augustus (1894–1973)
Australian Labour politician
Defending the deportation of a Chinese refugee who, Calwell claimed, was not eligible to become a permanent resident of Australia

> There are many Wongs in the Chinese community, but I have to say – and I am sure that the honourable member for Balaclava will not mind me doing so – that 'two Wongs do not make a White'.
>
> Commonwealth Parliamentary Debates, 1947

De Blank, Joost (1908–1968)
Dutch-born British churchman

> I suffer from an incurable disease – colour blindness.
>
> Attr.

Disraeli, Benjamin (1804–1881)
English statesman and writer

> All is race; there is no other truth.
>
> *Tancred* (1847)

Einstein, Albert (1879–1955)
German-born US mathematical physicist

> If my theory of relativity is proven successful, Germany will claim me as a German and France will declare that I am a citizen of the world. Should my theory prove untrue, France will say that I am a German and Germany will declare that I am a Jew.
>
> Address, c.1929

Fanon, Frantz (1925–1961)
West Indian psychoanalyst and philosopher

> For the black man there is only one destiny. And it is white.
>
> *Black Skin, White Masks*

Fisher, H.A.L. (1856–1940)
English historian

> Purity of race does not exist. Europe is a continent of energetic mongrels.
>
> *A History of Europe* (1935)

Forster, E.M. (1879–1970)
English writer, essayist and literary critic

> The so-called white races are really pinko-gray.
>
> *A Passage to India* (1924)

Goebbels, Joseph (1897–1945)
Nazi politician

> … mir in Bälde einen Gesamtentwurf über die organisatorischen, sachlichen und materiellen Vorausmassnahmen zur Durchführung der angestrebten Endlösung der Judenfrage vorzulegen.
> … to place before me soon a complete proposal for the organisational, practical and material preliminary measures which have to be taken in order to bring about the desired Final Solution to the Jewish question.
>
> Letter to Reinhard Heydrich, 1941

Gordimer, Nadine (1923–)
South African writer

> The force of white men's wills, which dispensed and withdrew life, imprisoned and set free, fed or starved, like God himself.
>
> *Six Feet of the Country* (1956)

Haggard, H. Rider (1856–1925)
English novelist

Umbopa to Quatermain
> We are men, you and I.
>> *King Solomon's Mines* (1885)

Hitler, Adolf (1889–1945)
German Nazi dictator, born in Austria
> *Was nicht gute Rasse ist auf dieser Welt, ist Spreu.*
> Whoever is not racially pure in this world is chaff.
>> *Mein Kampf* (1925)

Jackson, Jesse (1941–)
US clergyman and civil rights leader
> I hear that melting-pot stuff a lot, and all I can say is that we haven't melted.
>> *Playboy*, 1969

Jean-Baptiste, Marianne
English actress
> The old men running the industry just have not got a clue ... Britain is no longer totally a white place where people ride horses, wear long frocks and drink tea. The national dish is no longer fish and chips, it's curry.
>> *The Observer*, 1997

King, Martin Luther (1929–1968)
US civil rights leader and Baptist minister
> I want to be the white man's brother, not his brother-in-law.
>> *New York Journal – American*, 1962

> We must learn to live together as brothers or perish together as fools.
>> *Speech at St. Louis, March 22, 1964*

> I have a dream that my four little children will one day live in a nation where they will not be judged by the colour of their skin but by the content of their character.
>> *Speech, civil rights march, 1963*

Lee, Spike (1957–)
US film director
> The only thing I like integrated is my coffee.
>> *Malcolm X* (film, 1992)

Lessing, Doris (1919–)
British writer, brought up in Zimbabwe
> When a white man in Africa by accident looks into the eyes of a native and sees the human being (which it is his chief preoccupation to avoid), his sense of guilt, which he denies, fumes up in resentment and he brings down the whip.
>> *The Grass is Singing* (1950)

Referring to South Africa
> When old settlers say 'One has to understand the country', what they mean is, 'You have to get used to our ideas about the native.' They are saying, in effect, 'Learn our ideas, or otherwise get out; we don't want you.'
>> *The Grass is Singing* (1950)

Makeba, Miriam (1932–)
South African singer
> I look at an ant and I see myself: a native South African, endowed by nature with a strength much greater than my size so I might cope with the weight of a racism that crushes my spirit.
>> *Makeba, My Story* (1987)

Malcolm X (1925–1965)
US black leader
> If you're born in America with a black skin, you're born in prison.
>> *Interview, June 1963*

> Sitting at the table doesn't make you a diner, unless you eat some of what's on that plate. Being here in America doesn't make you an American. Being born here in America doesn't make you an American.
>> *Malcolm X Speaks*, 1965

> I believe in the brotherhood of all men, but I don't believe in wasting brotherhood on anyone who doesn't want to practise it with me.
>> *Speech, 1964*

> We never made one step forward until world pressure put Uncle Sam on the spot ... It has never been out of any internal sense of morality or legality or humanism that we were allowed to advance.
>> *Speech, 1964*

> The Negro problem has ceased to be a Negro problem. It has ceased to be an American problem and has now become a world problem, a problem for all humanity.
>> *Speech, Harvard Law School, 1964*

Mandela, Nelson (1918–)
South African statesman and President
> I have fought against white domination, and I have fought against black domination. I have cherished the ideal of a democratic and free society in which all persons will live together in harmony and with equal opportunities. It is an ideal which I hope to live for and achieve. But, if needs be, it is an ideal for which I am prepared to die.
>> *Statement in the dock, 1964*

Menand, Louis (1953–)
> The evil of modern society isn't that it creates racism but that it creates conditions in which people who don't suffer from injustice seem incapable of caring very much about people who do.
>> *The New Yorker*, 1992

Mencken, H.L. (1880–1956)
US writer, critic, philologist and satirist
> One of the things that makes a Negro

unpleasant to white folk is the fact that he suffers from their injustice. He is thus a standing rebuke to them.

Notebooks (1956)

Miller, Arthur (1915–)
US dramatist and screenwriter
> If there weren't any anti-semitism, I wouldn't think of myself as Jewish.

The Observer, 1995

Paton, Alan (1903–1988)
South African writer
> I have one great fear in my heart, that one day when they whites are turned to loving, they will find we blacks are turned to hating.

Cry, the Beloved Country (1948)

> It was on Wednesday 16 June 1976 that an era came to an end in South Africa. That was the day when black South Africans said to white, 'You can't do this to us any more.' It had taken three hundred years for them to say that.

Journey Continued (1988)

Plomer, William (1903–1973)
South African-born British writer and editor
> The warm heart of any human that saw the black man first not as a black but as a man.

Turbott Wolfe (1926)

Powell, Enoch (1912–1998)
English politician and scholar
On race relations in Britain
> As I look ahead I am filled with foreboding. Like the Roman I seem to see 'The River Tiber foaming with much blood.'

Speech, Birmingham, 1968

Pringle, Thomas (1789–1834)
Scottish poet
> But I brought the handsomest bride of them all – Brown Dinah, the bondmaid who sat in our hall …

> Shall the Edict of Mercy be sent forth at last, To break the harsh fetters of Colour and Caste?

Poetical Works (1838)

Sheridan, Philip Henry (1831–1888)
US general
> The only good Indian is a dead Indian.

Attr.

Smith, Ian (1919–)
Prime Minister of what was Rhodesia (now Zimbabwe)
> I don't believe in black majority rule in Rhodesia … not in a thousand years.

Speech, 1976

Sontag, Susan (1933–)
US critic and writer
> The truth is that Mozart, Pascal, Boolean algebra, Shakespeare, parliamentary

government, baroque churches, Newton, the emancipation of women, Kant, Marx, and Ballanchine ballets don't redeem what this particular civilisation has wrought upon the world. The white race is the cancer of human history.

Attr.

Tecumseh (d. 1812)
Native American chief of the Shawnees
> Where today are the Pequot? Where are the Narragansett, the Mohican, the Pokanoket, and many other once powerful tribes of our people? They have vanished before the avarice and the oppression of the White Man, as snow before a summer sun.

In Brown, *Bury My Heart at Wounded Knee* (1971)

Tomaschek, Rudolphe (b. c.1895)
German scientist
> Modern Physics is an instrument of Jewry for the destruction of Nordic science … True physics is the creation of the German spirit.

In Shirer, *The Rise and Fall of the Third Reich* (1960)

Tutu, Archbishop Desmond (1931–)
South African churchman and anti-apartheid campaigner
> It is very difficult now to find anyone in South Africa who ever supported apartheid.

The Observer, 1994

Zangwill, Israel (1864–1926)
English writer and Jewish spokesman
> The law of dislike for the unlike will always prevail. And whereas the unlike is normally situated at a safe distance, the Jews bring the unlike into the heart of every milieu, and must there defend a frontier line as large as the world.

Speech, 1911

▶▶ EQUALITY; FREEDOM; JEWS; PREJUDICE; SLAVERY; SOUTH AFRICA

radio

Carrott, Jasper
English comedian
> I am amazed at radio DJs today. I am firmly convinced that AM stands for Absolute Moron. I will not begin to tell you what FM stands for.

Attr.

Monroe, Marilyn (1926–1962)
US film actress and model
When asked if she really had nothing on during a calendar shoot
> I had the radio on.

Time, 1952

Wogan, Terry (1926–)
Irish radio and television presenter
> Television contracts the imagination and radio expands it.
>
> *The Observer*, 1984

reading

Addison, Joseph (1672–1719)
English essayist, poet, playwright and statesman
> Of all the diversions of life, there is none so proper to fill up its empty spaces as the reading of useful and entertaining authors.
>
> *The Spectator*, 1711

Augustine, Saint (354–430)
Numidian-born Christian theologian and philosopher
> *Tolle lege, tolle lege.*
> Take up and read, take up and read!
>
> *Confessions* (397–398)

Austen, Jane (1775–1817)
English writer
> Oh, Lord! not I; I never read much; I have something else to do.
>
> *Northanger Abbey* (1818)

Bacon, Francis (1561–1626)
English philosopher, essayist, politician and courtier
> Read not to contradict and confute, nor to believe and take for granted, nor to find talk and discourse, but to weigh and consider.
>
> 'Of Studies' (1625)

Baudelaire, Charles (1821–1867)
French poet, translator and critic
> *Hypocrite lecteur, – mon semblable, – mon frère!*
> Hypocrite reader, my likeness, my brother!
>
> *Les Fleurs du mal* (1857)

Bellow, Saul (1915–)
Canadian-born US Jewish writer
> With a novelist, like a surgeon, you have to get a feeling that you've fallen into good hands – someone from whom you can accept the anaesthetic with confidence.
>
> *The New York Times Book Review*, 1977

Birrell, Augustine (1850–1933)
English politician
> Reading is not a duty, and has consequently no business to be made disagreeable.
>
> *Obiter Dicta* (second series, 1887)

Chandler, Raymond (1888–1959)
US crime writer
> All men who read escape from something else … they must escape at times from the deadly rhythm of their private thoughts.
>
> *Atlantic Monthly* (1944)

Colton, Charles Caleb (c.1780–1832)
English clergyman and satirist
> Some read to think, – these are rare; some to unite, – these are common; and some to talk, – and these form the great majority.
>
> *Lacon* (1820)

Crabbe, George (1754–1832)
English poet, clergyman, surgeon and botanist
> Who often reads, will sometimes wish to write.
>
> *Tales* (1812)

Descartes, René (1596–1650)
French philosopher and mathematician
> *La lecture de tous les bons livres est comme une conversation avec les plus honnêtes gens des siècles passés.*
> The reading of all good books is like a conversation with the finest men of past centuries.
>
> *Discours de la Méthode* (1637)

D'Israeli, Isaac (1766–1848)
English literary critic; father of Benjamin Disraeli
> There is an art of reading, as well as an art of thinking, and an art of writing.
>
> *Literary Character* (1795)

Disraeli, Benjamin (1804–1881)
English statesman and writer
His customary reply to those who sent him unsolicited manuscripts
> Thank you for the manuscript; I shall lose no time in reading it.
>
> Attr.

Emerson, Ralph Waldo (1803–1882)
US poet, essayist, transcendentalist and teacher
> Tis the good reader that makes the good book.
>
> *Society and Solitude* (1870)

Flaubert, Gustave (1821–1880)
French writer
> *Mais ne lisez pas, comme les enfants lisent, pour vous amuser, ni comme les ambitieux lisent, pour vous instruire. Non, lisez pour vivre.*
> Do not read, as children do, for the sake of entertainment, or like the ambitious, for the purpose of instruction. No, read in order to live.
>
> Letter to Mlle Leroyer de Chantepie, 1857

Franklin, Benjamin (1706–1790)
US statesman, scientist, political critic and printer
On being asked what condition of man he considered the most pitiable
> A lonesome man on a rainy day who does not know how to read.
>
> In Shriner, *Wit, Wisdom, and Foibles of the Great*

Gibbon, Edward (1737–1794)
English historian, politician and memoirist
> My early and invincible love of reading, which I

would not exchange for the treasures of India.

Memoirs of My Life and Writings (1796)

Hamerton, P.G. (1834–1894)
British artist and writer

The art of reading is to skip judiciously.

The Intellectual Life (1873)

Handke, Peter (1942–)
Austrian playwright

Der gedankenloseste aller Menschen: der in jedem Buch nur blättert.
The most unthinking person of all: the one who only flicks through every book.

The Weight of the World. A Diary (1977)

Helps, Sir Arthur (1813–1875)
English historian and writer

Reading is sometimes an ingenious device for avoiding thought.

Friends in Council (1849)

Hobbes, Thomas (1588–1679)
Political philosopher

He was wont to say that if he had read as much as other men, he should have knowne no more than other men.

In Aubrey, Brief Lives (c.1693)

Johnson, Samuel (1709–1784)
English lexicographer, poet, critic, conversationalist and essayist

A man ought to read just as inclination leads him; for what he reads as a task will do him little good.

In Boswell, The Life of Samuel Johnson (1791)

Kraus, Karl (1874–1936)
Austrian scientist, critic and poet

Man muss alle Schriftsteller zweimal lesen, die guten und die schlechten. Die einen wird man erkennen, die anderen entlarven.
You must read all writers twice, both the good ones and the bad ones. You'll recognize the good ones and you'll unmask the others.

Sayings and Contradictions (1909)

Katherine, Mansfield (1888–1923)
New Zealand writer

The pleasure of all reading is doubled when one lives with another who shares the same books.

Letter, 1928

L'Amour, Louis (1908–1988)
US author

It is often said that one has but one life to live, but that is nonsense. For one who reads, there is no limit to the number of lives that may be lived, for fiction, biography and history offer an inexhaustible number of lives in all periods of time.

Reader's Digest, 1993

Mao Tse-Tung (1893–1976)
Chinese Communist leader

To read too many books is harmful.

The New Yorker, 1977

Milton, John (1608–1674)
English poet, libertarian and pamphleteer

Who reads
Incessantly, and to his reading brings not
A spirit and judgment equal or superior
(And what he brings, what needs he elsewhere seek)
Uncertain and unsettl'd still remains,
Deep verst in books and shallow in himself.

Paradise Regained (1671)

Orton, Joe (1933–1967)
English dramatist and writer

Reading isn't an occupation we encourage among police officers. We try to keep the paper work down to a minimum.

Loot (1967)

Penn, William (1644–1718)
English Quaker, founder of state of Pennsylvania

Much reading is an oppression of the mind, and extinguishes the natural candle, which is the reason of so many senseless scholars in the world.

'Advice to His Children' (1699)

Petronius Arbiter (d. AD 66)
Roman satirist

Scimus te prae litteras fatuum esse.
We know that you are mad with too much reading.

Satyricon

Quarles, Francis (1592–1644)
English poet, writer and royalist

I wish thee as much pleasure in the reading, as I had in the writing.

Emblems (1635)

Roscommon, Fourth Earl of (1633–1685)
Irish translator and poet

Choose an author as you choose a friend.

An Essay on Translated Verse (1684)

Ruskin, John (1819–1900)
English art critic, philosopher and reformer

But whether thus submissively or not, at least be sure that you go to the author to get at his meaning, not to find yours.

Sesame and Lilies (1865)

Russell, Bertrand (1872–1970)
English philosopher, mathematician, essayist and social reformer

There are two motives for reading a book: one, that you enjoy it, the other that you can boast about it.

The Conquest of Happiness (1930)

Schopenhauer, Arthur (1788–1860)
German philosopher
> To expect a man to retain everything that he has ever read is like expecting him to carry about in his body everything that he has ever eaten.
>
> *Parerga and Paralipomena* (1851)

Smith, Logan Pearsall (1865–1946)
US-born British epigrammatist, critic and writer
> People say that life is the thing, but I prefer reading.
>
> *Afterthoughts* (1931)

Smith, Sydney (1771–1845)
English clergyman, essayist, journalist and wit
> Live always in the best company when you read.
>
> In Lady Holland, *Memoir* (1855)

Solzhenitsyn, Alexander (1918–)
Russian writer, dramatist and historian
> Their teacher had advised them not to read Tolstoy's novels, because they were very long and would only confuse the clear ideas which they had acquired from reading critical studies about him.
>
> *The First Circle* (1968)

Steele, Sir Richard (1672–1729)
Irish-born English writer, dramatist and politician
> Reading is to the Mind, what Exercise is to the Body ... But as Exercise becomes tedious and painful when we make use of it only as the Means of Health, so Reading is apt to grow uneasy and burdensome, when we apply our selves to it only for our Improvement in Virtue.
>
> *The Tatler*, 47, 1710

Sterne, Laurence (1713–1768)
Irish-born English writer and clergyman
> Digressions, incontestably, are the sunshine; – they are the life, the soul of reading; – take them out of this book for instance, – you might as well take the book along with them.
>
> *Tristram Shandy*

Twain, Mark (1835–1910)
US humorist, writer, journalist and lecturer
> Persons attempting to find a motive in this narrative will be prosecuted; persons attempting to find a moral in it will be banished; persons attempting to find a plot in it will be shot.
>
> *The Adventures of Huckleberry Finn* (1884), Introduction

Waugh, Evelyn (1903–1966)
English writer and diarist
> Lady Peabury was in the morning room reading a novel; early training gave a guilty spice to this recreation, for she had been brought up to believe that to read a novel before luncheon was

one of the gravest sins it was possible for a gentlewoman to commit.

Work Suspended (1942)

Wilde, Oscar (1854–1900)
Irish poet, dramatist, writer, critic and wit
> I never travel without my diary. One should always have something sensational to read in the train.
>
> *The Importance of Being Earnest* (1895)

> Oh! it is absurd to have a hard-and-fast rule about what one should read and what one shouldn't. More than half of modern culture depends upon what one shouldn't read.
>
> *The Importance of Being Earnest* (1895)

▶▶ BOOKS; CRITICISM; FICTION; LITERATURE; WRITING

realism

Adams, Scott (1957–)
US cartoonist
> My reality check bounced.
>
> *The Dilbert Principle*

Bacon, Francis (1561–1626)
English philosopher, essayist, politician and courtier
> We are much beholden to Machiavel and others, that write what men do, and not what they ought to do.
>
> *The Advancement of Learning* (1605)

Bohm, David (1917–1992)
> There are no things, only processes.
>
> Attr.

Burgess, Anthony (1917–1993)
English writer, linguist and composer
> Reality is what I see, not what you see.
>
> *The Sunday Times Magazine*, 1983

Cervantes, Miguel de (1547–1616)
Spanish writer and dramatist
> *Mire vuestra merced ... que aquellos que allí se parecen no son gigantes, sino molinos de viento.*
> Look, your worship ... those things which you see over there are not giants, but windmills.
>
> *Don Quixote* (1605)

Connolly, Cyril (1903–1974)
English literary editor, writer and critic
> Everything is a dangerous drug to me except reality, which is unendurable.
>
> *The Unquiet Grave* (1944)

Dürrenmatt, Friedrich (1921–1990)
Swiss dramatist and writer
> Whoever is faced with the paradoxical exposes himself to reality.
>
> *The Physicists* (1962)

Eliot, T.S. (1888–1965)
US-born British poet, verse dramatist and critic
> Human kind
> Cannot bear very much reality.
>> *Four Quartets* (1944)

Fry, Christopher (1907–)
English verse dramatist, theatre director and translator
> There may always be another reality
> To make fiction of the truth we think we've
> arrived at.
>> *A Yard of Sun* (1970)

Hegel, Georg Wilhelm (1770–1831)
German philosopher
> *Was vernünftig ist; das ist wirklich: und was wirklich ist,*
> *das ist vernünftig.*
> What is rational is real, and what is real is
> rational.
>> *Basis of Legal Philosophy*
>> (1820)

Khrushchev, Nikita (1894–1971)
Russian statesman and Premier of the USSR
> If you cannot catch a bird of paradise, better
> take a wet hen.
>> Attr.

Murdoch, Iris (1919–1999)
Irish-born British writer, philosopher and dramatist
> We live in a fantasy world, a world of illusion.
> The great task in life is to find reality.
>> *The Times*, 1983

Pindar (518–438 BC)
Greek lyric poet
> Strive not, my soul, for an immortal life,
> but make the most of the possibilities open to
> you.
>> *Pythian Odes*

Twain, Mark (1835–1910)
US humorist, writer, journalist and lecturer
> Don't part with your illusions. When they are
> gone, you may still exist, but you have ceased to
> live.
>> *Pudd'nhead Wilson's Calendar*
>> (1894)

Wilde, Oscar (1854–1900)
Irish poet, dramatist, writer, critic and wit
> The nineteenth century dislike of Realism is
> the rage of Caliban seeing his own face in a
> glass.
>> *The Picture of Dorian Gray* (1891)

> *Cecily*: When I see a spade I call it a spade.
> *Gwendolen*: I am glad to say that I have never
> seen a spade. It is obvious that our social
> spheres have been widely different.
>> *The Importance of Being Earnest*
>> (1895)

reason

Chandler, Raymond (1888–1959)
US crime writer
> The more you reason the less you create.
>> *Raymond Chandler Speaking* (1962)

Dryden, John (1631–1700)
English poet, satirist, dramatist and critic
> Dim, as the borrowed beams of moon and stars
> To lonely, weary, wandering travellers
> Is reason to the soul.
>> *Religio Laici* (1682)

FitzGerald, Edward (1809–1883)
English poet, translator and letter writer
> You know, my Friends, with what a brave
> Carousel made a second Marriage in my house;
> Divorced old barren Reason from my Bed,
> And took the Daughter of the Vine to Spouse.
>> *The Rubáiyát of Omar Khayyám* (1879)

Fry, Christopher (1907–)
English verse dramatist, theatre director and translator
> I've begun to believe that the reasonable
> Is an invention of man, altogether in opposition
> To the facts of creation.
>> *The Firstborn* (1945)

Hodgson, Ralph (1871–1962)
English poet, illustrator and journalist
> Reason has moons, but moons not hers,
> Lie mirror'd on her sea,
> Confounding her astronomers,
> But, O! delighting me.
>> 'Reason Has Moons' (1917)

Kant, Immanuel (1724–1804)
German idealist philosopher
> *Büchergelehrsamkeit vermehrt zwar die Kenntnisse,*
> *aber erweitert nicht den Begriff und die Einsicht, wo*
> *nicht Vernunft dazukommt.*
> Book learning certainly increases knowledge, but
> does not broaden one's ideas and insight when
> it is not accompanied by reason.
>> *Pragmatic Anthropology* (1800)

Keats, John (1795–1821)
English poet
> I have never yet been able to perceive how any
> thing can be known for truth by consecutive
> reasoning – and yet it must be.
>> Letter to Benjamin Bailey, 22 November 1817

Powell, Sir John (1645–1713)
English judge
> Let us consider the reason of the case. For
> nothing is law that is not reason.
>> In Lord Raymond's *Reports*
>> (1765)

Rochester, Earl of (1647–1680)
English poet, satirist, courtier and libertine
> Reason, an ignis fatuus of the mind,
> Which leaving the light of nature, sense, behind …
> Then Old Age, and Experience, hand in hand,
> Lead him to Death, and make him understand,
> After a search so painful, and so long,
> That all his life he has been in the wrong.
> Huddled in dirt the reasoning engine lies,
> Who was so proud, so witty, and so wise.
>> 'A Satire Against Reason and Mankind' (1679)

Shaw, George Bernard (1856–1950)
Irish socialist, writer, dramatist and critic
> The man who listens to Reason is lost: Reason
> enslaves all whose minds are not strong enough
> to master her.
>> *Man and Superman* (1903)

Voltaire (1694–1778)
French philosopher, dramatist, poet, historian writer and critic
> Once the people start to reason, all is lost.
>> Letter to Damilaville, 1766

▶▶ ART

rebellion

Arendt, Hannah (1906–1975)
German-born US theorist
> The defiance of established authority, religious
> and secular, social and political, as a world-wide
> phenomenon may well one day be accounted
> the outstanding event of the last decade.
>> *Crises of the Republic* (1972)

Arnold, Thomas (1795–1842)
English historian and educator
> As for rioting, the old Roman way of dealing
> with that is always the right one; flog the rank
> and file, and fling the ringleaders from the
> Tarpeian rock.
>> Letter, written before 1828

Berlinguer, Enrico (1922–1984)
Italian political leader
> *Da ragazzo c'era in me un sentimento di ribellione.*
> *Contestavo, se vogliamo usare una parola di moda,*
> *tutto.*
> When I was a young man I felt within me a
> sentiment of rebellion. I used to challenge, to
> use a fashionable word, everything.
>> *The Geography of Italy* (1975)

Bradshaw, John (1602–1659)
English judge and republican
> Rebellion to tyrants is obedience to God.
>> In Randall, *Life of Jefferson* (1865)

Burke, Edmund (1729–1797)
Irish-born British statesman and philosopher
> Make the Revolution a parent of settlement, and
> not a nursery of future revolutions.
>> *Reflections on the Revolution in France*
>> (1790)

Camus, Albert (1913–1960)
Algerian-born French writer
> Every revolutionary ends as an oppressor or a
> heretic.
>> *The Rebel* (1951)

> What is a rebel? A man who says no.
>> *The Rebel* (1951)

> All modern revolutions have led to a
> reinforcement of the power of the State.
>> *The Rebel* (1951)

Conrad, Joseph (1857–1924)
Polish-born British writer, sailor and explorer
> The scrupulous and the just, the noble, humane,
> and devoted natures; the unselfish and the
> intelligent may begin a movement – but it
> passes away from them. They are not the
> leaders of a revolution. They are its victims.
>> *Under Western Eyes* (1911)

Durrell, Lawrence (1912–1990)
Indian-born British poet and writer
> No one can go on being a rebel too long
> without turning into an autocrat.
>> *Balthazar* (1958)

Engels, Friedrich (1820–1895)
German socialist and political philosopher
> The proletariat has nothing to lose but its chains
> in this revolution. It has a world to win. Workers
> of the world, unite!
>> *The Communist Manifesto* (1848)

George V (1865–1936)
King of the United Kingdom
On hearing Mr Wheatley's life story
> Is it possible that my people live in such awful
> conditions? … I tell you, Mr Wheatley, that if I
> had to live in conditions like that I would be a
> revolutionary myself.
>> In MacNeill Weir, *The Tragedy of Ramsay*
>> *MacDonald* (1938)

Hill, Reginald (1936–)
British writer and playwright
> The first thing revolutionaries of the left or right
> give up is their sense of humour. The second
> thing is other people's rights.
>> In Winks (ed.), *Colloquium on Crime*
>> (1986)

Jefferson, Thomas (1743–1826)
US Democrat statesman and President

A little rebellion, now and then, is a good thing, and as necessary in the political world as storms in the physical.

Letter to James Madison, January 30, 1787

Khrushchev, Nikita (1894–1971)
Russian statesman and Premier of the USSR
> If you feed people with revolutionary slogans alone they will listen today, they will listen tomorrow, they will listen the day after that, but on the fourth day they will say 'To hell with you!'.

Attr.

Lewis, Wyndham (1882–1957)
US-born British painter, critic and writer
> The revolutionary simpleton is everywhere.

Time and Western Man (1927)

Shakespeare, William (1564–1616)
English dramatist, poet and actor
> Rebellion lay in his way, and he found it.

Henry IV, Part 1, V.i

Storr, Dr Anthony (1920–)
British writer and psychiatrist
> It is harder to rebel against love than against authority.

Attr.

Trotsky, Leon (1879–1940)
Russian revolutionary and Communist theorist
> Insurrection is an art, and like all arts it has its laws.

History of the Russian Revolution (1933)

Vergniaud, Pierre (1753–1793)
French politician and revolutionary
Remark at his trial, 1793
> *Il a été permis de craindre que la Révolution, comme Saturne, dévorât successivement tous ses enfants.*
> There was reason to fear that the Revolution, like Saturn, would eventually devour all her children one by one.

In Lamartine, *Histoire des Girondins* (1847)

Weil, Simone (1909–1943)
French philosopher, essayist and mystic
> *On pense aujourd'hui à la révolution, non comme à une solution des problèmes posés par l'actualité, mais comme à un miracle dispensant de résoudre les problèmes.*
> Nowadays we think of revolution not as the solution to problems posed by current developments but as a miracle which releases us from the obligation to solve these problems.

Oppression and Freedom (1955)

Wellington, Duke of (1769–1852)
Irish-born British military commander and statesman
> Beginning reform is beginning revolution.

In Mrs Arbuthnot's Journal, 1830

▶▶ REVOLUTION

reconciliation

Mandela, Nelson (1918–)
South African statesman and President
> The time for the healing of the wounds has come.

Speech at his inauguration as President of South Africa, 1994

> True reconciliation does not consist in merely forgetting the past.

Speech, 1996

Whitman, Walt (1819–1892)
US poet and writer
> Beautiful that war and all its deeds of carnage must in time be utterly lost,
> That the hands of the sisters Death and Night incessantly softly wash again, and ever again, this soil'd world;
> For my enemy is dead, a man as divine as myself is dead,
> I look where he lies white-faced and still in the coffin – I draw near,
> Bend down and touch lightly with my lips the white face in the coffin.

'Reconciliation' (1865)

reform

Carlyle, Thomas (1795–1881)
Scottish historian, biographer, critic, and essayist
> All reform except a moral one will prove unavailing.

Critical and Miscellaneous Essays (1839)

Webb, Sidney (1859–1947)
English reformer, historian and socialist
> The inevitability of gradualness.

Presidential address to the annual conference of the Labour Party, 1923

regret

Cato the Elder (234–149 BC)
Roman statesman
> In all my life, I have never repented but of three things: that I trusted a woman with a secret, that I went by sea when I might have gone by land, and that I passed a day in idleness.

In Pliny, *Naturalis Historia*

Fonda, Jane (1937–)
US actress and political activist
On her visit to Hanoi in support of the Viet Cong during the Vietnam War

> I will go to my grave regretting the photograph of me on an anti-aircraft gun, which looks like I was trying to shoot at American planes. It galvanised hostility.
>
> *The Sunday Times*, 2000

Maugham, William Somerset (1874–1965)
English writer, dramatist and physician

> It's no use crying over spilt milk, because all the forces of the universe were bent on spilling it.
>
> *Of Human Bondage* (1915)

Rossetti, Dante Gabriel (1828–1882)
English poet, painter, translator and letter-writer

> Look in my face; my name is Might-have-been
> I am also called No-more, Too-Late, Farewell …
>
> Then shalt thou see me smile, and turn apart
> Thy visage to mine ambush at my heart
> Sleepless with cold commemorative eyes.
>
> *The House of Life* (1881)

Thompson, William Hepworth (1810–1886)
English Greek scholar
Of Seeley's inaugural lecture as Professor of History at Cambridge, following Charles Kingsley

> I never could have supposed that we should have had so soon to regret the departure of our dear friend the late Professor.
>
> In A.J. Balfour, *Chapters of Autobiography*

▶▶ APOLOGIES; MEMORY; MOURNING; NOSTALGIA; PAST; SORROW

religion

Addison, Joseph (1672–1719)
English essayist, poet, playwright and statesman

> We have in England a particular bashfulness in every thing that regards religion.
>
> *The Spectator*, August 1712, 458

Anonymous

> There was a young man from Dijon,
> Who had little, if any, religion.
> He said, 'As for me,
> I detest all three,
> The Father, the Son, and the Pigeon.'
>
> *The Norman Douglas Limerick Book* (1969)

Arnold, Matthew (1822–1888)
English poet, critic, essayist and educationist

> The true meaning of religion is thus not simply morality, but morality touched by emotion.
>
> *Literature and Dogma* (1873)

Ashford, Daisy (1881–1972)
English child author

> Bernard always had a few prayers in the hall and some whiskey afterwards as he was rarther pious but Mr Salteena was not very addicted to prayers so he marched up to bed.
>
> *The Young Visiters* (1919)

Barrie, Sir J.M. (1860–1937)
Scottish dramatist and writer

> One's religion is whatever he is most interested in, and yours is Success.
>
> *The Twelve-Pound Look*

Behan, Brendan (1923–1964)
Irish dramatist, writer and Republican

> Pound notes are the best religion in the world.
>
> *The Wit of Brendan Behan* (1968)

Belloc, Hilaire (1870–1953)
English writer of verse, essayist and critic; Liberal MP
Suggested rider to the Ten Commandments

> Candidates should not attempt more than six of these.
>
> Attr.

Bergman, Ingmar (1918–)
Swedish film director

> I hope I never get so old I get religious.
>
> Attr.

Blake, William (1757–1827)
English poet, engraver, painter and mystic

> I went to the Garden of Love,
> And saw what I never had seen:
> A Chapel was built in the midst,
> Where I used to play on the green.
>
> And the gates of this Chapel were shut,
> And 'Thou shalt not' writ over the door …
>
> And Priests in black gowns were walking their rounds,
> And binding with briars my joys & desires.
>
> 'The Garden of Love' (1794)

Brenan, Gerald (1894–1987)
English writer

> Religions are kept alive by heresies, which are really sudden explosions of faith. Dead religions do not produce them.
>
> *Thoughts in a Dry Season* (1978)

Browne, Sir Thomas (1605–1682)
English physician, author and antiquary

> At my devotion I love to use the civility of my knee, my hat, and hand.
>
> *Religio Medici* (1643)

> As for those wingy mysteries in divinity, and airy subtleties in religion, which have unhinged the brains of better heads, they never stretched the

pia mater of mine. Methinks there be not impossibilities enough in Religion for an active faith.

Religio Medici (1643)

Men have lost their reason in nothing so much as their religion, wherein stones and clouts make martyrs.

Hydriotaphia: Urn Burial (1658)

Persecution is a bad and indirect way to plant religion.

Religio Medici (1643)

Burke, Edmund (1729–1797)
Irish-born British statesman and philosopher
Nothing is so fatal to religion as indifference, which is, at least, half infidelity.

Letter to William Smith, 1795

Burton, Robert (1577–1640)
English clergyman and writer
One religion is as true as another.

Anatomy of Melancholy (1621)

Butler, Samuel (1835–1902)
English writer, painter, philosopher and scholar
To be at all is to be religious more or less.

The Note-Books of Samuel Butler (1912)

Charles II (1630–1685)
King of Great Britain and Ireland
He Charles II said once to myself, he was no atheist, but he could not think God would make a man miserable only for taking a little pleasure out of the way. He disguised his popery to the last.

In Burnet, *The History of His Own Time* (1724)

Of Presbyterianism
The king spoke to him Lauderdale to let that Presbytery go, for it was not a religion for gentlemen.

In Burnet, *The History of His Own Time* (1724)

Chesterfield, Lord (1694–1773)
English politician and letter writer
Religion is by no means a proper subject of conversation in a mixed company … It is too awful and respectable a subject to become a familiar one.

Letter to his godson, c.1766

Putting moral virtues at the highest, and religion at the lowest, religion must still be allowed to be a collateral security, at least, to virtue; and every prudent man will sooner trust to two securities than to one.

Letter to his son, 1750

Coleridge, Samuel Taylor (1772–1834)
English poet, philosopher and critic

Time consecrates; and what is grey with age becomes religion

Attr.

Colton, Charles Caleb (c.1780–1832)
English clergyman and satirist
Men will wrangle for religion; write for it; fight for it; anything but – live for it.

Lacon (1820)

Daly, Mary (1928–)
US feminist and theologian
Patriarchy is itself the prevailing religion of the entire planet, and its essential message is necrophilia.

Gyn/Ecology: the Metaethics of Radical Feminism (1979)

Diderot, Denis (1713–1784)
French philosopher, encyclopaedist, writer and dramatist
Wandering in a vast forest at night, I have only a faint light to guide me. A stranger appears and says to me: 'My friend, you should blow out your candle in order to find your way more clearly.' This stranger is a theologian.

Addition aux Pensées Philosophiques

Diogenes (the Cynic) (c.400–325 BC)
Greek philosopher
I do not know whether there are gods, but there ought to be.

In Tertullian, *Ad Nationes*

Disraeli, Benjamin (1804–1881)
English statesman and writer
'Sensible men are all of the same religion.' 'And pray what is that?' inquired the prince. 'Sensible men never tell.'

Endymion (1880)

Dix, George Eglington (1901–1952)
English Anglican monk, historian and scholar
It is no accident that the symbol of a bishop is a crook, and the sign of an archbishop is a double-cross.

Letter to *The Times*, 1977

Dryden, John (1631–1700)
English poet, satirist, dramatist and critic
Yet dull religion teaches us content;
But when we ask it where that blessing dwells,
It points to pedant colleges and cells.

The Conquest of Granada (1670)

Eddy, Mary Baker (1821–1910)
US founder of Christian Science
Christian Science explains all cause and effect as mental, not physical.

Science and Health, with Key to the Scriptures (1875)

Ellis, Havelock (1859–1939)
English sexologist and essayist
The whole religious complexion of the modern

world is due to the absence from Jerusalem of a lunatic asylum.

Impressions and Comments (1914)

Emerson, Ralph Waldo (1803–1882)
US poet, essayist, transcendentalist and teacher
The religions we call false were once true.

'Character' (1866)

Erasmus (c.1466–1536)
Dutch scholar and humanist
Of his failure to fast during Lent
I have a Catholic soul, but a Lutheran stomach.

Dictionnaire Encyclopédique

Fielding, Henry (1707–1754)
English writer, dramatist and journalist
When I mention religion, I mean the Christian religion; and not only the Christian religion, but the Protestant religion; and not only the Protestant religion but the Church of England.

Tom Jones (1749)

Fleming, Marjory (1803–1811)
Scottish child diarist
I hope I will be religious again but as for reganing my charecter I despare for it.

In Esdaile (ed.), *Journals, Letters and Verses* (1934)

Forster, E.M. (1879–1970)
English writer, essayist and literary critic
My law-givers are Erasmus and Montaigne, not Moses and St Paul.

Two Cheers for Democracy (1951), 'What I Believe'

Freud, Sigmund (1856–1939)
Austrian physicist; founder of psychoanalysis
Religion is an illusion and it derives its strength from the fact that it falls in with our instinctual desires.

New Introductory Lectures on Psychoanalysis (1933)

Gibbon, Edward (1737–1794)
English historian, politician and memoirist
The various modes of worship, which prevailed in the Roman world, were all considered by the people as equally true; by the philosopher, as equally false; and by the magistrate, as equally useful.

Decline and Fall of the Roman Empire (1776–88)

Goldsmith, Oliver (c.1728–1774)
Irish dramatist, poet and writer
As I take my shoes from the shoemaker, and my coat from the tailor, so I take my religion from the priest.

In Boswell, *The Life of Samuel Johnson* (1791)

Heinlein, Robert A. (1907–1988)
US science fiction writer
One man's theology is another man's belly laugh.

Notebooks of Lazarus Long

Hooton, Harry (1908–1961)
Australian philosopher and poet
Psychology is the theology of the 20th century.

'Inhuman Race'

Hope, Bob (1903–)
English-born US comedian
I do benefits for all religions. I'd hate to blow the hereafter on a technicality.

In Simon Rose, *Classic Film Guide* (1995)

Inge, William Ralph (1860–1954)
English divine, writer and teacher
To become a popular religion, it is only necessary for a superstition to enslave a philosophy.

Outspoken Essays

Jerrold, Douglas William (1803–1857)
English dramatist, writer and wit
Religion's in the heart, not in the knees.

The Devil's Ducat (1830)

Lucretius (c.95–55 BC)
Roman philosopher
Tantum religio potuit suadere malorum.
So potent a persuasion to evil was religion.

De Rerum Natura

Marlowe, Christopher (1564–1593)
English poet and dramatist
I count religion but a childish toy,
And hold there is no sin but ignorance.

The Jew of Malta (c.1592)

Marx, Karl (1818–1883)
German political philosopher and economist; founder of Communism
Religion … is the opium of the people.

A Contribution to the Critique of Hegel's Philosophy of Right (1844)

Melbourne, Lord (1779–1848)
English statesman
On listening to an evangelical sermon
Things have come to a pretty pass when religion is allowed to invade the sphere of private life.

In Russell, *Collections and Recollections* (1898)

Mencken, H.L. (1880–1956)
US writer, critic, philologist and satirist
We must respect the other fellow's religion, but only in the sense and to the extent that we respect his theory that his wife is beautiful and his children smart.

Notebooks (1956)

Montaigne, Michel de (1533–1592)
French essayist and moralist.
Our religion was made to root out vices; it covers them up, nourishes them, incites them.

Essais (1580)

Newman, John Henry, Cardinal (1801–1890)
English Cardinal, theologian and poet
> From the age of fifteen, dogma has been the fundamental principle of my religion: I know no other religion; I cannot enter into the idea of any other sort of religion; religion, as a mere sentiment, is to me a dream and a mockery.
>> *Apologia pro Vita Sua* (1864)

O'Casey, Sean (1880–1964)
Irish dramatist
> There's no reason to bring religion into it. I think we ought to have as great a regard for religion as we can, so as to keep it out of as many things as possible.
>> *The Plough and the Stars* (1926)

Runcie, Rosalind (1932–)
Wife of the Archbishop of Canterbury
> Too much religion makes me go pop.
>> In M. Duggan, *Runcie: The Making of an Archbishop* (1983)

Runciman, Sir Steven (1903–)
British scholar, historian and archaeologist
> Unlike Christianity, which preached a peace that it never achieved, Islam unashamedly came with a sword.
>> *A History of the Crusades* (1954)

Russell, Bertrand (1872–1970)
English philosopher, mathematician, essayist and social reformer
> Religion is based … mainly on fear … fear of the mysterious, fear of defeat, fear of death. Fear is the parent of cruelty, and therefore it is no wonder if cruelty and religion have gone hand in hand … My own view on religion is that of Lucretius. I regard it as a disease born of fear and as a source of untold misery to the human race. I cannot, however, deny that it has made some contributions to civilization. It helped in early days to fix the calendar, and it caused Egyptian priests to chronicle eclipses with such care that in time they became able to predict them. These two services I am prepared to acknowledge, but I do not know of any others.
>> *Why I Am Not a Christian and Other Essays*

Selden, John (1584–1654)
English historian, jurist and politician
> For a priest to turn a man when he lies a-dying, is just like one that has a long time solicited a woman, and cannot obtain his end; at length he makes her drunk, and so lies with her.
>> *Table Talk*

Sewell, Anna (1820–1878)
English writer
> There is no religion without love, and people may talk as much as they like about their religion, but if it does not teach them to be good and kind to man and beast, it is all a sham.
>> *Black Beauty* (1877)

Shaftesbury, Earl of (1621–1683)
English statesman
> 'People differ in their discourse and profession about these matters, but men of sense are really but of one religion.' … 'Pray, my Lord, what religion is that which men of sense agree in?' 'Madam,' says the earl immediately, 'men of sense never tell it.'
>> In Bishop Burnet's *History of His Own Time* (1823)

Shaw, George Bernard (1856–1950)
Irish socialist, writer, dramatist and critic
> There is only one religion, though there are a hundred versions of it.
>> *Plays Pleasant and Unpleasant* (1898)

> I can't talk religion to a man with bodily hunger in his eyes.
>> *Major Barbara* (1907)

> I am a sort of collector of religions; and the curious thing is that I find I can believe in them all.
>> *Major Barbara* (1907)

Shelley, Percy Bysshe (1792–1822)
English poet, dramatist and essayist
> Earth groans beneath religion's iron age,
> And priests dare babble of a God of peace,
> Even whilst their hands are red with guiltless blood.
>> *Queen Mab* (1813)

Sterne, Laurence (1713–1768)
Irish-born English writer and clergyman
> Whenever a man talks loudly against religion, – always suspect that it is not his reason, but his passions which have got the better of his creed.
>> *Tristram Shandy* (1759–67)

Swift, Jonathan (1667–1745)
Irish satirist, poet, essayist and cleric
> We have just enough religion to make us hate, but not enough to make us love one another.
>> *Thoughts on Various Subjects* (1711)

Tolstoy, Leo (1828–1910)
Russian writer, essayist, philosopher and moralist
Refusing to reconcile himself with the Russian Orthodox Church as he lay dying
> Even in the valley of the shadow of death, two and two do not make six.
>> Attr.

Webb, Beatrice (1858–1943)
English writer and reformer
> Religion is love; in no case is it logic.
>> *My Apprenticeship* (1926)

Wilde, Oscar (1854–1900)
Irish poet, dramatist, writer, critic and wit
> Religion does not help me. The faith that others give to what is unseen, I give to what one can touch, and look at.
>> *De Profundis* (1897)

Zangwill, Israel (1864–1926)
English writer and Jewish spokesman
> Let us start a new religion with one commandment, 'Enjoy thyself'.
>> *Children of the Ghetto* (1892)

▶▶ AFTERLIFE; ATHEISM; BELIEF; BIBLE; CHRISTIANITY; CHRISTMAS; CHURCH; DEVIL; GOD; HEAVEN; HELL; PRAYER; SAINTS; SUNDAY

repentance

The Bible (King James Version)
> I am not come to call the righteous, but sinners to repentance.
>> *Matthew*, 9:13

> Joy shall be in heaven over one sinner that repenteth, more than over ninety and nine just persons, which need no repentance.
>> *Luke*, 15:7

Dryden, John (1631–1700)
English poet, satirist, dramatist and critic
> Repentance is the virtue of weak minds.
>> *The Indian Emperor* (1665)

> Repentance is but want of power to sin.
>> *Palamon and Arcite* (1700)

FitzGerald, Edward (1809–1883)
English poet, translator and letter writer
> Come, fill the Cup, and in the Fire of Spring
> The Winter Garment of Repentance fling:
> The Bird of Time has but a little way
> To fly – and Lo! the Bird is on the Wing.
>> *The Rubáiyát of Omar Khayyám* (1859)

Scott, Sir Walter (1771–1832)
Scottish writer and historian
> But with the morning cool repentance came.
>> *Rob Roy* (1817)

Shakespeare, William (1564–1616)
English dramatist, poet and actor
> Well, I'll repent, and that suddenly, while I am in some liking; I shall be out of heart shortly, and then I shall have no strength to repent.
>> *Henry IV, Part 1*, III.iii

> If one good deed in all my life I did,
> I do repent it from my very soul.
>> *Titus Andronicus*, V.iii

Watts, Isaac (1674–1748)
English hymn-writer, poet and minister
> There's no repentance in the grave.
>> *Divine Songs for Children* (1715)

reputation

Beaverbrook, Lord (1879–1964)
Canadian-born British newspaper owner
Of Earl Haig
> With the publication of his Private Papers in 1952, he committed suicide twenty-five years after his death.
>> *Men and Power* (1956)

Burney, Fanny (1752–1840)
English diarist
> Nothing is so delicate as the reputation of a woman; it is at once the most beautiful and most brittle of all human things.
>> *Evelina* (1778)

Colette (1873–1954)
French writer
> *Ne porte jamais de bijoux artistiques, ça déconsidère complètement une femme.*
> Never wear artistic jewellery; it ruins a woman's reputation.
>> *Gigi* (1944)

Eliot, George (1819–1880)
English writer and poet
> 'Abroad', that large home of ruined reputations.
>> *Felix Holt* (1866)

Emerson, Ralph Waldo (1803–1882)
US poet, essayist, transcendentalist and teacher
> I trust a good deal to common fame, as we all must. If a man has good corn, or wood, or boards, or pigs, to sell, or can make better chairs or knives, crucibles, or church organs, than anybody else, you will find a broad, hard-beaten road to his house, though it be in the woods.
>> *Journals*, 1855

Hill, Reginald (1936–)
British writer and playwright
> The ultimate stage of reputation would be to have a name so powerful in market terms it would sell anything. Well, the money would be nice, but I don't know yet if I'm ready for the irresponsibility.
>> In Winks (ed.), *Colloquium on Crime* (1986)

Keynes, John Maynard (1883–1946)
English economist
> Wordly wisdom teaches that it is better for the

reputation to fail conventionally than to succeed unconventionally.

The General Theory of Employment, Interest and Money (1936)

Mitchell, Margaret (1900–1949)
US author

Until you've lost your reputation, you never realize what a burden it was or what freedom really is.

Gone with the Wind (1936)

Shakespeare, William (1564–1616)
English dramatist, poet and actor

Good name in man and woman, dear my lord,
Is the immediate jewel of their souls:
Who steals my purse steals trash; 'tis something, nothing;
'Twas mine, 'tis his, and has been slave to thousands;
But he that filches from me my good name
Robs me of that which not enriches him
And makes me poor indeed.

Othello, III.iii

The purest treasure mortal times afford
Is spotless reputation; that away,
Men are but gilded loam or painted clay.
A jewel in a ten-times barr'd-up chest
Is a bold spirit in a loyal breast.
Mine honour is my life; both grow in one;
Take honour from me, and my life is done.

Richard II, I.i

Twain, Mark (1835–1910)
US humorist, writer, journalist and lecturer

There was worlds of reputation in it, but no money.

A Yankee at the Court of King Arthur (1889)

Washington, George (1732–1799)
US general, statesman and President

Associate yourself with men of good quality if you esteem your own reputation; for 'tis better to be alone than in bad company.

Rules of Civility and Decent Behaviour

▶▶ CELEBRITY; CHARACTER; FAME

research

Adkins, Homer

Basic research is like shooting an arrow into the air and, where it lands, painting a target.

Nature, 1984

Green, Celia (1935–)

The way to do research is to attack the facts at the point of greatest astonishment.

The Decline and Fall of Science

Medawar, Sir Peter (1915–1987)
British zoologist and immunologist

If politics is the art of the possible, research is surely the art of the soluble. Both are immensely practical-minded affairs.

New Statesman, 1964

Pattison, Mark (1813–1884)

In research the horizon recedes as we advance, and is no nearer at sixty than it was at twenty. As the power of endurance weakens with age, the urgency of the pursuit grows more intense – And research is always incomplete.

Isaac Casaubon (1875)

Routh, Martin Joseph (1755–1854)
English divine and scholar

You will find it a very good practice always to verify your references, sir!

Attr.

Rutherford, Ernest (1871–1937)
English physicist

We haven't the money, so we've got to think!

In Bulletin of the Institute of Physics, 1962

▶▶ SCIENCE

respect

Accius, Lucius (170–86 BC)
Roman poet

Let them hate, so long as they fear.

Atreus

Churchill, Sir Winston (1874–1965)
English Conservative Prime Minister

We do not covet anything from any nation except their respect.

Broadcast to the French people, October 1940

Voltaire (1694–1778)
French philosopher, dramatist, poet, historian writer and critic

We owe respect to the living; to the dead we owe only truth.

Oeuvres, 'Premiere lettre sur Oedipe'

▶▶ COURTESY; MANNERS

responsibility

Quayle, Dan (1947–)
US Republican politician and Vice President

One word sums up probably the responsibility of any vice president, and that one word is 'to be prepared'.

Attr.

Saint-Exupéry, Antoine de (1900–1944)
French author and aviator
> *Tu deviens responsable pour toujours de ce que tu a apprivoisé. Tu es responsable de ta rose.*
> You become responsible, for ever, for what you have tamed. You are responsible for your rose.
> > *The Little Prince* (1943)

Semple, Robert (1873–1955)
New Zealand Labour politician
Allegedly said on the occasion of the Fordell tunnel botch, 1944
> As minister I accept the responsibility but not the blame.
> > In Richard Long, *Dominion* (1984)

Shakespeare, William (1564–1616)
English dramatist, poet and actor
> Our remedies oft in ourselves do lie,
> Which we ascribe to heaven.
> > *All's Well That Ends Well*, I.i

Truman, Harry S. (1884–1972)
US President
> The buck stops here.
> > Sign on his desk

retaliation

Marsden, Samuel (1792–1848)
English-born Australian churchman
On Christianity
> A hefty whaler, after some discussion with Marsden, remarked, 'Your religion teaches that if a man is hit on one cheek, he will turn the other.' And hit Marsden on the right cheek. Marsden obediently offered his left cheek and received a second blow. 'Now,' he said, 'I have obeyed my Master's commands. What I do next, he left to my own judgement. Take this.' And knocked the man down.
> > From Mrs P.R. Woodhouse, oral tradition

Parker, Dorothy (1893–1967)
US writer, poet, critic and wit
> It costs me never a stab nor squirm
> To tread by chance upon a worm.
> 'Aha, my little dear,' I say,
> 'Your clan will pay me back one day.'
> > *Sunset Gun*, 'Thoughts for a Sunshiny Morning'

▶▶ PUNISHMENT; REVENGE

retirement

Ali, Muhammad (1942–)
US heavyweight boxer

Announcing his retirement
> I want to get out with my greatness intact.
> > *The Observer*, 1974

Takayama, Hideko
> Husbands' inertia at home has made its mark on the language. Wives refer to their menfolk with fond exasperation as 'oversize' trash – and males sheepishly apply the term to themselves. A more recent coinage tags retired husbands as 'wet leaves': no matter how you try to sweep them out the door, they stick to the spot where they landed.
> > *Newsweek*, 1990

Thomson, James (1700–1748)
Scottish poet and dramatist
> An elegant sufficiency, content,
> Retirement, rural quiet, friendship, books.
> > *The Seasons* (1746)

▶▶ AGE; LONGEVITY

revenge

Atwood, Margaret (1939–)
Canadian writer, poet and critic
> An eye for an eye leads only to more blindness.
> > *Cat's Eye* (1988)

Bacon, Francis (1561–1626)
English philosopher, essayist, politician and courtier
> Revenge is a kind of wild justice, which the more man's nature runs to, the more ought law to weed it out.
> > 'Of Revenge' (1625)

> A man that studieth revenge keeps his own wounds green.
> > 'Of Revenge' (1625)

The Bible (King James Version)
> Vengeance is mine; I will repay, saith the Lord.
> > *Romans*, 12:19

> Life for life,
> Eye for eye, tooth for tooth, hand for hand, foot for foot,
> Burning for burning, wound for wound, stripe for stripe.
> > *Exodus*, 21:23–25

Cyrano de Bergerac, Savinien de (1619–1655)
French writer
> *Périsse l'Univers, pourvu que je me venge.*
> The universe may perish, so long as I have my revenge.
> > *La Mort d'Agrippine* (1654)

Ford, John (c.1586–c.1640)
English dramatist and poet

Revenge proves its own executioner.

The Broken Heart (1633)

Guitry, Sacha (1885–1957)
Russian-born French actor, dramatist and film director
When a man steals your wife, there is no better revenge that to let him keep her.

Elles et toi (1948)

Milton, John (1608–1674)
English poet, libertarian and pamphleteer
Revenge, at first though sweet,
Bitter ere long back on it self recoils.

Paradise Lost (1667)

Proverbs
Revenge is sweet.

Revenge is a dish that tastes better cold.

Scott, Sir Walter (1771–1832)
Scottish writer and historian
Vengeance, deep-brooding o'er the slain,
Had lock'd the source of softer woe.

The Lay of the Last Minstrel (1805), I

Shakespeare, William (1564–1616)
English dramatist, poet and actor
Let's make us med'cines of our great revenge
To cure this deadly grief.

Macbeth, IV.iii

Heat not a furnace for your foe so hot
That it do singe yourself.

Henry VIII, I.i

The rarer action is
In virtue than in vengeance.

The Tempest, V.i

▶▶ RETALIATION

revolution

Aristotle (384–322 BC)
Greek philosopher
Revolutions may spring from trifles, but their issues are far from trifling.

Politics, I

Boulez, Pierre (1925–)
French conductor and composer
Revolutions are celebrated when they are no longer dangerous.

The Guardian, 1989

Cezanne, Paul (1839–1906)
French painter
The day is coming when a single carrot, freshly observed, will set off a revolution.

Attr.

Disraeli, Benjamin (1804–1881)
English statesman and writer
I have been ever of opinion that revolutions are not to be evaded.

Coningsby (1844)

Emerson, Ralph Waldo (1803–1882)
US poet, essayist, transcendentalist and teacher
Here once the embattled farmers stood,
And fired the shot heard round the world.

Poems (1847)

Fox, Charles James (1749–1806)
English statesman and abolitionist
On the Fall of the Bastille
How much the greatest event it is that ever happened in the world! and how much the best!

Letter, 1789

Hoffman, Abbie (1936–1989)
US political activist
The first duty of the revolutionary is to get away with it.

Speech, 1966

Jefferson, Thomas (1743–1826)
US Democrat statesman and President
To attain all this universal republicanism, however, rivers of blood must yet flow, and years of desolation pass over; yet the object is worth rivers of blood, and years of desolation.

Letter to John Adams, 1823

Kafka, Franz (1883–1924)
Czech-born German-speaking writer
Every revolution evaporates, leaving behind only the slime of a new bureaucracy.

The Great Wall of China: Aphorisms 1917–1919

La Rochefoucauld-Liancourt, Duc de (1747–1827)
French social reformer and writer
In reply to Louis XVI's question 'C'est une révolte?' on hearing of the fall of the Bastille
Non, Sire, c'est une révolution.
No, Sire, it is a revolution.

Remark, 1789

Lenin, V.I. (1870–1924)
Russian revolutionary, Marxist theoretician and first leader of the USSR
The substitution of the proletarian for the bourgeois state is impossible without a violent revolution.

The State and Revolution (1917)

Lewis, Wyndham (1882–1957)
US-born British painter, critic and writer
The revolutionary simpleton is everywhere.

Time and Western Man (1927)

Linklater, Eric (1899–1974)
Welsh-born Scottish writer and satirist
There won't be any revolution in America ... The

people are too clean. They spend all their time changing their shirts and washing themselves. You can't feel fierce and revolutionary in a bathroom.

> *Juan in America* (1931)

Orwell, George (1903–1950)
English writer and critic
> Nine times out of ten a revolutionary is merely a climber with a bomb in his pocket.

> *New English Weekly*, 1939

Paine, Thomas (1737–1809)
English-born US political theorist and pamphleteer
> A share in two revolutions is living to some purpose.

> In Eric Foner, *Tom Paine and Revolutionary America* (1976)

Reed, John (1887–1920)
US radical journalist
Of the October Revolution in Russia
> Ten Days that Shook the World.

> Title of book, 1919

Seward, William (1801–1872)
US statesman
> I know, and all the world knows, that revolutions never go backward.

> Speech at Rochester on the Irrepressible Conflict, 1858

Sieyès, Abbé Emmanuel Joseph (1748–1836)
French churchman
Reply when asked what he did during the French Revolution
> *J'ai vécu.*
> I lived.

> In F.A.M. Mignet, *Notice historique sur la vie et les travaux de M. le Comte de Sieyès* (1836)

Talleyrand, Charles-Maurice de (1754–1838)
French statesman, memoirist and prelate
Of the French Revolution
> *Qui n'a pas vécu dans les années voisines de 1789 ne sait pas ce que c'est que le plaisir de vivre.*
> He who has not lived during the years around 1789 cannot know what is meant by the joy of living.

> In M. Guizot, *Mémoires pour servir à l'histoire de mon temps* (1858)

Trotsky, Leon (1879–1940)
Russian revolutionary and Communist theorist
> The revolution does not choose its paths, it makes its first steps towards victory under the belly of a Cossack's horse.

> *History of the Russian Revolution* (1933)

> Revolutions are always verbose.

> *History of the Russian Revolution* (1933)

> The fundamental premise of a revolution is that the existing social structure has become incapable of solving the urgent problems

connected with the development of the nation.

> *History of the Russian Revolution* (1933)

Ustinov, Sir Peter (1921–)
English actor, director, dramatist, writer and raconteur
> Revolutions have never succeeded unless the establishment does three-quarters of the work.

> *Dear Me* (1977)

Wordsworth, William (1770–1850)
English poet
> Bliss was it in that dawn to be alive,
> But to be young was very heaven.

> *The Prelude* (1850)

▶▶ REBELLION

rewards

Smith, F.E. (1872–1930)
English politician and Lord Chancellor
> The world continues to offer glittering prizes to those who have stout hearts and sharp swords.

> Rectorial Address, Glasgow University, 1923

> We have the highest authority for believing that the meek shall inherit the Earth; though I have never found any particular corroboration of this aphorism in the records of Somerset House.

> *Contemporary Personalities* (1924), 'Marquess Curzon'

Swift, Jonathan (1667–1745)
Irish satirist, poet, essayist and cleric
> These unhappy people were proposing schemes for persuading monarchs to choose favourites upon the score of their wisdom, capacity and virtue; of teaching ministers to consult the public good; of rewarding merit, great abilities and eminent services; of instructing princes to know their true interest by placing it on the same foundation with that of their people: of choosing for employments persons qualified to exercise them; with many other wild impossible chimeras, that never entered before into the heart of man to conceive, and confirmed in me the old observation, that there is nothing so extravagant and irrational which some philosophers have not maintained for truth.

> *Gulliver's Travels* (1726)

Waugh, Evelyn (1903–1966)
English writer and diarist
> Meanwhile you will write an essay on 'self-indulgence'. There will be a prize of half a crown for the longest essay, irrespective of any possible merit.

> *Decline and Fall* (1928)

rich and poor

The Bible (King James Version)
> It is easier for a camel to go through the eye of a needle, than for a rich man to enter into the kingdom of God.
>> *Mark*, 10:25

Disraeli, Benjamin (1804–1881)
English statesman and writer
> 'Two nations; between whom there is no intercourse and no sympathy; who are as ignorant of each other's habits, thoughts, and feelings, as if they were dwellers in different zones, or inhabitants of different planets; who are formed by a different breeding, are fed by a different food, are ordered by different manners, and are not governed by the same laws.'
> 'You speak of –' said Egremont, hesitatingly.
> 'THE RICH AND THE POOR.'
>> *Sybil* (1845)

Euripides (c.485–406 BC)
Greek dramatist and poet
> When a man's stomach is full it makes no difference whether he is rich or poor.
>> Attr.

Pound, Ezra (1885–1972)
US poet
> Come, let us pity those who are better off than we are.
> Come, my friend, and remember that the rich have butlers and no friends,
> And we have friends and no butlers.
>> 'The Garret' (1916)

Proverb
> There's one law for the rich, and another for the poor.

Shaw, George Bernard (1856–1950)
Irish socialist, writer, dramatist and critic
> I am a Millionaire. That is my religion.
>> *Major Barbara* (1907)

Smith, Adam (1723–1790)
Scottish economist, philosopher and essayist
> The rich only select from the heap what is most precious and agreeable. They consume little more than the poor, and in spite of their natural selfishness and rapacity … they divide with the poor the produce of all their improvements. They are led by an invisible hand to make nearly the same distribution of the necessaries of life, which would have been made, had the earth been divided into equal portions among all its inhabitants.
>> *The Theory of Moral Sentiments* (1759)

Smith, Logan Pearsall (1865–1946)
US-born British epigrammatist, critic and writer
> It is the wretchedness of being rich that you have to live with rich people.
>> *Afterthoughts* (1931)

> Eat with the rich, but go to the play with the Poor, who are capable of Joy.
>> *Afterthoughts* (1931)

> To suppose, as we all suppose, that we could be rich and not behave as the rich behave, is like supposing that we could drink all day and keep absolutely sober.
>> *Afterthoughts* (1931)

Stead, Christina (1902–1983)
Australian writer
> The rich take their time, the rich marry late so that property will be divided little and late, while the poor rush to marry and divide the little pay that one gets.
>> *For Love Alone* (1944)

Vidal, Gore (1925–)
US writer, critic and poet
> There's a lot to be said for being *nouveau riche* and the Reagans mean to say it all.
>> *The Observer*, 1981

Wilde, Oscar (1854–1900)
Irish poet, dramatist, writer, critic and wit
> We are often told that the poor are grateful for charity. Some of them are, no doubt, but the best amongst the poor are never grateful. They are ungrateful, discontented, disobedient, and rebellious. They are quite right to be so.
>> *The Fortnightly Review*, 1891

Woollcott, Alexander (1887–1943)
US writer, drama critic and anthologist
On being shown round Moss Hart's elegant country house and grounds
> Just what God would have done if he had the money.
>> Attr.

▶▶ MONEY AND WEALTH; POVERTY

ridicule

Albee, Edward (1928–)
US dramatist
> I have a fine sense of the ridiculous, but no sense of humour.
>> *Who's Afraid of Virginia Woolf?* (1962)

Hattersley, Roy (1932–)
British Labour politician and writer
> In politics, being ridiculous is more damaging

than being extreme.

The Observer, 1996

Napoleon I (1769–1821)

French emperor

Du sublime au ridicule il n'y a qu'un pas.

It is only one step from the sublime to the ridiculous.

In De Pradt, *Histoire de l'Ambassade dans le grand-duché de Varsovie en 1812* (1815)

Paine, Thomas (1737–1809)

English-born US political theorist and pamphleteer

The sublime and the ridiculous are often so nearly related, that it is difficult to class them separately. One step above the sublime, makes the ridiculous; and one step above the ridiculous, makes the sublime again.

The Age of Reason (1795)

Scott, Sir Walter (1771–1832)

Scottish writer and historian

Ridicule often checks what is absurd, and fully as often smothers that which is noble.

Quentin Durward (1823)

Voltaire (1694–1778)

French philosopher, dramatist, poet, historian writer and critic

I have never made but one prayer to God, a very short one: 'O Lord, make my enemies ridiculous.' And God granted it.

Letter to Damilaville, 1767

▶▶ CONTEMPT; SATIRE

right and wrong

Anonymous

In simple cases, presenting one obvious right way versus one obvious wrong way, it is often wiser to choose the wrong way so as to expedite subsequent revision.

Buffett, Warren (1930–)

US billionaire investment expert

It is better to be approximately right than precisely wrong.

Fortune, 1994

Churchill, Sir Winston (1874–1965)

English Conservative Prime Minister

Perhaps it is better to be irresponsible and right than to be responsible and wrong.

Party Political Broadcast, London, 1950

Clay, Henry (1777–1852)

US statesman

I had rather be right than be President.

Remark, 1839

Coleridge, Samuel Taylor (1772–1834)

English poet, philosopher and critic

The innumerable multitude of Wrongs
By man on man inflicted.

'Religious Musings' (1796)

Confucius (c.550–c.478 BC)

Chinese philosopher and teacher of ethics

To see what is right and not to do it is want of courage.

Analects

Cowper, William (1731–1800)

English poet, hymn and letter writer

A noisy man is always in the right.

'Conversation' (1782)

Emerson, Ralph Waldo (1803–1882)

US poet, essayist, transcendentalist and teacher

No law can be sacred to me but that of my nature. Good and bad are but names very readily transferable to that or this; the only right is what is after my own constitution, the only wrong what is against it.

Essays, First Series (1841)

Goldwyn, Samuel (1882–1974)

Polish-born US film producer

I am willing to admit that I may not always be right, but I am never wrong.

Attr.

Junius (1769–1772)

Pen-name of anonymous author of letters criticising ministers of George III

It is not that you do wrong by design, but that you should never do right by mistake.

Letters (1769–1771)

Kingsley, Charles (1819–1875)

English writer, poet, lecturer and clergyman

Some say that the age of chivalry is past, that the spirit of romance is dead. The age of chivalry is never past, so long as there is a wrong left unredressed on earth.

In Mrs C. Kingsley, *Life* (1879)

La Chaussée, Nivelle de (1692–1754)

French sentimental dramatist

Quand tout le monde a tort, tout le monde a raison.

When everyone is wrong, everyone is right.

La Gouvernante (1747)

Melbourne, Lord (1779–1848)

English statesman

Replying to someone who said he would support Melbourne so long as he was right

What I want is men who will support me when I am in the wrong.

In Lord David Cecil, *Lord M.* (1954)

Solon (c.638–c.559 BC)

Athenian statesman, reformer and poet

Wrongdoing can only be avoided if those who are not wronged feel the same indignation at it as those who are.

Attr.

▶▶ GOOD AND EVIL; MORALITY; PRINCIPLES

rights

Carlyle, Thomas (1795–1881)
Scottish historian, biographer, critic, and essayist
Surely of all 'rights of man', this right of the ignorant man to be guided by the wiser, to be, gently or forcibly, held in the true course by him, is the indisputablest.

Chartism (1839)

Condorcet, Antoine-Nicolas de (1743–1794)
French mathematician and academician
Either none of mankind possesses genuine rights, or everyone shares them equally; whoever votes against another's rights, whatever his religion, colour or sex, forswears his own.

In Vansittart (ed.), *Voices of the Revolution* (1989)

Jefferson, Thomas (1743–1826)
US Democrat statesman and President
We hold these truths to be self-evident: that all men are created equal; that they are endowed by their Creator with certain unalienable rights; that among these are life, liberty, and the pursuit of happiness.

Declaration of Independence, 1776

Johnson, Samuel (1709–1784)
English lexicographer, poet, critic, conversationalist and essayist
I have got no further than this: Every man has a right to utter what he thinks truth, and every other man has a right to knock him down for it. Martyrdom is the test.

In Boswell, *The Life of Samuel Johnson* (1791)

Magna Carta (1215)
Nullus liber homo capiatur, vel imprisonetur, aut disseisiatur, aut utlagetur, aut exuletur, aut aliquo modo destruatur, nec super eum ibimus, nec super eum mittemus, nisi per legale judicium parium suorum vel per legem terrae.
No free man shall be taken or imprisoned or dispossessed, or outlawed or exiled, or in any way destroyed, nor will we go upon him, nor will we send against him, except by the lawful judgement of his peers or by the law of the land.

Clause 39

Pankhurst, Emmeline (1858–1928)
English suffragette

Women had always fought for men, and for their children. Now they were ready to fight for their own human rights. Our militant movement was established.

My Own Story (1914)

Robespierre, Maximilien (1758–1794)
French revolutionary
Toute institution qui ne suppose pas le peuple bon, et le magistrat corruptible, est vicieuse.
Any institution which does not suppose the people good, and the magistrate corruptible, is a vicious one.

Déclaration des Droits de l'homme (1793), Article 25

Universal Declaration of Human Rights
All human beings are born free and equal in dignity and rights.

Article 1

Voltaire (1694–1778)
French philosopher, dramatist, poet, historian writer and critic
I disapprove of what you say, but I will defend to the death your right to say it.

Attr.

▶▶ EQUALITY; FEMINISM; FREEDOM; JUSTICE AND INJUSTICE

risk

Nixon, Richard (1913–1994)
US Republican politician and President
If you take no risks, you will suffer no defeats. But if you take no risks, you win no victories.

US News & World Report, 1987

Stevenson, Adlai (1900–1965)
US lawyer, statesman and United Nations ambassador
In America any boy may become President and I suppose it's just one of the risks he takes!

Speech, 1952

rivers

Burns, Robert (1759–1796)
Scottish poet and song writer
Ye banks and braes o' bonny Doon,
How can ye bloom sae fresh and fair?
How can ye chant, ye little birds,
And I sae weary fu' o' care?

'Ye Banks and Braes o' Bonny Doon' (1791)

Hammerstein II, Oscar (1895–1960)
US librettist and lyricist
Ol' man river, dat ol' man river,
He must know sumpin', but don't say nothin',

He jus' keeps rollin',
He jus' keeps rollin' along.

> 'Ol' Man River', song, 1927, from *Show Boat*

Kipling, Rudyard (1865–1936)
Indian-born British poet and writer
> The great, grey-green, greasy Limpopo River, all set about with fever-trees.
>
> *Just So Stories* (1902), 'The Elephant's Child'

rules

Ade, George (1866–1944)
US fabulist and playwright
> To ensure peace of mind ignore the rules and regulations.
>
> Attr.

Carroll, Lewis (1832–1898)
English writer and photographer
> 'That's not a regular rule: you invented it just now.'
> 'It's the oldest rule in the book,' said the King.
> 'Then it ought to be Number One,' said Alice.
>
> *Alice's Adventures in Wonderland* (1865)

> The rule is, jam to-morrow and jam yesterday – but never jam to-day.
>
> *Through the Looking-Glass (and What Alice Found There)* (1872)

Charles I (1600–1649)
King of Great Britain and Ireland
> I will end with a rule that may serve for a statesman, a courtier, or a lover – never make a defence or apology before you be accused.
>
> Letter to Wentworth, 1636

Clough, Arthur Hugh (1819–1861)
English poet and letter writer
> Thou shalt have one God only; who
> Would be at the expense of two? …
>
> Thou shalt not kill; but need'st not strive
> Officiously to keep alive.
> Do not adultery commit;
> Advantage rarely comes of it.
> Thou shalt not steal; an empty feat,
> When it's so lucrative to cheat …
> Thou shalt not covet; but tradition
> Approves all forms of competition.
>
> 'The Latest Decalogue' (1862)

Mayhew, Jonathan (1720–1766)
US clergyman and pamphleteer
> Rulers have no authority from God to do mischief.
>
> *A Discourse Concerning Unlimited Submission and Non-Resistance to the Higher Powers* (1750)

Melba, Dame Nellie (1861–1931)
Australian opera singer
> The first rule in opera is the first rule in life: see to everything yourself.
>
> *Melodies and Memories* (1925)

Molière (1622–1673)
French dramatist, actor and director
> *Je voudrais bien savoir si la grande règle de toutes les règles n'est pas de plaire.*
> I would like to know if, after all, the greatest rule of all is not to please.
>
> *L'Ecole des Femmes* (1662)

Rabelais, François (c.1494–c.1553)
French monk, physician, satirist and humanist
> Referring to the fictional Abbey of Thélème
> *En leur règle n'estoit que ceste clause: 'fay ce que vouldra.'*
> In their rules there was only this one clause: 'Do what you will.'
>
> *Gargantua* (1534)

Shaw, George Bernard (1856–1950)
Irish socialist, writer, dramatist and critic
> The golden rule is that there are no golden rules.
>
> *Man and Superman* (1903)

▶▶ REBELLION

russia

Anonymous
> An intelligent Russian once remarked to us, 'Every country has its own constitution; ours is absolutism moderated by assassination.'
>
> In Munster, *Political Sketches of Europe* (1868)

Burnham, Lord
On Russian policy
> The bear does not change his spots.
>
> *The Times*, 1999

Churchill, Sir Winston (1874–1965)
English Conservative Prime Minister
> I cannot forecast to you the action of Russia. It is a riddle wrapped in a mystery inside an enigma.
>
> Broadcast, October 1939

Lenin, V.I. (1870–1924)
Russian revolutionary, Marxist theoretician and first leader of the USSR
> Any cook should be able to run the country.
>
> In Alexander Solzhenitsyn, *The First Circle* (1968)

Nicholas I, Emperor of Russia (1796–1855)
> Russia has two generals in whom she can trust – Generals Janvier and Février.
>
> Attr.

Nixon, Richard (1913–1994)
US Republican politician and President
Urging more generous support for Russian leader Boris Yeltsin
> Without large-scale outside aid, Russia may turn to a new despotism, which could be a far more dangerous threat to peace and freedom than the old Soviet totalitarianism.
>
> *Remark at a Washington conference, 1992*

Putin, Vladimir (1952–)
President of Russia
> You would need to be heartless not to regret the disintegration of the Soviet Union. You would need to be brainless to attempt to restore it.
>
> *The Scotsman, 2000*

Reagan, Ronald (1911–)
US actor, Republican statesman and President
During a microphone test prior to a radio broadcast
> My fellow Americans, I am pleased to tell you that I have signed legislation to outlaw Russia for ever. We begin bombing in five minutes.
>
> *Audio recording, 1984*

Thurber, James (1894–1961)
US humorist, writer and dramatist
> The difference between our decadence and the Russians' is that while theirs is brutal, ours is apathetic.
>
> *The Observer, 1961*

Tolstoya, Tatyana
> In our country we are all great specialists in the irrational but not yet great specialists in the logical … Today in Russia there are as many sorcerers as militia men.
>
> Interview, Waterstones, Glasgow

Trotsky, Leon (1879–1940)
Russian revolutionary and Communist theorist
> From being a patriotic myth, the Russian people have become a terrible reality.
>
> *History of the Russian Revolution* (1933)

Yevtushenko, Yevgeny (1933–)
Russian poet
> No Jewish blood runs among my blood,
> but I am as bitterly and hardly hated
> by every anti-semite
> as if I were a Jew. By this
> I am a Russian.
>
> 'Babi Yar' (1961)

Zhirinovsky, Vladimir (1946–)
Russian politician
> The whole nation, I promise you, will experience an orgasm next year.
>
> In *Newsweek*, 1994

▶▶ COMMUNISM

S

sacrifice

Brooke, Rupert (1887–1915)
English poet
> Blow out, you bugles, over the rich Dead!
> There's none of these so lonely and poor of old,
> But, dying, has made us rarer gifts than gold.
> These laid the world away; poured out the red
> Sweet wine of youth, gave up the years to be
> Of work and joy, and that unhoped serene,
> That men call age; and those who would have
> been,
> Their sons, they gave, their immortality.
> > 'The Dead' (1914)

Ewer, William Norman (1885–1976)
English journalist
> I gave my life for freedom – This I know:
> For those who bade me fight had told me so.
> > Five Souls and Other Verses (1917)

Goethe (1749–1832)
German poet, writer, dramatist and scientist
> Deny yourself! You should deny yourself! That is
> the eternal song.
> > Faust, I (1808), 'Studierzimmer' ('Study')

Rosewarne, V.A. (1916–1940)
English airman
> The universe is so vast and so ageless that the
> life of one man can only be justified by the
> measure of his sacrifice.
> > Letter to his mother, 1940

Thackeray, William Makepeace (1811–1863)
Indian-born English writer
> That dismal pleasure which the idea of sacrificing
> themselves gives to certain women.
> > Pendennis (1848–1850)

Yeats, W.B. (1865–1939)
Irish poet, dramatist, editor, writer and senator
> Too long a sacrifice
> Can make a stone of the heart.
> > Easter, 1916 (1916)

▶▶ WAR

saints

Browne, Sir Thomas (1605–1682)
English physician, author and antiquary
> There are many (questionless) canonized on
> earth, that shall never be Saints in Heaven.
> > Religio Medici (1643)

Pope, Alexander (1688–1744)
English poet, translator and editor
> For Virtue's self may too much zeal be had;
> The worst of Madmen is a Saint run mad.
> > Imitations of Horace (1737–1738)

Proverb
> All are not saints that go to church.

Saki (1870–1916)
Burmese-born British writer
> There may have been disillusionments in the
> lives of the mediaeval saints, but they would
> scarcely have been better pleased if they could
> have foreseen that their names would be
> associated nowadays chiefly with racehorses and
> the cheaper clarets.
> > Reginald (1904)

▶▶ BELIEF; CHURCH; MIRACLES; RELIGION

satire

Lewis, Wyndham (1882–1957)
US-born British painter, critic and writer
> In its essence the purpose of satire – whether
> verse or prose – is aggression … Satire has a
> great big blaring target. If successful, it blasts a
> great big hole in the centre.
> > 'Note on Verse-Satire'

Macmillan, Harold (1894–1986)
British Conservative Prime Minister
> It is a good thing to be laughed at. It is better
> than to be ignored.
> > That Was The Week That Was, BBC TV, 1962

Montagu, Lady Mary Wortley (1689–1762)
English letter writer, poet, traveller and introducer of
smallpox inoculation
> Satire should, like a polished razor keen,
> Wound with a touch that's scarcely felt or seen.
> > 'To the Imitator of the First Satire of Horace'

Swift, Jonathan (1667–1745)
Irish satirist, poet, essayist and cleric
> Satire is a kind of glass, wherein beholders do
> generally discover everybody's face but their
> own.
> > The Battle of the Books (1704)

> Satire, by being levelled at all, is never resented
> for an offence by any.
> > A Tale of a Tub (1704)

▶▶ RIDICULE

sayings

Fuller, Thomas (1608–1661)
English churchman and antiquary
Definition of a Proverb
> Much matter decocted into a few words.
>> *The History of the Worthies of England* (1662)

Macaulay, Lord (1800–1859)
English Liberal statesman, essayist and poet
> Nothing is so useless as a general maxim.
>> *Collected Essays* (1843), 'Machiavelli'

Pembroke, Earl of (1734–1794)
English general
> Dr Johnson's sayings would not appear so extraordinary, were it not for his bow-wow way.
>> In Boswell, *The Life of Samuel Johnson* (1791)

Roosevelt, Theodore (1858–1919)
US Republican President
> There is a homely old adage which runs, 'Speak softly and carry a big stick; you will go far.'
>> Speech, 1903

scholars

Confucius (c.550–c.478 BC)
Chinese philosopher and teacher of ethics
> The scholar who cherishes the love of comfort, is not fit to be deemed a scholar.
>> *Analects*

Lippmann, Walter (1889–1974)
Canadian sociologist
> I doubt whether the student can do a greater work for his nation in this grave moment in its history than to detach himself from its preoccupations, refusing to let himself be absorbed by distractions about which, as a scholar, he can do almost nothing.
>> *The Scholar in a Troubled World* (1932)

Schopenhauer, Arthur (1788–1860)
German philosopher
> *Die Gelehrten aber, wie sie in der Regel sind, studieren zu dem Zweck, lehren und schreiben zu können. Daher gleicht ihr Kopf einem Magen und Gedärmen, daraus die Speisen unverdaut wieder abgehn.*
> Scholars, however, as a rule study with the aim of being able to teach and write. That is why their heads are like a stomach and intestines from which food passes out again undigested.
>> *Parerga und Paralipomena* (1851)

Swift, Jonathan (1667–1745)
Irish satirist, poet, essayist and cleric
> Then, rising with Aurora's light,
> The Muse invoked, sit down to write;

> Blot out, correct, insert, refine,
> Enlarge, diminish, interline …

> As learned commentators view
> In Homer more than Homer knew.
>> 'On Poetry' (1733)

Yeats, W.B. (1865–1939)
Irish poet, dramatist, editor, writer and senator
> Bald heads forgetful of their sins,
> Old, learned, respectable bald heads
> Edit and annotate the lines
> That young men, tossing on their beds,
> Rhymed out in love's despair
> To flatter beauty's ignorant ear.

> All shuffle there; all cough in ink;
> All wear the carpet with their shoes;
> All think what other people think;
> All know the man their neighbour knows.
> Lord, what would they say
> Did their Catullus walk that way?
>> In *Catholic Anthology 1914–1915*

▶▶ EDUCATION; KNOWLEDGE; LEARNING; SCHOOL; TEACHERS; WISDOM

school

Aitken, Jonathan (1942–)
English Conservative politician
On prison
> I lived at Eton in the 1950s and know all about life in uncomfortable quarters.
>> *The Times*, 1999

Anthony, Susan B. (1820–1906)
US reformer, feminist and abolitionist
> And yet, in the schoolroom more than any other place, does the difference of sex, if there is any, need to be forgotten.
>> In Theodore Stanton and Harriet Stanton Blatch (eds), *Elizabeth Cady Stanton* (1922)

Beerbohm, Sir Max (1872–1956)
English satirist, cartoonist, critic and essayist
> Not that I had any special reason for hating school … I was a modest, good-humoured boy. It is Oxford that has made me insufferable.
>> *More* (1899)

Clark, Lord Kenneth (1903–1983)
English art historian
On boarding schools
> This curious, and, to my mind, objectionable feature of English education was maintained solely in order that parents could get their children out of the house.
>> *Another Part of the Wood* (1974)

Connolly, Cyril (1903–1974)
English literary editor, writer and critic
> The ape-like virtues without which no one can enjoy a public school.
> > *Enemies of Promise* (1938)

Davies, Robertson (1913–1995)
Canadian playwright, writer and critic
> The most strenuous efforts of the most committed educationalists in the years since my boyhood have been quite unable to make a school into anything but a school, which is to say a jail with educational opportunities.
> > *The Cunning Man* (1994)

Dickens, Charles (1812–1870)
English writer
> EDUCATION. – At Mr Wackford Squeer's Academy, Dotheboys Hall, at the delightful village of Dotheboys, near Greta Bridge in Yorkshire, Youth are boarded, clothed, booked, furnished with pocket-money, provided with all necessaries, instructed in all languages, living and dead, mathematics, orthography, geometry, astronomy, trigonometry, the use of the globes, algebra, single stick (if required), writing, arithmetic, fortification, and every other branch of classical literature. Terms, twenty guineas per annum. No extras, no vacations, and diet unparalleled.
> > *Nicholas Nickleby* (1839)

Fielding, Henry (1707–1754)
English writer, dramatist and journalist
> Public schools are the nurseries of all vice and immorality.
> > *Joseph Andrews* (1742)

Forster, E.M. (1879–1970)
English writer, essayist and literary critic
Of public schoolboys
> They go forth into it the world with well-developed bodies, fairly developed minds, and undeveloped hearts.
> > *Abinger Harvest* (1936)

Greene, Graham (1904–1991)
English writer and dramatist
> I had left civilisation behind and entered a savage country of strange customs and inexplicable cruelties: a country in which I was a foreigner and a suspect, quite literally a hunted creature, known to have dubious associates. Was not my father the headmaster? I was like the son of a quisling in a country under occupation.
> > *A Sort of Life* (1971)

Lindsay, Sir David (c.1490–1555)
Scottish poet and satirist
> We think them verray naturall fules,

> That lernis ouir mekle at the sculis.
> > 'Complaynt to the King'

Neil, A.S. (1883–1973)
Scottish educational reformer
> 'Casting Out Fear' ought to be the motto over every school door.
> > *The Problem Child* (1926)

Orwell, George (1903–1950)
English writer and critic
> Probably the Battle of Waterloo was won on the playing-fields of Eton, but the opening battles of all subsequent wars have been lost there.
> > *The Lion and the Unicorn* (1941)

Parsons, Tony (1953–)
British journalist and author
> The death of the grammar schools – those public schools without the sodomy – resulted in state education relinquishing its role of nurturing bright young working class kids.
> > *Arena*, 1989

Patten, Brian (1946–)
British poet
> Before playtime let us consider the possibilities of getting stoned on milk.
> > *Grinning Jack* (1990)

Rifkind, Malcolm (1946–)
Scottish barrister and Conservative politician
> Every school needs a debating society far more than it needs a computer. For a free society, it is essential.
> > In Kamm and Lean (eds), *A Scottish Childhood* (1985)

Saki (1870–1916)
Burmese-born British writer
> But, good gracious, you've got to educate him first. You can't expect a boy to be vicious till he's been to a good school.
> > *Reginald in Russia* (1910)

Searle, Ronald William Fordham (1920–)
English cartoonist
> Though loaded firearms were strictly forbidden at St Trinian's to all but Sixth-Formers … one or two of them carried automatics acquired in the holidays, generally the gift of some indulgent relative.
> > *The Terror of St Trinian's* (1952)

Waugh, Evelyn (1903–1966)
English writer and diarist
> That's the public-school system all over. They may kick you out, but they never let you down.
> > *Decline and Fall* (1928)

> 'We class schools, you see, into four grades: Leading School, First-rate School, Good School,

and School. Frankly', said Mr Levy, 'School is pretty bad.'

Decline and Fall (1928)

Wellington, Duke of (1769–1852)
Irish-born British military commander and statesman
The battle of Waterloo was won on the playing fields of Eton.

Attr.

▶▶ EDUCATION; KNOWLEDGE; LEARNING; TEACHERS; WISDOM

science

Amis, Martin (1949–)
English writer
Not only are all characters and scenes in this book entirely fictitious; most of the technical, medical and psychological data are too. My working maxim here has been as follows: I may not know much about science but I know what I like.

Dead Babies (1975)

Anonymous
No experiment is reproducible.

Wyszowski's Law

When a distinguished but elderly scientist states that something is possible, he is almost certainly right. When he states that something is impossible, he is very probably wrong.

Clarke's First Law.

The limits of the possible can only be defined by going beyond them into the impossible.

Clarke's Second Law

Archimedes (c.287–212 BC)
Greek mathematician
Give me a place to stand, and I will move the Earth.

In Poppus Alexander, *Collectio*

Arnold, Thomas (1795–1842)
English historian and educator
Rather than have Physical Science the principal thing in my son's mind, I would rather have him think that the Sun went round the Earth, and the Stars were merely spangles set in a bright blue firmament.

In Alan L. Mackay, *The Harvest of a Quiet Eye* (1977)

Auden, W.H. (1907–1973)
English poet, essayist, critic, teacher and dramatist
The true men of action in our time, those who transform the world, are not the politicians and statesmen, but the scientists. Unfortunately, poetry cannot celebrate them, because their deeds are concerned with things, not persons

and are, therefore, speechless.

The Dyer's Hand (1963)

When I find myself in the company of scientists, I feel like a shabby curate who has strayed by mistake into a drawing-room full of dukes.

The Dyer's Hand (1963)

Bainbridge, Kenneth (1904–)
US nuclear physicist
Now we are all sons of bitches.

Remark after directing the first atomic test, 1945

Belloc, Hilaire (1870–1953)
English writer of verse, essayist and critic; Liberal MP
The Microbe is so very small
You cannot make him out at all …
Oh! let us never, never doubt
What nobody is sure about!

More Beasts for Worse Children (1897)

Bridie, James (1888–1951)
Scottish dramatist, writer and physician
Eve and the apple was the first great step in experimental science.

Mr Bolfry (1943)

Bronowski, Jacob (1908–1974)
British scientist, writer and TV presenter
Physics becomes in those years the greatest collective work of science – no, more than that, the great collective work of art of the twentieth century.

The Ascent of Man (1973)

That is the essence of science: ask an impertinent question, and you are on the way to the pertinent answer.

The Ascent of Man (1973)

Science has nothing to be ashamed of, even in the ruins of Nagasaki.

Science and Human Values

Bush, Vannevar (1890–1974)
US engineer and physicist
To pursue science is not to disparage the things of the spirit. In fact, to pursue science rightly is to furnish the framework on which the spirit may rise.

Speech, 1953

Chomsky, Noam (1928–)
US linguist and political critic
As soon as questions of will or decision or reason or choice of action arise, human science is at a loss.

Television interview, 1978

Clarke, Arthur C. (1917–)
English writer
When a distinguished but elderly scientist states that something is possible, he is almost certainly

right. When he states that something is impossible, he is very probably wrong. (Clarke's First Law.).

> *The New Yorker*, 1969

Technology, sufficiently advanced, is indistinguishable from magic.

> *The Times*, 1996

Cook, Captain James (1728–1779)
English navigator
Following Cook's experiences with the natural historians on his second voyage

Curse the scientists, and all science into the bargain.

> In J.C. Beaglehole (ed.), *The Voyage of the Resolution* (1961)

Crick, Francis (1916–)
British biologist
On the discovery of the structure of DNA, 1953

We have discovered the secret of life!

> In Watson, *The Double Helix* (1968)

Cronenberg, David (1943–)
Canadian film director

A virus is only doing its job.

> *Sunday Telegraph*, 1992

Curie, Marie (1867–1934)
Polish-born French physicist

After all, science is essentially international, and it is only through lack of the historical sense that national qualities have been attributed to it.

> *Memorandum*, 'Intellectual Co-operation'

Dagg, Fred (1948–)
Australian writer, actor and broadcaster

I can see … why a man who lives in Colorado is so anxious for all this nuclear activity to go on in Australia, an area famed among nuclear scientists for its lack of immediate proximity to their own residential areas.

> *Dagshead Revisited* (1989)

Dürrenmatt, Friedrich (1921–1990)
Swiss dramatist and writer

Unsere Wissenschaft ist schrecklich geworden, unsere Forschung gefährlich, unsere Erkenntnis tödlich.
Our science has become terrible, our research dangerous, our knowledge fatal.

> *The Physicists* (1962)

Eddington, Sir Arthur (1882–1944)
English astronomer, physicist and mathematician

We used to think that if we knew one, we knew two, because one and one are two. We are finding that we must learn a great deal more about 'and'.

> In Mackay, *The Harvest of a Quiet Eye* (1977)

Science is an edged tool, with which men play

like children, and cut their own fingers.

> Attr.

Einstein, Albert (1879–1955)
German-born US mathematical physicist

Why does this magnificent applied science which saves work and makes life easier bring us so little happiness? The simple answer runs: Because we have not yet learned to make sensible use of it.

> Address, California Institute of Technology, 1931

Science without religion is lame, religion without science is blind.

> *Science, Philosophy and Religion: a Symposium* (1941)

A theory can be proved by experiment; but no path leads from experiment to the birth of a theory.

> In Mackay, *The Harvest of a Quiet Eye* (1977)

When a man sits with a pretty girl for an hour, it seems like a minute. But let him sit on a hot stove for a minute – and it's longer than any hour. That's relativity.

> Attr.

Faraday, Michael (1791–1867)
English chemist and physicist
On his scientific research

It may be a weed instead of a fish that, after all my labour, I may at last pull up.

> Letter, 1831

Feyerabend, Paul (1924–1994)
Austrian philosopher

The time is overdue for adding the separation of state and science to the by now customary separation of state and church. Science is only one of the many instruments man has invented to cope with his surroundings. It is not the only one, it is not infallible, and it has become too powerful, too pushy, and too dangerous to be left on its own.

> *Against Method* (1975)

Haldane, J.B.S. (1892–1964)
British biochemist, geneticist and popularizer of science

Einstein – the greatest Jew since Jesus. I have no doubt that Einstein's name will still be remembered and revered when Lloyd George, Foch, and William Hohenzollern share with Charlie Chaplin that ineluctable oblivion which awaits the uncreative mind.

> *Daedalus or Science and the Future* (1924)

Heisenberg, Werner (1901–1976)
German theoretical physicist

Natural science does not simply describe and explain nature, it is part of the interplay between nature and ourselves.

> Attr.

Huxley, T.H. (1825–1895)
English biologist, Darwinist and agnostic
> The great tragedy of Science – the slaying of a beautiful hypothesis by an ugly fact.
>> *British Association Annual Report* (1870)

Jeans, Sir James Hopwood (1877–1946)
English mathematician, physicist and astronomer
> Science should leave off making pronouncements: the river of knowledge has too often turned back on itself.
>> *The Mysterious Universe* (1930)

Lamb, Charles (1775–1834)
English essayist, critic and letter writer
> In everything that relates to science, I am a whole Encyclopaedia behind the rest of the world.
>> *Essays of Elia* (1823)

Leary, Timothy (1920–1996)
US writer and psychologist
> Science is all metaphor.
>> Interview, 1980

Levin, Bernard (1928–)
British writer
> Those of our own-day scientists who stir the embers of fires that went out millions of years ago may believe their theories but can never know. It would be better for all of us if they said as much.
>> *The Times*, 1992

McCarthy, Mary (1912–1989)
US writer and critic
> In science, all facts, no matter how trivial or banal, enjoy democratic equality.
>> Attr.

Medawar, Sir Peter (1915–1987)
British zoologist and immunologist
> Scientific discovery is a private event, and the delight that accompanies it, or the despair of finding it illusory does not travel.
>> *Hypothesis and Imagination*

Montaigne, Michel de (1533–1592)
French essayist and moralist
> Science without conscience is but death of the soul.
>> In Simcox, *Treasury of Quotations on Christian Themes*

Needham, Joseph (1900–1995)
British biochemist
> *Laboratorium est oratorium.*
> The place where we do our scientific work is a place of prayer.
>> In Alan L. Mackay, *The Harvest of a Quiet Eye* (1977)

Newton, Sir Isaac (1642–1727)
English scientist and philosopher
> If I have seen further it is by standing on the shoulders of giants.
>> Letter to Robert Hooke, 1675–76

Oppenheimer, J. Robert (1904–1967)
US nuclear physicist
On the consequences of the first atomic test
> The physicists have known sin; and this is a knowledge which they cannot lose.
>> Lecture, 1947

Pasteur, Louis (1822–1895)
French chemist, bacteriologist and immunologist
> *Il n'existe pas de sciences appliquées, mais seulement des applications de la science.*
> There are no applied sciences, only applications of science.
>> Address, 1872

> *Dans les champs de l'observation, l'hasard ne favorise que les esprits préparés.*
> In the field of observation, chance favours only the prepared mind.
>> Lecture, 1854

Peacock, Thomas Love (1785–1866)
English writer and poet
> I almost think it is the ultimate destiny of science to exterminate the human race.
>> *Gryll Grange* (1861)

Pirsig, Robert (1928–)
US author
> Traditional scientific method had always been at the very best, 20-20 hindsight. It's good for seeing where you've been.
>> *Zen and the Art of Motorcycle Maintenance* (1974)

Popper, Sir Karl (1902–1994)
Austrian-born British philosopher
> Science must begin with myths, and with the criticism of myths.
>> In C.A. Mace (ed.), *British Philosophy in the Mid-Century* (1957)

> Science may be described as the art of systematic oversimplification.
>> *The Observer*, 1982

Porter, Sir George (1920–)
English chemist
> Should we force science down the throats of those that have no taste for it? Is it our duty to drag them kicking and screaming into the twenty-first century? I am afraid that it is.
>> Speech, 1986

Roux, Joseph (1834–1886)
French priest and epigrammatist
> Science is for those who learn; poetry, for those who know.
>> *Meditations of a Parish Priest* (1886)

Ruskin, John (1819–1900)
English art critic, philosopher and reformer
> The work of science is to substitute facts for appearances, and demonstration for impressions.
>> *The Stones of Venice* (1851)

Salk, Jonas (1914–1995)
US virologist
On being asked who owned the patent on his antipolio vaccine
> The people – could you patent the sun?
>> Attr.

Santayana, George (1863–1952)
Spanish-born US philosopher and writer
> If all the arts aspire to the condition of music, all the sciences aspire to the condition of mathematics.
>> *The Observer*, 1928

Smith, Sydney (1771–1845)
English clergyman, essayist, journalist and wit
Of William Whewell
> Science is his forte and omniscience is his foible.
>> In Isaac Todhunter, *William Whewell* (1876)

Snow, C.P. (1905–1980)
English writer, critic, physicist and public administrator
> A good many times I have been present at gatherings of people who, by the standards of the traditional culture, are thought highly educated and who have with considerable gusto been expressing their incredulity at the illiteracy of scientists. Once or twice I have been provoked and have asked the company how many of them could describe the Second Law of Thermodynamics. The response was cold: it was also negative.
>> *The Two Cultures and the Scientific Revolution* (1959)

Spencer, Herbert (1820–1903)
English philosopher and journalist
> Science is organized knowledge.
>> *Education* (1861)

Stenhouse, David (1932–)
English-born New Zealand zoologist and educationist
On the conservation of biological resources
> I know a man who has a device for converting solar energy into food. Delicious stuff he makes with it, too. Being doing it for years … It's called a farm.
>> *Crisis in Abundance* (1966)

Suzuki, David (1936–)
Japanese Buddhist scholar and main interpreter of Zen to the West
> Science is really in the business of disproving its current models or changing them to conform to new information. In essence, we are constantly

proving our latest ideas are wrong.
>> *Metamorphosis: Stages in a Life* (1987)

Szent-Györgyi, Albert von (1893–1986)
Hungarian-born US biochemist
> Discovery consists of seeing what everybody has seen and thinking what nobody has thought.
>> In Good (ed.), *The Scientist Speculates* (1962)

Tolstoy, Leo (1828–1910)
Russian writer, essayist, philosopher and moralist
> The highest wisdom has but one science – the science of the whole – and science explaining the whole creation and man's place in it.
>> *War and Peace* (1868–1869)

Valéry, Paul (1871–1945)
French poet, mathematician and philosopher
> *Il faut n'appeler 'Science' que l'ensemble des recettes qui réussissent toujours. – Tout le reste est littérature.*
> The term Science should only be given to the collection of the recipes that are always successful. All the rest is literature.
>> *Moralities*, 1932

Veblen, Thorstein (1857–1929)
US economist and sociologist
> The outcome of any serious research can only be to make two questions grow where only one grew before.
>> *The Place of Science in Modern Civilization* (1919)

▶▶ CULTURE; DISCOVERY; MATHEMATICS; NATURE; PROGRESS; TECHNOLOGY

scotland

Barrie, Sir J.M. (1860–1937)
Scottish dramatist and writer
> You've forgotten the grandest moral attribute of a Scotsman, Maggie, that he'll do nothing which might damage his career.
>> *What Every Woman Knows* (1908)

> There are few more impressive sights in the world than a Scotsman on the make.
>> *What Every Woman Knows* (1908)

Boorde, Andrew (c.1490–1549)
English traveller, physician and writer
> Trust your no Skott.
>> Letter to Thomas Cromwell, 1536

> The devellysche dysposicion of a Scottysh man, not to love nor favour an Englishe man.
>> Letter to Thomas Cromwell, 1536

Burns, Robert (1759–1796)
Scottish poet and song writer
> My heart's in the Highlands, my heart is not here,

My heart's in the Highlands a-chasing the deer,
A-chasing the wild deer and following the roe –
My heart's in the Highlands, wherever I go!

'My Heart's in the Highlands' (1790)

The story of Wallace poured a Scottish prejudice in my veins which will boil along there till the flood-gates of life shut in eternal rest.

Letter to Dr Moore, 1787

Cleveland, John (1613–1658)
English poet

Had Cain been Scot, God would have changed his doom,
Nor forced him wander, but confined him home.

'The Rebel Scot' (1647)

Connery, Sean (1930–)
Scottish actor

Scotland should be nothing less than equal with all the other nations of the world.

The Times, 1999

Ewart, Gavin (1916–1995)
English poet

The Irish are great talkers
Persuasive and disarming,
You can say lots and lots
Against the Scots –
But at least they're never charming!

The Complete Little Ones (1986)

Fawkes, Guy (1570–1606)
English conspirator

On being asked by the King whether he regretted his proposed plot against Parliament and the royal family

A desperate disease requires a dangerous remedy … one of my objects was to blow the Scots back again into Scotland.

Dictionary of National Biography

Forsyth, Michael (1954–)
Scottish Conservative politician

Attacking Scottish National Party policy on Europe

It is difficult to imagine how, if Scotland's identity is stifled as a nation of five million in an economic and monetary union of 58 million, it will somehow have more influence, more authority and more status in a European Union of 371 million.

Speech, 1999

Freed, Arthur (1894–1973)
US film producer and songwriter

Defending his decision to produce Brigadoon on the MGM lot

I went to Scotland and found nothing there that looks like Scotland.

In Halliwell, The Filmgoer's Book of Quotes (1973)

Galt, John (1779–1839)
Scottish writer and Canadian pioneer

From the lone shieling of the misty island

Mountains divide us, and the waste of seas –
Yet still the blood is strong, the heart is Highland,
And we in dreams behold the Hebrides!
Fair these broad meads, these hoary woods are grand;
But we are exiles from our fathers' land.

Attr. in Blackwoods Edinburgh Magazine, 1829

Lappin, Tom

Glasgow is not a melting pot; it's closer to a chip pan in which you've attempted to boil cream, the ingredients have separated, and neither element is palatable.

The Scotsman, 1999

Halliday, J. (1790–1867)

As sure as I'm a Scot
A redshank Norland haggis-eater.

Rustic Bard, quoted in F. Marian McNeill, The Scots Kitchen (1929)

Hamilton, Ian (1925–)
Lawyer and Scottish Nationalist

On the performance of Scottish National Party MPs in Westminster

Courage is a quality Scots lack only when they become MPs. They should be twisting the lion's tail until it comes out by the roots.

Daily Mail, 1996

Jenkins, Robin (1912–)
Scottish novelist

Football has taken the place of religion in Scotland.

A Would-Be Saint

Johnson, Samuel (1709–1784)
English lexicographer, poet, critic, conversationalist and essayist

I know not whether it be not peculiar to the Scots to have attained the liberal without the manual arts, to have excelled in ornamental knowledge, and to have wanted not only the elegancies, but the conveniences of common life.

A Journey to the Western Islands of Scotland (1775)

Boswell: I do indeed come from Scotland, but I cannot help it …
Johnson: That, Sir, I find, is what a very great many of your countrymen cannot help.

In Boswell, The Life of Samuel Johnson (1791)

Of the Scots

Their learning is like bread in a besieged town: every man gets a little, but no man gets a full meal.

In Boswell, The Life of Samuel Johnson (1791)

Oats. A grain, which in England is generally

given to horses, but in Scotland supports the people.

> *A Dictionary of the English Language* (1755)

Norway, too, has noble wild prospects; and Lapland is remarkable for prodigious noble wild prospects. But, Sir, let me tell you, the noblest prospect which a Scotchman ever sees, is the high road that leads him to England!

> In Boswell, *The Life of Samuel Johnson* (1791)

Much may be made of a Scotchman, if he be caught young.

> In Boswell, *The Life of Samuel Johnson* (1791)

Seeing Scotland, Madam, is only seeing a worse England. It is seeing the flower fade away to the naked stalk.

> In Boswell, *The Life of Samuel Johnson* (1791)

Joyce, James (1882–1941)
Irish writer

> Poor sister Scotland!
> Her doom is fell.
> She cannot find any more Stuarts to sell.
>
> *Chamber Music* (1907)

Keillor, Garrison (1942–)
US writer and broadcaster

> Lutherans are like Scottish people, only with less frivolity.
>
> *The Independent*, 1992

Lamb, Charles (1775–1834)
English essayist, critic and letter writer

> I have been trying all my life to like Scotchmen, and am obliged to desist from the experiment in despair.
>
> 'Imperfect Sympathies' (1823)

Leacock, Stephen (1869–1944)
English-born Canadian humorist, writer and economist
Of the Scots

> Having little else to cultivate, they cultivated the intellect. The export of brains came to be their chief item of commerce.
>
> *Humour* (1935)

Lincoln, Mary Todd (1818–1882)
Wife of US President Abraham Lincoln

> Beautiful, glorious Scotland, has spoilt me for every other country!
>
> Letter, 1869 in *The Mary Lincoln Letters* (1956)

Linklater, Eric (1899–1974)
Welsh-born Scottish writer and satirist

> While swordless Scotland, sadder than its psalms,
> Fosters its sober youth on national alms
> To breed a dull provincial discipline,
> Commerce its god and golf its anodyne.
>
> 'Preamble to a Satire'

Lockier, Francis (1667–1740)
English churchman

> In all my travels I have never met with any one Scotchman but what was a man of sense. I believe everybody of that country that has any, leaves it as fast as they can.
>
> In Spence, *Anecdotes* (1858)

MacDiarmid, Hugh (1892–1978)
Scottish poet

> A Scottish poet maun assume
> The burden o' his people's doom,
> And dee to brak' their livin' tomb.
>
> *A Drunk Man Looks at the Thistle* (1926)

> It's easier to lo'e Prince Charlie
> Than Scotland – mair's the shame!
>
> 'Bonnie Prince Charlie' (1930)

> The rose of all the world is not for me
> I want for my part
> Only the little white rose of Scotland
> That smells sharp and sweet – and breaks the heart.
>
> 'The Little White Rose'

Maugham, William Somerset (1874–1965)
English writer, dramatist and physician

> Scotchmen seem to think it's a credit to them to be Scotch.
>
> *A Writer's Notebook* (1949)

Nash, Ogden (1902–1971)
US poet

> No McTavish
> Was ever lavish.
>
> 'Genealogical Reflection' (1931)

Nicholson, Emma
British Liberal Democrat MEP

> England treats Scotland as if it was an island off the coast of West Africa in the 1830s.
>
> *Daily Mail*, 1996

North, Christopher (1785–1854)
Scottish poet, writer, editor and critic

> Minds like ours, my dear James, must always be above national prejudices, and in all companies it gives me true pleasure to declare, that, as a people, the English are very little indeed inferior to the Scotch.
>
> *Blackwood's Edinburgh Magazine*, 1826

Ogilvy, James (1663–1730)
Scottish politician and lawyer
On signing the Act of Union

> Now there's an end of ane old song.
>
> Remark, 1707

Piccolomini, Enea (1405–1464)
Pope 1458–64
Comment after a visit to Scotland in 1435

There is nothing the Scots like better to hear than abuse of the English.

Attr.

Ramsay, Allan (1686–1758)
> A Scots mist will weet an Englishman to the skin.
>> *A Collection of Scots Proverbs* (1737)

Robertson, Pat (1930–)
US fundamentalist Christian broadcaster and politician
> In Europe the big word is tolerance. Homosexuals are riding high in the media … and in Scotland, you can't believe how strong the homosexuals are.
>> *The Guardian*, 1999

Salmond, Alex (1955–)
Scottish nationalist politician
> There is not an anti-English bone in my body. I have forgotten more about English history than most Tory MPs ever learned.
>> *The Observer*, 1998

Scott, Sir Walter (1771–1832)
Scottish writer and historian
> O Caledonia! stern and wild,
> Meet nurse for a poetic child!
> Land of brown heath and shaggy wood,
> Land of the mountain and the flood,
> Land of my sires! what mortal hand
> Can e'er untie the filial band,
> That knits me to thy rugged strand!
>> *The Lay of the Last Minstrel* (1805)

> Still from the sire the son shall hear
> Of the stern strife, and carnage drear,
> Of Flodden's fatal field,
> Where shiver'd was fair Scotland's spear,
> And broken was her shield!
>> *Marmion* (1808)

Comment on the Union of Scotland with England in 1707
> We have become the caterpillars of the island, instead of its pillars.
>> Letter to the Editor of *The Edinburgh Weekly Journal*, 1826

Smith, Sydney (1771–1845)
English clergyman, essayist, journalist and wit
> It requires a surgical operation to get a joke well into a Scotch understanding. Their only idea of wit … is laughing immoderately at stated intervals.
>> In Holland, *A Memoir of the Reverend Sydney Smith* (1855)

Of Scotland
> That knuckle-end of England – that land of Calvin, oat-cakes, and sulphur.
>> In Holland, *A Memoir of the Reverend Sydney Smith* (1855)

Smollett, Tobias (1721–1771)
Scottish writer, satirist, historian, traveller and physician

The Scots have a slight tincture of letters, with which they make a parade among people who are more illiterate than themselves; but they may be said to float on the surface of science, and they have made very small advances in the useful arts.

Humphry Clinker (1771)

Vincent, John
English historian and journalist
On the falling birth rate in Scotland
> The Scottish people will one day become extinct.
>> *The Observer*, 1998

Witzel, Jean-Luc
Comment before a France–Scotland football match
> In Scotland – well, you know what the Scots are like. They booze, they smoke and they eat anything that comes to hand.
>> *Attr.*

Wodehouse, P.G. (1881–1975)
English humorist and writer
> It is never difficult to distinguish between a Scotsman with a grievance and a ray of sunshine.
>> *Blandings Castle and Elsewhere* (1935)

the sea

Aeschylus (525–456 BC)
Greek dramatist and poet
> The ceaseless twinkling laughter of the waves of the sea.
>> *Prometheus Bound*

Arnold, Matthew (1822–1888)
English poet, critic, essayist and educationist
> The sea is calm to-night,
> The tide is full, the moon lies fair
> Upon the straits.
>> 'Dover Beach' (1867)

> Sand-strewn caverns, cool and deep,
> Where the winds are all asleep;
> Where the spent lights quiver and gleam;
> Where the salt weed sways in the stream;
> Where the sea-beasts ranged all round
> Feed in the ooze of their pasture-ground…
> Where great whales come sailing by,
> Sail and sail, with unshut eye,
> Round the world for ever and aye.
>> 'The Forsaken Merman' (1849)

Belloc, Hilaire (1870–1953)
English writer of verse, essayist and critic; Liberal MP
> Everywhere, the sea is a teacher of truth. I am not sure that the best thing I find in sailing is not this salt of reality … There, sailing the sea, we

play every part of life: control, direction, effort, fate; and there can we test ourselves and know our state.

Quoted by Libby Purves, The Times, 1998

The Bible (King James Version)

They that go down to the sea in ships, that do business in great waters;
These see the works of the Lord, and his wonders in the deep.

Psalms, 107:23–24

Bridges, Robert (1844–1930)

English poet, dramatist, essayist and doctor

Whither, O splendid ship, thy white sails crowding,
Leaning across the bosom of the urgent West,
That fearest not sea rising, nor sky clouding,
Whither away, fair rover, and what thy quest?

'A Passer-by' (1890)

Byron, Lord (1788–1824)

English poet satirist and traveller

Roll on, thou deep and dark blue Ocean – roll!
Ten thousand fleets sweep over thee in vain;
Man marks the earth with ruin – his control
Stops with the shore.

Childe Harold's Pilgrimage (1818)

Dark-heaving – boundless, endless, and sublime,
The image of eternity.

Childe Harold's Pilgrimage (1818)

Campbell, Alistair Te Ariki (1925–)

New Zealand poet

Now it is water I dream of,
… lifting
casually on a shore
where yellow lions come out
in the early morning
and stare out to sea.

Collected Poems 1947–1981 (1981)

Carpenter, Joseph Edwards (1813–1885)

What are the wild waves saying
Sister, the whole day long,
That ever amid our playing,
I hear but their low lone song?

'What are the Wild Waves Saying' (song, 1850)

Carson, Rachel Louise (1907–1964)

US marine biologist and writer

In its mysterious past, it encompasses all the dim origins of life and receives in the end … the dead husks of that same life. For all at last return to the sea – to Oceanus, the ocean river, like the ever-flowing stream of time, the beginning and the end.

The Sea Around Us (1951)

Chopin, Kate (1851–1904)

US writer

The voice of the sea speaks to the soul. The touch of the sea is sensuous, enfolding the body in its soft, close embrace.

The Awakening (1899)

Clayton, Keith (1928–)

Professor of Environmental Sciences

Of sewage

You can do far worse than putting it into a deep and well-flushed sea. As far as poisoning the fish is concerned, that's rubbish. The sewage has probably kept the poor fish alive.

The Times, 1992

Coleridge, Samuel Taylor (1772–1834)

English poet, philosopher and critic

The fair breeze blew, the white foam flew,
The furrow followed free;
We were the first that ever burst
Into that silent sea.

'The Rime of the Ancient Mariner' (1798)

As idle as a painted ship
Upon a painted ocean.

'The Rime of the Ancient Mariner' (1798)

Water, water, every where,
And all the boards did shrink;
Water, water, every where
Nor any drop to drink.

'The Rime of the Ancient Mariner' (1798)

Conrad, Joseph (1857–1924)

Polish-born British writer, sailor and explorer

This could have occurred nowhere but in England, where men and sea interpenetrate, so to speak.

Youth (1902)

Cunningham, Allan (1784–1842)

Scottish poet, reporter and biographer

A wet sheet and a flowing sea,
A wind that follows fast
And fills the white and rustling sail
And bends the gallant mast …

'A Wet Sheet and a Flowing Sea' (1825)

Dekker, Thomas (c.1570–c.1632)

English dramatist

That great fishpond (the sea).

The Honest Whore (1604)

Dickens, Charles (1812–1870)

English writer

I want to know what it says … The sea, Floy, what it is that it keeps on saying?

Dombey and Son (1848)

'People can't die, along the coast,' said Mr Peggotty, 'except when the tide's pretty nigh out. They can't be born, unless it's pretty nigh in – not properly born, till flood. He's a going out with the tide.'

David Copperfield (1850)

Donne, John (1572–1631)
English poet
> The sea is as deepe in a calme as in a storme.
>> *Sermons*

Flecker, James Elroy (1884–1915)
English poet, orientalist and translator
> The dragon-green, the luminous, the dark, the serpent-haunted sea.
>> *The Golden Journey to Samarkand* (1913)

> A ship, an isle, a sickle moon –
> With few but with how splendid stars
> The mirrors of the sea are strewn
> Between their silver bars.
>> *The Golden Journey to Samarkand* (1913)

Homer (fl. c.8th century BC)
Greek epic poet
> The wine-dark sea.
>> *Iliad*

Joyce, James (1882–1941)
Irish writer
> The snotgreen sea. The scrotumtightening sea.
>> *Ulysses* (1922)

Keats, John (1795–1821)
English poet
> It keeps eternal whisperings around
> Desolate shores, and with its mighty swell
> Gluts twice ten thousand caverns.
>> 'On the Sea' (1817)

Kipling, Rudyard (1865–1936)
Indian-born British poet and writer
> What is a woman that you forsake her,
> And the hearth-fire and the home-acre,
> To go with the old grey Widow-maker?
>> 'Harp Song of the Dane Women' (1906)

> Oh, was there ever sailor free to choose,
> That didn't settle somewhere near the sea?
>> *The Years Between* (1919)

Longfellow, Henry Wadsworth (1807–1882)
US poet and writer
> 'Wouldst thou' – so the helmsman answered –
> 'Learn the secret of the sea?
> Only those who brave its dangers
> Comprehend its mystery!'.
>> 'The Secret of the Sea' (1904)

Masefield, John (1878–1967)
English poet, writer and critic
> I must go down to the seas again, to the lonely sea and the sky,
> And all I ask is a tall ship and a star to steer her by,
> And the wheel's kick and the wind's song and the white sail's shaking,
> And a grey mist on the sea's face and a grey dawn breaking …

> I must go down to the seas again, for the call of the running tide
> Is a wild call and a clear call that may not be denied …

> I must go down to the seas again, to the vagrant gypsy life,
> To the gull's way and the whale's way where the wind's like a whetted knife;
> And all I ask is a merry yarn from a laughing fellow rover,
> And a quiet sleep and a sweet dream when the long trick's over.
>> 'Sea Fever' (1902)

Parker, Martin (c.1600–c.1656)
English ballad writer
> You gentlemen of England
> Who live at home at ease,
> How little do you think
> On the dangers of the seas.
>> In J.O. Halliwell (ed.), *Early Naval Ballads* (1841), 'The Valiant Sailors'

Rimbaud, Arthur (1854–1891)
French poet
> *Je me suis baigné dans le Poème*
> *De la Mer, infusé d'astres, et lactescent,*
> *Dévorant les azurs verts.*
> I have bathed in the Poem
> Of the Sea, steeped in stars, milky,
> Devouring the green azures.
>> 'Le Bâteau ivre' (1870)

Rossetti, Dante Gabriel (1828–1882)
English poet, painter, translator and letter-writer
> The sea hath no king but God alone.
>> 'The White Ship'

Scott, Sir Walter (1771–1832)
Scottish writer and historian
> It's no fish ye're buying – it's men's lives.
>> *The Antiquary* (1816)

Swinburne, Algernon Charles (1837–1909)
English poet, critic, dramatist and letter writer
> I will go back to the great sweet mother,
> Mother and lover of men, the sea.
> I will go down to her, I and no other,
> Close with her, kiss her and mix her with me …
> I shall sleep, and move with the moving ships,
> Change as the winds change, veer in the tide;
> My lips will feast on the foam of thy lips,
> I shall rise with thy rising and with thee subside.
>> 'The Triumph of Time' (1866)

Synge, J.M. (1871–1909)
Irish dramatist, poet and letter writer
> 'A man who is not afraid of the sea will soon be drownded,' he said, 'for he will be going out on

a day he shouldn't. But we do be afraid of the sea, and we do only be drownded now and again.'

The Aran Islands (1907)

Uvavnuk
Inuit singer and shaman
    The great sea
    Has set me adrift
    It moves me as the weed in the river,
    Earth and the great weather
    Move me,
    Have carried me away
    And move my inward parts with joy.

In Rasmussen, *Intellectual Culture of the Igulik Eskimos* (1929)

Villiers, Alan John (1903–1982)
Australian naval commander
    Only fools and passengers drink at sea.

The Observer, 1957

Whiting, William (1825–1878)
English teacher, poet and hymn writer
    Eternal Father, strong to save,
    Whose arm hath bound the restless wave,
    … O hear us when we cry to Thee
    For those in peril on the sea.

Hymn, 1869

Xenophon (c.430–354 BC)
Greek historian, essayist and military commander
The joyful cry of his soldiers after their long march (1000 miles) back to the Aegean from the centre of Persia
    The sea! The sea!

Anabasis

▶▶ NAVY

the seasons

Adams, Richard (1920–)
English writer
    Many human beings say that they enjoy the winter, but what they really enjoy is feeling proof against it.

Watership Down (1974)

Andrewes, Bishop Lancelot (1555–1626)
English churchman
    It was no summer progress. A cold coming they had of it, at this time of the year; just, the worst time of the year, to take a journey, and specially a long journey, in. The ways deep, the weather sharp, the days short, the sun farthest off in *solstitio brumali*, the very dead of Winter.

Sermon 15, Of the Nativity (1629)

The Bible (King James Version)
    For, lo, the winter is past, the rain is over and gone;
    The flowers appear on the earth; the time of the singing of birds is come, and the voice of the turtle is heard in our land.

Song of Solomon, 2:11–12

Campion, Thomas (1567–1620)
English poet
    The Summer hath his joyes,
    And Winter his delights;
    Though Love and all his pleasures are but toyes,
    They shorten tedious nights.

The Third Booke of Ayres (1617)

Catullus (84–c.54 BC)
Roman poet
    Iam ver egelidos refert tepores.
    Now Spring brings back her gentle warmth.

Carmina

Coleridge, Samuel Taylor (1772–1834)
English poet, philosopher and critic
    Therefore all seasons shall be sweet to thee,
    Whether the summer clothe the general earth
    With greenness, or the redbreast sit and sing
    Betwixt the tufts of snow on the bare branch
    Of mossy apple-tree, while the nigh thatch
    Smokes in the sun-thaw; whether the eave-drops fall
    Heard only in the trances of the blast,
    Or if the secret ministry of frost
    Shall hang them up in silent icicles,
    Quietly shining to the quiet moon.

'Frost at Midnight' (1798)

    Summer has set in with its usual severity.

Letters of Charles Lamb (1888)

Cowper, William (1731–1800)
English poet, hymn and letter writer
    Our severest winter, commonly called the spring.

Letter to the Rev. W. Unwin, 1783

Holmes, Oliver Wendell (1809–1894)
US physician, poet, writer and scientist
    For him in vain the envious seasons roll
    Who bears eternal summer in his soul.

'The Old Player' (1861)

Hood, Thomas (1799–1845)
English poet, editor and humorist
    I saw old Autumn in the misty morn
    Stand shadowless like Silence, listening
    To silence.

'Ode: Autumn' (1823)

    No sun – no moon!
    No morn – no noon
    No dawn – no dusk – no proper time of day –
    No warmth, no cheerfulness, no healthful ease,
    No comfortable feel in any member –
    No shade, no shine, no butterflies, no bees,

No fruits, no flowers, no leaves, no birds, –
November!

Whimsicalities (1844), 'No!'

James I of Scotland (1394–1437)
King of Scotland

Worshippe, ye that loveris been, this May,
For of your blisse the Kalendis are begun,
And sing with us, away, Winter, away!
Come, Summer, come the sweet seasoun and
sun.

The Kingis Quair

Keats, John (1795–1821)
English poet

Four seasons fill the measure of the year;
There are four seasons in the mind of man.

'The Human Seasons' (1818)

Where are the songs of Spring? Ay, where are
they?
Think not of them, thou hast thy music too.

'To Autumn' (1819)

Kipling, Rudyard (1865–1936)
Indian-born British poet and writer

No one thinks of winter when the grass is green!

Rewards and Fairies (1910), 'A St Helena Lullaby'

Langland, William (c.1330–c.1400)
English poet

In a somer seson whan soft was the sonne.

The Vision of William Concerning Piers the Plowman

Nabokov, Vladimir (1899–1977)
Russian-born US writer, poet, translator and critic

Yes, I was right, spring and summer did happen
in Cambridge almost every year (that mysterious
'almost' was singularly pleasing).

The Real Life of Sebastian Knight
(1941)

Ransom, John Crowe (1888–1974)
US poet and critic

Two evils, monstrous either one apart,
Possessed me, and were long and loath at
going:
A cry of Absence, Absence, in the heart,
And in the wood the furious winter blowing –

Dear love, these fingers that had known your
touch,
And tied our separate forces first together,
Were ten poor idiot fingers not worth much,
Ten frozen parsnips hanging in the weather.

'Winter Remembered' (1945)

Rilke, Rainer Maria (1875–1926)
Austrian poet, born in Prague

Frühling ist wiedergekommen. Die Erde
ist wie ein Kind, das Gedichte weiss.
Spring has come again. The earth is like a child

who knows poems.

The Sonnets to Orpheus (1923)

Rossetti, Christina (1830–1894)
English poet

In the bleak mid-winter
Frosty wind made moan,
Earth stood hard as iron,
Water like a stone;
Snow had fallen, snow on snow,
Snow on snow,
In the bleak mid-winter,
Long ago.

'A Christmas Carol' (1875)

Santayana, George (1863–1952)
Spanish-born US philosopher and writer

To be interested in the changing seasons is, in
this middling zone, a happier state of mind than
to be hopelessly in love with spring.

Little Essays (1920)

Shakespeare, William (1564–1616)
English dramatist, poet and actor

At Christmas I no more desire a rose
Than wish a snow in May's new-fangled shows;
But like of each thing that in season grows.

Love's Labour's Lost, I.i

Shall I compare thee to a summer's day?
Thou art more lovely and more temperate.
Rough winds do shake the darling buds of May,
And summer's lease hath all too short a date.

Sonnet 18

Spenser, Edmund (c.1522–1599)
English poet

Fresh spring the herald of love's mighty king,
In whose cote armour richly are displayd
All sorts of flowers the which on earth do spring
In goodly colours gloriously arrayd.

Amoretti, and Epithalamion (1595),
Sonnet 70

Thompson, Francis (1859–1907)
English poet

Spring is come home with her world-wandering
feet.
And all things are made young with young
desires …

Let even the slug-abed snail upon the thorn
Put forth a conscious horn!

'From the Night of Forebeing' (1913)

Trollope, Anthony (1815–1882)
English writer, traveller and post office official

The comic almanacs give us dreadful pictures of
January and February; but, in truth, the months
which should be made to look gloomy in
England are March and April. Let no man boast
himself that he has got through the perils of

winter till at least the seventh of May.

Doctor Thorne (1858)

Tusser, Thomas (c.1524–1580)
English writer, poet and musician
Sweet April showers
Do spring May flowers.

Five Hundred Points of Good Husbandry (1557)

Walpole, Horace (1717–1797)
English writer and politician
The way to ensure summer in England is to have it framed and glazed in a comfortable room.

Letter to William Cole, 1774

▶▶ WEATHER

secrets

Acton, Lord (1834–1902)
English historian and moralist
Everything secret degenerates … nothing is safe that does not show how it can bear discussion and publicity.

Attr.

Adams, Franklin P. (1881–1960)
US writer, poet, translator and editor
Ninety-two percent of the stuff told you in confidence you couldn't get anyone else to listen to.

Attr.

Adler, Renata
US film critic and writer
No one ever confides a secret to one person only. No one destroys all copies of a document.

In Melissa Stein, The Wit & Wisdom of Women (1993)

Auden, W.H. (1907–1973)
English poet, essayist, critic, teacher and dramatist
At last the secret is out, as it always must come in the end,
The delicious story is ripe to tell to the intimate friend;
Over the tea-cups and in the square the tongue has its desire;
Still waters run deep, my dear, there's never smoke without fire …

For the clear voice suddenly singing, high up in the convent wall,
The scent of elder bushes, the sporting prints in the hall,
The croquet matches in summer, the handshake, the cough, the kiss,
There is always a wicked secret, a private reason for this.

Collected Poems, 1933–1938, 'Twelve Songs', VIII

Behn, Aphra (1640–1689)
English dramatist, writer, poet, translator and spy
Love ceases to be a pleasure, when it ceases to be a secret.

The Lover's Watch (1686)

Cervantes, Miguel de (1547–1616)
Spanish writer and dramatist
Mucho más dañan a las honras de las mujeres las desenvolturas y libertades públicas que las maldades secretas.
Brazenness and public liberties do much more harm to a woman's honour than secret wickedness.

Don Quixote (1615)

Clark, Alan (1928–1999)
British Conservative politician, historian and diarist
On being asked whether he had any embarrassing skeletons in the cupboard
Dear boy, I can hardly close the door.

The Observer, 1998

Congreve, William (1670–1729)
English dramatist
I know that's a secret, for it's whispered everywhere.

Love for Love (1695)

Crabbe, George (1754–1832)
English poet, clergyman, surgeon and botanist
Secrets with girls, like loaded guns with boys,
Are never valued till they make a noise.

Tales of the Hall (1819)

Dickens, Charles (1812–1870)
English writer
We never knows wot's hidden in each other's hearts; and if we had glass winders there, we'd need keep the shetters up, some on us, I do assure you!

Martin Chuzzlewit (1844)

Dryden, John (1631–1700)
English poet, satirist, dramatist and critic
For secrets are edged tools,
And must be kept from children and from fools.

Sir Martin Mar-All (1667)

Franklin, Benjamin (1706–1790)
US statesman, scientist, political critic and printer
Three may keep a secret, if two of them are dead.

Poor Richard's Almanac (1735)

Franks, Oliver, Baron (1905–1992)
English diplomat, lecturer and banker
It is a secret in the Oxford sense: you may tell it to only one person at a time.

Sunday Telegraph, 1977

Frost, Robert (1874–1963)
US poet

We dance round in a ring and suppose,
But the Secret sits in the middle and knows.

'The Secret Sits' (1942)

Haldeman, H.R. (1926–1993)
US President Nixon's Chief of Staff
Comment to John Dean on the Watergate affair, 1973

Once the toothpaste is out of the tube, it is
awfully hard to get it back in.

In Hearings Before the Select Committee on
Presidential Campaign Activities of US
Senate: Watergate and Related Activities
(1973)

Shakespeare, William (1564–1616)
English dramatist, poet and actor

But that I am forbid
To tell the secrets of my prison-house,
I could a tale unfold whose lightest word
Would harrow up thy soul, freeze thy young
blood,
Make thy two eyes, like stars, start from their
spheres,
Thy knotted and combined locks to part,
And each particular hair to stand an end,
Like quills upon the fretful porpentine.
But this eternal blazon must not be
To ears of flesh and blood. List, list, O, list!

Hamlet, I.v

Stephens, James (1882–1950)
Irish poet and writer

A secret is a weapon and a friend. Man is God's
secret, Power is man's secret, Sex is woman's
secret.

The Crock of Gold (1912)

Surtees, R.S. (1805–1864)
English writer

There is no secret so close as that between a
rider and his horse.

Mr Sponge's Sporting Tour (1853)

▶▶ GOSSIP

security

Mailer, Norman (1923–)
US writer

All the security around the American President is
just to make sure the man who shoots him gets
caught.

Sunday Telegraph, 1990

self

Arnold, Matthew (1822–1888)
English poet, critic, essayist and educationist

Resolve to be thyself; and know, that he,
Who finds himself, loses his misery!

'Self-Dependence' (1852)

Auden, W.H. (1907–1973)
English poet, essayist, critic, teacher and dramatist

Some thirty inches from my nose
The frontier of my Person goes,
And all the untilled air between
Is private pagus and demesne.
Stranger, unless with bedroom eyes
I beckon you to fraternize,
Beware of rudely crossing it;
I have no gun, but I can spit.

About the House, 'Prologue: the Birth of Architecture'

Aurelius, Marcus (121–180)
Roman emperor and Stoic philosopher

This whatever this is that I am is flesh and spirit,
and the ruling part.

Meditations

Bacon, Francis (1561–1626)
English philosopher, essayist, politician and courtier

It is a poor centre of a man's actions, himself.

'Of Wisdom for a Man's Self' (1625)

Barrie, Sir J.M. (1860–1937)
Scottish dramatist and writer

The tragedy of a man who has found himself
out.

What Every Woman Knows (1908)

Bhagavadgita
On the Self

He who considers this as a slayer or he who
thinks that this is slain, neither of these knows
the Truth. For it does not slay, nor is it slain.

Ch. II

Brontë, Emily (1818–1848)
English poet and writer

He is more myself than I am.

Wuthering Heights (1847)

Browne, Sir Thomas (1605–1682)
English physician, author and antiquary

There is another man within me, that's angry
with me, rebukes, commands, and dastards me.

Religio Medici (1643)

Burns, Robert (1759–1796)
Scottish poet and song writer

O wad some Power the giftie gie us
To see oursels as ithers see us!
It wad frae monie a blunder free us,
An' foolish notion:
What airs in dress an' gait wad lea'e us,
An' ev'n devotion!

'To a Louse' (1786)

Carlyle, Thomas (1795–1881)
Scottish historian, biographer, critic, and essayist

A certain inarticulate Self-consciousness dwells dimly in us … Hence, too, the folly of that impossible precept, Know thyself; till it be translated into this partially possible one, Know what thou canst work at.

Sartor Resartus (1834)

Chaplin, Charlie (1889–1977)
English comedian, film actor, director and satirist
You have to believe in yourself, that's the secret. Even when I was in the orphanage, when I was roaming the street trying to find enough to eat, even then I thought of myself as the greatest actor in the world. I had to feel the exuberance that comes from utter confidence in yourself. Without it, you go down to defeat.

My Autobiography (1964)

Cicero (106–43 BC)
Roman orator, statesman, essayist and letter writer
Mens cuiusque is est quisque.
The spirit is the true self.

De Republica

Compton-Burnett, Dame Ivy (1884–1969)
English novelist
'Know thyself' is a most superfluous direction. We can't avoid it. We can only hope that no one else knows.

A Family and a Fortune (1939)

Connolly, Cyril (1903–1974)
English literary editor, writer and critic
I have always disliked myself at any given moment; the total of such moments is my life.

Enemies of Promise (1938)

Emerson, Ralph Waldo (1803–1882)
US poet, essayist, transcendentalist and teacher
All sensible people are selfish, and nature is tugging at every contract to make the terms of it fair.

Conduct of Life (1860)

Fonteyn, Margot (1919–)
English dancer
The one important thing I have learned over the years is the difference between taking one's work seriously and taking one's self seriously. The first is imperative and the second is disastrous.

Margot Fonteyn: Autobiography (1976)

Goethe (1749–1832)
German poet, writer, dramatist and scientist
Ich kenne mich auch nicht und Gott soll mich auch davor behüten.
I do not know myself either, and may God protect me from that.

Gespräche mit Eckermann, 1829

Hillel, 'The Elder' (c.60 BC–c.10 AD)
If I am not for myself who is for me; and being for my own self what am I? If not now when?

In Taylor (ed.), Sayings of the Jewish Fathers (1877)

Huxley, Aldous (1894–1963)
English writer, poet and critic
There's only one corner of the universe you can be certain of improving, and that's your own self.

Time Must Have a Stop (1944)

Joad, C.E.M. (1891–1953)
English popularizer of philosophy
Whenever I look inside myself I am afraid.

The Observer, 1942

Kempis, Thomas à (c.1380–1471)
German mystic, monk and writer
Si non potes te talem facere qualem vis, quomodo poteris alium ad tuum habere beneplacitum?
If you cannot mould yourself to such as you would wish, how can you expect others to be entirely to your liking?

De Imitatione Christi (1892)

Humilis tui cognitio, certior via est ad Deum; quam profunda scientiae inquisitio.
The humble knowledge of thyself is a surer way to God than the deepest search after learning.

De Imitatione Christi (1892)

La Rochefoucauld (1613–1680)
French writer
On aime mieux dire du mal de soi-même que de n'en point parler.
One would rather speak ill of oneself than not speak of oneself at all.

Maximes (1678)

L'amour-propre est le plus grand de tous les flatteurs.
Self-love is the greatest flatterer of all.

Maximes (1678)

L'intérêt parle toutes sortes de langues, et joue toutes sortes de personnages, même celui de désintéressé.
Self-interest speaks every kind of language, and plays every role, even that of disinterestedness.

Maximes (1678)

Longfellow, Henry Wadsworth (1807–1882)
US poet and writer
Not in the clamour of the crowded street,
Not in the shouts and plaudits of the throng,
But in ourselves, are triumph and defeat.

'The Poets' (1876)

Lowell, James Russell (1819–1891)
US poet, editor, abolitionist and diplomat
He's been true to one party – an' thet is himself.

The Biglow Papers (1848)

SELF   636

McCarthy, Mary (1912–1989)
US writer and critic
> However much we reform our ways, grow a new self, we *are* our past; it lurks behind us, follows us, denounces us, tracks us down.
>> *Ideas and the Novel* (1980)

Mansfield, Katherine (1888–1923)
New Zealand writer
On human limitations
> To have the courage of your excess – to find the limit of yourself.
>> *Journal of Katherine Mansfield* (1954)

Marryat, Frederick (1792–1848)
English naval officer and writer
> We always took care of number one.
>> *Scenes and Adventures in the Life of Frank Mildmay* (1829)

Maugham, William Somerset (1874–1965)
English writer, dramatist and physician
> I recognize that I am made up of several persons and that the person that at the moment has the upper hand will inevitably give place to another. But which is the real one? All of them or none?
>> *A Writer's Notebook* (1949)

Molière (1622–1673)
French dramatist, actor and director
> *On doit se regarder soi-même un fort long temps,*
> *Avant que de songer à condamner les gens.*
> We should look long and carefully at ourselves before we consider judging others.
>> *Le Misanthrope* (1666)

Montaigne, Michel de (1533–1592)
French essayist and moralist
> *La plus grande chose du monde, c'est de savoir être à soi.*
> The greatest thing in the world is to know how to belong to oneself.
>> *Essais* (1580)

Pascal, Blaise (1623–1662)
French philosopher and scientist
> *Le moi est haïssable.*
> Self is hateful.
>> *Pensées* (1670)

Pinter, Harold (1930–)
English dramatist, poet and screenwriter
On being asked why he did not include a character representing himself in *The Birthday Party*
> I had – I have – nothing to say about myself, directly. I wouldn't know where to begin. Particularly since I often look at myself in the mirror and say 'Who the hell's that?'.
>> Attr.

Powell, Anthony (1905–2000)
English writer and critic
> He fell in love with himself at first sight and it is a passion to which he has always remained faithful. Self-love seems so often unrequited.
>> *The Acceptance World* (1955)

Proverb
> Every man for himself and the devil take the hindmost.

Rossetti, Dante Gabriel (1828–1882)
English poet, painter, translator and letter-writer
> I do not see them here; but after death
> God knows I know the faces I shall see,
> Each one a murdered self, with low last breath.
> 'I am thyself, – what hast thou done to me?'
> 'And I – and I – thyself', (lo! each one saith,)
> 'And thou thyself to all eternity!'.
>> *The House of Life*

Russell, Bertrand (1872–1970)
English philosopher, mathematician, essayist and social reformer
> Man is not a solitary animal, and so long as social life survives, self-realization cannot be the supreme principle of ethics.
>> *A History of Western Philosophy* (1946)

Shakespeare, William (1564–1616)
English dramatist, poet and actor
> This above all – to thine own self be true,
> And it must follow, as the night the day,
> Thou canst not then be false to any man.
>> *Hamlet*, I.iii

Shaw, George Bernard (1856–1950)
Irish socialist, writer, dramatist and critic
> It is easy – terribly easy – to shake a man's faith in himself. To take advantage of that to break a man's spirit is devil's work.
>> *Candida* (1898)

> Don't fuss, my dear, I'm not unhappy. I am enjoying the enormous freedom of having found myself out and got myself off my mind; it is the beginning of hope and the end of hypocrisy.
>> *On the Rocks*

Sitwell, Dame Edith (1887–1964)
English poet, anthologist, critic and biographer
> Why not be oneself? That is the whole secret of a successful appearance. If one is a greyhound, why try to look like a Pekingese?
>> 'Why I look the Way I do' (1955)

Tolstoy, Leo (1828–1910)
Russian writer, essayist, philosopher and moralist
> I am always with myself, and it is I who am my own tormentor.
>> *Memoirs of a Madman* (1943)

Trollope, Anthony (1815–1882)
English writer, traveller and post office official
> No man thinks there is much ado about nothing

when the ado is about himself.

The Bertrams (1859)

Never think that you're not good enough yourself. A man should never think that. My belief is that in life people will take you very much at your own reckoning.

The Small House at Allington (1864)

Twain, Mark (1835–1910)
US humorist, writer, journalist and lecturer
When people do not respect us we are sharply offended; yet deep down in his heart no man much respects himself.

Notebooks (1935)

White, Patrick (1912–1990)
English-born Australian writer and dramatist
I have never managed to escape being this thing, Myself.

The Eye of the Storm (1973)

Whitman, Walt (1819–1892)
US poet and writer
I celebrate myself, and sing myself,
And what I assume you shall assume …

'Song of Myself' (1855)

Behold, I do not give lectures or a little charity,
When I give I give myself.

'Song of Myself' (1855), 40

Wilde, Oscar (1854–1900)
Irish poet, dramatist, writer, critic and wit
Other people are quite dreadful. The only possible society is oneself.

An Ideal Husband (1895)

▶▶ APPEARANCE; PRIDE; VANITY

sentimentality

Carlyle, Thomas (1795–1881)
Scottish historian, biographer, critic, and essayist
The barrenest of all mortals is the sentimentalist.

Critical and Miscellaneous Essays (1839)

Greene, Graham (1904–1991)
English writer and dramatist
They had been corrupted by money, and he had been corrupted by sentiment. Sentiment was the more dangerous, because you couldn't name its price. A man open to bribes was to be relied upon below a certain figure, but sentiment might uncoil in the heart at a name, a photograph, even a smell remembered.

The Heart of the Matter (1948)

Jung, Carl Gustav (1875–1961)
Swiss psychiatrist and pupil of Freud
Sentimentality is a superstructure covering

brutality.

Reflections

Maugham, William Somerset (1874–1965)
English writer, dramatist and physician
Sentimentality is only sentiment that rubs you up the wrong way.

A Writer's Notebook (1949)

▶▶ FEELINGS

separation

Arnold, Matthew (1822–1888)
English poet, critic, essayist and educationist
A God, a God their severance ruled!
And bade betwixt their shores to be
The unplumb'd, salt, estranging sea.

'To Marguerite – Continued' (1852)

Bayly, Thomas Haynes (1797–1839)
English songwriter, writer and dramatist
Absence makes the heart grow fonder,
Isle of Beauty, Fare thee well!

'Isle of Beauty', song, 1830

Brennan, Christopher (1870–1932)
Australian poet
I am shut out of mine own heart
because my love is far from me.

'I Am Shut Out of Mine Own Heart' (1914)

Brooke, Rupert (1887–1915)
English poet
How that we've done our best and worst, and parted.

'The Busy Heart' (1913)

Bussy-Rabutin, Comte de (1618–1693)
French soldier and writer
L'absence est à l'amour ce qu'est au feu le vent; il éteint le petit, il allume le grand.
Absence is to love what the wind is to fire; it extinguishes the small, it kindles the great.

Histoire Amoureuse des Gaules (1665)

Cope, Wendy (1945–)
English poet
The day he moved out was terrible –
That evening she went through hell.
His absence wasn't a problem
But the corkscrew had gone as well.

'Loss' (1992)

Cornford, Frances Crofts (1886–1960)
English poet and translator
How long ago Hector took off his plume,
Not wanting that his little son should cry,
Then kissed his sad Andromache goodbye –
And now we three in Euston waiting-room.

'Parting in Wartime' (1948)

Cowper, William (1731–1800)
English poet, hymn and letter writer
> Absence from whom we love is worse than
> death.
>
> 'Hope, like the Short-lived Ray' (1791)

Dickinson, Emily (1830–1886)
US poet
> My life closed twice before its close –
> It yet remains to see
> If Immortality unveil
> A third event to me
>
> So huge, so hopeless to conceive
> As these that twice befell.
> Parting is all we know of heaven,
> And all we need of hell.
>
> 'My life closed twice before its close' (1896)

Donne, John (1572–1631)
English poet
> When I died last, and, Dear I die
> As often as from thee I go,
> Though it be but an hour ago,
> And Lovers' hours be full eternity.
>
> *Songs and Sonnets* (1611)

Drayton, Michael (1563–1631)
English poet
> Since there's no help, come let us kiss and part,
> Nay, I have done: you get no more of me,
> And I am glad, yea glad with all my heart,
> That thus so cleanly, I myself can free,
> Shake hands for ever, cancel all our vows,
> And when we meet at any time again,
> Be it not seen in either of our brows,
> That we one jot of former love retain;
> Now at the last gasp of love's latest breath,
> When his pulse failing, passion speechless lies,
> When faith is kneeling by his bed of death,
> And innocence is closing up his eyes,
> Now if thou wouldst, when all have given him
> over,
> From death to life, thou might'st him yet
> recover.
>
> 'Idea', 61 (1619)

Eliot, George (1819–1880)
English writer and poet
> In every parting there is an image of death.
>
> *Scenes of Clerical Life* (1858)

Gay, John (1685–1732)
English poet, dramatist and librettist
> O what pain it is to part!
>
> *The Beggar's Opera*
(1728)

Haraucourt, Edmond (1856–1941)
> *Partir c'est mourir un peu,*
> *C'est mourir à ce qu'on aime:*

> *On laisse un peu de soi-même*
> *En toute heure et dans tout lieu.*
> Leaving is dying a little,
> Dying to one's loves:
> One leaves behind a little of oneself
> At every moment, everywhere.
>
> *Seul* (1891)

Jago, Rev. Richard (1715–1781)
English poet
> With leaden foot time creeps along
> While Delia is away.
>
> *Absence*

Keats, John (1795–1821)
English poet
> I wish you could invent some means to make me
> at all happy without you. Every hour I am more
> and more concentrated in you; every thing else
> tastes like chaff in my Mouth.
>
> Letter to Fanny Brawne, 1820

Keppel, Lady Caroline (b. 1735)
> What's this dull town to me?
> Robin's not near.
> He whom I wished to see,
> Wished for to hear;
> Where's all the joy and mirth
> Made life a heaven on earth?
> O! they're all fled with thee,
> Robin Adair.
>
> 'Robin Adair' (c.1750)

King, Bishop Henry (1592–1669)
English royal chaplain; poet and sermonist
> We that did nothing study but the way
> To love each other, with which thoughts the day
> Rose with delight to us, and with them set,
> Must learn the hateful art, how to forget.
>
> 'The Surrender' (1651)

Maugham, William Somerset (1874–1965)
English writer, dramatist and physician
> When married people don't get on they can
> separate, but if they're not married it's
> impossible. It's a tie that only death can sever.
>
> *The Circle* (1921)

Patmore, Coventry (1823–1896)
English poet
> With all my will, but much against my heart,
> We two now part.
> My Very Dear,
> Our solace is, the sad road lies so clear.
> It needs no art,
> With faint, averted feet
> And many a tear,
> In our opposed paths to persevere.
>
> *The Unknown Eros* (1877)

> So, till to-morrow eve, my Own, adieu!
> Parting's well-paid with soon again to meet,

Soon in your arms to feel so small and sweet,
Sweet to myself that am so sweet to you!
The Unknown Eros (1877), 'The Azalea'

Pound, Ezra (1885–1972)
US poet

And if you ask how I regret that parting:
It is like the flowers falling at Spring's
end
Confused, whirled in a tangle.
What is the use of talking, and there is
no end of talking,
There is no end of things in the heart.
'Exile's Letter' (1915)

Proust, Marcel (1871–1922)
French writer and critic

It is seldom indeed that one parts on good
terms, because if one were on good terms one
would not part.
La Prisonnière (1923)

Rilke, Rainer Maria (1875–1926)
Austrian poet, born in Prague

So leben wir und nehmen immer Abschied.
And so we live and forever take our leave.
Duino Elegies (1923)

Rossetti, Christina (1830–1894)
English poet

Remember me when I am gone away,
Gone far away into the silent land …

Better by far you should forget and smile
Than you should remember and be sad.
'Remember' (1862)

Schopenhauer, Arthur (1788–1860)
German philosopher

*Jede Trennung gibt einen Vorschmack des Todes, – und
jedes Wiedersehen einen Vorschmack der
Auferstehung.*
Every separation gives a foretaste of death, –
and every reunion a foretaste of resurrection.
Parerga und Paralipomena (1851)

Shakespeare, William (1564–1616)
English dramatist, poet and actor

Parting is such sweet sorrow
That I shall say good night till it be morrow.
Romeo and Juliet, II.ii

Sterne, Laurence (1713–1768)
Irish-born English writer and clergyman

Every time I kiss thy hand to bid adieu, and
every absence which follows it, are preludes to
that eternal separation which we are shortly to
make.
Tristram Shandy (1759–1767)

Stevenson, Robert Louis (1850–1894)
Scottish writer, poet and essayist

But all that I could think of, in the darkness and
the cold,
Was that I was leaving home and my folks were
growing old.
Ballads (1890)

Swinburne, Algernon Charles (1837–1909)
English poet, critic, dramatist and letter writer

I remember the way we parted,
The day and the way we met;
You hoped we were both broken-hearted,
And knew we should both forget …

And the best and the worst of this is
That neither is most to blame,
If you have forgotten my kisses
And I have forgotten your name.
'An Interlude' (1866)

▶▶ ABSENCE

servants

Barham, Rev. Richard Harris (Thomas Ingoldsby) (1788–1845)
English clergyman and comic poet

A servant's too often a negligent elf;
– If it's business of consequence do it yourself!
The Ingoldsby Legends (1840–1847)

Belloc, Hilaire (1870–1953)
English writer of verse, essayist and critic; Liberal MP

In my opinion, Butlers ought
To know their place, and not to play
The Old Retainer night and day.
Cautionary Tales (1907)

Braxfield, Lord (1722–1799)
Scottish judge

To the butler who gave up his place because Lady Braxfield
was always scolding him

Lord! Ye've little to complain o': ye may be
thankfu' ye're no married to her.
In Cockburn, *Memorials* (1856)

Montaigne, Michel de (1533–1592)
French essayist and moralist

*Tel a été miraculeux au monde, auquel sa femme et son
valet n'ont rien vu de remarquable. Peu d'hommes ont
été admirés par leurs domestiques.*
Many a man has been a wonder to the world,
whose wife and valet have seen nothing in him
that was remarkable. Few men have been
admired by their servants.
Essais (1580)

Shakespeare, William (1564–1616)
English dramatist, poet and actor

Every good servant does not all commands.
Cymbeline, V.i

Shaw, George Bernard (1856–1950)
Irish socialist, writer, dramatist and critic
> When domestic servants are treated as human beings it is not worth while to keep them.
>> *Man and Superman* (1903)

Wodehouse, P.G. (1881–1975)
English humorist and writer
> Ice formed on the butler's upper slopes.
>> *Pigs Have Wings* (1952)

sex

Allen, Woody (1935–)
US film director, writer, actor and comedian
On bisexuality
> It immediately doubles your chances for a date on Saturday night.
>> *New York Times*, 1975

> Hey, don't knock masturbation! It's sex with someone I love.
>> *Annie Hall* (film, 1977)

> Is sex dirty? Only if it's done right.
>> *Everything You Always Wanted to Know About Sex* (film, 1972)

After sex
> It was the most fun I ever had without laughing.
>> *Annie Hall* (film, 1977)

> I finally had an orgasm, and then my doctor told me it was the wrong kind.
>> Attr. in *The Herald*, 1998

> The last time I was inside a woman was when I went to the Statue of Liberty.
>> *Crimes and Misdemeanors* (film, 1989)

Anonymous
> *Post coitum omne animal triste.*
> After coition every animal is sad.
>> Post-classical saying

> If ye want a boy, dae it wi' your boots on.
>> Traditional Scottish saying

Aubrey, John (1626–1697)
English antiquary, folklorist and biographer
> He loved a wench well: and one time getting up one of the maids of honour against a tree in a wood ('twas his first lady) who seemed at first boarding to be somewhat fearful of her honour, and modest, she cried, 'Sweet Sir Walter, what do you ask me? Will you undo me? Nay, sweet Sir Walter! Sir Walter!' At last as the danger and the pleasure at the same time grew higher, she cried in ecstasy, 'Swisser Swatter! Swisser Swatter!' She proved with child and I doubt not but this hero took care of them both, as also

that the product was more than an ordinary mortal.
>> *Brief Lives* (c.1693)

Bagnold, Enid (1889–1981)
English playwright
> The great and terrible step was taken. What else could you expect from a girl so expectant? 'Sex,' said Frank Harris, 'is the gateway to life.' So I went through the gateway in an upper room in the Café Royal.
>> *Enid Bagnold's Autobiography* (1969)

Bankhead, Tallulah (1903–1968)
US actress
To an admirer
> I'll come and make love to you at five o'clock. If I'm late start without me.
>> In Morgan, *Somerset Maugham* (1980)

Betjeman, Sir John (1906–1984)
English poet laureate
When asked if he had any regrets
> Yes, I haven't had enough sex.
>> *Time With Betjeman*, BBC TV, 1983

Boy George (1961–)
English singer
> I'd rather have a cup of tea than go to bed with someone – any day.
>> Remark, variously expressed, 1983

Bradbury, Malcolm (1932–)
English writer, critic and academic
> If God had meant us to have group sex, I guess he'd have given us all more organs.
>> *Who Do You Think You Are? Stories and Parodies* (1976)

Brome, Richard (c.1590–1652)
English dramatist
> *Doctor*: But there the maids doe woe the Batchelors, and tis most probable, The wives lie uppermost.
> *Diana*: That is a trim, upside-downe Antipodian tricke indeed.
>> *The Antipodes* (1638)

Browne, Sir Thomas (1605–1682)
English physician, author and antiquary
> I could be content that we might procreate like trees, without conjunction, or that there were any way to perpetuate the World without this trivial and vulgar way of coition: it is the foolishest act a wise man commits in all his life; nor is there any thing that will more deject his cool'd imagination, when he shall consider what an odd and unworthy piece of folly he hath committed.
>> *Religio Medici* (1643)

Burchill, Julie (1960–)
English writer

> Sex, on the whole, was meant to be short, nasty and brutish. If what you want is cuddling, you should buy a puppy.
>
> *Sex and Sensibility* (1992)

Campbell, Mrs Patrick (1865–1940)
English actress

> I don't mind where people make love, so long as they don't do it in the street and frighten the horses.
>
> Attr.

Cartland, Barbara (1901–2000)
English writer

> If a woman's going to leap into the bedroom waving a sex manual and demanding her rights to have 15 orgasms every five minutes, men are going to lose their pride and confidence. Do that to a man and he's finished.
>
> *The Guardian*, 2000

Chandler, Raymond (1888–1959)
US crime writer

> She gave me a smile I could feel in my hip pocket.
>
> *Farewell, My Lovely* (1940)

Chesterfield, Lord (1694–1773)
English politician and letter writer
On sex

> The pleasure is momentary, the position ridiculous, and the expense damnable.
>
> Attr.

Comfort, Alex (1920–2000)
British medical biologist and writer on sex

> A woman who has the divine gift of lechery will always make a superlative partner.
>
> Attr.

Connolly, Cyril (1903–1974)
English literary editor, writer and critic

> In the sex-war thoughtlessness is the weapon of the male, vindictiveness of the female.
>
> *The Unquiet Grave* (1944)

Coogan, Tim Pat (1935–)
Irish writer
Describing the rulings of the Catholic Church on matters of sexual morality

> It's rather like teaching swimming from a book without ever having got wet oneself.
>
> *Disillusioned Decades: Ireland, 1966–87* (1987)

Davies, Robertson (1913–1995)
Canadian playwright, writer and critic

> Sex that is not an evidence of a strong human tie is just like blowing your nose; it's not a celebration of a splendid relationship.
>
> Interview, 1974

Donne, John (1572–1631)
English poet

> Licence my roving hands, and let them go,
> Before, behind, between, above, below.
> O my America! my new-found-land,
> My kingdom, safeliest when with one man mann'd.
>
> 'To His Mistress Going to Bed' (c.1595)

Durrell, Lawrence (1912–1990)
Indian-born British poet and writer

> No more about sex, it's too boring.
>
> *Tunc* (1968)

Dworkin, Andrea (1946–)
US writer and feminist

> Sex exists on both sides of the law but the law itself creates the sides.
>
> *Intercourse* (1987)

> Intercourse as an act often expresses the power men have over women.
>
> *Intercourse* (1987)

> Seduction is often difficult to distinguish from rape. In seduction, the rapist often bothers to buy a bottle of wine.
>
> *The Independent*, 1992

Ekland, Britt (1942–)
Swedish actress

> I say I don't sleep with married men, but what I mean is that I don't sleep with happily married men.
>
> Attr.

Ephron, Nora (1941–)
US writer and screenwriter

> Women need a reason to have sex. Men need a place.
>
> *When Harry Met Sally* (film, 1989)

Fairbairn, Sir Nicholas (1933–1995)
Scottish Conservative MP and barrister

> Sex is a human activity like any other. It's a natural urge, like breathing, thinking, drinking, laughing, talking with friends, golf. They are not crimes if you plan them with someone other than your wife. Why should sex be?
>
> *The Independent*, 1992

> Most cases of rape are reported as an act of vengeance because the fellow has got himself another woman. Or guilt.
>
> *Daily Mail*, 1993

Fielding, Henry (1707–1754)
English writer, dramatist and journalist

> He in a few minutes ravished this fair creature, or at least would have ravished her, if she had not, by a timely compliance, prevented him.
>
> *Jonathan Wild* (1743)

Figes, Eva (1932–)
German-born British writer and critic
> When modern woman discovered the orgasm it was (combined with modern birth control) perhaps the biggest single nail in the coffin of male dominance.
>> In Morgan, *The Descent of Woman* (1972)

Flynt, Larry
US publisher of *Hustler* magazine
Defending President Bill Clinton
> People always lie about sex – to get sex, during sex, after sex, about sex.
>> *The Times*, 1999

Friedkin, William (1939–)
US film director
> I really think that sex always looks kind of funny in a movie.
>> Attr.

Fry, Stephen (1957–)
British comedian and writer
> A walk, a smile, a gait, a way of flicking the hair away from the eyes, the manner in which clothes encase the body, these can be erotic, but I would be greatly in the debt of the man who could tell me what could ever be appealing about those damp, dark, foul-smelling and revoltingly tufted areas of the body that constitute the main dishes in the banquet of love.
>> *Paperweight*

> I gave coitus the red card for utilitarian reasons: the displeasure, discomfort and aggravation it caused outweighed any momentary explosions of pleasure, ease or solace.
>> *Paperweight*

Fukuyama, Francis (1952–)
US historian
Arguing that women were more selective in choosing sexual partners than men (he later excepted certain kinds of seahorses and British women)
> For men, it is a notch on the belt; for women, it is a chance to draw men into a relationship of greater intimacy.
>> Lecture, 1997

Granville-Barker, Harley (1877–1946)
English actor and playwright
> But oh, the farmyard world of sex!
>> *The Madras House*

Greer, Germaine (1939–)
Australian feminist, critic, English scholar and writer
> No sex is better than bad sex.
>> Attr.

Herrick, Robert (1591–1674)
English poet, royalist and clergyman

> Night makes no difference 'twixt the Priest and Clark;
> Jone as my Lady is as good i' th' dark.
>> *Hesperides* (1648)

Hillingdon, Lady Alice (1857–1940)
English aristocrat
> I am happy now that Charles calls on my bedchamber less frequently than of old. As it is, I now endure but two calls a week and when I hear his steps outside my door I lie down on my bed, close my eyes, open my legs and think of England.
>> *Journal* (1912)

Huxley, Aldous (1894–1963)
English writer, poet and critic
> People will insist ... on treating the *mons Veneris* as though it were Mount Everest.
>> *Eyeless in Gaza* (1936)

> A million million spermatozoa,
> All of them alive:
> Out of their cataclysm but one poor Noah
> Dare hope to survive.
>> 'Fifth Philosopher's Song' (1918)

> Mr Mercaptan went on to preach a brilliant sermon on that melancholy sexual perversion known as continence.
>> *Antic Hay* (1923)

> 'Bed,' as the Italian proverb succinctly puts it, 'is the poor man's opera.'
>> *Heaven and Hell* (1956)

Keegan, Kevin (1951–)
English footballer and manager
> I came to Nantes two years ago and it's much the same today, except that it's totally different. The red light district is still the same mind you. Though it's a lot bigger and more expensive. I prefer Hamburg, more variety. There are these ladies there with fully formed moustaches, know what I mean.
>> Attr.

Kristofferson, Kris (1936–)
US singer and film actor
> Never go to bed with anyone crazier than yourself.
>> *The Observer*, 1999

Landers, Ann (1918–)
Famous 'agony aunt' and columnist
> Women complain about sex more often than men. Their gripes fall into two major categories: (1) Not enough (2) Too much.
>> *Ann Landers Says Truth Is Stranger Than ...* (1968)

Larkin, Philip (1922–1985)
English poet, writer and librarian
> Sexual intercourse began

In nineteen sixty-three
(Which was rather late for me) –
Between the end of the Chatterley ban
And the Beatles' first LP.

'Annus Mirabilis' (1974)

Lawrence, D.H. (1885–1930)
English writer, poet and critic
'It is sex,' she said to herself. 'How wonderful sex can be, when men keep it powerful and sacred, and it fills the world! Like sunshine through and through one! …'.

The Plumed Serpent (1926)

It's all this cold-hearted fucking that is death and idiocy.

Lady Chatterley's Lover (1928)

Lewis, Wyndham (1882–1957)
US-born British painter, critic and writer
The 'homo' is the legitimate child of the 'suffragette'.

The Art of Being Ruled (1926)

Longford, Lord (1905–)
English politician, social reformer and biographer
No sex without responsibility.

The Observer, 1954

Loren, Sophia (1934–)
Italian actress
Sex appeal is fifty percent what you've got and fifty percent what people think you've got.

In *Halliwell's Filmgoer's Companion* (1984)

Mackenzie, Sir Compton (1883–1972)
Scottish writer and broadcaster
From the days of Eve women have always faced sexual facts with more courage and realism than men.

Literature in My Time (1933)

I told him D.H. Lawrence that if he was determined to convert the world to proper reverence for the sexual act … he would always have to remember one handicap for such an undertaking – that except to the two people who are indulging in it the sexual act is a comic operation.

My Life and Times

Maclaine, Shirley (1934–)
US actress
The more sex becomes a non-issue in people's lives, the happier they are.

Attr.

Mikes, George (1912–1987)
Hungarian-born British writer
Continental people have sex life; the English have hot-water bottles.

How to be an Alien (1946)

Miller, Henry (1891–1980)
US writer
Sex is one of the nine reasons for reincarnation … The other eight are unimportant.

Big Sur and the Oranges of Hieronymus Bosch

Milton, John (1608–1674)
English poet, libertarian and pamphleteer
Into thir inmost bower
Handed they went; and eas'd the putting off
These troublesom disguises which wee wear,
Strait side by side were laid, nor turned I weene
Adam from his fair Spouse, nor Eve the Rites
Mysterious of connubial Love refus'd:
Whatever Hypocrits austerely talk
Of puritie and place and innocence,
Defaming as impure what God declares
Pure, and commands to som, leaves free to all.

Paradise Lost (1667)

Montgomery, Viscount (1887–1976)
English field marshal
Comment on a bill to relax the laws against homosexuals
This sort of thing may be tolerated by the French, but we are British – thank God.

Speech, 1965

Muggeridge, Malcolm (1903–1990)
English writer
An orgy looks particularly alluring seen through the mists of righteous indignation.

The Most of Malcolm Muggeridge (1966)

The orgasm has replaced the Cross as the focus of longing and the image of fulfilment.

The Most of Malcolm Muggeridge (1966)

Nash, Ogden (1902–1971)
US poet
Home is heaven and orgies are vile
But you need an orgy, once in a while.

'Home, Sweet Home' (1935)

Newbold, H.L. (1890–1971)
Sex is between the ears as well as between the legs.

Mega-Nutrients for Your Nerves

Newby, P.H. (1918–)
English writer and Director of the BBC
He felt that he could love this woman with the greatest brutality. The situation between them was electric. When he was in a room with her the only thing he could think of was sex.

A Journey to the Interior (1945)

Oddie, William
Editor of the *Catholic Herald*
If couples need Viagra, they shouldn't be getting married in the first place.

The Times, 1998

Orton, Joe (1933–1967)
English dramatist and writer

You were born with your legs apart. They'll send you to the grave in a Y-shaped coffin.

What the Butler Saw (1969)

Petronius Arbiter (d. AD 66)
Roman satirist

Foeda est in coitu et brevis voluptas
Et taedet Veneris statim peractae.
Pleasure in coupling is gross and brief. Once sated, desire begins to pall.

In A. Baehrens, *Poetae Latini Minores*

Pinter, Harold (1930–)
English dramatist, poet and screenwriter

I tend to believe that cricket is the greatest thing that God ever created on earth … certainly greater than sex, although sex isn't too bad either.

Interview in *The Observer*, 1980

Prior, Matthew (1664–1721)
English poet

No, no, for my virginity,
When I lose that, says Rose, I'll die;
Behind the elms last night, cry'd Dick,
Rose, were you not extremely sick?

'A True Maid' (1718)

Reuben, David (1933–)

Everything You Always Wanted to Know About Sex, But Were Afraid to Ask.

Title of book, 1969

Salinger, J.D. (1919–)
US writer

Sex is something I really don't understand too hot. You never know where the hell you are. I keep making up these sex rules for myself, and then I break them right away.

The Catcher in the Rye (1951)

Sayers, Dorothy L. (1893–1957)
English writer, dramatist and translator

As I grow older and older,
And totter towards the tomb,
I find that I care less and less
Who goes to bed with whom.

In Hitchman, *Such a Strange Lady* (1975)

Shakespeare, William (1564–1616)
English dramatist, poet and actor

Is it not strange that desire should so many years outlive performance?

Henry IV, Part 2, II.iv

Simenon, Georges (1903–1989)
Belgian writer

His wife later said: 'The true figure is no more than twelve hundred'

I have made love to ten thousand women.

Die Tat, 1977

Sophocles (496–406 BC)
Greek dramatist

Someone asked Sophocles, 'How do you stand in matters of love? Are you still able to have sex with a woman?' 'Quiet, man,' he replied, 'I've left all that behind me very gladly, as if I'd escaped from a mad and savage master.'

In Plato, *Republic*

Steinem, Gloria (1934–)
US writer and feminist activist
On transsexualism

If the shoe doesn't fit, must we change the foot?

Outrageous Acts and Everyday Rebellions (1984)

Stewart, Rod (1945–)
English rock singer
On his sexual partners

The most memorable is always the current one; the rest just merge into a sea of blondes.

Attr.

Suckling, Sir John (1609–1642)
English poet and dramatist

At length the candle's out, and now
All that they had not done they do:
What that is, who can tell?
But I believe it was no more
That thou and I have done before
With Bridget, and with Nell.

'A Ballad upon a Wedding' (1646)

Szasz, Thomas (1920–)
Hungarian-born US psychiatrist and writer

Masturbation: the primary sexual activity of mankind. In the nineteenth century it was a disease; in the twentieth, it's a cure.

The Second Sin (1973)

Traditionally, sex has been a very private, secretive activity. Herein perhaps lies its powerful force for uniting people in a strong bond. As we make sex less secretive, we may rob it of its power to hold men and women together.

The Second Sin (1973)

Thurber, James (1894–1961)
US humorist, writer and dramatist
On being accosted at a party by a drunk woman who claimed she would like to have a baby by him

Surely you don't mean by unartificial insemination!

Attr.

Tynan, Kenneth (1927–1980)
English drama critic, producer and essayist
When asked on live television if he would allow sexual intercourse on stage at the National Theatre

Oh, I think so, certainly. … I mean, there are few rational people in this world to whom the word 'fuck' is particularly diabolical or revolting or totally forbidden.

In Paul Ferris, Sex and the British *(1993)*

Vidal, Gore (1925–)
US writer, critic and poet
On being asked if his first sexual experience had been heterosexual or homosexual
I was too polite to ask.

Forum, 1987

Voltaire (1694–1778)
French philosopher, dramatist, poet, historian writer and critic
C'est une des superstitions de l'esprit humain d'avoir imaginé que la virginité pouvait être une vertu.
It is one of the superstitions of the human mind to have imagined that virginity could be a virtue.

'The Leningrad Notebooks' (c.1735–1750)

Waugh, Evelyn (1903–1966)
English writer and diarist
All this fuss about sleeping together. For physical pleasure I'd sooner go to my dentist any day.

Vile Bodies (1930)

Weldon, Fay (1931–)
British writer
Reading about sex in yesterday's novels is like watching people smoke in old films.

The Guardian, 1989

Yeats, W.B. (1865–1939)
Irish poet, dramatist, editor, writer and senator
The tragedy of sexual intercourse is the perpetual virginity of the soul.

Attr. in Jeffares, W.B. Yeats: man and poet *(1949)*

▶▶ ABSTINENCE; ADULTERY; CONTRACEPTION; PORNOGRAPHY; PROSTITUTION

shadows

Campion, Thomas (1567–1620)
English poet
Follow thy fair sunne, unhappy shadowe.

A Booke of Ayres (1601)

Cotton, Charles (1630–1687)
English poet
The shadows now so long do grow,
That brambles like tall cedars show,
Molehills seem mountains, and the ant
Appears a monstrous elephant.

'Evening Quatrains' (1689)

Lee, Nathaniel (c.1653–1692)
English dramatist

When the sun sets, shadows, that showed at noon
But small, appear most long and terrible.

Oedipus (1679)

Stevenson, Robert Louis (1850–1894)
Scottish writer, poet and essayist
I have a little shadow that goes in and out with me,
And what can be the use of him is more than I can see.

A Children's Garden of Verses (1885), 'My Shadow'

shakespeare

Arnold, Matthew (1822–1888)
English poet, critic, essayist and educationist
Others abide our question. Thou art free.
We ask and ask – Thou smilest and art still,
Out-topping knowledge.

'Shakespeare' (1849)

Aubrey, John (1626–1697)
English antiquary, folklorist and biographer
When he killed a calf he would do it in high style, and make a speech.

Brief Lives (c.1693)

He was a handsome, well-shaped man: very good company, and of a very ready and pleasant smooth wit.

Brief Lives (c.1693)

Austen, Jane (1775–1817)
English writer
We all talk Shakespeare, use his similes, and describe with his descriptions.

Mansfield Park (1814)

Browning, Elizabeth Barrett (1806–1861)
English poet; wife of Robert Browning
There, Shakespeare, on whose forehead climb
The crowns o' the world. Oh, eyes sublime,
With tears and laughters for all time!

A Vision of Poets (1844)

Chesterfield, Lord (1694–1773)
English politician and letter writer
If Shakespeare's genius had been cultivated, those beauties, which we so justly admire in him, would have been undisgraced by those extravagances and that nonsense with which they are frequently accompanied.

Letter to his son, 1748

Coleridge, Samuel Taylor (1772–1834)
English poet, philosopher and critic
Our myriad-minded Shakespeare.

Biographia Literaria (1817)

I believe Shakespeare was not a whit more

intelligible in his own day than he is now to an educated man, except for a few local allusions of no consequence. He is of no age – nor of any religion, or party or profession. The body and substance of his works came out of the unfathomable depths of his own oceanic mind: his observation and reading, which was considerable, supplied him with the drapery of his figures.

Table Talk (1835)

Condell, Henry (d. 1627)
English actor and editor of Shakespeare's plays

Who, as he was a happy imitator of Nature, was a most gentle expresser of it. His mind and hand went together: And what he thought, he uttered with that easiness, that we have scarce received from him a blot.

Preface to the First Folio Shakespeare, 1623

Darwin, Charles (1809–1882)
English naturalist

I have tried lately to read Shakespeare, and found it so intolerably dull that it nauseated me.

Autobiography (1877)

DiCaprio, Leonardo (1974–)
US film actor

Romeo was, like, a gigolo who falls for this girl Juliet, who says, 'Look, if you've got the balls, put them on the table.'

The Observer, 1998

Dryden, John (1631–1700)
English poet, satirist, dramatist and critic
Of Shakespeare

He was the man who of all modern, and perhaps ancient poets, had the largest and most comprehensive soul … He was naturally learn'd; he needed not the spectacles of books to read Nature: he looked inwards, and found her there … He is many times flat, insipid; his comic wit degenerating into clenches, his serious swelling into bombast. But he is always great.

Essay of Dramatic Poesy (1668)

Eliot, T.S. (1888–1965)
US-born British poet, verse dramatist and critic

We can say of Shakespeare, that never has a man turned so little knowledge to such great account.

Lecture, 1942

Emerson, Ralph Waldo (1803–1882)
US poet, essayist, transcendentalist and teacher

When Shakespeare is charged with debts to his authors, Landor replies: 'Yet he was more original than his originals. He breathed upon dead bodies and brought them into life.'

Letters and Social Aims
(1875)

Fuller, Thomas (1608–1661)
English churchman and antiquary
Comparing Shakespeare and Ben Jonson

Many were the wit-combats betwixt him and Ben Jonson, which two I behold like a Spanish great galleon, and an English man of war; Master Jonson (like the former) was built far higher in learning; solid but slow in his performances. Shakespeare was the English man of war, lesser in bulk, but lighter in sailing, could turn with all tides, tack about and take advantage of all winds, by the quickness of his wit and invention.

The History of the Worthies of England (1662)

Graves, Robert (1895–1985)
English poet, writer, critic, translator and mythologist

The remarkable thing about Shakespeare is that he is really very good – in spite of all the people who say he is very good.

The Observer, 1964

Gray, Thomas (1716–1771)
English poet and scholar
On Shakespeare

Far from the sun and summer-gale,
In thy green lap was Nature's Darling laid,
What time, where lucid Avon stray'd,
To him the mighty Mother did unveil
Her aweful face: The dauntless child
Stretch'd forth his little arms, and smiled.

'The Progress of Poesy' (1757)

Greene, Robert (1558–1592)
English dramatist and poet
Of Shakespeare

For there is an upstart Crow, beautified with our feathers, that with his Tyger's heart wrapt in a Player's hyde, supposes he is as well able to bombast out a blanke verse as the best of you: and being an absolute Iohannes fac totum, is in his owne conceit the onely Shake-scene in a countrey.

Greenes Groats-Worth of witte bought with a million of Repentance (1592)

Halsey, Margaret (1910–)
US writer

All of Stratford, in fact, suggests powdered history – add hot water and stir and you have a delicious, nourishing Shakespeare.

With Malice Toward Some (1938)

Isherwood, Christopher (1904–1986)
English novelist

I'll bet Shakespeare compromised himself a lot; anybody who's in the entertainment industry does to some extent.

In Jon Winokur, *Writers on Writing* (1990)

Johnson, Samuel (1709–1784)
English lexicographer, poet, critic, conversationalist and essayist

> Shakespeare never had six lines together without a fault. Perhaps you may find seven, but this does not refute my general assertion.
>
> > In Boswell, *The Life of Samuel Johnson* (1791)

Jonson, Ben (1572–1637)
English dramatist and poet

> Soul of the Age!
> The applause! delight! the wonder of our stage!
> My Shakespeare, rise; I will not lodge thee by
> Chaucer, or Spenser, or bid Beaumont lie
> A little further, to make thee a room:
> Thou art a monument, without a tomb,
> And art alive still, while thy book doth live,
> And we have wits to read, and praise to give.
>
> > 'To the Memory of My Beloved, the Author, Mr William Shakespeare' (1623)

> He was not of an age, but for all time!
>
> > 'To the Memory of My Beloved, the Author, Mr William Shakespeare' (1623)

> I remember the players have often mentioned it as an honour to Shakespeare that in his writing (whatsoever he penned) he never blotted out a line. My answer hath been 'Would he had blotted a thousand'. Which they thought a malevolent speech. I had not told posterity this, but for their ignorance, who chose that circumstance to commend their friend by wherein he most faulted; and to justify mine own candour: for I loved the man, and do honour his memory, on this side of idolatry, as much as any. He was (indeed) honest, and of an open and free nature; had an excellent phantasy, brave notions, and gentle expressions; wherein he flowed with that facility, that sometimes it was necessary he should be stopped: *sufflaminandus erat*, as Augustus said of Haterius. His wit was in his own power, would the rule of it had been so too ... But he redeemed his vices with his virtues. There was ever more in him to be praised than to be pardoned.
>
> > *Timber, or Discoveries made upon Men and Matter* (1641)

Keats, John (1795–1821)
English poet

> I have great reason to be content, for thank God I can read and perhaps understand Shakespeare to his depths.
>
> > Letter to John Taylor, 1818

> Shakespeare led a life of Allegory: his works are the comments on it.
>
> > Letter to George and Georgiana Keats, 1819

Lawrence, D.H. (1885–1930)
English writer, poet and critic

> When I read Shakespeare I am struck with wonder
> That such trivial people should muse and thunder
> In such lovely language.
>
> > *Pansies* (1929)

Olivier, Sir Laurence (1907–1989)
English actor and director

> Shakespeare – the nearest thing in incarnation to the eye of God.
>
> > Kenneth Harris *Talking To*: 'Sir Laurence Olivier'

Philip, Prince, Duke of Edinburgh (1921–)
Greek-born consort of Queen Elizabeth II

> A man can be forgiven a lot if he can quote Shakespeare in an economic crisis.
>
> > Attr.

Powys, John Cowper (1872–1963)
English writer and poet

> He combined scepticism of everything with credulity about everything ... and I am convinced this is the true Shakespearian way wherewith to take life.
>
> > *Autobiography*

Shaw, George Bernard (1856–1950)
Irish socialist, writer, dramatist and critic

> With the single exception of Homer, there is no eminent writer, not even Sir Walter Scott, whom I can despise so entirely as I despise Shakespeare when I measure my mind against his ... it would positively be a relief to me to dig him up and throw stones at him.
>
> > *Dramatic Opinions and Essays* (1906)

Smith, Dodie (1896–1990)
English dramatist

> For though he had very little Latin beyond 'Cave canem, ' he had, as a young dog, devoured Shakespeare (in a tasty leather binding).
>
> > *One Hundred and One Dalmatians* (1956)

Spillane, Mickey (1918–)
US author

> If the public likes you, you're good. Shakespeare was a common, down-to-earth writer in his day.
>
> > In Jon Winokur, *Writers on Writing* (1990)

Terry, Dame Ellen (1847–1928)
English actress, theatrical manager and memoirist

> Wonderful women! Have you ever thought how much we all, and women especially, owe to Shakespeare for his vindication of women in these fearless, high-spirited, resolute and intelligent heroines?
>
> > *Four Lectures on Shakespeare* (1932)

Walpole, Horace (1717–1797)
English writer and politician
> One of the greatest geniuses that ever existed, Shakespeare, undoubtedly wanted taste.
>> Letter to Christopher Wren, 1764

▶▶ CRITICISM; POETS; WRITERS

shame

Bentley, Edmund Clerihew (1875–1956)
English writer
> When their lordships asked Bacon
> How many bribes he had taken
> He had at least the grace
> To get very red in the face.
>> Baseless Biography (1939)

Blake, William (1757–1827)
English poet, engraver, painter and mystic
> Shame is Pride's cloke.
>> The Marriage of Heaven and Hell (c.1790–1793)

Shaw, George Bernard (1856–1950)
Irish socialist, writer, dramatist and critic
> We are ashamed of everything that is real about us; ashamed of ourselves, of our relatives, of our incomes, of our accents, of our opinions, of our experience, just as we are ashamed of our naked skins … The more things a man is ashamed of, the more respectable he is.
>> Man and Superman (1903)

Swift, Jonathan (1667–1745)
Irish satirist, poet, essayist and cleric
> I never wonder to see men wicked, but I often wonder to see them not ashamed.
>> Thoughts on Various Subjects (1711)

shopping

Bryson, Bill (1951–)
US travel writer
> My first rule of consumerism is never to buy anything you can't make your children carry.
>> The Lost Continent (1989)

Cato the Elder (234–149 BC)
Roman statesman
> Do not buy what you want, but what you need; what you do not need is dear at a farthing.
>> Reliquiae (Remains)

Evans, Dame Edith (1888–1976)
English actress
In Fortnum and Mason, to a salesgirl who insisted on giving her threepence change
> Keep the change, my dear. I trod on a grape as I came in.
>> In B. Forbes, Dame Edith Evans: Ned's Girl (1977)

Ginsberg, Allen (1926–1997)
US poet
Addressing Walt Whitman
> In my hungry fatigue, and shopping for images, I went into the neon fruit supermarket, dreaming of your enumerations!
> What peaches and what penumbras! Whole families shopping at night! Aisles full of husbands! Wives in the avocados, babies in the tomatoes! – and you, Garcia Lorca, what were you doing down by the watermelons?
>> 'A Supermarket in California'

Selfridge, Harry Gordon (1858–1947)
US-born British merchant
> The customer is always right.
>> Slogan in A.H. Williams, No Name on the Door; A Memoir of Gordon Selfridge (1956)

> There are — shopping days to Christmas.
>> In A.H. Williams, No Name on the Door: A Memoir of Gordon Selfridge (1956)

▶▶ CONSUMER SOCIETY

showbusiness

Allen, Woody (1935–)
US film director, writer, actor and comedian
> Showbusiness is dog eat dog. It's worse than dog eat dog. It's dog doesn't return other dog's phone calls.
>> Crimes and Misdemeanours (film, 1989)

Anonymous
> Can't act, can't sing, slightly bald. Can dance a little.
>> Comment by a Hollywood executive on Fred Astaire's first screen test

Barnes, Clive (1927–)
On Oh, Calcutta! (1969)
> This is the kind of show that gives pornography a bad name.
>> Attr.

Brooks, Mel (1926–)
US film actor and director
> That's it, baby, if you've got it, flaunt it.
>> The Producers (film, 1968)

Cameron, James (1954–)
US film director
Accepting the Oscars won by the film Titanic
> Does this prove, once and for all, that size does matter?
>> The Observer, 1998

Chandler, Raymond (1888–1959)

US crime writer

> You can live a long time in Hollywood and never
> see the part they use in pictures.
>
> *The Little Sister*

Chasen, Dave (1926–)

Hollywood restaurateur

> Bogart's a helluva nice guy until 11.30 p.m. After
> that he thinks he's Bogart.
>
> In Halliwell, The *Filmgoer's Book of Quotes* (1973)

Cher (1946–)

US singer and actress

> Mother told me a couple of years ago,
> 'Sweetheart, settle down and marry a rich man.'
> I said, 'Mom, I am a rich man.'
>
> *The Observer Review*, 1995

Cochran, Charles B. (1872–1951)

English showman and theatrical producer

> I still prefer a good juggler to a bad Hamlet.
>
> *The Observer*, 1943

Davis, Bette (1908–1989)

US film actress

Of a starlet

> I see – she's the original good time that was had
> by all.
>
> In Halliwell, *Filmgoer's Book of Quotes* (1973)

Davis Jnr., Sammy (1925–1990)

US entertainer and singer

> Being a star has made it possible for me to get
> insulted in places where the average Negro
> could never hope to get insulted.
>
> *Yes I can* (1965)

Dillingham, Charles Bancroft (1868–1934)

US theatrical producer

Said at the funeral of Harry Houdini, the escapologist, while
carrying his coffin

> I bet you a hundred bucks he ain't in here.
>
> Attr.

Garbo, Greta (1905–1990)

Swedish-born US film actress

> I never said, 'I want to be alone.' I only said, 'I
> want to be let alone.' There is all the difference.
>
> In Colombo, *Wit and Wisdom of the Moviemakers*

Garland, Judy (1922–1969)

US film actress and singer

> I was born at the age of twelve on a Metro-
> Goldwyn-Mayer lot.
>
> *The Observer*, 1951

Goldwyn, Samuel (1882–1974)

Polish-born US film producer

> Directors are always biting the hand that lays
> the golden egg.
>
> In Zierold, *Moguls* (1969)

> I'll give you a definite maybe.
>
> In Colombo, *Wit and Wisdom of the Moviemakers*

> In two words: im possible.
>
> Attr.; in Zierold, *Moguls* (1969)

> What we want is a story that starts with an
> earthquake and works its way up to a climax.
>
> Attr.

Grable, Betty (1916–1973)

US film actress and wartime 'pin-up'

> There are two reasons why I'm in show business,
> and I'm standing on both of them.
>
> Attr.

Grade, Lew (1906–1994)

Russian-born British film, TV and theatrical producer.

> All my shows are great. Some of them are bad.
> But they are all great.
>
> *The Observer*, 1975

Guinan, Texas (1884–1933)

Canadian actress

When she and her troupe were refused entry to France in 1931

> It goes to show that fifty million Frenchmen can
> be wrong.
>
> Attr.

Helpman, Sir Robert Murray (1909–1986)

Australian choreographer and director

After the opening night of *Oh, Calcutta!*

> The trouble with nude dancing is that not
> everything stops when the music stops.
>
> In *The Frank Muir Book*
> (1976)

Hill, Benny (1924–1992)

English comedian

> That's what show business is – sincere insincerity.
>
> *The Observer*, 1977

Hope, Bob (1903–)

English-born US comedian

> Clint Eastwood is a man who walks softly and
> carries a big percentage of the gross.
>
> In Simon Rose, *Classic Film Guide* (1995)

Levant, Oscar (1906–1972)

US pianist and autobiographer

> Strip the phony tinsel off Hollywood and you'll
> find the real tinsel underneath.
>
> In Halliwell, *Filmgoer's Book of Quotes*
> (1973)

Reed, Rex (1938–)

US film and music critic and columnist

> Cannes is where you lie on the beach and stare
> at the stars – or vice versa.
>
> Attr.

Richard, Cliff (1940–)

English singer

> There's no room in my life for drugs, fights,

divorce, adultery, sadism, unnecessary fuss and sex.

Daily Mail, 1996

Stars who debauch themselves, get addicted to drugs then kick them get all the praise. Wouldn't you think that people who have never been addicted should be praised all the more?

The Observer Review, 1996

Shaw, George Bernard (1856–1950)
Irish socialist, writer, dramatist and critic
> The trouble, Mr Goldwyn, is that you are only interested in art and I am only interested in money.

In Johnson, *The Great Goldwyn* (1937)

Skelton, Red (1913–1997)
US comedian
Commenting on the large crowds attending the funeral of Hollywood producer Harry Cohn
> It proves what they say, give the public what they want to see and they'll come out for it.

Remark, 1958

Southern, Terry (1924–1995)
US writer and screenwriter
> She says, 'Listen, who do I have to fuck to get off this picture?'

Blue Movie (1970)

Thomas, Irene (1920–)
English writer and broadcaster
> It was the kind of show where the girls are not auditioned – just measured.

Attr.

Tracy, Spencer (1900–1967)
US film actor
Explaining what he looked for in a script
> Days off.

Attr.

Welles, Orson (1915–1985)
US actor, director and producer
> I began at the top and I've been working my way down ever since.

In Colombo, *Wit and Wisdom of the Moviemakers*

▶▶ CELEBRITY; CINEMA; FAME; HOLLYWOOD

shyness

Bergman, Ingmar (1918–)
Swedish film director
> After years of playing with images of life and death, life has made me shy.

The Observer, 1997

silence

Anonymous
> Silence is one great art of conversation.

Austen, Jane (1775–1817)
English writer
> From politics, it was an easy step to silence.

Northanger Abbey (1818)

Bacon, Francis (1561–1626)
English philosopher, essayist, politician and courtier
> Silence is the virtue of fools.

Of the Dignity and Advancement of Learning (1623)

Bashó, Matsuo (1644–1694)
Japanese haiku poet
> The din of cicadas
> Seeps into the rock;
> the air rings with silence.

'Narrow Roads of Oku', 1703)

Carlyle, Thomas (1795–1881)
Scottish historian, biographer, critic, and essayist
> Under all speech that is good for anything there lies a silence that is better. Silence is deep as Eternity; speech is shallow as Time.

'Memoirs of the Life of Scott' (1839)

Dark, Eleanor (1901–1985)
> Silence ruled this land. Out of silence mystery comes, and magic, and the delicate awareness of unreasoning things.

The Timeless Land (1941)

Eliot, George (1819–1880)
English writer and poet
> Speech is often barren; but silence also does not necessarily brood over a full nest. Your still fowl, blinking at you without remark, may all the while be sitting on one addled nest-egg; and when it takes to cackling, will have nothing to announce but that addled delusion.

Felix Holt (1866)

Flecknoe, Richard (d. c.1678)
Irish priest, poet and dramatist
> Still-born Silence! thou that art
> Floodgate of the deeper heart.

'Invocation of Silence' (1653)

Goldsmith, Oliver (c.1728–1774)
Irish dramatist, poet and writer
> Silence is become his mother tongue.

The Good Natur'd Man (1768)

Holmes, Oliver Wendell (1809–1894)
US physician, poet, writer and scientist
> And silence, like a poultice, comes
> To heal the blows of sound.

'The Music-Grinders' (1836)

Hood, Thomas (1799–1845)
English poet, editor and humorist
> There is a silence where hath been no sound,
> There is a silence where no sound may be,
> In the cold grave – under the deep, deep sea,
> Or in the wide desert where no life is found.
>> 'Sonnet: Silence' (1823)

Huxley, Aldous (1894–1963)
English writer, poet and critic
> Silence is as full of potential wisdom and wit as the unhewn marble of great sculpture.
>> *Point Counter Point* (1928)

Jonson, Ben (1572–1637)
English dramatist and poet
> Calumnies are answered best with silence.
>> *Volpone* (1607)

La Rochefoucauld (1613–1680)
French writer
> *Le silence est le parti le plus sûr de celui qui se défie de soi-même.*
> Silence is the safest policy for the man who distrusts himself.
>> *Maximes* (1678)

Lincoln, Abraham (1809–1865)
US statesman and President
> Better to remain silent and be thought a fool than to speak out and remove all doubt.
>> Attr.

Mandelstam, Nadezhda (1899–1980)
Russian writer, translator and teacher
> If nothing else is left, one must scream. Silence is the real crime against humanity.
>> *Hope Against Hope* (1970)

Marceau, Marcel (1923–)
French mime artist
> Do not the most moving moments of our lives find us all without words?
>> *Reader's Digest*, 1958

Pascal, Blaise (1623–1662)
French philosopher and scientist
> *Le silence éternel de ces espaces infinis m'effraie.*
> The eternal silence of these infinite spaces terrifies me.
>> *Pensées* (1670)

Proverb
> Silence is golden.

Rossetti, Christina (1830–1894)
English poet
> Silence more musical than any song.
>> 'Rest' (1862)

Rossetti, Dante Gabriel (1828–1882)
English poet, painter, translator and letter-writer
> 'Tis visible silence, still as the hour-glass …

> Deep in the sun-searched growths the dragon-fly
> Hangs like a blue thread loosened from the sky: –
> So this winged hour is dropt to us from above.
> Oh! clasp we to our hearts, for deathless dower,
> This close-companioned inarticulate hour
> When twofold silence was the song of love.
>> *The House of Life* (1881)

Sainte-Beuve, Charles-Augustin (1804–1869)
French writer and critic
> *Le silence seul est le souverain mépris.*
> Silence is the supreme contempt.
>> 'Mes Poisons'

Sartre, Jean-Paul (1905–1980)
French philosopher, writer, dramatist and critic
> You get the impression that their normal condition is silence and that speech is a slight fever which attacks them now and then.
>> *Nausea* (1938)

Schleiermacher, F.E.D. (1768–1834)
German philosopher
Of a celebrated philologist
> He could be silent in seven languages.
>> Attr.

Sidney, Sir Philip (1554–1586)
English poet, critic, soldier, courtier and diplomat
> Shallow brookes murmur moste, Depe sylent slyde away.
>> *Old Arcadia* (1581), 'The Firste Eclogues'

Sitwell, Dame Edith (1887–1964)
English poet, anthologist, critic and biographer
> My personal hobbies are reading, listening to music, and silence.
>> Attr.

Smith, Sydney (1771–1845)
English clergyman, essayist, journalist and wit
Of Macaulay
> He has occasional flashes of silence, that make his conversation perfectly delightful.
>> In Holland, *A Memoir of the Reverend Sydney Smith* (1855)

Swinburne, Algernon Charles (1837–1909)
English poet, critic, dramatist and letter writer
> For words divide and rend;
> But silence is most noble till the end.
>> *Atalanta in Calydon* (1865)

Tucholsky, Kurt (1890–1935)
German satirist and writer
> *Es gibt vielerlei Lärme, aber es gibt nur eine Stille.*
> There are many sorts of noises, but there is only one silence.
>> *Scraps* (1973)

Tupper, Martin (1810–1889)
English writer, lawyer and inventor

Well-timed silence hath more eloquence than speech.

Proverbial Philosophy (1838)

Vega Carpio, Félix Lope de (1562–1635)
Spanish dramatist and poet
> *El más discreto hablar*
> *no es santo como el silencio.*
> The most wise speech
> is not as holy as silence.

The Stupid Lady (1613)

Vigny, Alfred de (1797–1863)
French writer
> *Seul le silence est grand; tout le reste est faiblesse …*
> *Fais énergiquement ta longue et lourde tâche …*
> *Puis, après, comme moi, souffre et meurs sans parler.*
> Silence alone is great; all else is weakness …
> Perform with all your heart your long and heavy task …
> Then, afterwards, as do I, suffer and die without a word.

'The Death of the Wolf' (1843)

Virgil (70–19 BC)
Roman poet
> *Tacitae per amica silentia lunae.*
> Through the friendly silence of the soundless moonlight.

Aeneid

Wittgenstein, Ludwig (1889–1951)
Austrian philosopher
> What can be said at all can be said clearly; and whereof one cannot speak, thereon one must keep silent.

Tractatus Logico-Philosophicus (1922)

▶▶ CONVERSATION

simplicity

Adams, Henry Brooks (1838–1918)
US historian and memoirist
> Simplicity is the most deceitful mistress that ever betrayed man.

The Education of Henry Adams (1918)

Douglas, Keith (1920–1944)
English war poet
> Remember me when I am dead
> And simplify me when I'm dead.

'Simplify me when I'm dead' (1941)

Einstein, Albert (1879–1955)
German-born US mathematical physicist
> Everything should be made as simple as possible, but not simpler.

Attr.

Kipling, Rudyard (1865–1936)
Indian-born British poet and writer
> Teach us Delight in simple things,
> And Mirth that has no bitter springs.

Puck of Pook's Hill (1906), 'The Children's Song'

Sassoon, Siegfried (1886–1967)
English poet and writer
> The simplicity that I see in some of the men is the one candle in my darkness. The one flower in all this arid sunshine.

Diary, April 1918

sin

Anonymous
> Would you like to sin
> With Elinor Glyn
> On a tiger-skin?
> Or would you prefer
> to err with her
> on some other fur?

Quoted in A. Glyn, *Elinor Glyn* (1955)

Auden, W.H. (1907–1973)
English poet, essayist, critic, teacher and dramatist
> All sin tends to be addictive, and the terminal point of addiction is what is called damnation.

A Certain World (1970)

The Bible (King James Version)
> Be sure your sin will find you out.

Numbers, 32:23

> He that is without sin among you, let him first cast a stone.

John, 8:7

> The wages of sin is death.

Romans, 6:23

Bulgakov, Mikhail (1891–1940)
Russian writer and dramatist
> Cowardice is, without a doubt, one of the greatest sins.

The Master and Margarita (1967)

Bunyan, John (1628–1688)
English preacher, pastor and writer
> One leak will sink a ship, and one sin will destroy a sinner.

The Pilgrim's Progress (1678)

Campbell, Thomas (1777–1844)
Scottish poet, ballad writer and journalist
> An original something, fair maid, you would win me
> To write – but how shall I begin?
> For I fear I have nothing original in me –
> Excepting Original Sin.

'To a Young Lady, Who Asked Me to Write Something Original for Her Album' (1843)

Coolidge, Calvin (1872–1933)
US President
On being asked what had been said by a clergyman who preached on sin
He said he was against it.

Attr.

Cowley, Abraham (1618–1667)
English poet and dramatist
Lukewarmness I account a sin
As great in love as in religion.

'The Request' (1647)

Donne, John (1572–1631)
English poet
Wilt thou forgive that sin, where I begun,
Which is my sin, though it were done before?
Wilt thou forgive those sins through which I run
And do them still, though still I do deplore?
When thou hast done, thou hast not done,
For I have more.

Wilt thou forgive that sin, by which I have won
Others to sin, and made my sin their door?
Wilt thou forgive that sin which I did shun
A year or two, but wallowed in a score?
When thou hast done, thou hast not done,
For I have more.

'Hymn to God the Father' (1623)

Eddy, Mary Baker (1821–1910)
US founder of Christian Science
Sin brought death, and death will disappear with the disappearance of sin.

Science and Health (1875)

Herbert, Sir A.P. (1890–1971)
English humorist, writer, dramatist and politician
Don't tell my mother I'm living in sin,
Don't let the old folks know:
Don't tell my twin that I breakfast on gin,
He'd never survive the blow.

Laughing Ann (1925)

Juliana of Norwich (c.1343–c.1429)
English mystic
Sin is behovely, but all shall be well and all shall be well and all manner of things shall be well.

Revelations of Divine Love (1393)

Juvenal (c.60–130)
Roman verse satirist and Stoic
Summum crede nefas animam praeferre pudori
Et propter vitam vivendi perdere causas.
Count it the greatest sin to put life before honour, and for the sake of life to lose the reasons for living.

Satires

Lawrence, D.H. (1885–1930)
English writer, poet and critic
There's nothing so artificial as sinning nowadays.
I suppose it once was real.

St Mawr (1925)

Molière (1622–1673)
French dramatist, actor and director
Le scandale du monde est ce qui fait l'offense,
Et ce n'est pas pécher que pécher en silence.
Public scandal is what constitutes offence; to sin in secret is no sin at all.

Tartuffe (1664)

Plomer, William (1903–1973)
South African-born British writer and editor
On a sofa upholstered in panther skin
Mona did research in original sin.

'Mews Flat Mona' (1960)

Quevedo y Villegas, Francisco Gómez de (1580–1645)
Spanish poet and writer
Tan ciego estoy a mi mortal enredo
que no te oso llamar, Señor, de miedo
de que querrás sacarme de pecado.
So blind am I to my mortal entanglement
that I dare not call upon thee, Lord, for fear
that thou wouldst take me away from my sin.

Christian Heraclitus (1613)

Roosevelt, Theodore (1858–1919)
US Republican President
The worst sin towards our fellow creatures is not to hate them, but to be indifferent to them: that's the essence of inhumanity.

The Devil's Disciple (1901)

Shakespeare, William (1564–1616)
English dramatist, poet and actor
Plate sin with gold,
And the strong lance of justice hurtless breaks;
Arm it in rags, a pigmy's straw does pierce it.

King Lear, IV.vi

Few love to hear the sins they love to act.

Pericles, Prince of Tyre, I.i

Nothing emboldens sin so much as mercy.

Timon of Athens, III.v

Smith, Sydney (1771–1845)
English clergyman, essayist, journalist and wit
Of boring sermons
They are written as if sin were to be taken out of man like Eve out of Adam – by putting him to sleep.

In J. Larwood, Anecdotes of the Clergy

Thomas, Dylan (1914–1953)
Welsh poet, writer and radio dramatist
You just wait, I'll sin till I blow up!

Under Milk Wood (1954)

SINCERITY

Wilde, Oscar (1854–1900)
Irish poet, dramatist, writer, critic and wit
> There is no sin except stupidity.
>> *Intentions* (1891), 'The Critic as Artist'

> It has been said that the great events of the world take place in the brain. It is in the brain, and the brain only, that the great sins of the world take place.
>> *The Picture of Dorian Gray* (1891)

▶▶ EVIL; VICE

sincerity

Maugham, William Somerset (1874–1965)
English writer, dramatist and physician
> I don't think you want too much sincerity in society. It would be like a girder in a house of cards.
>> *The Circle*

Shaw, George Bernard (1856–1950)
Irish socialist, writer, dramatist and critic
> It is dangerous to be sincere unless you are also stupid.
>> *Man and Superman* (1903), 'Maxims for Revolutionists'

Wilde, Oscar (1854–1900)
Irish poet, dramatist, writer, critic and wit
> A little sincerity is a dangerous thing, and a great deal of it is absolutely fatal.
>> *Intentions* (1891), 'The Critic as Artist'

▶▶ HONESTY

single life

Anonymous
> When you've got over the disgrace of the single life, it's more airy.
>> Irish woman, quoted in broadcasts by Joyce Grenfell

Ferber, Edna (1887–1968)
> Being an old maid is like death by drowning, a really delightful sensation after you cease to struggle.
>> In R.E. Drennan, *Wit's End* (1973), 'Completing the Circle'

Jacomb, C.E.
> The prevalence of men living alone has thus caused the coining of a new word in Australia: that word is 'baching'; and the word expresses vividly, if crudely, the ugly life it gives a name to.
>> *God's Own Country*

Lowry, L.S. (1887–1976)
English painter

> A bachelor lives like a king and dies like a beggar.
>> Attr.

▶▶ MARRIAGE

slavery

Burke, Edmund (1729–1797)
Irish-born British statesman and philosopher
> Slavery they can have anywhere. It is a weed that grows in every soil.
>> *Speech on Conciliation with America* (1775)

Gandhi (1869–1948)
Indian political leader
> The moment the slave resolves that he will no longer be a slave, his fetters fall. He frees himself and shows the way to others. Freedom and slavery are mental states.
>> *Non-Violence in Peace and War* (1949)

Garrison, William Lloyd (1805–1879)
US abolitionist and newspaper editor
> The compact which exists between the North and the South is 'a covenant with death and an agreement with hell'.
>> Resolution adopted by the Massachusetts Anti-Slavery Society, 1843

Gill, Eric (1882–1940)
English stonecarver, topographer and writer
> That state is a state of Slavery in which a man does what he likes to do in his spare time and in his working time that which is required of him.
>> 'Slavery and Freedom' (1929)

Johnson, Samuel (1709–1784)
English lexicographer, poet, critic, conversationalist and essayist
> How is it that we hear the loudest yelps for liberty among the drivers of negroes?
>> *Taxation No Tyranny* (1775)

Lincoln, Abraham (1809–1865)
US statesman and President
> In giving freedom to the slave, we assure freedom to the free – honourable alike in what we give and what we preserve.
>> Speech, 1862

Mackenzie, Sir Compton (1883–1972)
Scottish writer and broadcaster
> The slavery of being waited upon that is more deadening than the slavery of waiting upon other people.
>> *The Adventures of Sylvia Scarlett* (1918)

Morris, Wesley
US film critic
> ... the slaves, who are so cordial and upbeat

about having their lives and property gentrified in 1776 that you fear for the entire future of the blues.

> Review of the film *The Patriot* in the *San Francisco Examiner*, 2000

Stanton, Elizabeth Cady (1815–1902)

US suffragist, abolitionist, feminist, editor and writer

The prolonged slavery of woman is the darkest page in human history.

> In Anthony and Gage, *History of Woman Suffrage* (1881)

Wedgwood, Josiah (1730–1795)

English potter, manufacturer and pamphleteer

Am I not a man and a brother?

> Motto adopted by Anti-Slavery Society

▶▶ EQUALITY; FREEDOM; RACISM

sleep

Anonymous

Whilst Adam slept, Eve from his side arose:
Strange his first sleep should be his last repose.

> 'The Consequence'

Browne, Sir Thomas (1605–1682)

English physician, author and antiquary

Sleep is in fine, so like death, I dare not trust it without my prayers.

> *Religio Medici* (1643)

Nor will the sweetest delight of gardens afford much comfort in sleep; wherein the dullness of that sense shakes hands with delectable odours; and though in the bed of Cleopatra, can hardly with any delight raise up the ghost of a rose.

> *The Garden of Cyrus* (1658)

Sleep is a death, O make me try,
By sleeping what it is to die.
And as gently lay my head
On my grave, as now my bed.

> *Religio Medici* (1643)

Half our days we pass in the shadow of the earth; and the brother of death exacteth a third part of our lives.

> *Pseudodoxia Epidemica* (1646)

Burgess, Anthony (1917–1993)

English writer, linguist and composer

Laugh and the world laughs with you; snore and you sleep alone.

> *Inside Mr. Enderby* (1963)

Cervantes, Miguel de (1547–1616)

Spanish writer and dramatist

Bien haya el que inventó el sueño, capa que cubre todos los humanos pensamientos, manjar que quita la hambre, agua que ahuyenta la sed, fuego que calienta el frío, frío que templa el ardor, y, finalmente, moneda general con que todas las cosas se compran, balanza y peso que iguala al pastor con el rey y al simple con el discreto.

God bless whoever invented sleep, the cloak that covers all human thoughts. It is the food that satisfies hunger, the water that quenches thirst, the fire that warms cold, the cold that reduces heat, and, lastly, the common currency which can buy anything, the balance and compensating weight that makes the shepherd equal to the king, and the simpleton equal to the sage.

> *Don Quixote* (1615)

Coleridge, Samuel Taylor (1772–1834)

English poet, philosopher and critic

Oh sleep! it is a gentle thing
Beloved from pole to pole!
To Mary Queen the praise be given!
She sent the gentle sleep from Heaven,
That slid into my soul.

> 'The Rime of the Ancient Mariner' (1798)

Daniel, Samuel (1562–1619)

English poet, historian and dramatist

Care-charmer Sleep, son of the sable Night,
Brother to Death, in silent darkness born:
Relieve my languish, and restore the light,
With dark forgetting of my care return
And let the day be time enough to mourn
The shipwreck of my ill adventured youth:
Let waking eyes suffice to wail their scorn,
Without the torment of the night's untruth.

> *Delia* (1592)

De La Mare, Walter (1873–1956)

English poet

I met at eve the Prince of Sleep,
His was a still and lovely face,
He wandered through a valley steep,
Lovely in a lonely place.

> 'I Met at Eve' (1902)

Dekker, Thomas (c.1570–c.1632)

English dramatist

Golden slumbers kiss your eyes,
Smiles awake you when you rise:
Sleep, pretty wantons, do not cry,
And I will sing a lullaby:
Rock them, rock them, lullaby.

> 'Patient Grissil' (1603)

Dickens, Charles (1812–1870)

English writer

It would make any one go to sleep, that bedstead would, whether they wanted to or not.

> *The Pickwick Papers* (1837)

Fields, W.C. (1880–1946)
US film actor
> The best cure for insomnia is to get a lot of sleep.
>> Attr.

Fletcher, John (1579–1625)
English dramatist
> Care-charming Sleep, thou easer of all woes,
> Brother to Death.
>> *The Tragedy of Valentinian* (1647)

Golding, William (1911–1993)
English writer and poet
> Sleep is when all the unsorted stuff comes flying out as from a dustbin upset in a high wind.
>> *Pincher Martin* (1956)

Henri IV (1553–1610)
King of France
> *Les grands mangeurs et les grands dormeurs sont incapables de rien faire de grand.*
> Great eaters and great sleepers are not capable of doing anything great.
>> Attr.

Keats, John (1795–1821)
English poet
> O soft embalmer of the still midnight,
> Shutting, with careful fingers and benign,
> Our gloom-pleas'd eyes.
>> 'To Sleep' (1819)

Kleitman, Nathaniel (1895–1999)
US sleep scientist
> Tell me what the role of wakefulness is, and then I shall explain the role of sleep.
>> Obituary, *The Times*, 1999

Nietzsche, Friedrich Wilhelm (1844–1900)
German philosopher, critic and poet
> *Keine geringe Kunst ist schlafen: es tut schon not, den ganzen Tag darauf hin zu wachen.*
> Sleeping is no mean art: it is necessary to stay awake for it all day.
>> *Thus Spake Zarathustra* (1884)

Onassis, Aristotle (1906–1975)
Turkish-born Greek shipping magnate
> Don't sleep too much. If you sleep three hours less each night for a year, you will have an extra month and a half to succeed in.
>> *New York Times*

Proverb
> There will be sleeping enough in the grave.

Racine, Jean (1639–1699)
French tragedian and poet
> *Elle s'endormit du sommeil des justes.*
> She fell asleep and slept the sleep of the just.
>> *Abrégé de l'Histoire de Port Royal* (1742)

Sassoon, Siegfried (1886–1967)
English poet and writer
> Why do you lie with your legs ungainly huddled,
> And one arm bent across your sullen, cold
> Exhausted face? …
>
> You are too young to fall asleep for ever;
> And when you sleep you remind me of the dead.
>> 'The Dug-Out' (1918)

Shakespeare, William (1564–1616)
English dramatist, poet and actor
> Weariness
> Can snore upon the flint, when resty sloth
> Finds the down pillow hard.
>> *Cymbeline*, III.vi

> O sleep, O gentle sleep,
> Nature's soft nurse, how have I frighted thee,
> That thou no more wilt weigh my eyelids down,
> And steep my senses in forgetfulness?
> Why rather, sleep, liest thou in smoky cribs,
> Upon uneasy pallets stretching thee,
> And hush'd with buzzing night-flies to thy slumber,
> Than in the perfum'd chambers of the great,
> Under the canopies of costly state,
> And lull'd with sound of sweetest melody?
>> *Henry IV, Part 2*, III.i

> Methought I heard a voice cry 'Sleep no more;
> Macbeth does murder sleep' – the innocent sleep,
> Sleep that knits up the ravell'd sleave of care,
> The death of each day's life, sore labour's bath,
> Balm of hurt minds, great nature's second course,
> Chief nourisher in life's feast.
>> *Macbeth*, II.ii

> Not poppy, nor mandragora,
> Nor all the drowsy syrups of the world,
> Shall ever medicine thee to that sweet sleep
> Which thou owed'st yesterday.
>> *Othello*, III.iii

Sidney, Sir Philip (1554–1586)
English poet, critic, soldier, courtier and diplomat
> Come, Sleepe, O Sleepe, the certaine knot of peace,
> The bathing place of wits, the balm of woe,
> The poore man's wealth, the prysoner's release,
> The indifferent Judge betweene the hie and lowe.
>> *Astrophel and Stella* (1591), 38

Southey, Robert (1774–1843)
English poet, essayist, historian and letterwriter
> Thou hast been call'd, O Sleep! the friend of Woe,
> But 'tis the happy who have called thee so.
>> *The Curse of Kehama* (1810)

Tertz, Abram (1925–1997)
Russian writer and dissident
> Sleep is the watering place of the soul to which it hastens at night to drink at the sources of life. In sleep we receive confirmation … that we must go on living.
>> *A Voice From the Chorus* (1973)

Thomas, Dylan (1914–1953)
Welsh poet, writer and radio dramatist
> Sleeping as quiet as death, side by wrinkled side, toothless, salt and brown, like two old kippers in a box.
>> *Under Milk Wood* (1954)

Thomas, Edward (1878–1917)
English poet
> I have come to the borders of sleep,
> The unfathomable deep
> Forest where all must lose
> Their way, however straight,
> Or winding, soon or late;
> They cannot choose.
>> 'Lights Out' (1917)

Thomson, James (1700–1748)
Scottish poet and dramatist
> A pleasing land of drowsyhead it was.
>> *The Castle of Indolence* (1748)

Tyrrell, George (1861–1909)
Irish theologian
> I never quite forgave Mahaffy for getting himself suspended from preaching in the College Chapel. Ever since his sermons were discontinued, I suffer from insomnia in church.
>> In Oliver St John Gregory, *As I Was Going Down Sackville Street*

Young, Edward (1683–1765)
English poet, dramatist, satirist and clergyman
> Tir'd nature's sweet Restorer, balmy Sleep!
> He, like the World, his ready visit pays
> Where Fortune smiles; the wretched he forsakes.
>> *Night-Thoughts on Life, Death and Immortality* (1742–1746)

▶▶ BED; DEATH; DREAMS

smoking

Anonymous
> Oh no, thank you, I only smoke on special occasions.
>> Labour minister when asked, while dining with King George VI, if he would like a cigar

The British Medical Association
On claims that smoking can make men impotent
> The prospect that they could wreck their sex lives might just make them stop and think.
>> *The Times*, 1999

Burns, George (1896–1996)
US comedian
> I smoke 10 to 15 cigars a day, at my age I have to hold on to something.
>> Attr.

Calverley, C.S. (1831–1884)
English poet, parodist, scholar and lawyer
> How they who use fusees
> All grow by slow degrees
> Brainless as chimpanzees,
> Meagre as lizards:
> Go mad, and beat their wives;
> Plunge (after shocking lives)
> Razors and carving knives
> Into their gizzards.
>> 'Ode to Tobacco' (1861)

Charles, Prince of Wales (1948–)
Son and heir of Elizabeth II and Prince Philip
On the Prince of Wales
> I gave up smoking at the age of 11. I had one or two strong ones behind the chicken run at school.
>> *The Times*, 1998

Cowper, William (1731–1800)
English poet, hymn and letter writer
> The pipe, with solemn interposing puff,
> Makes half a sentence at a time enough;
> The dozing sages drop the drowsy strain,
> Then pause, and puff – and speak, and pause again.
>> 'Conversation' (1782)

> Pernicious weed! whose scent the fair annoys,
> Unfriendly to society's chief joys,
> Thy worst effect is banishing for hours
> The sex whose presence civilizes ours.
>> 'Conversation' (1782)

Doyle, Sir Arthur Conan (1859–1930)
Scottish writer and war correspondent
> A little monograph on the ashes of one hundred and forty different varieties of pipe, cigar, and cigarette tobacco.
>> 'The Boscombe Valley Mystery' (1892)

Elizabeth I (1533–1603)
Queen of England
To Sir Walter Raleigh
> I have known many persons who turned their gold into smoke, but you are the first to turn smoke into gold.
>> In Chamberlin, *The Sayings of Queen Elizabeth* (1923)

Helps, Sir Arthur (1813–1875)
English historian and writer

What a blessing this smoking is! perhaps the greatest that we owe to the discovery of America.

Friends in Council (1859)

James VI of Scotland and I of England (1566–1625)
King of Scotland from 1567 and of England from 1603

A branch of the sin of drunkenness, which is the root of all sins.

A Counterblast to Tobacco (1604)

Herein is not only a great vanity, but a great contempt of God's good gifts, that the sweetness of man's breath, being a good gift of God, should be wilfully corrupted by this stinking smoke.

A Counterblast to Tobacco (1604)

A custom loathesome to the eye, hateful to the nose, harmful to the brain, dangerous to the lungs, and in the black, stinking fume thereof, nearest resembling the horrible Stygian smoke of the pit that is bottomless.

A Counterblast to Tobacco (1604)

Jonson, Ben (1572–1637)
English dramatist and poet

Neither do thou lust after that tawney weed tobacco.

Bartholomew Fair (1614)

I do hold it, and will affirm it before any prince in Europe, to be the most sovereign and precious weed that ever the earth rendered to the use of man.

Every Man in His Humour (1598)

Ods me, I marvel what pleasure or felicity they have in taking their roguish tobacco. It is good for nothing but to choke a man, and fill him full of smoke and embers.

Every Man in His Humour (1598)

Kipling, Rudyard (1865–1936)
Indian-born British poet and writer

And a woman is only a woman, but a good cigar is a Smoke.

'The Betrothed' (1886)

Knebel, Fletcher (1911–1993)
US journalist and author

It is now proved beyond doubt that smoking is one of the leading causes of statistics.

Attr.

Lamb, Charles (1775–1834)
English essayist, critic and letter writer

This very night I am going to leave off tobacco! Surely there must be some other world in which this unconquerable purpose shall be realized. The soul hath not her generous aspirings implanted in her in vain.

Letter to Thomas Manning, 1815

Dr Parr ... asked him, how he had acquired his power of smoking at such a rate? Lamb replied, 'I toiled after it, sir, as some men toil after virtue.'

In Talfourd, *Memoirs of Charles Lamb* (1892)

May my last breath be drawn through a pipe and exhaled in a pun.

In Wintle and Kenin, *Dictionary of Biographical Quotations*

Lindsay, Norman (1879–1969)
Australian artist and writer

'You ain't got any tobacco,' he said scornfully to Bunyip Bluegum. 'I can see that at a glance, You're one of the non-smoking sort, all fur and feathers.'

The Magic Pudding (1918)

Napoleon III (1808–1873)
French emperor
On being asked to ban smoking

This vice brings in one hundred million francs in taxes every year. I will certainly forbid it at once – as soon as you can name a virtue that brings in as much revenue.

In Hoffmeister, *Anekdotenschatz*

Satie, Erik (1866–1925)
French composer

Mon médecin m'a toujours dit de fumer. Il ajoute à ses conseils: 'Fumez, mon ami: sans cela, un autre fumera à votre place.'
'My doctor has always told me to smoke. He explains himself thus: 'Smoke, my friend. If you don't, someone else will smoke in your place.'

Mémoires d'un amnésique (1924)

Shields, Brooke (1965–)
US film actress

Smoking kills. If you're killed, you've lost a very important part of your life.

Remark, quoted in *The Observer*, 1998

Toscanini, Arturo (1867–1957)
Italian conductor

I smoked my first cigarette and kissed my first woman on the same day. I have never had time for tobacco since.

The Observer, 1946

Twain, Mark (1835–1910)
US humorist, writer, journalist and lecturer
Saying how easy it is to give up smoking

I've done it a hundred times!

Attr.

Wilde, Oscar (1854–1900)
Irish poet, dramatist, writer, critic and wit

A cigarette is the perfect type of a perfect pleasure. It is exquisite, and it leaves one unsatisfied. What more can one want?

The Picture of Dorian Gray (1891)

▶▶ ABSTINENCE

snobbery

Lynes, J. Russel (1910–1991)

The true snob never rests: there is always a higher goal to attain, and there are, by the same token, always more and more people to look down upon.

Attr.

Proust, Marcel (1871–1922)
French writer and critic

His hatred of snobs was a derivative of his snobbishness, but made the simpletons (in other words, everyone) believe that he was immune from snobbishness.

Le Côté de Guermantes (1921)

Thackeray, William Makepeace (1811–1863)
Indian-born English writer

It is impossible, in our condition of Society, not to be sometimes a Snob.

The Book of Snobs (1848)

He who meanly admires mean things is a Snob.

The Book of Snobs (1848)

Ustinov, Sir Peter (1921–)
English actor, director, dramatist, writer and raconteur

Laughter would be bereaved if snobbery died.

The Observer, 1955

Wilde, Oscar (1854–1900)
Irish poet, dramatist, writer, critic and wit

Never speak disrespectfully of Society, Algernon. Only people who can't get into it do that.

The Importance of Being Earnest (1895)

Wilson, Sir Angus (1913–1991)
English author

I have no concern for the common man except that he should not be so common.

No Laughing Matter (1967)

▶▶ ARISTOCRACY; CLASS

snow

Bridges, Robert (1844–1930)
English poet, dramatist, essayist and doctor

When men were all asleep the snow came flying,
In large white flakes falling on the city brown,
Stealthily and perpetually settling and loosely lying,
Hushing the latest traffic of the drowsy town …

All night it fell, and when full inches seven
It lay in depth of its uncompacted lightness,
The clouds blew off from a high and frosty heaven;
And all woke either for the unaccustomed brightness
Of the winter dawning, the strange unheavenly glare …

Or peering up from under the white-mossed wonder,
'O look at the trees!' they cried, 'O look at the trees!'.

'London Snow' (1890)

Emerson, Ralph Waldo (1803–1882)
US poet, essayist, transcendentalist and teacher

The frolic architecture of the snow.

Poems (1847), 'The Snow-storm'

Hardy, Thomas (1840–1928)
English writer and poet

Every branch big with it,
Bent every twig with it;
Every fork like a white web-foot;
Every street and pavement mute:
Some flakes have lost their way, and grope back upward, when
Meeting those meandering down they turn and descend again.

'Snow in the Suburbs' (1925)

Southey, Robert (1774–1843)
English poet, essayist, historian and letterwriter

Their wintry garment of unsullied snow
The mountains have put on.

The Poet's Pilgrimage (1816)

Thomas, Dylan (1914–1953)
Welsh poet, writer and radio dramatist

I can never remember whether it snowed for six days and six nights when I was twelve or whether it snowed for twelve days and twelve nights when I was six.

A Child's Christmas in Wales (1954)

Thompson, Francis (1859–1907)
English poet

What heart could have thought you? –
Past our devisal
(O filigree petal!)
Fashioned so purely,
Fragilely, surely,
From what Paradisal
Imagineless metal,
Too costly for cost?

'To a Snowflake' (1913)

▶▶ SEASONS; WEATHER

socialism

Benn, Tony (1925–)

English Labour politician

On Tony Blair

> The paradox at the moment is that the Labour Party is cheering the leader because they think he'll win. The City and the press are cheering him because they think he's going to destroy socialism.
>
> *The Observer,* 1995

Bennett, Alan (1934–)

English dramatist, actor and diarist

> Why is it always the intelligent people who are socialists?
>
> *Forty Years On* (1969)

Bevan, Aneurin (1897–1960)

Welsh Labour politician, miner and orator

> The language of priorities is the religion of Socialism.
>
> Attr.

Cartland, Barbara (1901–2000)

English writer

> The trouble with half the Socialists is they're suffering from vitamin deficiency.
>
> Remark 1965, quoted in *The Guardian,* 2000

Connell, James M. (1852–1929)

Irish-born writer of socialist songs and poems

> The people's flag is deepest red;
> It shrouded oft our martyred dead,
> And ere their limbs grew stiff and cold,
> Their heart's blood dyed its every fold.
> Then raise the scarlet standard high!
> Within its shade we'll live or die.
> Tho' cowards flinch and traitors sneer,
> We'll keep the red flag flying here.
>
> 'The Red Flag' (1889)

Dubcek, Alexander (1921–1992)

Czechoslovak statesman; First Secretary of the Communist Party 1968–69

> In the service of the people we followed such a policy that socialism would not lose its human face.
>
> Attr.

Durant, Will (1885–1982)

US philosopher and writer

> There is nothing in Socialism that a little age or a little money will not cure.
>
> Attr.

Edward VIII (later Duke of Windsor) (1894–1972)

King of the United Kingdom; abdicated 11 December 1936

Quoting Sir William Harcourt

> We are all socialists now.
>
> Attr.

Hattersley, Roy (1932–)

British Labour politician and writer

> Since I was 16 I have held the view that the Sermon on the Mount was a better statement of democratic socialism than Clause 4, either old or new.
>
> *The Observer,* 1999

Keynes, John Maynard (1883–1946)

English economist

> Marxian Socialism must always remain a portent to the historians of opinion – how a doctrine so illogical and so dull can have exercised so powerful and enduring an influence over the minds of men, and, through them, the events of history.
>
> 'The End of Laissez-Faire' (1926)

Kinnock, Neil (1942–)

Welsh Labour politician

> The idea that there is a model Labour voter, a blue-collar council house tenant who belongs to a union and has 2.4 children, a five-year-old car and a holiday in Blackpool, is patronizing and politically immature.
>
> Speech, 1986

Lenin, V.I. (1870–1924)

Russian revolutionary, Marxist theoretician and first leader of the USSR

> We shall now proceed to construct the socialist order.
>
> Speech, 1917

> Under socialism all will govern in turn and will soon become accustomed to no one governing.
>
> *The State and Revolution* (1917)

Lindsay, Norman (1879–1969)

Australian artist and writer

On Melbourne socialists

> They were a bloodthirsty lot, those sentimentalists who wept for the sad lot of the working classes.
>
> *Bohemians of the Bulletin* (1965)

Orwell, George (1903–1950)

English writer and critic

> As with the Christian religion, the worst advertisement for Socialism is its adherents.
>
> *The Road to Wigan Pier* (1937)

> To the ordinary working man, the sort you would meet in any pub on Saturday night, Socialism does not mean much more than better wages and shorter hours and nobody bossing you about.
>
> *The Road to Wigan Pier* (1937)

Stoppard, Tom (1937–)
British dramatist
> Socialists treat their servants with respect and then wonder why they vote Conservative.
>> *Lord Malquist and Mr Moon* (1966)

Stretton, Hugh (1924–)
Australian political scientist and historian
> Most capacities for love develop (or don't) in childhood; the largest quantity of willing human cooperation occurs within and between households; cooperation there is the pattern, and has to be the continuing basis, for cooperation anywhere else. To put it in the most shocking possible language, socialism should cease to be the factory-floor and chicken-battery party, and become the hearth-and-home, do-it-yourself party.
>> *Capitalism, Socialism and the Environment* (1976)

Thatcher, Margaret (1925–)
English Conservative Prime Minister
> State socialism is totally alien to the British character.
>> *The Times*, 1983

Viera Gallo, José Antonio (1943–)
Chilean politician
> Socialism can arrive only by bicycle.
>> In Ivan Illich, *Energy and Equity* (1974)

Warren, Earl (1891–1974)
US lawyer and politician
> Many people consider the things which government does for them to be social progress, but they consider the things government does for others as socialism.
>> *Peter's Quotations*

▶▶ COMMUNISM

society

Aristotle (384–322 BC)
Greek philosopher
> A person who cannot live in society, or does not need to because he is self-sufficient, is either a beast or a god.
>> *Politics*

Aurelius, Marcus (121–180)
Roman emperor and Stoic philosopher
> What is not good for the beehive, cannot be good for the bees.
>> *Meditations*

Bacon, Francis (1561–1626)
English philosopher, essayist, politician and courtier
> Man seeketh in society comfort, use, and protection.
>> *The Advancement of Learning* (1605)

Berlin, Isaiah (1909–1997)
English philosopher
> The history of society is the history of the inventive labours that alter man, alter his desires, habits, outlook, relationships both to other men and to physical nature, with which man is in perpetual physical and technological metabolism.
>> *Karl Marx* (1978)

Cicero (106–43 BC)
Roman orator, statesman, essayist and letter writer
> *O tempora! O mores!*
> What times! What manners!
>> *In Catilinam*

Claudel, Paul (1868–1955)
French dramatist, poet and diplomat
> The only living societies are those which are animated by inequality and injustice.
>> *Conversations dans le Loir-et-Cher*

Counihan, Noel Jack (1913–1986)
Australian cartoonist and artist
> In human society the warmth is mainly at the bottom.
>> *Age*, 1986

Curry, George
English churchman
On the young people involved in the 1991 riots in Tyneside
> It's not sex and drug advice these kids need, so much as help in acquiring a world view, in motivating them to take responsibility and enabling them to build proper relationships. But if you say that sort of thing to the social work agencies, they just turn off and say: 'Oh, those are moral issues – we can't be going into those.' But we have to! Otherwise, we shall simply be raising generations of animals, of Calibans.
>> *Daily Mail*, 1996

Emerson, Ralph Waldo (1803–1882)
US poet, essayist, transcendentalist and teacher
> The virtues of society are the vices of the saint.
>> *Essays, First Series* (1841)

> Society everywhere is in conspiracy against the manhood of every one of its members.
>> 'Self-Reliance' (1841)

Fortune, T. Thomas (1856–1928)
US journalist and editor
> When a society fosters as much crime and destitution as ours, with ample resources to meet the actual necessities of every one, there must be something radically wrong, not in the society but in the foundation upon which society

is reared.

Black and White: Land, Labor and Politics in the South (1884)

Galbraith, J.K. (1908–)
Canadian-born US economist, diplomat and writer
In the affluent society, no sharp distinction can be made between luxuries and necessaries.

The Affluent Society (1958)

Gingrich, Newt (1943–)
US Republican politician
No society can survive, no civilization can survive, with 12-year-olds having babies, with 15-year-olds killing each other, with 17-year-olds dying of Aids, with 18-year-olds getting diplomas they can't read.

The Times, 1995

Hazlitt, William (1778–1830)
English writer and critic
I do not think there is anything deserving the name of society to be found out of London.

Table-Talk (1822)

Howkins, Alun (1947–)
British historian and writer
The English pub is, we are told from childhood, a unique institution. Nothing 'quite like it' exists anywhere else. That's true. The pub uniquely represents, even in metropolitan England, the precise inequalities of gender, race and class that construct our society. From the inclusive white, male and proletarian 'public' of many northern pubs to the parasitic blazer and cotton dress 'locals' of the home counties, our unique institution divides our society and our social life.

New Statesman and Society, 1989

Hume, Basil (1923–1999)
English Cardinal, Archbishop of Westminster
On the killing of London headmaster Philip Lawrence
We have really lost in our society the sense of the sacredness of life.

The Observer Review, 1995

Jenkins, Roy (1920–)
Welsh politician and writer
The permissive society has been allowed to become a dirty phrase. A better phrase is the civilized society.

Speech, 1969

Jospin, Lionel (1937–)
French politician and Socialist Prime Minister
Yes to the market economy. No to the market society.

The Observer, 1998

Mandela, Nelson (1918–)
South African statesman and President
We enter into a covenant that we shall build the society in which all South Africans, both black and white, will be able to walk tall, without any fear in their hearts, assured of their inalienable right to human dignity – a rainbow nation at peace with itself and the world.

Inaugural Address, 1994

Mencken, H.L. (1880–1956)
US writer, critic, philologist and satirist
A society made up of individuals who were all capable of original thought would probably be unendurable. The pressure of ideas would simply drive it frantic.

'Minority Report' (1956)

Mill, John Stuart (1806–1873)
English philosopher, economist and reformer
When society requires to be rebuilt, there is no use in attempting to rebuild it on the old plan.

Dissertations and Discussions (1859)

Roosevelt, Theodore (1858–1919)
US Republican President
The men with the muck-rakes are often indispensable to the well-being of society; but only if they know when to stop raking the muck.

Speech, 1906

Shakespeare, William (1564–1616)
English dramatist, poet and actor
Society is no comfort
To one not sociable.

Cymbeline, IV:ii

Smith, Adam (1723–1790)
Scottish economist, philosopher and essayist
No society can surely be flourishing and happy, of which the far greater part of the members are poor and miserable.

Wealth of Nations (1776)

Spencer, Herbert (1820–1903)
English philosopher and journalist
No one can be perfectly free till all are free; no one can be perfectly moral till all are moral; no one can be perfectly happy till all are happy.

Social Statics (1850)

Spinoza, Baruch (1632–1677)
Dutch philosopher and theologian
Homo sit animale sociale.
Man is a social animal.

Ethics (1677)

Tawney, R.H. (1880–1962)
British economic historian and Christian socialist
As long as men are men, a poor society cannot be too poor to find a right order of life, nor a rich society too rich to have need to seek it.

The Acquisitive Society (1921)

Thackeray, William Makepeace (1811–1863)
Indian-born English writer

It is impossible, in our condition of Society, not to be sometimes a Snob.

The Book of Snobs (1848)

Thatcher, Margaret (1925–)
English Conservative Prime Minister
> There is no such thing as society. There are individual men and women and there are families.
>
> Attr.

Thoreau, Henry David (1817–1862)
US essayist, social critic and writer
> Wherever a man goes, men will pursue him and paw him with their dirty institutions, and, if they can, constrain him to belong to their desperate oddfellow society.
>
> *Walden* (1854)

Wilde, Oscar (1854–1900)
Irish poet, dramatist, writer, critic and wit
Of society
> To be in it is merely a bore. But to be out of it simply a tragedy.
>
> *A Woman of No Importance* (1893)

Wilson, Harold (1916–1995)
English Labour Prime Minister
Referring to Christine Keeler
> There is something utterly nauseating about a system of society which pays a harlot 25 times as much as it pays its Prime Minister, 250 times as much as it pays its Members of Parliament, and 500 times as much as it pays some of its ministers of religion.
>
> Speech, 1963

▶▶ HUMANITY AND HUMAN NATURE; PARTIES; PEOPLE

solitude

Bacon, Francis (1561–1626)
English philosopher, essayist, politician and courtier
> It had been hard for him that spake it to have put more truth and untruth together, in a few words, than in that speech: 'Whosoever is delighted in solitude is either a wild beast, or a god.'
>
> 'Of Friendship' (1625)

Cowper, William (1731–1800)
English poet, hymn and letter writer
> I praise the Frenchman, his remark was shrewd –
> How sweet, how passing sweet, is solitude!
> But grant me still a friend in my retreat,
> Whom I may whisper – solitude is sweet.
>
> 'Retirement' (1782)

De Quincey, Thomas (1785–1859)
English writer

No man will ever unfold the capacities of his own intellect, who does not at least checker his life with solitude.

Suspiria de Profundis (1845)

Eco, Umberto (1932–)
Italian critic and writer
> Solitude is a kind of freedom.
>
> *The Observer Review*, 1995

Gibbon, Edward (1737–1794)
English historian, politician and memoirist
> I was never less alone than when by myself.
>
> *Memoirs of My Life and Writings* (1796)

Mann, Thomas (1875–1955)
German writer and critic
> *Einsamkeit zeitigt das Originale, das gewagt und befremdend Schöne, das Gedicht. Einsamkeit zeitigt aber auch das Verkehrte, das Unverhältnismässige, das Absurde und Unerlaubte.*
> Solitude gives rise to what is original, to what is daringly and displeasingly beautiful, to poetry. Solitude however also gives rise to what is wrong, excessive, absurd and forbidden.
>
> *Death in Venice* (1912)

Montaigne, Michel de (1533–1592)
French essayist and moralist
> *Il se faut réserver une arrière boutique toute nôtre, toute franche, en laquelle nous établissons notre vraie liberté et principale retraite et solitude.*
> We should keep for ourselves a little back shop, all our own, untouched by others, in which we establish our true freedom and chief place of seclusion and solitude.
>
> *Essais* (1580)

Pope, Alexander (1688–1744)
English poet, translator and editor
> Thus let me live, unseen, unknown;
> Thus unlamented let me die;
> Steal from the world, and not a stone
> Tell where I lie.
>
> 'Ode on Solitude' (c.1700)

Rostand, Jean (1894–1977)
French biologist
> *Etre adulte, c'est être seul.*
> To be an adult is to be alone.
>
> *Thoughts of a Biologist* (1939)

Sarton, May (1912–1995)
US poet and writer
> Loneliness is the poverty of self; solitude is the richness of self.
>
> *Mrs Stevens Hears the Mermaids Singing* (1993)

Sassoon, Siegfried (1886–1967)
English poet and writer
> Alone … The word is life endured and known.
> It is the stillness where our spirits walk

And all but inmost faith is overthrown.
The Heart's Journey (1928)

Schopenhauer, Arthur (1788–1860)
German philosopher
> *Einsamkeit ist das Los aller hervorragenden Geister: sie werden solche bisweilen beseufzen; aber stets sie als das kleinere von zwei ‹beln erwählen.*
> Solitude is the fate of all outstanding minds: it will at times be deplored; but it will always be chosen as the lesser of two evils.
> 'Aphorisms for Wisdom' (1851)

Schreiner, Olive (1855–1920)
South African writer
> She thought of the narrowness of the limits within which a human soul may speak and be understood by its nearest of mental kin, of how soon it reaches that solitary land of the individual experience in which no fellow footfall is ever heard.
> *The Story of an African Farm* (1884)

Thoreau, Henry David (1817–1862)
US essayist, social critic and writer
> I never found the companion that was so companionable as solitude.
> *Walden* (1854)

▶▶ LONELINESS

songs and singers

Beaumarchais (1732–1799)
French dramatist, essayist, watchmaker and spy
> *Aujourd'hui ce qui ne vaut pas la peine d'être dit, on le chante.*
> Today what is not worth saying is made into a song.
> *Le Barbier de Seville* (1775)

Claribel (Mrs C.A. Barnard) (1840–1869)
Engish ballad writer
> I cannot sing the old songs
> I sang long years ago,
> For heart and voice would fail me,
> And foolish tears would flow.
> 'The Old Songs' (1865)

Coleridge, Samuel Taylor (1772–1834)
English poet, philosopher and critic
> Swans sing before they die –'twere no bad thing
> Should certain persons die before they sing.
> 'Epigram on a Volunteer Singer' (1800)

Dylan, Bob (1941–)
US singer and songwriter
On being asked if he could say something about his songs
> Yeah, some of them are about ten minutes long, others five or six.
> Interview

> In writing songs I've learned as much from Cézanne as I have from Woody Guthrie.
> In Clinton Heylin, *Dylan: Behind the Shades* (1991)

Fletcher, Andrew, of Saltoun (1655–1716)
Scottish politician and reformer
> I knew a very wise man who believed that … if a man were permitted to make all the ballads, he need not care who should make the laws of a nation. And we find that most of the ancient legislators thought they could not well reform the manners of any city without the help of a lyric, and sometimes of a dramatic poet.
> *Letter to the Marquis of Montrose*, 1704

Freed, Arthur (1894–1973)
US film producer and songwriter
> I'm singing in the rain, just singing in the rain;
> What a wonderful feeling, I'm happy again.
> 'Singing in the Rain', 1929

Landor, Walter Savage (1775–1864)
English poet and writer
> There is delight in singing, tho' none hear
> Beside the singer.
> 'To Robert Browning' (1846)

Maugham, William Somerset (1874–1965)
English writer, dramatist and physician
> Music-hall songs provide the dull with wit, just as proverbs provide them with wisdom.
> *A Writer's Notebook* (1949)

Musset, Alfred de (1810–1857)
French dramatist and poet
> *Les plus désespérés sont les chants les plus beaux*
> *Et j'en sais d'immortels qui sont de purs sanglots.*
> The most despairing songs are the most beautiful, and I know of immortal ones which are pure tears.
> 'La Nuit de mai' (1840)

Saint-Lambert, Jean François, Marquis de (1716–1803)
French poet
> *Souvent j'écoute encor quand le chant a cessé.*
> Often I am still listening when the song has ended.
> *Les Saisons*, 'Le Printemps'

Sassoon, Siegfried (1886–1967)
English poet and writer
> Everyone suddenly burst out singing;
> And I was filled with such delight
> As prisoned birds must find in freedom
> Winging wildly across the white
> Orchards and dark green fields; on – on – and out of sight.
> 'Everyone Sang' (1919)

The song was wordless;
The singing will never be done.

'Everyone Sang' (1919)

Scott, Sir Walter (1771–1832)
Scottish writer and historian
The way was long, the wind was cold,
The Minstrel was infirm and old;
His wither'd cheek, and tresses gray,
Seemed to have known a better day.

The Lay of the Last Minstrel (1805), Introduction

Shakespeare, William (1564–1616)
English dramatist, poet and actor
I had rather be a kitten and cry mew
Than one of these same metre ballad-mongers.

Henry IV, Part 1, III.i

Stevens, Wallace (1879–1955)
US poet, essayist, dramatist and lawyer
For she was the maker of the song she sang.
The ever-hooded, tragic-gestured sea
Was merely a place by which she walked to sing.

'The Idea of Order at Key West' (1936)

Thompson, Francis (1859–1907)
English poet
Go, songs, for ended is our brief sweet play;
Go, children of swift joy and tardy sorrow:
And some are sung, and that was yesterday,
And some unsung, and that may be to-morrow.

'Envoy' (1913)

Wordsworth, William (1770–1850)
English poet
Behold her, single in the field,
Yon solitary Highland lass! …

Will no one tell me what she sings? –
Perhaps the plaintive numbers flow
For old, unhappy, far-off things,
And battles long ago.

'The Reaper' (1807)

Yeats, W.B. (1865–1939)
Irish poet, dramatist, editor, writer and senator
I made my song a coat
Covered with embroideries
Out of old mythologies
From heel to throat;
But the fools caught it,
Wore it in the world's eye
As though they'd wrought it.
Song, let them take it
For there's more enterprise
In walking naked.

Responsibilities (1914)

▶▶ MUSIC

the soul

Arnold, Matthew (1822–1888)
English poet, critic, essayist and educationist
We cannot kindle when we will
The fire which in the heart resides,
The spirit bloweth and is still,
In mystery our soul abides.

'Morality' (1852)

Bernard, Saint (1091–1153)
French abbot and founder of the Cistercian order
Liberavi animam meam.
I have freed my soul.

'Epistle 371'

The Bible (King James Version)
What is a man profited, if he shall gain the whole world, and lose his own soul?

Matthew, 16:26

Crabbe, George (1754–1832)
English poet, clergyman, surgeon and botanist
It is the soul that sees; the outward eyes
Present the object, but the mind descries.

The Lover's Journey

Dickinson, Emily (1830–1886)
US poet
The Soul selects her own Society –
Then – shuts the Door –
To her divine Majority –
Present no more …

I've known her – from an ample nation –
Choose One –
Then – close the Valves of her attention –
Like Stone.

'The Soul selects her own Society' (c.1862)

Donne, John (1572–1631)
English poet
Poor intricated soul! Riddling, perplexed, labyrinthical soul!

LXXX Sermons (1640)

Emerson, Ralph Waldo (1803–1882)
US poet, essayist, transcendentalist and teacher
When divine souls appear men are compelled by their own self-respect to distinguish them.

Journals

Hadrian (AD 76–138)
Roman emperor and patron of the arts
Ah fleeting Spirit! wand'ring Fire,
That long hast warm'd my tender Breast,
Must thou no more this Frame inspire?
No more a pleasing, cheerful Guest?

'Ad Animam Suam', trans.
Pope

Juvenal (c.60–130)
Roman verse satirist and Stoic

> *Mors sola fatetur*
> *Quantula sint hominum corpuscula.*
> Death only this mysterious truth unfolds,
> The mighty soul, how small a body holds.
>
> *Satires*

Keats, John (1795–1821)
English poet

> A man should have the fine point of his soul
> taken off to become fit for this world.
>
> Letter to J.H. Reynolds, 1817

Lewis, Wyndham (1882–1957)
US-born British painter, critic and writer

> The soul started at the knee-cap and ended at
> the navel.
>
> *The Apes of Gods* (1930)

Lucretius (c.95–55 BC)
Roman philosopher

> *Nil igitur mors est ad nos neque pertinet hilum,*
> *Quandoquidem natura animi mortalis habetur.*
> What has this bugbear death to frighten man
> If souls can die as well as bodies can?
>
> *De Rerum Natura*

McAuley, James Philip (1917–1976)
Australian poet and critic

> The soul must feed on something for its dreams,
> In those brick suburbs, and there wasn't much:
> It can make do with little, so it seems.
>
> 'Wisteria' (1971)

Meredith, George (1828–1909)
English writer, poet and critic

> There is nothing the body suffers the soul may
> not profit by.
>
> *Diana of the Crossways* (1885)

Pope, Alexander (1688–1744)
English poet, translator and editor

> It is with narrow-souled people as with narrow-
> necked bottles: the less they have in them, the
> more noise they make in pouring it out.
>
> *Miscellanies (1727)*, 'Thoughts on Various Subjects'

Raleigh, Sir Walter (c.1552–1618)
English courtier, explorer, military commander, poet,
historian and essayist

> Go, Soul, the body's guest,
> Upon a thankless arrant:
> Fear not to touch the best;
> The truth shall be thy warrant:
> Go, since I needs must die,
> And give the world the lie.
>
> 'The Lie' (1608)

Rimbaud, Arthur (1854–1891)
French poet

> *O saisons, ô châteaux!*

> *Quelle âme est sans défauts?*
> O seasons, O castles! What soul is without
> faults?
>
> 'O saisons, ô châteaux' (1872)

Shelley, Percy Bysshe (1792–1822)
English poet, dramatist and essayist

> The soul of man, like unextinguished fire,
> Yet burns towards heaven with fierce reproach.
>
> *Prometheus Unbound* (1820)

Smith, Logan Pearsall (1865–1946)
US-born British epigrammatist, critic and writer

> Most people sell their souls, and live with a
> good conscience on the proceeds.
>
> *Afterthoughts* (1931)

Socrates (469–399 BC)
Athenian philosopher

> A man should feel confident concerning his soul,
> who in his life has rejected those pleasures and
> fineries that go with the body as being alien to
> him, considering them to result more in harm
> than in good, and has eagerly sought the
> pleasures that go with learning and adorned his
> soul with no alien but rather with its own proper
> refinements, moderation and justice and
> courage and freedom and truth; thus he awaits
> his journey to the world below, ready whenever
> fate calls him.
>
> Attr. in Plato, *Phaedo*

Sterne, Laurence (1713–1768)
Irish-born English writer and clergyman

> I am positive I have a soul; nor can all the books
> with which materialists have pestered the world
> ever convince me to the contrary.
>
> *A Sentimental Journey* (1768)

Swift, Jonathan (1667–1745)
Irish satirist, poet, essayist and cleric

> The Manner whereby the Soul and Body are
> united, and how they are distinguished, is wholly
> unaccountable to us. We see but one Part, and
> yet we know we consist of two; and this is a
> Mystery we cannot comprehend, any more than
> that of the Trinity.
>
> 'On the Trinity'

Swinburne, Algernon Charles (1837–1909)
English poet, critic, dramatist and letter writer

> A little soul for a little bears up this corpse
> which is man.
>
> 'Hymn to Proserpine'
> (1866)

Webster, John (c.1580–c.1625)
English dramatist

> My soul, like to a ship in a black storm,
> Is driven, I know not whither.
>
> *The White Devil* (1612)

Wordsworth, William (1770–1850)
English poet
> Our birth is but a sleep and a
> forgetting.
> The Soul that rises with us, our life's Star,
> Hath had elsewhere its setting,
> And cometh from afar.
>> 'Ode: Intimations of Immortality' (1807)

►► IMMORTALITY

south africa

Campbell, Roy (1901–1957)
South African poet and journalist
> South Africa, renowned both far and wide
> For politics and little else beside:
> Where, having torn the land with shot and shell,
> Our sturdy pioneers as farmers dwell,
> And, 'twixt the hours of strenuous sleep, relax
> To shear the fleeces or to fleece the blacks.
>> *The Wayzgoose* (1928)

Mandela, Nelson (1918–)
South African statesman and President
> Let there be justice for all. Let there be peace
> for all. Let there be bread, water and salt for all.
> Let freedom reign. The sun shall never set on so
> glorious a human achievement.
>> *Independent on Sunday*, 14 May 1994

O'Rourke, P.J. (1947–)
US writer
On white South Africans
> They've never learned to stand up and lie like
> white men.
>> *The Weekend Guardian*, 1993

Paton, Alan (1903–1988)
South African writer
> It was on Wednesday 16 June 1976 that an era
> came to an end in South Africa. That was the
> day when black South Africans said to
> white, 'You can't do this to us any more.'
> It had taken three hundred years for them
> to say that.
>> *Journey Continued*
>> (1988)

Pringle, Thomas (1789–1834)
Scottish poet
> Afar in the desert I love to ride,
> With the silent Bush-boy alone by my side;
> Away, away in the wilderness vast,
> Where the white man's foot hath never passed …
>
> Man is distant, but God is near.
>> *African Sketches* (1834)

space

Addison, Joseph (1672–1719)
English essayist, poet, playwright and statesman
> The spacious firmament on high,
> With all the blue ethereal sky,
> And spangled heavens, a shining frame,
> Their great Original proclaim.
>> *The Spectator*, 1712

Alfonso X (1221–1284)
Spanish monarch
On the Ptolemaic system of astronomy
> If the Lord Almighty had consulted me before
> embarking upon Creation, I should have
> recommended something simpler.
>> Attr.

Armstrong, Neil (1930–)
US astronaut and first man on the moon
First words on lunar touch-down of space module during
Apollo XI mission
> Tranquillity Base here – the Eagle has landed.
>> TV coverage, 20 July 1969

On stepping on to the moon
> That's one small step for a man, one giant leap
> for mankind.
>> *New York Times*, 1969

The Bible (King James Version)
> The heavens declare the glory of God; and the
> firmament sheweth his handywork.
>> *Psalms*, 19:1

Brennan, Christopher (1870–1932)
Australian poet
> Where star-cold and the dread of space
> in icy silence bind the main
> I feel but vastness on my face
> I sit, a mere incurious brain,
> under some outcast satellite.
>> *Poems* (1914)

Byron, Lord (1788–1824)
English poet satirist and traveller
> Ye stars! which are the poetry of heaven!
>> *Childe Harold's Pilgrimage* (1812–18)

Campbell, Thomas (1777–1844)
Scottish poet, ballad writer and journalist
> The sentinel stars set their watch in the sky.
>> 'The Soldier's Dream'

Chesterton, G.K. (1874–1936)
English writer, poet and critic
> The cosmos is about the smallest hole that a
> man can hide his head in.
>> *Orthodoxy* (1908)

De Vries, Peter (1910–1993)
US novelist

Anyone informed that the universe is expanding and contracting in pulsations of eighty billion years has a right to ask, 'What's in it for me?'.

The Glory of the Hummingbird (1974)

Frost, Robert (1874–1963)
US poet

> They cannot scare me with their empty spaces
> Between stars – on stars where no human race is.
> I have it in me so much nearer home
> To scare myself with my own desert places.

'Desert Places' (1936)

Fuller, Richard Buckminster (1895–1983)
US architect and engineer

> I am a passenger on the spaceship, Earth.

Operating Manual for Spaceship Earth (1969)

Galilei, Galileo (1564–1642)
Italian scientist
Remark made after he was forced to withdraw his assertion that the Earth moved round the Sun

> *Eppur si muove.*
> But it does move.

Attr., 1632

Hardy, Thomas (1840–1928)
English writer and poet

> The sovereign brilliancy of Sirius pierced the eye with a steely glitter, the star called Capella was yellow, Aldebaran and Betelgueux shone with a fiery red.
> To persons standing alone on a hill during a clear midnight such as this, the roll of the world eastward is almost a palpable movement.

Far From the Madding Crowd (1874)

Holmes, Rev. John H. (1879–1964)
US Unitarian minister

> This universe is not hostile, nor yet is it friendly. It is simply indifferent.

A Sensible Man's View of Religion (1932)

Hopkins, Gerard Manley (1844–1889)
English Jesuit priest, poet and classicist

> Look at the stars! look, look up at the skies!
> Oh look at all the fire-folk sitting in the air!
> The bright boroughs, the circle-citadels there!

'The Starlight Night' (1877)

Joyce, James (1882–1941)
Irish writer

> The heaventree of stars hung with humid nightblue fruit.

Ulysses (1922)

O'Casey, Sean (1880–1964)
Irish dramatist

> I often looked up at the sky an' assed meself the question – what is the stars, what is the stars?

Juno and the Paycock (1924)

Shakespeare, William (1564–1616)
English dramatist, poet and actor

> Look how the floor of heaven
> Is thick inlaid with patines of bright gold;
> There's not the smallest orb which thou behold'st
> But in his motion like an angel sings,
> Still quiring to the young-ey'd cherubins.

The Merchant of Venice, V.i

Sidney, Sir Philip (1554–1586)
English poet, critic, soldier, courtier and diplomat

> With how sad steps O Moone thou clim'st the skyes,
> How silently, and with how meane a face,
> What may it be, that even in heavenly place,
> That busie Archer his sharpe Arrowes tryes?

Astrophel and Stella (1591)

Vidal, Gore (1925–)
US writer, critic and poet

> The astronauts! … Rotarians in outer space.

Two Sisters (1970)

Virgil (70–19 BC)
Roman poet

> *Nosque ubi primus equis Oriens adflavit anhelis,*
> *Illic sera rubens accendit lumina Vesper.*
> And when the rising sun has first breathed on us with his panting horses, over there the glowing evening-star is lighting his late lamps.

Georgics

Woolley, Richard
In 1956, one year before Sputnik

> Space travel is utter bilge.

In Martin Moskovits, *Science and Society*, 1995

Young, Andrew John (1885–1971)
Scottish poet, churchman and botanist

> But moon nor star-untidy sky
> Could catch my eye as that star's eye;
> For still I looked on that same star,
> That fitful, fiery Lucifer,
> Watching with mind as quiet as moss
> Its light nailed to a burning cross.

'The Evening Star' (1922)

▶▶ DISCOVERY; SCIENCE; STARS; TECHNOLOGY; UNIVERSE

speech

Clinton, William ('Bill') (1946–)
US Democrat President
Remembering an overlong speech

> It wasn't my finest hour. It wasn't even my finest half hour.

The Washington Post, 1988

Lloyd George, David (1863–1945)
British Liberal statesman

> The finest eloquence is that which gets things done; the worst is that which delays them.
>> Speech at Paris Peace Conference, 1919

Peacock, Thomas Love (1785–1866)
English writer and poet

> He remembered too late on his thorny green bed,
> Much that well may be thought cannot wisely be said.
>> *Crotchet Castle* (1831), 'The Priest and the Mulberry Tree'

Pepys, Samuel (1633–1703)
English diarist, naval administrator and politician

> Strange the difference of men's talk!
>> *Diary*, 1659–60

Perelman, S.J. (1904–1979)
US humorist, writer and dramatist

> You've a sharp tongue in your head, Mr Essick. Look out it doesn't cut your throat.
>> *The Rising Gorge*

Shakespeare, William (1564–1616)
English dramatist, poet and actor

> I do not much dislike the matter, but
> The manner of his speech.
>> *Antony and Cleopatra*, II.ii

▶▶ CONVERSATION

spirituality

Bukowski, Charles (1920–1994)
US writer and poet

> Show me a man who lives alone and has a perpetually clean kitchen, and eight times out of nine I'll show you a man with detestable spiritual qualities.
>> *Tales of Ordinary Madness* (1967)

sport and games

Ali, Muhammad (1942–)
US heavyweight boxer

> Float like a butterfly, sting like a bee.
>> Catchphrase

> Champions aren't made in gyms. Champions are made from something they have deep inside them – a desire, a dream, a vision. They have to have the skill, and the will. But the will must be stronger than the skill.
>> *The Greatest* (1975)

Anonymous
Plea to 'Shoeless' Joe Jackson, when he and seven other US baseball players were banned for life after being found guilty of throwing the World Series in 1920

> Say it ain't so, Joe. Please say it ain't so.

> Shooting is a popular sport in the countryside … Unlike many other countries, the outstanding characteristic of the sport has been that it is not confined to any one class.
>> The Northern Ireland Tourist Board, 1969

> They'll be dancing in the streets of Raith tonight.
> Falsely attributed to both Kenneth Wolstenholme and David Coleman, this reference to Raith Rovers fans dancing in a non-existent Scottish town – the team plays in Kirkcaldy – almost certainly originated in a BBC radio broadcast from London in 1963, after Raith Rovers defeated Aberdeen in a Scottish Cup tie

> 'Well, what sort of sport has Lord — had?'
> 'Oh, the young Sahib shot divinely, but God was very merciful to the birds.'
>> In Russell, *Collections and Recollections* (1898)

> [Alberto] Juantorena opens wide his legs and shows his class.
> British commentator at 1976 Montreal Olympics, probably Ron Pickering; wrongly ascribed to David Coleman

Archer, Mark

> In the case of almost every sport one can think of, from tennis to billiards, golf to skittles, it was royalty or the aristocracy who originally developed, codified and popularised the sport, after which it was taken up by the lower classes.
>> *The Spectator*, 1996

Barbarito, Luigi (1922–)
Papal emissary
Commenting on a sponsored snooker competition at a convent

> Playing snooker gives you firm hands and helps to build up character. It is the ideal recreation for dedicated nuns.
>> *The Daily Telegraph*, 1989

Bardot, Brigitte (1934–)
Comment on the 1998 World Cup, hosted by France

> It's a pity to see Paris, the world capital of thinking, devoting so much interest to a game played with feet.
>> *The Scotsman*, June 1998

Barnes, Simon (1951–)
English writer
On the use of drugs in sport

> Showbiz brings us people who change their superficial appearance, but sport brings us people who … change their bodies as we might change a shirt.
>> *The Times*, 1999

Sport is something that does not matter, but is performed as if it did. In that contradiction lies its beauty.

The Spectator, 1996

Belasco, David (1853–1931)
US theatre producer and playwright
> Boxing is showbusiness with blood.

Attr., 1915

Bennett, Alan (1934–)
English dramatist, actor and diarist
> If you think squash is a competitive activity, try flower arrangement.

Talking Heads (1988)

Bernhardt, Sarah (1844–1923)
French actress
Remark while watching a game of football
> I do love cricket – it's so very English.

Attr.

Best, George (1946–)
English footballer
On being named Footballer of the Century
> It's a pleasure to be standing up here. It's a pleasure to be standing up.

Speech, 1999

Blainey, Geoffrey Norman (1930–)
Australian writer
> We forget that the nineteenth century often turned work into sport. We, in contrast, often turn sport into work.

Victorian Historical Journal, 1978

Brown, Rita Mae (1944–)
US writer and poet
> Sport strips away personality, letting the white bone of character shine through.

Sudden Death (1983)

Byron, H.J. (1834–1884)
English dramatist and actor
> Life's too short for chess.

Our Boys

Canterbury, Tom
US basketball player
> The trouble with referees is that they just don't care which side wins.

The Guardian, 1980

Coleman, David (1926–)
English sports commentator and broadcaster
> That's the fastest time ever run – but it's not as fast as the world record.

In Fantoni, *Private Eye's Colemanballs (3)* (1986)

Connolly, Billy (1942–)
Scottish comedian and actor
> I love fishing. It's like transcendental meditation

with a punch-line.

Gullible's Travels

Connors, Jimmy (1952–)
US tennis player
> I hate to lose more than I love to win. I hate to see the happiness on their faces when they beat me.

New York Times, 1977

> New Yorkers love it when you spill your guts out there. Spill your guts at Wimbledon and they make you stop and clean it up.

The Guardian, 1984

Davis, Steve (1957–)
English snooker player
> Sport is cut and dried. You always know when you succeed … You are not an actor: you don't wonder 'did my performance go down all right?' You've lost.

Remark

Dempsey, Jack (1895–1983)
US boxer
> Kill the other guy before he kills you.

Motto

Disraeli, Benjamin (1804–1881)
English statesman and writer
> Yesterday at the racket court, sitting in the gallery among strangers, the ball … fell at my feet. I picked it up, and observing a young rifleman excessively stiff, I humbly requested him to forward its passage into the court, as I really had never thrown a ball in my life.

Letter to his father, quoted by André Maurois in *Disraeli: A Picture of the Victorian Age* (1927)

Durocher, Leo (1905–1991)
US baseball player and coach
Remark at a practice ground, 1946
> Nice guys finish last.

Attr.

Eubank, Chris (1966–)
British boxer
> Any boxer who says he loves boxing is either a liar or a fool. I'm not looking for glory … I'm looking for money. I'm looking for readies.

The Times, 1993

Fitzsimmons, Robert (1862–1917)
New Zealand world champion boxer
Remark before a boxing match, 1900
> The bigger they come, the harder they fall.

Attr.

Ford, Henry (1863–1947)
US car manufacturer
> Exercise is bunk. If you are healthy, you don't need it: if you are sick, you shouldn't take it.

Attr.

Fox, Dixon Ryan
US historian

> I listened to a football coach who spoke straight from the shoulder – at least I could detect no higher origin in anything he said.
>
> Attr.

Fuller, Thomas (1654–1734)
English physician

> It is a silly game where nobody wins.
>
> *Gnomologia* (1732)

Gascoigne, Paul (1967–)
English footballer

> I get on a train and sit in second class and people think, 'tight bastard. Money he's got and he sits in second class.' So I think, ' them' and I go in first class and then they say, 'look at that ing flash bastard in first class'.
>
> *Glasgow Herald*, 1995

Greaves, Jimmy (1940–)
English footballer and television commentator

> The only thing that Norwich didn't get was the goal that they finally got.
>
> In Fantoni, *Private Eye's Colemanballs (2)* (1984)

> The thing about sport, any sport, is that swearing is very much part of it.
>
> Attr.

Gummer, John (1939–)
English Conservative politician

> Extravagant hospitality, gifts and freebies have been part of the culture of the International Olympics Committee for years.
>
> *The Times*, 1999

Hemingway, Ernest (1898–1961)
US author

> Bullfighting is the only art in which the artist is in danger of death and in which the degree of brilliance in the performance is left to the fighter's honour.
>
> *Death in the Afternoon* (1932)

Huistra, Peter (1967–)
Dutch footballer

> Soccer in Japan is interesting, in Glasgow it's a matter of life and death.
>
> *Daily Mail*, 1996

Humphries, Barry (1934–)
Australian entertainer

> Sport is a loathsome and dangerous pursuit.
>
> *Sydney Morning Herald*, 1982

Ingham, Sir Bernard (1932–)
English government press officer and writer

> Blood sport is brought to its ultimate refinement in the gossip columns.
>
> Remark, 1986

Jacobs, Joe (1896–1940)
US boxing manager
Remark made after Max Schmeling, whom he managed, lost his boxing title to Jack Sharkey in 1932

> We was robbed!
>
> Attr.

Jerrold, Douglas William (1803–1857)
English dramatist, writer and wit

> The only athletic sport I ever mastered was backgammon.
>
> In W. Jerrold, *Douglas Jerrold* (1914)

John Paul II (1920–)
Polish pope
Replying to the suggestion that it was inappropriate for a cardinal to ski

> It is unbecoming for a cardinal to ski badly.
>
> Attr.

Johnson, Samuel (1709–1784)
English lexicographer, poet, critic, conversationalist and essayist

> I am sorry I have not learned to play at cards. It is very useful in life: it generates kindness and consolidates society.
>
> In Boswell, *Journal of a Tour to the Hebrides* (1785)

> Fly fishing may be a very pleasant amusement; but angling or float fishing I can only compare to a stick and a string, with a worm at one end and a fool at the other.
>
> Attr. in Hawker, *Instructions to Young Sportsmen* (1859)

King, Billie-Jean (1943–)
US tennis player

> It's really impossible for athletes to grow up. As long as you're playing, no one will let you. On the one hand, you're a child, still playing a game … But on the other hand, you're a superhuman hero that everyone dreams of being. No wonder we have such a hard time understanding who we are.
>
> *Billie-Jean* (1982)

Kinglake, Edward (1864–1935)

> Every Australian worships the Goddess of Sport with profound adoration, and there is no nation in the world which treats itself to so many holidays.
>
> *The Australian at Home*

Lamb, Charles (1775–1834)
English essayist, critic and letter writer

> Man is a gaming animal. He must always be trying to get the better in something or other.
>
> 'Mrs Battle's Opinions on Whist' (1823)

Louis, Joe (1914–1981)
US champion boxer
Referring to the speed of an opponent, Billy Conn

He can run, but he can't hide.

Attr.

Mays, Willie (1931–)
US baseball player
> I think I was the best baseball player I ever saw.

Newsweek, 1970

McEnroe, John (1959–)
US tennis player
To an umpire; this remark became a catchphrase in the early 1980s
> You cannot be serious.

Attr.

To an umpire at Wimbledon, 1981
> You are the pits of the world.

The Sunday Times, 1984

McGuigan, Barry (1961–)
British boxer
> The gladiators and champions through the ages confirm quite clearly that aggressive competition is part of the human makeup. For the sport of professional boxing to be banned would be the most terrible error.

The Observer, 1994

Mourie, Graham (1952–)
New Zealand rugby player
> Nobody ever beats Wales at rugby, they just score more points.

In Keating, *Caught by Keating*

Navratilova, Martina (1956–)
US tennis player
> The moment of victory is much too short to live for that and nothing else.

The Guardian, 1989

Nicol, Patricia
English journalist
On Scottish football fans
> Crowds of drunk, usually disappointed men are, I think, quite a frightening spectre for a woman. When they happen to be got up like some savage hybrid of Calum Kennedy, Papa Smurf and Chewbacca, I think a full-blown phobia is perfectly understandable.

The Sunday Times, 1999

O'Reilly, Tony (1936–)
Irish entrepreneur and international rugby player
Commenting on the voice of Winston McCarthy, the noted rugby commentator
> The love call of two pieces of sandpaper.

New Zealand Listener, 1984

O'Rourke, P.J. (1947–)
US writer
> The sport of skiing consists of wearing three thousand dollars' worth of clothes and equipment and driving two hundred miles in the snow in order to stand around at a bar and get drunk.

Modern Manners (1984)

Orwell, George (1903–1950)
English writer and critic
> Serious sport has nothing to do with fair play. It is bound up with hatred, jealousy, boastfulness, disregard for all rules and sadistic pleasure in witnessing violence; in other words it is war minus the shooting.

Shooting an Elephant (1950)

Ovett, Steve (1955–)
English athlete
> There is no way sport is so important that it can be allowed to damage the rest of your life.

Remark at the Olympic Games, 1984

Potter, Stephen (1900–1969)
English writer, critic and lecturer
> Gamesmanship or, The Art of Winning Games without actually Cheating.

Title of book, 1947

Rice, Grantland (1880–1954)
US writer
> For when the One Great Scorer comes to mark against your name,
> He marks – not that you won or lost – but how you played the Game.

'Alumnus Football' (1941)

Shaw, George Bernard (1856–1950)
Irish socialist, writer, dramatist and critic
An R.S.V.P. to an invitation to attend an athletic meeting at the Wangamui Domain
> I take athletic competitive sports very seriously indeed ... as they seem to produce more bad feeling, bad manners and international hatred than any other popular movement.

Auckland Star, 1934

Snagge, John (1904–1996)
British television broadcaster and commentator
> I don't know who's ahead – it's either Oxford or Cambridge.

Radio commentary on the Boat Race, 1949

Somerville, William (1675–1742)
English poet
> My hoarse-sounding horn
> Invites thee to the chase, the sport of kings;
> Image of war, without its guilt.

The Chase (1735)

Spencer, Herbert (1820–1903)
English philosopher and journalist
> It was remarked to me ... that to play billiards well was a sign of an ill-spent youth.

In Duncan, *Life and Letters of Spencer* (1908)

Tosatti, Giorgio (1740–1778)

Lo sport è sempre stato strumento di lotta politica.
Sport has always been an instrument for political
strife.

Corriere della Sera, 1994

Vukovich, Bill (1918–1955)
US racing driver
Explaining his success in the Indianapolis 500

There's no secret. You just press the accelerator
to the floor and steer left.

Attr.

Walton, Izaak (1593–1683)
English writer

Sir Henry Wotton … was also a most dear lover,
and a frequent practiser of the art of angling; of
which he would say, 'it was an employment for
his idle time, which was then not idly spent … a
rest to his mind, a cheerer of his spirits, a
diverter of sadness, a calmer of unquiet
thoughts, a moderator of passions, a procurer of
contentedness; and that it begat habits of peace
and patience in those that professed and
practised it.'

The Compleat Angler (1653)

We may say of angling as Dr Boteler said of
strawberries: 'Doubtless God could have made a
better berry, but doubtless God never did'; and
so (if I might be judge) God never did make a
more calm, quiet, innocent recreation than
angling.

The Compleat Angler (1653)

As no man is born an artist, so no man is born
an angler.

The Compleat Angler (1653)

White, Andrew Dickson (1832–1918)
US educator and diplomat
Refusing to allow the Cornell football team to visit Michigan
to play a match

I will not permit thirty men to travel four
hundred miles to agitate a bag of wind.

In D. Wallechinsky, *The People's Almanac*

Wodehouse, P.G. (1881–1975)
English humorist and writer

While they were content to peck cautiously at
the ball, he never spared himself in his efforts to
do it a violent injury.

The Heart of a Goof (1926)

The least thing upset him on the links. He
missed short putts because of the uproar of the
butterflies in the adjoining meadows.

The Clicking of Cuthbert (1922)

▶▶ CRICKET; FOOTBALL; GOLF

the state

Aristotle (384–322 BC)
Greek philosopher

Blessed is the state in which those in power
have moderate and sufficient means since where
some are immoderately wealthy and others have
nothing, the result will be extreme democracy or
absolute oligarchy, or a tyranny may result from
either of these extremes.

Politics

The final association composed of several
villages is the city state; it has now reached the
limit of virtual self-sufficiency, and so while it
comes into existence for the sake of life, it exists
for the good life.

Politics

Auden, W.H. (1907–1973)
English poet, essayist, critic, teacher and dramatist

There is no such thing as the State
And no one exists alone.
Hunger allows no choice
To the citizen or the police;
We must love one another or die.

Collected Poems, 1939–1947, 'September 1, 1939'

Boutros-Ghali, Boutros (1922–)
Secretary General of the United Nations

… the time of absolute and exclusive national
sovereignty has passed.

Scotland on Sunday, 1992

Burke, Edmund (1729–1797)
Irish-born British statesman and philosopher

A state without the means of some change is
without the means of its conservation.

Reflections on the Revolution in France (1790)

Cromwell, Oliver (1599–1658)
English general, statesman and Puritan leader

The State, in choosing men to serve it, takes no
notice of their opinions. If they be willing
faithfully to serve it, that satisfies.

Said before the Battle of Marston Moor,
1644

Dürrenmatt, Friedrich (1921–1990)
Swiss dramatist and writer

*Wir haben durch die Jahrhunderte hindurch so viel dem
Staat geopfert, dass es jetzt Zeit ist, dass sich der Staat
für uns opfert.*
Through the centuries we have sacrificed so much
for the state that it is now time for the state to
sacrifice itself for us.

Romulus the Great (1964)

Engels, Friedrich (1820–1895)
German socialist and political philosopher

Der Staat wird nicht 'abgeschafft', er stirbt ab.

The state is not abolished, it dies away.

Anti-Dühring (1878)

Inge, William Ralph (1860–1954)

English divine, writer and teacher

The nations which have put mankind and posterity most in their debt have been small states – Israel, Athens, Florence, Elizabethan England.

Outspoken Essays: Second Series (1922)

Landor, Walter Savage (1775–1864)

English poet and writer

States, like men, have their growth, their manhood, their decrepitude, their decay.

Imaginary Conversations (1876)

Lenin, V.I. (1870–1924)

Russian revolutionary, Marxist theoretician and first leader of the USSR

So long as the state exists there is no freedom. When there is freedom there will be no state.

The State and Revolution (1917)

Louis XIV (1638–1715)

King of France

L'État c'est moi.

I am the State.

Attr.

Mill, John Stuart (1806–1873)

English philosopher, economist and reformer

A State which dwarfs its men, in order that they may be more docile instruments in its hands even for beneficial purposes – will find that with small men no great thing can really be accomplished.

On Liberty (1859)

The worth of a State, in the long run, is the worth of the individuals composing it.

On Liberty (1859)

Plato (c.429–347 BC)

Greek philosopher

Our object in the establishment of the state is the greatest happiness of the whole, and not that of any one class.

Republic

It is the rulers of the state, if anybody, who may lie in dealing with citizens or enemies, for reasons of state.

Republic

Ruskin, John (1819–1900)

English art critic, philosopher and reformer

I hold it for indisputable, that the first duty of a State is to see that every child born therein shall be well housed, clothed, fed and educated, till it attain years of discretion.

Time and Tide by Weare and Tyne (1867)

Shelley, Percy Bysshe (1792–1822)

English poet, dramatist and essayist

The rich have become richer, and the poor have become poorer; and the vessel of the state is driven between the Scylla and Charybdis of anarchy and despotism.

A Defence of Poetry (1821)

Stalin, Joseph (1879–1953)

Soviet Communist leader

The state is a machine in the hands of the ruling class for suppressing the resistance of its class enemies.

Foundations of Leninism (1924)

Temple, William (1881–1944)

Anglican prelate, social reformer and writer

In place of the conception of the Power-State we are led to that of the Welfare-State.

Citizen and Churchman (1941)

▶▶ DEMOCRACY; GOVERNMENT

statistics

Asquith, Herbert (1852–1928)

English Liberal statesman and Prime Minister

On the reason for the three sets of figures kept by the War Office

One to mislead the public; another to mislead the Cabinet, and the third to mislead itself.

In Alastair Horne, *The Price of Glory* (1962)

Auden, W.H. (1907–1973)

English poet, essayist, critic, teacher and dramatist

Thou shalt not sit

With statisticians nor commit

A social science.

Collected Poems, 1939–1947, 'Under Which Lyre'

Out of the air a voice without a face

Proved by statistics that some cause was just

In tones as dry and level as the place.

The Shield of Achilles (1955)

Carlyle, Thomas (1795–1881)

Scottish historian, biographer, critic, and essayist

A witty statesman said, you might prove anything by figures.

Chartism (1839)

Disraeli, Benjamin (1804–1881)

English statesman and writer

There are three kinds of lies: lies, damned lies and statistics.

Attr.

Lloyd George, David (1863–1945)

British Liberal statesman

Advocating Tariff Reform

You cannot feed the hungry on statistics.

Speech, 1904

Nightingale, Florence (1820–1910)
English nurse

To understand God's thoughts we must study statistics, for these are the measure of his purpose.

Attr.

Stout, Rex (1886–1975)
US crime writer

There are two kinds of statistics, the kind you look up and the kind you make up.

Death of a Doxy

stories

Ford, Ford Madox (1873–1939)
English novelist

This is the saddest story I have ever heard.

The Good Soldier (1915), first sentence

Heine, Heinrich (1797–1856)
German lyric poet, essayist and journalist

It is an old story, yet it remains forever new.

Book of Songs (1822–1823)

Shakespeare, William (1564–1616)
English dramatist, poet and actor

An honest tale speeds best being plainly told.

Richard III, IV.iv

Sidney, Sir Philip (1554–1586)
English poet, critic, soldier, courtier and diplomat

With a tale forsooth he commeth unto you, with a tale, which holdeth children from play, and olde men from the Chimney corner.

The Defence of Poesie
(1595)

Steele, Sir Richard (1672–1729)
Irish-born English writer, dramatist and politician

I have often thought that a Story-teller is born, as well as a Poet.

The Guardian, 42, 1713

▶▶ BOOKS; FICTION; LITERATURE

strangers

The Bible (King James Version)

I was a stranger, and ye took me in: Naked, and ye clothed me: I was sick, and ye visited me: I was in prison, and ye came unto me.

Matthew, 25:35–36

Be not forgetful to entertain strangers: for

thereby some have entertained angels unawares.

Hebrews, 13:2

Punch

'Who's 'im, Bill?' 'A stranger!' ''Eave 'arf a brick at 'im.'

1854

Shakespeare, William (1564–1616)
English dramatist, poet and actor

I do desire we may be better strangers.

As You Like It, III.ii

Steele, Sir Richard (1672–1729)
Irish-born English writer, dramatist and politician

We were in some little Time fixed in our Seats, and sat with that Dislike which People not too good-natured, usually conceive of each other at first Sight.

The Spectator, 132, 1711

stress

Adams, Scott (1957–)
US cartoonist

I don't suffer from stress – I'm a carrier …

The Dilbert Priniciple

stupidity

Adams, Scott (1957–)
US cartoonist

You can never underestimate the stupidity of the general public.

The Dilbert Future

There's nothing more dangerous than a resourceful idiot.

Dilbert

Anonymous

Never attribute to malice that which is adequately explained by stupidity.

Hanlon's Razor

The probability of someone watching you is proportional to the stupidity of your action.

Hartley's First Law

Dickens, Charles (1812–1870)
English writer

He'd be sharper than a serpent's tooth, if he wasn't as dull as ditch water.

Our Mutual Friend
(1866)

Marx, Groucho (1895–1977)
US comedian

You've got the brain of a four-year-old boy, and I

bet he was glad to get rid of it.
Horse Feathers (film, 1932)

Muir, Frank (1920–1998)
English writer, humorist and broadcaster
I've examined your son's head, Mr Glum, and there's nothing there.
Take it from Here, with Dennis Norden, 1957

O'Rourke, P.J. (1947–)
US writer
Earnestness is just stupidity sent to college.
Attr. in *The Observer*, 1996

Proverb
Ask a silly question and you'll get a silly answer.

Wilde, Oscar (1854–1900)
Irish poet, dramatist, writer, critic and wit
There is no sin except stupidity.
Intentions (1891), 'The Critic as Artist'

▶▶ FOOLISHNESS; IGNORANCE

style

Arnold, Matthew (1822–1888)
English poet, critic, essayist and educationist
Nothing has raised more questioning among my critics than these words – noble, the grand style … I think it will be found that the grand style arises in poetry, when a noble nature, poetically gifted, treats with simplicity or with severity a serious subject.
On Translating Homer (1861)

Bailey, David (1938–)
English photographer
Commenting on dumbed-down 'Cool Britannia'
The avant-garde has gone to Tescos.
The Times, 1999

Buffon, Comte de (1707–1788)
French naturalist
Ces choses sont hors de l'homme, le style est l'homme même.
These things subject matter are external to the man; style is the essence of man.
'Discours sur le Style' (1753)

Camus, Albert (1913–1960)
Algerian-born French writer
Le style, comme la popeline, dissimule trop souvent de l'eczéma.
Style, like sheer silk, too often hides eczema.
The Fall (1956)

Colman, the Younger, George (1762–1836)
English dramatist and Examiner of Plays
Johnson's style was grand and Gibbon's elegant; the stateliness of the former was sometimes pedantic, and the polish of the latter was occasionally finical. Johnson marched to kettle-drums and trumpets; Gibbon moved to flutes and hautboys: Johnson hewed passages through the Alps, while Gibbon levelled walks through parks and gardens.
Random Records (1830)

Connolly, Cyril (1903–1974)
English literary editor, writer and critic
An author arrives at a good style when his language performs what is required of it without shyness.
Enemies of Promise (1938)

The Mandarin style … is beloved by literary pundits, by those who would make the written word as unlike as possible to the spoken one. It is the style of those writers whose tendency is to make their language convey more than they mean or more than they feel.
Enemies of Promise (1938)

Gibbs, Wolcott (1902–1958)
Parody of *Time* magazine style
Backward ran sentences until reeled the mind.
More in Sorrow (1958)

Renard, Jules (1864–1910)
French writer and dramatist
Un mauvais style, c'est une pensée imparfaite.
Poor style reflects imperfect thought.
Journal, 1898

Swift, Jonathan (1667–1745)
Irish satirist, poet, essayist and cleric
Proper words in proper places, make the true definition of a style.
Letter to a Young Gentleman Lately Entered Into Holy Orders (1720)

Voltaire (1694–1778)
French philosopher, dramatist, poet, historian writer and critic
Tous les genres sont bons hors le genre ennuyeux.
All styles are good except the tedious kind.
L'Enfant prodigue (1738)

Wesley, Samuel (1662–1735)
English churchman and poet
Style is the dress of thought; a modest dress,
Neat, but not gaudy, will true critics please.
'An Epistle to a Friend concerning Poetry' (1700)

Wilde, Oscar (1854–1900)
Irish poet, dramatist, writer, critic and wit
In matters of grave importance, style, not sincerity, is the vital thing.
The Importance of Being Earnest (1895)

▶▶ FASHION; TASTE

suburbia

Betjeman, Sir John (1906–1984)
English poet laureate
> Gaily into Ruislip Gardens
> Runs the red electric train,
> With a thousand Ta's and Pardon's
> Daintily alights Elaine –
> Well cut Windsmoor flapping lightly,
> Jacqmar scarf of mauve and green
> Hiding hair which, Friday nightly,
> Delicately drowns in Drene.
>> *A Few Late Chrysanthemums* (1954), 'Middlesex'

Macaulay, Lord (1800–1859)
English Liberal statesman, essayist and poet
> An acre in Middlesex is better than a principality in Utopia.
>> *Collected Essays* (1843), 'Lord Bacon'

Raphael, Frederic (1931–)
English author
> I come from suburbia – I don't ever want to go back. It's the one place in the world that's further away than anywhere else.
>> *The Glittering Prizes* (1976)

▶▶ CITIES

success

Aaron, Hank (1934–)
US baseball player
> I never doubted my ability, but when you hear all your life you're inferior, it makes you wonder if the other guys have something you've never seen before. If they do, I'm still looking for it.
>> *I Had a Hammer* (1992)

Adams, Joey (b. 1911)
US comedian and author
> Rockefeller once explained the secret of success. 'Get up early, work late – and strike oil.'
>> Attr.

Addison, Joseph (1672–1719)
English essayist, poet, playwright and statesman
> 'Tis not in mortals to command success,
> But we'll do more, Sempronius; we'll deserve it.
>> *Cato* (1713)

Ade, George (1866–1944)
US fabulist and playwright
> Anybody can win, unless there happens to be a second entry.
>> Attr.

Anonymous
> Success always occurs in private, and failure in full view.

Barrie, Sir J.M. (1860–1937)
Scottish dramatist and writer
> Every man who is high up loves to think that he has done it all himself; and the wife smiles, and lets it go at that. It's our only joke. Every woman knows that.
>> *What Every Woman Knows* (1908

Brookner, Anita (1928–)
English writer
On the myth of the tortoise and the hare
> In real life, of course, it is the hare who wins. Every time. Look around you. And in any case it is my contention that Aesop was writing for the tortoise market … Hares have no time to read. They are too busy winning the game.
>> *Hotel du Lac* (1984)

Browning, Robert (1812–1889)
English poet
> A minute's success pays the failure of years.
>> 'Apollo and the Fates' (1887)

Buffett, Warren (1930–)
US billionaire investment expert
> If at first you succeed, quit trying.
>> In Janet Lowe, *Warren Buffet Speaks*

Burke, Edmund (1729–1797)
Irish-born British statesman and philosopher
> The only infallible criterion of wisdom to vulgar minds – success.
>> *Letter to a Member of the National Assembly* (1791)

Cagney, James (1904–1986)
US film actor
> Made it, Ma! Top of the world!
>> *White Heat* (film, 1949)

Canetti, Elias (1905–1994)
Bulgarian-born English writer, dramatist and critic
> Success is the space one occupies in the newspaper. Success is one day's insolence.
>> *The Secret Heart of the Clock: Notes, Aphorisms, Fragments 1973-1985* (1991)

Churchill, Charles (1731–1764)
English poet, political writer and clergyman
> Where he falls short, 'tis Nature's fault alone;
> Where he succeeds, the merit's all his own.
>> *The Rosciad* (1761)

Confucius (c.550–c.478 BC)
Chinese philosopher and teacher of ethics
> In all things, success depends upon previous preparation, and without such preparation there is sure to be failure.
>> *Analects*

Dewar, Lord Thomas Robert (1864–1930)

Scottish Conservative politician and writer

> The road to success is filled with women pushing their husbands along.
>
> *Epigram*

Dickinson, Emily (1830–1886)

US poet

> Success is counted sweetest
> By those who ne'er succeed.
> To comprehend a nectar
> Requires sorest need.
>
> 'Success is counted sweetest' (c.1859)

Ebner-Eschenbach, Marie von (1830–1916)

Austrian writer

> *Die stillstehende Uhr, die täglich zweimal die richtige Zeit angezeigt hat, blickt nach Jahren auf eine lange Reihe von Erfolgen zurück.*
> The clock which has stopped but has twice daily indicated the right time can years later look back on a long line of successes.
>
> *Aphorisms* (1880)

Hill, Damon (1960–)

English racing driver

> Winning is everything. The only ones who remember you when you come second are your wife and your dog.
>
> *The Sunday Times*, 1994

Huxley, Aldous (1894–1963)

English writer, poet and critic

> Success – 'The bitch-goddess, Success,' in William James's phrase – demands strange sacrifices from those who worship her.
>
> *Proper Studies* (1927)

James, William (1842–1910)

US psychologist and philosopher

> The moral flabbiness born of the exclusive worship of the bitch-goddess success. That – with the squalid cash interpretation put on the word success – is our national disease.
>
> Letter to H.G. Wells, 1906

King, Stephen (1947–)

US writer

> Talent is cheaper than table salt. What separates the talented individual from the successful one is a lot of hard work.
>
> *Independent on Sunday*, 1996

La Rochefoucauld (1613–1680)

French writer

> *Pour s'établir dans le monde, on fait tout ce que l'on peut pour y paraître établi.*
> To succeed in the world we do all we can to appear successful.
>
> *Maximes* (1678)

Lehman, Ernest (1920–)

US screenwriter

> Sweet Smell of Success.
>
> Title of novel and film, 1957

Lerner, Alan Jay (1918–1986)

US lyricist and screenwriter

> You write a hit the same way you write a flop.
>
> Attr.

Meir, Golda (1898–1978)

Russian-born Israeli stateswoman and Prime Minister

> I can honestly say that I was never affected by the question of the success of an undertaking. If I felt it was the right thing to do, I was for it regardless of the possible outcome.
>
> In Syrkin, *Golda Meir: Woman with a Cause* (1964)

Parks, Gordon (1912–)

US photographer and film director

> Success can be wracking and reproachful, to you and those close to you. It can entangle you with legends that are consuming and all but impossible to live up to.
>
> *Voices in the Mirror* (1990)

Pater, Walter (1839–1894)

English critic, writer and lecturer

> To burn always with this hard, gemlike flame, to maintain this ecstasy, is success in life.
>
> *Studies in the History of the Renaissance* (1873)

Powell, Colin (1937–)

US military leader

> There are no secrets to success: don't waste time looking for them. Success is the result of perfection, hard work, learning from failure, loyalty to those for whom you work, and persistence.
>
> *Colin Powell* (1989)

Proverbs

> If at first you don't succeed, try, try, try again.
>
> Nothing succeeds like success.

Quayle, Dan (1947–)

US Republican politician and Vice President

> If we do not succeed, then we run the risk of failure.
>
> Attr.

Renoir, Jean (1894–1979)

French film director

> Is it possible to succeed without betrayal?
>
> *My Life and My Films* (1974)

Russell, Rosalind (1911–1976)

US actress

> Success is a public affair. Failure is a private funeral.
>
> *Life Is a Banquet* (1977)

Sassoon, Vidal (1928–)
English hairdresser
> The only place where success comes before
> work is a dictionary.
>> Quoting one of his teachers in a BBC radio broadcast

Springsteen, Bruce (1949–)
US singer and songwriter
> Your success story is a bigger story than
> whatever you're trying to say on stage…
> Success makes life easier. It doesn't make living
> easier.
>> Q magazine, 1992

Turner, Lana (1920–1995)
US actress
> A successful man is one who makes more money
> than his wife can spend. A successful woman is
> one who can find such a man.
>> Attr.

Turner, Tina (1938–)
US singer
> The real power behind whatever success I have
> now was something I found within myself –
> something that's in all of us, I think, a little piece
> of God just waiting to be discovered.
>> I, Tina (1986)

Vidal, Gore (1925–)
US writer, critic and poet
> It is not enough to succeed. Others must fail.
>> In Irvine, Antipanegyric for Tom Driberg (1976)

> Whenever a friend succeeds, a little something
> in me dies.
>> The Sunday Times Magazine, 1973

> In America, the race goes to the loud, the
> solemn, the hustler. If you think you are a great
> writer, you must say that you are.
>> In George Plimpton, Writers at Work (1981)

Virgil (70–19 BC)
Roman poet
> *Hos successus alit: possunt, quia posse videntur.*
> To these success gives heart: they can because
> they think they can.
>> Aeneid

▶▶ ACHIEVEMENT; FAILURE; VICTORY

suffering

Achebe, Chinua (1930–)
Nigerian writer, poet and critic
> When suffering knocks at your door and you say
> there is no seat for him, he tells you not to
> worry because he has brought his own stool.
>> Arrow of God (1967)

Anonymous
> Three things one does not recover from –
> oppression that knows the backing of brute
> force,
> poverty that knows the destitution of one's
> home,
> and being deprived of children.
>> Somali poem

Auden, W.H. (1907–1973)
English poet, essayist, critic, teacher and dramatist
> About suffering they were never wrong,
> The Old Masters: how well they understood
> Its human position; how it takes place
> While someone else is eating or opening a
> window or just walking dully along …
>
> They never forgot
> That even the dreadful martyrdom must run its
> course
> Anyhow in a corner, some untidy spot
> Where the dogs go on with their doggy life and
> the torturer's horse
> Scratches its innocent behind on a tree.
>> 'Musée des Beaux Arts'

Austen, Jane (1775–1817)
English writer
> One does not love a place the less for having
> suffered in it, unless it has all been suffering,
> nothing but suffering.
>> Persuasion (1818)

Bacon, Francis (1561–1626)
English philosopher, essayist, politician and courtier
> It is a miserable state of mind to have few things
> to desire and many things to fear.
>> 'Of Empire' (1625)

Barnard, Christiaan (1922–)
South African surgeon
> Suffering isn't ennobling, recovery is.
>> New York Times, 1985

Boethius (c.475–524)
Roman statesman, scholar and philosopher
> *In omni adversitate fortunae, infelicissimum est genus*
> *infortunii, fuisse felicem.*
> At every blow of fate, the worst kind of
> misfortune is to have been happy.
>> De Consolatione Philosophiae (c.524)

> *Nihil est miserum nisi cum putes; contraque beata sors*
> *omnis est aequanimitate tolerantis.*
> Nothing is miserable unless you think it so;
> conversely, every lot is happy to one who is
> content with it.
>> De Consolatione Philosophiae (c.524)

Bono, Edward de (1933–)
British physician and writer
> Unhappiness is best defined as the difference

between our talents and our expectations.

The Observer, 1977

Browning, Elizabeth Barrett (1806–1861)
English poet; wife of Robert Browning

> For frequent tears have run
> The colours from my life.

Sonnets from the Portuguese (1850)

Carlyle, Thomas (1795–1881)
Scottish historian, biographer, critic, and essayist

> Man's Unhappiness, as I construe, comes of his
> Greatness; it is because there is an Infinite in
> him, which with all his cunning he cannot quite
> bury under the Finite.

Sartor Resartus (1834)

Chaucer, Geoffrey (c.1340–1400)
English poet, public servant and courtier

> For of fortunes sharpe adversitee
> The worste kynde of infortune is this,
> A man to han ben in prosperitee,
> And it remembren, whan it passed is.

Troilus and Criseyde

Congreve, William (1670–1729)
English dramatist

> *Millamant:* I believe I gave you some pain.
> *Mirabel:* Does that please you?
> *Millamant:* Infinitely; I love to give pain.

The Way of the World (1700)

Corneille, Pierre (1606–1684)
French dramatist, poet and lawyer

> *A raconter ses maux, souvent on les soulage.*
> Telling one's sorrows often brings comfort.

Polyeucte (1643)

Cowper, William (1731–1800)
English poet, hymn and letter writer

> But misery still delights to trace
> Its semblance in another's case.

'The Castaway' (1799)

Dante Alighieri (1265–1321)
Italian poet

> *Nessun maggior dolore,*
> *Che ricordarsi del tempo felice*
> *Nella miseria.*
> No sorrow is deeper than the remembrance of
> happiness when in misery.

Divina Commedia (1307)

Dickinson, Emily (1830–1886)
US poet

> After great pain, a formal feeling comes –
> The Nerves sit ceremonious, like Tombs –
> The stiff Heart questions was it He, that bore,
> And Yesterday, or Centuries before? ...
>
> This is the Hour of Lead –
> Remembered, if outlived,

As Freezing persons, recollect the Snow –
First – Chill – then Stupor – then the letting go.

'After great pain, a formal feeling comes' (c.1862)

Dix, Dorothy (1870–1951)
US writer

> It is only the women whose eyes have been
> washed clear with tears who get the broad
> vision that makes them little sisters to all the
> world.

Dorothy Dix, Her Book (1926)

Éluard, Paul (1895–1952)

> *Adieu tristesse*
> *Bonjour tristesse*
> *Tu es inscrite dans les lignes du plafond.*
> Sadness, adieu, sadness, hello, you are engraved
> in the lines of the ceiling.

'Slightly Disfigured' (1932)

Gay, John (1685–1732)
English poet, dramatist and librettist

> A moment of time may make us unhappy
> forever.

The Beggar's Opera (1728)

Hazlitt, William (1778–1830)
English writer and critic

> The least pain in our little finger gives us more
> concern and uneasiness, than the destruction of
> millions of our fellow-beings.

Edinburgh Review, 1829

Hemingway, Ernest (1898–1961)
US author

> The world breaks everyone and afterward many
> are strong at the broken places.

A Farewell to Arms (1929)

Hogg, James (1770–1835)
Scottish poet, ballad writer and writer

> How often does the evening cup of joy lead to
> sorrow in the morning!

Attr.

Hopkins, Gerard Manley (1844–1889)
English Jesuit priest, poet and classicist

> No worst, there is none. Pitched past pitch of
> grief,
> More pangs will, schooled at forepangs, wilder
> wring.
> Comforter, where, where is your comforting? ...
>
> O the mind, mind has mountains; cliffs of fall
> Frightful, sheer, no-man-fathomed ...
>
> Here! creep,
> Wretch, under a comfort serves in a whirlwind:
> all
> Life death does end and each day dies with
> sleep.

'No Worst, there is None' (1885)

Hugo, Victor (1802–1885)
French poet, writer, dramatist and politician
Souffrons, mais souffrons sur les cimes.
Let us suffer if we must, but let us suffer on the heights.
Contemplations (1856)

James, William (1842–1910)
US psychologist and philosopher
There is no more miserable human being than one in whom nothing is habitual but indecision.
Principles of Psychology (1890)

Johnson, Samuel (1709–1784)
English lexicographer, poet, critic, conversationalist and essayist
I shall long to see the miseries of the world, since the sight of them is necessary to happiness.
Rasselas (1759)

There is no wisdom in useless and hopeless sorrow.
Letter to Mrs. Thrale, 1781

Depend upon it that if a man talks of his misfortunes there is something in them that is not disagreeable to him; for where there is nothing but pure misery there never is any recourse to the mention of it.
In Boswell, *The Life of Samuel Johnson* (1791)

Keats, John (1795–1821)
English poet
Is there another Life? Shall I awake and find all this a dream? There must be, we cannot be created for this sort of suffering.
Letter to Charles Brown, 1820

Kempis, Thomas à (c.1380–1471)
German mystic, monk and writer
Si libenter crucem portas portabit te.
If you bear the cross willingly, it will bear you.
De Imitatione Christi (1892)

Kierkegaard, Søren (1813–1855)
Danish philosopher
The Two Ways: One is to suffer; the other is to become a professor of the fact that another suffered.
In W.H. Auden, *Kierkegaard*

La Rochefoucauld (1613–1680)
French writer
On n'est jamais si malheureux qu'on croit, ni si heureux qu'on espère.
One is never as unhappy as one thinks, or as happy as one hopes to be.
Maximes (1664)
Nous avons tous assez de force pour supporter les maux d'autrui.

We are all strong enough to bear the sufferings of others.
Maximes (1678)

Lowell, James Russell (1819–1891)
US poet, editor, abolitionist and diplomat
The misfortunes hardest to bear are those which never come.
'Democracy' (1887)

Miller, Arthur (1915–)
US dramatist and screenwriter
Years ago a person, he was unhappy, didn't know what to do with himself – he'd go to church, start a revolution – something. Today you're unhappy? Can't figure it out? What is the salvation? Go shopping.
The Price (1968)

Montaigne, Michel de (1533–1592)
French essayist and moralist
Qui craint de souffrir, il souffre déjà de ce qu'il craint.
A man who fears suffering is already suffering from what he fears.
Essais (1580)

Neaves, Charles, Lord (1800–1876)
English jurist
We can't for a certainty tell
What mirth may molest us on Monday;
But, at least, to begin the week well,
Let us all be unhappy on Sunday.
Songs and Verses

Nietzsche, Friedrich Wilhelm (1844–1900)
German philosopher, critic and poet
Was eigentlich gegen das Leiden empört, ist nicht das Leiden an sich, sondern das Sinnlose des Leidens.
What actually fills you with indignation as regards suffering is not suffering in itself but the pointlessness of suffering.
On the Genealogy of Morals (1881)

Parker, Dorothy (1893–1967)
US writer, poet, critic and wit
Sorrow is tranquillity remembered in emotion.
Here Lies (1939)

Pascal, Blaise (1623–1662)
French philosopher and scientist
All the troubles of men are caused by one single thing, which is their inability to stay quietly in a room.
Pensées (1670)

Pope, Alexander (1688–1744)
English poet, translator and editor
I never knew any man in my life, who could not bear another's misfortunes perfectly like a Christian.
Miscellanies (1727)

Saki (1870–1916)
Burmese-born British writer
> He's simply got the instinct for being unhappy
> highly developed.
>> *The Chronicles of Clovis* (1911)

Shakespeare, William (1564–1616)
English dramatist, poet and actor
> When sorrows come, they come not single spies,
> But in battalions.
>> *Hamlet*, IV.v

> In sooth I know not why I am so sad.
> It wearies me; you say it wearies you;
> But how I caught it, found it, or came by it,
> What stuff 'tis made of, whereof it is born,
> I am to learn;
> And such a want-wit sadness makes of me
> That I have much ado to know myself.
>> *The Merchant of Venice*, I.i

> Misery acquaints a man with strange bedfellows.
>> *The Tempest*, II.ii

Shaw, George Bernard (1856–1950)
Irish socialist, writer, dramatist and critic
> The secret of being miserable is to have leisure
> to bother about whether you are happy or not.
>> *Misalliance* (1914)

Sinatra, Frank (1915–1998)
US singer and actor
> I'm for anything that can get you through the
> night, be it prayer, tranquillizers or a bottle of
> Jack Daniels.
>> Attr. in *The Herald*,
>> 1998

Thompson, Francis (1859–1907)
English poet
> Nothing begins and nothing ends
> That is not paid with moan;
> For we are born in others' pain,
> And perish in our own.
>> 'Daisy' (1913)

Tolstoy, Leo (1828–1910)
Russian writer, essayist, philosopher and moralist
> Pure and complete sorrow is just as impossible
> as pure and complete joy.
>> *War and Peace* (1869)

> He knew that people would be merciless for the
> very reason that his heart was lacerated. He felt
> that his fellow-man would destroy him, as dogs
> kill some poor cur maimed and howling with
> pain. He knew that his only salvation lay in
> hiding his wounds, and he had instinctively tried
> to do this for two days, but now he no longer
> had the strength to keep up the unequal
> struggle.
>> *Anna Karenina* (1875–1877)

Verlaine, Paul (1844–1896)
French poet and autobiographer
> *Il pleure dans mon coeur*
> *Comme il pleut sur la ville.*
> Tears fall in my heart as rain falls on the city.
>> *Romances sans paroles* (1874)

Vigny, Alfred de (1797–1863)
French writer
> I love the majesty of human suffering.
>> *The Shepherd's House* (1844)

Whittier, John Greenleaf (1807–1892)
US poet, abolitionist and journalist
> For all sad words of tongue or pen,
> The saddest are these: 'It might have been!'.
>> 'Maud Muller' (1854)

Wilde, Oscar (1854–1900)
Irish poet, dramatist, writer, critic and wit
> Where there is sorrow, there is holy ground.
>> *De Profundis* (1897)

Wolpert, Lewis
English biologist
> A useful … way of thinking about depression is
> in terms of malignant sadness. Sadness is to
> depression what normal growth is to cancer.
>> *Malignant Sadness* (1999)

▶▶ DESPAIR

suicide

Budgell, Eustace (1686–1737)
English writer
Lines found on his desk after his suicide
> What Cato did, and Addison approved
> Cannot be wrong.
>> Attr.

Greer, Germaine (1939–)
Australian feminist, critic, English scholar and writer
> Suicide is an act of narcissistic manipulation and
> deep hostility.
>> *The Observer Review*, 1995

Ibsen, Henrik (1828–1906)
Norwegian writer, dramatist and poet
Judge Brack, on Hedda Gabler's suicide
> People don't do such things!
>> *Hedda Gabler* (1890)

Nietzsche, Friedrich Wilhelm (1844–1900)
German philosopher, critic and poet
> *Der Gedanke an den Selbstmord ist ein starkes*
> *Trostmittel: mit ihm kommt man gut über manche böse*
> *Nacht hinweg.*
> The thought of suicide is a great comfort: it's a
> good way of getting through many a bad night.
>> *Beyond Good and Evil* (1886)

Parker, Dorothy (1893–1967)
US writer, poet, critic and wit
> Razors pain you;
> Rivers are damp;
> Acids stain you;
> And drugs cause cramp.
> Guns aren't lawful;
> Nooses give;
> Gas smells awful;
> You might as well live.
>
> 'Résumé' (1937)

Parkes, Sir Henry (1815–1896)
Australian politician, writer and poet
On William Nicholas Willis
> Ho! the honourable member for Bourke, who is
> believed to have committed every crime in the
> calendar, – except the one we could so easily
> have forgiven him – suicide.
>
> In Wannan, *With Malice Aforethought*

Rhys, Jean (1894–1979)
West Indian-born English writer
> Next week, or next month, or next year I'll kill
> myself. But I might as well last out my month's
> rent, which has been paid up, and my credit for
> breakfast in the morning.
>
> *Good Morning, Midnight* (1939)

Sanders, George (1906–1972)
Russian-born British film actor
> Dear World, I am leaving you because I am bored.
> I am leaving you with your worries. Good luck.
>
> Suicide note

Shakespeare, William (1564–1616)
English dramatist, poet and actor
> O, that this too too solid flesh would melt,
> Thaw, and resolve itself into a dew!
> Or that the Everlasting had not fix'd
> His canon 'gainst self-slaughter! O God! God!
> How weary, stale, flat, and unprofitable,
> Seem to me all the uses of this world!
>
> *Hamlet*, I.ii

Swift, Jonathan (1667–1745)
Irish satirist, poet, essayist and cleric
> In Church your grandsire cut his throat;
> To do the job too long he tarry'd,
> He should have had my hearty vote,
> To cut his throat before he marry'd.
>
> 'Verses on the Upright Judge' (1724)

Tennyson, Alfred, Lord (1809–1892)
English lyric poet
> Nor at all can tell
> Whether I mean this day to end myself,
> Or lend an ear to Plato where he says,
> That men like soldiers may not quit the post
> Allotted by the Gods.
>
> 'Lucretius' (1868)

▶▶ DEATH

sun

Beckett, Samuel (1906–1989)
Irish dramatist, writer and poet
> The sun shone, having no alternative, on the
> nothing new.
>
> *Murphy* (1938)

Bridges, Robert (1844–1930)
English poet, dramatist, essayist and doctor
> The day begins to droop, –
> Its course is done:
> But nothing tells the place
> Of the setting sun.
>
> 'Winter Nightfall' (1925)

Donne, John (1572–1631)
English poet
> Yesternight the sun went hence,
> And yet is here today,
> He hath no desire nor sense,
> Nor half so short a way:
> Then fear not me,
> But believe that I shall make
> Speedier journeys, since I take
> More wings and spurs than he.
>
> *Songs and Sonnets* (1611)

Douglas, Gavin (c.1474–1522)
Scottish poet and bishop
> And all small fowlys singis on the spray:
> Welcum the lord of lycht and lamp of day.
>
> *Eneados* (1553)

Thomas, Dylan (1914–1953)
Welsh poet, writer and radio dramatist
> *Mr Pritchard*: I must dust the blinds and then I
> must raise them.
> *Mrs Ogmore-Pritchard*: And before you let the
> sun in, mind it wipes its shoes.
>
> *Under Milk Wood* (1954)

Whitman, Walt (1819–1892)
US poet and writer
> Give me the splendid silent sun with all his
> beams full-dazzling!
>
> 'Give me the splendid silent sun' (1865)

▶▶ SEASONS; WEATHER

sunday

Abelard, Peter (1079–1142)
> *O quanta qualia sunt illa sabbata,*
> *Quae semper celebrat superna curia.*
> O how great and how glorious are those

sabbaths which the heavenly court for ever celebrates!

Hymnus Paraclitensis

Addison, Joseph (1672–1719)
English essayist, poet, playwright and statesman
Sunday clears away the rust of the whole week.

The Spectator, July 1711, 112

Carey, Henry (c.1687–1743)
English poet and musician
Of all the days that's in the week
I dearly love but one day –
And that's the day that comes betwixt
A Saturday and Monday.

'Sally in our Alley' (1729)

De Quincey, Thomas (1785–1859)
English writer
It was a Sunday afternoon, wet and cheerless: and a duller spectacle this earth of ours has not to show than a rainy Sunday in London.

Confessions of an English Opium Eater (1822)

Hoban, Russell (1925–)
US author
Sometimes there's nothing but Sundays for weeks on end. Why can't they move Sunday to the middle of the week so you could put it in the OUT tray on your desk?

The Lion of Boaz-Jachin and Jachin-Boaz

Rhys, Jean (1894–1979)
West Indian-born English writer
The feeling of Sunday is the same everywhere, heavy, melancholy, standing still. Like when they say, 'As it was in the beginning, is now, and ever shall be, world without end.'

Voyage in the Dark (1934)

Swift, Jonathan (1667–1745)
Irish satirist, poet, essayist and cleric
I always love to begin a journey on Sundays, because I shall have the prayers of the church, to preserve all that travel by land, or by water.

Polite Conversation (1738)

superiority and inferiority

Confucius (c.550–c.478 BC)
Chinese philosopher and teacher of ethics
The superior man is satisfied and composed; the mean man is always full of distress.

Analects

The superior man is distressed by his want of ability.

Analects

What the superior man seeks is in himself: what the small man seeks is in others.

Analects

Jung, Carl Gustav (1875–1961)
Swiss psychiatrist and pupil of Freud
Wherever an inferiority complex exists, there is a good reason for it. There is always something inferior there, although not just where we persuade ourselves that it is.

Interview, 1943

Nietzsche, Friedrich Wilhelm (1844–1900)
German philosopher, critic and poet
I teach you the Superman. Man is something that is to be surpassed.

Thus Spake Zarathustra

▶▶ EGOISM; EQUALITY;FAILURE; SNOBBERY; SUCCESS

superstition

Aubrey, John (1626–1697)
English antiquary, folklorist and biographer
Anno 1670, not far from Cirencester, was an apparition; being demanded whether a good spirit or a bad? returned no answer, but disappeared with a curious perfume and most melodious twang. Mr W. Lilly believes it was a fairy.

Miscellanies (1696)

Bacon, Francis (1561–1626)
English philosopher, essayist, politician and courtier
There is a superstition in avoiding superstition.

'Of Superstition' (1625)

Barrie, Sir J.M. (1860–1937)
Scottish dramatist and writer
Every time a child says 'I don't believe in fairies,' there is a little fairy somewhere that falls down dead.

Peter Pan (1904)

Berlin, Isaiah (1909–1997)
English philosopher
What men call superstition and prejudice are but the crust of custom which by sheer survival has shown itself proof against the ravages and vicissitudes of its long life; to lose it is to lose the shield that protects men's national existence, their spirit, the habits, memories, faith that have made them what they are.

'The Counter-Enlightenment'

Bohr, Niels Henrik David (1885–1962)
Danish nuclear physicist
Explaining why he had a horseshoe on his wall
Of course I don't believe in it. But I understand

that it brings you luck whether you believe in it or not.

Attr.

Browne, Sir Thomas (1605–1682)
English physician, author and antiquary
> For my part, I have ever believed, and do now know, that there are witches.

Religio Medici (1643)

Burke, Edmund (1729–1797)
Irish-born British statesman and philosopher
> Superstition is the religion of feeble minds.

Reflections on the Revolution in France (1790)

Cooper, James Fenimore (1789–1851)
US writer
> Ignorance and superstition ever bear a close and even a mathematical relation to each other.

Jack Tier

Goethe (1749–1832)
German poet, writer, dramatist and scientist
> *Der Aberglaube ist die Poesie des Lebens.*
> Superstition is the poetry of life.

'Literature and Language' (1823)

Hume, David (1711–1776)
Scottish philosopher and political economist
> We soon learn that there is nothing mysterious or supernatural in the case, but that all proceeds from the usual propensity of mankind towards the marvellous, and that, though this inclination may at intervals receive a check from sense and learning, it can never be thoroughly extirpated from human nature.

'Of Miracles' (1748)

> Opposing one species of superstition to another, set them a quarrelling; while we ourselves, during their fury and contention, happily make our escape into the calm, though obscure, regions of philosophy.

The Natural History of Religion (1757)

Johnson, Samuel (1709–1784)
English lexicographer, poet, critic, conversationalist and essayist
Of ghosts
> All argument is against it; but all belief is for it.

In Boswell, *The Life of Samuel Johnson* (1791)

▶▶ LUCK

surprise

Diaghilev, Sergei (1872–1929)
Russian arts impresario
Reply after Jean Cocteau's accusation that he rarely gave praise or encouragement
> *Étonne-moi.*

> Surprise me.

The Journals of Jean Cocteau (1956)

Priestley, J.B. (1894–1984)
English writer, dramatist and critic
> I am always surprised when I am told that somebody likes me.

Instead of the Trees: A Final Chapter of Autobiography (1977)

Tremain, Rose (1951–)
English author
> There is something about the unexpected that moves us. As if the whole of existence is paid for in some way, except for that one moment, which is free.

Sacred Country

Webster, Noah (1758–1843)
US lexicographer
Responding to his wife's comment that she had been surprised to find him embracing their maid
> No, my dear, it is I who am surprised; you are merely astonished.

Attr.

▶▶ ACCIDENTS; CHANCE; LUCK

survival

Arnold, Matthew (1822–1888)
English poet, critic, essayist and educationist
> Friends who set forth at our side,
> Falter, are lost in the storm,
> We, we only are left!

'Rugby Chapel' (1867)

Benson, E.F. (1867–1940)
English writer
Speaking of a fellow of King's College, Cambridge, who never emerged from his rooms except in the evening gloaming
> He then shuffled out on to the big lawn, with a stick in his hand, and he prodded with it at the worms in the grass, muttering to himself, 'Ah, damn ye: haven't got me yet.'

As We Were (1930)

Meir, Golda (1898–1978)
Russian-born Israeli stateswoman and Prime Minister
> We intend to remain alive. Our neighbours want to see us dead. This is not a question that leaves much room for compromise.

Reader's Digest, 1971

Scott, Ridley
English film director
> This is Ripley – last survivor of the *Nostromo* – signing off.

Alien (film, 1979)

Service, Robert W. (1874–1958)
Canadian poet
> This is the Law of the Yukon, that only the
> Strong shall thrive;
> That surely the Weak shall perish, and only the
> Fit survive.
> Dissolute, damned and despairful, crippled and
> palsied and slain,
> This is the Will of the Yukon, –
> Lo, how she makes it plain!
> > 'The Law of the Yukon' (1907)

▶▶ EVOLUTION

suspicion

Dickens, Charles (1812–1870)
English writer
> It was a maxim with Foxey – our revered father,
> gentlemen – 'Always suspect everybody.'
> > *The Old Curiosity Shop* (1841)

Macaulay, Lord (1800–1859)
English Liberal statesman, essayist and poet
> Ye diners-out from whom we guard our spoons.
> > Letter to Hannah Macaulay, 1831

Mtshali, Oswald (1940–)
South African poet
> I trudge the city pavements
> side by side with 'madam'
> who shifts her handbag
> from my side to the other.
> > *Sounds of a Cowhide Drum* (1971)

Roche, Sir Boyle (1743–1807)
Irish politician
> Mr Speaker, I smell a rat; I see him forming in
> the air and darkening the sky; but I'll nip him in
> the bud.
> > Attr.

Thurber, James (1894–1961)
US humorist, writer and dramatist
> Her own mother lived the latter years of her life
> in the horrible suspicion that electricity was
> dripping invisibly all over the house.
> > *My Life and Hard Times* (1933)

Tolstoy, Leo (1828–1910)
Russian writer, essayist, philosopher and moralist
> Don't trust your horse in the field, or your wife
> in the house.
> > *The Kreutzer Sonata* (1890)

Virgil (70–19 BC)
Roman poet
> *Equo ne credite, Teucri.*

> *Quidquid id est, timeo Danaos et dona ferentis.*
> Trust not the horse, Trojans. Whatever it is, I fear
> the Greeks even when they bring gifts.
> > *Aeneid*

switzerland

Coren, Alan (1938–)
British humorist, writer and broadcaster
Of Switzerland
> Since both its national products, snow and
> chocolate, melt, the cuckoo clock was invented
> solely in order to give tourists something solid
> to remember it by.
> > *The Sanity Inspector* (1974)

Nichol, Dave
Canadian businessman and environmentalist
Said at the Summit on the Environment, Toronto, 1989
> Incidentally, I've always heard what a practical
> people the Swiss are – I finally understood these
> comments when I found out how they dispose of
> their mercury batteries. They collect them, and
> then dump them down an abandoned mine shaft
> – in France!
> > Attr.

Russell, John (1919–)
British art critic
> Certain phrases stick in the throat, even if they
> offer nothing that is analytically improbable. 'A
> dashing Swiss officer' is one such.
> > *Paris* (1960)

Smith, Sydney (1771–1845)
English clergyman, essayist, journalist and wit
> I look upon Switzerland as an inferior sort of
> Scotland.
> > *Letters*, To Lord Holland, 1815

Stoppard, Tom (1937–)
British dramatist
> What a bloody country! even the cheese has got
> holes in it!
> > *Travesties* (1975)

Welles, Orson (1915–1985)
US actor, director and producer
> In Italy for thirty years under the Borgias they
> had warfare, terror, murder, bloodshed – they
> produced Michelangelo, Leonardo da Vinci and
> the Renaissance. In Switzerland they had
> brotherly love, five hundred years of democracy
> and peace, and what did they produce ...? The
> cuckoo clock.
> > *The Third Man* (film, 1949)

T

talent

Adler, Alfred (1870–1937)
Austrian psychiatrist and psychologist
> There is no such thing as talent. There is pressure.
> *Attr.*

Bailey, Pearl (1918–1990)
US singer and actress
> There are two kinds of talents, man-made talent and God-given talent. With man-made talent you have to work very hard. With God-given talent, you just touch it up once in a while.
> *Newsweek*, 1967

Blessington, Lady Marguerite (1789–1849)
Irish-born writer and socialite
> Talent, like beauty, to be pardoned, must be obscure and unostentatious.
> *Desultory Thoughts and Reflections* (1839)

Brontë, Anne (1820–1849)
English writer and poet
> All our talents increase in the using, and every faculty, both good and bad, strengthens by exercise.
> *The Tenant of Wildfell Hall* (1848)

Degas, Edgar (1834–1917)
French painter and sculptor
> Everybody has talent at twenty-five. The difficult thing is to have it at fifty.
> In Gammell, *The Shop-Talk of Edgar Degas* (1961)

Lerner, Alan Jay (1918–1986)
US lyricist and screenwriter
> Back home everyone said I didn't have any talent. They might be saying the same thing over here, but it sounds better in French.
> *An American in Paris* (film, 1951)

Stanislavsky, Konstantin (1863–1938)
Russian actor and director; developed the 'method' theory of acting in which the actor identifies with the role
> Talent is nothing but a prolonged period of attention and a shortened period of mental assimilation.
> *The Art of the Stage* (1950)

▶▶ GENIUS

taste

Adair, Gilbert
English author and critic
> The only tastes worth having are acquired tastes.
> *Attr.*

Adams, Henry Brooks (1838–1918)
US historian and memoirist
> Every one carries his own inch-rule of taste, and amuses himself by applying it, triumphantly, wherever he travels.
> *The Education of Henry Adams* (1918)

Bennett, Arnold (1867–1931)
English writer, dramatist and journalist
> Good taste is better than bad taste, but bad taste is better than no taste.
> *The Observer*, 1930

Dali, Salvador (1904–1989)
Spanish painter and writer
> It is good taste, and good taste alone, that possesses the power to sterilize and is always the first handicap to any creative functioning.
> *Diary of a Genius* (1966)

Fitzgerald, Edward (1809–1883)
English poet, translator and letter writer
> Taste is the feminine of genius.
> Letter to J.R. Lowell, 1877

Huxley, Aldous (1894–1963)
English writer, poet and critic
> The aristocratic pleasure of displeasing is not the only delight that bad taste can yield. One can love a certain kind of vulgarity for its own sake.
> *Vulgarity in Literature* (1930)

Johnson, Samuel (1709–1784)
English lexicographer, poet, critic, conversationalist and essayist
> Our tastes greatly alter. The lad does not care for the child's rattle, and the old man does not care for the young man's whore.
> In Boswell, *The Life of Samuel Johnson* (1791)

Reynolds, Sir Joshua (1723–1792)
English portrait painter
> Taste does not come by chance: it is a long and laborious task to acquire it.
> In Northcote, *Life of Sir Joshua Reynolds* (1818)

Valéry, Paul (1871–1945)
French poet, mathematician and philosopher
> *Le goût est fait de mille dégoûts.*
> Taste is created from a thousand distastes.
> *Unsaid Things*

Veblen, Thorstein (1857–1929)
US economist and sociologist
> The requirement of conspicuous wastefulness is not commonly present, consciously, in our

canons of taste, but it is none the less present as a constraining norm, selectively shaping and sustaining our sense of what is beautiful.

The Theory of the Leisure Class (1899)

▶▶ INDIVIDUALITY

taxes

Anonymous
Definition from the 'style invitational'
> *Intaxication*: euphoria at getting a tax rebate until you realize it was your money to start with.
> *Washington Post*

Bierce, Ambrose (1842–c.1914)
US writer, verse writer and soldier
> Out-of-Doors: That part of one's environment upon which no government has been able to collect taxes.
> *The Devil's Dictionary* (1911)

Burke, Edmund (1729–1797)
Irish-born British statesman and philosopher
> To tax and to please, no more than to love and to be wise, is not given to men.
> *Speech on American Taxation* (1774)

Camden, Lord (1714–1794)
English lawyer and Lord Chancellor
Arguing that the British parliament had no right to tax the Americans
> Taxation and representation are inseparable … whatever is a man's own, is absolutely his own; no man hath a right to take it from him without his consent either expressed by himself or representative; whoever attempts to do it, attempts an injury; whoever does it, commits a robbery; he throws down and destroys the distinction between liberty and slavery.
> *Speech, House of Lords, 1766*

Capone, Al (1899–1947)
Chicago gangster
Objecting to the US Bureau of Internal Revenue claiming large sums in unpaid back tax
> They can't collect legal taxes from illegal money.
> In Kobler, *Capone* (1971)

Dewar, Lord Thomas Robert (1864–1930)
Scottish Conservative politician and writer
> The only thing that hurts more than paying an income tax is not having to pay an income tax.
> Attr.

Dickens, Charles (1812–1870)
English writer
> 'It was as true,' said Mr Barkis, '… as taxes is. And nothing's truer than them.'
> *David Copperfield* (1850)

Franklin, Benjamin (1706–1790)
US statesman, scientist, political critic and printer
> But in this world nothing can be said to be certain, except death and taxes.
> *Letter to Jean Baptiste Le Roy, 1789*

Gibbon, Edward (1737–1794)
English historian, politician and memoirist
> All taxes must, at last, fall upon agriculture.
> *Decline and Fall of the Roman Empire* (1776–88)

Healey, Denis (1917–)
English Labour politician
> I warn you there are going to be howls of anguish from the 80,000 people who are rich enough to pay over 75% on the last slice of their income.
> *Speech, Labour Party Conference, 1973*

Helmsley, Leona (1920–)
Hotel tycoon during her trial for tax evasion
> We don't pay taxes. Only the little people pay taxes.
> *Remark, 1989*

Johnson, Samuel (1709–1784)
English lexicographer, poet, critic, conversationalist and essayist
> Excise. A hateful tax levied upon commodities.
> *A Dictionary of the English Language* (1755)

Lowe, Robert (Viscount Sherbrooke) (1811–1892)
English Liberal politician and lawyer
> The Chancellor of the Exchequer is a man whose duties make him more or less of a taxing machine. He is intrusted with a certain amount of misery which it is his duty to distribute as fairly as he can.
> *Speech, 1870*

O'Rourke, P.J. (1947–)
US writer
> Giving money and power to the government is like giving whiskey and car keys to teenage boys.
> Attr.

Otis, James (1725–1783)
US lawyer, politician and pamphleteer
> Taxation without representation is tyranny.
> Attr.

Reagan, Ronald (1911–)
US actor, Republican statesman and President
To the American Business Conference
> I have my veto pen drawn and ready for any tax increase that Congress might even think of sending up. And I have only one thing to say to the tax increasers. Go ahead – make my day.
> *Time, 1985*

Rogers, Will (1879–1935)
US humorist, actor, rancher, writer and wit

Income tax has made more liars out of American people than golf.

The Illiterate Digest (1924)

Shaw, George Bernard (1856–1950)
Irish socialist, writer, dramatist and critic

A government which robs Peter to pay Paul can always depend on the support of Paul.

Everybody's Political What's What (1944)

Smith, Adam (1723–1790)
Scottish economist, philosopher and essayist

In England the different poll-taxes never produced the sum which had been expected of them, or which, it was supposed, they might have produced, had they been exactly levied.

Wealth of Nations (1776)

There is no art which one government sooner learns of another than that of draining money from the pockets of the people.

Wealth of Nations (1776)

Smith, Sydney (1771–1845)
English clergyman, essayist, journalist and wit

The schoolboy whips his taxed top – the beardless youth manages his taxed horse, with a taxed bridle, on a taxed road: – and the dying Englishman, pouring his medicine, which has paid seven per cent., into a spoon that has paid fifteen per cent. – flings himself back upon his chintz bed, which has paid twenty-two per cent. – and expires in the arms of an apothecary who has paid a licence of a hundred pounds for the privilege of putting him to death.

Edinburgh Review, 1820, 'America'

Swift, Jonathan (1667–1745)
Irish satirist, poet, essayist and cleric
Responding to Lady Carteret's admiration for the quality of the air in Ireland

For God's sake, madam, don't say that in England for if you do, they will surely tax it.

In H. Pearson, *Lives of the Wits* (1962)

Wouk, Herman (1915–)
US novelist

Income tax returns: the most imaginative fiction written today.

Attr.

tea

Addison, Joseph (1672–1719)
English essayist, poet, playwright and statesman

The infusion of a China plant sweetened with the pith of an Indian cane.

The Spectator, 1711

Armour, G.D. (1864–1949)

Look here, Steward, if this is coffee, I want tea; but if this is tea, then I wish for coffee.

Punch, cartoon caption, July 1902

Chesterton, G.K. (1874–1936)
English writer, poet and critic

Tea, although an Oriental,
Is a gentleman at least;
Cocoa is a cad and coward,
Cocoa is a vulgar beast.

The Flying Inn (1914)

Cobbett, William (1762–1835)
English politician, reformer, writer, farmer and army officer

Resolve to free yourselves from the slavery of the tea and coffee and other slop-kettle.

Advice to Young Men (1829)

Cowper, William (1731–1800)
English poet, hymn and letter writer

Now stir the fire, and close the shutters fast,
Let fall the curtains, wheel the sofa round,
And, while the bubbling and loud-hissing urn
Throws up a steamy column, and the cups,
That cheer but not inebriate, wait on each,
So let us welcome peaceful ev'ning in.

The Task (1785)

Gladstone, William (1809–1898)
English statesman and reformer

The domestic use of tea is a powerful champion able to encounter alcoholic drink in a fair field and throw it in a fair fight.

Budget Speech, 1882

Johnson, Samuel (1709–1784)
English lexicographer, poet, critic, conversationalist and essayist

A hardened and shameless tea-drinker, who has for twenty years diluted his meals with only the infusion of this fascinating plant; whose kettle has scarcely time to cool; who with tea amuses the evening, with tea solaces the midnight, and with tea welcomes the morning.

Review in the *Literary Magazine*, 1757

Joyce, James (1882–1941)
Irish writer

When I makes tea I makes tea, as old mother Grogan said. And when I makes water I makes water ... Begob, ma'am, says Mrs. Cahill, God send you don't make them in the one pot.

Ulysses (1922)

Pain, Barry (1864–1928)
English humorist and writer

The cosy fire is bright and gay,
The merry kettle boils away
And hums a cheerful song.

I sing the saucer and the cup;
Pray, Mary, fill the teapot up,
And do not make it strong.

The Poets at Tea, 'Cowper'

Pour, varlet, pour the water,
The water steaming hot!
A spoonful for each man of us,
Another for the pot!

The Poets at Tea, 'Macaulay'

As the sin that was sweet in the sinning
Is foul in the ending thereof,
As the heat of the summer's beginning
Is past in the winter of love:
O purity, painful and pleading!
O coldness, ineffably gray!
O hear us, our handmaid unheeding,
And take it away!

The Poets at Tea, 'Swinburne'

'Come, little cottage girl, you seem
To want my cup of tea;
And will you take a little cream?
Now tell the truth to me.'
She had a rustic, woodland grin
Her cheek was soft as silk,
And she replied, 'sir, please put in
A little drop of milk.'

The Poets at Tea, 'Wordsworth'

Pinero, Sir Arthur Wing (1855–1934)
English dramatist
While there's tea there's hope.

The Second Mrs Tanqueray
(1893)

Priestley, J.B. (1894–1984)
English writer, dramatist and critic
Our trouble is that we drink too much tea. I see
in this the slow revenge of the Orient, which has
diverted the Yellow River down our throats.

The Observer, 1949

Smith, Sydney (1771–1845)
English clergyman, essayist, journalist and wit
Thank God for tea! What would the world do
without tea? How did it exist? I am glad I was
not born before tea.

Attr.

Thomas, Dylan (1914–1953)
Welsh poet, writer and radio dramatist
Here's your arsenic, dear.
And your weedkiller biscuit.
I've throttled your parakeet.
I've spat in the vases.
I've put cheese in the mouseholes.
Here's your – – nice tea, dear.

Under Milk Wood (1954)

teachers

Adams, Henry Brooks (1838–1918)
US historian and memoirist
A teacher affects eternity; he can never tell
where his influence stops.

The Education of Henry Adams (1907)

Anonymous
Headmaster's reference for a teacher he dismissed
He left us as he came to us, fired with
enthusiasm.

The Times, 1998

From a letter to *The Times*
You do not report daily that the sun rose in the
east. So why report annually that the National
Union of Teachers is opposed to reform of the
education system.

The Times, 1999

Armstrong, Dr John (1709–1779)
Scottish physician, poet and writer
Of right and wrong he taught
Truths as refin'd as ever Athens heard;
And (strange to tell!) he practis'd what he
preach'd.

The Art of Preserving Health (1744)

Auden, W.H. (1907–1973)
English poet, essayist, critic, teacher and dramatist
A professor is one who talks in someone else's
sleep.

Attr.

A professor is one who talks in someone else's
sleep.

Attr.

Berlioz, Hector (1803–1869)
French composer; founder of modern orchestration
Time is a great teacher, but unfortunately it kills
all its pupils.

Attr.

Brougham, Lord Henry (1778–1868)
Scottish politician, abolitionist and journalist
The schoolmaster is abroad, and I trust more to
him, armed with his primer, than I do to the
soldier in full military array, for upholding and
extending the liberties of his country.

Speech, 1828

Carlyle, Thomas (1795–1881)
Scottish historian, biographer, critic, and essayist
It were better to perish than to continue
schoolmastering.

In Wilson, *Carlyle Till Marriage* (1923)

Carroll, Lewis (1832–1898)
English writer and photographer
'We called him Tortoise because he taught us,'

said the Mock Turtle angrily. 'Really you are very dull!'.

Alice's Adventures in Wonderland (1865)

The Drawling-master was an old conger-eel, that used to come once a week: he taught Drawling, Stretching, and Fainting in Coils.

Alice's Adventures in Wonderland (1865)

Churchill, Sir Winston (1874–1965)
English Conservative Prime Minister
Headmasters have powers at their disposal with which Prime Ministers have never yet been invested.

My Early Life (1930)

Darling, Sir James (1899–)
Australian educationalist
If you are going to be any good, you have got to like the little swine.

Attr.

Defoe, Daniel (c.1661–1731)
English writer and critic
We lov'd the doctrine for the teacher's sake.

'Character of the late Dr S. Annesley' (1697)

Farquhar, George (1678–1707)
Irish dramatist
Charming women can true converts make,
We love the precepts for the teacher's sake.

The Constant Couple (1699)

Huxley, T.H. (1825–1895)
English biologist, Darwinist and agnostic
Some experience of popular lecturing had convinced me that the necessity of making things plain to uninstructed people was one of the very best means of clearing up the obscure corners of one's own mind.

Man's Place in Nature (1894)

Montessori, Maria (1870–1952)
Italian doctor and educationist
We teachers can only help the work going on, as servants wait upon a master.

The Absorbent Mind

Seneca (c.4 BC–AD 65)
Roman philosopher, poet, dramatist, essayist, rhetorician and statesman
Homines dum docent discunt.
Even while they teach, men learn.

Epistulae Morales

Shaw, George Bernard (1856–1950)
Irish socialist, writer, dramatist and critic
He who can, does. He who cannot, teaches.

Man and Superman (1903)

Stallone, Sylvester (1946–)
US actor
When I was in junior high school, the teachers voted me the student most likely to end up in the electric chair.

Attr.

Trollope, Anthony (1815–1882)
English writer, traveller and post office official
Of his headmaster
He must have known me had he seen me as he was wont to see me, for he was in the habit of flogging me constantly. Perhaps he did not recognize me by my face.

Autobiography (1883)

Waugh, Evelyn (1903–1966)
English writer and diarist
I expect you'll be becoming a schoolmaster, sir. That's what most of the gentlemen does, sir, that gets sent down for indecent behaviour.

Decline and Fall (1928)

We schoolmasters must temper discretion with deceit.

Decline and Fall (1928)

Assistant masters came and went … Some liked little boys too little and some too much.

A Little Learning (1964)

Wilde, Oscar (1854–1900)
Irish poet, dramatist, writer, critic and wit
Everybody who is incapable of learning has taken to teaching.

'The Decay of Lying' (1889)

Yeatman, Robert Julian (1897–1968)
English writer
For every person wishing to teach there are thirty not wanting to be taught.

And Now All This (1932)

▶▶ EDUCATION; LEARNING; SCHOLARS; SCHOOL; UNIVERSITY

technology

Adams, Scott (1957–)
US cartoonist
Technology: No Place for Wimps!

Dilbert

Boorstin, Daniel (1914–)
US librarian, historian, lawyer and writer
Technology is so much fun but we can drown in our technology. The fog of information can drive out knowledge.

New York Times, 1983

Carlyle, Thomas (1795–1881)
Scottish historian, biographer, critic, and essayist
Man is a tool-using animal.

Sartor Resartus (1834)

Clarke, Arthur C. (1917–)
English writer
> Any sufficiently advanced technology is indistringuisable from magic.
>> *Technology and the Future*

Frisch, Max (1911–1991)
Swiss dramatist, writer and architect
> Technology is the knack of so arranging the world that we do not experience it.
>> In Rollo May, *The Cry for Myth*

Harlow, Jean (1911–1937)
US actress
> *Harlow*: I was reading a book the other day … the guy said machinery is going to take the place of every profession.
> *Dressler*: Oh, my dear, that's something you'll never have to worry about.
>> *Dinner at Eight* (film, 1933)

Harrington, Michael (1928–1989)
US writer
> If there is a technological advance without a social advance, there is, almost automatically, an increase in human misery.
>> *The Other America* (1962)

Hayes, Rutherford B. (1822–1893)
US President
After participating in a trial telephone conversation, 1876
> That's an amazing invention [the telephone], but who would ever want to use one of them?
>> Attr.

Rilke, Rainer Maria (1875–1926)
Austrian poet, born in Prague
> The machine threatens all achievement.
>> *The Sonnets to Orpheus* (1923)

Sculley, John (1939–)
US business executive
> If we hadn't put a man on the moon, there wouldn't be a Silicon Valley today.
>> *US News & World Report*, 1992

Verne, Jules (1828–1905)
French novelist
> *Captain Nemo*: I wonder if you are familiar with utensils, Mr. Land?
> *Ned Land*: I'm indifferent to 'em.
>> *20,000 Leagues Under the Sea* (film, 1954)

Wright, Frank Lloyd (1869–1959)
US architect and writer
> If it keeps up, man will atrophy all his limbs but the push-button finger.
>> *New York Times Magazine*, 1953

▶▶ ARTIFICIAL INTELLIGENCE; COMPUTERS; INTERNET; PROGRESS; SCIENCE

television

Allen, Woody (1935–)
US film director, writer, actor and comedian
> Life doesn't imitate art. It imitates bad television.
>> *Husbands and Wives* (film, 1992)

Anonymous
> The human race is faced with a cruel choice: work or daytime television.

Bakewell, Joan (1933–)
British journalist and television presenter
> The BBC is full of men appointing men who remind them of themselves when young, so you get the same back-grounds, the same education, and the same programmes.
>> *The Observer*, 1993

Barnes, Clive (1927–)
English journalist and critic
> Television is the first truly democratic culture – the first culture available to everybody and entirely governed by what the people want. The most terrifying thing is what people do want.
>> *The New York Times*, 30 September 1969

Biagi, Enzo (1920–)
Italian writer
> *La televisione ha fatto per la nostra unità più di Garibaldi e Cavour, ha dato un linguaggio e un costume comuni.*
> Television has done more for the unification of Italy than Garibaldi and Cavour did; it has given us a communal custom and language.
>> *The Good and the Bad* (1989)

Birt, John (1944–)
Former Director-General of the BBC
> There is a bias in television journalism. It is not against any particular party or point of view – it is a bias against *understanding*.
>> *The Times*, 1975

Broadcasting Standards Commission
> We are concerned to remind broadcasters that 9pm is a watershed, not a waterfall.
>> *The Times*, 1999

Buchwald, Art (1925–)
US humorist
> Every time you think television has hit its lowest ebb, a new … program comes along to make you wonder where you thought the ebb was.
>> *Have I Ever Lied to You?* (1968)

Chayefsky, Paddy (1923–1981)
US playwright and screenwriter
> Television is democracy at its ugliest.
>> Attr.

Connery, Sean (1930–)
Scottish actor
On turning down a part in US sitcom *Friends*
> I didn't do it because your prestige in cinema tends to drop if you do television.
>> *The Times*, 1998

Coren, Alan (1938–)
British humorist, writer and broadcaster
> Television is more interesting than people. If it were not, we should have people standing in the corners of our rooms.
>> Attr.

Coward, Sir Noël (1899–1973)
English dramatist, actor, producer and composer
> Television is for appearing on, not looking at.
>> Attr.

Crisp, Quentin (1908–1999)
English writer, publicist and model
> If any reader of this book is in the grip of some habit of which he is deeply ashamed, I advise him not to give way to it in secret but to do it on television. No-one will pass him with averted gaze on the other side of the street. People will cross the road at the risk of losing their own lives in order to say 'We saw you on the telly'.
>> *How to Become a Virgin*

Cronkite, Walter (1916–)
US broadcast journalist
Criticising the quality of television news
> Everything is being compressed into tiny tablets. You take a little pill of news every day – 23 minutes and that's supposed to be enough.
>> *Newsweek*, 1983

Debray, Régis (1942–)
French writer
> The darkest spot in modern society is a small luminous screen.
>> *Teachers, Writers, Celebrities*

Eco, Umberto (1932–)
Italian critic and writer
> *La TV non offre, come ideale in cui immedesimarsi, il superman ma l'everyman. La TV presenta come ideale l'uomo assolutamente medio.*
> Television doesn't present, as an ideal to aspire to, the superman but the everyman. Television puts forward, as an ideal, the absolutely average man.
>> *Diario Minimo*

Eliot, T.S. (1888–1965)
US-born British poet, verse dramatist and critic
> It is a medium of entertainment which permits millions of people to listen to the same joke at the same time, and yet remain lonesome.
>> Attr.

Ford, Anna (1943–)
English television newscaster and reporter
> Let's face it, there are no plain women on television.
>> *The Observer*, 1979

Frost, David (1939–)
English broadcaster
> Television is an invention that permits you to be entertained in your living room by people you wouldn't have in your home.
>> Remark, 1971

Goldwyn, Samuel (1882–1974)
Polish-born US film producer
> Television has raised writing to a new low.
>> Attr.

Hanson, Lord James
English businessman
> Television exacerbates the concentration on personality and trivia at the expense of serious discussion and analysis, but its tendency to unbalance and to displace what really matters goes much further and is potentially very damaging to our lives and beliefs. It tends to destroy public trust.
>> *The Spectator*, 1996

Hitchcock, Alfred (1899–1980)
English film director
> Television has done much for psychiatry by spreading information about it, as well as contributing to the need for it.
>> Attr.

> Television has brought murder back into the home – where it belongs.
>> *The Observer*, 1965

Kovacs, Ernie
> Television – a medium. So called because it is neither rare nor well-done.
>> Attr.

Landers, Ann (1918–)
Famous 'agony aunt' and columnist
> Television has proved that people will look at anything rather than each other.
>> Attr.

McLuhan, Marshall (1911–1980)
Canadian communications theorist
> Television brought the brutality of war into the comfort of the living room. Vietnam was lost in the living rooms of America – not on the battle fields of Vietnam.
>> Montreal *Gazette*, 1975

Marx, Groucho (1895–1977)
US comedian
> I find television very educating. Every time

somebody turns on the set, I go into the other room and read a book.

Attr.

Muggeridge, Malcolm (1903–1990)
English writer
> I have had my TV aerials removed – it's the moral equivalent of a prostate operation.

In *Radio Times*, 1981

Paglia, Camille (1947–)
US academic and writer
> Television is actually closer to reality than anything in books. The madness of TV is the madness of human life.

Sex, Art, and American Culture (1992)

Parris, Matthew (1949–)
British Conservative politician and journalist
> Television lies. All television lies. It lies persistently, instinctively and by habit
> … A culture of mendacity surrounds the medium, and those who work there live it, breathe it and prosper by it …
> I know of no area of public life – no, not even politics – more saturated by professional cynicism.

The Spectator, 1996

Pasolini, Pier Paolo (1922–1975)
Italian film director
> It's through the spirit of television that the essence of the new power clearly shows itself.

From an essay in *Corriere della sera*, 1973

Scott, C.P. (1846–1932)
English newspaper editor and Liberal politician
> Television? The word is half Latin and half Greek. No good can come of it.

Attr.

Seinfeld, Jerry (1955–)
US comedian
> Men don't care what's on TV. They only care what else is on TV.

Attr.

Street-Porter, Janet (1946–)
English editor and writer
> A terminal blight has hit the TV industry nipping fun in the bud and stunting our growth. This blight is management – the dreaded Four M's: male, middle class, middle-aged and mediocre.

MacTaggart lecture, Edinburgh Television Festival, 1995

Thomson, Roy (1894–1976)
Canadian-born English newspaper and television magnate
To an Edinburgh neighbour just after the opening of Scottish Television, which Thomson had founded, in 1957
> You know, it's just like having a licence to print your own money.

In R. Braddon, *Roy Thomson of Fleet Street* (1965)

Welles, Orson (1915–1985)
US actor, director and producer
> I hate television. I hate it as much as peanuts. But I can't stop eating peanuts.

New York Herald Tribune, 1956

Wilder, Billy (1906–)
Austrian-born US film director, producer and screenwriter
> It used to be that we in film were the lowest form of art. Now we have something to look down on.

In A. Madsen, *Billy Wilder* (1968)

▶▶ MEDIA

temptation

Adams, Joey (b. 1911)
US comedian and author
> Do not worry about avoiding temptation. As you grow older it will avoid you.

Attr.

Anonymous
> The trouble with resisting temptation is it may never come your way again.

Korman's Law

Beckford, William (1760–1844)
English writer, collector and politician
> I am not over-fond of resisting temptation.

Vathek (1787)

Belloc, Hilaire (1870–1953)
English writer of verse, essayist and critic; Liberal MP
> The Devil, having nothing else to do,
> Went off to tempt My Lady Poltagrue.
> My Lady, tempted by a private whim,
> To his extreme annoyance, tempted him.

Sonnets and Verse (1923)

Dryden, John (1631–1700)
English poet, satirist, dramatist and critic
> Thou strong seducer, opportunity!

The Conquest of Granada (1670)

Graham, Clementina Stirling (1782–1877)
Scottish writer, lyricist and translator
> The best way to get the better of temptation is just to yield to it.

Mystifications (1859)

Hope, Anthony (1863–1933)
English writer, dramatist and lawyer
> 'You oughtn't to yield to temptation.'

'Well, somebody must, or the thing becomes absurd.'

The Dolly Dialogues (1894)

Jerrold, Douglas William (1803–1857)
English dramatist, writer and wit
Honest bread is very well – it's the butter that makes the temptation.

The Cat's Paw (1930)

Shaw, George Bernard (1856–1950)
Irish socialist, writer, dramatist and critic
I never resist temptation, because I have found that things that are bad for me do not tempt me.

The Apple Cart (1930)

Wilde, Oscar (1854–1900)
Irish poet, dramatist, writer, critic and wit
The only way to get rid of a temptation is to yield to it.

The Picture of Dorian Gray (1891)

I couldn't help it. I can resist everything except temptation.

Lady Windermere's Fan (1892)

theatre

Adamov, Arthur (1908–1970)
Russian-born French political dramatist
Remark at the International Drama Conference, Edinburgh, 1963
The reason why Absurdist plays take place in No Man's Land with only two characters is primarily financial.

Attr.

Addison, Joseph (1672–1719)
English essayist, poet, playwright and statesman
A perfect tragedy is the noblest production of human nature.

The Spectator, 1711

Agate, James (1877–1947)
English drama critic and writer
Theatre director: a person engaged by the management to conceal the fact that the players cannot act.

Attr.

Long experience has taught me that in England nobody goes to the theatre unless he or she has bronchitis.

Attr.

Aristotle (384–322 BC)
Greek philosopher
Tragedy, then, is the imitation of an action that is serious, has magnitude, and is complete in itself … through incidents arousing pity and fear it

effects a catharsis of these and similar emotions.

Poetics

The plot is the first principle and, as it were, the soul of tragedy; character comes second.

Poetics

Askey, Arthur (1900–1982)
English comic entertainer
On pantomime
Pantomimes – the smell of oranges and wee-wee.

Attr.

Bankhead, Tallulah (1903–1968)
US actress
It's one of the tragic ironies of the theatre that only one man in it can count on steady work – the night watchman.

Tallulah (1952)

Bernard, Tristan (1866–1947)
French writer and dramatist
In the theatre the audience want to be surprised – but by things that they expect.

Attr.

Boileau-Despréaux, Nicolas (1636–1711)
French writer
*Qu'en un lieu, qu'en un jour, un seul fait accompli
Tienne jusqu'á la fin le théâtre rempli.*
Let a single complete action, in one place, in one day, keep a full house till the end of the play.

L'Art Poétique (1674)

Brooks, Mel (1926–)
US film actor and director
Tragedy is if I cut my finger. Comedy is if I walk into an open sewer and die.

The New Yorker, 1978

Buckingham, Duke of (1628–1687)
English courtier and dramatist
What the devil does the plot signify, except to bring in fine things?

The Rehearsal (1663)

Burney, Fanny (1752–1840)
English diarist
'Do you come to the play without knowing what it is?' 'Oh, yes, sir, yes, very frequently. I have no time to read play-bills. One merely comes to meet one's friends, and show that one's alive.'

Evelina (1778)

Byron, Lord (1788–1824)
English poet satirist and traveller
All tragedies are finish'd by a death,
All comedies are ended by a marriage.

Don Juan (1824)

Cook, Peter (1937–1995)
English comedian and writer
> You know, I go to the theatre to be entertained
> … I don't want to see plays about rape, sodomy
> and drug addiction … I can get all that at home.
>> *The Observer*, cartoon caption, 1962

Coward, Sir Noël (1899–1973)
English dramatist, actor, producer and composer
On child star Bonnie Langford in a musical version of *Gone
with the Wind* (1972) when a horse defecated on stage
> If they'd stuffed the child's head up the horse's
> arse, they would have solved two problems at
> once.
>> In N. Sherrin, *Cutting Edge, or, Back in the Knife Box
>> Miss Sharp* (1984)

On a poor portrayal of Queen Victoria
> It made me feel that Albert had married beneath
> his station.
>> In D. Richards, *The Wit of Noël Coward*

Craig, Sir Gordon (1872–1966)
English actor, artist and stage designer
> Farce is the essential theatre. Farce refined
> becomes high comedy: farce brutalized becomes
> tragedy.
>> Attr.

Crisp, Quentin (1908–1999)
English writer, publicist and model
Description of his touring show
> [going about the country] preaching to the
> perverted.
>> Obituary, *The Times*, 1999

Dennis, John (1657–1734)
English critic and dramatist
Remark at a production of *Macbeth*, which used his new
technique for producing stage thunder
> See how the rascals use me! They will not let my
> play run and yet they steal my thunder!
>> Attr.

Evelyn, John (1620–1706)
English writer and diarist
> I saw Hamlet Prince of Denmark played: but now
> the old playe began to disgust this refined age.
>> *Diary*, 1661

Garrick, David (1717–1779)
English actor and theatre manager
> Prologues precede the piece – in mournful
> verse;
> As undertakers – walk before the hearse.
>> Prologue to Arthur Murphy's *The Apprentice*
>> (1756)

Gosse, Sir Edmund (1849–1928)
English literary critic
Referring to one of Swinburne's plays
> We were as nearly bored as enthusiasm would

permit.
>> In C. Hassall, *Biography of Edward Marsh*

Guinness, Sir Alec (1914–2000)
British actor
Vowing never to perform again in the West End when he saw
the blank faces of uncomprehending tourists
> I'd rather go to the provinces where they still
> speak English and not Japanese.
>> *Scotsman*, 1992

Hitchcock, Alfred (1899–1980)
English film director
> What is drama but life with the dull bits cut out?
>> *The Observer*, 1960

Hope, Anthony (1863–1933)
English writer, dramatist and lawyer
On the first night of J. M. Barrie's play *Peter Pan*
> Oh, for an hour of Herod!
>> In Birkin, *J. M. Barrie and the Lost Boys*

Huxley, Aldous (1894–1963)
English writer, poet and critic
> We participate in a tragedy; at a comedy we
> only look.
>> *The Devils of Loudun* (1952)

Johnson, Samuel (1709–1784)
English lexicographer, poet, critic, conversationalist and
essayist
> The stage but echoes back the public voice.
> The drama's laws the drama's patrons give,
> For we that live to please must please to live.
>> 'Prologue at the Opening of Drury Lane' (1747)

Kemble, John Philip (1757–1823)
English Shakespearian actor
Said during a play which was continually interrupted by a
crying child
> Ladies and gentlemen, unless the play is
> stopped, the child cannot possibly go
> on.
>> Attr.

Lloyd Webber, Andrew (1948–)
English composer
On the success of his *Phantom of the Opera*, 1995
> It doesn't stand up to huge intellectual scrutiny.
>> Attr.

Pavlova, Anna (1881–1931)
Russian ballet dancer
> Although one may fail to find happiness in
> theatrical life, one never wishes to give it up
> after having once tasted its fruits.
>> In Franks (ed.), *Pavlova: A Biography*

Peter, John
> Political theatre is by definition subversive:
> anything else is only propaganda.
>> Review, *Sunday Times*, 1998

Pinter, Harold (1930–)

English dramatist, poet and screenwriter

> I've never regarded myself as the one authority on my plays just because I wrote the damned things.
>
> *The Observer*, 1993

Rattigan, Terence (1911–1977)

English dramatist and screenwriter

> A nice, respectable, middle-class, middle-aged, maiden lady, with time on her hands and the money to help her pass it … Let us call her Aunt Edna … Aunt Edna is universal, and to those who might feel that all the problems of the modern theatre might be solved by her liquidation, let me add that … she is also immortal.
>
> *Collected Plays* (1953)

Reynolds, Frederic (1765–1841)

English playwright

> Now do take my advice, and write a play – if any incident happens, remember, it is better to have written a damned play, than no play at all – it snatches a man from obscurity.
>
> *The Dramatist* (1789)

Shaffer, Peter (1926–)

English dramatist

> Rehearsing a play is making the word flesh. Publishing a play is reversing the process.
>
> *Equus* (1973)

Shaw, George Bernard (1856–1950)

Irish socialist, writer, dramatist and critic

> An all-night sitting in a theatre would be at least as enjoyable as an all-night sitting in the House of Commons, and much more useful.
>
> *Saint Joan* (1924)

> You don't expect me to know what to say about a play when I don't know who the author is, do you? … If it's by a good author, it's a good play, naturally. That stands to reason.
>
> *Fanny's First Play* (1911)

Responding to a solitary boo amongst the mid-act applause at the first performance of *Arms and the Man* in 1894

> I quite agree with you, sir, but what can two do against so many?
>
> *Oxford Book of Literary Anecdotes*

Stoppard, Tom (1937–)

British dramatist

> We do on the stage the things that are supposed to happen off. Which is a kind of integrity, if you look on every exit being an entrance somewhere else.
>
> *Rosencrantz and Guildenstern Are Dead* (1967)

> I can do you blood and love without the rhetoric, and I can do you blood and rhetoric without the love and I can do you all three concurrent or consecutive but I can't do you love and rhetoric without the blood. Blood is compulsory – they're all blood you see.
>
> *Rosencrantz and Guildenstern Are Dead* (1967)

> The bad end unhappily, the good unluckily. That is what tragedy means.
>
> *Rosencrantz and Guildenstern Are Dead* (1967)

Victoria, Queen (1819–1901)

Queen of the United Kingdom

Giving her opinion of *King Lear*

> A strange, horrible business, but I suppose good enough for Shakespeare's day.
>
> Attr.

Voltaire (1694–1778)

French philosopher, dramatist, poet, historian writer and critic

When asked why no woman had ever written a tolerable tragedy

> The composition of a tragedy requires testicles.
>
> In a letter from Byron to John Murray, 1817

Winchell, Walter (1897–1972)

US drama critic, columnist and broadcaster

Referring to a show starring Earl Carroll

> I saw it at a disadvantage – the curtain was up.
>
> In A. Whiteman, *Come to Judgement*

▶▶ ACTING; ACTORS; CENSORSHIP; CRITICISM; LITERATURE; SHAKESPEARE

theft

Balzac, Honoré de (1799–1850)

French writer

Remark made on waking to find a burglar in his room

> I am laughing to think what risks you take to try to find money in a desk by night where the legal owner can never find any by day.
>
> Attr.

Cibber, Colley (1671–1757)

English actor, dramatist and poet

> Stolen sweets are best.
>
> *The Rival Fools* (1709)

Hunt, Leigh (1784–1859)

English writer, poet and literary editor

> Stolen sweets are always sweeter,
> Stolen kisses much completer,
> Stolen looks are nice in chapels,
> Stolen, stolen, be your apples.
>
> 'Song of Fairies Robbing an Orchard' (1830)

Moravia, Alberto (1907–1990)

Italian writer

> *Ho avuto la malattia del ladro … m'è venuta una crisi di furto. Cosa vuol dire una parola! Tirai avanti qualche*

giorno, disgustato e smanioso, finché una mattina, ricordai, ad un tratto: cleptomane. E mi sentii innocente.
I had the thief's sickness ... I had a thieving crisis. How much meaning there can be in a word! I went along for a few days feeling disgusted and restless, until one morning I suddenly remembered: kleptomaniac. And I felt innocent.

Roman Tales (1954)

Patten, Brian (1946–)
British poet
When I went out I stole an orange
It was a safeguard against imagining there was nothing
bright or special in the world.

'The stolen orange'

Peacock, Thomas Love (1785–1866)
English writer and poet
The mountain sheep are sweeter,
But the valley sheep are fatter;
We therefore deemed it meeter
To carry off the latter.

The Misfortunes of Elphin (1823)

▶▶ CRIME

therapy

Scruton, Roger (1930–)
English philosopher and critic
Therapy seems to be about making people feel good about their weaknesses and inadequacies. Religion is to do with making people feel bad about their weaknesses and inadequacies. We are therefore in a condition of social and spiritual chaos. Therapy enhances that chaos.

The Times, 2000

▶▶ ILLNESS; PSYCHIATRY

thought

Adams, John Quincy (1767–1848)
US lawyer, diplomat and President
Old minds are like old horses; you must exercise them if you wish to keep them in working order.

Attr.

Balzac, Honoré de (1799–1850)
French writer
Je préfère la pensée à l'action, une idée à une affaire, la contemplation au mouvement.
I prefer thought to action, ideas to events, meditation to movement.

Louis Lambert (1832)

Penser, c'est voir.
Thinking is seeing.

Louis Lambert (1832)

Bierce, Ambrose (1842–c.1914)
US writer, verse writer and soldier
Brain: An apparatus with which we think that we think.

The Cynic's Word Book (1906)

Blake, William (1757–1827)
English poet, engraver, painter and mystic
One thought fills immensity.

The Marriage of Heaven and Hell (c.1790–1793)

Confucius (c.550–c.478 BC)
Chinese philosopher and teacher of ethics
Learning without thought is labour lost; thought without learning is perilous.

Analects

Descartes, René (1596–1650)
French philosopher and mathematician
Cogito, ergo sum.
I think, therefore I am.

Discours de la Méthode (1637)

Emerson, Ralph Waldo (1803–1882)
US poet, essayist, transcendentalist and teacher
Beware when the great God lets loose a thinker on this planet. Then all things are at risk.

'Circles' (1841)

Goethe (1749–1832)
German poet, writer, dramatist and scientist
Alles Gescheite ist schon gedacht worden, man muss nur versuchen, es noch einmal zu denken.
Everything worth thinking has already been thought, our concern must only be to try to think it through again.

'Thought and Action' (1829)

Hazlitt, William (1778–1830)
English writer and critic
The most fluent talkers or most plausible reasoners are not always the justest thinkers.

Atlas (1830)

Heath, Sir Edward (1916–)
English Conservative Prime Minister
The real problem in life is to have sufficient time to think.

The Observer, 1981

Holmes, Oliver Wendell (1809–1894)
US physician, poet, writer and scientist
A thought is often original, though you have uttered it a hundred times.

The Autocrat of the Breakfast-Table (1858)

Horváth, Ödön von (1901–1938)
German-Hungarian writer
Denken tut weh.

Thinking hurts.

A Child of our Time (1938)

Huxley, Aldous (1894–1963)
English writer, poet and critic
> Thought must be divided against itself before it can come to any knowledge of itself.
>
> *Do What You Will* (1929)

James, William (1842–1910)
US psychologist and philosopher
> A great many people think they are thinking when they are merely rearranging their prejudices.
>
> Attr.

Johnson, Samuel (1709–1784)
English lexicographer, poet, critic, conversationalist and essayist
> Whatever withdraws us from the power of our senses; whatever makes the past, the distant, or the future, predominate over the present, advances us in the dignity of thinking beings.
>
> *A Journey to the Western Islands of Scotland* (1775)

Luther, Martin (1483–1546)
German Protestant theologian and reformer
> *Gedanken sind zollfrei.*
> Thoughts are not subject to duty.
>
> *On Worldly Authority* (1523)

Mill, John Stuart (1806–1873)
English philosopher, economist and reformer
> No great improvements in the lot of mankind are possible, until a great change takes place in the fundamental constitution of their modes of thought.
>
> *Autobiography* (1873)

Newton, Sir Isaac (1642–1727)
English scientist and philosopher
> If I have done the public any service, it is due to patient thought.
>
> Letter to Dr Bentley, 1713

Ortega y Gasset, José (1883–1955)
Spanish philosopher
> *Pensar es el afán de captar mediante ideas la realidad.*
> Thinking is the desire to gain reality by means of ideas.
>
> *The Dehumanization of Art* (1925)

Reith, Lord (1889–1971)
Scottish wartime minister, administrator, diarist and Director-General of the BBC
> You can't think rationally on an empty stomach, and a whole lot of people can't do it on a full one either.
>
> Attr.

Ruskin, John (1819–1900)
English art critic, philosopher and reformer
> The purest and most thoughtful minds are those

which love colour the most.

The Stones of Venice (1853)

Russell, Bertrand (1872–1970)
English philosopher, mathematician, essayist and social reformer
> People don't seem to realize that it takes time and effort and preparation to think. Statesmen are far too busy making speeches to think.
>
> In Harris, *Kenneth Harris Talking To:* (1971)

> Many people would sooner die than think. In fact they do.
>
> In Flew, *Thinking about Thinking* (1975)

Sainte-Beuve, Charles-Augustin (1804–1869)
French writer and critic
On the habit of literary men and politicians of constantly improvising and expressing their thoughts in public
> Thoughts which are born in front of everyone are like beautiful women who spend their lives at balls … they have no colouring. Try to produce thoughts which have their natural colour, their true colour, which is red.
>
> *Notebooks, 1834–1847*

Sartre, Jean-Paul (1905–1980)
French philosopher, writer, dramatist and critic
> My thought is me: that is why I cannot stop. I exist by what I think … and I can't prevent myself from thinking.
>
> *Nausea* (1938)

Shakespeare, William (1564–1616)
English dramatist, poet and actor
> There is nothing either good or bad, but thinking makes it so.
>
> *Hamlet*, II.ii

Shelley, Mary Wollstonecraft (1797–1851)
English writer
> Mrs Shelley was choosing a school for her son, and asked the advice of this lady, who gave for advice … Just the sort of banality, you know, one does come out with: 'Oh, send him somewhere where they will teach him to think for himself!' … Mrs Shelley answered: 'Teach him to think for himself? Oh, my God, teach him rather to think like other people!'.
>
> In Matthew Arnold, *Essays in Criticism* (1888)

Shelley, Percy Bysshe (1792–1822)
English poet, dramatist and essayist
> A single word even may be a spark of inextinguishable thought.
>
> *A Defence of Poetry* (1821)

Sheridan, Richard Brinsley (1751–1816)
Irish dramatist, politician and orator
> I don't know any business you have to think at all – thought does not become a young woman.
>
> *The Rivals* (1775)

Sidgwick, Henry (1838–1900)
English philosopher
> We think so because other people think so,
> Or because – or because – after all we do think
> so,
> Or because we were told so, and think we must
> think so,
> Or because we once thought so, and think we
> still think so,
> Or because having thought so, we think we will
> think so.
>> 'Lines Composed in his Sleep'

Smith, Sydney (1771–1845)
English clergyman, essayist, journalist and wit
> I never could find any man who could think for
> two minutes together.
>> *Sketches of Moral Philosophy* (1849)

Thackeray, William Makepeace (1811–1863)
Indian-born English writer
> There are a thousand thoughts lying within a
> man that he does not know till he takes up the
> pen to write.
>> *The History of Henry Esmond* (1852)

Thomson, James (1834–1882)
Scottish poet and dramatist
> … to cure the pain
> Of the headache called thought in the brain.
>> 'L'Ancien Régime' (1880)

Thomson, Roy (1894–1976)
Canadian-born English newspaper and television
magnate
> Thinking is work.
>> *After I Was Sixty: A Chapter of Autobiography*

Valéry, Paul (1871–1945)
French poet, mathematician and philosopher
> A gloss on Descartes: Sometimes I think: and
> sometimes I am.
>> *The Faber Book of Aphorisms* (1962)

Vanbrugh, Sir John (1664–1726)
English dramatist and baroque architect
> Thinking is to me the greatest fatigue in the
> world.
>> *The Relapse, or Virtue in Danger* (1696)

Vaughan, Henry (1622–1695)
Welsh poet and physician
> And yet, as Angels in some brighter dreams
> Call to the soul, when man doth sleep:
> So some strange thoughts transcend our wonted
> theams,
> And into glory peep.
>> *Silex Scintillans* (1650–1655), 'They Are All Gone'

Vauvenargues, Marquis de (1715–1747)
French soldier and moralist
> *Les grandes pensées viennent du coeur.*

> Great thoughts come from the heart.
>> *Réflexions et Maximes*
>> (1746)

Voltaire (1694–1778)
French philosopher, dramatist, poet, historian writer and
critic
> *Ils ne servent de la pensée que pour autoriser leurs*
> *injustices, et n'emploient les paroles que pour déguiser*
> *leurs pensées.*
> People use thought only to justify their
> injustices, and they use words only to disguise
> their thoughts.
>> *Dialogues* (1763)

Webster, John (c.1580–c.1625)
English dramatist
> There's nothing of so infinite vexation
> As man's own thoughts.
>> *The White Devil* (1612)

Wittgenstein, Ludwig (1889–1951)
Austrian philosopher
> In order to draw a limit to thinking, we should
> have to be able to think both sides of this limit.
>> *Tractatus Logico-Philosophicus*
>> (1922)

▶▶ BELIEF; IDEAS; INTELLECTUALS; INTELLIGENCE;
MIND; PHILOSOPHY

threats

Caligula (12–41)
Roman emperor
> *Utinam populus Romanus unam cervicem haberet!*
> I wish that the Roman people had only one neck!
>> In Suetonius, *Lives of the Caesars*

Crompton, Richmal (1890–1969)
English writer and teacher
> Violet Elizabeth dried her tears. She saw that
> they were useless and she did not believe in
> wasting her effects. 'All right,' she said calmly,
> 'I'll thcream then. I'll thcream, an' thcream, an'
> thcream till I'm thick.'
>> *Still William* (1925)

Elizabeth I (1533–1603)
Queen of England
To the leaders of her Council when they opposed her policy
on Mary Queen of Scots
> I will make you shorter by the head!
>> In F. Chamberlin, *The Sayings of Queen Elizabeth*
>> (1923)

Puzo, Mario (1920–)
US writer
> We'll make him an offer he can't refuse.
>> *The Godfather* (film, 1972)

time

Ace, Jane (1905–1974)
US comedian and radio personality
> Time wounds all heels.
>> Goodman Ace *The Fine Art of Hypochondria* (1966)

Aeschylus (525–456 BC)
Greek dramatist and poet
> Time brings all things to pass.
>> *The Libation Bearers*

Anonymous
> The only things that start on time are those that you're late for.
>> Cayo's Law

> It always takes longer than you expect, even when you take Hofstadter's Law into account.
>> Hofstadter's Law

Auden, W.H. (1907–1973)
English poet, essayist, critic, teacher and dramatist
> O let not Time deceive you,
> You cannot conquer Time.
>
> In the burrows of the Nightmare
> Where Justice naked is,
> Time watches from the shadow
> And coughs when you would kiss.
>
> In headaches and in worry
> Vaguely life leaks away,
> And Time will have his fancy
> To-morrow or to-day.
>
> Into many a green valley
> Drifts the appalling snow;
> Time breaks the threaded dances
> And the diver's brilliant bow.
> O plunge your hands in water,
> Plunge them in up to the wrist;
> Stare, stare in the basin
> And wonder what you've
> missed.
>
> The glacier knocks in the cupboard,
> The desert sighs in the bed,
> And the crack in the tea-cup opens
> A lane to the land of the dead …
>
> O stand, stand at the window
> As the tears scald and start;
> You shall love your crooked neighbour
> With your crooked heart.
>> *Collected Poems, 1933–1938*

Aurelius, Marcus (121–180)
Roman emperor and Stoic philosopher
> Time is like a river made up of the things which happen, and its current is strong; no sooner does anything appear than it is carried away, and another comes in its place, and will be carried away too.
>> *Meditations*

Bacon, Francis (1561–1626)
English philosopher, essayist, politician and courtier
> He that will not apply new remedies, must expect new evils; for time is the greatest innovator.
>> 'Of Innovations' (1625)

Bashó, Matsuo (1644–1694)
Japanese haiku poet
> Days and months are itinerants on an eternal journey; the years that pass by are also travellers.
>> 'Narrow Roads of Oku' (1703)

Beckett, Samuel (1906–1989)
Irish dramatist, writer and poet
> *Vladimir*: That passed the time.
> *Estragon*: It would have passed in any case.
> *Vladimir*: Yes, but not so rapidly.
>> *Waiting for Godot* (1955)

Belloc, Hilaire (1870–1953)
English writer of verse, essayist and critic; Liberal MP
> I am a sundial, and I make a botch
> Of what is done far better by a watch.
>> *Sonnets and Verse* (1938

Berlioz, Hector (1803–1869)
French composer; founder of modern orchestration
> Time is a great teacher, but unfortunately it kills all its pupils.
>> Attr.

The Bible (King James Version)
> To every thing there is a season, and a time to every purpose under the heaven:
> A time to be born, and a time to die …
> A time to love, and a time to hate; a time of war, and a time of peace.
>> *Ecclesiastes*, 3:1–8

> For a thousand years in thy sight are but as yesterday when it is past, and as a watch in the night.
>> *Psalms*, 90:4

Boucicault, Dion (1822–1890)
Irish dramatist, actor and theatrical manager
> Men talk of killing time, while time quietly kills them.
>> *London Assurance* (1841)

Browne, Sir Thomas (1605–1682)
English physician, author and antiquary
> The night of time far surpasseth the day, and who knows when was the equinox?
>> *Hydriotaphia: Urn Burial* (1658)

Carlyle, Thomas (1795–1881)

Scottish historian, biographer, critic, and essayist

> The illimitable, silent, never-resting thing called Time, rolling, rushing on, swift, silent, like an all-embracing ocean-tide, on which we and all the Universe swim like exhalations, like apparitions which are, and then are not.

> 'The Hero as Divinity' (1841)

Chesterfield, Lord (1694–1773)

English politician and letter writer

> I recommend to you to take care of minutes; for hours will take care of themselves.

> Letter to his son, 1747

Compton-Burnett, Dame Ivy (1884–1969)

English novelist

> 'Time has too much credit,' said Bridget. 'I never agree with the compliments paid to it. It is not a great healer. It is an indifferent and perfunctory one. Sometimes it does not heal at all. And sometimes when it seems to, no healing has been necessary.'

> Darkness and Day (1951)

Coward, Sir Noël (1899–1973)

English dramatist, actor, producer and composer

> Time is the reef upon which all our frail mystic ships are wrecked.

> Blithe Spirit (1941)

Disraeli, Benjamin (1804–1881)

English statesman and writer

> Time is the great physician.

> Henrietta Temple (1837)

Dobson, Henry Austin (1840–1921)

English poet, essayist and biographer

> Time goes, you say? Ah no!
> Alas, Time stays, we go.

> 'The Paradox of Time' (1877)

Duras, Marguerite (1914–1996)

French author and film-maker

> The best way to fill time is to waste it.

> Practicalities (1987)

Dylan, Bob (1941–)

US singer and songwriter

> Come mothers and fathers,
> Throughout the land
> And don't criticize
> What you can't understand.
> Your sons and your daughters
> Are beyond your command
> Your old road is Rapidly agin'
> Please get out of the new oneIf you can't lend your hand
> For the times they are a-changin'.

> 'The Times They Are A-Changing' (song, 1964)

Emerson, Ralph Waldo (1803–1882)

US poet, essayist, transcendentalist and teacher

To a person complaining that he had not enough time

> 'Well,' said Red Jacket, 'I suppose you have all there is.'

> 'Works and Days' (1870)

> A day is a miniature eternity.

> Journals

Frame, Janet (1924–)

New Zealand writer

> There is no past present or future. Using tenses to divide time is like making chalk marks on water.

> Faces in the Water (1961)

Franklin, Benjamin (1706–1790)

US statesman, scientist, political critic and printer

> Remember that time is money.

> Advice to a Young Tradesman (1748)

Goethe (1749–1832)

German poet, writer, dramatist and scientist

> Mein Erbteil wie herrlich, weit und breit!
> Die Zeit ist mein Besitz, mein Acker ist die Zeit.
> How marvellous, wide and broad is my inheritance!
> Time is my property, my estate is time.

> Wilhelm Meister's Wandering Years (1821)

Hodgson, Ralph (1871–1962)

English poet, illustrator and journalist

> Time, you old gypsy man,
> Will you not stay,
> Put up your caravan,
> Just for one day?

> 'Time, You Old Gypsy Man' (1917)

Larkin, Philip (1922–1985)

English poet, writer and librarian

> What are days for?
> Days are where we live
> They come they wake us
> Time and time over.
> They are to be happy in;
> Where can we live but days?

> 'Days' (1964)

Macaulay, Dame Rose (1881–1958)

English writer

> Decades have a delusive edge to them. They are not, of course, really periods at all, except as any other ten years would be. But we, looking at them, are caught by the different name each bears, and give them different attributes, and tie labels on them, as if they were flowers in a border.

> Told by an Idiot (1923)

Marx, Groucho (1895–1977)

US comedian

Time wounds all heels.

Attr.

Maxwell, Gavin (1914–1969)
British writer and naturalist
> Yet while there is time, there is the certainty of return.

Ring of Bright Water (1960)

McCarthy, Mary (1912–1989)
US writer and critic
> Every age has a keyhole to which its eye is pasted.

Attr.

McLuhan, Marshall (1911–1980)
Canadian communications theorist
> For tribal man space was the uncontrollable mystery. For technological man it is time that occupies the same role.

The Mechanical Bridge (1951)

Muir, Edwin (1887–1959)
Scottish poet, critic, translator and writer
> Over the sound a ship so slow would pass
> That in the black hill's gloom it seemed to lie
> The evening sound was smooth like sunken glass
> And time seemed finished ere the ship passed by.

'Childhood' (1952)

Pericles (c.495–429)
Athenian statesman, general, orator and cultural patron
> Wait for that wisest of counsellors, Time.

In Plutarch, *Life*

Plato (c.429–347 BC)
Greek philosopher
> Time brings everything.

Greek Anthology

Proverbs
> An hour in the morning is worth two in the evening.

> No time like the present.

> Time is a great healer.

Raleigh, Sir Walter (c.1552–1618)
English courtier, explorer, military commander, poet, historian and essayist
Written the night before his execution
> Even such is Time, which takes in trust
> Our youth, our joys, and all we have,
> And pays us but with age and dust;
> Who in the dark and silent grave,
> When we have wandered all our ways,
> Shuts up the story of our days.

Untitled poem (1618)

Rogers, Will (1879–1935)
US humorist, actor, rancher, writer and wit
> Half our life is spent trying to find something to

do with the time we have rushed through life trying to save.

New York Times, 1930

Sartre, Jean-Paul (1905–1980)
French philosopher, writer, dramatist and critic
> *Trois heures, c'est toujours trop tard ou trop tôt pour ce qu'on veut faire.*
> Three o'clock is always too late or too early for anything you want to do.

Nausea (1938)

Service, Robert W. (1874–1958)
Canadian poet
> Ah! the clock is always slow;
> It is later than you think.

'It is Later than You Think' (1921)

Shakespeare, William (1564–1616)
English dramatist, poet and actor
> Th' inaudible and noiseless foot of Time.

All's Well That Ends Well, V.iii

> But thoughts, the slaves of life, and life, time's fool,
> And time, that takes survey of all the world,
> Must have a stop.

Henry IV, Part 1, V.iv

> Time's glory is to calm contending kings,
> To unmask falsehood, and bring truth to light.

'The Rape of Lucrece'

> Come what come may,
> Time and the hour runs through the roughest day.

Macbeth, I.iii

> I wasted time, and now doth time waste me.

Richard II, V.v

> Time's thievish progress to eternity.

Sonnet 77

Sitwell, Sir Osbert (1892–1969)
English writer
> In reality, killing time is only the name for another of the multifarious ways by which time kills us.

'Milordo Inglese' (1958)

Slessor, Kenneth (1901–1971)
Australian poet and journalist
> All through the night-time, clock talked to clock,
> In the captain's cabin, tock-tock-tock,
> One ticked fast and one ticked slow,
> And Time went over them a hundred years ago.

'Five Visions of Captain Cook' (1931)

Spencer, Herbert (1820–1903)
English philosopher and journalist

Time: That which man is always trying to kill, but which ends in killing him.

Definitions

Stoppard, Tom (1937–)
British dramatist

Eternity's a terrible thought. I mean, where's it all going to end?

Rosencrantz and Guildenstern Are Dead (1967)

Thomas, Dylan (1914–1953)
Welsh poet, writer and radio dramatist

Oh as I was young and easy in the mercy of his means,
Time held me green and dying
Though I sang in my chains like the sea.

'Fern Hill' (1946)

Thoreau, Henry David (1817–1862)
US essayist, social critic and writer

Time is but the stream I go a-fishing in.

Walden (1854)

Virgil (70–19 BC)
Roman poet

Sed fugit interea, fugit inreparabile tempus.
But time meanwhile is flying, flying beyond recall.

Georgics

Watts, Isaac (1674–1748)
English hymn-writer, poet and minister

Time, like an ever-rolling stream,
Bears all its sons away;
They fly forgotten, as a dream
Dies at the opening day.

The Psalms of David Imitated (1719)

Young, Edward (1683–1765)
English poet, dramatist, satirist and clergyman

We take no note of Time
But from its Loss.

Night-Thoughts on Life, Death and Immortality (1742–1746)

Procrastination is the Thief of Time.

Night-Thoughts on Life, Death and Immortality (1742–1746)

▶▶ CHANGE; ETERNITY; FUTURE; LIFE; PAST; PRESENT

tolerance

The Bible (King James Version)

For ye suffer fools gladly, seeing ye yourselves are wise.

Paul, 3:67

Browne, Sir Thomas (1605–1682)
English physician, author and antiquary

No man can justly censure or condemn another, because indeed no man truly knows another.

Religio Medici (1643)

Burke, Edmund (1729–1797)
Irish-born British statesman and philosopher

There is, however, a limit at which forbearance ceases to be a virtue.

Observations on 'The Present State of the Nation' (1769)

Kennedy, John F. (1917–1963)
US Democrat President

If we cannot now end our differences, at least we can help make the world safe for diversity.

Speech, 1963

Pegler, Westbrook (1894–1969)
US journalist

Tolerance to my mind has been greatly overrated … I take as much pleasure in detesting the good brothers and sisters of the [Anti-Saloon] League as they have in hating me.

In Oliver Pilat, Pegler: Angry Man of the Press (1963)

Rostand, Jean (1894–1977)
French biologist

Il est dans la tolérance un degré qui confine à l'injure.
There is a degree of tolerance which borders on insult.

Thoughts of a Biologist (1939)

Sade, Marquis de (1740–1814)
French soldier and writer

La tolérance est la vertu du faible.
Tolerance is the virtue of the weak.

La nouvelle Justine (1797)

Smith, Thorne (1892–1934)
US humorous novelist

Steven's mind was so tolerant that he could have attended a lynching every day without becoming critical.

The Jovial Ghosts (1933)

Staël, Mme de (1766–1817)
French writer, critic, memoirist and hostess

Tout comprendre rend très indulgent.
Understanding everything makes one very tolerant.

Corinne (1807)

Sterne, Laurence (1713–1768)
Irish-born English writer and clergyman

So long as a man rides his hobby-horse peaceably and quietly along the King's highway, and neither compels you or me to get up behind him, – pray, Sir, what have either you or I to do with it?

Tristram Shandy (1759–1767)

Trollope, Anthony (1815–1882)
English writer, traveller and post office official
> It is because we put up with bad things that hotel-keepers continue to give them to us.
>> *Orley Farm* (1862)

toys

Franklin, Benjamin (1706–1790)
US statesman, scientist, political critic and printer
> Old boys have their playthings as well as young ones; the difference is only in price.
>> *Poor Richard's Almanac* (1752)

trade

Canning, George (1770–1827)
English Prime Minister, orator and poet
> In matters of commerce the fault of the Dutch
> Is offering too little and asking too much.
> The French are with equal advantage content,
> So we clap on Dutch bottoms just twenty per cent.
>> Coded dispatch to Sir Charles Bagot, English Ambassador to the Hague, 1826

Hoover, Herbert Clark (1874–1964)
US Republican President
Predicting the outcome if tariff protection were removed
> The grass will grow in the streets of a hundred cities, a thousand towns; the weeds will overrun the fields of millions of farms if that protection is taken away.
>> Speech, 1932

Schumacher, E.F. (1911–1977)
German-born British economist and essayist
> After all, for mankind as a whole there are no exports. We did not start developing by obtaining foreign exchange from Mars or the moon. Mankind is a closed society.
>> *Small is Beautiful, A Study of Economics as if People Mattered* (1973)

▶▶ ECONOMICS; BUYING AND SELLING

tradition

Bloom, Allan (1930–1992)
US academic and critic
> As soon as tradition has come to be recognized as tradition, it is dead.
>> *The Closing of the American Mind* (1987)

Hoffman, Abbie (1936–1989)
US political activist
> Sacred cows make the best hamburger.
>> Attr.

Mumford, Lewis (1895–1990)
US sociologist and writer
> Traditionalists are pessimists about the future and optimists about the past.
>> *Technics and Civilization* (1934)

▶▶ CUSTOM; HISTORY

tragedy

Aristotle (384–322 BC)
Greek philosopher
Of the dramatic form of tragedy
> A whole is that which has a beginning, a middle, and an end.
>> *Poetics*

Austen, Jane (1775–1817)
English writer
> One of Edward's Mistresses was Jane Shore, who has had a play written about her, but it is a tragedy and therefore not worth reading.
>> *The History of England* (1791)

Chaucer, Geoffrey (c.1340–1400)
English poet, public servant and courtier
> Tragedie is to seyn a certeyn storie,
> As olde bookes maken us memorie,
> Of hym that stood in greet prosperitee
> And is yfallen out of heigh degree
> Into myserie, and endeth wrecchedly.
>> *The Canterbury Tales* (1387)

Fyfe, Alistair (1961–)
Scottish artist
Explaining the obscurity of Glasgow architect Alexander 'Greek' Thomson compared with Charles Rennie Mackintosh
> Thomson was guilty of not having enough tragedy in his life.
>> *The Guardian*, 1999

Scott, Sir Walter (1771–1832)
Scottish writer and historian
> The play-bill, which is said to have announced the tragedy of Hamlet, the character of the Prince of Denmark being left out.
>> *The Talisman* (1825)

translation

Borges, Jorge Luis (1899–1986)
Argentinian writer, poet and librarian
On Henley's translation of Beckford's Vathek

El original es infiel a la traducción.
The original is not faithful to the translation.
Sobre el 'Vathek' de William Beckford (1943)

Borrow, George (1803–1881)
English writer and linguist
Translation is at best an echo.
Lavengro (1851)

Campbell, Roy (1901–1957)
South African poet and journalist
Translations (like wives) are seldom strictly faithful if they are in the least attractive.
Poetry Review, 1949

Denham, Sir John (1615–1669)
English poet, royalist and Surveyor-General
Such is our pride, our folly, or our fate,
That few, but such as cannot write, translate.
'To Richard Fanshaw' (1648)

Frost, Robert (1874–1963)
US poet
Poetry is what is lost in translation.
In Untermeyer, Robert Frost: a Backward Look (1964)

Johnson, Samuel (1709–1784)
English lexicographer, poet, critic, conversationalist and essayist
A translator is to be like his author; it is not his business to excel him.
Attr.

McMurtry, Larry
US author and screenwriter
All Native American orators, whatever their language group, are translated to sound either like Dr. Johnson, the prophet Isaiah, or … the Sioux wise man Black Elk.
The New York Review of Books, 1999

Sheridan, Richard Brinsley (1751–1816)
Irish dramatist, politician and orator
Not a translation – only taken from the French.
The Critic (1779)

Egad, I think the interpreter is the hardest to be understood of the two!
The Critic (1779)

travel

Anonymous
When the plane you are on is late, the plane you want to transfer to is on time.
The Airplane Law

When you are served a meal aboard an aircraft, the aircraft will encounter turbulence.
Gunter's First Law of Air Travel

The strength of the turbulence is directly proportional to the temperature of your coffee.
Gunter's Second Law of Air Travel

Tourists are terrorists with cameras. Terrorists are tourists with guns.

Arnold, Matthew (1822–1888)
English poet, critic, essayist and educationist
And see all sights from pole to pole,
And glance, and nod, and bustle by;
And never once possess our soul
Before we die.
'A Southern Night' (1861)

A wanderer is man from his birth.
He was born in a ship
On the breast of the river of Time.
'The Future'

Atwood, Margaret (1939–)
Canadian writer, poet and critic
The north focuses our anxieties. Turning to face north, we enter our own unconscious. Always, in retrospect, the journey north has the quality of dream.
Saturday Night, 1987, 'True North'

Baxter, James K. (1926–1972)
New Zealand poet and playwright
Upon the upland road
Ride easy, stranger:
Surrender to the sky
Your heart of anger.
'High Country Weather' (1945)

Boone, Daniel (1734–1820)
US pioneer
Reply on being asked if he had ever been lost
I can't say I was ever lost, but I was bewildered once for three days.
Attr.

Brien, Alan (1925–)
English writer
I have done almost every human activity inside a taxi which does not require main drainage.
Punch, 1972

Buchan, William (1822–1888)
Canadian trains did not rush and rock. They pounded steadily along, every so often giving a warning blast on their sirens. I remember those sirens blowing in the icy darkness of winter nights in Ottawa, the most haunting sound, at once melancholy and stirring, like the mourning of some strange, sad beast.
A Memoir

Burney, Fanny (1752–1840)
English diarist
Travelling is the ruin of all happiness! There's no looking at a building here after seeing Italy.
Cecilia (1782)

Cherry-Garrard, Apsley (1886–1959)
English explorer
> Polar exploration is at once the cleanest and most isolated way of having a bad time which has been devised.
>> *The Worst Journey in the World* (1922)

Chesterton, G.K. (1874–1936)
English writer, poet and critic
> Chesterton taught me this: the only way to be sure of catching a train is to miss the one before it.
>> In P. Daninos, *Vacances à tous prix* (1958), 'Le supplice de l'heure'

Clarkson, Jeremy
English motoring journalist
> To argue that a car is simply a means of conveyance is like arguing that Blenheim Palace is simply a house.
>> *Sunday Times*, 1999

Coleridge, Samuel Taylor (1772–1834)
English poet, philosopher and critic
> From whatever place I write you will expect that part of my 'Travels' will consist of excursions in my own mind.
>> *Satyrane's Letters* (1809)

Cook, Captain James (1728–1779)
English navigator
Of the *Endeavour* expedition
> Altho' the discoveries made in this Voyage are not great, yet I flatter myself that they are such as may merit the attention of their Lordships, and altho' I have failed in discovering the so much talk'd of southern Continent (which perhaps do not exist) and which I myself had so much at heart, yet I am confident that no part of the failure of such discovery can be laid at my Charge.
>> Letter, 1770

Cowper, William (1731–1800)
English poet, hymn and letter writer
> How much a dunce that has been sent to roam
> Excels a dunce that has been kept at home.
>> 'The Progress of Error' (1782)

Dewar, Lord Thomas Robert (1864–1930)
Scottish Conservative politician and writer
> Lord Dewar … made the famous epigram about there being only two classes of pedestrians in these days of reckless motor traffic – the quick, and the dead.
>> In George Robey, *Looking Back on Life*

Didion, Joan (1934–)
US writer
> Certain places seem to exist mainly because someone has written about them.
>> *The White Album* (1979)

Drew, Elizabeth (1887–1965)
English-born US writer and critic
> Too often travel, instead of broadening the mind, merely lengthens the conversation.
>> *The Literature of Gossip* (1964)

Eliot, T.S. (1888–1965)
US-born British poet, verse dramatist and critic
> The first condition of understanding a foreign country is to smell it.
>> Attr.

Emerson, Ralph Waldo (1803–1882)
US poet, essayist, transcendentalist and teacher
> Travelling is a fool's paradise. Our first journeys discover to us the indifference of places.
>> 'Self-Reliance' (1841)

Flanders, Michael (1922–1975) and **Swann, Donald** (1923–1994)
English comedians and songwriters
> If God had intended us to fly, he'd never have given us the railways.
>> 'By Air', 1963

Galbraith, J.K. (1908–)
Canadian-born US economist, diplomat and writer
> The Great Wall, I've been told, is the only man-made structure on earth that is visible from the moon. For the life of me I cannot see why anyone would go to the moon to look at it, when, with almost the same difficulty, it can be viewed in China.
>> *The Sunday Times Magazine*

George VI (1895–1952)
King of the United Kingdom
> Abroad is bloody.
>> In Auden, *A Certain World* (1970)

Godley, A.D. (1856–1925)
English classical scholar and satirist
> What is this that roareth thus?
> Can it be a Motor Bus?
> Yes, the smell and hideous hum
> Indicate Motorem Bum!
>> 'The Motor Bus', in a letter to C.R.L. Fletcher, 1914

Grahame, Kenneth (1859–1932)
English author
Toad's reaction to the motor-car which destroyed his gypsy caravan
> The real way to travel! Here today – in next week tomorrow! Villages skipped, towns and cities jumped – always somebody else's horizon! O bliss! O poop-poop! O my! O my!
>> *The Wind in the Willows* (1908)

Hazlitt, William (1778–1830)
English writer and critic
> One of the pleasantest things in the world is

going a journey; but I like to go by myself.

Table-Talk (1822)

Give me the clear blue sky over my head, and the green turf beneath my feet, a winding road before me, and a three hours' march to dinner – and then to thinking! It is hard if I cannot start some game on these lone heaths.

'On Going a Journey' (1822)

Heckels, David
In a letter to *The Times*

The money and effort Richard Branson has been expending on his balloon would have been better put towards making his trains run on time.

The Times, 1999

Johnson, Amy (1903–1941)
English aviator

Had I been a man I might have explored the Poles or climbed Mount Everest, but as it was my spirit found an outlet in the air ...

In Margot Asquith (ed.), *Myself When Young*

Johnson, Samuel (1709–1784)
English lexicographer, poet, critic, conversationalist and essayist

A man who has not been in Italy, is always conscious of an inferiority, from his not having seen what it is expected a man should see. The grand object of travelling is to see the shores of the Mediterranean.

In Boswell, *The Life of Samuel Johnson* (1791

Kerouac, Jack (1922–1969)
US writer and poet

The Road is life.

On the Road (1957)

Kilvert, Francis (1840–1879)
English curate and diarist

Of all noxious animals, too, the most noxious is a tourist. And of all tourists, the most vulgar, ill-bred, offensive and loathsome is the British tourist.

Diary, 1870

Kipling, Rudyard (1865–1936)
Indian-born British poet and writer

Down to Gehenna or up to the Throne,
He travels the fastest who travels alone.

'The Winners' (1888)

Macaulay, Dame Rose (1881–1958)
English writer

The great and recurrent question about abroad is, is it worth getting there?

Attr.

Mansfield, Katherine (1888–1923)
New Zealand writer

Whenever I prepare for a journey I prepare as

though for death. Should I never return, all is in order. That is what life has taught me.

Journal of Katherine Mansfield (1954)

Marx, Groucho (1895–1977)
US comedian

Captain Jeffrey Spaulding: You are going Uruguay, and I'm going my way.

Animal Crackers (film, 1930)

Masefield, John (1878–1967)
English poet, writer and critic

It is good to be out on the road, and going one knows not where,
Going through meadow and village, one knows not whither nor why.

'Tewkesbury Road' (1902)

McLuhan, Marshall (1911–1980)
Canadian communications theorist

The car has become the carapace, the protective and aggressive shell, of urban and suburban man.

Understanding Media (1964)

Moore, George (1852–1933)
Irish writer, dramatist and critic

A man travels the world over in search of what he needs and returns home to find it.

The Brook Kerith (1916)

Morris, Jan (1926–)
Welsh travel writer

Travel, which was once either a necessity or an adventure, has become very largely a commodity, and from all sides we are persuaded into thinking that it is a social requirement, too.

New York Times, 1985

Peary, Robert Edwin (1856–1920)
US Arctic explorer, admiral and writer

The Eskimo had his own explanation. Said he: 'The devil is asleep or having trouble with his wife, or we should never have come back so easily.'

The North Pole (1910)

Explaining how he knew he had reached the North Pole

Nothing easier. One step beyond the pole, you see, and the north wind becomes a south one.

Attr.

Proverbs

He travels fastest who travels alone.

Travel broadens the mind.

Ruskin, John (1819–1900)
English art critic, philosopher and reformer

There was a rocky valley between Buxton and Bakewell, ... divine as the vale of Tempe; you might have seen the gods there morning and evening, – Apollo and the sweet Muses of the

Light ... You enterprised a railroad, ... you blasted its rocks away ... And now, every fool in Buxton can be at Bakewell in half-an-hour, and every fool in Bakewell at Buxton.

Praeterita (1889)

Sackville-West, Vita (1892–1962)
English poet and novelist

Travel is the most private of pleasures. There is no greater bore than the travel bore. We do not in the least want to hear what he has seen in Hong-Kong.

Passenger to Tehran (1926)

Santayana, George (1863–1952)
Spanish-born US philosopher and writer
On being asked why he always travelled third class

Because there's no fourth class.

In Thomas, *Living Biographies of the Great Philosophers*

Scott, Robert Falcon (1868–1912)
English naval officer and Antarctic explorer
Of the South Pole

Great God! this is an awful place.

Journal, 1912

Had we lived, I should have had a tale to tell of the hardihood, endurance, and courage of my companions which would have stirred the heart of every Englishman. These rough notes and our dead bodies must tell the tale.

Message to the Public, 1912

Shenstone, William (1714–1763)
English poet, essayist and letter writer

Whoe'er has travell'd life's dull round,
Where'er his stages may have been,
May sigh to think he still has found
The warmest welcome, at an inn.

'At an Inn at Henley' (1758)

Slessor, Kenneth (1901–1971)
Australian poet and journalist

... The dark train shakes and plunges;
Bells cry out; the night-ride starts again.
Soon I shall look out into nothing but blackness,
Pale, windy fields. The old roar and knock of the rails
Melts into dull fury. Pull down the blind. Sleep. Sleep.
Nothing but grey, rushing rivers of bush outside.
Gaslight and milk-cans. Of Rapptown I recall nothing else.

'The Night-Ride'

Stark, Dame Freya (1893–1993)
French-born traveller and writer

The beckoning counts, and not the clicking latch behind you.

Sunday Telegraph, 1993

Sterne, Laurence (1713–1768)
Irish-born English writer and clergyman

The whole circle of travellers may be reduced to the following Heads:
Idle Travellers,
Inquisitive Travellers,
Lying Travellers,
Proud Travellers,
Vain Travellers,
Splenetic Travellers,
Then follow The Travellers of Necessity,
The delinquent and felonious Traveller,
The unfortunate and innocent Traveller,
The simple Traveller,
And last of all (if you please)
The Sentimental Traveller.

Sentimental Journey (1768)

I pity the man who can travel from Dan to Beersheba, and cry, 'tis all barren.

Sentimental Journey (1768)

I think there is a fatality in it – I seldom go to the place I set out for.

A Sentimental Journey (1768)

A man should know something of his own country too, before he goes abroad.

Tristram Shandy (1767)

Stevenson, Robert Louis (1850–1894)
Scottish writer, poet and essayist

Give to me the life I love,
Let the lave go by me,
Give the jolly heaven above
And the byway nigh me.
Bed in the bush with stars to see,
Bread I dip in the river –
There's the life for a man like me,
There's the life for ever.

Songs of Travel (1896)

Let the blow fall soon or late,
Let what will be o'er me;
Give the face of earth around
And the road before me.
Wealth I seek not, hope nor love,
Nor a friend to know me;
All I seek, the heaven above
And the road below me.

Songs of Travel (1896)

For my part, I travel not to go anywhere, but to go. I travel for travel's sake. The great affair is to move.

Travels with a Donkey in the Cévennes (1879)

To travel hopefully is a better thing than to arrive, and the true success is to labour.

Virginibus Puerisque (1881)

But all that I could think of, in the darkness and
the cold,
Was that I was leaving home and my folks were
growing old.

'Christmas at Sea' (1890)

Thomson, Joseph (1858–1895)
Scottish explorer, geologist and writer
His reply when J.M. Barrie asked what was the most
hazardous part of his expedition to Africa
Crossing Piccadilly Circus.

In Dunbar, J.M. Barrie

Twain, Mark (1835–1910)
US humorist, writer, journalist and lecturer
You feel mighty free and easy and comfortable
on a raft.

The Adventures of Huckleberry Finn (1884)

Vine, David
English television commentator
Here we are in the Holy Land of Israel – a Mecca
for tourists.

Attr.

Vizinczey, Stephen (1933–)
Hungarian-born writer, editor and broadcaster
I was told I am a true cosmopolitan. I am
unhappy everywhere.

The Guardian, 1968

White, E.B. (1899–1985)
US humorist and writer
Commuter – one who spends his life
In riding to and from his wife;
A man who shaves and takes a train,
And then rides back to shave again.

Poems and Sketches, 1982

▶▶ FOREIGNERS

treason

Bennett, Alan (1934–)
English dramatist, actor and diarist
Coral Browne to Guy Burgess
Outside Shakespeare the word treason to me
means nothing. Only, you pissed in our soup and
we drank it.

An Englishman Abroad (1989)

▶▶ BETRAYAL

trees

The Bible (King James Version)
And out of the ground made the Lord God to
grow every tree that is pleasant to the sight, and

good for food; the tree of life also in the midst
of the garden, and the tree of knowledge of
good and evil.

Genesis. 2:9

De La Mare, Walter (1873–1956)
English poet
Of all the trees in England,
Oak, Elder, Elm, and Thorn,
The Yew alone burns lamps of peace
For them that lie forlorn.

'Trees' (1913)

Herbert, George (1593–1633)
English poet and priest
Oh that I were an Orenge-tree,
That busie plant!
Then should I ever laden be,
And never want
Some fruit for him that dressed me.

The Temple (1633), 'Employment'

Kavanagh, P.J. (1931–)
English poet
I love trees revealed, the way
Light rinses fog from colours, opens out.

Collected Poems (1964), 'Edward Thomas in Heaven'

Keats, John (1795–1821)
English poet
In drear-nighted December,
Too happy, happy tree,
Thy branches ne'er remember
Their green felicity.

'In drear-nighted December' (1817)

As when, upon a trancèd summer-night,
Those green-rob'd senators of mighty woods,
Tall oaks, branch-charmèd by the earnest stars,
Dream, and so dream all night without a stir.

'Hyperion. A Fragment (1818)'

Kilmer, Alfred Joyce (1886–1918)
US poet
I think that I shall never see
A poem lovely as a tree …

Poems are made by fools like me,
But only God can make a tree.

'Trees' (1914)

Kipling, Rudyard (1865–1936)
Indian-born British poet and writer
Of all the trees that grow so fair,
Old England to adorn,
Greater are none beneath the Sun,
Than Oak, and Ash, and Thorn.

Puck of Pook's Hill (1906), 'A Tree Song'

Mander, Jane (1877–1949)
New Zealand novelist
On early North Auckland

Towering arrogantly above all else, on the crests and down the spurs, stood groups of the kauri, the giant timber tree of New Zealand, whose great grey trunks, like the pillars in the ancient halls of Karnak, shot up seventy and eighty feet without a knot or branch, and whose colossal heads, swelling up onto the sky, made a cipher of every tree near.

The Story of a New Zealand River (1920)

Morris, George Pope (1802–1864)
US journalist

Woodman, spare that tree!
Touch not a single bough!
In youth it sheltered me,
And I'll protect it now.

'Woodman, Spare That Tree' (1830)

Pound, Ezra (1885–1972)
US poet

The difference between a gun and a tree is a difference of tempo. The tree explodes every spring.

Criterion (1937)

Smith, Betty (1896–1972)
US writer

There's a tree that grows in Brooklyn. Some people call it the Tree of Heaven. No matter where its seed falls, it makes a tree which struggles to reach the sky.

A Tree Grows in Brooklyn (1943)

▶▶ COUNTRY; NATURE

trivia

Ashford, Daisy (1881–1972)
English child author

Oh I see said the earl but my own idear is that these things are as piffle before the wind.

The Young Visiters (1919)

Doyle, Sir Arthur Conan (1859–1930)
Scottish writer and war correspondent

You know my method. It is founded upon the observance of trifles.

The Adventures of Sherlock Holmes (1892), 'The Boscombe Valley Mystery'

It has long been an axiom of mine that the little things are infinitely the most important.

The Adventures of Sherlock Holmes (1892), 'A Case of Identity'

Pope, Alexander (1688–1744)
English poet, translator and editor

What dire offence from am'rous causes springs,

What mighty contests rise from trivial things, I sing.

The Rape of the Lock (1714)

trouble

Achebe, Chinua (1930–)
Nigerian writer, poet and critic

A man who makes trouble for others is also making trouble for himself.

Things Fall Apart (1959)

trust

Anonymous

Trust in Allah, but tie your camel.

Old Muslim Proverb

Caine, Michael (1933–)
English actor

Never trust anyone who wears a beard, a bow tie, two-toned shoes, sandals or sunglasses.

The Times, 1992; quoting his father

Camus, Albert (1913–1960)
Algerian-born French writer

It is very true that we seldom confide in those who are better than ourselves.

The Fall (1956)

Christie, Dame Agatha (1890–1976)
English crime writer and playwright

Where large sums of money are concerned, it is advisable to trust nobody.

Endless Night (1967)

Fielding, Henry (1707–1754)
English writer, dramatist and journalist

Never trust the man who hath reason to suspect that you know that he hath injured you.

Jonathan Wild (1743)

Greene, Graham (1904–1991)
English writer and dramatist

His smile explained everything; he carried it always with him as a leper carried his bell; it was a perpetual warning that he was not to be trusted.

England Made Me (1935)

Haskins, Minnie Louise (1875–1957)
English teacher and writer
Quoted by King George VI in his Christmas broadcast, 1939

And I said to a man who stood at the gate of the year: 'Give me a light that I may tread safely into the unknown.' And he replied: 'Go out into the darkness and put your hand into the hand of God. That shall be to you better than a light, and safer than a known way.'

The Desert (1908), 'God Knows'

Jefferson, Thomas (1743–1826)

US Democrat statesman and President

When a man assumes a public trust, he should consider himself as public property.

Remark, 1807

Pitt, William (1708–1778)

English politician and Prime Minister

I cannot give them my confidence; pardon me, gentlemen, confidence is a plant of slow growth in an aged bosom: youth is the season of credulity.

Speech, 1766

Rubin, Jerry (1936–)

US political activist

Don't trust anyone over thirty.

In S.B. Flexner, *Listening to America*

Santayana, George (1863–1952)

Spanish-born US philosopher and writer

Trust the man who hesitates in his speech and is quick and steady in action, but beware of long arguments and long beards.

Soliloquies in England (1922)

Sheridan, Richard Brinsley (1751–1816)

Irish dramatist, politician and orator

There is no trusting appearances.

The School for Scandal (1777)

Theodoric (c.445–526)

King of the Ostrogoths

Explaining why he had a trusted minister, who had said he would adopt his master's religion, beheaded

If this man is not faithful to his God, how can he be faithful to me, a mere man?

In E. Guérard, *Dictionnaire Encyclopédique*

Williams, Tennessee (1911–1983)

US dramatist and writer

We have to distrust each other. It's our only defence against betrayal.

Camino Real (1953)

truth

Adler, Alfred (1870–1937)

Austrian psychiatrist and psychologist

The truth is often a terrible weapon of aggression. It is possible to lie, and even to murder, for the truth.

Problems of Neurosis (1929)

Agar, Herbert Sebastian (1897–1980)

US writer

The truth which makes men free is for the most part the truth which men prefer not to hear.

A Time for Greatness (1942)

Agassiz, Louis (1807–1873)

Swiss-born US naturalist

Every scientific truth goes through three states: first, people say it conflicts with the Bible; next, they say it has been discovered before; lastly, they say they always believed it.

In Shulman and Asimov, *Isaac Asimov's Book of Science and Nature Quotations* (1988)

Angelou, Maya (1928–)

US writer, poet and dramatist

There's a world of difference between truth and facts. Facts can obscure truth.

I Know Why the Caged Bird Sings (1970)

Anonymous

Speak the truth, but leave immediately after.

Slovenian Proverb

Se non è vero, è molto ben trovato.

If it is not true, it is a happy invention.

16th century

Aristotle (384–322 BC)

Greek philosopher

Amicus Plato, sed magis amica veritas.

Plato is dear to me, but dearer still is truth.

Greek original attributed to Aristotle

Arnold, Matthew (1822–1888)

English poet, critic, essayist and educationist

Truth sits upon the lips of dying men.

'Sohrab and Rustum' (1853)

Bacon, Francis (1561–1626)

English philosopher, essayist, politician and courtier

What a man had rather were true he more readily believes.

The New Organon (1620)

Some in their discourse desire rather commendation of wit, in being able to hold all arguments, than of judgement in discerning what is true.

'Of Discourse' (1625)

This same truth is a naked and open daylight, that doth not show the masques and mummeries and triumphs of the world half so stately and daintily as candlelights.

'Of Truth' (1625)

Baldwin, Stanley (1867–1947)

English Conservative statesman and Prime Minister

A platitude is simply a truth repeated until people get tired of hearing it.

Attr.

Balfour, A.J. (1848–1930)

British Conservative Prime Minister

It is unfortunate, considering that enthusiasm moves the world, that so few enthusiasts can be trusted to speak the truth.

Letter to Mrs Drew, 1891

Berkeley, Bishop George (1685–1753)
Irish philosopher and scholar
> Truth is the cry of all, but the game of the few.

Siris (1744)

The Bible (King James Version)
> *Magna est veritas et praevalet.*
> Great is Truth, and mighty above all things.

Apocrypha, I Esdras, 4:41

> And ye shall know the truth, and the truth shall make you free.

John, 8:32

Blake, William (1757–1827)
English poet, engraver, painter and mystic
> Truth can never be told so as to be understood, and not be believ'd.

'Proverbs of Hell' (c.1793)

> A truth thats told with bad intent
> Beats all the Lies you can invent.

'Auguries of Innocence' (c.1803)

> When I tell any Truth it is not for the sake of Convincing those who do not know it but for the sake of defending those who Do.

Public address, from the *Notebook*, c.1810

Bolingbroke, Henry (1678–1751)
English statesman, historian and actor
> Plain truth will influence half a score of men at most in a nation, or an age, while mystery will lead millions by the nose.

Letter, 1721

> They make truth serve as a stalking-horse to error.

Letters on Study and Use of History (1752)

Bowen, Elizabeth (1899–1973)
Irish writer
> Nobody speaks the truth when there's something they must have.

The House in Paris (1935)

Braque, Georges (1882–1963)
French painter
> *La vérité existe; on n'invente que le mensonge.*
> Truth exists; only lies are invented.

Day and Night, Notebooks (1952)

Brooks, Thomas (1608–1680)
English Puritan divine
> For (*magna est veritas et praevalebit*) great is truth, and shall prevail.

The Crown and Glory of Christianity (1662)

Browne, Sir Thomas (1605–1682)
English physician, author and antiquary
> A man may be in as just possession of truth as

of a city, and yet be forced to surrender.

Religio Medici (1643)

Carroll, Lewis (1832–1898)
English writer and photographer
> What I tell you three times is true.

'The Hunting of the Snark' (1876)

Chaucer, Geoffrey (c.1340–1400)
English poet, public servant and courtier
> Trouthe is the hyeste thyng that man may kepe.

The Canterbury Tales (1387)

Cowper, William (1731–1800)
English poet, hymn and letter writer
> And diff'ring judgments serve but to declare
> That truth lies somewhere, if we knew but where.

'Hope' (1782)

Darling, Charles (1849–1936)
English judge and Conservative politician
> Much truth is spoken, that more may be concealed.

Scintillae Juris (1877)

> Perjury is often bold and open. It is truth that is shamefaced – as, indeed, in many cases is no more than decent.

Scintillae Juris (1877)

Dickinson, Emily (1830–1886)
US poet
> Tell all the Truth but tell it slant –
> Success in Circuit lies
> Too bright for our infirm Delight
> The Truth's superb surprise.

'Tell all the Truth but tell it slant' (c.1868)

Donne, John (1572–1631)
English poet
> On a huge hill,
> Cragged, and steep, Truth stands, and he that will
> Reach her, about must, and about must go;
> And what the hill's suddenness resists, win so.

Satire, no. 3 (c.1594)

Doyle, Sir Arthur Conan (1859–1930)
Scottish writer and war correspondent
> It is an old maxim of mine that when you have excluded the impossible, whatever remains, however improbable, must be the truth.

'The Beryl Coronet' (1892)

Dryden, John (1631–1700)
English poet, satirist, dramatist and critic
> I never saw any good that came of telling truth.

Amphitryon (1690)

Finey, George (1895–1987)
> The truth is always libellous.

Sydney Morning Herald, 1981

Frame, Janet (1924–)
New Zealand writer
> In an age of explanation one can always choose varieties of truth.
>> *Living in the Maniototo* (1979)

George, Henry (1839–1897)
US economist, editor and lecturer
> He who sees the truth, let him proclaim it, without asking who is for it or who is against it.
>> *The Land Question* (1881)

Guitry, Sacha (1885–1957)
Russian-born French actor, dramatist and film director
> What probably distorts everything in life is the fact that we are convinced we are telling the truth because we are saying what we think.
>> *Toutes réflexions faites*

Hamilton, Sir William (1788–1856)
Scottish metaphysical philosopher
> Truth, like a torch, the more it's shook it shines.
>> *Discussions on Philosophy* (1852)

Hare, Augustus (1792–1834)
English clergyman and writer
> Truth, when witty, is the wittiest of all things.
>> *Guesses at Truth* (1827)

Hellman, Lillian (1907–1984)
US dramatist and screenwriter
> Cynicism is an unpleasant way of saying the truth.
>> *The Little Foxes* (1939)

Huxley, T.H. (1825–1895)
English biologist, Darwinist and agnostic
> Irrationally held truths may be more harmful than reasoned errors.
>> *Science and Culture, and Other Essays* (1881)

> It is the customary fate of new truths to begin as heresies and to end as superstitions.
>> *Science and Culture, and Other Essays* (1881)

Ibsen, Henrik (1828–1906)
Norwegian writer, dramatist and poet
> A man should never have his best trousers on when he goes out to battle for freedom and truth.
>> *An Enemy of the People* (1882)

Jerome, Jerome K. (1859–1927)
English writer and dramatist
> It is always the best policy to speak the truth, unless of course you are an exceptionally good liar.
>> In *The Idler*, 1892

Johnson, Samuel (1709–1784)
English lexicographer, poet, critic, conversationalist and essayist
On sceptics
> Truth, Sir, is a cow which will yield such people no more milk, and so they are gone to milk the bull.
>> In Boswell, *The Life of Samuel Johnson* (1791)

La Bruyère, Jean de (1645–1696)
French satirist
> Il y a quelques rencontres dans la vie où la vérité et la simplicité sont le meilleur manège du monde.
> There are some circumstances in life where truth and simplicity are the best strategy in the world.
>> *Les caractères ou les moeurs de ce siècle* (1688)

Leacock, Stephen (1869–1944)
English-born Canadian humorist, writer and economist
> A half truth in argument, like a half brick, carries better.
>> In Flesch, *The Book of Unusual Quotations*

Le Gallienne, Richard (1866–1947)
English writer and critic
Of Oscar Wilde
> Paradox with him was only Truth standing on its head to attract attention.
>> *The Romantic 90s*

Lowell, James Russell (1819–1891)
US poet, editor, abolitionist and diplomat
> New occasions teach new duties:
> Time makes ancient good uncouth;
> They must upward still, and onward, who would keep abreast of Truth.
>> 'The Present Crisis' (1845)

Mill, John Stuart (1806–1873)
English philosopher, economist and reformer
> History teems with instances of truth put down by persecution … It is a piece of idle sentimentality that truth, merely as truth, has any inherent power denied to error, of prevailing against the dungeon and the stake.
>> *On Liberty* (1859)

Milton, John (1608–1674)
English poet, libertarian and pamphleteer
> Beholding the bright countenance of truth in the quiet and still air of delightfull studies.
>> *The Reason of Church-government Urg'd against Prelaty* (1642)

Newton, Sir Isaac (1642–1727)
English scientist and philosopher
> I do not know what I may appear to the world, but to myself I seem to have been only a boy playing on the sea-shore, and diverting myself in now and then finding a smoother pebble or a prettier shell than ordinary, whilst the great ocean of truth lay all undiscovered before me.
>> In Brewster, *Memoirs of the Life, Writings, and Discoveries of Sir Isaac Newton* (1855)

Nixon, Richard (1913–1994)
US Republican politician and President
> Let us begin by committing ourselves to the truth, to see it like it is and to tell it like it is, to find the truth, to speak the truth and live with the truth. That's what we'll do.
>> Nomination acceptance speech, 1968

Patmore, Coventry (1823–1896)
English poet
> For want of me the world's course will not fail:
> When all its work is done, the lie shall rot;
> The truth is great, and shall prevail,
> When none cares whether it prevail or not.
>> *The Unknown Eros* (1877)

Plato (c.429–347 BC)
Greek philosopher
> But, my dearest Agathon, it is truth which you cannot contradict; you can easily contradict Socrates.
>> *Symposium*

Proust, Marcel (1871–1922)
French writer and critic
> *Une vérité clairement comprise ne peut plus être écrite avec sincérité.*
> A truth which is clearly understood can no longer be written with sincerity.
>> 'Senancour c'est moi'

Proverbs
> Craft maun hae claes, but truth goes naked.
>> Scots proverb

> Many a true word is spoken in jest.

> Truth is stranger than fiction.

> Truth will out.

Samuel, Lord (1870–1963)
English Liberal statesman, philosopher and administrator
> A truism is on that account none the less true.
>> *A Book of Quotations* (1947)

Sand, George (1804–1876)
French writer and dramatist
> *Le vrai est trop simple, il faut y arriver toujours par le compliqué.*
> The truth is too simple, it must always be arrived at through complication.
>> Letter to Armand Barbès, 1867

Shakespeare, William (1564–1616)
English dramatist, poet and actor
> O, while you live, tell truth, and shame the devil!
>> *Henry IV, Part 1*, III.i

Schiller, Johann Christoph Friedrich (1759–1805)
German writer, dramatist, poet and historian
> *Die Wahrheit lebt in der Täuschung fort.*
> Truth lives on in deception.
>> *On the Aesthetic Education of Man* (1793–1795)

Shaw, George Bernard (1856–1950)
Irish socialist, writer, dramatist and critic
> All great truths begin as blasphemies.
>> *Annajanska* (1919)

Smith, Sydney (1771–1845)
English clergyman, essayist, journalist and wit
> It is the calling of great men, not so much to preach new truths, as to rescue from oblivion those old truths which it is our wisdom to remember and our weakness to forget.
>> Attr.

Solzhenitsyn, Alexander (1918–)
Russian writer, dramatist and historian
> When truth is discovered by someone else, it loses something of its attractiveness.
>> *Candle in the Wind*

> If decade after decade the truth cannot be told, each person's mind starts to roam irretrievably. One's fellow countrymen become harder to understand than Martians.
>> *Cancer Ward* (1968)

Thoreau, Henry David (1817–1862)
US essayist, social critic and writer
> It takes two to speak the truth, – one to speak, and another to hear.
>> *A Week on the Concord and Merrimack Rivers* (1849)

Twain, Mark (1835–1910)
US humorist, writer, journalist and lecturer
> When in doubt, tell the truth.
>> *Pudd'nhead Wilson's New Calendar*

> There was things which he stretched, but mainly he told the truth.
>> *The Adventures of Huckleberry Finn* (1884)

Whitehead, A.N. (1861–1947)
English mathematician and philosopher
> There are no whole truths; all truths are half-truths. It is trying to treat them as whole truths that plays the devil.
>> *Dialogues* (1954)

Wilde, Oscar (1854–1900)
Irish poet, dramatist, writer, critic and wit
> If one tells the truth, one is sure, sooner or later, to be found out.
>> *The Chameleon*, 1894

> The truth is rarely pure and never simple. Modern life would be very tedious if it were either, and modern literature a complete impossibility!
>> *The Importance of Being Earnest* (1895)

Williams, Rowan
Archbishop of Wales
> Words cannot be relied on to bury the truth. Even when the winners have rewritten history,

where a language and civilization have been destroyed – the buried truth finds its way in from the margins.

The Observer, 2000

Woolf, Virginia (1882–1941)
English writer and critic
> If you do not tell the truth about yourself you cannot tell it about other people.

The Moment and Other Essays

Wright, Frank Lloyd (1869–1959)
US architect and writer
> The truth is more important than the facts.

In Simcox, *Treasury of Quotations on Christian Themes*

Wycliffe, John (c.1329–1384)
English religious reformer
To the Duke of Lancaster, 1381
> I believe that in the end the truth will conquer.

In J.R. Green, *Short History of the English People*

Xenophanes (c.570–480 BC)
Greek philosopher and historian
> And of course the clear and certain truth no man has seen.

In J.H. Lesher, *Xenophanes of Colophon* (1992)

Yeltsin, Boris (1931–)
Russian statesman and President
> Truth is truth, and the truth will overcome the left, the right and the centre.

Interview in *Newsweek*, 1994

Zola, Emile (1840–1902)
French writer
Article on the Dreyfus affair
> *La vérité est en marche, et rien ne l'arrêtera.*
> Truth is on the move and nothing can stop it.

In *La Vérité en marche* (1901)

▶▶ ERROR; FACTS; HONESTY; LIES

tyranny

Arendt, Hannah (1906–1975)
German-born US theorist
> Under conditions of tyranny it is far easier to act than to think.

In Auden, *A Certain World* (1970)

Bellow, Saul (1915–)
Canadian-born US Jewish writer
> It is not inconceivable that a man might find freedom and identity by killing his oppressor. But as a Chicagoan, I am rather skeptical about this. Murderers are not improved by murdering.

'A World Too Much With Us' (1975)

Blake, William (1757–1827)
English poet, engraver, painter and mystic

> One law for the Lion & Ox is Oppression.

The Marriage of Heaven and Hell (c.1790–1793)

Browning, Robert (1812–1889)
English poet
> Oppression makes the wise man mad.

Luria (1846)

Burke, Edmund (1729–1797)
Irish-born British statesman and philosopher
> Bad laws are the worst sort of tyranny.

Speech at Bristol (1780)

Churchill, Sir Winston (1874–1965)
English Conservative Prime Minister
> Dictators ride to and fro upon tigers which they dare not dismount. And the tigers are getting hungry.

While England Slept (1936)

Defoe, Daniel (c.1661–1731)
English writer and critic
> And of all plagues with which mankind are curst,
> Ecclesiastic tyranny's the worst.

The True-Born Englishman (1701)

> Nature has left this tincture in the blood,
> That all men would be tyrants if they could.

'The Kentish Petition' (1713)

Herrick, Robert (1591–1674)
English poet, royalist and clergyman
> 'Twixt Kings & Tyrants there's this difference known;
> Kings seek their Subjects good: Tyrants their owne.

Hesperides (1648)

Inge, William Ralph (1860–1954)
English divine, writer and teacher
> The enemies of Freedom do not argue; they shout and they shoot.

End of an Age (1948)

Jung Chang (1952–)
Chinese author
> Mao had managed to turn the people into the ultimate weapon of dictatorship. That was why under him there was no real equivalent of the KGB in China. There was no need. In bringing out and nourishing the worst in people, Mao had created a moral wasteland and a land of hatred.

Wild Swans (1991)

Mandela, Nelson (1918–)
South African statesman and President
> Never, never and never again shall it be that this beautiful land will again experience the oppression of one by another and suffer the indignity of being the skunk of the world.

Inauguration speech, 1994

Mill, John Stuart (1806–1873)
English philosopher, economist and reformer
> Whatever crushes individuality is despotism, by whatever name it may be called.
>> *On Liberty* (1859)

> Protection, therefore, against the tyranny of the magistrate is not enough: there needs protection also against the tyranny of the prevailing opinion and feeling.
>> *On Liberty* (1859)

Niemöller, Martin (1892–1984)
German Lutheran theologian
> In Germany, the Nazis came for the Communists and I didn't speak up because I was not a Communist. Then they came for the Jews and I didn't speak up because I was not a Jew. Then they came for the trade unionists and I didn't speak up because I was not a trade unionist. Then they came for the Catholics and I was a Protestant so I didn't speak up. Then they came for me … By that time there was no one to speak up for anyone.
>> In Neil, *Concise Dictionary of Religious Quotations*

Plato (c.429–347 BC)
Greek philosopher
> Tyranny comes from no other form of government but democracy.
>> *Republic*

Seneca (c.4 BC–AD 65)
Roman philosopher, poet, dramatist, essayist, rhetorician and statesman
> *Victima haud ulla amplior*
> *Potest magisque opima mactari Iovi*
> *Quam rex iniquus.*
> There can be slain
> No sacrifice to God more acceptable
> Than an unjust and wicked king.
>> *Hercules Furens*

Thomas, Dylan (1914–1953)
Welsh poet, writer and radio dramatist
> The hand that signed the paper felled a city;
> Five sovereign fingers taxed the breath,
> Doubled the globe of death and halved a country;
> These five kings did a king to death …

> The hand that signed the treaty bred a fever,
> And famine grew, and locusts came;
> Great is the hand that holds dominion over
> Man by a scribbled name.
>> 'The hand that signed the paper' (1936)

Trotsky, Leon (1879–1940)
Russian revolutionary and Communist theorist
> Lenin's method leads to this: the party organization at first substitutes itself for the party as a whole. Then the central committee substitutes itself for the party organization, and finally a single dictator substitutes himself for the central committee.
>> In N. McInnes, *The Communist Parties of Western Europe*

▶▶ CENSORSHIP

U

uncertainty

Barnfield, Richard (1574–1627)
English poet
> Nothing more certain than incertainties;
> Fortune is full of fresh variety:
> Constant in nothing but inconstancy.
> *The Affectionate Shepherd* (1594)

Bissell, Claude T. (1916–)
Canadian writer
> I prefer complexity to certainty, cheerful
> mysteries to sullen facts.
> Address, University of Toronto, 1969

Boyd, William (1952–)
Scottish writer
> What now? What next? All these questions. All
> these doubts. So few certainties. But then I have
> taken new comfort and refuge in the doctrine
> that advises one not to seek tranquillity in
> certainty, but in permanently suspended
> judgement.
> *Brazzaville Beach* (1990)

Drabble, Margaret (1939–)
English writer
> When nothing is sure, everything is possible.
> *The Middle Ground* (1980)

▶▶ DOUBT; INDECISION

unconscious

Calvino, Italo (1923–1985)
Italian writer
> The unconscious is the ocean of the unsayable,
> of what has been expelled from the land of
> language, removed as a result of ancient
> prohibitions.
> *The Literature Machine* (1987)

unhappiness

Bono, Edward de (1933–)
British physician and writer
> Unhappiness is best defined as the difference
> between our talents and our expectations.
> *The Observer*, 1977

▶▶ SUFFERING

universe

Carlyle, Thomas (1795–1881)
Scottish historian, biographer, critic, and essayist
> *Margaret Fuller*: I accept the universe.
> *Carlyle*: Gad! she'd better!
> In William James, *Varieties of Religious Experience* (1902)

To Wm Allingham
> I don't pretend to understand the Universe – it's
> a great deal bigger than I am … People ought
> to be modester.
> In D.A. Wilson and D. Wilson MacArthur, *Carlyle in
> Old Age* (1934)

Cook, Peter (1937–1995)
English comedian and writer
> I am very interested in the Universe – I am
> specializing in the universe and all that
> surrounds it.
> *Beyond the Fringe*, 1962

Haldane, J.B.S. (1892–1964)
British biochemist, geneticist and popularizer of science
> My own suspicion is that the universe is not only
> queerer than we suppose, but queerer than we
> can suppose.
> *Possible Worlds and Other Essays* (1927)

▶▶ SPACE; WORLD

university

Archibald, John Feltham (1856–1919)
> I have nothing against Oxford men. Some of our
> best shearers' cooks are Oxford men.
> In R. H. Croll, *I Recall …*

Bacon, Francis (1561–1626)
English philosopher, essayist, politician and courtier
> Universities incline wits to sophistry and
> affectation.
> *Valerius Terminus of the Interpretation of Nature* (1603)

Bateson, Mary Catherine (1939–)
US anthropologist and writer
> Most higher education is devoted to affirming
> the traditions and origins of an existing elite and
> transmitting them to new members.
> *Composing a Life* (1989)

Betjeman, Sir John (1906–1984)
English poet laureate
> Balkan Sobranies in a wooden box,
> The college arms upon the lid; Tokay
> And sherry in the cupboard; on the shelves

The University Statutes bound in blue,
Crome Yellow, Prancing Nigger, Blunden, Keats.
Summoned by Bells (1960)

Chekhov, Anton (1860–1904)
Russian writer, dramatist and doctor
Liubov Andreevna: Are you really still a student?
Trofimov: I shall probably be a student forever.
The Cherry Orchard (1904)

Carlyle, Thomas (1795–1881)
Scottish historian, biographer, critic, and essayist
The true University of these days is a Collection
of Books.
On Heroes, Hero-Worship, and the Heroic in History (1841)

Congreve, William (1670–1729)
English dramatist
Aye, 'tis well enough for a servant to be bred at
an University. But the education is a little too
pedantic for a gentleman.
Love for Love (1695)

Esson, Louis (1879–1943)
Scots-born Australian dramatist
On Melbourne University
If the science professors knew as little about
their jobs as the literary ones the University
would have been blown up long ago!
In Vance Palmer, *Louis Esson and the Australian
Theatre* (1948)

Ewart, Gavin (1916–1995)
English poet
After Cambridge – unemployment. No one
wanted much to know.
Good degrees are good for nothing in the
business world below.
'The Sentimental Education'

Fry, Stephen (1957–)
British comedian and writer
The competitive spirit is an ethos which it is the
business of universities … to subdue and
neutralise.
Paperweight (1992)

Gibbon, Edward (1737–1794)
English historian, politician and memoirist
To the University of Oxford I acknowledge no
obligation; and she will as cheerfully renounce
me for a son, as I am willing to disclaim her for a
mother. I spent fourteen months at Magdalen
College: they proved the fourteen months the
most idle and unprofitable of my whole life.
Memoirs of My Life and Writings (1796)

Hodson, Peregrine
British author
He probably doesn't understand what he's
looking at but he's reluctant to ask, because this
is Japan and the student doesn't ask questions

but waits to be told by the teacher.
A Circle Round The Sun – A Foreigner in Japan

Illich, Ivan (1926–)
Austrian-born US educator, sociologist, writer and priest
Any attempt to reform the university without
attending to the system of which it is an integral
part is like trying to do urban renewal in New
York City from the twelfth storey up.
Deschooling Society (1971)

Johnson, Paul (1928–)
British editor and writer
In a growing number of countries everyone has a
qualified right to attend a university … The
result is the emergence of huge caravanserais …
where higher education is doled out rather like
gruel in a soup kitchen.
The Spectator, 1996

Lodge, David (1935–)
English writer, satirist and literary critic
Rummidge … had lately suffered the mortifying
fate of most English universities of its type (civic
redbrick): having competed strenuously for fifty
years with two universities chiefly valued for
being old, it was, at the moment of drawing
level, rudely overtaken in popularity and
prestige by a batch of universities chiefly valued
for being new.
Changing Places (1975)

Universities are the cathedrals of the modern
age. They shouldn't have to justify their
existence by utilitarian criteria.
Nice Work

McLuhan, Marshall (1911–1980)
Canadian communications theorist
The reason universities are so full of knowledge
is that the students come with so much and they
leave with so little.
Antigonish Review, 1988

Melville, Herman (1819–1891)
US writer and poet
A whale ship was my Yale College and my Harvard.
Moby Dick (1851)

Nabokov, Vladimir (1899–1977)
Russian-born US writer, poet, translator and critic
Like so many ageing college people, Pnin had
long ceased to notice the existence of students
on the campus.
Pnin (1957)

Newman, John Henry, Cardinal (1801–1890)
English Cardinal, theologian and poet
A university is an *alma mater*, knowing her
children one by one, not a foundry, or a mint, or
a treadmill.
Attr.

O'Connor, Flannery (1925–1964)
US writer

> Everywhere I go I'm asked if I think the university stifles writers. My opinion is that they don't stifle enough of them. There's many a bestseller that could have been prevented by a good teacher.
>
> In Fitzgerald, *The Nature and Aim of Fiction*

Osborne, John (1929–1994)
English dramatist and actor

> I don't think one 'comes down' from Jimmy's university. According to him, it's not even red brick, but white tile.
>
> *Look Back in Anger* (1956)

Ozick, Cynthia (1928–)
US writer

> It is the function of a liberal university not to give the right answers, but to ask right questions.
>
> 'Women and Creativity' (1969)

Peacock, Thomas Love (1785–1866)
English writer and poet

> He was sent, as usual, to a public school, where a little learning was painfully beaten into him, and from thence to the university, where it was carefully taken out of him.
>
> *Nightmare Abbey* (1818)

Smith, Adam (1723–1790)
Scottish economist, philosopher and essayist
Of universities

> Several of those learned societies have chosen to remain … the sanctuaries in which exploded systems and obsolete prejudices found shelter and protection, after they had been hunted out of every other corner of the world.
>
> *Wealth of Nations* (1776)

Spooner, William (1844–1930)
English churchman and university warden

> Sir, you have tasted two whole worms; you have hissed all my mystery lectures and have been caught fighting a liar in the quad; you will leave Oxford by the town drain.
>
> Attr.

Spring-Rice, Cecil Arthur (1859–1918)
English diplomat and hymn writer

> I am the Dean of Christ Church, Sir:
> There's my wife; look well at her.
> She's the Broad and I'm the High;
> We are the University.
>
> In Hiscock (ed.), *The Balliol Rhymes* (1939)

Trapp, Joseph (1679–1747)
English poet, pamphleteer, translator and clergyman

> The King, observing with judicious eyes,
> The state of both his universities,
> To Oxford sent a troop of horse, and why?
> That learned body wanted loyalty;
> To Cambridge books, as very well discerning,
> How much that loyal body wanted learning.
>
> Epigram on George I's donation of Bishop Ely's Library to Cambridge University

Walker, Alice (1944–)
US writer and poet

> Ignorance, arrogance and racism have bloomed as Superior Knowledge in all too many universities.
>
> *In Search of our Mothers' Gardens* (1983)

▶▶ EDUCATION; KNOWLEDGE; LEARNING; SCHOLARS; SCHOOL; TEACHERS

V

values

Montherlant, Henry de (1896–1972)
French novelist and dramatist
> *Les valeurs nobles, à la fin, sont toujours vaincues;
> l'histoire est le récit de leurs défaites renouvelées.*
> Noble values, in the end, are always overcome;
> history tells the story of their defeat over and
> over again.
>> *Le Maître de Santiago* (1947)

Sterne, Laurence (1713–1768)
Irish-born English writer and clergyman
> Honours, like impressions upon coin, may give
> an ideal and local value to a bit of base metal;
> but Gold and Silver will pass all the world over
> without any other recommendation than their
> own weight.
>> *Tristram Shandy* (1759–1767)

Thatcher, Margaret (1925–)
English Conservative Prime Minister
> Victorian values … were the values when our
> country became great.
>> Television interview, 1982

Ustinov, Sir Peter (1921–)
English actor, director, dramatist, writer and raconteur
> When Mrs Thatcher says she has a nostalgia for
> Victorian values I don't think she realises that 90
> per cent of her nostalgia would be satisfied in
> the Soviet Union.
>> *The Observer*, 1987

Woolf, Virginia (1882–1941)
English writer and critic
> It is the masculine values that prevail. Speaking
> crudely, football and sport are 'important'; the
> worship of fashion, the buying of clothes
> 'trivial'… This is an important book, the critic
> assumes, because it deals with war. This is an
> insignificant book because it deals with feelings
> of women in a drawing-room … everywhere and
> much more subtly the difference of values
> persists.
>> *A Room of One's Own* (1929)

▶▶ PRINCIPLES

vanity

The Bible (King James Version)
> Vanity of vanities, saith the Preacher, vanity of
> vanities; all is vanity.
>> *Ecclesiastes*, 1:2

Cowley, Hannah (1743–1809)
English dramatist and poet
> Vanity, like murder, will out.
>> *The Belle's Stratagem* (1780)

Ebner-Eschenbach, Marie von (1830–1916)
Austrian writer
> We are so vain that we are even concerned
> about the opinion of those people who are of no
> concern to us.
>> *Aphorisms* (1880)

Parris, Matthew (1949–)
British Conservative politician and journalist
> Being an MP feeds your vanity and starves your
> self-respect.
>> *The Times*, 1994

Stevenson, Robert Louis (1850–1894)
Scottish writer, poet and essayist
> Vanity dies hard; in some obstinate cases it
> outlives the man.
>> *Prince Otto*

Swift, Jonathan (1667–1745)
Irish satirist, poet, essayist and cleric
> 'Tis an old maxim in the schools,
> That vanity's the food of fools;
> Yet now and then your men of wit
> Will condescend to take a bit.
>> 'Cadenus and Vanessa' (c.1712)

Thackeray, William Makepeace (1811–1863)
Indian-born English writer
> Ah! *Vanitas Vanitatum*! Which of us is happy in
> this world? Which of us has his desire? or, having
> it, is satisfied? – Come, children, let us shut up
> the box and the puppets, for our play is played
> out.
>> *Vanity Fair* (1847–1848)

> Oh, Vanity of vanities!
> How wayward the decrees of Fate are;
> How very weak the very wise,
> How very small the very great are!
>> 'Vanitas Vanitatum'

Unamuno, Miguel de (1864–1936)
Spanish philosopher, poet and writer
> *Cúrate de la afección de preocuparte cómo aparezcas a
> los demás. Cuídate sólo de cómo aparezcas ante Dios,
> cuídate de la idea que de ti Dios tenga.*
> Cure yourself of the disease of worrying about
> how you appear to others. Concern yourself only
> with how you appear before God, concern
> yourself with the idea which God has of you.
>> *Vida de Don Quijote y Sancho* (1914)

▶▶ APPEARANCE; PRIDE; SELF

vegetarianism

Brown, A. Whitney

> I am not a vegetarian because I love animals; I am a vegetarian because I hate plants.

Attr.

Campbell, Mrs Patrick (1865–1940)

English actress

To Bernard Shaw, a vegetarian

> Some day you'll eat a pork chop, Joey, and then God help all women.

In Woollcott, While Rome Burns (1934)

Davis, Miles (1926–1991)

US jazz musician

On vegetarianism

> I figure if horses can eat green shit and be strong and run like motherfuckers, why shouldn't I?

In Ian Carr, Miles Davis: a Critical Biography (1982)

Lang, K.D. (1961–)

Canadian singer

> If you knew how meat was made, you'd probably lose your lunch. I'm from cattle country. That's why I became a vegetarian.

Attr.

Obis, Paul

Founder of *Vegetarian Times* on his decision to start eating meat, 1997

> Twenty-two years of tofu is a lot of time.

Attr.

▶▶ DIETS; DINING; FOOD

vice

Bankhead, Tallulah (1903–1968)

US actress

> Here's a rule I recommend. Never practice two vices at once.

Tallulah (1952)

Blessington, Lady Marguerite (1789–1849)

Irish-born writer and socialite

> The vices of the rich and great are mistaken for error; and those of the poor and lowly, for crimes.

Desultory Thoughts and Reflections (1839)

Crisp, Quentin (1908–1999)

English writer, publicist and model

> Vice is its own reward.

The Naked Civil Servant (1968)

Proverb

> Vice is often clothed in virtue's habit.

Shakespeare, William (1564–1616)

English dramatist, poet and actor

> Through tatter'd clothes small vices do appear;
> Robed and furr'd gowns hide all.

King Lear, IV.vi

▶▶ CRIME; EVIL; SIN; VIRTUE

victory

Alexander the Great (356–323 BC)

Macedonian king and conquering army commander

> I send you a kaffis of mustard seed, that you may taste and acknowledge the bitterness of my victory.

Letter to King Darius III

Caesar, Gaius Julius (c.102–44 BC)

Roman statesman, historian and army commander

On his triumphant Pontic campaign

> *Veni, vidi, vici.*
> I came, I saw, I conquered.

In Suetonius, Lives of the Caesars

Churchill, Sir Winston (1874–1965)

English Conservative Prime Minister

> You ask, what is our aim? I can answer that in one word: victory at all costs, victory in spite of all terror, victory however long and hard the road may be; for without victory there is no survival.

Speech, House of Commons, May 1940

Coppola, Francis Ford (1939–)

US film director

Colonel Killgore in the film *Apocalypse Now*

> I love the smell of Napalm in the morning … smells like victory.

Apocalypse Now (film, 1977)

Kennedy, John F. (1917–1963)

US Democrat President

> Victory has a thousand fathers but defeat is an orphan.

Attr.

Khrushchev, Nikita (1894–1971)

Russian statesman and Premier of the USSR

Of the Cuban missile crisis

> People talk about who won and who lost. Human reason won. Mankind won.

The Observer, 1962

MacArthur, Douglas (1880–1964)

US general

> In war there is no substitute for victory.

Speech to Congress, 1951

Marcy, William (1786–1857)

US Democrat politician

On the politicians of New York

They see nothing wrong in the rule, that to the victor belong the spoils of the enemy.

Speech, 1832

McLennan, Murdoch (fl. 1715)
Scottish poet

There's some say that we wan, some say that they wan,
Some say that nane wan at a', man;
But one thing I'm sure, that at Sheriffmuir
A battle there was which I saw, man:
And we ran, and they ran, and they ran, and we ran,
And we ran; and they ran awa', man!

In J. Woodfall Ebsworth (ed.), *Roxburghe Ballads* (1889)

Nelson, Lord (1758–1805)
English admiral
At the Battle of the Nile, 1798

Victory is not a name strong enough for such a scene.

In Robert Southey, *The Life of Nelson* (1860)

Southey, Robert (1774–1843)
English poet, essayist, historian and letterwriter

'And everybody praised the Duke,
Who this great fight did win.'
'But what good came of it at last?'
Quoth little Peterkin.
'Why that I cannot tell,' said he,
'But 'twas a famous victory.'

'The Battle of Blenheim' (1798)

▶▶ SUCCESS; WAR

violence

Ali, Muhammad (1942–)
US heavyweight boxer

Fighting is not the answer to frustration and hate. It is a sport, not a philosophy of life.

Interview, *TV Guide* magazine, 1999

Ascherson, Neal (1932–)
Scottish journalist

Rioting is at least as English as thatched cottages and honey still for tea.

The Observer, 1985

Asimov, Isaac (1920–1992)
Russian-born US scientist, academic and writer

Violence is the last refuge of the incompetent.

Foundation (1951)

Bramah, Ernest (1868–1942)

It has been said that there are few situations in life that cannot be honourably settled, and without loss of time, either by suicide, a bag of gold, or by thrusting a despised antagonist over

the edge of a precipice upon a dark night.

Kai Lung's Golden Hours (1922)

Brien, Alan (1925–)
English writer

Violence is the repartee of the illiterate.

Punch, 1973

Bright, John (1811–1889)
English Liberal politician and social reformer

Force is not a remedy.

Speech, 1880

Bronowski, Jacob (1908–1974)
British scientist, writer and TV presenter

The wish to hurt, the momentary intoxication with pain, is the loophole through which the pervert climbs into the minds of ordinary men.

The Face of Violence (1954)

Burke, Edmund (1729–1797)
Irish-born British statesman and philosopher

The use of force alone is but temporary. It may subdue for a moment; but it does not remove the necessity of subduing again: and a nation is not governed, which is perpetually to be conquered.

Speech on Conciliation with America (1775)

Eames, Dr Robin (1940–)
Referring to the Enniskillen bombing, 8 November 1987

'... I see,' he said with emphasis, 'the faces of the little children who have lost a father, as they walk behind the coffin with roses in their hands. I see the faces of good, honest, decent people who have never done wrong to anyone else, who have lost a loved one, blown to bits by a terrorist bomb. And of course I weep.'

The Observer, 1992

Horace (65–8 BC)
Roman lyric poet and satirist

Vis consili expers mole ruit sua.
Brute force without judgement collapses under its own weight.

Odes

Inge, William Ralph (1860–1954)
English divine, writer and teacher

A man may build himself a throne of bayonets, but he cannot sit upon it.

Philosophy of Plotinus (1923)

King, Martin Luther (1929–1968)
US civil rights leader and Baptist minister

A riot is at bottom the language of the unheard.

Chaos or Community (1967)

Koran

Let there be no violence in religion.

Chapter 2

La Fontaine, Jean de (1621–1695)

French poet and fabulist

> *La raison du plus fort est toujours la meilleure.*
> The reason of the strongest is always the best.
>
> *'Le loup et l'agneau'*

Laing, R.D. (1927–1989)

Scottish psychiatrist, psychoanalyst and poet

> We are effectively destroying ourselves by violence masquerading as love.
>
> *The Politics of Experience (1967)*

Mackenzie, Sir Compton (1883–1972)

Scottish writer and broadcaster

> There is little to choose morally between beating up a man physically and beating him up mentally.
>
> *On Moral Courage (1962)*

Milton, John (1608–1674)

English poet, libertarian and pamphleteer

> ... who overcomes
> By force, hath overcome but half his foe.
>
> *Paradise Lost (1667)*

Reading, the Dowager Duchess of

> We are a nation of yobs. Now that we don't have war, what's wrong with a good punch-up?
>
> *The Observer, 1998*

Trotsky, Leon (1879–1940)

Russian revolutionary and Communist theorist

> Where force is necessary, one should make use of it boldly, resolutely, and right to the end. But it is as well to know the limitations of force; to know where to combine force with manoeuvre, assault with conciliation.
>
> *What Next? (1932)*

Unamuno, Miguel de (1864–1936)

Spanish philosopher, poet and writer

Of Franco's supporters

> *Vencer no es convencer.*
> To conquer is not to convince.
>
> Speech, 1936

▶▶ CRUELTY; FORCE; WAR; WEAPONS

virtue

Alda, Alan (1936–)

US actor

> It's too bad I'm not as wonderful a person as people say I am, because the world could use a few people like that.
>
> Attr.

Aristotle (384–322 BC)

Greek philosopher

> Moral virtue is the child of habit.
>
> *Nicomachean Ethics*

> Moral virtues we acquire through practice like the arts.
>
> *Nicomachean Ethics*

Bacon, Francis (1561–1626)

English philosopher, essayist, politician and courtier

> Virtue is like a rich stone, best plain set.
>
> *'Of Beauty' (1625)*

Bagehot, Walter (1826–1877)

English economist and political philosopher

> Nothing is more unpleasant than a virtuous person with a mean mind.
>
> *Literary Studies (1879)*

The Bible (King James Version)

> Whatsoever things are true, whatsoever things are honest, whatsoever things are just, whatsoever things are pure, whatsoever things are lovely, whatsoever things are of good report; if there be any virtue, and if there be any praise, think on these things.
>
> *Philippians, 4:8*

Brecht, Bertolt (1898–1956)

German dramatist

> *Wenn es wo so grosse Tugenden gibt, das beweist, dass da etwas faul ist.*
> Whenever there are such great virtues, it's proof that something's fishy.
>
> *Mother Courage and her Children (1941)*

Browne, Sir Thomas (1605–1682)

English physician, author and antiquary

> There is no road or ready way to virtue.
>
> *Religio Medici (1643)*

Butler, Samuel (1835–1902)

English writer, painter, philosopher and scholar

> Virtue and vice are like life and death, or mind and matter: things which cannot exist without being qualified by their opposite.
>
> *The Way of All Flesh (1903)*

Colette (1873–1954)

French writer

> My virtue's still far too small, I don't trot it out and about yet.
>
> *Claudine at School (1900)*

Confucius (c.550–c.478 BC)

Chinese philosopher and teacher of ethics

> Fine words and an insinuating appearance are seldom associated with true virtue.
>
> *Analects*

> To be able to practise five things everywhere under heaven constitutes perfect virtue ... gravity, generosity of soul, sincerity, earnestness, and kindness.
>
> *Analects*

> Virtue is not left to stand alone. He who

practises it will have neighbours.

Analects

Congreve, William (1670–1729)
English dramatist
For 'tis some virtue, virtue to commend.

'To Sir Godfrey Kneller'

Du Maurier, George (1834–1896)
French-born English novelist
She had all the virtues but one.

Trilby (1894)

Fletcher, John (1579–1625)
English dramatist
'Tis virtue, and not birth that makes us noble:
Great actions speak great minds, and such
should govern.

The Prophetess (1647)

Goldsmith, Oliver (c.1728–1774)
Irish dramatist, poet and writer
The virtue which requires to be ever guarded, is
scarce worth the sentinel.

The Vicar of Wakefield (1766)

Hazlitt, William (1778–1830)
English writer and critic
The greatest offence against virtue is to speak ill
of it.

London Weekly Review, 1828

Herbert, George (1593–1633)
English poet and priest
Onely a sweet and vertuous soul,
Like season'd timber, never gives;
But though the whole world turn to coal,
Then chiefly lives.

The Temple (1633)

Huxley, Aldous (1894–1963)
English writer, poet and critic
Particulars, as everyone knows, make for virtue
and happiness. Generalities are intellectually
necessary evils.

Brave New World (1932)

Juvenal (c.60–130)
Roman verse satirist and Stoic
Nobilitas sola est atque unica virtus.
The one and only true nobility is virtue.

Satires

Kingsley, Charles (1819–1875)
English writer, poet, lecturer and clergyman
To be discontented with the divine discontent,
and to be ashamed with the noble shame, is the
very germ and first upgrowth of all virtue.

Health and Education (1874)

La Rochefoucauld (1613–1680)
French writer
Il faut de plus grandes vertus pour soutenir la bonne

fortune que la mauvaise.
Greater virtues are needed to sustain good
fortune than bad.

Maximes (1678)

Marlowe, Christopher (1564–1593)
English poet and dramatist
Virtue is the fount whence honour springs.

Tamburlaine the Great (1590)

Milton, John (1608–1674)
English poet, libertarian and pamphleteer
Most men admire
Vertue, who follow not her lore.

Paradise Regained (1671)

Molière (1622–1673)
French dramatist, actor and director
Il faut, parmi le monde, une vertu traitable.
Virtue, in this world, should be accommodating.

Le Misanthrope (1666)

Montaigne, Michel de (1533–1592)
French essayist and moralist
*La vertu refuse la facilité pour compagne ... elle
demande un chemin âpre et épineux.*
Virtue shuns ease as a companion. It needs a
rough and thorny path.

Essais (1580)

Persius Flaccus, Aulus (AD 34–62)
Roman satirical poet
Virtutem videant intabescantque relicta.
Let them see virtue and pine away for having
lost it.

Satires

Pope, Alexander (1688–1744)
English poet, translator and editor
When men grow virtuous in their old age, they
only make a sacrifice to God of the devil's
leavings.

Miscellanies (1727)

Shakespeare, William (1564–1616)
English dramatist, poet and actor
Assume a virtue, if you have it not.
That monster custom, who all sense doth eat,
Of habits devil, is angel yet in this.

Hamlet, III.iv

Men's evil manners live in brass: their virtues
We write in water.

Henry VIII, IV.ii

Virtue is bold, and goodness never fearful.

Measure For Measure, III.i

Dost thou think, because thou art virtuous, there
shall be no more cakes and ale?

Twelfth Night, II.iii

Shaw, George Bernard (1856–1950)
Irish socialist, writer, dramatist and critic

What is virtue but the Trade Unionism of the married?

Man and Superman (1903)

Skinner, Cornelia Otis (1901–1979)
US actress
> Woman's virtue is man's greatest invention.
> *Attr.*

Steele, Sir Richard (1672–1729)
Irish-born English writer, dramatist and politician
> Will Honeycomb calls these over-offended Ladies the outrageously virtuous.
> *The Spectator*, 266, 1712

Taine, Hippolyte Adolphe (1828–1893)
French writer and philosopher
> *Le vice et la vertu sont des produits comme le vitriol et le sucre.*
> Vice and virtues are products like sulphuric acid and sugar.
> *History of English Literature*, 1863)

Walpole, Horace (1717–1797)
English writer and politician
> Tell me, ye divines, which is the most virtuous man, he who begets twenty bastards, or he who sacrifices an hundred thousand lives?
> *Letter to Sir Horace Mann, 1778*

> Virtue knows to a farthing what it has lost by not having been vice.
> In Kronenberger, *The Extraordinary Mr. Wilkes* (1974)

Walton, Izaak (1593–1683)
English writer
> Good company and good discourse are the very sinews of virtue.
> *The Compleat Angler* (1653)

Washington, George (1732–1799)
US general, statesman and President
> Few men have virtue to withstand the highest bidder.
> *Moral Maxims*

White, Patrick (1912–1990)
English-born Australian writer and dramatist
> Virtue is … frequently in the nature of an iceberg, the other parts of it submerged.
> *The Tree of Man* (1955)

Williams, William Carlos (1883–1963)
US poet, writer and paediatrician
> no woman is virtuous
> who does not give herself to her lover
> – forthwith.
> Paterson (1946–1958)

Wotton, Sir Henry (1568–1639)
English diplomat, traveller and poet
> Virtue is the roughest way,
> But proves at night a bed of down.
> 'Upon the Imprisonment of the Earl of Essex'

▶▶ GOOD AND EVIL; GOODNESS; MORALITY; PRINCIPLES; VICE

wales

Thomas, Dylan (1914–1953)
Welsh poet, writer and radio dramatist
Referring to Wales
> The land of my fathers. My fathers can have it.
>> In John Ackerman, *Dylan Thomas* (1991)

Thomas, Edward (1878–1917)
English poet
> Make me content
> With some sweetness
> From Wales
> Whose nightingales
> Have no wings.
>> 'Words'

Thomas, Gwyn (1913–1981)
Welsh writer, dramatist and teacher
> I wanted a play that would paint the full face of sensuality, rebellion and revivalism. In South Wales these three phenomena have played second fiddle only to the Rugby Union which is a distillation of all three.
>> *Jackie the Jumper* (1962)

> There are still parts of Wales where the only concession to gaiety is a striped shroud.
>> *Punch*, 1958

Waugh, Evelyn (1903–1966)
English writer and diarist
> 'The Welsh,' said the Doctor, 'are the only nation in the world that has produced no graphic or plastic art, no architecture, no drama. They just sing,' he said with disgust, 'sing and blow down wind instruments of plated silver.'
>> *Decline and Fall* (1928)

war

Acheson, Dean (1893–1971)
US Democrat politician
Of the Vietnam war
> It is worse than immoral, it's a mistake.
>> Quoted on Alistair Cooke's radio programme
>> *Letter from America*

Adams, Charles Francis (1807–1886)
> It would be superfluous in me to point out to your lordship that this is war.
>> Dispatch to Earl Russell,
>> September 1863

Angell, Norman (1872–1967)
English writer and pacifist

> The Great Illusion.
>> Title of book, 1910, rejecting war as economically advantageous to a nation

Anonymous
> Friendly fire isn't.

> The most dangerous thing in the combat zone is an officer with a map.

> The quartermaster has only two sizes, too large and too small.

American officer on the town of Ben Tre, Vietnam, during the Tet offensive, 1968
> To save the town, it became necessary to destroy it.

On placards held by Belgraders celebrating the downing of a Nato Stealth plane
> Sorry, we didn't know it was invisible.
>> *The Times*, 1999

Armistead, Lewis (1817–1863)
US general
Spoken at Gettysburg, 1863
> Give them the cold steel, boys!
>> Attr.

Arnold, Matthew (1822–1888)
English poet, critic, essayist and educationist
> But now in blood and battles was my youth,
> And full of blood and battles is my age;
> And I shall never end this life of blood.
>> 'Sohrab and Rustum' (1853)

Asquith, Herbert (1852–1928)
English Liberal statesman and Prime Minister
> We shall never sheath the sword which we have not lightly drawn until Belgium recovers in full measure all and more than she has sacrificed, until France is adequately secured against the menace of aggression, until the rights of the smaller nationalities of Europe are placed upon an unassailable foundation, and until the military domination of Prussia is wholly and finally destroyed.
>> Speech, 1914

Auden, W.H. (1907–1973)
English poet, essayist, critic, teacher and dramatist
> O what is that sound which so thrills the ear
> Down in the valley drumming, drumming?
> Only the scarlet soldiers, dear,
> The soldiers coming …

> O it's broken the lock and splintered the door,
> O it's the gate where they're turning, turning;
> Their boots are heavy on the floor
> And their eyes are burning.
>> *Collected Poems, 1933–1938*

Austen, Jane (1775–1817)
English writer
Of the Battle of Albuera in 1811

> How horrible it is to have so many people killed!
> – And what a blessing that one cares for none of
> them!

*Letter to Cassandra Austen,
1811*

Baldwin, Stanley (1867–1947)
English Conservative statesman and Prime Minister

> I think it is well also for the man in the street to
> realise that there is no power on earth that can
> protect him from being bombed. Whatever
> people may tell him, the bomber will always get
> through. The only defence is in offence, which
> means that you have to kill more women and
> children more quickly than the enemy if you
> want to save yourselves.

Speech, 1932

Baruch, Bernard (1870–1965)
US financier, government advisor and writer

> Let us not be deceived – we are today in the
> midst of a cold war.

Speech, 1947

Beers, Ethel Lynn (1827–1879)
US poet

> All quiet along the Potomac to-night,
> No sound save the rush of the river,
> While soft falls the dew on the face of the dead –
> The picket's off duty forever.

In Harper's Magazine, 1861, 'The Picket Guard'

Bell, Martin
English war correspondent and politician
Comment on NATO's accidental bombing of the Chinese
Embassy in Belgrade

> The greatest military alliance in the world is
> becoming 'the gang that cannot shoot straight'.

*Speech, House of Commons,
May 1999*

Belloc, Hilaire (1870–1953)
English writer of verse, essayist and critic; Liberal MP

> Whatever happens, we have got
> The Maxim Gun, and they have not.

Modern Traveller (1898)

Bennett, Alan (1934–)
English dramatist, actor and diarist

> I have never understood this liking for war. It
> panders to instincts already catered for within
> the scope of any respectable domestic
> establishment.

Forty Years On (1969)

Bethmann Hollweg, Theobald von (1856–1921)
German statesman

> Just for a word – 'neutrality', a word which in
> wartime has so often been disregarded, just for

> a scrap of paper – Great Britain is going to make
> war.

Letter, 1914

Bethune, Frank Pogson (1877–1942)

> Special Orders to No. 1 Section
> 1. The position will be held, and the section will
>   remain here until relieved.
> 2. The enemy cannot be allowed to interfere
>   with the programme.
> 3. If the section cannot remain here alive, it will
>   remain here dead, but in any case it will
>   remain here.
> 4. Should any man, through shell shock or other
>   cause, attempt to surrender, he will remain
>   here dead.
> 5. Should all guns be blown out, the section will
>   use Mills grenades, and other novelties.
> 6. Finally, the position, as stated, will be held.

*An order issued by Bethune to his machine gun
section in France, 13 March 1918*

The Bible (King James Version)

> All they that take the sword shall perish with the
> sword.

Matthew, 26:52

Blacker, Valentine (1778–1823)
English lieutenant-colonel

> Put your trust in God, my boys, and keep your
> powder dry.

Oliver's Advice (1856)

Blair, Tony (1953–)
British Labour Prime Minister
On the war in Kosovo

> For every act of barbarity, every slaughter of the
> innocent, Slobodan Milosevic must be made to
> pay a higher and higher price.

The Times, 1999

Borges, Jorge Luis (1899–1986)
Argentinian writer, poet and librarian
On the Falklands War of 1982

> The Falklands thing was a fight between two
> bald men over a comb.

Time, 1983

Bosquet, Pierre François Joseph (1810–1861)
French general
Remark on witnessing the Charge of the Light Brigade, 1854

> *C'est magnifique mais ce n'est pas la guerre.*
> It is magnificent, but it is not war.

Attr.

Bradley, Omar (1893–1981)
US general
On General MacArthur's proposal to carry the Korean war into
China

> The wrong war, at the wrong place, at the wrong
> time, and with the wrong enemy.

Senate inquiry, 1951

The way to win an atomic war is to make certain it never starts.

The Observer, 1952

Brecht, Bertolt (1898–1956)

Hier ist zu lang kein Krieg gewesen.
It's too long since there's been a war here.

Mother Courage and her Children (1941)

Einen vollkommenen Krieg, wo man sagen könnt: an dem ist nix mehr auszusetzen, wirds vielleicht nie geben.
There'll perhaps never be a perfect war where you could say that there was nothing wrong with it.

Mother Courage and her Children (1941)

Der Krieg findet immer einen Ausweg.
War always finds a solution.

Mother Courage and her Children (1941)

Bright, John (1811–1889)
English Liberal politician and social reformer
Comment on the American Civil War
My opinion is that the Northern States will manage somehow to muddle through.

Attr.

Referring to the Crimean War
The angel of death has been abroad throughout the land; you may almost hear the beating of his wings.

Speech, 1855

Brooke, Rupert (1887–1915)
English poet
Now, God be thanked Who has matched us with His hour,
And caught our youth, and wakened us from sleeping …

Leave the sick hearts that honour could not move,
And half-men, and their dirty songs and dreary,
And all the little emptiness of love …

Naught broken save this body, lost but breath;
Nothing to shake the laughing heart's long peace there
But only agony, and that has ending;
And the worst friend and enemy is but Death.

'Peace' (1914)

Butler, Samuel (1612–1680)
English poet
An unjust Peace is to be preferr'd before a just War.

Two Speeches made in the Rump Parliament

Carlyle, Thomas (1795–1881)
Scottish historian, biographer, critic, and essayist

Referring to the American Civil War
There they are cutting each other's throats, because one half of them prefer hiring their servants for life, and the other by the hour.

Attr.

Chamberlain, Neville (1869–1940)
English Conservative Prime Minister
In war, whichever side may call itself the victor, there are no winners, but all are losers.

Speech, Kettering, 1938

This morning the British Ambassador in Berlin handed the German Government a final note, stating that, unless the British Government heard from them by eleven o'clock that they were prepared at once to withdraw their troops from Poland, a state of war would exist between us. I have to tell you now that no such undertaking has been received, and that consequently this country is at war with Germany.

Radio broadcast, 3 September 1939

We have resolved to finish it. It is the evil things we shall be fighting against – brute force, bad faith, injustice, oppression and persecution and against them I am certain that the right will prevail.

Radio broadcast, 3 September 1939

On the annexation by Germany of the Sudetenland
How horrible, fantastic, incredible, it is that we should be digging trenches and trying on gas-masks here because of a quarrel in a far-away country between people of whom we know nothing.

Speech, 1938

Christie, Dame Agatha (1890–1976)
English crime writer and playwright
One is left with the horrible feeling now that war settles nothing; that to win a war is as disastrous as to lose one!

An Autobiography (1977)

Churchill, Sir Winston (1874–1965)
English Conservative Prime Minister
We shall not flag or fail. We shall go on to the end. We shall fight in France, we shall fight on the seas and oceans, we shall fight with growing confidence and growing strength in the air, we shall defend our island, whatever the cost may be, we shall fight on the beaches, we shall fight on the landing grounds, we shall fight in the fields and in the streets, we shall fight in the hills; we shall never surrender.

Speech, June 1940

Let us therefore brace ourselves to our duties, and so bear ourselves that, if the British Empire and its Commonwealth last for a thousand years, men will still say, 'This was their finest hour'.

> Speech, June 1940

The battle of Britain is about to begin.

> Speech, July 1940

No one can guarantee success in war, but only deserve it.

> *The Second World War* (1948–1954)

Referring to Dunkirk

Wars are not won by evacuations.

> *The Second World War* (1948–1954)

On the ceremonial form of the declaration of war against Japan, 8 December 1941

When you have to kill a man it costs nothing to be polite.

> *The Second World War* (1948–1954)

Before Alamein we never had a victory. After Alamein we never had a defeat.

> *The Second World War* (1948–1954)

On RAF pilots in the Battle of Britain

Never in the field of human conflict was so much owed by so many to so few.

> Speech, 1940

Cicero (106–43 BC)
Roman orator, statesman, essayist and letter writer

Silent enim leges inter arma.
Laws are silent in war.

> *Pro Milone*

Nervos belli, pecuniam infinitam.
The sinews of war, unlimited money.

> *Philippic*

Clausewitz, Karl von (1780–1831)
German general and military philosopher

Der Krieg ist nichts als eine Fortsetzung des politischen Verkehrs mit Einmischung anderer Mittel.
War is nothing but a continuation of politics by other means.

> *On War* (1834)

Cleese, John (1939–)
British comedian, actor and writer
Addressing a German guest in the dining room

Fawlty: Is there something wrong?
Guest: Will you stop talking about the war.
Fawlty: Me? You started it.
Guest: We did not start it.
Fawlty: Yes you did – you invaded Poland.

> *Fawlty Towers* (BBC TV, 1975)

Clemenceau, Georges (1841–1929)
French Prime Minister and journalist

La guerre! C'est une chose trop grave pour la confier à des militaires.
War is much too serious a thing to be left to the military.

> In Suarez, *Sixty Years of French History: Clemenceau*

Daly, Dan (1874–1937)
Remark during Allied resistance at Belleau Wood, 1918

Come on, you sons of bitches! Do you want to live for ever?

> Attr.

D'Avenant, Sir William (1606–1668)

For I must go where lazy Peace
Will hide her drowsy head;
And, for the sport of Kings, increase
The number of the Dead.

> 'The Soldier Going to the Field' (1673)

Dawe, (Donald) Bruce (1930–)
Australian poet

All day, day after day, they're bringing them home,
they're picking them up, those they can find,
and bringing them home,
they're bringing them in, piled on the hulls of
Grants, in trucks, in convoys,
they're zipping them up in green plastic bags,
they're tagging them now in Saigon, in the
mortuary coolness,
they're giving them names, they're rolling them
out of
the deep-freeze lockers – on the tarmac at Tan
Son Nhut
the noble jets are whining like hounds,
they are bringing them home …

telegrams tremble like leaves from a wintering
tree
and the spider grief swings in his bitter
geometry
– they're bringing them home, now, too late, too
early.

> 'Homecoming' (1971)

Dayan, Moshe (1915–81)
Israeli general and politician

War is the most exciting and dramatic thing in life. In fighting to the death you feel terribly relaxed when you manage to come through.

> *The Observer*, 1972

Dryden, John (1631–1700)
English poet, satirist, dramatist and critic

All delays are dangerous in war.

> *Tyrannic Love* (1669)

War is the trade of kings.

> *King Arthur* (1691)

Eden, Anthony (1897–1977)
English Conservative Prime Minister

We are not at war with Egypt. We are in armed conflict.

> Speech, 1956

Elizabeth, the Queen Mother (1900–)
Queen of the United Kingdom and mother of Elizabeth II

After Buckingham Palace was bombed during the Blitz in 1940
> I'm glad we've been bombed. It makes me feel I can look the East End in the face.
>> Attr.

Ellis, Havelock (1859–1939)
English sexologist and essayist
> In many a war it has been the vanquished, not the victor, who has carried off the finest spoils.
>> *The Soul of Spain* (1908)

Erasmus (c.1466–1536)
Dutch scholar and humanist
> *Dulce bellum inexpertis.*
> War is sweet to those who do not fight.
>> *Adagia* (1500)

Foch, Ferdinand (1851–1929)
French marshal
Dispatch during the Battle of the Marne, 1914
> *Mon centre cède, ma droite recule, situation excellente. J'attaque!*
> My centre is giving way, my right is retreating; situation excellent. I shall attack.
>> Attr.

Fontenelle, Bernard (1657–1757)
French librettist, philosopher and man of letters
> I detest war: it ruins conversation.
>> In Auden, *A Certain World* (1970)

Forgy, Howell (1908–1983)
US navy chaplain
Remark at Pearl Harbour, 1941
> Praise the Lord and pass the ammunition.
>> Attr.

Goldwater, Barry (1909–1998)
US presidential candidate and writer
> You've got to forget about this civilian. Whenever you drop bombs, you're going to hit civilians.
>> Speech, 1967

Gorky, Maxim (1868–1936)
Russian writer, dramatist and revolutionary
On Germany's declaration of war against Russia
> One thing is clear; we are entering the first act of a world-wide tragedy.
>> Attr., 1914

Grey, Edward, Viscount of Fallodon (1862–1933)
English statesman and writer
To a caller at the Foreign Office in August 1914
> The lamps are going out all over Europe; we shall not see them lit again in our lifetime.
>> In *Twenty-five Years*

Haig, Douglas (1861–1928)
Scottish military commander
> Every position must be held to the last man: there must be no retirement. With our backs to the wall, and believing in the justice of our

cause, each one of us must fight on to the end.
>> Order to British forces on the Western Front, 1918

Hanrahan, Brian (1949–)
English journalist
Reporting the British attack on Port Stanley airport, during the Falklands war
> I'm not allowed to say how many planes joined the raid but I counted them all out and I counted them all back.
>> BBC report, 1 May 1982

Harkin, Thomas (1939–)
> The Gulf War was like teenage sex. We got in too soon and we got out too soon.
>> *Independent on Sunday*, 1991

Hirohito, Emperor (1901–1989)
Emperor of Japan
> The war situation has developed not necessarily to Japan's advantage.
>> Announcing Japan's surrender, 15 August 1945

Hitler, Adolf (1889–1945)
German Nazi dictator, born in Austria
Said in 1939
> In starting and waging a war it is not right that matters, but victory.
>> In Shirer, *The Rise and Fall of the Third Reich* (1960)

Hobbes, Thomas (1588–1679)
Political philosopher
> Force, and fraud, are in war the two cardinal virtues.
>> *Leviathan* (1651)

Hoffman, Abbie (1936–1989)
US political activist
> I believe in compulsory cannibalism. If people were forced to eat what they killed, there would be no more wars.
>> Attr.

Hoover, Herbert Clark (1874–1964)
US Republican President
> Older men declare war. But it is youth that must fight and die.
>> Speech, 1944

Jackson, Andrew (1767–1845)
US President
Order given during the Battle of New Orleans, American War of Independence
> Elevate them guns a little lower.
>> Attr.

Jarrell, Randall (1914–1965)
US poet, critic and translator
> From my mother's sleep I fell into the State,
> And I hunched in its belly till my wet fur froze.
> Six miles from earth, loosed from its dream of life,
> I woke to black flak and the nightmare fighters.

When I died they washed me out of the turret with a hose.

'The Death of the Ball Turret Gunner' (1969)

Johnson, Hiram (1866–1945)

US Republican politician

The first casualty when war comes is truth.

Speech, US Senate, 1917

Kennedy, G.A. Studdert (1883–1929)

Waste of Blood, and waste of Tears,
Waste of youth's most precious years,
Waste of ways the saints have trod,
Waste of Glory, waste of God,
War!

'Waste' (1919)

Key, Ellen (1849–1926)

Swedish feminist, writer and lecturer

Everything, everything in war is barbaric … But the worst barbarity of war is that it forces men collectively to commit acts against which individually they would revolt with their whole being.

War, Peace, and the Future (1916)

Formerly, a nation that broke the peace did not trouble to try and prove to the world that it was done solely from higher motives … Now war has a bad conscience. Now every nation assures us that it is bleeding for a human cause, the fate of which hangs in the balance of its victory … No nation will admit that it was only to insure its own safety that it declared war. No nation dares to admit the guilt of blood before the world.

War, Peace, and the Future (1916)

Khrushchev, Nikita (1894–1971)

Russian statesman and Premier of the USSR

Of the Cuban missile crisis

Only lunatics or suicides, who themselves want to perish and to destroy the whole world before they die, could want an atomic war.

The Independent, 1992

Lao-Tzu (c.604–531 BC)

Chinese philosopher

To joy in conquest is to joy in the loss of human life.

Tao Te Ching

Law, Bonar (1858–1923)

Canadian-born British statesman and Conservative MP

I said in 1911 that if ever war arose between Great Britain and Germany it would not be due to inevitable causes, for I did not believe in inevitable war. I said it would be due to human folly.

Speech, House of Commons, 1914

Lawrence, D.H. (1885–1930)

English writer, poet and critic

We have all lost the war. All Europe.

The Ladybird (1923)

Lee, Robert E. (1807–1870)

Confederate general during US Civil War

It is well that war is so terrible – we would grow too fond of it.

Remark after the Battle of Fredericksburg, 1862

Lloyd George, David (1863–1945)

British Liberal statesman

Referring to the popular opinion that World War I would be the last major war

This war, like the next war, is a war to end war.

Attr.

Low, Sir David (1891–1963)

New Zealand-born British political cartoonist

I have never met anybody who wasn't against war. Even Hitler and Mussolini were, according to themselves.

In Jonathon Green (ed.), A Dictionary of Contemporary Quotations (1982)

Lowell, Amy (1874–1925)

US poet

And the softness of my body will be guarded from embrace
By each button, hook, and lace.
For the man who should loose me is dead,
Fighting with the Duke in Flanders,
In a pattern called a war.
Christ! What are patterns for?

Men, Women and Ghosts (1916), 'Patterns'

Macaulay, Lord (1800–1859)

English Liberal statesman, essayist and poet

Of John Hampden

He knew that the essence of war is violence, and that moderation in war is imbecility.

Collected Essays (1843)

MacDonald, Ramsay (1866–1937)

Scottish Labour politician, Prime Minister

We hear war called murder. It is not: it is suicide.

The Observer, 1930

McNamara, Robert (1916–)

US politician and Secretary of Defence

On the war in Vietnam

I don't object to it's being called 'McNamara's War'… It is a very important war and I am pleased to be identified with it and do whatever I can to win it.

New York Times, 1964

Speech on the twentieth anniversary of the American withdrawal from Vietnam

We were wrong. We were terribly wrong.

Daily Telegraph, 1995

Manning, Frederic (1882–1935)

Australian writer

War is waged by men; not by beasts, or by gods. It is a peculiar human activity. To call it a crime against mankind is to miss half its significance; it is also the punishment of a crime.

Her Privates We (1929)

Mao Tse-Tung (1893–1976)
Chinese Communist leader
We are advocates of the abolition of war, we do not want war; but war can only be abolished through war, and in order to get rid of the gun it is necessary to take up the gun.

Quotations from Chairman Mao Tse-Tung

Marlowe, Christopher (1564–1593)
English poet and dramatist
Accurs'd be he that first invented war!

Tamburlaine the Great (1590)

Mary, Queen Consort (1867–1953)
Queen Consort of George V
Remark to soldier who had exclaimed 'No more bloody wars for me'
No more bloody wars, no more bloody medals.

Attr.

McAuliffe, Anthony (1898–1975)
US general
Response when surrounded by Germans and ordered to surrender during World War II
Nuts!

New York Times, 1944

McClellan, George (1826–1885)
US general
Said during the American Civil War
All quiet along the Potomac.

Attr.

Meir, Golda (1898–1978)
Russian-born Israeli stateswoman and Prime Minister
A leader who doesn't hesitate before he sends his nation into battle is not fit to be a leader.

I. and M. Shenker, *As Good as Golda* (1943)

Mencken, H.L. (1880–1956)
US writer, critic, philologist and satirist
War will never cease until babies begin to come into the world with larger cerebrums and smaller adrenal glands.

Notebooks (1956)

Michaelis, John H. (1912–1985)
US army officer
Said to the 27th Infantry (Wolfhound) Regiment during the Korean War
You're not here to die for your country. You're here to make those—die for theirs.

Attr.

Milosevic, Slobodan (1941–)
Serbian political leader
Warning NATO of the consequences of invading Serbia

The earth itself will burn under the occupiers' feet.

The Times, April 1999

Milton, John (1608–1674)
English poet, libertarian and pamphleteer
For what can Warr, but endless warr still breed.

'On the Lord Generall Fairfax at the seige of Colchester' (1648)

Mirabeau, Comte de (1749–1791)
French statesman
La guerre est l'industrie nationale de la Prusse.
War is Prussia's national industry.

Attr.

Moltke, Helmuth von (1800–1891)
German field marshal
Der ewige Friede ist ein Traum, und nicht einmal ein schöner und der Krieg ein Glied in Gottes Weltordnung … Ohne den Krieg würde die Welt in Materialismus versumpfen.
Eternal peace is a dream, and not even a pleasant one; and war is an integral part of the way God has ordered the world … Without war, the world would sink in the mire of materialism.

Letter to Dr J.K. Bluntschli, 1880

Monash, Sir John (1865–1931)
Australian military commander
In France, 1917
War is not a business in which one can take any pride or pleasure, or even pretend to. Its horror, its ghastly inefficiency, its unspeakable cruelty and misery has always appalled me, but there is nothing to do but to set one's teeth and stick it out as long as one can.

In Geoffrey Serle, *John Monash* (1982)

Montague, C.E. (1867–1928)
English writer and critic
War hath no fury like a non-combatant.

Disenchantment (1922)

Montgomery, Viscount (1887–1976)
English field marshal
On American policy in Vietnam
The US has broken the second rule of war. That is, don't go fighting with your land army on the mainland of Asia. Rule One is don't march on Moscow. I developed these two rules myself.

Speech, 1962

Napoleon I (1769–1821)
French emperor
In war, three-quarters depends on matters of character and morale; the balance of manpower and equipment counts only for the remaining quarter.

Correspondance de Napoléon I (1854–1869)

Referring to the carnage at the Battle of Borodino, 1812

It's the most beautiful battlefield I've ever seen.

Attr.

Napoleon III (1808–1873)
French emperor
After the narrow and bloody French victory at Solferino, 1859
> I don't care for war, there's far too much luck in it for my liking.

In E. Crankshaw, The Fall of the House of Habsburg

Nelson, Lord (1758–1805)
English admiral
At the Battle of Copenhagen, 1801
> Leave off action? Now, damn me if I do! ... I have only one eye – I have a right to be blind sometimes ... I really do not see the signal! ... Damn the signal!

In Southey, The Life of Nelson (1860)

Orwell, George (1903–1950)
English writer and critic
> The quickest way of ending a war is to lose it.

Polemic (1946)

Owen, Wilfred (1893–1918)
English poet
> What passing-bells for these who die as cattle?
> Only the monstrous anger of the guns.
> Only the stuttering rifles' rapid rattle
> Can patter out their hasty orisons.

'Anthem for Doomed Youth' (1917)

> My subject is War, and the pity of War. The Poetry is in the pity.

Quoted in Poems (1963), Preface

Pankhurst, Sylvia (1882–1960)
English suffragette, pacifist and internationalist
> I could not give my name to aid the slaughter in this war, fought on both sides for grossly material ends, which did not justify the sacrifice of a single mother's son. Clearly I must continue to oppose it, and expose it, to all whom I could reach with voice or pen.

The Home Front

Patton, George S. (1885–1945)
US general
> The object of war is not to die for your country, but to make the other bastard die for his.

Attr.

Plomer, William (1903–1973)
South African-born British writer and editor
> Out of that bungled, unwise war
> An alp of unforgiveness grew.

'The Boer War' (1932)

Prescott, William (1726–1795)
Command given at the Battle of Bunker Hill, 1775
> Don't fire until you see the whites of their eyes.

Attr

Pyrrhus (319–272 BC)
King of Epirus and army commander
After a hard-won battle
> If we are victorious against the Romans in one more battle we shall be utterly ruined.

In Plutarch, Lives

Rabelais, François (c.1494–c.1553)
French monk, physician, satirist and humanist
> *Guerre faicte sans bonne provision d'argent n'a qu'un souspirail de vigueur. Les nerfs des batailles sont les pécunes.*
> The strength of a war waged without a good supply of money is as fleeting as a breath. Money is the sinews of battle.

Gargantua (1534)

Rae, John (1931–)
English educationist and writer
> War is, after all, the universal perversion. We are all tainted: if we cannot experience our perversion at first hand we spend our time reading war stories, the pornography of war; or seeing war films, the blue films of war; or titillating our senses with the imagination of great deeds, the masturbation of war.

The Custard Boys (1960)

Reed, Henry (1914–1986)
English poet, radio dramatist and translator
> In a civil war, the general must know – and I'm afraid it's a thing rather of instinct than of practice – he must know exactly when to move over to the other side.

Not a Drum was Heard: The War Memoirs of General Gland (1959)

Repington, Lieut-Col. Charles A'Court (1858–1925)
> I saw Major Johnstone, who is here to lay the bases of an American History. We discussed the right name of the war. I said that we called it now The War, but that this could not last. The Napoleonic War was The Great War. To call it The German War was too much flattery for the Boche. I suggested The World War as a shade better title, and finally we mutually agreed to call it The First World War in order to prevent the millennium folk from forgetting that the history of the world was the history of war.

Diary entry for 10 September 1918, published in The First World War 1914–18 (1920)

Roosevelt, Franklin Delano (1882–1945)
US Democrat President
> More than an end to war, we want an end to the beginnings of all wars.

Speech, 1945

Rubens, Paul Alfred (1875–1917)
English dramatist and songwriter
> We don't want to lose you but we think you

ought to go.

'Your King and Country Want You', song, 1914

Russell, William Howard (1820–1907)
English journalist
Reporting the charge of the Russian cavalry on Sir Campbell's
Highland infantry during the Crimean War

The Russians on their left drew breath for a moment, and then in one grand line dashed at the Highlanders. The ground flies beneath their horses' feet; gathering speed at every stride, they dash on towards that thin red streak topped with a line of steel.

The Times, 1854

Sallust (86–c.34 BC)
Roman historian and statesman

Omne bellum sumi facile, ceterum aegaerrime desinere,
non in ejusdem potestate initium ejus et finem esse.
Every war is easy to begin but difficult to stop; its beginning and end are not in the control of the same person.

Jugurtha

Sandburg, Carl (1878–1967)
US poet, writer and song collector

Pile the bodies high at Austerlitz and Waterloo.
Shovel them under and let me work –
I am the grass; I cover all.

Cornhuskers (1918), 'Grass'

Sometime they'll give a war and nobody will come.

The People, Yes (1936)

Sassoon, Siegfried (1886–1967)
English poet and writer

Safe with his wound, a citizen of life,
He hobbled blithely through the garden gate,
And thought: 'Thank God they had to amputate!'.

'The One-Legged Man' (1916)

I'd like to see a Tank come down the stalls,
Lurching to rag-time tunes, or 'Home, sweet Home,' –
And there'd be no more jokes in Music-halls
To mock the riddled corpses round Bapaume.

'Blighters' (1917)

If I were fierce and bald and short of breath,
I'd live with scarlet Majors at the Base,
And speed glum heroes up the line to death …

And when the war is done and youth stone dead
I'd toddle safely home and die – in bed.

'Base Details' (1917)

From the statement sent to his commanding officer, July 1917

I am making this statement as an act of wilful defiance of military authority, because I believe that the War is being deliberately prolonged by

those who have the power to end it … I have seen and endured the sufferings of the troops, and I can no longer be a party to prolong these sufferings for ends which I believe to be evil and unjust.

Memoirs of an Infantry Officer (1930)

Schwarzkopf, Norman (1934–)
US general
Describing Saddam Hussein of Iraq, 1991

He is neither a strategist nor is he schooled in the operational arts, nor is he a tactician, nor is he a general. Other than that he's a great military man.

Attr.

Service, Robert W. (1874–1958)
Canadian poet

When we, the Workers, all demand: 'What are we fighting for?' …
Then, then we'll end that stupid crime, that devil's madness – War.

'Michael' (1921)

Shakespeare, William (1564–1616)
English dramatist, poet and actor

To th' wars, my boy, to th' wars!
He wears his honour in a box unseen
That hugs his kicky-wicky here at home,
Spending his manly marrow in her arms,
Which should sustain the bound and high curvet
Of Mars's fiery steed.

All's Well That Ends Well, II.iii

Once more unto the breach, dear friends, once more;
Or close the wall up with our English dead.
In peace there's nothing so becomes a man
As modest stillness and humility;
But when the blast of war blows in our ears,
Then imitate the action of the tiger:
Stiffen the sinews, summon up the blood,
Disguise fair nature with hard-favour'd rage;
Then lend the eye a terrible aspect.

Henry V, III.i

We few, we happy few, we band of brothers;
For he to-day that sheds his blood with me
Shall be my brother; be he ne'er so vile,
This day shall gentle his condition;
And gentlemen in England now a-bed
Shall think themselves accurs'd they were not here,
And hold their manhoods cheap whiles any speaks
That fought with us upon Saint Crispin's day.

Henry V, IV.iii

Sherman, William Tecumseh (1820–1891)
US general

There is many a boy here today who looks on

war as all glory, but, boys, it is all hell.

Speech, 1880

Spock, Dr Benjamin (1903–1998)
US pediatrician and psychiatrist
> To win in Vietnam, we will have to exterminate a nation.

Dr Spock on Vietnam (1968)

Strachey, Lytton (1880–1932)
English biographer and critic
Reply when asked by a Tribunal what he, as a conscientious objector, would do if he saw a German soldier trying to rape his sister
> I should try and come between them.

In Holroyd, *Lytton Strachey: A Critical Biography* (1968)

Struther, Jan (1901–1953)
English writer
> To abolish shooting before you had abolished war was rather like flecking a speck of dust off the top of a midden.

Mrs Miniver, quoted in *The Times*, 1993

Swift, Jonathan (1667–1745)
Irish satirist, poet, essayist and cleric
> Hobbes clearly proves, that every creature
> Lives in a state of war by nature.

'On Poetry' (1733)

Taber, Robert (20th century)
US writer
> The guerrilla fights the war of the flea, and his military enemy suffers the dog's disadvantages: too much to defend; too small, ubiquitous, and agile an enemy to come to grips with.

The War of the Flea

Talleyrand, Charles-Maurice de (1754–1838)
French statesman, memoirist and prelate
> War is much too serious to be left to the generals.

Attr.

Teller, Edward (1908–)
Hungarian-born US physicist
> Could we have avoided the tragedy of Hiroshima? Could we have started the atomic age with clean hands? No one knows. No one can find out.

Urey, Harold (1893–1981)
US chemist
> The next war will be fought with atom bombs and the one after that with spears.

The Observer, 1946

Virgil (70–19 BC)
Roman poet
> I see wars, dreadful wars, and the Tiber foaming with much blood.

Aeneid

Von Schlieffen, Alfred, Graf (1833–1913)
Prussian soldier
Referring to the Schlieffen plan, a German military strategy to enter France by first going through Belgium
> When you march into France, let the last man on the right brush the Channel with his sleeve.

In Barbara Tuchman, *The Guns of August 1914* (1964)

Vulliamy, Ed
British journalist and author
A pacifist until the war in Bosnia forced him to change his convictions
> Ironically, the horrors of war have taught me that there are things that are worse than war, and against them determined and careful war should be waged, in the name of the innocent and the weak.

The Weekend Guardian, 1992

Waugh, Evelyn (1903–1966)
English writer and diarist
> When the war broke out she took down the signed photograph of the Kaiser and, with some solemnity, hung it in the menservants' lavatory; it was her one combative action.

Vile Bodies (1930)

Giving his opinions of warfare after the battle of Crete, 1941
> Like German opera, too long and too loud.

Attr.

Wellington, Duke of (1769–1852)
Irish-born British military commander and statesman
> All the business of war, and indeed all the business of life, is to endeavour to find out what you don't know by what you do; that's what I called 'guessing what was at the other side of the hill'.

The Croker Papers (1885)

> I always say that, next to a battle lost, the greatest misery is a battle gained.

In Rogers, *Recollections (1859)*

Remark at Waterloo
> Hard pounding this, gentlemen; let's see who will pound longest.

In Sir Walter Scott, *Paul's Letters* (1816)

Refusing permission to shoot at Napoleon during the Battle of Waterloo
> It is not the business of generals to shoot one another.

Attr.

Wells, H.G. (1866–1946)
English writer
> The War That Will End War.

Title of book, 1914

White, Patrick (1912–1990)
English-born Australian writer and dramatist

But bombs are unbelievable until they actually fall.

> *Riders in the Chariot* (1961)

Wilde, Oscar (1854–1900)
Irish poet, dramatist, writer, critic and wit
> As long as war is regarded as wicked it will always have its fascination. When it is looked upon as vulgar, it will cease to be popular.
> *The Critic as Artist* (1890)

Wilson, Woodrow (1856–1924)
US Democrat President
> Once lead this people into war and they'll forget there ever was such a thing as tolerance.
> In Dos Passos, *Mr Wilson's War* (1917)

Young, Edward (1683–1765)
English poet, dramatist, satirist and clergyman
> One to destroy, is murder by the law;
> And gibbets keep the lifted hand in awe;
> To murder thousands, takes a specious name,
> War's glorious art, and gives immortal fame.
> *Night-Thoughts on Life, Death and Immortality*

▶▶ ARMY; DEFEAT; NAVY; NUCLEAR WEAPONS; PATRIOTISM; SACRIFICE; VICTORY; WAR AND PEACE

war and peace

Blake, William (1757–1827)
English poet, engraver, painter and mystic
> Sweet Prince! the arts of peace are great,
> And no less glorious than those of war.
> *Poetical Sketches* (1783)

Churchill, Sir Winston (1874–1965)
English Conservative Prime Minister
> Peace with Germany and Japan on our terms will not bring much rest ... As I observed last time, when the war of the giants is over the wars of the pygmies will begin.
> *The Second World War* (1948–1954)

> Those who can win a war well can rarely make a good peace and those who could make a good peace would never have won the war.
> *My Early Life* (1930)

> In war, resolution; in defeat, defiance; in victory, magnanimity; in peace, goodwill.
> *The Gathering Storm*

Clemenceau, Georges (1841–1929)
French Prime Minister and journalist
To General Mordacq, 11 November 1918
> We have won the war: now we have to win the peace, and it may be more difficult.
> In D.R. Watson, *Georges Clemenceau: a Political Biography* (1974)

Il est plus facile de faire la guerre que la paix.
It is easier to make war than to make peace.
> Speech, 1919

Cowper, William (1731–1800)
English poet, hymn and letter writer
> War lays a burden on the reeling state,
> And peace does nothing to relieve the weight.
> 'Expostulation' (1782)

Franklin, Benjamin (1706–1790)
US statesman, scientist, political critic and printer
> There never was a good war, or a bad peace.
> Letter to Josiah Quincy, 1783

Hardy, Thomas (1840–1928)
English writer and poet
> My argument is that War makes rattling good history; but Peace is poor reading.
> *The Dynasts* 1903)

Herbert, George (1593–1633)
English poet and priest
> He that makes a good war, makes a good peace.
> *Jacula Prudentum; or Outlandish Proverbs, Sentences &c.* (1640)

Kellogg, Frank B. (1856–1937)
US statesman
> The high contracting parties solemnly declare in the names of their respective peoples that they condemn recourse to war for the solution of international controversies, and renounce it as an instrument of national policy in their relations with one another. The high contracting parties agree that the settlement or solution of all disputes or conflicts of whatever nature or of whatever origin they may be, which may rise among them, shall never be sought except by pacific means.
> Peace Pact, 1928; possibly based on original text by Aristide Briand

Kettle, Thomas (1880–1916)
Irish writer and academic
> If I live, I mean to spend the rest of my life working for perpetual peace. I have seen war and faced artillery and know what an outrage it is against simple men.
> *Poems and Parodies*

Lawrence, D.H. (1885–1930)
English writer, poet and critic
> Loud peace propaganda makes war seem imminent.
> *Pansies* (1929)

Shakespeare, William (1564–1616)
English dramatist, poet and actor
> Let me have war, say I; it exceeds peace as far as day does night; it's spritely, waking, audible, and full of vent. Peace is a very apoplexy,

lethargy; mull'd, deaf, sleepy, insensible; a
getter of more bastard children than war's a
destroyer of men.

Coriolanus, IV.v

Stevenson, Adlai (1900–1965)
US lawyer, statesman and United Nations ambassador
> Making peace is harder than making war.

*Address to Chicago Council on Foreign Relations,
1946*

Tucholsky, Kurt (1890–1935)
German satirist and writer
> *Aber der Frieden ist undankbar, und weiss nie, dass er
> seinen Bestand nur dem Krieg dankt.*
> But peace is ungrateful and never knows it only
> owes its continued existence to war.

To Arno Holz (1913)

Vegetius Renatus, Flavius (fl. c.AD 375)
Latin military writer
> *Qui desiderat pacem, praeparet bellum.*
> Let him who desires peace be prepared for war.

Epitoma Rei Militaris

Wilder, Thornton (1897–1975)
US author and playwright
> When you're at war you think about a better life;
> when you're at peace you think about a more
> comfortable one.

The Skin of Our Teeth (1942)

▶▶ ARMY; DEFEAT; NAVY; NUCLEAR WEAPONS;
PATRIOTISM; VICTORY; WAR

water

The Bible (King James Version)
> I will give unto him that is athirst of the fountain
> of the water of life freely.

Revelation, 21:6

Bashó, Matsuo (1644–1694)
Japanese haiku poet
> Into the ancient pond
> A frog dives:
> A sound of the water.

'Haru-no-Hi' ('Spring Days', 1686)

Brooke, Rupert (1887–1915)
English poet
> Fish say, they have their stream and pond;
> But is there anything beyond? –
> One may not doubt that, somehow, good
> Shall come of water and of mud;
> And, sure, the reverent eye must see
> A purpose in liquidity.

'Heaven' (1913)

> The benison of hot water.

'The Great Lover' (1914)

Chesterton, G.K. (1874–1936)
English writer, poet and critic
> And Noah he often said to his wife when he sat
> down to dine,
> 'I don't care where the water goes if it doesn't
> get into the wine.' ...
>
> And water is on the Bishop's board and the
> Higher Thinker's shrine,
> But I don't care where the water goes if it
> doesn't get into the wine.

The Flying Inn (1914)

Coleridge, Samuel Taylor (1772–1834)
English poet, philosopher and critic
> Water, water, every where,
> And all the boards did shrink;
> Water, water, every where
> Nor any drop to drink.

'The Rime of the Ancient Mariner' (1798)

Fields, W.C. (1880–1946)
US film actor
His reason for not drinking water
> Fish fuck in it.

Attr.

Herbert, Sir A.P. (1890–1971)
English humorist, writer, dramatist and politician
> For any ceremonial purposes the otherwise
> excellent liquid, water, is unsuitable in colour
> and other respects.

Uncommon Law (1935)

Lawrence, D.H. (1885–1930)
English writer, poet and critic
> Water is H2O, hydrogen two parts, oxygen one,
> but there is also a third thing, that makes it
> water
> and nobody knows what it is.

Pansies (1929)

Robbins, Tom (1936–)
US writer
> Human beings were invented by water as a
> device for transporting itself from one place to
> another.

Another Roadside Attraction (1971)

Shakespeare, William (1564–1616)
English dramatist, poet and actor
> What, man! more water glideth by the mill
> Than wots the miller of.

Titus Andronicus, II.i

Slessor, Kenneth (1901–1971)
Australian poet and journalist
> The character and the life of Sydney are shaped
> continually and imperceptibly by the fingers of
> the Harbour, groping across the piers and
> jetties, clutching deeply into the hills, the water
> dyed a whole paint-box's armoury of colour with

every breath of air, every shift of light or shade, according to the tide, the clock, the weather and the state of the moon. The water is like silk, like pewter, like blood, like a leopard's skin, and occasionally merely like water.

Bread and Wine (1970)

Smith, Sydney (1771–1845)
English clergyman, essayist, journalist and wit
I am better in health … and drinking nothing but London water, with a million insects in every drop. He who drinks a tumbler of London water has literally in his stomach more animated beings than there are men, women, and children on the face of the globe.

Letter to Countess Grey, 1834

the weather

Austen, Jane (1775–1817)
English writer
What dreadful hot weather we have! It keeps me in a continual state of inelegance.

Letter, 1796

Campbell, David (1915–1979)
Australian poet, rugby player and wartime pilot
Sweet rain, bless our windy farm,
Stepping round in skirts of storm:
Amongst the broken clods the hare
Folds his ears like hands in prayer.

'Prayer for Rain' (c.1950)

Chekhov, Anton (1860–1904)
Russian writer, dramatist and doctor
He who doesn't notice whether it is winter or summer is happy. I think that if I were in Moscow, I wouldn't notice what the weather was like.

The Three Sisters (1901)

Congreve, William (1670–1729)
English dramatist
Is there in the world a climate more uncertain than our own? And, which is a natural consequence, is there any where a people more unsteady, more apt to discontent, more saturnine, dark and melancholic than our selves? Are we not of all people the most unfit to be alone, and most unsafe to be trusted with our selves?

Amendments of Mr Collier's False and Imperfect Citations (1698)

Ellis, George (1753–1815)
West Indian-born British satirist and poet
Snowy, Flowy, Blowy,
Showery, Flowery, Bowery,

Hoppy, Croppy, Droppy,
Breezy, Sneezy, Freezy.

'The Twelve Months'

Fish, Michael (1944–)
English meteorologist and weather presenter
Said during the weather forecast just prior to the storm of October 1987 which proved him disastrously wrong
A woman rang to say she'd heard there was a hurricane on the way – well don't worry, there isn't.

Sunday Telegraph, 1989

Gogarty, Oliver St John (1878–1957)
Irish poet, dramatist, writer, politician and surgeon
In my best social accent I addressed him. I said, 'It is most extraordinary weather for this time of year!' He replied, 'Ah, it isn't this time of year at all.'

It Isn't This Time of Year at All (1954)

Hardy, Thomas (1840–1928)
English writer and poet
This is the weather the cuckoo likes,
And so do I;
When showers betumble the chestnut spikes,
And nestlings fly:
And the little brown nightingale bills his best,
And they sit outside at 'The Travellers' Rest'.

'Weathers' (1922)

Johnson, Samuel (1709–1784)
English lexicographer, poet, critic, conversationalist and essayist
When two Englishmen meet, their first talk is of the weather.

The Idler (1758–1760)

Keats, John (1795–1821)
English poet
Of Devon
It is impossible to live in a country which is continually under hatches … Rain! Rain! Rain!

Letter to J.H. Reynolds, 1818

Lodge, David (1935–)
English writer, satirist and literary critic
The British, he thought, must be gluttons for satire: even the weather forecast seemed to be some kind of spoof, predicting every possible combination of weather for the next twenty-four hours without actually committing itself to anything specific.

Changing Places (1975)

Macaulay, Dame Rose (1881–1958)
English writer
Owing to the weather, English social life must always have largely occurred either indoors, or, when out of doors, in active motion.

'Life Among The English' (1942)

Pound, Ezra (1885–1972)
US poet
> Winter is icummen in,
> Lhude sing Goddamn,
> Raineth drop and staineth slop,
> And how the wind doth ramm!
> Sing: Goddamn.
>> 'Ancient Music' (1916)

Ruskin, John (1819–1900)
English art critic, philosopher and reformer
> There is really no such thing as bad weather,
> only different kinds of good weather.
>> Attr.

Sandburg, Carl (1878–1967)
US poet, writer and song collector
> The fog comes
> on little cat feet.
> It sits looking over harbor and city
> on silent haunches
> and then moves on.
>> Chicago Poems (1916), 'Fog'

Smith, Logan Pearsall (1865–1946)
US-born British epigrammatist, critic and writer
> Thank heavens, the sun has gone in, and I don't
> have to go out and enjoy it.
>> All Trivia (1933)

Smith, Sydney (1771–1845)
English clergyman, essayist, journalist and wit
Discussing the recent hot weather
> Heat, Ma'am! It was so dreadful here, that I
> found there was nothing left for it but to take
> off my flesh and sit in my bones.
>> In Holland, A Memoir of the Reverend Sydney Smith (1855)

Southey, Robert (1774–1843)
English poet, essayist, historian and letterwriter
> She has made me half in love with a cold
> climate.
>> Letter to his brother Thomas, 1797

Swift, Jonathan (1667–1745)
Irish satirist, poet, essayist and cleric
> Plaguy twelvepenny weather.
>> Journal to Stella, 1710

Twain, Mark (1835–1910)
US humorist, writer, journalist and lecturer
> Everybody talks about the weather but nobody
> does anything about it.
>> Attr.

▶▶ SEASONS

weddings

Behan, Brendan (1923–1964)
Irish dramatist, writer and Republican
> I think weddings is sadder than funerals,
> because they remind you of your own wedding.
> You can't be reminded of your own funeral
> because it hasn't happened. But weddings
> always make me cry.
>> Richard's Cork Leg (1972)

Lamb, Charles (1775–1834)
English essayist, critic and letter writer
> I was at Hazlitt's marriage, and had like to have
> been turned out several times during the
> ceremony. Anything awful makes me laugh. I
> misbehaved once at a funeral.
>> Letter to Southey, 1815

Lampton, William James (1859–1917)
> Same old slippers,
> Same old rice,
> Same old glimpse of
> Paradise.
>> 'June Weddings'

Lerner, Alan Jay (1918–1986)
US lyricist and screenwriter
> I'm getting married in the morning!
> Ding dong! the bells are gonna chime.
> Pull out the stopper!
> Let's have a whopper!
> But get me to the church on time!
>> My Fair Lady (1956)

Muir, Frank (1920–1998)
English writer, humorist and broadcaster
> It has been said that a bride's attitude towards
> her betrothed can be summed up in three
> words: Aisle. Altar. Hymn.
>> Upon My Word!, 'A Jug of Wine', with Dennis
>> Norden

▶▶ MARRIAGE

widows

Dickens, Charles (1812–1870)
English writer
> Take example by your father, my boy, and be
> wery careful o' widders all your life.
>> The Pickwick Papers (1837)

Gay, John (1685–1732)
English poet, dramatist and librettist
> The comfortable estate of widowhood, is the
> only hope that keeps up a wife's spirits.
>> The Beggar's Opera (1728), I

> I think, you must do like other widows – buy
> your self weeds, and be cheerful.
>> The Beggar's Opera (1728)

Guitry, Sacha (1885–1957)
Russian-born French actor, dramatist and film director

Responding to his fifth wife's jealousy of his previous wives
> The others were only my wives. But you, my dear, will be my widow.

Attr.

Hoffnung, Gerard (1925–1959)
British artist, illustrator and musician
> There is a French widow in every bedroom (affording delightful prospects).

Speech, Oxford Union debating society, 1958

Ibárruri, Dolores ('La Pasionaria') (1895–1989)
Basque Communist leader
> It is better to be the widow of a hero than the wife of a coward.

Speech, Valencia, 1936

Wycherley, William (c.1640–1716)
English dramatist and poet
> Well, a widow, I see, is a kind of sinecure.

The Plain Dealer (1677)

wind

The Bible (King James Version)
> They have sown the wind, and they shall reap the whirlwind.

Hosea, 8:7

> The wind bloweth where it listeth.

John, 3:8

Borrow, George (1803–1881)
English writer and linguist
> There's the wind on the heath, brother; if I could only feel that, I would gladly live for ever.

Lavengro (1851)

Burns, Robert (1759–1796)
Scottish poet and song writer
> Of a' the airts the wind can blaw
> I dearly like the west.

'Of a' the Airts' (1788)

Dickinson, Emily (1830–1886)
US poet
> There came a Wind like a Bugle –
> It quivered through the Grass.

'There came a Wind' (c.1883)

Edwards, Elwyn Hartley (1927–)
Translated from the writings of the Emir Abd-el-Kadr
> When God wanted to create the horse, he said to the South Wind, 'I want to make a creature of you. Condense.'

Horses: Their Role in the History of Man (1987), 'The First Progenitor'

Lawrence, D.H. (1885–1930)
English writer, poet and critic

> Not I, not I, but the wind that blows through me!

Look! We Have Come Through! (1917), 'Song of a man who has come through'

Lowell, Robert (1917–1977)
US poet and writer
> Here too in Maine things bend to the wind forever.
> After two years away, one must get used to the painted soft wood staying bright and clean,
> to the air blasting an all-white wall whiter,
> as it blows through curtain and screen
> touched with salt and evergreen.

For the Union Dead (1964), 'Soft Wood'

Masefield, John (1878–1967)
English poet, writer and critic
> It's a warm wind, the west wind, full of birds' cries;
> I never hear the west wind but tears are in my eyes,
> For it comes from the west lands, the old brown hills,
> And April's in the west wind, and daffodils.

'The West Wind' (1902)

Rossetti, Christina (1830–1894)
English poet
> Who has seen the wind?
> Neither you nor I:
> But when the trees bow down their heads,
> The wind is passing by.

'Who Has Seen the Wind?' (1872)

Selden, John (1584–1654)
English historian, jurist and politician
> Take a straw and throw it up into the air, you shall see by that which way the wind is.

Table Talk (1689), 'Libels'

Sterne, Laurence (1713–1768)
Irish-born English writer and clergyman
> God tempers the wind … to the shorn lamb.

A Sentimental Journey (1768), 'Maria'

Tusser, Thomas (c.1524–1580)
English writer, poet and musician
> Yet true it is, as cow chaws cud,
> And trees at spring do yield forth bud,
> Except wind stands as never it stood,
> It is an ill wind turns none to good.

Five Hundred Points of Good Husbandry (1557)

▶▶ SEASONS; WEATHER

wisdom

Achebe, Chinua (1930–)
Nigerian writer, poet and critic
> When old people speak it is not because of the

sweetness of words in our mouths; it is because we see something which you do not see.

No Longer At Ease (1961)

Aeschylus (525–456 BC)
Greek dramatist and poet
It is a fine thing even for an old man to learn wisdom.

Fragments

Aristophanes (c.445–385 BC)
Greek playwright
One may learn wisdom even from one's enemies.

Birds

Bacon, Francis (1561–1626)
English philosopher, essayist, politician and courtier
A wise man will make more opportunities than he finds.

'Of Ceremonies and Respects' (1625)

The Bible (King James Version)
Wisdom is the principal thing; therefore get wisdom: and with all thy getting get understanding.

Proverbs, 4:7

The fear of the Lord is the beginning of wisdom.

Psalms, 111:10

Blake, William (1757–1827)
English poet, engraver, painter and mystic
I care not whether a Man is Good or Evil; all that I care
Is whether he is a Wise Man or a Fool. Go! put off Holiness
And put on Intellect.

Jerusalem (1820)

Caxton, William (c.1421–1491)
It is notoriously known through the universal world that there be nine worthy and the best that ever were. That is to wit three paynims, three Jews, and three Christian men. As for the paynims they were ... the first Hector of Troy ... the second Alexander the Great; and the third Julius Caesar ... As for the three Jews ... the first was Duke Joshua ... the second David, King of Jerusalem; and the third Judas Maccabaeus.... And sith the said Incarnation... was first the noble Arthur.... The second was Charlemagne or Charles the Great ... and the third and last was Godfrey of Bouillon.

In Malory, *Le Morte d'Arthur* (1485)

Chaucer, Geoffrey (c.1340–1400)
English poet, public servant and courtier
Ful wys is he that kan hymselven knowe!

The Canterbury Tales (1387)

Chesterfield, Lord (1694–1773)
English politician and letter writer

Be wiser than other people if you can; but do not tell them so.

Letter to his son, 1745

Confucius (c.550–c.478 BC)
Chinese philosopher and teacher of ethics
Gravity is only the bark of wisdom's tree, but it preserves it.

Analects

The heart of the wise, like a mirror, should reflect all objects without being sullied by any.

Analects

Cowper, William (1731–1800)
English poet, hymn and letter writer
Knowledge dwells
In heads replete with thoughts of other men;
Wisdom in minds attentive to their own.

The Task (1785)

Knowledge is proud that he has
learn'd so much;
Wisdom is humble that he knows no more.

The Task (1785)

Emerson, Ralph Waldo (1803–1882)
US poet, essayist, transcendentalist and teacher
The wise through excess of wisdom is made a fool.

Essays, Second Series (1844)

Now that is the wisdom of a man, in every instance of his labor, to hitch his wagon to a star, and see his chore done by the gods themselves.

Society and Solitude (1870)

Fitzgerald, Edward (1809–1883)
English poet, translator and letter writer
With them the Seed of Wisdom did I sow,
And with mine own hand wrought to make it grow;
And this was all the Harvest that I reap'd –
'I came like Water, and like Wind I go'.

The Rubáiyát of Omar Khayyám (1859)

Fuller, Thomas (1608–1661)
English churchman and antiquary
Many have been the wise speeches of fools, though not so many as the foolish speeches of wise men.

The Holy State and the Profane State (1642)

Horace (65–8 BC)
Roman lyric poet and satirist
Dimidium facti qui coepit habet: sapere aude.
To have made a beginning is half of the business; dare to be wise.

Epistles

Hutcheson, Francis (1694–1746)
Scottish philosopher
Wisdom denotes the pursuing of the best ends

by the best means.

An Inquiry into the Original of our Ideas of Beauty and Virtue (1725)

Lévi-Strauss, Claude (1908–)
French anthropologist

Le savant n'est pas l'homme qui fournit les vraies réponses; c'est celui qui pose les vraies questions.
The wise man is not the man who gives the right answers; he is the one who asks the right questions.

The Raw and the Cooked

Marquis, Don (1878–1937)
US columnist, satirist and poet

How often when they find a sage
As great as Socrates or Plato
They hand him hemlock for his wage
Or take him like a sweet potato.

Taking the Longer View

Meredith, George (1828–1909)
English writer, poet and critic

In action Wisdom goes by majorities.

The Ordeal of Richard Feverel (1859)

Plato (c.429–347 BC)
Greek philosopher

That man is wisest who, like Socrates, has realized that in truth his wisdom is worth nothing.

The Apology of Socrates

Proverb

It is easy to be wise after the event.

Quarles, Francis (1592–1644)
English poet, writer and royalist

Be wisely worldly, not worldly wise.

Emblems (1635)

Roosevelt, Theodore (1858–1919)
US Republican President

Nine-tenths of wisdom is being wise in time.

Speech, 1917

Smollett, Tobias (1721–1771)
Scottish writer, satirist, historian, traveller and physician

Some folks are wise, and some are otherwise.

The Adventures of Roderick Random (1748)

Swift, Jonathan (1667–1745)
Irish satirist, poet, essayist and cleric

No wise man ever wished to be younger.

Thoughts on Various Subjects (1711)

Szasz, Thomas (1920–)
Hungarian-born US psychiatrist and writer

The stupid neither forgive nor forget; the naive forgive and forget; the wise forgive but do not forget.

The Second Sin (1973)

Thoreau, Henry David (1817–1862)
US essayist, social critic and writer

It is a characteristic of wisdom not to do desperate things.

Walden (1854)

Trollope, Anthony (1815–1882)
English writer, traveller and post office official

It may almost be a question whether such wisdom as many of us have in our mature years has not come from the dying out of the power of temptation, rather than as the results of thought and resolution.

The Small House at Allington (1864)

Wordsworth, William (1770–1850)
English poet

Wisdom doth live with children round her knees.

Sonnets Dedicated to Liberty and Order (1807)

Wisdom is oftimes nearer when we stoop
Than when we soar.

The Excursion (1814)

Young, Edward (1683–1765)
English poet, dramatist, satirist and clergyman

Be wise today, ' tis madness to defer.

Night-Thoughts on Life, Death and Immortality (1742–1746)

▶▶ INTELLIGENCE; KNOWLEDGE; WIT

wit

Adams, Joey (b. 1911)
US comedian and author

Of course, it's very easy to be witty tomorrow, after you get a chance to do some research and rehearse your ad libs.

Attr.

Dryden, John (1631–1700)
English poet, satirist, dramatist and critic

A thing well said will be wit in all languages.

Essay of Dramatic Poesy (1668)

Johnson, Samuel (1709–1784)
English lexicographer, poet, critic, conversationalist and essayist
Of Lord Chesterfield

This man I thought had been a Lord among wits; but, I find, he is only a wit among Lords.

In Boswell, The Life of Samuel Johnson (1791)

Mahaffy, Sir John Pentland (1839–1919)

My dear Oscar, you are not clever enough for us in Dublin. You had better run over to Oxford.

In H. Montgomery Hyde, Oscar Wilde: A Biography (1975)

Maugham, William Somerset (1874–1965)
English writer, dramatist and physician

Impropriety is the soul of wit.

The Moon and Sixpence (1919)

Pope, Alexander (1688–1744)
English poet, translator and editor

Some have at first for Wits, then Poets pass'd, Turned Critics next, and proved plain fools at last.

An Essay on Criticism (1711)

True Wit is Nature to advantage dress'd, What oft was thought, but ne'er so well express'd.

An Essay on Criticism (1711)

You beat your Pate, and fancy Wit will come; Knock as you please, there's nobody at home.

'Epigram' (1732)

Rogers, Thorold (1823–1890)

Sir, to be facetious it is not necessary to be indecent.

In John Bailey, *Dr Johnson and his Circle* (1913)

Russell, Lord John (1792–1878)
English Liberal Prime Minister and writer

A proverb is one man's wit and all men's wisdom.

In R.J. Mackintosh, *Sir James Mackintosh* (1835)

Shadwell, Thomas (c.1642–1692)

And wit's the noblest frailty of the mind.

A True Widow (1679)

Skelton, Robin (1925–)

Anything said off the cuff has usually been written on it first.

Attr.

Sterne, Laurence (1713–1768)
Irish-born English writer and clergyman

An ounce of a man's own wit is worth a ton of other people's.

Tristram Shandy (1759–1767)

▶▶ WISDOM

women

Addams, Jane (1860–1935)
US sociologist and writer

Old-fashioned ways which no longer apply to changed conditions are a snare in which the feet of women have always become readily entangled.

Newer Ideals of Peace (1907)

Addison, Joseph (1672–1719)
English essayist, poet, playwright and statesman

The woman that deliberates is lost.

Cato (1713)

I consider woman as a beautiful, romantic animal, that may be adorned with furs and feathers, pearls and diamonds, ores and silks.

Trial of the Petticoat

Agnew, Spiro T. (1918–1996)
US Vice President

Three things have been difficult to tame: the oceans, fools and women. We may soon be able to tame the oceans; fools and women will take a little longer.

Attr.

Alcott, Louisa May (1832–1888)
US writer

… girls are so queer you never know what they mean. They say No when they mean Yes, and drive a man out of his wits for the fun of it …

Little Women (1869)

Alexander, Sir William, Earl of Stirling
(c.1567–1640)
Scottish poet and statesman

The weaker sex, to piety more prone.

Doomsday (1614)

Anonymous

In particular, the State recognises that by her life within the home, woman gives to the State a support without which the common good cannot be achieved.

The Irish Constitution

Arnold, Matthew (1822–1888)
English poet, critic, essayist and educationist

With women the heart argues, not the mind.

Merope (1858)

Augustine, Saint (354–430)
Numidian-born Christian theologian and philosopher

Women should not be enlightened or educated in any way. They should, in fact, be segregated as they are the cause of hideous and involuntary erections in holy men.

Attr.

Austen, Jane (1775–1817)
English writer

Next to being married, a girl likes to be crossed in love a little now and then.

Pride and Prejudice (1813)

Where people wish to attach, they should always be ignorant. To come with a well-informed mind, is to come with an inability of administering to the vanity of others, which a sensible person would always wish to avoid. A woman especially, if she have the misfortune of knowing any thing, should conceal it as well as she can.

Northanger Abbey (1818)

In nine cases out of ten, a woman had better show more affection than she feels.

Letter

Bacall, Lauren (1924–)
US film actress
> I'm not a member of the weaker sex.
>> In Simon Rose, *Classic Film Guide* (1995)

Bagehot, Walter (1826–1877)
English economist and political philosopher
> Women – one half the human race at least – care fifty times more for a marriage than a ministry.
>> *The English Constitution* (1867)

Balanchine, George (1904–1983)
Russian-born US choreographer
> In my ballets, woman is first. Men are consorts. God made men to sing the praises of women. They are not equal to men: They are better.
>> *Time* 15 September 1980

Beauvoir, Simone de (1908–1986)
French writer, feminist critic and philosopher
> *On ne naît pas femme: on le devient.*
> One is not born a woman: one becomes a woman.
>> *The Second Sex* (1950)

Beerbohm, Sir Max (1872–1956)
English satirist, cartoonist, critic and essayist
> Most women are not so young as they are painted.
>> *The Works of Max Beerbohm* (1896)

> 'After all,' as a pretty girl once said to me, 'women are a sex by themselves, so to speak.'
>> *The Works of Max Beerbohm* (1896)

> Women who love the same man have a kind of bitter freemasonry.
>> *Zuleika Dobson* (1911)

Behn, Aphra (1640–1689)
English dramatist, writer, poet, translator and spy
> The soft, unhappy sex.
>> *The Wandering Beauty* (c.1694)

The Bible (King James Version)
> And the rib, which the Lord God had taken from man, made he a woman.
>> *Genesis*, 2:22

> Who can find a virtuous woman? for her price is far above rubies.
>> *Proverbs*, 31:10

> All wickedness is but little to the wickedness of a woman.
>> *Ecclesiasticus*, 25:19

Bridges, Robert (1844–1930)
English poet, dramatist, essayist and doctor
> All women born are so perverse
> No man need boast their love possessing.
> If nought seem better, nothing's worse:
> All women born are so perverse.
> From Adam's wife, that proved a curse

> Though God had made her for a blessing,
> All women born are so perverse
> No man need boast their love possessing.
>> 'Triolet' (1890)

Burnet, Sir Frank Macfarlane (1899–1985)
Australian medical researcher
> In an affluent society most healthy women would like to have four healthy children.
>> *Dominant Mammal* (1970)

Burns, Robert (1759–1796)
Scottish poet and song writer
> Auld nature swears, the lovely dears
> Her noblest work she classes, O:
> Her prentice han' she try'd on man,
> An' then she made the lasses, O.
>> 'Green Grow the Rashes' (1783)

Butler, Samuel (1612–1680)
English poet
> The souls of women are so small,
> That some believe they've none at all.
>> *Miscellaneous Thoughts*

Butler, Samuel (1835–1902)
English writer, painter, philosopher and scholar
> Brigands demand your money or your life; women require both.
>> Attr.

Byron, Lord (1788–1824)
English poet satirist and traveller
> There is something to me very softening in the presence of a woman, – some strange influence, even if one is not in love with them – which I cannot at all account for, having no very high opinion of the sex.
>> *Journal*, 1814

Catullus (84–c.54 BC)
Roman poet
> But what a woman says to her eager lover, she ought to write in the wind and the running water.
>> *Carmina*

Cervantes, Miguel de (1547–1616)
Spanish writer and dramatist
> *La mujer honrada, la pierna quebrada, y en casa; y la doncella honesta, el hacer algo es su fiesta.*
> An honest woman and a broken leg should be at home; and for a decent maiden, working is her holiday.
>> *Don Quixote* (1615)

Chandler, Raymond (1888–1959)
US crime writer
> It was a blonde. A blonde to make a bishop kick a hole in a stained glass window.
>> *Farewell, My Lovely* (1940)

Chaucer, Geoffrey (c.1340–1400)
English poet, public servant and courtier
> What is bettre than wisedoom? Womman. And what is bettre than a good womman? Nothyng.
>> *The Canterbury Tales* (1387)

Chekhov, Anton (1860–1904)
Russian writer, dramatist and doctor
> Women don't forgive failure.
>> *The Seagull* (1896)

Chesterfield, Lord (1694–1773)
English politician and letter writer
> Women, then, are only children of a larger growth; they have an entertaining tattle and sometimes wit; but for solid, reasoning good-sense, I never in my life knew one that had it, or who reasoned or acted consequentially for four-and-twenty hours together.
>> Letter to his son, 1748

Of women
> A man of sense only trifles with them, plays with them, humours and flatters them, as he does with a sprightly, forward child; but he neither consults them about, nor trusts them with, serious matters; though he often makes them believe that he does both.
>> Letter to his son, 1748

> Women are much more like each other than men; they have, in truth, but two passions, vanity and love; these are their universal characteristics.
>> Letter to his son, 1749

Chesterton, G.K. (1874–1936)
English writer, poet and critic
> She the elegant female was maintaining the prime truth of woman, the universal mother: that if a thing is worth doing, it is worth doing badly.
>> *What's Wrong with the World* (1910)

Chisholm, Caroline (1808–1877)
English-born Australian humanitarian
> For all the churches you can build, and all the books you can export, will never do much good without what a gentleman in that Colony very appropriately called 'God's police' – wives and little children – good and virtuous women.
>> *Emigration and Transportation Relatively Considered* (1847)

Congreve, William (1670–1729)
English dramatist
> Women are like tricks by slight of hand,
> Which, to admire, we should not understand.
>> *Love for Love* (1695)

> Heav'n has no rage, like love to hatred turned,
> Nor Hell a fury, like a woman scorn'd.
>> *The Mourning Bride* (1697)

Coward, Sir Noël (1899–1973)
English dramatist, actor, producer and composer
> Certain women should be struck regularly, like gongs.
>> *Private Lives* (1930)

Cowley, Hannah (1743–1809)
English dramatist and poet
> But what is woman?–only one of Nature's agreeable blunders.
>> *Who's the Dupe?* (1779)

Delaney, Shelagh (1939–)
English dramatist, screenwriter and writer
> Women never have young minds. They are born three thousand years old.
>> *A Taste of Honey* (1959)

Donne, John (1572–1631)
English poet
> Women are like the Arts, forc'd unto none,
> Open to all searchers, unpriz'd if unknown.
>> *Elegies* (c.1595)

Dyson, James
English inventor of the bagless vacuum cleaner
> I don't operate rationally. I think just like a woman.
>> *The Times*, 1999

Ekland, Britt (1942–)
Swedish actress
> As a single woman with a child, I would love to have a wife.
>> *The Independent*, 1994

Eliot, George (1819–1880)
English writer and poet
> I should like to know what is the proper function of women, if it is not to make reasons for husbands to stay at home, and still stronger reasons for bachelors to go out.
>> *The Mill on the Floss* (1860)

> A woman can hardly ever choose … she is dependent on what happens to her. She must take meaner things, because only meaner things are within her reach.
>> *Felix Holt* (1866)

Farquhar, George (1678–1707)
Irish dramatist
> There's some diversion in a talking blockhead; and since a woman must wear chains, I would have the pleasure of hearing 'em rattle a little.
>> *The Beaux' Stratagem* (1707)

Fitzgerald, Edward (1809–1883)
English poet, translator and letter writer
> Mrs Browning's death is rather a relief to me, I must say: no more Aurora Leighs, thank God! A woman of real genius, I know; but what is the upshot of it all? She and her sex had better

mind the kitchen and their children; and perhaps the poor: except in such things as little novels, they only devote themselves to what men do much better, leaving that which men do worse or not at all.

Letter to W.H. Thompson, 1861

Frayn, Michael (1933–)
English dramatist and writer
No woman so naked as one you can see to be naked underneath her clothes.

Constructions

Freud, Sigmund (1856–1939)
Austrian physicist; founder of psychoanalysis
The great question … which I have not been able to answer, despite my thirty years of research into the feminine soul, is 'What does a woman want?'.

In Robb, Psychiatry in American Life

Gay, John (1685–1732)
English poet, dramatist and librettist
Woman's mind
Oft' shifts her passions, like th' inconstant wind;
Sudden she rages, like the troubled main,
Now sinks the storm, and all is calm again.

Dione (1720)

I must have women. There is nothing unbends the mind like them.

The Beggar's Opera (1728

Gorman, Theresa
English Conservative politician
The Conservative establishment has always treated women as nannies, grannies and fannies.

The Observer, 1998

Granville, George (1666–1735)
English poet, dramatist and politician
Of all the plagues with which the world is curst,
Of every ill, a woman is the worst.

The British Enchanters

Greer, Germaine (1939–)
Australian feminist, critic, English scholar and writer
A man who is slovenly and untidy is considered normal. The woman who is either is a slut or a slommack or a sloven or a slag.

The Times, 1999

Hakim, Catherine
British sociologist
The unpalatable truth is that a substantial proportion of women still accept the sexual division of labour which sees home-making as women's principal activitiy and income-earning as men's principal activity in life.

The Observer Review, 1996

Haran, Maeve
British writer and journalist

The itemised telephone bill ranks up there with suspender belts, Sky Sports channels and *Loaded* magazine as inventions women could do without.

The Times, 1999

Harman, Sir Jeremiah (1930–)
British High Court judge
I've always thought there were only three kinds of women: wives, whores and mistresses.

Daily Mail, 1996

Home, John (1722–1808)
Scottish clergyman and dramatist
He seldom errs
Who thinks the worst he can of womankind.

Douglas (1756)

Irving, Washington (1783–1859)
US writer and diplomat
A woman's whole life is a history of the affections.

The Sketch Book (1820)

James I of Scotland (1394–1437)
King of Scotland
On being introduced to a young girl proficient in Latin, Greek, and Hebrew
These are rare attainments for a damsel, but pray tell me, can she spin?

Attr.

Johnson, Samuel (1709–1784)
English lexicographer, poet, critic, conversationalist and essayist
Sir, a woman's preaching is like a dog's walking on his hinder legs. It is not done well; but you are surprised to find it done at all.

In Boswell, The Life of Samuel Johnson (1791)

Kipling, Rudyard (1865–1936)
Indian-born British poet and writer
'Tisn't beauty, so to speak, nor good talk necessarily. It's just IT. Some women'll stay in a man's memory if they once walked down a street.

Traffics and Discoveries (1904)

Knox, John (1505–1572)
Scottish religious reformer
The First Blast of the Trumpet Against the Monstrous Regiment of Women.

Title of pamphlet, 1558

To promote a Woman to bear rule, superiority, dominion or empire, above any Realm, Nation, or City, is repugnant to Nature; contumely to God, a thing most contrarious to his revealed will and approved ordinance; and finally it is the subversion of good Order, of all equity and justice.

'The First Blast of the Trumpet Against the Monstrous Regiment of Women', 1558

Knox, Vicesimus (1752–1821)

English churchman and writer

Can anything be more absurd than keeping women in a state of ignorance, and yet so vehemently to insist on their resisting temptation?

Liberal Education (1780)

Lerner, Alan Jay (1918–1986)

US lyricist and screenwriter

There is no greater fan of the opposite sex than me, and I have the bills to prove it.

Attr.

I'd be equally as willing
For a dentist to be drilling
Than to ever let a woman in my life.

My Fair Lady (1956)

Lewis, C.S. (1898–1963)

Irish-born English academic, writer and critic

She's the sort of woman who lives for others—you can always tell the others by their hunted expression.

The Screwtope Letters (1942)

Loos, Anita (1893–1981)

US writer and screenwriter

So this gentleman said a girl with brains ought to do something with them besides think.

Gentlemen Prefer Blondes (1925)

Mackenzie, Sir Compton (1883–1972)

Scottish writer and broadcaster

Women do not find it difficult nowadays to behave like men; but they often find it extremely difficult to behave like gentlemen.

Literature in My Time (1933)

Mailer, Norman (1923–)

US writer

You don't know a woman until you've met her in court.

The Observer, 1983

Mansfield, Katherine (1888–1923)

New Zealand writer

On women's ambition

Most women turn to salt, looking back.

In John Middleton Murry (ed.), *Journal of Katherine Mansfield* (1954)

Marlowe, Christopher (1564–1593)

English poet and dramatist

Like untun'd golden strings all women are
Which long time lie untouch'd, will harshly jar.

Hero and Leander (1598)

Masefield, John (1878–1967)

English poet, writer and critic

To get the whole world out of bed
And washed, and dressed, and warmed, and fed,
To work, and back to bed again,
Believe me, Saul, costs worlds of pain.

'The Everlasting Mercy' (1911)

Maugham, William Somerset (1874–1965)

English writer, dramatist and physician

A woman will always sacrifice herself if you give her the opportunity. It is her favourite form of self-indulgence.

The Circle (1921)

McCarthy, Abigail (c.1914–)

US writer

For those of us whose lives have been defined by others – by wifehood and motherhood – there is no individual achievement to measure, only the experience of life itself.

Private Faces/Public Places (1972)

Mencken, H.L. (1880–1956)

US writer, critic, philologist and satirist

When women kiss, it always reminds me of prize-fighters shaking hands.

Attr.

Milton, John (1608–1674)

English poet, libertarian and pamphleteer

… nothing lovelier can be found
In Woman, than to studie household good,
And good works in her Husband to promote.

Paradise Lost (1667)

O why did God,
Creator wise, that peopl'd highest Heav'n
With Spirits Masculine, create at last
This noveltie on Earth, this fair defect
Of Nature?

Paradise Lost (1667)

Reply when asked if he would allow his daughters to learn foreign languages

One tongue is sufficient for a woman.

Attr.

Moore, Thomas (1779–1852)

Irish poet

Disguise our bondage as we will,
'Tis woman, woman, rules us still.

Miscellaneous Poems (1840), 'Sovereign Woman'

Morissette, Alanis (1974–)

US singer

I want to walk through life instead of being dragged through it.

Attr.

Mulkerns, Val (1925–)

Irish writer

On the last day of his life Dan decided that women who haunted you were not those whom you had enjoyed or even known remotely well, but strangers who had at one time or another troubled you with the most transient flicker of desire.

Loser

Nash, Ogden (1902–1971)
US poet
Women would rather be right than reasonable.

'Frailty, Thy Name is a Misnomer' (1942)

Nietzsche, Friedrich Wilhelm (1844–1900)
German philosopher, critic and poet
Alles am Weibe ist ein Rätsel, und alles am Weibe hat eine Lösung: sie heisst Schwangerschaft.
Everything to do with women is a mystery, and everything to do with women has one solution: it's called pregnancy.

Thus Spake Zarathustra (1884)

Nin, Anais (1903–1977)
French-born US writer
Women (and I, in this Diary) have never separated sex from feeling, from love of the whole man.

Delta of Venus (1977)

Noble, Emma
English model
I think any woman who becomes successful is demonised by the media because they can't possibly be attractive, intelligent, nice and genuine. It's just too scary for a woman to be all these things.

The Times, 1999

Otway, Thomas (1652–1685)
English dramatist and poet
What mighty ills have not been done by woman!
Who was't betrayed the Capitol? – A woman!
Who lost Mark Antony the world? – A woman!
Who was the cause of a long ten years' war,
And laid at last old Troy in ashes? – Woman!
Destructive, damnable, deceitful woman!

The Orphan (1680)

Oh woman! lovely woman! Nature made thee
To temper man: we had been brutes without you;
Angels are painted fair, to look like you;
There's in you all that we believe of heav'n,
Amazing brightness, purity, and truth,
Eternal joy, and everlasting love.

Venice Preserv'd (1682)

Ovid (43 BC–AD 18)
Roman poet
Whether they give or refuse, women are glad that they have been asked.

Ars Amatoria

Paglia, Camille (1947–)
US academic
There is no female Mozart because there is no female Jack the Ripper.

Attr. in *The Observer*, 1996

Pericles (c.495–429)
Athenian statesman, general, orator and cultural patron
The greatest glory of a woman is to be least talked about by men, in praise or blame.

In Thucydides, *Histories*

Pope, Alexander (1688–1744)
English poet, translator and editor
Most Women have no Characters at all.

'Epistle to a Lady' (1735)

Woman's at best a Contradiction still.

'Epistle to a Lady' (1735)

Racine, Jean (1639–1699)
French tragedian and poet
Elle flotte, elle hésite; en un mot, elle est femme.
She wavers, she hesitates; in a word, she is a woman.

Athalie (1691)

Renan, J. Ernest (1823–1892)
French philologist, writer and historian
La femme nous remet en communication avec l'éternelle source où Dieu se mire.
Woman puts us back into communication with the eternal spring in which God looks at his reflection.

Souvenirs d'enfance et de jeunesse (1883)

Rochester, Earl of (1647–1680)
English poet, satirist, courtier and libertine
Love a woman? You're an ass!

'Song' (1680)

Rowland, Helen (1875–1950)
US writer
It takes a woman twenty years to make a man of her son, and another woman twenty minutes to make a fool of him.

Reflections of a Bachelor Girl (1909)

Rubinstein, Helena (1872–1965)
Polish-born US cosmetician and businesswoman
There are no ugly women, only lazy ones.

My Life for Beauty (1965)

Schopenhauer, Arthur (1788–1860)
German philosopher
One needs only to see the way she is built to realise that woman is not intended for great mental labour.

Attr.

Scott, Sir Walter (1771–1832)
Scottish writer and historian
O Woman! in our hours of ease,

Uncertain, coy, and hard to please,
And variable as the shade
By the light quivering aspen made;
When pain and anguish wring the brow,
A ministering angel thou!

Marmion (1808)

Woman's faith, and woman's trust –
Write the characters in dust.

The Betrothed (1825)

Shakespeare, William (1564–1616)
English dramatist, poet and actor
Do you not know I am a woman? When I think, I
must speak.

As You Like It, III.ii

Frailty, thy name is woman!

Hamlet, I.ii

She's beautiful, and therefore to be woo'd;
She is a woman, therefore to be won.

Henry VI, Part 1, V.iii

A woman mov'd is like a fountain troubled –
Muddy, ill-seeming, thick, bereft of beauty.

The Taming of the Shrew, V.ii

Sharif, Omar (1932–)
Egyptian film actor
The truth is I worship women … the kind who
can use both intelligence and femininity. The
woman must give the impression that she needs
a man.

In Spada, S*treisand: The Intimate Biography* (1995)

Shaw, George Bernard (1856–1950)
Irish socialist, writer, dramatist and critic
The fickleness of the women I love is only
equalled by the infernal constancy of the women
who love me.

The Philanderer (1898)

The one point on which all women are in furious
secret rebellion against the existing law is the
saddling of the right to a child with the
obligation to become the servant of a man.

Getting Married (1911)

Sheridan, Richard Brinsley (1751–1816)
Irish dramatist, politician and orator
Here's to the maiden of bashful fifteen;
Here's to the widow of fifty;
Here's to the flaunting, extravagant quean;
And here's to the housewife that's thrifty.
Let the toast pass –
Drink to the lass –
I'll warrant she'll prove an excuse for the glass!

The School for Scandal (1777)

Southey, Robert (1774–1843)
English poet, essayist, historian and letterwriter
What will not woman, gentle woman, dare,

When strong affection stirs her spirit up?

Madoc (1805)

Steinem, Gloria (1934–)
US writer and feminist activist
One day, an army of grey-haired women may
quietly take over the earth.

Outrageous Acts and Everyday Rebellions (1984)

Stocks, Mary, Baroness (1891–1975)
English educationist, broadcaster and biographer
It is clearly absurd that it should be possible for
a woman to qualify as a saint with direct access
to the Almighty while she may not qualify as a
curate.

Attr.

Tennyson, Alfred, Lord (1809–1892)
English lyric poet
The woman is so hard
Upon the woman.

The Princess (1847)

Vanbrugh, Sir John (1664–1726)
English dramatist and baroque architect
Once a woman has given you her heart you can
never get rid of the rest of her.

The Relapse, or Virtue in Danger (1696)

Ward, Artemus (1834–1867)
US humorist, journalist, editor and lecturer
The female woman is one of the greatest
institooshuns of which this land can boste.

Artemus Ward, His Book (1862), 'Woman's Rights'

Waugh, Auberon (1939–)
English writer and critic
It is one of the tragedies of our time to see
women making a nuisance of themselves as
welfare officers when they could be employed as
nursery maids.

The Independent on Sunday, 1994

Wells, H.G. (1866–1946)
English writer
There's no social differences – till women come
in.

Kipps: the Story of a Simple Soul (1905)

Wolff, Charlotte (1904–1986)
German-born British psychiatrist and writer
Women have always been the guardians of
wisdom and humanity which makes them
natural, but usually secret, rulers. The time has
come for them to rule openly, but together with
and not against men.

Bisexuality: A Study

Woolf, Virginia (1882–1941)
English writer and critic
Women have served all these centuries as
looking-glasses possessing the magic and
delicious power of reflecting the figure of man

at twice its natural size.

A Room of One's Own (1929)

Wynne-Tyson, Esme (1898–1972)
British actress and writer
Scheherazade is the classical example of a woman saving her head by using it.

Attr.

▶▶ FEMINISM; MEN AND WOMEN

words

Aeschylus (525–456 BC)
Greek dramatist and poet
Words are physic to the distempered mind.

Prometheus Bound

Ashdown, Paddy (1941–)
Former leader of the UK Social and Liberal Democrat Party
Lord, make my words sweet and reasonable. Some day I may have to eat them.

The Observer, 1998

Bacon, Francis (1561–1626)
English philosopher, essayist, politician and courtier
The ill and unfit choice of words wonderfully obstructs the understanding.

The New Organon (1620)

The Bible (King James Version)
Man shall not live by bread alone, but by every word that proceedeth out of the mouth of God.

Matthew, 4:4

Brown, George MacKay (1921–1996)
Scottish novelist, poet and playwright
We who deal in words must strive to keep language pure and wholesome; and it is hard work, as hard almost as digging a stony field with a blunt spade.

Time in a Red Coat (1984)

Carlyle, Thomas (1795–1881)
Scottish historian, biographer, critic, and essayist
Be not the slave of Words.

Sartor Resartus (1834)

Carroll, Lewis (1832–1898)
English writer and photographer
'When I use a word,' Humpty Dumpty said in rather a scornful tone, 'it means just what I choose it to mean – neither more nor less.'

Through the Looking-Glass (and What Alice Found There) (1872)

You see it's like a portmanteau – there are two meanings packed up into one word.

Through the Looking-Glass (and What Alice Found There) (1872)

Confucius (c.550–c.478 BC)
Chinese philosopher and teacher of ethics
Without knowing the force of words, it is impossible to know men.

Analects

De La Mare, Walter (1873–1956)
English poet
Until we learn the use of living words we shall continue to be waxworks inhabited by gramophones.

The Observer, 1929

Eliot, T.S. (1888–1965)
US-born British poet, verse dramatist and critic
Words strain,
Crack and sometimes break, under the burden,
Under the tension, slip, slide, perish,
Decay with imprecision, will not stay in place,
Will not stay still.

Four Quartets (1944)

Emerson, Ralph Waldo (1803–1882)
US poet, essayist, transcendentalist and teacher
Words are also actions, and actions are a kind of words.

'The Poet' (1844)

Farquhar, George (1678–1707)
Irish dramatist
Grant me some wild expressions, Heavens, or I shall burst … Words, words or I shall burst.

The Constant Couple (1699)

France, Anatole (1844–1924)
French writer and critic
Il fut des temps barbares et gothiques où les mots avaient un sens; alors les écrivains exprimaient des pensées.
It was in the times, barbarous and gothic, when words had a meaning; in those days, writers would express thoughts.

La Vie Littéraire (1888)

Hardy, Thomas (1840–1928)
English writer and poet
Dialect words – those terrible marks of the beast to the truly genteel.

The Mayor of Casterbridge (1886)

Hobbes, Thomas (1588–1679)
Political philosopher
Words are wise men's counters, they do but reckon by them; but they are the money of fools.

Leviathan (1651)

Holmes, Oliver Wendell (1809–1894)
US physician, poet, writer and scientist
I am omniverbivorous by nature and training. Passing by such words as are poisonous, I can

swallow most others, and chew such as I cannot swallow.

The Autocrat of the Breakfast-Table (1858)

Huxley, Aldous (1894–1963)

English writer, poet and critic

Words can be like X-rays, if you use them properly – they'll go through anything.

Brave New World (1932)

Thanks to words, we have been able to rise above the brutes; and thanks to words, we have often sunk to the level of the demons.

Adonis and the Alphabet (1956)

James, Henry (1843–1916)

US-born British writer, critic and letter writer

Summer afternoon – summer afternoon; to me those have always been the two most beautiful words in the English language.

In Edith Wharton, A Backward Glance (1934)

Joyce, James (1882–1941)

Irish writer

I fear those big words, Stephen said, which make us so unhappy.

Ulysses (1922)

Kipling, Rudyard (1865–1936)

Indian-born British poet and writer

Words are, of course, the most powerful drug used by mankind.

Speech, 1923

Landor, Walter Savage (1775–1864)

English poet and writer

How many verses have I thrown
Into the fire because the one
Peculiar word, the wanted most,
Was irrevocably lost.

'Verses Why Burnt'

I hate false words, and seek with care, difficulty, and moroseness, those that fit the thing.

Imaginary Conversations (1853)

Lydgate, John (c.1370–c.1451)

English monk, poet and translator

Woord is but wynd; leff woord and tak the dede.

'Secrets of Old Philosophers'

Madden, Samuel (1686–1765)

Irish writer

Words are men's daughters, but God's sons are things.

Boulter's Monument (1745)

Massinger, Philip (1583–1640)

English dramatist and poet

All words,
And no performance!

The Parliament of Love (1624)

Ogden, C.K. (1889–1957) and **Richards, I.A**. (1893–1979)

English critics and poets

The belief that words have a meaning of their own account is a relic of primitive word magic, and it is still a part of the air we breathe in nearly every discussion.

The Meaning of Meaning (1923)

Parker, Dorothy (1893–1967)

US writer, poet, critic and wit

Giving her version of the two most beautiful words in the English language

Check enclosed.

Attr.

Plautus, Titus Maccius (c.254–184 BC)

Roman comic dramatist

Dictum sapienti sat est.

A word to the wise is enough.

Persa

Pope, Alexander (1688–1744)

English poet, translator and editor

Words are like leaves; and where they most abound,
Much fruit of sense beneath is rarely found.

An Essay on Criticism (1711)

Roscommon, Fourth Earl of (1633–1685)

Irish translator and poet

But words once spoke can never be recall'd.

Horace's Art of Poetry Made English (1680)

Scott, Sir Walter (1771–1832)

Scottish writer and historian

There is a southern proverb, – fine words butter no parsnips.

A Legend of Montrose (1819)

Shadwell, Thomas (c.1642–1692)

Words may be false and full of Art,
Sighs are the natural language of the heart.

Psyche (1675)

Shakespeare, William (1564–1616)

English dramatist, poet and actor

Men of few words are the best men.

Henry V, III.ii

But words are words: I never yet did hear
That the bruis'd heart was pierced through the ear.

Othello, I.iii

Sheridan, Richard Brinsley (1751–1816)

Irish dramatist, politician and orator

You shall see them on a beautiful quarto page, where a neat rivulet of text shall murmur through a meadow of margin.

The School for Scandal (1777)

Spencer, Herbert (1820–1903)

English philosopher and journalist

> How often misused words generate misleading thoughts.

Principles of Ethics (1879)

Spender, Sir Stephen (1909–1995)

English poet, editor, translator and diarist

> The word bites like a fish.
> Shall I throw it back, free
> Arrowing to that sea
> Where thoughts lash tail and fin?
> Or shall I pull it in
> To rhyme upon a dish?

'Word'

Stevenson, Robert Louis (1850–1894)

Scottish writer, poet and essayist

> Man is a creature who lives not upon bread alone, but principally by catchwords.

Virginibus Puerisque (1881)

Wesley, John (1703–1791)

English theologian and preacher

On preaching to 'plain people'

> We should constantly use the most common, little, easy words (so they are pure and proper) which our language affords.

In R. Southey, *Life of Wesley* (1820)

▶▶ CONVERSATION; LANGUAGE

work

Acheson, Dean (1893–1971)

US Democrat politician

Remark made on leaving his post as Secretary of State, 1952

> I will undoubtedly have to seek what is happily known as gainful employment, which I am glad to say does not describe holding public office.

Attr.

Adams, Scott (1957–)

US cartoonist

> Be careful that what you write does not offend anybody or cause problems within the company. The safest approach is to remove all useful information.

Building a Better Life by Stealing Office Supplies: Dogbert's Big Book of Business (1991)

> In Japan, employees occasionally work themselves to death. It's called Karoshi. I don't want that to happen to anybody in my department. The trick is to take a break as soon as you see a bright light and hear dead relatives beckon.

The Dilbert Principle (1996)

Alley, Rewi (1897–1987)

New Zealand reformer and educationist

The motto of the Chinese Industrial Co-operatives Association

> Gung Ho!
> Work Together!

In Chapple, *Rewi Alley of China* (1980)

Anonymous

> *Laborare est orare.*
> Work is prayer.

> If you tell the boss you were late for work because you had a flat tyre, the next morning you will have a flat tyre.

Cannon's Law

> The working class can kiss my arse –
> I've got the boss's job at last.

Australian Labor movement, traditional folk saying, sung to the tune of the 'Red Flag'

Bach, Richard (1936–)

> The more I want to get something done, the less I call it work.

Illusions: Reflections of a Reluctant Messiah

Bacon, Francis (1909–1993)

Irish-born expressionist artist

> How can I take an interest in my work when I don't like it?

Attr.

Baldwin, James (1924–1987)

US writer, dramatist, poet and civil rights activist

> The price one pays for pursuing any profession or calling is an intimate knowledge of its ugly side.

Nobody Knows My Name (1961)

Benchley, Robert (1889–1945)

US essayist, humorist and actor

> I do most of my work sitting down; that's where I shine.

Attr.

> Anyone can do any amount of work, provided it isn't the work he is supposed to be doing at the moment.

In Robert E. Drennan, *The Algonquin Wits* (1968)

Bennett, Arnold (1867–1931)

English writer, dramatist and journalist

> The test of a first-rate work, and a test of your sincerity in calling it a first-rate work, is that you finish it.

Things That Have Interested Me (1921–1925)

> Habit of work is growing on me. I could get into the way of going to my desk as a man goes to whisky, or rather to chloral.

Journals (1932)

The Bible (King James Version)

> The labourer is worthy of his hire.

Luke, 10:7

If any would not work, neither should he eat.

II Thessalonians, 3:10

The husbandman that laboureth must be first partaker of the fruits.

II Timothy, 2:6

Burns, Robert (1759–1796)
Scottish poet and song writer
> We labour soon, we labour late,
> To feed the titled knave, man,
> And a' the comfort we're to get,
> Is that ayont the grave, man.

'The Tree of Liberty' (1838)

Butler, Samuel (1835–1902)
English writer, painter, philosopher and scholar
> Every man's work, whether it be literature or music or pictures or architecture or anything else, is always a portrait of himself.

The Way of All Flesh (1903)

Carlyle, Thomas (1795–1881)
Scottish historian, biographer, critic, and essayist
> Be no longer a Chaos, but a World, or even Worldkin. Produce! Produce! Were it but the pitifullest infinitesimal fraction of a Product, produce it, in God's name!'Tis the utmost thou hast in thee: out with it, then. Up, up! Whatsoever thy hand findeth to do, do it with thy whole might.

Sartor Resartus (1834)

> Blessed is he who has found his work; let him ask no other blessedness.

Past and Present (1843)

> Work is the grand cure of all the maladies and miseries that ever beset mankind.

Speech, 1886

Cervantes, Miguel de (1547–1616)
Spanish writer and dramatist
> Diligence is the mother of good fortune; and the goal of a good intention was never reached through its opposite, laziness.

Don Quixote (1615)

Chekhov, Anton (1860–1904)
Russian writer, dramatist and doctor
> The time has come, something huge is approaching us, a refreshing, powerful storm is brewing ... Soon it will blow away all the laziness, indifference, prejudice against work and decaying boredom from our society ... I'm going to work, and in some twenty-five or thirty years' time every one will be working. Every one!

The Three Sisters (1901)

Churchill, Jennie Jerome (1854–1921)
US-born English hostess and author
> You seem to have no real purpose in life and won't realize at the age of twenty-two that for a

man life means work, and hard work if you mean to succeed.

Letter to Winston Churchill, 1897

Cicero (106–43 BC)
Roman orator, statesman, essayist and letter writer
> *Vulgo enim dicitur: 'iucundi acti labores'.*
> For it is commonly said: 'hard tasks are pleasant when they are finished'.

De Finibus

Clarke, John (fl. 1639)
English scholar
> He that would thrive
> Must rise at five;
> He that hath thriven
> May lie till seven.

Paraemiologia Anglo-Latina (1639)

Cluff, Algy
British businessman
On the controversy over whether the inhabitants of Hong Kong should be allowed to enter Britain
> Energy, brains and hard work made Hong Kong. If only a few of its people would come here.

Daily Mail, 1996

Coghill, Anna Louisa (1836–1907)
> Work, for the night is coming,
> When man works no more.

Hymn, 1854

Coleridge, Samuel Taylor (1772–1834)
English poet, philosopher and critic
> Work without hope draws nectar in a sieve,
> And hope without an object cannot live.

'Work Without Hope' (1828)

Collingwood, R.G. (1889–1943)
English philosopher, archaeologist and historian
> Perfect freedom is reserved for the man who lives by his own work and in that work does what he wants to do.

Speculum Mentis (1924)

Coward, Sir Noël (1899–1973)
English dramatist, actor, producer and composer
> Work is much more fun than fun.

The Observer, 1963

Cumberland, Bishop Richard (1631–1718)
English philosopher, divine and translator
> It is better to wear out than to rust out.

In Horne, *The Duty of Contending for the Faith* (1786)

Curie, Marie (1867–1934)
Polish-born French physicist
> One never notices what has been done; one can only see what remains to be done ...

Letter to her brother, 1894

Davidson, John (1857–1909)
Scottish writer

'My time is filched by toil and sleep;
My heart,' he thought, 'is clogged with dust;
My soul that flashed from out the deep,
A magic blade, begins to rust.'

'A Ballad of a Workman' (1894)

Davis, Bette (1908–1989)
US film actress

This became a credo of mine ... attempt the impossible in order to improve your work.

Attr.

Edward VIII (later Duke of Windsor) (1894–1972)
King of the United Kingdom; abdicated 11 December 1936
Of steel works in South Wales where 9,000 men had been made unemployed

These works brought all these people here. Something must be done to find them work.

Speech, 1936

Emmons, Margaret

If while you are in school, there is a shortage of qualified personnel in a particular field, then by the time you graduate with the necessary qualifications, that field's employment market is glutted.

Attr.

France, Anatole (1844–1924)
French writer and critic

Man is so made that he can only find relaxation from one kind of labour by taking up another.

The Crime of Sylvestre Bonnard (1881)

George, Henry (1839–1897)
US economist, editor and lecturer

The man who gives me employment, which I must have or suffer, that man is my master, let me call him what I will.

Social Problems (1884)

Gilman, Charlotte Perkins (1860–1935)
US writer, social reformer and feminist

There's a whining at the threshold
There's a scratching at the floor.
To work! To work! In Heaven's name!
The wolf is at the door.

Attr.

Hood, Thomas (1799–1845)
English poet, editor and humorist

With fingers weary and worn,
With eyelids heavy and red,
A Woman sat, in unwomanly rags,
Plying her needle and thread –
Stitch! stitch! stitch!
In poverty, hunger, and dirt ...

O! Men with Sisters dear!
O! Men with Mothers and Wives!

It is not linen you're wearing out,
But human creatures' lives! ...

Oh! God! that bread should be so dear,
And flesh and blood so cheap! ...

No blessed leisure for Love or Hope,
But only time for Grief!

'The Song of the Shirt' (1843)

Jerome, Jerome K. (1859–1927)
English writer and dramatist

I like work; it fascinates me. I can sit and look at it for hours. I love to keep it by me: the idea of getting rid of it nearly breaks my heart.

Three Men in a Boat (1889)

Jerrold, Douglas William (1803–1857)
English dramatist, writer and wit

The ugliest of trades have their moments of pleasure. Now, if I were a grave-digger, or even a hangman, there are some people I could work for with a great deal of enjoyment.

Wit and Opinions of Douglas Jerrold (1859)

Johnson, Samuel (1709–1784)
English lexicographer, poet, critic, conversationalist and essayist

I have protracted my work till most of those whom I wished to please have sunk into the grave, and success and miscarriage are empty sounds; I therefore dismiss it with frigid tranquillity, having little to fear or hope from censure or praise.

In Boswell, *The Life of Samuel Johnson (1791)*

Joliot-Curie, Irène (1897–1956)
French nuclear physicist
Recalling the advice of her mother, Marie Curie

That one must do some work seriously and must be independent and not merely amuse oneself in life – this our mother has told us always, but never that science was the only career worth following.

In Mary Margaret McBride, *A Long Way from Missouri*

Katzenberg, Jeffrey (1951–)
US film producer

If you don't show up for work on Saturday, don't bother coming in on Sunday.

Attr.

Kerouac, Jack (1922–1969)
US writer and poet

We're really all of us bottomly broke. I haven't had time to work in weeks.

On the Road (1957)

Kollwitz, Käthe (1867–1945)
German painter, sculptor and graphic artist

For the last third of life there remains only work.

It alone is always stimulating, rejuvenating, exciting and satisfying.

Diaries and Letters (1955)

Lang, Ian (1940–)
Scottish Conservative politician
Job insecurity is a state of mind.

The Observer Review, 1995

Larkin, Philip (1922–1985)
English poet, writer and librarian
Why should I let the toad *work*
Squat on my life?
Can't I use my wit as a pitchfork
And drive the brute off?

'Toads' (1955)

Levi, Primo (1919–1987)
Italian writer, poet and chemist; survivor of Auschwitz
The bond between a man and his profession is similar to that which ties him to his country; it is just as complex, often ambivalent, and in general it is understood completely only when it is broken … by retirement in the case of a trade or profession.

Other People's Trades (1989)

London, Jack (1876–1916)
US writer, sailor, socialist and goldminer
In an English ship, they say, it is poor grub, poor pay, and easy work; in an American ship, good grub, good pay, and hard work. And this is applicable to the working populations of both countries.

The People of the Abyss (1903)

Lowell, James Russell (1819–1891)
US poet, editor, abolitionist and diplomat
No man is born into the world, whose work
Is not born with him; there is always work,
And tools to work withal, for those who will:
And blessèd are the horny hands of toil!

'A Glance Behind the Curtain' (1844)

Montaigne, Michel de (1533–1592)
French essayist and moralist
The unceasing labour of your life is to build the house of death.

Essais (1580)

Morris, William (1834–1896)
English poet, designer, craftsman, artist and socialist
All their devices for cheapening labour simply resulted in increasing the burden of labour.

News from Nowhere (1891)

Neilson, John Shaw (1872–1942)
Australian poet
Work should begin with wine and generous joking,
And in the place of penalties for smoking

Let us have fines for platitudes and croaking.

Collected Poems (1934), 'To a Blonde Typist'

Parkinson, C. Northcote (1909–1993)
English political scientist and historian
Work expands so as to fill the time available for its completion.

Parkinson's Law (1958)

The rise in the total of those employed is governed by Parkinson's Law and would be much the same whether the volume of work were to increase, diminish or even disappear.

Parkinson's Law (1958)

Peter, Laurence J. (1919–1990)
Canadian educationist and writer
In a hierarchy every employee tends to rise to his level of incompetence.

The Peter Principle – Why Things Always Go Wrong (1969)

Philip, Prince, Duke of Edinburgh (1921–)
Greek-born consort of Queen Elizabeth II
Replying to a query as to what nature of work he did
I am self-employed.

Attr.

Proverbs
All work and no play makes Jack a dull boy.

Many hands make light work.

Reagan, Ronald (1911–)
US actor, Republican statesman and President
They say hard work never hurt anybody, but I figure why take the chance.

Attr.

Reynolds, Sir Joshua (1723–1792)
English portrait painter
If you have great talents, industry will improve them: if you have but moderate abilities, industry will supply their deficiency.

Discourses on Art (1769)

Rhodes, Zandra (1940–)
English fashion designer
I was lucky to always have a work ethic. Relationships end, men fail, but your work will never let you down.

The Observer, 1998

Roosevelt, Theodore (1858–1919)
US Republican President
I wish to preach not the doctrine of ignoble ease, but the doctrine of the strenuous life.

Speech, 1899

No man needs sympathy because he has to work … Far and away the best prize that life offers is the chance to work hard at work worth doing.

Address, 1903

Rowland, Helen (1875–1950)
US writer
> When you see what some girls marry, you realize
> how they must hate to work for a living.
>> *Reflections of a Bachelor Girl* (1909)

Ruskin, John (1819–1900)
English art critic, philosopher and reformer
> Which of us … is to do the hard and dirty work
> for the rest – and for what pay? Who is to do
> the pleasant and clean work, and for what pay?
>> *Sesame and Lilies* (1865)

> Labour without joy is base. Labour without
> sorrow is base. Sorrow without labour is base.
> Joy without labour is base.
>> *Time and Tide by Weare and Tyne* (1867)

> Life without industry is guilt, and industry
> without art is brutality.
>> *Lectures on Art* (1870)

Russell, Bertrand (1872–1970)
English philosopher, mathematician, essayist and social
reformer
> One of the symptoms of approaching nervous
> breakdowns is the belief that one's work is
> terribly important. If I were a medical man, I
> should prescribe a holiday to any patient who
> considered his work important.
>> Attr.

Sargeson, Frank (1903–1982)
New Zealand writer
A notice to callers, said to be on his house door
> Frank Sargeson works in the mornings. Do you?
>> *Islands*, 1978

Scott, Sir Walter (1771–1832)
Scottish writer and historian
> I live by twa trades, sir, … fiddle, sir, and spade;
> filling the world, and emptying of it.
>> *The Bride of Lammermoor* (1819)

Shakespeare, William (1564–1616)
English dramatist, poet and actor
> The labour we delight in physics pain.
>> *Macbeth*, II.iii

Shaw, George Bernard (1856–1950)
Irish socialist, writer, dramatist and critic
> A day's work is a day's work, neither more nor
> less, and the man who does it needs a day's
> sustenance, a night's repose, and due leisure,
> whether he be painter or ploughman.
>> *An Unsocial Socialist* (1887)

Smith, Adam (1723–1790)
Scottish economist, philosopher and essayist
> It is the interest of every man to live as much at
> his ease as he can; and if his emoluments are to
> be precisely the same whether he does, or does
> not perform some very laborious duty, it is

certainly his interest, at least as interest is
vulgarly understood, either to neglect it
altogether, or, if he is subject to some authority
which will not suffer him to do this, to perform it
in as careless and slovenly a manner as that
authority will permit.
>> *Wealth of Nations* (1776)

Southerne, Thomas (1660–1746)
Irish dramatist
> And when we're worn,
> Hack'd, hewn with constant service, thrown
> aside
> To rust in peace, or rot in hospitals.
>> *The Loyal Brother* (1682)

Spacey, Kevin (1959–)
US actor
As the disaffected Lester Burnham
> My job requires mostly masking my contempt
> for the assholes in charge, and, at least once a
> day, retiring to the men's room so I can jerk off
> while I fantasize about a life that doesn't so
> closely resemble Hell.
>> *American Beauty* (film, 1999)

Spooner, William (1844–1930)
English churchman and university warden
> You will find as you grow older that the weight
> of rages will press harder and harder upon the
> employer.
>> In W. Hayter, *Spooner* (1977)

Stanton, Elizabeth Cady (1815–1902)
US suffragist, abolitionist, feminist, editor and writer
> Woman has been the great unpaid laborer of the
> world.
>> In Anthony and Gage, *History of Woman Suffrage*
>> (1881)

Tebbitt, Norman (1931–)
English Conservative politician
Of his father who had grown up during the 1930s
> He didn't riot. He got on his bike and looked for
> work and he kept looking till he found it.
>> Speech, 1981

Thoreau, Henry David (1817–1862)
US essayist, social critic and writer
> For more than five years I maintained myself
> thus solely by the labor of my hands, and I
> found, that by working about six weeks in a
> year, I could meet all the expenses of living.
>> *Walden* (1854)

Twain, Mark (1835–1910)
US humorist, writer, journalist and lecturer
> Work consists of whatever a body is obliged to
> do.
>> *The Adventures of Tom Sawyer*
>> (1876)

Voltaire (1694–1778)
French philosopher, dramatist, poet, historian writer and critic

> *Le travail éloigne de nous trois grand maux: l'ennui, le vice et le besoin.*
> Work keeps away those three great evils: boredom, vice, and poverty.
>
> *Candide* (1759)

> When man was put in the garden of Eden, he was put there to work; that proves that man was not born for rest. Let us work without reasoning – that is the only way to make life bearable.
>
> *Candide* (1759)

Watts, Isaac (1674–1748)
English hymn-writer, poet and minister

> In works of labour, or of skill,
> I would be busy too;
> For Satan finds some mischief still
> For idle hands to do.
>
> 'Against Idleness and Mischief' (1715)

Whitehorn, Katherine (1926–)
English writer

> The best careers advice to give to the young is 'Find out what you like doing best and get someone to pay you for doing it.'
>
> *The Observer*, 1975

Wilde, Oscar (1854–1900)
Irish poet, dramatist, writer, critic and wit

> Work is the curse of the drinking classes.
>
> In Pearson, *Life of Oscar Wilde* (1946)

Yeats, W.B. (1865–1939)
Irish poet, dramatist, editor, writer and senator

> The intellect of man is forced to choose
> Perfection of the life, or of the work.
>
> 'The Choice' (1933)

▶▶ CAREERS

the world

Arnold, Matthew (1822–1888)
English poet, critic, essayist and educationist

> Ah, love, let us be true
> To one another! for the world, which seems
> To lie before us like a land of dreams,
> So various, so beautiful, so new,
> Hath really neither joy, nor love, nor light,
> Nor certitude, nor peace, nor help for pain;
> And we are here as on a darkling plain
> Swept with confused alarms of struggle and flight
> Where ignorant armies clash by night.
>
> 'Dover Beach' (1867)

Balfour, A.J. (1848–1930)
British Conservative Prime Minister

> This is a singularly ill-contrived world, but not so ill-contrived as all that.
>
> Attr.

Bennett, Arnold (1867–1931)
English writer, dramatist and journalist

> Well, my deliberate opinion is – it's a jolly strange world.
>
> *The Title* (1918)

Breton, Nicholas (c.1545–c.1626)
English writer and poet

> A Mad World, My Masters.
>
> Title of dialogue, 1603

Bronowski, Jacob (1908–1974)
British scientist, writer and TV presenter

> The world is made of people who never quite get into the first team and who just miss the prizes at the flower show.
>
> *The Face of Violence* (1954)

Brontë, Anne (1820–1849)
English writer and poet

> There is always a 'but' in this imperfect world.
>
> *The Tenant of Wildfell Hall* (1848)

Browne, Sir Thomas (1605–1682)
English physician, author and antiquary

> For the world, I count it not an inn, but an hospital, and a place, not to live, but to die in.
>
> *Religio Medici* (1643)

Buckingham, Duke of (1628–1687)
English courtier and dramatist

> The world is made up for the most part of fools and knaves.
>
> 'To Mr. Clifford, on his Humane Reason'

Butler, Samuel (1835–1902)
English writer, painter, philosopher and scholar

> The world will, in the end, follow only those who have despised as well as served it.
>
> *The Note-Books of Samuel Butler* (1912)

Carlyle, Thomas (1795–1881)
Scottish historian, biographer, critic, and essayist

> But the world is an old woman, and mistakes any gilt farthing for a gold coin; whereby being often cheated, she will thenceforth trust nothing but the common copper.
>
> *Sartor Resartus* (1834)

Chaucer, Geoffrey (c.1340–1400)
English poet, public servant and courtier

> This world nys but a thurghfare ful of wo,
> And we been pilgrymes, passynge to and fro.
> Deeth is an ende of every worldly soore.
>
> *The Canterbury Tales* (1387)

Clough, Arthur Hugh (1819–1861)

English poet and letter writer
> This world is bad enough, may-be,
> We do not comprehend it;
> But in one fact can all agree,
> God won't, and we can't mend it.
>> *Dipsychus* (1865)

Cowley, Abraham (1618–1667)
English poet and dramatist
> The world's a scene of changes, and to be
> Constant, in Nature were inconstancy.
>> *The Mistress: or ... Love Verses* (1647)

De La Mare, Walter (1873–1956)
English poet
> What is the world, O soldiers?
> It is I:
> I, this incessant snow,
> This northern sky;
> Soldiers, this solitude
> Through which we gols I.
>> 'Napoleon' (1906)

Dickinson, Emily (1830–1886)
US poet
> How much can come
> And much can go,
> And yet abide the World!
>> 'There came a Wind' (c.1883)

Diderot, Denis (1713–1784)
French philosopher, encyclopaedist, writer and dramatist
> *Oh! que ce monde-ci serait une bonne comédie si l'on*
> *n'y faisait pas un rôle.*
> What a fine comedy this world would be if one
> did not play a part in it!
>> Letters to Sophie Volland

Emerson, Ralph Waldo (1803–1882)
US poet, essayist, transcendentalist and teacher
> As there is a use in medicine for poisons, so the
> world cannot move without rogues.
>> *Conduct of Life* (1860)

Firbank, Ronald (1886–1926)
English writer
> The world is disgracefully managed, one hardly
> knows to whom to complain.
>> *Vainglory* (1915)

Gracián, Baltasar (1601–1658)
Spanish writer
> *La metad del mundo se está riendo de la otra metad,*
> *con necedad de todos.*
> Half the world is laughing at the other half,
> which shows how foolish everyone is.
>> *Handbook-Oracle and the Art of Prudence* (1647)

Hardy, Thomas (1840–1928)
English writer and poet
> Well, World, you have kept faith with me,
> Kept faith with me;

> Upon the whole you have proved to be
> Much as you said you were.
>> 'He Never Expected Much, A Consideration on My
>> Eighty-Sixth birthday (1928)'

Hazlitt, William (1778–1830)
English writer and critic
> If the world were good for nothing else, it is a
> fine subject for speculation.
>> *Characteristics* (1823)

Hemingway, Ernest (1898–1961)
US author
> The world is a fine place and worth the fighting
> for.
>> *For Whom the Bell Tolls* (1940)

Johnson, Samuel (1709–1784)
English lexicographer, poet, critic, conversationalist and
essayist
> This world where much is to be done and little
> to be known.
>> In G.B. Hill (ed.), *Johnsonian Miscellanies* (1897)

Kafka, Franz (1883–1924)
Czech-born German-speaking writer
> *Im Kampf zwischen dir und der Welt sekundiere der*
> *Welt.*
> In the struggle between you and the world,
> support the world.
>> *Reflections on Sin, Sorrow, Hope and the True Way* (1953)

Keats, John (1795–1821)
English poet
> Call the world if you Please 'The vale of Soul-
> making'.
>> Letter to George and Georgiana Keats,
>> 1819

Koestler, Arthur (1905–1983)
British writer, essayist and political refugee
> One may not regard the world as a sort of
> metaphysical brothel for emotions.
>> *Darkness at Noon* (1940)

Lloyd George, David (1863–1945)
British Liberal statesman
> The world is becoming like a lunatic asylum run
> by lunatics.
>> *The Observer*, 1953

MacNeice, Louis (1907–1963)
Belfast-born poet, writer, radio producer, translator and
critic
> World is crazier and more of it than we think,
> Incorrigibly plural. I peel and portion
> A tangerine and spit the pips and feel
> The drunkenness of things being various.
>> 'Snow' (1935)

Marquis, Don (1878–1937)
US columnist, satirist and poet
> Ours is a world where people don't know what

they want and are willing to go through hell to get it.

> In *Treasury of Humorous Quotations*

Marx, Karl (1818–1883)
German political philosopher and economist; founder of Communism

> The philosophers have merely interpreted the world in various ways; the point, however, is to change it.
>
> *Theses on Feuerbach* (1845, published 1888)

O'Casey, Sean (1880–1964)
Irish dramatist

> Th' whole worl's in a terrible state o' chassis!
>
> *Juno and the Paycock* (1924)

Oppenheimer, J. Robert (1904–1967)
US nuclear physicist

> The optimist thinks that this is the best of all possible worlds and the pessimist knows it.
>
> *Bulletin of Atomic Scientists*, 1951

Owen, Robert (1771–1858)
Welsh social and educational reformer
To W. Allen, on dissolving their business partnership

> All the world is queer save thee and me, and even thou art a little queer.
>
> Attr., 1828

Patten, Brian (1946–)
British poet

> and I understood
> how there is nothing complicated in the world
> that is not of my own making.
>
> 'turning the pages'

Sartre, Jean-Paul (1905–1980)
French philosopher, writer, dramatist and critic

> *Le monde peut fort bien se passer de la littérature.*
> *Mais il peut se passer de l'homme encore mieux.*
> The world can survive very well without literature. But it can survive even more easily without man.
>
> *Situations*

Scott, Sir Walter (1771–1832)
Scottish writer and historian

> The ae half of the warld thinks the tither daft.
>
> *Redgauntlet* (1824)

Shakespeare, William (1564–1616)
English dramatist, poet and actor

> O, how full of briers is this working-day world!
>
> *As You Like It*, I.iii

> I hold the world but as the world, Gratiano –
> A stage, where every man must play a part,
> And mine a sad one.
>
> *The Merchant of Venice*, I.i

> How many goodly creatures are there here!
> How beauteous mankind is! O brave new world

That has such people in't!

> *The Tempest*, V.i

Shaw, George Bernard (1856–1950)
Irish socialist, writer, dramatist and critic

> Nothing is ever done in this world until men are prepared to kill one another if it is not done.
>
> *Major Barbara* (1907)

Smith, Sydney (1771–1845)
English clergyman, essayist, journalist and wit

> Bishop Berkeley destroyed this world in one volume octavo; and nothing remained, after his time, but mind; which experienced a similar fate from the hand of Mr Hume in 1739.
>
> *Sketches of Moral Philosophy* (1849)

Smollett, Tobias (1721–1771)
Scottish writer, satirist, historian, traveller and physician

> I consider the world as made for me, not me for the world: it is my maxim therefore to enjoy it while I can, and let futurity shift for itself.
>
> *The Adventures of Roderick Random* (1748)

Stevens, Wallace (1879–1955)
US poet, essayist, dramatist and lawyer

> In my room, the world is beyond my understanding;
> But when I walk I see that it consists of three or four hills and a cloud.
>
> 'Of the Surface of Things' (1923)

Stevenson, Robert Louis (1850–1894)
Scottish writer, poet and essayist

> The world is so full of a number of things,
> I'm sure we should all be as happy as kings.
>
> *A Child's Garden of Verses* (1885), 'Happy Thought'

Thatcher, Margaret (1925–)
English Conservative Prime Minister

> It's a funny old world.
>
> *The Sunday Telegraph*, 1990

Thompson, Francis (1859–1907)
English poet

> O world invisible, we view thee,
> O world intangible, we touch thee,
> O world unknowable, we know thee,
> Inapprehensible, we clutch thee!
>
> 'The Kingdom of God' (1913)

Traherne, Thomas (c.1637–1674)
English religious writer and clergyman

> You never enjoy the world aright, till the sea itself floweth in your veins, till you are clothed with the heavens, and crowned with the stars: and perceive yourself to be the sole heir of the whole world, and more than so, because men are in it who are every one sole heirs as well as you. Till you can sing and rejoice and delight in God, as misers do in gold, and kings in sceptres,

you can never enjoy the world.

Centuries of Meditations

Walpole, Horace (1717–1797)
English writer and politician
This world is a comedy to those that think, and a tragedy to those that feel.

Letter to Anne, Countess of Upper Ossory, 1776

Ward, Nathaniel (1578–1652)
English Puritan divine
The world is full of care, much like unto a bubble;
Women and care, and care and women, and women and care and trouble.

Epigram (1647)

Wordsworth, William (1770–1850)
English poet
The world is too much with us; late and soon,
Getting and spending, we lay waste our powers.

'The world is too much with us' (1807)

Not in Utopia – subterranean fields, –
Or some secreted island, Heaven knows where!
But in the very world, which is the world
Of all of us, – the place where, in the end
We find our happiness, or not at all!

The Prelude (1850)

Wotton, Sir Henry (1568–1639)
English diplomat, traveller and poet
When we meet, all the world to nothing we shall laugh; and, in truth Sir this world is worthy of nothing else.

Letter to Sir Edmund Bacon, 1614

Yeats, W.B. (1865–1939)
Irish poet, dramatist, editor, writer and senator
This pragmatical, preposterous pig of a world.

In *The Exile*, 1928

Young, Edward (1683–1765)
English poet, dramatist, satirist and clergyman
To know the World, not love her, is thy point;
She gives but little, nor that little long.

Night-Thoughts on Life, Death and Immortality (1742–45)

▶▶ UNIVERSE

worrying

Asaf, George (1880–1951)
US songwriter
What's the use of worrying?
It never was worth while,
So, pack up your troubles in your old kit-bag,
And smile, smile, smile.

'Pack up Your Troubles in Your Old Kit-bag' (song, 1915)

Inge, William Ralph (1860–1954)
English divine, writer and teacher
Worry is interest paid on trouble before it is due.

The Observer, 1932

Longfellow, Henry Wadsworth (1807–1882)
US poet and writer
The cares that infest the day
Shall fold their tents, like the Arabs,
And as silently steal away.

'The Day is Done' (1844)

Middleton, Thomas (c.1580–1627)
English dramatist
I never heard
Of any true affection, but 'twas nipt
With care.

Blurt, Master-Constable (1602)

Schulz, Charles (1922–2000)
US cartoonist
I've developed a new philosophy – I only dread one day at a time.

Attr.

worship

The Bible (King James Version)
O come, let us sing unto the Lord; let us make a joyful noise to the rock of our salvation.
Let us come before his presence with thanksgiving, and make a joyful noise unto him with psalms.
For the Lord is a great God, and a great King above all gods.
In his hand are the deep places of the earth: the strength of the hills is his also.
The sea is his, and he made it: and his hands formed the dry land.
O come, let us worship and bow down: let us kneel before the Lord our maker.

Psalms, 95:1–6

Carlyle, Thomas (1795–1881)
Scottish historian, biographer, critic, and essayist
Worship is transcendent wonder.

On Heroes, Hero-Worship, and the Heroic in History

Coward, Sir Noël (1899–1973)
English dramatist, actor, producer and composer
Everybody worships me, it's nauseating.

Present Laughter (1943),

Keats, John (1795–1821)
English poet
Rich in the simple worship of a day.

'Ode to May. Fragment' (1818)

Runcie, Robert (1921–2000)
Archbishop of Canterbury 1980–91

I am temperamentally against clappy-and-happy, huggy-and-feely worship, which seems to reduce God to a puppet.

The Guardian, 2000

writers

Addison, Joseph (1672–1719)

English essayist, poet, playwright and statesman

Thus I live in the world rather as a spectator of mankind, than as one of the species, by which means I have made myself a speculative statesman, soldier, merchant, and artisan, without ever meddling with any practical part in life.

The Spectator, March 1711

Anonymous

A member of the Soviet Writers' Union, after the decision to urge publication of *The Gulag Archipelago*, in reply to Vladimir Karpov's comment 'I have never seen such unanimity among us'

At least, not since we voted to expel Solzhenitsyn.

The Independent, 1989

Arnold, Matthew (1822–1888)

English poet, critic, essayist and educationist

Of Chaucer

He lacks the high seriousness of the great classics, and therewith an important part of their virtue.

Essays in Criticism (1888)

Dryden and Pope are not classics of our poetry, they are classics of our prose.

Essays in Criticism (1888)

Aubrey, John (1626–1697)

English antiquary, folklorist and biographer

How these curiosities would be quite forgot, did not such idle fellows as I am put them down.

Brief Lives (c.1693)

Auden, W.H. (1907–1973)

English poet, essayist, critic, teacher and dramatist

No poet or novelist wishes he were the only one who ever lived, but most of them wish they were the only one alive, and quite a number fondly believe their wish has been granted.

The Dyer's Hand (1963)

Austen, Jane (1775–1817)

English writer

I think I may boast myself to be, with all possible vanity, the most unlearned and uninformed female who ever dared to be an authoress.

Letter to James Stanier Clarke, 1815

Bagehot, Walter (1826–1877)

English economist and political philosopher

Writers, like teeth, are divided into incisors and grinders.

'The First Edinburgh Reviewers' (1858)

A man who has not read Homer is like a man who has not seen the ocean. There is a great object of which he has no idea.

Literary Studies (1879)

Barlow, Jane (1860–1917)

Irish novelist

That old yahoo George Moore ... His stories impressed me as being on the whole like gruel spooned up off a dirty floor.

Letter, 1914

Beauvoir, Simone de (1908–1986)

French writer, feminist critic and philosopher

L'écrivain original, tant qu'il n'est pas mort, est toujours scandaleux.

Writers who stand out, as long as they are not dead, are always scandalous.

The Second Sex (1950)

Bellow, Saul (1915–)

Canadian-born US Jewish writer

If one yearns to live dangerously, is it not as dangerous to persist in the truth as to rush to the barricades? But then it is always more agreeable to play the role of a writer than to be a writer. A writer's life is solitary, often bitter. How pleasant it is to come out of one's room, to fly about the world, make speeches, and cut a swath.

Critical Enquiry, 1975

Bennett, Alan (1934–)

English dramatist, actor and diarist

We were put to Dickens as children but it never quite took. That unremitting humanity soon had me cheesed off.

The Old Country (1978)

Bernard, Jeffrey (1932–1997)

British columnist

Writers as a rule don't make fighters, although I would hate to have to square up to Taki or Andrea Dworkin.

The Spectator, 1992

Brenan, Gerald (1894–1987)

English writer

Of Henry Miller

Miller is not really a writer but a non-stop talker to whom someone has given a typewriter.

Thoughts in a Dry Season (1978)

Brontë, Charlotte (1816–1855)

English writer

Novelists should never allow themselves to

weary of the study of real life.

The Professor (1857)

Brontë, Rev. Patrick (1777–1861)
English clergyman; father of the Brontës
> Girls, do you know Charlotte has been writing a
> book, and it is much better than likely?

In Elizabeth Gaskell, *Life of Charlotte Brontë* (1857)

Browne, Coral (1913–1991)
English actress
To a Hollywood writer who had criticized the work of Alan
Bennett
> Listen, dear, you couldn't write fuck on a dusty
> venetian blind.

Attr., in *The Sunday Times Magazine*, 1984

Campbell, Roy (1901–1957)
South African poet and journalist
> You praise the firm restraint with which they
> write –
> I'm with you there, of course:
> They use the snaffle and the curb all right,
> But where's the bloody horse?

Adamastor (1930)

Canetti, Elias (1905–1994)
Bulgarian-born English writer, dramatist and critic
> *Er legt Sätze wie Eier, aber er vergisst, sie zu bebrüten.*
> He lays sentences like eggs, but he forgets to
> incubate them.

The Human Province. Notes from 1942 to 1972

Carlyle, Thomas (1795–1881)
Scottish historian, biographer, critic, and essayist
> O thou who art able to write a Book, which once
> in the two centuries or oftener there is a man
> gifted to do, envy not him whom they name
> City-builder, and inexpressibly pity him whom
> they name Conqueror or City-burner!

Sartor Resartus (1834)

> Literary men are … a perpetual priesthood.

Critical and Miscellaneous Essays (1839)

On Ralph Waldo Emerson
> A hoaryheaded and toothless baboon.

Collected Works (1871)

Caxton, William (c.1421–1491)
First English printer
> The worshipful father and first founder and
> embellisher of ornate eloquence in our English, I
> mean Master Geoffrey Chaucer.

Epilogue to Caxton's edition (c.1478) of Chaucer's
translation of Boethius, *The Consolacion of
Philosophie*

Chateaubriand, François-René (1768–1848)
French writer and statesman
> *L'écrivain original n'est pas celui qui n'imite personne,*
> *mais celui que personne ne peut imiter.*
> The original writer is not the one who refrains

from imitating others, but the one who can be
imitated by none.

The Beauties of Christianity (1802)

Chesterton, G.K. (1874–1936)
English writer, poet and critic
> Mr Shaw is (I suspect) the only man on earth
> who has never written any poetry.

Orthodoxy (1908)

> Jane Austen was born before those bands which
> (we are told) protected woman from truth, were
> burst by the Brontës or elaborately untied by
> George Eliot. Yet the fact remains that Jane
> Austen knew much more about men than either
> of them.

The Victorian Age in Literature (1913)

> Hardy went down to botanise in the swamp,
> while Meredith climbed towards the sun.
> Meredith became, at his best, a sort of daintily
> dressed Walt Whitman: Hardy became a sort of
> village atheist brooding and blaspheming over
> the village idiot.

The Victorian Age in Literature (1913)

Clark, Manning (1915–1991)
> All writers are liars, and there is not the slightest
> chance that any writer will get into heaven.

Speech, Melbourne, 1987

Cocteau, Jean (1889–1963)
French dramatist, poet, film writer and director
> *Victor Hugo … un fou qui se croyait Victor Hugo.*
> Victor Hugo … a madman who thought he was
> Victor Hugo.

Opium (1930)

Coleridge, Samuel Taylor (1772–1834)
English poet, philosopher and critic
> Until you understand a writer's ignorance,
> presume yourself ignorant of his understanding.

Biographia Literaria (1817)

> Swift was *anima Rabelaisii habitans in sicco* – the
> soul of Rabelais dwelling in a dry place.

Table Talk (1835)

> When I was a boy, I was fondest of Aeschylus; in
> youth and middle-age I preferred Euripides; now
> in my declining years I prefer Sophocles. I can
> now at length see that Sophocles is the most
> perfect. Yet he never rises to the sublime
> simplicity of Aeschylus – a simplicity of design, I
> mean – nor diffuses himself in the passionate
> outpourings of Euripides.

Table Talk (1835)

> I believe the souls of five hundred Sir Isaac
> Newtons would go to the making up of a
> Shakespeare or a Milton.

Letter to Thomas Poole, 1801

Condon, Richard (1915–)

> Writers are too self-centred to be lonely.
>
> > Attr.

Connolly, Cyril (1903–1974)

English literary editor, writer and critic

> An author arrives at a good style when his language performs what is required of it without shyness.
>
> > *Enemies of Promise* (1938)

> Better to write for yourself and have no public, than write for the public and have no self.
>
> > In Pritchett (ed.), *Turnstile One*

Of George Orwell

> He would not blow his nose without moralizing on conditions in the handkerchief industry.
>
> > *The Evening Colonnade* (1973)

Delillo, Don (1936–)

US author

> Years ago I used to think it was possible for a novelist to alter the inner life of the culture. Now bomb-makers and gunmen have taken that territory. They make raids on human consciousness. What writers used to do before we were all incorporated.
>
> > *Mao II*

Didion, Joan (1934–)

US writer

> Writers are always selling somebody out.
>
> > *Slouching Towards Bethlehem* (1968)

Disraeli, Benjamin (1804–1881)

English statesman and writer

> An author who speaks about his own books is almost as bad as a mother who talks about her own children.
>
> > Speech at Banquet given in Glasgow on his installation as Lord Rector, 1873

Dryden, John (1631–1700)

English poet, satirist, dramatist and critic

> Our author by experience finds it true,
> 'Tis much more hard to please himself than you.
>
> > *Aureng-Zebe* (1675)

Emerson, Ralph Waldo (1803–1882)

US poet, essayist, transcendentalist and teacher

> Talent alone cannot make a writer. There must be a man behind the book.
>
> > 'Goethe; or, the Writer' (1850)

Faulkner, William (1897–1962)

US writer

> The writer's only responsibility is to his art … If a writer has to rob his mother, he will not hesitate; the 'Ode on a Grecian Urn' is worth any number of old ladies.
>
> > *Paris Review*, 1956

On Henry James

> The nicest old lady I ever met.
>
> > In E. Stone, *The Battle and the Books* (c.1964)

Of Ernest Hemingway

> He has never been known to use a word that might send the reader to the dictionary.
>
> > Attr.

Frost, Robert (1874–1963)

US poet

> No tears in the writer, no tears in the reader.
>
> > *Collected Poems* (1939)

Goldsmith, Oliver (c.1728–1774)

Irish dramatist, poet and writer

> As writers become more numerous, it is natural for readers to become more indolent.
>
> > *The Bee* (1759)

Gordimer, Nadine (1923–)

South African writer

> The tension between standing apart and being fully involved; that is what makes a writer.
>
> > *Selected Stories* (1975)

Guedalla, Philip (1889–1944)

English historian, writer and lawyer

> The work of Henry James has always seemed divisible by a simple dynastic arrangement into three reigns: James I, James II, and the Old Pretender.
>
> > *Collected Essays* (1920)

Hazlitt, William (1778–1830)

English writer and critic

Of Sir Walter Scott

> He writes as fast as they can read, and he does not write himself down.
>
> > *The Spirit of the Age* (1825)

> His worst is better than any other person's best.
>
> > *The Spirit of the Age* (1825)

> His works (taken together) are almost like a new edition of human nature. This is indeed to be an author!
>
> > *The Spirit of the Age* (1825)

Hemingway, Ernest (1898–1961)

US author

Of James Joyce

> And when you saw him he would take up a conversation interrupted three years before. It was nice to see a great writer in our time.
>
> > *Green Hills of Africa* (1935)

In response to a jibe by William Faulkner

> Poor Faulkner. Does he really think big emotions come from big words? He thinks I don't know the ten-dollar words. I know them all right. But there are older and simpler and better words,

and those are the ones I use.

Attr.

Hill, Reginald (1936–)
British novelist and playwright
When asked in America why all the great crime writers of the 1920s were female
> Because the men were all dead.

Hobbes, Thomas (1588–1679)
Political philosopher
> The praise of ancient authors, proceeds not from the reverence of the dead, but from the competition, and mutual envy of the living.

Leviathan (1651)

Hughes, Ted (1930–1998)
English poet
> The progress of any writer is marked by those moments when he manages to outwit his own inner police system.

In Wendy Cope, Making Cocoa for Kingsley Amis (1986)

Irving, Washington (1783–1859)
US writer and diplomat
> I am always at a loss to know how much to believe of my own stories.

Tales of a Traveller (1824)

Johnson, Samuel (1709–1784)
English lexicographer, poet, critic, conversationalist and essayist
> The greatest part of a writer's time is spent in reading, in order to write: a man will turn over half a library to make one book.

In Boswell, The Life of Samuel Johnson (1791)

> The chief glory of every people arises from its authors.

A Dictionary of the English Language (1755)

> It is the fate of those who toil at the lower employments of life … to be exposed to censure, without hope of praise; to be disgraced by miscarriage, or punished for neglect … Among these unhappy mortals is the writer of dictionaries … Every other author may aspire to praise; the lexicographer can only hope to escape reproach.

A Dictionary of the English Language (1755)

> The reciprocal civility of authors is one of the most risible scenes in the farce of life.

Life of Sir Thomas Browne (1756)

Joseph, Michael (1897–1958)
English publisher and writer
> Authors are easy to get on with – if you're fond of children.

The Observer, 1949

Koestler, Arthur (1905–1983)
British writer, essayist and political refugee

A writer's ambition should be … to trade a hundred contemporary readers for ten readers in ten years' time and for one reader in a hundred years' time.

New York Times Book Review, 1951

Lamb, Lady Caroline (1785–1828)
English writer and poet
Of Byron
> Mad, bad, and dangerous to know.

Journal, 1812

Landor, Walter Savage (1775–1864)
English poet and writer
> Clear writers, like clear fountains, do not seem so deep as they are; the turbid look the most profound.

Imaginary Conversations (1824)

Lincoln, Abraham (1809–1865)
US statesman and President
On meeting Harriet Beecher Stowe
> So you're the little woman who wrote the book that made this great war!

Attr.

MacDiarmid, Hugh (1892–1978)
Scottish poet
> Our principal writers have nearly all been fortunate in escaping regular education.

The Observer, 1953

MacManus, Michael (1888–1951)
> But my work is undistinguished
> And my royalties are lean
> Because I never am obscure
> And not at all obscene.

'An Author's Lament'

Pascal, Blaise (1623–1662)
French philosopher and scientist
> When we see a natural style, we are quite surprised and delighted, for we expected to see an author and we find a man.

Pensées (1670)

Saki (1870–1916)
Burmese-born British writer
> Sherard Blaw, the dramatist who had discovered himself, and who had given so ungrudgingly of his discovery to the world.

The Unbearable Bassington (1912)

Sartre, Jean-Paul (1905–1980)
French philosopher, writer, dramatist and critic
> The writer, a free man addressing free men, has only one subject – freedom.

What Is Literature?

Singer, Isaac Bashevis (1904–1991)
Polish-born US Yiddish writer
> When I was a little boy they called me a liar but

now that I am a grown up they call me a writer.
The Observer, 1983

Solzhenitsyn, Alexander (1918–)
Russian writer, dramatist and historian
> No regime has ever loved great writers, only minor ones.
> *The First Circle* (1968)

Stevenson, Robert Louis (1850–1894)
Scottish writer, poet and essayist
> Though we are mighty fine fellows nowadays, we cannot write like Hazlitt.
> *Virginibus Puerisque* (1881)

Tynan, Kenneth (1927–1980)
English drama critic, producer and essayist
> William Congreve is the only sophisticated playwright England has produced; and like Shaw, Sheridan, and Wilde, his nearest rivals, he was brought up in Ireland.
> *Curtains* (1961)

Vidal, Gore (1925–)
US writer, critic and poet
> American writers want to be not good but great; and so are neither.
> *Two Sisters* (1970)

Waugh, Evelyn (1903–1966)
English writer and diarist
> No writer before the middle of the 19th century wrote about the working classes other than as grotesque or as pastoral decoration. Then when they were given the vote certain writers started to suck up to them.
> *Paris Review*, 1963

Wellington, Duke of (1769–1852)
Irish-born British military commander and statesman
> In my situation as Chancellor of the University of Oxford, I have been much exposed to authors.
> In G.W.E. Russell, *Collections and Recollections* (1898)

Whitlam, Gough (1916–)
Australian Labor statesman and Prime Minister
> The challenge for the writer is to adapt his ancient and difficult craft to a generation that is largely insensitive to its virtues and to a popular audience increasingly distracted by the pace, immediacy and materialism of contemporary life.
> Speech, 1975

Yeats, W.B. (1865–1939)
Irish poet, dramatist, editor, writer and senator
> It's not a writer's business to hold opinions.
> Attr.

> A good writer should be so simple that he has no faults, only sins.
> *The Death of Synge and other Passages from an Old Diary* (1928)

▶▶ CRITICISM; POETS; WRITING

writers (individual)

Anonymous
Of Irvine Welsh
> '… he is quite distinctive being bald, Scottish and ugly.'
> *Daily Record*, 1999

Bainbridge, Beryl (1934–)
English novelist
Message on her answering machine
> Beryl is getting down to her new novel. She can't accept social engagements as they inevitably lead to getting tired and emotional.
> *The Observer*, 1999

Johnson, Samuel (1709–1784)
English lexicographer, poet, critic, conversationalist and essayist
> Why, Sir, if you were to read Richardson for the story, your impatience would be so much fretted, that you would hang yourself. But you must read him for the sentiment, and consider the story as only giving occasion to the sentiment.
> In Boswell, *The Life of Samuel Johnson* (1791)

Of Thomas Gray
> He was dull in a new way, and that made many people think him great.
> In Boswell, *The Life of Samuel Johnson* (1791)

Of Goldsmith
> No man was more foolish when he had not a pen in his hand, or more wise when he had.
> In Boswell, *The Life of Samuel Johnson* (1791

Lamb, Mary (1764–1847)
English prose writer
Of Henry Crabb Robinson
> He says he never saw a man so happy in three wives as Mr Wordsworth is.
> Letter to Sarah Hutchinson, 1816

Lehmann, Rosamond (1901–1990)
English novelist
> The trouble with Ian Fleming is that he gets off with women because he can't get on with them.
> Borrowing a line from Elizabeth Bowen, quoted in J. Pearson, *The Life of Ian Fleming* (1966)

Lenin, V.I. (1870–1924)
Russian revolutionary, Marxist theoretician and first leader of the USSR
Of Bernard Shaw
> A good man fallen among Fabians.
> In Arthur Ransome, *Six Weeks in Russia in 1919* (1919)

Leverson, Ada Beddington (1862–1936)
English writer
Of Oscar Wilde
> The last gentleman in Europe.
>> *Letters to the Sphinx* (1930)

Mitford, Mary Russell (1787–1855)
English writer
> I have discovered that our great favourite, Miss Austen, is my country-woman … with whom mamma before her marriage was acquainted. Mamma says that she was then the prettiest, silliest, most affected, husband-hunting butterfly she ever remembers.
>> Letter to Sir William Elford, 1815

Of Jane Austen
> Perpendicular, precise and taciturn.
>> In *Life and Letters of Mary R. Mitford* (1870)

Muggeridge, Malcolm (1903–1990)
English writer
Of Evelyn Waugh
> He looked, I decided, like a letter delivered to the wrong address.
>> *Tread Softly For You Tread on My Jokes* (1966)

O'Casey, Sean (1880–1964)
Irish dramatist
Of P.G. Wodehouse
> English literature's performing flea.
>> In P.G. Wodehouse, *Performing Flea* (1953)

O'Conor, Roderic (1860–1940)
On Somerset Maugham
> A bedbug on which a sensitive man refuses to stamp because of the smell and squashiness.
>> Attr. in Larry Powell, 'The Discovery of a New Master, Roderic O'Conor', *Etudes Irlandaises*, 1933

Ruskin, John (1819–1900)
English art critic, philosopher and reformer
> Thackeray settled like a meat-fly on whatever one had got for dinner, and made one sick of it.
>> *Fors Clavigera* (1871–1884)

Scott, Sir Walter (1771–1832)
Scottish writer and historian
> The blockheads talk of my being like Shakespeare – not fit to tie his brogues.
>> *Journal*, 11 December 1826

Sherwood, Robert Emmet (1896–1955)
US writer and dramatist
> It is disappointing to report that George Bernard Shaw appearing as George Bernard Shaw is sadly miscast in the part. Satirists should be heard and not seen.
>> Reviewing a Shaw play

Shorthouse, J.H. (1834–1903)
> In all probability 'Wordsworth's standard of intoxication was miserably low.'
>> Remark

Sitwell, Dame Edith (1887–1964)
English poet, anthologist, critic and biographer
Of Virginia Woolf
> I enjoyed talking to her, but thought nothing of her writing. I considered her 'a beautiful little knitter'.
>> Letter to G. Singleton, 1955

Smith, Sydney (1771–1845)
English clergyman, essayist, journalist and wit
Of Macaulay
> He is like a book in breeches.
>> In Holland, *A Memoir of the Reverend Sydney Smith* (1855)

Walpole, Horace (1717–1797)
English writer and politician
> Lord Rochester's poems have much more obscenity than wit, more wit than poetry, more poetry than politeness.
>> *Catalogue of Royal and Noble Authors* (1758)

Ward, Artemus (1834–1867)
US humorist, journalist, editor and lecturer
> It is a pity that Chawcer, who had geneyus, was so unedicated. He's the wuss speller I know of.
>> *Artemus Ward in London* (1867)

Waugh, Evelyn (1903–1966)
English writer and diarist
Remark to Graham Greene, who was planning to write a political novel
> I wouldn't give up writing about God at this stage if I was you. It would be like P.G. Wodehouse dropping Jeeves half-way through the Wooster series.
>> In Christopher Sykes, *Evelyn Waugh*

> I put the words down and push them a bit.
>> Obituary, *New York Times*, 11 April 1966

Wells, H.G. (1866–1946)
English writer
Of Henry James
> The thing his novel is about is always there. It is like a church lit but without a congregation to distract you, with every light and line focused on the high altar. And on the altar, very reverently placed, intensely there, is a dead kitten, an egg-shell, a bit of string.
>> *Boon* (1915)

Yeats, W.B. (1865–1939)
Irish poet, dramatist, editor, writer and senator
Of George Eliot
> She is magnificently ugly – deliciously hideous … now in this vast ugliness resides a most powerful beauty which, in a very few minutes steals forth and charms the mind.
>> Attr.

▶▶ CRITICISM; POETS; SHAKESPEARE; WRITING

writing

Adams, Franklin P. (1881–1960)
US writer, poet, translator and editor

> Having imagination, it takes you an hour to write a paragraph that, if you were unimaginative, would take you only a minute. Or you might not write the paragraph at all.
>
> *Attr.*

Addison, Joseph (1672–1719)
English essayist, poet, playwright and statesman
Of the difference between his conversational and writing abilities

> I have but ninepence in ready money, but I can draw for a thousand pounds.
>
> In Boswell, *The Life of Samuel Johnson* (1791)

> Authors have established it as a kind of rule, that a man ought to be dull sometimes; as the most severe reader makes allowances for many rests and nodding-places in a voluminous writer.
>
> *The Spectator*, July 1711

Ade, George (1866–1944)
US fabulist and playwright

> After being turned down by numerous publishers, he decided to write for posterity.
>
> *The Fable of the Bohemian who had Hard Luck* (1899)

Albee, Edward (1928–)
US dramatist

> Good writers define reality; bad ones merely restate it. A good writer turns fact into truth; a bad writer will, more often than not, accomplish the opposite.
>
> *Saturday Review*, 1966

Aldiss, Brian (1925–)
English writer

> Why had I become a writer in the first place? Because I wasn't fit for society; I didn't fit into the system.
>
> In Jon Winokur, *Writers on Writing* (1990)

Anonymous

> Inspiration is the act of drawing up a chair to the writing desk.

Arnold, Matthew (1822–1888)
English poet, critic, essayist and educationist

> People think that I can teach them style. What stuff it all is! Have something to say, and say it as clearly as you can. That is the only secret of style.
>
> In Russell, *Collections and Recollections* (1898)

Ascham, Roger (1515–1568)
English scholar, educationist and archer

> He that will write well in any tongue, must follow this counsel of Aristotle, to speak as the common people do, to think as wise men do; and so should every man understand him, and the judgment of wise men allow him.
>
> *Toxophilus* (1545)

Atwood, Margaret (1939–)
Canadian writer, poet and critic

> Once upon a time I thought there was an old man with a grey beard somewhere who knew the truth, and if I was good enough, naturally he would tell me that this was it. That person doesn't exist, but that's who I write for. The great critic in the sky.
>
> In Earl G. Ingersoll (ed.), *Margaret Atwood: Conversations* (1990)

> Writing … is an act of faith: I believe it's also an act of hope, the hope that things can be better than they are.
>
> *Attr.*

Austen, Jane (1775–1817)
English writer

> … the little bit (two inches wide) of ivory on which I work with so fine a brush, as produces little effect after much labour.
>
> Letter, 1816

> Let other pens dwell on guilt and misery.
>
> *Mansfield Park* (1814)

Benjamin, Walter (1892–1940)
German writer, philosopher and critic

> Work on good prose has three steps: a musical stage when it is composed, an architectonic one when it is built, and a textile one when it is woven.
>
> *One-Way Street* (1928)

Bentham, Jeremy (1748–1832)
English writer and philosopher

> Prose is when all the lines except the last go on to the end. Poetry is when some of them fall short of it.
>
> In Packe, *Life of John Stuart Mill* (1954)

Boileau-Despréaux, Nicolas (1636–1711)
French writer

> He who does not know how to limit himself does not know how to write.
>
> *L'Art Poétique* (1674)

Brittain, Vera (1893–1970)
English writer and pacifist

> The idea that it is necessary to go to a university in order to become a successful writer, or even a man or woman of letters (which is by no means the same thing), is one of those phantasies that surround authorship.
>
> *On Being an Author* (1948)

Brown, Rita Mae (1944–)
US writer and poet
> Show me a writer, any writer, who hasn't
> suffered and I'll show you someone who writes
> in pastels as opposed to primary colors.
>> *Starting From Scratch* (1988)

Bulwer-Lytton, Edward (1803–1873)
English novelist and politician
> Beneath the rule of men entirely great
> The pen is mightier than the sword.
>> *Richelieu* (1839)

Burchill, Julie (1960–)
English writer
> Writing is more than anything a compulsion, like
> some people wash their hands thirty times a day
> for fear of awful consequences if they do not. It
> pays a whole lot better than this type of
> compulsion, but it is no more heroic.
>> *Sex and Sensibility* (1992)

Burgess, Anthony (1917–1993)
English writer, linguist and composer
> The trouble began with Forster. After him it was
> considered ungentlemanly to write more than
> five or six novels.
>> *The Guardian*, 1989

Capote, Truman (1924–1984)
US writer
> Writing has laws of perspective, of light and
> shade just as painting does, or music. If you are
> born knowing them, fine. If not, learn them.
> Then rearrange the rules to suit yourself.
>> *Writers at Work* (1958)

Carlyle, Thomas (1795–1881)
Scottish historian, biographer, critic, and essayist
> After two weeks of blotching and blaring I have
> produced two clear papers.
>> Attr.

Cartland, Barbara (1901–2000)
English writer
On the publication of her 217th book
> As long as the plots keep arriving from outer
> space, I'll go on with my virgins.
>> *New Yorker*, 1976

Chandler, Raymond (1888–1959)
US crime writer
> A good story cannot be devised; it has to be
> distilled.
>> *Raymond Chandler Speaking* (1962)

> What greater prestige can a man like me (not
> too gifted, but very understanding) have than to
> have taken a cheap, shoddy and utterly lost kind
> of writing, and have made of it something that
> intellectuals claw each other about?
>> *Raymond Chandler Speaking* (1962)

Cheever, John (1912–1982)
US novelist
> I can't write without a reader. It's precisely like a
> kiss – you can't do it alone.
>> *Christian Science Monitor*, 1979

Dickens, Charles (1812–1870)
English writer
> I hold my inventive faculty on the stern condition
> that it must master my whole life, often have
> complete possession of me … and sometimes
> for months together put everything else away
> from me.
>> *The Letters of Charles Dickens*

Doctorow, E. L. (1931–)
US writer
> Writing is like driving at night in the fog. You can
> only see as far as your headlights, but you can
> make the whole trip that way.
>> In George Plimpton, *Writers at Work* (1988)

> Writing is a socially acceptable form of
> schizophrenia.
>> In George Plimpton, *Writers at Work* (1988)

Eliot, T.S. (1888–1965)
US-born British poet, verse dramatist and critic
On his ideal of writing
> The common word exact without vulgarity, the
> formal word precise but not pedantic, the
> complete consort dancing together.
>> *Sunday Telegraph*, 1993

Etherege, Sir George (c.1635–1691)
English Restoration dramatist
> Writing, Madam, is a mechanic part of wit; a
> gentleman should never go beyond a song or a
> billet.
>> *The Man of Mode* (1676)

Fanon, Frantz (1925–1961)
West Indian psychoanalyst and philosopher
On 'native' writers trying to rid themselves of European
influences
> It is always easier to proclaim rejection than to
> reject.
>> *Les damnées de la terre* (1961)

Faulkner, William (1897–1962)
US writer
> If a writer has to rob his mother, he will not
> hesitate; the 'Ode on a Grecian Urn' is worth
> any number of old ladies.
>> In Malcolm Cowley, *Writers at Work* (1958)

Fitzgerald, F. Scott (1896–1940)
US writer
Referring to his novel *This Side of Paradise*
> To write it, it took three months; to conceive it –
> three minutes; to collect the data in it – all my life.
>> 'The Author's Apology' (1920)

Frame, Janet (1924–)
New Zealand writer

> Writing a novel is not merely going on a shopping expedition across the border to an unreal land: it is hours and years spent in the factories, the streets, the cathedrals of the imagination.
>
> *The Envoy from Mirror City* (1985)

Frost, Robert (1874–1963)
US poet

> Writing free verse is like playing tennis with the net down.
>
> Address, 1935

Galsworthy, John (1867–1933)
English writer and dramatist

> I do wish I had the gift of writing. I really think that it is the nicest way of making money going.
>
> Letter to Monica Sanderson, c.1894

Glendinning, Victoria (1937–)
English writer

> There's no greater bliss in life than when the plumber eventually comes to unblock your drains. No writer can give that sort of pleasure.
>
> *The Observer*, 1993

Golding, William (1911–1993)
English writer and poet

> Novelists do not write as birds sing, by the push of nature. It is part of the job that there should be much routine and some daily stuff on the level of carpentry.
>
> 'Rough Magic' lecture, 1977

Gorky, Maxim (1868–1936)
Russian writer, dramatist and revolutionary

> You must write for children just as you do for adults, only better.
>
> Attr.

Gray, Thomas (1716–1771)
English poet and scholar

> Any fool may write a most valuable book by chance, if he will only tell us what he heard and saw with veracity.
>
> Letter to Horace Walpole, 1768

Hellman, Lillian (1907–1984)
US dramatist and screenwriter

> If I had to give young writers advice, I would say don't listen to writers talking about writing or themselves.
>
> *New York Times*, 1960

Hemingway, Ernest (1898–1961)
US author

> Prose is architecture, not interior decoration, and the Baroque is over.
>
> *Death in the Afternoon* (1932)

Johnson, Samuel (1709–1784)
English lexicographer, poet, critic, conversationalist and essayist

> A man may write at any time, if he will set himself doggedly to it.
>
> In Boswell, *The Life of Samuel Johnson* (1791)

> What is written without effort is in general read without pleasure.
>
> In William Seward, *Biographia* (1799)

> The only end of writing is to enable the readers better to enjoy life, or better to endure it.
>
> *Works* (1787)

> No man but a blockhead ever wrote, except for money.
>
> In Boswell, *The Life of Samuel Johnson* (1791)

Juvenal (c.60–130)
Roman verse satirist and Stoic

> *Tenet insanabile multos*
> *Scribendi cacoethes et aegro in corde senescit.*
> The incurable itch for writing takes hold of many and becomes chronic in their distempered brains.
>
> *Satires*

Keats, John (1795–1821)
English poet

> I have come to this resolution – never to write for the sake of writing or making a poem, but from running over with any little knowledge or experience which many years of reflection may perhaps give me; otherwise I will be dumb.
>
> Letter to B.R. Haydon, 8 March 1819

> I am convinced more and more day by day that fine writing is next to fine doing, the top thing in the world.
>
> Letter to J. H. Reynolds, 1819

La Bruyère, Jean de (1645–1696)
French satirist

> *Tout est dit, et l'on vient trop tard depuis plus de sept mille ans qu'il y a des hommes et qui pensent.*
> Everything has been said already; we come too late after more than seven thousand years in which men have lived and thought.
>
> *Les caractères ou les moeurs de ce siècle* (1688)

Lawrence, D.H. (1885–1930)
English writer, poet and critic

> I like to write when I feel spiteful: it's like having a good sneeze.
>
> Letter to Lady Cynthia Asquith, 1913

Le Carré, John (1931–)
English writer

> Writing is like walking in a deserted street. Out of the dust in the street you make a mud pie.
>
> *Time*, 1964

Lerner, Alan Jay (1918–1986)
US lyricist and screenwriter
> You write a hit the same way you write a flop.
>
> Attr.

Lynes, J. Russel (1910–1991)
> Every journalist has a novel in him, which is an excellent place for it.
>
> Attr.

Mansfield, Katherine (1888–1923)
New Zealand writer
> Better to write twaddle, anything, than nothing at all.
>
> Attr.

Maugham, William Somerset (1874–1965)
English writer, dramatist and physician
> You don't just get a story … You have to wait for it to come to you. I've never written a story in my life. The story has come to me and demanded to be written.
>
> In Robin Maugham, *Conversation with Willie* (1978)

Mencken, H.L. (1880–1956)
US writer, critic, philologist and satirist
> I write in order to attain that feeling of tension relieved and function achieved which a cow enjoys on giving milk.
>
> *The Delights of Reading*

Metalious, Grace (1924–1964)
US writer; author of *Peyton Place*
> I'm a lousy writer; a helluva lot of people have got lousy taste.
>
> In Jon Winokur, *Writers on Writing* (1990)

Michener, James (1907–1997)
US writer
> The really great writers are people like Emily Brontë who sit in a room and write out of their limited experience and unlimited imagination.
>
> *New York Times*, 1985

Morrison, Toni (1931–)
US writer
> If there's a book you really want to read but it hasn't been written yet, then you must write it.
>
> Attr.

Murdoch, Iris (1919–1999)
Irish-born British writer, philosopher and dramatist
> Writing is like getting married. One should never commit oneself until one is amazed at one's luck.
>
> *The Black Prince* (1989)

Orwell, George (1903–1950)
English writer and critic
> Good prose is like a window pane.
>
> 'Why I Write' (1946)

Rules for writing good English
> Never use a metaphor, simile or other figure of speech which you are used to seeing in print. Never use a long word where a short one will do. If it is possible to cut a word out, always cut it out. Never use the passive where you can use the active. Never use a foreign phrase, a scientific word or a jargon word if you can think of an everyday English equivalent. Break any of these rules sooner than say anything outright barbarous.
>
> 'Politics and the English Language' (1950)

Pascal, Blaise (1623–1662)
French philosopher and scientist
> *La dernière chose qu'on trouve en faisant un ouvrage, est de savoir celle qu'il faut mettre la première.*
> The last thing one finds out when constructing a work is what to put first.
>
> *Pensées* (1670)

Pinter, Harold (1930–)
English dramatist, poet and screenwriter
> Writing is for me a completely private activity, a poem or a play, no difference … What I write has no obligation to anything other than to itself.
>
> Speech to student drama festival, 1962

Piron, Alexis (1689–1773)
Discussing Voltaire's *Sémiramis* with him after its poor reception on the first night
> I think you would have been very glad if I had written it.
>
> In K. Arvine, *Cyclopaedia of Anecdotes*

Pope, Alexander (1688–1744)
English poet, translator and editor
> 'Tis hard to say, if greater want of skill
> Appear in writing or in judging ill.
>
> *An Essay on Criticism* (1711)

> True ease in writing comes from art, not chance,
> As those move easiest who have learn'd to dance.
> 'Tis not enough no harshness gives offence,
> The sound must seem an echo to the sense.
>
> *An Essay on Criticism* (1711)

Pound, Ezra (1885–1972)
US poet
> O God, O Venus, O Mercury, patron of thieves,
> Give me in due time, I beseech you, a little tobacco-shop …
> And a pair of scales not too greasy,
> And the whores dropping in for a word or two in passing,
> For a flip word, and to tidy their hair a bit.
>
> O God, O Venus, O Mercury, patron of thieves,
> Lend me a little tobacco-shop,
> or install me in any profession
> Save this damn'd profession of writing,

where one needs one's brains all the time.

'The Lake Isle' (1916)

Pratchett, Terry (1948–)
English writer

I don't think I am writing books for people too stupid to wear their baseball caps the right way round.

The Times, 1998

Renard, Jules (1864–1910)
French writer and dramatist

The profession of letters is, after all, the only one in which one can make no money without being ridiculous.

Journal

Rushdie, Salman (1947–)
Indian-born English author

Writers and politicians are natural rivals. Both groups try to make the world in their own images; they fight for the same territory.

The Observer, 1989

Scott, Sir Walter (1771–1832)
Scottish writer and historian
On Jane Austen

The Big Bow-Wow strain I can do myself like any now going; but the exquisite touch, which renders ordinary commonplace things and characters interesting, from the truth of the description and the sentiment, is denied to me.

Journal, 14 March 1826

But no one shall find me rowing against the stream. I care not who knows it – I write for the general amusement.

The Fortunes of Nigel (1822)

Sheridan, Richard Brinsley (1751–1816)
Irish dramatist, politician and orator

You write with ease, to show your breeding;
But easy writing's vile hard reading.

'Clio's Protest' (1771)

Sidney, Sir Philip (1554–1586)
English poet, critic, soldier, courtier and diplomat

Byting my tongue and penne, beating my selfe for spite:
'Foole,' saide My muse to mee, 'looke in thy heart and write'.

Astrophel and Stella (1591)

Simenon, Georges (1903–1989)
Belgian writer

Writing is not a profession but a vocation of unhappiness.

Writers at Work (1958)

Steinbeck, John (1902–1968)
US writer
Accepting the Nobel prize for literature

The profession of book writing makes horse racing seem like a solid, stable business.

Quoted in *Newsweek*, 1962

Stephen, James Kenneth (1859–1892)
English writer and poet

Will there never come a season
Which shall rid us from the curse
Of a prose which knows no reason
And an unmelodious verse …
When there stands a muzzled stripling,
Mute, beside a muzzled bore:
When the Rudyards cease from kipling
And the Haggards ride no more.

Lapsus Calami (1891)

Sterne, Laurence (1713–1768)
Irish-born English writer and clergyman

Writing, when properly managed, (as you may be sure I think mine is) is but a different name for conversation.

Tristram Shandy (1759–1767)

Stoppard, Tom (1937–)
British dramatist

You can only write about what bites you.

The Observer, 1984

Stowe, Harriet Beecher (1811–1896)
US writer and reformer
Of *Uncle Tom's Cabin*

I did not write it. God wrote it. I merely did his dictation.

Attr.

Trollope, Anthony (1815–1882)
English writer, traveller and post office official

Three hours a day will produce as much as a man ought to write.

Autobiography (1883)

Weldon, Fay (1931–)
British writer

I think if you had ever written a book you were absolutely pleased with, you'd never write another. The same probably goes for having children.

The Guardian, 1991

▶▶ BOOKS; CRITICISM; FICTION; INSPIRATION; LITERATURE; POETRY; READING; WRITERS

Y

youth

Asquith, Herbert (1852–1928)
English Liberal statesman and Prime Minister
> Youth would be an ideal state if it came a little later in life.
>> *The Observer*, 1923

Atwood, Margaret (1939–)
Canadian writer, poet and critic
> I've never understood why people consider youth a time of freedom and joy. It's probably because they have forgotten their own.
>> *Ms*, 1976

Borrow, George (1803–1881)
English writer and linguist
> Youth will be served, every dog has his day, and mine has been a fine one.
>> *Lavengro* (1851)

Bulwer-Lytton, Edward (1803–1873)
English novelist and politician
> In the lexicon of youth, which Fate reserves
> For a bright manhood, there is no such word
> As – fail!
>> *Richelieu* (1839)

Cartland, Barbara (1901–2000)
English writer
> Being 18 is like visiting Russia. You're glad you've had the experience but you'd never want to repeat it.
>> Comment 1978, quoted in *The Guardian*, 2000

Chanel, Coco (1883–1971)
French couturier and perfumer
> Youth is something very new: twenty years ago no one mentioned it.
>> In Haedrich, *Coco Chanel, Her Life, Her Secrets* (1971)

Conrad, Joseph (1857–1924)
Polish-born British writer, sailor and explorer
> I remember my youth and the feeling that will never come back any more – the feeling that I could last for ever, outlast the sea, the earth, and all men; the deceitful feeling that lures us on to perils, to love, to vain effort – to death; the triumphant conviction of strength, the heat of life in the handful of dust, that glow in the heart that with every year grows dim, grows cold, grows small, and expires – and expires, too soon, too soon – before life itself.
>> *Youth* (1902)

Crisp, Quentin (1908–1999)
English writer, publicist and model
> The young always have the same problem – how to rebel and conform at the same time. They have now solved this by defying their parents and copying one another.
>> *The Naked Civil Servant* (1968)

Cunard, Lady (**Maud**) **'Emerald'** (1872–1948)
Granddaughter-in-law of Samuel Cunard, shipowner
Reply to Somerset Maugham, when said he was leaving early 'to keep his youth'
> Then why didn't you bring him with you? I should be delighted to meet him.
>> In D. Fielding, *Emerald and Nancy: Lady Cunard and her Daughter* (1968)

Denham, Sir John (1615–1669)
English poet, royalist and Surveyor-General
> Youth, what man's age is like to be doth show;
> We may our ends by our beginnings know.
>> 'Of Prudence' (1668)

Disraeli, Benjamin (1804–1881)
English statesman and writer
> Almost everything that is great has been done by youth.
>> *Coningsby* (1844)

> The Youth of a Nation are the Trustees of Posterity.
>> *Sybil* (1845)

> Youth is a blunder; Manhood a struggle; Old Age a regret.
>> *Coningsby* (1844)

Fitzgerald, Edward (1809–1883)
English poet, translator and letter writer
> Alas, that Spring should vanish with the Rose!
> That Youth's sweet-scented Manuscript should close!
> The Nightingale that in the Branches sang,
> Ah, whence, and whither flown again, who knows!
>> *The Rubáiyát of Omar Khayyám* (1859)

Gay, John (1685–1732)
English poet, dramatist and librettist
> Youth's the season made for joys,
> Love is then our duty.
>> *The Beggar's Opera* (1728)

Herbert, Edward (1583–1648)
English statesman, poet and philosopher
> Now that the April of your youth adorns
> The Garden of your face.
>> 'Ditty in imitation of the Spanish Entre tantoque L'Avril' (1665)

Ibsen, Henrik (1828–1906)
Norwegian writer, dramatist and poet

Youth will come here and beat on my door, and force its way in.

The Master Builder (1892)

Jagger, Mick (1943–)
English rock musician

People have this obsession. They want you to be like you were in 1969. They want you to, because otherwise their youth goes with you… It's very selfish, but it's understandable.

The Observer, 1993

Johnson, Samuel (1709–1784)
English lexicographer, poet, critic, conversationalist and essayist

Young men have more virtue than old men; they have more generous sentiments in every respect.

In Boswell, *The Life of Samuel Johnson* (1791)

Jowett, Benjamin (1817–1893)
English scholar, translator, essayist and priest

Young men make great mistakes in life; for one thing, they idealize love too much.

Life and Letters of Benjamin Jowett (1897)

Kingsley, Charles (1819–1875)
English writer, poet, lecturer and clergyman

When all the world is young, lad,
And all the trees are green;
And every goose a swan, lad,
And every lass a queen;
Then hey for boot and horse, lad,
And round the world away:
Young blood must have its course, lad,
And every dog his day.

Song from *The Water Babies* (1863), 'Young and Old'

Longworth, Alice Roosevelt (1884–1980)
US writer

I've always believed in the adage that the secret of eternal youth is arrested development.

Conversations with Alice Roosevelt Longworth

Medici, Lorenzo de' (1449–1492)
Florentine ruler

Quant'è bella giovinezza
che si sfugge tuttavia!
Chi vuol esser lieto, sia:
di doman non c'è certezza.
How lovely is youth, which is always slipping away! Let him be glad who will be so: for tomorrow has no certainty.

'Trionfo di Bacco ed Arianna'

Melville, Herman (1819–1891)
US writer and poet

In youth we are, but in age we seem.

Pierre (1852)

Osborne, John (1929–1994)
English dramatist and actor

I keep looking back, as far as I can remember, and I can't think what it was like to feel young, really young.

Look Back in Anger (1956)

Parsons, Tony (1953–)
British journalist and author

Funky royals, coked-out old men and streaking BA stewardesses make me nostalgic for an age when people knew youth was just a stage you passed through, like acne.

The Observer, 1999

Pitt, William (1708–1778)
English politician and Prime Minister

The atrocious crime of being a young man … I shall neither attempt to palliate nor deny.

Speech, House of Commons, 1741

Porter, Cole (1891–1964)
US songwriter

They have found that the fountain of youth
Is a mixture of gin and vermouth.

The Fountain of Youth (song, 1928)

Porter, Hal (1911–1984)
Australian writer, dramatist and poet

How ruthless and hard and vile and right the young are.

The Watcher on the Cast-iron Balcony (1963)

Roosevelt, Franklin Delano (1882–1945)
US Democrat President

I confess to pride in this coming generation. You are working out your own salvation; you are more in love with life; you play with fire openly, where we did in secret, and few of you are burned!

Address, 1926

Shakespeare, William (1564–1616)
English dramatist, poet and actor

My salad days,
When I was green in judgment, cold in blood,
To say as I said then.

Antony and Cleopatra, I.v

He capers, he dances, he has eyes of youth, he writes verses, he speaks holiday, he smells April and May.

The Merry Wives of Windsor, III.ii

I would there were no age between ten and three and twenty, or that youth would sleep out the rest; for there is nothing in the between but getting wenches with child, wronging the ancientry, stealing, fighting.

The Winter's Tale, III.iii

Shaw, George Bernard (1856–1950)
Irish socialist, writer, dramatist and critic

Youth, which is forgiven everything, forgives itself nothing: age, which forgives itself everything, is forgiven nothing.

Man and Superman (1903)

It's all that the young can do for the old, to shock them and keep them up to date.

Fanny's First Play (1911)

On youth

Far too good to waste on children.

Attr. in Copeland, *10,000 Jokes, Toasts, & Stories* (1939)

Smith, Logan Pearsall (1865–1946)
US-born British epigrammatist, critic and writer

The old know what they want; the young are sad and bewildered.

'Last Words' (1933)

Stevenson, Robert Louis (1850–1894)
Scottish writer, poet and essayist

Youth is the time to go flashing from one end of the world to the other both in mind and body; to try the manners of different nations; to hear the chimes at midnight; to see sunrise in town and country; to be converted at a revival; to circumnavigate the metaphysics, write halting verses, run a mile to see a fire, and wait all day long in the theatre to applaud *Hernani.*

Virginibus Puerisque (1881)

Thatcher, Margaret (1925–)
English Conservative Prime Minister

Young people ought not to be idle. It is very bad for them.

The Times, 1984

Thomas, Dylan (1914–1953)
Welsh poet, writer and radio dramatist

Now as I was young and easy under the apple boughs
About the lilting house and happy as the grass was green ...

Oh as I was young and easy in the mercy of his means,
Time held me green and dying

Though I sang in my chains like the sea.

'Fern Hill' (1946)

Thompson, William Hepworth (1810–1886)
English academic
Comment on Junior Fellow of Trinity

We are none of us infallible – not even the youngest.

Attr.

Virgil (70–19 BC)
Roman poet

In youth alone, unhappy mortals live;
But oh! the mighty bliss is fugitive:
Discoloured sickness, anxious labours, come,
And age and death's inexorable doom.

Georgics

Wever, Robert (fl. 1550)
British poet

In a harbour grene aslepe whereas I lay,
The byrdes sang swete in the middes of the day,
I dreamèd fast of mirth and play:
In youth is pleasure, in youth is pleasure.

'Lusty Juventus'

Whitman, Walt (1819–1892)
US poet and writer

Youth, large, lusty, loving – youth full of grace, force, fascination,
Do you know that Old Age may come after you with equal grace, force, fascination?

'Youth, Day, Old Age and Night' (1855)

Wilde, Oscar (1854–1900)
Irish poet, dramatist, writer, critic and wit

The old-fashioned respect for the young is fast dying out.

The Importance of Being Earnest (1895)

Wilson, Woodrow (1856–1924)
US Democrat President

Generally young men are regarded as radicals. This is a popular misconception. The most conservative persons I ever met are college undergraduates.

Speech, 1905

▶▶ AGE; CHILDREN

INDEX OF AUTHORS